THE OXFORD HANDBOOK OF

COMPOSITIONALITY

OXFORD HANDBOOKS IN LINGUISTICS

THE OXFORD HANDBOOK OF APPLIED LINGUISTICS
Second edition
Edited by Robert B. Kaplan

THE OXFORD HANDBOOK OF CASE
Edited by Andrej Malchukov and Andrew Spencer

THE OXFORD HANDBOOK OF COGNITIVE LINGUISTICS
Edited by Dirk Geeraerts and Hubert Cuyckens

THE OXFORD HANDBOOK OF COMPARATIVE SYNTAX
Edited by Gugliemo Cinque and Richard S. Kayne

THE OXFORD HANDBOOK OF COMPOUNDING
Edited by Rochelle Lieber and Pavol Štekauer

THE OXFORD HANDBOOK OF COMPUTATIONAL LINGUISTICS
Edited by Ruslan Mitkov

THE OXFORD HANDBOOK OF COMPOSITIONALITY
Edited by Markus Werning, Edouard Machery, and Wolfram Hinzen

THE OXFORD HANDBOOK OF FIELD LINGUISTICS
Edited by Nicholas Thieberger

THE OXFORD HANDBOOK OF GRAMMATICALIZATION
Edited by Heiko Narrog and Bernd Heine

THE OXFORD HANDBOOK OF JAPANESE LINGUISTICS
Edited by Shigeru Miyagawa and Mamoru Saito

THE OXFORD HANDBOOK OF LABORATORY PHONOLOGY
Edited by Abigail C. Cohn, Cécile Fougeron, and Marie Hoffman

THE OXFORD HANDBOOK OF LANGUAGE EVOLUTION
Edited by Maggie Tallerman and Kathleen Gibson

THE OXFORD HANDBOOK OF LANGUAGE AND LAW
Edited by Lawrence Solan and Peter Tiersma

THE OXFORD HANDBOOK OF LINGUISTIC ANALYSIS
Edited by Bernd Heine and Heiko Narrog

THE OXFORD HANDBOOK OF LINGUISTIC INTERFACES
Edited by Gillian Ramchand and Charles Reiss

THE OXFORD HANDBOOK OF LINGUISTIC MINIMALISM
Edited by Cedric Boeckx

THE OXFORD HANDBOOK OF LINGUISTIC TYPOLOGY
Edited by Jae Jung Song

THE OXFORD HANDBOOK OF TRANSLATION STUDIES
Edited by Kirsten Malmkjaer and Kevin Windle

THE OXFORD HANDBOOK OF

COMPOSITIONALITY

Edited by

MARKUS WERNING,
WOLFRAM HINZEN,

and

EDOUARD MACHERY

OXFORD
UNIVERSITY PRESS

OXFORD
UNIVERSITY PRESS

Great Clarendon Street, Oxford, OX2 6DP,
United Kingdom

Oxford University Press is a department of the University of Oxford.
It furthers the University's objective of excellence in research, scholarship,
and education by publishing worldwide. Oxford is a registered trade mark of
Oxford University Press in the UK and in certain other countries

Published in the United States of America by Oxford University Press
198 Madison Avenue, New York, NY 10016, United States of America

British Library Cataloguing in Publication Data
Data available

Library of Congress Cataloging in Publication Data
Data available

ISBN 978–0–19–954107–2

Contents

PART I   HISTORY AND OVERVIEW

PART II   COMPOSITIONALITY IN LANGUAGE

PART III   COMPOSITIONALITY IN FORMAL SEMANTICS

PART IV   LEXICAL DECOMPOSITION

PART V   THE COMPOSITIONALITY OF MIND

PART VI EVOLUTIONARY AND COMMUNICATIVE SUCCESS

PART VII NEURAL MODELS OF COMPOSITIONAL REPRESENTATION

LIST OF ABBREVIATIONS

A	adjective
ACG	Abstract Categorial Grammar
AI	artificial intelligence
an	adjective–noun
ASL	American Sign Langugage
CARIN	competition among relations in nominals (model)
CE	clarification ellipsis
CG	Construction Grammar
CM	catious monotonicity
CP	Context Principle
CPL	compositional (view of) protolanguage
CPM	composite prototype model
CTF	cognitive transititon function
CTM	Computational Theory of Mind
DC	Direct Compositionality
DC	dynamical cognition (framework)
DCTF	diachronic cognitive-transition function
DP	determiner phrase
DP	default inheritance of prototypical properties
DRS	Discourse Representation Structure
DRT	Discourse Representation Theory
DS	default to the compositional stereotype strategy
E(CTM)	(Essential) Computational Theory of Mind
EEG	electroencephalograph
EFL	English as a Formal Language (Montague 1970a)
E-language	externalized language
ERPs	event-related brain potentials
GQT	Generalized Quantifier Theory
GRC	Generalized Reflexion Principle
HCH	hybrid content hypothesis
HPL	holophrastic (view of) protolanguage
HPSG	head-driven phrase structure grammar
HSS	Homomorphy of syntactic and semantic composition
iff	if and only if

IL	Intensional Logic
I-language	internalized language
i.n.s.	in the narrow sense
i.w.s.	in the wide sense
LAN	Lexicalized Adicity Number
LCS	Lexical Conceptual Structure
LDG	Lexical Decomposition Grammar
LF	logical form
LFP	Local Field Potential
lhs	left-hand side
LIF	leaky integrate-and-fire (neurons)
LISA	Learning and Inference with Schemas and Analogies
LOT	Language of Thought
LPN	lexical proper noun
M(CTM)	(Minimal) Computational Theory of Mind
MEG	magnetoencephalograph
MTS	model-theoretic semantics
N	noun
NEF	Neural Engineering Framework
NP	noun phrase
NSM	Natural Semantic Metalanguage
OSV	object–subject–verb [word order]
PC	Principle of Compositionality
PCA	principal component analysis
PDR	probability default reasoning
PF	phonetic form
POSSE	Property of Smallest Sentential Entourage
PTQ	The Proper Treatment of Quantification in Ordinary English (Montague, 1973)
PTW	Partee, ter Meulen, and Wall (1990)
RCA	Retrieval, Composition, and Analysis
rhs	right-hand side
RM	rational monotonicity
SCAN	Semantic Composition Adicity Number
SDRT	Segmented Discourse Representation Theory
SEL	sense enumerative lexical [model]
SF	semantic form
TCS	total cognitive state
UG	Universal Grammar
V	verb
VP	verb phrase
VSA	vector symbolic architecture
VSO	verb–subject–object [word order]
wrt	with respect to

Acknowledgements

Bringing a project as comprehensive, voluminous, and protracted as this Handbook to a successful end would not have been possible without the constant encouragement and the helping hands of many people. First of all, we would like to thank John Davey of OUP, who, when approached by us some years ago with the idea and a preliminary table of contents for an anthology on compositionality (no more than 250 pages then), told us that it 'almost looked like a handbook'. He tripled the number of pages and he gave us the opportunity to publish a comprehensive handbook on compositionality in the prestigious 'Oxford Handbook of ...' series. From the beginning, our intention was to take a cross-disciplinary stance toward the project and to treat the debate on compositionality as virtually including the whole of cognitive science. Authors from all the disciplines composing cognitive science were invited so that a plurality of perspectives on compositionality is now presented here. We would like to thank all those authors. We are grateful also to an armada of anonymous reviewers whose comments significantly improved the quality of each chapter.

Helping hands were also indispensable for bringing this volume together. We all have to thank Christopher Topp, who in Bochum diligently kept track of the various manuscript versions and assisted us in formatting them. We have also been supported by Aenne Petersen, our Bochum secretary. At OUP Elmandi du Toit and Kim Allen were in charge of copy-editing and deserve to be thanked here.

Financially, work in the context of this Handbook was supported by grants from the German Research Foundation DFG (FOR 600) and the Mercator Foundation on behalf of MW as well as by grants from NWO (360-20-150) and AHRC (AH/H50009X/1) on behalf of WH.

Bochum, Durham, & Pittsburgh in July, 2011
MW, WH, & EM

The Contributors

Michael Arbib is a University Professor at the University of Southern California, and is known for his contributions to the mathematical study of systems and computation, to computational and cognitive neuroscience, and—most recently—to the Mirror System Hypothesis for the evolution of the language-ready brain. His 38 books range from *Brains, Machines and Mathematics* (1964) to *How the Brain Got Language* (OUP, 2012).

Sharon Lee Armstrong is Associate Professor of Psychology at La Salle University. She is also Associate Faculty Member at Rutgers University Center for Cognitive Science, Adjunct Scientist at Moss Rehabilitation Research Institute, and Research Associate at the Selective Mutism Research Institute. Her specializations within Cognitive Science are psycholinguistics, reasoning, and metacognition, with some applications to special populations.

Giosuè Baggio is a Post-doctoral Fellow at the International School for Advanced Studies in Trieste. His research combines electrophysiology and modelling at different levels of analysis to study the cortical dynamics of language comprehension, in particular semantics.

Andrew C. Connolly is a Post-doctoral Fellow at Dartmouth College, Department of Psychological and Brain Sciences. He earned his Ph.D. in Psychology at the University of Pennsylvania. His interests include the representation of concepts and categories, especially the relationship between sensation, perception, and conception, the role of concepts in language comprehension, and the neural basis of visual category representation in the human visual cortex.

Chris Eliasmith holds a Canada Research Chair in Theoretical Neuroscience and is the director of the Centre for Theoretical Neuroscience at the University of Waterloo. He wrote the book Neural Engineering with Charles H. Anderson (MIT Press, 2003) and is currently working on a book for OUP called *How to Build a Brain*.

Andreas K. Engel is Professor of Physiology and head of the Department of Neurophysiology and Pathophysiology at the University Medical Center Hamburg-Eppendorf. He studied medicine and philosophy and graduated in medicine at the Technical University Munich in 1987. From 1987 to 1995, he worked as a staff scientist at the Max Planck Institute for Brain Research in Frankfurt, where he developed a long-standing interest in the dynamics of sensory processing, intermodal and senso-rimotor integration, and theories of perception, action, attention, and consciousness. In 1996, he established an independent group at the Max Planck Institute for Brain Research funded by the Heisenberg Program of the German Research Foundation (DFG). In 2000, he moved to the Research Center Jülich to set up the newly established Cellular Neurobiology Group at the Institute for Medicine. In 2002, he was appointed to the Chair of Neurophysiology at the University Medical Center, Hamburg-Eppendorf.

Tim Fernando has been a lecturer at Trinity College Dublin since October 1999, having earned his Ph.D. under Solomon Feferman and Jon Barwise at Stanford University, and been a post-doctoral associate of Hans Kamp in Stuttgart.

Lila R. Gleitman is Professor Emerita at the University of Pennsylvania (Department of Psychology) and Rutgers University (RUCCS), and she was co-Director of Penn's Institute for Research in Cognitive Science from 1982 to 2000. She is a Past President of the Linguistic Society of America and of the Society for Philosophy and Psychology. She has written extensively on language acquisition, the mental lexicon, and the putative effects of language on perception and cognition.

Peter Hagoort is Professor of Cognitive Neuroscience at the Radboud University Nijmegen, director of the Donders Institute for Brain, Cognition, and Behaviour, Centre for Cognitive Neuroimaging and director of the Max Planck Institute for Psycholinguistics. His group studies the way complex language skills such as reading, listening, and speaking are fixed in the human brain.

James Hampton read Natural Sciences at Cambridge, and has a Ph.D. from University College London. Based at City University London, he has also held visiting posts at Stanford, Cornell, Chicago (as a Senior Fulbright Scholar), Yale, ENS Paris, and NYU. He has published over 50 articles on the psychology of concepts and categorization. He has long been associated with the development of prototype theory and its application to problems of conceptual combination, vagueness, and reasoning.

Heidi Harley is Professor in the Linguistics department at the University of Arizona. She works on lexical semantics, syntax, and the syntax/morphology interface, and has published on these topics in English, Japanese, Irish, Italian, and Hiaki (Yaqui). Her work has appeared in *Linguistic Inquiry*, *Language*, and *Lingua*, among others.

Wolfram Hinzen is Professor of Philosophy at the University of Durham. Before that he was an assistant professor at Regensburg University and a senior lecturer at the University of Amsterdam. He is the author of *Mind Design and Minimal Syntax* and *An Essay on Names and Truth* (OUP, 2006 and 2007).

Wilfrid Hodges taught mathematics at London University (Bedford College and Queen Mary) from 1968 to 2006. He has published five textbooks and over 100 papers and articles in mathematical logic and related areas, mainly in mathematical model theory and formal aspects of semantics. He now works on medieval Arabic discussions of logic and semantics. He is a Fellow of the British Academy.

Terry Horgan has been Professor of Philosophy at the University of Arizona since 2002. He writes articles in metaphysics, epistemology, mind, and metaethics. His publications include, with J. Tienson, *Connectionism and the Philosophy of Psychology* (MIT Press, 1996) and, with M. Potrc, *Austere Realism: Contextual Semantics Meets Minimal Ontology* (MIT, 2008).

Pauline Jacobson is Professor of Cognitive and Linguistic Sciences at Brown University. She has also held visiting appointments at Ohio State University and Harvard University. Her books include *The Syntax of Crossing Coreference Sentences* (Garland, 1980), *The Nature of Syntactic Representation,* co-edited with G. K. Pullum (Reidel, 1982), and *Direct Compositionality* co-edited with Chris Barker (OUP, 2007).

Theo M. V. Janssen (ILLC, University of Amsterdam) studied mathematics, with logic as a specialization, and general linguistics as a second subject. His dissertation was about Montague grammar, a framework for dealing in a compositional way with the semantics of natural language. His research falls in the interdisciplinary field of logic, natural language semantics, computer science, and the philosophy of language and has compositionality as leading theme.

Martin L. Jönsson is a philosopher of language. He received his Ph.D. from Lund University where his dissertation 'On Compositionality' was awarded the King Oscar II's scholarship for best dissertation in the humanities. He is also a Fulbright Alumnus, having spent a year at Rutgers University. His main research interests are compositionality and expressive power. His general interests also include metaphysics, logic, and categorization.

Simon Kirby is Professor of Language Evolution at the University of Edinburgh where he co-founded the Language Evolution and Computation Research Unit which has pioneered the application of computational, mathematical, and experimental techniques to traditional issues in language acquisition, change, and evolution. The overall goal is to develop a theory of language as a complex adaptive system operating on multiple timescales. To this end, he has developed the Iterated Learning framework for language evolution.

Marcus Kracht obtained his Ph.D. in mathematical logic at the Free University of Berlin in 1992. He was appointed Assistant Professor of Computational and Mathematical Linguistics at UCLA in 2002 where be became Associate Professor in 2006. Since 2008 he has been Professor of Computational and Mathematical Linguistics at Bielefeld University. He is the author of *Interpreted Languages and Compositionality* (Springer, 2011).

Michiel van Lambalgen is Professor of Logic and Cognitive Science at the University of Amsterdam. His main research interest is in logical modelling of cognitive processes, especially language comprehension and infant cognition. He is co-author, with Fritz Hamm, of *The Proper Treatment of Events* (Wiley, 2004) and, with Keith Stenning, of *Human Reasoning and Cognitive Science* (MIT Press, 2008).

Lisa Lederer is a Ph.D. student in the Department of History and Philosophy of Science at the University of Pittsburgh, where she is also pursuing a Master's in Bioethics. Her work is currently focused on the history and philosophy of psychology, especially as they relate to ethical issues in psychology and neuroscience research.

Sebastian Löbner first graduated in mathematics and then took a Ph.D. in General Linguistics at Düsseldorf University. He is now Professor at the Department of General Linguistics there. His main field of research is linguistic semantics; he has published on the semantics of NPs, quantification and negation, intensional verbs and dual operators, and on semantics in general. Löbner is heading the interdisciplinary Coordinated Research Centre 991 on 'The Structure of Representations in Language, Cognition, and Science' financed by the Deutsche Forschungsgemeinschaft.

Edouard Machery is Associate Professor in the Department of History and Philosophy of Science at the University of Pittsburgh, a resident fellow of the Center for Philosophy of Science (University of Pittsburgh), a member of the Center for the Neural Basis of Cognition (CMU and Pittsburgh), and an associate editor of the *European Journal for Philosophy of Science*. He is the author of *Doing without Concepts* (OUP, 2009).

Alexander Maye studied computer science in Dresden and Berlin, where his interest in computational models of vision developed. In his graduate studies he investigated the dynamics of models of neuronal oscillations, and received his Ph.D. in 2002 from the Institute of Technology in Berlin. After working on brain atlases at the Zuse Institute in Berlin, he went to the University Medical Center Hamburg-Eppendorf to combine computational modelling and electrophysiological studies of the human brain.

Peter Pagin received his Ph.D. in 1987 at Stockholm University, where he has been Professor of Philosophy since 2002. He has published papers on compositionality, vagueness, assertion, and other topics in the philosophy of language.

Francis Jeffry Pelletier was Mellon Chair in Cognitive Science at the University of Rochester, 1990–2; Professor of Philosophy and Computing Science at the University of Alberta, 1992–2003; and Canada Research Chair in Cognitive Science and Professor of Philosophy and Linguistics at Simon Fraser University from 2003 until 2009. He now teaches at the University of Alberta and writes on issues of the philosophy of language and logic, formal semantics, cognitive science, and artificial intelligence, as well as some specific topics that overlap with these areas (e.g., mass terms and generics).

Martina Penke is Professor of Psycholinguistics at the University of Cologne. She obtained her doctoral degree in linguistics at the University of Düsseldorf and has held positions at the Universities of Düsseldorf, Hamburg, Konstanz, and Ghent. Her research focuses on phonology, morphology, and syntax in normal/impaired language acquisition, language disorders, and language processing as well as on issues regarding the mental/neural representation of language. She has coordinated and is involved in several research projects.

Paul M. Pietroski is Professor of Linguistics and Philosophy at the University of Maryland. His interests lie at the intersection of the two fields. He is the author of *Causing Actions* (OUP 2000) and *Events and Semantic Architecture* (OUP 2005). He is currently working on a book (also for OUP) currently entitled *Semantics without Truth Values*.

Jesse Prinz is a Distinguished Professor of Philosophy at the Graduate Center of the City University of New York and an Adjunct Professor at the University of North Carolina, Chapel Hill where he taught until 2009. He has research interests in cognitive science, philosophy of psychology, philosophy of language, moral psychology, and aesthetics. His books include *Gut Reactions: A Perceptual Theory of Emotion* (OUP, 2004) and *The Emotional Construction of Morals* (OUP, 2007). He also has two forthcoming titles: *Beyond Human Nature* (London: Penguin; New York: Norton, 2011) and *The Conscious Brain* (OUP, 2011). He has published numerous articles on concepts, emotions, morals, consciousness, and other topics.

James Pustejovsky holds the TJX/Feldberg Chair in Computer Science at Brandeis University, where he conducts research in the theoretical and computational modelling of language, specifically: computational semantics; lexical meaning; knowledge representation; temporal and event reasoning; and spatial semantics. He also directs the Laboratory of Linguistics and Computation and is Chair of the Language and Linguistics Program. His work in Generative Lexicon Theory explores the computational nature of compositionality in natural language, while focusing on the interface between lexical semantics and compositional mechanisms in language. Pustejovsky has been active in developing semantic annotation standards for temporal and event information in natural language, and is the chief architect of TimeML. He is currently involved in spatial reasoning and annotation and is editor of the ISO work item, ISO-Space.

François Récanati is the Director of Institut Jean-Nicod (Ecole Normale Supérieure, Paris). He is also a research fellow at CNRS and a professorial fellow at EHESS and the University of St Andrews. He has taught in several major universities around the world. His recent publications include *Literal Meaning* (CUP, 2004), *Perspectival Thought* (OUP, 2007), and *Truth-Conditional Pragmatics* (OUP, 2010). He is General Editor of the OUP series, *Context and Content*.

Gabriel Sandu is currently Professor of Theoretical Philosophy at the University of Helsinki. He has been a Research Director (CNRS, Paris) and Professor of Philosophy at Paris 1, Sorbonne. His publications include *On the Methodology of Linguistics*, co-authored with Jaakko Hintikka (Blackwell, 1991), *Entre Logique et Langage*, co-authored with François Rivenc (Vrin, 2009), *Logic, Games and Computation: A strategic approach* *to IF-languages*, co-authored with Allen Mann and Merlijn Sevenster (CUP, 2011), and numerous articles on the connection between games and language.

Gerhard Schurz is Chair of Theoretical Philosophy at the University of Düsseldorf. Having studied chemistry and philosophy at the University of Graz he received his Habilitation in Philosophy in 1989 at the University of Salzburg, where he was first Assistant and then Associate Professor of Philosophy. He has been a visiting professor at the University of California at Irvine and at Yale University. His research areas are philosophy of science, logic, and cognitive science.

Kenny Smith is a lecturer in the School of Philosophy, Psychology, and Language Sciences, University of Edinburgh, with interests in the evolution of communication, human language, and the human capacity for language.

Terrence C. Stewart is a Post-doctoral Fellow at the Centre for Theoretical Neuroscience at the University of Waterloo, where he is developing scalable methods for implementing high-level cognition using biologically realistic spiking neurons. He received his Ph.D. in Cognitive Science from Carleton University (specializing in the role of computational modelling within cognitive science) and his M.Phil. from the School of Cognitive and Computing Sciences (COGS) at the University of Sussex.

Zoltán Gendler Szabó received his Ph.D. from the Massachusetts Institute of Technology and is currently Professor of Philosophy at Yale University. He works primarily on philosophy of language. He is author of *Problems of Compositionality* (Garland, 2000), editor of *Semantics versus Pragmatics* (OUP, 2005) and wrote numerous articles on the interpretation of descriptions, tense, aspect, modality, and propositional attitudes.

Markus Werning is Professor of Philosophy of Language and Cognition at the Ruhr University Bochum. He received his Ph.D. from the Heinrich-Heine University Düsseldorf and Master degrees in Philosophy and Physics from the Free University of Berlin. In his work he unites various perspectives on compositionality and theories of meaning in general, including philosophy of language, formal semantics, logic, neural modelling, and neuro-semantics. He is author of the book *The Compositional Brain: A Unification of Conceptual and Neuronal Perspectives* (Mentis, 2011).

Dag Westerståhl is Professor of Theoretical Philosophy and Logic at Stockholm University. He received his Ph.D. at the University of Gothenburg under the supervision of Per Lindström. His research areas are model theory, formal semantics, generalized quantifiers, and philosophy of logic, language, and mathematics. He is author, together with Stanley Peters, of *Quantifiers in Language and Logic* (OUP, 2006, 2008).

Edward Wisniewski is Professor of Cognitive Science at the University of North Carolina at Greensboro, USA. He was an Associate Editor of the *Journal of Experimental Psychology: Learning, Memory, and Cognition*. His research focuses on people's mental representations or concepts of everyday things. It addresses a number of interrelated issues associated with people's concepts, especially how people combine familiar concepts to produce new one.

Jing Wu was formerly Associate Professor of contrastive and cognitive linguistics at the School of Foreign Languages, Soochow University, China. Currently, she is an instructor of Chinese at the University of North Carolina at Greensboro, USA.

Dieter Wunderlich obtained a Ph.D. for his thesis 'Tense and time reference in German' at the Technische Universität, Berlin, 1969. From 1973 to 2002, he held the chair of General Linguistics in Düsseldorf. He was co-founder and first president of the German Linguistic Society 1978, and initiated, among others, the Collaborative Research Center on the Theory of the Lexicon in Düsseldorf. He developed Lexical Decomposition Grammar and Minimalist Morphology, and wrote articles and books in a number of linguistic fields.

Thomas Ede Zimmermann graduated from Konstanz University in 1987 and has since held academic positions at various universities. Since 1999, he has been Professor of Formal Semantics in the Linguistics Department of Goethe University, Frankfurt. He has made various descriptive and foundational contributions to formal semantics. His main areas of research include intensional constructions, the theory of reference, and the formal aspects of semantic complexity.

INTRODUCTION

WOLFRAM HINZEN, MARKUS WERNING,
AND EDOUARD MACHERY

THE notion of compositionality was first introduced as a constraint on the relation between the syntax and the semantics of languages (Frege, 1914; Montague, 1970b). In this context compositionality demands that the meaning of every syntactically complex expression of a language (save, maybe, for idioms) be determined by the meanings of its syntactic parts and the way they are put together. Compositionality was later postulated as an adequacy condition also for other representational systems such as structures of mental concepts (see, e.g., Fodor's (1975, 1998a, 2008) Language of Thought), computer programmes (Janssen, 1986), and even neural architectures (Fodor and Pylyshyn, 1988; Smolensky, 1990/1995b). Various mathematical frameworks for compositionality have been provided (Partee et al., 1990; Hodges, 2001), and stronger and weaker versions have been formulated (Szabó, 2000a, this volume). Although the force and justification of compositionality as a requirement for representational systems is still disputed, it is fair to say that compositionality today is widely recognized as a key issue all over the cognitive sciences and remains a challenge for various models of cognition that are in an apparent conflict with it.

This Handbook brings together chapters on the issue of compositionality from formal-logical, semantic, psychological, linguistic, philosophical, and neuroscientific points of view. Our emphasis has been on the breadth of approaches to the notion, illustrating its key status in the study of language and mind today, and the need for strong interdisciplinarity in investigating it. Often regarded as a virtually defining feature for the discipline of formal semantics, compositionality has led to myriad controversies in regards to its scope, formulation, and psychological reality. This Handbook aims to provide an inroad into these controversies, by covering almost every major aspect of these controversies (with the exception of a few questions, particularly in the domain of comparative cognition, where the degree of systematicity and compositionality of the non-human animal mind is an important ongoing problem; see e.g. McGonigle and Chalmers, 2006).

All our contributors have been asked to do more than just give an overview of the issues raised by compositionality in their domain of expertise: They were invited to take a particular, perhaps even controversial, stance towards it. It is our hope that this Handbook will find an audience in the broader cognitive science community, including philosophy, linguistics, psychology, neuroscience, computer science, modelling, and logic. In the rest of the introduction, we give brief sketches of the individual contributions and their interconnections.

1 HISTORY AND OVERVIEW

Part I of this Handbook collects four contributions that introduce the debate on compositionality from historical, formal-semantical, philosophical, and linguistic points of view, respectively. The history of the notion in the nineteenth and twentieth centuries is reviewed by **Janssen**, while **Kracht** extends this history, starting from Montague's work in the 1970s and subsequent developments in semantic theory today. As Janssen shows, in the nineteenth-century, Frege's discussion of compositionality and its apparent opposite, namely contextuality, was richly embedded in nineteenth-century German discussions among psychologists, linguists, and logicians such as Trendelenburg, Wundt, and Lotze. The Principle of Contextuality maintained that, even though judgements are composed of concepts, these have meaning only in the context of the judgements. Though nowadays widely replaced by the principle of compositionality, Frege himself never quite abandoned the Principle of Contextuality. Compositionality in its contemporary form is rather a creation of Frege's student, Carnap (1947), and, later, of Montague (1970*a*, 1970*b*, 1973). Montague's seminal work, in particular, here reviewed by **Kracht**, was based on Carnap's extension–intension distinction, which replaced Frege's sense–reference distinction. **Janssen** shows that, although compositionality is a widely accepted principle in linguistic and logical practice, reasons for endorsing it are not so much principled as practical or pragmatic. **Kracht**, too, illustrates that compositionality as a method in formal-logical analysis was not a principled decision for Montague, and that it is not always clear whether his analyses were fully compositional.

Szabó, adopting a more philosophical point of view, discusses the formulation of the principle of compositionality, a difficult issue in itself. A standard formulation is (C):

(C)   The meaning of a complex expression is a function of the meanings of its constituents and the way they are combined.

As **Szabó** points out, the moment we look at this formulation, questions arise. Does 'is a function of' mean 'is determined by'? Is it meanings that are being combined, or is it syntactic constituents? Are we talking about the meanings that constituents have individually, or that they have when taken together? One sensible disambiguation of C yields a principle that, Szabó argues, makes for a useful empirical hypothesis in the study of natural language meaning: It says that, once we have fixed the individual meanings of syntactic constituents in a given expression, and have fixed its syntactic structure, there is nothing else that determines meaning. However, relevant notions involved in its formulation will themselves have to be clarified when the hypothesis is investigated. Moreover, when this hypothesis has entered various research agendas in philosophy, linguistics, and psychology, it has always been strengthened, and its strengthenings are not entirely equivalent to one another.

Zimmermann illustrates the role that compositionality has played as a constraint on semantic analysis in linguistic practice via a number of case studies, such as quantified noun phrases in object position and intensional arguments. Such problems are encountered when, given some syntactic whole that has a semantic value, the question arises what the semantic values of its immediate parts must be, if the meaning of the whole is to come out from their combination. **Zimmermann** gives an account of a number of generic strategies that have been used to overcome these problems so as to maintain compositionality. For example, the syntactic tree structure is re-analysed in such a way that the expression as a whole has different parts than it initially seemed.

2 COMPOSITIONALITY IN LANGUAGE

The primary concern of the 'linguists' principle of compositionality', as **Szabó** describes it in his contribution, is the relationship between meaning and structure. Although compositionality is very widely assumed as a constraint for this relationship, linguists and philosophers have fundamentally disagreed on whether the principle is empirically valid, and in what form it can be maintained. *Direct Compositionality* (DC) in the sense of **Jacobson**, in particular, wants to set a 'gold standard' for what this relationship is like: this standard is that the mapping of syntactic form to semantic content exploits no 'hidden' level of syntactic representation from which semantic interpretation is read off (such as the level of logical form or 'LF' explored by generative grammarians in the 1980s: see e.g. Huang, 1995). Instead, semantics reads off interpretations from the surface form of expressions directly: these (and potentially the context of use) provide all the information that is required. Cases of linguistic expressions whose meaning has been thought to require a hidden (or more abstract) level of representation are solved by assigning a more complex semantic type to the word or constituent that causes the problem. In Jacobson's view, a compositional semantics and a compositional syntax are minimally required to understand languages. Syntax is compositional in that it builds more complex well-formed expressions recursively, on the basis of smaller ones, while semantics is compositional in that it constructs the meanings of larger expressions on the basis of the meanings of smaller ones (ultimately words, or rather morphemes). Unless empirical linguistic or psychological evidence were to require it (which she argues it doesn't) nothing *else* should be needed to understand language. She proposes that the strategy of assigning a more complex semantic type to the troublesome constituent shows that one can make do with only a compositional semantics and syntax.

A quite different dimension of the compositionality problem has to do with the relations between language and thought. It is widely assumed that language expresses thought and that thoughts are made up of mental concepts under a certain mode of composition—an assumption revisited by **Hinzen** and **Pietroski** later in the volume. However, how does the composition of concepts in thought and the composition of linguistic meanings relate? **Pietroski**, adopting a Chomskyan internalist linguistic perspective, suggests that the 'adicities' (number of argument places) of concepts might differ from those of the lexical meanings of the words that label these concepts. He speculates that the lexical meanings are uniformly monadic, requiring saturation by a single argument, and that syntax, by combining the words with these meanings, simply conjoins them. In this way, language 're-formats' concepts in accordance with its own structural resources, and so as to fulfil the demands of semantic composition. For example, there are no polyadic concepts such as POKED(E,X,Y) in language, where E is a variable over events. Language rather 'decomposes' this concept into three conjoined predicates: POKED(E) & THEME(E,Y) & AGENT(E,X), where THEME and AGENT are special thematic predicates.

Traditionally, the term compositionality is used in opposition with various forms of *holism*, with which compositionality is often said to be inconsistent. Thus, if in a system the identity and properties of an object are partially determined through their relations to other objects and properties, as the holist claims, then, in an intuitive sense, the system won't be compositional—it won't be 'made up' of its parts, in such a way that the parts do not in turn depend on the whole of which they form a part. **Pelletier** surveys this important debate and distinguishes an older, ontological and metaphysical debate, on whether there are wholes that cannot be thought of as individuals or combinations of them, from the more recent debate on how some properties of wholes such as sentences are a *function* of properties of their parts (such as their meanings). Potentially, the holist's challenge is only severe when posed to the latter of the two debates just mentioned. Other problems remain for the holistic view, from a psychological and language acquisition perspective.

Holism is just one potential threat to the compositional analysis of language or thought. *Contextualism* is another, and Jerry Fodor has long argued that contextualism is inconsistent with compositionality. **Récanati** sorts out for which notions of contextualism and compositionality this is so. For example, is the same meaning of 'cut' involved in 'cutting the grass' and 'cutting the cake', which is then contributed compositionally to the content? As **Récanati** notes, the activity seems different in both cases, but then again, in a somewhat unusual context, it might actually be the same. So does context need to enter as an argument into the composition function, and will that preserve a sensible notion of compositionality? According to **Récanati**, this does indeed seem to be the case, yet not in the sense in which indexicals such as 'here' depend on context: While indexicals depend for their semantic evaluation on a process of 'saturation', the meaning of a word, though pragmatically modulated, does not depend on such a process. Yet if we factor the pragmatically modulated meanings of the parts of expressions into our notion of compositionality, a sensible version of the latter can be preserved.

Kaplan style semantics—a notion introduced by **Westerståhl** to subsume a certain class of semantic theories—takes the idea seriously that certain kinds of semantic values may depend on extra-linguistic contexts. Those semantics have in common that they permit a distinction between contexts of utterance and circumstances of evaluation. In agreement with Kaplan (1989) and Lewis (1980), their basic truth relation is the following: A sentence s is true at context c in circumstance d. For the three main kinds of semantic values, viz. characters, contents, and extensions, together with their interrelations, two versions of Kaplan style semantics are formally developed: The truth-functional version treats the contents of sentences as functions from circumstances to truth-values. The structural version, by contrast, regards the contents of sentences as structured entities, in which properties, individuals, and the like literally occur. In both versions the primary semantic value of an expression is its character: a function from contexts to contents. The evaluation of an expression at a circumstance is now relative to a context where the context of utterance determines the circumstance of evaluation. With these notions at hand, **Westerståhl** shows how even problematic phenomena like indexicals, unarticulated constituents, modulation, or pragmatic intrusion (see **Récanati**) may be dealt with in a strictly compositional, contextually compositional, or weakly contextually compositional way. The strength of the compositionality property employed depends on the kind of semantic values chosen. The only remaining challenge to the compositionality of content from the point of view of context dependence are so-called monsters.

The classical model of composition in model-theoretic semantics (Montague 1970*a*, 1973) assumes that a lexicon provides a set of basic expressions that are each assigned a lexical meaning corresponding to one of a restricted set of semantic types, to which the rules of semantic composition then apply. It could, however, be that if we have two autonomous systems of syntactic and semantic composition, the types that are respectively combined in each system do not *match*. This can happen in at least two ways. First, some lexical items don't correspond to non-decomposed meanings: They have a non-overt underlying structure from which their meaning is composed. Second, some syntactic construction types do not correspond to a single way of combining the semantic types assigned to its constituents. The first possibility is called *lexical decomposition* and is the topic of the next sub-part. As for the second possibility, **Löbner** calls it *sub-compositionality*. He argues that it is frequently instantiated in natural languages. Assuming compositionality as a methodological principle prevents us from seeing this empirical fact. Using gradation of German verbs with *sehr* ('very', 'a lot') as a case study, he shows that semantic patterns of gradation divide syntactic types of verbs into several semantic sub-types with their own sub-rules of composition, which depend on the type of lexical meaning of the verb. Having distinct syntactic sub-types corresponding to the semantic sub-types is not plausible in these instances. In line with the older evidence that Montague's (1973) definition of NPs as generalized quantifiers ignores important syntactic and semantic differences among these constructions, **Löbner**'s chapter provides new evidence that a homomorphy of composition operations in the syntactic and semantic domains, which would rule out sub-compositionality as a priori incompatible with the design of grammar, cannot be assumed.

3 COMPOSITIONALITY IN FORMAL SEMANTICS

Compositionality is frequently debated not only in philosophical and linguistic semantics, but also in theoretical psychology as well as classical and connectionist computer science, partly because it can be formalized. A number of mathematical results that link the principle of compositionality to other formal semantic principles can thus be proven. It is fair to say that compositionality is one of the most important principles of what is now called 'formal semantics'. Part III illustrates the role that the principle of compositionality plays in formal semantics and discusses some of the formal results in this field.

As a synopsis of many of the articles in this Handbook illustrates, there is no universally accepted formal definition of compositionality. However, compositionality in formal semantics is typically understood as a property of a relation, function, or morphism between the syntax and the semantics of a language. In this light, the expression 'syntactic compositionality'—sometimes used in the literature to refer to the property of languages to allow for syntactic combinations—is an oxymoron. The most widely used formal definitions of compositionality treat the syntax of a language as a single-sorted or multi-sorted algebra. In the single-sorted approach, only one carrier set—the set of terms—is assumed, and syntactic rules correspond to *partial* functions from Cartesian products of the set of terms into the set of terms. By contrast, the multi-sorted approach uses a multitude of carrier sets for the different syntactic categories. In this case, a syntactic rule corresponds to a *total* function from a product of typically two (or more than two) syntactic categories, for example the set of adjectives and the set of nouns, into some syntactic category, for example the set of noun phrases. In both the single-sorted and the multi-sorted approach, compositionality is then defined in terms of a homomorphism between the syntax algebra and a semantic algebra (see Janssen, 1986; Partee et al., 1990; Hodges, 2001; Werning, 2005b). The latter is again single-sorted—one set of meanings as carrier set—or multi-sorted—a carrier set for each semantic category. It is crucial to see here that semantic compositionality is not a property of the structure of meanings, the semantic algebra, taken in isolation. Rather, it is a property that characterizes the interaction between syntax and semantics.

Saying more about this interaction is **Hodges**'s goal in Chapter 11. The chapter has two parts—a historical one and a formal one. In the historical part, the roots of the idea of compositionality are traced back to the Aristotelian theory of meaning—as we have received it via medieval Arab philosophers like Ibn Sina and Al-Farabi. It is indeed astonishing to see how close certain passages from Al-Farabi and from the French medieval philosopher Abelard are to well-known formulations of the principle of compositionality by Frege. Returning to modern times, **Hodges** discusses various notions of a constituent or constituent structure—for example Bloomfield's (1933)—to come up with his own account in terms of frames (roughly speaking, complex expressions). His notion of a constituent is then used to define what he calls PTW compositionality ('PTW' is a reference to Partee, ter Meulen, and Wall, 1990). It is the property that an equivalence relation on frames possesses if and only if it is invariant with regard to the substitution of equivalent constituent expressions. Aside from ambiguity and metaphor, **Hodges** discusses whether *tahrifs* are a threat to PTW compositionality: This Arab word refers to the phenomenon that the occurrence of a word in a sentence has its meanings changed by its context in the sentence. How does this phenomenon relate to Frege's Principle of Contextuality that the meaning of a word is what it contributes to the meaning of a sentence? This question leads **Hodges** to the so-called extension problem: Given that one has already assigned meanings to some subset of the set of expressions in a language by some meaning function, what are the conditions under which one can extend this original meaning function to the rest of the language? Hodges's (2001) famous extension theorem states that there exists an up-to-equivalence unique extension if the following conditions are fulfilled: (i) The subset is cofinal in the total set of expressions of the language: Every expression of the total set is a constituent of some expression of the subset. (ii) The original and the extended meaning function are compositional. (iii) The original and the extended meaning function are Husserlian: No two synonyms belong to different semantic categories. (iv) The extended meaning function is fully abstract with regard to the original meaning function: For every pair of non-synonymous expressions of the total set, there exists a witness for their meaning difference in the subset. Such a witness is a complex expression that contains one of the non-synonymous expressions as a constituent and its substitution by the other would either change the meaning of the complex expression or render it meaningless (Werning, 2004).

Together with other formal questions on compositionality, the extension problem is also discussed by **Sandu** in Chapter 12. **Sandu** begins with a number of equivalent formulations of the principle of compositionality and critically reviews a number of formal triviality results associated with it. The chapter then focuses on the relation of the principle of compositionality to the Principle of Contextuality before presenting a number of compatibility and incompatibility results. The former, for example, show how one can devise a compositional interpretation that agrees with assumed facts about the meanings of complex noun phrases. He illustrates this strategy with problem cases such as the extensions of combinations with non-intersecting adjectives like 'big' (see also Récanati's contribution to this Handbook) or the prototypes of certain noun–noun compositions like 'pet fish' (see also Prinz's and Wisnewski's contributions). The incompatibility results turn on the question of whether the principle of compositionality is consistent with other semantic principles. The sling shot argument (Gödel, 1944; Davidson, 1984; Neale, 1995), for example, purports to show that compositionality conflicts with the assumption that two sentences, though both true, may well denote distinct facts. In the case of Independent Friendly Logics (Hintikka and Sandu, 1997), it can be shown that compositionality and the semantic assumption that every formula is associated with a set of assignments cannot be reconciled. Finally, **Sandu** considers the question of equivalent compositional interpretations in the context of the debate between Lewis (1980) and Stalnaker (1999) on the problem of indexicals.

In Chapter 13, **Fernando** extends the notion of compositionality beyond the sentence level and applies it to discourses. At the level of discourses, compositionality seems in tension with the idea that the meaning of a sentence is intimately related, if not identical, to its truth-conditions. If one substitutes truth-conditionally equivalent sentences in a discourse, the referents of anaphors may change or get lost. This would result in a change of the meaning of the discourse even though compositionality grants that synonymous sentences should be substitutable *salva significatione*. Anaphor resolution is not the only problem in the attempt to give a compositional semantics for discourses. Discourses also create a new kind of ambiguity that is neither lexical nor syntactic: A sequence of two or more sentences may, for example, be interpreted as a temporal succession or a causal explanation. Fernando gives an overview of a number of formal-semantic theories for discourses and proposes to shift from a model-theoretic treatment of Discourse Representation Theory (DRT, Kamp and Reyle, 1993) to a proof-theoretic account.

4 LEXICAL DECOMPOSITION

Although compositionality as understood in most formal-semantic approaches concerns the contribution of words and syntactic constituents to the determination of the meaning of a complex expression, there is also a question about the determination of the meanings of the lexical constituents themselves. Since Generative Semantics in the early 1970s (Lakoff, 1970; McCawley, 1971; Ross, 1972), many theories have proposed that words such as 'kill' are internally complex, and that their relations to other words such as the relation of 'kill' to 'dead', depends on the internal structure of these words. According to these theories, most lexical items and particularly verbs are decomposed both syntactically and semantically. The lexical atomism of Fodor (1970) and Fodor and Lepore (2002) famously contradicts this idea, yet this part of this Handbook shows that variants of the original decompositional position are very much alive.

The major approaches that have tried to improve on the original ideas of the generative semanticists are surveyed by **Wunderlich**. These approaches make various syntactic and architectural assumptions, and differ on what the true atoms of semantic composition are taken to be. Among these theories, one finds Montague's (1960, 1970b) and Dowty's (1979) meaning-postulate approach, Jackendoff's (1990) conceptual semantics, which proposes atoms such as EVENT, STATE, ACTION, PLACE, PATH,

PROPERTY, and AMOUNT, Generative Lexicon Theory (Pustejovsky, 1995; this volume), which aims to account for the multiplicity of readings of polysemous words, Lexical Decomposition Grammar (Gamerschlag, 2005; Wunderlich, 1997*b*), which distinguishes between semantic form (SF) and conceptual structure in Jackendoff's sense and decomposes lexical concepts in complex hierarchical structures or templates, Lexical Conceptual Structure as elaborated in the work of Levin and Rappaport Hovav (1991, 1995), the Natural Semantic Metalanguage (NSM) account of Wierzbicka (see e.g. Goddard and Wierzbicka 2002), which analyses concepts/words by reductive paraphrases using a small collection of universal semantic primes, the Neo-Davidsonian account (Krifka, 1989; Davidson, 1967*a*; Pietroski, 2002, this volume), and the more strongly syntactocentric approach of Hale and Keyser (2002). All of these theories stand in contrast to the strictly atomist position of Fodor and Lepore (1998, 1999), which objects to every form of lexical decomposition and takes the meaning of every morpheme as primitive.

Wunderlich offers a number of empirical arguments in favour of the Lexical Decomposition Grammar (LGD) approach. For example, it elegantly accounts for lexical alternative, as when intransitive verbs like 'break' or 'gallop' have transitive and causative variants: In the causative variant, an additional, non-overt, CAUSE (or ACT) predicate is arguably present in the underlying meaning of the verb. Another advantage is that the arguments of a verb cross-linguistically appear to be *hierarchically ordered*: A decomposition like the Neo-Davidsonian one, which is 'flat' in the sense that it merely adds a number of conjoined predicates to a given event variable, cannot account for such hierarchies. A further argument is provided through the behaviour of denominal verbs such as 'saddle', 'box', or 'shelve'. In these cases, the incorporated noun provides a lexical root meaning that enters into one of a number of templates restricting the verbs that can be formed from such nouns as well as their possible meanings. The complementarity of manner and result in possible verb meanings is also predicted, as is the near-equivalence of Possession and Location in many languages: For instance, a house can be said to *have* three bathrooms, while the bathrooms can also be said to be *in* the house.

Like Wunderlich, **Harley** is convinced that there is extensive cross-linguistic empirical evidence against the atomist approach, and hence for some form of lexical decomposition. Taking a more syntax-centred approach rooted in recent minimalist syntax, **Harley** lays out a framework meant to make Generative Semantics finally work. As she notes, if words of categories N, V, and A are not semantic primitives, a first problem affecting lexical atomism is solved: that it is not clear how structureless atoms can ever be learned. However, this problem returns (and remains unsolved) with the irreducible meanings of the lexical roots: the decompositional buck has to stop somewhere. Once entering a syntactic derivation, the syntactic category of such roots is only gradually determined as the derivation proceeds, and syntactic dependents are introduced by additional, phonologically empty syntactic heads: For instance, the transitive verb 'kill' acquires its transitive status through a silent syntactic head translatable as 'CAUSE' or 'MAKE' (as in MAKE John BECOME dead). Arguably, this syntactic decomposition, which is not visible in the surface form of the word 'kill' in English, is overtly manifest in the morphosyntax of many languages. With more fine-grained distinctions between syntactic heads and their projections at our disposal, an ambiguity in sentences like 'John opened the door for 5 minutes' can now be accounted for in purely structural terms. **Harley** also presents case studies of the decompositions of 'have', 'give', and 'get'. Surveying all of Fodor's classical arguments against such an approach, **Harley** concludes that these objections can be successfully met.

Hinzen, taking a slightly different stance, argues that the debate for or against lexical decomposition nonetheless continues. He picks up a topic addressed by **Pietroski** as well, namely the relation between lexical decomposition in language and the atomicity of concepts in human thought. If language were a guide to the structure of concepts, the theory of syntax might be a theory of what structures our concepts have. If so, concepts that the computational system of language treats as atomic or structureless, should be structureless at the level of thought as well. **Hinzen** argues that evidence for the syntactic decomposition of lexical verbs is very considerable; however, classical evidence leading to the conclusion that lexicalized concepts in general are not internally structured remains powerful as well. This presents us with a dilemma: Syntactic decomposition appears to be real, and we expect the relevant syntactic decompositions to be compositionally interpreted; but this conflicts with the classical evidence Fodor provides for lexical atomism in semantics. **Hinzen** suggests that only rethinking the architecture of grammar will address this problem.

The part closes with a survey by **Pustejovsky** of the approach to 'co-composition', a term that refers to the process of how compositional processes determined by the phrasal structure of an expression are supplemented by additional interpretive mechanisms at the interface between lexicon and syntactic structure. These concern productive ways in which meaning can be determined systematically even when the semantic types of particular ambiguous predicates are fixed. For example, **Pustejovsky** notes that the verb 'throw' has different senses in different grammatical contexts, in which it can have the senses of 'propel' (as in 'Mary threw the ball to John'), or of 'organize' (as in 'John threw a party'), or of 'create' (as in 'Mary threw breakfast together quickly'). But even when such senses each correspond to unique semantic types that can as such enter compositional processes of function application, there is an abundant number of cases in language where predicates are coerced to change their types, as in *Mary began the book*, where *begin* selects an event rather than an object. Generative lexicon theory accounts for meaning determination in such cases by positing a structure of 'Qualia' inside lexical items, which act as operators shifting the types of predicates in systematic and compositional ways. The co-compositional approach also generalizes to a number of other otherwise problematic constructions, such as subjects interpreted as agentive when they normally are not, or the various senses that a verb such as 'to open' can have, depending on what kind of objects it takes as its complement.

5 THE COMPOSITIONALITY OF MIND

Part V of the Handbook focuses on the psychology of concept combination. In psychology, concepts are those bodies of knowledge used in the processes underlying higher-cognitive competencies, such as categorization, induction, or analogy-making (see Machery, 2009 for discussion). For about thirty years, psychologists have examined whether in addition to the concepts that are permanently stored in long-term memory (e.g. DOG, WATER, GOING TO THE DENTIST) people are able to produce new concepts on the fly by combining the concepts they already possess. Such a process is typically called 'concept combination'. For instance, psychologists wonder whether people are able to combine their bodies of knowledge about Harvard graduates and about carpenters to create a body of knowledge about Harvard graduates who are carpenters (Kunda et al., 1990) that could be used to make inductive inferences about Harvard graduates who are carpenters or to explain their behaviour.

Part V reviews the findings about concept combination as well as the models that have been developed to explain these. The first two chapters, respectively by **James Hampton** and **Martin Jönsson** and by **Edward Wisniewski** and **Jing Wu**, review the most important findings about concept combination and propose two distinct models to account for them. The two following chapters focus on a well-known criticism of the field of concept combination in the psychology of concepts. **Lila Gleitman, Andrew Connolly**, and **Sharon Armstrong** argue that prototype theories of concepts are inadequate to explain how concepts combine, while **Jesse Prinz** defends the psychological research on concept combination against a range of criticisms. Finally, **Edouard Machery** and **Lisa Lederer** argue that psychologists have overlooked a range of ways in which concepts might combine in a fast and frugal manner.

In 'Typicality and compositionality: the logic of combining vague concepts', **Hampton** and **Jönsson** endorse the prototype theory of concepts, and they review a range of important findings suggesting that prototypes compose. It appears that people's judgements about whether an object belongs to the interpart of two classes A and B does not depend on whether it is judged to belong to these two classes; rather, it is a function of its similarity to a prototype resulting from the combination of the prototypes of A and B. Furthermore, **Hampton** and **Jönsson** describe in detail the model of prototype combination developed by Hampton in an important series of articles starting in the 1980s. Finally, they discuss Connolly et al.'s (2007) recent work on concept combination, which has challenged the claim that prototypes combine (this work is also discussed in Gleitman and colleagues', Prinz's, and Machery and Lederer's chapters).

Wisniewski and **Wu**'s chapter, 'Emergency!!!! Challenges to a compositional understanding of noun–noun combinations', examines how speakers interpret novel noun–noun combinations (e.g. 'zebra football' or 'roller coaster dinner') with a special focus on speakers of English and Chinese. Wisniewski and Wu show that speakers typically attribute to the members of the extension of novel noun–noun combinations (e.g. 'zebra football') 'emergent properties' (see also Hampton and Jönsson's chapter)—viz. properties that are not attributed to the members of the extensions of the nouns (e.g. 'zebra' and 'football'). They then review the model of concept combination developed by Wisniewski in a series of groundbreaking articles before showing that this model can account for the phenomenon of emergent features.

In 'Can prototype representations support composition and decomposition?' **Gleitman, Connolly,** and **Armstrong** challenge the prototype theory of concepts, arguing especially that the prototype theory of concepts fails to predict how complex expressions such as 'quacking ducks' are interpreted. They review and elaborate on the recent findings by Connolly et al. (2007) that have been influential in the recent debates about concept combination.

Prinz's 'Regaining composure: a defence of prototype compositionality' defends the claim that prototypes combine against the philosophical objections developed by Jerry Fodor and the more empirical criticisms developed by Connolly, Gleitman, and Armstrong. While Fodor gives numerous examples of complex concepts (e.g. PINK TENNIS BALLS SILKSCREENED WITH PORTRAITS OF HUNGARIAN CLOWNS) that do not seem to involve complex prototypes produced out of other prototypes, Prinz argues that Fodor's argument can be blocked by distinguishing the claim that prototypes can be combined from the claim that prototypes are always combined. Appealing to the model of prototype combination developed in *Furnishing the Mind* (Prinz, 2002), which draws in part on Hampton's research, he then shows how prototypes can be combined.

In 'Simple heuristics for concept combination', **Machery** and **Lederer** review critically three influential models of concept combination (Smith et al.'s (1988*b*); Hampton's, and Costello and Keane's). They note that these models have not paid much attention to the reason why complex concepts are produced (to categorize, to draw an induction, etc.), and they propose that complex concepts might be produced differently depending on the context in which they are produced. They also note that many of the hypothesized processes of concept combination are complex and resource-intensive. By contrast, taking their cue from the Fast-and-Frugal-Heuristics research programme (Gigerenzer et al., 1999), **Machery** and **Lederer** argue that concept combination is likely to be underwritten by several distinct processes, each of which produces complex concepts in a fast and frugal way, and they describe several such processes.

6 EVOLUTIONARY AND COMMUNICATIVE SUCCESS OF COMPOSITIONAL STRUCTURES

Part VI is concerned with the evolution of compositional linguistic systems and the utility of compositional systems. On the basis of the communicative systems found in living primates, it is natural to speculate that the systems of signs used by our ancestor species during the evolution of hominins were either non-compositional (see, e.g., Cheney and Seyfarth, 1990 on the signs used by baboons) or had only a primitive form of compositionality (recent research by Arnold and Zuberbühler, 2006, suggests that putty-nosed monkeys can combine some sounds in a meaningful way; see also Ouattara et al., 2009, on Campbell's monkeys; and see McGonigle and Chalmers, 2006 for general discussion). The compositionality of human languages raises the question of how compositionality evolved and of what benefits compositionality brings about.

This part reviews the main controversies about the evolution of compositionality and introduces some new hypotheses about the utility of compositional systems. The first two chapters are mostly focused on the evolution of compositionality. **Michael Arbib** describes the holophrasis–compositionality debate for protolanguage, while **Kenny Smith** and **Simon Kirby** describe two possible mechanisms that explain the evolution of compositional languages, the first of which appeals to biological evolution and the second to cultural evolution. The following two chapters are concerned with the utility of compositional systems. **Peter Pagin** examines the benefits brought about by compositional linguistic systems, while **Gerhard Schurz** explains why people possess prototypes and combine them by appealing to the natural evolution of species and the cultural evolution of artefacts.

In 'Compositionality and holophrasis: from action and perception through protolanguage to language', **Arbib** argues that natural languages are not properly said to *be* compositional; rather, they *have* compositionality. While the meanings of component expressions contribute to the meaning of the expressions that contain them (e.g. sentences), they do not determine it entirely. He then moves on to discuss the status of compositionality in the hypothesized protolanguage. Protolanguage is the system of signs used by hominids before the evolution of natural languages. According to what **Arbib** calls 'the compositional view', prototolanguages were made of words, but lacked syntax. Protolanguages were thus quite similar to pidgins, where words are merely juxtaposed. The evolution of compositional languages merely consisted in adding syntax to already existing words. By contrast, the 'holophrastic view', which is defended by **Arbib**, holds that in protolanguages communicative acts were unitary words and could not be decomposed into concatenated words.

Smith and **Kirby**'s chapter, 'Compositionality and linguistic evolution', compares two approaches to the evolution of compositionality—one that appeals to biological evolution, one that focuses on cultural evolution. They first discuss critically Pinker and Bloom's (1990) approach to biological evolution. By contrast, they hypothesize that compositionality is socially learned, and they then review numerous models explaining how cultural evolution could have selected for compositional languages.

Pagin's 'Communication and the complexity of semantics' begins by challenging the traditional idea that compositionality is required for a language to be learnable. This challenge immediately raises the following question: If the function of compositionality is not to make languages learnable, why are languages compositional? **Pagin** proposes that the main benefit of compositionality is to enable speakers to interpret complex expressions quickly and efficiently, while quick interpretation is needed for successful communication (see Machery and Lederer's chapter in Part V for a related discussion of simplicity and speed). To support this hypothesis, he argues that compositional semantics tend to minimize computational complexity.

In 'Prototypes and their composition from an evolutionary point of view', **Schurz** explains why, given the (biological or cultural) evolution of species and artefacts, prototypes are an efficient way of representing classes, and he extends this argument to the combination of prototypes. **Schurz's** argument for the existence and utility of prototypes should be read in conjunction with the discussion of prototypes in Part V (see, particularly, Hampton and Jönsson's, Gleitman and colleagues', and Prinz's chapters).

7 NEURAL MODELS OF COMPOSITIONAL REPRESENTATION

In his programmatic article 'On the proper treatment of connectionism', Smolensky (1988a) made the provocative claim that connectionism does not only provide us with a good biological model of information flow among single neurons or larger groups of neurons, but may well give explanations on the cognitive level of information processing. However, it needed Fodor and Pylyshyn's (1988) empathic reply to define the agenda for a new debate—the debate between classicism and connectionism. It continues to this day. The crucial questions are: (i) What are the defining features of the 'cognitive level' of information processing? (ii) How close do connectionist architectures in principle come to fulfilling these features? (iii) Are the connectionist architectures in question really biologically plausible? And (iv) what is the surplus value that connectionist models contribute to the explanation of cognitive processes? A mere implementation of classical architectures would be too little. Fodor and Pylyshyn argue that information processes on the cognitive level have to be accounted for by reference to a representational structure that is compositional, productive, and systematic. Defenders of the connectionist perspective on cognition have since either denied or weakened one or more of those structural requirements or they have tried to show how connectionist architectures might fulfil them.

In Chapter 27, **Horgan** introduces a non-classical notion of compositionality and argues that a dynamical-cognition framework satisfying non-classical compositionality might provide a foundation for cognitive science. The kind of compositionality **Horgan** has in mind is non-classical in at least two respects: First, compositional structure in the system of representations need not be tractably computable. Second, compositional structure does not require separately tokenable constituent-representations. **Horgan's** notion of non-classical compositionality thus does not primarily contrast with the formal notion of compositionality used, for example, in formal semantics, where compositionality just implies the existence of a homomorphous mapping between syntax and semantics. It rather addresses something that one might call 'Fodorian compositionality', a cluster of ideas that not only involves the notion that the semantic value of a complex representation is a structure-dependent function of the semantic values of its constituents, but also the postulate that representational constituents be separately tokenable and processes over representations be tractably computable. The dynamical-cognition framework treats cognition in terms of total occurrent cognitive states that are mathematically realized as points in a high-dimensional dynamical system. These mathematical points, in turn, are physically realized by total-activation states of a neural network with specific connection weights. **Horgan**'s dynamical-cognition framework opposes the classicist assumption that cognitive-state transitions conform to a tractably computable transition over cognitive states. **Horgan** has in mind systematically content-sensitive cognitive-state transitions that accommodate lots of relevant information without explicitly representing it during cognitive processing.

A psycholinguistic test case for the controversy between classicism and connectionism, analysed by **Penke** in Chapter 28, are the different processing models of linguistic inflections, such as the past tense formation in English (Pinker, 1999). According to the classical symbolic view, morphologically complex word forms are structurally composed out of component parts by the application of a mental rule that combines a word stem (*laugh*) with an affix (*-ed*). Connectionist approaches deny that regular inflection is based on a compositional mental operation assuming instead that regular inflected forms are stored in an associative network structure. In the classical picture a dual mechanism is postulated for regular and irregular verb forms, viz. semantic composition and, respectively, associative memory. The challenge for connectionism is to provide a unified model for both regular and irregular verb forms and so demonstrate its superiority over classicist models.

In Chapter 29, **Stewart** and **Eliasmith** discuss the biological plausibility of recent proposals for the implementation of compositionality in local and distributed connectionist networks. In particular Hummel and Holyoak's (2003) LISA architecture and the neural blackboard architectures of van der Velde and de Kamps (2006) are reviewed. **Stewart** and **Eliasmith** then turn to their own model, which combines a vector symbolic architecture (VSA) with a neural engineering framework. The core idea of vector symbolic architectures, which goes back to Smolensky's (1995*b*) Integrated Connectionist Symbolic Architecture, is to map a semantic structure into a vector algebra by a homomorphism. The vector algebra contains role and filler vectors. The filler vector corresponds to lexical concepts and the role vectors to thematic roles. An operation of binding is achieved by some kind of multiplication of a role vector and a filler vector and encodes the fact that a certain lexical concept fills a certain thematic role (e.g. the agent or theme role of an event). An operation of merging, typically vector addition, allows the generation of a complex role-filler structure where various lexical concepts play different thematic roles. This operation of binding and merging are recursive and thus warrant productivity. The homomorphous mapping guarantees compositionality. The different VSAs mainly differ in the choice of the merging operation. While Smolensky uses tensor multiplication, **Stewart** and **Eliasmith** argue for the better biological plausibility of cyclic convolution. The model remains symbolic since a semantic constituent relation can be defined for the vector algebra using an operation of unbinding.

The idea of neuro-emulative semantics is a radically different, non-symbolic proposal of how to achieve compositionality in connectionist networks. It is based on the mechanism of neural synchronization. Building on empirical evidence on object-related neural synchrony in the cortex and topologically structured cortical feature maps, presented by **Engel** and **Maye** in Chapter 30, **Werning** develops the idea of neuro-emulative semantics in Chapter 31 (see also Werning, 2003*a*, 2005*a*). The approach incorporates the Gestalt principles of psychology and uses oscillatory recurrent neural networks as a mathematical model. The semantics to be developed is structurally analogous to model-theoretical semantics. However, unlike model-theoretical semantics, it regards meanings as set-theoretical constructions not of denotations, but of their neural counterparts, their emulations. Objects are emulated by oscillatory network activity induced by bottom-up or top-down mechanisms. These oscillations are able to track and represent objects in the environment. The fact that objects have certain properties is emulated by the fact that those oscillations pertain to various cortical features maps. On these maps, neurons encode properties of various attribute dimensions like colour, orientation, direction of movement, etc. Synchronous oscillatory activity provides a mechanism of binding and allows for the emulation of one and the same property bundle, whereas anti-synchronous oscillatory activity corresponds to the emulation of distinct property bundles and hence distinct objects. Exploiting the isomorphism between model-theoretical semantics and neuro-emulative semantics, compositionality theorems can be proven.

The Handbook concludes with a neurolinguistic outlook presented in Chapter 32 by **Baggio, van Lambalgen**, and **Hagoort**. Can we reformulate compositionality as a processing principle such that we will be in a position to test it empirically? Does the comprehension of sentences by humans really proceed in a compositional way? **Baggio, van Lambalgen**, and **Hagoort** take the main motivation for compositionality to be an easing in the burden of storage. They review a number of empirical data that include neurolinguistic EEG experiments and involve among others semantic illusions, the difference between world knowledge and semantic knowledge, fictional discourse, semantic attraction, and coercion. To account for those data, **Baggio, van Lambalgen**, and **Hagoort** argue, it is often necessary to postulate an increase of storage if one wants to stick to compositionality as a processing principle. This, however, goes against the main motivation of compositionality. They concede that compositionality remains effective as an explanation of cases in which processing complexity increases due to syntactic factors only. However, it apparently falls short of accounting for situations in which complexity arises from interactions with the sentence or discourse context, perceptual cues, and stored knowledge.

PART I

HISTORY AND OVERVIEW

CHAPTER 1

....

COMPOSITIONALITY: ITS HISTORIC CONTEXT

....

THEO M. V. JANSSEN

1.1 INTRODUCTION

....

The *principle of compositionality*, reads, in a formulation that is standard nowadays (Partee, 1984: 281):

> The meaning of a compound expression is a function of the meanings of its parts and of the way they are syntactically combined.

One finds a principle like this in all fields of science that deal with language and its relation with meaning. It is found in philosophy, logic, computer science, psychology, and most prominently in the field of semantics of natural language.

   If the principle is attributed to somebody, then this is, without exception, the German mathematician, logician, and philosopher Gottlob Frege (1848–1925). Therefore, the principle is often called 'Frege's principle'. This attribution is illustrated below by quotes from respectively a philosopher, a logician, and from linguists; for many more quotes see Pelletier (2000*a*).

> Dummett (1981*b*: 152): [In a chapter titled 'Some Theses of Frege's on Sense and Reference'. The first thesis is:] The sense of a complex is compounded out of the senses of the constituents.
>   Cresswell (1973: 19) These rules reflect an important general principle which we shall discuss later under the name *Frege's Principle*, that the meaning of the whole sentence is a function of the meanings of its parts.
>   Gazdar, Klein, Pullum, and Sag (1985: 8): Apart from such general scientific canons as maximizing the simplicity and generality of the statements in the theory, model-theoretic semanticists have attempted to adhere to a principle of compositionality, attributed to Frege, which requires that the meaning of a complex expression should be a function of the meaning of its component parts.

The aim of this contribution is to investigate the line from the nineteenth century, through Frege's works, to the appearance of the principle of compositionality in modern sciences. Some questions are: who is the source of the principle; is the attribution to Frege correct; why was compositionality introduced in the different sciences; which motivation was given?

The search for the source of the principle immediately brings us into a controversy. There is another principle, viz. 'the principle of contextuality', that can be directly traced back to Frege, and that is called 'Frege's principle' as well. It appears in the introduction of his 'Foundations of arithmetic': (Frege, 1884: x^e):

> Never ask for the meaning of a word in isolation, but only in the context of a sentence.

Pelletier (2001) describes the two (disjoined!) philosophical communities in which the name *Frege's principle* is used (for these different principles). This situation is remarkable because there is a clear tension between the two principles, and, under straightforward interpretations, they seem to exclude each other. What was Frege's position in the tension between the two principles, did he accept both principles, did he do so at the same time, or did his opinion change at some moment? Is it correct to attribute 'compositionality' to him? The answer that will be given in this chapter is not the standard one, and therefore a careful argumentation and an investigation of his original writings is required.

The organization of this chapter will mainly be chronological, since that will exhibit developments best. The first part of the article concerns the period before Frege. The nineteenth-century philosophical landscape in Germany will be sketched (of course, only as far as compositionality is concerned), and special attention will be given to some authors who were influential in those days: Trendelenburg, Lotze, and Wundt. In the second part, the papers of Frege which are important in the discussion concerning his position are investigated, and, again Wundt. The arguments that are used in the literature are put to test, and in some cases, rejected (this is a summary of the extensive discussion in Janssen (2001)). It will be argued that there is development in the way Frege speaks about these issues, and that his development reflects a development in the field. The third part starts with the work of Frege's student Rudolf Carnap because he played an important role in the history of compositionality. In the twentieth century logic, linguistics, and psychology became separate disciplines. The introduction of compositionality in the first two fields will be investigated (I have no expertise in psychology). Then authors such as Tarski, Hintikka, Ryle, Wittgenstein, Davidson, and Montague will be considered. The story ends with computer science: in that field the concept of meaning and its relation to language is as important as in the other fields.

Our aim implies certain limitations:

1. Although the principle of contextuality will mentioned frequently, we do not investigate the history of contextuality. For an extended history of that principle, see Scholz (1999).

2. We are interested in the line of history that brought compositionality to modern times, and we will therefore neglect interesting work that was not acknowledged by history. For instance, Hodges (1998) discovered compositionality in the works of Husserl (end of the nineteenth century) and formalized one of his ideas. Husserl's work will not be discussed, because his ideas about compositionality seem to have had no impact (until recently).

3. We will not provide a formalization of the principle of compositionality, but rather use a minimal interpretation. We assume that it requires that there are expressions (we do not say how abstract they may be) and these have parts (we do not say whether the parts should be visible in the expression, nor whether it should be consecutive chunks): the syntax should somehow define what the parts of an expression are. Each expression and subexpression (part) should have a meaning (but what meanings can be, is unspecified). Furthermore, there are functions that build compound expressions from expressions, and functions that build new meanings from meanings (but what functions can do is left open). The main aspect of the interpretation is, of course, that if the meaning of the compound expression is *not* a function of the meaning of its parts (e.g. because some parts have no meaning), then the proposal does *not* obeys the principle of compositionality.

4. We are not hunting for old occurrences. The principles are so immediate and general that they can be found in the writings of several authors from many periods. The internet source Wikipedia says that the idea appears already among Indian philosophers of grammar such as Ya-ska, and in Plato's *Theaetetus*. Hodges (this handbook) discovered that a tenth-century Arab author proposed compositionality, and he argues that the Arabs must have found it in the third-century commentaries on Aristotle. Wundt (1880: 80) gives a connection with the founder of logic himself (Metaphysik V 17). The philosopher Dalgarno (*c.*1626–87) developed an artificial language in such a way that it might be conceived as compositional. Leibniz (1646–1716) introduced a principle that is very similar to compositionality (see Section 1.7). A discussion of such sources falls outside the scope of our story.

PART I BEFORE FREGE

1.2 GERMANY,
EARLY NINETEENTH CENTURY

In the eighteenth and nineteenth centuries there was in Germany a growing interest in analysing thinking and language. An important theme was the question what is primary, concept or thought? Are concepts associated with words and are thoughts formed from these concepts, or are thoughts grasped and can concepts then be distinguished within the thoughts? One notices the ideas of compositionality and contextuality.

In the nineteenth century the disciplines logic, psychology, and linguistics were not yet separated, and the issues under discussion could by a single author be considered from several points of view. So a book with *Logic* in its title, might for instance deal with ontology, metaphysics, investigate natural language use, and speak about the human mind. In any case, it will not contain any symbolic logic, because that emerged only at the end of the nineteenth century; one of the pioneering works was *Begriffsschrift* (Frege, 1879).

Immanuel Kant (1724–1804) taught the primacy of the judgement against the concept in his *Critique of Pure Reason* (Kant, 1781). According to him, judgements possess an initial transcendental unity out of which we gain concept by analysis. Hence, the parts inherit their interpretation from the judgement. Sluga (1980: 55) informs us that Kant's late nineteenth-century argument became the standard argument in anti-naturalistic theories of knowledge, and that Sigwart and Lotze used it this way.

F. D. E. Schleiermacher (1768–1834) was an influential philosopher in the nineteenth century. In his hermeneutical writings, he makes the suggestion that the semantic value of a word is not a completely determined content, but rather something determinable, a *schema* that only gets determined in the larger context of a sentence, text, etc. (for details, see Scholz (2001a: 279–80)). Modern authors transformed these ideas into the schema of a hermeneutic circle (note that our summary describes not a circle, but a mutual dependency). Recently proposals are made in which, using ideas from hermeneutics (especially the hermeneutic circle), the principles of compositionality and contextuality work together in order to achieve understanding (see Rott, 2000; Prosoporov 2005).

This sketch illustrates that both the ideas of contextuality and of compositionality were discussed at the beginnings of the nineteenth century, but that contextuality was the favoured one. In the next section, we will consider in more detail the ideas concerning compositionality and contextuality of two predecessors of Frege: Trendelenburg and Lotze. Thereafter the first edition of Wundt's book on logic will considered, in a later section a comparison with the second edition will exhibit a development in the field.

1.3 1840, TRENDELENBURG: *LOGICAL INVESTIGATIONS*

Trendelenburg (1802–72), a well-known philosopher in nineteenth-century Germany, wrote *Logische Untersuchungen* (Trendelenburg 1840), a book that every German philosopher knew, and that influenced Frege's ideas (according to Sluga (1980: xi, 48–9)).

In Trendelenburg's work the two directions between thought and reality, viz. contextuality and compositionality, arise (Trendelenburg 1840, Bd. I: 365):

> Since there is such a unity between thinking and being, it is not only the case that things determine a thought in such a way that the thought reconstructs them as concepts in the mind. And in case it is already realized, it recovers itself. The thought can also determine the things, in such a way that they represent it physically. In that case the thought exists before the representation, and the parts arise from the whole, and not, as in other cases where the whole comes from the parts.

Neither of the two directions seems favoured (Trendelenburg 1840, Bd. II: 367):

> As in reality the substance originates from the activity, and the activity on its turn from the substance, concepts originate from judgements, and judgements from concepts.

Nevertheless, he also mentions a reason why contextuality should be more basic (Trendelenburg 1840, Bd. II: 145), the reference he gives is Gruppe (1834: 48, 80):

> Recently Gruppe has shown that every concept is founded in a judgement, and that therefore it is incorrect to treat the judgement after the concept, with the concept as origin.

In order to explain the relation between part and whole Trendelenburg (1840, Bd. I: 83) uses a metaphor that illustrates the role of contextuality:

> It is the essence of abstraction that the elements of the thought, which originally are closely grown together, are violently kept apart. What is isolated in the abstract situation, has to aim at a return from this enforced situation. Since it is torn off as part from a whole, it must have the traces of the fact that it only is a part. That is, it has to require a completion.

Frege would use the same metaphor of unsaturedness much later. An example is a quote from *Gedankengefüge* concerning negated thoughts (Frege, 1923a: 55–6):

> The whole owes its unity to the fact that the thought satisfies the unsatisfied part, or as one may say, completes the part that needs a completion.

One might consider this resemblance of the metaphors as an indication that Frege had read Trendelenburg.

The metaphor played a role in the discussion concerning the position of Frege. Resnik (1979) claims that the first appearance of this metaphor in Frege's writings dates to 1891 and that it supersedes Frege's principle of contextuality from *Grundlagen* (Frege 1884). As we have seen, for Trendelenburg there was no conflict: the metaphor explains contextuality. Moreover, there was no conflict for Frege: Dummett (1981b: 557) has refuted Resnik's argument by pointing to an occurrence of the metaphor in a letter that Frege wrote in 1882, so before he wrote *Grundlagen*. There is no conflict with contextuality because the unsatisfied part is obtained (violently) from a *given* thought, so the part is considered within the context of a sentence. Another argument by Resnik's for his point will be considered in Section 1.8.

Concluding: forty-five years before Frege wrote about contextuality, the ideas of compositionality and contextuality were known in the field, and contextuality was considered more fundamental.

1.4 1874, LOTZE: *LOGIC*

Lotze was philosopher at the University of Göttingen when Frege arrived in 1871 to study there as preparation for his thesis. In 1874 Lotze published his *Logik*, which Heidegger called 'the most fundamental book of modern logic' (witness Sluga (1980: 53)). Lotze extensively discusses the contextual and the compositional method. His style gives the impression that he is attacking or defending positions taken by others, which would indicate that the methods were well-known, but, unfortunately, he gives no references at all.

There is a controversy between Sluga and Dummett about Lotze's position with respect to contextuality. According to Sluga (1980: 55), it was due to Lotze that Frege became a proponent of contextuality, but according to Dummett (1981b: 538) Lotze was, on the contrary, an opponent of contextuality. We will investigate the source.

Sluga refers to the following quote in which Lotze argues for the necessary priority of judgements (Lotze 1874: 509, in 2nd edn, p. 521):

> Previously we have used rules, i.e. sentences which express a connection between different elements, as examples which make clear what it means to hold in contrast with what it is to be; only with half as much clarity can this expression be transferred to independent concepts; of these it can only be said that they mean something; *but they only mean something because propositions are true of them.* [my emphasis T.J.]

Another fragment where Lotze argues for starting with judgements is Lotze (1874: 255):

> … it will essentially not be upon the analysis of our concepts and their reduction to fundamental concepts, *but upon the analysis of our judgements and their reduction to simple axioms,* that the evolving fixation of our convictions, now unsure about so much, must be based. [my emphasis T.J.]

Here Lotze seems to be a proponent of contextuality. However, Dummett argues for the opposite, and gives the quote (Lotze 1874: 23):

> This… has given rise to the statement that the theory of judgements should be placed before the treatment of concepts….I consider this statement as overhasty….

This is indeed a negative remark about contextuality. However, I consider Dummett's conclusion that Lotze rejected contextuality as overhasty, because the quote continues as follows:

> I consider this statement as overhasty because it originates from an interchange of the aims of pure logic with applied logic …

This shows that Lotze is not absolutely against contextuality: it depends on the aim one has.

On the next page, Lotze makes clear that logic has to balance between the two approaches (Lotze 1874: 24):

> Without doubt, pure logic has to give the form of concepts preference over the form of judgements; applied logic should first learn how for the formation of certain concepts judgements can be used which consist in simpler concepts.

On the first page of his book Lotze presents an analogy for building thoughts; it expresses his appreciation for both methods (Lotze 1874: 14):

> It is easy to build a heap from balls only if it does not matter how they are arranged, but the building of a regular form is possible only by means of building blocks that have been given a shape with surfaces fitting for reliable connecting and stacking.

Concluding: Lotze had definite opinions on contextuality and compositionality: they are separated methods, each has its role in logic, depending on the purpose one has, but they may profit from each other's results.

1.5 1880, WUNDT: *LOGIC*

In 1880, Wundt published a work called *Logik*, comprising two volumes, which evolved to the German standard text on logic (of course, logic in the broad nineteenth-century sense). As a logician, he seems to be completely forgotten, but he is still honoured nowadays as one of the founding fathers of psychology. Wundt's book had four editions; we will consider here the first edition, and in Section 1.9 the second edition. It will be interesting to see the change in his opinion on the compositional and the contextual method.

In the first edition, Wundt considers many of the arguments concerning this issue. An example is (Wundt 1880: 88):

> If the concepts are the elements of our logical thinking, then it is the obvious consequence that the construction of logic has to start with them. But it is equally true that the perfect concepts of science presuppose other logical functions.

There are problems with the compositional approach and one option is:

> ... that one reverts the customary order of investigation by putting the study of judgement function before the concepts.

and another option is:

> One could with Schleiermacher postulate a two-sided dependency in which the judgement by its nature assumes the concept, and the concept in the same way assumes the judgement ...

Wundt considers several arguments and he concludes (p. 89):

> [...] therefore, it is not a contradiction if the concepts are considered on the one hand as ingredients and on the other hand as results of the process of acquiring knowledge.

Concluding: for Wundt compositionality and contextuality are separated methods; deliberations and care are required to let them cooperate.

PART II THE PERIOD OF FREGE

1.6 1884, FREGE:
FOUNDATIONS OF ARITHMETIC

In the nineteenth century, there were enormous developments within calculus, and remarkable results were obtained. For instance, imaginary numbers, as the name says, strange numbers, turned out to be very useful, the infinity was counted by Cantor, and a curve was discovered that in no point had a tangent. Many notions that previously seemed obvious now required fundamental investigations. In this situation, Frege wrote *Grundlagen der Arithmetik* (Frege, 1884). It was preceded by many other publications on foundations of mathematics; he mentions thirteen publications from the preceding thirty years.

As an example of Frege's argumentation, we paraphrase his discussion of Mill (1843). Mill was in those days the most discussed philosopher and politician, both in England and in Germany (witness Wundt (1880: VII)). Frege summarizes Mill's approach as follows (Frege (1884: §7), all translations are from the English edition by Austin).

According to John Stuart Mill, all knowledge is empirical. His definitions of numbers are not definitions in the logical sense, because they do not only state the meaning of an expression, but also express empirical facts. For instance the number 3 consists, according to Mill, 'in this that collections of objects exists, which while they impress the senses thus * $\star$ *, may be separated into two parts, thus $\star$ $\star$ $\star$' (Frege, 1884: 9^e).

Frege comments as follows: 'What a mercy that not everything in the world is nailed down; for if it were, we should not be able to bring off this separation, and 2+1 would not be 3!'. Frege considers this approach to be ridiculous: 'On Mill's view we could actually not put $1, 000, 000 = 999, 999 + 1$ unless we observed a collection of things split up in precisely this particular way' (Frege, 1884: 11^e).

The discussion of Mill is one of the sharpest discussions in *Grundlagen*. The kernel of Frege's objection (Frege, 1884: §8) is that if we call a proposition empirical on the ground that we must have made observations in order to become conscious of its content, then we are making a psychological statement, which concerns solely the content of the proposition; the question of its truth is not touched. This exhibits Frege's main motivation for his book: to save the objective truth of mathematics.

In the introduction to his book, Frege discusses psychologism (the movement in those days that tried to base the foundations of logical and mathematical knowledge on psychology). He says, 'But this account makes everything subjective. And if we follow it through to the end, it does away with truth' (Frege, 1884: vii^e). Therefore, mathematics should refuse all assistance from the direction of psychology (Frege, 1884: ix^e). This shows that Frege's aim was to defend the objectivity of mathematics against the influence of psychologism. In order to reach this aim, he keeps three principles for his investigations (Frege, 1884: x^e):

1. always to separate sharply the psychological from the logical, the subjective from the objective;
2. never ask for the meaning of a word in isolation, but only in the context of a sentence;
3. never lose sight of the distinction between concept and object.

From the previous discussion, we understand why the first point is mentioned: it is his main theme. And 'If the second point is not observed, one is almost forced to take as the meanings of words mental pictures or acts of the individual mind, and so to offend against the first principle as well. As to the third point, it is a mere illusion to suppose that a concept can be made an object without altering it' (Frege, 1884: x^e).

Note that the only argument Frege presents in favour of the principle of contextuality is that its consequences suit him. It is remarkable that he does not give any further argument for the correctness of the principle (Hacker (1979: 223) makes the same observation); in a polemic discussion about these consequences that seems not a strong position. However, after the preceding sections, we understand this: Frege used an idea that was well-known to his readers.

What then was Frege's solution? He explains it in §60 with an analogy. 'Even so concrete a thing as the Earth we are unable to imagine as we know it to be.' It is too large; there is no way to have a conception of it. Accordingly, any word, 'for which we can find no mental picture appears to have no content.' However, 'That we can form no idea of its content is... not a reason for excluding it from our vocabulary'. 'It is enough if the sentence as a whole has a sense; by this also its parts get content'. This is the approach that he uses to clarify the mathematical concepts. About numbers: 'The self-subsistence I claim for number, is *not* taken to mean that a number word signifies something when removed from the context of a sentence.' In §62 he says: 'Therefore the point is to explain the sense of a sentence in which a numeral occurs'. About infinity (∞) §84: 'That we cannot form any idea of an infinite number of objects is absolutely of no importance'. About infinitesimals (infinitely small units), which arise in calculus, for example in $df(x) = g(x)dx$: 'The problem is not, as might be thought, to produce a segment bounded by two distinct points whose length is dx, but rather to define the sense of an identity of the type $df(x) = g(x)dx$' 'we ought always to keep before our eyes a complete sentence. Only therein do the words really have a meaning.'

Concluding: Frege presented (in 1884) contextuality as his basic principle, his solution of the foundational problems is based upon it, he meant the principle literally, and would have rejected compositionality.

1.7 1892, FREGE:
ON SENSE AND REFERENCE

In his paper 'Über Sinn und Bedeutung' (Frege, 1892) the distinction between sense and reference is introduced. Frege's aim is to explain the difference between the informative sentence $b = a$ and the a priori true sentence $a = a$. Even if the names a and b designate the same object, they do so in a different way. For the-way-of-presentation, Frege introduced the name *sense*. Whereas the referents of a and b are the same in the first sentence, their senses are different, and therefore the first equation is informative. However, in reported speech the situation is different: then the referent of a word is what in normal speech is its sense (Frege, 1892: 28).

Frege hypothesizes the assumption that the reference of a sentence is its truth value and investigates as follows (Frege, 1892: 35):

> If our supposition that the reference of a sentence is its truth value is correct, the latter must remain unchanged when a part of the sentence is replaced by an expression with the same reference. And this is indeed the case.

The next step is (Frege, 1892: 35):

> But we have not yet considered the case that the expression for which we substitute is a sentence itself. If our insight is correct, then the truth value of a sentence which has another one as part must remain unchanged if we replace the subsentence by another one which has the same truth value.

These statements are used to argue that Frege now adhered to compositionality of reference. That, however, is not justified, as will be explained below.

Frege describes here what is known nowadays as the substitution principle: two expressions have the same meaning if the one can be substituted for the other without changing the truth value of the whole. This principle is known in philosophy as *Leibniz's law*, formulated by Leibniz as 'Eadem sunt quorum, quae mutuo substitui possunt, salva veritate' (Frege, 1892: 35). It is obvious that if compositionality holds, the substitution property also holds. Vice versa, if the substitution property holds, then we may form the equivalence classes consisting of expressions that are intersubstitutable, and attribute the same meaning to all expressions in a class. A proof of the equivalence of the two notions is given by Hodges (2001); it requires that some tidiness conditions be satisfied. So for the equivalence of substitutivity and compositionality, it is required that there are sets of expressions that are intersubstitutable.

That is, however, *not* the case in Frege's theory: two expressions may be intersubstitutable in some contexts, in other contexts not. Frege repeatedly says that there are exceptions to the substitution property. About a sentence embedded after *believes that*, Frege (1892: 37) says:

> In these cases, it is not allowed to replace in the subordinate clause an expression by another one that has the same customary meaning, but only by one which has the same indirect meaning, i.e. its customary sense.

Above it is shown that Frege did not accept the notion *the reference of an expression*, instead his approach is based upon the notion *the reference of an expression in a given sentence*. So Frege did not accept a notion comparable with *the meaning of an expression*. Within a given sentence a version of compositionality can be found, but the units in that analysis cannot be put into other sentences because the reference of an expression depends on the complete sentence. This is not a minor point, but an essential aspect; it will return later, especially in Sections 1.12 and 1.14.

Concluding: (in 1892) Frege adhered to contextuality, he discerned a compositional structure within a *given* sentence, but would certainly not accept the principle of compositionality.

1.8 1880/1893, FREGE: BOOLE'S CALCULATING LOGIC AND THE CONCEPT-SCRIPT

Some authors claim that Frege abandoned the principle of contextuality because it makes no appearance in Frege's writings after *Grundlagen* (e.g. Dummett (1973: 192), Resnik (1967: 46), and Resnik (1979)), whereas other authors deny this (e.g. Currie, 1982; Sluga, 1971, 1975, 1977). In this section, we will investigate a paper that played a role in this discussion; a remarkable story comes with it.

Frege's *Posthumous Writings* appeared in 1969 (Hermes, Kambartel, and Kaulbach, 1969), the English translation appeared ten years later (Hermes, Kambartel, and Kaulbach, 1979). Sluga wrote a review of the German edition (1971). He remarks that contextuality is repeated several times therein, and points to two papers. The first one is *Booles rechnende Logik und die Begriffsschrift*, which is considered here, and the other one is a note Frege wrote in 1919 (that is considered in Janssen (2001)).

Frege writes (German: Hermes et al., 1969: 204, English: Hermes et al., 1979: 17):

> And so instead of putting the judgement together out of an individual as subject, and an already previously formed concept as predicate, we do the opposite and arrive at a concept by splitting up the content of a possible judgement.

Here Frege describes the contextual method. In a footnote, he mentions one of the dangers of the opposite method: it would lead to unpleasant discussions about negative concepts, such as *non-triangle*. A few lines later Frege warns us that the contextual method (letting the thought fall apart) is *not* a way to obtain isolated properties or relations, and paraphrases the contextuality principle:

> But it does not follow from this that the ideas of these properties and relations are formed apart from entities. ... Hence, in the concept-script [=Begriffsschrift] their designations never occur on their own, but always in combinations that express contents of possible judgement. I could compare this with the behaviour of the atom: we suppose an atom never to be found on its own, but only combined with others, moving out of one combination only in order to enter immediately into another.

Resnik published a second paper (Resnik (1976), after the review by Sluga) in which he repeats his opinion that Frege rejected contextuality after *Grundlagen*. He seems to accept the above quote as a formulation of contextuality, but says 'that it is clearly not relevant because it was written *before* the *Grundlagen*' (Resnik, 1976: 47). Here he seems to have a point, *Grundlagen* is from 1884, and Frege wrote the paper under discussion in 1880. It remained unpublished; Frege submitted it several times in vain. However, this is not the whole story.

Above we quoted Frege's metaphor about atoms. Frege has a footnote attached to the last sentence of the quotation, reading 'As I have seen since, Wundt uses in his *Logik* the same image in a similar way'. The authors of the German version inform us that this picture of parts as atoms does *not* occur in the first edition of Wundt's book (dating from 1880), but in the third edition (dating from 1906). This is not quite correct: the picture of parts as atoms already occurs in the second edition from 1893 with almost the same formulations as in the third edition. The dates prove that Frege cannot have added the footnote before 1893, so that he adhered to contextuality at least until 1893. Although the *English* version of the *Posthumous Writings* did not incorporate the German editorial footnote, this cannot explain Resnik's ignorance of the reference to Wundt because Resnik's paper appeared three years earlier than the English translation.

By the way, in the next section we will see that Frege in fact misunderstood Wundt's intention.

Concluding: due to the added footnote, we know that Frege adhered to contextuality both before and 10 years after *Grundlagen*.

1.9 1893, WUNDT: *LOGIC*

The second edition of Wundt's book was extensively revised and grew to two volumes of about 650 pages each. The spread of subjects is extended considerably. It is surprising to see that contextuality and compositionality now even arise in the context of chemistry: analytic chemistry as a version of contextuality, and synthetic chemistry as a version of compositionality. However, we will restrict our discussion to the case of language and thought. The third edition (1909) grew to three huge volumes; the fragments we will discuss below occur almost unchanged in it.

It is interesting that Wundt gives many references, but none to Frege, so he considered Frege not to have made an important contribution to the issue, or he did not read him.

Wundt's statements about contextuality and compositionality are much more pronounced than in the first edition. He now explicitly mentions the context principle (Wundt, 1893: 96):

> The real thinking consists of thoughts, and separated from a thought in which it enters a concept has no existence. The same holds for an isolated word in ordinary language when used as a sign for a concept; it has reality only in the context of a sentence.

This is a formulation of contextuality that seems even stronger than Frege's formulation ('not exist' vs. 'do not ask').

Wundt describes the late nineteenth-century scientific landscape as follows (Wundt, 1893: 97):

> The fact that logical concepts are not independently given, but are obtained from judgements, was a reason for many logicians to give the investigation of judgements preference over the investigation of concepts. As soon as we get rid of the still widespread opinion that real thinking consists in a linking of originally independently existing concepts or representations, one will hardly give this question any other value than a didactical one.

From this passage we learn that:

1. The idea of contextuality was well known at the end of the nineteenth century ('many logicians give the investigation of judgements preference').
2. The idea of compositionality ('the still widespread opinion') was well-known in those days.
3. Although Wundt completely agrees with the contextuality principle, he nevertheless does not appreciate the approach based on it ('hardly any value than a didactical one').

Wundt prefers *not* to start with the analysis of judgements. His arguments are:

> On the other hand, it cannot be denied that the logical analysis of judgements must be based upon the investigation of properties of its concept-elements. Logic is here in the same situation as other branches of science that are compelled to similar abstractions. Although a word does not occur in isolation, grammarians study the formation of sentences from words. Although chemical elements only occur in compounds, chemists study the properties of elements. And also for logicians it will be better to follow the same order. The old methodological rule that one has to start with the simple, in order to understand the combination, still has its value, even when it is true that in real experience only the combination is given.

This expresses that the requirements of research compel logicians to give investigation of parts a primary role, so as to follow the compositional method. Note that Wundt uses the metaphor of parts-as-atoms to convey the opposite of what Frege said about the picture (cf. Section 1.8): Frege used it to emphasize contextuality, whereas Wundt used it to defend the compositional approach as a necessary abstraction in science.

Concluding: due to arguments from practice, Wundt shifted from a position in-between the two principles (first edition) towards a position in favour of compositionality (second and third editions).

1.10 1896, FREGE: LETTER TO PEANO

We now turn to a quote from a letter that Frege wrote to Peano in reaction to his favourable review of *Grundgesetze der Arithmetik*. The quote played an important role in the discussion of whether Frege at a certain moment abandoned the principle of contextuality or not.

Frege makes some remarks about using concepts in proofs, and mentions the inscrutability of vernacular languages. Then he says (German: Gabriel, Hermes, Kambartel, Thiel, and Veraart, 1976: 183; English: Gabriel, Hermes, Kambartel, Thiel, and Veraart, 1980: 115) [my translation, T.J.]:

> The case is different when inferences have to be drawn: then it is essential that in two sentences the same expression occurs, and that it has exactly the same meaning in both. It must therefore have a meaning for its own that is independent of the other parts of the sentence.

The point Frege makes in the above quote would nowadays be formulated by the requirement that the expression is used 'unambiguously', that is that only one meaning of the word is used. Frege, however, uses a more complex formulation. He speaks about the meaning which the expression has within the two sentences ('it has the same meaning *in both*' [my emphasis T.J.]), and not just about its meaning taken in isolation. His formulation takes sentences as the starting point, and thus he conforms to contextuality.

Resnik used another translation of the above quote and states that it is an explicit rejection of the context principle by Frege. The original German text reads 'Er muss also für sich eine Bedeutung haben, die unabhängig ist von den anderen Theilen des Satzes.' Resnik translates this as (Resnik, 1967: 362): 'Therefore, it must have a reference by itself which is independent of the parts of the sentence.'

On two points I disagree with this translation. The first is that 'für' is not translated into 'for' (or 'of' as in Gabriel et al. (1980)) but into 'by'; the second point is that 'anderen' ('other') is not translated. Nevertheless, this translation must be as intended: nine years later, he uses almost the same translation (Resnik, 1976: 46). The translation 'by itself' suggests that the meaning originates from the expression itself, and thus excludes that it comes from some other source (in this case: derived from the sentence meaning). So Resnik's translation lacks an important indication of contextuality. With this indication the text is, as we have seen, in accordance with contextuality.

In addition, Dummett (1981b: 543) does not consider the quote as an explicit rejection of contextuality (although the formulation conforms to his opinion—based on other grounds—that Frege has rejected it). Dummett interprets it as stating that each word should have the same sense in every context (cf. Section 1.7). That asks too much because the paragraph concerns only the two sentences involved in drawing a conclusion.

1.11 1923, FREGE: *COMPOUND THOUGHTS*

Frege uses several times in his later writings the argument from creativity of language: how is it possible that we understand sentences we have never heard before? Several authors base their opinion concerning the relation between Frege and compositionality on those statements.

The first occurrence is in 1914 in a draft for a letter to Jourdain (German: Gabriel et al., 1976: 127; English: Gabriel et al., 1980: 79); it is the letter with mounts Ateb and Aphla. In fact, Frege rejected the draft, it was never sent, and the letter he actually sent to Jourdain has no comparable passages. Therefore it is remarkable that it is used without any hesitation in the literature: one might expect an explication why Frege did not send the letter, or at least an argumentation that his considerations for not sending had nothing to do with what he said about the subject under discussion. Below, a *published* paper will be considered in which the argument from creativity is used, for a discussion of the letter to Jourdain, see Janssen (2001).

The first sentence of *Gedankengefüge* (Frege, 1923) in the translation by Geach and Stoothoff (1977: 55) reads:

> It is astonishing what language can do. With a few syllables it can express an incalculable number of thoughts, so that even a thought grasped by a terrestrial being for the very first time can be put into a form of words which will be understood by someone to whom the thought is entirely new. This would be impossible, were we not able to distinguish parts in the thoughts corresponding to the parts of a sentence, so that the structure of the sentence serves as the image of the structure of the thoughts.

This fragment has been used to show that Frege abandoned contextuality and adopted compositionality (e.g. Resnik, 1976: 47). There are several arguments why that is not a correct conclusion.

The most important argument is that the last sentence of the quote ('distinguish parts in the thought') does not speak about the formation of the sense of a sentence from the senses of its parts. It says that we start from a thought and then go to the parts of the thought. That direction is *contextuality*. The fact that within a *given* sentence a compositional structure can be conceived is not the same as *compositionality* (we have seen this in Section 1.7).

The second argument concerns the translation of the second sentence. It contains the phrase 'a thought...can be put into a form of words which will be understood by someone...'. One has to read this as 'the form...is understood', but it seems possible to parse this as 'words which will be understood' and think that first words are understood, and from that the sentence and the thought are formed. However, this option is created by the translation. The original German version reads: 'eine Einkleidung findet, in der ihn ein anderer erkennen kann...'. A more literal translation would be: 'the thought finds an outfit in which someone else can recognize it'. So in the original the word *Wort* does not occur, and the referent of *ihn* can only be the thought. So Frege said that the thought is recognized, and *not* that (as a first step) words are understood.

Third, the quote concerns only *compound thoughts*, that is thoughts that have a thought as part. Frege warns us that not all sentences composed from a sentence provide a serviceable example, for example relative clauses are not an example 'because they do not express a thought (we cannot tell what the relative pronoun is supposed to refer to)'. So the argument was not intended as a universally valid statement, let alone as a principle.

The paper has another passage from which we can conclude Frege's position with respect to compositionality. He gives a systematic discussion of all compound thoughts made up from two thoughts using negation and conjunction. When considering compound thoughts of the form *Not [...and ...]*, Frege says (1923: 61):

> By filling the gaps with expressions of thoughts, we form the expression of a compound thought of the second kind. But we really should not talk of the compound thought as originating in this way, for it is a thought, and a thought does not originate.

So by the line of his argumentation Frege is almost forced to say that a compound thought of the form *Not [...and ...]* is formed from two other thoughts, thus following the compositional approach. That is a way of speaking which he cannot accept. Thoughts are objective (recall *Grundlagen*), we can only grasp or recognize them, but they do not originate. So Frege explicitly denies in this published paper that thoughts are formed, and therefore he would deny compositionality as well.

Concluding: Frege consequently takes the whole thought as starting point, and that within that one may distinguish a compositional structure. His research brings him close to compositionality, but that last step is, for basic reasons, not acceptable to him. Therefore, throughout his whole career, Frege advocated contextuality and never accepted compositionality.

PART III AFTER FREGE

1.12 1947, CARNAP:
MEANING AND NECESSITY

Since the principle of compositionality cannot be traced back to Frege, the question arises: where does the attribution *Frege's principle* come from? There must have been an influential source for the attribution. Following a suggestion by Pelletier Hodges found the passage; it will be given below.

Carnap was a student of Frege, and one of the three students in his class *Begriffsschrift-II* (Kreiser, 2001: 278). In 1947 he published a book, *Meaning and Necessity* (Carnap, 1947) that presents a new method for analysing the meaning of natural language: his method of intension and extension. A substantial part (1947: 96–144) concerns the analysis of Frege's theory in *Sense and Reference*. That theory had been forgotten for fifty years, until Church argued on several occasions for the sense–reference distinction and developed its formalization.

Carnap makes Frege's aims explicit, investigates carefully his arguments and gives a step-by-step reconstruction that explains Frege's statements. He shows that Frege's argument on substitutivity should be taken as a basic principle and called it *Frege's principle*. A word on terminology: Carnap translates Frege's *Bedeutung* by *nominatum*, and, following Frege, he regards a sentence as a complex name (for a truth value). The relevant quote is (Carnap, 1947: 120–1):

> In order to understand the specific sense in which Frege means his terms, we have to look not so much at his preliminary explanations as at the reasoning by which he reaches his results. When we do this, we find that Frege makes use of certain assumptions as if they were self-evident or at least familiar and plausible, without formulating them explicitly as the basic principles of his method. These assumptions can be formulated as principles of interchangeability in the following way:
>
> **Frege's Principles of Interchangeability**
> Let ... A_j ... be a complex name containing an occurrence of the name A_j, and ... A_k ... the corresponding expression with the name A_k instead of A_j.
> **28-6** *First principle.* If A_j and A_k have the same nominatum, then ... A_j ... and ... A_k ... have the same nominatum. In other words, the nominatum of the whole expression is a function of the nominata of the names occurring in it.
> **28-7** *Second principle.* If A_j and A_k have the same sense, then ... A_j ... and ... A_k ... have the same sense. In other words, the sense of the whole expression is a function of the senses of the names occurring in it.

The heading reads *Frege's principle*, and when we substitute *meaning* for *sense* (or for *nominatum*) in the second sentence of the principle, we obtain the well-known formulation 'the meaning of the whole is a function of the meaning of the parts'. As Carnap explains, Frege has to regard certain cases (e.g. occurrences in indirect speech) as exceptions to these principles, and thereby Frege has to make his whole scheme rather complicated.

Carnap gives the following characterization of the differences between his and Frege's method (Carnap, 1947: 125):

> A decisive difference between our method and Frege's consists in the fact that our concepts, in distinction to Frege's, are independent of the context. An expression in a well-constructed language system always has the same extension and the same intension: but [in Frege's theory] in some contexts it has its ordinary nominatum and its ordinary sense, in other contexts its oblique nominatum and its oblique sense.

Carnap (1947: 128–9) emphasizes that there is no contradiction between the two theories, only a practical competition or conflict. He is cutting the cake in a different way.

Carnap explains the disadvantages of Frege's theory. He shows that it is a consequence of Frege's theory that an infinite hierarchy of names and senses is needed: a sentence has a sense, and in order to speak about that sense a name is needed, that name has a sense, and so on. Furthermore, with a single expression an infinite hierarchy of references has to be associated. His example is the sentence *Scott is human* occurring in the contexts such as *It is possible that Scott is human*, *John believes that it is possible that Scott is human*, *It is not necessary that John believes that it is possible that Scott is human*. Carnap mentions yet more disadvantages, discusses proposals by others (Church, Russell, Quine), and shows the advantages of his own method, in which with an expression one intension and one extension are associated.

Davidson (1968: 99) explains that it is this feature of Frege's language that prohibits a truth definition meeting Tarski's standards.

> What stands in the way in Frege's case is that every referring expression has an infinite number of entities it may refer to, depending on the context, and there is no rule that gives the reference in more complex contexts based on the reference in more simpler ones.

Concluding: the relevant point for us is that in Carnap's work the principles hold without exceptions. Indeed, Montague's successful work is based upon Carnap's intension–extension distinction, and not on Frege's sense–reference distinction. Carnap was the first to give a formulation of what *he* called 'Frege's principle'. This formulation is closely related with the principle of compositionality, and if we adopt Carnap's notion of intension, then we have the principle as we know it today. Therefore the name 'Carnap's principle' would be more appropriate for the principle of compositionality.

1.13 COMPOSITIONALITY AND LOGIC

In the period before Tarski, logics were regarded as deductive theories. Tarski made an important step with his paper on 'Truth in formalized languages' (Tarski, 1933, in Polish) in which he characterized the notion of a true sentence in a purely semantic way. Hodges (2008*b*) describes extensively the road Tarski had to follow; the next paragraph is based on that paper.

At some time before 1930, Tarski became interested in metamathematics and aimed at defining concepts such as definability, entailment, and truth. It has been suggested that Tarski took the idea of induction on the complexity of formulas from quantifier elimination theory. In fact there some *other* induction was used, so he had to invent a variant of the method, a process that took at least four years. In fact Tarski:

- had no program for defining semantics;
- wouldn't have known what to try if he had had such a programme;
- reached his truth definition by purely technical manipulations of other things in the Warsaw environment.

Finally the paper appeared (Tarski, 1933), first in Polish, soon followed by a German translation.

For us the crucial information is that Tarski did not have the aim of designing a compositional semantics. That also becomes clear from a detail of his truth definition. The clause for the existential quantifier reads (in our terminology): '$[\![\exists x \phi(x)]\!]^g$ is true if and only if there is an $h \sim_x g$ such that $[\![\phi(x)]\!]^h$'. So the definition it is not of the form $\mathcal{M}(\exists x \phi) = \mathcal{F}(\mathcal{M}(\phi))$; the meaning of the compound is not obtained by application of a function on the meaning of its parts. A prominent researcher in the semantics of computer science once said (Pratt, 1979: 55): 'there is no such function $\mathcal{F}$ that the meaning of $\forall x \phi$ can be specified with a constraint of the form $\mathcal{M}(\forall x \phi) = \mathcal{F}(\mathcal{M}(\phi))$'. In linguistic circles, this objection has been raised against the claim that Montague grammar would be compositional, and therefore Janssen (1997: 423) and Dowty (2007: 49) had to explain the solution (see below). The philosopher Davidson (1967b: 24) noted the fundamental difference between a recursive definition of satisfaction (that is what Tarski represented) and a compositional meaning assignment, but, as Davidson remarked, there is an obvious connection.

A reformulation of Tarski's definition is possible in which the compositional character is evident (because a closed form is used). He provided this himself, when he, around 1960, became interested in the application of methods from algebra in logic (Henkin, Monk, and Tarski, 1971). It requires a shift of perspective to appreciate the formulation. The meaning of a formula is defined as the set of assignments for which the formula is true. Then, for example, $\mathcal{M}(\phi \wedge \psi) = \mathcal{M}(\phi) \cap \mathcal{M}(\psi)$. The clause for the existential quantifier reads $\mathcal{M}(\exists x \phi) = \{h \mid h \sim_x g \text{ and } g \in \mathcal{M}(\phi)\}$. Graphically represented, this makes out of sets of assignments a cylinder, therefore this operation on $\mathcal{M}(\phi)$ is called a cylindrification. This definition can be found in some textbooks on logic (e.g. Monk, 1976; Kreisel and Krivine, 1976), and it is the basis of the theory of cylindric algebras (Henkin et al., 1971). However, usually Tarski's definition of satisfaction is followed.

Compositional semantics is not the only way to deal with the semantics of logics. We present four examples.

1. For modal logics the only way to define their semantics was for a long time by a proof system (until Kripke semantics was discovered), and it still is a standard way.

2. Some propositional logics are only characterized by a proof system or in another non-compositional way (e.g. relevance logics).

3. For predicate logic an alternative is the substitutional interpretation of quantifiers: $\exists x \phi(x)$ is true if and only if there is a substitution a for x such that $\phi(a)$ is true.

The substitutional interpretation can be found especially in proof theory and in philosophical logic. A proponent of proof theory is Schütte (1977). According to his syntax $\forall x \phi(x)$ is formed from $\phi(a)$, where a can be an arbitrary name (the expression $\phi(x)$ does not belong to his language). Therefore, the formula $\forall x \phi(x)$ is syntactically ambiguous: there are as many derivations as there are expressions of the form $\phi(a)$. It is not possible to define the interpretation of $\forall x \phi(x)$ from one of its derivations because $\phi(a)$ might be true for the chosen a whereas $\forall x \phi(x)$ is false. In philosophical logic, an advocate of substitutional semantics is Marcus (1962). She argues that one may believe *Pegasus is a winged horse* without believing *There exists at least one thing that is a winged horse*. At the same time she accepts that from the first sentence it follows that $\exists x$ [x *is a winged horse*]. The substitutional interpretation of the quantifier allows for this conclusion and at the same time avoids the ontological commitment.

Kripke (1976) gives a mathematical discussion of the approach. According to the syntax he presents, $\forall x \phi(x)$ is formed from $\phi(x)$, whereas the interpretation is the substitutional one. Regarding this matter, Kripke (1976: 330) says: 'Formulae which are not sentences will be assigned no semantic interpretation'. Therefore, the meaning of $\forall x \phi(x)$ cannot be a function of the meaning of $\phi(x)$, which according to the syntax is a part of $\forall x \phi(x)$. Therefore this substitutional interpretation is not compositional.

4. Hintikka introduced a variant of predicate logic, Independence Friendly logic (in short: IF-logic) and defined its semantics in a non-compositional way. An example of a sentence in IF-logic is $\forall x \exists y /_x \phi(x, y)$. Here the second quantifier expresses that the y should be independent of the x. The interpretation is defined by means of a game between two players. The first player chooses a value for x, say c. This choice is hidden from the other player, who next chooses a value for y, say d. Finally, $\phi(c, d)$ is evaluated. This is not a compositional interpretation because the meaning of $\exists y /_x \phi(x, y)$ is not defined in terms of the meaning of $\phi(x, y)$, furthermore, the interpretation proceeds in the direction outside inside. In fact, for open formulas no interpretation is defined at all.

Hintikka claimed that it would not be possible to design a compositional semantics for IF-logic, and argued that to be a virtue. An example of his viewpoint is (Hintikka, 1996: 110):

> Since I am in this chapter showing the very important limitations of Tarski-type definitions, I am ipso facto exposing certain serious theoretical shortcomings of the principle of compositionality.

He even published an article with the title: 'Tarski's guilty secret: compositionality' (Hintikka and Sandu 1999).

Challenged by Hintikka's claim, Hodges (1997a) provided a compositional semantics. The interpretation of a formula is a set of sets (of values for free variables). This semantics was not acceptable for Hintikka because of the higher order ontology (Sandu and

Hintikka, 2001). However, a variant of the compositional semantics enabled Caicedo, Dechesne, and Janssen (2009) to prove properties of IF-logic, for example a normal form theorem.

Concluding: the compositional method was not introduced in logic due to some principle, but because it was technically a good method. Although it has become a standard method, it is not the only method that is used.

1.14 COMPOSITIONALITY AND NATURAL LANGUAGE

Ryle (1957) gives an overview of theories of meaning in the British philosophical tradition. He lets the story begin with Mill (late nineteenth century), and says (1957: 242) that Mill started with the idea 'that the meanings of sentences are compound of the components, which are the meanings of their ingredient words'. However, according to Ryle, 'that was a tragically false start', because (1957: 294):

> Word-meanings do not stand to sentence meanings as atoms to molecules or as letters of the alphabet to the spellings of words, but more nearly as the tennis-racket stands to the strokes which are or may be made with it. . . . Their significances are their roles inside actual and possible sayings.

This describes the opinion of many British philosophers. An example is Wittgenstein. Frege's principle of contextuality appears, virtually word for word, in the *Tractatus* (Wittgenstein, 1921: 3.3): 'Only the sentence has sense; a name has a meaning only in the context of a sentence'. It also occurs, thirty years later, in the *Philosophical Investigations*. Wittgenstein (1953: §49) considers a situation in which someone introduces names for squares occurring in a given figure, and explains then:

> naming is a preparation for description. Naming is so far not a move in the language game. We may say: *nothing* has so far been done, when a thing has been named. It has not even *got* a name except in the language game. That was what Frege meant, too, when he said that a word had meaning only as part of a sentence.

Dummett (1973: 193–4) gave an interpretation of Frege's contextuality principle that reconciles it with compositionality: to consider the meaning of a word as a self-contained matter and then proceed to some unrelated topic makes no sense; it only makes sense as preparation for considering a larger context. That interpretation seems to be the same as the one by Wittgenstein. However, as we have seen, Frege could not have accepted this: according to him, the meaning of a sentence should always be the point of departure. Therefore, although Wittgenstein uses the same words as Frege, it differs from Frege's intentions. Scholz (2001b: 177–8) characterizes, with more examples, Wittgenstein's statements as a liberal reinterpretation of Frege.

Davidson's opinion on compositionality was positive. He presents a classical argument in favour of it, the argument from learnability (Davidson, 1965: 8):

> When we regard the meaning of each sentence as a function of a finite number of features of the sentence, we have an insight not only into what there is to be learnt; we also understand how an infinite aptitude can be encompassed by finite accomplishments. For suppose that a language lacks this feature; then no matter how many sentences a would-be speaker learns to produce and understand, there will remain others whose meanings are not given by the rules already mastered.

He attributes the idea to Frege (Davidson, 1967b: 19–20):

> If we want a theory that gives the meaning . . . of each sentence, we must start with the meaning . . . of its parts. . . . Up to here we have been following Frege's footsteps; thanks to him the path is well known and even well worn.

Davidson had his own requirement for a theory: it should satisfy Tarski's *convention T* and give an account of truth. Davidson (1973: 68) says:

> Convention T defines a goal irrelevant to much contemporary work in semantics. Theories that characterize or define a relativized concept of truth (truth in a model, . . . valuation, or possible world) set out from the start in a direction different from that proposed by Convention T.

So although Davidson accepts a compositionality in his theory, he cannot be considered as an advocate of compositionality of semantics. But, just as in Section 1.13 there was a connection between Tarski's definition of satisfaction and a compositional interpretation of logic, there is a connection between a theory of truth and a theory of meaning. After a long discussion Davidson (1967b: 23) says:

> The path to this point has been tortuous, but the conclusion may be stated simply: a theory of meaning for a language L shows 'how the meanings of sentences depend upon the meanings of words' if it contains a (recursive) definition of truth-in-L. And so far at least, we have no other idea how to turn the trick.

The first author in linguistics who presents compositionality of meaning as the leading principle of his approach seems to be Katz (1966: 152):

> The hypothesis on which we will base our model of the semantic component is that the process by which a speaker interprets each of the infinitely many sentences is a compositional process in which the meaning of any syntactically compound constituent of a sentence is obtained as a function of the meanings of the parts of the constituent.

Katz does not attribute the idea to Frege; his motivation is of a practical nature (Katz, 1966: 152):

> Accordingly, we again face the task of formulating a hypothesis about the nature of a finite mechanism with an infinite output.

The issue of compositionality became prominent due to the work of Montague. He was a mathematical logician, specializing in set theory and modal logic, and he was dissatisfied with the fact that semantics was neglected by the theory of transformational grammar. In his most influential work, 'The proper treatment of quantification in ordinary English' (Montague 1973), the compositional method is exemplified: for each basic expression a meaning is given, and for each syntactic rule there is a corresponding semantic rule that describes how the meanings of the parts have to be combined in order to obtain the meaning of the expression formed by the syntactic rule. Thus the semantics mirrors exactly the syntax.

An important factor that made this framework possible was that Montague, following Carnap, associated with an expression one meaning, instead of an infinity of meanings (see Section 1.12). However, Carnap's solution had problems that were caused by the fact that he identified possible worlds with models. To overcome these, Montague (1970*b*: 233) introduced *intensional logic* in which these problems do not arise.

The principle of compositionality was for Montague not a subject of deliberation or discussion, because for him, as a mathematical logician, it was a standard way to proceed: he described his method of assigning meanings to expressions in side remarks with phrases like 'following Tarski', or 'following Frege', without ever calling it a principle. His view is expressed as follows (Montague, 1970*b*: 222):

> There is in my opinion no important theoretical difference between natural languages and the artificial languages of logicians; indeed I consider it possible to comprehend the syntax and semantics of both kinds of languages with a single natural and mathematically precise theory.

In later years, the principle of compositionality was mentioned as the cornerstone of Montague's work in several discussions. We consider three causes.

The first was that phenomena were studied that did not easily fit in the framework of Montague (1970*b*) or Montague (1973). Relaxations were proposed, and that raised the question what the essential ingredients of the approach were, and which aspects could be changed without losing the kernel.

The second cause was that a non-compositional alternative arose. In Chomsky's transformational grammar, semantics eventually received a corner. With each sentence a so-called deep structure was associated, and that structure was the input of a process that gradually transformed it into something that was called 'logical form'. So the sentence has to be completed before this semantic process can take place. Therefore the process is not compositional.

The third cause was a challenge of a principled nature. All phenomena considered by Montague (and his first successors) concern sentences in isolation. But what about discourse? Compositionality suggests that a discourse should be treated by analysing each sentence on its own. How could one then account for discourse phenomena, such as discourse pronouns, or the tense structure of a story? The first treatment of these phenomena was introduced by Kamp (1981) in the form of Discourse Representation Theory, henceforth DRT. On the one hand, it sprung from Montague's approach because it used model theoretic semantics; on the other hand, it was a deviation because (discourse) representations were an essential ingredient. A new semantics for binding free variables in logic had to be developed in order to treat discourse within Montague semantics (Groenendijk and Stokhof, 1991), and the solution allowed more phenomena to be dealt with than did DRT. Nowadays there are several compositional reformulations of DRT, for example those by van Eijck and Kamp (1997), Zeevat (1989), or Muskens (1989).

These discussions evoked fundamental questions. Why should we obey compositionality? What is the status of the principle of compositionality? Is it possible at all to give a compositional semantics for natural languages? What are the essential aspects of Montague's approach? Some authors considered it to be a principle that could be empirically tested (for a discussion see Dowty (2007)), others authors as a methodological principle that better be obeyed because deviations yield inferior proposals (for arguments, see Janssen (1997)).

In these discussions, the mathematical results about compositionality were relevant. A mathematical description of compositionality is that syntax and semantics are algebras, and meaning assignment is a homomorphism from syntax to semantics (see Montague, 1970b; Janssen, 1986). A proof that any language can be given a compositional semantics if one is willing to accept an unnatural grammar is given in Janssen (1997). On the other hand, Zadrozny (1994) argues that if one accepts rather complex meanings (using non-well-founded set theory), compositionality can always be achieved, even with a syntax consisting of concatenation rules. In both cases, the resulting grammar deviates from what one would like to have as a result. Hodges (2001) presented another formal result. He investigated under which conditions a compositional semantics for a given fragment can be extended to a semantics for the whole language.

Concluding: the compositional method is used because it appeared, due to linguistic or mathematical arguments, to be the best method. However, when complications arose, there was not much hesitation in relaxing it as far as needed.

1.15 COMPOSITIONALITY
AND COMPUTER SCIENCE

Programs are texts written to instruct computers. In the middle of the twentieth century these grew so complex that the need was felt to develop tools to keep control. The earliest occurrence of the idea that one needs a form of compositionality, was, according to de Roever et al. (2001), formulated in a note by Dijkstra (1969):

> if we ever want to be able to compose large programs reliable, we need a discipline such that the intellectual effort E (measured in some loose sense) needed to understand a program does not grow more rapidly than proportional to the length L . . ..

Compositionality evidently is a method to achieve this goal. Other authors mention compositionality explicitly. Milner (1975: 167):

If we accept that any abstract semantics should give a way of composing the meanings of the parts into the meaning of the whole . . .

Mazurkiewicz (1975: 75) says:

One of the most natural methods of assigning meanings to programs is to define the meaning of the whole program by the meaning of its constituents.

As motivation he gives a practical argument:

The designer of a computing system should be able to think of his system as a composite of behaviours, in order that he may factor his design problem into smaller problems. . . .

Note that here is no awareness that in philosophy a *principle* of compositionality is known. The first publication in the field of the semantics of programming languages that mentions this connection is probably Janssen and van Emde Boas (1977*a*).

The computers from the 1960s can be regarded as calculating machines with a single processing unit. The programs were written in an imperative language (FORTRAN or Algol) that instructed the machines precisely what to do. Issues in semantics were questions of correctness (does the program calculate the intended function?) and termination (does the program never go into an infinite loop?). Later other types of programming languages were developed, and computers are nowadays units in a large network and operate concurrently. In those situations, the semantical issues are different. The role of compositionality will be illustrated with two examples concerning the early situation; thereafter its role in the field of semantics of concurrency will be sketched.

A very simplified view of a computer program is that it consists of a sequence of instructions p_1, p_2, p_3 that are performed in order, where each action changes the internal state of the computer. A prominent approach to the semantics of programming languages is the Floyd–Hoare approach. States are characterized by predicates, and the meaning of an instruction is given by describing how a predicate about the state before the action is related to a predicate about the state after the action.

The first illustration concerns the assignment statement. It is an instruction that changes the value of an identifier (something like a variable). For instance, $v := v + 1$ expresses that the value v in the next state of the computer has to be one more than the current value of v. The predicate transformer for the assignment instruction $x := t$ reads $\{[t/x]P\}\, x := t\, \{P\}$. This says that in order to guarantee that P holds after the assignment, it is necessary and sufficient that $[t/x]\,P$ holds before the assignment (where $[t/x]$ indicates that in P every occurrence of x has to be replaced by t). Consider the assignment $x := w + 1$, where $x > 9$ has to hold afterwards. The rule says that then initially $[w + 1/x](x > 9)$ has to hold, so $w + 1 > 9$, i.e. $w > 8$.

The predicate transformer just given is a proof rule, and not a (compositional) definition of meaning. This is a characteristic of computer science: since the aim is to prove properties, insights are formulated as proof rules. Of course, at the background there should be an abstract model of the computer (needed to define notions such as correctness and completeness of the proof system). In most cases, proof rules can easily be reformulated as defining a meaning (only for *recursive* procedures this is not immediate). For the case of the assignment statement, the meaning is denoted by the predicate transformer $\lambda P \cdot [t/x] \, P$, that is a mapping from sets of states to sets of states. One detail requires attention. The substitution operator does not belong to the logic itself, but to the metalanguage, and in order to let the expression denote a meaning, the substitution should have a semantic interpretation as well. It can be seen as a tense operator: it shifts the state with respect to which its argument is interpreted, from the current moment to the one in which the value assigned to x equals t. This interpretation is given by Janssen and van Emde Boas (1977b), and, in a different context, by Müller-Olm (1997: 30–2). The semantic version of the predicate transformer for the assignment statement is a very general formulation, and can be applied to pointers as well. Thus the requirement of compositionality has led towards a generalization of the rule.

The second illustration concerns the semantics of procedures with arguments. A procedure can be seen as a *name* for a series of instructions; this name can be used on several places in the program whereas the relation between the name and the instructions is defined only once. An example is *sqrt* that yields as result the positive square root of its argument, so $sqrt(4) = 2$. This procedure needs the *value* of its argument as input; therefore, this treatment of the argument bears the name *call by value*. A variant of this procedure, say *sq*, can be defined that has the effect that the resulting value is assigned to its argument, so $sq(w)$ has the same effect as $w := sqrt(w)$. In this case, the procedure needs to know *which variable* is the argument. This treatment of arguments is known as *call by name*. There is yet another mechanism for the treatment of arguments: *call by reference*.

In a compositional approach, the meaning of the entire construction (procedure with given argument) has to be obtained by combining the meaning of the procedure with the meaning of the argument. Tennent expressed this in a discussion (Neuholt, 1978: 163) by: 'Your first two semantics are not "denotational" ... because the meaning of the procedure call constructs is not defined in terms of the meanings of its components'. But what are the meanings of the parts of the construction? The semantics of the *call by name* construction was for a long time given as a syntactic substitution of the argument in the description of the procedure, and that is something one would prefer not to do in a semantic analysis. A compositional analysis is given by Hung and Zucker (1991) using Montague's intensional logic. Their abstract semantic approach enabled semantics for all three kinds of treatments of arguments, and for many types of arguments.

Finally a relativizing remark. Although compositional semantics and proof rules are important in the field of the semantics of programs, it is not the only method. Alternatives are, for instance, model checking and (non-compositional) deductive systems. And in practice the standard approach to show correctness seems to be testing, or trial and error.

Nowadays computers are part of a system with several other units (scanner, printer, storage, other computers), and each unit has computing power. These units operate in parallel, but have to communicate and work together. In this context new issues arise, such as guaranteeing fairness (each unit gets its turn for access to a resource) and avoidance of deadlock (the situation that every unit is waiting for an action by another unit, so nothing is happening anymore). The following description of the field of semantics for concurrency is based upon the introductions of de Roever et al. (2001) and de Roever, Langmaack, and Pnueli (1998) (the latter bears the suggestive title *Compositionality. The significant difference*).

Concurrency is difficult to understand: several published algorithms for concurrency are incorrect. A striking example concerns a bug in the Pentium FD-IV chip: it cost Intel 475 million dollars to cover up the costs evoked by this error (since then, they have a team that verifies designs by formal methods). Methods like model checking, deductive systems, or modelling by finite automata are suitable for small systems, but for large systems their complexity explodes: if there are 80 components with 10 possible states, then the state space to be considered is 10^{80}. Using compositional methods, the parallel process can be specified using *conjunction* instead of product. 'However, the measure of success of a compositional process is its simplicity' (de Roever et al., 1998: 14), and there are situations where compositionality does not make the description simpler. The textbook by de Roever et al. (2001: 62) presents both compositional and non-compositional proof methods, and he says about them:

> Summarizing, compositional reasoning should be applied whenever it successfully solves the problems of specifier, prover and implementor alike—such is the case for instance with formalisms for synchronous constructs. However, there are many cases where the formulation of the problem at hand (developing a program preserving a certain invariant), the inherent semantic complexity of the semantics of a program construct (e.g. one requiring nine-tuples for its compositional characterization), or the tight coupling of the processes . . . prevents a practical solution.

Concluding: compositional methods are considered attractive, not for principled reasons, but for a practical reason: they reduce the complexity of controlling the whole process. However, in situations where parts are highly intertwined, non-compositional methods have to be used.

1.16 CONCLUSION

We have seen that halfway the nineteenth century compositionality and contextuality were regarded as two methods that each had their role. Towards the end of that century compositionality became, due to its practical advantages, the favourite. Frege was a strong advocate of contextuality, but even he came, at the end of his career, close to compositionality. So his development reflected the development of the field. Frege's distinction between *sense* and *reference* originally was a context dependent distinction, but in the middle of the twentieth century a compositional formalization was developed by Carnap and successfully applied by Montague.

In the nineteenth century, the study of thought was a united science, but in the twentieth century logic, linguistics, and psychology became separate sciences. The history of compositionality in the first two fields and in the new field of computer science was investigated. In all those fields compositionality is a widely accepted methodology, if not the standard one. But it cannot be said that it is the only one, or the one favoured for principled reasons. Sometimes ontological considerations cause a different approach to be advocated, and, more frequently, in cases where a phenomenon is studied in which there is a strong influence from context, non-compositional methods are used without hesitation.

Generally speaking, the wide support for compositionality is not for principled, but for practical reasons. This motivation can be expressed using an old wisdom, often attributed to Julius Caesar, but probably from Philippus of Macedonia (father of Alexander the Great): compositionality implements the rule *divide et impera*.[1]

[1] I am indebted to the anonymous referees and the editors of this Handbook for their comments on the previous version of this chapter. I thank Wouter Beek, Johan van Benthem, Wilfrid Hodges, Dick de Jongh, Peter Pagin, Jeff Pelletier, Martien Rijk, and Hans Rott for their comments on earlier versions of this chapter or during my research on this subject.

CHAPTER 2

COMPOSITIONALITY IN MONTAGUE GRAMMAR

MARCUS KRACHT

2.1 INTRODUCTION

As is well-known, Montague not only wrote about the Principle of Compositionality but also produced concrete grammars to show that a compositional account of quantification (and other phenomena) is indeed possible. The papers now known as PTQ ('The Proper Treatment of Quantification in Ordinary English'—Montague, 1973), UG ('Universal Grammar'—Montague, 1970b) and EFL ('English as a Formal Language'—Montague, 1970a) have been eye openers for the linguistic community. They mark the birth of formal semantics. Not that there has not been any formal semantics before and not that there have not been any similar proposals on the table, but these papers demonstrated the possibility of this approach beyond doubt. Montague's papers have been collected in Montague (1974), where R. Thomason also wrote quite a readable introduction. Furthermore, Dowty, Wall, and Peters (1981) has further helped to disseminate the ideas of Montague.

In the wake of the new interest in formal semantics, much new research has been initiated. Further refinement of the semantics has led to an expansion of the basic ontology. Over time, new kinds of entities have been introduced and studied (events, situations, plurals, degrees, and so on). Other research has questioned the particular treatment of elements; should, for example, sentences be translated into propositions, that is, closed expressions, or would it be more appropriate to allow for free variables? Furthermore, there is research that takes issue with the overall framework itself. It is the latter that shall interest us here. Montague defines a translation into some logical language called IL (Intensional Logic). However, it is not possible to translate the meanings of most words like /talk/, /run/, and so on, into such a language. It is expressively weak. A simple remedy would be to add enough constants, like talk', run'. However the price to be paid is that many inferences do not come out as logical inferences. For example, it is held that the inference from /John is a bachelor./ to /John is a man./ is true in virtue of its meaning alone; so it should be a matter of logical form. But how can this come about if both are simply translated by some constant? There are two solutions: one is to simply define 'bachelor' using among other the primitive 'man'. The other is to introduce a meaning postulate. One such example is Montague's analysis of 'seek' as 'try to find'. Other people have taken issue with the idea that Montague allows the use of deletion (see e.g. Hausser, 1984). Still others wish to generalize the modes of composition. In this chapter I shall pinpoint some of these developments. However, first I give a brief introduction into PTQ (Section 2.2) and then into UG and the general ideas behind the programme (Section 2.3). After that I review the historical development (Section 2.4) before discussing problematic aspects of the theory (Section 2.5).

2.2 A VERY SHORT INTRODUCTION TO PTQ

The system known as PTQ is explained in great detail in Dowty et al. (1981). Here I give a quick overview based on Dowty et al. (1981), simplifying matters to a great extent. Intensionality will be ignored as it is not essential in understanding the architecture of the theory.

To illustrate the theory, let us see how it analyses the sentence

(2.1)   John talks.

This sentence has two parts, each of which are taken as primitive. One of them is /talks/. Montague Grammar assigns this expression a **category**, in this case IV, the category of intransitive verbs. Actually, Montague assumes that the inflected form /talks/ is not basic but rather derived from the infinitive /talk/. This expression is assigned a meaning. The meaning is expressed by a typed λ-expression. Since the interest is not in understanding what it is to talk, the expression is simply the constant talk'. This expression has the **type** $\langle e, t \rangle$, by which we mean that it is a function from individuals to truth values. Given an individual it tells us whether the individual talks. By convention, 1 stands for 'true' and 0 stands for 'false'. Given an individual c, $\mathsf{talk}'(c) = 1$ simply means that c talks; $\mathsf{talk}'(c) = 0$ means that c does not talk. We may also rewrite talk' in the following form.

(2.2) $\lambda x.\mathsf{talk}'(x)$

The λ operator binds the variable x. It forms the function that assigns to x the value $\mathsf{talk}'(x)$. By the laws of λ-calculus we have

(2.3) $f = \lambda x.f(x)$

The other part of the sentence is the proper name /John/. The ordinary assumption is that proper names are constants and denote individuals. Assume that the individual denoted by /John/ is j. Then in order to know whether or not /John talks./ is true we just have to compute the value $\mathsf{talk}'(j)$. However, Montague takes a different route. Rather than taking the name to denote an individual, he takes it to denote a function, the function J.

(2.4) $J := \lambda P.P(j)$

By definition, this is the function that takes some object g and applies it to j. Thus, rather than the subject being the argument of the intransitive verb it is the verb that is the argument of the subject. Let us see how that works. /John talks./ denotes

(2.5) $J(\mathsf{talk}') = (\lambda P.P(j))(\mathsf{talk}') = \mathsf{talk}'(j)$

We are now ready to introduce the first grammar. We use the notation and numbering of Dowty et al. (1981), which occasionally differs from PTQ. Rules come in pairs; one half of the rule is responsible for generating expressions and the other half takes care of the meanings.

S4.   If $a \in P_T$ and $\delta \in P_{IV}$ then $F_4(a, \delta) \in P_t$ where $F_4(a, \delta) = a\delta'$ where δ' is the result of replacing δ by its third person singular form.

Here P_c is the set of expressions of category c. The expressions of category t are the sentences. So, $F_4(\mathsf{John}, \mathsf{talk}) = \mathsf{John\ talks}$. (Concatenation is thought to introduce a blank. The period is not accounted for.)

T4.   If $a \in P_T$ and $\delta \in P_{IV}$ and a, δ translate into a', δ', respectively, then $F_4(a, \delta)$ translates into $a'(\delta')$.

Thus, by T4, /John talks/ translates into $J(\mathsf{talk}') = \mathsf{talk}'(j)$. This is 1 iff the sentence is true and 0 otherwise.

    To see the need for treating proper names in this roundabout way let us look at the treatment of quantification. A common noun, /man/, denotes objects of the same type as verbs, namely functions from individuals to truth values. Syntactically, their category is given as CN; thus common nouns are different syntactically but not semantically from intransitive verbs. The word /every/ gets the category T/CN. The slash says the following: 'if given an expression of category CN to my right, we shall together be an expression of category T'. In general, the notation a/β is used for expressions that will form an expression of category a when combined with an expression of category β to their right.

S2.   If $a \in P_{T/CN}$ and $\delta \in P_{CN}$ then $F_2(a, \delta) \in P_T$, where $F_2(a, \delta) = a\delta$.

The meaning of /every/ is

(2.6) $\lambda P.\lambda Q.(\forall x)(P(x) \rightarrow Q(x))$

(I follow here Dowty et al. (1981) rather than the original PTQ, where /every/ is still treated syncategorematically.)

T2.   If $a \in P_{T/CN}$ and $\delta \in P_{CN}$ translate into a' and δ', respectively, then $F_2(a, \delta)$ translates into $a'(\delta')$.

This allows the generation, via S2, of the expression /every man/, which by T2 has the meaning:

$$(2.7) \quad \begin{aligned} & (\lambda P.\lambda Q.(\forall x)(P(x) \to Q(x)))(\mathrm{man}') \\ & = \lambda Q.(\forall x)(\mathrm{man}'(x) \to Q(x)) \end{aligned}$$

By S4, /every man talks/ is an expression of category t. By T4 it has the meaning:

$$(2.8) \quad \begin{aligned} & (\lambda Q.(\forall x)(\mathrm{man}'(x) \to Q(x)))(\mathrm{talk}') \\ & = (\forall x)(\mathrm{man}'(x) \to \mathrm{talk}'(x)) \end{aligned}$$

For the sake of simplicity I shall not discuss intensionality. Let me instead illustrate by way of example some more rules that each show some aspects of the theory that have later been found problematic.

S11a.   If $\alpha \in P_t$ and $\delta \in P_t$ then $F_8(\alpha, \delta) \in P_t$, where $F_8(\alpha, \delta) := \alpha$ and δ.

T11a.   If $\alpha, \delta \in P_t$ denote α' and δ', respectively, then $F_8(\alpha, \delta)$ denotes $\alpha' \wedge \delta'$.

Rule S11a introduces the word /and/ into the expression. Thus, in PTQ English /and/ is actually not a basic word but is introduced by the rule. This is expressed by saying it is **syncategorematic** in S11a.

The next rules are quite difficult to understand in their full complexity. Nevertheless, they have been so important in the discussion that we have to include them here. Montague first of all assumes that for each natural number n there are basic expressions /he$_n$/ and /him$_n$/ with meaning $\lambda P.P(x_n)$. The indices are, however, never allowed to surface and there are rules that allow for them to be removed. Here is one, known as the **rule of quantifying in.**

S14.   If $\alpha \in P_T$ and $\delta \in P_t$ then $F_{10,n}(\alpha, \delta) \in P_t$, where either (i) α does not have the form /he$_n$/, and $F_{10,n}(\alpha, \delta)$ comes from δ by replacing the first occurrence of /he$_n$/ or /him$_n$/ by α and all other occurrences of /he$_n$/ or /him$_n$/ by he/she/it or him/her/it, respectively, according to whether the gender of the B_{CN} or B_T in α is masculine/feminine/neuter, or (ii) $\alpha = $ he$_k$, and $F_{10,n}(\alpha, \delta)$ comes from replacing all occurrences of /he$_n$/ or /him$_n$/ by /he$_k$/ or /him$_k$/, respectively.

T14.   If $\alpha \in P_T$ and $\delta \in P_t$ translate into α' and δ', respectively, then $F_{10,n}(\alpha, \delta)$ translates into $\alpha'(\lambda x_n.\delta')$.

2.3 MONTAGUE'S GENERAL THEORY

In this section I shall present the version of Montague (1970*b*), henceforth UG. In it Montague proposed an abstract theory of semantics for language. Before I begin with the outline proper, I shall describe a few problems that the theory is designed to solve. The first is: what are the mechanisms for combining meanings? The second, clearly related question is: what linguistic intuitions is the theory supposed to explain?

It is perhaps best to start with the second question. One of the most solid intuitions we have is that of logical inference. We know for example (perhaps after some reflection) that the first inference is valid and the second is not.

(2.9)
Every man walks and talks.
John is a man.
∴ John talks.

(2.10)
Every man loves some woman.
Mary is a woman.
∴ Some man loves Mary.

Now why is that so? One answer is that an inference is valid because of its logical form. For example, formalizing the sentences of (2.9) as given in (2.11) makes the argument valid due to the meaning of the logical elements alone.

(2.11)
$(\forall x)(\text{man}'(x) \rightarrow \text{walk}'(x) \wedge \text{talk}'(x))$
$\text{man}'(j)$
$\therefore \text{talk}'(j)$

This reasoning has been used among others by Davidson (1967a). In this view the logical form is supposed to transparently show why an inference is valid. This presupposes a distinction that has frequently been made between logical constants ('$\forall$', '$\wedge$', '$\rightarrow$') and nonlogical constants ('man', 'talk'). The validity of the inference (2.11) is independent of the particular meaning of the nonlogical words. Therefore, if (2.11) is the logical form of (2.9) the validity of the latter is accounted for by appeal to the validity of the former. And that in turn is done by appeal to standard predicate logic.

The second answer to the question is that the inference is valid simply because the words mean what they mean. For example, assume that /man/, /talks/, and /walks/ denote subsets of the set E of entities. Let these be M, T, and W, respectively. So, M is the set of all men, T the set of all talking things, and W the set of all walking things. Then the sentence /Every man walks and talks./ is true if $M \subseteq W \cap T$. Now let /John/ denote a single object, say j. Then /John is a man./ is true if and only if $j \in M$. It now follows that $j \in W \cap T$, and so $j \in T$, which is true if and only if /John talks./ is true. Let us also see why the second inference fails. Here we construct a particular situation. Let $E := \{j, c, m\}$ be a set of entities. Assume that the meaning of /woman/ is $\{c, m\}$, and the meaning of /man/ is $\{j\}$. Finally, the meaning of /loves/ is the relation $\{\langle j, c \rangle\}$. Then every man loves some woman (namely c), but no one loves m.

One should note that the second approach is somewhat superior to the first. For appeal to the logical form in itself is not sufficient. After all, we can raise the same question with respect to the logical form itself: why is it that the inference (2.11) is valid? Surely, it must be because of what the formulas mean. From a practical point of view, though, we do not need to decide between the two. Montague clearly preferred the second view (inferences are valid because of what the words effectively mean) but used a logical language (the typed λ-calculus over predicate logic) to encode the meanings.

Montague never asked what meanings *are*. He has been agnostic about them, as he has been about syntax. He only cared about how meanings functioned. That he used the typed λ-calculus was mere convenience on his part; he could have chosen something else as long as the basic properties are preserved. The question, however, is why we should choose a logical language when we already have a natural language. The answer is that natural language sentences are ambiguous. One problematic sentence was supplied by Chomsky.

(2.12) `Visiting relatives can be a nuisance.`

There are two ways to understand this: the nuisance is caused by the relatives that are visiting, or by visiting the relatives. Given that the concept of visit involves two arguments, a subject and an object, we would like to be clear about who is visiting. There are many more such examples (/clever children and parents/, where either only the children are clever, or both children and parents). Since natural language is full of such ambiguities, one aim of the translation into a logical language is to be crystal clear about what a given sentence means and what it does not mean. In translation, the sentences are neither vague nor ambiguous. Ignoring vagueness we must ask: how is it that an ambiguous sentence is translated into an unambiguous sentence? Should the meaning of (2.13) be rather (2.14) or (2.15)?

(2.13) `Every man loves a woman.`

(2.14) $(\forall x)(\mathrm{man}'(x) \rightarrow (\exists y)(\mathrm{woman}'(y) \wedge \mathrm{love}'(x, y)))$

(2.15) $(\exists y)(\mathrm{woman}'(y) \wedge (\forall x)(\mathrm{man}'(x) \rightarrow \mathrm{love}'(x, y)))$

The answer that Montague gives is that meanings are not assigned to sentences but to disambiguations. Disambiguations are abstract objects which can be spelled out in two ways: as a sentence of English and as a formula of a logical language. A sentence has as many translations as it has disambiguations.

In syntax the disambiguation is done by means of structure. Something similar happens here. We think of the constituent /visiting relatives/ as formed from the elements /visiting/ and /relatives/ in two different ways. We can represent these ways abstractly by binary function symbols, say f and g, and write as follows: f(visiting, relatives), and g(visiting, relatives). We say f and g are *modes of composition*. This presupposes, of course, that the words in this example are basic. If not, they should in turn be composed using some modes of combination. However, even if they are basic it is not always advisable to use the words themselves as objects. For there can be homonyms (say /bank/) and in order to prevent lexical ambiguity we need to separate them, too. We can do this by introducing two arbitrary lexical constants, say b_0 and b_1. These shall be 'spelled out' as /bank/. (This is done by the ambiguation relation, see below.) Finally, we observe that the constituents are of different kind, called *category*. Words of identical category can be coordinated, those of different category cannot (see Keenan and Faltz (1985) for an elaborate semantic theory of boolean meanings):

```
man and woman    : (N & N)
walk and talk    : (V & V)
green and blue   : (A & A)
in and out       : (P & P)
if and when      : (C & C)
*man and out     : (*N & P)
*green and if    : (*A & C)
```

The categories will also have different kinds of meanings associated with them.

Montague therefore started with an abstract language that serves to define the syntactic objects, which then get spelled out, both in terms of sound and meaning. The abstract language already uses categories, which reflect the syntactic categories seen above but, as we shall see, indirectly also the semantics categories, or types. The key notion is that of a *disambiguated language*. This is a quintuple $\langle A, \langle F_\gamma : \gamma \in \Gamma \rangle, \langle X_\delta : \delta \in \Delta \rangle, S, \delta_0 \rangle$ such that the following holds.

(1) A is the least set containing all X_δ and is closed under all operations. It is the set of proper expressions.

(2) Δ is a list of *categories*.

(3) For every $\delta \in \Delta$, X_δ is the set of basic expressions of category δ.

(4) $\delta_0 \in \Delta$ is a designated category (that of declarative sentences).

(5) For every $\gamma \in \Gamma$, F_γ is an operation on the set A.

(6) For every $\gamma, \gamma' \in \Gamma$ and elements x_i, $i < m$, and y_j, $j < n$, $F_\gamma(x_1, \cdots, x_m) = F_{\gamma'}(y_1, \cdots, y_n)$, if and only if $\gamma = \gamma'$, $m = n$ and $x_i = y_i$ for all $1 \leq i \leq n$; also, $F_\gamma(x_1, \cdots, x_m) \notin X_\delta$ for every $\delta \in \Delta$.

(7) S is a subset of $\{F_\gamma : \gamma \in \Gamma\} \times \Gamma^* \times \Gamma$. This is the type assignment for the function symbols.

Here, Γ is an arbitrary of indices. We put $X := \bigcup_{\delta \in \Delta} X_\delta$. We have $X \subseteq A$ though equality need not hold. Every expression can be given a unique category $\delta \in \Delta$. For either it is in X_δ, and its category is δ; or it has the form $y = F_\gamma(x_1, \cdots, x_n)$ and if x_i belongs to δ_i and $\langle F_\gamma, \langle \delta_1, \cdots, \delta_n \rangle, \eta \rangle \in S$ then y has category η. Let A_δ denote the expressions of category δ; then $A = \bigcup_{\delta \in \Delta} A_\delta$. So, A is the carrier set of an algebra, the algebra $\mathfrak{A} := \langle A, \langle F_\gamma : \gamma \in \Gamma \rangle \rangle$. This algebra is what is known as the *algebra freely generated by X*. (This is a slight simplification. $\mathfrak{A}$ is free as a many sorted algebra.) It has the property that any map $h : X \to B$, where B is the carrier set of an algebra $\mathfrak{B} = \langle B, \langle G_\gamma : \gamma \in \Gamma \rangle \rangle$ can be uniquely extended to a homomorphism $\overline{h} : \mathfrak{A} \to \mathfrak{B}$, that is, a map satisfying

(2.16) $h(F_\gamma(x_1, \cdots, x_n)) = G_\gamma(h(x_1), \cdots, h(x_n))$

This definition shall be simplified as follows. A *many sorted signature* is a triple $\langle F, \Sigma, \Omega \rangle$, where F is the set of *function symbols*, Σ the set of *sorts* and $\Omega : F \to \Sigma^+$ a map assigning to each function symbol a sequence $\langle s_0, \cdots, s_n \rangle$ of sorts. An algebra of this signature is a pair $\langle\{A_s : s \in \Sigma\}, I\rangle$ where A_s is a set for each $s \in \Sigma$, and $A_s \cap A_{s'} = \emptyset$ if $s \neq s'$; and, furthermore, if $\Omega(f) = \langle s_0, \cdots, s_n\rangle$ then $I(f) : A_{s_0} \times \cdots \times A_{s_{n-1}} \to A_{s_n}$. (Montague allows polymorphism, that is, he allows a set of sequences to be assigned to a function symbol. That can be accommodated by introducing enough new function symbols.)

The disambiguated language is thus a polymorphic many-sorted algebra. Ω is the signature. Notice that the basic expressions can be identified with 0-ary functions. It is easy to see that each member of A is the (disjoint) union of certain sets A_δ. Namely, we put $F_\gamma(x_1, \cdots, x_n) \in A_\delta$ just in case $\Omega(\gamma) = \langle\delta_0, \cdots, \delta_{n-1}, \delta\rangle$. The set A_δ additionally contains the expressions of category A_δ; thus, $X_\delta \subseteq A_\delta$.

A *language*, finally, is a pair $\langle\mathcal{L}, R\rangle$, where $\mathcal{L}$ is a disambiguated language and R a so-called ambiguation relation. For example, R may contain the pairs $\langle b_0, \text{bank}\rangle$ and $\langle b_1, \text{bank}\rangle$. In that case, both b_0 and b_1 will be spelled out as /bank/. Another example is the following. $\mathcal{L}$ generates fully bracketed arithmetical expressions, like this: $(((3+5)*7)+1)$. Then put $\zeta R \zeta'$ if ζ is a fully bracketed expression and ζ' results from ζ by erasing all brackets. Then $(((3+5)*7)+1) R 3+5*7+1$, but also $((3+(5*7))+1) R 3+5*7+1$. Likewise, the expressions that Montague generates for English have plenty of brackets and variables in them which are 'deleted' in the ambiguation process.

Meanings are not assigned to elements of the language but to elements of the disambiguated language, and thus ζ' has meaning m in virtue of being an ambiguation of ζ that has meaning m. The semantics is provided by an algebra $\mathfrak{B} = \langle B, \langle G_\gamma : \gamma \in \Gamma\rangle, f\rangle$, where f is a map from the basic expressions to B. This map can be uniquely extended to a map h satisfying

$$(2.17) \quad h(F_\gamma(x_1, \cdots, x_n)) = G_\gamma(h(x_1), \cdots, h(x_n))$$

Here, no sorts are added. Montague calls h *Fregean* if in addition h is a homomorphism modulo category-to-type correspondence. This is to say that the semantic algebra is not a many sorted algebra with the same sorts, and so the notion of a homomorphism cannot be employed. Rather, each sort τ of the syntactic algebra, called *category*, is mapped to a sort $\sigma(\tau)$ of the semantic algebra, also called *type*. The sortal structure of the semantic algebra is simply an image under σ of the syntactic algebra. If $\Omega(F_\delta) = \langle s_0, \cdots, s_n\rangle$ then $\Omega'(G_\delta) = \langle\sigma(s_0), \cdots, \sigma(s_n)\rangle$.

2.4 HISTORY AND INFLUENCE OF MONTAGUE GRAMMAR

It is not the aim of this chapter to give a full history of Montague Grammar as such. Nevertheless, in this section I shall outline some developments so as to put the subsequent discussion into proper context.

At the time of the publication of Montague's papers the most popular version of linguistic semantics was Generative Semantics (as proposed by Jackendoff, Katz, McCawley, and others). Generative Semantics did semantics essentially in a syntactic fashion: meanings were bits of representation, like CAUSE, BECOME, and RED and were combined in a tree that was subject to transformations. Thus, the sentence /John dies./ would be generated as follows. First, a structure like this is generated:

(2.18)   [BECOME [NOT [ALIVE *John*]]]

Then two transformations rearrange these elements as follows

(2.19)   [[BECOME [NOT ALIVE]] *John*]

The constituent [BECOME [NOT ALIVE]] is spelled out as /dies/ (modulo suitable morphological manipulations). Generative Semantics never bothered to elucidate the meanings of the upper-cased expressions in any detail; it was more concerned with lexical decompositions and capturing semantic regularities (active–passive, and so on).

Montague by contrast was not concerned with syntax; he was interested in getting the meanings right. Moreover, unlike Generative Semanticists he explicated the meanings using models. The lectures and seminars by Montague have had an immediate influence. Cresswell's (1973) book was written after Cresswell had visited UCLA. Similarly, Partee had been taught by Montague and then continued to explore the potential of this theory in natural language semantics (see the collection Partee (2004)). Dowty et al. (1981) was instrumental in popularizing Montague Grammar. Dowty (1979), in which he compares Montague Grammar with Generative Semantics, arguing that there is no incompatibility between them, was also influential. It is possible to assign a model-theoretic meaning to the primitives in Generative Semantics, and it is likewise possible to perform lexical decompositions within Montague Grammar.

Soon it emerged that there is even a compositional treatment of Government and Binding Theory through a mechanism that is now known as the Cooper storage (R. Cooper, 1975). The classic source for generative grammar today—Heim and Kratzer (1998)—uses Montague's ideas. A formal semantics for the Minimalist Program in that direction has been given by Kobele (2006). Today, nearly all branches of formal semantics use techniques inspired by Montague's work.

Montague's use of categorial grammar also led to a rediscovery of the work of Ajdukiewicz, Bar-Hillel, and Lambek, and a return of categorial syntax. The fact that categorial syntax was easily paired with a semantic analysis made it extremely attractive. This is interesting since it was Chomsky who had earlier convinced both Lambek and Bar-Hillel that phrase structure grammars were superior to categorial grammars. Categorial Grammars were explored in particular in Amsterdam, where among others Theo Janssen and Reinhard Muskens promoted the new research agenda of *compositionality* (see Janssen (1983) and Muskens (1995), based on his 1989 dissertation). It is nevertheless necessary to emphasize that the use of categorial grammar does not automatically mean that the grammar is compositional. Not all developments within Categorial Grammar directly address this issue and often the relationship with semantics is not always clearly stated. The mechanism of decomposition employed in Steedman (1990), for example, is incompatible. A similar problem has been noted by Calcagno (1995) with respect to Moortgat's (1993) analysis of quantifier scope. In both cases a string is first formed and then split into components.

Categorial Grammar couples phrase structure with category, and, via the category-to-type mapping also with meanings. This is not without problems. In standard categorial grammars there is no uniform treatment of VSO or OSV languages, since the OV-constituent cannot be formed. One answer to this problem is to relax the correspondence between hierarchical structure and linear order. This has been advocated in Abstract Categorial Grammar ((ACG) de Groote (2001), similar proposals can be found in Muskens (2001) and Kracht (2003)). ACGs treat the phonology in the same way as the semantics: expressions are no longer just strings, they are λ-terms over the algebra of strings. There are precedents for this, for example Bach and Wheeler (1983), Oehrle (1988). A different solution is to allow for discontinuous constituents, for example in the form of Linear Context Free Rewrite Systems (see Calcagno (1995)).

2.5 DISCUSSION OF MONTAGUE'S FRAMEWORK

Montague's proposals were also seen as problematic in various respects. In this section I shall discuss some aspects of his theory that have been subject to criticism in the literature.

2.5.1 Some technical remarks

Montague did not discuss the motivations for his proposals to a large extent, except in the form of exegetical remarks and an occasional example. It is, however, necessary to ask what his overall system achieves and what it does not. We shall highlight a few points where criticism has been raised of Montague's treatment and which have led to further development. Before we can enter a detailed discussion, we shall fix a few terms of discussion. Since the formal apparatus is different from Montague's, we shall have to start again with some basic definitions. The main difference with Montague's setup is that we do not assign meanings to terms of some abstract language but generate sound meaning pairs directly.

A language is defined as a set of signs. Signs are pairs $\sigma = \langle e, m \rangle$, where e is the *exponent* and m the *meaning* of σ. A *grammar* is a finite set of partial functions on signs. There is no need to have sorts; however, functions are from now on partial by default.

A zeroary function is also called a *constant* (and is never partial, since that makes no sense). The lexicon is part of the grammar; it is the set of zeroary functions. Thus the lexicon may contain entries of the form $\langle\text{run}, \text{run}'\rangle$. A *mode of composition* or *mode* is a function that is not zeroary.

> Let S be a set of signs and F a set of partial functions. Then $\langle S\rangle_F$ is the least set such that if $f \in F$ is an n-ary function and $\sigma_i, i < n$, are in $\langle S\rangle_F$ then also $f(\sigma_0, \cdots, \sigma_{n-1}) \in \langle S\rangle_F$ (if defined).

Notice that $\langle\varnothing\rangle_F = \varnothing$ unless F contains constants. The language generated by the grammar F is simply the set $\langle\varnothing\rangle_F$.

F is *compositional* if for all $f \in F$ there is a function f^μ such that for all signs $\langle e_i, m_i\rangle$, $i < n$, if $f(\langle e_0, m_0\rangle, \cdots, \langle e_{n-1}, m_{n-1}\rangle)$ exists then there is an exponent $\vec{y}$ such that:

$$(2.20) \quad f(\langle e_0, m_0\rangle, \cdots, \langle e_{n-1}, m_{n-1}\rangle) = \langle \vec{y}, f^\mu(m_0, \cdots, m_{n-1})\rangle$$

In general, for every function f there are functions f^ε and f^μ such that

$$(2.21) \quad f(\langle e_0, m_0\rangle, \cdots, \langle e_{n-1}, m_{n-1}\rangle) = \langle f^\varepsilon(\vec{e}, \vec{m}), f^\mu(\vec{e}, \vec{m})\rangle$$

Thus, a grammar is compositional if the f^μ are independent of the exponents. It is the mirror image of autonomy, which requires the f^ε to be independent of the meanings (cf. Kracht 2003).

Often, signs are considered to be triples $\langle e, c, m\rangle$, where c is the category. A standard formulation of such grammars assumes independence of the categories on the exponents and meanings; (Kracht, 2003). This is the most popular format used, but contrary to popular opinion there is not much need for the additional category (see Kracht (2011) for arguments). Notice that there is no start symbol. This is no accident. Although it is possible to distinguish different kinds of expressions, the language is not simply the collection of its sentences and associated meanings. If it were, the principle of compositionality would be meaningless. There would be no way we can explain the meaning of /A man talks./ in terms of more primitive elements since these are not sentences and therefore would have no meaning in the language.

2.5.2 Type raising and flexibility

One problem area of Montague Grammar is the idea of type raising. Type raising works as follows. If A is an expression of category a (and meaning m) it can also be assigned the category $\beta/(a\backslash\beta)$ with meaning $\lambda n.n(m)$ or—alternatively—the category $(\beta/a)\backslash\beta$ with meaning $\lambda n.n(m)$. (I use the notation $\gamma\backslash\delta$ for the constituents that look for a γ to their left to form a δ.) The rationale is this. Suppose that B is a constituent of category $a\backslash\beta$ with meaning n. Then $[A\ B]$ is well-formed and a constituent of category β with meaning $n(m)$. Now, suppose that in place of A we are given the category of B and its meaning, m, and the category of the entire constituent, β and its meaning, $n(m)$. Then

A may be either a or $\beta/(a\backslash\beta)$. If we choose the latter, and given that the meaning of the entire constituent is $n(m)$ we must choose $\lambda n.n(m)$ for the meaning of A. Similarly if B is a constituent of category β/a with meaning n we end up with A being of category $(\beta/a)\backslash\beta$ and meaning $\lambda n.n(m)$ so that $[B\,A]$ is a constituent with meaning $n(m)$. Thus, categorially, **type raising** is the pair of rules

$$(2.22) \quad \frac{a}{\beta/(a\backslash\beta)} \qquad \frac{a}{(\beta/a)\backslash\beta}$$

Montague did not think of raising as rules; he rather assumed raised types to begin with. In order to allow names to be coordinated with ordinary NPs Montague assumed that the semantics of names is similar to that of NPs. Thus, /John/ is taken to denote not the individual John but rather the set of properties true of John. This is clearly motivated by the desire to have uniform types for all NPs. This strategy of raising types so as to harmonize the type assignment has become known as 'raising to the worst case'.

In a standard model (where we allow quantifying over all subsets) there is a biunique correspondence between the individuals of the domain and the set of all subsets of the domain containing that individual (such sets are also called **principal ultrafilters**). Partee (1986) has taken a somewhat different approach. The idea there is that we allow grammars to raise (or lower) a type on need. So we pass from an individual to the corresponding ultrafilter or from the ultrafilter to the individual if the type assignment mandates this. This proposal has been widely adopted. Also, Categorical Grammar has adopted a similar strategy to overcome the inflexibility of categories. Rather than multiplying the base categories of words, it may allow the category of a word to be changed on need using the rules of raising as above. This was the proposal made by Geach (1972). Using standard techniques one can associate a canonical semantics with these new constituents. The Geach Rule, for example, corresponds exactly to function composition. Namely, let A, B, and C be constituents of category a/β, β/γ, and γ, respectively. Then, according to standard categorial grammar, the constituents can be put together only like this: $[A\,[B\,C]]$ (assuming, of course, that $\beta \neq \gamma$). However, there are circumstances where we would want the structure $[[A\,B]\,C]$, though with identical meaning. If A, B, and C have meanings m, n, and o, then $[A\,[B\,C]]$ has meaning $m(n(o))$, and this should also then be the meaning of $[[A\,B]\,C]$. Geach proposes a syntactic rule to combine a/β and β/γ into a/γ. Its semantic correlate is $\circ$. For $(m \circ n)(o) = m(n(o))$, whence $m \circ n = \lambda x.m(n(x))$. In natural language, the need for this rule arises rather frequently. Certain adjectives, say /Greek/ or /bald/ are properties of individuals, but can be applied also to relational nouns. The intended meaning of /Greek neighbour/ is 'person, who is Greek and is a neighbour'.

The Lambek Calculus can be seen as the end result of this procedure. In the Lambek Calculus, any continuous sub-part of a constituent can be a constituent again and can be given a semantics compatible with the overall structure. An exposition can be found in Morrill (1994).

2.5.3 Surface compositionality

The analysis offered by Montague uses some non-standard mechanisms for handling strings. One is arbitrary insertion (as in the use of syncategorematic expressions), and the other is the use of deletion. Here is an example, the derivation of /a man walks and he talks/.

(2.23)   1. /man/, basic expression
2. /a/, basic expression
3. /some man/, from 1. and 2. using S2
4. /walk/, basic expression
5. /talk/, basic expression
6. /he$_5$/, basic expression
7. /he$_5$ walks/, from 6. and 4. using S4,
8. /he$_5$ talks/, from 6. and 5. using S4,
9. /he$_5$ walks and he$_5$ talks/, from 7. and 8. using S11a,
10. /a man walks and he talks/, from 3. and 9. using S14.

In this analysis, the word /and/ is not a constituent of the sentence, not even a part. Similarly, the agreeing form /walks/ is created by magic, no further analysis is given. Second, the numbers subscripted to the pronouns, $_5$, are deleted, and sometimes also the pronouns themselves. This means that they are not part of the surface string.

Hausser (1984) objects to this analysis; he coined the phrase 'surface compositionality' for the property that he favoured instead. Surface compositionality analyses strings as being composed completely and exhaustively from their actual parts. This can be stated as follows. The lexicon contains basic expressions, and every complex expression is made from basic expressions through concatenation. Since constituents may be discontinuous, this boils down to the following: basic expressions are tuples of strings, and modes can only concatenate these parts to form the parts of the tuple. (It seems that mild uses of duplication may be necessary.) If expressions are strings then we can formulate the principle as follows. Consider the expressions to be members of the algebra of strings $\langle A^*, \cdot \rangle$, with A the alphabet, and $\cdot$ the operation of concatenation. A *term* $t(x_1, \cdots, x_n)$ is as usual a well-formed expression made from the variables using $\cdot$ and no constants. A *term function* is a function that is the extension of a term (see Burris and Sankappanavar (1981)).

Surface Compositionality. For every mode f the function f^ϵ is a term function of the string algebra.

The formal details are worked out in Kracht (2003).

The use of syncategorematic expressions is mostly unproblematic. We can at no cost introduce basic expressions of the desired kind and formulate a corresponding semantics. Also, empty pronouns have been argued for in many places, most prominently Government and Binding Theory. However, from the standpoint of Surface Compositionality the overt reflex of /he$_n$/ must be taken to be either /he/ or the empty word, and thus we can have only one or two such pronouns. There are essentially two solutions to this problem. One is to renounce the use of free variables altogether. This is the route that P. Jacobson (1999) has taken. Another is to face the use of free variables head on. We shall discuss this problem below, after we have discussed the development of DRT.

2.5.4 DRT

Discourse Representation Theory (DRT) presented a challenge to Montague Grammar. If the interpretation of a sentence is a proposition, then reference to objects introduced in that sentence should be impossible, contrary to fact.

(2.24) Some man walks. He talks.

This is the problem that is raised in Kamp (1981). The theory proposed in that paper and developed further in Kamp and Reyle (1993, among much other work) is that of partial maps into a model. As in Montague Grammar, pronouns carry indices, so what gets effectively interpreted is not (2.24) but something like (2.25).

(2.25) Some$_1$ man$_1$ walks$_1$. He$_1$ talks$_1$.

To be exact, the interpretive algorithm works on surface sentences. It proceeds via construction rules that replace surface strings with semantic structures. However, this algorithm is not compositional, and it still needs to choose variable names when translating pronouns. For a bottom-up translation, we must choose the indexation beforehand.

The second sentence is interpreted against a partial map that makes the first true. This is a partial map β that sends x_1 to some man that walks. A Discourse Representation Structure (DRS) is a pair $D = [V : \Delta]$, where V is a finite set of variables, and Δ a set of formulae or DRSs. There are various constructors, such as a binary constructor $\Rightarrow$ to create complex DRSs. A partial function β makes D true if there is a V-variant β' of β such that all clauses of Δ are true. Here a V-variant β' of β is a partial map such that if $x \notin V$ then β' is defined on x if and only if β is, and they have the same value; and if $x \in V$ then β' is defined on x even if β is not (no condition on its value). A formula is true under a partial map if all variables are assigned a value and the formula is true in the standard sense. $[V : \Delta] \Rightarrow [W : \Sigma]$ is true under β if for every V-variant β' of β that makes Δ true there is a W-variant that makes Σ true. So, unlike standard quantification that has no side effects, the assignment is kept and the second sentence is interpreted using that assignment. It is true therefore if $\beta(x_1)$ also talks.

DRT was originally thought to exemplify the non-compositional nature of natural language meanings. Yet, later Zeevat (1989) proposed a compositional interpretation. Basically, a compositional account is possible in the same way as it can be given in predicate logic: the meaning of a formula is not truth under an assignment, rather, it is a set of assignments. For then the interpretation of a quantifier, say $\exists x_n$, can be given as follows:

(2.26) $[(\exists x_n)\varphi] = \{\beta : \text{there is } \beta' \text{ with } \beta' \sim_n \beta \text{ and } \beta' \in \varphi\}$

Define the map C_n on sets of assignments by

(2.27) $C_n(A) := \{\beta : \text{there is } \beta' \text{ with } \beta' \sim_n \beta \text{ and } \beta' \in A\}$

Then

(2.28) $[(\exists x_n)\varphi] = C_n([\varphi])$

This allows λ-abstraction to be interpreted as well. Zeevat notes, however, that the arrow $\Rightarrow$ is not interpreted properly. His own solution is to take as meaning the pair $\langle V, C \rangle$, where C is the set of satisfying assignments and V the set of main discourse referents.

2.5.5 The problem of variable names

The rule of quantifying not only has the weakness of eliminating indices. There is another issue hidden behind it: how is the correct index actually chosen? The theoretical answer is that any index may be chosen, and there is only one condition, a surface filter: the surface string may not contain any index. The (intended) result of this system is that quantifiers may take scope with respect to each other in any conceivable way. Montague has used this to derive, for example, two different readings of:

(2.29)   Every man loves some woman.

The trick is to derive first

(2.30)   he₃ loves he₇

and then use either first S14 with /every man/ replacing /he₃/ and then S14 with /some woman/ replacing /he₇/ or first S14 with /some woman/ replacing /he₇/ and then S14 with /every man/ replacing /he₃/. (Other indices would do equally well.)

Apart from the fact that it is not surface compositional there are basically two problems with this idea. The first is that it generates way too many readings. There is no mechanism to restrict the scope of quantifiers. The other has to do with the issue of choosing names for variables. Montague takes no precaution against choosing the same variable in subject and object position. Thus if we start with

(2.31)   he₃ loves he₃

a single application of S14 yields

(2.32)   Every man loves him.

This is a grammatical sentence; however, it associates the following meaning to it.

(2.33) $(\forall x_3)(\text{man}'(x_3) \rightarrow \text{love}'(x_3, x_3))$

This is clearly incorrect. One major theme of Government and Binding Theory has been the distribution of pronouns and anaphors and thus, indirectly, refining the rules in such a way as to exclude these incorrect readings (see Heim and Kratzer (1998)).

2.5.6 Meaning postulates and logical form

A somewhat disregarded theme in Montague Grammar is the use of meaning postulates. A discussion is found in Dowty (1979) and Zimmermann (1999). Meaning postulates go back at least to Carnap. Montague introduces them for a specific purpose. One consisted in the analysis of 'seek' as 'try to find'. This resulted in a reduction of the number of primitives and illustrated why 'seek' is not extensional in the object.

The strategy of raising to the worst case introduces too many degrees of freedom. For example, if names are now on a par with proper nouns, their interpretation can be any set of individual concepts. But that is not what names are supposed to denote; they are more specific. They are such sets of individual concepts that are true of a single object. Also, Montague noted the following problematic inference.

(2.34)
$$\frac{\text{The temperature rises.}}{\text{The temperature is ninety degrees.}}$$
$$\therefore \text{Ninety rises.}$$

A proper analysis must take into account that /rise/ is a property not of individuals but of individual concepts. A temperature can rise since it is a function from worlds to numbers, a particular number cannot rise. Montague therefore opted to intensionalize all arguments of a verb. This excludes the dubious inference, but it also excludes inferences that are nevertheless valid.

(2.35)
$$\frac{\text{The president talks.}}{\text{Nicolas Sarkozy is the president.}}$$
$$\therefore \text{Nicolas Sarkozy talks.}$$

The solution is to add a meaning postulate to the effect that /talks/ is transparent with respect to its subject.

In its strictest definition a meaning postulate is simply a definition, as the definition of 'seek' as 'try to find'. The virtue of such a decomposition is not apparent at first sight. However, as rules of quantification allow intermediate scopes, having a single primitive expression is not the same as having a composition of several of them. Also, as is emphasized in Generative Semantics, the choice of primitives may reveal something about the underlying semantic regularities of a language. Dowty (1979) argues in a similar way.

At the other extreme, a meaning postulate is any formula constraining the meaning of some primitive. This means that a meaning postulate is nothing but an axiom in the ordinary sense. It is, however, not clear whether this should be held against Montague Grammar. For it is clear that even an analysis in terms of a logical language relies ultimately on axioms to secure a minimum of material content to its symbols, logical or not.

2.6 CONCLUSION

Montague Grammar has inspired several generations of formal semanticists. It has paved the way to a precise formulation of semantic problems and solutions. Montague has shown that it is possible to do highly rigorous work and yet make substantial progress at the same time. What it certainly is not, however, is the last word on matters. Especially when it comes to compositionality there is no consensus whether Montague has supplied a fully compositional approach. This has nothing to do with a lack of precision; it has more to do with the question whether the abstract formulation is a good rendering of our initial intuitions. In many ways, Montague looks more like a technician than a theoretician; he prefers something that works over something that has intrinsic virtues. Forty years on, the ideas have been substantially modified. We seem to have a much more profound notion of what is a compositional semantics for natural languages.

CHAPTER 3

THE CASE FOR
COMPOSITIONALITY

ZOLTÁN GENDLER SZABÓ

A standard, theory-neutral way to state the principle of compositionality is as follows:

(C_0)   The meaning of a complex expression is a function of the meanings of its constituents and the way they are combined.

The principle is always understood as involving a tacit 'that's all' clause—it states that the meaning of a complex expression is a function of the meanings of its constituents, the way they are combined, and nothing else besides.[1] (C_0) tacitly quantifies over expressions of a language.[2] It holds for most formal languages, which is no great surprise given the extent to which it facilitates metalinguistic proofs. The question is whether we can find this nice feature in languages we did not design. Stated in full generality, (C_0) is taken to be the claim that the meaning of any expression in any natural language is a function of the meanings of the constituents of that expression in that language, and the way they are combined in that language.

Conventional wisdom regarding (C_0) is that it is reasonably clear, fairly trivial, and more or less indispensable in semantic theorizing.[3] I think conventional wisdom is wrong on all three accounts. First, there are significant ambiguities in (C_0). More-over, no matter how the ambiguities are resolved, there is no familiar argument that

---

[1] The principle presupposes that the expressions it quantifies over are unambiguous. There are several ways to extend the principle to expressions with multiple meanings. For the sake of simplicity, I will set this issue aside.

[2] 'Language' can be understood broadly, encompassing systems of symbols that permit the construction of complex symbols. Talk of compositionality in the realm of thoughts presupposes that thoughts make up a language of some sort.

[3] Some philosophers regard compositionality as analytic. While this strikes me as a rather implausible claim, for the sake of this paper I propose to set it aside. What matters is not whether compositionality is analytic, but whether it is self-evident. It clearly is not. Someone who assented to 'Some bachelors are married' is arguably confused about the meaning of 'bachelor' or the meaning of 'married', someone who assented to 'Some natural languages are not compositional' is not plausibly accused of linguistic incompetence.

adequately supports the truth of the principle. The usual considerations speak in favour of a considerably weaker thesis only. Finally, the compositionality principles discussed in philosophy, linguistics, and psychology tend to differ from one another and they are all significantly stronger than (C_0). Since our grounds for accepting (C_0) are already shaky, the stronger principles have at best the standing of methodological assumptions. In other words, despite widespread enthusiasm, the case for compositionality is surprisingly weak.

This is not to say that we should give up on compositionality. It is an interesting hypothesis and it has led to some important discoveries in semantics. My recommendation is only that we should acknowledge that it is on a par with other bold hypotheses, such as that all syntactic operations are binary, that lexical categories are universal, that logical form and syntactic structure are intimately related, and so on.

3.1 AMBIGUITIES

One complaint often voiced against (C_0) is that short of an explicit theory of meaning and a detailed set of constraints on modes of composition it is hopelessly vague. As Barbara Partee puts it:

> if the syntax is sufficiently unconstrained and the meanings sufficiently rich, there seems no doubt that natural languages can be described compositionally. Challenges to the principle generally involve either explicit or implicit arguments to the effect that it conflicts with other well-motivated constraints on syntax and/or on the mapping from syntax to meaning.[4]

Because of this, (C_0) is typically considered but a rough statement of compositionality. Textbooks tend not to dwell on it—rather they proceed quickly with more specific principles which incorporate a number of assumptions about meaning and grammar.

Partee's point can be illustrated with a classic example regarding quantifier scope. Sentences involving multiple quantifiers are often intuitively ambiguous: 'An ambassador was sent to every country' could mean that an ambassador is such that she was sent to every country or that every country is such that an ambassador was sent to it. At the same, the sentence appears to have a single grammatical structure: its subject is 'an ambassador', its predicate 'was sent to every country', the object within the predicate 'every country'. There is no independent evidence for significant lexical ambiguity either—whatever dictionaries tell us about the words within this sentence

---

[4] Partee (1984: 153). Compositionality is a demonstrably empty principle if one completely neglects syntactic and lexical constraints. Janssen (1983) has a proof that we can turn an arbitrary meaning assignment on a recursively enumerable set of expressions into a compositional one, as long as we are allowed to replace the syntactic operations with different ones. Zadrozny (1994) has shown that this can also be done by replacing the old meanings with new ones from which they are uniformly recoverable. For critical discussion of these triviality results, see Westerståhl (1998) and Dever (1999).

seems irrelevant to the ambiguity under discussion. The sentence presents us with a clear *prima facie* counterexample to (C_0): the meaning of 'An ambassador was sent to every country' does not seem to be a function of merely the meanings of its constituents and the way they are combined. Something else makes a difference.

Most of us these days are ready to give up on at least one of these appearances. Some deny that the sentence is ambiguous: they think it has a unitary meaning underspecified with respect to scope relations.[5] Some deny that it has a unique grammatical structure: they think that the reading where the object takes scope over the subject is generated through a movement that remains invisible on the surface.[6] And some deny that the sentence is free of lexical ambiguities: they account for the scope possibilities by assigning multiple (but systematically related) meanings of different types to both the subject and the object.[7] If we are willing to bracket some pre-theoretical intuitions, (C_0) can be smoothly accommodated.[8]

On the other hand, if one has set views on meaning and grammar one might find the challenge scope raises for compositionality insurmountable. The early Russell was, for example, strongly attracted to the view that the meaning of a sentence is literally built up from the meanings of the words within the sentence, and that the way simpler meanings compose into more complex ones tracks the grammatical structure of the sentence. In the face of scope ambiguities he gave up on (C_0), and opted instead for the substantially weaker (C_0'):

(C_0')   If a complex expression has only meaningful constituents then its meaning is a function of the meanings of its constituents and of the way they are combined.

Russell famously denied that quantifying phrases have meaning, so for him (C_0') came out as vacuously true for sentences involving such expressions.[9] One may reasonably wonder how sentences containing meaningless expressions end up meaning something. Russell's response to this challenge was the obvious one: not all meaninglessness is the same. A quantifying phase, like 'an ambassador' is associated with a semantic rule that specifies what larger expressions mean that contain it as a constituent. When we have more than one quantifying phrase, there is a question as to what order the rules are to be applied, and depending on this order we may end up with different meanings. This is how scope ambiguities arise.[10]

---

[5] Cf. Kempson and Cormack (1981) and Bach (1982).

[6] Cf. May (1977) and Heim and Kratzer (1998).

[7] Cf. R. Cooper (1975) and Hendriks (1993).

[8] Some appeals to type-shifting rules are not comfortably described as postulations of lexical or grammatical ambiguities. Still, if there are multiple ways of deriving the surface structure of a sentence due to different applications of type shifting rules and if these different applications lead to different meanings, then it remains natural to say that there is more than one way to build up the meaning of this sentence. So, (C_0) is accommodated.

[9] If we replace the quantifying phrases in 'An ambassador was sent to every country' with logically proper names (expressions that are guaranteed to have meaning) we get sentences for which (C_0') is no longer vacuous. According to Russell, such sentences don't give rise to scope ambiguity.

[10] Cf. Russell (1905).

Russell abandoned compositionality only because he was wedded to his assumptions about meaning and grammar; had he been more flexible he could have preserved compositionality by following one of the paths taken by present day semanticists. But the fact that (C_0) has bite only in conjunction with further commitments does not mean that the principle is in need of further clarification. Consider a claim that is formally analogous to (C_0):

(P$_0$)   The physical properties of an ordinary object are a function of the physical properties of its parts and of the way they are combined.

One may reasonably complain that the notion of a physical property is vague and that there are different views about how parts of ordinary objects are combined. Still, it would be a mistake to declare (P$_0$) obscure on this basis. We may not know exactly which properties are physical or what laws underlie material composition but we still have a grip on these notions. (We certainly know that being ectoplasm is not a physical property and that elementary particles don't compose larger objects by falling in love with one another.) Similarly, despite our disagreements about meaning and structure we know well enough what these are. (We certainly know that the 'cat' and 'not' have different kinds of meanings and that 'John kissed' is not a constituent of 'John kissed Mary'.) In fact, we know enough to see that scope ambiguities are a genuine (albeit not insurmountable) challenge to (C_0). Whether we opt for scope-neutral meanings, quantifier-movement, or type-shifting rules to respond to it, we have to acknowledge that such manœuvres go against the appearances, and have to justify them accordingly.

So, I don't think the open-endedness of the notions of meaning and structure should count as a legitimate complaint against (C_0). Still, there are other reasons for maintaining that the principle is unclear. (C_0) contains three crucial ambiguities that should be brought to light. The source of the first is the word 'function', the source of the second is the phrase 'the meanings of its constituents', and the source of the third is the pronoun 'they'. They are all ordinary lexical or structural ambiguities, not the contrivances of philosophers. I will discuss them in order.

3.1.1 '... is a function of ...'

Among the various meanings of the word 'function' dictionaries tend to distinguish between one that indicates a dependency relation and another—the mathematical sense—that does not. The construction '...is a function of...' is most naturally taken in the former sense but can, perhaps, be understood in the latter as well. When we say that height is a function of age (among other things), we tend to read this as something stronger than the bland claim that there is a function from age (and other things) to height. So, we need to distinguish between the following two principles:

The meaning of a complex expression is *determined by* of the meanings of its constituents and of the way they are combined.

There is a function to the meaning of complex expressions from the meanings of their constituents and of the way they are combined.

The first of these entails the second, but not the other way around. There is a long tradition of reading (C_0) in the weaker fashion. But it is unclear whether the official reading always conforms to our intuitions about what compositionality should demand.

One way to see this is to consider the possibility of there being two languages that are almost identical: they have the same expressions, the same syntax, and the same meanings for all expressions except for an arbitrary sentence S. In other words, S has different meanings in these languages, even though it has the same structure and all its constituents mean the same. The weaker reading is not in conflict with this possibility: there may be different functions in the different languages that map the meanings of S's constituents and the way they combine to S's meaning. The stronger reading, however, rules this out. The meaning of S is not determined bottom up, for it *can* mean different things even if we hold the meanings of all its constituents and the way they are combined fixed.[11]

Another way to see the contrast between these two readings of (C_0) is to consider linguistic change. Suppose we have a language that undergoes some very limited meaning change. The change is manifested in one obvious way: sentence S that once meant one thing now means something completely different. At the same time, suppose we have no evidence of any change in grammar. Under these conditions, I submit, we would assume that some constituent or other within S also changed its meaning. Why? One might say that because we tend to think that meaning is compositional, and it remains compositional as meaning changes. This is exactly what the stronger reading would allow us to say. But if natural languages are compositional only in the weaker sense the explanation is illegitimate: S could change its meaning in accordance with compositionality even if its constituents and the way they are combined remain the same. This, I think, is a fairly good indication that the weak reading—despite being the standard one employed in semantics textbooks—is unreasonably weak.

3.1.2 '...the meanings of its constituents ...'

Plural definite descriptions exhibit a collective/distributive ambiguity and 'the meanings of its constituents' within (C_0) is no exception. Consider the sentence 'The wealth of a country is a function of the wealth of its citizens.' In its distributive reading this sentence makes a rather controversial claim, namely, that the individual wealth of citizens fixes the wealth of nations. The collective reading permits the wealth of nations to be a

---

[11] In Szabó (2000b), I argued that the stronger reading of (C_0) could be spelled out as the claim that there is a single function *across all possible human languages* to the meaning of complex expressions from the meanings of their constituents and of the way they are combined. Thus understood, the stronger reading entails that at most one of the two languages mentioned above is a possible human language. One of them is not learnable in the ordinary fashion, as a first language. It would have to be acquired by acquiring the other language first and then learning a special translation rule for S.

function of what its citizens own collectively (including what they own as singleton groups, i.e. what they own individually). If there are roads or parks jointly owned by entire communities they are allowed to influence the wealth of nations on the second, but not on the first reading. We have thus the following two principles:

The meaning of a complex expression is a function of the meanings its constituents have *individually* and of the way they are combined.

The meaning of a complex expression is a function of the meanings its constituents have *collectively* and of the way they are combined.

Opting for the weaker principle allows the possibility of non-structurally encoded semantic relations in a compositional language. Consider, for example, the classic contrast between 'Cicero is Cicero' and 'Cicero is Tully'. The semantic literature has been torn by such examples: on the one hand it is very plausible to think that these two sentences are not synonyms (for the former seems analytic but the latter does not), and on the other hand it is also very plausible that the meaning of proper names is nothing but their referent (for the point of having proper names in a language does not seem to go beyond the labelling of objects). The stronger reading forces us to give up one of these views: otherwise we would have a difference in meaning between the sentences without a difference in the individual meanings of constituents or a difference in the way they are combined. But if we think that the meanings the constituents have collectively in these sentences depend not only on what 'Cicero' and 'Tully' mean but also on the presence or absence of *semantically encoded coreference* between the names, we can explain how 'Cicero is Cicero' can mean something other than 'Cicero is Tully'.[12]

Another way to think of this proposal is to bring in the notion of indices. Sameness of indices encodes coreference. The difference between 'Cicero is Cicero' and 'Cicero is Tully' is that of indexing: the former is represented as 'Cicero$_1$ is Cicero$_1$', the latter as 'Cicero$_1$ is Tully$_2$'.[13] If the meanings of these sentences depend on the individual meanings of constituents and the way they are combined, *as well as on indexing*, the difference in meaning between these sentences can be accounted for. If we think of the indexing as a feature of the collective meaning of the constituents the account is compatible with the collective reading of (C$_0$).

3.1.3 '...they...'

The pronoun 'they' in (C$_0$) can have two different antecedents: 'its constituents' or 'the meanings of its constituents'. The two readings can be paraphrased as follows:

---

[12] For details, see Fine (2007). He argues that natural languages are compositional only in the collective reading of the principle.

[13] This sort of proposal can be found in Fiengo and May (1994).

The meaning of a complex expression is a function of the meanings of its constituents and of the way *those constituents* are combined.

The meaning of a complex expression is a function of the meanings of its constituents and of the way *those meanings* are combined.

The difference is subtle but significant. It is syntactic structure that encodes how the constituents of a complex expression are combined, so according to the first reading, complex meaning is a function of constituent meanings and syntax. The second, on the other hand, permits the existence of non-synonymous complex expressions with identical syntactic structure and pairwise synonymous constituents, as long as we have different semantic rules associated with the same syntactic rules.

Here is an example to illustrate the difference between the two readings. Assume that meaning is truth-conditional content, that 'every man' has a single syntactic structure, that 'every' and 'man' each have a single determinate truth-conditional content, and that the truth-conditional content of 'every man' includes some contextual restriction on the domain of quantification. Given the first reading, we have a violation of compositionality. But the second yields no such verdict: if the syntactic rule which combines the quantifier and the noun is associated with a context-sensitive semantic rule, we can still maintain that in every context the meaning of 'every man' is a function of the meanings of its constituents and the way those meanings are combined in that context.[14]

The first reading of (C_0) is rather restrictive. Compare, for example the expressions 'red apple' and 'pink grapefruit'. As competent speakers know, a red apple is red on the outside, while a pink grapefruit is pink on the inside. Here we seem to have complex expressions whose meanings are combined in different ways from the meanings of their lexical constituents, even though the syntactic mode of composition is the very same. Defenders of the first reading of (C_0) would have to argue for a hidden constituent in the structure of these expressions, and providing independent motivation for such a hidden constituent might be a tall order. Alternatively, they might try to deny that our knowledge of which part of a red apple is red and which part of a pink grapefruit is pink is part of our linguistic competence.[15] This might be more promising, but when carried to the extreme in responding to a great many similar examples, it eventually leads to an uncomfortably narrow conception of meaning.

By contrast, the second reading of (C_0) is rather permissive. Instead of a semantic rule that looks at the context in determining the meaning of a quantifier phrase in order to associate with it a domain, we could have one that says: 'Flip a coin—if it lands on tails then the domain of the quantifier phrase is the set of blue things; otherwise it is the set of red things.' If languages that allow such rules count as compositional one surely loses sight of all intuitive motivation behind adopting the principle. I am not suggesting that

---

[14] See Stanley and Szabó (2000) and Pelletier (2003). The former subscribe to the stronger reading, the latter to the weaker one.

[15] If I don't know which part of a red apple must be red I am probably unable to tell which apples are red. But—barring verificationism—there is no quick argument from this premise to the conclusion that I do not know what 'red apple' means.

those who announce the second reading as their way of understanding compositionality would want to allow such rules: they all have explicit or tacit restrictions on what counts as a legitimate way of combining meanings. It is those restrictions that carry the theoretical weight.[16]

3.1.4 Fixing meaning

The three ambiguities in (C_0) give us eight possible readings. Which of them best deserves the title 'the principle of compositionality'? I suggest that we opt for the strongest one, (C):

(C)   The meaning of a complex expression is determined by the meanings its constituents have individually and of the way those constituents are combined.

What this says is that once you fix the meanings of the constituents of an expression and its syntactic structure, you have fixed what the expression means. If we assume that the *constituent-of* relation is irreflexive, asymmetric, and transitive, and that every expression has but finitely many constituents the claim can be further strengthened: once you fix the meanings of lexical items within an expression and its syntax, you have no more leeway as to what the expression means. We all know that the meaning of complex expressions can depend on the lexicon and on syntax—what (C) says is that it does not depend on anything else.

It is important that (C) does not rule out that the meaning of phrases, clauses, sentences, paragraphs, entire novels, etc. should depend on all sorts of odd things. All it says is that *if* the meaning of a complex expression depends on, say, the price of copper on the stock market, then so does *either* the meaning of some lexical item within that expression *or* the syntactic structure of that expression. (C) poses absolutely no restriction on what lexical meanings could be.[17]

All other readings of (C_0) besides (C) permit non-lexical non-syntactic sources for multiplicity of meaning in complex expressions. If we construe 'is a function of' as merely requiring the existence of a function we allow differences in meaning in complex expressions across languages or stages of developments of languages. If we construe 'the meanings of its constituents' collectively we allow differences in meaning in complex expressions due to semantic relations among constituents. If we construe 'they' as anaphoric to 'the meanings of its constituents' we allow differences in meaning in complex expressions different due to different semantic operations associated with the same syntactic operations.

---

[16] Compare: 'The wealth of a country is a function of the wealth of its citizens and the way the wealth of the citizens is combined.' If this is to be a substantive claim there should be constraints on what counts as a way of combining individual wealth.

[17] This is in conflict with the main thrust of a number of papers in Fodor and Lepore (2002). For a more extensive criticism of the idea that compositionality is a substantive constraint on lexical meaning see Szabó (2004).

(C) is both the strongest and the most natural reading of (C_0). It deserves to be called the principle of compositionality. If it turns out to be too strong, we have the other versions to fall back upon.

3.2 ARGUMENTS

There are three more or less traditional considerations for compositionality. The first two are rarely stated explicitly—to some extent I am reading between the lines when I call them traditional. They are also obviously inconclusive. The third—the argument from understanding—is frequently evoked and is widely accepted to be sound. This argument comes in two flavours, one emphasizing the productivity, the other the systematicity of understanding. Each argument has significant weaknesses.

3.2.1 Intrinsicness

Consider a golden ring and its particular mass. Could an object have a different mass if it were made up of the same sort of particles arranged in the same manner as this ring? There is a strong intuition that it could not. Could an object made up of the same particles in the same manner as this ring have a different price? Clearly yes—if such a ring had once belonged to Nefertiti it would surely be worth a fortune. Whence the difference between mass and price? Taking the same sort of particles as the ones that a particular ring comprises and arranging them in the manner they are arranged in that ring amounts to a duplication of the ring. Properties that duplicates share are intrinsic, and mass, unlike price, strikes us as an intrinsic property.[18]

Perhaps one of the reasons we are drawn to compositionality is that we are prone to view meaning as somehow intrinsic to its bearer. Why? The idea is that if e and e' are duplicate expressions then they must be tokens of the same expression type, and (setting aside indexicals) tokens of the same expression type are synonyms (if they have meaning at all).[19] So, meaningful non-indexical duplicate expressions must share their meanings.[20] The intuition behind the intrinsicness of meaning can be brought out by considering pictures. A perfect copy of a picture shares its representational properties

---

[18] The precise distinction between intrinsic and extrinsic properties is an elusive matter. For a good survey of the problems and the headway already made, see Weatherson (2006).

[19] The claim that linguistic expressions are individuated semantically is fairly widely held among philosophers. This entails that linguistic expressions cannot change their meanings. What we ordinarily call meaning change is a (perhaps gradual) replacement of one expression with another that sounds just the same. Those who think that the proposition that 'Snow is white' means that snow is white is a necessary truth are all committed to this.

[20] If by meaning we mean something like Kaplan's notion of character then indexicals of the same type turn out to be synonyms across contexts of use. If, on the other hand, by meaning we mean something like Kaplan's notion of content, this does not hold.

with the original: if the Mona Lisa is depicts a woman with a mysterious smile, so do all its countless reproductions. Of course, the original relates to its object in a way the copies do not, but this is supposed to be a non-representational difference. To the extent that meaning is anything like pictorial representation, the analogy carries some weight. Let's call this the *intrinsicness argument*.

The argument is, of course, deeply problematic. We know that the sort of intuition that underlies it is sometimes deceptive—physics has taught us that we must distinguish between inertial and gravitational mass, and it may well turn out that neither is genuinely intrinsic. More importantly, we know that meaning isn't intrinsic *tout court*— clearly, some meaning is conventional and conventions are external to bearers of meaning. These are important caveats, but I don't think they fully undermine the underlying intuitions. Perhaps mass is an extrinsic property of elementary particles (e.g. because mass depends on frame of reference); still, it remains intuitively plausible (and physically uncontested) that duplicates of objects whose elementary particles have the same mass themselves have the same mass. That is, mass remains intrinsic *modulo* elementary mass. Similarly, although meaning is an extrinsic feature of lexical items (e.g. because meaning depends on social conventions); still, it remains intuitively plausible (and undefeated by mere platitudes) that duplicates of sentences whose lexical components have the same meaning themselves have the same meaning. That is, for all we know meaning is intrinsic *modulo* lexical meaning. Still, this is no solid ground for accepting any form of compositionality.

3.2.2 Induction

Convincing counterexamples to compositionality are hard to come by.[21] In linguistic semantics, compositionality has been a central assumption for at least half a century. Accordingly, a great many putative counterexamples had been offered: adjectives, negative polarity items, propositional attitude contexts, cross-sentential anaphora, conditionals, etc. Some of these are more convincing than others, but none has convinced many. For each of these phenomena, several compositional accounts have been proposed. As things stand, linguists tend to stick with a hypothesis that has worked. Let's call this the *inductive argument*.

The strength of the inductive argument should not be overestimated. For one thing we don't really have satisfactory semantic theories for anything more than small fragments of ordinary languages. The fixes semanticists come up with when faced with putative counterexamples to compositionality are often complicated and lack independent motivation.

---

[21] Actually, quoted expressions are plausible counterexamples to compositionality. The English words 'woodchuck' and 'groundhog' are synonyms but the English phrases 'the word "woodchuck"' and 'the word "groundhog"' are not. It seems entirely *ad hoc* to blame the meaning differences on different modes of composition. However, this example can be dismissed by claiming that quotation marks are devices for demonstrating an expression type whose token they surround, i.e. that quoted expressions are indexicals.

What would be a clear violation of compositionality for, say, English? Imagine if the sentence 'Grass is green' were to mean that grass is green during the week, and that grass is *not* green on weekends. Then surely the meaning of this sentence would depend on something other than the meanings of its constituent words and the way those words are combined—what day of the week it is would make a difference. Except, of course, if the change in meaning is coupled with a corresponding change in the lexicon or in syntax. If on weekends 'green' means what 'not green' does on weekdays or an unpronounced negation pops into the structure of 'Grass is green' we have no violation of compositionality. To make sure that any given putative counterexample to compositionality is genuine, one must make sure that one has a pair of complexes with different meanings that are built up from synonymous simples in a parallel fashion. Given the rudimentary state of our knowledge of meaning and structure, this is a tall order.

3.2.3 Understanding

Here is the argument most of us would fall back on in defence of compositionality: the meanings of complexes must be determined by the meanings of their constituents and the way they are combined, since we in fact understand them by understanding their parts and their structure. Call this the *argument from understanding*.

There are two problems with this, as it stands. First, the argument presupposes something rather controversial, namely, that understanding is a matter of grasping the meaning of that which is understood. This is certainly not right in general: to understand a problem, an idea, or a proof is not the same as grasping the meaning of the problem, the meaning of the idea, or the meaning of the proof (whatever *those* might be). Of course, one might try to stipulate that the required equivalence holds in the case of language—that to understand a *linguistic expression* is nothing more or less than grasping what it means. But such a stipulation is by no means innocent. There are many conceptions of meaning for which it is a rather bad fit. It is certainly false, in general, that understanding a linguistic expression is a matter of grasping its extension— so there is no argument from understanding in favour of the claim that extensional semantic theories should be compositional. But richer notions of meaning employed in semantics are also problematic in this context. Take for example the standard view according to which the meaning of a declarative sentence is the set of possible worlds where the sentence is true. Should proponents of this standard view be taken to embrace the idea that understanding a declarative sentence requires that we grasp a set of possible worlds? What sort of grasping would that be? Does it require the ability to tell of any particular possible world whether it is a member of the set? Or take the view according to which the meaning of a proper name is its bearer. Should someone who thinks this also accept that understanding a proper name is a matter of grasping its bearer? What does that amount to? Does it require that one be able to single out the name-bearer? Many semanticists recoil at these suggestions—they would prefer to stay neutral on what are arguably substantive psychological questions. But without taking a stand on the relationship between meaning and understanding, the argument from understanding gives no support to the principle of compositionality.

Let us then simply assume that understanding a linguistic expression is grasping its meaning. Even so, there remains the second problem with the argument from understanding. Its central premise—that we understand complex expressions by understanding their parts and their structure—is not obvious. *How* we understand phrases and clauses is not open to reflection—if it were, psycholinguistics would presumably be a far less perplexing field of inquiry. Convincing arguments for compositionality must focus on some feature of language understanding we are certain of. There are two such features that have been emphasized—productivity and systematicity.

3.2.3.1 *Productivity*

The argument from productivity goes as follows. It is a fact that competent speakers can understand complex expressions they never encountered before.[22] There must therefore be something competent speakers know (perhaps tacitly) on the basis of which they can determine what those complex expressions mean. What can this knowledge be? It seems that the only thing we can plausibly point at is knowledge of the structure of the complex expression and knowledge of the meanings of its lexical constituents. Having this knowledge must be sufficient to understanding a complex expression, which means that the structure of the expression, together with the meanings of its simple constituents must determine what the expression means.[23]

An important caveat must be added: the argument is unable to screen out isolated counterexamples. The counterexamples are usually labelled *idioms* and swept under the rug. There is nothing wrong with this, as long us we have an independent characterization of what it is to be an idiom. And—since idioms must presumably be acquired one-by-one—we cannot allow for more than finitely many of them in any given natural language.

A more important problem with the productivity argument is that there are infinitely many complex expressions *nobody* has ever heard. How does the alleged fact that syntax plus lexicon determines the meanings of complex expression we do hear support the claim that syntax plus lexicon determines the meanings of all the other complex expressions as well? This is not just the general Humean worry about induction—we have good reasons to doubt that the complex expressions we hear form an unbiased sample of all complex expressions. For if there were complex expressions whose meaning we could not determine in the usual way we would presumably want to stay away from them.

---

[22] This should be fairly uncontroversial—everyone can come up with sentences they have never heard before. Another way to see that this must be so is to call attention to the fact that we can understand infinitely many distinct complex expressions whose meanings all differ from one another. A plain example of this is the sequence of sentences 'Ann's father is bold', 'Ann's father's father is bold', 'Ann's father's father's father is bold', … etc.

[23] '… the possibility of our understanding sentences which we have never heard before rests evidently on this, that we can construct the sense of a sentence out of parts that correspond to words' (Frege, 1980: 79 (English translation)).

Another worry concerns the claim that we *already* understand certain expressions
we have never heard before. What is the evidence for this? The fact that when we hear
them we understand them shows nothing more than that the information necessary to
determine what they mean is available to us immediately *after* they have been uttered.
If there are features of the context of utterance we can invariably rely on, those features
may well play a role in interpreting novel complex expressions. And there may well be
such features. For example, consider a case when a speaker utters a sentence that means
one thing in the language of the conversation, and another thing in another language
that the hearer also knows. The hearer will then rely on her knowledge of which language
is being spoken in interpreting the sentence, even though this information isn't part of
the lexicon or the syntax of that language.

One can also wonder whether we always rely on syntax in interpreting novel expressions. In the case of numerals one might reasonably doubt this. It is plausible that syntax
writes numerals right-to-left—that is that the syntactic constituents of 'five hundred
eighty two' include 'eighty two' but not 'fifty eight'. At the same time, by far the simplest
algorithm for identifying the referent of numerals (something that may well be crucial
for grasping the meaning of these expressions) reads the numerals left-to-right—that
is 'five hundred eighty two' refers to ten times what 'fifty eight' refers to plus what 'two'
refers to, etc. If in interpreting numerals we do rely on this simple algorithm then we
must discern in these expressions a structure distinct from their syntactic structure.[24]

In sum, I think the argument from productivity supports at best the cautious claim
that by and large the meanings of complex expressions are determined by the meanings
of their simple constituents, by some familiar pattern into which we can arrange those
meanings (which may or may not be the syntactic structure of the complex expression),
and, perhaps, by familiar and predictable features of the context in which the complex
expression is used. This is a far cry from (C).

3.2.3.2 *Systematicity*

The argument from systematicity states that anyone who understands a number of
complex expressions $e_1, \ldots, e_n$ understands all other complex expressions that can be
built up from the constituents of $e_1, \ldots, e_n$ using syntactic rules employed in building
up their structures. Since this is so, there must be something competent speakers know
(perhaps tacitly) on the basis of which they can determine what the complex expressions
built through such recombination mean. What can that be? The only plausible assumption seems to be that it is the structure of the original complex expressions $e_1, \ldots, e_n$
and the meanings of their simple constituents. Having this knowledge must be sufficient
to understanding the recombined complex expression, which means that its structure
together with the meanings of its simple constituents must determine what it means.

Like the argument from productivity, this is an argument to the best explanation.
It too needs a caveat to dismiss idioms and is also subject to the worry whether it is

[24] For further discussion of this example, see Szabó (2000a: 77–80).

syntactic structure (as opposed to some other structure) that we rely on in interpreting complex expressions. In addition, it has problems of its own.

First, it is not entirely clear whether the phenomenon it seeks to explain is real. Although it is fairly obvious that anyone who understands 'brown dog' and 'black cat' also understands 'brown cat' and 'black dog', the intuition becomes rather weak once we start considering more complex cases. Is the fact that someone understands 'red car' and 'tall building' enough to show that he must understand 'red building' and 'tall car'? One might argue that to understand 'red building' one has to know which parts of a red building are supposed to be red, and to understand 'tall car' one would need to know how to compare cars in terms of height. Neither of these is something one must obviously know in order to understand 'red car' and 'tall building'.

There is also the problem that the argument shows less than it claims to. If we run the argument for the pair of sentences 'apples are red' and 'bananas are yellow' we can conclude that the meanings of 'apples', 'bananas', 'are red', and 'are yellow' plus predication determine the meaning of 'Bananas are red'. It does *not* follow that the meanings of 'bananas' and 'are red' plus predication do that.

It is also worth emphasizing that the systematicity argument seeks to prove not only compositionality but also its converse. For the best explanation for recombination is supposed to be that we can decompose complex expressions into their simple constituents and then use the material to compose new ones. If we know how to do this in general then, presumably, the meanings of complex expressions are not only *determined by* but also *determine* their structure and the meanings of their simple constituents.[25]

3.3 STRENGTHENINGS

Debates in philosophy, linguistics, and psychology focus on related but significantly stronger claims. Whatever interest there is in compositionality derives from the fact that it is the common core of the stronger claims. I will identify these claims and call them the philosopher's principle, the linguist's principle, and the psychologist's principle. In so doing, I do not wish to suggest that they are widely accepted within those respective fields.

3.3.1 The philosopher's principle

Philosophers are not in the business of designing semantic theories for natural languages, although they are certainly interested in general questions about what shape such theories could take. Philosophers are interested in *what* expressions mean instrumentally (to clarify various philosophical problems), but they are first and foremost

---

[25] Cf. Fodor and Lepore (2002: 59); Pagin (2003: 292).

interested in *why* expressions mean what they do. To address this latter problem they need to figure out what is explanatorily prior, the meanings of simple expressions or the meanings of complex ones. A strengthening of (C) offers an answer to this:

(Φ)   Complex expressions have their meanings in virtue of the meanings their constituents have individually and in virtue of the way those constituents are combined.

It is clear that (Φ) entails (C)—if X holds in virtue of Y and Z then X is determined by Y and Z. The converse does not hold because explanatory priority is asymmetric, while determination need not be. (According to Newton's second law of motion, for example, given the mass of an object, the applied force and the acceleration mutually determine each other.) When philosophers state compositionality as the principle according to which the meanings of complex expressions are *defined in terms of* or *derived from* the meanings of their constituents, or when they say that complex expressions *get their meaning* from the meanings of their constituents they most likely have (Φ) and not (C) in mind. They commit themselves to the idea that the wholes have meaning because their parts do, and not the other way around.

In section 60 of the *Foundations of Arithmetic* Frege declares 'it is enough if the sentence as whole has meaning; thereby also its parts obtain their meanings'.[26] This has come to be called the *context principle*. The idea is presumably that we should think of the meanings of constituent expressions as abstractions from the entire sentence meaning, which in turn can be taken to mean that words and phrases mean what they do *because* what the sentences in which they occur as constituents mean. On pain of circularity in the explanatory account of meaning one cannot hold on to both (Φ) and the context thesis.

Many philosophers believe that the meaning of sentences is explanatorily prior to the meanings of all other expressions.[27] One might hold this because one thinks that linguistic expressions get their meanings from mental states (paradigmatically, beliefs) that they are used to express, or from speech acts (paradigmatically assertions) that they are used to perform, and because one thinks that those relevant mental states or speech-act must have propositional content. But there are all sorts of mental states and speech-acts that are *prima facie* non-propositional—to imagine a unicorn, to hope for rain, to refer to an object, or to alert someone are but a few obvious examples. Proponents of sentential primacy must argue either that these are not as central in grounding linguistic meaning as propositional beliefs and assertions, or that despite appearances to the contrary these too have propositional content.[28]

---

[26] Frege (1884: section 60). The translation in the standard English edition is misleading; the translation here is mine.

[27] See Davis (2003: 175, fn. 16) for a representative list of defenders of this view. Davis himself rejects sentential primacy.

[28] One might even challenge the assumption that belief and assertion always have propositional content. For the former, see Szabó (2003), for the latter Buchanan and Ostretag (2005).

3.3.2 The linguist's principle

Linguists, at least the ones I tend to meet, don't have strong views on what makes words and sentences meaningful. They tend to focus on the relationship between structure and meaning. Even in lexical semantics, most of the action is in identifying the structural features that are supposed to underlie lexical categorization, not in trying to explain the meaning-differences within categories. (C) does not make a particularly strong claim about how structure constrains meaning; the principle that holds real interest for linguists is (Λ):

(Λ)   The meaning of a complex expression is determined by its immediate structure and the meanings of its immediate constituents.

Proposition (C) says that the meaning of a complex expression is determined by its *entire* structure and the meanings of *all* its constituents. In assigning meaning to a complex expression (C) allows us to look at the meanings of constituents deep down the tree representing its syntactic structure, while (Λ) permits looking down only one level.

It is important to note that it is this stronger principle that gets often formalized and stated in textbooks as 'the principle of compositionality'. When we demand of compositional meaning assignments that they establish a homomorphism between the syntactic and semantic algebras, we demand that (Λ) should hold for the language in question.[29] (Λ) pushes theorists towards rich conceptions of meaning. If we are not allowed to look deep inside complex expressions to determine what they mean we had better make sure that whatever semantic information is carried by an expression is projected to larger expressions in which they occur as constituents. There is nothing in the traditional arguments in favour of compositionality that yields support to (Λ).[30]

3.3.3 The psychologist's principle

From the psychological perspective what matters is how we actually understand complex expressions. (Ψ) formulates a rather straightforward hypothesis about this matter:

(Ψ)   We understand a complex expression by understanding its structure and its constituents.

Proposition (C) guarantees that one could—cognitive limitations aside—determine the meanings of complex expressions on the basis of their structure and the meanings of their constituents. According to (Ψ), this is in fact how we always proceed.[31]

---

[29] For detailed presentations of such formal statements, see Montague (1970*b*), Janssen (1983), and Westerståhl (1998).

[30] An example of a semantics that violates this locality constraint is the treatment of propositional attitudes in Carnap (1947).

[31] Horwich (1998: 155) thinks that something like (Ψ) is true by definition. This strikes me as a rather unfortunate stipulation in that it seems neither to accord with the ordinary meaning of 'understanding', nor to create a theoretically useful novel term.

The fact that we understand complex expressions we never heard before is a reason to think that *sometimes* we do understand complex expressions in this way. But there is no reason to assume that this is how we *always* proceed. In the case of complex expressions we hear all the time we may not have to go through all that. They may be understood as if they were idioms, even if they are not. (Ψ) seems to be an implausibly strong hypothesis that receives no support from the traditional arguments for compositionality.

3.4 SUMMARY

I have argued for three main claims. The first one is that the usual statement of the compositionality principle is massively ambiguous. One of the eight available readings rules out all sources of multiplicity in meaning in complex expressions besides the lexicon and the syntax. Others are more permissive—how much more is not always clear. The second claim is that traditional considerations in favour of compositionality are less powerful than is often assumed: the intrinsicness argument and the inductive argument are inconclusive; the two arguments based on facts of language understanding have a number of shortcomings. In the end, compositionality is best construed as an empirical hypothesis on meanings expressed in natural languages. Finally, the third claim is that even if compositionality is true, most of the debates in philosophy, linguistics, and psychology surrounding compositionality will remain open. These debates tend to be about significantly stronger theses.

CHAPTER 4

....

COMPOSITIONALITY PROBLEMS AND HOW TO SOLVE THEM

....

THOMAS EDE ZIMMERMANN

WHETHER by methodological principle or by empirical hypothesis, theories of formal semantics usually seek to account for the meanings of complex expressions in a compositional way. Nevertheless, in semantic practice the *Principle of Compositionality* is known to lead to occasional problems. The aim of the present, largely descriptive and taxonomic survey is to exemplify and classify the kinds of problems caused by the demand of compositionality as well as common strategies that have been used to solve them. The first section will provide some general background on the perspective taken on semantic theory in general and the role of compositionality in particular. Section 4.2 presents a classification of compositionality problems based on a certain, broadly Fregean strategy of identifying meanings and, more generally, semantic values. Solution strategies are discussed in the third and final section.

4.1 COMPOSITIONALITY...

....

Semantic theories account for the literal, conventional meanings of linguistic expressions, and they tend to do so by assigning them one or more *semantic values*: extensions, intensions, characters, etc.[1] Lest semantics should be a *cul-de-sac*, at least some of these values must be interpretable from the outside. It is commonly assumed that semantics inputs to pragmatics (and possibly other cognitive disciplines). In particular, *semantic values*, are supposed to figure in accounts of preconditions of utterances and their communicative effects, contributing *aspects* of their literal meaning. For instance, the

---

[1] Cf. T. E. Zimmermann (forthcoming) for more on the very role of semantic values in semantics and its interfaces.

extensions of terms (names, descriptions, personal pronouns,...) correspond to their *referents*; the *intension* of a declarative sentence goes proxy for its *propositional content*; the (semantic) *presuppositions* of an expression determine *appropriateness conditions* on its use; etc. And, to be sure, reference, propositional content, appropriateness, etc. play central roles in speech act theory and other areas of pragmatics. Thus pragmatics relies on semantics to determine some of these factors, and semantics usually does so by providing corresponding values. The external identifiability of these values may constrain their nature: extensions of terms must be, if not identical with, then at least naturally connected to, their referents; intensions of declarative sentences must some-how encode the information making up their propositional content; presuppositions must be at least truth-valuable in order to constrain appropriate use; etc. However, not all semantic values serve as input to pragmatics (or other disciplines, for that matter). Typically, pragmatic explanations relate to semantic aspects—and thus corresponding values—of sentences, terms, and sometimes certain predicates, but not to those of, say, conjunctions, determiners, or quantified noun phrases.[2] The vast majority of semantic values is purely theory-internal and thus not subject to external constraints. But there may be internal constraints imposed on them. Most prominent among them is the demand for *compositionality*, in a sense to be explained now.

A truism has it that speakers of a natural language master an unlimted number of expressions most of which have never been uttered. Part of this mastery is the faculty of associating with each linguistic form the meaning it has in their language. Grammatical theories may be seen as reconstructing this faculty in a systematic, and usually modular, fashion. In particular, syntax seeks to individuate the forms of expressions in terms of abstract structures that serve as the input to semantics, which in turn determines their (literal) meanings. Typically, semantic theories proceed systematically by mapping their syntactic input to one or more *semantic values*, adhering to one or more instances of a:

Generalized Principle of Compositionality
The *V* of a complex expression functionally depends on the *V*s of its immediate parts and the way in which they are combined.

where the exact nature of the semantic value(s) *V* depends on the particular theory. The following instances of the Generalized Principle of Compositionality are cases in point:[3]

Ordinary Principle of Compositionality
The meaning of a complex expression functionally depends on the meanings of its immediate parts and the way in which they are combined.

---

[2] Sometimes their logical properties and relations between them may become relevant though, as in the derivation of scalar implicatures in Gazdar (1979) or the treatment of elliptic answers in von Stechow and Zimmermann (1984).

[3] The first of these principles may be found in Montague (1970b). The Extensional Principle of Compositionality has its roots in Frege's work, particularly Frege (1892). The third version is part and parcel of Kaplan's (1989) theory of meaning and reference, and particularly of his prohibition against monsters (1989: 510ff); cf. T. E. Zimmermann (1991: 166ff) and Westerståhl (this volume) for more on compositionality within Kaplan's framework.

Extensional Principle of Compositionality
The extension of a complex expression functionally depends on the extensions of its immediate parts and the way in which they are combined.

Intensional Principle of Compositionality
The content of a complex expression functionally depends on the contents of its immediate parts and the way in which they are combined.

In the following, the part-whole structure of linguistic expressions referred to in the Principle of Compositionality, will be indicated by way of tree graphs like:

(4.1)   John loves Mary

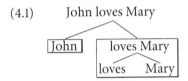

According to (4.1), the English sentence **John loves Mary** has five parts, all but one—viz. (4.1) itself—are *proper*; three of which are *ultimate*—**John**, **loves**, and **Mary**; and two of which are *immediate*—viz. the highlighted subtrees representing (the structure of) subject and predicate. Only the latter two are relevant when it comes to determining the (pertinent) semantic value of (4.1) in a compositional way. In particular, the values of the (ultimate) parts **loves** and **Mary** only matter for the value of (4.1) inasmuch as they influence the value of the predicate; but they need not—indeed: must not—be taken into account separately. As a consequence, the semantic value of (4.1) must be the same if either of its immediate parts is replaced by an expression with the same value, irrespective of how this value has been determined and what the internal structure of this part is. If, for example, **John** has the same extension as **the boss** and **loves Mary** shares its extension with **snores**, then the Extensional Principle of Compositionality predicts that (4.1) has the same extension as:

(4.2)   The boss is snores

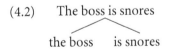

Thus compositionality imposes a more severe restriction on the determination of semantic values than it would if the values of arbitrary—and not just: immediate—parts of expressions could be taken into account.[4] On the other hand, compositionality does not require the value of a complex expression to be determined by the values of its immediate parts alone. In particular, it is consistent with there being different ways of combining the same input expressions (or expressions with the same values), but with different

---

[4] To prove the point, one may consider an artificial function f assigning numerical values to expressions so that for any (binary) branching of the form

outcomes. In other words, the combinations of values is not determined by the values to be combined, as would be the case in the more restrictive framework of *type-driven interpretation*.[5]

Semantic values are assigned to expressions, not to surface strings. Unlike the latter, the former are unambiguous. The disambiguation of surface strings usually shows in the part-whole structure of the underlying expressions. This is most clearly illustrated in *bracketing ambiguities*. Thus the surface string **John or Jane and Mary** stands for (at least) two distinct expressions that differ in what their parts are and thus allow for different compositional interpretations:

(4.3)   John or Jane and Mary

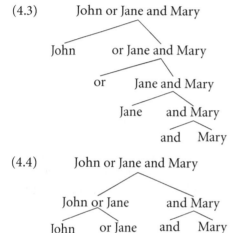

(4.4)   John or Jane and Mary

Following common syntactic practice, (4.3) and (4.4) analyse coordination as (post-)modification. As a side-effect, ternarity gives way to binarity. In fact, throughout this article, we will make the (possibly simplifying) assumption that syntactic analysis trees are always binary.

The semantically relevant parts of an expression need not be determined according to its surface structure. Rather, there is a specific level of syntactic analysis—sometimes

we have it that:

(*) $f(WHOLE) = \begin{cases} f(LEFT) + f(RIGHT), & \text{if } |LEFT| > |RIGHT| \\ f(LEFT) \times f(RIGHT), & \text{otherwise} \end{cases}$

where $|T|$ is the number of nodes of a tree T. Clearly, according to (*), the value $f(T)$ of any expression depends on the nodes of (all) of its parts and the way they are combined: any two (binarily branched) expressions with the same arrangement of parts are isomorphic (trees) and receive the same value as soon as their ultimate parts do. However, the value assignment (*) does not conform to the Generalized Principle of Compositionality (where values are fs) if, say, $f(the) = f(loves) = 1, f(boss) = f(John) = 2$, and $f(Mary) = f(snores) = 3$; for although the immediate parts of (4.1) and (4.2) coincide in their respective values (viz. 4.2 and 4.3), the whole expressions do not (obtaining 6 vs. 5).

[5] Cf. Klein and Sag (1985); the standard textbook account is Heim and Kratzer (1998). Type-driven interpretation rests on the observation that the combinations are usually predictable from the values to be combined, counterexamples either being somewhat artificial—like the 'rules of tense and sign' in Montague (1973: 234)—or else accountable by *Redefining Input* (in the sense to be explained in Section 4.3).

called *Logical Form* (*LF*)—which defines the syntactic input to semantic analysis. In fact, the compositional treatment of an expression may call for otherwise unmotivated structuring. The ambiguity of indefinites in referentially opaque positions is a case in point:

(4.5)   John seeks a unicorn

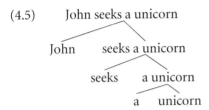

(4.6)   John seeks a unicorn

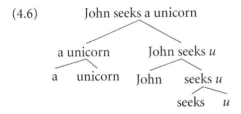

According to standard analyses,[6] the straightforward bracketing (4.5) of **John seeks a unicorn** underlies an unspecific reading according to which no particular unicorn is sought, whereas (4.6) is interpreted as implying the existence of unicorns, at least one of which is the specific object of John's search.

The combinations of the parts mentioned in the Principle of Compositionality ought to be understood as *syntactic constructions*—in a fine enough sense so as to allow for semantically motivated distinctions like that between (4.5) and (4.6), which are understood as involving distinct combinations; in particular, syntactic constructions do not necessarily combine surface material by juxtaposition. As usual, we will think of constructions as (binary) functions Δ which, like its immediate parts, are uniquely determined by the expression itself.[7] That the semantic value of an expression *depends* on those of its immediate parts, then, is to be understood as there being a function Γ corresponding to the construction at hand, Δ, and assigning the value of the expression to the pair consisting of the values of the parts. It should be noted that this condition does not render Γ unique: different such Γ may have different domains, even though all include the pairs of the values of the immediate parts combined; and even though Γ is unique if restricted to the semantic values of the (immediate) parts, the combinations actually employed in semantics are usually much more general, also applying to entities that do not happen to be the values of particular expressions. The reason for this is threefold:

[6] See Section 4.3 for references.

[7] The usual algebraic way of putting this condition is that linguistic expressions form a *term algebra*, or (absolutely) *free algebra*; cf. Montague (1970: 376f) and the expositions, refinements, and revisions in Janssen (1983, 1997), Hendriks (2001), Hodges (2001), and Fernando (2005).

(1) Grammatical constructions appear to have the same meaning across different languages, and across (historical, regional, …) varieties of the same language. However, it is not obvious that these (variants of) languages also share precisely the same semantic values. In particular, if an expression is added to a language (e.g. a neologism), its semantic value may not coincide with that of any existing expression; still the addition would not seem to bear on grammatical meaning. The problem is avoided if the combinations Γ are 'idealized' beyond the combination of actual semantic values of the object language.

(2) Given the potential infinity of expressions and their values entering a construction, the corresponding combination Γ must be accounted for in general and systematic terms. Any such account calls for some finite specification of Γ, which preferably avoids reference to the expressions themselves (to satisfy compositionality), but does make general reference to their values. In general, such specifications will (have to) treat the values to be combined in general terms, e.g. as objects of a certain kind, without necessarily being values *of* any particular expressions. As a case in point, combinations of truth-values are defined without taking them to be the truth-values of any sentences (which they need not be in very poor languages, or in multi-valued systems).

(3) The combinations Γ encode grammatical meaning, which is known to be much more restricted than ordinary, lexical meaning. Although there is no agreement about the possible combinations of semantic values that correspond to gram-matical constructions, present approaches usually characterize them as general operations whose domains (and ranges) stretch far beyond the values found in any particular language.[8]

4.2 Problems…

When it comes to determining semantic values that are not externally constrained, semanticists from Frege onward usually apply a *top-down heuristics* that rests on the assumption that (at least) the semantic values of sentences have been determined before-hand and that every expression occurs in some sentence.[9] The heuristics for determin-ing semantic values then takes sentences as its starting point and gradually descends

---

[8] For instance, in order to be predictable from the values of the parts combined, the combinations Γ allowed in type-driven interpretation (cf. fn. 5), are taken from a small universal inventory. Other char-acterizations have been given in logical (definability) and algebraic (invariance) terms; cf. van Benthem (1995) for a thorough and general survey of the methods involved.

[9] As pointed out in Hodges (2001: 16), this means that, algebraically speaking, the sentences form a cofinal class of expressions (with respect to part–whole structure). The strategy goes back to Frege (1891), where sentences and terms are used as starting points; cf. T. E. Zimmermann (2c11: 767f) for a more thorough account.

their syntactic trees down to their ultimate consitutents. At any stage of this (ideal-ized) non-deterministic process, some grammatical construction is taken into account, by means of which (assuming binarity) two expressions combine into a complex expression:

(4.7)   WHOLE
         ⌢
    LEFT   RIGHT

Thanks to the top-down direction of the process, the value of the *WHOLE* may be assumed to have been determined before; otherwise the analysis of the particular con-struction represented (but not mentioned) in (4.7), will have to await a later occasion. The values of the parts, *LEFT* and *RIGHT*, may have been determined before, too— but they need not be. Accordingly, there are three types of stages the processes of value determination may be in when entering the analysis of a construction as represented in (4.7). In a *Type 0* situation, neither part has a known value, that is one that has already been determined; in a *Type 1* situation, exactly one of them does; and in a *Type 2* situation, both do. The three types of situation may be represented graphically by decorating the nodes in (4.7) according to whether the values of the corresponding parts expressions are known ('√') or not ('?')—and where the ubiquitous '?' to the left of the top node indicates that, though its value is known (due to the top-down direction of the heuristics), it is not known how it comes about by combining the values of the two immediate parts:

(4.8) *Type 0:*

                  ? WHOLE √
                 ⌢
            LEFT ?   RIGHT ?

    Type 1:

    a)   or: b)

              ? WHOLE √   ? WHOLE √
             ⌢   ⌢
        LEFT   RIGHT ?   LEFT ?   RIGHT √

    Type 2:

                  ? WHOLE √
                 ⌢
            LEFT √ RIGHT √

The trees in (4.7) and (4.8) represent *constructions*, not particular expressions. Hence, *WHOLE*, *LEFT*, and *RIGHT* are syntactic *categories*, and the trees stand for families of expressions of the form $\Delta(LEFT_i, RIGHT_j)$ and with surfaces $WHOLE_{ij}$, where Δ is the particular construction involved. Consequently, a '√' on a daughter node indicates that the values of *all* expressions of that category have been *determined*; and a '?' means that *none* of them has a *known* value.[10] It should also be noted that for the values to count as determined, it suffices for them to be fully determined relative to the given initial values. Thus, for example, if the latter include the truth-values of all declarative sentences (as they do in the case of extensions), these need not be known to the semanticist following the top-down strategy; and the ensuing values may crucially depend on them. Still, values that are determined relative to truth-values (or any other initial values) may be ticked off.

The ideal situations in (4.8) correspond to three kinds of problems in determining semantic values following the top-down strategy. In each case, the meaning of a complex expression (construction) is known, but not how it comes about compositionally. The aim is to obtain the values of the *WHOLE* mother expression by combining the values of the corresponding *LEFT* and *RIGHT* daughters, that is to specify a function Γ that assigns the value of the *WHOLE* to the pair of values of the *LEFT* and *RIGHT* part. *Type 0* and *1* situations pose the additional problem that the latter have to be determined in the first place, and in such a way that they can be combined in the desired way. In *Type 2* situations the problem totally reduces to the specification of a suitable operation Γ.

The situations depicted in (4.8) thus present different types of challenges encountered in determining compositional semantic values by the usual top-down strategy. In the remainder of this section a sample of such *compositionality problems* will illustrate each of the cases under (4.8). It is important to realize that these problems only arise in the course of constructing a semantic theory and are usually immediately resolved by one of the strategies to be presented in Section 4.3. To a large part, the following account is based on a reconstruction of this process.

According to a widespread doctrine,[11] declarative sentences are the only expressions with externally constrained values. Following this lead, the top-down strategy immediately encounters *Type 0* problems once non-compound sentences are considered—and no matter what the (relevant) values of sentences may be. For concreteness, let us look at *simple predications* (declarative sentences consisting of a singular term and a predicate), like (4.9a) and let their *contents* be the points (in the Logical Space *I* of world-time pairs) that they describe:

(4.9)   a. $[\![\textbf{Mary is coughing}]\!] = \{(w, t) |$ Mary is coughing in world w at time $t\}$
      b. $[\![\textbf{The boss is laughing}]\!] = \{(w, t) |$ whoever is the boss in w at t, is laughing in w at $t\}$

In general, we thus have:

(4.9)   c. $[\![\textit{Sentence}]\!] \subseteq I$

---

[10] In principle, the top-down strategy can also lead to situations in which the values of some parts have been determined; however, these appear to be of no importance in practice and will thus be left out of consideration.

[11] Cf. Williams (2005) for a critical survey of the literature on the *inscrutability of reference*.

Then the objective is to find suitable values ('contents') of subject terms and predicates and a combination Γ such that (4.10a,b) and, more generally, all equations of type (4.10c) hold:

(4.10) a. $[\![\text{Mary is coughing}]\!] = \Gamma([\![\text{Mary}]\!], [\![\text{is coughing}]\!])$
        b. $[\![\text{The boss is laughing}]\!] = \Gamma([\![\text{the boss}]\!], [\![\text{is laughing}]\!])$
        c. $[\![Sentence]\!] = \Gamma([\![Term]\!], [\![Predicate]\!])$

Obviously, this is a *Type 0* situation:

(4.11)   ? *Sentence* √

    Term ?   *Predicate* ?

Type 0 problems are frequently solved by reducing them to *Type 1* problems. In partic-ular, one strategy for solving (4.11) consists in identifying suitable values for (at least some) terms, arriving at the following *Type 1* situation:

(4.12)   ? *Sentence* √

    Term √   *Predicate* ?

Situation (4.12) ensues if the values of terms are their referents as depending on points (w, t) in Logical Space:[12]

(4.13) a. $[\![\text{Mary}]\!](w, t) = \text{Mary}$
        b. $[\![\text{the boss}]\!](w, t) = \text{the boss in } w \text{ at } t$
        c. $[\![Term]\!] : I \to U$

where U is the *U*niverse of all individuals. The most straightforward solution to (4.12) assigns to predicates the world-time dependent sets of the individuals satisfying them:

(4.14) a. $[\![\text{is coughing}]\!](w, t) = \{x \mid x \text{ is coughing in } w \text{ at } t\}$
        b. $[\![\text{is laughing}]\!](w, t) = \{x \mid x \text{ is laughing in } w \text{ at } t\}$
        c. $[\![Predicate]\!] : I \to \wp(U)$

With these values at hand, an operation Γ satisfying the equations in (4.10) is eas-ily found:

(4.15) $\Gamma([\![Term]\!], [\![Predicate]\!]) = \{(w, t) \mid [\![Term]\!](w, t) \in [\![Predicate]\!](w, t)\}$

The solution of (4.11) and (4.12) can then be used to define a new *Type 1* problem, (4.17), presented by sentences like:

(4.16) **Everyone is shouting.**

---

[12] This is basically the strategy taken by Frege (1892), where the senses of terms are the *modes of presentation* of their referents. It should be noted that this approach requires syntax to specify a category of [*individual*]*terms* that includes proper names, personal pronouns, and definite descriptions but excludes quantificational noun phrases, which will be dealt with separately.

(4.17)

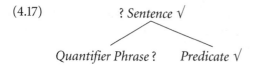

Obviously, the initial *Type 0* problem in (4.12) can be avoided by starting with externally determined semantic values for terms or predicates. In the realm of extensions, the former option boils down to a variant of the above strategy, starting with term extensions as individuals, and leading to predicate extensions as satisfaction sets of individuals; the details are left to the reader. Alternatively, one may start with predicates. Generalizing the latter, one may take the extension of an n-valent verb to be the n-ary relation holding between its satisfiers:

(4.18)   a. $[\![\mathbf{kill}]\!] = \{(x, y) \in U^2 | \ x \text{ kills } y\}$
         b. $[\![\mathbf{introduce}]\!] = \{(x, y, z) \in U^3 | \ x \text{ introduces } z \text{ to } y\}$
         c. $[\![\mathbf{Verb}_n]\!] \subseteq U^n$

In the limiting case $n = 0$, the extensions of sentences come out as their truth-values.[13] As a result, simple subject predicate constructions now present a *Type 1* problem:

(4.19)   a. $[\![\text{John loves Mary}]\!] = \Gamma([\![\text{John}]\!], [\![\text{loves Mary}]\!]) = 1$
         b. $[\![\text{Nobody loves Mary}]\!] = \Gamma([\![\text{nobody}]\!], [\![\text{loves Mary}]\!]) = 0$
         c. $[\![\textit{Sentence}]\!] = \Gamma([\![\textit{NounPhrase}]\!], [\![\textit{Verb}_1]\!]) \subseteq \{\emptyset\}$

(4.20)   ? *Sentence* √

                 NounPhrase ?   *Verb*₁ √

A straightforward solution to (4.20) has the extensions of (subject) noun phrases come out as generalized quantifiers (= sets of sets of individuals) as in (4.21), combining them with the predicate in the obvious way (4.22):

(4.21)   a. $[\![\text{John}]\!] = \{X \subseteq U| \ \text{John} \in X\}$
         b. $[\![\text{nobody}]\!] = \{\emptyset\}$
         c. $[\![\textit{NounPhrase}]\!] \subseteq \wp(U)$

(4.22) $\Gamma([\![\textit{NounPhrase}]\!], [\![\textit{Predicate}]\!]) = \begin{cases} 1, \text{ iff } [\![\textit{Predicate}]\!] \in [\![\textit{NounPhrase}]\!] \\ 0, \text{ iff } [\![\textit{Predicate}]\!] \notin [\![\textit{NounPhrase}]\!] \end{cases}$

Although this strategy avoids the particular problem in (4.11) about subject–predicate constructions, it does not avoid *Type 0* problems altogether. In fact, the top-down strategy almost inevitably leads to a *Type 0* situation when it comes to the internal structure

---

[13] Since an n-valent predicate is an expression that needs n (nominal) constituents to form a full (declarative) sentence, a sentence is a 0-ary predicate, its extension being a set of 0-tuples, of which there is only one, viz. $\emptyset$. Hence the extension of a sentence is either $\{\emptyset\}$ or $\emptyset$, depending on whether $\emptyset$ satisfies it, i.e. whether it is true or false. As is usual in set theory, we identify these values with the (von Neumann ordinal) numbers 1 and 0. —To avoid notational overkill, throughout this article semantic brackets '$[\![\cdot]\!]$' will be used for whatever semantic values happen to be at stake; similarly, the symbol 'Γ' represents whatever combination of values is needed.

of quantified noun phrases. For instance, the extension of **every semanticist**, which contains the superset of the set S of all semanticists, will be 'dissected' into extensions of determiners and count nouns, thus creating:

(4.23) $[\![\text{every semanticist}]\!] = \{X \subseteq U \mid S \subseteq X\} = \Gamma([\![\text{every}]\!], [\![\text{semanticist}]\!])$

(4.24)   ? *QuantifierPhrase* √

  Determiner ?   *Noun* ?

The standard solution to (4.24) is to identifiy the extension of a *Noun* with its corresponding (unary) predicate **be a** *NOUN*, thus reducing (4.24) to a *Type 1* problem, which in turn is solved by having determiners act as binary quantifiers (relations between sets of individuals).

The reduction of *Type 0* to *Type 1* problems is particularly fruitful, because a large class of the latter have canonical solutions, to which we will come in the next section. However, a *Type 1* problem does not always prove as simple as the ones considered so far. Staying in the realm of extensions, the analysis of speech and attitude reports as in (4.25) is known to be rather recalcitrant:

(4.25)   a. **John says it is raining.**
         b. **Most experts believe Mary will win the election.**

Since the extensions of the (unary) predicate and the embedded clause are known to be sets of individuals and truth values, respectively, sentences of this form present a *Type 1* problem to be solved by finding suitable extensions of *clause embedding verbs*:

(4.26)   ? *Verb₁* √

  Verb_{ce} ?   *Sentence* √

A solution to (4.26) requires the following equations to be solved:

(4.27)   a. $[\![\text{says it is raining}]\!] = \Gamma([\![\text{says}]\!], [\![\text{it is raining}]\!])$
         b. $[\![\text{believe Mary will win}]\!] = \Gamma([\![\text{believe}]\!], [\![\text{Mary will win}]\!])$
         c. $[\![\textit{Verb}_1]\!] = \Gamma([\![\textit{Verb}_{ce}]\!], [\![\textit{Sentence}]\!])$

However, a classical substitution argument shows that no combination Γ of extensions satisfies (4.27): otherwise replacing the embedded clause by any one with the same truth value, would have to result in a co-extensional predicate.[14] We will return to this observation at the beginning of the next section.

A different kind of problem is posed by post-nominal modifiers of quantifier phrases:

(4.28)   **no linguist from India**

In the absence of an analysis of the modifiers, the following *Type 1* situation arises:[15]

---

[14] The argument originates with Frege (1892: 37f).
[15] The primes are only meant to distinguish different *occurrences* of the same category within the tree.

(4.29)

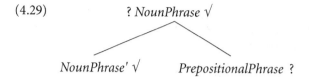

Again a substitution argument shows that no operation Γ satisfies the equations in (4.30) or (4.31)—no matter what the values of the modifiers may be:

(4.30) a. $\llbracket$**no linguist from India**$\rrbracket = \Gamma(\llbracket$**no linguist**$\rrbracket, \llbracket$**from India**$\rrbracket)$
         b. $\llbracket$**every pope from India**$\rrbracket = \Gamma(\llbracket$**every pope**$\rrbracket, \llbracket$**from India**$\rrbracket)$
         c. $\llbracket NounPhrase \rrbracket = \Gamma(\llbracket NounPhrase' \rrbracket, \llbracket PrepositionalPhrase \rrbracket)$

Given that there exists precisely one pope, the extension of **every pope** coincides with that of **some pope**, and consists of all sets containting the (one and only) pope as its member:

(4.31) $\llbracket$**every pope**$\rrbracket = \{X \subseteq U \mid \{p\} \subseteq X\} = \{X \subseteq U \mid \{p\} \cap X \neq \emptyset\} =$
         $\llbracket$**some pope**$\rrbracket$

With (4.30), **every pope from India** would thus have to be coextensional with **some pope from India**—which is absurd, because the former but not the latter leads to trivial truth in subject position. The problem is usually presented as a *Type 2* problem, assuming some independently motivated value of the modifier (which may also be a relative clause);[16] the above reasoning shows that it is quite independent of any such assumption. The standard solution resorts to re-bracketing; we will return to the issue in the third section.

The *Type 2* problems are compositionality problems in the narrowest sense. A textbook case arises when the above strategy of finding extensions hits upon quantified noun phrases in object position:[17]

(4.32)   ? *Verb*$_1$ √
           ⟋‾‾‾‾‾‾╲
      Verb$_2$ √   *QuantifierPhrase* √

As it turns out, compositionality can be achieved by a somewhat tricky combination of extensions:

(4.33) $\Gamma(\llbracket Verb_2 \rrbracket, \llbracket QuantifierPhrase \rrbracket)$
        $= \{x \in U \mid \{y \in U \mid (x, y) \in \llbracket Verb_2 \rrbracket\} \in \llbracket QuantifierPhrase \rrbracket\}$

Some motivation for this particular solution to (4.32) can be derived from formalization in (extensions of) predicate logic. In fact, an alternative solution *(Quantifier Raising)* comes even closer to logical notation; it will be discussed in due course.

---

[16] See Heim and Kratzer (1998: 82f) and the literature cited there. A more recent variation of this argument shows that, on its unspecific reading, the subject of **Most screws are missing** cannot be analysed as a quantifier over ordinary physical objects; cf. T. E. Zimmermann (2010).

[17] Cf. Heim and Kratzer (1998: 178ff).

The combination in (4.33) does not cover all cases of transitive verbs. In particular, when it comes to *referentially opaque* verbs, which allow for unspecific readings of indefinite objects, (4.33) only captures their specific readings:

(4.34)   a. **Jones is looking for a sweater.**
         b. **Jones painted a unicorn.**

Finally, the celebrated problem of *donkey sentences* should be mentioned, which come in two varieties:[18]

(4.35)   a. **If a farmer owns a donkey, he beats it.**
         b. **A farmer owns a donkey.**
         c. **He beats it.**

(4.36)   a. **Every farmer who owns a donkey beats it.**
         b. **every farmer who owns a donkey**
         c. **beats it**

The problem is to derive the value of (4.35a) under the assumption that the **if**-clause has the ordinary semantic value of (4.35b), no matter what the value of the 'open' sentence (4.35c) may be; and to derive the value of (4.36a) under the assumption that the subject has the ordinary value of the quantifier phrase (4.36b), no matter what the value of the 'open' predicate (4.36c) may be. In the present classification, both varieties of donkey sentences thus present a *Type 1* problem.

4.3 ... AND HOW TO SOLVE THEM

This final section takes a look at the major strategies of solving compositionality problems. The reader should be warned that these are strategies, not recipes: they give the direction in which a solution ought to be found, but they are neither blindly applicable nor infallible. And none of them is without alternative. In fact, it turns out that most of the above sample problems allow for different solutions complying with different strategies.

It should also be kept in mind that the compositionality problems to be solved arise in the context of the top-down heuristics of determining semantic values. By its very nature, the latter is non-deterministic: at any given point, the decision which construction to look at next is open to the semanticist. If one such construction presents a problem of the kind envisaged here, one option is always to delay the solution and treat it only after other constructions have been dealt with that may shed light on the problem at hand, or even change its *Type*. One instance of this *Deferring* strategy has already been mentioned in connection with (4.24) above: it is convenient to determine the semantic values of nouns in predicative positions, before analysing complex quantifier phrases,

---

[18] The problem was first described in Geach (1962: 117ff, 128f).

thus turning the initial *Type 0* problem they pose to a *Type 1* problem. Since *Deferring* does not directly solve or even reduce a given compositionality problem but merely serves to steer the top-down process, it will not be regarded as a solution strategy *sui generis*. But it is important to realize that it is often an option.

Although the situations described in (4.8) cover all compositionality problems addressed by the strategies, there is an (almost) orthogonal way of classifying the former, which is crucial for understanding the scope of the latter. A compositionality problem may be called *solvable* just in case there is a way of replacing all **?** by $\sqrt{}$ without changing any $\sqrt{}$. More precisely, solvability means that the assignment of (known) semantic values can be extended to a function assigning values $[\![WHOLE_{ij}]\!]$, $[\![LEFT_i]\!]$, and $[\![RIGHT_j]\!]$ to all expressions $WHOLE_{ij}$, $LEFT_i$, and $RIGHT_j$ (of the respective categories *WHOLE*, *LEFT*, and *RIGHT*) in such a way that these values behave compositionally, that is such that there is some function Γ satisfying the following equation:

(4.37) $[\![WHOLE_{ij}]\!] = \Gamma([\![LEFT_i]\!], [\![RIGHT_j]\!])$

The above three types of compositionality problems behave differently with respect to solvability. In particular, it is not hard to see that *Type 0* problems are always solvable. Thus, for example, the identity function on the expressions of categories *LEFT* and *RIGHT* presents an obvious solution, with Γ mapping any pair $([\![LEFT_i]\!], [\![RIGHT_j]\!]) = (LEFT_i, RIGHT_j)$ to the (uniquely determined) semantic value of the (uniquely determined) result $WHOLE_{ij}$ of combining them by the syntactic construction Δ at hand:

(4.38) $\Gamma([\![LEFT_i]\!], [\![RIGHT_j]\!])$
$= \Gamma(LEFT_i, RIGHT_j)$
$= [\![\Delta(LEFT_i, RIGHT_j)]\!]$
$= [\![WHOLE_{ij}]\!]$

In the light of the criteria listed at the end of Section 4.1, this solution is of no particular interest, but it does suffice to render the *Type 0* problem solvable in the sense intended here.

Type 1 problems, on the other hand, turn out to be solvable just in case (*) the substitution of equivalent known parts preserves equivalence of the whole expression, that is if (a) $[\![LEFT_i]\!] = [\![LEFT_k]\!]$ implies $[\![WHOLE_{ij}]\!] = [\![WHOLE_{kj}]\!]$, or (b) $[\![RIGHT_j]\!] = [\![RIGHT_k]\!]$ implies $[\![WHOLE_{ij}]\!] = [\![WHOLE_{ik}]\!]$, depending on whether the known parts are (a) the *LEFT* ones or (b) the *RIGHT* ones. Clearly, if condition (*) is not met, there is no hope for finding a function Γ satsfying (4.37): if (a) $[\![LEFT_i]\!] = [\![LEFT_k]\!]$ but $[\![WHOLE_{ij}]\!] \neq [\![WHOLE_{kj}]\!]$, then whatever $[\![RIGHT_j]\!]$ may be, $\Gamma([\![LEFT_i]\!], [\![RIGHT_j]\!])$, would have to be the same as $\Gamma([\![LEFT_k]\!], [\![RIGHT_j]\!])$, contradicting the generalization of (4.37); and similarly for case (b). If (*) does hold, the *Type 1* problem is solvable by a canonical construction (to which we will soon get), removing the **?** and (partially) determining Γ.

Substitutivity is also relevant to *Type 2* problems: it is readily seen that they are solvable precisely if both of the above alternative conditions are met, that is if $[\![LEFT_i]\!] = [\![LEFT_k]\!]$ implies $[\![WHOLE_{ij}]\!] = [\![WHOLE_{kj}]\!]$, and $[\![RIGHT_j]\!] = [\![RIGHT_k]\!]$ implies $[\![WHOLE_{ij}]\!] = [\![WHOLE_{ik}]\!]$. In this case, the most obvious combination Γ satisfying (4.37) is the function mapping all pairs $([\![LEFT_i]\!], [\![RIGHT_j]\!])$ to the corresponding values $[\![WHOLE_{ij}]\!]$—all of which may be assumed to have been determined beforehand.

The most general strategies of solving compositionality problems apply to all problems alike, including unsolvable ones (in the sense envisaged). Two of these general strategies will be considered. Both consist in redefining the syntactic input and may be regarded as syntagmatic and paradigmatic varieties of *syntactic approaches* to compositionality problems.

- *Restructuring* [applicable to compositionality problems of any *Type*]
  Reset part–whole division!
- *Recategorizing* [applicable to compositionality problems of any *Type*]
  Delimit range of expressions!

A classical example for *Restructuring* is the *Type 1* problem about post-nominal quantification (4.29).[19] After the substitution argument (4.31) proved it unsolvable, the kind of bracketing illustrated in (4.39) offers a fresh perspective:

(4.39)   no linguist from India

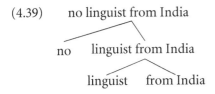

Generalizing from the example, the strategy for solving (4.29) may be summed up as follows:

(4.40)   *Restructuring: post-nominal modification*
          From: (*Type 1*, unsolvable)

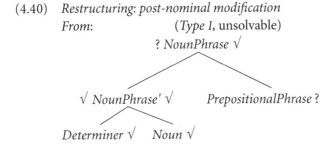

---

[19] More recently, starting with unpublished work by Richard Larson, Restructuring has been proposed to account for the semantic non-locality of certain attributive adjectives; cf. the analyses of *occasional* and *wrong* in M. Zimmermann (2003) and Schwarz (2006), respectively.

to:

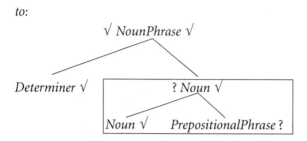

As the annotation indicates, Restructuring leads to another (boxed) *Type 1* problem. Unlike the starting point, however, this one is solvable; two straightforward solutions will be discussed in connection with other strategies.[20]

Restructuring may also be applied to reset the stage for solvable compositionality problems. The classical case is the *Type 2* problem, (4.32), about quantificational objects, where Restructuring helps in avoiding the somewhat idiosyncratic value combination (4.33). A standard solution replaces the surface bracketing with something like:[21]

(4.41)

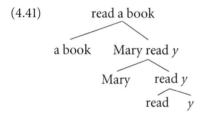

More generally this application of *Restructuring* may be described as follows:

(4.42)   *Restructuring: object linking*
             From: (*Type 2*, solvable)

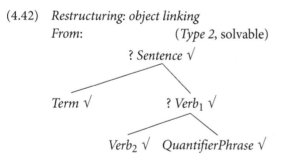

---

[20] Given its limitation to (quantificational) noun phrases of the form **Det Noun**, (4.39) does not immediately cover post-nominal modifications like **everybody from India**. The obvious (and standard) way to fill this gap is by *decomposing* **everybody** into the determiner **every** and an underlying noun (synonymous with **person**)—which constitutes another application of *Restructuring*.

[21] The constellation in (4.41) goes back to Montague (1973) and is known as *Quantifier Raising*. It was originally designed as optional, motivated by scope ambiguity and bound readings of pronouns—and leading to 'spurious ambiguity' in cases like (4.41); further motivation and references can be found in Heim and Kratzer (1998: 193ff).

to:

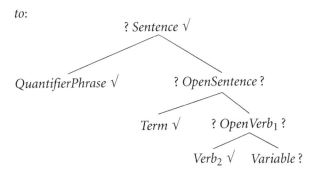

Once more, Restructuring leads to new compositionality problems, viz. a *Type 1* problem about values of natural language analogues of open formulae, as well as the *Type 0* and *Type 1* problems waiting further down the tree. We will not go into the compositionality of variable binding here and must refer the reader to the pertinent literature.[22]

The other variety of the syntactic approaches to compositionality proceeds by reassigning the categories of some of the expressions involved while leaving the original part–whole structure untouched. The sentential starting point may be seen as a result of applying Recategorization to simple subject–predicate constructions, distinguishing between terms and quantificational noun phrases. And it may itself be subject to this strategy if the categories of terms is further split up into proper names and others, thereby singling out a special case of predication, replacing the original (solvable) *Type 0* problem (4.11) by a narrower *Type 0* problem, one that allows for a particularly simple solution:

(4.43)   *Recategorizing: terms, names, quantifiers*

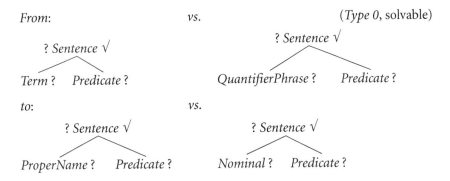

According to (4.43), any term that does not happen to be a proper name, will be treated separately as a nominal (or *denoting phrase*); in particular, this applies to definite descriptions. We will return to this issue in due course.

---

22 See Hodges (2001: 25ff & *passim*) for a general discussion of the compositionality of variable binding.

Like Restructuring, Recategorizing may be applied to escape unsolvable compositionality problems. One case has already been mentioned: the combination of referentially opaque (transitive) verbs with their direct objects, which a simple substitution argument proves unsolvable on the level of extensions:

(4.44)   a. **Jones is looking for a <u>vegetarian restaurant in Schweinfurt</u>.**
         b. **Jones is looking for an <u>Indian restaurant in Schweinfurt</u>.**

Under the (unconfirmed) assumption that the underlined complex nouns are coextensional, so would have to be the direct objects and, in fact, the two sentences, extensional compositionality prevailed. Yet, clearly, either may be true without the other.[23] In particular, then, extensional combinations should be prevented from applying in this particular case—as they will be if opaque verbs are categorized separately from ordinary transitives:

(4.45)   *Recategorizing: transitive verbs and their objects*

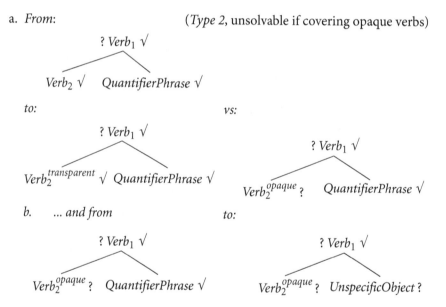

By delimiting the scope of the syntactic construction to transparent verbs, *Recategorizing* helps to interpret direct object linking in terms of extensions, as indicated in the left branch of (4.45a). However, as far as referentially opaque verbs are concerned, it merely creates another, obviously unsolvable *Type 1* Problem—which in turn may be subjected to *Recategorizing*, as in (4.45b)—to which we will return.

---

[23] According to standard analyses originating with Quine (1956), this applies to the unspecific (or notional) readings of these sentences.

Recategorizing may also be seen at work in the classical approach to the unsolvable *Type 1* problem (4.26) of clausal embedding:[24]

(4.46)   *Recategorizing: clausal embedding*
    From: to:

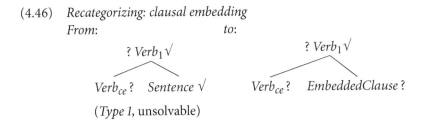

      (*Type 1*, unsolvable)

Given that the starting points are unsolvable, (4.45) and (4.46) withdraw one of the assumptions, thus making the purportedly known value of the embedded clause subject to revision: the substitutivity argument carries over from the initial situation in (4.46) to the resulting *Type 0* problem, and so any solution to the latter will have to introduce finer-grained values for the expressions. The upshot is that embedded clauses cannot get the same values as unembedded sentences, which means that their category is sensitive to their environment. Just which values they should be assigned instead, is a matter of solving the *Type 0* problem to which (4.46) leads.

The original (extensional) values being replaced by more complex and possibly more dubious entities, the particular kinds of *Recategorizing* in (4.45b) and (4.46) are frequently presented as parts of *ontological* approaches to the *Type 1* problem posed by embedded clauses. For the sake of uniformity, we stick to the present classification, which subsumes ontological approaches to compositionality problems under the syntactic ones.

Before we move on to other strategies, a word of warning is in order. It has already been mentioned that the strategies discussed here are usually not unique. This is true of all the examples presented so far; some alternatives will come up as we move along. Moreover, none of the five above cases completely settles the issue raised by the original problem. This is typical of syntactic approaches, which cannot offer semantic solutions all by themselves. But they do pave the way for solutions to be reached by employing additional strategies. Finally, whether or not a syntactic approach should be chosen to solve a given compositionality problem is usually not up to the semanticist alone, let alone as an arbitrary decision. Independent evidence over and above compositionality issues is called for; otherwise, tampering with the individuation of linguistic expressions may have unwelcome consequences. This is why syntactic approaches to compositionality problems tend to be met with scepticism unless they are supported by additional arguments.

The other strategies to be discussed address specific types of solvable compositionality problems, each *Type n* coming with its own *Strategy n*.

____

[24] Frege (1892).

- *Strategy 0* [applicable to any solvable *Type 0* problem]
  Assign representatives of substitution classes to **LEFT** *[or* **RIGHT***]*
  ...*to get from:*   *to:*

? WHOLE √	? WHOLE √
LEFT ? RIGHT ?	LEFT √ RIGHT ?

  [...or from: *to:*

? WHOLE √	? WHOLE √
LEFT ? RIGHT ?	LEFT ? RIGHT √]

- *Strategy 1* [applicable to any solvable *Type 1* problem]
  Define $[\![RIGHT]\!]$ *as function from* $[\![LEFT]\!]$ *to* $[\![WHOLE]\!]$ ... *and*
  $\Gamma([\![LEFT]\!], [\![RIGHT]\!]) = [\![RIGHT]\!]([\![LEFT]\!])$
  ...*to get from:*   *to:*

? WHOLE √	√ WHOLE √
LEFT √ RIGHT ?	LEFT √ RIGHT √

  [or:
  Define $[\![LEFT]\!]$ *as function from* $[\![RIGHT]\!]$ *to* $[\![WHOLE]\!]$ ... *and*
  $\Gamma([\![LEFT]\!], [\![RIGHT]\!]) = [\![LEFT]\!]([\![RIGHT]\!])$
  ...*to get from:*   *to:*

? WHOLE √	√ WHOLE √
LEFT √ RIGHT ?	LEFT √ RIGHT √]

- *Strategy 2* [applicable to any solvable *Type 2* problem]
  Find pattern in the dependence of $[\![WHOLE]\!]$ *on* $[\![LEFT]\!]$ *and* $[\![RIGHT]\!]$
  ...*to get from*   *to:*

? WHOLE √	√ WHOLE √
LEFT ? RIGHT √	LEFT √ RIGHT √

It is important to realize that each *Strategy n* requires the *Type n* problem at hand to be solvable. Due to the potential infinity of the expressions entering a given construction, it is not always easy to decide whether this is the case. As a result, what looks like an application of some *Strategy n* may turn out to be a false generalization.[25]

Strategy 0 proceeds by picking out one of the two (families of) expressions with unknown values, partition them into substitution classes and find some natural representatives for the latter—where the substitution class consists of those immediate parts (of the correct category) that may replace each other without thereby affecting the value of the whole expression. Again, (4.11) is a case in point. It has already been mentioned that one of the standard ways out reduces the *Type 0* problem to a *Type 1*

---

[25] See T. E. Zimmermann (1999: 552ff) for examples and (failed) attempts to save them by imposing meaning postulates.

problem by assigning the terms in subject position their referents as depending on Logical Space. In hindsight, this solution may be seen as the result of applying *Strategy 0* after observing that a subject term may safely (i.e. always) replace another without affecting the proposition expressed, just in case the two terms coincide in their reference conditions.[26]

(4.47)   *Strategy 0: subjects in Fregean predications*
         Put: $[\![Term]\!] : I \rightarrow U$ [=(4.13c)]
         ...*to get from* [(4.11)=]:   *to*:

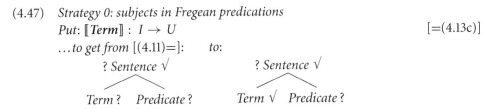

The application (4.43) of *Recategorizing* offers an alternative way out of (4.11). One of its outcomes is perfectly suited to act as an input to *Strategy 0*. Since the proposition expressed by a sentence with a proper name in its subject position does not change when the subject is replaced with a coreferential name,[27] the substitution classes consist of names with the same bearers. The latter thus constitute a simple and highly natural system of representatives. Identifying the (relevant) value of a proper name with its bearer then reduces the original *Type 0* problem to a solvable *Type 1* problem:[28]

(4.48)   *Strategy 0: subjects in Russellian predications*
         Put: $[\![Proper\ Name]\!] \in U$
         ...*to get from*:   *to*:

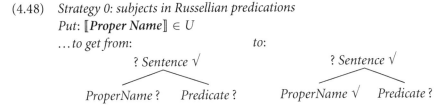

Given that the initial situation is solvable, the value of a predication with a particular predicate ***Predicate**_j* depends only on the value of the subject: if $[\![Name_i]\!] = [\![Name_k]\!]$, then $[\![Sentence_{ij}]\!] = [\![Sentence_{kj}]\!]$. Hence, for any ***Predicate**_j* there is a function f_j assigning the proposition expressed by ***Sentence**_{ij}* to the value of the subject, that is the bearer of the name ***Name**_j*:

(4.49) $f_j : [\![Name_i]\!] \mapsto [\![Sentence_{ij}]\!]$),

Example (4.49) shows that the *Type 1* problem (4.48) leads to, is solvable by assigning f_j to ***Predicate**_j* and then combining the values of the two parts by *functional application*. However, as a semantic value of the predicate, f_j is not general enough in that it crucially depends on which individuals happen to have names: after all, the meaning of a (lexical)

---

[26] But for the modelling of content in terms of Logical Space, this observation goes back to Frege (1892).

[27] From Frege (1892) onward, this has been debated in view of sentences of the form *NN is NN* vs. *MM is NN* (with distinct coreferential names *NN* and *MM*). Arguably, though, the difference between them could be explained in pragmatic terms, e.g. along the lines of Stalnaker (1978).

[28] But for the modelling of content in terms of Logical Space, this is the approach to predication taken in Russell (1905).

predicate does not appear to change when a name is added to, or dropped from, a language—but its semantic value would have to, which is hard to reconcile with the fact that semantic values somehow reconstruct literal meaning. On the other hand, if f_j is generalized so as to include arbitrary *potential* name bearers in its domain, then the idea behind (4.49) can be saved:

(4.50) $f_j \subseteq [\![Predicate_j]\!]$

If the semantic value of **Predicate**$_j$ can be determined in line with (4.50), then (4.49) guarantees compositionality:

(4.51) $\Gamma([\![Name_i]\!], [\![Predicate_j]\!]) = [\![Predicate_j]\!]([\![Name_i]\!])$

How, then, can (4.50) be guaranteed? In the case of a lexical predicate, this may be done by specifying the value that the function $[\![Predicate_j]\!]$ takes for any given individual x, independently of x's name or, indeed, whether x has a name at all. Such a specification may take the form of a definitional equation:

(4.52) $[\![grumbles]\!](x) := \{(w, t) \mid x \text{ grumbles in } w \text{ at } t\}$

If **Predicate**$_j$ is itself a complex expression, then the values of its immediate parts would have to be designed so that (4.50) comes out; this in turn means that the compositional treatments of all constructions involved in building up the predicate would have to conspire to make (4.50) come out true. In any case it must be stressed that (4.50) in itself does not constitute a specification of the unknown value of the predicate; but it does indicate the direction further analyses should take and may thus be regarded as a strategy for solving the *Type 1* problem posed by (4.49). In fact, it is an instance of the standard strategy of solving such problems:

(4.53)   *Strategy 1: predicates in Russellian predications*
         Put: $[\![Predicate]\!]: U \to \wp(I)$
         ...*to get from:*   *to:*

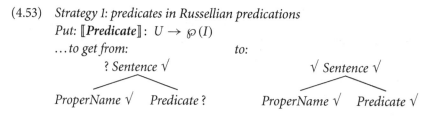

In general, then, *Strategy 1* proceeds by generalizing the function taking the known values of one of the parts to the corresponding (known) values of the whole expression. That such a (uniquely determined) function exists is a consequence of solvability. Generalization means that its domain is extended beyond the actual semantic values (of expressions of the relevant category), and it has the welcome effect that the resulting value will not depend on accidental features of the particular language described, or indeed any language at all.

   Strategy 1 can also be applied to solve the situation created by (4.47), whereupon the semantic values of predicates come out as slightly more complex, viz. as functions assigning propositions to term intensions instead of individuals. The obvious and natural way to systematize and generalize these functions beyond the semantic values of actual terms is to define them for arbitrary individual concepts θ (= functions from Logical Space to individuals). For illustration, a typical value assignment to a lexical predicate comes out as in:

(4.54) $[\![\mathbf{grumbles}]\!](\theta) := \{(w, t) \mid \theta(w, t) \text{ grumbles in } w \text{ at } t\}$

As before, the values assigned by the constructions building up non-lexical predicates then have to make sure that the latter receive analogous values. We thus arrive at the following picture:

(4.55) *Strategy 1: predicates in Fregean predications*
        Put: $[\![\mathbf{Predicate}]\!]: [\![W \times T]\!] \to U] \to \wp(I)$
        ...*to get from:*   *to:*

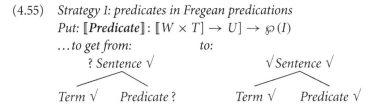

Finally, (4.55) can be followed up by a further application of *Strategy 1* to arrive at a full analysis of subject predicate constructions:

(4.56) *Strategy 1: Russellian quantification*
        Put: $[\![\mathbf{Nominal}]\!]: [U \to \wp(I)] \to \wp(I)$
        ...*to get from:*   *to:*

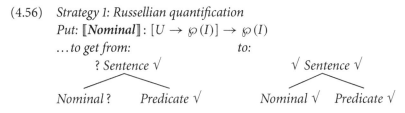

In principle, the same route could be taken from (4.53), arriving at a rather gruesome and redundant semantic evaluation of quantifier phrases in terms of functions from predicate intensions to propositions. The more common alternative is to account for the compositionality of quantification on an extensional level and derive intensions from there. Once more *Strategy 1* is of help here if the extensions of the predicates have already been identified with sets of individuals; we thus arrive at a restricted variant of (4.21c), which also covered proper names and definite descriptions:

(4.57) *Strategy 1: Fregean quantification*
        Put: $[\![\mathbf{QuantifierPhrase}]\!]: \wp(U) \to \{0, 1\}$
        ...*to get from:*   *to:*

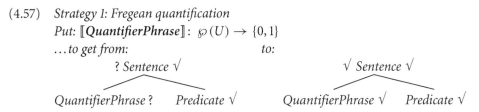

The Russellian approach (4.56) has the values of definite descriptions come out as functions defined on predicate values whereas the Fregean one assimilates them to proper names. At the end of the day though, both approaches can accommodate the same facts concerning the propositions expressed by sentences. Hence if sentence meaning is all that counts, they may be regarded as equivalent.[29]

---

[29] Cf. T. E. Zimmermann (forthcoming) for the relevant notion of equivalence and Kaplan (1975) for the intertranslatability of the Fregean and the Russellian approaches to semantic analysis. It should be

Another rather straightforward application of *Strategy 1* leads to a compositional treatment of post-nominal modification after *Restructuring* according to (4.40):

(4.58)   *Strategy 1: post-nominal modification*
Put: $[\![PrepositionalPhrase]\!]$: $\wp(U) \to \wp(U)$
...to get from: to:

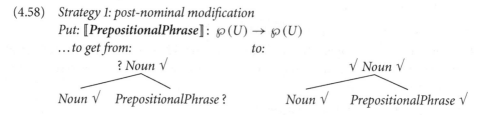

Strategy 1 also turns out to be of help in solving the intricate compositionality problem posed by the unspecific readings of indefinite objects.[30] Example (4.45) showed that *Recategorization* turns this unsolvable *Type 1* problem into the following (solvable) *Type 0* problem, which is thus in principle accessible to *Strategy 0*:

(4.59)   ? $Verb_1$ √

$Verb_2^{opaque}$?   UnspecificObject ?

In order to actually apply *Strategy 0* to this case, appropriate substitution classes for one of the parts would have to be found (keeping the other part fixed). The key observation is that for most, if not all, referentially opaque verbs, paraphrases can be found in terms of infinitival embeddings,[31] as in:

(4.60)

a. Jones is looking for $\left\{ \begin{array}{c} \text{a sweater} \\ \text{a book} \\ \text{a unicorn} \\ \cdots \\ UnspecificObject_i \end{array} \right\}$.

b. Jones is trying to find $\left\{ \begin{array}{c} \text{a sweater} \\ \text{a book} \\ \text{a unicorn} \\ \cdots \\ Indefinite_i \end{array} \right\}$.

Deferring the solution to (4.59) until after the compositional treatment of (4.60b) will endow each *Indefinite* with a value that contributes to the extension of the predicate in (4.60b). But then any two equivalent *Indefinites* may be substituted in (4.60b) due to compositionality, and so they may also be substituted as *UnspecificObjects* in (4.60a) without affecting the extensions of the predicates, given their (assumed) synonymy.

pointed out, though, that according to Frege (1892), reference conditions (including truth conditions) are regarded as externally determined.

[30] The basic idea was first expressed in Montague (1969: 174ff).

[31] The observation is due to Quine (1956). Various potential counterexamples are discussed in Forbes (2000, 2006).

Hence whatever the values assigned to the objects in (4.60b), these same values may play the role of the extensions of the *UnspecificObject*s in (4.60a). We thus have:

(4.61)   *Strategy 0: unspecific objects*
          Put: $[\![UnspecificObject_i]\!] = [\![Indefinite_i]\!]$
          …to get from: *to:*

$$\text{? } Verb_1 \; \checkmark \qquad\qquad\qquad \text{? } Verb_1 \; \checkmark$$

$$Verb_2^{opaque}\text{ ? } \quad UnspecificObject\text{ ? } \qquad Verb_2^{opaque}\text{ ? } \quad UnspecificObject \; \checkmark$$

At this point *Strategy 1* may be applied to solve the ensuing *Type 1* problem by assigning the opaque verb a value that naturally extends the function mapping each $[\![UnspecificObject_i]\!]$ to the corresponding $[\![\text{seek } UnspecificObject_i]\!]$.

A combination of strategies may also be seen at work in certain solutions to the problem of donkey sentences like (4.35a) and (4.36a), repeated here exclusively for the readers' convenience:

(4.35)   a. **If a farmer owns a donkey, he beats it.**

(4.36)   a. **Every farmer who owns a donkey beats it.**

Deferring (4.36a), the unsolvable *Type 1* problem about (4.35a) may be attacked by *Recategorizing* the conditional clause as an *OpenSentence* and interpreting it as expressing the binary relation of Owning among farmers and donkeys. Using the same categorization on the main clause and interpreting it as expressing the relation of Beating, the whole sentence can then be interpreted as subsuming O under B. By a tricky variation of the above theme, the contribution of the complex noun **farmer who owns a donkey** and the predicate of (4.36a) may then be interpreted as also expressing O and B respectively, whence the determiner **every** takes over the part of expressing the subsumption relation. For reasons of space, we leave it at that and refer the reader to the relevant literature.[32]

Far beyond the samples presented here, *Strategy 1* has been applied in the semantic analysis of a large variety of constructions, and mostly with success. In fact, present-day formal semantics owes much of its flavour to the result of defining semantic values as functions obtained following this strategy. The widespread use of (various varieties of) *logical types* is a clear indication of this trend: they help to determine the domains of the very values *Strategy 1* is after.[33]

---

[32] The basic idea underlying this so-called *dynamic* approach to conditional donkey sentences like (4.35a) originated with Lewis (1975) and has first been transferred to cases like (4.36a) in Heim (1982); a similiar analysis was independently developed in Kamp (1981). See Hamm and Zimmermann (2002: 155ff) for a more explicit exposition along the above lines. Haida (2007) has adapted the dynamic approach to solve a compositionality problem about indirect questions, discussed and attacked by *Restructuring* in Groenendijk and Stokhof (1982: 204f) and proved unsolvable in T. E. Zimmermann (1985: 433f).

[33] Logical types have become popular among semanticists mainly on account of Montague (1970*b*, 1973). The place of *Strategy 1* within the top-down approach to finding semantic values is discussed in T. E. Zimmermann (2011: 767f); both can be traced back to Frege (1981).

Given that a solvable *Type 2* problem consists in finding a way of systematically accounting for the value of the **WHOLE** in terms of the known values of the **LEFT** and **RIGHT** parts, *Strategy 2* is little more than a reformulation of the problem itself. An inspection of different cases shows that following it sometimes is very easy, whereas at other times it may require some ingenuity on the semanticist's part. The easy cases can be illustrated by post-nominal prepositional modifiers again. *Deferring* the determination of *PrepositionalPhrase* extensions to their occurrences in predicative positions (as in **be from India**), these extensions are readily identified as sets of individuals. Turning to their post-nominal use and *Restructuring* as in (4.40), then poses a *Type 2* problem. Inspection of typical cases reveals that the extensions of the two parts combine by intersection:

(4.62)   ⟦linguist from India⟧ = ⟦linguist⟧ ∩ ⟦from India⟧

Generalizing from this kind of example one thus arrives at:

(4.63)   *Strategy 2: post-nominal modification*
          Put: Γ(⟦*Noun*⟧) = ⟦*Noun′*⟧ ∩ ⟦*PrepositionalPhrase*⟧
          …*to get from:*   *to:*

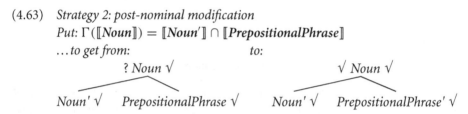

As observed above, quantificational objects call for a less obvious combination, which is repeated here just for the record:

(4.64)   *Strategy 2: object linking*
          Put: Γ(⟦*Verb₂*⟧, ⟦*QuantifierPhrase*⟧)   [= (4.33)]
          = $\{x \in U \mid \{y \in U \mid (x, y) \in$ ⟦*Verb₂*⟧$\} \in$ ⟦*QuantifierPhrase*⟧$\}$
          …*to get from:*   *to:*

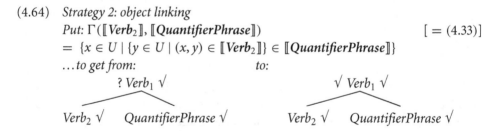

As mentioned above, the pattern in (4.64) is readily detected by generalizing a set-theoretic formulation (4.65c) of the predicate logic formalization (4.65b) of (schematic) sentences like (4.65a):[34]

(4.65)   a. *x sees everything*
          b. $(\forall y)$ See(x,y)
          c. $\{y \mid$ See$(x, y)\} \in \forall [= \{U\}]$

[34] For critical comments I am indebted to audiences at the universities of Hyderabad, Nantes and Frankfurt, and especially to Berit Gehrke, Louise McNally, Cécile Meier, Orin Percus, Gillian Ramchand, and Gautam Sengupta. Thanks are also due to an anonymous reviewer and to the editors of the Handbook.

PART II

COMPOSITIONALITY IN LANGUAGE

CHAPTER 5

....

DIRECT COMPOSITIONALITY

....

PAULINE JACOBSON

5.1 INTRODUCTION

....

Although there is considerable (albeit not universal) agreement among researchers working on the semantics of natural language that the semantics must be, in some sense, compositional, what is much more controversial is just what kind of object (or, level) is compositionally assigned a meaning, and how this object (or level) is related to the actual sentences of a language. It is, after all, generally quite easy to take a sentence of, say, English, and assign it a compositional interpretation if what is feeding the compositional semantics is not that sentence at all, but some other representation whose relation to the actual English sentence can be quite remote. Matters become even murkier if no explicit procedure for relating the two are spelled out, since then we do not have a theory which actually specifies how it is that the compositional semantics assigns a meaning to the sentence in question.[1]

This chapter will discuss and defend the hypothesis of Direct Compositionality (hereafter, DC). This is the hypothesis that there is actually no 'level of representation' which feeds into the compositional semantics. Rather, the syntactic combinatory system and the semantic combinatory system work in tandem. The syntax can be seen as a recursive system which proves the well-formedness of expressions in a language (the base of the system being of course the words, or—more accurately—the morphemes). DC claims each syntactic rule/principle which proves an expression well-formed is coupled with a semantics which specifies the meaning of that expression.

---

[1] To be fair, most theories which posit that English sentences are mapped into some other representation which is compositionally interpreted *do* assume that of course there is such a procedure. But, to be equally fair, in actual practice the relevant rule(s) are not always fully spelled out; making it difficult to evaluate the overall complexity of the theory.

I begin (Section 5.3) with a more detailed definition of DC, where I distinguish a few different subtheories which are compatible with this general hypothesis. (For related discussion, see Jacobson, 2002). Section 5.4 argues that DC is a priori preferable to non-DC theories in terms of its commitments: it offers the simplest conception both of the overall architecture of the grammar and of how it is that the grammar can hook into a model of human sentence processing. As such, this hypothesis should be abandoned only in the face of strong evidence to the contrary. Be that as it may, much literature has claimed (or assumed) that there *is* strong evidence to the contrary; there is a huge body of literature arguing for (or assuming) a conception of grammar whereby structured sentences map into another level of Logical Form (LF) which is compositionally interpreted. Section 5.4, therefore, addresses a few of these arguments. Obviously space precludes a detailed discussion of the vast literature of relevance, but my strategy will be to pick a few of the more typical arguments for LF, and show that these simply do not withstand scrutiny.[2]

5.2 DEFINING DIRECT COMPOSITIONALITY

As noted above, the hypothesis of direct compositionality is the hypothesis (familiar from, e.g. Montague 1970*a*, 1973[3]) that the syntax and the semantics work 'in tandem'. The syntax builds expressions (strings and/or more complex representations); the semantics works to assign meanings (model-theoretic objects) to the representations as they are built in the syntax. Among other things, DC entails that there are no syntactic expressions of any sort which do not have a meaning (in the sense of a model-theoretic interpretation). Compare this to a theory in which the syntax first 'builds' syntactic objects such as trees which have no interpretation, and where these are then 'sent' to the semantics for interpretation. (Note that here and elsewhere I use the term *builds* simply as a metaphor for 'proves well-formed'.) Under that view, there is an initial stage of the

----

[2] Chris Potts points out that it is misleading to phrase the debate as if DC and the LF view discussed here were the only two competitors. Indeed, the landscape of competing theories regarding the syntax/semantics interface is far richer than this would suggest. However, obvious considerations of space preclude a comparison across a number of other theories (among those which I will not discuss are Lexical Functional Grammar, Head Driven Phrase Structure Grammar, and many others). My point of comparison here is a group of theories which agree on a number of very fundamental premises (compositionality, model-theoretic interpretation). And, more narrowly, these theories agree (more or less) on what type of object is the final semantic interpretation of a sentence. Thus the theories discussed here make use of (basically) the same inventory of semantic types and the same notion of semantic types. Holding these points constant makes for a much easier comparison and one which is doable within the space here.

[3] The architecture of the grammar in Montague (1973) did make use of an intermediate representation of Intensional Logic (IL). The role of IL, however, was inessential and the theory was still a Direct Compositional one in the sense that each syntactic expression was assigned a model-theoretic interpretation as 'built' in the syntax; this is discussed below. Montague (1970*a*) did not make use of the intermediate representation.

syntax where the trees—and in fact each local tree within a tree—have no meaning; the meaning is assigned to the output of the syntactic computation. The difference between DC and the 'syntax-builds-then-semantics-interprets' view is even more striking under the by now fairly widespread conception (due originally to Chomsky, 1976 and May, 1977) according to which the syntax builds one level of representation which is subsequently mapped into another level (a level of 'Logical Form', or LF) which is then interpreted. (For textbook expositions of this view, see Chierchia and McConnell-Ginet (1990) and Heim and Kratzer (1998).) The subexpressions of a surface sentence might, then, have no meaning at any stage of the computation. This is because meaning is assigned only to syntactic constituents of LF, and the constituents at LF can be quite different than the surface expressions which specify the well-formed (surface) syntactic object.

Before continuing, it is worth clearing up one misleading terminological point. In speaking of DC—or something like it—many authors use the terminology of a theory in which 'surface *structures* are interpreted'. Similarly, one can find works which raise the question as to 'what *level* of structure feeds the semantics'. Strictly speaking, under DC, there is no sense in which any 'level' is computed and interpreted. The semantic interpretation always proceeds along with the syntactic proof of the well-formedness of some expression. It thus makes no sense, under this view, to ask what 'level' inputs the compositional semantics.

That said, there are a variety of ways to implement DC—where the differences depend on how rich is the set of operations available to the syntax. To clarify what is at stake, I will define four versions of DC (surely others could be imagined, too). I will call the first Type 1 Direct Compositionality (what in Jacobson, 2002, I called Strong Direct Compositionality). This view maintains that the syntax keeps no track at all of structure; the grammar sees only strings, not structured representations of any sort. Thus, take any linguistic expression to be (only) a triple of <sound; syntactic category; meaning>. Assume that the grammatical rules take one or more such triples as input and yield a triple as output—and that when two or more expressions are in the input, the phonology can do nothing more than concatenate the two phonological inputs. Notice that this view does not require that all rules take two or more expressions as input to return a single expression as output; there can certainly be rules mapping a single expression into another. (Such rules often go under the rubric of 'type shift' rules in the semantics literature but this is potentially misleading since there is no a priori reason to restrict unary rules only to ones which shift the semantic type. There could be rules shifting the syntactic category but not the meaning. Or, there could be rules shifting the meaning but not affecting the type.) As long as there are also a finite number of syntactic categories used in the grammar, the syntax is equivalent to a context free phrase structure grammar. Thus, for example, any rule concatenating more than one expression to give an output expression of category A boils down to a phrase structure rule of the form $A \rightarrow \omega$ where the material on the right is the string of categories of the concatenated input expressions. These rules would also be supplemented with a semantic part, specifying how the meaning of the mother is put together from the meaning of the daughters. A unary rule would be a phrase structure rule of the form A → B (where it could be that B = A if the only change were a semantic one); again the semantic supplement to this would specify the meaning of the mother in terms of the meaning of the single daughter.

Something along these lines is assumed in various versions of Categorial Grammar—where here the rules are stated in a highly generalized format (thus what is listed is a very general rule schemata). The view above was also the theory taken in Generalized Phrase Structure Grammar (Gazdar et al. 1985). Under any kind of Type 1 DC, not only is the semantics not fed by any kind of structured representation, but indeed the *syntax* also makes no reference to structure. A tree structure is simply a representation of how the rules worked to prove something well-formed. It can also be taken as a (rough and underspecified) representation of how the compositional semantics puts things together.[4] I will use the slogan that under such a view, grammars never 'see' structure.

There is one issue worth addressing before continuing. An anonymous referee points out that the claim that grammars never 'see' structure—only strings—is meaningful only when coupled with constraints on what sorts of objects we can use as the syntactic category. After all, one could have a sufficiently rich inventory of categories that these encode the entire information that is encoded in a tree—or even in a sequence of trees. Imagine, for example, that a tree—or a sequence of trees—actually *is* the category label. Then of course all of the information available in a structure is something that the grammar could 'see'. I am, therefore, assuming that the claim here can be coupled with a view of syntactic categories which is not that rich. It is true that a certain amount of information on category labels has indeed played a large role in the statement of grammatical processes in some of the strong direct compositional theories, most notably GPSG but also some versions of Categorial Grammar. And so ultimately the inventory of possible categories needs to be carefully spelled out. But I will continue to assume here that we can keep our theory of categories sufficiently impoverished as to disallow categories whose richness is equivalent to full trees and/or sequences of trees.

But it is by now well established that the syntactic operations of natural languages cannot be just those which can be expressed by context-free phrase structure rules (see, e.g., Shieber 1985). Thus a slight retreat from Type 1 DC supplements the range of possible syntactic operations with an infixation operation—whereby one string is infixed into another. (See, e.g., discussion of 'Wrap' operations within the Categorial Grammar and related literature, which includes Bach, 1979, 1980; Dowty, 1982, 2007; Pollard, 1984; Vijay-Shanker, Weir, and Joshi, 1986; Jacobson, 1987, 1992a; etc.) There are a variety of ways to formalize this and we will leave it open here as to the best way to do so. Suffice it to say that under this view—which I will call Type 2 DC—it is not correct

---

[4] It is underspecified because, for example, when there is more than one daughter the tree itself does not specify how the meanings of each of the daughter expressions combine. And, when there is a unary rule, all that is represented by the tree is the syntactic category of the input and of the output, but no representation of how the meaning of the output is derived from that of the input in cases where there is a change. Of course there could be other principles in the grammar that predict this in terms of the categories involved, but a tree itself does not show this.

that there is *no* structure that the grammar 'sees'. Since infixation is possible, the input to the rules cannot be simple strings, but strings which at least contain some information about an infixation point. But, by Type 2 DC, I mean a theory in which this is the only non-concatenative syntactic operation. While there are substantive differences between Types 1 and 2 DC, I will generally lump them together in the subsequent discussion, and refer to the two together as Strong(ish) DC.

Much of the work within classical Montague Grammar took a yet richer view of the syntax, and allowed a variety of other operations besides just infixation. Such operations included substitution and deletion. The idea here is that the *syntax* could 'see' objects with as rich a structure as a tree, and these trees could therefore be manipulated in various ways by the rules. Nonetheless there is no 'level' which gets interpreted: the syntactic rules map syntactic objects (one or more input trees) into syntactic objects (an output tree), where each such mapping is coupled with a semantics that spells out the model-theoretic content of the output. Thus, while structures are real and visible to the syntax, they are not what feeds the compositional semantics; the semantics again runs 'in tandem' with the syntax rather than being read off of a representation computed by a separate system. The point is made forcefully in Partee (1976). I will refer to this view as Type 3 Direct Compositionality.

To clarify the remarks so far, consider the case of quantified NPs in object position as in (5.1):

(5.1)   Some candidate visited every small town in Pennsylvania.

First the question arises as to why quantified NPs can occur in object position at all. If *visit* expects an individual in object position (an argument of type e) how can it occur with a quantified NP here? (I am making the usual assumption that these quantified NPs denote functions characterizing sets of sets of individuals—that is, they are of type $<< e, t >, t >$.)[5] This problem has gone under the rubric of there being a 'type mismatch'. The meaning of *visit*—notated hereafter as [[visit]]—wants an e-type argument in object position, but here it combines in the syntax with a generalized quantifier; that is something with a meaning of type $<< e, t >, t >$. Under Strong(ish) DC there are a variety of possible answers, but they generally boil down to challenging the assumption that there really is a type mismatch here. Thus one way to implement this is to challenge the view that [[visit]] needs an argument of type e (see, for example, Montague, 1973).

A particularly ingenious version of this solution is due to Hendriks (1993)—which builds on work by Partee and Rooth (1983) which work in turn builds on Montague's work. This solution assumes that *visit* in the lexicon is of type $< e, < e, t >>$ (it denotes—in 'Curry'ed form'—a relation between two individuals). But it can shift its meaning into a fancier package. Thus, there is a general shift rule defined which allows any e-argument position to shift into one expecting a generalized quantifier (a meaning

---

[5] For readers unfamiliar with the type notation as used in linguistic semantics, I use $< a,b >$ to mean any function in $a \times b$. e is the set of individuals, t the set of truth values, and i the set of times. To say that the 'type' of an expression of category A is $< a, b >$ means that expressions of this category have meanings which are functions in $a \times b$.

of type $<< e, t >, t >$) in that position. What is especially ingenious here is that Hendriks defines things in such a way that both the subject and object position can shift (this being one way of allowing quantified NPs to occur in either or both positions), and the order in which they shift determines the scope possibilities. Thus this simultaneously answers the question of what allows for object quantified NPs in general, and what gives both scopal possibilities in (5.1). Notice that Hendrik's 'shift' rule is a unary rule; it takes a triple (in this case a single word) and maps it into a new word with the same phonology and a different meaning. (Whether or not the syntactic category of the word shifts actually depends on the details of one's theory of syntax.) This is of course compatible with strong(ish) DC.

What about Type 3 Direct Compositionality? A solution compatible with this can be illustrated using a variant of Montague's Quantifying In rule (Montague, 1973). It should be noted that I am taking considerable liberties with Montague's actual proposal in that he used both a higher type for [[visit]] and a Quantifying In rule, and I will here simplify his proposal and use only the second. Thus here the syntactic and semantic combinatory rules can build up an expression of the form x_1 visited x_2, whose meaning is a function from the set of assignments G (each of which is a function from variable names to individuals) to a proposition, such that for any g, the proposition expressed is that $g(x_1)$ visited $g(x_2)$. Call the syntactic category of this expression S, and allow a rule which maps this expression into another expression with category Λ, with no phonological change, but whose meaning is a function from the set of assignments G to the set of individuals which visited $g(x_2)$. The semantics of this operation of course needs to be spelled out in full generality which we will not do here as this is just meant for illustration (it is just the semantics of 'lambda-abstraction'). The key step is the next step, where the expression of category Λ with the above meaning can combine in the syntax with a generalized quantifier *some candidate*. The interesting point here is what it means to 'combine' them—they do not concatenate, but rather the expression *some candidate* is substituted for the subject variable x_1. (Montague actually used an indexed pronoun.)[6] The compositional semantics which goes hand in hand with this substitution operation is the predictable one: for each assignment g, we get the proposition that the set denoted by Λ is a member of the set of sets denoted by the generalized quantifier (on g). The same process happens again for the object; we map the S to something of category Λ, give it the meaning which (on any assignment g) characterizes the set of individuals such that there is some candidate who visited it, and then apply this to the generalized quantifier *every town in Pennsylvania*. The derivation that I spelled out here is the one which ultimately gives wide scope to the object. But the 'Quantifying-In' steps could have just as easily happened in the opposite order, which would give narrow scope to the object. (Again, then, what allows for quantified NPs in

---

[6] The syntax needs some way to ensure that the *right* indexed variable (or pronoun) is substituted onto—it has to be the one that the semantics 'abstracted over' in the preceding step. This can be ensured in a variety of mechanical ways, such as having an index (in this case 1) on the node Λ which is abstracted over in the step above, and using this index in the full definition of the syntax of the substitution operation.

object position in general—if generalized to quantified NPs in subject position—gives both scopal possibilities.) Notice that the semantics is entirely direct compositional; the 'trick' is that the syntax allows a substitution operation. One could use what has been called an 'analysis tree' as an illustration of the order of steps in the syntactic and semantic combinatorics. But there is no sense in which the generalized quantifier is ever a 'sister' to the S node into which it is substituted. So, for example, it would make no sense to ask whether it is on the left or on the right of the rest of the sentence with which it combines at the 'level' before it combines. (See also fn. 9 for additional discussion of this point.) There is no such level.

Finally, there is (at least) one other possible DC view which I will call here Type 4 DC (what I called 'Deep Direct Compositionality' in Jacobson 2002). This view is roughly compatible (although not exactly identical to) the view taken within the theory in the 1960s and 1970s known as Generative Semantics (see in particular, Bach, 1968; McCawley, 1970; Lakoff, 1971). Suppose that there is a kind of two-stage syntax. The first consists only of phrase structure rules (hence, only concatenative operations), but where the representations built are not just strings but trees that can therefore be referred to by later grammatical operations (hence, structure is something that the grammar 'sees' and keeps track of *in the syntax*). The compositional semantics works in tandem with the phrase structure rules to provide a model-theoretic interpretation of each constituent as it is 'built' in the syntax, exactly as in Type 1 DC. Suppose further, though, that there are additional 'unary rules' which map an entire tree into another tree and leave the semantics intact. One can see these as rules which take a triple as input—a tree-structured sound representation, a syntactic category, and a meaning; change the structure (and perhaps the category) but return the same meaning in the input as in the output. (See Partee, 1976 for similar discussion.) This architecture is entirely compatible with the treatment of object-wide scope quantification in, for example, Bach (1968), McCawley (1970), Lakoff (1971), and others, where the actual pronounced surface structures were derived by a rule of Quantifier Lowering. Thus the phrase structure rules would build up a structure of the form in (5.2) (I deliberately model these roughly after the LFs of Heim and Kratzer, 1998). (I have called the root node F rather than S here to predict that such a structure is not an actual sentence of the language.)

(5.2) $[_F[_{QP}$ every city in Pennsylvania$][_\Lambda 8[_F[_{QP}$ some candidate$]$
        $[_\Lambda 7[_{Sx7}$ visited $_{x8}]]$

The compositional semantics builds up the interpretation of this in tandem with its building up in the syntax, and does so in a way exactly analogous to the semantic procedure spelled out above for the Type 3 DC Quantifying In approach. The difference between this and that approach is that here quantified NPs are not directly introduced into the syntax by a substitution operation but are introduced into a syntactic representation where they are attached higher in the tree. (Thus here, for example, it becomes a meaningful question to ask whether the quantified NP is to the left or to the right of its sister; notated here as a node with the label Λ.) The second stage of rules works in such a way as to map this into the final surface sentence in (5.1), presumably by two occurrences of 'Quantifier Lowering' which lower the material labelled QP onto the variable labelled with the integer which is the daughter of the Λ node which is sister to the QP. Each such syntactic operation is a mapping from a full triple to another, but what is changed is the phonology and syntactic category; the meaning remains intact. Note that, of course, the two QPs could have been reversed in the pre-lowering tree which would be the end product of a semantic composition which built up the meaning with the reverse scope (subject having wide scope). The final surface sentence would be the same, hence the ambiguity. While this view does make use of an abstract level in the syntax (that is, syntactic operations map trees to trees), it is still the case that there is no sense in which a 'level' is interpreted; the interpretation proceeds hand in hand with the phrase structure rules.

Within the general landscape of theories being considered here, the 'received' modern view on a sentence like (5.1) is essentially the backwards version of the Type 4 DC view given above (the 'modern' view due originally to May, 1977). Here, the surface sentence is mapped into the LF in (5.2) (or something similar) by a rule of 'Quantifier Raising'. Thus the syntax first builds the surface structure, and assigns it no interpretation. That structure is then mapped into a structure like (5.2) (or the similar one with the QPs reversed), and that structure itself is then 'sent' to the semantics for compositional bottom-up interpretation along the lines spelled out above. The difference, though, is that the operations supplying the compositional semantics are not linked to the operations which proved this to be a well-formed tree of LF; that part happened earlier and in a separate system. As such, the QR solution is in no sense compatible with DC. What I will argue below is that—even if there is some good reason to believe in the existence of (5.2) as a syntactic object—the Type 4 DC approach is still far simpler than the 'modern' surface-to-LF approach. But for the most part I will be concerned with defending the stronger view: there is no real reason to abandon even Type 2 DC.[7]

While perhaps not taken entirely for granted, the feasibility of DC was certainly hoped for in much of the work within classical 'Montague grammar' especially work in the 1970s and early 1980s. (Interestingly, one can argue about whether the influential work of Montague (1973, The Proper Treatment of Quantification in Ordinary English) maintained a complete DC architecture; the answer to this depends on the precise

---

[7] One argument sometimes given for the 'modern' approach centres on the notion of Type Driven interpretation. The idea is that the grammar need not contain a list of construction-specific rules specifying how the meanings of expressions combine (or, how the meaning of a single expression is mapped into the meaning of another). Rather, much of this can be deduced from the types of the inputs combined with the type of the output. In fact, though, the issue of having the semantics stated in terms of very general principles is completely orthogonal to the question of a DC or a non-DC architecture. One can have any of the DC architectures sketched above and still have the semantics associated with the syntactic combinatory rules follow from very general statements (and, in fact, the syntax itself can be stated in very general terms, as in most versions of a Categorial Grammar). Space precludes detailed demonstration of this here, but suffice it to point out that the original notion of 'type driven' interpretation was actually formulated within the purely Type 1 DC architecture of Generalized Phrase Structure Grammar; see Klein and Sag (1985). There the idea was that the grammar listed (in general and schematic form) phrase structure rule schemata, and the semantics associated with each schema was predictable in terms of the semantic types.

definition of DC. The system there used a two step semantic procedure: each expression built in the syntax was, in tandem, mapped into a representation in the language of Intensional Logic (IL), and each expression of IL—that is each expression that was the output of that first computation—was assigned a model-theoretic interpretation. Hence, every syntactic expression was indeed assigned a model-theoretic interpretation as it was built in the syntax. In that sense the system is a DC one, even though it did contain a 2-step procedure and hence use of an intermediate 'representation' of IL. But, that representation is obviously dispensable; it plays no essential role in the system for it is not mapped into any other representation, the grammar contains no constraints or 'filters' on this representation, and so forth. Note too that the system of Montague (1970a) uses no such level and directly paired syntactic expressions with meanings.) During that period, there was some discussion as to whether a DC architecture could be maintained, or would there instead need to be a level with its own properties on which, for example, might be stated certain constraints about the representations? See, for example, Partee and Bach (1981) for relevant discussion of just this point. But while the question was unsettled, it is clear that a DC architecture was certainly taken to be the 'gold standard' in this period in history—at least within much of the work in formal semantics within linguistics. I have argued elsewhere (Jacobson, 2002) that the shift away from this position (where many researchers now simply take surface-to-LF mapping as axiomatic) was motivated more by sociological than by scientific concerns. While I do not have space to demonstrate this here, I will now turn to the related claim that DC *should* indeed be taken as the gold standard, and should be abandoned only in the face of very strong evidence to the contrary.

5.3 THE A PRIORI SIMPLEST HYPOTHESIS

There are several reasons to hope that Direct Compositionality is the correct hypothesis. As will be elaborated on below, it is both the simplest conception of the architecture of the grammar and the one with the best chance of hooking into a theory of human sentence processing. As such, it is a hypothesis that should be rejected only in the face of strong evidence to the contrary. Of course there are many challenges to the DC, so I will return to a few of these briefly in Section 5.3 to argue that the hypothesis of DC is often much too hastily abandoned.

The first argument for DC is perhaps a conceptual one, but nonetheless seems quite compelling. This is that of course any theory needs a compositional syntax—that is, a recursive rule system which proves the well-formedness of expressions, often proving the well-formedness of larger output expressions based on the well-formedness of smaller ones. At the base of the system are the words (or, really, morphemes) which are just listed. And any system needs a compositional semantics to predict the meanings of larger expressions based on the meanings of smaller ones—and again the base of the system is the meanings of the smallest units—the words (or morphemes). The minimal hypothesis is that the two work in tandem, rather than being divorced. Indeed it would seem like a somewhat perverse architectural design to have one system run divorced from the other. One might think that these remarks concern only a (subjective) aesthetic preference, but by generally accepted standards of simplicity the DC architecture is simplest. After all, it contains no additional machinery beyond that which every theory needs; it has no extra types of rules, no extra levels, etc. (Of course it could be that this ultimately leads to more complex statements and would need to be rejected; the claim here is simply that all other things being equal, this is the simpler view—and so the burden of proof should be on the more complex architecture.) Second, if meanings are computed on representations which are the output of the syntactic computation, then there is a certain amount of duplication of information. Those representations need to be referred to twice: once as output of the syntactic rules and then again as input to the semantic rules. (For a more detailed discussion, see Jacobson, 2002.)

A third argument in favour of a DC architecture concerns the locality of the rules for the compositional semantics. As pointed out above, under any of the versions of DC there is no actual level which is interpreted; the interpretation process is not fed by some tree. Consider instead the view according to which a surface syntactic representation is mapped into a tree which is then interpreted. Under this view, a full tree is the input to the semantic computation. Nonetheless, it is assumed by most researchers that the compositional semantics proceeds in a *local* fashion; each node in a tree is assigned a meaning in virtue of the meanings only of the daughter expression. (See Heim and Kratzer, 1998 for an explicit statement of this.) But under such a view, the locality of interpretation is a pure accident and follows from nothing else in the system and hence requires an extra stipulation. After all, if full trees are the input to the semantics, why *shouldn't* there be rules which interpret large chunks of trees? But under DC, the locality of interpretation is no accident. While trees might be visible to the *syntax* under some of the weaker DC theories, they are not visible to the semantics. Rather the semantic combinatorics works in tandem with the local syntactic combinatorics (under all of the versions sketched above), and the locality effect could not be any other way.

Of course there are some apparent challenges to the locality hypothesis—and hence to direct compositionality—the most notable such case being the interpretation of apparently non-compositional idioms. While the correct treatment of idioms remains an open question, merely saying that they are interpreted in a non-local fashion does not really provide any sort of theory for their actual behaviour. Note first that there are a few truly 'non-separable' idioms like *kick the bucket*. But since here the parts cannot be separated and there cannot be internal modification, there is little evidence that these actually have kind of internal structure rather than having these listed as a single unit.[8]

---

[8] There is, however, an open question about the interaction of the morphology with the syntax and semantics—the morphology must have access to some internal information in that *kick* receives the normal verbal inflections. But the only sense in which these seem to have internal structure is in terms of the information accessible to the morphology.

Thus the challenge to locality (and hence direct compositionality) would come from cases where it appears that the idiom has internal structure but is not compositionally interpreted. To put this in terms of direct relevance to the direct compositionality hypothesis, the challenge would come if the syntax allowed pieces of an idiom to occur in different spots while the semantics had to somehow 'collect' these up into a unit; it is difficult to see how this could be reconciled with the view that the syntax and semantics work in tandem. And indeed almost from the beginning of work within generative grammar (and perhaps earlier) it has been assumed that there are many such cases; notably cases along the lines of, for example, (5.3):

(5.3)   a. The cat was let out of the bag. ('idiom' is *let the cat out of the bag*)
          b. The strings that he pulled got me my job. ('idiom' is *pull strings*)

(Example (5.3b) is a particularly interesting case because it has been used to argue that the head noun of a relative clause must be interpreted only inside the relative clause; the idea here is that *strings* has no interpretation other than as object of *pull*.) But it is far from self-evident that calling these idioms non-compositional accounts for the facts. After all, claiming that *strings* in (5.3b) has no interpretation except as the object of *pull* leaves it a mystery as to what is being interpreted as the agent of the job-getting event. Moreover, McCawley (1981) pointed out that these cases can be turned upside down since things like (5.4) are fine too:

(5.4)   He pulled the strings that got me my job.

If relative clause heads are interpreted only internally—as the non-compositional 'idiom' account of *pull strings* is forced to assume—then how is (5.4) interpreted? Similar points can be made regarding internal modification as in *He let that highly confidential cat out of the bag*. Most 'idioms' do indeed allow for their parts to be modified—but what could be the interpretive process if the parts have no interpretation of their own? Obviously there are co-occurrence restrictions that need to be accounted for in these cases, but the assumption that these are interpreted as a unit with no meaning to the internal parts is at odds with the very fact that the parts do combine semantically with other material as in the examples above. For one view on how to actually treat separable 'idioms' compositionally, see Nunberg, Sag, and Wasow (1994).

Note that all three of the arguments given above for DC speak directly to the choice between even as 'weak' a DC theory as Type 4 DC and the surface-to-LF-to-interpretation view. Suppose that we could find evidence against the stronger DC theories, and evidence that a syntactic level of LF representation (which differs significantly from the surface structures) is necessary. This would still not require an abandonment of DC, for such evidence would also be compatible with Type 4 DC where the syntactic rules that construct LF go hand-in-hand with the model-theoretic interpretation.[9] And while it might at first glance appear as if the surface-to-LF view and a Type 4 DC are just

---

[9] A referee raises the question of whether there really is any significant difference between Type 3 DC and an LF view, given that a Type 3 DC contains (or can contain) the sort of 'analysis trees' of, e.g., classical Montague grammar. (One can similarly ask whether Type 3 DC and Type 4 DC are different

'notational variants' where the directionality of the mapping is inconsequential, this is incorrect. The surface-to-LF view involves a more complex view of the architecture of the grammar than does a Type 4 DC, for the reasons discussed just above.

Finally, and a fact which I think should be taken very seriously—it seems extremely difficult to reconcile anything but a (fairly strong) direct compositional architecture with the fact that humans process sentences incrementally and online (see, e.g., Sedivy, Tanenhaus, Chambers, and Carlson, 1999). By processing online I do not mean that they come up with some representation (indeed, what sort of representation they may or may not come up with is very difficult to determine). But the results cited above show that humans reason and make inferences based on what they hear before they reach the end of a sentence—inferences which arguably can be arrived at only as the result of reasoning processes combined with an actual (presumably, model-theoretic) interpretation of what they have heard. One can make sense of this under the following picture: the meanings (model-theoretic objects) of partial expressions are being computed with each incoming word (or at least, very small chunk). Of course these meanings (under a certain set of assumptions) will not generally be full propositions if they are being computed in the middle of a sentence, but they could be some kinds of functions into propositions, and those functions could be available to the reasoning system for use in making various inferences. In other words, the pragmatics is 'at work' throughout the process of a hearer processing an incoming speech stream, and if pragmatic inferences are the result of applying rationality to meaning, this means that meanings are being computed online as well.

Note that the remarks here assumed something like the classical Gricean view of the interaction of semantics and pragmatics: which is that the semantics feeds the pragmatics—meaning is computed, and the meaning of an expression combined with principles of reasoning give rise to pragmatic inferences. To stress again a point made above, this view does *not* require a commitment to the view that a listener must wait until the end of the sentence in order to compute its meaning and then 'send it' off to the pragmatics—indeed this is exactly the claim that we are challenging above. Rather, if we do assume that the semantics feeds the pragmatics then we can assume that model-theoretic objects—albeit incomplete propositions—must be computed online in order for reasoning to take place about these (model-theoretic) objects. But it should be noted

for this same reason.) But there are several differences between these 'analysis trees' and the LFs of any theory with such a level. In the first place, these analysis trees are merely representations of how the syntax worked and have no role in the grammar itself. There could not, for example, be any constraints stated on these representations. But theories with LFs often employ constraints on the syntax of the LFs. A second related point (discussed above) is that the analysis trees have only a hierarchical structure and, because they are not actual syntactic representations, they contain no notion of linear order. To illustrate this point, consider the Montague-style analysis trees under the Quantifying-In approach in a Type 3 DC and LFs with either Quantifier Lowering (Type 4 DC) or Quantifier Raising (the surface-to-LF view). Under the latter two types, we can (and people have) asked the question of whether the material *every small town in Pennsylvania* is at LF adjoined to the left or to the right. Under Type 3 DC—even with analysis trees to illustrate the semantic composition—this question is meaningless. (Of course someone who feels that there is something at stake in this question would take this as an argument *for* an LF; I give this here just to illustrate that there really is a difference in these kinds of representations.)

that this picture of the interaction of semantics and pragmatics has recently been challenged. There has recently emerged a competing view according to which the pragmatic computation is actually a part of the semantic computation (see, e.g., Chierchia, 2004). I am not endorsing this view here, and think that it has been well refuted in, for example, Russell (2006), but I bring it up to forestall a potential misunderstanding regarding online processing. That is, even if the view that traditional Gricean inferences are in some sense a part of the compositional semantic computation turns out to be correct, it would not affect the main point at issue here. For the fact that pragmatic inferences are available online would of course still entail that meaning (and along with it, the pragmatic computation) is computed online.

What would it take to explain the phenomenon of online computation of meaning? It would appear to be incompatible with the view that meanings are computed off of LFs which themselves are not computed until the entire surface structure has been assigned a representation which is mapped into the LF. (It is conceivable that one could have a theory of partial surface computation—which is mapped to a partial LF—which is assigned some kind of meaning as it is computed, but no such theory has ever been put forth, and it is hard to see how to implement this for actual cases.) Does a Strong(ish) DC architecture fare any better? The actual answer is not necessarily: we indeed need to make some additional assumptions. But those assumptions can be made. Thus if we have a DC architecture in which the 'bottom-up' syntactic and semantic composition also goes right to left, then the ability of humans to construct an online understanding remains equally mysterious. In other words, consider a sentence such as *Porky tricked Wolf*. If our syntactic/semantic composition theory requires *tricked* and *Wolf* to first combine into a syntactic expression with a meaning where only then can *tricked Wolf* combine with *Porky*, the DC architecture is of no help here. But it is well-known that there are various versions of Categorial Grammar and related theories in which any set of rules which allow a right-to-left syntactic and semantic computation can also be converted into rules which allow a left-to-right computation.[10] The syntax will thus prove well-formedness as each new word is encountered, and the DC architecture will map each well-formed expression into a meaning.[11]

---

[10] There is a caveat here: this is true for a theory with Type 1 DC, but it is not in all cases clear what are the consequences of the addition of an infixation operation. Still, even Type 2 DC can be tweaked in conceivable ways to account for the online results; it is difficult to imagine even getting off the ground with a surface-to-LF view.

[11] An anonymous referee objects to the force of this argument by pointing out that it presupposes 'not only that grammar is psychologically real, but also that its reality concerns processing'. While acknowledging that there are open questions about the way in which the grammars that we write feed into a theory of processing, it seems to me to be somewhat uncontroversial that there must be *some* such link—and the closer a theory is to being able to elucidate this link, the better. We can put this in different terms. Suppose we have a theory of processing which is entirely divorced from our theory of 'grammar' but which provides a full model in which the input is a string and the output is a meaning (as must be the case in processing). Then we might as well have that be our model of the compositional semantics in general.

5.4 THE CHALLENGES TO DIRECT COMPOSITIONALITY

I have argued above that DC is the a priori simplest theory. But can it be maintained? There is certainly a large body of literature arguing for a level of LF—much of it claiming (or assuming) such a level makes the statement of the compositional semantics easier. Obviously such arguments need to be addressed—since DC is tenable only if it does not create undue complications elsewhere in the grammar.

In the brief space here I can only scratch the surface of some of these arguments, but I will touch upon two points. First, observe that arguments which assume LF and show that the compositional semantics is easier to state off of this level can be evaluated *only* once we also have a formulation of the rules that pair the surface representations with LFs. There is a common practice to simply not formulate these rules (or to do so rather informally). But it is quite likely that once such rules are fully formalized there is nothing simpler about the LF solutions over a competing DC solution; I consider one such case study in Section 5.4.1. (Of course—at the risk of being repetitive—note that such arguments at best argue only against Strong(ish) DC: such phenomena can trivially be handled under either Type 3 or Type 4 DC, both of which are still simpler than the surface-to-LF mapping view.) Second, many of the arguments for a level of LF are based on other assumptions which are often taken as axiomatic in syntactic and semantic theory, but which actually have no serious motivation (see Section 5.4.2)

5.4.1 When things can 'only be interpreted in places other than where they sit in the syntax'

One of the most common type of arguments for a level of LF (and hence against Strong(ish) DC) is based on the assumption that certain words are not of the right type to combine in the semantics with their syntactic sister(s), and thus must move to a different position at LF before interpretation can take place. Typical examples are phenomena like negation, certain auxiliaries, tenses, etc.—things which are assumed to operate on propositions, but which tend to sit in English in the VP or in fact combine with even smaller things, such as verbs (tense being the most extreme, as it is just expressed as a morpheme which combines with a verb stem).

By way of illustration, consider the English auxiliary *will*. Let us assume a (possibly oversimplified) semantics but crucially one in which the meaning of *will* maps propositions to propositions. Ignoring worlds here, we take a proposition to be a function from times to truth values—that is of type $<i,t>$ (for i the set of times). Hence [[will]] under this view is $\lambda p[\lambda I[\exists I'[I' > I \ \& \ p(I')]]]$ (for p a variable over propositions and I, I' variables over times, and $>$ meaning later than). It is thus a function of type $<<i,t>,<i,t>>$; in prose, it maps a proposition to be true at time I if there is a time later than *I* at which that proposition is true. But in the syntax, it combines with a VP to give a VP. Assume for discussion that a VP is a function from individuals to propositions; its meaning is of type $<e, <i,t>>$, and we do not have a proposition to be an argument of [[will]] until a subject is introduced. Given all of this, consider a sentence like *Porky will grunt*. [[will]] is not of the right type to combine with [[grunt]]. Enter the existence of LF as a solution: we could assume that the actual level which inputs the semantics is not the same as the (visible) syntax, but rather that *will* is raised to be a sister of the S *Porky grunt* whose meaning is a set of times, and [[will]] thus combines in the semantics with [[Porky grunt]] to give back a new set of times (a new proposition).[12]

But the case here is perfectly compatible with Strong(ish) DC. For rather than positing a raising rule, we can just perfectly easily revise the type of [[will]], to be a function from VP type meanings (call this a property) to VP type meanings. Thus its meaning is of type $<<e, <i,t>>, <e, <i,t>>>$. Using P to mean some property and x any individual, its meaning is $\lambda P[\lambda x[\lambda I[\exists I'[I' > I \& P(x)(I')]]]]$. This is a simple mutation on the meaning given above. Informally, [[will]] takes an incomplete proposition (a function from individuals into propositions) and returns an incomplete proposition (again, a function from individuals into propositions), holding off on the individual slot. The core of the meaning is the same as on the propositional theory, it simply has a slightly different argument structure.

Is there any benefit to the view in which [[will]] takes propositional arguments but raises at LF to the competing Strong(ish) DC view—whereby it has a slightly more complex meaning but no raising rule is needed? It is difficult to see what could possibly be the advantage of the first view. True, the meaning under DC is a bit more complex— but no extraordinary changes have been made to the theory of the types of meanings that words can have. We are still building meanings from the same 'stuff' as in the LF account. In fact, the verdict has to come down on the side of the more complex meaning. For if the trade-off were only between a more complex meaning vs. a movement rule then it would be hard to decide between them. But once we consider the commitments that each view makes to the entire architecture of the grammar, it seems clear that the overall simplicity is on the side of DC.

Let me ward off one potential objection to the reasoning here. It is often assumed in the surface-to-LF view that—while some principle must be stated allowing an item to raise—it at least is not the case that such a principle refers to specific items; it can be stated quite generally. The idea is that the raising of an item in the mapping from a surface representation to LF happens 'to resolve type mismatch'. In the case at hand then, the idea is that it is an accidental property of the syntax of English that *will* is a sister to a VP, but its semantics is the propositional operator given above. Therefore,

---

[12] This example is for illustrative purposes only; many proponents of an LF theory actually advocate a different solution to the apparent type mismatch here, one which does not require raising *will* at LF. This solution is to say that VPs themselves have meanings of type $<i,t>$; they have subjects which have raised (in the syntax) from a position internal to the VP to be sister to *will*. Thus at the relevant level, there is no mismatch between the type of [[will]] and its syntactic sister. This solution was actually originally proposed in Ross (1969). However, the remarks above regarding the raising of *will* are typical of other such cases, and thus serve to make the general points here.

its syntactic position is such that the compositional semantics could not proceed as its meaning could not combine with that of its VP sister (again, recall that for the sake of discussion here we are assuming that VP meanings are of type $< e, < i, t >>$). Thus the fact that it raises is an automatic consequence of this type mismatch, and it will raise until it finds the appropriate type of sister, presumably S. Note that at best this just means the above mentioned movement rule is general rather than referring to a specific item—but the hidden agenda behind this argument is that the surface-to-LF view can systematically predict and explain what undergoes raising to LF, as opposed to having lexical items listed whose complex meaning is an idiosyncratic property. No special rule needs to refer to *will* here.[13]

But consider what it takes to formalize this idea. The conversion from a surface representation to an LF is a conversion from an uninterpreted syntactic object to another object, and interpretation proceeds only on the output of this conversion. The syntactic rules themselves have no access to meanings, only syntactic configurations. Thus if the mapping process were driven by 'type mismatch', this means that the semantic types must be taken to be syntactic objects—annotations, perhaps, on the syntactic categories visible to the syntax. Conceivable, perhaps, but a strange duplication: since words do have meanings, the minimal assumption is that the types are just a consequence of the meanings and not something listed as a separate bit of information in the syntax. Alternatively, one might propose that the rules mapping representations into LFs work in such a way that they are interspersed with the semantic computation of the meaning of a (partial) LF. But how this should be spelled out is unclear. As far as I can see, it entails a theory in which an LF-like representation is compositionally interpreted, bottom-up, in the usual fashion, until a type mismatch is found. This representation is then mapped into another one (where something raises). But does the semantic computation procedure then have to 'go back' and recompute meanings bottom-up on the new structure? Or is the output of this some mix of representation and meanings? Until this is spelled out, it is hard to take the 'movement happens to repair type mismatch' slogan as a particularly illuminating way to view the workings of the system.

---

[13] Actually, this kind of reasoning in no way speaks to the choice between an LF-to-surface vs. a DC architecture. The same kind of reasoning given above could be taken in a DC view. Thus, one could imagine a DC theory in which *will* has the simpler meaning given above (its meaning is of type $<< i, e >, < i, t >>$) and where its syntactic category is such that it can only combine in the syntax with a VP. However, there could be general combinatory principles (in a type-driven system) to resolve type-mismatch (just as under the surface-to-LF view we are envisioning raising rules to resolve type mismatch). Then, a type-driven syntax/semantics correspondence (of the type proposed in, e.g., Klein and Sag, 1985) can have a principle which would force function composition rather than functional application here. More generally, when there is a 'type mismatch' such that functional application is impossible, there would be rules for other combinatorics—just like in the non-DC view a raising rule instead takes over. (The entire system needs to be formulated with some care due to the case of a quantified NP in object position combining with a transitive verb. If the transitive verb had the simple $< e, < e, t >>$ type disaster would result if function composition were allowed here, since then a sentence like *Mitka chased every squirrel* would end up meaning that every squirrel chased Mitka; we leave verification of this to the reader.) The point, though, is that one *can* formulate a set of rules to 'repair type mismatch' under DC.

5.4.2 The interaction of quantified NPs in object position and antecedent contained deletion

The remarks above focus on a simple example of an argument used against DC centring on apparent type mismatch; we have seen that it is possible instead to recast the meanings of the words so that there is no type mismatch. As discussed earlier, this is also one of the strategies available to Strong(ish) DC to solve the problem of the interpretation of quantified NPs in object position (as well as the scopal ambiguity). Thus quantifiers in object position—often taken to be one of the signature cases for an argument for 'raise material to create an LF' view—are, as we have seen, perfectly compatible with DC.

But the story regarding quantified NPs in object position does not end just with the observations about type mismatch. There is a more sophisticated argument—due originally (though in a slightly different form) to Sag (1976) which has become standard fare, and which purports to show that there must be a rule of QR mapping surface structures into abstract LFs. To elucidate, we turn first to the phenomenon of 'VP Ellipsis' illustrated in (5.5):

(5.5)   John will vacation on Martha's Vineyard, and Bill will too.

Of interest here is the understanding of this sentence in which we conclude that Bill will also vacation on Martha's Vineyard, which understanding I will indicate with the strike-through notation:

(5.6)   John will vacation on Martha's Vineyard, and Bill will ~~vacation on Martha's Vineyard~~ too.

There are any number of accounts of this phenomenon. On one, there is actual material in the position of the 'ellipsis site' (the position following *will*) which contributes to the compositional semantics in the usual way, and there is some process by which this material is either silent or deleted on the basis of identity of form and/or meaning with the material in the first clause. This view is difficult to reconcile with a Strong(ish) DC architecture—not because we could not have rules in the syntax which suppress the phonology of some expression—but because the identity condition is not a *local* property of the 'silenced' material. A second view (see, among others, Hardt, 1993; Jacobson, 2003) is that there is nothing in the syntax or in the compositional semantics following *will*. Here, the 'missing meaning' is supplied by the listener and is not grammatically encoded. In the particular implementation of this idea in Jacobson (2003), the entire sentence does not denote a proposition but rather a function from properties to propositions. In order to extract propositional information, the listener applies this to some contextually salient property; here the property of vacationing on Martha's Vineyard is of course quite contextually salient. While this view does not require that there be an overt linguistic expression whose meaning supplies the 'missing property', let us assume that usually (for reasons which remain unclear) the property is made salient in virtue of having been mentioned. This general view is in fact compatible with DC, although a full demonstration of this fact would take too much space here (see Jacobson, 2003 for details).

Despite the fact that the first view (that there is silent material in the ellipsis site) is difficult to reconcile with a Strong(ish) DC architecture, I will nonetheless use it in the rest of this exposition. This is purely for convenience; thinking of the ellipsis site as actually having material in place (and material which needs to find an identical antecedent elsewhere) considerably simplifies the exposition.

Of interest here are sentences like (5.7) which are called cases of 'Antecedent Contained Deletion' (I will treat *vote for* as a single complex verb):

(5.7)   Mary will vote for every candidate that Bill will ~~vote for~~.

To develop the argument, consider first the parallel sentence where there is overt material after the auxiliary:

(5.8)   Mary will vote for every candidate that Bill will vote for.

Before proceeding, we need to make some decision regarding [[will]]. Again, for expository convenience, assume that it is indeed of the 'fancier' meaning discussed above—it directly combines with the meaning of VPs rather than being raised at LF. (In truth, this is not the standard account of its meaning, but that debate is somewhat orthogonal to the points here.)

There is a very deeply held view on the syntactic and semantic composition of cases like this—a view which has guided much of the research in syntactic and semantic theory since the inception of Transformational Grammar and which has persisted in various forms to this day in much of the 'standard' literature on this. This is the view that—to put it in semantic terms—functions (or at least those which are the meanings of verbs) always get their arguments during the course of the semantic composition: all (or at least in general) functions must be 'saturated'. This means, in essence, that verbs have to combine with their arguments by functional application. It also means that no verb can have a meaning which takes a function as argument. (Note that this in itself would rule out the analysis of [[will]] discussed above, but again we are mixing theories only to keep the point simple.) What does that mean for the analysis of *vote-for*? It means that it must combine with an object. But there is no obvious object in the surface syntax. Hence it is usual to posit that there is actually something there in the syntax—a trace, which semantically is interpreted as an indexed variable (say, x_8). Thus the meaning of *vote for* t_8 is—on some assignment function g—the set of individuals who voted for $g(x_8)$. That then occurs as argument of [[will]] which in turn takes the meaning of the subject as argument. The result is that the expression *(that) Bill will vote for* t_8 has as its meaning the open proposition which, for any assignment g, is the proposition that Bill will vote for $g(x_8)$. This then maps into the property of being an x who Bill votes for (i.e. a function which characterizes the set of Bill votees); that then intersects with the set denoted by *candidate* and the rest of the composition proceeds in the expected way.

What happens, then, in a case like (5.7) where there is an ellipsis site after *will*? The assumption is that here the semantic composition has to proceed in exactly the same way. But herein lies the rub. What is needed in the ellipsis site is a VP type meaning. Why? Because it is assumed that [[will]] combines only with VP type meanings, and so that is the kind of argument it is looking for.[14] But—assuming that some other expression has to have a meaning which is identical to the elided meaning—the problem is that there *is* no other VP which can supply the meaning. It appears that it could not be the matrix VP because this contains the ellipsis site; if we try to supply that as the meaning we thus run into an infinite regress. LF comes to the rescue. If one posits that there is a level at which the object NP is raised out of the sentence, than in fact the matrix VP can also be of the form (roughly) *vote for t8* with the appropriate meaning, and this can be the meaning at the ellipsis site.

The fallacy here is that the entire argument rests on the premise that *vote for* in a sentence like (5.8) has to combine with an object. So, since there is no actual object, the theory supplies it with a variable. But none of this is necessary if we simply abandon the view that functions must be saturated (as well as the weaker view that functions themselves can never be arguments). In fact, such a requirement follows from nothing else—and would require an additional stipulation. Suppose it is untrue. Then there are other ways to put together the meanings in (5.8). One is developed in, among others, Steedman (1987). In (5.8), [[vote-for]]—which is an (unsaturated) function of type $< e, < e, t >>$ (that is, a 2-place relation between individuals)—function composes with the meaning of *will*. In turn, this combines with the meaning of the subject *Bill* (let [[Bill]] be a generalized quantifier which function composes with [[will vote for]]), with the result that *(that) Bill will vote for* denotes the set of individuals that Bill will vote for. Note that this is exactly the meaning ultimately posited for this expression in the standard view too—the difference is only in how we arrived at this. Here there was no use of a trace or a variable; function composition directly puts the meanings together in such a way that we end up with a set. That set then intersects with the set of candidates, exactly as above.

The consequences of this view for the ACD argument are dramatic. As first noted in Cormack (1984) and subsequently in Evans (1988), Jacobson, (1992b), and others, we now have no reason to think that the 'missing' meaning in the ACD case in (5.7) is something like [[vote for t_8]]. Neither traces nor variables are needed. Rather, the 'missing' meaning is simply the transitive verb (phrase) [[vote-for]]—which function composes with [[will]] exactly as in the composition of (8).[15] But if all that is needed in order to put the meanings together is the simple 2-place relation [[vote-for]], then there is no argument for 'pulling' the object out of the matrix to create the VP-meaning [[vote for t_8]] in order to supply the 'missing' VP meaning for (5.7). Rather, all we need for (5.7) is a transitive verb (phrase) meaning, and so the meaning of *vote for* is sufficient. The key to this alternative story has simply been the abandonment of the view that functions

[14] If *will* were instead raised at LF the ultimate argument would be the same, it would just be made with a few extra steps.
[15] Note again that this way of phrasing the story uses the view that the elided material is actually there in the syntactic and semantic composition. Again, though, this is for exposition only, and the interested reader can consult Jacobson (2003) to see a fully DC version of this worked out.

must always be saturated. Hence ACD provides no argument for LF and it is perfectly compatible with Strong(ish) DC.[16]

As with all interesting cases, this is hardly the end of the story. There are many additional facts about ACD which need to be accounted for; I have addressed a number of these in Jacobson (2003, 2007, and to appear). Moreover, Koster-Moeller, Varvoutis, and Hackl (to appear) have recently argued for the QR approach as against the 'transitive verb (phrase) ellipsis' approach on the basis of some online processing facts. I must leave a reply to this as a promissory note for the future. Suffice it to note here, however, that any argument for something like QR using online processing is somewhat difficult to reconcile with known results about processing. The Koster-Moeller et al. explanation for the results that they found assumes that what is being computed online is a *representation*—not a meaning. Since the LF representations of the sort that they posit do not feed into the model-theoretic computation (and hence the system of understanding) until *after* these representations are constructed (after which they are interpreted compositionally bottom-up), the actual online comprehension of sentences is mysterious in this view. One might try to have a view in which partial representations are computed and assigned meanings online, but how this would actually work step by step in the cases they look at—and how this would actually explain their results—is not at all clear. It is thus difficult to see how any results about online understanding could possibly be taken to support the view that representations are constructed.

5.5 CONCLUSION

I have argued in this paper that DC is the simplest among competing theories of the architecture of the grammar, and I have tried to give a taste for the kinds of answers that can be given to claims that a non-DC architecture is necessary. Obviously there are many additional pieces of evidence which have been put forth against DC, so the remarks here should be taken simply as programmatic and as suggestions for further research.[17]

---

[16] An anonymous referee points out that the DC approach to ACD 'leads to a more complicated notion of semantic interpretation (in which the semantics of the sentence as determined by the syntax is essentially incomplete and has to be completed by a different form of semantic interpretation'. But this does not in fact represent any new notion of semantic interpretation. Just about all theories allow for, e.g., 'free pronouns' whose value is ultimately not fixed by the semantics alone, but by taking an incomplete meaning and completing it via context. (The technical details of how this happens differ from theory to theory, but the basic idea that there are cases like 'free pronouns' is fairly standard.) The view of ACD here is no different: it merely takes the 'missing' material to be treated much like free pronouns are in general. For further discussion, see Hardt (1993) and Jacobson (2003).

[17] I would like to thank Chris Potts and two anonymous referees for comments on an earlier version of this. This work was partially supported by NSF Grant BCS 0646081.

CHAPTER 6

....

SEMANTIC MONADICITY
WITH CONCEPTUAL
POLYADICITY

....

PAUL M. PIETROSKI

How are meanings of expressions in a natural human language related to concepts? And how is semantic composition related to conceptual composition? I assume that concepts are mental symbols that can be combined in certain ways (see, e.g., Fodor, 1975, 1986, 2003), and that children lexicalize concepts in acquiring a language (see, e.g., Bloom, 2000).[1] Many concepts, which can be constituents of thoughts, are somehow indicated with words that can be constituents of sentences. But this assumption is compatible with many hypotheses about the concepts lexicalized, linguistic meanings, and the relevant forms of composition.

One familiar suggestion is that lexical items simply *label* the concepts they lexicalize, and that composition of lexical meanings mirrors composition of the labeled concepts, which exhibit diverse *adicities*. This makes it tempting to say that names label singular concepts—mental tags for particular things—which can *saturate* the concepts labeled with verbs, where these predicative (unsaturated) concepts may be monadic or polyadic. As we'll see, while the adicities of lexicalized concepts are not obvious, there are many ways of developing the familiar suggestion in detail. But attending to these details invites an alternative proposal according to which (i) lexicalization is a more creative process in which available concepts are used to *introduce* formally distinct concepts that are uniformly *monadic*, and (ii) phrases signify *conjunction* of monadic concepts, as opposed to saturation of one concept by another.

---

[1] These concepts may not be fully integrated and recursively combinable, in the sense that any two can be constituents of a third; see note 9. But many animals have representations that can be combined with others, in some interesting sense; for reviews, see Gallistel (1990), Margolis and Laurence (1999a), Gallistel and Gibbon (2002). And infants can presumably tether at least some of these representations to words.

From this perspective, semantic composition is rooted in a conjunctive operation that may be available to other animals, but lexicalization is not simply a matter of pairing concepts with perceptible signals (and/or certain grammatical information). This proposal may initially seem odd. But perhaps it should be our null hypothesis, given that young humans have a distinctive talent for lexicalization.[2]

6.1 BACKGROUND: COMPLICATIONS FOR LABELLING AND SATURATING

In light of Frege's (1879, 1884, 1891) seminal work, as developed by Church (1941) and many others, one might begin with the following idea: a name like 'Caesar' labels a singular concept; an intransitive verb like 'arrived' labels a monadic concept, which can be saturated by a singular concept to form a thought like the one expressed with 'Caesar arrived'; and a transitive verb like 'poked' labels a dyadic concept that can be saturated once to form a complex monadic concept, which can be expressed with 'poked Caesar' and saturated to form a thought expressed with (6.1).

(6.1)   Brutus poked Caesar

The posited concepts/thoughts can be represented as follows, in small capitals, with order of saturation indicated right to left: CAESAR, ARRIVED(X), ARRIVED(CAESAR), POKED(X, Y), POKED(X, CAESAR), BRUTUS, and POKED(BRUTUS, CAESAR).

Of course, verbs are not the only predicative words, and such words need not combine with names. If 'red' and 'stick' label monadic concepts, RED(X) and STICK(X), then an obvious hypothesis is that 'red stick' expresses a conjunction of these concepts. A sentence like (6.2)

(6.2)   Every stick is red

may express a thought—for example EVERY[RED(X), STICK(X)]—in which a *second-order* concept is saturated by two first-order concepts whose variables are thereby quantificationally bound. But perhaps combining lexical items always signifies an operation that applies to the labelled concepts, and often, the signified operation combines a concept of adicity n with a saturater to form a concept of adicity $n - 1$.[3] In this

---

[2] I have argued elsewhere that a 'Conjunctivist' semantics can be descriptively adequate while still explaining various phenomena concerning the meanings of adverbial, causal, plural, quantificational, and speech report constructions; see Pietroski (2002, 2006a), drawing on many others, including Davidson (1967a, 1985), Castañeda (1967), Carlson (1984), Higginbotham (1985), Taylor (1985), Parsons (1990), Schein (1993), Larson and Segal (1995). See also Hobbs (1985), Williams (2005), Schein (forthcoming), and for interesting discussion in the context of language evolution, Hurford (2007). Here, I suppress many compositional details to focus on issues concerning the basic operations of composition and how they constrain lexicalization.

[3] Thoughts can be viewed as sentential concepts of adicity zero, or instances of the truth-evaluable type $< t >$. I return to the idea that combining expressions *always* signifies saturation, and that RED(X) is used to introduce a higher-order concept, $\lambda X.\text{RED}(X) \& Xx$.

section, I discuss some complications that together motivate an alternative defended in Section 6.2: verbs, nouns (including names), and modifiers are uniformly devices for fetching monadic concepts that are often introduced in lexicalization.

6.1.1 Robust polyadicity

By hypothesis, POKED(X, Y) is not merely a mental symbol that can combine with two singular concepts to form a thought. One can imagine concepts that are 'minimally dyadic' in this sense, yet *cannot* be combined with one concept to form a monadic concept like POKED(X, CAESAR). Indeed, one can imagine a mind stocked with concepts like POKED($< 1, 2 >$) that are satisfied by ordered pairs of singular concepts, though with no possibility of leaving exactly one slot unfilled. And there is no guarantee that children come equipped with all the 'robustly polyadic' concepts required for saturation to be a common operation of semantic composition. But if a lexical item *labels* a concept C that is only minimally polyadic, yet *fetches* a concept C′ that is robustly polyadic in this sense, then perhaps C was used to introduce C′.

The requisite reformatting is now so familiar—see Frege (1891), Church (1941), Montague (1974)—that it is easily ignored. Given a capacity to represent truth values and mappings, from representables to representables, a mind with the concept POKED($< 1, 2 >$) might be able to introduce the following concept: $\lambda 2.\lambda 1.$TRUE if POKED($< 1, 2 >$) and FALSE otherwise; or abbreviating, POKED(X, Y). If this mind is also constrained to treat a phrase like 'poked Caesar' as an instruction to saturate a concept fetched via the verb, with a concept fetched via the name, then merely labelling POKED($< 1, 2 >$) with 'poked' will preclude execution of this instruction. This might trigger the capacity to create POKED(X, Y), which could then be retrieved via 'poked'. Similarly, even if competent speakers fetch the concept EVERY$_x$ [$\Phi(x)$, $\Psi(x)$] upon hearing 'every', this concept may have been introduced in terms of a minimally dyadic concept that cannot itself be saturated once to form EVERY$_x$[$\Phi(x)$, STICK(x)]. So those who appeal to saturation, in describing semantic composition, should *welcome* the idea that lexicalized concepts can be used to introduce formally distinct but analytically related concepts, which can be combined via the operation(s) signified by combining lexical items.

That said, let's henceforth ignore any differences between concepts like POKED($< 1, 2 >$) and their robustly polyadic counterparts of matching adicity. If lexicalization always introduces monadic concepts, lexicalized concepts and their introduced counterparts often *differ* in adicity. And by way of easing into this idea, let's consider the apparent complexity of tensed verbs.

6.1.2 Event variables

Instead of saying that 'arrived' labels an atomic concept ARRIVED(X), one might say that the lexical item 'arrive' labels ARRIVE(E, X). Saturating this concept once would yield a concept like ARRIVE(E, CAESAR), which applies to an *event* if and only if it is (tenselessly) an arrival of Caesar. This complex monadic concept can be existentially closed, or conjoined with concepts that may be context-sensitive: PAST(E), TODAY(E), $\exists x[\text{WITH}(E, x) \& \text{STICK}(x)]$, etc.[4] While ARRIVE(E, x) is formally dyadic, it may not be a concept of a genuine relation—like UNDER(x, y) or BEFORE(E, F)—since an event of *x* arriving is not independent of *x*. In any case, one can hypothesize that 'arrive' labels a concept that has an event variable. But given this twist on the original hunch that 'arrived' labels ARRIVED(x), lexicalization may not be mere labelling.

Perceptual reports like (6.3) suggest that 'arrive' is somehow linked to an eventish concept;

(6.3)   Brutus saw Caesar arrive

see Higginbotham (1983). If the untensed clause expresses ARRIVE(E, CAESAR), one can say that 'saw Caesar arrive' expresses $\exists y[\text{SEE}(E, x, y) \& \text{PAST}(E) \& \text{ARRIVE}(y, \text{CAESAR})]$, thereby accommodating both readings of 'saw Caesar arrive with a spyglass': $\exists y\{\text{SEE}(E, x, y) \& \text{PAST}(E) \& \text{ARRIVE}(y, \text{CAESAR}) \& \exists z[\text{WITH}(E/y, z) \& \text{SPYGLASS}(z)]\}$; where things seen, corresponding to the variable '*y*', include both events and individuals. If 'see' labels a formally *tri*adic concept, perhaps 'poke' labels POKE(E, x, y), and 'give' labels a formally tetradic concept GIVE(E, x, y, z) variables for events, givers, things given, and recipients.

One can still retain the idealization that 'arrived' labels a monadic concept of those who arrived. But the underlying truth may be that a sentence like (6.4a) expresses a thought like (6.4b),

(6.4)   a. Caesar arrived
         b. $\exists E[\text{ARRIVE}(E, \text{CAESAR})]$

and that abstracting away from the contribution of 'Caesar' leaves a complex monadic concept: $\exists E[\text{ARRIVE}(E, x)]$. We cannot just intuit the adicity of a concept lexicalized (or retrieved) with a word. Hypotheses about the relevant conceptual adicities must be evaluated in the light of available evidence, especially given the possibility of covertly closing covert variables. And prima facie, infants have many concepts with event variables (see Leslie, 1984; Scholl and Tremoulet, 2000). On the other hand, concepts like ARRIVE(E, x)/POKE(E, x, y)/GIVE(E, x, y, x) need not be available for labelling independently of lexicalization, since 'eventish' concepts may be introduced along the following lines: $\forall x\{\exists E[\text{ARRIVE}(E, x) \& \text{PAST}(E)] \equiv \text{ARRIVED}(x)\}$.[5]

---

[4] See Davidson (1967*a*). Initially, one might speculate that 'arrive' labels ARRIVE(x, T), with a variable for *times*. But Taylor (1985) reviews an argument, due to Gareth Evans, for appealing to event variables that permit simultaneous events. Suppose that at noon, Brutus poked Caesar softly with a red stick and sharply with a blue stick. It doesn't follow that Brutus poked Caesar softly with a blue stick, or sharply with a red stick, because there were *two* pokes of Caesar by Brutus: a soft one done with a red stick, and a sharp one with a blue stick. And note that if the event variable is the *first* one saturated/bound—as in POKE(x, y, E)—it is hard to explain the adverbial modifications corresponding to the implications that Brutus poked Caesar softly, with a red stick, sharply, and with a blue stick; cp. Higginbotham (1983), Pollock (1989).

[5] Or perhaps the concept initially *lexicalized* is ARRIVED(x, T), with a variable for times, and $\forall x \forall T\{\text{ARRIVE}(x, T) \equiv \exists E[\text{ARRIVE}(E, x) \& \text{AT}(E, T)]\}$. Any such introduction of concepts raises delicate

Correlatively, semanticists can appeal to concepts like POKE(E, X, Y) and GIVE(E, X, Y, z), even if infants do not have such concepts to lexicalize. But those who posit such concepts—perhaps along with the idea that combining a verb and a name signifies saturation of a polyadic concept—should also welcome the following idea: lexicalizing a concept C often involves using C to introduce a formally distinct concept C′ that meets certain conditions imposed by whatever aspects of human cognition support semantic composition. For example, one might speculate that labelling POKED(X, Y) triggers the introduction of POKE(E, X, Y) given the need to accommodate tense and/or adjunction. But this speculation invites others.

If lexical items can be linked to polyadic concepts like POKE(E, X, Y), they can be linked to monadic concepts like POKE(E), given independently motivated appeal to 'thematic' concepts: $\forall E\{AGENT(E, X) \ \& \ POKE(E) \ \& \ PATIENT(E, X) \equiv POKE(E, X, Y)\}$; where this generalization can reflect the introduction of POKE(E) in terms of the other concepts (cp. Castañeda's (1967) response to Davidson (1967a)). While a concept like PATIENT(E, x) is formally dyadic, it may not be a concept of a genuine relation: an event with x as its patient is not independent of x. In any case, one can hypothesize that 'poke' is a device for fetching POKE(E), yet deny that this monadic concept was available for lexicalization. The concept lexicalized is presumably polyadic. Indeed, it may be tetradic—POKE(E, X, Y, z)—with a variable for the 'instrument' with which y is poked by x in e; in which case, lexicalization is not mere labelling if 'poke' is a device for fetching POKE(E, X, Y).

As this last point illustrates, one needs evidence for the hypothesis that the concept *lexicalized* with 'poke' has an adicity that *matches* the number of saturaters (or quantificational binders) indicated in sentences where 'poke' takes a grammatical subject and object. Observing that instrumental adjuncts like 'with a stick' are optional, in such sentences, does not establish that the lexicalized concept has no variable for instruments—just as the passive/nominal uses of 'poke' in (6.5) do not show that the lexicalized concept has no variable for agents/patients.

(6.5)   Caesar was poked. Brutus gave him a good poke with a red stick.

But such examples do invite a speculation. Perhaps the concept *fetched* with 'poke', for purposes of semantic composition, has no variable for agents/patients/instruments.[6]

---

issues—beyond the scope of this chapter—concerning the relations among logic, truth, and existential commitment. But Frege's (1884) discussion of number and 'contextual' definitions are relevant, as is his idea that languages are tools for introducing concepts that let us re-present thoughts in fruitful ways; see Horty (2007).

[6] See Parsons (1990). Moreover, if 'poke' labels a polyadic concept with an event variable, we need to explain why 'That Brutus poked Caesar' cannot be used to say that the demonstrated event was a poke of Caesar by Brutus. If the answer is that the event variable must be covertly bound, then one cannot insist that the number of grammatical arguments in a sentence reveals the adicity of the concept lexicalized with the matrix verb. I return to these issues. Kratzer (1996) argues—stressing subject/object asymmetries revealed in passivization and especially idioms (see Marantz, 1984)—that while agent variables are 'severed' from the semantic contribution of verbs like 'poke', this contribution is still polyadic: combination with an object indicates saturation of a variable, yielding a concept like POKE(E, CAESAR); see also Harley (2006). But this presupposes some kind of creative lexicalization, unless the hypothesis is that

Of course, one wants to know what would drive any mismatch between the adicities of lexicalized concepts and the concepts introduced in lexicalization. Other things equal, one might expect a polyadic concept of adicity n to be lexicalized with a predicate that can and must combine with n arguments to form a sentence, at least if children can acquire languages that allow for such predicates. But correlatively, in so far as polyadic concepts fail to be so lexicalized, one wonders if there are relevant constraints on acquisition. And suppose, for a moment, that saturation is *not* available as an operation to be signified by phrasal syntax in a natural human language (as opposed to a Fregean *Begriffsschrift*).

If a phrase must be understood as an instruction to conjoin monadic concepts that correspond to the constituents, with 'red stick' being illustrative, lexicalization must be a process in which non-monadic concepts are used to introduce monadic analogues. But given such analogues, along with some thematic concepts, conjunctions can mimic the effect of saturating polyadic concepts. For example, 'poke Caesar' can be analysed as an instruction to build the following concept: POKE(E) & ∃x[PATIENT(E, x) & CAESARED(x)]; where CAESARED(x) is a concept of the relevant Caesar. I return to names, which may harbour covert demonstratives (cp. Burge, 1973), in Section 6.3. For now, pretend that CAESARED(x) is introduced in terms of a mental tag for a certain individual: ∀x[CAESARED(x) ≡ (CAESAR = x)] (cp. Quine, 1963).

This is compatible with a restricted kind of semantic composition based on operations that require monadic inputs: the concepts POKE(E) and PAST(E) can, like RED(x) and STICK(x), be the inputs to an operation that (only) conjoins pairs of monadic concepts; and CAESARED(x) can be the input to a 'variable-change' operation that (only) converts one monadic concept into another—for example ∃x[PATIENT(E, x) & CAESARED(x)]—via conjunction with a thematic concept and existential closure of the original variable. One can posit a small number of such variable-change operations as the semantic correlates of certain grammatical relations (like being the object of a certain kind of verb), prepositions, and other functional ('closed class') vocabulary items.[7]

(1) concepts like POKE(E, x) are available for labelling, *and* (2) concepts of higher adicity are not. So absent independent arguments for (1) and (2), one might blame the relevant asymmetry on cognitive factors independent of semantic composition, instead of positing distinct composition operations for subjects and objects: language-independent cognition may prefer POKE(E, x) to POKE(E)—perhaps a variable for individuals helps 'locate' the events—even if both concepts are introduced via POKE(E, x, y) or POKE(E, x, y, z). Williams' (2007) defends such a diagnosis by offering independent arguments for severing patients (see also Schein, 1993, forthcoming; Pietroski, 2002), and a rebuttal of Kratzer's specific arguments to the contrary.

[7] Existential closure of a 'matrix' event variable can also be viewed as an operation that converts a monadic concept into C(E)—for example ∃x[AGENT(E, x) & BRUTUSED(x)] & POKE(E) & PAST(E) & ∃x[PATIENT(E, x) & CAESARED(x)]—into another monadic concept that is satisfied by everything or nothing: everything if C(E) is satisfied by something, and otherwise nothing. And since negation can be viewed as an operation that converts one 'universal-or-empty' concept into another, appeal to truth-values (as entities of type < t >) may be unneeded; cp. Tarski (1933). For further discussion, see Pietroski (2011).

6.1.3 Composition and Procedures

Let me conclude this introductory section by framing the proposal explicitly in the context of a psychological conception of naturally acquirable human languages (like spoken English or ASL).

Following Chomsky (1986), let's identify these languages with states of a mental faculty that supports the acquisition of certain *implemented procedures* that connect human linguistic signals with mental representations. Chomsky speaks of 'I-languages' to highlight their intensional/procedural character (cp. Church, 1941). By contrast, 'E-languages' are *sets* of expressions. Expressions of an I-language can be described as generable pairs of instructions—PFs and LFs, or more neutrally, PHONs and SEMs— via which the language faculty interfaces with articulatory/perceptual systems and conceptual/intentional systems (see Chomsky, 1995). These '*i*-expressions' exhibit relations of homophony and rhyme, synonymy and entailment. Focusing on understanding, as opposed to speech production, lexical and phrasal *i*-expressions can be viewed as instructions to fetch and combine concepts.

Each child acquires at least one I-language, in addition to the one or more mental languages that provide lexicalizable concepts. Once acquired, an I-language can be used in both thought and communication. But *i*-expressions have *inherited significance*, as indicators of concepts with which we (and perhaps other animals) can think about things more directly. And the concepts fetched with lexical *i*-expressions need not have been the concepts lexicalized, since the former may have been introduced via the latter.

From an I-language perspective, issues about semantic composition concern the operations invoked by a certain biologically implemented mental faculty. It can sometimes be useful to speak of an unspecified determination relation—as when we say that the meaning of a sentence is somehow determined by its structure and (the meanings of) the constituent words—or an abstract supervenience relation: expressions that differ in meaning differ, somehow, with respect to their structure and/or constituents (see Szabó, 2000*b*). But this abstract relation must be implemented by specific operations (cp. Marr, 1982), like saturation or conjunction, with implications for the kinds of concepts that can be so combined.[8]

Regarding potential differences between lexicalized and introduced concepts, my focus here is on adicity. But there is a more general point concerning respects in which lexicalized concepts vary formally: lexicalization must somehow efface any such variation that cannot be tolerated by the composition operations that I-languages can invoke.

---

[8] There is, of course, more than one conjunction operation. Given the usual conventions, ampersands indicate an operation that can combine sentences with *any* number of variables left open. By contrast, the operation I have in mind can only take two kinds of inputs: a pair of monadic concepts, or a monadic concept and one of a few available (formally dyadic) thematic concepts; and in the second case, conjunction must be followed immediately by existential closure of the monadic concept's variable. Correlatively, the closure operation need not be applicable to an open sentence of arbitrary adicity; it just needs to target the variable of any monadic concept in its scope. In this sense, using '&' and '∃' may *exaggerate* the composition operations required. But I will retain the usual notation.

Correlatively, the available 'i-operations' impose limits on the kind(s) of variation that fetchable concepts can exhibit.

For example, semantic composition may require variables that are neutral with regard to a plural/singular distinction—permitting combination, perhaps via conjunction, with PLURAL(x) or ~PLURAL(x)—while at least many lexicalizable concepts are essentially singular or essentially plural (Boolos, 1998; Schein, 1993, 2001; Pietroski, 2002, 2006a). If so, intrinsically 'numbered' concepts may be used to create number-neutral analogues. More generally, even if a lexicalized concept is monadic, 'formatting' may be required for the purposes of semantic composition, depending on which operations are available to I-languages. But if lexicalization is a tool for creating concepts that *abstract* from certain formal distinctions exhibited by prior concepts, this may help explain the remarkable combinability of human concepts.[9]

In any case, as I have been stressing, this idea is not peculiar to any one conception of semantic composition. An old idea is that if phrasal syntax always signifies saturation, phrases like 'red stick' can be accommodated as follows: 'red' lexicalizes RED(x), which can be used to create the higher-order concept $\lambda Y.\lambda x.RED(x)$ & $Y(x)$, which can be saturated by STICK(x) to yield RED(x) & STICK(x) (Parsons, 1970; Montague, 1974; Kamp, 1975). The required type-lifting operation can be posited in semantic composition or in lexicalization. On the latter hypothesis, 'red' fetches *either* the core concept of type <e, t>—associated with a monadic function from entities to truth-values—*or* the adjusted concept of type <<e, t>, <e, t>>, associated with a function from monadic functions to (conjunctively specified) monadic functions, depending on its syntactic role as the main predicate or adjunct. But instead of saying that monadic concepts are often type-lifted for purposes of saturation, one can say that non-monadic concepts are paired (in lexicalization) with monadic analogues. And instead of viewing 'red stick' as a non-transparent instruction to saturate, one can view 'saw Caesar' as a non-transparent instruction to conjoin.[10]

[9] While animals have composable concepts, animal thoughts may not satisfy Evans's (1982) Generality Constraint; cp. Spelke (2002), Carruthers (2002). A creature might have more than one mental language, each associated with one or more modules, with the following result: the creature has analogues of 'Fa' and 'Gb' in one mental language, and an analog of 'Γαβ' in another; within each mental language, substituting expressions of the same type preserves well-formedness; so the creature can form analogues of 'Gb', 'Fa', and 'Γβα'; yet it cannot form analogs of 'Fa' or 'Γab'. In this sense, an animal's concepts may not be fully integrated. One can insist that concepts count as Concepts only if they exhibit a certain (independently specified) kind of integration that may turn out to be distinctly human. But then humans may acquire Concepts in the course of acquiring a 'second nature' that supplements a less unique but still sophisticated animal nature. Terminology aside, humans do have many mental representations that compose as easily as the words in a phrase; cp. Fodor and Pylyshyn (1998), Fodor and Lepore (2002). But this raises the question of how words can combine so easily, yet still interface with so many disparate cognitive systems. One wants to know *how* humans came to have Concepts and a correspondingly *unified* language of thought; cp. Fodor (1983, 2003). But perhaps lexicalizing concepts introduces new concepts that abstract from formal differences that hinder the combinabilty of prior concepts. For discussion, see Pietroski (forthcoming).

[10] Examples like 'big ant' show that some cases of adjunction invoke more than *mere* conjunction of concepts. But a big ant is still an ant that meets a further condition; and 'big', which presumably lexicalizes a genuinely relational concept, may contain a covert anaphoric element. So perhaps 'big ~~one~~ ant' is an

With this background in place, my central point is easily summarized. *If* the human language faculty allows for a range of lexical types corresponding to conceptual types, then other things equal, one expects the adicity of the concept fetched with a lexical item to *match* the adicity of the concept lexicalized—perhaps modulo an 'extra' (event) variable to accommodate tense and adjunction. If infants can simply label concepts with words, perhaps modulo the minimal kind of reformatting needed for robust polyadicity with event variables, one would expect lexicalization to take this form. And one expects each variable in a concept fetched with a lexical item to correspond to a saturater (or binder) in sentences where the lexical item appears. But if these expectations are massively violated, in ways which suggest that the human language faculty allows for only a narrow range of lexical types, we should look for a conception of semantic composition that predicts the corresponding constraints on lexicalization.

6.2 CONCEPTUAL ADICITY VS. LEXICAL VALENCE

In the rest of this chapter, I review some well-known considerations that together suggest a striking constraint: non-monadic concepts are regularly lexicalized with expressions that are used to fetch monadic concepts, as if semantic composition required such concepts as inputs. Section 6.2.2 focuses on singular concepts and proper nouns like 'Caesar'. Later subsections focus on polyadic concepts and various corresponding linguistic devices. But let me first introduce a caveat.

6.2.1 Opaque adicities

As already noted, we cannot just intuit the adicities of lexicalized concepts.

Let's assume that for a normal child acquiring English, 'triangle' lexicalizes an available concept. Is this concept monadic, triadic, or other? (Might there be variation across lexicalizers?) Since 'is a triangle' combines with exactly one grammatical argument to form a sentence, we can say—borrowing terminolgy from nineteenth-century chemistry—that the copular phrase has a 'grammatical valence' of −1. But even if the word 'triangle' also has this valence, there are various possibilities for the concept fetched—TRIANGLE(X), TRIANGLE(X, T) with a variable for times, TRIANGULARITY(S)

instruction to form the following monadic concept: $\exists Y[\text{BIG-ONE}(X, Y)^\wedge\text{THEANTS}(Y)]$; where BIG-ONE (X, Y) is a formally dyadic concept satisfied by a thing, x, and some things, the Ys, such that x is both a Y and a big one. See Higginbotham (1985) on 'autonymous' theta-marking and Pietroski (2006b) for elaboration in a Conjunctivist account of plural and comparative constructions, drawing on Boolos (1998). Other kinds of examples require different analyses. But note that if x is a fake diamond, there was an event of faking whose intentional content was (roughly) that x seem to be a diamond; see Pietroski (2002) on events and contents.

with a variable for states that hold at times (cp. Parsons, 1990)—and still more for the concept lexicalized: TRIANGLE(X, Y, Z) with variables for lines, or perhaps points, that exhibit a certain relation; TRIANGLE(X, Y, Z, T); TRIANGLE(G, X, Y, Z) with a variable for geometric figures that have points/lines as 'participants'; TRIANGLE(G, X, Y, Z, T); etc.

Note that 'mortal', a classical example of monadicity, arguably lexicalizes a concept that *relates* individuals to events of death. We can speak of mortals, who fall under the concept MORTAL(X). But this monadic concept may not be primitive. And in any case, we can speak of mortal wounds. Talk of quartets hardly shows that the concept QUARTET(X) is available for—as opposed to a product of—lexicalization; and likewise for SQUARE(X). More generally, I don't know how to determine the adicities of concepts lexicalized with common nouns, even setting aside issues about temporal/eventish variables. So I see no reason to assume that these concepts are regularly monadic, modulo some 'special cases' like 'sister' and other familial terms.

Of course, ignorance is not an argument *against* the idea that common nouns typically conform to the generalization that lexical valence matches the adicity of the concept lexicalized. But we should not be seduced into assuming such conformity, absent independent evidence concerning the concepts lexicalized. Similar issues arise for verbs. So while I assume that many verbs result from lexicalizing polyadic concepts, I remain agnostic about the details.

Consider 'eat'. We surely have a polyadic concept—perhaps EAT(X, Y) or EAT(E, X, Y)—with which we can think about the relation an eater bears to the eaten. But we may also have a concept akin to GRAZE(E, X) with which we can think about those who eat; compare DINE(E, X). Moreover, (6.6–6.9) suggest that 'eat' indicates a concept that is somehow normative.

(6.6)   John ate a tack

(6.7)   John ate something

(6.8)   John had a snack

(6.9)   John ate

Note that (6.6) implies (6.7), on a 'purely existential' reading of (6.7) that does not follow from (6.8); and so read, (6.7) does not imply (6.9). In this sense, (6.7) and (6.9) differ in meaning. Likewise, (6.6) does not imply (6.9), unless it is assumed that tacks are edible for John (see Chomsky, 1986).

So even if 'eat' has a valence of −2, and takes a covert object in (6.9), the concept lexicalized may lack a variable for the consumed—as in NUTRIFY(E, X) or REFUEL(E, X)—though it may have an additional variable for the relevant norm. More generally, even given assumptions about lexical valence, confirming a 'matching' hypothesis requires independent evidence concerning the relevant conceptual adicities for specific words. By contrast, as I'll now argue, disconfirming evidence is available given the general assumption that we lexicalize some singular and polyadic concepts.

6.2.2 Singular concepts and proper nouns

Sentences like (6.10–6.13) suggest that the lexical item 'Caesar' can be used to fetch a monadic concept, and that in this respect, a *lexical proper noun* (LPN) is like the common noun 'tyrant'.[11]

(6.10)   Every Caesar I saw was a tyrant

(6.11)   Every tyrant I saw was a Caesar

(6.12)   There were three Caesars at the party

(6.13)   That Caesar stayed late, and so did this one, but the other Caesar left early

Of course, the subject and object of (6.1) are not mere LPNs, and (6.14) is not a sentence of English.

(6.1)   Brutus poked Caesar

(6.14)   *Tyrant arrived

But while the subject and object of (6.1) are *names*, these expressions may be complex, consisting of an LPN and a determiner akin to 'That' in (6.13), where this determiner, covert in English, combines with LPNs but not common nouns. On this view, the sound of 'Caesar' can be either the sound of a lexical item, or the sound of a determiner phrase whose head is silent.

This hypothesis is not *ad hoc*, given overt analogues of the posited determiner in other languages. For example, Spanish allows for both 'Juan' and 'El Juan' as devices for referring to a certain Juan.[12] And even English allows for 'our John' ('my John', etc.) as a way of referring to a certain John who is suitably related to the speaker.

I return to alternative diagnoses of the facts. But if LPNs are used to fetch monadic concepts, this presents a puzzle if these nouns *could* be used as labels for singular concepts like CAESAR. For if lexicalizers could simply label such concepts with distinctive nouns, and thereby acquire names that can combine with a predicate that has valence n to form a predicate that has valence $n − 1$ (treating sentences as predicates with valence 0), one might expect lexicalizers to do so. Such children would become adults for whom examples like (6.10–6.13) would be defective; phrases like 'Every Caesar' would be like the nonsensical '$\forall x:c$', where 'c' is a logical constant.

We were not such children. So assuming that we had singular concepts, and often used them to think about named individuals, lexicalizing these concepts was evidently

---

[11] See Burge (1973) and many others, e.g., Katz (1994), Longobardi (1994), Elbourne (2005), Matushansky (2006).

[12] Similar remarks apply to Basque, German, Scandanavian languages, many dialects of Italian, and Greek (discussed below). I won't try to defend a specific proposal about the posited covert functional element. But to illustrate, and stress that complex names can be used to designate rigidly, imagine an indexed determiner D_i with the following character: relative to any assignment **A** of values to variables, every entity e is such that (1) e is a value of D_i iff e is the value assigned to the index i, and (2) e is a value of $D_i \wedge Tyler$ iff e is a value of both D_i and the noun *Tyler*. Such an analysis might be extended to pronouns $(D_i \wedge she)$ and demonstratives $(D_i \wedge this)$; though cf. Segal (2001).

not a simple matter of labelling them with LPNs. On the contrary, such lexicalization led to the acquisition of nouns like 'Caesar' that can appear in sentences like (6.10–6.11). And such nouns, like their common counterparts, show all the signs of being devices for fetching monadic concepts. They can be pluralized as in (6.12), or constituents of complex demonstratives, as in (6.13); and note that 'one', as it appears in (6.13), is ordinarily a pro-form for nouns that are *not* singular terms.

This leaves room for various views about the specific meanings of LPNs. The earlier pretense, of treating 'Caesar' as a device for fetching a concept of things identical with a certain individual, is inadequate. But if the LPN is satisfied by individuals called (with the sound of) 'Caesar', then (6.10–6.13) should mean what they do mean. So if the singular concept CAESAR is initially labelled with the phonological form of 'Caesar'— PF:'Caesar'—then a mind with access to the relational concept CALLED(x, y) might form thoughts like CALLED(CAESAR, PF:'Caesar') and CALLED(JULIUS, PF:'Caesar'). Such a mind might come to use the LPN to fetch the complex monadic concept CALLED(x, PF:'Caesar'). And various facts suggest that we have such minds.

Example (6.15) is most naturally heard as a claim about some people who share a surname.

(6.15)   The Tylers are coming to dinner

But as surnames remind us, even overt 'surface' considerations suggest that many names are *not* grammatically atomic. The direct object of (6.16) seems to have two words as parts.

(6.16)   At noon, I saw Tyler Burge

Prima facie, 'Tyler Burge' is *semantically* related to 'Tyler' and 'Burge', roughly as 'red ball' is to 'red' and 'ball': a Tyler Burge is both a Tyler and a Burge—that is someone called 'Tyler' *and* called 'Burge'. Of course, a Burge need not be a Tyler Burge. But in a context where the only Tyler is also the only Burge, one can use (6.17) or (6.18) to say what one says with (6.16).[13]

(6.17)   I saw Tyler at noon

(6.18)   I saw Burge at noon

These 'monadic uses' tell against the idea that LPNs are labels for singular concepts. Of course, one can posit ambiguities. Perhaps speakers who use 'Caesar' to talk about two people—say, Julius and Romero—have *three* homophonous LPNs, used to fetch the concepts JULIUS, ROMERO, and CALLED(x, PF: 'CAESAR'). This posits 'saturating LPNs' *and* 'monadic-LPNs'. Such ambiguity hypotheses are notoriously hard to refute

---

[13] We also want a systematic account of why certain inferences are compelling: 'Tyler Burge is a philosopher' seems to follow from (6.16) and 'Every Tyler I saw was a philosopher'. But this inference shouldn't be good if 'Tyler Burge' is semantically like 'Mark' or 'Samuel'. For then 'Tyler Burge' is as semantically distinct from 'Tyler' as 'Twain' is from 'Clemens'. Titles, as in 'Professor Tyler Burge and Doctor Tyler Smith are both philosophers', raise similar issues.

(see Kripke, 1979). But given examples like (6.10–6.18) it seems clear that for each name-sound, there is a monadic LPN. And positing additional LPNs, with meanings of another type, is unattractive in several respects.

Since many I-languages permit complex names, in which monadic LPNs combine with a determiner, one cannot assume that English *forbids* a complex-name analysis of (6.4).

(6.4)   Caesar arrived

Yet if such an analysis is available for children, positing an analysis with 'Caesar' as a saturating LPN makes (6.4) strangely ambiguous: 'Caesar' might be an instruction to fetch the monadic concept CALLED(x, PF:'Caesar'), or an instruction to fetch any of several singular concepts; and the posited singular meanings can be plausibly redescribed in terms of the monadic meaning.

Relatedly, appeal to saturating LPNs makes 'noun' a disjunctive grammatical category, and not just because of the two semantic types: saturating LPNs would not head *phrases*, much less phrases of their own type. (Why posit such lexical items if one can account for the data without them?) A similar point applies to acquisition. The human language faculty supports the acquisition of I-languages in which complex names, with monadic LPNs as constituents, appear regularly. So we must ask if this faculty *also* supports the acquisition of saturating LPNs.

For example, Greek names typically *must* be complex: bare LPNs—as in analogues of (6.4), without an overt determiner—are anomolous, like (6.14) (see Giannakidou and Stavrou, 1999).

(6.14)   *Tyrant arrived

Any child can acquire such a language. And if English has saturating LPNs, along with monadic LPNs, any child can acquire such a language. Innate assumptions must be compatible with each actual language. So *if* the ambiguity hypothesis for English is correct: experience with English leads every normal acquirer to a lexicon with *enough* LPN entries, despite homophony and the grammatical possibility of monadic LPN analyses that would shorten the lexicon; and experience with Greek leads every normal acquirer to a lexicon without *too many* entries, despite the possibility of ambiguity and saturating LPN analyses that would lengthen the lexicon.

Usually, children treat lexical sounds as ambiguous only when given reason to do so. So one might expect children to treat LPNs as uniformly monadic, absent evidence of ambiguity. But what would lead children to conclude that English name sounds are ambiguous? One can conjecture that not hearing the determiner, in examples like (6.1), lets children know that English has lexical names. On this view, children use 'negative' evidence to *dis*confirm that English names are complex. But the use of such evidence in acquisition remains unattested (see, e.g., Crain and Pietroski, 2001). Worse, a special lexical type must be posited to let children use negative evidence to acquire a grammar that admits theoretically superfluous ambiguities.

In short, many considerations converge to suggest that there are no saturating LPNs, even though children plausibly lexicalize many singular concepts with LPNs. Hence, if these nouns are used to fetch monadic concepts, that tells against the idea that combining names with verbs signifies saturation. With this in mind, let me turn to cases in which the lexicalized concepts are plausibly *polyadic* while the concepts fetched still seem to be monadic.

6.2.3 Supradyadic concepts: adicity >2

If there are no 17-place concepts to lexicalize, the absence of verbs with valence −17 tells us little. But animal navigation apparently requires polyadic representations (Gallistel, 1990). And humans, who can distinguish selling from giving, seem to have concepts that are at least tetradic—for example SELL(x, y, z, w) as opposed to GIVE(x, y, z) with 'w' as a variable for what z transfers to x in exchange for y, ignoring any event variables for simplicity. So why doesn't lexicalization of tetradic concepts result in verbs with valence −4?

We could invent a language in which (6.19a) is a sentence with the meaning of (6.19b).

(6.19)   a. *Barry sold ten dollars Peter the wine
         b. Barry sold the wine to Peter for ten dollars

But in English, (6.19a) is anomolous, and 'sell' can combine with *two* arguments as in (6.20).

(6.20)   Barry sold the wine

The hypothesis that 'sold' really takes four saturating arguments, with two often being covert, is strained—especially if part of a proposal that eschews a covert constituent of names in English. And then what is wrong with (6.19a)? Similar remarks apply to 'bought'. But note that that (6.21) is roughly synonymous with (6.22), which has a 'benefactive' implication, unlike (6.23).[14]

(6.21)   Professor Plum bought Miss Scarlet the knife

(6.22)   Plum bought the knife for Scarlet

(6.23)   Plum bought the knife for ten dollars

More generally, few if any 'supradyadic' concepts seem to be lexicalized with verbs of matching valence. Initially, examples like (6.24) make it tempting to posit verbs with valence −3,

(6.24)   Scarlet gave Plum the money

corresponding to triadic concepts like GIVE(x, y, z). But (6.24) is roughly synonymous with (6.25),

---

[14] And presumably, the valence of 'bought' is not reduced by combination with 'Scarlet' in (6.22).

(6.25)   Scarlet gave the money to Plum

whose prepositional phrase is plausibly analysed as a conjunct in a neo-Davidsonian event description, as opposed to a saturating argument that is case-marked by a semantically null preposition. And famously, while (6.26a) is fine, (6.26b) is odd—suggesting that the verb does *not* fetch a concept that is saturated by correlates of three grammatical arguments (see also Schein, 1993).

(6.26)   a. Scarlet donated the money to Oxfam
          b. *Scarlet donated Oxfam the money

Moreover, even if the oddity of (6.26b) can be explained away, the acceptability of (6.27) is puzzling if 'give' has valence −3.

(6.27)   Scarlet gave the money away, and Plum gave at the office.

Correlatively, ditransitive *constructions* like (6.24) invite analysis in terms of a verb whose 'indirect object' is understood as part of a semantically optional modifying phrase, as opposed to a grammatical reflection of a recipient variable in the concept fetched.[15] The mere existence of such constructions cannot show that 'give' has valence −3, else (6.28) would show that 'kick' has the same valence, making a puzzle of the synonymous (6.29), which implies (6.30).

(6.28)   Plum kicked Scarlet the knife

(6.29)   Plum kicked the knife to Scarlet

(6.30)   Plum kicked the knife

Likewise, we don't usually think of 'cooked' or 'sang' as taking three arguments or lexicalizing concepts with variables for recipients/beneficiaries. But consider (6.31–6.33).

(6.31)   Mrs White cooked, while Colonel Mustard sang

(6.32)   White cooked an egg for Mustard, while he sang a lullaby to the baby

(6.33)   White cooked Mustard an egg, while he sang the baby a lullaby

The number of noun/determiner phrases that combine with a verb to form a sentence can be lower or higher than the adicity of the lexicalized concept. In particular, ditransitive constructions tell *against* the idea that triadic concepts are labelled and fetched with predicates of valence −3. Given the absence of tetradic concepts labelled and fetched with predicates of valence −4, along with the reasons for doubting that lexical proper nouns label and fetch singular concepts, this suggests that lexicalization introduces concepts that exhibit a limited range of adicities.

---

[15] See Larson (1988). Of course, the concept lexicalized can have a variable for recipients. For discussion in the context of Chomsky's (1995) Minimalist Program and its relation to neo-Davidsonian semantics; see Pietroski (2003), drawing on Baker (1988, 1997), Dowty (1991), Hale and Keyser (1993), and many others.

One can hypothesize that 'supratransitive' verbs are disallowed for reasons stemming from the underlying *syntax* of I-languages. But this fits ill with the idea that combining expressions often signifies saturation. If a mode of composition can be employed twice in a sentence, why not thrice or more? And if saturation is not available as a *recursive* mode of composition, why appeal to it, given the neo-Davidsonian alternative?

Indeed, examples like (6.34) suggest that 'give' fetches GIVE(E),

(6.34)   Even though Scarlet gave until it hurt, not enough was given

a concept with no variable for thing given or the giver. One can say that 'gave' is like a passive verb, as in 'Caesar was stabbed (by Brutus)', with the active voice subject in an optional prepositional phrase (Baker, Johnson, and Roberts, 1989). But while analogies between ditransitive and passive constructions may be apt, passives present further puzzles for adicity/valence-matching hypotheses. If 'poked' indicates a concept with a variable corresponding to pokers, then one wants to know why (6.35) is understood as a full sentence.

(6.35)   Caesar was poked

Moreover, verbs are not the only devices for indicating supradyadic relations. We understand (6.36a), and surely have a triadic concept BETWEEN(X, Y, Z).

(6.36)   a. Plum was between Scarlet and White

But this concept cannot be lexicalized with verb 'bewtixt' as in (6.37b).

(6.36)   b. *Plum betwixted Scarlet White

On the contrary, (6.36b) sounds like a report of something Plum did to a certain Scarlet White. This is puzzling if, but only if, the lexicon of a natural language *can* include predicates of valence −3 that fetch supradyadic concepts. In this light, note that 'jimmied' takes *two* arguments.

(6.37)   a. Mister Green jimmied the lock (with a screwdriver)
         b. *Mister Green jimmied the lock with a screwdriver

Any reference to an implement must appear as a modifying adjunct as in (6.37a), not a third argument as in (6.37b).[16] Yet the concept lexicalized presumably has a variable for an implement with which the jimmier jimmies the jimmied.

---

[16] I am indebted to Alexander Williams for this example, and more importantly, for a series of conversations that deeply influenced the development of this chapter—and the next few paragraphs in particular. He has discussed closely related matters in Williams (2005, 2007). Note that if 'He jimmied me the lock' has a meaning, it is that he jimmied the lock *for* me, as opposed to he jimmied the lock with me, and likewise for 'He jimmied the screwdriver the lock'.

6.2.4 Dyadic concepts: adicity = 2

If singular and supradyadic concepts are lexicalized in mismatching ways, with symptoms of monadicity, one wonders if *any* lexical items inherit their valences from non-monadic concepts.

I readily grant that certain dyadic concepts can be fetched via (contextualized uses of) prepositions. From a neo-Davidsonian perspective, many closed class expressions are functional devices for introducing relations like FROM(x, y). But in examples like (6.38a),

(6.38)   a. Plum is from Devon

the prepositional phrase combines with a copula to form a tensed monadic predicate. We can imagine a language with a corresponding semantically dyadic verb, as in (6.38b).

(6.38)   b. *Plum froms Devon

But for naturally acquirable human I-languages, it seems that the relational concept indicated with '(is) from' cannot be lexicalized directly with a verb of matching adicity.

Circumlocution is required, as in (6.38a) or (6.39). Similarly, we use (6.40a), not (6.40b),

(6.39)   Plum hails from Devon

(6.40)   a. Plum is taller than Green
         b. *Plum talls Green

as if relational concepts cannot be lexicalized with open-class monomorphemic expressions. So perhaps dyadic concepts like FROM(x, y) and TALLER(x, y) *cannot* be labelled/fetched with verbs, not even verbs that take two grammatical arguments.[17] Note that given standard accounts of causatives, according to which the verb in (6.41a) also appears in (6.42), the verbs in many transitive *constructions* do not label/fetch concepts like BREAK(x, y).

(6.41)   a. Green broke the glass

(6.42)   The glass broke

On such views, (6.41a) reflects a combination of (1) an overt verb that does *not* fetch a concept that has a variable for the breaker with (2) a covert functional 'causativizing' element that is covert in English but overt in many other languages. The relevant structure is shown in (6.41b).[18]

(6.41)   b. [Green [[*v* broke] [_ [the glass]]]]]

<hr/>

[17] One might reply that 'tall' is of this type, with a relation holding between entities like Plum and abstracta like heights; cp. Kennedy (1999). But while I agree that 'tall' is used to signify a relation, in a way that invites talk of heights (or degrees thereof), circumlocution is still required. We can say 'Plum is that tall', but not 'Plum talls that'.

[18] See, e.g., Chomsky (1995) and Kratzer (1996), drawing on Baker's (1988) revival of an old idea. For further references and discussion in a neo-Davidsonian context, see Pietroski (2003).

Advocates of adicity/valence-matching can say that the concept lexicalized with 'broke' is—perhaps modulo an event variable—a monadic concept of broken things, not a dyadic concept of a causal relation. But it is hard to see how the judgement expressed with (6.41a) can be analysed in terms of any such monadic concept and a plausible correlate of 'v' (see Fodor, 1970; Fodor and Lepore, 2002). And my proposal does not require that the verbs in causative constructions lexicalize monadic concepts from which the corresponding causal concepts are built. On the contrary, a neo-Davidsonian mind might use BREAK(X, Y) or BREAK(E, X, Y) to introduce BREAK(E)—a concept of causal processes that have agents and patients—and then a second monadic concept BREAK(F) such that: $\exists$F[BREAK(F) & TERMINATOR(E, F)] $\equiv$ BREAK(E); where BREAK(F) applies to events of something breaking, regardless of the cause, and TERMINATOR(E, F) is a concept of a whole-to-part relation that processes bear to their final parts.[19]

Once causative constructions are set aside, we need to ask how many verbs remain that plausibly lexicalize dyadic concepts *and* have a valence of −2. For even if a verb must combine with two arguments in a sentence with active voice, such a verb can be described as one that fetches a monadic concept but *also* imposes a lexically specified restriction on which thematic role bearers must accompany the verb in sentences. This risks missing generalizations (Levin and Rappaport, 1995, 2005). But the question is whether there is *enough* motivation for adicity/valence matching hypotheses, despite the difficulties that such hypotheses face. If nouns like 'Caesar' and verbs like 'give'/'sell'/'break' tell against such hypotheses, one cannot just assume that there is a generalization for matching hypotheses to capture.

To be sure, strings like (6.43a) and (6.44a) are anomalous. But given (6.43b) and (6.44b),

(6.43)   a. *Brutus sent
         b. Brutus sent for help

(6.44)   a. *Caesar put the cup
         b. The cup stayed put

one might well say that 'send' and 'put' fetch SEND(E) and PUT(E), adding that 'sent' typically requires the specification of a patient, while 'put' also typically requires the specification of a location. Given the range of facts noted above, it seems that for at least

---

[19] Cf. Levin and Rappaport (1995). See Pietroski (1998, 2003, 2002) for discussion of TERMINATOR (E, X), its relation to PATIENT(E, X), and the extensive literature on these topics. And for present purposes, we can be neutral about whether BREAK(E) should be replaced with BREAK(E, X), on the grounds that verbs are always saturated by internal arguments; see Kratzer (1996). The points about adicity mismatches remain even if verbs are always relational in this limited neo-Davidsonian sense (and the potentially related sense of Hale and Keyser, 1993).

Put another way, our causal concept of one thing breaking another *may* be complex: CAUSR(X, BREAK (E, Y)); where CAUSR(X, Φ(E)) corresponds to the much discussed relation of causing Φ-ish events 'in the right way'. But many concepts—of moving, boiling, surprising, drenching, etc.—are intuitively causal. And there is no independent evidence that all these relational *concepts* fit a common pattern of analysis by decomposition; see Fodor (2003). Though pace Fodor, this does not tell against the following idea: (6.41a) implies (6.42), because (6.41a) has the grammatical structure indicated in (6.41b).

many verbs, any view will require a distinction between the 'Semantic Composition Adicity Number' (SCAN) of a lexical predicate—the adicity of the concept fetched— from the 'Lexicalized Adicity Number' (LAN), which may be a better indication of a lexical predicate's 'Property of Smallest Sentential Entourage' (POSSE), corresponding to the number of grammatical arguments and/or mandatory adjuncts that must appear with the predicate in an acceptable (active voice, declarative) sentence.

Given some such distinction, one can hypothesize that while SCANs are uniformly monadic, POSSEs vary in part because LANs vary (see Pietroski, forthcoming). As noted above, passive constructions already suggest that no SCAN is supramonadic. And the ubiquity of 'nominalization', in languages like English, points in the same direction (Chomsky, 1970; Marantz, 1984; Borer, 2005; Ramchand, 2008). One can cut to the chase, expect an onsides kick, or give someone a break. So prima facie, 'chase', 'kick', and 'break' fetch monadic concepts. Instead of positing a single lexical item that can appear in diverse constructions, one can posit 'SCAN-reducing operations' that create one kind of lexical item from another. But this is hardly costless. And why posit a process that creates a noun that fetches CHASE(E), from a verb that fetches CHASE(X, Y) or CHASE(E, X, Y), given the independent reasons for thinking that the homophonic verb also fetches a monadic concept of events? The relevant kind of reformatting may be a common byproduct of lexicalizing concepts, as opposed to nominalizing verbs.

Note too that paradigms of polysemy, like 'book', often exhibit a clear sense of semantic monadicity despite being used to indicate a range of relational concepts. One can book a ticket or a criminal. And upon reflection, even the 'core' concept lexicalized with 'book' may be relational, having something to do with authors. As a final illustration of argument flexibility, consider the concept of marriage. Whatever its adicity, this concept can be indicated with a noun. Yet each of (6.45–6.49) might be used to describe the same wedding.

(6.45)   Scarlet married Plum, but their marriage was doomed

(6.46)   Scarlet got married to Plum, with the Reverend Green officiating

(6.47)   With reservations, Green married Plum and Scarlet

(6.48)   Plum and Scarlet married, and they got married in a hurry

(6.49)   It was Scarlet's first marriage, though Plum married for third time

This suggests that given three acting participants—Scarlet, Plum, and Green—we can describe various events of marrying that fall under a monadic concept (of marriage) that a competent speaker has given the word 'marry', which lexicalizes a relational concept.

6.3 CONCLUDING REMARKS

I do not deny that verbs are associated, at least statistically, with a 'canonical' number of arguments. These associations presumably reflect, in part, the adicities of lexicalized concepts. But they may also reflect complicated *interactions* of grammatical principles with various contingencies of actual language use. We should not assume that the concepts fetched with verbs vary in adicity, much less that this variation helps explain why verbs vary with regard to the number of arguments they require. An alternative point of departure, for purposes of explanation, is that open class lexical items fetch semantically monadic concepts that may have been introduced via prior concepts that exhibit diverse adicities.

From this perspective, lexical items efface conceptual adicity distinctions, making it possible to treat a recursive combination of expressions as a sign of monadic predicate conjunction. This conception of semantic composition helps explain the otherwise puzzling massive monadicity of natural language. This conception of lexicalization may also help explain why humans have concepts that combine so rapidly and easily. For if our prelexical concepts (with roots in various modules) are analytically related to some concepts that are systematically composable, via simple operations like predicate conjunction, then we can begin to explain how humans might use I-languages to think in systematic ways.[20]

[20] For helpful comments and discussion, my thanks to an anonymous referee, Barry Smith, Norbert Hornstein, and Alexander Williams.

CHAPTER 7

HOLISM AND COMPOSITIONALITY

FRANCIS JEFFRY PELLETIER

7.1 INTRODUCTION

A brief acquaintance with the web shows that the terms 'holism'[1] and 'compositionality' are used in many different fields, both academic and non-academic. And given any two academic fields, it is usually not obvious that the terms mean the same to the practitioners. Even just within philosophy and linguistics it seems that rather different conceptions are in play when we read any two different authors. We start, therefore, with a brief survey of some of the senses in which these terms are used. A little later we will make some more careful remarks about the notions.

7.1.1 Two kinds of compositionality

A recent interdisciplinary conference revealed that there are (at least) two different things that are thought of when the issue of compositionality is considered. One concerns a (generalized) notion of 'what is a complex item (of my theory) made of?' Here are a few places where this notion arose:

---

[1] 'Whole', and presumably also 'hole', is derived from the Greek ὅλος. As a word first formed in the English language (after the fifteenth century, when *wh* and *h* were separated), 'holism' ought to be the belief in holes, perhaps along the lines argued for and against in Lewis and Lewis (1970, 1996); Casati and Varzi (1994)—or maybe the belief in holiness. But that's not the way it is. The *Oxford English Dictionary* cites Smuts (1926) as the originator of this term. In this work 'holism' was defined as 'the theory which makes the existence of "wholes" a fundamental feature of the world. It regards natural objects, both animate and inanimate, as wholes and not merely as assemblages of elements or parts.' Evolutionary forces act on species, rather than individuals, with the consequence that 'evolution aims at more perfect wholes'. The *OED* also cites Boodin (1939) as the originator of 'wholism': 'Two conceptions...namely, creative synthesis (or emergence), and wholism (or gestaltism). . . .'.

PROTOTYPES: Current prototype theory says that a prototype is a structure that has a number of attribute–value pairs. A question of interest in this area is: Given that prototype-1 has a structure [A: value-a; B: value-b; ...] and that prototype-2 has the structure [C: value-c; D: value-d ...], is the prototype of the 'combined prototypes' (that is, the conceptual combination of the two prototypes) made up only from the material in the two component prototypes, that is, from the attribute–value pairs that are in one or the other of the prototypes? The discussion at the conference said 'yes' to this question, characterizing this as the *compositional* view of prototypes. As an example, it was said that the prototype of PET FISH *was* made up compositionally from the prototypes of PET and FISH because all the 'relevant material' could be found in these smaller prototypes.

EXPLANATION: Given hypothesis-1 that explains phenomenon-1 and hypothesis-2 that explains phenomenon-2, is the best explanation of a phenomenon that is intuitively some mixture or combination of phenomena-1-and-2 to be constructed only from the elements of hypotheses-1-and-2? If the answer is 'yes', then it is a compositional explanation.

NEURAL ACTIVITY: Suppose assemblage-1 of neurons is active during task-1 and assemblage-2 is active during task-2. Now consider a 'supertask' which intuitively involves doing task-1 and task-2 as parts. Then: is the assemblage of neurons involved in this supertask made up out of, and only of, those neurons involved in either task-1 or task-2? Or does the new supertask bring an entirely new assemblage of neurons to bear on the new task? The claim by the authors was that, at least after the new supertask becomes a learned, repetitive action, there is a new group of neurons responsible. And thus, motor neural accounts are *not* compositional.

Underlying this type of compositionality is the slogan:

Definition 1. *A whole in a compositional system is built up solely from materials in the parts.*

And accordingly, we call this 'the building block version of compositionality'.

A second view of compositionality comes (mostly) from linguistic semantics.[2] In this conception the question is whether there is a certain relationship that holds amongst the *properties* of members of a structure. The background presumption is that the structure is compositional (in the sense just given in Definition 1 to the term); this is usually put in terms of a 'part of' relation—for instance in the language case, we might be given in advance some notion of 'syntactic part', so that we know what are the syntactic parts of a whole in some structure. The question now is whether some property of arbitrary members of this structure can be defined in terms of the possession of the same type of property by the parts of that member, together with information about how these

---

[2] The first occurrence of the word 'compositionality' more or less in the sense under discussion here seems to be in Katz and Fodor (1963), although in this paper those authors appear to be most interested in some sort of 'lexical composing'.

parts are syntactically combined. In the language case, the property that is usually of interest is *the meaning* of arbitrary members of the syntactically given structure. And the question is whether there is a way to define this property—the meaning—of all complex items solely in terms of the meanings of the syntactically given parts of the complex item and their syntactic method of combination. A 'yes' answer to this for every complex member signals that the semantic theory is said to assign meanings compositionally. One might note that in this kind of compositional theory, there is a second structure (in the language case, it would be 'the meanings') which is a kind of mirror of the first (syntactic) structure. So another way of asking whether a semantic theory is compositional in this sense is to ask whether there is a homomorphic mapping between the syntactic structures and the semantic structures.

In the language case, this mapping is called 'the meaning function', which I will symbolize μ. So, $X = \mu(A)$ means that (i) A is some element of the first structure (e.g., A is some syntactic item), and (ii) that X is the item in the meaning structure that is paired up with A (i.e. X is the meaning of A). Then this second conception of compositionality asserts that, there is a function f such that whenever A is composed (in the sense of Definition 1) of B, C, D ...by means of syntactic method X, then $\mu(A)$ is f applied to $\mu(B), \mu(C), \mu(D), \ldots \mu(X)$. That is: the system is compositional if and only if, there is a function f such that for every (syntactically) complex item A in the syntactic system, its meaning $\mu(A)$ is a function of, and only of, the meanings of A's syntactic parts, together with the way they are comined. If NP_1 and VP_1 make up the entirety of S_1 and they are combined by rule-X to do so, then $\mu(S_1) = f(\mu(NP_1), \mu(VP_1), \mu(X))$. Underlying this type of compositionality is the slogan:

Definition 2. *The μ of a whole is a function of the μs of its parts and the ways those parts are combined.*

And accordingly, we call this 'the functional version of compositionality'.

A difference between the two notions of compositionality concerns whether some 'whole' can contain things not in the parts. According to the building-block view, no; but according to the functional version, yes. For, the first notion allows the whole to contain only what is in the parts, possibly re-arranged in some manner. But the second allows the thing associated with a whole (in the linguistic case: the meaning of a complex whole) to be a *function* of the things associated with the parts (in the linguistic case: a function of the meanings of the syntactic parts and syntactic mode of combination). There is nothing to stop such a function from introducing new material into the thing associated with the whole—that is, the function can make the meaning of a whole contain many new and radically different things than are contained in the meanings of the parts. Indeed, it could introduce *all* new material, and contain *none* of the properties of the subparts. According to Definition 2, all that is required is that this be a function— which merely means that it must introduce this same material every time it is faced with the same parts and manner of combination. In the case of describing the neurons active in the complex task, the function f need not pick out any of the neurons that are active in the subtasks ...but it would still be compositional.

This means that one cannot deny compositionality of this second sort merely with the claim that some whole is 'more than the sum of its parts'; for, even if that is true, we haven't thereby denied that there is some function that can define the whole from the parts. (This is the result of confusing the two types of compositionality. In the first type, the 'building block' theory, the only things in the whole are re-arrangements of the building blocks. But this does not apply to compositionality of the second sort, wherein there might be a function that transmogrifies properties of building blocks into some entirely different things or stuff.)

Now, one might argue that the distinction between the two conceptions of compositionality merely reflects a difference between 'ontological compositionality' and 'semantic compositionality'. But a closer inspection shows that those proposing the differing conceptions do not view it in that way. The prototype example, for instance, shows that those with interests in 'the meaning of mental items' can use the 'building block' notion. And of course, the prototype conception of meaning is rife within some linguistic theories, such as those advocated by Ron Langacker, Len Talmy, and perhaps Ray Jackendoff.[3] Various other authors have proposed still different theories of meaning that are compositional in the first sense. Using the notion of a 'semantic differential', Osgood, Suci, and Tannenbaum (1957) propose a finite number of 'dimensions of meaning', and every lexical item is said to have some value along each dimension. For example, along a *pleasant–unpleasant* dimension, each lexical item receives some numerical value; along an *active–passive* dimension they each receive some numerical value; and so on. All meanings of more complex items are seen as being constructed from the values, and they too will have their own vector of meaning defined by their [dimension:value] set of pairs. In general, *any* theory that postulates a finite vocabulary of primitives and a finite number of ways to evaluate a primitive will be compositional in this first sense so long as the ways of combining the part-values is unique—that is, there is no way to get two different complexes when given the same parts combined the same way. For example, the notion of universal (cross-cultural) semantic primitives is like this (Wierzbicka, 1996), as is the notion of basic conceptual dependencies (Schank, 1972), and most semantic decomposition models, for example Jackendoff (1990) among others. The idea is that all one can use in constructing a complex will already be present in the parts. The construction can of course differ if the parts are 'put together' differently, just as a combination of two building blocks differs depending on whether they are laid side-by-side or one-atop-the other. (For the example of combining prototypes, a building-block compositional theory distinguishes 'flea circus' from 'circus flea', 'gun grease' from 'grease gun', 'school teacher' from 'teacher school', and so forth, in this manner.)

So, I do not think it useful to distinguish the two notions of compositionality as merely being due to applying the same concept in different areas of inquiry. Instead, there just are two very different notions, of course with some overlap in conception,

---

[3] See, e.g., Langacker (1987a); Talmy (2000); Jackendoff (2002), even though these theorists don't all think their theories are compositional.

that yield very different accounts of and rationales for views about how complexes are to be understood.

7.1.2 Two kinds of holism

The same conference that revealed a difference in understanding of the term 'compositionality' also displayed a basic difference between two ways of understanding 'holism'. The fundamental idea behind holism is to give some sort of priority to a 'whole' in preference to the 'parts' of that whole, and of course this plays out differently in different areas where the term is used. But there is a basic difference between 'holism' as describing the view that there are objects ('wholes') that need to be referenced in some realm of inquiry, and 'holism' as describing the view that properties of the individuals under consideration require reference to properties of other individuals before the original properties can be fully defined or explained. The first sort of holism concerns what entities have basic existence:

Definition 3. *Some properties can only be attributed to entities that are not individuals.*

and accordingly, we call this 'ontological holism'.

Ontological holism is raised in very many fields of enquiry, especially in the social sciences and humanities. Businesses and corporations, for instance, might have duties and obligations (etc.) that are not duties or obligations of any individual within the business. They might similarly have legal rights and legal constraints that do not devolve to any individual. Nations might have properties that are not properties of any members or collections of members of the nation. They can declare war, or decree that their borders be closed; but no individual in the nation can do so, not even the leader. Thus there must be these entities, call them 'wholes', that are distinct from, and not 'reducible to', the set of individuals that make them up.

Something similar to this is sometimes postulated within some sciences. Such a scientific holism is the view that some scientific laws must make reference to populations/species/etc. The type of example that is often given[4] concerns the interaction of two populations:

> Suppose we have an ecological system composed of seals and cod. There are periodic fluctuations in their population levels. Seals eat cod to the point that there are too few cod to sustain the seal population, so they begin to die out. But this allows the cod to multiply. And in turn this provides food enough for the seal population so they can multiply … and so on, cyclically.

The claim is that this is a type of scientific law that cannot be rephrased in terms of individual seals and cod, but makes essential reference to the notion of a 'population' or (perhaps) to species. Quantum holism is another area that introduces wholes of this type. Here, the view is that an 'entangled pair' of quantum particles form a unity

---

[4] This example is inspired by Garfinkel (1981: ch. 2).

that is distinct from the individual particles that constitute the 'whole'. Further issues concerning compositionality in science come from consideration of theoretical terms, which seem to be holistic in that they are defined only by the axioms of the theory that introduce them. For discussion, see Schurz (2005b: esp. §5).

Contrasted with ontological holism is talk about properties that are somehow interconnected:

Definition 4. *Some properties of an object are defined in terms of the same type of property of some other object(s), and these properties of the other object(s) are in turn defined by means of the first property.*

and accordingly, we call this 'property holism'.

The 'partiality' inherent in this definition of property holism is difficult to overcome, for proponents of property holism do not believe that there are any 'independent' properties from which one can start and thereby develop an account of all the holistically-related properties. And similarly, the appearance of circularity is mandated by the fact that such holists do not think that any of these properties can be described independently of any others. For, they would say, this is just what it means to be holistic. (We return to this issue of 'the direction of explanation' below, in the next section.)

Definition 4 could describe just a very small holistic system containing but two objects and some property they each have. But of course the main cases of interest are where there are very many such objects and they each have a property that is defined in terms of that same category of property as manifested by all the other objects that make up this group. As examples, perhaps 'beautiful' is (partially) defined by reference to the meaning of 'ugly', which in turn is (partially) defined by the meaning of 'beautiful'. Or, it might be claimed that the meaning of 'aggression' is (partially) defined in terms of the meaning of 'defence' and (partially) in terms of the meaning of 'instigate' and partially in terms of other words of this nature. They in turn are defined (partially) by the word 'aggression'.

A natural conclusion to draw from Property Holism is that a 'whole' is formed from the items which are related by having some property of each of them be defined in terms of the others. That is, a whole of the sort envisaged by Definition 3. Although this might be a natural conclusion, I think it is not inevitable. For example, the letter of Definition 4 makes the properties remain as properties of the individual items, and does not demand that they be attributed to any yet further whole, as would be required by Definition 3. Keeping these two notions of holism separate may shield the believers in one or the other types of holism from criticisms levelled at the other type, in much the same way that keeping the two notions of compositionality separate can protect the believers of one type from criticisms levelled at the other type.

It can also be noted that the two distinctions—one within compositionality and the other within holism—are really quite similar. Definition 1 in effect denies the ('primary') existence of wholes; Definition 3 affirms it. Definition 2 clams that properties of wholes can be functionally computed from the similar properties of their parts;

Definition 4 denies this. The Definition 1 vs. Definition 3 dispute is about the existence of (kinds of) entities; the Definition 2 vs. Definition 4 dispute concerns how properties of objects are to be understood or defined. The Definition 1 vs. Definition 3 dispute is the age-old conflict between *atomism* vs. *wholism* (with a 'w').[5] The Definition 2 vs. Definition 4 dispute is a newer conflict about how properties of objects are best explained, and this dispute is usually called *compositionality* vs. *holism*. And while there are connections between the atomism and compositionality, and other connections between wholism and holism, it does none of the four positions good to have it conflated with some other position to which they are not committed.[6] So, I will use the four names 'atomism', 'wholism', 'compositionality', and 'holism' for the remainder of the chapter.

7.2 ATOMISM AND WHOLISM

The dispute between atomism and wholism is fundamentally ontological: Are there non-individual items in the world? Of course, such a dispute turns crucially on what is meant by '(non-)individual', and so it is rather surprising to find that many of the disputants agree on what is meant, or at least, do not seem to challenge each other about this. The kinds of argumentation in this dispute instead range from the explanatory abilities of (natural and social) scientific laws to psychological phenomena to issues in 'the direction of explanation'.

As part of their belief in the existence of wholes that cannot be defined in terms of their parts ('the whole is more than the sum of its parts')—primitive wholes, let's call them—wholists also believe

(7.1)   A primitive whole determines the nature of its parts.

(7.2)   The parts cannot be understood when considered in isolation from the primitive whole of which it is a part.

And they usually also add

(7.3)   The parts of a primitive whole are dynamically interrelated and interdependent.

(7.4)   Analysis as a methodology fails in the case of primitive wholes.

And conversely, atomists deny these four claims.

Since the central topic of this chapter is the compositionality–holism dispute, we cannot go deeply into a discussion of the atomism–wholism dispute. However, it seems

---

[5] Yes, there is also a quasi-religious movement called 'wholism', not to be confused with what followers of Definition 3 believe.

[6] For instance, there is unending argumentation between atomists and wholists over the correctness and applicability of 'reduction'. But this sort of consideration is just beside the point in the dispute between compositionalists and holists.

apposite to say a few words nonetheless, since there are people who confuse the considerations relevant only to this issue with those relevant to the other debate. For instance,
compositionalists will admit of wholes that are not defined entirely in terms of their
parts. In the case of language, for example, they hold that sentences (and other syntactic
units) are more than a set of words—sentences are wholes that take a set of words and
form a unity by blending them together in accordance with some syntactic rules. And
this is a different sort of entity—a whole—that is not to be identified with the set of
words that comprise it. The various wholes that are formed in compositional systems
of language *cannot* be identified with the set of the words comprising the whole; that
is why the formulations of compositionality in language always look like 'the meanings
of its parts *and* the way these parts are combined'. Nonetheless, when arguing against
compositionality, wholists/holists will claim that wholes cannot be identified with their
parts, and they will give examples from many different fields where this is alleged to
be clearly true. But as an argument against compositionality in language, this claim just
misses the mark, since the compositionalists *are* committed to their own sorts of wholes.
Their differences with holism lie elsewhere.

Sometimes wholists bring forward considerations of gestalt theory and emergent
properties to bolster the claim that there are primitive wholes. (Recall the earlier quotation from Boodin (1939) who identified wholism and gestaltism.) The square that
is formed when very heavily-blackened cut-out corners are drawn is one such gestalt
figure that is common in the literature. 'Surely,' it is claimed, 'the square is *not at all*
to be analyzed as those four heavily-blackened cut-out corners.' But equally surely, the
atomist never claimed any such thing. Rather, the square requires that the corners be
placed *exactly so* in relation to one another to make the square appear. The square
could be claimed by atomists to be a function of the heavy corners plus their method of
arrangement or combination.

Similar remarks can be made about emergent properties, that is, properties that the
wholes have that are not possessed by any of the parts. For example, hydrogen and
oxygen combining to give off energy and to produce water. The claim of wholists is
that such properties are not 'sums' of the properties of the initial hydrogen and oxygen.
And since they are not 'sums' of the properties of the initial parts, it has seemed to some
that this calls for a new whole that possesses this property. But we can see that such
considerations do not really play a role here. An atomist would attribute the property to
the *juxtaposition* of the hydrogen and oxygen (plus whatever else is needed to initiate
the reaction).[7]

According to points (7.1) and (7.2), the whole *determines* the nature of its parts, a
doctrine which is interpreted by wholists as entailing that the whole determines the
properties that the parts have. Phillips puts the view's rationale like this:

[7] In fact, historically this seems to be the initial purpose in introducing emergent properties—to avoid
having to postulate some new force that operates 'on a different level from' the ordinary objects. This was
pretty successful in eliminating 'the vital force' from accounts of life in the late 1800s and early 1900s. See
McLaughlin (1992) for an historical account along these lines, but also see O'Connor and Wong (2006)
for an opposing view of the history of emergentism.

In effect, [Bradley] maintained that when entity A enters into a relationship with entity B or C, it gains some property or characteristic, *p*, as a result of this relationship. Without the relationship, and hence without property *p*, Bradley argues, A would be different, or not-A. Any relation at all between A and another entity necessarily determines some property of A, without which A would not be what it is. This is the heart of the theory of internal relations: entities are *necessarily* altered by the relations into which they enter. (Phillips, 1976: 8)

When some entities form a whole, this theory claims that their defining characteristics will be determined at least in part by the relational properties they thus possess. If the whole were different by containing some further item, then the old members would themselves be different in their essential qualities. So, parts cannot be understood in isolation from the whole in which they are parts.

So far as points (7.1) and (7.2) go, Phillips (1976) says that these claims make sense only against the backdrop of a theory of 'internal relations'. And, since Phillips also thinks that this theory is intellectually bankrupt, he concludes that these wholistic doctrines cannot stand. The doctrine of internal relations claims that (apparent) relational properties which two or more items bear to one another are actually intrinsic properties of those items. If A is taller than B, this 'taller than B' is one of A's inherent properties (and 'shorter than A' is one of B's inherent properties). The history of philosophy has not been kind to this doctrine. If it is an inherent property of A that he is 175cm tall, and an inherent property of B that she is 160cm tall, this still does not adequately characterize the tallness-in-A-and-B, for it does not tell us that the relation of taller-than is asymmetric, irreflexive, and transitive. And these properties of *the relation*, taller, cannot be captured by monadic properties of individuals. G. E. Moore and Bertrand Russell were instrumental in disposing of internal relations more than a century ago. Modern wholists seem to forget that this aspect of their position requires them to adopt a notion of internal relations.

An important feature of much reasoning by most wholists is a concentration on 'failures of analysis'. It is claimed that no one could predict the behaviour of a certain mass of gas, for example, looking merely at the intrinsic properties of the atoms that describe it; and thus there is a failure of analysis as a methodological principle. As Phillips (1976: 12) says, however, this overlooks the fact that any proponent of methodological analysis would say that the laws of the system had first to be known, and that the initial conditions of the system had to be described. In fact, a wholist will be in the same condition, will s/he not? If the 'whole' is the mass of gas and its behaviour, it seems implausible that anyone could predict the items that make up the whole without the laws of the system—regardless of whether they are atomists or wholists.

Some wholists are also attracted to the argument that, methodologically, one wants to eschew reductionism; and there is usually presented at this stage a number of shortcomings of reductionism. But saying that 'from knowledge of the parts only one cannot predict the properties of the whole' is quite different from saying that *after* knowledge of the whole has somehow been attained, *then* this cannot be reduced to, or explained in terms of, the atomic parts. And surely this latter notion of analysis is that to which the atomists are committed.

In any case, though, it seems to me that all these arguments start from the wrong point. Isn't the atomist committed only to saying that *in reality* the wholes are sums of their parts? Surely whether or not we *know how to construct* the wholes from their parts is irrelevant to this, and doesn't at all impugn atomism. Aren't these epistemic considerations completely beside the point in the atomism–wholism dispute about ontology?

I have concentrated in this section on the ontological issues of atomism and wholism because they often seep into discussions of compositionality and holism. I hope this discussion now makes clear the sorts of considerations that are *not* relevant to our discussion in the next section, where we *will* talk about compositionality and holism. And although I have been concentrating, in this section, on the ways that an atomist can respond to the charges that wholists make in favour of their theory and against the opposed atomist theory, this shows only that the wholist has not adequately cinched his/her case. It is not thereby shown that the atomistic position is proved, and in fact I do not believe it has been. It has long seemed to me that atomism and wholism are 'structurally identical' theories, differing only in starting points. Intuitively, an atomistic theory postulates a set of basic entities and defines wholes by combining these entities in certain prescribed ways, generating bigger and bigger wholes, all of which are non-primitive. A wholist postulates[8] an all-encompassing primitive whole and defines smaller and smaller wholes based on prescribed ways of decomposing, some of which will be primitive and others not. If it is true that these theories are structurally identical, then there is no difference between them other than their names, and what they choose to name items in their self-same theory. But a discussion of these issues must await a different venue.

7.3 COMPOSITIONALITY AND HOLISM

7.3.1 Is there a conflict?

The definitions given earlier for compositionality and holism were:

A system is **compositional with respect to property** μ if and only if there is a function f such that the μ of any complex object in the system is that function of the μs of its parts.

A system is **holistic with respect to property** μ if and only if the μs of complex objects in the system are defined partially in terms of the μs of some other objects of the system, and the μs of these other objects are in turn defined partially by means of the μs of the first object.

---

[8] Or at least, the type of wholist I am imagining.

This chapter is for the most part concerned with the use of these notions in semantics, and so μ is interpreted as 'the meaning of', and it is in that sense that I will be concerned with compositional and holistic systems when I speak of them without further qualification. The systems themselves are collections of syntactically-defined objects, and the notion of 'part' is therefore understood as being a syntactic part. The key notions used in defining compositional and holistic systems could use some further explication and perhaps some tidying-up. But on an intuitive level, the two types of systems are supposed to be in conflict. Thus, my explications will be aimed at making compositional and holistic semantic systems be contrary to each other, after which we will see which side of the conflict seems a more viable approach to semantics.

It will not have escaped the reader's notice that there has been rather a lot of 'slack' in the accounts offered for compositionality and holism. And, therefore, many writers have been moved to show that the two are compatible. And certainly they are, if one picks the right definitions. If one focuses on the

Slogan: The meaning of a word is its contributions to the sentences in which it occurs. More generally, the meaning of any expression is the contribution it makes to all the larger wholes of which it is a part.

it will then seem that the two are equivalent, for this slogan can be seen as a description of *both* compositionality and holism (especially to those holists who focus on 'contextualism'). I do not here go into a discussion of how the two theories can both have this Slogan as a consequence, but readers of the literature can find numerous examples. So, this Slogan does not set compositionality apart from holism, and for this reason we do not consider it any further because it cannot show the 'conflict' that is supposed to hold between the two viewpoints. At least, it is my view that the two are opposed notions in most theorists' minds and I therefore wish to discover an interpretation of the notions that makes this happen.

Other ways of using the 'play' in the terms that are used to define 'holism' and 'compositionality' to show that they are after all compatible can be found in discussions of Frege. When addressing their beliefs that Frege both held to compositionality and to holism (the latter in virtue of his 'Don't ask for the meaning of a word except in the context of a sentence' (Frege, 1884: §60)), scholars such as Dummett, Currie, Haaparanta, and Hintikka[9] have gone to extraordinary lengths to show that Frege was not being simply inconsistent. In this same vein, although not in the context of Fregean exegesis, Pagin (1997: 13) is concerned to find a *'reasonable* interpretation of [Holism]...which is compatible with Compositionality.'[10]

My goal here is rather the opposite: to show why holism and compositionality are opposed theories. I take interpretations of the terms that make them be compatible as evidence against these interpretations. I want to know why the issue of holism vs. compositionality actually divides theorists of language; I'm not interested in explanations to

---

[9] See Dummett (1981a, 1981b); Currie (1982); Hintikka (1984); Haaparanta (1985); Baker and Hacker (1980). These (and many others) are discussed in Pelletier (2000a).

[10] Although on most other issues I am in broad agreement with Pagin (1997, 2006).

the effect that 'you're both right, just about different things'. Of course there might be very many interpretations that make them out to be incompatible, just as there are many interpretations that make them be compatible, but I will focus on what is offered in the literature. Once we can come up with an interpretation of this nature, we will then be in a position to evaluate compositionality as against holism.

7.3.2 Further characterization of compositionality

Many scholars think that the notion of compositionality is much clearer than that of holism, and perhaps they are right. But there are nonetheless many things about Definition 2 that could stand to be more carefully delineated. The issues fall generally into three categories: What is it to be a function of the sort under consideration? What are meanings and their parts? What restrictions are there on the underlying syntax? There is the further, very general issue concerning the idea that compositionality, as opposed to holism, is supposed to be a theory of *local* meaning. But the characterization of compositionality in Definition 2 says only that there is *some mathematical function* that relates the parts to the more complex. In itself, this does not build in any notion of locality vs. globality; that was, in fact, one of the morals to be drawn from the earlier discussion of how some characterizations of compositionality can be made compatible with holism. Once a system is characterized in whatever way, then there can very often be a mathematical function that relates the complex items with the simple ones; but that does not explain the intuitive notion of *depends upon*, which is supposed, in turn, to tell us about *the order of explanation* inherent in compositionality, and which is supposed to be different in holism.

So, I wish to understand this 'functional relationship' in an ontological way. The function is supposed to correspond to the way that the meaning of complexes *really depend* on the meanings of their parts. Even adopting this understanding of function, there are some things that ought to be cleared up in our talk about functions. When one says that X is a function of Y, they might be talking either mathematically or informally. In the latter case they just mean that in one way or another Y is important for X. I am presuming that our compositional theorists are not talking informally, but rather that they mean their function to be one in the mathematical sense, augmented by a notion of 'depends on'. I believe that the intent of compositionalists is to say that the meaning of the complex item is a function of, *and only of*, the meanings of its parts and manner of composition.[11] But even if we tighten up in this way, then there can be unwanted cases,

[11] Hintikka (1980); Partee (1984) both think, contrary to what I have just said, that the common intent of compositionality is to allow factors other than the meaning of the parts as possible influences on the meaning of the complex. Hintikka calls having the meaning of all wholes be completely determined by the meanings of the parts the *determinacy thesis*. Partee thinks that there are a number of cases that cast doubt on the determinacy thesis. It seems to me that compositionalists have *always* had the determinacy thesis in mind when advocating compositionality. After all, *opponents* argue *against* compositionality by

some of which are surveyed in Pelletier (1994*a*). I am presuming here that these niceties are taken care of.

Some disputes about compositionality turn on what is meant by 'meaning.' For instance, if the syntactic form of the part is considered to be an aspect of the meaning of the part, then it can be shown that 'any semantics can be made to be compositional'.[12] Thus, theories that take the meaning of a word to be the pair consisting of the actual word and its word-meaning as normally understood, and use this information to construct the meaning of a next-most-complex unit, which meaning is also a pair consisting of this syntactic description of the item plus a second element computed from the word meanings, are susceptible to the charge of triviality. Westerståhl (1998) considers other proofs that purport to have much the same upshot—that compositionality is 'trivial' or 'a methodological matter' (meaning that it is merely a theoretician's preference to work with a theory of that nature than with a theory of some other nature, but which has no empirical consequences). Westerståhl brings out the sort of presuppositions these proofs make, and argues that they are all implausible assumptions.

One direction not considered by Westerståhl, but which seems related to theories that build the syntactic form into the meaning (a kind of 'structured meaning' approach, perhaps), are theories that want meaning functions to operate not only on the meanings of the parts, but also on the parts of these parts, and so on. Thus, the meaning function takes as arguments not only the *immediate* syntactic constituents, but on their subconstituents. This distinction is mentioned in Partee (1984), and in Larson and Segal (1995) it is called the difference between 'strictly local' and 'non-local' compositionality. To see the difference, suppose the meaning of some node in a syntax tree is a set of possible worlds.[13] A strictly local compositional semantic rule would use this set of possible worlds (plus information about the way its syntactic value is combined with another meaning) to compute the meaning of the parent node. But a non-local rule could have access to information such as *which part of that set comes from which subpart of the syntactic item*, and this in turn seems very close to the above-rejected picture of meaning where the syntactic form is considered a part of the meaning.

In a similar vein, if we are given a language—a syntax plus semantics—where the semantics is non-compositional, and if one is allowed to change freely the syntactic structure assigned to the elements of the language, then the same semantic values can be assigned to the sentences (strings of words, now having a different structure) of the language as before but in a compositional way.[14] For example, if one is allowed to introduce two syntactic forms where there used to be just one in the original language,

trying to show that there are *some* features other than the parts which are relevant; they do not think they have to show that the parts *never* play a role.

[12] See Westerståhl (2004: 551–2). I believe Putnam (1954) was the first to suggest this as a way to save compositionality in the face of Mates-type examples (Mates, 1950).

[13] Just suppose. You don't have to believe it.

[14] See the discussion in Westerståhl (1998) for proofs of this and related matters. See also Westerståhl (2004) for discussion of the conditions under which a compositional partial semantics can be extended to an entire language.

then (some) violations of compositionality can be given a compositional treatment. But surely this sort of change is quite different from the charge that compositionality itself is vacuous. In the case of creating new syntactic forms, we need to have some *syntactic* evidence for this; and if we do have it that is our evidence for a compositional treatment, and if we don't have it that is our evidence against compositionality for this language's semantics. (Of course, if the desire for compositionality is the *only* motivation for such syntactic changes in every case, then we might indeed accuse the theoretician of treating compositionality as a methodological principle. But this does not mean that the general notion of compositionality is itself vacuous, only its employment in this particular case.)

We have just seen that some versions of compositionality are vacuous because they define meaning in such a way as to encode all the lexical and syntactic information, or they allow the meaning function to have access to the way that meanings of parts was computed, or they allow otherwise unmotivated changes to the underlying syntactic part–whole relation. And as a consequence, it always becomes possible to re-code a non-compositional semantics as a compositional one. But ignoring these sorts of features and tricks, one might ask, is the whole notion still vacuous? Is it, maybe, just that semantic theoreticians are drawn to the 'neat and tidy' picture that compositionality offers—the issue of compositionality vs. non-compositionality in semantics is perhaps just an aesthetic taste?

The answer to this is no: there do seem to be non-compositional features of natural languages. I am not going to discuss these here: they are the 'argument from synonymy' and the 'argument from ambiguity' discussed in Pelletier (1994*a,b*, 2000*b*). Perhaps further investigation will yield evidence that these features are best described in some other ways that do not generate non-compositionality. But this further evidence needs to be independent from the desire to retain compositionality, or else the principle truly is 'merely methodological' in linguistics.

7.3.3 Further characterization of holism

Much of the opposition between holism and compositionality comes from considerations that are lumped together under the banner of *direction of explanation*. In a holistic system, it is the 'whole' that is considered primary and it is this whole that is the 'cause' or 'explanation' of the meaning of the words. In a compositional system, on the other hand, the words are primary, and it is they (plus their modes of combination with other words) that 'cause' or 'explain' why larger units like sentences have the meaning they do.

The sort of holism that I am interested in—the sort that is *really* opposed to compositionality—is expressed in Saussure (1916). It is a complex explanation, but the various aspects of this explanation will illustrate many of the features in holism that compositionalists claim to be faulty. Let us start with his general characterization (Saussure, 1916: 114). He distinguishes 'value', or 'content', from 'meaning'; it is the notion of value that I wish to focus on.

[A word's] value is therefore not determined merely by that concept or meaning for which it is a token. It must also be assessed against comparable values, by contrast with other words. The content of a word is determined in the final analysis not by what it contains but by what exists outside it....

The French word *mouton* may have the same meaning as the English word *sheep*; but it does not have the same value. ...The difference in value between *sheep* and *mouton* hinges on the fact that in English there is another word *mutton* for the meat, whereas *mouton* in French covers both.

In a given language, all the words which express neighbouring ideas help define one another's meaning. Each of a set of synonyms like 'to dread', 'to fear', 'to be afraid' has its particular value only because they stand in contrast with one another. If 'to dread' did not exist, its content would be shared out among its competitors. ...So the value of any given word is determined by what other words there are in that particular area of the vocabulary. ...No word has a value that can be identified independently of what else there is in its vicinity. (Saussure, 1916: 114)

(Since I'm using Saussure merely to give a feel for the type of view that I want to call holism, I propose to delete any reference to Saussure's notion of meaning and just talk about his notion of value—although I will feel free to call it 'meaning'.)

Like most semantic holistic theories, however, Saussure's theory focuses on the lexical items and not on sentences. On the surface—and maybe deep down inside—this seems to be a shortcoming, since pretty much all theories of language think of sentences, or even longer stretches of discourse, as defining 'language'. (Or alternatively, they think of language as the ability to generate these longer items.) Can it really be the case that a language is holistic if its lexical items are given meaning in the way indicated by Saussure? Perhaps; let's see.

The presumption apparently made by these holists who focus on the lexical interpenetration of each meaning by all other members of the lexicon is that this same interpenetration will infect sentences as well. It might be noted that many of the semantic rules that such a holist could propose might be of a form that compositionalists would like—they could combine two or more lexically interpenetrated meanings in some specified way—and the result would nonetheless be considered objectionably holistic by the compositionalist's lights. For, these complexes will also have interpenetrated meanings: for example, no sentence's meaning can be understood without understanding all the various interpenetrations that this sentence has with other items. And this now means not only the rest of the lexical items, but also all the sentences in which these lexical items can occur. And that pretty much means the entire language, doesn't it? So, to understand any sentence at all, one needs to understand every sentence in the language. So, the apparent ability to combine a holistic lexicon with a compositionally-acceptable set of semantic rules does not remove the offensive feature from the holist's theory. It still exhibits what anti-holists find most objectionable: the direction of explanation and understanding.

Unlike most other semantic holist theories, Saussure's is not individualistic. Instead, he seems to be thinking of 'the French lexicon in the abstract', and how its basic units are assigned values. Most other theories start with an individual's *mental* lexicon, and argue that the way these items are acquired dictates that their meanings are all defined in terms of others in their lexicon. As we will see later, a consequence of making this holism be a matter of individuals' private lexicons is that such theories become vulnerable to the charge that interpersonal communication is impossible because each person learns their meanings differently. But a theory like Saussure's trades this difficulty in for a difficulty in understanding how one can 'learn the lexicon of French' at all—another topic to which we will return.

Saussure also thinks that the claims one can make about 'the French language' are identical to those we can make about any (native?) speaker of the French language. In more up-to-date terminology, he thinks that the semantic facts concerning the 'external', independent-of-people, French language are identical to the 'internal' semantic facts of a (native?) speaker of French. Saussure says:

> Psychologically, setting aside its expression in words, our thought is simply a vague, shapeless mass. . . . In itself, thought is like a swirling cloud, where no shape is intrinsically determinate. No ideas are established in advance, and nothing is distinct, before the introduction of linguistic structure.
>
> But do sounds, which lie outside this nebulous world of thought, in themselves constitute entities established in advance? No more than ideas do. The substance of sound is no more fixed or rigid than that of thought. It does not offer a ready-made mould, with shapes that thought must inevitably conform to. It is a malleable material which can be fashioned into separate parts in order to supply the signals which thought has need of. So we can envisage the linguistic phenomenon in its entirety— the language, that is—as a series of adjoining subdivisions simultaneously imprinted both on the plane of vague, amorphous thought, and on the equally featureless plane of sound. . . .
>
> Just as it is impossible to take a pair of scissors and cut one side of paper without at the same time cutting the other, so it is impossible in a language to isolate sound from thought, or thought from sound. To separate the two for theoretical purposes takes us into either pure psychology or pure phonetics, not linguistics.
>
> Linguistics, then, operates along this margin, where sound and thought meet. *The contact between them gives rise to a form, not a substance.* (Saussure 1916: 110–11)

Focusing on what Saussure calls the 'value' of words, let's look a little more closely at what this theory would say about more modern issues. First note that the view is *not* epistemic: it is not merely that we can't *know* the value of a word without knowing the values of words that are its competitors, but that the word *doesn't have* a value without these oppositions. Saussure's holism is bound up with the view that lexical items are defined 'by contrast' with others in the same neighbourhood. Although Saussure talks about such 'closely related' lexical items, surely the effect can't be so easily localized. The 'semantic field' of the terms Saussure used in his example are also related to items in the 'motivational semantic field', and to those in the 'moral semantic field', and so on indefinitely. And these relations or 'interpenetrations' can't really just be 'contrast', unless this term is taken very generally indeed. Most theorists, both holists and anti-holists, would like to include *any* epistemic liaison there may be between two items. And I suspect that Saussure would want his liaisons to be broader than the 'contrast' he mentions—at least, that's the type of holism I am interested in opposing to compositionality.

As I remarked, Saussure's view is that the 'external language' is itself holistic. And the entire language, with all its sentences and other structures, is holistic because the lexical items are defined by means of liaisons with one another.[15] Although Saussure, like other holists, discusses only lexical items and not sentences, he nonetheless differs from the more usual take by holists, for whom the whole is restricted to an individual's lexicon. Most holist theorists (unlike Saussure's) do not hold that all people 'tap into' the same independent-of-an-individual lexicon.[16] To my mind, it is no accident that most holistic theories have the feature of being lexically oriented, for there simply is no sense in the notion of a *sentence* being 'admitted' into the language without any further restrictions. (One possible such further restriction is that the sentence be true, or considered true; but this move in the direction of confirmation holism does not capture *meaning* holism, in the sense that most holists want.[17]) The two features are related: once you see that there is no such independently specifiable whole as 'all the possible meanings in the language', then you will choose to work with the (finite) lexicon and find your holism there. But if you start there, you most naturally are attracted to how an individual acquires the lexicon, thereby making your holism individualistic. Saussure is an exception in this last regard, and this is why I chose his view as my exemplar of semantic holism that is really at odds with compositional treatments of language.

Once one therefore fixes on lexical items, it seems that the most natural direction to take is to think of each person's subjective lexicon as separate wholes, and deny that they are *sub-parts* of some larger, social whole, or somehow *manifestations* of such a larger whole. In Section 7.3.4.1 we will look at a case where we *do* talk of a whole as being comprised of sentence meanings. But it will not form the sort of holism we seek here.

7.3.4 Compositionality vs. holism

Given how popular the doctrine is, it is rather surprising that there are not very many arguments that support semantic compositionality directly. Most arguments from compositionalists on the general topic of holism and compositionality *assume* compositionality to be true and then go on to show that such-and-so alternative position can't be

---

[15] It might further be noted that the meaning of a word is *not* characterized as its contributions to all the sentences in which it occurs.

[16] There are some who think people can tap into 'how society uses language' or 'a form of life'. These do not seem any more clear than tapping into 'the French lexicon' in the abstract.

[17] Some Davidsonians think otherwise. They think that a theory can leverage the notion of 'accepted true' to escape the internalism or individualism that holism seems committed to. But I won't follow up this strand in my discussion. I'll discuss my own take on the issue of true sentences in Section 7.3.4.1, but it will not involve Davidsonian considerations. Some further Davidsonian issues will come out in Section 7.3.4.2.

right.[18] In the linguistics literature there is, to be sure, some argumentation concerning the proper form of a linguistic theory; and in that milieu, semantic compositionality is praised for its clarity and transparency. But these 'methodological' (aesthetic?) considerations don't really count as direct arguments in favour of the position, in my mind.

This article on holism is not the place to review the considerations that have been put forward both for and against (semantic) compositionality,[19] but we should look at what Jerry Fodor calls 'the sword of compositionality',[20] since it is usually seen as decisive against (semantic) holism.

These main considerations in favour of the semantic compositionality of language in the sense of Definition 2 come from a series of similar 'arguments' that we might collectively call 'The Infinity of Language'.

[**Argument from understanding**] We can *understand* an infinite number of novel sentences, so long as they employ words we already understand. We understand sentences and other combinations that we have never encountered. So, language must be 'compositional': it must start with a finite stock of words/morphemes and put these together in a finite number of different ways, but using an unlimited recursive method.

[**Argument from productivity/creativity**] We can *create* new sentences that we have never heard or used before, and we know that they are appropriate to the situation in which we use them. This can only happen if language is 'compositionally' organized, so that we learn some finite base of words and rules, but know how to combine them recursively so as to produce totally new descriptions.

[**Argument from learnability**] We are finite creatures who are exposed to a finite amount of information concerning our language. Nonetheless we can *learn* a system that is capable of infinite expression. The only way this can happen is if what we learn has a finite basis of terms and rules, but the rules themselves allow for arbitrarily complex 'composition'.

As I see it, there are three threads interwoven in the arguments:

1. that language is something special (infinite, or novel, or creative, or whatever);
2. that people manage to use/learn/understand language despite their being 'finite';
3. that one (the only?) way to do this is if language exhibited a compositional framework.

Clearly Descartes was especially impressed by (1). But he did not follow the above argumentation, and (apparently) concluded instead that people are somehow 'not finite',

---

[18] I think it not unfair to characterize much of Fodor's argumentation to be along these lines. He is famous for remarks like 'Compositionality is, as they say in Britain, non-negotiable' and 'So non-negotiable is compositionality that I am not even going to tell you what it is'. Of course, there are other places where he does put forward some more serious considerations.

[19] Many of these are discussed in Pelletier (1994a), to which the reader is directed.

[20] (Fodor, 1998a: 98) 'Compositionality is a sharp sword and cutteth many knots'.

unlike other animals. Leibniz and others around him (see Wilson, 1989: 28–32) envisaged constructing a 'universal language' that could be learned very easily (because it exhibited a compositional structure?). But (apparently) these thinkers did not see natural languages as having the same properties, for, natural languages were not easy to learn and they did not represent the composition of reality in the language.

The simultaneous bringing together of (1) and (2) occurs in the opening paragraph of Frege (1923), and can also be found in an earlier draft, Frege (1914). There is also a strong hint that he believes (3) is the explanation of it all. Russell might also have had such a view. In Russell (1918: 193–5) there is recognition of the fact that (3) would/does explain (1), but it is not clear whether this is a recommendation for a perfect language or a description of natural language. And others of the same time had similar thoughts, such as Wittgenstein (*Tractatus* 4.027–4.03) and Schlick (1918). None of these authors cite any earlier thinkers for this general argument/observation; so, although the thought seems to have been very much in the air at the time, perhaps it is true that Frege (1923) is the first time that (3) was used as a unifying explanation. I've not seen any earlier ones.[21] Related to the Infinity of Language is also the consideration that is often called 'systematicity', perhaps first raised in the context of an argument against connectionism in Fodor and Pylyshyn (1988). This consideration is usually put: 'if a speaker can understand "Cats chase rats" they can also understand "Rats chase cats".' Some part of this consideration seems plausible, although I think that part is already contained in one or another of the Infinity of Language arguments. But the failures of this argument in a number of other cases make me think that whatever remains after the part covered by the earlier arguments is best forgotten. (See Johnson, 2004a; Pullum and Scholz, 2007, for comments.)

7.3.4.1 *Holism pro*

I emphasized earlier that holistic semantic theories tended to the view that holism starts in the lexicon and that a holistic language (taken as a set of sentences) is a byproduct of this lexical phenomenon. And I said that this was in part due to the difficulties in specifying what a whole might be in the case of 'all the possible meanings there are'. But there can be some sense where one talks of a whole as a group of the sentence-meanings. The natural examples of this are *theories*—a set of meanings/sentences that are taken to be true of, or constitute an understanding of, some area of knowledge (e.g. scientific theories). Note that we do *not* have here a set of 'all possible meanings', but rather a set of meanings that are presumed to be well-behaved with respect to one another (e.g. are not contradictory). In this sort of case we can talk of a different type of holism:

Definition 5. *Confirmation Holism is the view that a hypothesis within a theory cannot be confirmed (or disconfirmed) in isolation from the remainder of the theory.*

---

[21] Wilfrid Hodges likes to point to medieval Arabic scholars as precursors, see Hodges (2006a). And Brendan Gillon likes to point to Pāṇini as an earlier example, see Gillon (2007). Hodges also gives Husserl (1900: Lecture 4) as a source, and has speculated that it is maybe possible that Frege had got his formulation from here.

Note that this is a picture of how an entire theory, viewed as a collection of statements, works—as opposed to anyone's grasp of this theory. Is it holism in the sense(s) previously discussed? Does the meaning of any sentence in the theory 'depend on the meaning of all the other sentences of the theory'?

In a standard picture of a (scientific) theory, a hypothesis together with other auxiliary statements (perhaps some other hypotheses, perhaps statements about the immediate surroundings) can 'generate a prediction', which sometimes can be evaluated against the facts of the world. Confirmation holism, as characterized in Definition 5, points out that the 'prediction' is in fact 'generated' by the entire theory and thus it is this entire theory that is being evaluated against the facts, and not just the hypothesis that has been singled out. The point is usually put like this: experience confronts the theory as a whole; recalcitrant experiences can be accommodated either by denying the hypothesis that appeared to generate its negation or by suitably changing other parts of the theory.[22]

Note that, as stated, confirmation holism is about the *truth* (or truth-in-the-theory), not about meaning. It would require yet another principle that brings the two notions together, to yield meaning holism. With confirmation holism we arguably have an ontological entity—a theory—and a claim about the 'direction of explanation' which is the criterion for admission into the theory. Can we view language in the same way? This seems less clear, since the criteria for admission to a language is not at all so well-defined as confirmation in a theory. But maybe it is possible to talk about how an entire society employs language, and this will be the 'whole' against which the meanings of individual sentences vie for membership? This seems a possible viewpoint, but it requires a considerable amount more of background work to make it clear than has hitherto been done.

Once we have the picture of an independent-of-people theory, and what confirmation holism would look like, we can analogously consider the similar 'individualistic' picture:

Definition 6. *Doxastic Holism is the view that one should believe what coheres with the majority of that which the person believes. The acceptance or rejection of a possible belief is due to the entire set of beliefs.*

Once again, this becomes an account of what *should* be in a theory—that is what *should* be believed. It takes yet further principles to turn this into semantic holism. As with confirmation holism, we then test sentences for possible membership into the believed set. The two types of holism are quite similar, as we can see. Confirmation holism presumes an independently-existing body of theory and evidence; doxastic holism presumes an individual with a set of believed propositions.

It should be made clear that confirmation holism and doxastic holism are not kinds of semantic holism;[23] for one thing, they rely on the idea that the 'whole' is circumscribed

---

[22] Confirmation holism is usually attributed to Duhem (1906); Hempel (1950); Quine (1951).

[23] Even the opponents of semantic holism (e.g., Fodor and Lepore, 1992: 37) seem happy enough to embrace pure confirmation and doxastic holism.

in one way or another (e.g. by consistency) so that it gives a criterion for some meanings *not* being in this whole. And so they are not semantic holism by pretty much anyone's definition. (Well, they are sometimes still called semantic holism, but only when that notion is broadened or disjunctified so as to include this other notion, as in Heal (1994). Heal requires that if one has a belief, then there are many other beliefs the person must have. But she denies that these beliefs have to be the usually-proffered sort of epistemic liaisons with items in the first belief. These other beliefs need not be further elucidations of the meaning of any terms in the first belief. It's just that there need to be some further beliefs.) Although confirmation and doxastic holism are not semantic holism, some have thought that semantic holism can be generated from epistemic holism by means of some further premise(s). The most common suggestion for such a premise is (some form or other of) verificationism.[24]

The most influential semantic theory that gives a motivation for semantic holism is inferential role semantics. So influential is this theory that it is often just taken to *be* semantic holism.

Definition 7. *Inferential Role Semantics is the view that the semantic content of terms is given by their liaisons with other terms.*

There are two relevant ways to understand the 'liaisons' that are mentioned in Definition 7. The first, less common way is to think of them as being the connections given by antecedently-given meanings, inferences, and truths. For example, many people hold that the meaning of 'bovine' entails having hollow horns,[25] and that this is so independently of any particular person's beliefs/knowledge of this fact about the meanings of zoological terms. Such people believe in a distinction between this type of fact and such facts as that the most common bovine in North America is the domestic cow. The former type of fact (they say) is about meanings, the latter is empirical. If all liaisons are given by inferences/truths of the meaning sort, then we might claim to have a non-individualistic meaning holism. It's a holism in an intuitive sense: the meaning of a term consists in these meaning liaisons. But of course, it also presumes these meaning liaisons to be given independently, and therefore seems to be a type of meaning atomism.

But of course, the distinction between meaning facts and empirical facts is widely thought to have been conclusively refuted by Quine (1951). And so the liaisons mentioned in Definition 7 are mostly thought to be those generated by an individual, and

---

[24] Quine (1951) seemed to hold that semantic holism followed from confirmation holism plus verificationism, and Fodor and Lepore (1992: 216–17) also cite Harman (1974), P. M. Churchland (1984); P. S. Churchland (1986) as others who think this is right. Fodor and Lepore (1992) deny that confirmation holism plus verificationism will lead to semantic holism. On the other hand, however, Harrell (1996) and Okasha (2000) deny that Quine's version would generate any conclusion that falls afoul of Fodor/Lepore's problems with semantic holism. We will not delve into this dispute, referring the reader to the papers cited here.

[25] Rather: being an individual member of a ruminant species whose typical horned members have hollow horns.

not to have any distinction between the person's 'necessary' meaning liaisons and his 'empirical' meaning liaisons—rather, they *all* form parts of the meaning of a lexical item. This is the more classical semantic holism—which is individualistic in nature. The meaning of any lexical item is the set of these liaisons—but as we saw earlier, this entails that the lexical items that thereby occur in this meaning will also in turn have this word's meaning as a part. Additionally, these lexical items in the liaisons will have liaisons with yet different lexical items, and so these further meanings too would be a part of the meaning of the first one. Ultimately, it is often said, the meaning of all lexical items is a part of the meaning of any lexical item. And so 'meaning forms a unified whole' (as the holist would put it) or 'the entire theory is circular' (as a compositionalist might say). As I indicated above, these liaisons would persist when lexical items are combined into larger syntactic groups, and so it would seem that every sentence would bring with it all the liaisons that any word in it contained. But since the lexical items in these liaisons have many other liaisons, these further liaisons will also be a part of the meaning of any sentence. Or to put it more broadly, the meaning of any sentence contains the meanings of all sentences.

This individualistic holism is supported by two 'master arguments'. The first is a plausible account of how children learn word meanings: it is a gradual process and children incorporate small parts of the meaning as to how the terms interact with what terms they already have grasped to some extent. They learn that broccoli is food, but that it is different in shape from asparagus, but that they are both vegetables and different from chicken; that it makes Daddy happy when the child eats it, that it can come with cheese on top and still be broccoli; and so on. Plausibly, all these liaisons, and innumerable others, form a part of the meaning of 'broccoli' for the child language-learner. And what reason is there to say that they do not remain in adult meanings?

The second master argument is a slippery-slope-like argument from the apparent truism that part of the meaning of, say, 'gold', is that it is a metal. But that's not all there is to the meaning of 'gold': gold is also either yellow or white; gold is different from silver and from helium; gold is valuable; gold is what pirates bury on Caribbean islands; gold has started many wars; .... It seems that one cannot stop, once you get started. (Well, you might stop if you had some way to distinguish 'important meaning-relations' from mere 'accidental associations', along the lines mentioned earlier in a non-individualistic inferential role semantics. But here, as there, the Quinean denial of an analytic–synthetic distinction (Quine, 1951) is brought forward to assert that there is no such difference.)

Given these as the only positive arguments for meaning holism, holistic theorists have been put on the defensive, especially since the publication of Fodor and Lepore (1992) (and earlier works of Fodor's) that attacked these two considerations. Currently, straightforward arguments in favour of holism have become rare as holists instead attempt to rebut the arguments raised in Fodor's works. It seems that the attitude is that meaning holism is the correct default position, and all that is needed for establishing it is to answer the relevant pesky considerations raised in Fodor and Lepore (1992). In this regard meaning holism joins Whorfianism as 'the hypothesis that just won't die'—don't give positive arguments, just rebut the contrary arguments and allow the underlying correctness of the view to shine through.

7.3.4.2 *Holism con*

Most who advocate holism think of the individualistic version, where it is the lexical meanings within each individual that rely for their meaning on their liaisons with other lexical items within that individual. As I remarked above, this is different from the version of holism I was suggesting as forming the 'real' conflict with compositionality, and which I attributed to Saussure. In this version, it is the public lexicon *of the language in the abstract* that has this property. The sorts of considerations that are brought against holism need to distinguish these two variants, since most of them do not hold with equal force against the two.

There seem to be two reasons that holists have gravitated toward the individualistic version. The first, a rather non-academic reason, is that it allows each person 'to have their own meanings'. It just is a matter of fact that many holists are drawn to some sort of individualistic relativism, and they think that the individualistic holism is a manifestation or vindication of this. The phrase 'That's true for you' can be cashed out as 'Your mental lexicon admits of a way to allow this to be true' (while retaining the idea that in my mental lexicon there is no such way). I don't propose to dwell on this feature, but I do think that anyone could walk around to the bastions of holism— many wings in philosophy departments, and '*almost* everybody in AI and cognitive psychology; and …absolutely everybody who writes literary criticism in French', as it is put in Fodor and Lepore 1992: 7 (they could have added English departments and Humanities departments)—and ask why some member believes holism, this will be one of the answers.[26]

The second reason is due to the picture of child language learning put forward above. The incremental nature of learning that seems to accompany parental correction, especially with contrast ('No Jimmy, that's not a ball, it's called a pyramid—you see, it doesn't roll on the floor like a ball does, it just sits there') gives a reason to think that all this becomes part of the child's mental lexicon. And thus, all the liaisons form a part of the meaning of each mental item.

Against the individualistic version of holism there have been raised many arguments. What seems amazing to non-holists is that there should be any holists left, after they have had these arguments presented to them. As I said a few paragraphs ago, maybe this is to be explained on 'non-cognitive grounds': holism is just the right view for a (post-)postmodern humanist, and no 'cognitive' consideration will ever dislodge it. (Of course, there are many who keep to holism for other reasons, and they try to show that the arguments are not as strong as they seem. Furthermore, these are arguments against *individualistic* holism, and not against the 'public' version, and it is often not appreciated by non-holists that there is this other route to holism.) In this final section I present the standard arguments against individualistic holism but will not give holists the opportunity to respond. I note those that do not hold against the non-individualistic

---

[26] On this particular issue, one might compare what is said in Fodor and Lepore (1992: xiii).

version, and will then present some considerations against that version also … and again will not allow its proponents to answer.

The list of anti-holism arguments directed against the individualistic version is large indeed. It is first noted that the theory predicts it to be extraordinarily likely that different people will have had different language-learning experiences, and therefore according to individualistic holism will have different liaisons among their lexical items. In turn, this means they do not speak the same language as one another. It furthermore follows that they do not mean the same thing as one another even when they utter the same word, phrase, or sentence. But then, when they (think they) agree with one another, or disagree with one another, they are in fact not doing so. Any evidence one has that you disagree with your conversational partner is, according to the theory, better evidence that you are talking about different things, and not disagreeing at all.

It is tempting to say, and many individualistic holists have, that communication does not require 'absolute identity' of the corresponding mental lexicons but only that they be 'similar enough'. But this can't really be made out in a non-circular way, it seems to me. The hypothesis that two different minds are 'similar enough' with respect to their understanding of some term—say, 'democracy'—has no empirical content other than the belief that the two people are understanding what each other says when they talk, despite their differences in acquisition of the relevant concepts. But that was precisely the (alleged) fact that the 'similarity' was hypothesized to explain. The very nature of individualistic holism makes it impossible to give an independent criterion of 'similar enough'.

It is also often pointed out that, not only is communication with others an impossibility according to the theory's own features, but also one cannot communicate with oneself from one year to the next, one day to the next, one hour to the next, …. For, in the intervening time period the person would have new experiences and (except in very special cases where the person is comatose) these will impact the class of liaisons that impinge on the meanings of his lexicon. Although one *thinks* one remembers that the bark of eucalyptus trees peels off yearly, there is no justification for this, according to the theory. Over the year when you last had that thought, many of your liaisons have been altered—or at least, it is most likely to have happened—and thus your last-year-thoughts have no necessary connection with this-year-thoughts.

Indeed, an individualistic holist can't change his mind about anything! For, the very act of getting new information makes it be a different thing, and hence it is *not* a case of changing one's mind about concept X. The old concept X is no longer there to have a new opinion about. Not only is it impossible to disagree with another person, as I remarked above, but it is impossible to disagree with the past. We think that we have learned that Anaxagoras was wrong when he said that the unevenness of the moon's surface is due to the mixture of earthy matter with cold. But individualistic holism is committed to claiming that we are in fact not at all disagreeing with him. We can't disagree. We can't agree either. We've just changed the subject.

The preceding arguments were directed against the individualistic or internalist version of holism. But we also considered a more 'public' version, as put forward by (our version of) Saussure. In this sort of holism, it is not an individual's internal epistemic liaisons that determine the meaning of a term, but rather these liaisons are features of some external reality. However, such a position seems to diminish the first of the arguments in favour of holism—those considerations based on how an individual child's language learning is based on corrections with contrasts. For, those corrections are by their nature unique to individuals, and can't realistically be mapped onto any 'external reality'. Indeed, one might wonder what such an external reality could possibly be. We've seen that Saussure seems to think of it as 'the French lexicon in the abstract'. Could it be some sort of social entity—the language endorsed by the people in my community, or some similar definition, such as a Form of Life?

Although this version of holism seems to lose the support from the intuitive picture of language learning, it gains some support because it avoids the criticisms based on individuals' having different liaisons. For, in this picture of meaning, the liaisons are an *external-to-individual-people* matter of fact. For example, in the French lexicon is the fact that *mouton* is both farmed and petted as well as eaten, while *redouter, craindre*, and *avoir peur* have some specified value in terms of their contrasts with each other. This is not affected by how an individual learns these words. Plurality in French, Saussure says, has a different value from plurality in Sanskrit because unlike French, Sanskrit has a third category, dual (Saussure, 1916: 114). In this version of holism, meaning is not contained in, nor constrained by, how any individual learns. The object that is learned exists independently.

Notwithstanding this advantage, there still seem to be problems with this version of holism. For one thing, it is not clear how language change can be accommodated. Any attempt to allow for it seems to make the theory become susceptible to the same sort of objection we levelled against the individualistic version of holism: if the liaisons change, so that the values of the words change, then what we are saying now differs from what was said before the change—even if the same words are being used.

It is also very difficult to see how language learning works on this picture. As children, we all get pieces of this independently-existing structure; and presumably our further education gets our internal representations closer and closer to the external original. But our learning process is fraught with individual variation—just as the individualistic holists say. So, when is it that we actually learn the language? How can we learn this antecedently existing 'lexicon of French' with all its inbuilt liaisons? And what relation does it have to our internal lexicons?

It seems to me that externalist versions of holism need to articulate a clearer notion of what the external reality is—that is, of what ontological status 'the lexicon of a language' has. And they need to further explicate the relation between what an individual learns and this external item. Once this is done, there needs to be a further discussion concerning whether the external item actually plays any role in holism, or whether this externalist holism merely transfers its claims to the learned internal representations.

7.4 LEFTOVERS, AND CONCLUSION

One main message of this survey is that there is a fundamental cleavage both within the 'compositionality' camp and the 'holist' camp between an ontological version of their doctrine and a property-oriented version. And, almost all the arguments that holists have mounted against the compositionalists are actually directed against the ontological version and have a very much reduced or even non-existent applicability to the property-based version. Yet, it is the property-oriented version that is of interest in philosophy of language and linguistic semantics.

Another point worthy of notice is that most versions of semantic holism are individualistic in nature. But this in turn brings up a host of problems concerning communication, belief change, understanding, and the like. I featured a non-individualistic version of semantic holism, drawing on Saussure. But this doctrine seems to have problems in formulating a way that such a language could be acquired. Generally speaking, both types of holism run afoul of the considerations that follow from the Infinity of Language.

Finally, because of my focus on versions of holism and compositionality that are opposed to one another, I have not discussed attempts to bring them together. For further thoughts along this line, one should consult Pagin (1997, 2006).[27]

[27] I am quite grateful for comments on an earlier version of this chapter from Chris Gauker, Peter Pagin, and Markus Werning. I wish I could have more adequately dealt with all of them. I also acknowledge comments and discussions over the years on the general topic of compositionality with Brendan Gillon, Mike Harnish, Jim Higginbotham, Wilfrid Hodges, Theo Janssen, Ali Kazmi, Ernie Lepore, Bernard Linsky, Peter Pagin, Barbara Partee, Len Schubert, Markus Werning, and Dag Westerståhl. I also acknowledge (Canadian) NSERC grant 5525 for its support over the years.

CHAPTER 8

COMPOSITIONALITY, FLEXIBILITY, AND CONTEXT DEPENDENCE

FRANÇOIS RECANATI

To the memory of L. Jonathan Cohen (1923–2006)

8.1 TWO TYPES OF RULE

The compositionality idea is the idea that semantic interpretation proceeds in two steps. Simple expressions are interpreted by means of *lexical rules*, which assign meanings to them directly. Complex expressions are interpreted by means of *compositional rules*, which assign meanings to them indirectly, as a function of the meanings of their parts.

For any simple expression a, the associated lexical rule says that the interpretation of a is a certain entity m:

(8.1) $I(a) = m$

There will be as many rules of this sort as there are simple expressions (or, rather, readings of simple expressions[1]) in the language. Since the number of simple expressions and the number of readings which an ambiguous expression has are both finite, it is, in principle, possible for a finite mind to get to know the meanings of all simple expressions of the language by learning each of the lexical rules that are associated with them in this way.

The syntax of natural language is such that (because of recursivity) the number of complex expressions is *not* finite: for any expression of whatever complexity it is always possible to construct a more complex expression. So it would not be possible for a finite

---

[1] For the purposes of applying the interpretation function, an ambiguous expression a endowed with n readings counts as several homonymous expressions $a_1, a_2 \ldots a_n$, each of which is interpreted by means of a rule like (8.1).

mind to get to know the meaning of all expressions of the language, simple *or* complex, by learning that meaning directly. If we only had rules like (8.1) to interpret a linguistic expression, there would have to be an infinite number of them, and we could not learn them. So we need a different type of rule than (8.1) for interpreting complex expressions.

Just as the number of simple expressions is finite, the number of ways in which distinct expressions can be put together so as to yield a complex expression of the language is finite. In other words, there is a finite number of syntactic rules, through which an infinite number of complex expressions can be generated. The solution, then, is to pair each syntactic rule with a semantic rule of a new sort—a compositional rule. A compositional rule is something like:

(8.2) $I(a*\beta) = f(I(a),\ I(\beta))$

where '$*$' stands for an arbitrary mode of combination. The rule says that the interpretation of the complex expression $a * \beta$ is the value of a certain function f when it takes as arguments the interpretation of a and the interpretation of β.

A compositional rule associates with a particular way of combining two expressions a and β a function whose arguments are the meanings (interpretations) of a and β, and whose value is the resulting meaning (interpretation) for the complex expression $a * \beta$. Thanks to rules of this sort, it is possible to compute the meaning of an expression of whatever degree of complexity on the basis of the meanings of its parts. If the parts are simple, their meanings $I(a)$ and $I(\beta)$ will be given directly by lexical rules such as (8.1). If the parts are themselves complex, their meanings will themselves be derivable via compositional rules such as (8.2).

In this framework, interestingly, the meaning of a complex expression only depends upon two things: the meanings of its immediate constituents (the simpler expressions into which it can be analysed), and the way they are put together. Nothing else counts. In particular, the meaning of an expression does not depend upon the meanings of other expressions that are not its constituents, even if they occur in the same sentence or discourse. Nor can the meaning of a given expression depend upon the meaning of a more complex expression in which *it* occurs as a constituent. Or at least, this is standardly considered to be a consequence of compositionality. In a compositional language, we are told, the meaning of an expression depends upon the meanings of its parts, in a bottom-up fashion, but it does not depend upon the meaning of the whole to which it belongs, nor upon the meanings of the other parts of that same whole. 'Top-down' or 'lateral' influences on meaning are ruled out by the compositional procedure. Yet, according to some authors, such influences are precisely what we observe.

8.2 SEMANTIC FLEXIBILITY

A language exhibits *semantic flexibility* if the following condition is satisfied: in that language, the meaning of a word may vary from occurrence to occurrence, and it may vary, in particular, as a function of the other words it combines with. Through semantic flexibility, the meaning of an expression may well depend upon the meaning of the complex in which it occurs (top-down influence), and it may also depend upon the meaning of the other words that occur in the same complex (lateral influence).

One of the authors who has insisted that natural languages exhibit semantic flexibility is Jonathan Cohen in a series of papers in which he criticizes mainstream approaches in semantics. He gives examples such as the following:

> Consider 'drop' . . . in the sentences
>
> (8.3)   Most students here drop geography in their final year
>
> (where 'drop' means 'drop studying'),
>
> (8.4)   Most students here drop geography lectures in their final year
>
> (where 'drop' means 'drop attending'),
>
> (8.5)   Most students here drop geography lectures reading assignments in their final year
>
> (where 'drop' means 'drop executing')
>
> (8.6)   Most students here drop geography lectures reading assignments library-fees in their final year
>
> (where 'drop' means 'drop paying'), and so on indefinitely. If we accept that a sentence can be as long as we please, then there seems no predictable end to the variety of expressions that we can put meaningfully after 'drop', so as to impose a series of different meanings on the latter word. (Cohen, 1986: 227–8)

According to Cohen, the verb 'drop' takes on a different meaning in each of (8.3) to (8.6), and one of the things that determines the meaning it takes on is the noun phrase it combines with.

A similar type of example is provided by John Searle:

> The sort of thing that constitutes cutting the grass is quite different from, e.g., the sort of thing that constitutes cutting a cake. One way to see this is to imagine what constitutes obeying the order to cut something. If someone tells me to cut the grass and I rush out and stab it with a knife, or if I am ordered to cut the cake and I run over it with a lawnmower, in each case I will have failed to obey the order. (Searle, 1980: 222–3)

According to Searle, 'cut' means something different—has different satisfaction conditions—in 'cut the grass' and in 'cut the cake'; and that is because the meaning which the verb 'cut' takes on in a particular occurrence depends, inter alia, upon what is said to be cut. Similarly, the verb 'like' takes on a different meaning in (8.7) and (8.8):

(8.7)   he likes my sister

(8.8)   he likes roasted pork

The first sentence talks about 'affective' liking and the second about 'culinary' liking. There is as much difference between the two kinds of state as there is between the processes of cutting involving grass and cakes respectively.

The examples I have given so far all involve a transitive verb, the (exact) meaning of which depends upon the noun phrase that serves as its complement. An even more productive class of examples involves adjectives, the (exact) meaning of which depends upon the noun they modify. A good car is not good in exactly the same sense in which a good house is; a piece of luggage is not light in exactly the same sense in which a sound is light; a big mouse's way of being big differs, to some extent, from the way in which a big elephant is big; a pink grapefruit is not pink in the same way—under the same aspect—as a pink raincoat; a fast typist's way of being fast is not the same as a fast runner's way of being fast; and so on and so forth. In all cases the basic meaning of the adjective is fleshed out differently according to the noun it modifies.

Semantic flexibility and compositionality, as I have characterized them, seem to be mutually exclusive properties. As Jerry Fodor puts it,

> The compositionality thesis says that complex representations inherit their content from simple ones, *not vice versa*. But the [flexibility] thesis says that the content of a simple [representation] depends (inter alia?) on which complex [representation] it's embedded in. Clearly, it can't be that both are true. Something's gotta give. (Fodor, 2003: 96–7)

So, if we take natural languages to be compositional, for the reasons adduced above, it seems that we must re-analyse the alleged examples of semantic flexibility, so as to make them compatible with the compositionality thesis. I will pursue that line below. But we may also, following Cohen, give up the standard, 'insulationist' approach to semantic composition assumed by Fodor in favour of an alternative, 'interactionist' approach:

> According to the insulationist account the meaning of any one word that occurs in a particular sentence is insulated against interference from the meaning of any other word in the same sentence. On this view the composition of a sentence resembles the construction of a wall from bricks of different shapes. The result depends on the properties of the parts and the pattern of their combination. But just as each brick has exactly the same shape in every wall or part of a wall to which it is moved, so too each standard sense of a word or phrase is exactly the same in every sentence or part of a sentence in which it occurs. . .
>
> Interactionism makes the contradictory assertion: in some sentences in some languages the meaning of a word in a sentence may be determined in part by the word's verbal context in that sentence. . . . On this view the composition of a sentence is more like the construction of a wall from sand-bags of different kinds. Though the size, structure, texture and contents of a sand-bag restrict the range of shapes it can take on, the actual shape it adopts in a particular situation depends to a greater or lesser extent on the shapes adopted by other sand-bags in the wall, and the same sand-bag might take on a somewhat different shape in another all or in a different position in the same wall. (Cohen, 1986: 223)

According to Cohen 1986: 230), 'we cannot construct a semantics for any natural language along the same lines as a semantics for a formal system of any currently familiar kind. Projects like Davidson's or Montague's cannot succeed.' They cannot succeed precisely because 'artificial languages satisfy an insulationist account whereas natural languages require an interactionist one' (Cohen, 1986: 224).

Whatever Cohen may have had in mind in his talk of 'interactionist semantics', it is not clear to me that we have to depart from the standard compositional framework inherited from Davidson and Montague if we are to account for semantic flexibility. In this chapter, I will question the assumption that semantic flexibility is incompatible with compositionality, as Fodor claims in the above passage. I think it is not. It is true that, in a compositional language, the meaning of a complex expression only depends upon the meanings of its immediate constituents and the way they are put together: nothing else counts. This seems to rule out top-down and lateral influences of the sort the interactionist describes, but, I will argue, it does not really. When Fodor writes, 'The compositionality thesis says that complex representations inherit their content from simple ones, *not vice versa*', he overstates his case. It may well be that complex representations inherit their contents from simple ones, in a strictly bottom-up fashion, while *at the same time* simple representations have their contents determined, in part, by the complex expressions in which they occur. Or so I will argue. If this is true, then a language can exhibit both compositionality and semantic flexibility.

8.3 STANDING MEANING VS. OCCASION MEANING

In all the examples of semantic flexibility I have given, it is possible and desirable to draw a distinction between the *standing meaning* of the expression (verb or adjective) as fixed by the semantic conventions of the language, and the *occasion meaning* which the expression assumes on a particular occurrence. Thus 'cut' has a standing meaning in English, and that standing meaning is carried by all non-idiomatic occurrences of the word; yet we need not deny that 'cut' takes on a different occasion meaning in 'cut the grass' and in 'cut the cake'. Likewise for all the other examples: in all cases we can draw a distinction between standing meaning and occasion meaning. Note that the distinction does not apply to truly ambiguous expressions: in the case of 'bank', for example, there is no standing meaning which the word-type itself carries, whether it is taken in the financial or in the other sense. Rather, there are two distinct word-types, each with its own (standing) meaning.[2]

The standing meaning is the meaning which the word (type) has in isolation, in virtue of the conventions of the language. The occasion meaning is the meaning which an

---

[2] What about 'polysemous' expressions like 'light'? Here, I would argue, there is a standing meaning which the word 'light' carries in the language, even if the various senses the word can take in various environments ('light sound', 'light luggage', etc.) happen to be conventionalized and somehow pre-compiled in the lexicon. It would be a mistake, in the case of 'light', to treat the multiplicity of readings as a multiplicity of words (homonymy).

occurrence of the word takes on in a particular linguistic context. What varies as a function of the other words in the sentence is the occasion meaning, not the standing meaning. Does this variation, and the existence of both top-down and lateral influences on occasion meaning, conflict with compositionality? Arguably not.

Consider the 'cut' example. The word 'cut' has a certain meaning in the language. It also takes on a certain occasion meaning in the phrase 'cut the grass'. Let us assume, with Searle, that the meaning of 'cut the grass' is something like MOW THE GRASS. Thus the occasion meaning of 'cut' is the sense MOW, and it takes on this occasion meaning as a result of lateral/top-down influences. But this is compatible with compositionality, because—one may argue—the occasion meaning of 'cut' is nothing but *an aspect of the meaning of the complex verb phrase 'cut the grass'*. Now the meaning of the verb phrase depends upon the meaning of its various constituents, *including the complement 'the grass'*. Hence it is no surprise that the occasion meaning of 'cut' (*qua* aspect of the meaning of the verb phrase) depends upon the meaning of the determiner phrase that completes the verb, just as it depends upon the (standing) meaning of the verb itself, since both the verb and its complement are constituents of the verb phrase.

Following a suggestion which Searle traces to Ed Keenan,[3] let us assume that the standing meaning of 'cut' is a function from objects of cutting (the sorts of things one cuts: cakes, grass, etc.) to specific cutting operations relevant to those objects: mowing, slicing, etc. Let us assume, further, that the argument of the function is determined by the grammatical object of 'cut', and that the value of the function (the specific cutting operation at stake) is the occasion meaning of the verb in the verb phrase. Since the value of the function depends both upon the function and its argument, it is no surprise that the occasion meaning of 'cut' depends, in part, upon the object that is said to be cut. On this analysis the meaning of the complex 'cut the grass' depends upon the (standing) meanings of its parts in a strictly bottom-up manner. The phrase 'cut the grass' represents a certain process (mowing) operating on a certain object (the grass). The semantic contribution of the verb 'cut' is not directly the process of mowing but something more abstract, namely a function which takes that process as value for a given argument (the grass). The complement 'the grass' contributes both the argument to the function and the object the mowing process operates on. So what I called the occasion meaning of 'cut' is not *really* the meaning of the word 'cut', on this analysis: it is an aspect of the meaning of the complex phrase, contributed jointly by the verb 'cut' and its complement. The lateral/top-down dependence of the occasion meaning of 'cut' on the meaning of 'the grass' is nothing but a side effect of the compositional, bottom-up dependence of the meaning of the complex 'cut the grass' upon the (standing) meanings of its parts.

---

[3] According to Keenan's suggestion, as stated by Searle, 'just as . . . some mathematical functions take different interpretations depending on whether they take an even or an odd number as argument, so the word 'cut' has different interpretations . . . but these different interpretations are determined by the different arguments—grass, hair, cake, skin and cloth. . . . On this account it is the word "cut", together with the literal meaning of "grass", that determines that in "cut the grass" "cut" has a different interpretation from the literal meaning of "cut" in "cut the cake" ' (Searle, 1980: 224).

One way of fleshing out the suggested analysis would be to assign the following standing meaning to 'cut':

$$\lambda X\, \lambda x\, \lambda y\, [X(y)\ \&\ (\text{CUT IN THE MANNER OF } X)\, (x, y)]$$

The occasion meaning is what we get when the grammatical object of 'cut' provides a value for the higher order variable 'X'. If the object of cutting is said to be grass, we get:

$$\lambda x\, \lambda y\, [\text{GRASS}(y)\ \&\ (\text{CUT IN THE MANNER OF GRASS})\, (x, y)]$$

Thus 'cut' means CUT IN THE MANNER OF GRASS when its object is a y such that GRASS (y), and it means CUT IN THE MANNER OF CAKES when its object is a y such that CAKE (y). If I order someone to cut the grass, I order him to cut the grass in a specific manner, namely, in the manner one cuts grass (by mowing it). The order will not be satisfied if, as Searle imagines, my addressee rushes out and stabs the lawn with a knife.

The same sort of analysis applies to the other examples. Consider 'big mouse': a big mouse is not big in the same sense in which a big elephant is; for an elephant just as big as a big mouse would not count as a big elephant. The occasion meaning of 'big' clearly depends upon the noun it modifies. But this can be accounted for by assuming that the constant meaning of 'big' is a function the value of which is the occasion meaning of 'big'. That constant meaning can be represented as an open predicate, BIG FOR AN X, where the free higher order variable stands for the argument of the function; the occasion meaning will be the predicate we get when the free variable is assigned a particular value, which value will be determined by the noun which the adjective modifies.

Standing meaning of 'big'
$$\lambda X\, \lambda x\, [X(x)\ \&\ (\text{BIG FOR AN } X)\, (x)]$$

On this analysis the occasion meaning of 'big' (e.g. BIG FOR A MOUSE in 'big mouse', or BIG FOR AN ELEPHANT in 'big elephant') is nothing but an aspect of the (standing) meaning of the complex noun phrase 'big mouse' or 'big elephant':

Standing meaning of 'big mouse'
$$\lambda X\, \lambda x\, [X(x)\ \&\ (\text{BIG FOR AN } X)\, (x)]\, (\text{MOUSE}) = \lambda x\, [\text{MOUSE}\, (x)\ \&\ (\text{BIG FOR A MOUSE})\, (x)]$$

That explains why, like the standing meaning of the complex noun phrase, the occasional meaning of the adjective depends, in part, upon the meaning of the noun it modifies.

8.4 COUNTEREXAMPLES

As usual, the devil is in the details, and a lot of details would have to be provided to make the suggested analysis worthy of serious consideration (especially when it comes to the verb–object construction). But the effort can be spared because, evidently, the analysis does not work. Even if we fix the linguistic environment (i.e. the modified noun, or the object of the verb), the occasion meaning of 'big' or 'cut' may still vary; this shows that the variation is not due merely to the linguistic environment, contrary to what the analysis claims. If we maintain a functional analysis of the standing meaning of 'big' and 'cut', and represent that meaning by means of an open predicate BIG FOR AN X or in CUT IN THE MANNER OF X as suggested, we must acknowledge that the value of the free variable is not fully determined by the linguistic context, but may be overriden by extralinguistic (or extrasentential) information.

Heim and Kratzer give the following example to show that a small elephant is not necessarily an elephant that is small for an elephant:

> Imagine we had first introduced a scenario populated with an army of monsters like King Kong. We might then have said something like 'Jumbo doesn't have a chance; he's only a small elephant', and this could have been true even if Jumbo were as large as or even larger than most other elephants. (Heim and Kratzer 1998: 71)

In this context the implicit comparison class for 'small' is the class of monsters of the relevant sort, not the class of elephants, even if the noun which 'small' modifies is 'elephant'. This shows that the domain of the function is not the class of objects denoted by the modified noun, but a comparison class determined by the context. In central cases that comparison class will be the class of objects denoted by the modified noun, but there are other possible cases in which it is not.

Searle also provides counterexamples to the analysis:

> It is easy to imagine circumstances in which 'cut' in 'cut the grass' would have the same interpretation it has in 'cut the cake', even though none of the semantic contents of the words has changed. Suppose you and I run a sod farm where we sell strips of grass turf to people who want a lawn in a hurry. . . . Suppose I say to you, 'Cut half an acre of grass for this customer'; I might mean not that you should *mow* it, but that you should slice it into strips as you could cut a cake or a loaf of bread. (Searle, 1980: 224–5)

'Cut the grass' here does not mean CUT THE GRASS IN THE MANNER OF GRASS, as it would under the suggested analysis. This shows that the value of the free variable in the open predicate CUT THE GRASS IN THE MANNER OF X (or, more straightforwardly perhaps, CUT THE GRASS IN MANNER m) need not be determined by the linguistic object of the verb: it is determined pragmatically and may but need not correspond to the linguistic object of the verb. Searle gives a parallel example in which 'cut the cake' would mean something like MOW THE CAKE:

> Suppose we run a bakery where due to our super yeast strain our cakes grow upwards uncontrollably. 'Keep cutting those cakes!', I shout to the foreman, meaning not that he should slice them up but that he should keep trimming the tops off. (Searle, 1980: 225)

Similar counterexamples can be constructed for all the cases of semantic flexibility I have mentioned. Thus, in an appropriate context, 'he likes my sister' might be interpreted in the culinary sense of 'like' (if the referent of 'he' is a cannibal); or 'good car' in the sense of a car that is a good place to inhabit (if the speaker is a homeless person).

I conclude that semantic flexibility is ultimately a matter of *context dependence*. The linguistic context plays the role it does because it is a prominent aspect of the context in which the expression occurs; but non-linguistic aspects of the context are also relevant, as the examples show.

8.5 CONTEXT DEPENDENCE

To deal with indexicals and other context-sensitive expressions, we need to revise, or rather enrich, the framework set up at the beginning of this chapter. In some cases the content of an expression cannot be assigned directly by means of a lexical rule such as (8.1), repeated below :

(8.1) $I(a) = m$

The content of a context-sensitive expression depends on the context of utterance, so what we need is a context-sensitive lexical rule such as (8.1*)

(8.1*) $I(a)_c = f(c)$

The constant meaning, or 'character', of the expression a determines a function f which, given a context c, returns a certain content $f(c)$ as semantic value for the expression. For example, the character of 'I' maps the context of utterance to what Kaplan calls the agent of the context, namely the speaker. Similarly, the character of a demonstrative d determines a function which, given a (non-defective) context c, returns the object demonstrated/intended by the user of d in c as semantic value. In all such cases, we need (something like) the Kaplanian distinction between 'character' and 'content'. The character is the constant meaning of the expression, represented as a function from contexts to contents, and the content, represented in (8.1*), is the value which the character determines given a particular context.[4]

Instead of two types of rules, (8.1) and (8.1*), covering the cases which are and those which are not context-sensitive, we can use a single type of rule, namely (8.1*), by considering the function f as a constant whenever the expression a at issue is not context-sensitive. Thus if a means m in a context-independent manner, $I(a)_c = f(c) = m$, for all contexts c.

---

[4] In addition to lexical context sensitivity, we may also need to make room for *constructional* context sensitivity, i.e. for cases in which the mode of combination maps the contents of the parts to the content of the whole only with respect to the context of utterance. Noun–noun compounds in English provide a prima facie case of that sort. Even if we know what a burglar is and what a nightmare is, we don't yet know, out of the blue, what a burglar nightmare is, for the value of the complex phrase 'burglar nightmare' depends upon the context in addition to the contents of its parts. A burglar nightmare is a nightmare that bears a certain relation R to burglars. What the relevant relation R is depends upon the context and the speaker's intentions. To keep things simple, I will ignore constructional context sensitivity in what follows. See Weiskopf (2007) for a treatment of compound nominals in the spirit of the present chapter.

If, as I suggested at the end of Section 8.4, semantic flexibility is a matter of context dependence, the distinction between standing meaning and occasion meaning turns out to be a particular case of the Kaplanian distinction between character and content. On this approach, we can still treat the standing meaning of an expression such as 'big' or 'cut' as functional, as it was in the previous account, but the argument of the function no longer corresponds to the linguistic expression with which the expression at issue combines; rather, the function takes the context (or some aspect of the context) as argument. In the case of 'small' or 'big', the argument to the function is a comparison class provided by the context. The standing meaning of 'big' can still be represented as BIG FOR AN X, but now 'X' will be assigned a value in context much as a demonstrative or a free pronoun is assigned a value in context.

Let us call this new approach the contextual theory. How different is it from the previous approach? Both draw a distinction between standing meaning and occasion meaning, but they treat the occasion meaning differently:

- The first theory says that the occasion meaning is not (really) the meaning of the expression at issue, but rather an aspect of the meaning of the complex phrase in which that expression occurs. Thus the predicate BIG FOR A MOUSE is not contributed by the word 'big' in 'big mouse' but by the complex phrase 'big mouse' itself. In 'big mouse', 'big' contributes BIG FOR AN X and 'mouse' contributes both the value of 'X' and the predicate MOUSE, in such a way that the complex phrase contributes the conjunctive predicate MOUSE & BIG FOR A MOUSE. (I assume that adjectival modification is interpreted by means of predicate conjunction.) The predicate BIG FOR A MOUSE here is an aspect or part of the meaning of the complex phrase 'big mouse', determined by the meanings of its various constituents, including the expression with which the adjective 'big' combines in the phrase.

- The contextual theory sees the occasion meaning as the context-dependent content of the expression, determined by (1) the standing meaning (character) of the expression and (2) the context of the utterance. Here the predicate BIG FOR A MOUSE is truly contributed by the adjective 'big' in 'big mouse', but it is contributed in a context-dependent manner. The standing meaning or character of 'big' is a function mapping a contextually provided comparison class to the property of being big for that class, that is, bigger than most members of the class. That property is the content which the adjective carries in context. Now the relevant comparison class may be contextually provided by *linguistic* means. The noun 'mouse' denotes the class of mice and makes that class highly salient. Unless an alternative comparison class is made more salient by extralinguistic or extrasentential means (as in the Heim–Kratzer scenario), 'big' in 'big mouse' will be contextually interpreted as contributing the predicate BIG FOR A MOUSE. Since 'mouse' contributes MOUSE and adjectival modification is interpreted by means of predicate conjunction, the complex phrase 'big mouse' contributes the conjunctive predicate MOUSE & BIG FOR A MOUSE.

In this theory the content of the complex phrase is a function of the contents of its parts, in a strictly bottom-up manner; but the content of the parts is, or may be, context-dependent, and the linguistic context in which an expression occurs is an aspect of the context which may influence its content. Lateral and top-down influences are therefore possible—the content carried by a particular expression may depend upon the other expressions with which it combines—but this is compatible with the fact that the content of the whole depends upon the contents of its parts in a strictly bottom-up manner: indeed, on the picture I have sketched, the content of the whole depends upon the contents of its parts (and their mode of combination) *and nothing else*.

8.6 SATURATION AND MODULATION

Though it is on the right track, the contextual theory as stated above suffers from a serious limitation. It unduly restricts the phenomenon of semantic flexibility to a small range of expressions that are indexical-like in the sense that their linguistic meaning is 'gappy' and stands in need of contextual completion. Indexicals need to be contextually assigned a value, and so do under-specified expressions such as 'burglar nightmare': the intended relation R needs to be contextually specified. In all such cases the standing meaning of the expression may be represented as involving a free variable to which a value must be contextually assigned, and the expression carries a definite content only with respect to such a contextual assignment. It is plausible that adjectives like 'small' fall into that category and involve covert reference to a comparison class or standard, but what about 'cut'? Do we really want to say that the meaning of 'cut' in English is gappy and involves an implicit reference to a contextually given manner of cutting? Is the word 'cut' in English covertly indexical?

I do not think it is. I assume that the standing meaning of 'cut' is something like EFFECT A LINEAR SEPARATION AFFECTING THE INTEGRITY OF (SOME OBJECT) BY MEANS OF AN EDGED INSTRUMENT. There is no free variable here. To be sure, the context may specify all sorts of aspects of the cutting operation and flesh it out in various ways (as in the Searle examples), yet I doubt that the lexical meaning of the expression conventionally singles out a particular dimension (a 'manner of cutting') such that the context *must* provide a definite value on that dimension.

Consider, as an analogy, the Rumelhart example I discuss in *Literal Meaning* (Recanati 2004: 73, 105–6):

(8.9)   The policeman stopped the car

We naturally interpret this as meaning that the policeman stopped the car by addressing an appropriate signal to the driver, just as we naturally interpret 'John cut the cake' as meaning that John sliced it. As Rumelhart points out, however, a different interpretation emerges if we imagine a context in which the policeman *is* the driver of the car: such a context provides for a totally different 'manner of stopping the car' on the policeman's part. Do we want to say that the transitive verb 'stop' in English covertly refers to a manner of stopping which the context is to specify? Of course not. Transitive 'stop' means CAUSE TO STOP, and this can be fleshed out in all sorts of ways, yet the fleshing out process is different from the saturation process mandated by indexicals and other expressions whose standing meaning is gappy and requires contextual completion. Indeed we can construct a context in which (8.9) would mean that the policeman stopped the car *in some way or other*, indifferently. No such option exists for indexicals or under-specified expressions, which do not carry a definite content unless the free variable is assigned a definite value in context.

In the Rumelhart example the context suggests a particular manner of stopping on the agent's part. If the contextual suggestion is conveyed by linguistic means—as it is in (8.9), where the phrase 'the policeman' is what evokes the traffic-regulation frame and thereby makes the relevant manner of stopping cars salient—we have a case of semantic flexibility: the interpretation of 'stop' is affected by the subject of the verb. That it is is established by the contrast between (8.9) and (8.10) when both are taken out of context:

(8.10)   The driver stopped the car

So there is semantic flexibility in these examples; yet I do not want to treat transitive 'stop' as indexical or semantically under-specified. And the same thing holds for 'cut'. Abstract though it is, the linguistic meaning of these verbs is not gappy in the way in which the meaning of an indexical or under-specified expression is.

Of course, I may be wrong about 'stop' or 'cut'. But my point is more general. I think there may be semantic flexibility even if the expression whose occasion meaning is affected by the neighbouring words is not context-sensitive in the way in which indexicals and semantically under-specified expressions are. Consider another example I discuss in *Literal Meaning* (Recanati 2004: 34–6):

(8.11)   The city is asleep

Because of the apparent category violation (a city is not the sort of thing that sleeps) either 'asleep' must be interpreted in a metaphorical or extended sense as meaning QUIET AND SHOWING LITTLE ACTIVITY, or 'the city' has to be interpreted metonymically as referring to the inhabitants of the city. Either way, how we interpret one expression depends upon how we interpret the other. This is semantic flexibility once again, but of course we do not want to account for that type of example in terms of context sensitivity and the character/content distinction. Rather, we take this case to involve a departure from literal meaning, resulting from some form of coercion. Let us assume that (8.11) is interpreted by giving to 'asleep' the extended sense QUIET AND SHOWING LITTLE ACTIVITY. That is not the literal sense of 'asleep'. The literal sense of 'asleep' is ASLEEP, and there is nothing fancy about it (no hidden indexical, no free variable, etc.). In this particular case, the proper way of cashing out the distinction between standing meaning and occasion meaning is not by means of the distinction between the expression's character and its context-dependent content, but, rather, by means of the distinction between the expression's meaning in the language and the non-literal sense it takes on through coercion in the context at hand.

In *Literal Meaning* and elsewhere I drew a systematic distinction between two types of contextual process possibly affecting truth-conditions: the (mandatory) process of 'saturation' through which indexicals and free variables in logical form are assigned a contextual value, and the (optional) process of 'modulation' through which the meaning *m* of an expression is mapped to a distinct meaning *g(m)*, where '*g*' is a pragmatic function. Metaphorical and metonymical interpretations result from the operation of such pragmatic functions, and the argument to the function may be the meaning of *any* expression, whether or not it is 'context-sensitive' in the standard sense in which indexicals and semantically under-specified expressions are. Another type of pragmatic function, involved in so-called 'free enrichment', maps the meaning of an expression to a more specific meaning. One way of accounting for the 'stop' and 'cut' cases would be to argue that the standing meaning of the verb (CAUSE TO STOP; EFFECT A LIN-EAR SEPARATION, ETC.) is understood in context in a more specific sense, through the provision of a particular manner of stopping or of cutting. On this view the context is indeed what makes the relevant manner of stopping or cutting salient and forces it into the interpretation, but the contextual process at issue in the generation of that occasion meaning is not saturation, but modulation. Again, I may be wrong about 'cut' and 'stop', but my point is more general and can be put as follows: we may get the sort of contextual influence on the interpretation of a lexical item which gives rise to the phenomenon of semantic flexibility even if the expression whose interpretation contextually varies in this way is not indexical or context-sensitive in the standard sense. If semantic flexibility is to be accounted for by appealing to contextual processes, as I have suggested (Section 8.5), there is no reason to restrict the type of contextual process at issue to saturation. Modulation plays exactly the same role: just as the value contextually assigned to an indexical or free variable may be influenced by the linguistic context, the modulated value which a given expression takes in context may also be influenced by the linguistic environment, that is, by the other words with which the expression combines, as in (8.9).

8.7 COMPOSITIONALITY AND MODULATION

Where does this leave us with respect to the compositionality issue? If the foregoing is correct, we cannot maintain that the meaning of a complex phrase is (wholly) deter-mined by the meanings of its parts and their mode of combination. As Searle points out, the satisfaction conditions of the imperative sentence 'cut the grass!' may vary even though the standing meanings *and* Kaplanian contents of all the words in that sentence are fixed, as well as their mode of combination. So the interpretation of the complex— insofar as it determines satisfaction conditions—is not a function of the 'meanings' (in one of the standard senses: character or content) of its parts and their mode of combination.

At this point there are two main options, corresponding to two positions in the philosophy of language: minimalism and contextualism. For the minimalist, there is a sharp distinction between semantic meaning (including Kaplanian 'content') and speaker's meaning. Insofar as modulation—hence speaker's meaning—enters into the determination of satisfaction conditions, it is not incumbent upon semantics to account for satisfaction conditions and the content of speech acts more generally: the compositional machinery is only supposed to deal with semantic meaning. (See Cappelen and Lepore (2005) for an articulation of this defeatist position.) For the contextualist, on the contrary, we should do our best to account for the intuitive truth- and satisfaction-conditions of utterances, and to that effect we may have to liberalize the notion of meaning/content to the point of blurring the semantics/pragmatics distinction.

The compositional framework as presented so far only makes room for those forms of semantic flexibility which arise from (lexical or constructional) context-sensitivity. Since these are not the only forms of semantic flexibility we have to account for, the right thing to do, it seems to me, is to revise/enrich the framework once again, in the spirit of the contextualist position. Examples like Searle's defeat compositionality (by showing that the interpretation of the complex is not a function of the meanings of its parts and their mode of combination) provided we take 'the meanings of the parts' in one of the standard senses (character or content). Why not, then, take the meanings of the parts to be their *modulated* meanings, and attempt to preserve compositionality in this manner?

Let us define a function *mod* taking as argument an expression *e* and the context *c* in which it occurs: the value of *mod* is the particular modulation function *g* that is contextually salient/relevant/appropriate for the interpretation of that expression in that context. For example, in (8.11), we can easily imagine that the context *c* in which the expression 'the city' occurs renders a certain metonymic function g_{513} from cities to their inhabitants salient and relevant to the interpretation of that expression. With respect to such a context we get:

mod ('the city', c) = g_{513}
mod ('the city', c) $(I(\text{'the city'})_c)$ = g_{513} (THE CITY) = THE INHABITANTS OF THE CITY

The suggestion, then, is that we should take the modulated meaning of an expression a in context c, viz. *mod* (a, c) $(I (a)_c)$, as the building block which our compositional machinery requires to deliver the correct interpretations for complex expressions.[5] Accordingly, we can keep the type of lexical rule we have worked with so far, viz:

(8.1*) $I(a)_c = f(c)$ (where '*f*' is the character of expression a)

---

[5] This suggestion can be traced back to Sag (1981; and to Nunberg's ideas, which Sag attempted to formalize).

but we must change the format of compositional rules so as to make room for modulation. Instead of

(8.2) $I(\alpha * \beta)_c = f(I(\alpha)_c, I(\beta)_c)$

we should use something like

(8.2*) $I(\alpha * \beta)_c = f(mod(\alpha, \ c^1)(I(\alpha)_{c^1}), mod(\beta, \ c^2)(I(\beta)_{c^2})) = f(g_1(I(\alpha)_{c^1}), g_2$
          $(I(\beta)_{c^2}))$

Here 'c^1' and 'c^2' correspond to sub-parts of the context c in which the complex expression $\alpha * \beta$ is used. (I assume that if a complex expression $\alpha * \beta$ is used in a context c, each of its constituents is used in a sub-part of c, e.g. α in c^1 and β in c^2). The gs correspond to pragmatic modulation functions which the context makes salient. If no modulation is contextually appropriate and the expression receives its literal interpretation, the value of *mod* will be the identity function: literalness is treated as a special case of (zero-) modulation. Thus understood, the formula says that *the interpretation (content) of a complex expression $\alpha * \beta$ is a function of the modulated meanings of its parts and the way they are put together (and nothing else).*

For simple expressions there is a clear distinction between their content $I(\alpha)_c$ determined by lexical rules such as (8.1*) and their modulated meaning $mod(\alpha, \ c)(I(\alpha)_c)$. What about complex expressions such as $\alpha * \beta$? Does the distinction between content and modulated meaning apply to them as well? Of course: a complex expression e can be a constituent in a more complex expression e+, and we need the modulated meaning of e to serve as a building block in constructing a content for e+. We must therefore generalize the notion of modulated meaning to all expressions. To reach the right level of generality, Pagin suggests that we define a function of modulated-interpretation M recursively.[6] This can be done as follows:

$M(e, c) = mod(e, c) \ (I(e)_c)$

Since the content $I(e)_c$ of a complex expression $e = {}^*(e_1, \ldots, \ e_n)$ is a function of the modulated meanings of its parts, this definition of modulated meaning entails the recursive clause

$M({}^*(e_1, \ldots, \ e_n), \ c) = mod({}^*(e_1, \ldots, \ e_n), \ c) \ (f(M(e_1, \ c^1), \ldots, \ M(e_n, \ c^n)))$

As before, * is a syntactic mode of combination, and f is the composition function of the ordinary sort corresponding to that mode of combination. The recursive clause says that the modulated meaning of a complex expression results from applying a contextually appropriate modulation function to the result of composing the modulated meanings of its parts. So the distinction between content and modulated meaning applies to complex expressions as well as to simple ones: the content of a complex expression is a function of the modulated meanings of its parts, and the modulated meaning of the expression results from modulating the content thus determined.

---

[6] See Pagin and Pelletier (2007: 46–50) for an elaboration.

In this framework, do we really achieve compositionality? Not in the strong sense in which compositionality is standardly understood. As we have seen, the *content* of a complex is a function of the *modulated meanings* of its parts (and the way they are put together), but it is not a function of the *contents* of its parts (and the way they are put together). Similarly, the *modulated meaning* of the complex is not a function of the *modulated meanings* of its parts (and the way they are put together): for a given complex with a given content (determined by the modulated meanings of its parts and they way they are put together) can still be modulated in different ways.

Still, as Pagin (2005) and Westerståhl (this volume) point out, there is a sense in which a weak form of compositionality is achieved. Take the modulated meaning of the complex: we can say that it is a function of the modulated meanings of the parts (and the way they are put together) *plus, in addition, the context which determines how the content of the whole itself is modulated.* The same trick—letting the composition function take the context as extra argument—works for the contents of expressions as well as for their modulated meanings: we can say that the content of a complex expression $\alpha * \beta$ is a function of the contents of its parts (and the way they are put together) *plus the context* which provides for the modulation of these contents (Westerståhl, this volume). As Pagin puts it, 'having the context itself as an extra argument cannot be objected to as violating compositionality, since the meaning function takes a context argument to begin with' (Pagin 2005: 313).

8.8 IS CONTEXTUALISM A THREAT TO COMPOSITIONALITY?

Jerry Fodor has argued that contextualism threatens compositionality. His argument runs as follows. Even though the sense of an equivocal expression depends upon the linguistic context (e.g. the sentence) in which it occurs, this does not prevent it from serving as a building block in the construction of the meaning of that sentence, as compositionality requires. The expression *has* a definite sense, which the context reveals, and that sense has the stability required to serve as a building block. An insuperable problem arises, however, as soon as we generalize this type of context-dependence, as the contextualist does. Take an expression α and assume its modulated meaning depends (inter alia) upon the meaning of its complex host. The meaning of the host itself is liable to vary, because of modulation, depending on *its* host: and so on indefinitely (as Cohen argues in the passage quoted in Section 8.2). So the meaning of α will never stabilize: there is unending equivocation, 'equivocation that can't be resolved', and it 'undermine[s] the compositionality of English' (Fodor, 2003: 99).

Insofar as I understand the argument, it does not go through. Contextual modulation provides for *potentially* unending meaning variation, but never gives rise to any *actual* unending meaning variation. Meaning eventually stabilizes, making compositionality possible, because the (linguistic as well as extralinguistic) context, however big, is always finite.

The contextualist emphasizes the unending potential for variation in order to point out that the (modulated) meaning of an expression always depends upon the context and cannot be fixed simply by complexifying the expression and 'making everything explicit'. Thus the contextualist gives the following sort of example in support of the irreducibly contextual character of the interpretation process. 'John took out his key and opened the door' is interpreted in such a way that John is understood to have opened the door *with the key*; this we get through modulation of 'open the door' which is understood via the contextual provision of a specific manner of opening. Can we make that explicit in the sentence, so as to get rid of the context dependence? Not quite: If we say 'he opened the door with the key' the new material gives rise to new underdeterminacies because it, too, can be variously modulated. The key may have been used as an axe to break the door open as well as inserted into the keyhole (Searle, 1992: 182). And if we make the way of using the key explicit, further indeterminacies will arise, and different meanings will emerge through modulation. However, when language is actually used and something is said, there is a definite context (both linguistic and extralinguistic) and it is finite. In virtue of the context, the various expressions used in it get a definite meaning. No instability is to be feared and, *pace* Fodor, contextualism is perfectly compatible with the demands of compositionality.[7]

[7] Since 2004 I have had opportunities to present the material in this paper in conferences, workshops or colloquia in many places, including Gargnano, Paris, Montreal, Kingston, Oxford, Geneva, Lisbon, Stanford, Cadiz, St Andrews, and Lund. I am indebted to the organizers of those events for inviting me, to those who attended for their questions and objections, to the editors of this volume and the anonymous referees for their comments, and, last but not least, to the European Research Council for supporting my research in this area and providing funding under the European Community's Seventh Framework Programme (FP7/2007–2013/ERC grant agreement no. 229 441—CCC). I am especially grateful to Gennaro Chierchia, Peter Pagin, Josh Armstrong, Martin Jönsson, and Dag Westerståhl for comments and discussions which inspired me.

....

CHAPTER 9

COMPOSITIONALITY IN KAPLAN STYLE SEMANTICS

....

DAG WESTERSTÅHL

9.1 INTRODUCTION

....

At first sight, the idea of compositionality doesn't seem to sit well with a semantics taking (extralinguistic) context seriously. The semantic value (meaning, content, extension, etc.) of the whole is supposed to be determined by the values of the immediate parts and the mode of composition, but what if input from context is required? It would appear that—unless context is *fixed*—compositionality could only apply to rather abstract semantic values, themselves functions from contexts to other values. However, the notion of compositionality *generalizes* to cases where the value is assigned to a syntactic item *and* a contextual item. In fact, it does so in two natural but distinct ways.

The last observation is implicit in some of the literature, and explicit in a few places.[1] Here I present it in a systematic way, within the framework of what I shall call *Kaplan style semantics*. This framework—despite the label—is not strictly tied to Kaplan's particular way of doing semantics (cf. Kaplan, 1989); rather, it is a *format* that covers his as well as many other theorists' preferred accounts of context-dependent meaning. For example, besides the abstract semantic values mentioned above, which essentially are what Kaplan called *character*, it applies when taking intermediate levels of (functional or structured) *content* or *intension* as values, as well as *extensions*.

The setup can furthermore be adapted to recent *relativist* modifications of Kaplan's original framework. It also applies, perhaps surprisingly, to the (controversial) phenomenon of *unarticulated constituents*, and to so-called *modulation* or *pragmatic intrusion*

---

[1] Notably Pagin (2005), Pagin and Pelletier (2007), Pagin and Westerståhl (2010a), and Recanati (this volume). See also footnote 28.

(Recanati, this volume). In addition, *situation semantics* can be made to fit this format, as can several other early or recent ideas about context dependence (in a wide sense) from the literature.[2]

Within this general format there are thus several ways of associating semantic values with expressions (and contexts), preferred by different theorists. *For each of these*, the issue of compositionality can be raised. My aim here is not to suggest any particular way of doing semantics, or to judge which kind of semantics is likely to be compositional, but only to map out the possibilities, and the logical relations between them.[3]

9.2 KAPLAN STYLE SEMANTICS

9.2.1 Context and circumstance

By *Kaplan style semantics* I mean a semantic theory permitting (but not necessitating) a distinction between two kinds of contextual factors: in Kaplan's terminology, used here, *contexts* (of utterance) and *circumstances* (of evaluation). Formally, I assume that a set

CU

of utterance contexts and a set

$CIRC$

of circumstances are given. Exactly what goes into the two compartments varies. Kaplan's (1989) Logic of Demonstratives associates with each context c in CU a quadruple $\langle c_A, c_T, c_P, c_W \rangle$ of the *agent, time, position*, and *world of c*, and circumstances are pairs of times and worlds: $CIRC = T \times W$. For Lewis (1980) circumstances—which he calls *indices*—are also tuples of times, worlds, locations, etc., whereas contexts are possible situations in which (normally) someone says something: parts of worlds, rich in structure and not reducible to tuples of independently specifiable parameters.

Kaplan and Lewis agreed that both factors are needed: their basic truth relation is

φ is true at context c in circumstance d.

Indeed, most semanticists in the model-theoretic tradition since Montague have found some such distinction necessary, including Montague himself (1970*b*: 228). A common criterion for putting a feature in *CIRC* is that it is *shiftable*: some linguistic operator 'shifts' the time or world, say, of the context to another time or world, as the perfect past tense and the modal 'necessary' in English can be taken to do. But some features

---

[2] Recanati (2007) mentions Aristotle, the Stoics, Bar-Hillel, Prior, Hintikka, Evans, Dummett, Stalnaker, Barwise, and Perry, among others, as well as participants in the recent debate about contextualism vs. relativism; see Section 9.4.5 below.

[3] As noted, I only deal with extralinguistic context here. For a treatment of linguistic context along similar lines, see Pagin and Westerståhl (2010*c*).

of context, such as the agent/speaker or position/location denoted by the indexicals 'I' and 'here', respectively, cannot be shifted; to take Kaplan's example, even if I try, I cannot make

(9.1)   In some contexts it is true that I am not tired now.

say that some other person than me is not tired at some other time than the time of my speaking. I come back to this issue in Section 9.6.3.

A related point often made is that features of contexts cannot be arbitrarily replaced by other features of the same kind. If you replace the *time*, say, of a context *c* with another time but change nothing else, you may not end up with a context at all; for example if the new time is one when the *speaker* of *c* wasn't born. Kaplan's contexts, even though theoretical constructs, are *proper* in this sense: the speaker must *exist* in the world of the context and be *at* the place of the context. Circumstances, on the other hand, are not required to obey such constraints.

Other formats impose no restrictions. *Two-dimensional* accounts, introduced in semantics in Kamp (1971) and systematized in Segerberg (1973), often identify *CU* and *CIRC*. For example, with both equal to a set T of time points, one can express that 'sentence φ uttered at t_1 is true at t_2', where $t_1, t_2 \in T$. Two- or multi-dimensional accounts are now a well established tool in intensional logic and formal semantics, not only as a means of dealing with context-dependence; cf. García-Carpintero and Macia (2006).

In this chapter, the point is not how contexts and circumstances are distinguished, but the semantic import of the distinction. The contrast is with what is sometimes called *index semantics*, where all contextual factors are lumped together (say, in one long tuple of features) and play the same role.[4] It will be important, however, that shiftable features (in the above sense) go into the circumstances.[5]

9.2.2 Content and character

Once the distinction between the two kinds of contextual factors is made, it is possible—though not obligatory—to identify a level of *content*, as that which you obtain by fixing the utterance context, but not the circumstances. I use Kaplan's term here, and likewise I will use *character* for the function taking expressions to contents.

Again, this terminology is meant to cover a host of related notions. There are Carnap's *intensions*; originally used for functions from worlds to extensions but often extended

---

[4] This was the advice of Scott (1970), though, as noted, not many semanticists have followed it (at least not for very long). But even index semantics could be seen as compatible with the framework here: just let one of *CU* and *CIRC* contain exactly one fixed element.

[5] Following Kaplan and Lewis, Stanley (2005: 147–52) argues that *only* shiftable features should go into the circumstances. MacFarlane (2009) disagrees, and indeed relativists place judges or standards, which are not thought to be shiftable, in that compartment; cf. Section 9.4.5. My concern here is with the inverse claim: that *all* shiftable contextual factors belong to the circumstances. As we will see in Section 9.6.3, this is not just a terminological matter.

to take other contextual factors as arguments.[6] Another terminology adapts Quine's (1960) distinction between standing and occasion sentences to *standing* and *occasion meaning*.[7] Recanati (2007) uses the Stoic *lekton* for propositional content, but also Barwise's term *Austinian proposition* (Barwise and Etchemendy, 1987). This marks a distinction *within* the notion of content, which requires a comment.

Kaplanian contents are *incomplete* in the sense that you need a circumstance to arrive at the *extension*—in the propositional case, a truth value. This was also true of the Stoic *lekta*: a *time* was needed for a truth value. But it contrasts starkly with Frege's thoughts or Russell's propositions, which are absolutely true or false. So it seems we should simply distinguish *complete* and *incomplete* propositions, and similarly for subsentential contents.

But there appears to be a complication: many regard propositions where only the *world* is not fixed as already complete, whereas if also a time, or a location, or a standard of taste, is required to obtain a truth value, the proposition is incomplete. It is an interesting issue what, if anything, gives worlds such a privileged status, but it is not one we need to resolve here.[8] *By definition*, contents are incomplete, precisely in the sense that you (normally) need a circumstance to get an extension (or, in the structured case, to get something that *has* an extension), even if that circumstance is just a world.

Note that although character and content *can* depend on context and circumstance, respectively, they don't have to. There will usually be expressions, such as proper names or mathematical predicates, whose extension is *independent* of one or both kinds of contextual factors. In the present setup, these are represented as *constant* functions (or structured objects without any 'holes'; see Section 9.3.2). In this sense we can think of Fregean or Russellian semantics, where *all* expressions are treated in this way, as a limiting case of Kaplan style semantics (see also Section 9.5.2).

To repeat, what I call Kaplan style semantics is *not* a formalization of any particular semantic theory. It is a framework that *fits* many different accounts. The fit may be more or less rough, but (I claim) for the discussion of context-dependent forms of compositionality, the distinctions made in this framework are all you need.

---

[6] The subject index of the volume mentioned above (García-Carpintero and Macia, 2006) lists 18 different kinds of intension.

[7] 'Standing meaning', essentially for character, is used, for example, in Heck (2001), Pagin (2005), King and Stanley (2005), and Recanati, this volume.

[8] Most semanticists in the possible worlds tradition regard functions from possible worlds to truth-values as complete, in particular, as entities that can be the objects of propositional attitudes. For example, Recanati's *lekta* are called incomplete, whereas Austinian propositions are complete, but can be true in one world and false in another. One argument is that you get an absolute truth value by plugging in the *actual* world (cf. Evans, 1985), the idea being that there is just one actual world but lots of available times. To a *presentist*, on the other hand, the actual time has the same status as the actual world. And some theorists (e.g. MacFarlane, 2007) consider speakers' utterances in non-actual worlds. Glanzberg (2009) attempts a general argument that worlds aren't really an important part of the semantic analysis. He says (his footnote 2), however, that a similar argument would go through for world-time pairs, whereas the issue here is whether worlds have a different status than, e.g., times.

9.2.3 Extensions and models

I also assume there is a given set

M

of *extensions*. Usually, formal semantics employs the notion of a *model* which, besides supplying the sets *CU*, *CIRC*, and a domain M_0 of individuals, also *interprets* the non-logical atomic expressions of the language. For example, the name *Saul* could denote a fixed element of M_0, in all contexts and under all circumstances, and the predicate *red* might be interpreted, in all contexts, as a certain function from *CIRC* to the power set of M_0 (i.e. as having a fixed content).

For almost all of this chapter, it is not necessary to mention models (the exception is Claim (III) in Section 9.6.2). We may think of a model $\mathcal{M}_0$ as *fixed*, and M as the set of all semantic objects (over M_0) that expressions can refer to in this model. For example, M could be a type-theoretic universe built up from M_0.

9.3 CONTENT

To repeat, a *content* yields, by definition, for each $d \in CIRC$, an extension in M. There are two main ways in which it is supposed to do this.

9.3.1 Contents as functions

The simplest notion of content is that of a *function* from *CIRC* to M. I use $[X \longrightarrow Y]$ for the set of functions from X to Y. Thus,

(9.2) $CONT = [CIRC \longrightarrow M]$

In particular, if extensions of sentences are truth-values, the set of *propositions* is

(9.3) $PROP = [CIRC \longrightarrow \{T, F\}] \subseteq CONT$

Contents that are independent of circumstance (e.g. for expressions that, in a given context, *directly refer* to something in M, such as indexicals like *I, you, here, tomorrow*, and deictic third-person pronouns) are treated as constant functions.

9.3.2 Structured contents

For certain tasks, functional contents are too coarse. Most dramatically, there are no distinctions among necessarily true propositions: there is just one function taking the value T for all $d \in CIRC$. For example, there would be just one true mathematical theorem on this account. More subtly, as Kaplan points out, there is no principled distinction between a directly referential term, like I, and a singular term that just happens to denote one and the same object in every circumstance, like *the smallest natural number*: their content (in a given context) will both be *constant* functions from *CIRC*.

This can be avoided by using instead some kind of *structured contents*. The idea goes back to Frege and Russell; for an overview of its motivation and its most common implementations, see King (2011). For our purposes, it suffices to think of a structured proposition, or in general a structured content, as something like a list or a tree, where (complex) properties, descriptions, etc., but also individuals, may literally *occur*.

We need not choose here between Frege style propositions, belonging wholly to the realm of thought, and Russell style propositions, in which worldly objects can occur, and which fit into Kaplan's theory of direct reference. I will simply use the following picture: incomplete propositions have 'holes' that can be 'filled' by elements of *CIRC*, resulting in Frege or Russell style structured propositions. Similarly for other kinds of structured contents. So there is a set

$$SCONT = I\text{-}SCONT \cup C\text{-}SCONT$$

of *structured contents*, partitioned into two disjoint subsets of *incomplete* and *complete* structured contents, respectively. I indicate that $p \in SCONT$ has a 'hole' by writing $p = p[\ ]$, and letting $p[d] \in C\text{-}SCONT$ be the result of 'filling' that hole with $d \in CIRC$. Also, there is a function

ref

from *C-SCONT* to M, reflecting the fact that complete contents have unique referents (extensions). The result is that for each $p \in I\text{-}SCONT$ we have a corresponding functional content $p^* \in [CIRC \longrightarrow M]$ given by

$$(9.4) \quad p^*(d) = ref(p[d])$$

That p^* is more coarse-grained than p means that we can have $p_1{}^* = p_2{}^*$ even though $p_1 \neq p_2$, that is that the function $*$ need not be one–one (e.g. when p_1 and p_2 are two distinct but true mathematical claims, or two distinct definite descriptions of the same object, etc.).

In fact, we can extend the function $*$ to all of *SCONT*: for the content of circumstance-independent expressions we still write $p = p[\ ]$, but nothing happens when one 'fills' with d: $p[d] = p$. Then p^* is a constant function,

$$p^*(d) = ref(p)$$

for all $d \in CIRC$, just as it should be.

9.4 THE GENERAL FORMAT

9.4.1 The circumstance of the context

Contexts play a double role in Kaplan style semantics. On the one hand, $c \in CU$ fixes the extension of indexicals and demonstratives. On the other hand, most theorists in this tradition hold that *utterances*, or *occurrences* of sentences in utterance contexts, can be true or false.[9] Since a circumstance is needed besides the context to obtain a truth value, the context must be taken to *determine* a particular circumstance, such as a world or a time. In many accounts, such as those of Kaplan and Lewis mentioned in Section 9.2.1, this is just the world, the time, etc. *of* the utterance.

However, this could be relaxed. Consider Perry's example of his son, who is standing in Perry's house in Palo Alto, and talking on the phone to his brother in Murdock. Perry asks *What's the weather like?*, and his son replies *It's raining*, meaning that it is raining in Murdock (Perry, 1986). The location *of* that utterance context is Palo Alto, while the location used to evaluate what is said is Murdock. Similarly, situation semantics, say in the format of Barwise and Etchemendy (1987), uses a basic distinction between the situation (circumstance) an utterance *is about*, and the one it is *in*. We capture all of this by just assuming that there is a given function

$$circ: CU \longrightarrow CIRC$$

that picks out a circumstance in each context.[10]

9.4.2 Semantics as assignments of values

Let us say that a *semantics* assigns meanings, or other semantic values, to expressions. In other words, it is a function

---

[9] Israel and Perry (1996) argue that utterances are the primary truth bearers, not tokens, because utterances are acts. MacFarlane (2007) says just the opposite: if seen as acts, utterances are *not* bearers of truth (he suggests using *accurate* for utterances instead of *true*). Kaplan (1989: 524, 546) claims that when doing semantics, not speech act theory, we should take *occurrences* of expressions *in* contexts to have extensions. (Occurrences are a little more specific than tokens: a written token can be 're-used' in another context.) These distinctions are not very important here, but for definiteness, I will use occurrences as Kaplan does.

[10] This may need refinement. First, the chosen circumstance may depend on the expression, so that *circ* is a function from $E \times CU$ to $CIRC$. I ignore that here since it plays no role in what follows. Second, in MacFarlane (2008), there can be more than one circumstance associated with a context; I disregard that too. Note also that I am not taking a stance in the debate about whether the circumstance determined by the context can *ever* be distinct from the circumstance *of* the context. Recanati (2007) calls the claim that it cannot the *Generalized Reflexion Principle* (GRC), and devotes the final part of his book to questions concerning the GRC. *circ* covers both: if you believe in the GRC, *circ* always picks out the circumstance of the context.

$\mu : E \longrightarrow X$

where E is a set of *structured expressions* and X is a set of *values*. But we will also consider functions taking contexts or circumstances as additional arguments; such functions too will be called *semantics*.

In principle, the elements of E are *types* of syntactic objects, *occurrences* of which may be used in acts such as utterances. Most writers follow Kaplan in taking character to apply to types, and content to occurrences. This makes good sense: the character of an expression assigns it a content in every context of utterance. Character reflects linguistic rules, what a speaker of the language must know. However, the character of a type transfers immediately to any occurrence of that type (cf. footnote 9). If we want to compare distinct assignments of semantic values, they had better apply to the same kinds of arguments. So I shall take all of these semantic functions to apply to *occurrences* of expressions.

9.4.3 Four semantic functions

If character is seen as the basic semantic function, we obtain the following picture.[11] I use e, c, and d (sometimes with subscripts) for elements of E, CU, and $CIRC$, respectively. Recall that $CONT = [CIRC \longrightarrow M]$.

(9.5) **Kaplan style semantics 1** (functional case)
   a. *char*: $E \longrightarrow [CU \longrightarrow CONT]$ is a given semantics.
   b. *cont*: $E \times CU \longrightarrow CONT$ is defined by $cont(e, c) = char(e)(c)$; the *content of e at c*.
   c. *ext*: $E \times CU \longrightarrow M$ is defined by $ext\,(e, c) = cont(e, c)(circ(c))$; the *extension of e at c*.
   d. *poe-sem*: $E \times CU \times CIRC \longrightarrow M$ is   defined   by $poe\text{-}sem\,(e, c, d) = cont(e, c)(d)$; the value of e at the *point of evaluation (c, d)*.

Thus, with each expression-in-context, *cont* associates a unique content in $CONT$, and *ext* a unique extension in M, via the circumstance picked out by *circ*. Points of evaluation are in a sense theoretical constructs, but when a formal semantics is given for a language fragment, one invariably starts with the point of evaluation semantics (*poe-sem*), and defines the others in terms of it. From this perspective, we begin at the other end, and get the following picture:[12]

---

[11] I omit here the *assignments* of individuals to variables required for handling quantification. The reader familiar with standard Tarskian semantics will see how a set of assignments can be added to the picture; cf. also Section 9.6.2.

[12] MacFarlane (2003) uses the term *point of evaluation* (taken from Belnap); Montague (1968) uses *point of reference*. MacFarlane (2003) calls μ the 'semantics proper', and μ_{ext} the 'post-semantics', since, for sentences, μ ('truth at a point') is the semantics needed in the recursive truth definition, whereas μ_{ext} ('truth at a context of utterance') is what comes closest to our normal use of 'true'.

(9.6)   **Kaplan style semantics 2** (functional case, alt. formulation)
   a. $\mu: E \times CU \times CIRC \longrightarrow M$ is a given semantics.
   b. $\mu_{cont}: E \times CU \longrightarrow CONT$ is defined by $\mu_{cont}(e, c)(d) = \mu(e, c, d)$.
   c. $\mu_{char}: E \longrightarrow [CU \longrightarrow CONT]$ is given by $\mu_{char}(e)(c)(d) = \mu(e, c, d)$.
   d. $\mu_{ext}(e, c) = \mu_{cont}(e, c)(circ(c))$

Here is a version of (9.5) for structured contents:

(9.7)   **Kaplan style semantics 3** (structured case)
   a. $char_s: E \longrightarrow [CU \longrightarrow SCONT]$ is a given semantics.
   b. $cont_s: E \times CU \longrightarrow SCONT$ is as before: $cont_s(e, c) = char_s(e)(c)$.
   c. Via the mapping * (recall (9.4) in Section 9.3.2) we get corresponding functional versions of character and content:

$$cont(e, c) = cont_s(e, c)^*$$
$$char(e)(c) = cont(e, c)$$

   d. *ext* and *poe-sem* are then defined from *cont* as in (9.5c,d).

This time, however, there is no obvious way to go in the other direction, from a semantics for points of evaluation to a content-assigning semantics, since the former has nothing to say about structured contents.

9.4.4 Propositions and truth

A sentence (occurrence) φ is true at $c \in CU$ if the proposition it expresses at c is true at c:

(9.8)   **Truth of propositions and sentences**
   a. A proposition p—in the functional case, a function from $CIRC$ to $\{T,F\}$, and in the structural case, an element of $SCONT$—is *true at* $d \in CIRC$ iff $p(d) = T$ (respectively, $p^*(d) = T$).
   b. φ *expresses* p at c iff $p = cont(\varphi, c)$ (resp. $p = cont_s(\varphi, c)$).
   c. φ is *true at* c iff *ext* $(\varphi, c) = T$.

To illustrate, suppose I produce an occurrence φ of

(9.9)   I am sitting.

The context c provides a referent for the indexical *I*, so φ expresses the proposition $cont(\varphi, c) = that$ Dag is sitting, which can be true or false at various circumstances, and which happens to be true at the circumstance of my utterance. If circumstances are world-time pairs as in Kaplan (1989), and we adopt the functional view, it is that function p_1 from $CIRC$ to truth-values such that $p_1(w, t) = T$ iff Dag is sitting in w at t. Fixing (w, t) to the *actual* circumstance, $circ(c) = (w_c, t_c)$, we get $ext(\varphi, c) = T$.

On one (of several) structural account, the proposition expressed could be something like $cont_s(\varphi, c) = p_2[\,] = \langle \text{SITTING}[\,], \text{Dag}\rangle$. Supplying the actual circumstance gives $p_2[w_c, t_c] = \langle \text{SITTING}[w_c, t_c], \text{Dag}\rangle$; again $ext(\varphi, c) = (p_2)^*(w_c, t_c) = \text{T}$.

If you don't accept propositions like p_1 or p_2 your must regard t_c, or both w_c and t_c, as fixed in the proposition. In the latter case, you get directly to T with the functional version, and to something like $p_2[w_c, t_c]$ with the structural version. In the former case, the actual world must be plugged in.[13]

Finally, a model-theoretic semanticist accounts for (9.9) using *poe-sem*, without resorting to either character or content: $poe\text{-}sem(\varphi, c, w, t) = \text{T}$ iff the speaker at c is sitting in w at t.

Consider also

(9.10)   I am sitting now.

On one natural view, (9.10), uttered in the same circumstance c, corresponds to a slightly different proposition, namely, one where the time has been fixed to t_c via the indexical *now*. This is (in the functional case) the function p_3 such that $p_3(w, t) = \text{T}$ iff Dag is sitting in w at t_c, that is essentially the same proposition that (9.9) expresses if only worlds are taken to be circumstances of evaluation (so on that view, the difference between (9.9) and (9.10) disappears at the propositional level). Here the time argument plays no role, but the world argument does, since I could be standing at t_c in some $w \neq w_c$. But the utterance fixes w to the actual world, so the truth value of the two utterances is of course the same.[14]

9.4.5   Variants: dealing with assessment

The truth-value of some sentences seems to depend on an irreducibly *subjective* element, for example, claims about taste, beauty, morals, about what is funny, what is likely, etc. A recent debate in the philosophy of language concerns how such claims (and

---

[13] Note that while t_c might be said to correspond to the present progressive tense in (9.9), nothing in the sentence corresponds to w_c. In this sense, the world would be an *unarticulated constituent*; see also Section 9.5.2 below.

[14] An alternative is to take *now* to be a temporal operator, setting t to the actual time. The sentence then has the form 'Now(I am sitting)'. On the functional view of content—but not on the structural view—the corresponding proposition would still be the same as when *now* is a simple indexical.

An *eternalist* about time lets the time parameter be fixed by the context of utterance; so that different propositions (still incomplete wrt worlds) are expressed by different utterances. This is compatible with the increasingly popular idea that tenses, in, say,

(i) Dag will be standing.

are not to be handled, as Kaplan did following Prior, by tense operators but rather by quantification over times. See King (2003) for arguments, and Recanati (2007: ch. 6), for a defence of the Prior–Kaplan treatment. Nothing of what I say here turns on this issue.

disagreements about them) should be treated within a Kaplan style framework.[15] For simplicity, think of all such claims as needing an *assessor* or a *judge*.[16]

A *contextualist* account fits directly into Kaplan style semantics as defined so far: simply consider the assessor as a feature of the context of an utterance, which thus helps determine which proposition is expressed. So if I say *Moby Dick is a funny novel* and you deny this, we are simply making claims about ourselves (so there is no real disagreement), or, if the contexts happen to single out other assessors, claims about what these assessors find funny.

According to *relativists* (about truth), this misses the disagreement aspect of such exchanges. Instead, they place the assessor among the circumstances. On one account, the utterance context still determines the assessor, but the proposition expressed needs not only a time, a world, etc. to yield a truth value, but also an assessor.[17] Now you and I can be said to dispute the *same proposition* in the above exchange (i.e. the proposition which is true at an ordinary circumstance d and an assessor a iff *Moby Dick* is funny for a in d), although both our utterances may be true, since the respective contexts, via the function *circ*, may determine different assessors (so-called *faultless* disagreement).

Other relativists see assessment as *independent* of the original utterance, that is, not determined by the utterance context.[18] This context still fixes the assessment-relative proposition expressed, but not the truth-value of the utterance or of any assessment of it; for that an independently chosen assessor (or a context of assessment) is required.

Yet another variant is relativist about *content* instead of truth.[19] That is, propositions do not take assessors as argument (in this sense, this approach is still contextualist), but in order to determine which proposition is expressed you need an assessor, which can be independent of the utterance context.

What I have said so far is not enough to even begin to discuss the hotly debated pros and cons of these various approaches, but it should be sufficient, I hope, for seeing that they all can be made to fit—in the relativist cases with slight adjustments—into Kaplan style semantics.

9.4.6 Does the choice of semantics matter?

μ_{cont} and μ_{char} in (9.7) are simply obtained by *currying* μ, and inversely, *cont* and *poe-sem* are simply obtained by *uncurrying* the function *char* (see Section 9.5.2 for definitions). From a mathematical point of view, these functions are often simply *identified*. So how can their differences matter semantically? That depends on what you want them to model or explain. For example, if you think *propositions* are important, say, as the objects

---

[15] For the current state of this debate consult, for example, the collection García-Carpintero and Kölbel (2008), the *Synthese* issue (2009), the 2008 issue of *Philosophical Perspectives*, or Cappelen and Hawthorne (2009).

[16] Alternatively, a *standard* of taste, or of what is funny, or a moral or epistemic standard.

[17] For example, Kölbel (2004) and Brogaard (2009).

[18] Notably, MacFarlane (2005) and Lasersohn (2005).

[19] Cappelen (2008).

of attitudes, you need something like *cont*. If *utterance truth* is what 'truth' in ordinary language stands for, *ext* provides a useful rendering of it. If your ambition is, to the contrary, to get by without propositions in our sense, you may focus on *poe-sem* or on *char* instead.

The differences also surface in notions of logical or necessary truth and consequence tied to the various semantic formats. Famously, Kaplan was able to account for the strong intuition that a sentence like

(9.11)   I am here.

is contextually true (true whenever uttered), but still not necessary (since I might have been somewhere else).[20]

Regardless of these issues in the philosophy of language, it turns out that for compositionality, the choice of values matters a great deal. This was observed by Lewis (1980). He argued that for most purposes the choice between (what I have called) *cont* and *poe-sem* is a matter of taste: a 'distinction without a difference', precisely because you can go between the two at will. But he also noted that with the wrong choice of arguments, contents may become non-compositional (and thereby, according to him, disqualified as semantic values). We will now see how compositionality fares in the presence of contextual factors. In particular, I will explain and generalize (in Section 9.6) Lewis's point about content.

9.5 COMPOSITIONALITY AND CONTEXT

We introduced four semantic functions, and noted that recursive truth definitions usually appear at the point of evaluation level. So it is natural to ask at which levels compositionality applies, and how compositionality of one of the semantic functions is related to that of the others.

9.5.1 Standard compositionality

To formulate compositionality, we must make explicit how expressions in *E* are *structured*. There are various ways to do this. Here, I shall simply assume that there is a

---

[20] Just restricting attention to *proper* contexts (Section 9.2.1) isn't enough, according to Kaplan: it makes (9.11) true in every context, but it also makes

(i) Necessarily, I am here.

true. But if context first fixes the reference of *I* and *here*, and necessity means that the *resulting* proposition is true at all circumstances, then (i) is false. In hindsight, however, the same distinction is available, though less obviously, to one who uses only *poe-sem* and *circ*.

set Σ of functions from E^n to E ($n \geq 1$) that *generate* E from some given set $A \subseteq E$ of *atoms*.[21] That is, every expression is either an atom or obtained from atoms by repeated applications of functions in Σ. If μ is a semantics for E, that is:

$$\mu \colon E \longrightarrow X$$

for some set X of semantic values, standard compositionality of μ means that the value of any complex expression is *determined* by the values of its immediate constituents and the rule applied. In other words:

Funct(μ)   For every syntactic rule a there is an operation r_a such that for all $e_1, \ldots, e_n \in$
E, $\mu(a(e_1, \ldots, e_n)) = r_a(\mu(e_1), \ldots, \mu(e_n))$.[22]

This is the *functional* version of compositionality, expressing directly the 'determination' idea. There is an equivalent *substitutional* version, saying that appropriate replacement of synonymous (not necessarily immediate) constituents preserves meaning; see Pagin and Westerståhl (2010*a*) for details. Here I will use the functional version.

9.5.2 Compositionality for incomplete meanings

Standard compositionality applies only to character: Funct(*char*) makes immediate sense, since character assigns a semantic value directly to expressions. For semantic functions taking contextual arguments, the notion of compositionality must be revised. Abstractly, we have a function

$$F \colon E \longrightarrow [Y \longrightarrow Z]$$

and its *uncurried* version:[23]

$$F_{uc} \colon E \times Y \longrightarrow Z$$

---

[21] Thus, I ignore (lexical and structural) *ambiguity*, the occurrence of which requires one to assign semantic values to *derivations* of expressions rather than the expressions themselves. This can be done by means of a *term algebra* corresponding to (E, A, Σ); see Hendriks (2001) for an account using *many-sorted* term algebras, Hodges (2001) for an account with *partial* term algebras, and Westerståhl (2004) for some remarks on the relation between the two. All notions and results here can easily be reformulated for this more accurate setting.

[22] The function μ may be *partial* (if not all well-formed expressions are meaningful), in which case one should add the condition that $\mu(a(e_1, \ldots, e_n))$ is defined. I ignore this in what follows.

[23] Equivalently, start from

$$\mu \colon E \times Y \longrightarrow Z$$

and apply *currying*:

$$\mu_{curr} \colon E \longrightarrow [Y \longrightarrow Z]$$

where $\mu_{curr}(e)(y) = \mu(e, y)$. The two operations are *inverses* to each other:

$$(F_{uc})_{curr} = F \text{ and } (\mu_{curr})_{uc} = \mu$$

The task is to reformulate the compositionality condition for F_{uc}. In fact, there are *two* natural ways to do this, depending on whether or not the choice of semantic operation is itself context-dependent:

C-Funct(F_{uc})   For every syntactic rule a there is an operation r_a such that for all $e_1, \ldots, e_n \in E$ and all $y \in Y$,

$$F_{uc}(a(e_1, \ldots, e_n), y) = r_a(F_{uc}(e_1, y), \ldots, F_{uc}(e_n, y)).$$

C-Funct(F_{uc})$_w$ For every syntactic rule a there is an operation r_a such that for all $e_1, \ldots, e_n \in E$ and all $y \in Y$,

$$F_{uc}(a(e_1, \ldots, e_n), y) = r_a(F_{uc}(e_1, y), \ldots, F_{uc}(e_n, y), y)$$

When C-Funct(F_{uc}) (C-Funct(F_{uc})$_w$) holds, I will say that F is (*weakly*) *contextually compositional*. Also, I will say that F is (weakly, contextually) a-*compositional* when the corresponding condition above holds for a particular $a \in \Sigma$.

The seemingly small difference between the two variants—that the contextual element is an argument of the semantic operation in the weak but not the strong version—is in fact significant, and corresponds to different accounts of how contextual elements interact with meaning. Here is one illustration:

(9.12)   John's books are thick.

requires a 'possessor relation' fixed by the utterance context: it might be the books he owns, or has borrowed, or authored, or sold, or the ones he is standing on to reach the upper shelf. But *John* doesn't single out such a relation, and neither does *books* or the possessive *'s*. The possessive *'s* indicates the presence of a 'possessor relation' R, but doesn't by itself specify which one. Consider a context c_1 where R is 'authored by' and another context c_2 where it is 'standing on to reach the upper shelf', but otherwise similar to c_1. One natural analysis (others are possible) has $cont(John, c_1) = cont(John, c_2)$, $cont('s, c_1) = cont('s, c_2)$ (using a free parameter for R), and also $cont(John's, c_1) = cont(John's, c_2)$. Furthermore, $cont(books, c_1) = cont(books, c_2)$, but at the next level the value of R could be specified, and so $cont(John's\ books, c_1) \neq cont(John's\ books, c_2)$.[24] If so, C-Funct($cont$) fails, but C-Funct($cont$)$_w$ may still hold.

This example illustrates what Pagin (2005) calls *context shift failure*: the failure of compositionality does not arise from substituting synonymous expressions, but merely from changing the context: all immediate subexpressions have the same value in both contexts, but the complex expression in question doesn't.

The same situation may apply if *unarticulated constituents* occur. Consider

(9.13)   It is raining.

---

[24] I am assuming that *John's books* contains *John's* and *books* as immediate parts, and *John's* is formed from *John* and the genitive *'s*. One reason not to fix R from the start in the context comes from cases with relational nouns like *John's bride*: this could be his spouse but also the bride he has been assigned to escort on some occasion. Until the level where *John's* and *bride* are combined, the former relation is not 'available'.

If one argues that *it* and *rain* have no location argument but (9.13) does, we have a case of unarticulated constituents that yields the same kind of counterexample to C-Funct(*cont*)—but not to C-Funct(*cont*)$_w$—as above. Indeed, unarticulated constituents are allowed by C-Funct(*cont*)$_w$ (a point noted and discussed in detail in Pagin (2005)).

This can be generalized. When Recanati (this volume) argues that phenomena like *modulation* falsify a principle of compositionality that only allows 'indexical-like' forms of context dependence, he is in effect claiming that C-Funct(*cont*) fails.[25] He discusses a proposal from Pagin and Pelletier (2007) (recursively using contextually modulated meanings as building blocks of meaning) that in a weak sense salvages compositionality. But he also observes that if the context itself is taken to be an argument of the composition function, modulation is straightforwardly covered. After all, the idea is precisely that *context* influences the build-up of the meaning of an expression, sometimes in ways not predictable solely from the (possibly context-dependent) meanings of its parts and the mode of composition.

The relations between our three notions of compositionality are as follows:[26]

Lemma 1. *C-Funct*(F_{uc}) $\Longrightarrow$ *C-Funct*(F_{uc})$_w$ $\Longrightarrow$ *Funct*(*F*), *but none of these arrows can be reversed.*

Proof. Clearly, C-Funct(F_{uc}) entails C-Funct(F_{uc})$_w$. Suppose C-Funct(F_{uc})$_w$ holds. We have:

$$F(a(e_1,\ldots,e_n))(y) = F_{uc}(a(e_1,\ldots,e_n),y)$$

$$= r_a(F_{uc}(e_1,y),\ldots,F_{uc}(e_n,y),y)$$

$$= s_a(F(e_1),\ldots,F(e_n))(y)$$

where $s_a : [Y \longrightarrow Z]^n \longrightarrow [Y \longrightarrow Z]$ is defined by

$$s_a(f_1,\ldots,f_n)(y) = r_a(f_1(y),\ldots,f_n(y),y)$$

for $f_1,\ldots,f_n \in [Y \longrightarrow Z]$ and $y \in Y$. The third equality above then follows, and since the argument holds for any $y \in Y$, we have

---

[25] '...[W]e cannot maintain that the meaning of a complex phrase is (wholly) determined by the meanings of its parts and their mode of combination', where the latter meanings are taken to be 'standing meanings (*and* Kaplanian contents)'. (p. 187) A typical example of modulation appears in

(i) The policeman stopped the car.

where we get different meanings depending on whether the policeman was outside the car or driving it, and where that variation is not attributable—so the story goes—to an implicit parameter for 'ways of stopping cars' or indeed to anything linguistic.

[26] This result, mentioned in my Kista talk (see footnote 35), is also proved in Pagin (2005: Appendix 1).

$$F(a(e_1, \ldots, e_n)) = s_a(F(e_1), \ldots, F(e_n))$$

Thus, Funct(F) holds.

Counterexamples to the converse of the first implication were just given. The following counterexample to the converse of the second implication is instructive, and will be generalized in Section 9.6.2. Consider a language for propositional modal logic, with atomic formulas $p_1, p_2, \ldots$ and complex formulas of the forms $\neg\varphi$, $\varphi \wedge \psi$, and $\Box\varphi$. A given model assigns, for every world $w \in W$, a truth-value $F(p_i)(w)$ to each p_i ($F(\varphi)(w) = T$ is usually written $w \models \varphi$). Truth-values to complex formulas in worlds as assigned in the usual (S5) way, in particular,

$$F(\Box\varphi)(w) = T \text{ iff for all } w' \in W, F(\varphi)(w') = T.$$

We may think of the meaning $F(\varphi)$ of a formula φ as the set of worlds where φ is true. Clearly, Funct(F) holds. But C-Funct(F_{uc})$_w$ normally fails. Specifically, suppose p_1 is true in all worlds, but there are worlds w' and w'' such that p_2 is true in w' but false in w''. Then $F_{uc}(p_1, w') = F_{uc}(p_2, w') = T$, but $F_{uc}(\Box p_1, w') = T$ and $F_{uc}(\Box p_2, w') = F$. So there can be no operation r that computes the truth value of $\Box\varphi$ in w from just the truth value of φ in w, and possibly w itself.   □

It will be convenient for applications to formulate a slightly more general version of this lemma. Suppose

$$G: E \times X \longrightarrow [Y \longrightarrow Z]$$

is given, with its uncurried version

$$G_{uc}: E \times X \times Y \longrightarrow Z$$

as usual: $G_{uc}(e, x, y) = G(e, x)(y)$. Both G_{uc} and G take contextual arguments. The proof of the following lemma is a minor variation of the proof of the first implication in Lemma 1 (which can be obtained as a special case of Lemma 2, taking X as a singleton).

Lemma 2. *C-Funct(G_{uc}) $\Longrightarrow$ C-Funct(G), and similarly for the weak case.*

Sometimes it is natural to *fix* the context, thus transforming a semantics F taking contextual arguments to one taking only expressions. That is, for some fixed $y_0 \in Y$, one considers $F_{y_0}: E \longrightarrow Z$ given by

$$F_{y_0}(e) = F(e)(y_0)$$

Much of classical formal semantics is done under such a *fixed context assumption*. We have the following result:[27]

Fact 3. *C-Funct(F_{uc})$_w$ is equivalent to the requirement that for all $y \in Y$, Funct(F_y) holds.*

---

[27] See also Pagin (2005: footnote 11).

Proof: Suppose that for all y in Y, $\text{Funct}(F_y)$. We then have, for each y,

$$F_{uc}(a(e_1,\ldots,e_n),y) = F_y(a(e_1,\ldots,e_n))$$

$$= r_{a,y}(F_y(e_1),\ldots,F_y(e_n)) \quad \text{(for some operation } r_{a,y})$$

$$= s_a(F_{uc}(e_1,y),\ldots,F_{uc}(e_n,y),y)$$

where

$$s_a(p_1,\ldots,p_n,y) = r_{a,y}(p_1,\ldots,p_n)$$

The converse direction is even simpler.   □

So weak contextual compositionality is equivalent to the condition that ordinary compositionality holds *however* the contextual argument is fixed (for an application, see Section 9.6.6).

Without a fixed context assumption it will still be the case that *some* expressions e are *context-independent* in the sense that $F(e)$ is a constant function. One may think of Frege style semantics as claiming that *all* expressions are context-independent. Then, unsurprisingly, the three notions of compositionality collapse into one. I leave the straightforward verification of the following fact as an exercise.

Fact 4. *If $Y = \{y_0\}$ or, more generally, if all expressions are context-independent, then $\text{Funct}(F) \Longrightarrow \text{C-Funct}(F_{uc})$.*

9.6 COMPOSITIONALITY IN KAPLAN STYLE SEMANTICS

9.6.1 The general picture

Notions of contextual compositionality apply directly to the functional version of the setup in Section 9.4, where we started with the function *char*, and defined the other semantics from it.[28] Let $char_0$ be the function from E to $[CU \times CIRC \longrightarrow M]$ obtained by currying both contextual arguments of *poe-sem*:

(9.14) $char_0(e)(c,d) = poe\text{-}sem(e,c,d)$

---

[28] Kaplan's principle (F1) (1989: 507), is the substitutional equivalent of Funct(*char*). His (F2) appears to be intended as a substitutional equivalent of C-Funct (*cont*), but it isn't; in fact C-Funct (*cont*) has no simple such equivalent. Indeed (F2) seems mistaken, but if it is reformulated for one context instead of two, it becomes equivalent to C-Funct (*cont*)$_w$. Kaplan dees not discuss these matters, however. Lewis (1980) implicitly uses context-dependent compositionality when discussing requirements on semantic values, but without explicit formulations.

It ought to make little or no difference whether one thinks of character in terms of *char* or *char* $_0$; the result below confirms this. The following picture results.

Proposition 5.

$$C\text{-}Funct(poe\text{-}sem) \Longrightarrow C\text{-}Funct(poe\text{-}sem)_w \Longrightarrow Funct(char_0)$$

$$\Downarrow \qquad\qquad\qquad \Downarrow \qquad\qquad\qquad \Updownarrow$$

$$C\text{-}Funct(cont) \quad \Longrightarrow \quad C\text{-}Funct(cont)_w \quad \Longrightarrow Funct(char)$$

Proof: The rightmost horizontal arrow in the lower row is an instance of Lemma 1, with $Z = CONT = [CIRC \longrightarrow M]$. The one in the upper row follows from the same lemma with $Y = CU \times CIRC$. The two leftmost downward implications follow from Lemma 2. Suppose Funct($char_0$) holds. To prove Funct(*char*) we calculate:

$$(9.15) \quad char(a(e_1, \ldots, e_n))(c)(d) = char_0(a(e_1, \ldots, e_n))(c, d)$$

$$= r_a(char_0(e_1), \ldots, char_0(e_n))(c, d)$$

$$= s_a(char(e_1), \ldots, char(e_n))(c)(d)$$

where, for any $f_1, \ldots, f_n : CU \longrightarrow CONT$, $c \in CU$, and $d \in CIRC$,

$$s_a(f_1, \ldots, f_n)(c)(d) = r_a((f_1)_{uc}, \ldots, (f_n)_{uc})(c, d)$$

Here, as before, $(f_i)_{uc}(x, y) = f_i(x)(y)$. Since we have

$$(char(e_i))_{uc} = char_0(e_i)$$

it follows that the last equality of (9.15) holds. This shows

$$char(a(e_1, \ldots, e_n)) = s_a(char(e_1), \ldots, char(e_n))$$

The proof that Funct(*char*) entails Funct($char_0$) is similar (using the curryings of the functions $m_1, \ldots, m_n : CU \times CIRC \longrightarrow M$). $\square$

Thus, the point of evaluation semantics is indeed basic: if it is (weakly) compositional, so is the content semantics, and the character semantics. None of the unidirectional arrows in Proposition 5 can be reversed in general. We show in Section 9.6.4 that under a certain natural condition, some of the arrows reverse. First, however, an important comment to Proposition 5 is required.

9.6.2 Compositional vs. recursively defined semantics

The pleasant symmetric picture in Proposition 5 is in many cases somewhat illusory, since it often happens that the point of evaluation semantics has a *recursive truth definition* but is *not even weakly contextually compositional*. Tarski's truth definition for first-order logic is a familiar example: it recursively specifies when an *assignment* (of individuals to variables) satisfies a *formula* in a *model*. Regarding the model as fixed, and thinking of assignments as contexts, the clause for the existential quantifier is:

(9.16) $\mu(\exists x\varphi, f) = T$ iff for some a, $\mu(\varphi, f(a/x)) = T$

where $f(a/x)$ is like f except that it assigns a to x. The clause is recursive in that the right-hand side of (9.16) uses the value of μ for an expression of lower complexity. But the assignment argument is not the same as on the left-hand side, and precisely for that reason, μ is *not* (weakly) contextually compositional. Suppose, for example, that (in the given model) P denotes the empty set but R doesn't, and that f assigns to x an individual which is not in the denotation of R. Then $\mu(Px, f) = \mu(Rx, f) = F$, but $\mu(\exists xPx, f) \neq \mu(\exists xRx, f)$. So $\mu(\exists xPx, f)$ cannot be calculated from $\mu(Px, f)$ and f.

Should we say that Tarski's definition is not compositional? But it is a familiar fact that if we take semantic values of formulas to be *sets of assignments* instead, we regain compositionality: the set of assignments satisfying $\exists x\varphi$ can be calculated (indeed using the clause (9.16)) from the set of assignments satisfying φ. This is another way of saying that the *currying* of μ is compositional. (In fact, the latter mode of expression is more general, since it covers not only formulas but subexpressions of formulas, e.g. individual constants.)

I will state some facts about the general situation, without attempting full detail or formal precision. In this setting, a recursive definition is best thought of as defining a *relation S*—so that in the case of a function we define its *graph*—by means of a sentence Φ in some suitable (usually first-order) interpreted metalanguage, in which one can also talk about the syntactic objects in E. When (the graph of) a semantics F is being defined, Φ is usually a disjunction of *base clauses* (for atomic expressions) and *inductive clauses* for the operators (elements of Σ in our case). I restrict attention here to the case of sentence operators Δ. With Φ_Δ as the corresponding disjunct, we may then have

(9.17) $F(\Delta\varphi, c, d, w) = T$ iff $\Phi_\Delta(F(\varphi, c, t[d], w), c, d, w)$

Here c, d, w are parameters, varying over C, D, W, respectively. Think of c as a *context parameter* and w as a *circumstance parameter*, for example a world. I will call d a *shifted parameter*, since it is changed on the right-hand side: in its place there is a term constructed from d and possibly other terms, such as bound variables.[29] So F is a point of evaluation semantics. In particular cases some of the parameters can be missing; for example, in (9.16) above both d and w are absent, and $\Phi_\Delta(F(\varphi, t[f]), f)$ is, roughly, $\exists v F(\varphi, f(v/x)) = T$.[30]

---

[29] This conforms to the usual notion of 'shiftiness' in the literature, e.g. in Lewis (1980), but not to Recanati (2007), who instead uses the term for cases when (in our terms) $circ(c)$ is not the circumstance *of c*; see Section 9.4.1.

[30] I.e. $t[f]$ describes how the assignment $f(v/x)$ is formed from f by assigning v to the object language variable x.

Various more abstract semantics, or notions of *content*, are obtainable by currying. Let F_w be the semantics obtained by currying w, $F_{d,w}$ by also currying the shifted parameter d, and F_d by currying only d:

$$F_w(\psi, c, d)(w) = F(\psi, c, d, w) = F_{d,w}(\psi, c)(d)(w) = F_d(\psi, c, w)(d)$$

We can now state various facts about the compositionality of F and its curried versions. To begin,

(I) F_d *is at least weakly contextually compositional. Hence, so is* $F_{d,w}$.

The second claim follows from the first by Lemma 2. The following argument is not a strict proof of the first claim, but gives the idea. Consider an operator Δ with defining clause as in (9.17), and let r_Δ be an operation taking functions g in $Z = [D \longrightarrow \{T, F\}]$ and $c \in C$ and $w \in W$ to functions in Z, defined by

$$r_\Delta(g, c, w)(d) = T \text{ iff } \Phi_\Delta(g(t[d]), c, d, w)$$

Then

$$r_\Delta(F_d(\varphi, c, w), c, w)(d) = T \Leftrightarrow \Phi_\Delta(F_d(\varphi, c, w)(t[d]), c, d, w)$$
$$\Leftrightarrow \Phi_\Delta(F(\varphi, c, t[d], w), c, d, w)$$
$$\Leftrightarrow F(\Delta\varphi, c, d, w) = T$$
$$\Leftrightarrow F_d(\Delta\varphi, c, w)(d) = T$$

Since this holds for all d,

$$F_d(\Delta\varphi, c, w) = r_\Delta(F_d(\varphi, c, w), c, w)$$

and we have weak (if c or w occurs in Φ_Δ; otherwise strong) contextual Δ-compositionality for F_d.   □

Recall that in Proposition 5, $cont = poe\text{-}sem_{curr}$. Here w is absent, or treated as part of the shifted d parameter. Thus, when *poe-sem* is recursively definable but not (contextually) compositional, so that Proposition 5 doesn't apply, (I) claims that *cont* is nevertheless (contextually) compositional. In this sense, the general picture given by Proposition 5 is still valid.

Next, I will call the shift in (9.17) *trivial* if

(9.18)   for all c, d, w, if $t[d] \neq d$, then $\Phi_\Delta(T, c, d, w) \Leftrightarrow \Phi_\Delta(F, c, d, w)$

For example, Kaplan (1989) defines a sentential operator *yesterday* (Y):

$$F(Y\varphi, d) = T \text{ iff } F(\varphi, d - 1) = T$$

Here the contextual parameter varies over *days*, representable as integers. So the day parameter is non-trivially shifted with $t[d] = d - 1$ (since today ≠ yesterday and $T = T$

is not equivalent to $T = F$). Likewise, the shifts occurring in (9.16) above, and in the modal example from the proof of Lemma 1, are non-trivial.

(II)   *If the contextual parameter is only trivially shifted in the inductive clause for the operator Δ, then F is weakly contextually Δ-compositional. Hence, so is F_w.*

The second statement uses (the proof of) Lemma 2. For the first statement, suppose (9.18) holds. We claim that

(9.19) $\Phi_\Delta(F(\varphi, c, t[d], w), c, d, w) \iff \Phi_\Delta(F(\varphi, c, d, w), c, d, w))$

For if $t[d] = d$ this is obvious, and if $t[d] \neq d$, the claim follows from triviality. (9.19) means that

$$F(\Delta\varphi, c, d, w) = T \iff \Phi_\Delta(F(\varphi, c, d, w), c, d, w)$$

But then it is clear that F is weakly contextually Δ-compositional.   □

(III)   *If the d-parameter is non-trivially shifted in a recursive definition of F, then F_w is not weakly contextually compositional. As before, it follows that neither is F.*

This time we need to assume something—the only occasion in this chapter—about how F relates to models; roughly, that one can always choose interpretations of primitive symbols to attain relevant semantic values. Suppose, then, that there is an operator Δ satisfying (9.17) for which (9.18) fails, so that there are c_0, d_0, w_0 such that $t[d_0] \neq d_0$ and, say, $\Phi_\Delta(T, c_0, d_0, w_0)$ but not $\Phi_\Delta(F, c_0, d_0, w_0)$. Our assumption is that we can find a model and sentences φ and φ' such that

$$F(\varphi, c_0, d_0) = F(\varphi', c_0, d_0)$$

and

$$F(\varphi, c_0, t[d_0], w_0) = T$$
$$F(\varphi', c_0, t[d_0], w_0) = F$$

Since $\Phi_\Delta(T, c_0, d_0, w_0) \not\iff \Phi_\Delta(F, c_0, d_0, w_0)$, $F(\Delta\varphi, c_0, d_0, w_0) \neq F(\Delta\varphi', c_0, d_0, w_0)$, and hence $F_w(\Delta\varphi, c_0, d_0) \neq F_w(\Delta\varphi', c_0, d_0)$. This contradicts weak contextual Δ-compositionality for F_w.   □

These observations generalize the remark by Lewis (1980) mentioned in Section 9.4.6. He noted that if *location* is shifted by some operator, but content doesn't take location as an argument, then content will not be compositional: the content of *Somewhere the sun is shining* at the location of c will depend on the content of *The sun is shining* at some other location. This is an instance of (III), with d as the location parameter and w as a world parameter (assuming the point of evaluation semantics can be recursively defined). Indeed, neither the point of evaluation semantics nor the one treating contents as functions from worlds to truth-values is (weakly contextually) compositional. Lewis's point was precisely that the latter kind of content would not be compositional if the location parameter is shifted.

Fact (II) generalizes the inverse claim, that if you *don't* shift the location parameter, (weak contextual) compositionality of content obtains. And (I) observes that if you curry shifted parameters, compositionality of the corresponding notion of content is guaranteed.

9.6.3 Compositionality and monsters

Semanticists in the tradition focused on here agree that the point of evaluation semantics provides the truth value of φ at context c in circumstance d, but differ as to what separates contexts from circumstances (Section 9.2.1). But since a context always *determines* a circumstance (via the function *circ*), an abstract picture could be:

context c: $\langle speaker_c, time_c, location_c, world_c, \ldots \rangle$
circumstance d: $\langle judge_d, time_d, world_d, \ldots \rangle$

(I have included an optional judge for the relativist's sake; cf. Section 9.4.5). A further point of agreement is that *shiftable* parameters belong to the circumstances. In view of (I) above, if *poe-sem* can be recursively defined, we have an *argument* for this:

(IV)   *Circumstance parameters allow content to be compositional.*

Note that (IV) doesn't prevent non-shiftable parameters like judges from being placed among the circumstances. But shiftable parameters must *not* go in the context. In Kaplan's terminology, that would create *monsters*. He claimed that monsters don't exist in English, in fact, that 'none could be added' (1989: 510). The claim has been debated,[31] but we can use (III) to find a rationale for the quoted phrase in terms of compositionality:

(V)   *Monsters destroy the compositionality of content.*

Given that compositionality of content is desirable, monsters are not. If you discover a monstrous contextual feature, relegate it to the circumstances.

9.6.4 Extensional composition

We have talked about *poe-sem*, *cont*, and *char*, but what about the semantics *ext*, that is in the case of sentences, the notion of truth at a context? MacFarlane (2003: 328–9) adapts a counterexample by Kaplan:

---

[31] Israel and Perry (1996) argue that even if there are no English monsters of the kind Kaplan considers ('metaphysical monsters'), this is at most an empirical fact, not a principled one. Moreover, they claim that a proper treatment of propositional attitudes requires context-shifting operators. Schlenker (2003) argues that various languages, including English, do have monsters (*two days ago* is said to be an example). Other putative counterexamples, noted by Kaplan too, involve quotation contexts. Finally, consider the following title of an art exhibition in Göteborg (Konsthallen, fall 2008): 'Tomorrow always belongs to us.' This sentence is not about the day after any particular day.

(9.20)   a. It is always the case that I am here.
         b. It is always the case that $2 + 2 = 4$.

Clearly, $ext(\text{'I am here'}, c) = ext(\text{'2 + 2 = 4'}, c) = \text{T}$ for all c, but in most contexts, (9.20a) is false and (9.20b) is true. So ext need not be even weakly contextually compositional, even when $poe\text{-}sem$ (and hence $cont$ and $char$) is.

    Note that the counterexample involves an intensional (in this case temporal) operator. Is this essential? To appreciate the situation, let us lay down the following terminology.

(9.21)   **Extensional semantic operations**
         a. An operation $r: [X \longrightarrow Y]^n \longrightarrow [X \longrightarrow Y]$ is *extensional* iff $f_i(x) = f_i'(x')$,
            $i = 1, \ldots, n, \implies r(f_1, \ldots, f_n)(x) = r(f_1', \ldots, f_n')(x')$.

         b. $r: [X \longrightarrow Y]^n \times C \longrightarrow [X \longrightarrow Y]$ is *extensional* iff for every $c \in C$, r_c
            defined by $r_c(f_1, \ldots, f_n) = r(f_1, \ldots, f_n, c)$ is extensional.

Consider

(9.22)   The president is sitting.

Calculating the content of (9.22) at a context c only requires extensional operators: $cont(\text{the president}, c)$ is a function f which for each circumstance d selects an individual $f(d)$ in M_0, $cont(\text{sitting}, c)$ is a function P such that each $P(d)$ is a subset of M_0,[32] and $cont((9.22), c) = r(f, P)$, where

$$r(f, P)(d) = \text{T} \text{ iff } f(d) \in P(d)$$

Clearly, the operation r is extensional. But as we just saw, the presence of intensional operators in the language changes the situation. In such a language, we may expect *content* to be contextually compositional with extensional composition operations only for restricted fragments. Proposition 7 below confirms this expectation.

    What about *character*? By Proposition 5, this is the weakest form of compositionality, and one certainly expects it to hold, but with what kind of composition operations? Suppose the speaker in c is the addressee in c', and the character of *sitting* is constant. Then *I am sitting* expresses the same (functional or structured) proposition in c as *You are sitting* does in c'. Again the simple example is perfectly extensional. But now recall Kaplan's injunction against monsters: no operators shift context. If so, there is no way to produce a counterexample like the previous one. So could we always require character compositionality to use extensional composition operators?

    Not if there are context shift failures as in the case of *John's books*, described in Section 9.5.2. This was a counterexample to C-Funct($cont$), but in fact shows that Funct($char$) (which holds by Proposition 5, provided C-Funct($cont$)$_w$ holds) cannot use extensional operations. The following result explains the situation.

---

[32] Assuming for simplicity that (9.22) expresses a temporal proposition (so c is irrelevant) and that the domain of individuals is the same in all circumstances.

Proposition 6. *C-Funct(cont) is equivalent to Funct(char) holding with extensional composition operations. So in that case, the four conditions Funct($char_0$), Funct(char), C-Funct(cont), and C-Funct(cont)$_w$ are all equivalent.*

Proof. One direction follows from the proof of Lemma 1. Assuming C-Funct(*cont*) with composition operations r_a, we in effect showed that Funct(*char*) holds with operations s_a defined by

$$s_a(f_1, \ldots, f_n)(y) = r_a(f_1(y), \ldots, f_n(y))$$

Clearly, the s_a are extensional. In the other direction, suppose Funct(*char*) holds with extensional composition operations r_a. We have

$$cont(a(e_1, \ldots, e_n), c) = char(a(e_1, \ldots, e_n))(c)$$
$$= r_a(char(e_1), \ldots, char(e_n))(c)$$
$$= r'_a(char(e_1)(c), \ldots, char(e_n)(c)) \quad \text{(for some } r'_a)$$
$$= r'_a(cont(e_1, c), \ldots, cont(e_n, c))$$

The existence of r'_a in the third equality is guaranteed by the extensionality of r_a: just define, for $p_1, \ldots, p_n \in [CIRC \longrightarrow M]$, $r'_a(p_1, \ldots, p_n)$ to be equal to $r_a(f_1, \ldots, f_n)(c)$ if there exist $f_1, \ldots, f_n \in [CU \longrightarrow [CIRC \longrightarrow M]]$ and $c \in CU$ such that $p_i = f_i(c)$, for $1 \le i \le n$ (undefined or arbitrary otherwise). This definition works (is independent of which f_i and c are chosen) precisely because r_a is extensional. Thus, C-Funct(*cont*) holds. □

Note that the first half of the proof doesn't go through if only C-Funct(*cont*)$_w$ is assumed. In that case, s_a was defined by

$$s_a(f_1, \ldots, f_n)(y) = r_a(f_1(y), \ldots, f_n(y), y)$$

and hence need *not* be extensional.

Here are the consequences of (contextual) *content* compositionality with extensional composition operators:

Proposition 7. *If C-Funct(cont) holds with extensional composition operators, then C-Funct(poe-sem) and C-Funct(ext) both follow. Similarly for the weak variants.*

Proof. Assume C-Funct(*cont*) with extensional operations r_a. We have

$$poe\text{-}sem(a(e_1, \ldots, e_n), c, d) = cont(a(e_1, \ldots, e_n), c)(d)$$
$$= r_a(cont(e_1, c), \ldots, cont(e_n, c))(d)$$
$$= s_a(cont(e_1, c)(d), \ldots, cont(e_n, c)(d)) \quad \text{(for some } s_a)$$
$$= s_a(poe\text{-}sem(e_1, c, d), \ldots, poe\text{-}sem(e_n, c, d))$$

The existence of s_a in the third equality is again guaranteed by the extensionality of r_a. So C-Funct(*poe-sem*) holds. Also, since $ext(e, c) = poe\text{-}sem(e, c, circ(c))$,

(9.23)   C-Funct(*poe-sem*) implies C-Funct(*ext*).

The proof in the weak case is analogous, using (9.21b).   □

   We saw in Section 9.6.2 that, even if *poe-sem* can be recursively defined, it is (given a few assumptions) weakly contextually compositional exactly when no operators in the language shift circumstances. So as soon as there are such operators, C-Funct(*cont*)$_w$ cannot hold with extensional composition operations, although, by (I), it does hold with non-extensional operations. Also, although the implication (9.23) cannot in general be reversed, in practice C-Funct(*ext*) will fail when C-Funct(*poe-sem*) does, and similarly for the weak version.

9.6.5 Compositionality with structured contents

Recall, from Section 9.3.2 and (9.7) in Section 9.4.3, that in this case we started with a character semantics *char$_s$*—or *cont$_s$* in its uncurried version—and then defined corresponding versions *char* and *cont* for functional contents via the mapping * (where $p^*(d) = ref(p[d])$, for $p \in SCONT$), from which we got the semantics *ext* and *poe-sem* in the usual way.
   This already says a lot about how the various notions of compositionality involved are related. A small extra assumption gives us a little more. When *cont$_s$* is contextually compositional, think of *SCONT* as structured by the corresponding semantic operations r_a. Then we can require that the operation * is compositional too, that is that there exist operations s_a such that

(9.24)   a. $r_a(p_1, \ldots, p_n)^* = s_a\left(p_1^*, \ldots, p_n^*\right)$,
           b. and in the weak case, $r_a(p_1, \ldots, p_n, c)^* = s_a\left(p_1^*, \ldots, p_n^*, c\right)$

This gives us the following picture.

Proposition 8.

C-Funct(poe-sem) $\Longrightarrow$ C-Funct(poe-sem)$_w$ $\Longrightarrow$ Funct(char$_0$)

⇓   ⇓   ⇕

C-Funct(cont) $\Longrightarrow$ C-Funct(cont)$_w$ $\Longrightarrow$ Funct(char)

⇑   ⇑

C-Funct(cont$_s$) $\Longrightarrow$ C-Funct(cont$_s$)$_w$ $\Longrightarrow$ Funct(char$_s$)

Proof: Note that the upper part of the diagram is exactly as in Proposition 5, and it is proved in exactly the same way, since the relations between the semantic functions involved are the same, even when these functions are derived from the given *char$_s$*. Moreover, the lower horizontal implications are again instances of Lemma 1. Next, let us show that C-Funct(*cont$_s$*) implies C-Funct(*cont*):

$$cont(a(e_1,\ldots,e_n),c) = cont_s(a(e_1,\ldots,e_n),c)^* \quad \text{(by definition)}$$

$$= r_a(cont_s(e_1,c),\ldots,cont_s(e_n,c))^*$$

$$= s_a(cont(e_1,c)^*,\ldots,cont(e_n,c)^*) \quad \text{(by 9.24a)}$$

$$= s_a(cont(e_1,c),\ldots,cont(e_n,c))$$

Finally, the weak case is analogous, using (9.24b). □

Relevant parts of the results in Sections 9.6.2–9.6.4 carry over more or less directly to structured contents; I will not pursue this further here.[33] Likewise, I will not go into the adjustments that various forms of relativist semantics (Section 9.4.5) require for the results of this section to carry over.

9.6.6 An application: Do characters compose?

King and Stanley (2005) argue that speakers don't seem to use the character of *complex* expressions. Rather, they say, speakers use the character of the *simple* subexpressions, then plug in the contextual elements, and *then* compose to get the *content* of the complex expression. This part of the argument concerns the processing of meaning in speakers' minds. Another of their arguments is that it makes no difference for the end result whether characters are composed or not.

It is natural to take this is as a claim that semantic composition is done under the assumption of a fixed context, say c_0, so that, as in Section 9.5.2, *cont* turns into a function (*char$_{c_0}$*) taking only expressions as arguments. However, if King and Stanley's

---

[33] Except to note the following. Recanati (2007) gives a functional account of content (the *lekton* for sentential content), but interposes 'Austinian content' between this and the extensions in M, in the form of *pairs* of contents and circumstances. In other words, he uses a function *acont* from $E \times CU \times CIRC$ to $ACONT = CONT \times CIRC$ defined by

(i) $acont(e,c,d) = \langle cont(e,c),d \rangle$

This is intermediate between a functional and a structured account. But since *acont* doesn't apply the content to the circumstance but only lists the two, one expects it to be (contextually) compositional just when *cont* is. The proof of the following fact is left as an exercise.

Fact 5. *C-Funct(acont) is equivalent to C-Funct(cont), and similarly for the weak versions.*

reasoning is valid, it must surely be independent of any particular context chosen. By Fact 3, we then see that the claim that content is compositional however the context is fixed amounts exactly to weak contextual compositionality for *cont*. That is, although King and Stanley only talk about standard compositionality, their claim in effect expresses one of the versions of contextual compositionality. Interestingly, it is the weak version.

Furthermore, it follows, as we have seen, that King and Stanley's claim *entails* standard compositionality for character. So from the perspective of descriptive semantics, there is no opposition between their proposal and the claim that characters compose. This is of course compatible with the claim that in terms of psychological processing, speakers in fact do not compose character, a claim I will not try to assess here.[34]

9.7 CONCLUSIONS

The pervasive context dependence of natural languages, in all its forms, may seem to conflict with compositionality, or systematicity. Hopefully, the observations in this chapter can alleviate such worries, or at least clarify the issues at stake. We have seen that compositionality and context dependence are not incompatible, indeed that contextual compositionality of content, far from being opposed to traditional compositionality of character or standing meaning, in fact *entails* it, and that the strong and weak versions of contextual compositionality relate to how semantic theories deal with things like context shift failure, unarticulated constituents, modulation, etc.

Furthermore, I have stated, albeit in a rough way, how the presence of a recursive truth definition for the model theorist's basic form of semantics relates to the compositionality of that same semantics, and to more abstract semantics (for content or character) obtainable from it. I also analysed the effect of intensional operators on compositionality, with applications to the distinction between context and circumstance, to so-called monsters, and to the conditions under which extension (*Bedeutung*) can be compositional. Finally, I indicated how these facts extend to semantic accounts that posit structured contents.

---

[34] But note that King and Stanley will have to tell a plausible story about what speakers do when context doesn't allow them to fix the reference of indexicals. Suppose I hear through my hotel room wall someone shouting 'You don't love me anymore!', or I find a note on the sidewalk saying 'Please help, I am locked in the basement since yesterday!'. If the answer is that discourse referents or something similar are introduced as referents of *me, you*, etc. so that composition of content can be performed, that doesn't seem very different from forming the complex character of those sentences.

In sum, the results here, though not surprising or mathematically deep, show in what forms and for which kinds of semantic values one may reasonably raise the issue of compositionality, when extralinguistic context is taken seriously.[35]

[35] An early version of the observations here was presented at the Cognitive Science Symposium in Kista, Stockholm, June 2003. Much later did I realize that they might be useful in the current debate on various forms of context-sensitive semantics. I am grateful to the editors of this volume for allowing me to present them here, as well as to those who made comments or suggestions, in Kista and later, on my attempts in this area; in particular, Alexander Almér, Denis Bonnay, Elisabet Engdahl, Jerry Fodor, Ragnar Francén, Ernie Lepore, Larry Moss, François Recanati, Barry C. Smith, Jason Stanley, and two anonymous referees. Particular thanks go to my constant interlocutor and co-worker on matters compositional, Peter Pagin. The work was made possible by a grant from the Swedish Research Council.

CHAPTER 10

....

SUB-COMPOSITIONALITY

....

SEBASTIAN LÖBNER

10.1 RULES IN COMPOSITIONAL SEMANTICS

....

10.1.1 The Principle of Compositionality

This chapter will be based on the following version of the Principle of Compositionality (PC):

Principle of Compositionality
The meaning of a complex expression is a function of the lexical meanings of its components and the syntactic structure of the whole.

I will use the term 'construction' for morphosyntactically complex expressions, much as the term is used in Construction Grammar, but to the exclusion of lexical expressions, and without committing to any particular assumptions on grammar and language made in this approach. For the sake of convenience, the formation of morphologically or syntactically complex expressions will just be called 'syntactic composition', while the term 'semantic composition' will refer to the composition of meaning.

10.1.2 Regularity of composition

PC is usually considered necessary for explaining the apparent ability of human language users to interpret arbitrary regular complex expressions efficiently and uniformly. The explanation tacitly presupposes the assumption that the semantic operations involved in composition follow rules.

Regularity of semantic composition
The meaning of a syntactically regular expression derives from the meanings of its components in a regular way.

What does it mean for semantic composition to be regular? There must be rules that define syntactically regular expressions; and there must be rules that describe the way in which the meanings of regular complex expressions are derived from the meanings of their respective component expressions. These methods of derivation must apply uniformly to different individual cases and they must apply generally. Therefore the rules must apply to types of cases, in this context: types of expressions. Types of expressions subsume different individual cases, and they represent general categories. If a rule applies, for example, for a specified type of construction, the number of concrete instances is in principle open. In this sense, rules of syntactic or semantic composition capture general patterns. This is how PC is implicitly understood: we assume that compositionality rests on the availability of a limited number of patterns of syntactic and semantic composition. Thus, the condition of regularity of composition roughly means the following:

(10.1)   For all complex expressions of a given *type*, the *same* semantic operation yields its meaning out of the meanings of their components.[1,2]

This condition does not entail that different semantic operations apply to different types of cases. Indeed in all actual accounts of composition like those of model-theoretic semantics (MTS) in the tradition of Montague a small number of semantic operations are assumed to apply to a considerably larger set of types of constructions.

10.1.3 Types of expressions

Any given lexical expression is not just of a certain type, but belongs to hierarchies of types in the sense of Carpenter (1992). The possible types form a semi-lattice ordered by the partial ordering relation of subsumption; some types are sub-types of others, that is they are more specific.[3] The most specific, or minimal, type consists of solely an individual lexical expression. The most general type comprises all lexical expressions indiscriminately. Let us consider some types to which the German intransitive verb *bluten* 'bleed' belongs (names of non-minimal types are written in small capitals in order to distinguish types from instances of the type):

---

[1] An aspect which will be ignored here is the fact that one complex expression may belong to different types and thereby receive different compositional meanings.
[2] The types mentioned here, of course must not be minimal types that consist of just one individual case.
[3] An ordering is partial iff some, but not necessarily all, pairs of cases can be compared with respect to the ordering. For example, of the types 1-PLACE VERB and 2-PLACE VERB neither subsumes the other.

(10.2) Type   Other expressions of the same type
        LEXICAL EXPRESSION   *für* 'for', *bald* 'soon'
        PREDICATE TERM   *Ausdruck* 'expression', *geben* 'give'
        1-PLACE PREDICATE TERM   *Buch* 'book', *grün* 'green'
        1-PLACE VERB   *schlafen* 'sleep', *sitzen* 'sit', *arbeiten* 'work'
        GRADABLE 1-PLACE VERB   *schmerzen* 'ache', *lachen* 'laugh'
        VERB OF EMISSION   *strahlen* 'radiate', *stauben* 'give off dust'
        VERB OF SECRETION   *schwitzen* 'transpire', *fetten* 'give off grease'
        bluten   (none)

The types in (10.2) are ordered decreasingly by subsumption. They include traditional syntactic categories such as 1-PLACE VERB. The more specific types are based on semantic characteristics which are usually not considered significant for syntax.

For the unlimited set of lexical or complex expressions of a given language, systems of types can be set up under various aspects. Any such aspect, for example syntactic behaviour, defines a type hierarchy of its own. We will say that two types (out of arbitrary systems) coincide iff they represent the same class of expressions.

10.1.4 Syntax and semantics

For the question of compositionality two systems of types are relevant. In order to define syntactically regular expressions, a system of morphosyntactic rules is to be assumed. These rules define morphosyntactic types of expressions: t is a morphosyntactic type iff there is a morphosyntactic rule that has t as its (maximum) range of application. For example, VERB in English constitutes a morphosyntactic type since verbs constitute the range of application for the rules of verb inflection. In general, the morphosyntactic types correspond to the constituent categories of the morphosyntactic system of the language.

Analogously, the system of rules of semantic composition gives rise to another type system: t is a semantic type iff there is a semantic composition rule that has t as its (maximum) range of application. For example, 1-PLACE PREDICATE TERM has been considered a candidate semantic type, being the range of application of the rule which combines a predicate with its argument.[4]

In view of these considerations, one fundamental question for any theory of composition is this: Do the respective systems of syntactic types and of semantic types match? Are the same categories relevant for both syntactic and semantic composition? Or are the two systems, at least to some degree, incongruous? Traditional wisdom assumes that the two systems match. All formal work on compositionality is based on this assumption. Some authors even consider it part of the very notion of compositionality. Janssen (1997: 426f) goes as far as stating, in a list of assumptions 'implicit in it [i.e. the principle of compositionality, S.L.]', '[f]or each syntactic rule there is a semantic rule that

---

[4] It will be argued below that 1-PLACE VERB does not constitute a uniform semantic type, whence 1-PLACE PREDICATE TERM doesn't either.

describes its effect. In order to obtain this correspondence, the syntactic rules should be designed appropriately. For instance, semantic considerations may influence the design of syntactic rules.'

From this point of view, PC has the status of a methodological principle: trying to construct a formal description of natural language with a 'syntax' and a 'semantics' that match in this sense. However, whether such a description actually constitutes an implementation of PC, would depend on the question whether the 'syntax' and 'semantics' components really constitute a syntax and a semantics, respectively.[5] Consequently, this kind of approach does not aid the decision of whether or not human language actually is compositional. This, however, is a very important question for any theory of language—and it is not settled. The argument based on the fact that regular complex human language sentences can be interpreted effectively and uniformly provides strong evidence in favour of PC, but it does not prove it.

The only way, it appears, of providing an empirical proof of PC would consist in a successful description of syntactic and semantic composition in accordance with PC. The description of syntactic composition would have to be in accordance with syntactic theory and methodology, that is adequately 'autonomous'. Certainly, the notion of designing syntax so as to meet the requirements of semantics is not necessarily compatible with this requirement. Likewise, a theory of semantic composition would have to take into account syntactic structure but may have 'autonomous' perspectives, too. Only when both accounts of composition, syntactic and semantic, are sufficiently elaborated, will it be possible to settle the question as to whether or not the two type systems match.

10.1.5 Sub-compositionality

What kind of mismatch could possibly arise between the type systems of syntactic and semantic composition? Given what we know about language, the major syntactic and semantic constituent categories seem to match at least partially. Syntactic types such as PROPER NAME, PROPER NOUN, 1-PLACE VERB, 2-PLACE VERB appear to exhibit homogeneous compositional behaviour—for the prototypical cases, ignoring relational nouns, intensional verbs, non-intersecting adjectives, and similar exceptions. According to theories of language acquisition that assume either semantic or syntactic bootstrapping,[6] it is the match of the central instances of syntactic and semantic types that crucially helps the acquisition of syntactic rules and lexical knowledge.

Yet there is still room for mismatch. The same syntactic construction might have developed to host different patterns of semantic composition: such as intersecting adjectives alongside non-intersecting ones, extensional verbs along with intensional

[5] See Kracht (2007) for an in-depth discussion of this point. Kracht argues convincingly that the question of compositionality for a given description, and therefore the observation of PC in general, crucially depends on a proper separation of syntactic and semantic aspects of grammar.
[6] For example Pinker (1984, and later work) on semantic bootstrapping, Gleitman (1990) on syntactic bootstrapping.

verbs, definite NPs as well as indefinites and genuinely quantifying NPs. While all the examples just quoted may turn out to in fact involve different *syntactic* types, in principle a situation might arise where a syntactic type is semantically heterogeneous. Assume a syntactic construction that consists of two expressions, of syntactic type Y1 and Y2, respectively. Let one of the types, say Y2, be syntactically minimal in the sense that there are no syntactic sub-types of Y2 that could be justified by merely morphosyntactic regularities. The expressions of Type Y2 might nevertheless exhibit differing compositional behaviour, forcing a distinction between semantic sub-types E1, E2 ... within the class of expressions of Type Y2. I will call such a construction **sub-compositional**. In general, a syntactic construction is sub-compositional if there is no uniform rule of semantic composition for it. Thus, there would be distinct semantic types with uniform syntactic behaviour.

A stronger mismatch would result if certain semantic categorizations cut across several syntactic types. For example, the gradability of adjectives is a property that would probably not be considered relevant for syntax, as there is nothing syntactically wrong with graded ungradables, such as in *he is more married than his wife*. Gradability, however, clearly matters for semantic composition, and it cuts across syntactic distinctions of adjective types such as 1-PLACE vs. 2-PLACE ADJECTIVE. Below in Section 10.3 it will be argued that gradation of German verbs with *sehr* ('very, a lot') constitutes this type of phenomenon: across syntactic types of verbs, semantic patterns of gradation divide syntactic types of verbs into several semantic sub-types with their own sub-rules of composition.

In Section 10.2 the classical Montagovian approach to compositionality will be briefly reviewed with respect to its attitude towards the matching of syntax and semantics. It will be argued that the analyses proposed for the central NP–VP construction fail to appropriately deal with the actual varieties of compositional patterns, the failure being due to the attempt at matching syntactic and semantic composition for this construction in general. In Section 10.3 data will be presented that strongly suggest that gradation of verbs in German represents a phenomenon which is irreducibly sub-compositional. Section 10.4 will reflect on the consequences of sub-compositionality for a general theory of composition.

10.2 SEMANTIC REGULARITY IN CLASSICAL IMPLEMENTATIONS OF COMPOSITIONALITY

10.2.1 The classical scheme

The classical model of composition was developed in model-theoretic semantics (MTS for short), such as Montague Grammar (Montague 1970*b*, 1973) and its later developments and derivatives. In a nutshell, its basic design is as follows. A lexicon provides a set of basic expressions. These are assigned a lexical meaning, one or more syntactic types (categories) that figure in the syntactic composition rules, and a logical type. The logical type, such as FIRST-ORDER 1-PLACE PREDICATE, is the same for all instances of a syntactic type. This is the first constraint that makes sure that syntactic and semantic types match. Rules of syntactic composition define the ways in which regular complex expressions can be formed. According to a syntactic rule, expressions of specified syntactic types can be combined by means of a syntactic operation such as concatenation to form a complex expression of a specified type. The meaning of a complex expression is determined by rules of semantic composition. According to these rules the meaning of a regular complex expression is defined as the value that a semantic operation such as functional application yields for the meanings of the component expressions. For each syntactic rule there is a rule of semantic composition. This is the second constraint that makes syntactic and semantic composition match: the rules of semantic composition apply to the meanings of syntactic types of input expressions.

This design straightforwardly implements PC: the meaning of a complex expression is a function of the meanings of its component expressions, where the choice of that function is determined by the syntactic rule used to form the expression. According to this model, the meaning assignment is what is called a homomorphism. The syntactic structure of complex expressions is mirrored by the way in which their meanings are calculated.

Homomorphy of syntactic and semantic composition (HSS)
For every complex expression of a particular syntactic composition, the same rule of semantic composition applies.[7]

HSS rules out sub-compositionality a priori. However, central linguistic constructions such as subject+predicate have been considered semantically heterogeneous ever since. Therefore their apparent sub-compositionality was one of the main challenges to a formal theory of composition from the very beginning. Montague's (1973) approaches in 'The proper treatment of quantification in ordinary English' (PTQ) and his earlier work can be seen as attempts at overcoming the intuitive sub-compositionality of the NP–VP construction (among other problems). The NP–VP construction is intuitively heterogeneous with respect to the NP position in that it harbours NPs of apparently different logical nature, such as proper names, pronouns, definites, and indefinites along with genuinely quantifying NPs. A second point of sub-compositionality concerns the VP position; it allows for a verb with an intensional subject argument (*the temperature rises*) as well as for an ordinary verb with extensional subject argument (*the sun rises*). The meanings of these two semantic sub-types of verbs combine differently with the meanings of their subject NP. In the following we will have a closer look at the ways in which the classical theory dealt with issues of potential sub-compositionality.

---

[7] Janssen (1997: 427) puts it this way: 'The meaning of an expression is determined by the way in which it is formed from its parts. The syntactic production process, therefore, is the only input to the process determining its meaning.'

10.2.2 General strategies of evading sub-compositionality

Never aiming at a complete coverage of composition, MTS approaches use the method of 'fragments'. The fragmentariness of these accounts is two-fold. First, only a limited set of construction types is dealt with. Second, the lexical elements within the syntactic categories included are always just very small sets of representative items. This offers the opportunity, heavily made use of, to exclude cases from the syntactic categories to which the proposed analysis would not apply. As a result, sub-compositional constructions are reduced to semantically homogeneous sub-constructions.

Another strategy, permissible in MTS, would consist in artificially distinguishing in syntax between sub-types with equal syntactic, but different compositional behaviour (cf. the quote from Janssen (1997) above). According to the definition of syntactic and semantic types given above, this would mean actually defining syntactic rules in terms of semantic types. Proceeding in such a way undermines HSS at its very root; there is no sense in talking of a match of syntax and semantics if the two systems of composition are not defined independently.

The most problematic strategy, however, is what was dubbed 'generalization to the worst case': a method of subsuming less complex cases under cases of higher complexity by exploiting logical equivalences. The discussion to follow will focus on this strategy.

10.2.3 The 'uniform analysis' of NPs

In PTQ, Montague presented a uniform analysis of singular quantificational, indefinite, and definite NPs, including proper names and third person personal pronouns. The treatment was taken over by MTS in general and considerably elaborated in Generalized Quantifier Theory (GQT) initiated by Barwise and Cooper (1981). GQT extended the uniform treatment to non-logical quantifiers such as *many* or numerals. NPs are considered to be composed of an expression of type DET—*a, the, some, every, each, all, no, both, neither, many, few, most, a few, one, two, …*[8]—and an expression of type NOUN; proper names and singular third person personal pronouns are considered lexical NPs. Leaving aside technical and notational details and ignoring tense and mood, the uniform treatment in this approach is essentially this: a sentence of the form 'NP–VP' is analysed as 'the property expressed by the VP is one of the properties of "NP"'. For example,

(10.3)   a. *every boy is hungry* **every(boy) (hungry)**[9]
$$= \textbf{hungry} \in \{p1 \mid \forall x (x \in \textbf{boy} \rightarrow x \in p)\}$$

---

[8] List from Barwise and Cooper (1981: 171).
[9] We are using the notation of Barwise and Cooper (1981: 171) rather than Montague's original notation which would be in need of more explanation.

b. *Paul is hungry* **Paul(hungry)**

$$= \textbf{hungry} \in \{p \mid \textbf{paul} \in p\}$$

In (10.3a), **hungry** and **boy** denote one-place first-order predicates, or sets,[10] the lexical meanings of *hungry* and *boy*, respectively. **every** is an operator which takes two first-order one-place predicates, first a noun meaning and then a VP meaning; thus **every** itself is second-order. The result of combining the determiner meaning with the noun meaning, in this case **every(boy)**, is a second-order one-place predicate, that is a quantifier in the technical sense. It predicates of the VP meaning that it is true of every boy. **Paul** in (10.3b), with a capital P, also denotes a second-order predicate, namely the predicate that is true of all properties of Paul. It predicates of the VP meaning that it is true of Paul. Thus, the meanings of both types of NPs are uniformly treated as second-order predicates that apply to the predicate denoted by the VP. Both sentences in (10.3) are treated as instances of second-order predication.

A simple set-theoretical transformation shows that (10.3b) is equivalent to (10.3c), where **paul** with a lower case **p** is a simple individual term that denotes Paul.

(10.3)   c. *Paul is hungry*   ⇔   **paul** ∈ **hungry** or **hungry(paul)**

Unlike the formula in (10.3b) this is a simple first-order predication; the formula says that Paul belongs to the set of the hungry, or equivalently, that the predicate of being hungry applies to Paul. Note the crucial fact that the simple formula in (10.3c) is equivalent to the meaning of the sentence *Paul is hungry*, but is *not* the meaning proper that PTQ and GQT assign. The meaning proper is a second-order predication about the property of being hungry.

This treatment of NPs is problematic, for syntactic, semantic, and external reasons (Section 10.2.5 for the latter). As to syntax, it can be argued that the elements treated as determiners do not form a uniform syntactic type; for example *many*, *few*, and the numerals can be preceded by the definite article and possessive pronouns, but not by the other elements of the set; they would more adequately be analysed as a sub-type of adjectives. Furthermore, it can be shown that definite NPs, including personal pronouns and proper names do not possess scope, whence their syntax is different from genuinely quantifying NPs containing, for example, *every* or *all*. Due to the scopelessness of definites the distinction of external (sentence) negation and internal (VP) negation does not apply in their case; sentence negation coincides with VP negation, the only negation available: *Paul is not hungry*. By contrast, the distinction matters for genuinely quantifying NPs such as *every boy*: cf. *not every boy is hungry* vs. *every boy is not hungry*.[11] Similarly, indefinite 'determiners' such as *no, some, many, a few*, and the numerals have scope only under marked contextual conditions (i.e. in partitive or generic readings).[12]

---

[10] The difference between properties, predicates, and sets is of no relevance here.

[11] See Löbner (2000: §1–3) for an extensive discussion of this point), also Krifka (1992a).

[12] See Krifka (1999) and Löbner (1987, 1990: §3) on indefinites. For general non-quantificational theories of indefinites and definites see Heim's (1982) File Change Semantic and Kamp's Discourse Representation Theory DRT (Kamp and Reyle, 1993).

More severely, the analysis is inadequate from a semantic point of view. The uniform treatment of definite NPs such as proper names and genuinely quantifying NPs disregards the semantic differences between the two types of NPs. Treating first-order predications such as in (10.3b) as second-order predications cannot be justified in an adequate account of compositionality.[13] Since proper name meanings combine with the VP meaning in one way—the VP meaning constitutes a predicate over the NP referent—and the meanings of quantifying NPs in another way—the NP meaning constitutes a predicate over the VP denotation—the two sub-types of NPs require different composition rules.

10.2.4 The 'uniform analysis' of verb arguments

The technique of generalizing to the worst case (GWC), illustrated for the NP position, has also been applied for coping with semantic sub-regularities concerning the VP position. For example, the verb *rise* is used in (10.4a) for predicating about the extension of its subject NP (extensional use), while the predication in (10.4b) is about the intension of the subject (intensional use).

(10.4)   a. *the sun is rising*
          b. *the temperature is rising*

Montague in PTQ presents an analysis that treats both, intensional and extensional verbs, as predications over the intension of the subject argument, that is over the temperature function that assigns a temperature value to indices of world and time and the (constant) sun function that assigns the sun to every such index. While this is adequate for intensional verbs, it is problematic for the extensional cases. It can be considered somehow logically admissible as a border-line case: a predication over an extension can be considered a trivial case of predicating over the intension, namely over the one value the intension takes for the given world and time. This treatment does not, however, capture the logical property of extensional predication that an argument term can be replaced *salva veritate* by a term with the same extension. In Montague's treatment, this shortcoming is remedied by additional meaning postulates for individual verbs that permit the logical reduction of the intensional interpretation to an equivalent extensional predication.

The remedy, however, leads into a dilemma. If the primary output of the compositional system, the intensional interpretation, is considered the meaning proper, the account fails to capture the logical behaviour of extensional verbs and is hence semantically inadequate. Alternatively, if the meaning proper is the result of a two-step procedure which first produces the intensional interpretation and then reduces it to its extensional version by applying the individual meaning postulate for the verb involved, the

---

[13] Even third-order treatments of ordinary NP–VP sentences have been proposed, see Keenan and Faltz (1985: 87ff).

result will be properly extensional. However, the total process of meaning assignment for extensional instances of NP–VP now violates the requirement of regularity since the result of composition depends on the presence or absence of a meaning postulate which declares the verb an individual exception.

10.2.5 Constraints on a theory of composition, and the principal inappropriateness of generalizing to the worst case

As can be seen from the two cases discussed, the strategy of GWC is highly problematic. The very idea of GWC contradicts the objective of an adequate theoretical account of semantic differences since the notion obviously presupposes that there are *different* cases to be subsumed under one 'uniform' treatment. These cases may differ with respect to syntactic and/or semantic composition. What makes the method even more problematic is the fact that the 'worst cases' are given the status of paradigm cases although, as a rule, they are rather marginal due to their unusual semantic complexity.[14]

From a logical point of view, GWC generally fails to accurately account for the properties of the less than worst cases. As a central feature of its conception, predicate logic distinguishes orders of predication. Consequently, if a case of predication logically behaves like first-order rather than second-order predication, then the semantic analysis ought to reproduce this property of the construction. A similar distinction applies to extensional vs. intensional verbs: intensions are entities of higher logical order than their respective extensions.

In addition to these objections, GWC violates reasonable external constraints on a theory of semantic composition. One such constraint derives from the concern that a theory of semantic composition should be plausible from the point of view of cognitive processing. This would be the case if the semantic operations could be considered as corresponding to cognitive processes that are actually carried out during semantic processing. Even if not yet really understood, these processes are constrained by requirements of economy, executability, and learnability. Processing definite NPs such as personal pronouns and proper names as second-order predicates would be obviously uneconomic when a simple first-order treatment is functionally equivalent.

A second objection derives from the perspective of language acquisition. It appears plausible that the acquisition of semantic composition is to a considerable extent monotone: central rules of semantic composition are unlikely to be replaced once they have received sufficient and persistent confirmation. Children acquire definite NPs,

---

[14] As for the NP–VP construction, only a very small percentage of NPs in actual language use is genuinely quantificational. Intensional subject constructions such as *the temperature is rising* appear to be even more infrequent. See Löbner (1979) for a lexical exploration of intensional verb constructions in German.

such as personal pronouns, proper names, and definite descriptions, much earlier than genuine quantifiers like 'every'. Consequently, they build up a composition rule for verbs with definite NP subjects which has the referents of the NP as arguments of simple first-order predication. It is extremely implausible that this composition rule should later be replaced by a quantifier interpretation of definite NP arguments. In Löbner (2000: 253–76) it is shown how quantification proper can be conceived of as a modification of an underlying first-order predication. This kind of account is more in accordance with the course of language acquisition than GQT.

Similar considerations apply to the case of extensional verbs. From the point of view of processing it appears implausible that for extensional verbs first an intensional inter-pretation should be generated only to be reduced to the simpler extensional variant in a second step. The type of construction represented by *the temperature is rising* involves some sort of abstraction, the formation of a functional concept that assigns varying temperature values to different times. This is not involved in the case of extensional predication. As for acquisition, extensional verbs are, of course, acquired much earlier than intensional verbs like *rise* as used in *the temperature is rising*. In fact there seem to be languages where this type of construction is not available at all.[15]

As a result, generalization to the worst case should be dismissed altogether as an admissible method in a theory of semantic composition since it conceals, rather than reveals the actual mechanisms of semantic composition. A theory aiming at a proper understanding of the interplay of syntactic and semantic composition should distin-guish what is actually different.

10.2.6 Summary of the classical account of the English NP–VP construction

The discussion shows that *if* the English NP–VP construction is considered a syntac-tically uniform type *then* it must be considered severely sub-compositional, both with respect to the subject position and the VP position. In the classical account, the sub-compositionality is not adequately dealt with. The 'uniform treatment' of the construc-tion is achieved only at the expense of violating vital constraints on any appropriate linguistic theory of composition. These include:

- independent syntactic foundation of the rules of morphosyntactic composition;
- independent semantic foundation of the rules of semantic composition;
- plausibility of the rules of composition from the perspective of cognitive processing;
- plausibility of the rules of composition from the perspective of language acquisition.

---

[15] This seems to be the case, for example, in Lakhota which apparently lacks functional nouns such as 'temperature' altogether (Robert Van Valin, p.c.).

The discussion of the classical accounts of the NP–VP construction does not necessarily mean that a treatment in accordance with these constraints would invalidate HSS. Still, properly determined sub-types of NPs and VPs might turn out to coincide with the semantic types that are to be distinguished. Nevertheless, the discussion is worthwhile in this context, as it helps to make clear what would make up an adequate account of composition.

We will now turn to a semantic phenomenon which seems to represent a genuine, irreducible case of sub-compositionality, gradation of verbs in German.[16] The construction GRADADV–VERB, with an unspecific grading adverb GRADADV combined directly with a verb, hosts quite a few different patterns of semantic composition, depending on the semantic sub-type of verb. Unlike the semantic sub-types in the English NP–VP construction, the respective semantic verb-types do not seem to coincide with syntactic sub-types.

10.3 A CASE STUDY IN SUB-COMPOSITIONALITY: GRADATION OF VERBS IN GERMAN

10.3.1 Gradation of verbs in general

Verb gradation as such is a phenomenon not much investigated, but gaining momentum in recent years.[17] Bolinger (1972) presented a descriptive account of verb gradation in English in terms of types of grading; but he did not attempt a semantic analysis.[18] Usually considered a phenomenon associated with adjectives, gradation in the case of verbs is in fact quite common, although usually not by morphological means. Bolinger distinguishes two types of gradation, extent intensification and inherent intensification. Extent intensification contributes a quantity specification of the event, or events, referred to. The quantity specification concerns the temporal dimension: frequency, duration, or temporal proportion. With agentive verbs it can be roughly paraphrased as 'spend [X] time with V-ing':

(10.5)   *I use my cell phone a lot*

---

[16] There is nothing particular about German; other languages will be quite similar.

[17] The research on German verb gradation was financed by the Deutsche Forschungsgemeinschaft in the project LO 454/1 'Verbgraduierung' (verb gradation).

[18] Tsujimura (2001) offers a first, but incomplete account of degree gradation in Japanese. Recent work by Kennedy et al. investigates a closed-scale gradation in depth, but this type is complementary to open-scale gradation considered here (Hay, Kennedy, and Levin, 1999; Kennedy and McNally, 2005).

Table 10.1 Standard adjective and verb intensifiers

	Adjective intensification (positive form)	Verbs: degree intensification	Verbs: extent intensification
German	*sehr* groß	wächst *sehr*	arbeitet *viel*
Russian	*očen* bolšoy	*očen* rastët	*mnogo* rabotaet
Hungarian	*nagyon* nagy	*nagyon* nő	*sokat* dolgozik
Japanese	*totemo* ôkii	*totemo* hueru	*takusan* hataraku
Italian	*molto* grande	cresce *molto*	lavora *molto*
Spanish	*muy* grande	crece *mucho*	trabaja *mucho*
French	*très* grand	grandit *beaucoup*	travaille *beaucoup*
English	*very* big	grows *a lot*[19]	works *a lot*

This type of modification requires an atelic verb phrase, that is an activity or state term in Vendler's (1967) classification. Since the gradation concerns the time argument common to all verbs, the construction receives a fairly uniform compositional interpretation across atelic verbs; its compositional interpretation does not require a deep analysis of verb meaning.

The phenomenon of interest here is Bolinger's 'inherent' intensification, for which the term 'degree intensification' will be preferred here. The adverb specifies some degree, or gradable aspect, of the situation referred to.

(10.6)   German

> er   hat sehr gelitten
> he   has very suffered

'he suffered/was suffering/has suffered a lot'

It is not the temporal extent that is specified in (10.6), but the intensity of suffering. We follow Bolinger in calling verbs that permit degree intensification 'degree verbs'. Degree verbs can be telic or atelic, static or dynamic; they occur in all Vendler classes and with any arity. This does not mean, of course, that all verbs are degree verbs; which verbs are, is an open question. Examples of non-degree verbs are *sit, sleep, eat, die, mean, constitute*.

For upgrading, the standard case of intensification, German has separate adverbs for extent intensification and degree intensification, *viel* ('much') and *sehr* ('very'), respectively. An analogous distinction exists, for example, in Russian, Hungarian, and Japanese. By contrast, English, French, and Spanish use the same intensifier for extent and degree intensification, but a different one for adjective intensification. Italian uses *molto* in all three cases (see Table 10.1).

The following discussion is confined to German *sehr*. It should be added that this type of intensifier is confined to adjectives, adverbs, and verbs that are related to open scales,

---

[19] According to Bolinger (1972: 221), *to like* is the only English verb that takes *very* as intensifier.

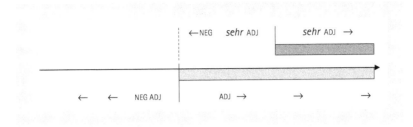

FIGURE 10.1 Scale diagram for *sehr* ADJ

that is scales without an absolute maximum. For closed scales, other intensifiers such as *ganz* ('wholly', 'completely') are used.[20]

10.3.2 The German degree intensifier *sehr* with adjectives

The German adverb *sehr* (a cognate of English *sore*) is the standard adverb for upgrading adjectives; it expresses a degree that is markedly higher than what is required for using the bare adjective. The intensifier can be used with all gradable adjectives and adverbs in the positive.[21]

(10.7)   a. *das Buch ist sehr schön/ dick/ teuer/   unterhaltsam*
              the book is   very nice/ thick/ expensive/ entertaining
         b. re-interpretation necessary
              das Buch ist (!) sehr englisch
              the book is   very English

The basic logical properties of *sehr* with adjectives can be captured by the following meaning postulates (for ADJ the respective adjective is to be inserted):

(10.8)   a. if *x* is 'sehr ADJ', then *x* is ADJ
         b. *x* may be ADJ but not 'sehr ADJ'
         c. if *x* is ADJ but not 'sehr ADJ' and *y* is 'sehr ADJ', then *y* is more ADJ than *x*

Given that all gradable adjectives relate to a scale and denote some interval of marked degree on that scale, the combination of *sehr* with an adjective would denote an extra marked part of the scale within the marked part denoted by the bare positive.[22] The function of *sehr* ADJ can be illustrated as in Fig. 10.1.

---

[20] See Kirschbaum (2002: §2.2, §3) for an elaborate account of types of adjective intensification in German. It would carry over, mutatis mutandis, to the gradation of verbs.

[21] Note that closed-scale adjectives such as *complete*, which cannot be modified with *very*, are basically not gradable. If used graded or modified with *sehr*, they undergo re-interpretation by way of coercion.

[22] For an analysis of *sehr*–ADJ implementing the postulates in (10.8) see Bierwisch (1989: 166, 177); an analysis of gradable adjectives in terms of markedness on a scale is proposed in Löbner (1990: §8).

10.3.3 *sehr* with degree verbs: examples

The meaning postulates for *sehr* with adjectives carry over, mutatis mutandis, to degree verbs. For example, if something grows a lot, it grows; it may grow, but not a lot; and if it grows a lot, it grows more than what just grows, but not a lot. Let me give a few representative examples with different semantic types of verbs. The collection of types is not exhaustive.

(10.9) a. *sie fror   sehr*   verb of sensation
          she was-cold very   *frieren*

       b. *ihre Pupille hat sich sehr geweitet*   degree achievement verb on a
          her pupil   has REFL very widened   specific scale *sich weiten*

       c. *die Erfahrung hat ihn sehr verändert*   degree achievement verb on an
          the experience has him very changed   unspecific scale *sich verändern*

       d. *er fürchtet   ihn sehr*   verb of emotional attitude
          he is afraid of him very   *fürchten*

       e. *das schockierte ihn sehr*   verb of emotional effect
          that shocked   him very   *schockieren*

       f. *er blutete sehr*   verb of substance emission
          he bled   very   *bluten*

       g. *er hat sich sehr verfahren*   verb of wrong action
          he has REFL very lost his way   *sich verfahren*

       h. *sie hebt   sich sehr von den andern ab* verb of comparison
          she stands REFL very from the others out *sich abheben von*

       i. *er stottert sehr*   verb of marked behaviour
          he stutters very   *stottern*

       j. *sie schlugen ihn sehr*   gradable verb of action
          they beat   him very   *schlagen*

10.3.4 Syntax

Although these examples trivially represent different constructions, due to the respective argument structures of the verbs, the grading adverb invariably modifies the verb itself prior to its combination with any arguments. Aspect does influence the interpretation of the gradation for certain types of verbs (see the next subsection) while tense obviously does not. Consequently the gradation applies between aspect and tense. What matters for the semantic composition is the syntactic combination of the adverb with the verb (plus aspect) itself. Syntactically, the hosting construction does not select degree adverbs; rather degree adverbs share the position with manner adverbs. Nor does the verb position select gradable verbs. Thus the GRADADV–VERB construction is a semantic type that does not match with any syntactic type. Consequently, the semantic type of degree verb intersects with various syntactic types of verbs.[23]

In addition, many degree verbs exhibit systematic alternation. For example the verb *ärgern* 'annoy, irritate, tease' of emotional effect occurs in the following constructions:

(10.10)   a. *sie   ärgert   ihre Schwester   sehr*   causative agent
               she   annoys   her   sister   very

           b. *das   ärgert   ihre Schwester   sehr*   causative source
               that annoys   her   sister   very

           c. *ihre Schwester   ärgert sich   sehr   (darüber)*   reflexive
               her   sister   is angry   very   about that

The gradation invariably relates to the degree of anger of the experiencer argument. In general, gradation affects the same aspect of the situation, independent of the way in which the varying argument structure of the verb is mapped into syntax.

10.3.5   Determining the scale of grading

With adjectives as well as with verbs, the intensification expressed by *sehr* relates to a certain scale. In the case of graded adjectives, the scale is provided by the adjective.[24] Notably, *sehr* itself does not provide a scale[25] although it is itself gradable (its suppletive comparative form is *mehr* 'more', its superlative *am meisten* 'most'). In this respect it resembles English *very* or French *très*. Therefore, in the case of combining *sehr* with a verb, the scale which *sehr* is to be related to has to be provided by the lexical meaning of the verb. Unlike gradable adjectives, however, most types of degree verbs do not semantically specify a particular prominent scale. Hence the question arises as to how the scale of intensification is compositionally determined. The following will not offer a formal account—which is not yet available—but just illustrate the type of problem a compositional account is facing.

10.3.5.1   *Verbs of sensation*

Stative intransitive verbs of sensation or emotion like *frieren* 'be cold', *schwitzen* 'be warm, hot' (one meaning variant of *schwitzen*, besides 'sweat, transpire'), *sich freuen* 'be glad', *sich ärgern* 'be angry' are semantically close to adjectives; in fact the respective state predications are lexicalized as adjectives in many languages (cf. the English equivalents,

---

[23] One would not even want to syntactically distinguish gradable verbs from non-gradable ones. Even non-gradable verbs can be syntactically combined with *sehr* or other intensifiers; the verb meaning is then coerced into a gradable reading.

[24] The scale of grading to which *sehr* relates is not just the scale the adjective in its positive form relates to, but the derived scale of the extent to which the minimum value for 'being ADJ' is exceeded (as illustrated in Fig. 10.1); for a formal account see Bierwisch (1989: 166, 177).

[25] In this regard *sehr* crucially differs from the large set of scale-specific gradable manner adverbs such as 'slowly', 'skilfully', etc.

but also corresponding adjectives in Korean or Japanese.) The state expressed is subjectively perceived in varying degrees and hence takes values on a scale. The individual verb determines a condition of the experiencer, for example felt temperature or joy, and predicates of the subject argument that it feels this condition to a certain degree. The addition of *sehr* specifies this degree as high. In a Davidsonian account of verb meaning, the verb would refer to a situation e of a certain type, which is characterized by the fact that there is an experiencer $\text{EXP}(e)$,[26] syntactically specified by the subject of the construction; a certain bodily or emotional condition COND of the experiencer, that is $\text{COND}(\underline{\text{EXP}}(e))$ is lexically specified and said to take some value other than normal. Intensification by *sehr* relates to the scale of possible degrees of $\text{COND}(\underline{\text{EXP}}(e))$.

10.3.5.2 *Verbs of degree achievement on a specific scale*

The numerous verbs of this type usually come in an intransitive variant and a causative variant, like *sich verbessern* 'become better' and *verbessern* 'make better'. In German, most of them are deadjectival, deriving either from the positive or the comparative form, but invariably meaning 'become/make more ADJ', where ADJ is the source of derivation. The adjective underlying degree achievement verbs is gradable, related to an open scale. The pattern is near-productive, seemingly only constrained by morphological conditions such as the exclusion of past participle forms as a source. Usually the intransitive version is the reflexive form of the causative one: *(sich) ver-eng-en* ('to narrow', > *eng* 'narrow'), *(sich) ver-kleiner-n* ('to become/make smaller', > *klein-er*, comparative of *klein* 'small'), etc. Some verbs of this type are not derived from adjectives: *wachsen* 'grow', *steigen* 'rise', *spreizen* 'spread out, force apart', or *dehnen* 'stretch'. Verbs of this semantic type refer to events which consist in (the causation of) a change in time of a specific attribute of the theme argument such as its *size*, *length*, etc. The addition of *sehr* to the predication specifies that change as big. Thus, the scale to which the intensification relates is the extent of $\text{VCHG}(\underline{\text{THEME}}(e))$, where VCHG represents the change of the theme with respect to the dimension of change specified by the verb, that is the difference between the value the theme argument occupies on the scale before the event and the value afterwards; this holds both for the intransitive and the causative verb variants.

10.3.5.3 *Verbs of degree achievement on an unspecific scale*

This type of verb is maybe less productive, but still not rare. Prototypical members are reflexive or causative *(sich) ändern*, *(sich) verändern* 'change, become different', *umformen* 'reshape', *überarbeiten* 'rework', *umstrukturieren* 'restructure', *modifizieren* 'modify', *mutieren* 'mutate', and many others. The pattern of *um-* prefixation is productive with verbs of producing, shaping, etc. The meaning of the verbs is similar to the previous type: they express a change of the theme argument in some respect, and intensification by *sehr* relates to the extent of the change. But the verbs of this type do not lexically

---

[26] In the following, roles of verbs that are part of the argument structure of the verb are underlined. Roles and attributes that do not surface grammatically are not underlined.

specify the dimension of change. The scale relevant for the intensification is the extent of some unspecific change the theme argument undergoes, $\text{CHG}(\underline{\text{THEME}}(e))$.

10.3.5.4 *Verbs of emotional attitude*

Verbs of emotional attitude such as *fürchten* 'be afraid of' are similar to the verbs of bodily or emotional attitudes. They denote a specific emotional attitude of the experiencer specified by the subject of the construction towards a specified source argument: $\text{ATT}(\underline{\text{EXP}}(e),\underline{\text{SRC}}(e))$. Intensification relates to the intensity of that attitude.

10.3.5.5 *Verbs of emotional effect*

This group is large and exhibits manifold alternation (cf. (10.10)): They express events involving a specific emotional effect on the part of the experiencer. Intensification by means of *sehr* specifies this effect as strong. The dimension involved is thus the intensity of $\text{EMO}(\underline{\text{EXP}}(e))$, with EMO the emotional effect on the experiencer.

10.3.5.6 *Verbs of substance emission*

Verbs of substance emission are mostly derived from nouns denoting some kind of substance; the verbs are intransitive and roughly mean 'emit/give off N', where N denotes that substance: *bluten* ('bleed', > *Blut* 'blood'), *schwitzen* ('sweat', > *Schweiß* 'sweat'), *stauben* ('send out dust', > *Staub* 'dust'), *haaren* ('lose hair', > *Haar* 'hair'), *dampfen* ('steam', > *Dampf* 'steam'), *nässen* ('wet', > *nass* (adj.) 'wet') and many more. These verbs have an implicit argument, which may occasionally surface, such as in *Blut und Wasser schwitzen*, 'to sweat blood and water'; let us call it EMI, for emitted substance. The intensification relates to the quantity of the substance emitted, that is $\text{QUANT}(\text{EMI}(e))$.

10.3.5.7 *Verbs of wrong action*

The pattern *sich ver-V*, meaning roughly 'to V with a wrong outcome', is very productive in German; almost any action verb, transitive or intransitive, can enter the pattern. It means to do what the source verb expresses with a result that erroneously differs from the intended result: taking the wrong way (*sich verlaufen* > *laufen* 'run, go'), miswriting (*sich verschreiben* > *schreiben* 'write'), dialling the wrong number, or the number wrong, *sich verwählen* (> *wählen* 'dial'), making a mistake *sich vertun* (> *tun* 'do'). Intensification relates to the extent of the difference between the intended result INTRES and the actual result RES of the action e, something like $\text{DIFF}(\text{INTRES}(e), \text{RES}(e))$.

10.3.5.8 *Verbs of comparison*

Verbs of comparison include *sich abheben* 'stand out', *sich unterscheiden* 'differ', or *sich ähneln* 'be similar'. They are usually non-transitive two-place verbs with an oblique object, some of them with reciprocal uses; they express some sort of general comparison stating an unspecific difference or similarity. The scale relevant for *sehr* intensification with verbs of differing is $\text{DIFF}(\underline{c1}(e),\ \underline{c2}(e))$, where C1 and C2 are the two roles surfacing in the construction, and DIFF the degree in which they differ in some unspecified respect. The difference is expressed to be great if *sehr* is added. There do not seem to be many verbs that relate to a difference in some specific dimension such as the verbs of the productive English type represented by *outnumber, outweigh, outlast, outrank*, etc.; one German example would be *überwiegen* 'outweigh, outbalance, prevail'.

10.3.5.9 *Verbs of marked behaviour*

This group of verbs denotes actions, or conditions, that differ from the unmarked way of performance in a specific respect, for example volume of speech, speed of motion, evenness of walking, etc. *sehr* with this type of verbs marks that difference as great. The type includes cases such as *schreien* 'shout, cry out', *flüstern* 'whisper', *stottern* 'stutter', *hinken* 'limp', *rennen* 'run', *schielen* 'squint', and many others. Intensification concerns the extent of deviation from the unmarked.

10.3.5.10 *Gradable verbs of action*

Finally, there is a big residue of verbs of action which do not seem so far to fit into a clear pattern. For example *schlagen* 'beat' can be intensified with *sehr*, with the result of at least two readings. Intensification may apply to the effort the agent invests into the beating, resulting in markedly many and/or heavy strokes; it may as well relate to the effect it has on the victim, in terms of pain or harm. It is not clear which transitive action verbs qualify for intensification with *sehr*. One sub-type consists of verbs that denote an action that leaves some effect on the patient; this type includes beneficiary verbs such as *helfen* 'help' or *schaden* 'damage, harm'; here *sehr* concerns the extent of the effect of action. Other verbs just denote some sort of action with intensification relating to some attribute of the agent, for example *sich anstrengen* 'exert o.s.'

For some but not all types of gradable verbs, the scale of grading interacts with aspect. For the verbs of substance emission, more substance is emitted the longer the event is continued. If the aspect of the verb is imperfective (in the sense of Comrie (1976)), gradation relates to the rate of emission. If verbal aspect is perfective, perfect, or prospective, that is if reference is to the total event, the quantity grading may also refer to the total amount of substance emitted. Analogous conditions hold for degree achievements on specific or unspecific scales.

10.3.6 Rules of composition and logical entailments

The observed variety of compositional patterns corresponds with varying types of logical entailments and equivalences ($\Leftrightarrow$), for example:

(10.11) a. *sie fror sehr*   ⟺   *ihr war sehr kalt* (adj.)
                                          'she (lit. to her) was very cold'

         b. *sich sehr weiten*   ⟺   *viel weiter* (adj. comp.) *werden*
                                          'become much wider'

         d. *sich sehr fürchten vor* ⟺   *große Furcht* (noun) *haben vor*
                                          'have great fear of'

         f. *sehr bluten*   ⟺   *viel Blut* (noun) *verlieren*
                                          'lose much blood'

         g. *sich sehr verwählen*   ⟺   *sehr falsch wählen*
                                          'dial very wrong'

         h. *sich sehr abheben*   ⟺   *sehr anders* (adj.) *sein*
                                          'be very different'

         i. *sehr stottern*   ⟺   *sehr stockend* (adv.) *sprechen*
                                          'speak very haltingly'

Logical equivalences like these constitute semantic evidence and data to be explained. The fact that they differ in form and cannot be unified to one general pattern provides strong evidence for the sub-compositionality of verbal degree intensification. If a uniform rule of interpretation were assumed, it seems impossible to derive all these different types of equivalences from it.

10.3.7 Summary on verb gradation

These data may suffice to show that there are considerable differences in compositional behaviour across various semantic types of verbs. It appears that an account of verb gradation can only be satisfactory if it is able to uncover the varying ways in which intensification finds its scale in the complex lexical meaning of the verb. Some cases concern implicit dimensions of overt arguments, others dimensions of implicit arguments; in yet other cases, the crucial scale is a scale of differences with respect to varying components of the verb meaning. Although the resulting picture of semantic composition is diverse and complex, there appear to be sub-rules that apply homogeneously for each type of gradable verb. These rules are grounded in the type of lexical meaning of the verb—and therefore general rules.

A promising framework for decomposition appears to be a frame semantics for verbs, or equivalent means such as the attribute–value structures used in formal linguistics. Frames[27] can be used to represent the attributes of events (which include explicit and implicit arguments) and, recursively, their respective attributes and hence the possible dimensions of intensification. Different instances of the same semantic type of verb

---

[27] For an appropriately elaborate frame conception see Barsalou (1992); Petersen (2007) offers a formalization of Barsalou's notions.

would share the same general frame structure, but differ in individual specifications of certain frame components. Instances of the same type of verb frame would interact with a grading adverb in a uniform way.

A frame analysis into verb meanings appropriate for a systematic compositional account of verb gradation would lead beyond those parts of verb frames that were elaborated in earlier theories such as Fillmore's. These accounts were essentially restricted to the representation of explicit (and sometimes implicit) verb arguments, that is those attributes of events which directly surface in syntax. Gradation of degree verbs, by contrast, concerns attributes of arguments rather than attributes of the event itself. Thus, the determination of the relevant scale of gradation reveals deeper elements of verb meaning.

10.4 CONCLUSION

If the existence of sub-compositional constructions is to be acknowledged, what does that mean for a theoretical account of compositionality? First of all, it does not mean abandoning the Principle of Compositionality. As long as semantic composition follows rules and does not draw on extra-linguistic information, it is in accordance with PC. Sub-compositionality, however, requires a revision of HSS, the notion that semantic composition is homomorphic to syntactic composition. While the classical approach assumes that the function that yields the meaning of the whole is determined by syntactic structure alone, we are now faced with cases where, in addition, the finer semantic types of the component expressions may matter. Note that this possibility, too, is covered by the phrasing of PC in its classical version. If the theory of compositional semantics is extended to more and more data, it might well turn out that sub-compositionality and the need for deep lexical decomposition is the rule rather than the exception. Other basic constructions that host a variety of sub-compositional sub-types may display a similar picture, for example the A–N construction. In fact, such constructions have led to similar considerations about the role of the lexicon in the determination of compositional regularities, for example Pustejovsky's conception of co-composition (this volume).

For the actual practice of doing analysis of semantic composition this means that it is no longer possible to more or less neglect lexical meanings, as has been common practice in MTS. Rather the analysis of composition has to be based, at least for some constructions, on a systematic decomposition of lexical meanings. This decompositional analysis would have to establish types of lexical meanings, and representations thereof, that allow an explanation of their compositional behaviour.

Such an approach is well in accordance with a cognitive perspective on composition. In actual semantic processing, lexical meanings are, of course, not only available as idiosyncratic units of knowledge, but rather as instances of more general patterns of concepts. Thus, the information available for processing is not confined to individual lexical meaning plus some level of syntactic type. Rather it includes qua the structure of the lexical meaning the whole hierarchy of semantic types the lexical entry belongs to—and this information can naturally be fed into the semantic processing.

P A R T III

COMPOSITIONALITY IN FORMAL SEMANTICS

CHAPTER 11

FORMALIZING THE RELATIONSHIP BETWEEN MEANING AND SYNTAX

WILFRID HODGES

INTRODUCTION

We will build a formalism for studying the relationship between meaning and syntax. Accounts of this relationship go back many centuries, and the last fifty years have no monopoly of insight. But the earlier work, particularly when it tried to rise above individual phenomena and give a general picture, too often relied on vagueness, metaphor, and even evasion. Today we try to separate the precise from the vague by formalizing. Research in semantics has moved steadily in this direction for some decades now, and it seems there is some way still to go.

I report some history and some mathematics; the mathematics builds on the history. I should have given more supporting evidence and arguments, but lack of space forced me to fall back on references. The referees very helpfully identified places where I needed to be more explicit.

11.1 ARISTOTELIAN COMPOSITIONALITY

11.1.1 The basic Aristotelian theory

The roots of the idea of compositionality lie in the Aristotelian theory of meaning—not so much Aristotle's own theory, rather the theory built up by the commentators on his writings. Versions of this theory prevailed in Western Europe, and among the philosophers of the medieval Arab empire, up until Frege and early Russell. For the sake of definiteness I mainly cite the eleventh-century Persian-Arabic writer Ibn Sīnā, although similar things can be found in many other authors. (With luck, translations of the relevant works of Ibn Sīnā will be available before long, but meanwhile Inati (1984) can serve as an introduction.)

The backbone of the Aristotelian theory of meaning, as it appears in Ibn Sīnā, consists of two clauses:

1. *Single words.* Certain words (for example 'horse', 'rational', 'moves') are true of certain things and not true of others. Each of these words has a corresponding mental object, its meaning or concept (*ma^{c}nā*), which governs its use. The *ma^{c}nā* is a many-faceted structure; for our purposes its main aspect is the essence (*dhāt*), which serves as a criterion to determine what things the word is true of.

2. *Constructions.* When words have a *ma^{c}nā*, they can be combined in certain ways so that the resulting expression has its own *ma^{c}nā* derived from those of the words. For example the criterion for 'rational animal' to be true of something is that the thing meets the criterion for 'rational' and the criterion for 'animal'. The criterion for 'Some animal is rational' to be true is that something satisfies the criterion for 'rational animal'. In these cases the criteria for the two words are 'parts' of the criterion for the whole phrase. (In what sense are they 'parts'? At this point Ibn Sīnā, like virtually all Aristotelians, hides behind metaphors and analogies.)

Several writers formulate (2) as a general rule. For example Al-Fārābī (tenth-century Arab):

(11.1)   [We] compose sentences of expressions signifying parts of the compound affair signified by the sentence. … the imitation of the composition of *ma^{c}nā*'s by the composition of expressions is by [linguistic] convention. (Zimmermann, 1981: 43, Zimmermann's translation slightly adjusted.)

Or Abelard (twelfth-century French):

(11.2)   For when [two phrases] have the same order of construction and the [corresponding] spoken words have the same meanings, it seems that the sense of the constructed phrase would be the same. (Abaelardus, 1970:125 l. 22ff, my trans.; see also Rosier-Catach 1999.)

Or Frege (early twentieth century):

(11.3)   Our ability to understand sentences that we have never heard before obviously rests on the fact that we build the sense of a sentence out of parts that correspond to the words. (Gabriel et al., 1976: 127, Letter to Jourdain, my trans.)

The common theme of these three quotations is that we understand phrases by building up a step-by-step correlation between their parts and the parts of their meanings. We can refer to this theme as *Aristotelian compositionality.* Since there is no known line of influence from Al-Fārābī to Abelard, it seems likely that similar formulations existed in the writings of their common source, namely the Aristotelian commentators of the late Roman Empire.

11.1.2 Extensions of the Aristotelian theory

Certainly not all words have meanings that we could describe by truth criteria as in (1). For example the word 'every' doesn't classify things in the world into those it is true of and those it isn't true of. The Aristotelians made some important progress towards describing meanings for some of these other words.

A typical example is the mainstream Aristotelian theory about 'every'. According to this theory, 'every' combines with other words w which do have meanings as in (1), so as to create meaningful phrases $P(w)$, and we can explain 'every' by saying how the meanings of these phrases $P(w)$ depend on those of the meaningful words w. Thus Ammonius (Alexandria, early sixth century):

(11.4) Determiners ... combine with the subject terms and indicate how the predicate relates to the number of individuals under the subject; ... 'Every man is an animal' signifies that 'animal' holds of all individuals falling under 'man'. (Ammonius, 1897: 89, my trans.)

Bertrand Russell rediscovered this account of quantifiers in his paper 'On denoting' (Russell 1905: 480):

(11.5) *everything* [is] to be interpreted as follows: C(everything) means '$C(x)$ is always true'.

The same style of explanation was used for some other expressions. For example Ibn Sīnā tells us that

(11.6) The senses of 'in' and 'not' become complete only through a link [with another meaning]. (Ibn Sīnā, 2002: Method i, Remark on atomic and compound expressions)

Frege took the revolutionary view that even the criterion for being a horse can be explained in terms of the criteria for sentences like 'Red Rum is a horse' to be true. This is presumably part of what he meant by his famous *Grundsatz*:

(11.7) The meanings of the words should be sought in the interconnections of the sentence (*im Satzzusammenhange*) ...

(Frege, 1884: Einleitung, my trans. In case the translation seems unfamiliar, note in particular that Frege is describing *where* one should look for the meaning, not *when*.) Ibn Sīnā was happy to say that this kind of analysis does give a 'sense' to the words in question, and Frege seems to agree.

By contrast the Aristotelians made very little progress towards extending (2) to other syntactic constructions. Constructions with the genitive gave them particular difficulties. For example, Ibn Sīnā notes the Arabic construction that yields the phrases 'thrower of stones' and 'herder of sheep' (his examples, Ibn Sīnā, 1970: 12.14), but he gives no hint of how the meanings of these phrases are constructed from the meanings of 'thrower', 'stones', 'herder', and 'sheep'. Some 650 years later, Leibniz (Couturat, 1903: 287) still struggles with the semantics of 'reading of poets'.

Their inability to handle more than a few constructions should have worried the Aristotelians more than it did. Aristotelian compositionality was essentially their only candidate for an explanation of how I transfer my thoughts into your mind by speaking to you.

Linguists had a different reason to be dissatisfied with the limited treatment of constructions in Aristotelian theory. Namely, each language has its own constructions, and we should be prepared to explain the semantics of any one of these constructions, not just those that fit a convenient theory. Already in the fourteenth century the Arabic grammarian Abu Ḥayyān was making this point:

(11.8)   Are Arabic constructions different from the words in the dictionary? ... All these matters are subject to convention, and matters of convention require one to follow the practice of the speakers of the relevant language. The difference between syntax and lexicography is that syntax studies universal rules, whereas lexicography studies items one at a time.

For further details of this text see Hodges (2006a). It seems that the 'rules' include rules of meaning corresponding to the syntax.

11.1.3 Some marks of the Aristotelian theory

The Aristotelian theory of meaning still has its influence, probably more among philosophers and cognitive scientists than among linguists. It may be helpful to list some distinctive features of the Aristotelian theory, before we turn to modern compositionality (i.e. PTW (Partee, ter Meulen, and Wall, 1990) compositionality—see Definition 4 below for the definition and the name).

1. *Parts of meanings.* On the Aristotelian theory, the meaning of a sentence has parts that correspond to the syntactic parts of the sentence. We will see that PTW compositionality doesn't assume that meanings have parts. In fact the PTW formalism allows two sentences with completely different syntax to have the same meaning.

2. *Words 'on their own' can have meanings.* Many Aristotelians have expressed the difference between words like 'horse' and words like 'every' by saying that 'horse' has a meaning 'by itself' or 'in isolation' or 'on its own account' or 'per se'. (Russell

(1905) uses all four expressions.) The idea is that one can describe the meaning of 'horse' without referring to how 'horse' relates to other words. This distinction is irrelevant to PTW compositionality.

3. *Taḥrīf*. This convenient term comes from Ibn Sīnā (e.g. Ibn Sīnā, 1970: 31.10); there seems to be no Western equivalent. *Taḥrīf* is the phenomenon that an occurrence of a word in a sentence has its meaning changed (*munḥarif*) by its context in the sentence. This notion makes sense if, like Ibn Sīnā, we think of the language user as setting up in her mind a correlation between occurrences of meanings and occurrences of expressions when she speaks or listens. If we don't think of the language user this way, we will need some other ways of describing the phenomena that Ibn Sīnā would count as examples of *taḥrīf*. We will return to this in Section 11.2.4.

11.2 MODERN (PTW) COMPOSITIONALITY

11.2.1 Some twentieth-century linguists

It was only in the twentieth century that linguists started to handle the semantics of linguistic constructions with the proper generality. Here I pick up the thread with Leonard Bloomfield's (1933) book *Language*.

Bloomfield considers a particular language, say *L*. A 'phonetic form' of *L* is a string of sounds which is 'pronounceable' in *L*; a 'linguistic form' of *L* is a phonetic form which 'has a meaning' (Bloomfield, 1933: 138). The meaning of a linguistic form is 'the [kind of] situation in which the speaker utters it and the response which it calls forth in the hearer' (Bloomfield, 1933: 139). (We need to add 'kind of' to Bloomfield's definition because a linguistic form is a part of the language; it's not limited to one situation.)

Bloomfield approaches the notion of a construction via the notion of a constituent. A 'constituent' of a linguistic form *e* is a linguistic form which occurs in *e* and also in some other linguistic form. It is an 'immediate constituent' of *e* if it appears at the first level in the analysis of the form into ultimate constituents. Bloomfield adds the significant remark that 'Any English-speaking person who concerns himself with this matter' can spot the immediate constituents of simple sentences and phrases (Bloomfield, 1933: 160f). A 'construction' combines two or more linguistic forms as immediate constituents of a more complex form (Bloomfield, 1933: 169—Bloomfield omits the word 'immediate', but it seems to be implied).

Bloomfield's definitions raise a number of problems. Let me discuss two.

(a) *Sentence meanings vs. word meanings*. There are good arguments for taking the meaning of a *sentence* in terms of the kinds of situation where it's appropriate to use the sentence and the appropriate responses to the sentence. This fills an obvious gap in the Aristotelian account, which had no separate notion of meanings for sentences. But problems arise as soon as we try to apply Bloomfield's account of meaning to single words. What kind of situation corresponds to 'apple'? Bloomfield himself notes that 'people very often utter a word like *apple* when no apple at all is present' (Bloomfield, 1933: 141). In short, Bloomfield repairs the Aristotelian account at the level of sentences, but he loses all the Aristotelian insights at the level of descriptive words. Since there is no natural way to combine kinds of situation into a complex kind of situation, the notion of compositionality drops out of the picture.

(b) *Meaningful vs. grammatical.* Bloomfield's notion of a 'pronounceable' string of sounds is purely phonetic. So the entire work of distinguishing grammatical from ungrammatical expressions of the language L rests on the question whether they are 'meaningful'. But I think the overwhelming consensus is that we can coherently ask (1) whether all grammatical expressions are meaningful, and (2) whether all meaningful expressions are grammatical.

The answers to both questions (1) and (2) are bound to depend on one's notion of meaningfulness. As to the first, in Section 11.3.1 below I prove a theorem to the effect that on one notion of meaning, which I call *fregean value*, any constituent of any sentence does have a meaning. Section 11.3.2 will note some features that fregean values have and your favourite notion of meaning might well not have.

As to the second question above, we obviously do manage to understand ungrammatical sentences all the time. In my youth I read somewhere the sentence 'Them's awkward things to drive, one man so many of them, is a pig, very'. (I'd be grateful to know where it came from. Dorothy Sayers?) But—as noted by James Higginbotham (2007)—the formalism later in this chapter will ignore all meanings except those of 'expressions' of the language. Since I intend that one possible interpretation of 'expression' in this formalism is your favourite notion of grammatical phrase, I should say why I think the restriction of meanings to grammatical expressions is not a disaster. Briefly, the assignment of meanings to ungrammatical expressions is parasitic on their assignment to grammatical ones. We assign a meaning to an ungrammatical utterance when we think we can reconstruct a grammatical sentence that the speaker could have intended. But first, the possibility of this reconstruction depends on a range of things, not all of them in the language; for example we give more charity when we know that the speaker is not a native speaker of the language, or that the utterance was a text message sent from a mobile phone. And second, the same charity sometimes makes us give to a completely grammatical sentence a meaning which really belongs to another similar sentence, if we think the speaker has confused the two sentences; so feeding the results of charity into the notion of meaning is going to result in some false meanings of grammatical expressions. But if you are still unconvinced, you can read 'meaning' in the later parts of this chapter as 'meaning of grammatical expression'.

The moral of problem (b) is that we need a definition of 'constituent' that doesn't depend on meaning. Bloomfield's observation about 'any English-speaking person' suggests taking it as a raw datum that users of a language know how to split sentences down into their constituent phrases. In the next generation after Bloomfield, some linguists (for example Wells (1947) and Chomsky (1975a: ch. 8 from 1955)) proposed criteria for determining the constituents of a phrase without any appeal to the notion of meaning.

Subsequent work has made it clear that the intuitions of Bloomfield's 'English-speaking person' are a poor guide to the general situation. For example in heavily inflected languages without fixed word order, low-level syntactic constructions don't arrange their immediate constituents in an order; instead they add inflections to them. The resulting phrase need not even be a connected segment of the sentence containing it. Further analysis of this situation led Joan Bresnan and Ronald Kaplan (Kaplan and Bresnan, 1982, Bresnan, 2001) to propose Lexical Functional Grammar, a formalism where sentences have two different kinds of constituent. In their formalism a sentence has 'c-structure' constituents reflecting 'the superficial arrangement of words and phrases' (Kaplan and Bresnan, 1982: 175), and a hierarchical 'f-structure' which 'encodes its meaningful grammatical relations and provides sufficient information for the semantic component to determine the appropriate predicate–argument formulas' (Kaplan and Bresnan, 1982: 176). Other linguists have proposed other formalisms with their own notions of constituent.

When there are various notions of constituent to choose between, a natural response is to axiomatize the basic features of constituents. Compare the formalization of 'bare grammar' by Keenan and Stabler (2003). In fact one can read off a constituent structure (in the sense of Definition 1 below) from any bare grammar in the sense of Keenan and Stabler, in at least two ways (Hodges, submitted). The formalization in the next subsection could have been derived from the ideas of Bloomfield and Chomsky above— though in fact it came from analysing the term-algebra formalism used in Hodges (2001) and removing unnecessary assumptions.

11.2.2 Constituents

Definition 1.

(a) By a *constituent structure* we mean an ordered pair of sets $(\mathbb{E}, \mathbb{F})$, where the elements of $\mathbb{E}$ are called the *expressions* and the elements of $\mathbb{F}$ are called the *frames*, such that the four conditions below hold. (Here and below, e, f, etc. are expressions; $F, G(\xi)$ etc. are frames.)

1. $\mathbb{F}$ is a set of nonempty partial functions on $\mathbb{E}$.

   (A partial function $F(\xi_1, \ldots, \xi_n)$ on $\mathbb{E}$ is a thing that yields a member of $\mathbb{E}$, namely $F(e_1, \ldots, e_n)$, if you put suitable expressions e_1 for ξ_1, e_2 for ξ_2 and so on. 'Nonempty' means that there is at least one collection of suitable expressions $e_1, \ldots, e_n$. 'Partial' means that we don't assume every n-tuple $(e_1, \ldots, e_n)$ is suitable for every frame $F(\xi_1, \ldots, \xi_n)$.)

2. (Nonempty Composition) If $F(\xi_1, \ldots, \xi_n)$ and $G(\eta_1, \ldots, \eta_m)$ are frames, $1 \leqslant i \leqslant n$ and there is an expression

$$F(e_1, \ldots, e_{i-1}, G(f_1, \ldots, f_m), e_{i+1}, \ldots, e_n),$$

then

$$F(\xi_1, \ldots, \xi_{i-1}, G(\eta_1, \ldots, \eta_m), \xi_{i+1}, \ldots, \xi_n)$$

is a frame.

(For example suppose $H(\xi, \eta)$ is $F(\xi, G(\eta))$. Then $H(e, f)$ is the expression found as follows: take the expression $G(f)$ (call it f'); then $H(e, f)$ is $F(e, f')$. If $G(f)$ or $F(e, f')$ don't exist, then neither does $H(e, f)$. Hidden in this is an important implication: If the expression $H(e, f)$ exists then so does the expression $G(f)$. The condition that 'there is an expression' etc. is necessary to ensure that the composed frame is a nonempty function.)

3. (Nonempty Substitution) If $F(e_1, \ldots, e_n)$ is an expression, $n > 1$ and $1 \leqslant i \leqslant n$, then

$$F(\xi_1, \ldots, \xi_{i-1}, e_i, \xi_{i+1}, \ldots, \xi_n)$$

is a frame.

4. (Identity) There is a frame $1(\xi)$ such that for each expression e, $1(e) = e$.

(b) We say that an expression e is a *constituent* of an expression f if f is $G(e)$ for some frame G; e is a *proper constituent* of f if e is a constituent of f and $e \neq f$.

(c) We say that a set Y of expressions is *cofinal* if every expression of L is a constituent of an expression in Y.

The definitions of *expression*, *constituent*, etc. apply to a language L when we fix a constituent structure for L.

In the next definition and later discussions, we distinguish a set X of expressions. In most applications X is the set of sentences. But see for example Werning (2004), Leitgeb (2005), and Kupffer (2008) where X is the set of observation sentences in the sense of Quine; or Hodges (2007) where X is a set of games and $\mathbb{E}$ is a set of parts of the games in X.

Definition 2. Let X be a set of expressions. We define the relation $\sim_X$ on the set of expressions by:

(11.9) $e \sim_X f \Leftrightarrow$ for every frame $H(\xi)$, $H(e) \in X \Leftrightarrow H(f) \in X$.

The relation $\sim_X$ is clearly an equivalence relation. Related informal definitions appear quite often in the linguistic literature. An example is Bloomfield's 'class-meanings' (Bloomfield, 1933: 146).

Lemma 3. *Suppose $F(e_1, \ldots, e_n)$ is a constituent of some expression in X, and for each i, $e_i \sim_X f_i$. Then:*

(a) $F(f_1, \ldots, f_n)$ *is an expression.*

(b) $F(e_1, \ldots, e_n) \sim_X F(f_1, \ldots, f_n)$.

Proof: By Nonempty Substitution we can make the replacements one expression at a time. So it suffices to prove the lemma when $n = 1$, thus. For (a), assume $F(e)$ is an expression, $H(F(e)) \in X$ and $e \sim_X f$. By Nonempty Composition $H(F(\xi))$ is a frame $G(\xi)$. Since $e \sim_X f$ and $G(e) \in X$, we have $G(f) \in X$. But $G(f)$ is $H(F(f))$; so $F(f)$ is an expression. Given (a), the proof of (b) is similar but doesn't use the assumption that $F(e)$ is a constituent of an expression in X. □

Lemma 3 gives us our first example of PTW compositionality.

Definition 4.

(a) Let $\simeq$ be an equivalence relation on the set of expressions. We say that $\simeq$ is *(PTW) compositional* if for every pair of expressions $F(e_1, \ldots, e_n)$ and $F(f_1, \ldots, f_n)$,

if $e_1 \simeq f_1$ and $\ldots$ and $e_n \simeq f_n$ then $F(e_1, \ldots, e_n) \simeq F(f_1, \ldots, f_n)$.

(b) Let ϕ be a function defined on the set of expressions. We say that ϕ is *(PTW) compositional* if for each expression $F(e_1, \ldots, e_n)$, the value

$$\phi(F(e_1, \ldots, e_n))$$

is determined by F and the values $\phi(e_i)$.

The letters PTW stand for Partee, ter Meulen, and Wall in view of Partee, ter Meulen, and Wall (1990: 318); see the end of the next subsection for some history. For the rest of this chapter we generally drop the prefix PTW. Lemma 3 said that the relation $\sim_X$ is compositional.

Note that the function ϕ in Definition 4(b) is compositional if and only if the equivalence relation $\phi(e) = \phi(f)$ is compositional in the sense of Definition 4(a). Also ϕ is compositional if and only if for each frame $F(\xi_1, \ldots, \xi_n)$ there is a function χ_F such that whenever $F(e_1, \ldots, e_n)$ is an expression,

(11.10) $\phi(F(e_1, \ldots, e_n)) = \chi_F(\phi(e_1), \ldots, \phi(e_n))$.

11.2.3 Semantics and the logicians' input

From the mid-nineteenth century, some logicians had been meditating on the notion of an artificial language in which we can carry out inferences by following purely syntactic rules. By the 1920s logicians had come to appreciate that a formal language is built up recursively, and that theorems about it can be proved 'by recursion on syntax'. This realization was a stimulus to greater precision; in fact by 1930 Alfred Tarski was able to give absolutely precise descriptions of formal languages for higher order logic.

Tarski did more. If L is one of his languages, then for each formula ϕ of L he showed how to define, by recursion on the complexity of ϕ, the class $\mu(\phi)$ of those assignments (of objects to the free variables of ϕ) which satisfy ϕ. This was a stage in the development of his famous truth definition, which he published in full in Tarski (1933); an English translation is in Tarski (1983: 152–278). (The function μ is buried deep in Tarski (1931), and he doesn't call it μ; see Hodges (2008b) for this and other aspects of the development of Tarski's truth theory.)

In an abstract sense of 'meaning', one can think of $\mu(\phi)$ as the 'meaning' of ϕ. If one gives Tarski's logics a constituent structure where expressions are formulas, then the function μ is a semantics in the sense of the following definition.

Definition 5. In the context of the definitions above, a *semantics* for the language L is a function whose domain is the set $\mathbb{E}$ of expressions of L. A *partial semantics* for L is a function whose domain is a subset of $\mathbb{E}$.

Tarski's truth definition has some other features that will be important for us. First, he defines his syntax precisely and without any reference to meaning. Also without any appeal to meaning, he defines the 'atomic formulas', and lists the constructions for building up complex formulas from simpler ones—he calls these constructions the 'fundamental operations' (Tarski, 1983: 213). So we have a purely syntactical definition of the constituents of a formula: they are the parts that are built up from atomic formulas by application of the fundamental operations.

Now suppose ϕ is a formula with immediate constituents ψ and θ, so that ϕ is $F(\psi, \theta)$ for some fundamental operation F. Tarski shows (in effect, but not in this notation) that there is a function χ_F depending only on F, such that $\mu(\phi)$ is $\chi_F(\mu(\psi), \mu(\theta))$. In short, Tarski shows that μ is compositional. (Appendix B of Chiswell and Hodges (2007) presents Tarski's semantics for the language of first-order logic with uninterpreted primitives, in a notation which guarantees its compositionality. This is actually not one of the languages that Tarski considered in the 1930s, though the difference is irrelevant to compositionality.)

Tarski was the first person to show results of this kind. So the idea of PTW compositionality—though not of course Definition 4—should be credited to Tarski. In MIT in the early 1960s, Tarski's truth definition was certainly known, thanks to Quine and perhaps others. But also the linguists in Chomsky's group believed, like Tarski for his languages, that the syntax of natural languages could be described without reference to meaning. The reasons were different, but the formal similarity allowed Tarski's framework to be carried over bodily. Chomsky had said (Chomsky, 1957: 102) 'we should like the syntactic framework of the language that is isolated and exhibited by the grammar to be able to support semantic description'. Katz and Fodor (1963: 183) worked out this proposal in terms of 'projection rules' which yield the meaning of a phrase from the meanings of its component words by recursion on the constituent structure tree of the phrase. They proposed the name 'compositionality' for a semantic theory of this kind (1963: 191*f*). Partee, ter Meulen, and Wall (1990) sharpened the definition of compositionality in the light of the work of Richard Montague (who was a very loyal student of Tarski). Janssen (1997) has given the PTW definition wide publicity.

11.2.4 Ambiguity, metaphor and *taḥrīf*

Some expressions have more than one meaning. Katz and Fodor (1963: 184, 193) suggested that the lexicon and projection rules should assign to each expression a set of alternative meanings. Thus (to take an example from Bar-Hillel, 1964: 175) the English word 'pen' can mean pen for writing, but it can also mean playpen. Then the semantics would assign to the sentence 'The box was in the pen' a pair of meanings, one of them the meaning of 'The box was in the writing-pen' and the other the meaning of 'The box was in the playpen'. Bar-Hillel's reason for giving this example is that both meanings are possible within the language, and one needs real-world information to see that in most contexts the intended meaning could hardly be the first.

Alternatively one could count 'pen' meaning writing-pen as a different expression from 'pen' meaning playpen—many dictionaries do this. But this option is hard to carry through when a word has several related meanings. One kind of example is where a range of meanings shade into each other; the word 'game' is often given as an example. (But Wierzbicka (1996: 157–60) argues that the phenomenon has never been properly established, and in particular that 'game' has just one meaning in normal usage.) Another kind of example is where there is a primary meaning, but regularities in the language allow other meanings to be derived. For example names of animals can be used metaphorically in some contexts, to ascribe points of character conventionally associated with those animals: 'She's a bitch', 'He's a stallion'.

The playpen meaning of 'The box was in the pen' is completely independent of the other meaning. So if these meanings are calculated compositionally, the two calculations are quite separate. Saying that the two meanings are each calculated compositionally is stronger than saying that the pair of meanings of the whole sentence is calculated compositionally from the sets of possible meanings of the words. By contrast in the case of families of related meanings, one might want to argue that the whole range of meanings of the word enters into the compositional calculation. The formalism above doesn't recognize this distinction, and wasn't intended to. If you want to add further formalism to deal with it, please feel free.

Some writers of an Aristotelian bent have suggested that in a sentence like 'He's a stallion', the context changes the meaning of the occurrence of 'stallion' from the name of the animal to a description of characteristics. This is *taḥrīf*. PTW compositionality makes no provision for changing meanings of occurrences. But before we call *taḥrīf* a threat to compositionality, we should analyse more closely just what is happening in this example.

On any account, both meanings of 'He's a stallion' are available, the literal and the metaphorical. If we count the metaphorical meaning of 'stallion' as available in the lexicon, then both meanings of the sentence can be derived compositionally, just like the two meanings of 'The box was in the pen'.

But if for some reason we want the word 'stallion' to contribute only the literal meaning to the sentence, then we need to say how the metaphorical meaning is derivable alongside the literal one. The simplest explanation would be that the frame 'He's ξ' is ambiguous and has two corresponding semantic functions. The first function takes the meaning of 'an e' to the literal meaning of 'He's an e'; the second takes it to the metaphorical meaning of 'He's an e'. Both derivations are compositional, and there is no point at which the meaning of an occurrence of an expression is changed during a derivation.

So there is no need to invoke *taḥrīf* here. There are at least two ways of doing without it, and the only embarrassment is to find a reason for using one way rather than the other. Various things are relevant to the choice. Your general view of the lexicon is one. Another is the question whether the same metaphorical meaning is also available for the sentence 'He's an uncastrated male horse'.

There is certainly more to be said about other putative examples of *taḥrīf*. For example a full account should explain up-casting of variables in Java (Pierce, 2002: 193ff); this differs from the stallion example because only the cast meaning is available. There is also Frege's explanation of the semantics of belief sentences in terms of a *taḥrīf* of Bedeutung in Frege (1892)—though in my view this is more a question about Frege than about belief sentences.

11.3 THE FREGEAN COVER

11.3.1 The fregean cover exists

Is there a coherent notion of 'meaning' that includes both the meanings of words (as recorded in the dictionary, say) and the meanings of sentences (say in terms of their appropriate use in situations)?

In this section I attack this question as follows. We assume we are given the meanings of sentences; or in terms of the formalism, we assume given a partial semantics μ (cf. Definition 5 above) whose domain is the set X (a subset of $\mathbb{E}$). We make no assumptions at all about μ, but we will need to assume that X is cofinal.

We adopt the guiding idea that

(11.11)   Two expressions e and f have the same meaning if and only if they make the same contribution to the meanings of sentences containing them as constituents.

See Hodges (2005) for comparison with a famous principle in Frege (1884).

Let L be a language with a constituent structure $(\mathbb{E}, \mathbb{F})$, and X a subset of $\mathbb{E}$. Given that the relation of 'having the same meaning' has to be an equivalence relation, there seems to be only one candidate for a formalization of the relation 'making the same contribution to the meanings of sentences containing them as constituents'. Namely:

Definition 6. Let e, f be expressions of L and μ any function with domain X. We write $e \equiv_\mu f$ if for every 1-ary frame $G(\xi)$,

    (i) $G(e)$ is in X if and only if $G(f)$ is in X;
    (ii) if $G(e)$ is in X then $\mu(G(e)) = \mu(G(f))$.

We say e, f have *the same $\equiv_\mu$-value*, or for short *the same fregean value*, if $e \equiv_\mu f$. Note that the condition (i) says that $e \sim_X f$.

The relation $\equiv_\mu$ is clearly an equivalence relation. Assuming some choice of labels for its equivalence classes, we write $|e|_\mu$ for the label of the equivalence class of the expression e. (The choice made will be irrelevant for us.) We call $|e|_\mu$ the *fregean value* of e. The function $|.|_\mu$ is defined on all expressions, so it is a semantics in the sense of Definition 5 above. I call it the *fregean semantics* (or when talking to computer scientists, the *fully abstract* semantics); it is the *fregean cover* of μ.

The fregean cover of μ always exists, thanks to Definition 6. The next two lemmas show that the fregean cover is always compositional, provided only that X is cofinal. (The lemmas generalize Theorem 14 in Hodges, 2001.)

Lemma 7 (Lifting Lemma). *Suppose $F(e_1, \ldots, e_n)$ is a constituent of some expression in X, and for each i, $e_i \equiv_\mu f_i$. Then $F(f_1, \ldots, f_n)$ is an expression, and $F(e_1, \ldots, e_n) \equiv_\mu F(f_1, \ldots, f_n)$.*

Proof: This builds on Lemma 3 above, with a similar proof. For more details see Hodges (2008a or submitted).   □

Lemma 8. *Suppose the domain X of μ is cofinal (Definition 1(c)). Then the relation $\equiv_\mu$ is compositional, and hence there is, for each n-ary frame F, a n-ary map $h_F : V^n \to V$, where V is the class of $\equiv_\mu$-values, such that whenever $F(e_1, \ldots, e_n)$ is an expression,*

$$|F(e_1, \ldots, e_n)|_\mu = h_F(|e_1|_\mu, \ldots, |e_n|_\mu).$$

Proof: This follows from Lemma 7.   □

The map h_F of the lemma is essentially unique; its values are determined on all n-tuples that actually occur as values of the constituents $e_1, \ldots, e_n$ of an expression $F(e_1, \ldots, e_n)$. We call this map the *Hayyan function* of F, in view of (11.8) above.

The next lemma justifies the description of the fregean value as a 'cover' of μ.

Lemma 9. *Suppose $e \equiv_\mu f$ and e is an expression in X. Then f is in X and $\mu(e) = \mu(f)$.*

Proof: This is immediate from the definition, by applying the identity frame $1(\xi)$.   □

It follows from Lemma 9 that there is a function p_μ such that for every expression e in X, $\mu(e) = p_\mu(|e|_\mu)$. This function p_μ is uniquely determined in a similar sense to the Hayyan functions. We will call it the *read-out function* of μ.

Lemma 10. *The following are equivalent:*

(a) *For all e,f in X, $e \equiv_\mu f$ if and only if $\mu(e) = \mu(f)$.*
(b) *For all e,f in X and every frame $F(\eta)$,*

$$\mu(e) = \mu(f) \text{ and } F(e) \in X$$
$$\Rightarrow F(f) \in X \text{ and } \mu(F(e)) = \mu(F(f)).$$

Proof: Again this is immediate from the definition.   □

When the conditions of Lemma 10 hold, we can assume that the representatives $|e|_\mu$ with e in X were chosen so that $|e|_\mu = \mu(e)$. The read-out function p_μ is then the identity function, and the fregean value function is an extension of the function μ.

Our next result needs a further assumption on the constituent structure.

Definition 11. We say that the constituent structure is *well-founded* if there are no infinite sequences of expressions

$$e_0, e_1, e_2, \ldots$$

where for every n, e_{n+1} is a proper constituent of e_n.

In a well-founded constituent structure there is a natural notion of complexity of expressions. (Namely, the complexity of an expression e is the least ordinal strictly greater than the complexities of all proper constituents of e.) We call an expression an *atom* if it has no proper constituents; otherwise it is *complex*.

The following theorem generalizes Tarski's truth definition.

Theorem 12 (Abstract Tarski Theorem). *Let L be a language with a well-founded constituent structure, and μ a function whose domain is a cofinal set X of expressions of L. Then μ has a definition of the following form. A function v is defined on all expressions of L by recursion on complexity. The basis clause is*

• $v(e) = |e|_\mu$ *for each atom e.*

The recursion clause is

• $v(F(e_1, \ldots, e_n)) = h_F(v(e_1), \ldots, v(e_n))$
   for each complex expression $F(e_1, \ldots, e_n)$.

Then for each expression e in X,

$$\mu(e) = p_\mu(v(e)).$$

(Here h_F, p_μ are as in the preceding discussion.)

This is as far as I take the mathematics in this chapter. The papers Hodges (2001 and submitted) have further information on how extending the language affects fregean values. Broadly the effect is:

Proposition 1. *Suppose the language L' comes from the language L by adding new expressions and/or frames, and the notion of meaning μ' on sentences of L' extends the notion of meaning μ on sentences of L. If e and f are expressions of L, then $|e|_{\mu'} = |f|_{\mu'}$ (for L') implies $|e|_{\mu} = |f|_{\mu}$ (for L), but in general the implication in the other direction fails.*

Frege himself noted this effect when a language is extended so as to express tenses or beliefs (Frege, 1892). The extreme case is where one adds quotation marks to a language; unless one does this in an unusually subtle way, the effect is that any two distinct words have distinct fregean values. But even leaving on one side beliefs and quotations, the evidence from computational linguistics seems to be that the more you expand the language, the smaller the fregean equivalence classes become, and there is no sign of there being a level where they stabilize. (See for example the section of Bullinaria and Levy (2007) on dependence on corpus size: 'even for corpora of around 90 million words, the TOEFL and semantic clustering results are still clearly improving with increased corpus size'.) One moral is that in linguistics, just as in physics, there are some parts of the theory that behave themselves only when they are applied to bounded systems.

Westerståhl (2004) and Fernando (2005) prove that under certain conditions a compositional partial semantics (in the sense of Definition 5) defined on a set X that is closed under constituents extends to a compositional semantics on all expressions. Their conditions are stronger than those above, and it is not yet clear whether they can be weakened.

As noted earlier, Fregean values are determined only up to the equivalence relation $\equiv_{\mu}$. In practice this is less of a deficiency than one might think. First, the exact identity of meanings is hardly ever an issue; two different semantics can contain the same information but assign completely different objects as meanings. Second, in any concrete case, pinning down $\equiv_{\mu}$ generally involves identifying the information that needs to be encoded in the meaning, regardless of how it is encoded.

11.3.2 Fregean values vs. meanings

Most of the standard formal languages of logic come with a Tarski-style semantics. For these languages, if we adopt a reasonable constituent structure and take two sentences to have the same meaning if they are true in the same models (or whatever corresponds for the kind of logic in question), then it almost always turns out that the standard semantics is the fregean value semantics. Also the fregean value semantics agrees with the Aristotelian criterion-meanings on relation symbols, and with the Aristotelian meanings-but-not-in-isolation on connectives, quantifiers, and so forth. This shouldn't cause any surprise—these languages grew from a logic whose roots are in the Aristotelian tradition. (See Hodges (2008a) for a discussion of some book-keeping matters for lining up Tarski-style semantics with fregean values.)

There is one rather un-Aristotelian formal language which we know has a compositional semantics, thanks to the Abstract Tarski Theorem above, but we have no idea how to give an explicit description of this semantics. This language is the double-slash language of Hintikka (1996: 53); see Hodges (2001) for its compositional semantics.

On the other hand, if we take a natural language L and give it a reasonable constituent structure with set of sentences X, and a reasonable notion of meaning μ for sentences, there is no reason a priori why the resulting fregean values should agree with your or my favourite intuitive notion of meaning (say ν) for all expressions of X. But we should ask what the discrepancies could look like.

There are three ways that the equivalence of $|e|_\mu = |f|_\mu$ and $\nu(e) = \nu(f)$ could fail for a pair of expressions e, f:

- Type I failure: $\nu(e) \neq \nu(f)$ but $|e|_\mu = |f|_\mu$.
- Type II failure: $\nu(e) = \nu(f)$ but $e \not\sim_X f$.
- Type III failure: $\nu(e) = \nu(f)$ and $e \sim_X f$ but $|e|_\mu \neq |f|_\mu$.

Following Hodges (2001), we say that the semantics ν is $(X\text{-})husserlian$ if there are no failures of type II.

There are methodological reasons why failures of types I and III are likely to be rare or uninteresting. In the case of type III, the reason is that when two expressions e and f are $\sim_X$-equivalent, a standard way of showing that they have different meanings is to give an example of a sentence s containing an occurrence of e, where the sentence changes from true to false in some situation if we replace this occurrence of e by one of f. So when $e \sim_X f$, the condition $|e|_\mu \neq |f|_\mu$ is almost a criterion for e and f to have different meanings. There are some reservations here, and the main one is that no linguist is going to invoke a sentence s where e is in quotation marks, and I don't recall seeing any example where e is in the scope of 'believes that'. This is one of the places where the theory works best if we confine ourselves to a manageable part of the language.

Likewise we shouldn't expect any interesting failures of type I. Here the reason is the intuition that if e and f have different meanings but $e \sim_X f$, then there must surely be some sentence that distinguishes between the meanings as in the previous paragraph. If there isn't, then we must have taken too limited a vocabulary or too coarse a notion of sentence meaning. (See Hodges submitted for a fuller discussion of these two types of failure.)

So the search for clashes between fregean values $|e|_\mu$ and intuitive meanings $\nu(e)$ sends us naturally to look at failures of the husserlian property. Some examples are discussed in Hodges (2008a, submitted). Here is a quick sample.

1. Two words express the same thing but require to be put in different places in the sentence. Compare 'She won prizes galore' and 'She won myriad prizes'.
2. Two words express the same thing in certain contexts, but one of the words is restricted to a smaller range of contexts. Thus 'He kept order' with 'He maintained order', but 'He kept her photo in his wallet' with (?)'He maintained her photo in his wallet'.
3. Two noun phrases describe the same class of things (and so have the same Aristotelian meaning), but differ in their optional arguments or their anchors for anaphora. For an Aristotelian, 'murderer' means 'person who has killed someone'; but contrast 'A person who has killed someone most often already knew him or her' with 'A murderer most often already knew him or her'.

In the example of (1) I think most people's intuition will be that the difference of fregean value is a purely syntactic phenomenon. It might be possible to finesse the definition of fregean value to eliminate such examples.

For examples like those in (2) and (3), there are some grounds for arguing that the difference in the fregean value does point to a semantic difference. (For example Jackendoff (1990: 26) discusses the behaviour of 'keep' in (2) in terms of 'semantic field features'.) People who have their own clear idea of what counts as meaning and what doesn't will no doubt have more to say about these cases.

11.3.3 Wrapping up

The main result of Section 11.3.1 was that under certain mild conditions, any partial semantics defined on the sentences of a language extends in a canonical way to a compositional semantics on all expressions of the language. I suspect that some semi-conscious awareness of this fact may be responsible for the very widespread feeling that meanings ought to be compositional but we can't quite say why. But it would need a very subtle cognitive experiment to confirm this suspicion.

There is certainly more to be said about the relationship between fregean values and various semantics that are in the literature. For example the relation between Hayyan functions and categorial or lambda-calculus operations needs to be clarified. Also there are good reasons for adjusting Frege and saying that the meaning of an expression is what it contributes to the meanings of dialogues involving it. I don't know how well the formalism above behaves if one takes $\mathbb{E}$ to include stretches of dialogue; but I do have the impression that the main difficulties in carrying this through are fundamental problems about meaning, and not just glitches in the formalism.

CHAPTER 12

COMPOSITIONALITY AND THE CONTEXT PRINCIPLE

GABRIEL SANDU

12.1 THE FORMULATION OF THE PRINCIPLE

The Principle of Compositionality (PC) has been informally spelled out in different, alternative ways:

> A central working premise of Montague's theory...is that the syntactic rules that determine how a sentence is built up out of smaller syntactic parts should correspond one-to-one with the semantic rules that tell how the meaning of a sentence is a function of the meanings of its parts. This idea is not new in either linguistics or philosophy; in philosophy it has its basis in the work of Frege, Tarski, and Carnap. (Partee, 1975: 203)

> Like Frege, we seek to do this...in such a way that...the assignment to a compound will be a function of the entities assigned to its components. (Montague, 1970a: 217)

> [Terms and sentences with the same meaning] ought to be substitutable salva veritate in all contexts obeying Frege's principle that the meaning of a phrase is a function of the meanings of its parts. (Thomason, 1974b: 55)

In order to see that these formulations are equivalent, we fix a (partial) interpretation μ which associates with expressions of a language L semantic values. An expression is said to be μ-meaningful if it is in the domain of μ. Technically speaking, expressions are built up out of atomic expressions and a set of partial operations (syntactic rules) O, each of which comes endowed with a natural number, its arity. Thus when $e_0, \ldots, e_{m-1}$ are (grammatical) expressions, and O is an m-ary syntactic operation, then if O is defined on $e_0, \ldots, e_{m-1}$, $O(e_0, \ldots, e_{m-1})$ is a (complex) expression of L.

Here are several alternative formulations of PC (Hodges, 2001):

(a) There is a function r such that for every complex μ-meaningful expression $s = O(e_0, \ldots, e_{m-1})$ we have

$$\mu(s) = r(O, \mu(e_0), \dots, \mu(e_{m-1}))$$

(b)   There is a function b and for each syntactic rule O, a function r_O such that for every μ-meaningful expression s we have

$$\mu(s) = \begin{cases} b(s), \text{ if } s \text{ is atomic} \\ r_O(\mu(e_0), \dots, \mu(e_{m-1})), \text{ if } s = O(e_0, \dots, e_{m-1}) \end{cases}$$

(c)   If s and s' are two expressions that differ only in that occurrences of $p_0, \dots, p_{n-1}$ in s are replaced by $q_0, \dots, q_{n-1}$ in s', both s and s' are μ-meaningful, and in addition, for each i, $\mu(p_i) = \mu(q_i)$ (i.e. p_i and q_i are μ-synonymous), then $\mu(s) = \mu(s')$.

Hodges (2001) shows that (a), (b), and (c) are equivalent. The proof is straightforward and will not be given here.

Formulation (a) represents the functional dependence interpretation of PC: the meaning of a complex expression is a function of the meanings of its parts together with their mode of composition (cf. the second quotation above.)

Formulation (b) represents the rule by rule interpretation of PC: for each syntactical operation, there is a corresponding semantical operation which yields the meaning of the compound in terms of the meanings of the parts and their mode of composition (cf. the first quotation.)

Finally (c) represents the substitutivity account of PC.

In practice (b) is handier to use, especially for those bits of language whose expressions are explicitly introduced via derivational trees. Consider, for instance, the sentence 'John reads a book'.

Suppose that a syntactic rule, say O_1, forms 'a book' out of the indefinite 'a' and the common noun 'book'; that a second rule, O_2, forms 'reads a book' out of 'reads' and 'a book'; and that finally a rule O_3 forms 'John reads a book' out of 'John' and 'reads a book'. Let μ be an interpretation function which assigns semantic values $\mu(s)$ to each expression s. If μ is compositional in sense (b), then there will be, on the semantic side, the operations r_1, r_2, and r_3 corresponding to O_1, O_2, and O_3 respectively, and a function b assigning interpretations to the atomic building blocks of the language such that the following hold:

$\mu(\text{John reads a book}) =$
$r_3(\mu(\text{John}), \mu(\text{reads a book})) =$
$r_3(\mu(\text{John}), r_2(\mu(\text{reads}), \mu(\text{a book}))) =$
$r_3(\mu(\text{John}), r_2(\mu(\text{reads}), r_1(\mu(\text{a}), \mu(\text{book})))) =$
$r_4(b(\text{John}), r_2(b(\text{reads}), r_1(b(\text{a}), b(\text{book}))))$

Whenever μ is compositional in the sense of either (a) or (b) above, one can show that the meaning function μ induces a semantic algebra, that is a set of objects M, called meanings, and a set of partial operations G_δ on M. Then, if the syntax is cast in the form of a syntactic algebra $\mathbb{A} = (A, (F_\gamma)_{\gamma \in \Gamma})$, where A is a set of expressions and each F_γ is a partial operation on A, one can show that for every m-ary syntactic operation

F there is a m-ary partial function G on M (i.e. a homomorphism) such that whenever $F(e_0, \dots, e_{m-1})$ is defined, we have

$$\mu(F(e_0, \dots, e_{m-1})) = G(\mu(e_0), \dots, \mu(e_{m-1}))$$

The presentation of PC as the existence of a homomorphism from a syntactic to a semantic algebra is due to Montague.

12.2 OTHER FORMAL REQUIREMENTS

Besides compositionality, some other formal requirements may be imposed on an interpretation function. Four of them have been particularly significant in all systems of formal semantics since the work of Tarski and Montague. All of them are discussed in Hodges (2001).

For a fixed interpretation μ, we say that the expressions e and e' belong to the same μ category, if for any substitution instances $O(e)$ and $O(e')$, one is μ-meaningful if and only if the other is.

(d)   An interpretation function μ is called *Husserlian* if, whenever two expressions e, e' are μ-synonymous, then they belong to the same μ category.

Hodges proves that if μ is Husserlian, then the principles (a),(b), and (c) in the previous section are equivalent to the following variant of (c) in which one considers only one-term sequences:

(e)   1-*compositionality*: If a subexpression of a meaningful expression e is replaced by a μ-synonymous expression, and the result of the replacement, say e' is again μ-meaningful (i.e. it is defined), then e and e' are synonymous.

(Notice that (e) is a logical consequence of (c); Husserlianity is needed only for the other direction.)

The Substitutivity Condition (c) or its consequence (e) provides a straightforward method for testing whether an interpretation is compositional or not. Let us apply it to a very rudimentary language L that contains three lexical elements, a, b, c and two compound ones, formed by concatenation: $a \frown c, b \frown c$. Let μ be the meaning function which associates natural numbers with expressions:

$\mu(a) = 1, \mu(b) = 1, \mu(c) = 2$
$\mu(a \frown c) = 3, \mu(b \frown c) = 4$

Since a and b are μ−synonymous, but $\mu(a \frown c) \neq \mu(b \frown c)$, then μ is not compositional.

Here are two more principles:

(f)   An μ-meaningful expression is necessarily grammatical.

In other words, ungrammatical expressions are not meaningful. This principle has been the pillar of all formal models of compositionality.

(g)   *The 'Tarskian' principle* (Tarski, 1983: 215f): If there is a context in which the result of the insertion of e is μ-meaningful if and only if the result of the insertion of e' is meaningful, then e, e' must belong to the same category.

Notice that (g) is stronger than the Husserlian condition (d): the latter requires only that two synonymous expressions be assigned to the same category.

Hodges favours (d) over (g) as a condition on a grammar of English. I first state his argument and then present a counter-argument to it in the next section, due to Higginbotham.

Hodges uses the following examples to show that English grammar cannot fulfil (g) (the examples are from Gazdar et al. (1985):

(12.3)   It is likely that Alex will leave

(12.4)   It is probable that Alex will leave

(12.5)   Alex is likely to leave

(12.6)   *Alex is probable to leave.

Suppose that the grammar is Hussserlian. In the context 'It is ... that Alex will leave', both the result of the insertion of 'likely' and that of the insertion of 'probable' lead to meaningful results. But now the antecedent of the Tarskian condition is satisfied, whence 'likely' and 'probable' should be assigned to the same category, which, by definition means that for every context, the result of the insertion of 'likely' in that context is meaningful iff the result of the insertion of 'probable' is meaningful. But the context provided by the pair (12.5) and (12.6) is a counterexample to this claim.

On the other side, (12.3)–(12.6) do not necessarily constitute a counterexample to the weaker, Husserlian condition (d): It is enough to treat 'likely' and 'probable' as non-synonymous. (Hodges, 2001: 11).

12.3 MEANINGFULNESS WITHOUT GRAMMATICALITY

We do not need to endorse the conclusion just reached. One may still want to treat 'likely' and 'probable' as synonymous, and yet not give up the Husserlian principle (d). Higginbotham (manuscript) endorses such a view: he argues that (12.5) and (12.6) are both meaningful and synonymous and so are 'likely' and 'probable'. But (12.6) is ungrammatical, although meaningful (p. 8) In other words, we reject (f), the slogan being: Semantics is indifferent to questions of grammaticality.

So far so good. One still may wonder though, how, given the synonymity of 'likely' and 'probable' (12.5) is grammatical while (12.6) is not. This is so, Higginbotham argues, because the two words have different *formal features*. The notion of formal feature would require a paper of its own, but a couple of examples should suffice for the purposes of this paper. The expressions 'probable' and 'likely' are synonymous but they do not share the same formal features: the former, unlike the latter does not admit subject-to-subject raising. Another illustrative pair is 'autobiography' and 'history of the life of its own author'. Both are synonymous although 'John's autobiography' is not synonymous with 'John's history of the life of its own author'. The latter is ungrammatical and meaningless. Again, the explanation may be found in the difference of their formal features: the former is relational (i.e. it takes one argument) while the latter is a one place predicate, that is, it enters into constructions of the form: 'That book is a history of the life of its own author'.

Higginbotham proposes an alternative, local model of compositionality, apparently more adequate for natural languages, which takes into account the formal features of expressions. We cannot do it full justice here. Roughly, it is formulated in terms of the existence of a function f_G which is such that for every syntactic structure (syntactic tree) T licensed by the grammar, and every constituent $X = Y - Z$, (Y and Z are possibly complex, and X is possibly embedded in a larger structure W), the family $M(X)$ of meanings borne by X is the result of applying f_G to the ordered triple $(F, M(X), M(Z))$, where F comprises the formal features associated with X, Y, Z, and $M(X)$ and $M(Y)$ are the families of meanings borne by X and Y. It is to be emphasized that this model does not require that whenever the meaning of the root Y of T_1 is the same as that of the root Y' of T_1' the meaning of the root X' of $T' = T_1' - T_2$ should be the same as that of the root X of $T = T_1 - T_2$. In fact, the example with 'autobiography' and 'history of the life of its own author' is meant to show that it is perfectly possible for Y and Y' to have the same meaning, but different formal features. In this case, for that reason alone or because the roots X and X' receive different formal features, meaning may not be preserved.

12.4 RESTORING COMPOSITIONALITY

There have been several results in the literature to the effect that a compositional semantics is always available.

Janssen (1986) proves a theorem which shows how to make any meaning function for a language L compositional. The problem with this result is that the devised compositional semantics does not respect the syntactical structure of L (cf. Westerståhl, 1998.)

Van Benthem (1986) observes that whenever we have available a class of lexical items, then any arbitrary connection of the syntactic operators with semantic operators with the same number of arguments is uniquely extendable to a homomorphism, as required by PC. This way of implementing PC respects the syntactic structure of the original language L. Again, Westerståhl (1998) points out that this result is not very useful for the semanticist, as only the meanings of the lexical items have been fixed in advance.

The same remarks apply to Horwich (1998). His setting is less technical than that of van Benthem, but his argument is essentially the same. He considers a fragment of English which contains proper names ('John', 'Peter', etc.), common nouns ('dogs', 'cows', etc.) and verb phrases ('talks', 'walks', 'bark', etc.) as primitive expressions together with few syntactic (grammatical) operations on them. For simplicity, we assume that predication (marked by concatenation) is the only such operation. The syntax will contain clauses of the form:

If 'n' is a proper name and 'v' is a verb phrase, then 'n v' is a complex expression.

On the semantic side, Horwich assumes that a domain of entities is given to serve as the intended meanings of the proper names and verbs phrases (they will be marked by capitals) plus a semantic operation (usually functional application) to correspond to (syntactic) predication. The relevant semantic clauses have now the form:

The interpretation of 'n v' is the result of the functional application of the entity assigned to 'v' to 'n'.

Thus the interpretation of the sentence 'John talks' is the result of the functional application of TALKS to JOHN. This interpretation is trivially compositional in the same sense as the previous one: the interpretation of every compound 'n v' is freely generated from the lexical meanings of 'n' and 'v' and the semantic operation. Horwich is certainly right in claiming that this brand of compositionality 'places no constraint at all on how the meaning properties of words are constituted' (Horwich, 1998: 154) but the problem lies elsewhere. (See Dever, 2006; and Janssen, 1997; Sandu and Hintikka, 2001, for similar remarks.)

Zadrozny (1994) gives us a method for producing a compositional semantics v for a given language L which agrees with an already given interpretation μ. More exactly v is devised to satisfy the following two conditions:

For every $e : v(e)(e) = \mu(e)$
For every $e, e' : v(e \frown e') = v(e)(v(e'))$

Thus the meaning $v(e)$ of the expression e is a function, which, when applied to e, agrees with the original semantic value of e. This is ensured by the first condition. The second condition ensures PC.

Finding v is a matter of solving a class of simultaneous equations given by

$$v(e) = \{\langle e, \mu(e)\rangle\} \cup \{\langle v(e), v(e \frown e')\rangle\} : e \frown e' \in L\}$$

For an easy application consider the rudimentary language L of the first section which violates the substitutivity condition (and hence PC). To find a compositional interpretation which agrees with the given one, we need to solve the following equations:

(a) $v(a) = \{\langle a, 1\rangle, \langle v(c), v(a \frown c)\rangle\}$
(b) $v(b) = \{\langle b, 1\rangle, \langle v(c), v(b \frown c)\rangle\}$
(c) $v(c) = \{\langle c, 2\rangle\}$
(d) $v(a \frown c) = \{\langle a \frown c, 3\rangle\}$
(e) $v(b \frown c) = \{\langle b \frown c, 4\rangle\}$

The last three clauses yield semantic values for the compound expressions and for c. We still need semantic values for a and b, which is a matter of replacing $v(c), v(a \frown c)$ and $v(b \frown c)$ with their new values as given by (a) and (b) respectively:

$$v(a) = \{\langle a, 1\rangle, \langle\{\langle c, 2\rangle\}, \{\langle a \frown c, 3\rangle\}\rangle\}$$
$$v(a) = \{\langle b, 1\rangle, \langle\{\langle c, 2\rangle\}, \{\langle b \frown c, 4\rangle\}\rangle\}$$

As a result, v is compositional, but the old semantic values $\mu(e)$ are replaced with new ones $v(e)$ (although the old values are recoverable from the new ones.) In addition, unlike μ, there are no v-synonyms, and thereby the Substitutivity Principle is trivially satisfied. This way of implementing PC can hardly be of any interest, although it has led some philosophers and logicians to claim that PC is methodologically empty. The problem with it is that the values of lexical and compound expressions can be settled in a too arbitrary way. Actually it has been pointed out that there are many ways to build up an interpretation function C which is both compositional and allows recovering the old semantic values. Here are two ways of doing this (Dever, 1999):

• Define for all e: $C(e) = \{\langle e, \mu(e)\rangle : e \in L\}$.
• Define for all e: $C(e) = \langle\mu(e), e\rangle$.

In the first case, the semantic value of each expression in the language encodes the old values of every expression in the language. In the second case no two expressions are synonymous, and thus the Substitutivity Principle is trivially satisfied. (Cf. Westerståhl, 1998.)

12.5 COMPOSITIONALITY AND THE CONTEXT PRINCIPLE (CP)

In two of our earlier examples (van Benthem and Horwich), the semantic values of complex expressions are freely generated from those of the lexicon through the application of the semantic operations which are the semantic values of the relevant syntactic operations. This is typically the case with artificial languages which are specially designed to satisfy PC. In applications to natural language though, the meaning of complex expressions, or facts about them, are fixed in advance, and any compositional interpretation is subservient to them. Historically the most significant illustration of this fact is provided by the so-called *Context Principle* (CP) associated with Frege:[1]

> First [Frege] propounded as a salient principle of his analysis that a word has a meaning or content (signifies something) only in the context of a sentence. This principle is evidently associated with his insistence upon the priority of judgments over concepts for purposes of logical analysis, viz. that we view concepts as derived by functional decomposition of judgments, rather than viewing judgments as synthesized from antecedently given concepts (subject and predicate). (Baker and Hacker, 1984: 35)

For the working semanticist, CP is bound to say that the meanings of sentences is independently understood and prior to the semantic values of non-sentences. The challenge is to find a compositional interpretation of the latter which will match the former. The passage below spells this view out in more detail:

> ...a compositional grammar must associate with each expression an entity that I shall call its *semantic value*. ...These play a twofold role. First, the semantic value of some expressions, the *sentences*, must enter somehow into determining whether truth-in-English would be achieved if the expression were uttered in a given context. ...The semantic values of non-sentences have only one job: to do their bit toward determining the semantic values of the sentences. (Lewis, 1970: 25–6; his italics)

Lewis is not the only semanticist to think so. Davidson (1984) and many others share the same view: sentences are the real meaning carrying units in the language. Accordingly, one has more or less free hands in designing an interpretation for non-sentences, provided it agrees with the independently given meanings of sentences. Apart from a computational role, non-sentential semantic values have only an instrumentalistic function in the manner of theoretical terms in empirical sciences. In what follows we shall understand CP in a rather liberal way: the priority of judgements (sentences) over concepts (formulas) and that of complex expressions over their sub-parts. We shall review two kinds of results:

(1) Results showing how, starting from antecedently fixed facts about the meanings of complex noun phrases, one can devise a compositional interpretation which agrees with them.
(2) Impossibility results which show that independent facts about the meaning of sentences are incompatible with PC and other semantic facts about the meanings of sub-sentences.

---

[1] For an elaboration of this point, see Pelletier (2001).

12.5.1 Semantic flexibility

One of the standard examples is that of *non-intersective adjectives*. It is known that it is not straightforward to get the meaning of 'large cheese' out of the meanings of 'large' and 'cheese', for that appropriate standards of largeness may vary on the type of objects in question. Thus something which instantiates large cheese must be a cheese but it may be quite small for a person. It is then obvious that the meaning of large cheese cannot be given through the meanings of 'large' and 'cheese' through conjunction or set intersection, but it can be so built up in another way. Here is one proposal (Dever, 2006):

$\|\text{cheese}\| = \{x : x \text{ is a cheese}\}$
$\|\text{large}\| = f, f(X) = \{x \in X : x \text{ is larger than the average size of } X\}$

In this case the meaning of 'large cheese' can be derived compositionally through functional application, but at the price of complicating lexical semantics.

The case of non-intersective adjectives is part of the larger phenomenon of *semantic flexibility* discussed by Recanati in this volume. It is an umbrella term which covers all the cases in which the meaning of a word varies as a function of the other words it combines with. Recanati discusses the contextual behaviour of 'big'. A big mouse is not the same thing as a big elephant. Fodor and others have invocated semantic flexibility as a natural language example violating compositionality. Recanati restores it using the same device as above: he takes a second-order function whose arguments are sets (properties) to be the *constant meaning* of 'big', and the result of the application of the function to an argument X to be its *occasion meaning* (p. 11).

12.5.2 Prototype semantics

Another example often invoked is that of *prototype semantics*. Empirical psychologists have argued that lexical concepts have prototype structure, that is, roughly, their constituents express properties that items in their extension tend to have. Fodor (1990) and Fodor and Lepore (1992) have criticized prototype theory on account of the fact that it is incompatible with compositionality. The well-known example is 'pet fish'. Fodor cannot see any way in which the prototype of 'pet fish' can be functionally composed out of the prototype for 'pet' and the prototype for 'fish'. This argument has been found wanting for many reasons. However, from the point of view of the present chapter we can see that in order for Fodor's conclusion to follow, one has to assume that both the interpretations of 'pet' and 'fish' and that of the complex expression 'pet fish' must be prototypes.[2] We can restate Fodor's argument in the form of an impossibility claim: PC is incompatible with the meanings of both simple and complex

[2] Lawrence and Margolis (1999) identify this assumption in Fodor's argument.

concept-words being prototypes. In this case one does not have available the kind of move that helped to restore PC in the previous examples.

12.5.3 Gödel's slingshot

There is an argument due to Gödel which purports to show that if a true sentence stands for a fact, then one has to give up PC or else the idea that definite descriptions are singular terms. Gödel displayed his argument in few lines:

> An interesting example of Russell's analysis of the fundamental logical concepts is his treatment of the definite article 'the'. The problem is: what do the so-called descriptive phrases (i.e., phrases as, e.g., 'the author of Waverley' or 'the king of England') denote or signify [footnote: I use the term 'signify' in the sequel because it corresponds to the German word 'bedeuten' which Frege, who first treated the question under consideration, first used in this connection.] and what is the meaning of sentences in which they occur? The apparently obvious answer that, e.g., 'the author of Waverley' signifies Walter Scott, leads, to unexpected difficulties. For, if we admit the further apparently obvious axiom, that the signification of a complex expression, containing constituents which have themselves a signification, depends only on the signification of these constituents (not on the manner in which this signification is expressed), then it follows that the sentence 'Scott is the author of Waverley' signifies the same thing as 'Scott is Scott'; and this again leads almost inevitably to the conclusion that all true sentences have the same signification (as well as the false ones). Frege actually drew this conclusion; and he meant it in an almost metaphysical sense, reminding one somewhat of the Eleatic doctrine of the 'One'. 'The True'—according to Frege's view—is analysed by us in different ways in different propositions; 'the True' being the name he uses for common signification of all true propositions (Gödel, 1944: 128–9)

To explicitate the argument, let us extend the syntax of first-order logic with expressions of the form '$\iota x \varphi$'. Syntactically they are singular terms, and semantically they stand for the unique object satisfying φ (if it exists, or are undefined, otherwise.) Thus '$\iota x(x = a \wedge Fx)$' represents the definite description 'the unique x such that x is identical to a and x is F'.

Gödel hints at the proof of his argument in a footnote:

> The only further assumption one would need in order to obtain a rigorous proof would be: [G1] that '$\varphi(x)$' and the proposition 'a is the object which has the property φ and is identical to a' mean the same thing and [G2] that every proposition 'speaks about something', i.e. can be brought to the form $\varphi(a)$. Furthemore one would have to use the fact that for any two objects a, b, there exists a true proposition of the form $\varphi(a, b)$ as e.g., $a \neq b$ or $a = a, b = b$. (Gödel, 1944: 129)

An elaborate discussion of these assumptions, and of their philosophical signification may be found in Neale (1995). For our purposes it suffices to say the following. (G1) seems rather obvious in the light of what Gödel has in mind by 'signifies' (cf. the main quotation). (G2) is bound to say that every sentence which stands for a fact can be put into the subject–predicate form. Without that assumption, the slingshot can be carried out only for atomic sentences. As for the argument itself, here it goes.[3]

Assume that the following three atomic sentences are all true.

1. $F(a)$
2. $a = b$
3. $G(b)$

Let the facts for which they stand be f_1, f_2, and f_3, respectively. By (G1) the sentence

4. $a = \iota x(x = a \wedge F(x))$

also stands for f_1. By a similar reasoning, the sentence

5. $a = \iota x(x = a \wedge x \neq b)$

stands for f_2. Since the defining descriptions $\iota x(x = a \wedge F(x))$ and $\iota x(x = a \wedge x \neq b)$ stand for the same object, that is the unique individual which is identical with a, then by the Principle of Compositionality (4) and (5) stand for the same fact, that is, $f_1 = f_2$. A similar argument shows that $f_2 = f_3$, whence all the three sentences stand for the same fact. The argument can be generalized to show that all true sentences stand for the same fact.

The purpose of Gödel's argument was to show that Russell, who adopted an ontology of facts, and a correspondence theory of truth, had a good reason to contextually eliminate definite descriptions: if he treated them as Frege did, that is as contributing with the unique individual which satisfies each of them, then all true sentences would have corresponded to one true fact, an absurdity for a correspondence theorist.

One should notice at this point that Gödel's argument can be cast in the form of an impossibility result: certain assumptions about the interpretations of sentences (i.e. they are facts, that is, complexes of entities) and about the meanings of other expressions (definite descriptions) are incompatible with PC.

12.5.4 The extension problem

Our next example is a language in which one has a well-defined intended interpretation for certain complex expressions of a language, but not for all their sub-expressions.

---

[3] The argument below follows closely Neale (1995).

Let X and Y be two sets of expressions, $X \subseteq Y$, such that every expression in Y is a subexpression of an expression in X. The typical example is the one in which Y is a set of formulas and X is the set of sentences of Y. We suppose we already have a compositional interpretation μ defined on X. The challenge is to find a compositional interpretation for the expressions in Y which agrees with the interpretation μ on the expressions in X. We have here a typical combination of PC with CP: an expression has a meaning only in the context of a sentence. The combination has been largely explored in the work of Frege and in Davidson's theory of meaning which assumes the form of a theory of truth. Davidson takes whole sentences to be the meaning carrying units in language and truth to be a primitive, undefinable semantic property which is independently understood. Being undefinable, the strategy applied above which ensured a trivial implementation of PC is no longer available. Instead, PC acquires the status of a methodological constraint on an empirical theory of truth for the target language: The division of a sentence into parts and their association with appropriate semantic entities in a compositional theory is a theoretical business which has no other role except to show how they contribute to the computation of the truth of the sentences of the target language in which they occur.

The Context Principle does the real work in this case. Suppose the expression e occurs in a complex expression $O(e)$ whose meaning is fixed by μ. Then the interpretation $v(e)$ we are looking for must reflect the contribution that e makes to $\mu(O(e))$. One way to spell this out is to require that v-synonymity be designed in such a way that μ-synonymity is not affected. This is technically expressed in the following requirements.

(a1) If e and e' are v-synonyms, then their substitution in expressions of X preserves μ-meaningfulness: If $O(e)$ is μ-meaningful, $O(e')$ is also μ-meaningful.
(a2) If e and e' are v-synonyms and both $O(e)$ and $O(e')$ are μ-meaningful, then $O(e)$ and $O(e')$ are μ-synonyms.

If e and e' are not v-synonyms, then

Either

(b1) There is an expression $O(x)$ such that exactly one of $O(e)$, $O(e')$ is not μ-meaningful,
or
(b2) both are meaningful and $\mu(O(e)) \neq \mu(O(e'))$.

Once we have constrained v-synonymity to fulfil (a1)–(b2), we can define the compositional interpretation itself: for any expression in Y, take its meaning to consist of the class of expressions v-synonmous with it.

Hodges' *Extension Theorem* shows that any partial interpretation μ (defined on X) which is Husserlian and 1-compositional, has a unique compositional extension to Y, which satisfies the conditions (a1)–(b2).

12.5.5 A case study: IF languages

Hodges' Extension Theorem is perfectly designed for the kind of extension problem of PC which arises in the so-called *IF* languages, introduced by Hintikka and Sandu (1989, 1997). These languages satisfy the conditions of the application of the Extension Theorem. They are extensions of standard first-order languages closed under:

- Atomic and negations of atomic formulas.
- Disjunctions and conjunctions of *IF*-formulas.
- Formulas of the form $(\exists x_n/V)\varphi$, $(\forall x_n/V)\varphi$, for φ and *IF*-formula.

Thus $\exists x_4/\{x_1, x_2\}\varphi$, $\forall x_3 \exists x_4/\{x_1, x_2\}\varphi$, $\exists x_2 \forall x_3 \exists x_4/\{x_1, x_2\}\varphi$ are formulas but $\forall x_1 \exists x_2 \forall x_3 \exists x_4/\{x_1, x_2\}\varphi$ is a sentence. A game-theoretical interpretation has been given by Hintikka and Sandu (1997). It is formulated only for sentences. The idea is that in the game associated with $\forall x_1 \exists x_2 \forall x_3 \exists x_4/\{x_1, x_2\}\varphi$, the universal and existential player choose individuals from the universe of discourse. In the last choice, corresponding to $\exists x_4/\{x_1, x_2\}\varphi$, the existential player does not 'know' the choices prompted by $\forall x_1$ and $\exists x_2$. The sentence is true exactly when there is a winning strategy for the existential player, that is there exist two (Skolem) functions f and g such that for all elements a and b chosen by the universal player, $(a, f(a), b, g(b))$ satisfies φ.

As the background model interprets the primitive predicate symbols of the language, the game-theoretical interpretation provides an interpretation for all sentences of the language, atomic or otherwise. Let Y be the set of formulas of an IF language, and X the set of its sentences. We can now check that every expression in Y is a sub-expression of an expression in X.

There are basically three results on IF logic related to compositionality. Hodges (1997) answers a challenge launched by Hintikka:

> there is no realistic hope of formulating compositional truth-conditions for [sentences of *IF*], even though I have not given a strict impossibility proof to that effect. (Hintikka, 1996: 110ff.)

Hodges (1997) provided a compositional interpetation for IF languages which agrees with the Hintikka–Sandu interpretation on sentences. The interpretation is essentially a second-order one. A formula is interpreted by a set X of sets assignments, and the slash '/' is interpreted by an equivalence relation on sequences of elements of the universe of the background model.

Hodges (2001) generalizes the extension theorem to bear on all languages which satisfies certain constraints. The result was mentioned in section 2.4 of Hodges (2001). The existence of a compositional interpretation for IF languages follows now from this more general result.

Cameron and Hodges (2001) show (Corollary 12) that the compositional interpretation given in Hodges (1997a) does not have a first-order equivalent: there is no compositional interpretation for IF formulas which associates with every IF formula a set of assignments, and which agrees with the Hintikka–Sandu interpretation on IF sentences. We have here an impossibility result of the same kind as the one in the slingshot argument.

12.6 EQUIVALENT COMPOSITIONAL INTERPRETATIONS

12.6.1 One-index theory

Hodges's extension theorem shows that when certain conditions are satisfied, a language has a unique (total) compositional interpretation which agrees with the initially given partial one. Accordingly any two such compositional interpretations must be formally equivalent. But the fact that two interpretations are formally equivalent doesn't mean that they are equally useful from an empirical or explanatory point of view. The history of formal semantics provides plenty of illustrative examples to the contrary. We review one of the most debated cases.

It is known that a compositional semantics for a language with quantifiers relativizes truth to satisfaction, in the Tarskian manner. The relevant clauses are:

- $\forall x\varphi$ is true relative to the assignment g if and only if for every assignment g' which differs from g at most in the value it gives to x, φ is satisfied by g'.

The presence of modal operators relativizes truth to both assignments and possible worlds. The clauses which interest us are:

- $\forall x\varphi$ is true relative to $\langle w,g\rangle$ if and only if for every assignment g' which differs from g at most in the value it gives to x, φ is satisfied by $\langle w,g'\rangle$.
- $\Box\varphi$ is true relative to $\langle w,g\rangle$ if and only if for every possible world w' which is accessible from g, φ is satisfied by $\langle w',g\rangle$.

And the story did not stop here:

> we must have several *contextual coordinates* corresponding to familiar sorts of dependence on features of contexts. ... We must have a *time coordinate*, in view of tense sentences and such sentences like 'Today is Tuesday'; a *place coordinate* in view of such sentences like 'Here there are tigers'; a *speaker coordinate*, in view of such sentences as 'I am Porky'; an audience coordinate in view of such sentences as 'You are Porky'; an *indicated-objects coordinate* in view of such sentences as 'That pig is Porky' or 'Those men are Communists'; and a *previous discourse coordinate* in view of such sentences as 'The aforementioned pig is Porky'. (Lewis, 1970: 7)[4]

---

[4] The references are to Partee (1975).

All this is well-known: it is nothing else than the generalization of extensional semantics started by Carnap. It led to the gradual refinement of the notion of intension as
the semantic value of a sentence. Carnapian intensions were functions from possible
worlds (state descriptions) to truth-values (Carnap, 1947), but work by Montague (1968),
Scott (1970), and Lewis (1970) encoded intensions into functions from *indices* to extensions. Indices, or points of reference as they have been alternatively called, are finite
sequences of various items, as in the quotation above, which may enter into determining
extensions. Further expansions may be needed with sentences like '*This* is older than
this' where the demonstratives point to two distinct objects. Following a suggestion by
Kaplan, Lewis replaces the indicated-objects coordinate by an infinite sequence of sets,
such that $this_n$ refers to the an object in the nth set.

12.6.2 The double-index theory

The merging of possible worlds with contextual parameters in one index met two main
opponents, Stalnaker (1970, 1999) and Kaplan (1977, 1989). Both felt the need to differentiate the components of an index according to their contribution: some of them
determine what is expressed by a sentence in a context (i.e. content or proposition),
while the others determine whether what is expressed is true or false.

12.6.2.1 *Stalnaker*

Stalnaker (1970) defends an account which does not merge context and indices but has
propositions as intermediate semantic values. That is, the semantic value of a sentence
in a context is a proposition, represented by a function from possible worlds into truth-
values. He recognizes that the one index account is simpler but thinks nevertheless that
propositions have some independent interest, as objects of our propositional attitudes
and illocutionary acts:

> It is a simpler analysis than the one I am sketching; I need some argument for the
> necessity or desirability of the extra step on the road from sentences to truth-values.
> The step is justified only if the middlemen—the propositions—are of some indepen-
> dent interest, and only if there is some functional difference between contexts and
> possible worlds. The independent interest in propositions comes from the fact that
> they are the objects of illocutionary acts and propositional attitudes. A proposition
> is supposed to be the common content of statements, judgements, promises, wishes
> and wants, questions and answers, things that are possible or probable. The mean-
> ings of sentences, or rules determining truth-values directly from contexts, cannot
> plausibly represent these objects. (Stalnaker, 1970, 1999: 36)[5]

Stalnaker provides several examples to justify his claims. Here are two of them.

The simpler example involves the typically Fregean notion of common thought shared
by the parties in a conversation. Somebody asks: 'Are you going to the party?' and you
answer 'Yes, I am going'. Your answer is appropriate because it expresses the proposi-

---

[5] The references are to Stalnaker (1999).

COMPOSITIONALITY AND THE CONTEXT PRINCIPLE

tional content of the question. On the simpler, Montagovian analysis, there is nothing to be the common content of question and answer, except a truth-value. As the propositions are expressed from different points of reference, they are different propositions. The only thing which is shared is a truth-value, but that is not enough to be what is commonly entertained.

In the second example, O'Leary says at the party 'I didn't have to be here, you know' by which he means something like: it was not necessary that O'Leary be at that party. The words *I* and *here* contribute to the determination of a proposition, one that O'Leary declares not to be necessary. But if the proposition declared not to be necessary were to be identified with the meaning of the sentence, then O'Leary would be mistaken, since the sentence 'I am here' is true from all points of reference, and hence necessarily true on the simpler analysis.

Lewis (1980, 1998) has criticized this account on the ground that it is not compositional. Consider, for instance, the sentence 'Somewhere in Paris I saw a Japanese garden'. In the context in which Gabriel utters it, it expresses the proposition which is the meaning of the sentence 'Somewhere in Paris Gabriel saw a garden'. But acording to Lewis, the propositional content of this sentence cannot be recovered compositionally, if the only relevant indices are possible worlds. We need both spatial locations and moments of time as shiftable features. True enough, Stalnaker does suggest at some point that possible worlds should be replaced with world–time pairs, but Lewis has another objection which connects with our earlier remarks on constraints on semantic values. In a compositional analysis, 'Sometimes in Paris Gabriel saw a garden' is parsed roughly as 'Somewhere(Past(Gabriel sees a garden))'. First 'Somewhere' shifts the location and next the temporal operator shifts the time of evaluation. On this account, the proposition expressed by 'Gabriel sees a garden' changes its truth-value from one index to the other. Lewis phrases his objection in terms of a question: 'If propositions are reconstrued so that they may vary in truth from one time to another, are they still suitable for propositional attitudes?' (Lewis, 1998: 39).

We know that the answer to this question is debatable. Frege held that propositions do not change in truth-value, while Prior, among others, thought the contrary. In a footnote added in 1996, Lewis seems to think that the two views are compatible (Lewis, 1998: 39).

12.6.2.2 *Kaplan*

Kaplan (1977) separates the indices which contribute to the semantic value of a sentence into those that make the *the context of utterance*, and those that constitute the *circumstances of evaluation*. The former determine *what is said* (i.e. content, proposition) and the latter determine whether what is said is true or false. For instance the sentence 'I am here now' expresses the proposition that Gabriel is in Paris when uttered by Gabriel in Paris. On the other side, in the counterfactual situation in which it is uttered by John in Berkeley, it would express the proposition that John is in Berkeley. But the proposition expressed by 'Descartes died in 1650' is the same in the actual and the counterfactual world. Kaplan's theory has a semantic layer which represents propositions, in virtue of which all these distinctions can be made. Even more, the sentence 'I am here now' seems to express a kind of a priori truth, which is different from the necessary truth associated traditionally with analytic or tautological truth. This distinction is easily accounted for on Kaplan's double-index theory. The proposition is expressed by 'I am here now' in every context of utterance, is true, although not necessary. Necessity shifts the circumstances of evaluation, not the context of utterance.

Let us take stock.

On the Montague–Lewis one-stage picture, grammar takes us to functions from indices to truth-values. On the Stalnaker–Kaplan, two-stage picture, grammar takes us from a sentence to a character. The character combines with a context and gives us a content, which in turn combines with a circumstance of evaluation to give us a truth-value. On this view, the content (proposition) expressed varies with the context. Both interpretations ar compositional, provided that indices are rich enough. Lewis (1980) calls the second semantic values constant but complicated, and the first ones variable but simple. But where Lewis (1970) defends the one-index, constant but complicated semantic values theory, Lewis (1980) observes that the two interpretations are formally equivalent: one can be defined in terms of the other and thus one sort of semantic value can be converted into the other. For this reason he seems to be indifferent as to the choice between them:

> Given the ease of conversion, how could anything of importance possibly turn on the choice between our two options?. . . How could the choice between the options possibly be a serious issue? (Lewis, 1980: 35)[6]

But in the end Lewis ends up by advocating 'solidarity for ever'. He has become convinced that useful distinctions between necessity and a priori of the kind contemplated by Kripke and Kaplan, might be missed by treatments that take the semantic values to be constant but complicated. Formally equivalent compositional interpretations are far from being equivalent from an explanatory point of view.

[6] The references are to Lewis (1998).

CHAPTER 13

....

COMPOSITIONALITY IN DISCOURSE FROM A LOGICAL PERSPECTIVE

....

TIM FERNANDO

13.1 INTRODUCTION

....

As a piece of language that can span several sentences, discourse goes beyond the expressions to which the Principle of Compositionality (PC) is commonly applied.

(PC)   The meaning of a complex expression e is determined by the meaning of its parts and how those parts are put together to form e.

The Principle of Compositionality is often contrasted with the Context Principle (X) of Frege (e.g. Janssen, 2001).

(X)   The meaning of a word w can only be given in the context of a sentence where w appears.

We can relate (X) roughly to (PC) if we take a complex expression to be a sentence, and its parts to be the words in it. Turning to discourse, we shall see that we must step beyond sentences in isolation, and that as we do, various notions of meaning break down under the weight of compositionality (PC). To understand how and why this should be the case, we shall appeal to a perspective on (PC) that brings (PC) in line with a broad construal (X') of (X).

(X')   The meaning of an expression e can only be given in the context of a discourse where e appears.

The passage from (PC) to (X') is, in a nutshell, what the present chapter is about, its bones. We flesh out these bones with material scattered in the *Handbook of Logic and*

Language (van Benthem and ter Meulen, 1997), the obvious reference for the logical perspective on natural language,[1] and with further empirical considerations.

13.1.1 Scope

Let us start with what we take the scope of compositionality in discourse to be in the present chapter. (PC) describes an interpretation with 'a complex expression' fed as input, and 'meaning' returned as output. Discourse aside, bounds are, in practice, imposed on these PC-inputs and PC-outputs. For instance, in Montague Grammar,

(a1)   PC-inputs are drawn from a 'disambiguated language' (with ambiguities that plague natural language resolved away)

and

(a2)   PC-outputs are confined to truth-conditional aspects (to be supplemented, for example, by Gricean implicatures).

Both assumptions (a1) and (a2) abstract away important features of natural language— ambiguity in the case of (a1), and non-literal meaning in the case of (a2). But as neither assumption is forced by (PC), either can be challenged when applying (PC) to discourse.

With respect to (a2), there is a well-known minimal pair attributed to Barbara Partee that is generally employed as an argument that truth conditional meaning is too coarse for pronoun reference.

(13.1)   a. I dropped ten marbles and found all of them, except for one. It is probably under the sofa.
          b. I dropped ten marbles and found only nine of them. #It is probably under the sofa.

The first sentences in (13.1a) and (13.1b) are truth-conditionally equivalent, but as two-sentence discourses, (13.1a) and (13.1b) differ. One way to account for this difference is to recognize (13.1a) as a legal PC-input, but not (13.1b). (This way we need not worry further about (PC).) Otherwise, if (13.1a) and (13.1b) are both subject to compositional interpretation, then their difference in meaning must (by (PC)) be traced to a difference in the meanings of their parts or a difference in the way these parts are put together to form (13.1a) and (13.1b). Some leeway is available here because PC-inputs may go beyond strings of English words and punctuation symbols displayed in (13.1). Under (a1), for instance, the PC-input for (13.2) must fix what *can be fun*: relatives who are visiting, or visits to relatives.

(13.2)   Visiting relatives can be fun.

---

[1] No less than five chapters in that Handbook are directly relevant to compositionality in discourse— namely, those written by (i) Partee with Hendriks, (ii) van Eijck and Kamp, (iii) Janssen, (iv) Muskens, van Benthem, and Visser, and (v) Beaver.

Of course, explaining the difference observed in (13.1) through the structure of PC-inputs need not commit us to preserving a truth-conditional picture (a2) of meaning. It is natural to expect more complicated outputs from more complicated inputs. Indeed, what better motivation can there be to complicating the inputs than that we demand more from the outputs? That said, we may demand more from the outputs precisely to avoid complicating the inputs—whence the tendency to construe (13.1) as an invitation to step beyond truth-conditions.

It is a purely technical question whether or not to count (13.1a) but not (13.1b) among the allowed PC-inputs. The more substantive problem is the possibility of truth-value gaps. This possibility looms over sentences such as (13.3), if not (13.4).

(13.3) He beats his donkey.

(13.4) If Pedro owns a donkey, he beats his donkey.

To assign a truth-value to (13.3), we must specify who *he* and *his donkey* are. Under an anaphoric reading of (13.4), *he* is *Pedro*, and *his donkey* is *a donkey Pedro owns*. Analyses of such a reading and also of (13.1) and (13.3) have been developed that expand conceptions of meaning from truth-conditions to context change. These are reviewed in Section 13.2 below, where context change is shown to support (among other things) the assignment of truth-values to suitably disambiguated inputs.

These disambiguated inputs, as in (a1), take anaphor(a) resolution for granted. A classic illustration of the complexity of anaphor resolution is the minimal pair (13.5) due to Winograd (1972).

(13.5) a. The authorities denied the marchers a permit because they feared violence.
        b. The authorities denied the marchers a permit because they advocated vio-
           lence.

Common sense suggests that in (13.5a) *they* are *the authorities* whereas in (13.5b) *they* are *the marchers*. Aside from the piece of 'world knowledge' that between authorities and marchers, the former can be expected to fear violence and the latter to advocate it, there is our understanding of the word *because*, which in a sentence of the form *S because S'* offers *S'* as an explanation of *S*. In practice, the word *because* is at times dropped and (13.6a) understood as (13.6b), with the danger that (13.6a) could instead be read as say, (13.6c).

(13.6) a. *S.S'*.
        b. *S because S'*.
        c. *S and then S'*.

An example analysed at length in Asher and Lascarides (2003) is (13.7).

(13.7) a. Max fell. Mary pushed him.
        b. Max fell because Mary pushed him.

The tendency to read (13.7a) as (13.7b) reflects a certain familiarity with stories of pushes leading to falls. If we change the second sentence *S'* as in (13.8), then (13.6a) is more likely to be read as (13.6c).

(13.8)   Max fell. Mary helped him get up.

Jumping from (13.6a) to (13.6b) is a leap that we should be prepared to reconsider, as illustrated by (13.9).

(13.9)   Max fell. Mary pushed him. Lying on the ground, he was unable to resist her push.

Why not avoid such leaps by restricting interpretation in (PC) to that which is explicit?
   Because (very briefly) a discourse is seldom, if ever, fully explicit and PC-inputs generally go beyond the surface forms that are explicitly given. By mentioning 'parts' and 'how those parts are put together to form e', (PC) raises the possibility of non-explicit parts and of any number of ways to put those parts together. At one extreme, we note that parts are all explicit and can only be put together one way in

Example PL: Discourse as a theory in predicate logic A discourse here is a set of sentences, where a sentence φ is evaluated against a suitable model M by a satisfaction relation $\models$. Relative to a set $\mathcal{M}$ of such models, the meaning $[\![D]\!]_{\mathcal{M}}$ of a discourse D is defined to be the set of models in $\mathcal{M}$ that $\models$-satisfy every sentence in D

$$[\![D]\!]_{\mathcal{M}} = \{M \in \mathcal{M} \mid (\forall \varphi \in D)\, M \models \varphi\}$$

so that compositionality in discourse comes down to the equation

$$[\![D]\!]_{\mathcal{M}} = \bigcap_{\varphi \in D} [\![\{\varphi\}]\!]_{\mathcal{M}}\,.$$

Example PL misrepresents natural language discourse in at least three ways. First of all, for pronouns and many other 'holes' filled by context, it is useful to form a discourse from formulas with free variables, pairing a model M with a variable assignment f in M before applying $\models$ to the formula φ. In connection with compositionality, it is worth noting that f constitutes a notion of context that is allowed to vary when defining

$$(M, f) \models \varphi$$

by induction on a formula φ. Secondly, if, for instance, the free variables are to be interpreted appropriately, then simply throwing the parts together in a set will not do for compositional interpretation. At the very least, the order of English sentences in a text is significant. (Consider just about any two-sentence English text where the first sentence introduces an entity referred to by a pronoun in the second sentence.) In addition, there is the possibility of putting the parts together using words such as *because* and *and then*. This brings us to the third problem with Example PL as a model of discourse. The parts of a natural language discourse should not be limited to sentences but must range also over subsentential units such as connectives between sentences (including perhaps *if . . . then . . .*, which figures in the donkey sentence (13.4) above). These three problems taken together suggest that discourse processing is far more than interpreting a discourse compositionally against pairs (M, f) of models M and variable assignments f in M.

A good deal of work must go to fashioning discourse into a structure that can serve as a PC-input. These structures are called *Discourse Representation Structures* (DRSs) in *Discourse Representation Theory* (DRT, Kamp and Reyle, 1993). The construction of DRSs from natural language text is distinguished from the model-theoretic interpretation of DRSs (the latter being what interpretation in (PC) is traditionally identified with). It is noteworthy that early on, Kamp should write that

> it seems to me that the rules for the construction of discourse representations have at least as good a claim to being constitutive of meaning as the clauses that make up the definition of truth. (Kamp, 1979: 409)

and that after about a decade of work, he should declare

> the principal challenge to DRT, experience indicates, is the exact formulation of the construction algorithm. (Kamp, 1990: 37)

The challenge in formulating the construction algorithm has to do in no small measure with semantic reasoning within the algorithm.[2] Take, for example, the simple variant (13.10) of (13.4).

(13.10)   If Pedro owns a donkey, he beats the quadruped.

We can link *the quadruped* to *a donkey Pedro owns* if we can infer the latter is a quadruped. In (13.7), repeated below, a straightforward deduction (or induction) will not do to leap from (13.7a) to (13.7b).

(13.7)   a. Max fell. Mary pushed him.
        b. Max fell because Mary pushed him.

For any fall, we can expect many more pushes to temporally precede it than cause it (to say nothing of pushes after the fall). The plausibility of (13.7b), given (13.7a), depends on the manner in which (13.7a) reports the push immediately after the fall. We must draw on knowledge not only about the world of pushes and falls but also about how language is used to describe that world. A common view concerning language use is that the sentences in a discourse must relate to each other so as to form a coherent whole (Halliday and Hasan, 1976; Hobbs, 1979; Polanyi, 1985; Grosz and Sidner, 1986; Mann and Thompson, 1988; Asher and Lascarides, 2003; Webber, Stone, Joshi, and Knott, 2003; Kehler, 2002). The concrete issue for a two-sentence discourse is how to present it as a PC-input: as (13.6a) or as some complex such as, for example, (13.6b) or (13.6c) that specifies how *S* is related to *S'*?

(13.6)   a. *S.S'*.
        b. *S* because *S'*.
        c. *S* and then *S'*.

---

[2] By contrast, in ordinary predicate logic, the formation of predicate logic formulas depends in *no* way on the subsequent semantic manipulations of these formulas (in accordance with their model-theoretic interpretation). The crucial difference is that the DRS construction algorithm starts from natural language input with much information necessary for interpretation left implicit.

An instantiation of the sequence (13.6a) can be described as incoherent insofar as it is unclear how S is related to S' in it. Consider

(13.11)   Pat bought a hamster in 1996. Three is a prime number.

There is no denying the oddness of (13.11). But is it un-interpretable? The two sentences are separately interpretable, and we might hope that a context can be found for combining them coherently. One attempt (albeit feeble) is

(13.12)   Pat bought a hamster in 1996. Three is a prime number. These are the first two facts about Pat and three which spring to mind.

The last sentence in (13.12) presupposes a topic (viz., *the first two facts about Pat and three which spring to mind*) that an interpreter is asked to take for granted. Two questions arise. First, can we, in general, render two otherwise disconnected sentences into a coherent discourse by forming a topic around the conjunction of their subjects? And second, can the incremental interpretation of a coherent discourse involve the interpretation of parts that are not coherent (when not considered in full; e.g. (13.11))? An affirmative answer to the first question would appear to neuter the constraints on discourse that a notion of coherence is designed to impose. An affirmative answer to the second would imply that we should not require every PC-input to be coherent, even if we require the whole combination at the end to be coherent. As tempting as it may be to subject discourse structure to scrutiny under compositionality (PC), we need not insist that all that structure be present in a PC-input or even in a PC-output. Some of that structure might emerge only through further processing. We are, after all, free to apply (PC) to any of a number of processes for interpreting discourse; these processes diverge, to varying degrees, from assumptions (a1) and (a2).

(a1)   PC-inputs are drawn from a disambiguated language.
(a2)   PC-outputs are confined to truth-conditional aspects.

In place of these assumptions, we explore two below for discourse

(b1)   PC-inputs have enough structure to associate truth-conditions with them

and

(b2)   PC-outputs feed into the interpretation of further PC-inputs.

Assumptions (b1) and (b2) are somewhat modest departures from (a1) and (a2), compared to the contention from Ginzburg and Cooper (2004: 297) that for dialogue, 'the updates resulting from utterances cannot be defined in purely semantic terms', destroying the Montagovian picture of compositionality as a homomorphism from a syntactic to a semantic algebra. We will return to Ginzburg and Cooper briefly below (in Section 13.4.2). Until then, we will concern ourselves with challenges of the sort illustrated above, arising in discourse that, short of dialogue, consists of declarative sentences.

13.1.2 Outline

Behind assumptions (b1) and (b2) is the truism that there is more to discourse than the succession of sounds we hear (or symbols we read), making discourse interpretation all about what structures we associate with these sounds. Compositionality (PC) is a constraint on transformations of these structures that yield what can be called (perhaps rather too loosely) meanings. There is a tradition in formal semantics of basing compositionally derived meanings on a 'reality' external to the heads of language users, employing model-assignment pairs (M,f) for this purpose (Jackendoff, 1996; Hamm, Kamp, and Lambalger, 2006). In Section 13.2, we proceed from such pairs (M,f) to a conception of PC-outputs that captures both external and internal aspects of meaning. That conception is closely tied to assumption (b2), and depends on a notion of context against which to understand PC-inputs and PC-outputs. Contexts and PC-outputs are reformulated proof-theoretically in Section 13.3, construing formulas as types (e.g. Troelstra and Schwichtenberg, 2000).

In Section 13.4, we look more closely at PC-inputs and turn to assumption (b1). Whereas Section 13.2 starts from model-assignment pairs (M,f), Section 13.4 revolves around representations that express in PC-inputs both the explicit (verbal) and implicit (non-verbal) components of discourse. (Representing enough implicit information to interpret what is made explicit is arguably the main challenge in discourse processing.) The implications of these representations for meanings are considered, including a notion of *part* distinct from (but related to) that mentioned in (PC). If there is a tendency to view PC-outputs as pertaining to a reality outside the mind, there is equally a temptation to regard PC-inputs as representations that somehow record internal cognitive processes.

13.2 MEANING AND CONTEXT

This chapter would not be written from a logical perspective if it did not (to put it very mildly) link meaning to truth. The standard picture of truth in logic is that of satisfaction $\models$ of a well-formed formula φ relative to a model M and a variable assignment f in M. For example, we may associate with (13.13) the formula $admire(x_{spk}, p, x_{now})$ built from variables x_{spk} and x_{now} (for the speaker and speech time) and constant p (for *Pat*), and interpreted according to (13.14).

(13.13) I admire Pat.

(13.14) $(M,f) \models admire(x_{spk}, p, x_{now})$ iff $admire^M(f(x_{spk}), p^M, f(x_{now}))$

Inspecting (13.14), one may ask: why separate out the variable assignment f from M? It is a trivial matter to eliminate talk of variable assignments by

1. reconstruing free variables (which we can assume never occur bound, renaming bound variables if necessary) as fresh constants;

and then

2. reconceptualizing (M,f) as a model over an enlarged vocabulary with additional constants.

In the case of (13.14), we reconstrue x_{spk} and x_{now} as fresh constants s and n, to be interpreted over an expansion M_f of M with $s^{M_f} = f(x_{spk})$ and $n^{M_f} = f(x_{now})$ so that

$$M_f \models admire(s, p, n) \text{ iff } admire^{M_f}(s^{M_f}, p^{M_f}, n^{M_f})$$

$$\text{iff } (M,f) \models admire(x_{spk}, p, x_{now}).$$

For natural language applications, one reason not to bury f in a model (over an enlarged vocabulary) comes from so-called two-dimensional semantics (Kaplan, 1975). We discuss this below before reformulating all constants as variables, resulting in pairs (M,f) where the vocabulary of M has been stripped of all constants and the domain of f has been expanded to record the interpretations of these constants. This elimination of constants paves the way for a notion of context against which to understand the assumption (b2) that PC-outputs feed into PC-inputs. PC-inputs are constructed throughout this section from formulas φ, while PC-outputs are derived (one way or another) from pairs (M,f).

13.2.1 Variable assignments as contexts

As every speaker of English knows, the claim made by a sentence such as (13.13) depends on who utters it and when. Change the circumstances of its utterance and the claim changes. A way to capture these systematic variations is to associate variables with pertinent aspects of the utterance such as the speaker and the speech time, and formulate an utterance as a variable assignment f that specifies speaker $f(x_{spk})$, speech time $f(x_{now})$, etc. We can then bring out the dependence of the meaning of (13.13) on its utterance by presenting (13.13) as the formula $admire(x_{spk}, p, x_{now})$ (rather than $admire(s, p, n)$). Next, let us fix some set $\mathcal{M}$ of models, each of which we regard as a *possible world*. Then an utterance f of a formula φ picks out a set of possible worlds—or in possible worlds semantics, a *proposition*. That is, borrowing terminology from Kaplan (1979), the $\mathcal{M}$-*content* of φ at f is the proposition

$$\text{content}_{\mathcal{M}}(\varphi, f) = \{M \in \mathcal{M} \mid (M,f) \models \varphi\}$$

consisting of models in $\mathcal{M}$ that, paired with f, satisfy φ. Abstracting over the utterance f, the function mapping f to $\text{content}_{\mathcal{M}}(\varphi, f)$ is the $\mathcal{M}$-*character* of φ

$\text{character}_{\mathcal{M}}(\varphi) = (\lambda f \in F_{\mathcal{M}})\ \text{content}_{\mathcal{M}}(\varphi, f)$

where $F_{\mathcal{M}}$ is the set of variable assignments in models from $\mathcal{M}$. A member f of $F_{\mathcal{M}}$ is called an $\mathcal{M}$-*context*, and is understood to be fixed when speaking of $\mathcal{M}$-content. We let f vary over $F_{\mathcal{M}}$ to reveal the $\mathcal{M}$-character of a formula. Contextual factors such as the speaker and speech time (in f) are not strictly part of *what* content is (understood as a subset of $\mathcal{M}$) although they determine *how* that content is expressed by constituting an input f to the character of a formula.

Turning now to compositionality (PC), we have two obvious candidates for the meaning of an expression φ, namely $\text{content}_{\mathcal{M}}(\varphi, f)$ and $\text{character}_{\mathcal{M}}(\varphi)$. These notions are progressive abstractions over the Fregean idea that a sentence refers to one of two truth-values. These truth-values are relativized to possible worlds by content, which amounts to the Carnap–Montague conception of intension as a function mapping a possible world to reference

φ is true at M iff $M \in \text{content}_{\mathcal{M}}(\varphi, f)$.

Character recognizes a further layer, namely that of utterances. The step from reference to content and the step from content to character both allow variations in a parameter previously held fixed; a possible world M is fixed for reference, while an utterance f is fixed for content. As we will see next, however, the problem is that λ-abstracting over utterances and possible worlds does not on its own account for certain changes observed in interpreting discourse.

13.2.2 Context change

A crucial component of context that is especially obvious when processing a discourse consisting of more than one sentence is the surrounding text, also known as co-text. Co-text can plug truth-value gaps associated with presupposition failure. Consider

(13.15) a. Pat's car is yellow.
b. Pat has a car. It is yellow.
c. Pat has a car. Pat's car is yellow.
d. If Pat has a car, it/Pat's car is yellow.

Neither (13.15a) nor the negation of (13.15a) can be said to be true if Pat has no car. This possibility is ruled out in (13.15b) and (13.15c) and side-stepped in (13.15d). The idea, roughly, is that an indefinite description (such as *a car*) introduces a *discourse referent* (Karttunen, 1976) that a pronoun (such as *it*) or a definite description (such as *the car*) can subsequently pick up.

In DRT,[3] discourse referents are treated as variables that may or may not be in the domain of a variable assignment f. That is, a variable assignment f is understood to specify not only contextual factors such as the speaker and speech time, but also

---

[3] A cousin of DRT with about the same age and features is *File Change Semantics* (Heim, 1982).

'familiar' discourse referents that have been previously introduced in the discourse. A useful annotation on texts is to hang variables as superscripts when they are introduced (in which case they are said to be 'novel'), and to attach them as subscripts where they are required to be familiar.

(13.16)   a. (Pat's car)$_x$ is yellow.
        b. Pat has (a car)^x. It$_x$ is yellow.
        c. Pat has (a car)^x. (Pat's car)$_x$ is yellow.
        d. If Pat has (a car)^x, it$_x$/(Pat's car)$_x$ is yellow.

The upshot is that a sentence can add discourse referents and/or conditions on discourse referents. Accordingly, a PC-input in DRT, called a DRS (for Discourse Representation Structure), is taken to be a pair (U, C) of a set U of discourse referents, and a set C of conditions. The old picture of satisfaction $\models$ applies to conditions (in C), but a DRS as a whole can be conceived, relative to a model M, as a programme with inputs and outputs that range over variable assignments in M. A DRS (U, C) that is fed a variable assignment f in M as input can return a variable assignment g in M as output if g extends f to the discourse referents in U and (M, g) satisfies every condition in C. More precisely, we encode the input/output behaviour of (U, C) in M as a binary relation $[\![(U, C)]\!]_M$ between variable assignments f and g in M such that

$$f[\![(U, C)]\!]_M g \text{ iff } f \subseteq g \text{ and } domain(g) = domain(f) \cup U$$

$$\text{and for each } \varphi \in C, (M, g) \models \varphi.$$

A condition φ can be turned into the DRS $(\emptyset, \{\varphi\})$, from which the $\mathcal{M}$-content of φ can be extracted

$$M \in \text{content}_{\mathcal{M}}(\varphi, f) \text{ iff } (M, f) \models \varphi$$

$$\text{iff } f[\![(\emptyset, \{\varphi\})]\!]_M f$$

for $M \in \mathcal{M}$. For any DRS K, we assume *the negation $\neg K$ of K* is a condition that is satisfied by (M, f) precisely if f falls outside the domain of $[\![K]\!]_M$

$$(M, f) \models \neg K \text{ iff there is no } g \text{ such that } f[\![K]\!]_M g.$$

The relations $[\![K]\!]_M$ are not unlike the input/output interpretations of programmes in *Quantified Dynamic Logic* (Harel, 1984), with $\neg K$ amounting to the dynamic logic formula $[K]\bot$ saying that some contradictory formula $\bot$ holds whenever K terminates (which is to say: K cannot terminate). Starting with Barwise (1987), various systems of 'dynamic semantics' mixing DRT and dynamic logic have been proposed, such as *Dynamic Predicate Logic* (DPL, Groenendijk and Stokhof, 1991). An example commonly mentioned as motivation for such systems is Geach's 'donkey sentence' (13.17).

(13.17)   If (a farmer)^x owns (a donkey)^y he$_x$ beats it$_y$.

To analyse a conditional such as (13.17), DRT builds a condition $K \Rightarrow K'$ from DRSs K and K', which is satisfied by a pair (M, f) exactly if the domain of $[\![K']\!]_M$ includes every $[\![K]\!]_M$-output on input f

$$(M, f) \models K \Rightarrow K' \text{ iff } (\forall g \text{ such that } f[\![K]\!]_M g)(\exists h)\, g[\![K']\!]_M h.$$

Example (13.17) is then translated as the DRS condition

$$(\{x, y\}, \{\text{farmer}(x), \text{donkey}(y), \text{own}(x, y)\}) \Rightarrow (\emptyset, \{\text{beat}(x, y)\}).$$

We can also define $\Rightarrow$ in terms of negation $\neg$, treating $(U, C) \Rightarrow K'$ as an abbreviation of $\neg(U, C \cup \{\neg K'\})$. In DPL, this reduction can be put quite perspicuously as the equivalence between the material conditional $\varphi \Rightarrow \psi$ and $\neg(\varphi \wedge \neg\psi)$, familiar from Boolean logic. The crucial difference is that in dynamic semantics, a formula φ is interpreted as an input/output relation $r(\varphi)$ with $\wedge$ expressing relational composition $\circ$

$$r(\varphi \wedge \psi) = r(\varphi) \circ r(\psi)$$
$$= \{(a, b) \mid (\exists c)\, a\, r(\varphi)\, c \text{ and } c\, r(\psi)\, b\}.$$

In DRT, the obvious way to conjoin two DRSs (U, C) and (U', C') is through the binary operation *merge* $\uplus$ that unions together the respective components

$$(U, C) \uplus (U', C') = (U \cup U', C \cup C').$$

For example,

$$(U, C) = (U, \emptyset) \uplus (\emptyset, C)$$

and for any model M,

$$[\![(U, C)]\!]_M = [\![(U, \emptyset)]\!]_M \circ [\![(\emptyset, C)]\!]_M.$$

A case in which

$$[\![K \uplus K']\!]_M \neq [\![K]\!]_M \circ [\![K']\!]_M$$

is given by $K = (\emptyset, \{x = x\})$ and $K' = (\{x\}, \emptyset)$. To rule out such examples, let us define (U', C') to be (U, C)-*novel* if *no* discourse referent in U' belongs to U or appears in a condition in C. Clearly, if K' is K-novel, then

$$[\![K \uplus K']\!]_M = [\![K]\!]_M \circ [\![K']\!]_M .$$

Notice that the input/output interpretation $[\![K]\!]_M$ of a DRS K depends on the choice of a model M. We can abstract over such choices by collecting possibilities (M, f) as follows. An *information state* is a set σ of pairs (M, f) of models M and variable assignments f in M. A DRS K can then be interpreted as a function K-update on information states that maps σ to the information state

$$K\text{-update}(\sigma) = \bigcup_{(M, f) \in \sigma} \{(M, g) \mid f[\![K]\!]_M g\}$$

gathering the $[\![K]\!]_M$-outputs on input f, for (M,f) ranging over σ. The intuition behind an information state σ is that each (M,f) in σ is a possibility, and that an information state σ' carries at least as much information as σ, notated $\sigma \sqsubseteq \sigma'$, precisely if every possibility in σ' fleshes out one in σ

$$\sigma \sqsubseteq \sigma' \text{ iff } (\forall (M,f') \in \sigma')(\exists f \subseteq f') \, (M,f) \in \sigma$$

(where (M',f') *fleshes out* (M,f) if $M = M'$ and $f' \supseteq f$.) The two components U and C in a DRS $K = (U, C)$ represent two different ways of adding information—by expanding the domain of a variable assignment (to include a discourse referent in U), and by eliminating a possibility (if it fails to satisfy a condition in C). K increases the information content in an information state σ in that

$$\sigma \sqsubseteq K\text{-update}(\sigma)$$

because

$$\text{whenever } f[\![K]\!]_M g, f \subseteq g$$

for all M. By contrast, information need not increase in systems of dynamic semantics (such as DPL) that use random assignment $x := ?$ (in place of the DRS $(\{x\}, \emptyset)$) with a relational interpretation $r(x := ?)$ given by

$$f \, r(x := ?) \, g \text{ iff } domain(g) = domain(f) \cup \{x\} \text{ and}$$

$$(\forall y \in domain(g) - \{x\}) \, f(y) = g(y)$$

that does not require $f \subseteq g$. In practice, however, it is unclear that a random assignment $x := ?$ is ever applied to a variable x that has already been assigned a value. For instance, when interpreting a pair of DRSs K and K' in sequence (representing say, a two-sentence text), it is natural to assume K' is K-novel. For the record,

Proposition 1. *Given DRSs K and K', if K' is K-novel, then*

$$[\![K \uplus K']\!]_M = [\![K]\!]_M \circ [\![K']\!]_M$$

for any model M, and so

$$(K \uplus K')\text{-update}(\sigma) = K'\text{-update}(K\text{-update}(\sigma))$$

for any information state σ.

The significance of Proposition 1 lies in its relevance to the basic intuition behind DRT: a discourse consisting of a sequence $S_1 \ldots S_n$ of sentences is processed one sentence at a time from left to right, by constructing (for $1 \leq i \leq n$) a DRS K_i representing sentence S_i in the context of representations $K_1 \cdots K_{i-1}$ of the preceding sequence $S_1 \ldots S_{i-1}$. For the discourse referents in K_i to be novel, we require that K_i be $(K_1 \uplus K_2 \uplus \cdots \uplus K_{i-1})$-novel. Let us call $K_1 K_2 \cdots K_n$ an *admissible DRS sequence* if this holds for all $i > 1$ and $\leq n$. Now, it is immediate from Proposition 1 that an admissible DRS sequence $K_1 \cdots K_n$ can be $\uplus$-merged for sequential interpretation against a model M

$$[\![K_1 \uplus K_2 \uplus \cdots \uplus K_n]\!]_M = [\![K_1]\!]_M \circ [\![K_2]\!]_M \cdots \circ [\![K_n]\!]_M$$

or against information states σ

$$(K_1 \uplus \cdots \uplus K_n)\text{-update}(\sigma) = K_n\text{-update}(\cdots K_1\text{-update}(\sigma) \cdots).$$

Evidently, compositionality (PC) holds for a complex expression given by an admissible DRS sequence $K_1 \cdots K_n$ with parts K_i (for $1 \leq i \leq n$), and meanings

$$[\![K_1 \uplus \cdots \uplus K_n]\!]_M \text{ and } [\![K_i]\!]_M$$

(if we can single out a model M) or (failing that) meanings

$$(K_1 \uplus \cdots \uplus K_n)\text{-update and } K_i\text{-update}$$

(Table 13.1). Each part K_i can, in turn, be conceived as a complex expression subject to compositionality, under the clauses for $\models$ and $[\![\cdot]\!]_M$. Compositionality in this case, however, pertains not so much to discourse-as-a-sequence-of-sentences, but rather to subsentential structure.

By the associativity of $\uplus$ and $\circ$, we can parenthesize $K_1K_2K_3$ either as $(K_1K_2)K_3$ (in accordance with the aforementioned intuition behind DRT) with parts K_1K_2 and K_3, or as $K_1(K_2K_3)$ with parts K_1 and K_2K_3. Implicit in the choice of parts K_i in Table 13.1 is the use of a multi-ary operation (of multiple arities $n \geq 1$) that can be derived from iterations of a binary operation under any system of parenthesization. Indeed, we might extend DRSs with a sequential connective; interpreted as relational composition $\circ$

$$[\![K; K']\!]_M = [\![K]\!]_M \circ [\![K']\!]_M$$

but at the cost of losing the decomposition of *every* DRS to a pair (U, C) of sets of discourse referents and conditions. Our restriction to admissible sequences KK' (where K' is K-novel) allows us to retain the uniform picture of a DRS as a pair (U, C) by flattening $K_1; K_2; \cdots ; K_n$ to $K_1 \uplus K_2 \uplus \cdots \uplus K_n$.

The novelty requirement in admissible DRS sequences captures only part of what assumption (b2) is about.

(b2)   PC-outputs feed into the interpretation of further PC-inputs.

Complementing novelty is familiarity, which for a sequence $(U, C)(U', C')$ of DRSs and an initial DRS (U_0, C_0) comes to the clause

(†)   every discourse referent appearing in C' but not in U' is in U and every discourse referent appearing in C_0 is in U_0.

Table 13.1 C–inputs and C–outputs in § 2.2

C-input	admissible DRS sequence $K_1 \cdots K_n$ with parts K_i
C-output	$[\![K_1 \uplus \cdots \uplus K_n]\!]_M$ (relative to a fixed model M)
	$(K_1 \uplus \cdots \uplus K_n)$-update (collecting different M's)

To make (†) concrete, let us return to (13.16a), (13.16b), and (13.16c), repeated below.

(13.16) a. (Pat's car)$_x$ is yellow.
  b. Pat has (a car)^x. It$_x$ is yellow.
  c. Pat has (a car)^x. (Pat's car)$_x$ is yellow.

Let us assign (13.16b) the admissible DRS sequence (U, C) $(\emptyset, \{yellow(x)\})$ where $x \in U$. (†) then holds in (13.16b) but not in (13.16a) or in (13.18).

(13.18) Not all cars have dull colours. (Pat's car)$_x$ is yellow.

As the first sentence in (13.18) fails to *make x* familiar, (13.18) can only be interpreted in a context where x is already familiar. Both (13.16a) and (13.18) *presuppose* an x that is *Pat's car* (Beaver, 1997). By contrast, both (13.16b) and (13.16c) assert *Pat has a car x*, which we might assume qualifies x to be *Pat's car*. Between (13.16a)/(13.18) and (13.16b)/(13.16c) are discourses such as (13.19) where a discourse referent y is assumed familiar that intuitively can be linked but not equated with a familiar discourse referent x (Clark, 1975; Asher and Lascarides, 2003).

(13.19) Pat has (a car)^x. (The engine)$_y$ needs repair.

In general, satisfying definite descriptions can be a difficult task involving implicit information from any number of sources, including the visual scene. Often presuppositions must simply be accommodated (Lewis, 1979), such as that represented by the proper name *Pat* in (13.16), (13.18) and (13.19). In DRT, *Pat* is treated as a unary relation, rather than a constant, leading to the translation (13.20) of the first sentence of (13.16b), (13.16c) and (13.19).

(13.20) Pat$_u$ has (a car)^x.
    $(\{u, x\}, \{pat(u), car(x), has(u, x)\})$

In (13.20), the presupposed discourse referent u (appearing as a subscript) is included in the DRS's set of discourse referents (alongside the variable x in superscript). A wide-ranging account of presuppositions is given in van der Sandt (1992) that treats presupposition triggers as anaphoric. Inasmuch as anaphora resolution lies outside compositional interpretation, however, this puts presuppositions beyond the scope of compositional semantics.

13.3 A PROOF-THEORETIC PERSPECTIVE

The crucial notion distinguishing a DRS K from an ordinary formula φ is that of a discourse referent, analysed in the step from content$_\mathcal{M}(\varphi,f)$ and character$_\mathcal{M}(\varphi)$ in Section 13.2.1 to the meanings $[\![K]\!]_M$ and K-update in Section 13.2.2. Instead of moving to DRSs, we can extract discourse referents from more or less ordinary formulas φ if we trade in model-theoretic semantics (centered around $\models$) for a proof-theoretic perspective (involving types).

13.3.1 Dependent types, t-contexts, and records

The idea of interpreting a formula φ as a type $[\varphi]$ is that

(i) the type $[\varphi]$ consists of 'constructive' proofs of φ

where

(ii) a type is defined relative to a finite sequence of variables paired with types

as in Martin-Löf type theory (Sundholm, 1986 Ranta, 1994).
   Let us explain (i) and (ii) in turn.
   The type constructs we require for (i) introduce dependencies in Cartesian products $A \times B$ and function spaces $A \to B$. Recall that $A \times B$ consists of pairs $\langle a, b \rangle$ of members a of A and b of B

$$A \times B = \{\langle a, b \rangle \mid a \in A \text{ and } b \in B\}$$

while $A \to B$ consists of functions mapping members a of A to members b of B

$$A \to B = \{f \mid f \text{ maps } a \in A \text{ to } b \in B\}.$$

Now, for dependencies, we allow the second type B to depend on an object of A, writing $B_{x/a}$ for the type obtained from B by instantiating x as a. We can then form the type $(\Sigma x \in A)B$ of pairs $\langle a, b \rangle$ consisting of members a of A and b of $B_{x/a}$

$$(\Sigma x \in A)B = \{\langle a, b \rangle \mid a \in A \text{ and } b \in B_{x/a}\}$$

as well as the type $(\Pi x \in A)B$ of functions mapping members a of A to members of $B_{x/a}$

$$(\Pi x \in A)B = \{f \mid f \text{ maps } a \in A \text{ to } b \in B_{x/a}\}.$$

We can express universal quantification through Π, and existential quantification through Σ, as illustrated in (13.21) and (13.22), respectively.

(13.21) Every ant bites.
         $(\Pi x \in \text{ant}) \text{bites}(x)$

(13.22) There is an ant that bites.
         $(\Sigma x \in \text{ant}) \text{bites}(x)$

Given a pair $\langle a, b \rangle$ from $(\Sigma x \in A)B$, we can apply *left* and *right* projections l and r to extract the left component

$$l\langle a, b \rangle = a$$

and the right component

$$r\langle a, b \rangle = b.$$

Noting that we can encode two variables in one (via pairing $\langle \cdot, \cdot \rangle$), let us return to Geach's donkey sentence (13.17), expressing implication through Π.[4]

(13.17)   If (a farmer)^x owns (a donkey)^y he$_x$ beats it$_y$.

The antecedent, (*a farmer*)^x *owns* (*a donkey*)^y, is translated to the type

$(\Sigma x \in \text{farmer})(\Sigma y \in \text{donkey})\text{owns}(x, y)$

using Σ to existentially bind the variables in the type expression owns(x, y). We connect the antecedent to the consequent through Π, turning (13.17) into the type

$(\Pi z \in (\Sigma x \in \text{farmer})(\Sigma y \in \text{donkey}) \text{ owns}(x, y))\text{beats}(lz, l(rz))$

where the subscripts x and y in (13.17) become terms lz and $l(rz)$ built from the left and right projections l and r. Navigating with l and r undeniably obscures the variable co-indexing in (13.17).

We can improve transparency by reformulating Σ in terms of records, as advocated in Cooper (2005), so that the type for (13.17) becomes

$(\Pi z \in \begin{bmatrix} x : \text{farmer} \\ y : \text{donkey} \\ s : \text{owns}(x, y) \end{bmatrix})\text{beats}(z.x, z.y)$

with : in place of $\in$, and with dotted projections $z.x$ and $z.y$ in place of lz and $l(rz)$. Within records, x and y above are called *labels*, rather than variables. But the variable/label distinction is a purely technical one that we can ignore as soon as we understand it, in much the same way that we can confuse variables with constants so as to construe the pair (M, f) of a model M and variable assignment f as a model expanding M. Treating labels as variables, a record type

$\begin{bmatrix} x_1 : T_1 \\ x_2 : T_2(x_1) \\ \vdots \\ x_n : T_n(x_1, x_2, \ldots, x_{n-1}) \end{bmatrix}$

amounts to a finite sequence (13.23) of variables paired with types, as mentioned in (ii) above.

(13.23) $x_1 : T_1, x_2 : T_2(x_1), \ldots x_n : T_n(x_1, x_2, \ldots, x_{n-1})$

Martin-Löf type theory builds particular sequences of the form (13.23), called *contexts*. To avoid confusion with other notions of context, let us refer to these as *t-contexts*. We take the empty sequence as a t-context (assigning no variable a type), and generate t-contexts inductively according to

---

[4] Similarly, conjunction can be expressed through Σ (inasmuch as a proof of $A \wedge B$ is a pair consisting of a proof of A and a proof of B).

(∗)   given a t-context Γ and a variable x not already assigned a type by Γ, we can form
the t-context

$\Gamma, x : T$

(assigning x the type T) provided that T is a type relative to Γ.

Let us agree to write

$\Gamma \vdash T$ type

to express the proviso in (∗) that T is a type relative to the t-context Γ. We have, for Q
equal to Σ or Π, the rule

$$\frac{\Gamma \vdash A \text{ type} \qquad \Gamma, x : A \vdash B \text{ type}}{\Gamma \vdash (Qx \in A)B \text{ type}} \quad x \text{ not in } \Gamma$$

stating that if

A is a type relative to Γ and B is a type relative to $\Gamma, x : A$

then $(Qx \in A)B$ is a type relative to Γ. Consider again (13.16).

(13.16)   a. (Pat's car)$_x$ is yellow.
b. Pat has (a car)^x. It$_x$ is yellow.
c. Pat has (a car)^x. (Pat's car)$_x$ is yellow.
d. If Pat has (a car)^x, it$_x$/(Pat's car)$_x$ is yellow.

Assuming

$x_1 : (\Sigma x \in \text{car})$ pat-has$(x) \vdash$ yellow(lx_1) type

we can derive

$\vdash (\Pi x_1 \in (\Sigma x \in \text{car})$ pat-has$(x))$ yellow(lx_1) type

for (13.16d), or

$\vdash (\Sigma x_1 \in (\Sigma x \in \text{car})$ pat-has$(x))$ yellow(lx_1) type

for a conjunctive form

Pat has (a car)^x, and it$_x$ is yellow

of (13.16b), or

$x_1 : (\Sigma x \in \text{car})$ pat-has$(x), x_2 :$ yellow(lx_1)

for (13.16bc).[5]

---

[5] For simplicity, we ignore here the difference between pronouns and definite descriptions. The interested reader is referred to Fernando (2001) for a more detailed proof-theoretic treatment of presupposition, linked to conservativity of generalized quantifiers.

It follows from $(*)$ that t-contexts of the form (13.23) satisfy

(nov) $x_i \neq x_j$ for $i \neq j$

and

(fam)   if x_i occurs in T_j then $i < j$

for i and j ranging over $\{1, 2, \ldots, n\}$. The consequences (nov) and (fam) correspond respectively to novelty and familiarity requirements on discourse referents, and together support a DRT-like treatment of anaphora. But whereas a string $K_1 \cdots K_n$ of DRSs K_i representing an n-sentence text $S_1 \ldots S_n$ is flattened by merge $\uplus$ to a single DRS

$$K_1 \uplus \cdots \uplus K_n = (U, C)$$

consisting of a set U of discourse referents and a set C of conditions, the sequential structure $S_1 \ldots S_n$ is preserved if we represent each sentence S_i by a type $T_i(x_1, \ldots, x_{i-1})$ relative to a t-context

$$x_1 : T_1, \ldots, x_{i-1} : T_{i-1}(x_1, \ldots, x_{i-2}).$$

Under this formulation, discourse referents arise as terms assembled from the t-context relative to which a type is defined. The t-context can include assumptions such as

all cars have engines
$(\Pi y \in \text{car})(\Sigma z \in \text{engine}) \text{ has}(y, z)$

allowing us to form a term for the engine mentioned in (13.19).

(13.19)   Pat has (a car)^x. (The engine)$_y$ needs repair.
$\quad\quad\quad x_0 : (\Pi y \in \text{car})(\Sigma z \in \text{engine}) \text{ has}(y, z),$
$\quad\quad\quad x_1 : (\Sigma x \in \text{car}) \text{ pat-has}(x),$
$\quad\quad\quad x_2 : \text{needs-repair}(l(x_0(lx_1)))$

Terms formed from such proofs (based on additional assumptions) may far outstrip the discourse referents enumerated in a DRS, and must be formed with restraint if we are to avoid overgeneration.

13.3.2 Denotations and instances

To instantiate the variables in a t-context, we interpret type expressions alongside t-contexts. More precisely, for each t-context Γ and type expression T such that $\Gamma \vdash T$ type, we define the notion of an *instance s of* Γ and the *denotation* T_s *of* T *relative to s* as follows.

(a) For Γ equal to the empty sequence, there is exactly one instance of Γ, the empty map $\emptyset$.

(b) T_s is the type obtained from the type expression T by replacing every variable x_i in T by $s(x_i)$.

(c) If Γ does *not* assign a variable x a type, then an instance of $(\Gamma, x : T)$ is an instance s of Γ expanded to map x to some object a in T_s.

Implicit in (b) and (c) is the assumption that T_s is a well-defined set whenever $\Gamma \vdash T$ type and s is an instance of Γ.[6] For T's built with neither Σ nor Π, various choices can be made (just as a DRS can be interpreted against any number of models). Fixing some such choice, let char(T) be the function that maps an instance s of a t-context Γ such that $\Gamma \vdash T$ type to the denotation

$$\text{char}(T)(s) = T_s$$

of T relative to s. The similarity between char(T) and character$_\mathcal{M}(\varphi)$ from Section 13.2.1 is unmistakable (see Table 13.2). Two important differences, however, should be noted. First, whereas content$_\mathcal{M}(\varphi, f)$ in Section 13.2.1 does not incorporate additions to f (arising from discourse referents φ takes to be novel), the denotation T_s encodes these additions directly into its objects (proofs).[7] Secondly, the notion of a t-context Γ structuring char(T) abstracts away the particular choices (M, f) in Section 13.2.1 and 13.2.2, providing a model-free semantic account. Familiar constructs in typed programming languages, typings of variables (in a t-context) are hypothetical until they are executed (as programmes are intended). Although t-contexts allow us to steer clear of models, a notion of reference is crucial for hooking up type expressions with an external reality. Situation semantics is linked, for instance in Cooper (2005), to Martin-Löf type theory on the basis of the following reading of Austin (1961) in Barwise and Perry (1983)

Table 13.2 Section 13.2.1 vs. Section 13.3.2

Section 13.2.1	Section 13.3.2
formula φ	type T
character$_\mathcal{M}(\varphi)$	char(T)
content$_\mathcal{M}(\varphi, f)$	denotation T_s relative to s
variable assignment f	instance s of a t-context

[6] The notion of set here can be understood in the sense of ordinary set theory (e.g. ZFC) under classical logic, assuming we formulate the dependent types $(\Sigma x \in A)B$ and $(\Pi x \in A)B$ as in, e.g., Feferman (1975).

[7] In programming language terms applied to 'apparently noncompositional phenomena in natural languages' in Shan (2005), the introduction of a discourse referent is a *side-effect* of evaluating an existential formula under dynamic formulations of DRT (based on quantified dynamic logic). By contrast, the type-theoretic approach considered here incorporates witnesses into the (constructive) proofs of an existential formula (Σ-type), and does so within a declarative rather than an imperative (assignment-based) programming language.

a statement is true when the actual situation to which it refers is of the type described by the statement. (Barwise and Perry, 1983: 160)

Austin distinguishes *demonstrative conventions* that determine reference from *descriptive conventions* that yield, in the present framework, type expressions. Without fixing either the demonstrative or descriptive conventions of a language, instances s of t-contexts together with denotations T_s of type expressions T give us a foothold by specifying which descriptions apply to which references. These specifications are compositional insofar as (PC) holds for a t-context as a PC-input, and its set of instances as a PC-output. That is, we may represent a sequence of n sentences not by a string $K_1 \cdots K_n$ of n DRSs (as in Table 13.1, Section 13.2.2) but by a t-context of the form (13.23).

(13.23) $x_1 : T_1, x_2 : T_2(x_1), \ldots x_n : T_n(x_1, x_2, \ldots, x_{n-1})$

Let us define the *interpretation* $[\![\Gamma]\!]$ *of* a t-context Γ to be its set of instances. By definition,

Proposition 2. *Whenever* $\Gamma \vdash T$ type *and x is a variable,*

$$[\![\Gamma, x : T]\!] = \{s \cup \{(x, a)\} \mid s \in [\![\Gamma]\!] \text{ and } a \in T_s\}$$

provided Γ does not assign x a type.

An immediate corollary of Proposition 2 is that the interpretation $[\![\Gamma]\!]$ of a t-context Γ is compositional. In accordance with assumption (b2) from Section 13.1.1, the PC-output s feeds into the interpretation of the PC-input $\Gamma, x : T$ (or more specifically, the type expression T). By linking meanings ever more tightly with contexts, we blur the line between semantics and pragmatics, bringing phenomena such as presupposition within the compass of compositional interpretation. One of the pay-offs in taking (13.23), rather than $K_1 \cdots K_n$, as a PC-input is the perspicuous representation of anaphoric connections by occurrences of x_i in T_j for $1 \leq i < j \leq n$.

13.4 REPRESENTATION AND STRUCTURE

Discourse interpretation in the previous sections proceeds from a representation of a sequence $S_1 \ldots S_n$ of n sentences by a string of $K_1 \cdots K_n$ of n DRSs (in Section 13.2.2) or (in Section 13.3.1) by a t-context of the form (13.23) with length n. The obvious question is how well does either picture represent discourse? For example, some instances of (13.6a) are, as noted in the introduction above, often analysed as (13.6b) or as (13.6c).

(13.6)   a. *S.S′.*
     b. *S* because *S′.*
     c. *S* and then *S′.*

We turn in the present section to conceptions of discourse structure beyond that suggested by the sequence $S_1 \ldots S_n$. As it happens, (13.23) can encode more structure than that exploited in the previous section. Indeed, (13.23) can serve as a representation of texts of m sentences where m differs from the length n in (13.23). This has consequences for denotations of type expressions that we explore below.

13.4.1 PC-inputs constrained and reconstrued

One reason for preferring (13.6b) or (13.6c) to (13.6a) is the intuition that *not* every sequence of interpretable sentences constitutes a coherent discourse, but that at the very least, the sentences in the sequence must have something to do with each other. Just what that something is is spelled out in (13.6b) and (13.6c), and represented in (13.24) through a type expression in which a variable from the t-context occurs.

(13.24)   a. *S*. That is because *S'*.
                 $x : T$, $x' : T'$-explaining(x)
              b. *S*. After that, *S'*.
                 $x : T$, $x' : T'$-following(x)

The type expressions T and T' in (13.24) correspond to the sentences S and S' respectively (according to what Austin calls descriptive conventions). Without worrying for the moment about how to choose a type expression, let us focus on the occurrence of a variable in it. Given a t-context Γ of the form

$$x_1 : T_1, \ldots, x_n : T_n$$

(as in (13.23)), let us collect all pairs (i, j) of indices such that x_i occurs in T_j in

$$\text{Link}_\Gamma = \{(i, j) \mid 1 \le i, j \le n \text{ and } x_i \text{ occurs in } T_j\} .$$

It follows from familiarity (one of the consequences of assuming Γ is a t-context)

(fam)   if x_i occurs in T_j then $i < j$ (where $1 \le i, j \le n$)

that $i < j$ whenever $\text{Link}_\Gamma(i, j)$. Next, let Conn_Γ be the symmetric, transitive closure of Link_Γ. Conn abbreviates *connected*, the idea being that $\text{Conn}_\Gamma(i, j)$ holds precisely when the sentences S_i and S_j represented in Γ are connected by variables occurring in type expressions. The requirement that the sentences in a coherent discourse are connected corresponds (in the representation Γ) to the constraint

(con)   whenever $1 \le i < j \le n$, $\text{Conn}_\Gamma(i, j)$.

The t-contexts Γ in (13.24a) and (13.24b) respect (con). Notice that every prefix of a t-context is a t-context but that a prefix of a t-context respecting (con) need not respect (con). (For an illustration, recall lines (13.11) and (13.12), as discussed in the introduction.) Accordingly, we should be careful about imposing (con) on every PC-input, leaving (con) instead as a final check once the sequence is complete. Otherwise, an incremental interpretation of (13.23) that processes typings $x_i : T_i$ one at a time from $i = 1$ to $i = n$ may fail.

That said, there are ways of building t-contexts from (13.23) other than by appending a typing

$$x_{n+1} : T_{n+1}$$

to its right. For an illustration, consider the discourse (13.25), analysed in Asher and Lascarides (2003) using *Segmented DRT* (SDRT).

(13.25)   a. John had a lovely evening.
        b. He had a great meal.
        c. He ate salmon.
        d. He devoured lots of cheese.
        e. He won a dancing competition.

SDRT extends DRSs to *Segmented DRSs* with rhetorical relations such as *Narration* and *Elaboration* linking *discourse segments*. Reformulating the SDRT analysis of (13.25) in terms of t-contexts and types, the five sentences are individually assigned type expressions T_a, T_b, T_c, T_d, and T_e that combine *not* into a flat 5-variable t-context of the form

$$x_a : T_a, \ x_b : T_b', \ x_c : T_c', \ x_d : T_d', \ x_e : T_e'$$

(decorating T_b, T_c, T_d, and T_e with primes to allow for modifications by rhetorical relations) but instead into a 3-variable t-context

$$x_a : T_a, \ y_b : U_b, \ z_b : Elaboration(x_a, y_b)$$

where U_b is the record type

$$U_b = \begin{bmatrix} x_b : T_b \\ y_c : \begin{bmatrix} x_c : T_c \\ x_d : T_d\text{-}Narration(x_c) \end{bmatrix} \\ z_c : Elaboration(x_b, y_c) \\ x_e : T_e\text{-}Narration(x_b) \end{bmatrix}$$

representing the discourse segment (13.25b)–(13.25e). Discourse segments of more than one sentence arise from *subordinating* rhetorical relations such as *Elaboration*, as opposed to *coordinating* rhetorical relations such as *Narration*. The typing

$$z_b : Elaboration(x_a, y_b)$$

relates (13.25a) to the discourse segment (13.25b)–(13.25e) by *Elaboration*, just as in U_b, the typing

$$z_c : Elaboration(x_b, y_c)$$

relates (13.25b) to the discourse segment (13.25c)–(13.25d) by *Elaboration*. In U_b, *Narration* links (13.25c) to (13.25d), and (13.25b) to (13.25e). Note that a simple narrative sequence $S_1 \ldots S_n$ would result in a flat t-context

$$x_1 : T_1, \ x_2 : T_2\text{-}Narration(x_1), \ \ldots \ x_n : T_n\text{-}Narration(x_{n-1})$$

of the same length n. Subordinating rhetorical relations introduce a hierarchical structure (built above with variables/labels y_b, z_b, y_c, and z_c) that strongly violates the associativity in flat sequences.[8] The t-context for (13.25) grows incrementally from

$$x_a : T_a$$

after (13.25a), to

$$x_a : T_a, \ y_b : [x_b : T_b], \ z_b : Elaboration(x_a, y_b)$$

after (13.25b), to

$$x_a : T_a, \ y_b : \begin{bmatrix} x_b : T_b \\ y_c : [x_c : T_c] \\ z_c : Elaboration(x_b, y_c) \end{bmatrix}, z_b : Elaboration(x_a, y_b)$$

after (13.25c), to

$$x_a : T_a, \ y_b : \begin{bmatrix} x_b : T_b \\ y_c : \begin{bmatrix} x_c : T_c \\ x_d : T_d\text{-}Narration(x_c) \end{bmatrix} \\ z_c : Elaboration(x_b, y_c) \end{bmatrix}, z_b : Elaboration(x_a, y_b)$$

after (13.25d) and finally to

$$x_a : T_a, \ y_b : U_b, \ z_b : Elaboration(x_a, y_b)$$

after (13.25e). Without necessarily increasing the length of the (outer) t-context by
one, each sentence adds to the overall structure according to a so-called *right frontier
constraint*. SDRT appeals to this constraint, for instance, to explain the unacceptability
of continuing (13.25a)–(13.25e) with (13.25f).

(13.25)   f. $^?$It was a beautiful pink.

Because the salmon is not on the right frontier, it is not available for the pronoun *it* in
(13.25f). A definite description can, however, access it (using, as van der Sandt (1992)
observes, its greater descriptive content).

(13.25)   f′. The salmon gave him all the energy he needed.

Exactly what discourse constraints hold when is a delicate matter subject to debate.
Discourse adverbials such as *then*, *instead*, and *otherwise* are argued in Webber et al.
(2003) to be anaphors exempt from constraints on 'structural' conjunctions such as *and*,
but, and *although*. It is straightforward to represent discourse adverbials in the framework of t-contexts. The framework is neutral on the question of what constraints to
impose or of precisely what rhetorical relations to use (e.g. Kehler, 2002), if any (as some
semanticists are loathe to use them). Beyond restricting the domain of compositional
interpretation in discourse,[9] such questions have consequences for the interpretation

---

[8] Notice that the constraint (con) above ensuring that the sentences in a discourse are connected must
be modified to account for the hierarchical structure.
[9] Recall from the introduction that one way to account for example (13.1) without fiddling with
PC-outputs is to restrict PC-inputs.

of subsentential units, crossing (and thereby challenging) the divide between multi-sentential and subsentential processing. It is a trivial matter to turn the analysis (13.24a) of two sentences into one for the single sentence (13.6b), S *because* S',

$$y : \begin{bmatrix} x : T \\ x' : T'\text{-explaining}(x) \end{bmatrix}$$

(or perhaps

$$y : \begin{bmatrix} x : T \\ y' : [x' : T'] \\ z' : Explanation(x, y') \end{bmatrix}$$

with a subordinating rhetorical relation *Explanation*). But it is far from obvious that t-contexts and the dependent type constructs Π and Σ (perhaps reformulated in terms of records) suffice for discourse, in its multi-sentential and subsentential splendour. Even so, it is worth noting how far they go in satisfying a minimal assumption about PC-inputs stated in Section 13.1.1.

(b1)   PC-inputs have enough structure to associate truth-conditions with them.

Beyond representing anaphoric connections by occurring in type expressions, the variables in a t-context serve as useful labels (written $\pi, a, \ldots$ in Asher and Lascarides (2003)) through which to express various abstract objects that figure in PC-outputs. We turn to some of these next.

13.4.2 Decomposing PC-outputs

What exactly does a variable x_i in a t-context (13.23) represent? Consider again (13.24a).

(13.24)   a. S. That is because S'.

$$x : T, \ x' : T'\text{-explaining}(x)$$

It is natural to assume that part (if not all) of what x and x' represent are semantic entities e_x and $e_{x'}$ such that the relation of explanation between x and x' can be cashed out as a causal relation between e_x and $e_{x'}$. The semantic entities e_x and $e_{x'}$ are called situations *characterized by* S and *by* S' (respectively) in Schubert (2000). To account for causation, Schubert argues that not only must a sentence be true in a situation it characterizes, but that the sentence must be about the situation as a whole, with no part of the situation extraneous to the sentence. (For instance, a situation characterized by the sentence 'Pat walked to the train station' should not include any subsequent train rides that Pat took.) As a consequence, possible worlds are ruled out as characterized situations. That is, situations are used as finer grained alternatives to total (fully fleshed out) worlds (much in the spirit of, for example, situation semantics, Barwise and Perry (1983)).

The tight fit between a situation and a sentence that characterizes it is similar to that assumed between an event and a predicate on the event in event semantics (e.g. Davidson, 1967a; Parsons, 1990). Indeed, the situations e_x and $e_{x'}$ are called the *main eventualities of x and x'* (respectively) in SDRT, with 'eventualities' understood to cover events, states, and the like. The semantic significance of a rhetorical relation typically comes down to some relation between the corresponding main eventualities. If the semantic content of z such that

$z : Explanation(x, y)$

is that the main eventuality e_y of y causes the main eventuality e_x of x, then for

$z : Elaboration(x, y)$

it is that e_y is part of e_x (Asher and Lascarides, 2003: 160). The notions of causation and part-of are not straightforward, and have potentially far-reaching ramifications for compositionality in discourse, especially if discourse structure is to stretch from the multi-sentential to the subsentential.

In Reichenbach's (1947) influential analysis of tense and aspect, the event time E is compared not only to the speech time S, but also to a reference time R, which is used, for instance, to distinguish the simple past from the present perfect (e.g. Steedman, 2000).

(13.26)   a. Pat left Dublin but is back.
          b. Pat has left Dublin ?but is back.

PC-outputs for discourse might similarly encode not only the main eventuality (described by Asher and Lascarides, (2003) as 'the semantic index of a clause' in head-driven phrase structure grammar (HPSG)) but also discourse analogues of S and of R pertaining to utterance and information structure, respectively. Information structure has to do with *how* content (or denotation, as in Table 13.2, Section 13.3.2 above) is packaged, negotiated, or managed through focus, topic, questions, and the like. It turns out that a sentence's truth-conditional content may depend on focus, which in turn is tailored to the question it is understood to answer (Rooth, 1985).

(13.27)   a. Mary only introduced $[Bill]_F$ to Sue.
             (a reply to: Who did Mary introduce to Sue?)
          b. Mary only introduced Bill to $[Sue]_F$.
             (a reply to: Who did Mary introduce Bill to?)

Focus is indicated in (13.27) by the subscript F, which marks an argument to a predicate that when replaced (i.e. abstracted out) by a variable, suitably restricted, induces the question answered (or 'background'), under a *structured meaning* account (e.g. Krifka, 2001b). The λ-abstraction involved here can be carried out in the type-theoretic framework of t-contexts, although the proper treatment of focus remains controversial (e.g. Beaver and Clark, 2003), as does that of questions (e.g. Ginzburg and Sag, 2000).

If information structure is analogous to Reichenbach's reference time R (just as the main eventuality is analogous to Reichenbach's event time E), what about speech time S? Ginzburg and Cooper argue that the semantics of dialogue requires utterances given by an

Utterances as events hypothesis: Utterances are spatio-temporally located events involving the sequential enunciation of one or more words. (Ginzburg and Cooper, 2004: 298)

For data, they point to *clarification ellipsis* (CE), as in (13.28), which appears as (4) in Ginzburg and Cooper (2004).

(13.28) a. A: Did Bo finagle a raise?
                B: (i) Bo?/(ii) Finagle?
            b. **Clausal reading**: Are you asking if BO (of all people) finagled a raise/Bo FINAGLED a raise (of all actions).
            c. **Constituent reading**: Who is Bo?/ What does it mean to finagle?

To analyse CEs, Ginzburg and Cooper propose a

Hybrid content hypothesis: the content which is updated in dynamic semantics consists of structure expressing detailed relationships between the content and the formal properties (syntax, phonology, etc.) of the various parts of an utterance. (Ginzburg and Cooper, 2004: 298)

The hybrid content hypothesis, HCH, is a far cry from the assumption (a2) that confines meaning to truth conditions (or indeed from the modest steps away from (a2) taken in DRT). Meanings under HCH are far richer, but then so are the expressions that have these meanings. Ginzburg and Cooper (2004: 306) require utterance representations that are 'fractally heterogeneous' in that 'the requisite representation format needs to contain heterogeneous (viz. phonological, syntactic, semantic, and contextual) information and, moreover, this applies uniformly as the parts get smaller and smaller'.

Notice that in a CE, a previous utterance forms part of the reality that language is about. This is surprising only to the extent that we are accustomed to a clean separation between language and the world, despite the existence of words (such as 'aforementioned' and 'latter') and phrases (such as 'that said' or 'replacing the second syllable of the last mentioned word by the third syllable of the first') that treat language as part of the world language describes or queries. Lest we dismiss such metalinguistic constructions as marginal, Ginzburg and Cooper (2004: 299) point out that CEs 'are commonplace in human conversation'. That said, there is more to the world that language is about than language. And even when language enters into that world (and knowledge of language becomes part of world knowledge, which is used say, to interpret definite descriptions or rhetorical connections between sentences), it may well prove helpful to distinguish language as a means of communication from language as what communication is about. In any case, the temptation to push some form of Montogovianism as far as it will go continues to be irresistible for many formal semanticists. And the proper integration of world knowledge and linguistic knowledge remains a vexed question.[10]

---

[10] My thanks to my referees for their helpful criticisms and advice.

PART IV

....

LEXICAL
DECOMPOSITION

....

CHAPTER 14

··

LEXICAL DECOMPOSITION
IN GRAMMAR

··

DIETER WUNDERLICH

14.1 OVERVIEW AND GENERAL ISSUES
··

Under a naive view, simple (underived) lexical items (or 'roots') such as *house, man, die* constitute the atoms of meaning which combine syntactically, forming structured utterances. Such a view could be supported by the role of simple words in human categorization. In the hierarchy of conceptual categories there is a privileged level of abstraction, called the basic level (Rosch et al., 1976*b*). It is the level at which the subjects are fastest at identifying category members, at which conceptual priming most easily obtains, at which information is most easily remembered over time, and at which a single mental image can reflect the entire category. Basic-level categories tend to be the first ones acquired by young children, and also tend to be expressed by the simplest words. 'In general, the basic level of abstraction in a taxonomy is the level at which categories carry the most information, possess the highest cue validity, and are, thus, the most differentiated from one another.' (Rosch et al. 1976*b*: 383f.). For example, in (14.1), *house* is at the basic level, while the composite noun *courthouse* is more specific, and the derived noun *building* is more general.

(14.1)   *building*
                   house
      courthouse   dwelling house

Under a more sophisticated view, however, even simple lexical items could be seen as internally complex, consisting of more atomic pieces of meaning. Given the number of fairly simple nouns referring to specific types of houses (such as *barracks, cabin, castle, hostel, hut, lodge, palace, villa*), one could either infer that the basic level is in fact lower than *house*, or that these nouns have HOUSE as one of their components.

(In the following, italics refer to words, while small capitals refer to concepts or parts of meaning.)

Componential analysis (Nida, 1951) aims at analysing the conditions under which semantically related words are differentially used, for example in determining the components by which *barracks, cabin*, etc. are more specific than *house*. Turning to another, often-discussed example, the word *bachelor* obviously relates to an unmarried man. The respective components, listed in (14.2a), are, of course, more general than the prime concept, so that they can be held to be entailed (14.2b). A decomposition is not necessarily a definition in the sense that it is exhaustive.

(14.2)   a. *Bachelor*: ADULT, HUMAN, MALE, UNMARRIED.
   b. If x is a bachelor, then x is an unmarried adult human male. (Katz, 1972: xviii, xxi)

If there is a set of intuitively related words that can be contrasted in pairs, componential analysis yields a semantic paradigm such as (14.3) for a very simple set of words, here ordered along the two independent dimensions of species and gender.

(14.3)   Names of domestic animals

	MALE	FEMALE
HORSE	*stallion*	*mare*
CHICKEN	*rooster*	*hen*

Some of the more atomic concepts could be universal because they are triggered by the biological nature of human beings, while others are culturally determined, such as UNMARRIED. This feature also plays a role for *widow*, denoting a female person who was married to a man who died, so a certain history of that person becomes relevant, see (14.4).[1]

(14.4)   WIDOW(x, t_0) : $\lambda x \lambda t_0 [\text{FEMALE}(x) \& \exists y \exists t_1 [\text{MARRIED}(x, y)(t_1) \& \text{DEAD}(y)(t_0)]]$, with $t_1 < t_0$.

Various approaches have been developed to deal especially with verbs, which, as the basis of grammatical clauses, are more structured than nouns. Generative Semantics (Lakoff, 1970; McCawley, 1968, 1971; Morgan, 1969; Ross, 1972) explored the idea that the inherent structure of verbs conforms to the syntactic structure of sentences, and therefore should be studied by means of complex paraphrases. For example, McCawley (1971) proposed that *persuade* (14.5a) should be decomposed into a structure built from predicates such as DO, CAUSE, BECOME, and INTEND, conforming to the paraphrase in (14.5b). By a series of prelexical transformations (corresponding to head movement in more recent terminology) the bundle of predicates in (14.5c) is obtained, and it is checked whether there is a single word corresponding to it. The corresponding semantic representation is shown in (14.5d).

[1] One might add a clause expressing that x is not married at t_0; however, if x remarries, x still remains the *widow of y*. In any case, the example demonstrates that the semantic components of a word can be highly structured.

(14.5)   a. Sally persuaded Ted to bomb the Treasury Building.
         b. What Sally did was cause Ted to get the intention to bomb the Treasury
            Building.
         c. [$_V$ DO [$_V$ CAUSE [$_V$ BECOME [$_V$ INTEND]]]]
         d. *persuade*: $\lambda P\, \lambda y\, \lambda x\, \exists\phi\, [\text{DO}(x, \phi)\ \&\ \text{CAUSE}\, (\phi, \text{BECOME}\, (\text{INTEND}(y, P)))]$

One argument in favour of decomposition was that an adverbial can have scope over
some internal structure (Morgan, 1969). The sentence (14.6a) can have several readings,
among them (14.6b) with external scope, and (14.6c) with the innermost scope of *almost*,
which are clearly distinct. Therefore, some internal part of the verb's meaning must be
visible for the adverb.

(14.6)   a. Sally *almost* persuaded Ted to go dancing.
         b. What Sally *almost* did was persuade Ted to go dancing.
         c. What Sally did was cause Ted to *almost* get the intention to go dancing.

Von Stechow (1995, 1996) and Rapp and von Stechow (1999) took up this argument. In
order to analyse internal scope of 'again' and 'almost', they opted for syntactic decomposition in a more recent framework. Problems of this account have been noted by Jäger
and Blutner (2000), and Wunderlich (2001). Hale and Keyser (1993, 1997) advocate a
minimalist syntactic decomposition, the atoms of which, however, remain more or less
undefined semantically.

   A different way of reflecting syntactic realization was proposed by Katz (1972), who
used complex syntactic indices for the argument variables occurring in a semantic
decomposition. In his representations, however, some of the components are merely
listed, as, for example, the three subcomponents PHYSICAL, MOVEMENT, and PUR-
POSE, characterizing *x*'s activity of chasing more narrowly in (14.7a), slightly simplified from Katz (1972: 106). Apart from the high-ranked predicates that could be taken
from a general type hierarchy, Katz's analysis of *chase* thus amounts to what is given
in (14.7b).

(14.7)   a. *chase*: [ACTIVITY [PHYSICAL, MOVEMENT [SPEED:FAST [FOLLOWING y^{obj}]]],
            PURPOSE [TO CATCH y^{obj}]]] $x^{\text{subj}}_{\text{animal}}$
         b. *chase*: $\lambda y\, \lambda x\, [\text{FAST}(\text{FOLLOW}(x, y))\ \&\ \text{TRY}(x,\ \lambda u\, \text{CATCH}(u, y))]$

Within the logical literature, decomposition is usually performed by means of meaning
postulates. An early example is found in Montague (1960, 1974: 167), who analysed the
verb *seek* into TRY and FIND by the meaning postulate in (14.8).

(14.8)   NEC $\forall x \forall y\, [\text{SEEK}(x, y) \Leftrightarrow \text{TRY}(x,\ \lambda u\, \text{FIND}(u, y))]$

Dowty (1979) clarified and further elaborated the insights of Generative Semantics
within Montague Grammar, an influential semantic framework at those times. In particular, he characterized the Vendler (1967) classes of verbs by means of generally available
predicates, such as DO for activities, BECOME for achievements, and CAUSE BECOME for
accomplishments (Dowty 1979: 124).

Jackendoff's (1990) Conceptual Semantics proposes a number of basic conceptual categories such as EVENT, STATE, ACTION, PLACE, PATH, PROPERTY, and AMOUNT, as well as formation rules that combine these categories. Lexical items are interpreted by a conceptual structure built with these rules. The decomposition can be rather fine-grained, as the example for *drink* in (14.9) shows, meaning 'cause a liquid to go into one's mouth' (Jackendoff, 1990: 53).

(14.9)   *drink*: [$_{event}$ CAUSE ([$_{thing}$]$_i$, [$_{event}$ GO ([$_{thing}$ LIQUID]$_j$,

[$_{path}$ TO ([$_{place}$ IN ([$_{thing}$ MOUTH OF ([$_{thing}$]$_i$)])])])])]

Jackendoff also includes an action tier, which describes the affectedness relation between individuals, and thus reconstructs the semantic notions of agent and patient. Example (14.10b) shows a slightly simplified representation of the sentence (14.10a) (Jackendoff, 1990: 143; INCH for 'inchoative', AFF for 'affect').

(14.10)   a. The car hit the tree.

b. *hit*:   [INCH [BE (CAR, AT [TREE])]]

AFF (CAR, TREE)

The lexical semantic structures proposed in Pinker (1989), as well as in the work of many other authors, are influenced by Jackendoff's view of conceptual structure.

Generative Lexicon Theory (Pustejovsky, 1991, 1995) aims to account for the multiplicity of readings of polysemic words (such as *apple*: a tree or fruit, *opera*: a building, an ensemble or a piece of music, etc.). It rejects the idea of an exhaustive decomposition of lexical items, and instead proposes partial functions that map the meaning of a word onto several representation levels such as argument structure, event structure, and qualia structure.

Lexical Decomposition Grammar (LDG; Gamerschlag, 2005; Kaufmann and Wunderlich, 1998; Stiebels, 1996; Wunderlich, 1997*a,b*, 2000) distinguishes between semantic form (SF) and conceptual structure, following proposals by Bierwisch (1983, 1997) and Bierwisch and Lang (1989). The SF of a lexical item is intended to capture only those aspects of its meaning that are grammatically relevant, in particular argument structure, and omits information that can be inferred from more general resources, so SF is a partial semantic structure. In contrast, conceptual structure is enriched by contextual information of various kind, and can be made more fine-grained in any direction that matters. Jackendoff's representations in (14.9) and (14.10b) are certainly not part of SF. The last three approaches, Jackendoff's, Pustejovsky's, and LDG, are compared in Wunderlich (1996*a*).

Lexical Conceptual Structure (LCS), proposed by Guerssel et al. (1985) and further elaborated in the work of Levin and Rappaport Hovav (1991, 1995, 1999) is similar to SF in that it serves to capture only those facets of meaning that determine the grammatical behaviour of (classes of) verbs, including argument alternations. An LCS representation consists of a general 'event type' structure, characteristic for a class of verbs and formed by a few primitive predicates, in which the respective root, representing the idiosyncratic meaning of the word, instantiates the variable position; see (14.11), in which *BROKEN* substitutes for the variable *STATE* (Levin and Rappaport Hovav, 1995: 94).

(14.11)   a. Causative verb: [[x DO-SOMETHING] CAUSE [y BECOME *STATE*]]
           b. *break*:   [[x DO-SOMETHING] CAUSE [y BECOME *BROKEN*]]

Different from all these approaches is the Natural Semantic Metalanguage (NSM) account (Wierzbicka, 1972, 1996; Goddard and Wierzbicka, 2002), which analyses concepts/words by reductive paraphrases using a small collection of semantic primes (*plants*: {living things, these things can't feel something, these things can't do something}; *sky*: {something very big, people can see it, . . . }). The inventory of these primes, believed to be present in all human languages, includes, among others, mental predicates such as THINK, KNOW, WANT, FEEL, SEE, HEAR, eventive predicates such as DO, HAPPEN, MOVE, PUT, GO, LIVE, DIE, SAY, existence THERE_IS, possession HAVE, temporal relations such as NOW, AFTER, BEFORE, spatial relations such as ABOVE, BELOW, FAR, NEAR, INSIDE, and also the 'logical' concept BECAUSE. Most of the decompositions proposed by other accounts could in principle also be described in NSM; a major difference, however, is that NSM aims to give a set of explicative paraphrases, while other approaches are looking for more formal representations that allow inferences to be made regarding parts of the meaning.

In Davidson (1967), as well as in the various versions of a neo-Davidsonian account (Krifka, 1989, and others), the verbal predicate itself is used as an undecomposed name of an event, while all information concerning number and type of arguments is delegated to extra predicates. Hence, transitive *watch* is represented by (14.12) rather than as WATCH(x, y).

(14.12)   *watch*: $\lambda e\, \lambda x\, \lambda y$ [WATCH(e) & AGENT(e, x) & THEME(e, y)]

A different take is to assume that every verb has an eventive argument, so that one gets RAIN(e) for a weather verb, DANCE(e, x) for an intransitive verb, and WATCH(e, x, y) for a transitive verb. This eventive argument is usually bound by the mood or tense operator applying on verbs. The individual subpredicates of a decomposition structure can often be related to subevents; for instance, three of the four predicates in (14.5d), namely DO, BECOME, and INTEND, relate to different subevents. We will return to this view in the next section, in which the status of CAUSE is clarified.

As might have become clear, the model of lexical decomposition to be chosen essentially depends on the goal one is pursuing. Semantic properties of the verb determine to a large degree the syntactic realization of arguments and the ability to take part in valency alternations. They also determine selectional restrictions for arguments, the co-occurrence with particular types of adverbials, and the possible scope behaviour of adverbs. Moreover, they determine how the verb contrasts with items of the same semantic field. A particular decomposition of the verb can usually satisfy only some of the goals, even if one concedes that the type of the respective components is independently given. It is, however, always possible to add information in the same way as in (14.12); for instance, if one wants to state that the entailment (14.13a) follows from the fact that a catch-event always contains a grasp-event as a proper part, one can use the neo-Davidsonian framework, as in (14.13b).

(14.13)   a. 'Stefan caught the ball' entails 'Stefan grasped the ball'.
           b. catch: $\lambda e\, \lambda x\, \lambda y\, [\text{CATCH}(e)\ \&\ \text{AG}(e,x)\ \&\ \text{TH}(e,y)\ \&\ \exists e_1\, [e_1 \subset e\ \&\ \text{GRASP}(e_1)$
              $\&\ \ldots]]$

However, this is not decomposition in the strict sense. One would still need a further meaning postulate for inferring 'Stefan had the ball'.

   Fodor and Lepore (1998, 1999, objecting to Pustejovsky's and Hale and Keyser's work, respectively) are sceptical about all approaches to lexical decomposition which aim at supporting inferences about the semantic structuring of the lexicon. They assume that lexical meaning only specifies denotations and not senses, and therefore must be atomic. What they might accept is lexical decomposition in the syntax. To Hale and Keyser's (1993) claim that the denominal verb *to cow* (as used in *It cowed a calf*, meaning 'A cow had a calf') is impossible because the derivation of this verb violates syntactic rules, Fodor and Lepore (1999) object that *to cow* could be a primitive lexical item, not violating those rules. Mateu (2005), however, accepting both Hale and Keyser's syntactic view and Fodor and Lepore's point of criticism, argues that *to cow* cannot be a primitive item because it has a relational meaning. It is important for this argument that lexical items are decomposed only for their argument structure; while the noun *cow* is primitive, the respective verb is not (see also Section 14.6).

14.2 CAUSATIVE VERBS

Lexical items such as *dead, die,* and *kill* have in common that they are related to the concept DEAD, although they are increasingly complex. *Dead* is a simple stative predicate, while both *die* and *kill* are transition predicates entailing the result of being dead. Their argument structure differs: *die* has only one argument (the patient or undergoer), while *kill* has an additional actor argument. Similar triples can be easily found; words such as *open* and *empty* allow for all three functions, as shown in (14.14).[2]

(14.14)   a. The bear is dead.   The door is open.   The pool is empty.
           b. The bear died.   The door opened.   The pool emptied.
           c. Mary killed the bear.   Mary opened the door.   Mary emptied the pool.

In view of these similarities and differences, the following representational ingredients are reasonable:

---

[2] It is a contingent property of English that *kill–die–dead* are maximally distinct. Mateu (2005) claims that *kill* should be decomposed into $[x\ [\text{CAUSE}\ [y\ [\text{TCR}\ (=\ \text{BECOME})\text{KILL}]]]]$. Such an option is particular for English; in Basque, both 'die' and 'kill' are expressed by the same verb (*hil* in the perfect), so that KILL would be identical with DIE (which is absurd). Moreover, KILL is not a predicate referring to a state, and the alternative KILLED is a derived predicate. Therefore, DEAD is the best corresponding 'root' predicate for *kill*.

(14.15)   Semantic Form (SF)

a.	statives:	*dead*:	λy	λt		DEAD(y)	(t)
b.	inchoatives:	*die*:	λy	λe	BECOME	DEAD(y)	(e)
c.	causatives:	*kill*:	$\lambda y \lambda x \lambda e$ [ACT(x) &		BECOME	DEAD(y)]	(e)

BECOME is the transition operator. Roughly, BECOME(p) is true at a time interval t at whose initial bound $\neg p$ holds and at whose final bound p holds (Dowty, 1979: 140). A representation such as (14.16) (simplified from Katz, 1972: 358) is unnecessarily complex.

(14.16)   *open* (intrans.): (at t_1 : x is positioned to prevent passage between inside and outside)

(at t_2 : x is positioned to allow passage between inside and outside), with $t_1 < t_2$.

ACT(x) is an activity predicate. Roughly, ACT(x) is true in e if there is some subevent of e which is instigated and controlled by x. ACT is similar to DO (Ross, 1972; Dowty, 1979: 118), but relates to an event rather than to what is done. Pietroski (1998) distinguishes between grounding and culminating events. In this sense, ACT(x) in (14.15c) is a grounding subevent, while BECOME P(y) is a culminating (and temporally terminating) subevent. Conceptually, these two subevents are integrated by the assumption that they stand in a causal relation, with the grounding subevent as the causal factor, and the culminating one as the effect.

In (14.15), however, the causal relationship between ACT(x) and BECOME(p) is not expressed. How does this reading come about? Note first that '&' is considered to be asymmetric ([ACT(x) [& BECOME(p)]]), thus, '&' is possibly stronger than logical 'and' and can be incremented by additional information. Second, there should be a principle under which '&' can achieve a CAUSE-reading contextually.

Such a principle in fact is needed for independent reasons. It is generally felt that a verb can denote only a coherent event, with respect to both the timescale and the participants involved (Kaufmann, 1995b; Pustejovsky, 1995: 186). Concerning the timescale, the idea is that the components of a single event must be 'available' for each other, either because they are situated in the same time-slot or because one component triggers the other.[3] This is formulated in (14.17) (Kaufmann and Wunderlich 1998).

(14.17)   COHERENCE: A lexical SF conjunction is either contemporaneously or causally interpreted.

Interestingly, the debate of what is possibly expressed in a verb–verb compound or in a serial verb construction, and what is not, centres around a concept of event coherence similar to (14.17). Differently from what one observes for verbs simpliciter, the coherence of a verb–verb construction also includes cases in which the second conjunct is not really caused by the first one (as in 'buy and eat a fish'), but is the natural and commonly expected consequential action of it (Gamerschlag, 2005: 82, 206). Thus, most important is not causation itself but whether something 'belongs together'.

---

[3] In the latter case, the parts of the event don't need to be temporally adjacent, e.g., cause and effect of a poisoning event can be separated temporally.

How does COHERENCE determine the causative reading of (14.15c)? ACT denotes an activity extended in time, and BECOME denotes a transition; these different types of events clearly cannot be contemporaneous, so their relationship must be causal. It is therefore ruled out that 'Mary killed the bear' is true if Mary did some arbitrary action (such as blowing her nose) and the bear died. Mary's action must have been a causal factor: if she had not done it, the bear wouldn't have died. (Of course, there could be other events, even simultaneous ones, that bring the bear to death.)

The two options offered by COHERENCE can effectively be studied in the case of secondary predication. Consider the sentence in (14.18), where the adjective *hot* is added to a transitive verb expressing an activity. In principle, *hot* could be predicated of either one of the arguments, x or y, and the time span at which $\text{HOT}(a)$ holds can overlap the beginning or the end of the activity. In the latter case, the change predicate BECOME has to be added. Which of these interpretational alternatives is chosen highly depends on context and world knowledge. Reading (14.18a) is true in traditional ironworks, (14.18c) is favoured if one thinks of producing heat or sparks by hammering on metal, and (14.18b) is possible in a context of high emotion. Only (14.18d) seems to be out; usually a reflexive is used to trigger such a reading (*Max hammered himself hot*).

(14.18)   Max hammered the metal hot.
    a. 'Max hammered the metal, when it was hot.' $\text{HAMMER}(x, y)$ & $\text{HOT}(y)$
    b. ?'Max hammered the metal, when he was hot.' $\text{HAMMER}(x, y)$ & $\text{HOT}(x)$
    c. 'Max hammered the metal, and it became hot.' $\text{HAMMER}(x, y)$ & BEC $\text{HOT}(y)$
    d. *'Max hammered the metal, and he became hot.' $\text{HAMMER}(x, y)$ & BEC $\text{HOT}(x)$

In verb–verb compounds (14.19a), as well as in serial verb constructions (14.19b,c) across the world, one often finds an (intransitive or transitive) activity verb combined with an inchoative verb, which yields a causal relationship. There is no linker visible, and none of the verbs includes CAUSE in its meaning. One can conclude that CAUSE is inferred from COHERENCE, which independently checks whether such a verb–verb combination is possible.

(14.19)   a. Verb–verb compound in Japanese (Gamerschlag 2005: 44)
        Watasi wa   haikingu de   tyotto   aruki-tukare-ta.
        I   TOP   hike   AT   a.little walk-become.tired-past
        'I became tired from walking at the hike.' $\text{WALK}(x)$ & $\text{BECOME TIRED}(x)$
    b. Serial verb construction in Edo (Stewart 2001: 15)
        Òzó dé wú.
        Ozo fall die
        'Ozo fell, and (so he) died.' $\text{FALL}(x)$ & $\text{DIE}(x)$
    c. Serial verb construction in Vietnamese (Kuhn 1990: 279)
        Giáp   ðung cái   to: be:.
        Giap   push CLASSIF bowl   break
        'Giap pushed the bowl, and (so it) broke.' $\text{PUSH}(x, y)$ & $\text{BREAK}(y)$

There is a continuing debate about whether lexical decomposition is a legitimate means of semantic analysis; Fodor (1970) was the first who denied this. One of his arguments was that the decompositional paraphrase can be true, while the sentence with the non-decomposed verb is false. Consider the case in which Mary gave the bear some poisoned food on Monday, so that the bear died the next day. In this case, (14.20b) is true, while either variant of (14.20a) is false.

(14.20)   a. Mary killed the bear {$^{(on\ Monday),\ (on\ Tuesday)}$}.
           b. What Mary did $^{(on\ Monday)}$ caused the bear to die $^{(on\ Tuesday)}$.

Syntactic paraphrasing allows for each of the involved subevents to be specified separately, which results in *two* events rather than *one* event. COHERENCE, however, requires that *kill* expresses only *one* event (to be specified by a temporal expression only once). The difference between *kill* (14.20a) and *cause to* die (14.20b) is often described as one between direct and indirect causation. This effect is explained by COHERENCE; the most direct influence is possible in a single coherent event, while in an event chain (i.e. causal chain) many other factors can intervene.

To another counterargument of Fodor (1970), saying that semantic decomposition of words might be costly for the processing of words, Jackendoff (1990: 38) replied that lexical complexity is learned just as any other sensomotoric complexity and so does not increase the processual expense. I would like to suggest that the one-event-restriction by COHERENCE, going hand in hand with the one-word restriction, facilitates the processing of complex words vis-à-vis their corresponding paraphrases.

In contrast to the representations given in (14.15c) and (14.18c), most researchers assume that CAUSE must occur in the decomposition of a causative verb (see also (14.11) above). Bierwisch (2002) argues that CAUSE belongs to the repertoire of SF because words such as *cause* and *because* have to be described by CAUSE anyway; although that is true, there is still no necessity for specifying verbs such as *kill* by CAUSE. These verbs are probably much older than the complementizer, so they can have worked without an explicit notion of cause.

Nevertheless, let us ask how the representations would look like if CAUSE were added. Lewis (1973) and Dowty (1979: 99–110) consider causation primarily as a relation between events. Roughly, CAUSE(e_1, e_2) is true if and only if both e_1 and e_2 occur, and if e_1 had not occurred then e_2 would not have occurred. Since this counterfactual analysis needs propositions rather than events, Lewis uses the occurrence predicate O(e), alternatively 'sentences' as complex names of events. Relying on Lewis' work and considering a number of intricate problems not to be discussed here, Dowty determines the truth conditions for CAUSE(p, q) in three steps: (i) whether q depends causally on p (by means of the counterfactual); (ii) whether p is a causal factor for q (by means of a series p, $p_1, \ldots p_n$, q, in which each member depends causally on the previous one); (iii) whether p is the most adequate causal factor for q (by means of similarities between possible worlds).

In any case, CAUSE is incremental on AND, with something like the counterfactual CF being added under certain conditions (14.21a). However, the verb *cause* can use an individual term as subject; the same is found in many decompositions of the literature;

in this case, one can define the related notion DO-CAUSE instead (14.21b) (Bierwisch 1997: 241), see also (14.11).

(14.21)   a. CAUSE$(p,q) \Leftrightarrow p \& q \& CF(\neg p, \neg q)$
          b. DO-CAUSE$(x,q) = df\ \exists\varphi$ CAUSE$(\varphi(x),q)$

In order to see how CAUSE fits into a more complex structure, let us consider the resultative sentence (14.22a), in which the subject's action is specified by the verb *water* (whereas it was unspecified in *kill* above). Representations such as (14.22b) (simplified from Jackendoff 1990: 232) and (14.22c) (Pustejovsky 1991: 65) are unnecessarily complex because BY is just a variant of CAUSE. So (14.22d) might be more appropriate. In (14.22e), the type of relation between WATER and BECOME FLAT is left unspecified, so it can and must be specified conceptually due to COHERENCE.

(14.22)   a. Max watered the tulips flat.
          b. *to water flat*: CAUSE$(x,$ INCH $[$BE$(y,$ AT $[$FLAT$])])$
               AFF(x,y)
               BY CAUSE$(x,$ INCH $[$BE$($WATER, ON$[y])])$
               AFF(x,y)
          c. *to water flat*: $\lambda y\, \lambda x\, \lambda e$ [CAUSE(ACT(x,y), BECOME FLAT(y)) BY WATER(x,y)]
             (e)
          d. *to water flat*: $\lambda y\, \lambda x\, \lambda e$ [CAUSE(WATER(x,y), BECOME FLAT(y))] (e)
          e. *to water flat*: $\lambda y\, \lambda x\, \lambda e$ [WATER(x,y) & BECOME FLAT(y)] (e)

Note that Jackendoff's (14.22b) includes an analysis of the verb *water* by means of the nominal concept WATER, meaning that Max pours water on the tulips (but see Section 14.7). Now, if WATER(x,y) itself is decomposed by means of CAUSE, (14.22c) turns into (14.23a), and (14.22d) into (14.23b).

(14.23)   a. ... [CAUSE (CAUSE (ACT(x), BECOME (WATER ON y)), BECOME FLAT(y))] (e)
          b. ... [[ACT(x) & BECOME (WATER ON y)] & BECOME FLAT(y)] (e)

The latter rightly shows the chain of events that matter in this case, while (14.23a) is inappropriate for obvious reasons: since CAUSE(p,q) itself doesn't relate to an event, it cannot be an argument of CAUSE. Therefore, (14.22d) must be rejected as well. Example (14.23a) could be improved by introducing subevents that are causally connected, as in (14.24).

(14.24)   ... $\exists e_1\, \exists e_2\, \exists e_3$ [[CAUSE(e_1, e_2) & ACT$(x)(e_1)$ & BECOME(WATER ON y) (e_2)]
          & CAUSE(e_2, e_3) & BECOME FLAT$(y)(e_3)$]

There could, however, be alternative readings, namely that x's action is the causal factor for e_3, too, or that the state brought about by x's action (that there is too much water on the tulips) is the causal factor for e_3. (Dowty (1979: 103) admits the possibility of 'stative' causatives). Given the multiplicity of readings of the actual causal chain, it is questionable whether CAUSE belongs to the lexical knowledge of the items or constructions considered here. It seems more reasonable to assume that the lexical items contribute something that is unspecified for CAUSE, such as (14.23b). For deriving a more fully specified conceptual structure, one needs at least the following preparations: (i) Each predicate is part of a type hierarchy, and so gets assigned a proper event type; (ii) The subevents are arranged according to their temporal order, and COHERENCE checks whether there are subevents that are causally connected. For example, the two occurrences of BECOME in (14.23b) can be ordered simultaneously: then ACT(x) is the common causal factor; or they are ordered sequentially: then either these two transitions are causally connected, or the first result state causes the second transition.

Note that our account is also able to deal with duality. Dual items such as *become/remain* and *make/let* differ from each other by a combination of outer and inner negation. The inventory of primitives can therefore be reduced, as shown in (14.25).

(14.25)   a. The door remained open: ¬∃e BECOME ¬OPEN(*the door*)(*e*)
          b. Anna let the door open: ¬∃e [ACT(*Anna*) & BECOME ¬OPEN(*the door*)](*e*)

By coherence one gets the more articulated reading 'Anna did nothing which caused the door to get closed'.

14.3 LEXICAL ALTERNATIONS

The lexical decomposition account has advantages in dealing with various lexically-triggered alternations. Cross-linguistically, it can explain why languages that widely differ in their vocabulary nevertheless have the capacity to express similar states of affairs, namely because they share the same semantic templates. Intra-linguistically, it can explain why certain verbs behave similarly in that they systematically vary in the types of constructions they allow for. For instance, intransitive verbs are often paired with a causative variant, which can, but does not need to, be marked explicitly. The unmarked causative alternation, illustrated in (14.26), can be accounted for by the assumption that an additional CAUSE (or a corresponding ACT) either is present or is not present in the meaning of the verb. The causative alternation is much more frequent with inchoative (non-agentive) verbs (14.26a) than with agentive verbs (14.26b). The latter is a marked option because there is already an agent present, while a theme is missing.

(14.26)   Causative alternation
          a. The stick broke.
             John broke the stick.

          b. The horse galloped.
             John galloped the horse.

Several other types of alternations can be dealt with by the assumption that the lexical meaning is enriched in the more articulated variants; an additional lexical predicate either introduces a further argument to be expressed (as in the causative alternation) or leads to a different argument realization. Consider briefly the strong resultative alternation in (14.27b) vs. (14.27a) (Levin and Rappaport Hovav, 1995: 37; Washio, 1997; Kaufmann and Wunderlich, 1998), in which a result predicate together with a new argument is added, which is not selected by the verb. The result can be passivized (*the wine cellar was drunk empty*); in German it is also possible to further add a dative beneficiary (14.27c), which comes about by an additional POSS. (When I was affected by the guests drinking the wine cellar empty, I was in a sense the possessor of the wine (cellar).) The German example can also undergo *kriegen*-passive (14.27d).

(14.27) Strong resultative alternation
   a. The guests drank all of the wine. $\mathrm{DRINK}(x, y)$
   b. The guests drank the wine cellar empty.   ... & BECOME $P(z)$;
                                                                           $P = \mathrm{EMPTY}$
   c. Die Gäste tranken *mir* den Weinkeller leer.   ... ... & POSS(u, z)
   d. Ich kriegte den Weinkeller leer getrunken.
      lit. 'I got drunk the wine cellar empty.'
   e. $\lambda P\ \lambda z\ \lambda u\ (\lambda y)\ \lambda x[[\mathrm{DRINK}(x, y)\ \&\ \mathrm{BECOME}\ P(z)]\ \&\ \mathrm{POSS}(u, z)];\ P = \mathrm{EMPTY}$

The combination of resultative and benefactive yields something like (14.27e) as a quite enriched meaning of 'drink'. On the basis of this formula, the argument roles z, u, x are predicted to be realized by accusative, dative, and nominative, in this order, while u (the stuff drunk) cannot be realized,[4] according to the principles of LDG (Wunderlich, 1997a,b). In particular, y is blocked from the structural case because it doesn't satisfy the condition for structural arguments in (14.28) (Wunderlich, 1997a: 41; Wunderlich 2006b: 31).

(14.28) STRUCTURAL ARGUMENT.
   An argument is structural only if it is either the lowest argument or (each of its occurrences) lexically commands the lowest argument.

Intuitively, this condition minimizes the number of structural arguments, and simultaneously guarantees that each predicate of the complex formula is made visible in the argument structure realized. Other decompositional approaches would have to invoke semantic (or syntactic) reasons to explain why the object of the simple verb *drink* is blocked in the resultative, which, however, are hard to identify. Carrier and Randall (1992) observed that the verb must allow an unspecified object, which clearly is only a precondition and not the triggering factor.

   Another type of alternation is the *wipe* alternation shown in (14.29) (see also Levin, 1993: 53, 125). In (14.29a), *wipe* combines with a locative PP that adds a certain piece of

---

[4] In the default reading one can, however, infer that the guests drank whatever occupied the wine cellar (probably wine), although more marked readings are possible, as usual.

meaning syntactically, that is *wipe* is subcategorized for some general locative predicate P (e.g. *wipe the crumbs away*). When the locative information, more specifically, is incorporated into the verb (14.29b), one is again confronted with the situation that the new argument role (z) must be realized, while the previous argument role (y) is blocked from realization, according to (14.28). Finally, (14.29c) derives from (14.29b) by adding a result predicate.

(14.29)   Wipe alternation
     a. Marga wiped the crumbs from the table.   WIPE(x, y) & P(y)
     b. Marga wiped the table.   ...   & BECOME ¬LOC(y, AT z)
     c. Marga wiped the table clean.   ... ... & BECOME CLEAN(z)

Similar to the case just discussed is what is called locative alternation, shown in (14.30) (see Levin, 1993: 49, 117). In (14.30a), the directional locative information is realized by a syntactic PP, while it is incorporated into the verb in (14.30b). Again, the previous object role cannot get structural case, it can, however, be realized obliquely (which is not excluded by (14.28)).

(14.30)   Locative alternation
     a. The peasant loaded the hay on the wagon.   LOAD(x, y) & P(y)
     b. The peasant loaded the wagon with hay.   ... & BECOME LOC(y, AT z)

An even stronger piece of evidence for lexical decomposition comes from examples in which the role of a recipient alternates with that of a goal, leading to different argument realizations. The recipient role, realized as the primary object in a double object construction (14.31a), is described by BECOME POSS, while the goal role, realized as a prepositional object (14.31b), is described by BECOME LOC (Krifka, 2004; Wunderlich, 2006*a*).

(14.31)   'Dative' alternation
     a. Oscar sent the publisher his manuscript.   (double object, DO)
     b. Oscar sent his manuscript to the publisher.   (prepositional object, PO)

In order to see the relevance of this distinction, one first has to look at POSS and LOC in more detail.

14.4 POSS AND LOC

Nearly every language provides means to express the two most general stative relations, namely location (LOC) and possession (POSS). LOC can, for instance, be instantiated by local prepositions, see (14.32). *The book is on the table* means that the book can be found within a certain neighbourhood region of the table, let's call it the ON*-region. Each preposition defines its own type of neighbourhood region; if the language at hand only has one general local preposition, the region can be abbreviated as AT*. The Japanese construction in (14.33) shows the decomposition into a relational marker (LOC) and a region-forming operator such as ON* most clearly, because ON* is here explicitly expressed by a region noun.

(14.32)   a. The book is on the table / under the table / in the library.
          b. LOC(*the book*, ON*[*the table*]/UNDER*[*the table*]/IN*[*the library*])

(14.33)   Locative construction in Japanese ((TOP = topic, GEN = genitive)
          a. Hon   wa   teeburu   no   ue/shita   ni   aru.
             book   TOP   table   GEN   on-/under-region   LOC   be
             lit. 'The book is located in the on-region/under-region of the table.'

          b. Hon   wa   tosho-kan   no   naka   ni aru.
                           library   GEN   in-region
             lit. 'The book is located in the in-region of the library.'

The possession relation (POSS) holds between two individuals if the first one, often animate, disposes of or has control over the second one. Thus, POSS includes ownership, the part–whole relationship, as well as other, more contingent relations. POSS is quite generally expressed by means of possessor affixes or possessive pronouns, and sometimes also by rather specific syntactic constructions.

Interestingly, POSS and LOC-AT often alternate with each other. Several languages express possession, besides using possessive pronouns, by means of a locative construction, among them Russian.

(14.34)   Possessive construction in Russian
          a. U   menja   kniga.
             at   me.GEN   book
                  'I have a/the book.'
          b. U   nego   bylo   mnogo   druzej.
             at   him.GEN   was   many   friends.GEN
                  'He had many friends.'

This suggests that LOC and POSS could be converse to each other. In German or English, one can indeed find a free alternation in the expression of the part–whole relationship.

(14.35)   POSS ≈ LOC alternation in German and English
          Das Haus hat drei Bäder.   ≈   Drei Bäder sind im Haus.
          The house has three bathrooms.   ≈   There are three bathrooms in
                                                     the house.

That POSS(x,y) and LOC-AT(y,x) are at least weakly equivalent can intuitively be justified. If x controls y, or has some ownership on y, then y must be located near to x for being able to exert control. Conversely, if y is located near to x then x is enabled to achieve control over y. The choice of construction is determined by various factors such as topic and focus (which are preferentially matched with subject vs. object), definiteness, and animacy. There are certainly circumstances under which POSS(x, y) and LOC-AT(y, x) are equivalent.

14.5 TWO TYPES OF DITRANSITIVE VERBS, AND THE DO–PO ALTERNATION

Ditransitive verbs typically express an action that leads to a change of state, either change of possession (POSS) or change of location (LOC). Change of possession verbs (such as *give, lend, buy*) have a recipient argument, usually realized by dative in a case language like German. English has the double object (DO) construction in (14.36); note that *buy* can also be used transitively, so the BECOME POSS extension is optional.

(14.36)   a. Anna gave Max a book.
           b. Anna bought Max a book.
           c. *give*: $\lambda z\, \lambda y\, \lambda x\, \lambda e\, [\text{ACT}(x)\; \&\; \text{BECOME POSS}(y,z)](e)$
              buy: $\lambda z\, \lambda y\, \lambda x\, \lambda e\, [\text{BUY}(x,z)\; \&\; \text{BECOME POSS}(y,z)](e)$

Change of location verbs (such as *throw, put, dip, splash, glue*) usually require a prepositional phrase (PP) to realize the goal argument. In a sentence such as (14.37a), the goal is an argument of the preposition (*behind*), while the directional PP is an argument of the verb *throw*, so the goal is only 'indirectly' linked to the verb. Example (14.37b) shows the composition of the phrase.

(14.37)   a. He threw the book behind the tree.

      b. *throw*: $\lambda P\, \lambda y\, \lambda x\, \lambda e\, [\text{THROW}(x,y)\&P(y)](e)$
         behind the tree: $\lambda u\; \text{BECOME LOC}(u,\; \text{BEHIND}^*[\textit{the tree}]),$
                             BECOME is optional
        throw behind the tree: $\lambda y\, \lambda x\, \lambda e[\text{THROW}(x,y)\; \&\; \text{BEC LOC}(y,\; \text{BEH}^*[\textit{the tree}])](e)$

If LOC is incorporated, the goal becomes a direct argument of the verb, as in *enter* (BECOME LOC $(x, \text{AT } y)$). However, in alternating verbs of English like *give* (*Anna gave Max the book*; *Anna gave the book to Max*), the preposition is fixed to *to*, which functions as an oblique marker for goals. The DO–PO alternation ('dative' alternation) is found rather frequently, only few ditransitive verbs do really resist. The DO construction often is possible only with a pronominal receiver, for example in verbs of imparting a force (*push, pull, carry, lift, lower*) and in verbs of communication (*whisper, yell, mumble, mutter*), see (14.38), (14.39). Conversely, there are verbs that allow the PO construction only with a pronominal theme, see (14.40). (All examples are from Bresnan and Nikitina, 2007.)

(14.38)   Verbs of imparting a force
          a. *Susan pushed John the box.
          b. Susan pushed the box to John.
          c. Susan pushed **him** the chips.

(14.39)   Verbs of communication
          a. *Susan whispered Rachel the news.

      b. Susan whispered the news to Rachel.

      c. Susan whispered **me** the answer.

(14.40) Verbs of 'prevention of possession'

      a. The car cost Beth $5,000.

      b. *The car cost $5,000 to Beth.

      c. It would cost **nothing** to the government.

Similar observations have been made with respect to definiteness, topic-hood, length of expression, etc. The more definite, topical, or shorter the expression is for the recipient, the better it fits with the DO construction. This follows from the recipient's position in the decomposition structure. If one assumes that the DO construction conforms to the change of possession template and the PO construction to the change of location template (Pinker, 1989; Krifka, 2004; Wunderlich, 2006a), then recipient/goal and theme exchange their positions in the hierarchy of arguments; consider y and z in (14.41). This semantic difference does not need to concern the truth conditions because POSS and LOC-AT *can* be equivalent when they exchange their arguments.

(14.41) a. DO: $\lambda z\, \lambda y\, \lambda x\, \lambda e\, [\text{ACT}(x)\ \&\ \text{BECOME POSS}(y, z)](e)$ $x > y > z$

      b. PO: $\lambda y\, \lambda z\, \lambda x\, \lambda e\, [\text{ACT}(x)\ \&\ \text{BECOME LOC}(z,\ \text{AT } y)](e)$ $x > z > y$

Barss and Lasnik (1986) proposed several tests for argument hierarchy. Binding is one of them: A quantifier in the higher argument can bind the possessor of a lower argument, but not conversely. Usually this test is applied to the relation between subject and object, however, it also works in the relation between the higher and lower object of a ditransitive verb (Larson, 1988). Example (14.42) shows that the recipient binds the possessor of the theme in the DO construction. Conversely, the theme binds the possessor of the recipient/goal in the PO construction, shown in (14.43).

(14.42) a. They gave every woman$_i$ her$_i$ baby.

      b. *They gave its$_i$ mother every baby$_i$.

(14.43) a. They gave every baby$_i$ to its$_i$ mother.

      b. *They gave her$_i$ baby to every woman$_i$.

Another test is markedness, which came under consideration only when differential object marking was discussed (Aissen, 2003). In a number of dimensions, the higher argument preferably realizes the more prominent semantic value, so it is more frequently animate, definite, a 1st or 2nd person, a pronoun, or the topic than the lower argument. This holds for the relation between subject and object, but also for the relation between higher and lower object. According to markedness, a linguistic construction might only be tolerated if it realizes the higher argument pronominally rather than nominally; exactly this was observed in (14.38) to (14.40) above. Therefore, if the semantic values are given, one has to make a choice between two constructions. The choice predicted in (14.44) has been proved to be overwhelmingly true in Standard English (Collins, 1995).

(14.44) DO–PO competition:[5]

    a. If the Recipient is less marked than the Theme, the DO construction is chosen (alternatively, PO is blocked).

    b. If the Recipient is more marked than the Theme, the PO construction is chosen (alternatively, DO is blocked).

In the Kwa languages of West Africa, the DO construction alternates with a serial verb construction (14.45).

(14.45) DO–SV alternation in Fongbe (Kwa)

    a. Ùn   xlɛ   Kofí   fòtóò.

       1sg   show   Kofi   picture

       'I showed Kofi a picture.'

    b. Ùn   só   fòtóò   xlɛ   Kofí.

       1sg   take   picture show   Kofi

       I showed the picture to Kofi.'

Lefebvre and Brousseau (2002: 455, 463) show that these constructions behave similarly to the English ones with respect to binding, so that one can conclude that the serial verb construction (14.45b) is an instance of change of location. Sedlak (1975) contributed data from Akan, a related language, in which the DO construction is preferred with a nominal or indefinite theme, while the serial verb construction requires the theme to be pronominal or definite.

    A neo-Davidsonian account doesn't say anything about the hierarchy of arguments, so it must be stated separately. An advantage of a strictly guided decomposition account is that it entails argument hierarchy.

14.6 REGULARITIES IN THE FORMATION OF DENOMINAL VERBS

One of the strongest arguments for lexical decomposition comes from denominal verbs. Sortal nouns such as (a) *box*, *cage*, *shelter*, referring to an individual thing, or (b) *butter*, *fuel*, *salt*, referring to a substance, canonically can have only one argument (BOX(x), ...), while when these words are used as verbs, they not only instead refer to an event or action, but can also have more arguments than one. Consider the verbs *box* and *butter* in (14.46); what types of actions are they referring to?

(14.46) a. Jane boxed the bagels.   (location verb)

       b. Jane buttered the bagels.   (locatum verb)

---

[5] If one of the constructions can be blocked with a certain distribution of semantic values one expects it to be a property that is sensitive to particular subclasses of ditransitive verbs, which indeed is the case (Rappaport Hovav and Levin, 2008).

Obviously, these verbs must contain the concepts BOX or BUTTER as one of their components. All other components must be inferred, in virtue of the context in which the verb is used, and in considering what the noun is usually used for ('if an action is named after a thing, it involves a canonical use of the thing', as Kiparsky (1997) noted). Boxes are containers—something can be put into them, thus, (14.46a) seems to express that the bagels are put into a box. The box becomes a location for the bagels, therefore, *box* is called a location verb here. In contrast, a substance such as butter can be located somewhere, or something can be provided with it; therefore, *butter* in (14.46b) is called a locatum verb.

The best view on the formation of denominal verbs is that the respective noun is incorporated into an abstract verbal template. Following a general requirement of functional application, the noun then has to realize the lowest (most deeply embedded) argument role available (Kiparsky, 1997, Stiebels, 1998). Transitive denominal verbs like those in (14.46) therefore correspond to a ditransitive template. The verb *box*, as it is used in (14.46a), can be represented by (14.47a) because z is the lowest argument role in this formula. The verb *butter* in (14.46b), however, cannot be represented by the same template (because then it would have to realize a non-lowest argument role), rather a predicate in which the argument roles are reversed has to be chosen, as in (14.47b).

(14.47) a. *box*: $\lambda z\, \lambda y\, \lambda x\, \lambda e\ [\text{ACT}(x)\ \&\ \text{BECOME LOC}(y, \text{AT } z)](e)$, with $z \approx$ BOX
  b. *butter*: $\lambda z\, \lambda y\, \lambda x\, \lambda e\ [\text{ACT}(x)\ \&\ \text{BECOME POSS}(y, z)](e)$, with $z \approx$ BUTTER

In general, if one wants to know what a denominal verb means, one needs a complex event (or action) predicate in which the referent of the noun functions as the lowest (or verb-nearest) participant. Therefore, a particular denominal verb can have more than one reading, while, simultaneously, the set of possible readings must be severely restricted. Examples (14.48a,b) show *shelve* as a verb with either the location or the locatum reading. It is not possible to get a mixture of these readings, nor can a context overwrite the particular decomposition.

(14.48) a. Paul shelved his books.   (Paul put his books onto shelves.)
  b. Paul shelved his study.   (Paul equipped his study with shelves.)

The number of possible denominal verb types is indeed very restricted. A noun can be predicative or referential, thus, a noun can saturate either a predicative or an individual role of a template. Denominal verbs with predicative nouns can have copula (14.49), inchoative (14.50), or causative readings (14.51).

(14.49) Paul gardenered the whole day.   (He behaved temporarily as a gardener.)
  $\lambda x\, \lambda t\ \textbf{\textit{GARDENER}}(x)(t)$

(14.50) The woodwork splintered.   (The woodwork turned into splints.)
  $\lambda x\, \lambda e\ \text{BECOME } \textbf{\textit{SPLINTER}}(x)(e)$

(14.51) Paul bundled the sticks.   (He made the sticks to form a bundle.)
  $\lambda y\, \lambda x\, \lambda e\ [\text{ACT}(x)\ \&\ \text{BECOME } \textbf{\textit{BUNDLE}}(y)](e)$

The incorporated noun can also saturate an individual argument, which then is existentially bound. The above-mentioned location and locatum verbs, as well as instrumental verbs, belong to this major type. Within each class a certain variation is possible: a location verb can have the IN- or ON- reading (14.52), a locatum verb can have the reading of adding or removing (14.53), an instrumental verb can be intransitive or transitive (14.54), etc.

(14.52)   a. Anne cellared the wine.
$$\lambda y\, \lambda x\, \lambda e\, \exists z\, [\text{ACT}(x)\ \&\ \text{BECOME LOC}(y,\ \text{IN}^*z)\ \&\ \textit{CELLAR}(z)](e)$$

      b. Anne shouldered the bundle.
$$\lambda y\, \lambda x\, \lambda e\, \exists z\, [\text{ACT}(x)\ \&\ \text{BECOME LOC}(y,\ \text{ON}^*z)\ \&\ \textit{SHOULDER}(z)](e)$$

(14.53)   a. Anne saddled the horse.
$$\lambda y\, \lambda x\, \lambda e\, \exists z\, [\text{ACT}(x)\ \&\ \text{BECOME POSS}(y,z)\ \&\ \textit{SADDLE}(z)](e)$$

      b. Anne scaled the fish.
$$\lambda y\, \lambda x\, \lambda e\, \exists z\, [\text{ACT}(x)\ \&\ \text{BECOME}\ \neg\text{POSS}(y,z)\ \&\ \textit{SCALE}(z)](e)$$

(14.54)   a. Anne biked.
$$\lambda x\, \lambda e\, \exists z\, [\text{MOVE}(x)\ \&\ \text{INSTRUMENT}(z)\ \&\ \textit{BIKE}(z)](e)$$

      b. Anne mopped the floor.
$$\lambda y\, \lambda x\, \lambda e\, \exists z\, [\text{MANIPULATE}(x,y)\ \&\ \text{INSTRUMENT}(z)\ \&\ \textit{MOP}(z)](e)$$

A decompositional account makes clear predictions about possible and impossible readings. For example, *saddle the horse* cannot mean 'put a saddle on the horse' (even if a saddle usually is put on the back of a horse) because then a non-lowest argument role would be saturated—in fact, a horse wouldn't be said to be saddled, if the saddle were just placed anyhow or anywhere on the horse. (Even more obvious is the case with *bridle*, a structurally and functionally similar verb; one doesn't just put a bridle on the horse.) Similarly, *church the money* cannot mean 'provide the church with money', but it can mean 'put the money into a church' (see also Hale and Keyser, 1993). It is hard to see how a neo-Davidsonian account (with a flat argument structure) could achieve those insights.

14.7 MANNER AND RESULT

Talmy (1985: 70, 63) observed that in the Romance languages it is preferable for the direction of motion to be specified in a simple verb of motion (e.g. Spanish *entar* 'move in', *salir* 'move out', *pasar* 'move by', *subir* 'move up', *bajar* 'move down', *cruzar* 'move across'), while in the Germanic languages it is the manner of motion (*swim, run, roll, slide, float, blow, kick*). None of the languages does both in a simple verb. This does not exclude that English also has simple verbs of motion specifying the direction or goal rather than the manner of motion (*cross, enter, arrive, come*).

Considering the general template (14.55a), it seems that a verbal root can only specify either ACT or the result state (including direction), as expressed in (14.55b).

(14.55)   a. $[\text{ACT}(x) \ \& \ \text{BECOME} < \text{result state} >](e)$

      b. Lexicalization constraint: 'A given root can modify ACT or be an argument of BECOME, but cannot do both within a single event structure.' (Levin and Rappaport Hovav, 2007)

Both manner verbs and instrumental verbs specify ACT, leaving open what type of result (or direction) can occur; for example *roll* is a verb that entails movement, but does not specify where. By contrast, verbs that specify the type of result state leave open what type of action has to be done (*open, empty, box, saddle*). Verbs such as *poison, strangle, stab* specify various ways of bringing someone to death, however, they do not entail that the person dies, whereas *kill*, which entails death, does not specify by which action. A potential counterexample could be *whisper*, which clearly specifies ACT but is also used in specific result constructions (see (14.39) above); the possibility of DO–PO alternation in fact neutralizes any specificity of the result. Note that derivational elements such as prefixes (German *ver-giften, er-würgen, er-dolchen*), as well as syntactic complements (*roll into the box; wipe the table clean*), are able to specify the respective complementary aspect of an event.

Levin and Rappaport Hovav (2007) argued that the complementarity of manner and result is a constraint of possible verb meanings that limits the complexity of verb meanings. Kaufmann (1995*a*: 221) suggested that in a decomposition structure such as [A & B & C . . .], any subsequent element can only specify the preceding one. Thus, BECOME(p) can specify the result of ACT, but it cannot specify a manner expressed in *roll, float, swim* more narrowly, while if ACT is left unspecified and BECOME(p) is added, then p can be specified more narrowly.

The exact nature and scope of those constraints have still to be studied. Whatever they may look like, if something of such a restriction exists, it strongly supports the lexical decomposition account.

14.8 SUMMARY

Concerning verbs, most linguists plead for lexical decomposition, serving to predict grammatical behaviour, especially argument structure. A decomposition can be a flat ('neo-Davidsonian') or a more hierarchical structure; the latter is more restrictive and therefore preferred if it can be done consistently. Verb classes share the same type of decompositional structure ('template'), which often (but not necessarily) includes an idiosyncratic *root* signalling the simplest use of the predicate in question; rather general verbs such as 'kill' and 'give' (in contrast to 'crucify' or 'donate') might be decomposed without such an idiosyncratic rest. Many *roots* can potentially occur in several, increasingly complex templates. Lexical decomposition thus allows for relating argument alternations to a single core meaning, placed into various contexts. It does not define a word meaning exhaustively (so there could be another level of meaning, conceptually more articulated). The components of a template can be viewed as semantic primitives, available to all languages, or, in approaches of syntactic decomposition, as 'light' verbs, which have a special status in that they contribute more structure than meaning. Denominal verbs (such as *to shelve*, *to bridle*) most clearly show the function of those templates, and therefore can be taken as a probe into the inventory of templates: to find the reading of a denominal verb, one necessarily has to look for a template. Despite many debates about details, various lines of research converge in the view that linguistic meaning is structured and hence not purely denotational. Proponents of an atomistic view of meaning (notably Fodor and Lepore) have to live against this insight as a minority.

CHAPTER 15

....

LEXICAL DECOMPOSITION IN MODERN SYNTACTIC THEORY

....

HEIDI HARLEY

In the past fifteen years, lexical decomposition has become an accepted fact among syntacticians and semanticists working in the Chomskyan framework, particularly among those studying verbal argument structure, and particularly with respect to change-of-state verbs. Many of the analyses of verbal syntax and semantics that are now accepted without much comment are essentially modernized versions of the long-discredited proposals of the Generative Semanticists.[1] For example, change-of-state verbs that exhibit the inchoative/causative alternation—*The screen cleared; John cleared the screen*—are now routinely treated as containing the equivalent of a formative BECOME in the intransitive version (roughly, [BECOME [THE SCREEN [CLEAR]]]) and an equivalent to CAUSE in their transitive version (roughly, [JOHN [CAUSE [THE SCREEN [CLEAR]]]]). English ditransitive verbs that occur in the double-object frame—*give John a book, pass Mary the salt*—are treated as syntactically complex, containing formatives CAUSE and HAVE in an embedding structure ([CAUSE [JOHN [HAVE [A BOOK]]]]). In some ways, then, the rather rapid transformation of the syntactic landscape has rolled back the clock. Progress is not retrograde, however: many of the most cogent empirical objections to the decompositional project have been answered, and there are at least some inklings of the explanations for others. The net result is that modern theories can capture many of the morphological, syntactic, and semantic generalizations that motivated the original proposals in the first place, which were difficult to capture in the Lexicalist frameworks that dominated the field from the

[1] For some comments from a related viewpoint on why the modern approach is distinct in important ways from the Generative Semantics approach, see Hale and Keyser (1992).

1970s to the 1990s. The proposals also have serious scientific legs, in that they have made predictions and captured cross-linguistic generalizations that would have been impossible to contemplate without them. In this chapter, I will first take some time to systematically address the status of some of the original empirical objections to the decompositional project, given a particular set of assumptions about how decomposition works in a modern framework. I will then quickly survey some decompositional proposals with an eye to conveying the breadth and depth that the approach has developed. I will focus primarily on English data, since that has been at the centre of the debate for philosophers of language, but I will touch on some of the key points from unrelated languages which have particular relevance to the claims, from a linguist's point of view.

In the end, however, I feel that the central philosophical issues remain largely untouched by this revolution. Although it has become clear that the notion of an atomic 'word' is misguided, where 'word' is understood to refer to linguistic entities of category N, V, A, or P, the problem is just one of granularity. The modern linguistically-motivated syntactic decomposition proposals just take the argument one level down: the problem of understanding the conceptual semantics of syntactically unanalysable linguistic entities ('Roots') remains, and, in my opinion, the argumentation developed by Fodor against the conceptual decomposition of these true atoms remains unassailable.

15.1 THE BASIC PICTURE

In this approach, the external argument of an agentive verb does not compose with the verb itself. Rather, it composes with an independent predicate (notated as v°) which relates the external argument to the verbal event. This independent predicate contributes the notion that the external argument is the Agent or Cause of the event. The verb composes directly only with its internal arguments. So, for example, the syntactic structure of the sentence *John will open the door* would be roughly represented as follows (to be refined below):

(15.1)

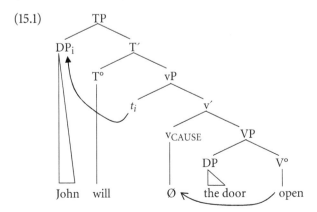

Here, the subject DP *John* has been base-generated in the specifier of v_{CAUSE}, as an argument of the v_{CAUSE} head; it has moved to the specifier of TP to check its nominative case, leaving a trace or copy in Spec-vP. The VP *the door open* is the complement of v_{CAUSE}; the V° head moves up and incorporates into v°, to the left of *the door*. Since the portion of the phrase structure tree that is of interest to us here is the structure beginning at vP and below, I will leave out the functional projections above vP in diagrams below (unless relevant), and will not indicate subject movement; I assume throughout, however, that these projections are present and doing their usual syntactic and semantic jobs.

The CAUSE formative is not realized in this English case by a visible morpheme or independent verb; it is here represented by the usual symbol for a null morpheme, Ø. This null morpheme contributes the semantic content associated with v° in the same way that a null plural morpheme contributes the semantic content of PLURAL in a sentence like *The sheep are sick*. In many, probably in most, languages, the CAUSE formative with lexical causatives such as this and/or its companion the BECOME formative in the intransitive counterpart are clearly associated with overt morphemic content (for examples, see Section 15.4 below).[2]

In the semi-neo-Davidsonian semantics for such structures proposed in Kratzer (1993, 1996), both predicates denote a relationship between an individual and an eventuality, and a compositional operation of Event Identification applies to ensure that the two event variables are coindexed and bound by the same operator. At the vP boundary, an existential quantifier is introduced which binds the open event argument.

(15.2) $\lambda e[\text{CAUSE}(\text{John}, e) \ \& \ \text{OPEN}(\text{the door}, e)]$

The Tense node contains an ordering predicate which encodes the temporal relationship between speech time and the timecourse of the event denoted by the vP, now modified by two predicates, along the lines proposed by Zagona (1995), among others.

The proposal captures the usual properties that motivated the adoption of its ancestors in the Generative Semantics literature. The fact that *John opened the door* entails *The door opened* falls out for the same reasons that *Mary made John sick* entails *John got sick*: the same predicative subconstituent is present in both sentences, composing with the upstairs causative predicate and thus contributing its meaning compositionally to the meaning of the whole. The existence of repetitive and restitutive scopes for adverbials like *again* (15.3a), and the existence of high-scope and low-scope readings for temporal adverbials like *for five minutes* (15.3b) is due to the fact that both vP and VP are legitimate adjunction sites for these adverbials. The high-scope reading in (15.3b) requires a certain amount of imagination to access, but it is certainly available:

(15.3)   a. John opened the door again.

> **Restitutive:** The door had been open before, and John reopened it.
>
> **Repetitive:** John had opened the door before, and he did it again.

---

[2] Even in English, v_{CAUSE} and its relative v_{BECOME} are sometimes realized by overt morphology; in *clar-ify*, *caramel-ize* and *em-bitter*, for example, the morphemes *-ify*, *-ize*, and *em-* are plausibly realizations of the causative v° head.

b. John opened the door for five minutes.

Low-scope: The door spent a five-minute period being open.

High-scope: John spent a five-minute period in the act of opening the door.

These two readings correspond to the string-identical but structurally distinct syntactic representations below, where (15.4a) represents the structure which compositionally provides the lower scope reading and (15.4b) the higher scope reading:[3]

(15.4) a.

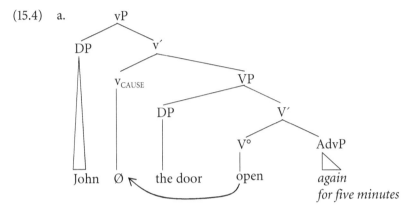

Reading: λe[CAUSE(John, e) & OPEN-AGAIN(the door, e)]
$\qquad\quad$ λe[CAUSE(John, e) & OPEN-FOR-FIVE-MINUTES (the door, e)]

b.

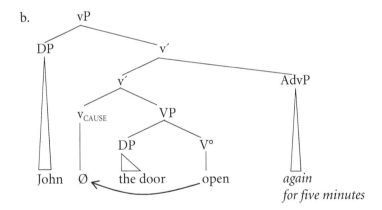

---

[3] Assuming cyclic, bottom-up semantic composition, in the low-scope structure, the composition of the lower predicate *open* and *again* or *for five minutes* will happen before Event Identification identifies the event variable the lower VP with that of the upper vP. I assume that predicates like *again* have a higher type and compose with the unsaturated *OPEN* predicate via Function Application. I indicate the notion that Event Identification applies after the VP has already composed with its modifiers and arguments by using the hyphenation notation, *OPEN-AGAIN* (the door, e), for the predicate-of-events denoted by the VP. Event identification is triggered when the interpretation function reaches and integrates the vCAUSE predicate; subsequent composition via function-application with other modifiers (as in the high-scope interpretation) will then necessarily modify the entire predicate created by Event Identification. Consequently, subsequent modification via adjunction to vP cannot target the CAUSE predicate alone; see also footnote 6.

Reading: λe[CAUSE(John, e) & OPEN(the door, e) & AGAIN(e)]
λe[CAUSE(John, e) & OPEN(the door, e) & FOR-FIVE-MIN-UTES(e)]

On this analysis, these ambiguities result from exactly the same structural options that produce the same ambiguities in the sentences *Mary made John sick again* and *Mary made John sick for five minutes* (note, again, that the high-scope reading requires some contextual coercion to be felicitous but that it is certainly available). Producing tree diagrams that reflect the two interpretations available for *Mary made John sick again* is an exercise for a Linguistics 101 class; no one contemplates anything other than a structural source for that ambiguity. The vP analysis of *John opened the door again* makes these two ambiguities essentially identical. Von Stechow (1995) argues that the typeshifting operations required to interpret *again* with two scopes in a model-theoretic semantics in which change-of-state verbs are *not* syntactically decomposed would complicate the interpretive system to an unacceptable degree; a system in which these distinct readings can be directly derived from their syntactic composition, then, is much to be desired from a purely theory-internal viewpoint.[4]

15.2 THE RIGHT WAY TO ANALYSE *KILL* AS *CAUSE TO DIE*

What of the counter-arguments against such an approach, perhaps most famously articulated in Fodor (1970)? Let us consider the empirical arguments he presents against decomposition of change-of-state verbs into a CAUSE predicate and an inchoative verbal predicate.[5]

First, the temporal locations of the causing eventuality and the door-open eventuality must be identical in *John opened the door*, but need not be identical in *John caused the door to open*, as illustrated by the fact that *on Saturday* and *on Sunday* may both occur in the latter but not the former:

(15.5)   a. *John caused the automatic door to open on Sunday by programming it on Saturday*
          b. *#John opened the automatic door on Sunday by programming it on Saturday.*

If the embedded and matrix events can be modified by independent temporal predicates (*on Sunday* for the embedded event and *on Saturday* for the matrix event) in the clausal paraphrase in (15.5a), then why cannot each subevent be so modified in (15.5b)? The

---

[4] Jäger and Blutner (2000) have proposed alternatives to von Stechow's argument from an anti-decompositional viewpoint; von Stechow has replied to the reply in von Stechow (2003).

[5] The perspective on these data offered here is a more developed version of that offered in Harley (1995: 87–8); similar replies to Fodor's remarks have been outlined elsewhere within other decompositional proposals; see, e.g. Pietroski (2003), Travis (2000), among others.

very natural answer lies in the fact that (15.5a) involves an embedding of an entire TP (itself containing its own vP and VP) under the matrix *cause* verb, which has its own independent T° head, while the causative structure in (15.5b) involves the embedding of only a VP under the causative v°.

In the periphrastic causative in (15.5a), each of the matrix and embedded events are related to separate Tense heads and each has its own independent existential closure operator, associated with the two separate vPs contained within the two separate clauses. The embedded (infinitival) Tense head (realized as *to* in *to open on Sunday*) expresses a relationship between the event denoted by the vP *open on Sunday* and some other event—one plausible analysis suggests that the infinitival T inherits a [+past] semantic value via sequence-of-tense from the matrix Tense head, thus locating the embedded event at some time prior to the speech time. The matrix event is located by its own [+past] Tense head to some time prior to speech time. At no point do the two events undergo Event Identification, and consequently there is no semantic contradiction involved in asserting that the embedded event occupies a distinct temporal location from the matrix event, as long their respective temporal locations respect the semantics of causation, such that that effect follows cause.

In contrast, in (15.5b), the CAUSE event and the event denoted by the VP *have* been coindexed by Event Identification, *are* bound by the same existential operator. The single event which they both modify is ordered relative to speech time by a single Tense operator. Consequently the two eventualities may not occupy separate temporal locations without contradiction. Asserting that a single event is temporally located both ON SUNDAY and ON SATURDAY poses the same problem that spatial modifiers which locate a single NP in two separate places pose, whatever that problem is—the ill-formedness of (15.5b) is analogous to the ill-formedness of the DP #*the big dog in the house on the lawn*, on the reading in which *on the lawn* and *in the house* are both understood to be predicated of the single dog (not the reading where *on the lawn* modifies *house*, rather than *dog*): a single spatially bounded entity cannot simultaneously occupy two locations. Similarly, a single temporally bounded event cannot occupy two temporal locations.[6]

---

[6] To present the argument in more detail: Suppose that ON-SUNDAY adjoins to VP and composes with OPEN via function application, as AGAIN did in (15.4a). The denotation of the VP will then be (i):

(i) $\lambda e[\text{OPEN-ON-SUNDAY}(door, e)]$

Upon the addition of the v$_{\text{CAUSE}}$ head, $\lambda x \lambda e[\text{CAUSE}(x, e)]$, Event Identification will apply to unify the functions denoted by the VP and the v° head by coindexing their event variables, to give the denotation of the v′ in (ii)

(ii) $\lambda x \lambda e[\text{CAUSE}(x, e)\ \&\ \text{OPEN-ON-SUNDAY}(door, e)]$

Imagine, then, that this predicate of entities and events is then modified by ON SATURDAY, adjoined to v′. The result is that the single event is asserted to be both an OPEN-ON-SUNDAY event and an ON-SATURDAY event, resulting in contradiction.

Note that it is impossible for the vP-adjoined ON-SATURDAY to compose solely with the v$_{\text{CAUSE}}$ head, since composition is cyclic and bottom-up; the v$_{\text{CAUSE}}$ head will be integrated into the interpretation via Event Identification before the ON-SATURDAY predicate can apply. That is, the structure

(iii)   [[v$_{\text{CAUSE}}$ [the door [open on Sunday]]] on Saturday]

The second argument adduced by Fodor against the decompositional analysis of causative verbs requires a bit more exposition, and a slight revision to the analysis outlined above. It relies on the observation that sentential subjects may control the null subjects of certain adjoined gerunds, but objects may not. In particular, *by*-phrases containing a gerund are controlled by the agent argument, if there is one—even if that agent argument is syntactically absent, as in the passive (15.6b)

(15.6)   a. John$_i$ tested the milk by PRO$_i$ sniffing.
      b. The milk$_j$ was tested by PRO$_{i/*j}$ sniffing.
          ($_i$ coindexed with the unspecified Agent argument of *test*)

In (15.6a), the subject of *tested* controls the null subject of *sniffing*. In the passive (15.6b), the controller of *sniffing*'s subject is still the understood agent argument of the main verb, not the derived subject *milk*.

When there is no agent argument at all, however, as in the case of unaccusative predicates (including inchoatives), then the derived subject argument can indeed control a PRO in a *by*-phrase:

(15.7)   a. Bill$_i$ died by PRO$_i$ swallowing his tongue.
      b. The milk$_i$ spoiled by PRO$_i$ sitting in the sun.

Now, compare the control possibilities in the unaccusative, the periphrasitic causative and the lexical causative below:

(15.8)   a. The milk$_i$ spoiled by PRO$_i$ sitting in the sun.   (= 15.7b)
      b. John$_i$ caused the milk$_j$ to spoil by PRO$_{i/j}$ sitting in the sun.
      c. John$_i$ spoiled the milk$_j$ by PRO$_{i/*j}$ sitting in the sun.

The important datum here is (15.8c), which demonstrates that the object of a change-of-state verb behaves like any object—it cannot control PRO in an adjoined gerund. If that object were really the subject of an embedded verb *spoil*, under a null CAUSE predicate, it should be able to control PRO, just as it does in (15.8a) and just as it can in (15.8b). In (15.8b), there are two potential subject controllers, and both readings are available: implausible though it is, on one reading, the matrix subject *John* could be sitting in the sun, and thereby cause the milk to spoil; on the other reading, the infinitival version of (15.8a) is embedded under *cause*, and the embedded subject *the milk* controls the

---

cannot be interpreted so that ON-SATURDAY modifies just the CAUSE predicate alone, producing CAUSE-ON-SATURDAY, before Event Identification applies. In order for that to happen, i.e. in order to arrive at the non-contradictory LF

(iv) $\lambda x \lambda e$[CAUSE-ON-SATURDAY(x, e) & OPEN-ON-SUNDAY$(door, e)$],

ON-SATURDAY would have to compose with v$_{\text{CAUSE}}$ before v$_{\text{CAUSE}}$ composed with the VP. The structure for v$'$ would have to be as follows:

(v)   [[v$_{\text{CAUSE}}$[on Saturday]$_{\text{ADVP}}$]$_{v^\circ}$ [the door [open on Sunday]]$_{\text{VP}}$]$_{v'}$

Standard structural assumptions bar phrases from adjoining directly to heads, however, and so such a structure would be syntactically ill-formed and never reach LF.

PRO subject of *sitting*, just as it does in (15.8a).[7] The argument should be clear: if the derivation of (15.8c) involves embedding (15.8a) under a null CAUSE predicate, then why isn't the embedded subject of *spoil* able to control PRO, just as it is in (15.8b)?[8]

Fodor's examples with *kill* and *cause to die* illustrate the same phenomenon much more cleverly, involving a gerundive clause with very particular content:

(15.9)   a. Bill$_i$ died [by PRO$_i$ swallowing his tongue].
         b. John$_i$ caused Bill$_j$ to die [by PRO$_{\#i/j}$ swallowing his tongue]
         c. John$_i$ killed Bill$_j$ [by PRO$_{\#i/*j}$ swallowing his tongue]

Because tongues are inalienably possessed, and located in the mouth, the action *swallowing one's tongue* most naturally gets a reflexive reading, where the swallower and the tongue-owner are one and the same. In (15.9b), because there are two structural subjects, either John or Bill can, in principle, control PRO and be the agent of the swallowing action. If John is the controller of PRO, then the sentence is about John causing Bill to die by swallowing his own, John's, tongue, which is pretty difficult to imagine. If Bill is the controller, as he is in (15.9a), then the sentence is about John causing Bill to die from Bill swallowing Bill's tongue, which is much more sensible; (15.9b) therefore has a plausible reading as well as a very implausible one. In the sentence in (15.9c), however, because only structural subjects can be controllers, only John can be the agent of swallowing his tongue, which means that (15.9c) only has the difficult-to-imagine reading in which John swallows John's tongue and as a result Bill dies, and thus rates a * from Fodor.[9] The plausible reading, where Bill is the controller of PRO and swallows his own tongue, is unavailable.

Thus, in (15.9c), *Bill* cannot control PRO. But if *kill* decomposes in such a way that it contains the predicate *die*, with *Bill* as its subject, then there should be no reason why Bill couldn't control PRO in (15.9c). Hence, Fodor concludes, analyses that treat *kill* as *cause to die* (or *spoil* as *cause to spoil*) make the incorrect predictions.

Consider, however, an alternative proposal concerning the lower portion of the decomposed verb phrase. Suppose the lower VP denotes a state, rather than an inchoa-

---

[7] In the classic GB analysis, it receives accusative case via Exceptional Case Marking from the matrix predicate here, hence behaving as a matrix object; in Minimalist treatments it raises through Spec-TP to a case-assigning specifier position in the matrix clause; as far as the central argument here goes, however, the main point is that at some point it occupies Spec-TP and hence is a structural subject and possible controller.

[8] Appealing to Event Identification will not help us here; nothing would prevent modifying the event of the embedded VP with *by sitting in the sun* and subsequently employing Event Identification to coindex that complex event with the event of CAUSE(John, *e*)—indeed, this is precisely what happens with the low-scope interpretation of *again* or *for five minutes*.

[9] It is important to recognize, however, that the problem here is pragmatic, not syntactic. (15.9c) should receive a #, for semantic infelicity, rather than a *. Given the right peculiar context—perhaps Bill has been shrunk, *Fantastic Voyage*-style, and is clinging to John's tongue, and is then killed when John swallows his own tongue—it's possible to interpret (15.9c) as written (or try, *Moby Dick$_i$ killed Ahab by swallowing his$_i$ tongue*). Alternatively, one could adopt an alienable-possession reading of *his*, and imagine a context in which John is a ghoul. Ghoul John attacks Bill and swallows Bill's tongue, thereby killing him, hence *John killed Bill$_i$ by swallowing his$_i$ tongue*.

tive event. Causative verbs are crucially change-of-state verbs. Imagine, then, that the appropriate paraphrases simply embed a stative predication under the causative predicate, describing the resultant state that characterizes the event. A periphrastic example of such a caused-state structure would be *John made [Mary happy]*. On this approach, transitive *spoil* would decompose as *MAKE (something) SPOILT*; intransitive *spoil* would be *BECOME SPOILT*. Similarly, if *kill* decomposes, it would decompose as *MAKE (something) DEAD*, not *MAKE (something) DIE*.[10]

Interestingly, if we assume a cause+state decomposition, rather than cause+event, it turns out that the controlled gerund test makes the correct predictions in the periphrastic examples. Subjects of stative predicates can never be controllers of *by*-gerunds (or any adjoined gerunds, for that matter):

(15.10)   a. *Mary$_i$ was happy by PRO$_i$ singing.
          b. John$_i$ made [Mary$_j$ happy] by PRO$_{i/*j}$ singing.
          c. *John$_i$ was sick by PRO$_i$ eating too much.
          d. Mary$_i$ made [John$_j$ sick] by PRO$_{i/*j}$ eating too much.

In (15.10a), we see that the subject of the stative predicate *(be) happy* cannot control an adjoined *by*-gerund; in (15.10b), the matrix subject of the verb *make* can control the gerund but the embedded subject of the stative small clause *Mary* still cannot. In (15.10c), although eating too much is a likely cause of sickness, we find that the stative subject *John* cannot control the gerund *by eating too much*; in (15.10d) we see a causative embedding the stative small clause [John sick], and again, despite the fact that it is the least plausible reading, we find that the only available controller for the *by*-gerund is the matrix subject of the causative verb *make*, that is *Mary*, not the embedded subject of the stative small clause.

Consequently, if the decomposed causative verbs involve a null CAUSE or MAKE predicate with a state-denoting small clause complement, the decompositional analysis makes the correct predictions concerning potential controllers of *by*-gerunds: Subjects of embedded stative predicates cannot control *by*-gerunds; *by*-gerunds must modify an eventive predicate.

Let us re-visit our structure from (15.1) for *John opened the door*, and also propose a structure for *The door opened*, treating the result of the causation as a state, rather than an event:

---

[10] Technically, in order to maintain the notion that the lexical-semantic core of the root KILL is present in this representation, the result state should be actually a target-state semantic primitive such as KILLED; I use DEAD here instead for shorthand so as not to get into debates concerning the construction of participles and the semantics/morphology relationship in roots. See Mateu (2005) and Kayne (2008) for arguments that such target-state primitives are constructed from a null P and the root. Alternatively, see Harley (2005) for a Hale and Keyser-based approach to transitive verbs like *kill* or *push* which have a nominal event-denoting counterpart (*a kill, a push*) which takes the homophony between the verb and the noun seriously.

(15.11)

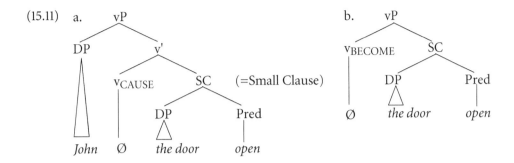

The verb root, now treated as a stative predicate, will incorporate into v°, and the incorporated complex of *open-Ø* is the transitive or inchoative verb *open*. Of course, the highest available DP moves to Spec-TP, resulting in the order *The door open(ed)* in (15.11b). The *by*-gerund adjoins to and modifies the vP, in each case; it may not modify the small clause. Consequently, in *John spoiled the milk by sitting in the sun*, the *by*-phrase may not attach to the small clause [MILK SPOILT] and have PRO controlled by MILK; rather, it may only attach to the vP, and be controlled by the c-commanding DP *John*.[11]

Finally, let us consider Fodor's third argument, and see if it applies to our revised analysis, with a stative predicate rather than an inchoative predicate embedded under the causative predicate. Sentences containing the paraphrase *cause to die* provide an antecedent that licenses an elided VP referring back to the embedded *die* event (15.12a), while sentences containing *kill* do not (15.12b):

(15.12)   a. John caused Mary to die, and it surprised me that she did so [=DIED].
          b. *John killed Mary, and it surprised me that she did so [=DIED].

Of course, if *kill Mary* here is really CAUSE MARY TO DIE, containing a concealed predicate DIE, then it is surprising that the concealed VP may not antecede a *do-so* elision. Here, appealing to Event Identification will not help; the LF, roughly equivalent to *There was an event, which was caused by John, and which was an event of Mary dying*, could license the semantic reconstruction of an appropriate VP *Mary die* in the interpretation of *do so* (certainly the paraphrase of the LF given above could be continued ... *and it surprised me that she did so*). Consequently the ill-formedness of (15.12b) must have another source.[12]

---

[11] In the inchoative variant, *The milk spoiled by sitting in the sun* attaches to the vP headed by BECOME, and *the milk*, a derived subject, can control PRO from Spec-TP in the absence of any more local appropriate controller.

[12] In Fodor's judgement, the transitive variant of inchoative/causative alternators does allow an interpretation in which the antecedent for elided VP is the intransitive inchoative, rather than the transitive causative. It also licenses a pronominal referent:

(i) a. Floyd melted the glass, and it [=the fact that the glass melted] surprised me.
    b. Floyd melted the glass, and I was surprised that he/it would do so.

The syntactic constraints on the licensing of verb-phrase ellipsis are relevant. That is, *do-so* ellipsis is categorically restricted in English; its antecedent must be a whole vP. Stative small clauses do not license *do-so* ellipsis:

(15.13) a. *John made Mary$_i$ happy and it surprised me that she$_i$ did so.
         b. *Mary made John$_i$ sick and it surprised me that he$_i$ did so.

Note that as soon as an explicit inchoative verb is included in the complement to *make*, the ellipsis is well-formed:

(15.14) a. John made Mary$_i$ become happy and it surprised me that she$_i$ did so.
         b. Mary made John$_i$ get sick and it surprised me that he$_i$ did so.

We see, then, that treating causative change-of-state predicates as including only a causing event and a result state predicts that *do-so* ellipsis targeting the stative result component of the predicate should be ill-formed; treating causative change-of-state predicates as including a causative event and an inchoative (BECOME) event makes the incorrect prediction.[13]

Note that the proposed analysis position fits better with the key adverbial modification evidence presented in (15.3) above. Temporal modifiers like *again* and *for five minutes* can modify stative predicates:

(15.15) a. The door was open again.
         b. The door was open for five minutes.

And these modifiers, on the low-scope reading with causative predicates, modify the result state of the causative event. The low-scope interpretation of *John opened the door for five minutes* involves modification of the result state, not the duration of the inchoative event of the door opening.

To recap the three points in reverse order: Stative eventualities cannot antecede *do-so* ellipsis, and hence the stative eventuality sub-part of causative change-of-state verbs cannot do so. Similarly, subjects of stative eventualities cannot control PRO in *by*-gerunds, and hence the object of a change-of-state verb (the subject of the embedded

Consequently, this example could be taken as an argument in *favour* of including the inchoative eventive verb in the decomposition of alternating verbs, at least, although it is a clear challenge to account for the contrast with *kill*; if we adopted this notion, however, it would be a puzzle how to cope with the *by*-gerund control facts. I tentatively suggest an appeal to the process of *Inchoative Coercion*; see discussion below. For evidence for the psychological reality of this process, see Brennan and Pylkkänen (2008).

[13] A reviewer notes that although the account outlined above does correctly capture the failure of *do-so* ellipsis in these contexts, the failure of adjectival predicate ellipsis under *be* then becomes a puzzle. One can say *John made Mary sick, and it surprised me that she was ____*, where the elided constituent is presumably *sick*, but it is decidedly off to say # *Mary killed John and it surprised me that he was ____*, with an understood 'dead' or 'killed' in the elided position. However, for deadjectival change-of-state verbs like *open*, the adjectival ellipsis is considerably better; *John opened the door at 2:00, (but I didn't know, so when I came in) it surprised me that it was ____*. This is presumably relevant to the question raised in footnote 10 concerning the actual identity of the downstairs root predicate which incorporates into *CAUSE* to create *kill*—it's probably in fact not DEAD, per se.

stative eventuality) cannot do so. Finally, Event Identification ensures that the stative eventuality and the causative eventuality are coindexed, each modifying the same single event argument, of which only a single temporal location can be predicated.

It is worth noticing that the proposed analysis accounts for one additional important fact concerning inchoative/transitive alternating verbs, namely, that they are morphologically related to each other. In most cases in English the relationship is one of zero-derivation, because the $v°$ head is realized by a null morpheme (though not in cases like *realize*), but they are nonetheless related not just semantically but morphologically. The claim that they are derived from a common root with a core stative meaning explains the formal identity of the causative and inchoative form, and, in cases of deadjectival verbs like *open*, the state-denoting adjective.

15.3 CASE STUDIES IN DECOMPOSITION: *HAVE, GIVE, GET, WANT*

One particularly fruitful line of analysis builds on the work of Freeze (1992) and Kayne (1994), which proposes to decompose the predicate *have* into a combination of the predication relation BE and with a relational function, which I will notate P_{HAVE}, which expresses a possession relation between two DPs, what Hale and Keyser (1993) term 'central coincidence' relation. That is, expressions like *John has a book* are derived from the following argument structure:

(15.16)

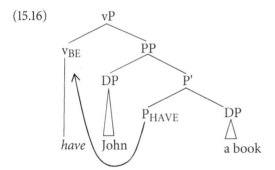

The verb *have* is the realization of the combination of the relational element P_{HAVE} incorporated into the stative verbal head v_{BE}; as usual, the highest DP in the structure, in this case *John*, will move up to Spec-TP to check nominative case and become the subject of the sentence. The proposal accounts cross-linguistically for variation in the expression of possession relations; in many languages, *John has a book* is expressed via a structure with the copula and a preposition, along the lines of *a book is with/at/to John*.

Assuming the existence of such a relational function, it is natural to look for other constructions in which it plays a part. One obvious possibility is that this P_{HAVE} relation is the nucleus of a small clause under v_{CAUSE} in the representation of English

double-object constructions, again reviving the essence of a Generative Semantics proposal according to which *Mary gave John a book* is underlyingly *Mary CAUSE John
HAVE a book*, with the structure illustrated below:

(15.17)

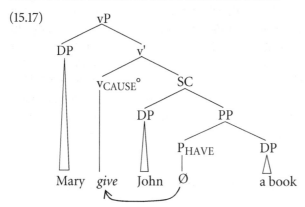

There are several converging lines of evidence that suggest this analysis, which I will
briefly sketch; for a more detailed presentation of these and related arguments, see
Harley (1995, 2003).

Several subtle semantic constraints on verbal *have* also apply to the relationship
between the Goal and Theme objects of *give* in the double-object structure (though
not in the *to*-dative structure), many of which were first noted by Oehrle (1976) and
Green (1974). For example, the subject of *have* constructions must be animate when
the possession relation is alienable; *have* can only have an inanimate subject when the
possession relation is inalienable (see Belvin (1996) for a thorough discussion of this
effect).

(15.18)   a. John has a book.   (alienable possession, animate subject)
          b. John has a big nose.   (inalienable possession, animate subject)
          c. *The bookcase has a book.   (alienable possession, inanimate subject)
          d. The bookcase has five shelves (inalienable possession, inanimate subject)

The same effects are observed with double-object constructions—inanimate Goal
objects cannot appear in the double-object structure unless the resulting possession
relation is inalienable:

(15.19)   a. *Mary gave the bookcase a book.
          b. Mary gave the bookcase five shelves (e.g. while building or repairing it)

In double-object constructions, though not in *to*-dative constructions, a kind of possession entailment is present:

(15.20)   a. Mary taught the students French.   (The students know some French)
          b. Mary taught French to the students. (The students may or may not)

It is worth noting that the possession entailment that follows from a double-object
construction does not necessarily require physical possession. It has repeatedly been
noted, for example, that double-object continuations like those in (15.21) are fine:

(15.21)   a. Mary sent John a letter, but he never received it.
          b. Mary baked John a cake, but it burned, so he never saw it.

If John never received the letter, or never saw the cake, it seems prima facie odd to say that he 'has' or 'had' them.

The key to reconciling this objection with the CAUSE-HAVE hypothesis is the observation that the possession relation does not necessarily entail enduring, physical, possession. If A wills a parcel of land or some deeds or a book to B, then upon the death of A, B can be said to have the land, deed, or book, even if he has never seen them or been physically close to them. Similarly, after the event in the sentence *Mary sent John a letter*, the letter can clearly be designated as *John's letter*, even if he never received it. The same is true in (15.21b): the burned cake was John's cake, even though he never tasted a bite. Mary can report the event in (15.21b) as, 'I burned John's cake!', even though John may not even know that the cake was designated as his. The relation that P_{HAVE} expresses can be momentaneous, it need not endure—see the discussion of *give X the boot* and *want a kiss* below—but its existence is asserted by ditransitive verbs in the double-object frame.[14]

Further support for the *give* as CAUSE-HAVE hypothesis comes from the resultant-state modification possibilities with temporal adverbials, which are the same as observed above for transitive change of state verbs. Again, this effect was first remarked on in the Generative Semantics literature, but has recently received a detailed updated treatment in Beck and Johnson (2004). Adverbial *again* has a both repetitive and a restitutive reading, where what is restored in the restitutive reading is a previous state of the Goal having the Theme. Similarly, temporal adverbials like *for a week* are most naturally taken to modify the result state denoted by P_{HAVE}, not the event of giving:

(15.22)   a. Mary gave John the car again
             Restitutive: *John had had the car before, and Mary caused him to have it again.*
             Repetitive: *Mary had given John the car before, and she did so again*
          b. Mary gave John the car for a week. ⇒ *John had the car for a week*

Again, these facts receive a natural explanation if the lower SC predicate is available as an adjunction site for these adverbials.

Finally, Richards (2001) advances a new argument in favour of decomposition of ditransitive double-object structures into something like CAUSE-HAVE: There are

---

[14] A reviewer reminds me that there are ditransitive verbs which semantically encode the *negation* of possession, as in *John denied Mary her rights*. Presumably this would entail that the downstairs predicate is *NOT-HAVE*, rather than *HAVE*. It is possible that the negation is syntactically decomposed and heads its own projection within the structure, but it is equally possible that *NOT-HAVE* is a primitive counterpart to *HAVE*. An analysis which includes *NOT* independently in the syntactic projection should potentially entail variable scope effects with negation and quantification, which seem not to be present. For example *John denied Mary every right she asked for*, if negation is decomposed, should have two readings analogous to those of *John caused Mary not to have every right she asked for*, which can be true if he refused just one of the rights she asked for but granted the others, as well as true in a situation where he refused all the rights she asked for. However, with *deny*, only the wide-scope reading for the negative element is available— *John denied Mary every right she asked for* means that Mary received no rights—so it seems implausible that the *NOT* element is present in syntactically independent fashion.

idiomatic expressions where the idiom consists of *give-Theme* whose idiomatic interpretation carries over to expressions with *have-Theme*, but is not present with other similar verbs like *own* or *possess* or *experience*.

(15.23) a. Mary gave me the creeps/willies.
        b. (It's so spooky in here,) I have the creeps/the willies.
        c. #I possess/own/am experiencing/feel the creeps/the willies.

This suggests that the constituent which receives the idiomatic interpretation is present in both the *give* cases and the *have* cases, namely, the P_{HAVE} + Theme constituent.

    An interesting corollary emerges from this analysis. In the analysis of causative/inchoative alternating verbs above, we claimed that the change from causative to inchoative argument structure was accomplished by changing the matrix little v° from causative, eventive v_{CAUSE} to eventive but not causative v_{BECOME}. Here we have proposed a third v°, stative v_{BE}. The relational P_{HAVE} can compose with both v_{CAUSE} and v_{BE}; it also seems reasonable to think it should be able to compose with v_{BECOME}. Such a verb would lack an external Agent argument; it would rather mean something like COME to HAVE. In fact, it seems clear that the corresponding English verb is *get* with a Goal/Recipient argument in subject position—if this analysis is correct, the Goal/Recipient is a derived subject (see Pesetsky (1995) for the first version of this proposal that I know of). The argument structure would be as follows:

(15.24)

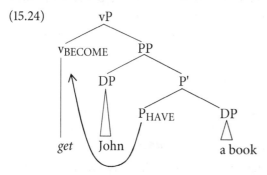

If this is correct, we should see animacy/alienability effects and result-state scope readings, as well as P_{HAVE} idioms, carrying over from *have* and *give*; in fact, we see all of these:

(15.25) a. Animacy/alienability effects:
          (i) John got the book.
          (ii) #Philadelphia got the book.[15]
          (iii) Philadelphia got a new freeway.

---

[15] The intended context is one in which the book was sent in the mail to Philadelphia, where Philadelphia just refers to the city as a location. Famously, this improves if 'Philadelphia' is understood to refer to some animate/intentional collective entity, like the Philadelphia office of a corporation; the same effect is seen in #*John sent Philadelphia the book* vs. *John sent the book to Philadelphia*. Since freeways are inalienable subconstituents of a city, (iii) is fine.

b. Scope of adverbials only over P$_{\text{HAVE}}$ state, not over *getting* event:

(i) John got his balance again

Restitutive: (i) can be true in a case where John never lost his balance before in his life, so he had never gotten his balance before, since he'd never lost it. In such a situation, (i) expresses the notion that what is happening again is the state of John having his balance, not that he is undergoing a second event of getting his balance.

(ii) John got the car for a week

Low-scope: What lasts a week is the state of John having the car, not the event of him getting it.

c. I got the creeps/willies

An interesting issue concerning some of the idioms cases discussed by Richards is that there are idioms which are acceptable with *give* and *get* but not with *have*, such as the following:

(15.26)   a. Mary gave John the boot.
            b. John got the boot.
            c. #John has the boot.

Again, the problem has to do with duration entailments contributed to the *have* verb by the v$_{\text{BE}}$ head which composes with the stative P$_{\text{HAVE}}$ predicate. *Give* and *get* are punctual Achievements; the resultant state which they create can last (as in *Mary gave John the car for three weeks*) but need not. This is especially the case when the Theme denotes an event, rather than a thing, as in *Mary gave John a kiss* or *John got a kiss*; the kiss John got was John's kiss, all right, but one couldn't say at the end of the event that *John has a kiss*. The idiomatic referent of *the boot* in the idiom P$_{\text{HAVE}}$ *the boot* is similarly an event; consequently the idiom can be used when P$_{\text{HAVE}}$ *the boot* is embedded under eventive v° (producing *give* or *get*), but not when it's embedded under v$_{\text{BE}}$.[16]

This effect, which appears when P$_{\text{HAVE}}$ composes with an event-denoting DP, can also be seen in a third case in which a null 'have' relation seems to be well-motivated, namely, in cases where a verb like *want* or *need*, which usually takes some kind of propositional complement, composes with a theme DP. The idea is that *John wants an apple* contains a null semantic component roughly similar to *have*; it's equivalent to *John wants to have an apple*. In the present framework, as outlined in Harley (2004),

---

[16] The P$_{\text{HAVE}}$ is necessary for the phrase *the boot* to refer to the event of firing, however, so the idiom is still definitely P$_{\text{HAVE}}$ *the boot*, not just a homosemous/metaphorical interpretation assigned to *the boot* in any old context. Compare *the Big Apple*, which can refer to New York no matter what verb it composes with; *the boot*, in contrast, needs *give* or *get*—*the boot* cannot refer to a firing event in something like *The boot has really depressed John*, which is not equivalent to *Getting the boot has really depressed John*.

the proposal would be that the complement to *want* in *John wants an apple* would be something like *PRO_i P_HAVE DP*. (I remain agnostic here concerning the substructure within the verb *want* itself, notating it V, but I assume it decomposes into at least stative v_{BE} and a root, as usual[17]):

(15.27)

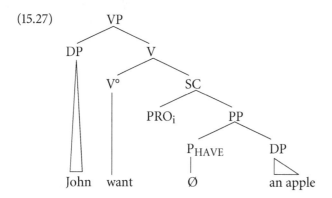

This proposal has been advanced many times in the literature in one form or another, including in Quine (1960), Bach (1968), McCawley (1974), Partee (1974), and Dowty (1979), and more recently in Den Dikken et al. (1997) and Fodor and Lepore (1998).[18] It accounts for a wide range of facts about *want DP* constructions, of a familiar type. For example, when *want DP* is modified by a temporal adverbial, a low-scope reading is available in which the adverbial modifies the length of the desired possession state, rather than the time that the wanting itself took; similarly, *again* can modify the having of the DP, rather than the wanting:

(15.28) a. John wants the car again. = *John wants to have the car again.*
   Low-scope: John has had the car in the past—perhaps without ever wanting to have it—and now he would like the state of him having the car to recur.
   b. John wants the car for a week. = *John wants to have the car for a week.*
   Low-scope: John wants his state of having a car to last a week.

Similarly, many subtly idiosyncratic interpretations available with *have DP* also surface with *want DP*:

---

[17] Harley (1995: 208) proposes that in fact all psychological state roots are nominal in character and are related to their experiencer argument by (another) P_HAVE relation: *John fears dogs* is decomposed into [v_{BE} [JOHN [HAS [√FEAR (of) DOGS]]]]; *John wants apples* presumably would work the same way: [v_{BE} [JOHN_i [HAS [√WANT [PRO_i [HAVE APPLES]]]]]]. The downstairs P_HAVE is the one at issue here, though, rather than the one that composes with the root and v_{BE} to form the surface verb, so the lexical decomposition of *want* itself is left moot for now.

[18] The general picture has recently received some indirect support from Harves and Kayne (2008), who show in a survey of a large number of Indo-European languages, that languages with verbal *have* have a *need DP* construction, while languages without *have* do not allow a *need DP* construction.

(15.29)   a.   John had Mary.   (can have a sexual interpretation)
           b.   John wants Mary.   (similarly can have a sexual interpretation)
           c.   John has a car.   (he has permanent possession of a car)
           d.   John wants a car.   (he wants permanent possession of a car)
           e.   John has the car.   (he has temporary possession of the car)
           f.   John wants the car.   (he wants temporary possession of the car)

So far we have not seen any reason why the complement to *want* couldn't simply be a covert verb *have*, rather than a covert P_{HAVE}. However, when the DP denotes a punctual event, like *a compliment*, or *a kiss*, paraphrases with *have* are infelicitous and paraphrases with *get* are much better:

(15.30)   a.   John wants a kiss.   *#John wants to have a kiss.*
                                        John wants to get a kiss.
           b.   John wants a compliment.   *#John wants to have a compliment.*
                                          John wants to get a compliment.

These facts indicate that the concealed complement to *want* cannot be the actual verb *have*. Nor can it be the actual verb *get*; sentences like *John wants Mary* are not appropriately paraphrased as *John wants to get Mary*.[19] The effect, in fact, is the same as we have seen above in the discussion of *get the boot*: event-denoting DPs are not comfortable with the verb *have*, but are fine with *give* and *get*, and, here, *want*. In the case of *give* and *get*, the P_{HAVE} relation composes with an eventive $v°$; here it composes with *want*; taken together, I conclude that the concealed 'have' relation in *want DP* structures is P_{HAVE}, rather than the actual verb *have*.[20]

---

[19] A reviewer rightly notes that an alternative to the P_{HAVE} analysis would suggest that *want* might take a covert *have* complement in some cases, and a covert *get* complement in some other cases, depending on the semantic content of the DP; this possibility is rejected on conceptual grounds by Fodor and Lepore (1998) and the present argument is predicated on the necessity of that rejection. If one proposed a Pustejovsky (1995)-style approach where 'univocality' for a given lexical item is not a desideratum, then this alternative possibility could be entertained.

[20] This has the added benefit of meaning that we need not explain why *have* is unpronounced in *want DP* sequences; P_{HAVE} is a null morpheme in all the English contexts in which we have seen it so far.

    Wechsler (2008) argues against this proposal on the grounds that the DP complement to *want* behaves like a standard accusative direct object of *want*, rather than like the object of a prepositional complement to *want*, with respect to all the usual tests which distinguish the two in English. Presumably the same objection could be raised with respect to *John gave Mary [$_{PP}$ Ø the book]*, in which *the book* is the object of a null preposition but behaves like a direct object, and *Mary got [$_{PP}$ Ø the book]*, with the same issues. I assume in all cases that P_{HAVE} incorporates into the verbal head which selects for it, so that in fact the element which is assigning case to the Theme object in all these cases is the [$v°$ + P_{HAVE}] complex (or in the case of *want*, the [*want* + P_{HAVE}] complex); consequently we expect the usual Adjacency Condition on English accusative case assignment to hold between these complex elements and the DP which is receiving Case from them, and for these DPs to behave in all relevant respects like direct objects. The situation is analogous to verb–particle combinations, such as, e.g., *John uploaded the file*, which I assume is derived from *John loaded [$_{PP}$ up the file]*, with subsequent incorporation of *up* into *load*. The object *the file* is subject to the adjacency condition after P incorporation, so that it cannot be separated from the P + V complex by an adverbial, e.g.: **John uploaded quickly the file*.

15.4 MORPHOLOGY, SYNTAX, AND COMPOSITIONALITY

I have focused on English data so far, but it is worth briefly outlining the kinds of facts from other languages which have led to the widespread adoption of this kind of decompositional analysis of verbs among linguists. Verbal structures quite broadly show the kind of bipartite structure that the vP analysis predicts—change-of-state verbs, certainly, but also verbs of other event classes, such as activities and semelfactives.

For example, here are a few examples of Japanese and Hiaki (Yaqui) change-of-state verbs which have a clear morphological structure that corresponds to their causative or inchoative interpretation. Assuming that the root remains constant, the changing morphology is a visible reflex of the change from vCAUSE to vBECOME in the causative/inchoative alternation. Both of these lists extend to include hundreds of verb pairs (see Jacobsen, 1981; Jelinek, 1998); the pattern is very robust in these languages.

(15.31)   Japanese inchoative/causative alternating morphology

Inchoative variant		*Causative variant*		
ag-**ar**-u	'rise'	ag-**e**-ru	'raise'	ag-
aratam-**ar**-u	'improve'	aratam-**e**-ru	'improve'	aratam-
ama-**r**-u	'remain'	ama-**s**-u	'remain'	ama-
hita-**r**-u	'soak'	hita-**s**-u	'soak'	hita-
arawa-**re**-ru	'show'	arawa-**s**-u	'show'	arawa-
hana-**re**-ru	'separate'	hana-**s**-u	'separate from'	hana-
ka-**ri**-ru	'borrow'	ka-**s**-u	'lend'	ka-
ta-**ri**-ru	'suffice'	ta-**s**-u	'supplement'	ta-
bak-**e**-ru	'turn into'	bak-**as**-u	'turn into/bewitch'	bak-
bar-**e**-ru	'come to light'	bar-**as**-u	'bring to light'	bar-
ak-**i**-ru	'tire'	ak-**as**-u	'tire'	ak
dek-**i**-ru	'come into being'	dek-**as**-u	'bring into being'	dek-
horob-**i**-ru	'fall to ruin'	horob-**os**-u	'ruin'	horob-
ok-**i**-ru	'get up'	ok-**os**-u	'get up'	ok-

. . .

(15.32)   Hiaki (Yaqui) inchoative/causative alternating morphology

bwase	'cook, ripen'	bwasa	'cook'	bwas-
chakukta	'bend'	chakukte	'bend'	chakuk-
chakte	'leak'	chakta	'drip'	chak-
chihakte	'shatter'	chihakta	'smash'	chihak-
hamte	'break'	hamta	'break'	ham-

heokte	'melt'	heokta	'melt'	heok-
chu'akte	'adhere'	chu'akta	'stick on'	chu'ak-
chukte	'come loose'	chukta	'cut loose'	chuk-
chupe	'come to end'	chupa	'finish'	chup-
ko'okte	'come undone'	ko'okta	'pull apart'	ko'ok-
kowiikte	'get crooked'	kowiikta	'make crooked'	kowiik-
kitokte	'shrivel'	kitokta	'deform'	kitok-
kotte	'break'	kotta	'break'	kot-

. . .

Indeed, one can see from the fact that many of the English translation equivalents are also morphologically related (usually identical) that the pattern of morphological relatedness between causative/inchoative pairs of verbs is robust in English as well.

In Malagasy and Tagalog, the verbal alternation is also extremely general: essentially any verb with an Agent argument in its argument structure has a particular *pag-* prefix attached; the same verb, without the prefix, is not agentive. The Tagalog examples given here are from Travis (2000). Note the inchoative version of the verb root is divided into two by an irrelevant infix in the left-most column; in fact, the verb roots are identical from column to column; the *pag-* prefix is the main difference between them:

(15.33)   Tagalog alternating verbs:

t-um-**umba**	'fall down'	m-pag-**tumba**	'knock down'
s-um-**abog**	'explode'	m-pag-**sabog**	'scatter'
l-um-**uwas**	'go into the city'	m-pag-**luwas**	'take into the city'
s-um-**abit**	'be suspended'	m-pag-**sabit**	'hang'
s-um-**ali**	'join'	m-pag-**sali**	'include'

In Tagalog and Malagasy, even non-alternating verbs with an Agent argument show the *pag* morpheme, illustrating the presence of v_{CAUSE} even in cases where alternation does not provide evidence of its independence; in such verbs v_{CAUSE} is part of a fixed structure associated with that root. Travis (2000) gives the following Tagalog example; in (15.34a) although *-halo* is clearly the root component of the verb *mix (transitive)*, prefixed with *pag-*, which occupies v° and selects for the Agent argument, there is no corresponding inchoative form:

(15.34)   a. m-pag-**halo**'   mix in (causative)
          b. *h-um-alo'   *incorporate by itself, mix in by itself

The prevalence of morphological alternations of this type, cross-linguistically, suggests the universality of this bipartite structure for verbs; indeed, it is this type of evidence that initially motivates this type of analysis in Hale and Keyser (1993). It is important to recognize, however, that the fact that these morphemes are contained within a single phonological word has no relevance to the question of their independence or dependence on the verb root, or their compositional or non-compositional nature. Essentially the same phenomena are observed in languages like Persian, with one key difference: In

Persian the element occupying the v° position and the contentful predicative element which it selects for are not morphologically dependent on each other the v° is an independent phonological word from its complement. This phenomenon is referred to descriptively as 'complex predication', since the linguistic forms which are the translation equivalents of monomorphemic verbs in English are syntactically complex, made up of multiple words.

Persian has only about 80–100 monomorphemic verbs of the English type; all other verbs are syntactically complex, consisting of a lexically contentful nominal, verbal, or adjectival element and one of ten or twelve light verbs, which Folli, Harley, and Karimi (2005) argued were realizations of v°. Folli et al. (2005) give the following examples as some typical illustrations of the complex predicates which characterize the Persian verbal lexicon. First, some illustrations of the form that inchoative/causative alternating predicates take; notice that the verbal portion changes while the lexically contentful non-verbal component remains the same:

(15.35) a. sabok shodan   sabok kardan
            light becoming   light making
            'degrade (intr)'   'degrade (tr)'

         b. pahn shodan   pahn kardan
            wide becoming   wide making
            'spread (intr)'   'spread (tr)'

         c. kotak xordan   zadan kotak
            beating colliding   beating hitting
            'to get beaten'   'to beat'

         d. xar shodan   xar kardan
            donkey becoming   donkey doing
            'to get fooled'   'to fool'

Non-alternating predicates are structurally complex in the same way, although the verb portion of the predicate in these cases is fixed:

(15.36) a. derâz keshidan
            long pulling
            'to nap, to lie down'

         b. birun kardan
            out doing
            'to dismiss, to fire (someone)'

         c. bâlâ keshidan
            up pulling
            'to steal'

         d. be yâd dâshtan
            to memory have
            'to remember (stative)'

    e. bejâ âvardan
       to.place bringing
       'to recognize'

These phrases are not distinguishable prima facie from idiomatically interpreted phrasal expressions; some are more compositional, some less, but all are clearly syntactically complex.

Although in most of the above I have focused on cases where semantic considerations clearly motivate decomposition, the claim that the erstwhile VP decomposes into a vP and a non-verbal root or lexical predicate complement extends even to cases where the independent semantic contributions of the two components out of which the verb is made are not independently obvious. Most Root +v° combinations have an idiomatic interpretation. It's only in cases like *to open* where the semantic contributions of each subcomponent are clearly encapsulated and independently characterizable.[21] The likelihood that a given syntactically complex constituent is an idiom varies with the size of the component. Root morphemes (together with the first functional item with which they compose, see Arad (2005)) are guaranteed to require a listed, 'idiomatic' interpretation, however, since they are the ultimate Saussurean sign.

Because the motivation for (morpho)syntactic decomposition stops at the level of the Root morpheme, however, the playing field for the central debate concerning lexical semantic decomposition remains essentially unchanged. Are the meanings contributed by Root morphemes atomistic? Or are they composed of more primitive lexical-semantic features? No answer to this issue will emerge from the kind of decomposition of word-sized items in the syntax advocated here. The evidence for a syntactically present CAUSE or BECOME or HAVE terminal node, sometimes realized by a null morpheme, sometimes by an overt morpheme or even an independent phonological word, does not prove anything one way or the other about the broader project of determining what meanings are—whether they are feature complexes or prototypes or meaning networks, or conceptual atoms. An atomist could perfectly seriously accept the conclusions of the present work and retain the atomistic position. Only the assumption about the nature of the particular irreducible morphosyntactic unit which is attached to the conceptual atom would change. The various conceptual arguments advanced over many years, especially by Fodor and Lepore, against the notion that concepts are anything but atoms, are not called into question by the conclusions presented here. The present analysis only rebuts the specific claim that apparently monomorphemic verbs should never be analysed as containing a null CAUSE or BECOME morpheme. It

---

[21] Importantly, however, the functional content, independent of the idiomatic component, which is contributed by the v° and the predicate in idioms and in the bipartite V, is always compositionally interpreted. McGinnis (2002) shows that the aspectual interpretation of a phrase, which is determined by the formal characteristics of its functional structure, remains consistent across literal and idiomatic interpretations. So, for example, *kick the bucket* is a punctual achievement predicate in both its literal and idiomatic interpretations.

seems clear that they can contain such a morpheme, but this is no more a challenge to the atomistic position than the observation that there are words containing null PLURAL morphemes is (*The sheep-PL are restless*). There is a fact of the matter about the correct syntactic analysis of English verb phrases, but once it is determined, we will still need to know the nature of the semantic content of the subconstituent terminals. The decompositional buck will have to stop at the Root morphosyntactic terminal node.

CHAPTER 16

....

SYNTAX IN THE ATOM

....

WOLFRAM HINZEN

16.1 INTRODUCTION

....

The question of lexical decomposition is the question of whether units of language that look simple on the surface—words like *bachelor*, *kill*, *have*, *get*, or even the plural morpheme *-s*—are simple in their underlying semantic representations as well. The considerable attention and excitement that this question has evoked in philosophy indicates its deep epistemological and metaphysical dimensions. In particular, if we hold that the structure of language is a good indicator for the structure of thought, then one would expect that what is structurally simple, at least superficially, such as mono-morphemic words, is structurally simple at the level of thought (or at the level of 'semantic representation') as well. That is, lexical semantics should not be *compositional*: the meaning of a word should not have to be determined on the basis of its internal structure. Yet, if there are nearly as many simple, non-structured concepts as there are morphemes (minimally meaningful linguistic units), how are we to learn them? If we can learn a new concept only on the basis of its internal structure (i.e. by constructing it), concepts without such a structure are not learnable. As for the metaphysical dimension of this problem: a non-decompositional theory of word meaning seems to commit us to strange, atom-like semantic entities (simple concepts) that are not analysable either structurally or functionally (Hinzen, 2006*b*). What are we to make of this ontology? What part of reality do such meaning-atoms inhabit?

This chapter addresses this philosophical debate in the way it has developed in the context of empirical findings in generative linguistic theory (Fodor, 1970, 1998*a*; Fodor and Lepore, 1998, 1999; Jackendoff, 2002; Richards, 2001; Harley, 2004, this volume; Johnson, 2004*b*). I will be arguing for a view according to which the initial question posed above is a pseudo-problem arising from a dissociation between thought and language that is conceptually obscure and empirically unmotivated: nothing can be decomposed in thought, when it is not decomposed in language. I will follow standard philosophical and linguistic practice and use small capitals when we intend to talk about concepts (putative entities in the world of 'thought'), while using linguistic expressions (entities in the world of 'language'), when intending to talk about language. The above question then is, to take a trivial example: If MET THIS MAN is a 'complex concept', as it presumably is, are MET and MAN complex concepts, too?

Well, how do we *know* that MET THIS MAN is a complex concept? Plainly, we simply *look*: the complex concept in question is clearly phrasal. It contains a verbal phrase and a noun phrase standing in particular syntactic and logical relations. However, this cannot be quite right, for MET THIS MAN was supposed to be a 'conceptual structure', not a linguistic expression, and conceptual structures, on rather standard philosophical (Fodor, 1998a) or linguistic (Jackendoff, 2002) assumptions, are not syntactic phrases: they don't contain verbal or nominal phrases, determiners, etc., in specific syntactic relations. If they did, their supposed independence from the syntactic organization of language, axiomatic within both Fodor's and Jackendoff's systems, would be hard to explain. But, then, if conceptual structures involve a different ontology than linguistic expressions and are independent of these, how would we determine, even in principle, whether a concept was simple or structured? Close conceptual connections between words, be they definitional or statistical, like between *kill* and *dead*, *man* and *animate*, etc., are, in particular, not sufficient to establish the structural complexity of a concept, let alone its compositionality. For example, it can be a necessary fact that anyone who has been killed is also dead, without it thereby also being the case that when we think or access the concept expressed by 'kill', we thereby also think or access the concept expressed by 'dead'.

There may well be complex thought of *some* sort without language. Yet, much of it is not relevant in this discussion, which targets structured, systematic, and compositional thought of the sort we express in language. If the identity of the exact concept MET THIS MAN and its ways of systematically combining with other concepts is the issue, it seems rather obscure how this concept could possibly be the one it is, in the absence of the exact syntactic-categorial resources and syntactic relations that plainly make it up. If all we are doing when making claims about the complexity of a concept, however, is trivially mapping conceptual structures from linguistic ones, the proposal that there are simple concepts is no more substantive or surprising than the insight that there are things treated as atoms by the syntactic generator. Nothing as trivial as capitalization should confuse us into believing that there is a distinct ontology there, a world of non-linguistic 'thought' and 'concepts', to which language and the forms which it provides are somehow 'mapped' or 'respond'. If, on the other hand, conceptual structure is trivially syntactic, then we can be quite certain what the answer is to the question of whether MAN is a complex concept. Presumably, the syntax is not sensitive to whether MAN contains BIPEDAL, say (in the way it is, when it generates the structure *a man is bipedal*). Syntactically, then, or in the way it is cognitively manipulated in systematic ways, *man* is an atom: the computational system carries it through a derivation like a locked suitcase. On this view, atomic is by definition what the computational system of language treats as such—this being in turn an entirely empirical question.

This conclusion would be in line with the broad framework proposed by Hinzen (2006a, 2007), where there isn't a computational system of 'thought' independent of the linguistic one which equally operates over discrete units and generates complex constituents from them in systematic ways, interpreted compositionally and in line with their internal hierarchical structure. Looking at syntax, on this view, is not merely an onerous and unfortunate detour that we have to take to get to the 'real thing', the thoughts themselves, which for some contingent reason we cannot look at directly, lacking some sort of non-linguistic or purely logical telescope. Syntax *is* the thing itself. The question, then, whether a thought or concept is an atom or not *can* only be the question of whether the syntactic component of language treats it as decomposed or not. This at least sets a methodologically clear and sound agenda for the decomposition debate: it consists in asking *which* aspects of the semantics of an expression the syntax *is* sensitive to.

My answer will be that the syntax *does* treat some lexical atoms as structurally complex, in ways that engender as well as explain systematic lexical entailments: implicational relations between lexical items. All viable semantic decomposition, in other words, is (i) syntactic; and (ii) there is lexical decomposition; yet, (iii), the semantics of lexical atoms is not compositional, in the above sense, ever. Where there is syntactic atomicity, there cannot be semantic compositionality (decomposition 'at a semantic level') either: syntax and semantics align. This will ultimately point us into a new direction, where we use syntax as a long-missing *cognitive theory*, a theory that tells us what our concepts are like, and why: for universal syntactic constraints will apply to their formation. As apparently impossible words guide us to these constraints, I will begin right here.

16.2 Impossible words

The organization of words into phrases and sentences is what we traditionally associate with syntax: the 'syntagmatic' ('horizontal') combinatoriality in human language. Yet, as Hinzen and Uriagereka (2006) note, it has always been clear that there are paradigmatic ('vertical') regularities among words as well. These have traditionally fallen under the rubric of the 'parts of speech', and it has long been noted (at least since the late medieval ages, see Covington, 2009), that not merely the syntagmatic connections but the paradigmatic ones as well are heavily constrained: syntactic interactions *cannot* solely be based on the combination of the idiosyncratic or 'atomic' parts of speech.

In the 1960s, generative semanticists (Lakoff, 1970; McCawley, 1968, 1971; Ross, 1972) asked a question that speaks to this issue: If the word literally was an atom—a structureless unit, with no syntax in it—what would explain why there don't seem to be possible verbs like the ones italicized in (16.1)?

(16.1) a. John **glarfed* Mary [meaning: John V-ed <u>someone and</u> Mary]
      b. John **marfoed* Harry [meaning: John killed Harry, <u>or</u> Harry died]
      c. Chris **laughed* Mary [meaning: Chris made Mary laugh]

    d. Mary *shelved the books on [meaning: Mary put the books on the shelf]

    e. We *got the pigs mud on the wall [meaning: We made the pigs get mud on
the wall]

If, they argued, there existed a word-internal syntax paralleling sentence-syntax and subject to similar constraints, the data in (16.1) could all be explained. In terms of the previous section, this means that a notion of a 'possible lexical concept' might be given a generative characterization. In (16.1a) we would say that the existence of such a lexical concept would violate the coordinate structure constraint, now holding *inside* lexical items; in (16.1b), that 'kill' really means CAUSE + COME ABOUT + BE + DEAD, hence contains the 'state' of Harry's being dead as an argument in its very underlying phrasal architecture; in (16.1c), that 'laugh' really projects the argument-structure [V [N laugh]] (as in *do a laugh*), which projects no Agent argument, hence cannot take one (cf. Hale and Keyser, 2002); in (16.1d), that the surface form *shelve* is really derived from the source structure *X put Y on the shelf* through successive incorporations of *the shelf* (first into the Preposition *on*, then into the verb *put*), and hence that (16.1d) leaves out *on* (and leaves it stranded) on its path to *put*; in (16.1e), that ditransitive *get*, if it existed, would have the structure AGENT + CAUSE + AGENT + CAUSE + V, and there are no such recursive argument structures in human language.

    Since surface syntax does obviously not mirror such lexical decompositions, generative semanticists concluded that syntactic representations ('deep structures') of such constructions were very abstract. But largely semantically motivated decompositions of this kind were a road to failure—a theme I will pursue throughout this chapter. As Newmeyer (1996) points out, what centrally brought down generative semantics was the syntax it posited: ever more unmotivated 'transformations' between hypothesized underlying 'semantic representations' and surface forms, without seeing these syntactic operations systematically accompanied by semantic effects.

    Since the syntax of generative semantics did not respect the morphemic boundary as semantically or conceptually relevant, the natural question arose why a linguistic level of 'deep structure' should not be abolished altogether, in favour of starting a syntactic derivation from a wholly abstract 'semantic' level, which would characterize the 'thought' expressed in a sentence directly:

(16.2)   Thought

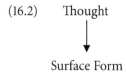

    Surface Form

Here, thought is a system *not* constrained (or explained by) syntactic or linguistic rules, and language merely consists in 'mapping' language-independent thoughts to phonetic representations. Surface language, crucially including word formation, is a mere 'expression' of deep thought, and whatever word-level regularities can be found ought to be studied as regularities of thought (by means of logic) unmediated by lexical expression. This, in essence, is what Fodor and Lepore (2001) have identified as 'Sam's theme'—a theme they don't want to have replayed. But there is no doubt that syntactic theory has been replaying it time and again. Re-tuning this theme, as I will here, leads to a quite different message: the organization of syntax, above and below the lexicon, is part of the *aetiology* of human thought rather than an arbitrary way in which thought is expressed for communicative purposes.

16.3 SAM'S THEME

While the excitement about generative semantics came to a quick end by the early 1970s, the idea that deep down, syntax is really or ideally should be semantics, or at least is to be in the service of it, has survived in various shapes and sizes. In a sense, the idea is a founding assumption of much of the philosophy of language, philosophical logic, formal semantics, and cognitive linguistics: here language is looked at as an arbitrary and deficient medium for the expression of thought. On the basis of this axiom, much of twentieth-century philosophy of language has become an exercise in 'translation': trading natural language for the 'regimented' representations of a formal language which would depict the semantic structure of a thought in line, not with grammatical constraints, but logical ones.

The question is how to study 'thought' empirically—especially if the lexical decompositions posed at a posited 'semantic level' simply behave as if they were not there: As Fodor noted at the time (Fodor, 1970), whereas Bill could, at noon, *cause Jim to die at midnight* (say by tampering with his telephone at noon and having someone give him a ring at midnight, causing an explosion), we couldn't felicitously express this fact by saying that *Bill killed Jim at noon*. If, therefore, 'kill' contains a lower verbal layer (BECOME DEAD), it is not transparent to interpretation: no separate modifier can attach to it. So why assume it is there? Similarly, Bill could *cause Jim to die by pulling the trigger of his pistol*, and then either Bill or Jim could be the ones pulling the trigger. However, if we say that *Bill killed Jim by pulling the trigger of his pistol*, the possibility that Jim is pulling the trigger is excluded. Again, then, why posit a lower verb ('die') in the underlying representation of 'kill', whose 'subject' Jim should then be able to control the subject of 'pull'? Finally, if there is an underlying embedded VP 'at the semantic level', why can't we elide it, which we clearly can in the decomposed version? Thus, for example, while *John caused Mary to die, and it surprised me that she did so* is fine, *John killed Mary, and it surprised me that she did so* is clearly not.

These objections are addressed by contemporary forms of lexical decomposition, but remain surprisingly recalcitrant. Harley's (this volume, pp. 334–6) explanation of the first Fodorian point above, in particular, is that the two verbal layers are not separately modifiable because 'Event Identification' has taken place in the 'synthetic' versions of the verbs in question (the ones where we have a single lexical verb). But this, one could reply, while yielding the right result, is the very problem to be explained. Regarding the second objection, she argues that if 'kill' is decomposed into $v +$ Adjective (DEAD) rather than $v + V$ (DIE), we can explain why the embedded 'PRO'-subject of the gerund cannot be controlled by Jim: compare 'John' controlling PRO in $Mary_i[_v made[John_j sick]]$ by $[PRO_{i/*j}[_V eating\ too\ much]]$. In short, CAUSE-plus-STATE decompositions (rather than CAUSE-plus-EVENT ones) make the behaviour that Fodor noted in regards to by-gerunds entirely expected. However, it is now *still* the case that the putative constituent concept DEAD cannot be separately modified in the synthetic form *kill*, whereas it can in the analytic one. This we see when we take a state modifier rather than an event modifier: Whereas *John made Bill dead by the time he reached the hospital* is ok, the same intended meaning is unavailable or unnatural in *John killed Bill by the time he reached the hospital*. As for the third Fodorian objection, *John made Mary happy and it surprised me that she was* is fine, just as *John made Mary dead and it surprised me that she was* is. However, *John killed Mary and it surprised me that she was* is clearly not. Moreover, although the *j*-option in $Mary_i made[John_j sick]$ by $PRO_{i/*j}$ *eating too much* is quite bad, *Mary sickened John by eating too much*, with the same interpretation, is a lot worse.

This evidence suggests that a word like *kill*, after all, is not only syntactically but also semantically simple—it is a semantic atom—contrary to complex phrases like *cause to die* or *make dead*, which contain *cause* or *dead* as parts and whatever meaning these words have in English (call them CAUSE and DEAD). Something that does not *seem* to have constituents, like *kill*, does not have them 'covertly', or at some 'semantic level of representation', either.

Even though, as a result of such empirical and methodological difficulties, the simplest model of grammar in (16.2) was abandoned, impossible word facts nonetheless remained where they were in the 1970s and 1980s, as did generalizations about word-internal paradigmatic complexity. Also, the empirical data against lexical decompositions are ultimately less clear than one would like. For example, (16.3) clearly has a reading (preferred, in fact) where the adjunct does modify an embedded state ('being in Munich') rather than the travel, suggesting there is an embedded verbal phrase, hidden under the syntactic surface:

(16.3)   I went to Munich for a week

Yet, Fodor (1998*a*) continues to take a hard-core 'atomistic' view of the lexicon, denying essentially any attempt to explain the semantic properties of lexical items by making them internally complex in the style of a compositional or 'inferential role' semantics (Fodor and Lepore, 2002, 2005). The word 'kill', on this view, does not contain the constituents 'die' or 'dead' any more than the number 6 contains the number 3 as a constituent (even though it can be factored into 2 times 3) (Fodor and Pylyshyn, 1988). Still, Fodor hasn't given us an alternative account of either impossible word facts or paradigmatic regularities: why, say, does killing Bill entail Bill's dying (see (16.1b)), or the presence of *a lamb* (qua individual object) entail *lamb*, the substance or mass (i.e. meat) that makes it up? Nor is it clear in principle what should give that account if, other than syntax, 'there is no obvious slice of reality (physics, biology, psychology, . . .) that is sensitive to matters of this sort. Insisting on the claim that there is nothing (for semantics or for anything) to explain here won't make the facts go away' (Hinzen and Uriagereka, 2006 p. 82–3). Neither does it bring us closer to what was called a cognitive theory of concepts above.

Meanwhile Chomsky, though engaged in the task of finding the ultimate 'vocabulary of syntax' (its unanalysable features) (see e.g. Chomsky, 1995), has had little to say about paradigmatic cuts in language, focusing on the horizontal dimension of merging words into phrases. Just as in his (1970), nouns and verbs are still often analysed in terms of '+/ − N' and '+/ − V' features. To this date very few have even worried about how these features truly relate or what they mean. A genuine theory of lexical categories is barely just beginning (Baker, 2003).

On Jackendoff's approach, in turn, there is a different grammar for syntax and for semantics (for that matter phonology too), and we get productivity and systematicity of a different kind in each of these domains (Jackendoff, 2002). Yet, emptying syntax of its semantic content will not explain why the two systems are so well-aligned. In fact, the autonomy (or independent generativity) of syntax with regards to semantics, which Jackendoff's approach writes into the very architecture of the linguistic system, has been largely abandoned in generative grammar, where it has become entirely normal to study semantic phenomena in syntactic terms and the very conceptual distinction between syntax and semantics is often obscure in linguistic practice.

16.4 Sam's theme replayed

16.4.1 Polysemy

Polysemy is one of the crucial phenomena that have motivated a comeback of lexical decomposition and lexical semantics (which the atomist position virtually pre-empts). For example, does 'bake' mean the same in 'bake a cake' and 'bake a potato'? The feeling is that the verb is univocal, yet its meaning is systematically different in the two contexts, with the former version exhibiting a 'creation' feature which the latter lacks. Pustejovsky (1995) posits that what enters the compositional process is the 'qualia-structure' of the NP (involving semantic features such as +/–ARTEFACT, etc.), which in a process called 'co-composition' determines the meaning of the VP. The immediate problem with this is the fact that the analytic–synthetic distinction breaks down at the level of the semantics of the lexicon. No lexical decomposition of a lexical item such as *paint, bake,* or *cow* is known that would preserve synonymy, making it unclear what exactly the semantic relation between the lexical atom and its putative decomposition is supposed to be (Fodor, 1998*a*).

Another problem, as Fodor and Lepore (1999) note, is that, in theory and maybe even in practice one can bake an already existing cake in much the same way that one can bake a potato. Although the opposite case, where we are creating a potato when we bake it, is somewhat harder to imagine, we could imagine a possible world in which precisely that happens (perhaps with an artificial potato) and the sentence 'John is baking a potato' would be entirely felicitous in describing it. Has the verb that occurs in it then changed its meaning? Why not say the opposite, that it contributes exactly the same meaning to the compositional process in these cases and that whatever other information enters the final interpretation is added contextually and non-compositionally (i.e. in ways that linguistic form does not determine)? How do we *determine* whether the verb *keep*, say, doesn't simply always mean the same, no matter whether we see it occurring in 'John kept the gift', 'John kept his face clean', or in 'John kept the wine elsewhere'?

Suppose to the contrary that which meanings verbs contribute to the composition of the meaning of the complex expressions in which they enter does depend on context. Then one needs to know the context to know the meanings of complex expressions containing the relevant verb. Therefore, one's knowledge of meaning won't be fully systematic. But if knowledge of language has unbounded productivity—there is no non-arbitrary finite limit to what expressions we can produce or understand—knowledge of meaning has to exhibit considerable systematicity properties (Fodor and Lepore, 2002). It could be replied that on Pustejovsky's decompositional view, knowledge of meaning would still be systematic and compositional in the sense that in all contexts, the same co-compositional processes can take place. However, assume the lexical decompositions of 'bake' or 'keep', whatever they may be, are given. Then the conceptual elements occurring in them (CAUSE, STAY, etc.) will either themselves be polysemous or not. If they are, then the lexical decomposition won't explain the intuitive *univocality* of the verb in question, or the fact that it is the 'same' lexical item in both kinds of contexts (unlike ambiguous words like *bank*). So suppose they are not polysemous. Then it is not clear why the verb in question is polysemous in the first place, and no explanation for its intuitive polysemy is needed (Fodor, 1998a: 50–2).

The irony here seems to be that the decompositional view only makes sense if there is, ultimately, no polysemy, and the abstract constituents of lexical decomposition—CAUSE, CREATE, BECOME, or whatever they may be—are atoms in the strictest sense, which are combined as such. When asked to tell what the meanings of these abstract atomic constituents of complex concepts are, we couldn't do better than to specify them purely denotationally: their meaning is given by their reference, and there is no more to say. Since avoiding this very move was among the motivations for adopting lexical decomposition, it is not clear how much we have gained. If a purely denotational semantics for abstract conceptual constituents is necessary, why could we not have adopted it in the first place for the surface words in question?

Having briefly zoomed into the polysemy discussion, let us zoom out of it again and instead return to verbal argument structure—though not before noting that the case for decomposition just reviewed again rests on decomposing the lexical atom *without* consulting an independently motivated syntax *first*: what we looked at was decomposition on a basically purely semantic motivation, a semantics not feeding from a syntactic source. Shortly (Section 16.4.3), we will turn this order of priorities around.

16.4.2 Argument-structure

Baker (1997), though a somewhat remote descendant of the generative semanticists, proposes a lexical decomposition of verbs motivated quite explicitly in semantic terms. Verb-internal syntactic structure is said to be supported by a (non-syntactic) 'conceptual structure' as provided in a 'lexical semantics' of the very sort Jackendoff proposes (e.g. Jackendoff, 2002: 337–9). Baker argues, specifically, that the *conceptual* structure in (16.4) rationalizes the *syntactic* structure in (16.5) (cf. Larson, 1988):

(16.4)   [X CAUSE [Y be/become PREDICATE]]

(16.5)

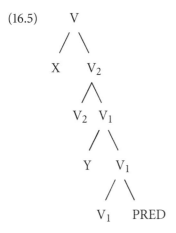

In (16.5), the agent argument, X, is the argument of the higher verb shell, V_2, while the Theme is the argument of the embedded one, V_1. Taking the articulated semantic structure in (16.4) to be independently given on semantic grounds—an assumption that may well strike one as circular, given that the structure of (16.4) is plainly syntactic itself—Baker writes:

> it is very attractive to identify the causative part of the lexical semantic representation [16.4] with the higher verb of the Larsonian shell, and the be/become+PREDICATE part with the lower verb position. (Baker, 1997: 123, see similarly Chomsky, 1995: 315–16)

Baker defends that 'syntactic structure is a projection of gross lexical semantic structure':

> On the semantic version of the Larsonian structure, the agent NP is not generated in the higher VP shell because there is no room for it in the lower VP; rather, it is generated there because it is the argument of a CAUSE verb (or configuration), and hence an agent by definition. (Baker, 1997: 124; see also Baker, 2003: 79–81)

In short, the Agent appears where it appears because *v* (or V₂ in our representation above) means CAUSE—the meaning, that is, of the English lexical word *cause*, a real constituent figuring as an interpretively relevant primitive in the underlying structure, on this view. Agents, by definition, are things that do such causing.

Uriagereka (2008: ch. 2), however, in a different context, asks how we know what *v* means. We cannot simply *intuit* what the sublexical constituents of verbs like *cut*, *roll*, or *laugh* are. The empirical syntactic evidence on the strength of which the existence of *v* can be made plausible is *not* also what supports this 'semantic version' of the Larsonian shell analysis. And what, in fact, does it show that some languages sport overt versions of *v*? On the face of it, *v* is not a word expressing CAUSE. Where it appears overtly (as in Japanese or even in English morphemes like *-ize*, as in *maximize*), it might be a mere syntactic formative that marks the transitivity of a causative verb, but does not as such carry a particular semantic interpretation—or not that of the English word *cause*.

Baker's proposal improves things in that it links a semantic decomposition with a plausible syntax, which is a very different enterprise from claiming that *food* means SUBSTANCE + ARTIFACT + EDIBLE + SOMETHING ELSE, say. But the improvement derived from replacing intuited conceptual structures by semantically relevant syntactic ones disappears once this kind of syntactic decomposition is again grounded in controversial lexical semantic decompositions. Thus, Baker argues that *laugh* really is a monadic predicate of events, meaning that laughter happened. Specifically, *John laughed* is said to mean that *John was the immediate cause of an instance of an event of laughter happening*. But this raises the old questions. Is John *causing*, in some literal sense, his laughter at all? And when, in general, is causation really 'immediate'? These are questions to be addressed if it is supposed to matter that *v* means CAUSE and its argument is a causer, in some determinate and conceptually defined sense.

16.4.3 Conceptual structure as syntax

Hale and Keyser (1993) is a particularly important contribution to the question of whether, and in what sense, conceptual structure *is* syntax, after all. In that case it would be nothing non-linguistic or 'thought'-like that is then somehow 'mapped' to syntax or 'coded' by it, as on the generative semantics picture. In the latter picture, as we saw, there is no D-structure component that provides linguistic constraints which the organization of conceptual structure has to adhere to. If conceptual structure is organized by *independent* principles, though, why would it be so tightly constrained? As Massimo Piattelli-Palmarini remarks (p.c.):

> by means of adjunctions we can optionally specify any 'thematic' information we want (source, composition, common/exceptional, effortless/effortful etc.) but the kind of mandatory information given by theta roles is fixed and universal, even when

more of the same kind can be recursively inserted. It's not too far fetched (though evidence is hard to be found) to imagine that some animal species can have some concepts of source, composition, effort etc. but the emergence of the machinery of language constrained this in us quite severely, making some conceptualizations mandatory and structurally fixed while others are optional and expressible only by means of adjunction.

This expresses well the fact that having concepts (if these are non-linguistic things) as such implies little for how they would be organized or constrained. We think that a typical transitive event must have an Agent and Theme, but it is equally true that it must have duration, say, or be either social or not. But these are not the kind of obligatorily specified 'thematic roles' that we find in human conceptual structure. It is not even clear why, in conceptual structure as viewed non-linguistically, there should be such a thing as an argument–adjunct *distinction*. If we witness an event of Bill killing a buffalo, say, clearly the buffalo is a salient element of the visual scene that we see. But this does not at all make it an argument as opposed to an adjunct, in the relevant syntactic senses of these words. Indeed, since this is a syntactically defined distinction, it is hard to see how it could originate in a non-syntactic 'conceptual structure'. A related concern is a structure like (16.6):

(16.6)   Bill loves

To the extent that this is grammatical and can be assigned an interpretation, it is likely to be interpreted to mean that Bill loves *someone*. What kind of constraint does this reflect? One answer is that it reflects a constraint at a syntactic level of representation, similar to the old D-structure level: there, one theta-role, that of the internal argument, is not discharged, and the Theta Criterion, according to which all arguments need to receive theta-roles and all theta-roles need to be discharged, is violated. Another answer is that (16.6) is grammatically well-formed, in fact, and the insertion of the object 'someone' follows from the semantics, or 'thought'. In that case, it is a *conceptual* constraint that derives the Theta Criterion. However, we don't know in this case why it should hold. Again, semantically, or conceptually, it is equally necessary that a loving event has duration. The constraint that this duration be specified is as predicted from 'conceptual structure', if the latter is viewed without linguistic prejudices, as the constraint that there is a beloved.[1] We feel that the existence of a direct object is somehow more necessary than the specification of duration. But *why* we have that intuition is precisely the question. It may restate a syntactic difference, between dependents that are 'selected' by the verb, and those that are not.

If we further assume that thematic roles that actually exist essentially reduce to three and that these biuniquely correspond to syntactic positions (Baker, 1997), a real and intriguing possibility arises, that crucial features of conceptual structure can actually be studied in syntactic terms. That is, the Agent–Theme–Goal roles are not primarily 'conceptual' notions, but inherently structural ones, which we simply like to express in

---

[1] Note also there is nothing *conceptually* impossible about most of the impossible verbs in (16.1), above. Language-independent semantics does not predict these facts.

fancy conceptual terms. Instead of 'Agent', say, we should talk more technically about 'Specifier of v'. If the reader wants to deny this, he or she might want to try to define what an Agent, say, is, without using sentences in which these Agents appear in specific structural positions. On this view, the fact that there is an argument–adjunct distinction relevant to conceptual structure derives from the accident of natural history that some adjuncts became fixed structural configurations in phrase structure, while others did not.

Hale and Keyser (1993) pursue this very idea: 'Argument structure is syntactic, necessarily, since it is to be identified with the syntactic structures projected by lexical heads' (Hale and Keyser, 1993: 55). On their view, moreover, the configurational position that an argument ends up in may be the result of syntactic processes that are subject to standard syntactic constraints such as locality—lending support to the inherently syntactic character of conceptual structures of the basic thematic kind, as well as to lexical decomposition, as we shall see. In this framework, theta-roles are theoretically redundant—it's not that they are not for real, but rather that they fall out from properties of the grammar.[2]

Hale and Keyser further make an explicit and bold proposal for *why* relations of lexical entailment obtain, viewed as entailment relations driven by linguistic form, hence 'analytic' ones, such as the entailment of (16.7b) by (16.7a):

(16.7)   a. Joe boiled the soup.
         b. The soup boiled.

Like Baker, above, they propose that the underlying structure of (16.7a) involves two verbal layers, the lower being the one we see isolated and separated from the higher one, in (16.7b). Each verbal layer correlates with an event. They note that the higher verbal head asymmetrically c-commands the lower verbal head, and propose:

> Corresponding to this syntactic relation, there is a similarly asymmetric (semantic) relation between the two events, a relation we will take to be that of *implication*. Accordingly, the matrix event 'implicates' the subordinate event . . ., a relation that makes perfect sense if the syntactic embedding corresponds to a 'semantic' composite in which the subordinate event is a proper part of the event denoted by the structure projected by the main [the light] verb. (Hale and Keyser, 1993: 68–9)

In other words, there is a direct mapping between the syntactic architecture of the biclausal structure of (16.7a) and its semantic structure, which has one event appearing as an inherent part of another: semantic relations are trivially mapped from syntactic ones (part–whole to part–whole, see Uriagereka (2008) on this). This is similar to, yet different from what we saw in Baker's case: there the semantics was more clearly in the driver's seat. Yet, there are problems, as we shall now see.

---

[2] This would explain a fact noted by Pietroski and Uriagereka (Uriagereka 2002: ch. 14): theta-roles are never a part of any natural object-language (they are not formatives in it): 'Theme', 'Agent', and 'Goal' become *formal* notions, following trivially from the structural architecture of the system itself.

16.5 A NEW TUNE

The 'correspondences' that Hale and Keyser posit are ultimately mere stipulations, or axioms, and as such they are not explained, natural as they may seem (indeed, this naturalness is what we need to explain).[3] We can identify three problems in particular. First, there should be something about the part–whole structure of our syntactic representations that justifies or motivates mapping them into the right part–whole relation in the semantic representation, without arbitrariness. Second, how would such mere correspondences make sense of the *necessity* of lexical entailments and paradigmatic regularities (as when propositions entail eventualities, events entail states, individuals entail masses, accomplishments entail achievements entail activities, etc.) (Hinzen and Uriagereka, 2006)? Third, in the last quote above the authors explicitly talk about *two* events. However, it is a prime moral of the famous counterexamples to the generative semanticists rehearsed in Section 16.2 that the denotation of a transitive causative verb crucially is a *single* event. Intuitively, there is *one* event—in two *parts*—that we talk about when we claim that *Anton boiled the soup*, not *two* events, and the question to ask is how we *derive* this very result. Something has to account for the fact that if there is internal structure in the lexical atom and a sentence is doubly headed by two verbs, ultimately these heads are interpreted as if they have 'fused'. Put differently, even if decomposition holds, atomism does, too.

A first step to a solution of these problems is a principled account of *why* the syntactic structures are the ones they are, independent of the semantic use to which we wish to put them. After that, we can try motivating these semantic uses as well. Hale and Keyser's later work can be understood as an attempt to carry out this first step. I present this idea here, not because I think the assumptions are necessarily correct, but to give an indication of how the relevant conceptual structures *could* follow from independently motivated structures in syntax—it's then the degree of this independent motivation one would need to discuss.

Let us assume that heads can, though need not, take both complements and specifiers, and that all possible argument structures must be structurally unambiguous, in the sense that there is always one head and at most one complement in a binary branching structure. Then we predict that we will firstly find argument structures that consist of a head alone, secondly structures that consist of a head and a complement alone,

---

[3] Neo-Davidsonian lexical decomposition, which I can't tackle here for reasons of space, arguably face similar explanatory problems and the syntax-to-semantics mapping is equally unmotivated, ultimately. 'Auxiliary assumptions' need to be introduced, to get it right: such that the two event variables introduced by the two verbal components of a complex event are identified and become the same event (though in two phases). Similarly, where arguments are assimilated to adjuncts and sentences are predicates of events joined by logical conjunctions (as per Pietroski, 2005), the right kind of part–whole relations cannot emerge in a natural way. Conjunction is a flat relation, inept to capture 'hierarchical' relations like that obtaining between an achievement and the resultant state that is achieved (see Uriagereka, 2008, ch. 2, on these matters)

and thirdly ones which consist of a head and a complement and a specifier. The first configuration is paradigmatically realized in English by nouns (H = head):

(16.8)   a. H   e.g.: *trouble*

The second is a pattern of the form H-XP, paradigmatically realized in English by the category, V:

(16.8)   b.   H
              / \   e.g. : [$_V$*make trouble*]
             H XP

The third is a structure YP-[H-XP], canonically realized in English by prepositions. This configuration we may view, more generally, as being organized around a 'relational' head, R, whose complement can also be an adjective, A:

(16.8)   c.   H
              / \
             Y H   e.g.: (pound) [$_P$*the nails*] [$_P$*into* [$_{NP}$*the wall*]]];
                / \   (make) [$_R$ *the leaves*] [$_R$*turn* [$_A$*red*]]]
               H X/H

The latter case also realizes the fourth a priori possibility, that we have a head and a specifier alone, for this is precisely what adjectives in this system are: heads requiring a specifier (though they need a mediating head to take one).

   Finally, there should be a 'free' option of *combining* the previous lexical representation structures (though not necessarily recursively). In particular, if we plug the third configuration (16.8c) as a whole into the complement position of the second (16.8b), we obtain the doubly-headed configuration $H_1 - [Y - [H_2 - X/A]]$, in which the specifier of the lower head (H_2), that is Y, has now become the object of the higher head H_1:

(16.9) H_1
          / \
        H_1 H_2
              / \   e.g. : [$_V$*pound* [$_P$*the nails*] [$_P$*into*[*the wall*]]]]
            Y H_2 [$_{V2}$*make* [$_{V1}$*the leaves*] [$_{V1}$*turn* [*red*]]]]
              / \
           H_2 X/H

If these are the only lexical argument structures that can be projected under the restrictive assumptions provided, we can make principled sense of restrictions in argument structure that we empirically observe.[4] Note further that the process of building argument-structure that we have described is structurally very specific, and contains

---

[4] Interestingly, these lexical conceptual structures exclude the external argument (EA), which Hale and Keyser, with Koopman and Sportiche (1991), take to be an adjunct to the full verbal projection: it

linguistically-specific terms, such as complement and specifier, predication, verb, and argument. It is hard to see how the same structures, with the same necessary syntactic relations, might be fabricated in a 'parallel' computational system which lacked all of these syntactically specific elements, yet would be subject to the same empirically observable restrictions on argument-structure configurations. It is not clear at all what it should be in the non-linguistic (semantic, visual, sensorimotor, etc.) domain that would account for similar such severe limitations on which thoughts we can think in the initial D-structural phase of a syntactic derivation. It therefore appears to be a sensible conclusion that these configurations in fact constrain how we can think about events in our experience, at least as long as we use arguments rather than adjuncts (or else mere associations) to do so. Put differently, syntax creates an ontology.

Conflation (Hale and Keyser, 2002) arises when the upper verbal head in a structure like (16.9) is phonologically empty at the level of lexical syntax. Empty phonological matrices of this kind are not possible at the level of sentences, so they trigger a process of fusion, which *supplies* the phonological matrix needed by taking it from the lower lexical head. This leads to the 'surface form' of, for example, (16.10), where the surface form *turn* is the conflation of the two verbal heads in (16.9):

(16.10)   The autumn turned the leaves red

In a bare phrase structure framework (Chomsky, 1995), this process will always go from the direct complement of the selecting higher head V_1 to this very head, and be strictly local. Specifically, on the theory of labelling of Chomsky (1995), at the point in the derivation where V_2 merges with the configuration projected by V_1, the lower head V_2 is strictly all that the computational system (i.e. Merge) 'sees': it represents all the information that is syntactically relevant about the lower event. If V_2 is then conflated, we obtain forms like (16.11) derived through a sequence of conflations in strictly local head-complement relations:

(16.11)   The autumn reddened the leaves.

First of the adjective conflates into V_2, then the conflated V_2 merges with the empty upper V_1. NPs may conflate too, as in intuitively denominal verbs such as (16.12):

(16.12)   a. *bag, bank, bottle, can, shelve,* etc.
            b. *bandage, bar, butter, saddle, spice,* etc.

The NP, for example *shelf*, conflates with the empty head P, which projects, and in turn conflates with the V, to yield the surface structure *shelve the books*:[5]

---

occupies no complement or specifier position within that lexical projection. More specifically, EA and *v*P are adjoined in a Small Clause relation, which arguably conceptually expresses a predication (Moro, 2000). The EA thus ends up as a sentence-syntactic subject in a way that is still enforced by principles of lexical projection: a fully specified *v*P with internal arguments specified is intrinsically a predicate, which as such, if Full Interpretation holds, requires a subject.

[5] I assume, following Uriagereka (2008: ch. 2), that contrary to what Hale and Keyser themselves propose the lexical representation structures for (16.12a) and (16.12b) are identical, on the lines of (16.13).

(16.13)

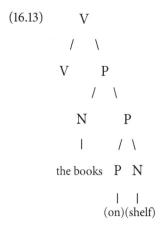

Semantically, the default relational head P corresponds to a relation of 'coincidence': the books undergo a path of motion which ends with books being *on* the shelf (the saddle on the horse, the butter on the bread, etc.), which is their terminal location. What will interest us in the rest of this chapter is the role of conflation in the syntax–semantics 'correspondences' discussed above.

One immediate answer might be: none. That would be so if the synthetic forms of these derived verbs are neither syntactically nor semantically different from their analytic counterparts in (16.14):

(16.14)   a. put the books on the shelf
           b. put the saddle on the horse

Hale and Keyser themselves are as explicit as one would like that conflation is a purely morpho-phonological process that is semantically inert. The shift of the phonetic signature of the conflated items is invisible to the syntax, to which phonetic signatures are 'irrelevant': 'conflation leaves the entire structure intact, unchanged, in respect to syntactic and semantic structure' (Hale and Keyser, 2002: 70). But this, if we wish to avoid the pitfalls of generative semantics, is precisely the conclusion we have to avoid. Sublexical syntactic structure is precisely not, at least in the general case, transparent to the overt sentential syntax and subject to a compositional interpretation. The fusion of heads therefore *has* to have a crucial semantic consequence. Let us say that it creates what is in effect a novel *name* for a more complex event than we had before, a new lexical item. This would fundamentally cohere with the fact that denominal verbs are strictly *lexical* ones in this theory: they are *words* listed in the lexicon which have to be *learned*. Every lexical item, indeed, has features of a name: taken on its own, it doesn't describe anything and it doesn't quantify over what it denotes: syntax is needed for any of this. So they irreducibly 'name' their denotation, hence rigidly, given their absence of descriptive and quantificational potential. This is almost, but not quite, what Hale and Keyser say:

> In reality, all verbs are to some extent phrasal idioms, that is, syntactic structures that must be learned as the conventional 'names' for various dynamic events. (Hale and Keyser, 1993: 96; see also Marantz, 1996)

On the other hand, idioms also have systematic and compositional aspects. McGinnis (2002) in particular argues that the Aspect of idioms behaves completely systematically: it is their encyclopedic content which is 'atomic', 'encapsulated', or 'opaque'. We therefore need something stronger than the creation of an idiomatic name to truly eradicate phrasal complexity in a conflated verb. Conflation *must* have a semantic potential.

Suppose it did. Then we now arrive at a view where semantic atomicity and syntactic complexity ('being derived') are not mutually exclusive. Syntax gives us a semantically and compositionally interpreted structure internal to the atom by providing the relevant configurations; and it is syntax again, through the device of creating a name, which makes this internal structure inaccessible to semantic interpretation. The atomist is thus deeply right, but so is the decompositionalist. We have an answer to the atomist's charge that decomposition at a purely semantic level is unreal: if there is something like the creation of a new meaning through the creation of a name that can denote it, syntax and semantics align again. Moreover, we give the following answer to the Fodorian atomist query why all of our 'derived' concepts could not simply be primitives: because then, we say, we wouldn't have a systematic theory of concepts at all from which data about possible and impossible concepts derive. 'Impossible word' facts would remain where they were (cf. Johnson, 2004*b*: 339–43). That result, admittedly, depends on how principled our derivation of possible argument structure configurations above really was, and that is an issue for the theory of syntax: but explaining the restrictions of syntax is a task on anyone's account.

16.6 EXPLODING THE LEXICAL ATOM

For all that, interesting problems remain. An event of Jack's boiling the soup entails an event of the soup's boiling, an event of shelving books entails a state of the books being 'on' the shelf, etc. We wanted to *explain* these entailments, as conceptually *necessary* ones. Neither the earlier 'correspondences' *nor* the creation of lexical 'names' in the sense above, however, in fact give us quite what is needed. If lexical items do not have internal structure that is semantically visible, because they are names, what can now explain these entailments? We can't have it both ways: If we say that creating a name eradicates an underlying compositional semantic structure, we can't also appeal to that underlying structure to explain a name's lexical entailments. Somehow, either atomicity or complexity has to go. And yet the problem is: none of them may.

I shall finish with a highly speculative suggestion for how a solution to this problem is *conceptually possible*, and perhaps even necessary (see further Hinzen and Uriagereka, 2006). The question, recall, is what makes it happen that a separate verbal head that by itself conceptually or semantically expresses, say, a state, comes to specify an inherent (final) *part* of another event, instead of denoting a separate event all by itself. If this is to follow in a motivated way from the nature of the syntactic representations involved, what must these representations be formally like?

Uriagereka (1995) answers that they must be *multi-dimensional*. Although creating a name won't turn the trick of generating a necessary entailment between any two such names, this stops to be so the moment that these names are generated at different layers of a multi-dimensional conceptual edifice. Suppose that (i) the syntactic processor can create lexical concepts at different such layers, (ii) the layers are 'recursively' built so as to asymmetrically entail or contain one another in virtue of their intrinsic architecture, and (iii) infants start out as lexical decompositionalists while settling eventually on a systems of names that can denote objects at different layers of this conceptual hierarchy: *then* subevent entailments will become conceptually possible, and indeed necessary, on purely formal grounds, or by the architecture of the system itself (see Uriagereka, 1995, 2002; Hinzen and Uriagereka, 2006; Hinzen, 2009).

In a standard vector space, the algebraic dimension of a space is the number of independent variables needed to specify the elements in that space; this number is also the number of vectors in the space's 'basis'. Thus, for example, the natural number line is a mathematical object that has dimensionality one, as a single vector suffices to generate all objects on the line by scalar multiplication. Higher-dimensional objects may now be further built on the basis of lower-dimensional ones. Thus, for example, while the space of the naturals is linearly generated from a single vector, the whole numbers are generated from the naturals by defining a null element and applying an inverse operation (subtraction). The rationals, in turn, are generated by applying inverse functions to the whole numbers (divisions), while the real numbers are generated by applying inverse functions to the rationals, and so on for the complex and hyper-complex numbers. In a geometric interpretation of these hierarchical entailments, higher-dimensional spaces entail lower-dimensional ones as parts in the purely formal or architectural way above, much as (and as necessarily as) the earth (qua planet) contains a two-dimensional surface, which in turn contains geodesic lines. A planet thus has a 'compositional' structure of sorts, but the notion of compositionality or part–whole structure involved, being dimensional, is not the one we are used to when we decompose the meaning of a whole sentence into the sum of its parts: the independent meanings of all syntactic constituents and a minimal way of relating them structurally (for example mere conjunction, on the model of Pietroski, 2005, or Merge, on the model of Chomsky, 1995, 2008). Syntactic combinatorial complexity may not merely be a linear progression of a sequence of the same objects but involve 'jumps' in representational complexity, with asymmetric entailments following from the operations recursively applied to lower-dimensional objects.

Our problem above, how a lexical item newly created in the course of a conflation process can engender a necessary asymmetric entailment would then be solved: language would have, in addition to its linear aspect (which is captured by Merge in minimalist syntax), a hierarchical (or non-linear) one as well. Two lexical 'names' that entail each other could do so (and do so necessarily) by being generated in different algebraic dimensions that are recursively constructed. But this requires a syntax that does not merely and arbitrarily merge syntactic objects, all in the same dimension, like the natural numbers, as in Chomsky (2008). Ultimately, indeed, it *has* to generate categorial hierarchies as well, with the associated entailments, if nothing else in the linguistic system does.

The claim here is that this solution is of the right *form* to solve the problem we started with, and I don't know of any other way, if we ultimately want to accommodate the insights of both the atomists and decompositionalists. Only in this way can we generate the standard syntagmatic regularities as much as the vertical ones, with the same syntactic principles operative in both domains. This effectively upgrades syntax into a cognitive theory, a theory of (possible) human concepts—which is lacking in the essentially metaphysical theory of concepts that the atomist offers (Fodor, 1998a: chs 6–7). The reason that the vertical and horizontal syntactic systems differ, as the atomist notes, does not lie in how they operate, but when the naming device, however it works, kicks in. As Uriagereka (2008) notes, children become lexical atomists only late on their path of acquisition, while behaving as decompositionalists before: the two systems, sub- and supra-lexical syntax, develop in the organism (or get expressed) at different rates: argument structure configurations may 'crystallize' as lexical names only at later stages, having been architecturally transparent to the child's mind before. It takes *time* for a word to become, truly, an atom.

16.7 CONCLUSIONS

We began from semantically motivated lexical decompositions that prioritize a philosophical abstraction, 'thought', over the concrete syntactic forms of language that we can see and empirically study in the world's languages. Fundamental empirical and methodological problems ensue. Nonetheless, paradigmatic regularities and impossible word facts motivating the decompositions in question have to be accounted for. As theoretical frameworks tackling these questions obtained a more syntactic spin, more principled decompositional theories with real explanatory potential were proposed. In particular, if internally complex lexical items function syntactically as names, the fact that their internal structure generates no compositional semantic interpretations is explained. Yet, paradigmatic regularities will not be. Also that problem can be solved if we allow a departure from a model of syntax that views the algebra of syntax as maximally simple—too simple for lexical entailments to arise. There are no empirical reasons why syntax cannot be formally multidimensional, in such a way that an object denoted by a lexical 'name' in one dimension may inherently entail another object located at a lower dimension, since the latter is a part of the former and inherent to its form of internal complexity. In that case there *is* something about the part–whole structure of our standard syntactic representations that justifies mapping them into a part–whole relation in the semantic representation, without arbitrariness: for a causative verb is not merely generated higher in the syntactic tree than verbs denoting mere states (or results); they are generated in a different syntactic dimension. Now an event, denoted by a name, can contain a state, denoted by another name, in the same way in which a sphere necessarily contains a surface, or a complex number necessarily contains a real.[6]

[6] I wish to thank Heidi Harley and an anonymous referee for generous comments on an early draft. Funding from the following grants, which enabled this research, is gratefully acknowledged: 'The Origins of Truth' (NWO 360-20-150) and 'Un-Cartesian Linguistics' (AHRC/DFG, AH/H50009X/1).

....

CHAPTER 17

CO-COMPOSITIONALITY
IN GRAMMAR

....

JAMES PUSTEJOVSKY

17.1 BASIC MECHANISMS OF SELECTION

....

Co-compositionality is a semantic property of a linguistic expression in which all constituents contribute functionally to the meaning of the entire expression. As a result, it extends the conventional definition of compositionality. The principle of compositionality in linguistics (cf. Janssen, 1983; Thomason, 1974a) and in philosophy (cf. Werning, 2004) involves the notion that the meanings of complex symbols are systematically determined by the composition of their component parts. In order to understand the theoretical motivation behind the theory of co-compositionality, it is necessary to understand where conventional theories of compositionality are unable to explain the meaning of certain natural language constructions. Since these issues are addressed in more detail by other chapters in this Handbook (non-compositionality), the present chapter will focus on the role that compositionality plays in mapping from the lexicon to syntactic form.

At the outset, it should be stated that co-compositonality is not the result of a failure of compositionality, and hence to be viewed as involving non-compositional processes. Rather, as the name would suggest, it entails at least conventional compositional mechanisms for the expressions involved, along with additional interpretive mechanisms not always exploited within a phrasal composition. In order to understand what these are, we first review conventional modes of argument selection in language.

While it is impossible to say how many meanings we create for a particular word in normal language use, we can reasonably ask how many meanings we have stored for that word in our mental lexicon. This is where linguists differ broadly in assigning responsibility for whether meaning shifts occur at all and, if so, how. As a result of this divide, the role that compositionality plays in structuring not only the grammar but also the lexicon is significant.

For example, in conventional models of language meaning, a verb is thought to have several different word senses. For each sense, the verb acts on its parameters (its arguments in syntax) in a compositional manner. This means that the semantics of the result of application of the verbal function to its argument is determined by the semantics of the function itself, a process referred to as *function application*. Consider, for example, the way in which the verbs *throw* and *kill* each have several distinct senses.

(17.1)   a. Mary threw the ball to John. (PROPEL)
        b. They threw a party for Bill. (ORGANIZE)
        c. Mary threw breakfast together quickly. (CREATE)

The use of *throw* in each sentence above illustrates a true verbal ambiguity, one that requires separate senses, each with specific subcategorization and semantic selection as illustrated. Likewise, the verb *kill* as used in (17.2c) below, demonstrates a systematic sense distinction as well.

(17.2)   a. John killed the plant.
        b. Mary killed the conversation.
        c. John killed the evening watching TV.

As with the verb *throw*, each of these senses has a regular and productive distribution in the language, exemplified below.

(17.3)   a. Mary killed the fish.
        b. The President killed any attempt at dialogue with Cuba.
        c. John killed the day reading.

Verb senses like these are distinct, semantic units, perhaps related to each other, but stored separately in the lexicon. Because they have distinct subcategorization and type selection frames, the semantic computation involving these senses in the syntax can be performed compositionally.

These examples with the verbs *throw* and *kill* illustrate that lexical forms may be truly ambiguous, and as such, can be modelled adequately by a sense enumerative lexical (SEL) model (cf. Pustejovsky, 1995). In such a model, each sense of a word, as in (17.2) above, would be strongly typed, illustrated in (17.4) below, where the intended sense is glossed as a relation with its appropriate argument types.

(17.4)   a. kill_1: CAUSE-TO-DIE(THING, ANIMATE)
        b. kill_2: TERMINATE(HUMAN, EVENT)
        c. kill_3: SPEND(HUMAN, TIME, EVENT)

Given distinct lexical types for these three senses of *kill*, compositional mechanisms in the semantics can compute the sentences in (17.2) as cases of function application. For this particular example, *function application* assumes that the verb *kill* applies to its arguments in discrete steps. For example, consider the derivation of (17.2) as a sequence of function applications, simplifying the arguments (HUMAN, TIME, EVENT) from (17.4) as numbered variables.

(17.5)   a. John killed the day reading.
   b. *kill*(Arg_1, Arg_2, Arg_3)
   c. Apply *kill*(Arg_1, Arg_2, Arg_3) to 'reading'
    $\Longrightarrow$ *kill*($Arg_1, Arg_2, [reading]$)
   d. Apply *kill*($Arg_1, Arg_2, [reading]$) to 'the day'
    $\Longrightarrow$ *kill*($Arg_1, [day], [reading]$)
   e. Apply *kill*($Arg_1, [day], [reading]$) to 'John'
    $\Longrightarrow$ *kill*($john, [day], [reading]$)

This derivation has a successful computation because the verb sense for *kill* selected in (17.5) has the appropriate typing. If we had tried using the type associated with kill-2, the sentence would not have an interpretation. As we see, compositional operations reflect the ontological and lexical design decisions made in the grammar.

 Treating the functional behaviour of composition formally, we can state this procedure as an operation over the types of expressions involved, as expressed in (17.6):

(17.6)   Function Application (FA):
   If a is of type a, and β is of type $a \rightarrow b$, then $\beta(a)$ is of type b.

Returning to the example derivation in (17.5), we can see FA at work on the last application step in (17.5e), where e stands for any of the specific types mentioned earlier (e.g. THING, HUMAN, TIME, EVENT) and t stands for the propositional type.

(17.7)   a. *kill*($Arg_1, [day], [reading]$) is of type $e \rightarrow t$;
   b. *john* is of type e;
   c. FA results in applying $e \rightarrow t$ to e;
    $\Longrightarrow$ *kill*($[john], [day], [reading]$), of type t, i.e., a sentence.

Hence, by enumerating separate senses for ambiguous predicates, we can ensure strong (unique) typing on the arguments expected by a verb (function), and thereby maintain compositionality within these constructions.

 If function application as described above were inviolable, then we would not expect to encounter examples of type mismatch between verb and argument. But, of course, such data are ubiquitous in language, and involve a process characterized as *type coercion* (Pustejovsky, 1995; Copestake and Briscoe, 1995; Partee and Rooth, 1983). This is an operation that allows an argument to change its type, if it does not match the type requested by the verb. For example, for one of its senses, the aspectual verb *begin* selects for an event as its internal argument:

(17.8)   Mary began [reading the book]*event*.

The same sense is used, however, when *begin* selects for a simple NP direct object, as in (17.9).

(17.9)   Mary began [the book]*event*.

In such configurations, the verb is said to 'coerce' the NP argument into an event interpretation (cf. Pustejovsky, 1991a, 1995). Under such an analysis, the NP actually denotes
a salient event that involves the book in some way, for example reading it, writing it,
and so on. This is schematically represented below, where the NP *the book* has been
reinterpreted through coercion, as some relation, R, involving the book.

(17.10)

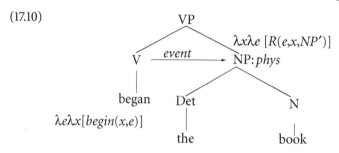

Our knowledge of the world associates conventional activities, such as reading and
writing, with books. This knowledge can be lexically encoded through the use of *Qualia
Structure* (Pustejovsky, 1995), thereby providing a mechanism for preserving compositionality in the construction above. In Generative Lexicon Theory (Pustejovsky, 1995), it
is assumed that word meaning is structured on the basis of four generative factors (the
qualia roles) that capture how humans understand objects and relations in the world and
provide the minimal explanation for the linguistic behaviour of lexical items (these are
inspired in large part by Moravcsik's (1975, 1990) interpretation of Aristotelian *aitia*).
These are: the FORMAL role: the basic category that distinguishes the object within a
larger domain; CONSTITUTIVE role: the relation between an object and its constituent
parts; the TELIC role: its purpose and function; and the AGENTIVE role: factors involved
in the object's origin or 'coming into being'. Qualia structure is at the core of the generative properties of the lexicon, since it provides a general strategy for creating new
types.

   The qualia act as type shifting operators, that can allow an expression to satisfy new
typing environments. Every expression, a, has some set of operators available to it,
that provide such type shifting behaviour. Let us refer to this set as Σ_a. Then we can
characterize function application under such conditions as follows:

(17.11)   Function Application with Coercion (FA$_c$):
          If α is of type c, and β is of type $a \rightarrow b$, then,

          (i) if type $c = a$ then $\beta(a)$ is of type b.
          (ii) if there is a $\sigma \in \Sigma_a$ such that $\sigma(a)$ results in an expression of type a, then
               $\beta(\sigma(a))$ is of type b.
          (iii) otherwise a type error is produced.

Such phenomena are quite common in language, and when viewed as a lexically-
triggered operation, coercion allows us to maintain a compositional treatment of argument selection in the grammar.

17.2 CO-COMPOSITIONAL MECHANISMS

With the additional mechanism of function application with coercion (FA_c), we are able to account for a larger range of data that would otherwise not have been modelled as compositional in nature. But there are many constructions in language which appear to be outside the scope of conventional compositional operations. In this section, we see how these can be analysed co-compositionally.

As stated above, co-compositionality is a semantic property of a linguistic expression in which all constituents contribute functionally to the meaning of the entire expression. As with compositionality, the notion of co-compositionality is a characterization of how a system constructs the meaning from component parts. It is a mistake to think that an expression in a language is inherently co-compositional or compositional. Rather, it is the set of computations within a specific system that should be characterized as co-compositional for those expressions. To make this distinction clear, consider the verb *run* as it is used in the contexts of (17.12)–(17.13) below.

(17.12)   a. John ran.
          b. John ran for twenty minutes.
          c. John ran two miles.

(17.13)   a. John ran to the store.
          b. John ran the race.

There are two senses of *run* that emerge in context with these examples:

(17.14)   a. run-1: manner-of-motion activity, as used in (17.12);
          b. run-2: change-of-location transition, as used in (17.13);

We can choose to design our semantics and the accompanying lexicon for these cases according to the null hypothesis, and create separate senses, as illustrated in (17.14). With two separate entries, they will select differently because they will have different types and argument structures. In this case, we say that the data are accounted for compositionally through sense enumeration. What is left unexplained, however, is any logical relation between the senses, a major drawback; this can be overcome, however, with lexical rules that explicitly specify this relationship as a redundancy rule or meaning postulate.

Similar remarks hold for verbs such as *wax* and *wipe* in (17.15)–(17.16), which are contextually ambiguous between a process reading and a transition reading, depending on the presence of a resultative adjectival. Normally, lexicons would have to enter both forms as separate lexical entries (cf. Levin and Rappaport, 1995).

(17.15)   a. Mary *waxed* the car.
          b. Mary *waxed* the car clean.

(17.16)   a. John *wiped* the counter.
        b. John *wiped* the counter dry.

Clearly, the local context is supplying additional information to the meaning of the predicate that is not inherently part of the verb's meaning; namely, the completive aspect that inheres in the resultative constructions (cf. Goldberg, 1995; Jackendoff, 2002).

    A related phenomenon of extended word sense in context is what Atkins et al. (1988) refer to as 'overlapping senses', and it is exhibited by cooking verbs such as *bake, fry*, as well as by activities such as *carve*, shown below.

(17.17)   a. John *baked* the potato.
        b. John *baked* the cake.

(17.18)   a. Mary *fried* an egg.
        b. Mary *fried* an omelette.

(17.19)   a. John *carved* the stick.
        b. John *carved* a statue.

These examples illustrate that strict lexical typing (preserving compositionality) does not explain when and how verb senses will overlap or be en tailed by another sense. Clearly, something is not being captured by the semantic theory with such data. The notion of co-compositionality was introduced to characterize just this type of phenomenon (cf. Pustejovsky, 1991, 1995), In particular, this construction has been referred to as *co-specification*, since the argument being selected by the predicate, seems to have a semantic familiarity with the predicate, and hence, *specifies* the governing predicate.

    Informally, we can view co-compositionality as the introduction of new information to an expression by the argument, beyond what it contributes as an argument to the function within the phrase. Hence, it can be considered an *ampliative* operation, relative to the function application. Returning to the examples considered above, let us see how this characterization fits the data. First, consider the shift from the process interpretation of *run* to the accomplishment sense in (17.12)–(17.13). The sense of the verb *run* in (17.13b) clearly overlaps (indeed, it entails) the sense exploited in (17.12a). We say that the NP *the race* in (17.13b) co-specifies the predicate selecting it, repeated below in (17.20).

(17.20)   John ran the race.

The semantic composition results in an interpretation entailing the activity of running, which is either quantified by a measure phrase with a specific distance (as in (17.12c) with *two miles*), or entails the completion of a specific course or event (as in (17.20) with *the race*).

    With the verbs *wax* and *wipe*, similar extensions to the basic meaning are at play in (17.15b) and (17.16b). What is still unclear is how the extended meaning is first licensed and then how it is computed formally through compositional mechanisms.

To better understand the mechanisms involved in the ampliative interpretations that result in such constructions, we examine the relationship between the core and derived senses of the verb *bake*, as presented above in (17.17). In the context of particular objects, the verb *bake* assumes the interpretation of a *creation* predicate, while with other objects, it maintains the underlying *change-of-state* predicate meaning. Certain NPs are said to *co-specify* the verb selecting it, as does the noun *cake* in its agentive qualia value. That is, the type structure for *cake* references the predicate selecting it as an argument. With this, the activity of baking assumes a resultative interpretation when combined with co-specifying arguments.

Assume that the lexical semantics for the change-of-state sense of *bake* is given as in (17.21), where the qualia roles are abbreviated as F (Formal), C (Constitutive), T (Telic), and A (Agentive).

$$
(17.21) \quad \lambda y \lambda x \lambda e
\begin{bmatrix}
\text{bake} \\
\text{AS} = \begin{bmatrix} \text{A1} = x : phys \\ \text{A2} = y : phys \end{bmatrix} \quad \text{ES} = \begin{bmatrix} \text{E1} = e : process \end{bmatrix} \\
\text{QS} = \begin{bmatrix} \text{A} = bake\_act(e, x, y) \end{bmatrix}
\end{bmatrix}
$$

The lexical representation for an artifactual concept such as the noun *cake* is shown below in (17.22).

$$
(17.22) \quad \lambda x \exists y
\begin{bmatrix}
\text{cake} \\
\text{AS} = \begin{bmatrix} \text{ARG1} = x : phys \\ \text{D-ARG1} = y : mass \end{bmatrix} \quad \text{QS} = \begin{bmatrix} \text{F} = cake(x) \\ \text{C} = made\_of(x, y) \\ \text{T} = \lambda z, e[eat(e, z, x)] \\ \text{A} = \exists w, e[bake(e, w, y)] \end{bmatrix}
\end{bmatrix}
$$

Notice that the Agentive qualia value for the noun *cake* makes reference to the very process within which it is embedded in the sentence in (17.17) (i.e. *bake a cake*), which is a case of co-specification.

We now define the conditions under which the derivation of an expression is said to be *co-compositional*. Ignoring the event structure for discussion, according to the type structure for the predicate *bake*, function application, as defined above, applies as expected to its argument *a cake*.[1] But the direct object co-specifies the verb selecting it,

---

[1] We also ignore the type shifting involved for the predicate to take the generalized quantifier *a cake* as its argument. For discussion, we assume the indefinite is treated as a discourse variable denoting an individual type.

since its type structure makes reference to the governing verb, *bake*. This is illustrated graphically in (17.23).

(17.23)

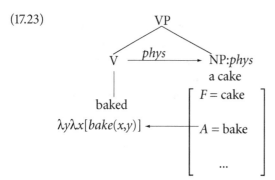

From the underlying process *change-of-state* sense of *bake*, the *creation* sense emerges when combined with the triggering NP *a cake*. This results in a logical form such as that shown in (17.24).

(17.24) $\exists e_1 \exists e_2 \exists x \exists y [bake(e_1, j, y) \wedge cake(e_2, x) \wedge made\_of(x, y) \wedge e_1 \leq e_2]$

The operation of co-composition results in a qualia structure for the VP that reflects aspects of both constituents. These include:

1. the governing verb *bake* applies to its complement;
2. the complement co-specifies the verb;
3. the composition of qualia structures results in a derived sense of the verb, where the verbal and complement AGENTIVE roles match, and the complement FORMAL quale becomes the FORMAL role for the entire VP.

The derived sense is computed from an operation called *qualia unification*, introduced in Pustejovsky (1995). The conditions under which this operation can apply are stated in (17.25) below:

(17.25)   FUNCTION APPLICATION WITH QUALIA UNIFICATION: For two expressions, α, of type <a, b>, and β, of type a, with qualia structures QS_α and QS_β, respectively, then, if there is a quale value shared by α and β, $[_{QS_\alpha} \ldots [Q_i = \gamma]]$ and $[_{QS_\beta} \ldots [Q_i = \gamma]]$, then we can define the qualia unification of QS_α and QS_β, $QS_\alpha \sqcap QS_\beta$, as the unique greatest lower bound of these two qualia structures. Further, $\alpha(\beta)$ is of type b with $QS_{\alpha(\beta)} = QS_\alpha \sqcap QS_\beta$.

The composition in (17.23) can be illustrated schematically in (17.26) below.

(17.26) $\begin{bmatrix} V A = bake \end{bmatrix} \sqcap \begin{bmatrix} NP \begin{matrix} F = cake \\ A = bake \end{matrix} \end{bmatrix} = \begin{bmatrix} VP \begin{matrix} F = cake \\ A = bake \end{matrix} \end{bmatrix}$

17.3 FURTHER EXTENSIONS
OF CO-COMPOSITION

Further examination of the derivation above suggests that co-composition involves a more general process, where conventional function application from an anchor function (e.g. the governing verb), is supplemented with ampliative information supplied by a triggering argument type. These properties can be summarized as follows in (17.27).

(17.27)   Properties of Co-compositional Derivations:

    a. Within an expression, α, consisting of two subexpressions, α_1 and α_2, i.e., $[_\alpha\ \alpha_1\ \alpha_2]$, one of the subexpressions is an *anchor* that acts as the primary functor;

    b. Within the argument expression, there is explicit reference to the anchor or the anchor's type (i.e., the complement co-specifies the functor);

    c. The composition of lexical structures results in a derived sense of the functor, within α.

This can be formalized as follows:

(17.28)   Co-compositionality:

    a. The derivation for an expression α, is *co-compositional* with respective to its constituent elements, α_1 and α_2, if and only if one of α_1 or α_2 applies to the other, $\alpha_i(\alpha_j)$, $i \neq j$, and $\beta_j(\alpha_i)$, for some type structure β_j within the type of α_j, i.e., $\beta_j \sqsubseteq type(\alpha_j)$.

    b. $[\![\alpha]\!] = \alpha_i(\alpha_j) \sqcap \beta_j(\alpha_i)$.

For the example at hand, the overall expression α is *bake a cake*. The anchor functional term is the verb *bake* (α_1), and the ampliative interpretation comes from the Agentive Qualia value for the NP (β_j). Given this formulation of co-composition, it is now clear when co-composition is licensed. If any component of the type of the argument in a construction makes reference to the anchor functional term in a construction, then co-composition should be permitted. This is, in fact, what we see in all the cases of co-specification we encountered above.

With the more general characterization of composition given above, we can now analyse a number of constructions as co-compositional in nature. These include, among others, subject-derived agentive interpretations (*subject-induced coercion*) and certain light verb constructions, for example *functionally dependent verbs*. For example, it has long been noted that certain classes of predicates select for non-agentive subjects, but allow agentive interpretations in the appropriate context, as illustrated in the examples below (cf. Wechsler, 1995).

(17.29)   a. The storm killed the deer.

    b. An angry rioter killed a policeman.

(17.30)   a. The glass touched the painting.
          b. The curious child touched the painting.

(17.31)   a. The ball rolled down the hill.
          b. John rolled down the hill as fast as he could.

(17.32)   a. The room cooled off quickly.
          b. John cooled off with an iced latte.

We will refer to these as *subject-induced coercions*, since, in each of these pairs, the subject in the (b)-sentence introduces agency or intentionality towards the predicated event. Rather than suggesting that each of these verbs is ambiguous between agentive/non-agentive readings, we can view the computation in the (b)-sentences as co-compositional, where an agentive subject introduces the appropriate intentional component to the interpretation of the VP. For the present discussion, let us characterize 'agency', in terms of Qualia Structure, as referring to the potential to act towards a goal. For a cognitive agent, such as a *human*, this amounts to associating a set of particular activities, $\mathcal{A}$, as the value of the Agentive role, and a set of goals, $\mathcal{G}$, associated with the Telic role in the Qualia for that concept, as illustrated below in (17.33).

$$(17.33)\quad \lambda x \begin{bmatrix} \text{human\_agent} \\ \text{QS} = \begin{bmatrix} \text{F} = human(x) \\ \text{T} = \lambda e'[\mathcal{G}(e',x)] \\ \text{A} = \lambda e[\mathcal{A}(e,x)] \end{bmatrix} \end{bmatrix}$$

Consider how this composition is instantiated for the subject-induced coercion in (17.29b). Causative verbs such as *kill* denote transitions from one state to a resulting state, by virtue of a causing event. This can be represented as the lexical structure given in (17.34).

$$(17.34)\quad \lambda y \lambda x \lambda e_2 \lambda e_1 \begin{bmatrix} \text{kill} \\ \text{AS} = \begin{bmatrix} \text{A1} = x : phys \\ \text{A2} = y : phys \end{bmatrix} \text{ES} = \begin{bmatrix} \text{E1} = e_1 : process \\ \text{E2} = e_2 : state \end{bmatrix} \\ \text{QS} = \begin{bmatrix} \text{F} = dead(e_2, y) \\ \text{A} = kill\_act(e, x, y) \end{bmatrix} \end{bmatrix}$$

Co-composition of the subject with the VP results in an agentive predicate replacing the underspecified predicate (i.e. *kill_act*) in the VP's agentive Qualia Structure. The resulting interpretation is shown in (17.35).

(17.35) $\exists x, y, e_1, e_2[rioter(e_1, x) \wedge \mathcal{A}(e_1, x, y) \wedge police(y) \wedge dead(e_2, y) \wedge e_1 \leq e_2]$

In fact, most cases of subject-induced coercion can be characterized in the manner defined above, as ampliative readings resulting from co-composition (cf. Pustejovsky (2011) for further discussion).

Another interesting case of co-composition can be seen in certain light verb constructions (Rosen, 1997; Goldberg, 1995; Butt, 1997; Mohanan, 1997), where much of the semantic content of the predicate is contributed by the complement meaning. Of particular interest to the current discussion are *functionally dependent verb* readings (Pustejovsky, 1995). These involve a range of verb classes, characterized by the verb's dependence on the specific *function* of the complement selected. Included in this class are the verbs *open, close, break*, and *fix*. The problem for compositionality for light verb constructions in general, and this class in particular, is the recurring issue of sense specificity. That is, can the different uses of *open*, for example, in (17.36), be captured with one verb meaning or are multiple senses required?

(17.36)   a. Mary opened the letter from her mother.
          b. The rangers opened the trail for the season.
          c. John opened the door for the guests.
          d. Mary opened up the application.
          e. She then opened a window and started writing.

Viewed as a co-compositional operation, in each case above, the sense of the verb *open* has been enriched through the context of the meaning associated with a specific object type. As with subject-induced coercions, the resulting VP meaning is ampliative relative to the function application of the verb over its object. This additional inference is derived from the complement itself. Briefly, we can view the verb *open* as bringing about a change of state, one which *enables* the activities associated with the complement's TELIC role. These are spelled out, somewhat informally in the glosses for each of the cases in (17.36e) below.

(17.37)   a. The letter can now be *read*.
          b. The trail can now be *walked on*.
          c. The door can be *walked through*.
          d. The application is *running*.
          e. The application window is *ready to use*.

17.4 FUTURE DIRECTIONS

In this chapter we have defined the general characteristics associated with co-compositional analyses of a modest range of linguistic phenomena. It is obvious that there is much still to study with the behaviour of co-compositionality in language. For example, there are clearly *degrees* of co-compositionality in the cases we have reviewed, and even more with cases we have not presented here. Current research on these areas focuses on broadening the definition of co-composition to include both finer degrees of sense modulation (cf. Pustejovsky and Rumshisky, 2010; Pustejovsky and Jezek, 2008), and deeper sense extensions to metaphorical shifts of meaning (cf. Pustejovsky and Rumshisky, 2010).

PART V

COMPOSITIONALITY OF MIND

CHAPTER 18

TYPICALITY AND COMPOSITIONALITY: THE LOGIC OF COMBINING VAGUE CONCEPTS

JAMES A. HAMPTON AND MARTIN L. JÖNSSON

18.1 THE PRINCIPLE OF COMPOSITIONALITY

The principle of compositionality (PC) is usually understood in the following way:

(PC)   The meaning of a complex expression is completely determined by the meaning of its parts and their mode of combination.

According to (PC), the meaning of the expression 'John loves spinach', for example, depends on the meanings of the three words that it contains, and the Subject–Verb–Object syntactic structure that relates them, *and nothing else*.

As expressed above, (PC) is a statement about the semantics of expressions. It can also be framed slightly differently so that it becomes a principle about the content of complex concepts. This chapter concerns this principle, and reasons for deviating from it. We will review several decades of psychological research on typicality effects and non-logical reasoning that suggest that explanations can be given for a wealth of phenomena if concepts are understood as prototypes (broadly construed). However the evidence also shows that the combination of prototypes is rarely compositional in the sense of (PC). Instead the evidence suggests that the combination of prototypes follows a principle corresponding to something like (PC′) rather than (PC).[1]

---

[1] The relative merits of principles such as (PC) and (PC′) are discussed further in Jönsson (2008).

(PC′) The content of a complex concept is completely determined by the contents of its parts and their mode of combination, *together with general knowledge*.

The reviewed evidence gives us good reason to think that this way of thinking about concepts (that many of them are prototypes) and conceptual combination (that concepts combine according to (PC′)) is the most productive in leading to scientific understanding.[2]

Research into typicality effects sprang from the observation that members of most conceptual categories differ in how representative they are of their categories (Rosch and Mervis, 1975). Robins are more typical birds than penguins, hammers are more typical tools than knifes, and apples are more typical fruits than coconuts. Typicality effects were found to affect a wide range of psychological tasks such as the learning of novel categories (Rosch, Simpson, and Miller, 1976), the speed and accuracy of categorizing items in common semantic categories like fruits or vehicles (Hampton, 1979), and the strength of inductive inferences (Rips, 1975). The explanation for all of these effects was the proposal that concepts are represented mentally as prototypes, where a prototype is a structured set of descriptive properties that captures what a cluster of items of some category typically have in common and what differentiates them from other kinds of thing (Hampton, 1995).[3] Early prototype models suggested a representation in terms of feature lists (Hampton, 1979; Rosch, 1975) such as 'flies', 'has a beak', 'hatches from an egg'. More recently, evidence about the importance of causal relations amongst such features has led to more powerful representational mechanisms such as frames or schemas being proposed (Barsalou and Hale, 1993; Murphy, 2002). Hampton (2006) argued that we should nonetheless consider such more powerful representations as prototypes, for the simple reason that they continue to exhibit typicality and vagueness, contain rich descriptions of typical properties and yet lack clearly expressible definitions. The notion of a prototype has also been employed with great success in different domains of linguistics, including lexical semantics, morphology, syntax, and phonology (Taylor, 2003).

Differences in typicality need to be distinguished from differences in degrees of membership (Kamp and Partee, 1995; Osherson and Smith, 1997). Both robins and ostriches are indisputably birds, but robins are more typical birds than ostriches. Nonetheless it seems that in many conceptual categories that show typicality effects, membership also comes in degrees so that it is indeterminate whether something belongs to a certain category or not. Whether carpets and clocks are furniture, for instance, seems to be

---

[2] This conclusion is not reached by a priori arguments similar to those that have been presented in favour of why natural languages or thought have to be compositional (e.g. Fodor and Lepore, 1991, 1996), why natural language doesn't have to be compositional (e.g. Schiffer, 1987), why natural languages in fact are not compositional (e.g. Lahav, 1989; Pelletier, 1994b, 2000b) or why thought is not compositional (Schiffer, 2003). The situation is, rather, that a certain approach to conceptual combination has (experimentally) shown itself to be extraordinarily revealing with respect to matters of typicality and non-logical reasoning and that this approach presupposes a non-compositional understanding of concepts.

[3] For a review of recent work on prototypes see Hampton (2006).

indeterminate in this way. In effect semantic categorization often shows vagueness (Keefe and Smith, 1997), with some statements being neither clearly true nor clearly false.

To explain the twin phenomena of vagueness and typicality, and their close correspondence it is most parsimonious to suppose that both arise from an underlying dimension of similarity to a prototype (Hampton, 1998, 2007). The closer an item is to the prototype representation of a concept, then the more frequently and quickly it will be judged as falling under that concept, the more typical it will be judged to be, the stronger will be inductive arguments from item to category, and the more similar it will be to other category items.

By invoking prototypes we can also provide explanations of how the typicality structure of complex concepts is related to that of their constituents, and why a considerable part of our reasoning appears to violate logical and statistical laws. The next two sections will substantiate these two claims. Section 18.4 will address some philosophical arguments that have been advanced against prototype theory in virtue of it being non-compositional. While we concede that prototypes are non-compositional in a strict sense, we maintain that they can perform the same explanatory work that concepts that behave compositionally can. This claim is corroborated by a closing discussion of the productivity and systematicity of our conceptual competence, phenomena which are often held to underlie the conviction that concepts have to be compositional.

18.2 How to combine prototypes

Let us take the simplest case for combining two concepts—the formation of a complex concept that refers to their conjunction, as in when the concepts PET and FISH are combined to form PET FISH. Prima facie one may suppose that this should be a paradigm case for compositional combination—the concept of PET FISH should just be the concept that refers to the class of things that are both pets and fish.[4]

But what of the prototypes of these concepts and the typicality of different items within them? When two concepts are combined into a conjunction, how does the typicality of an instance of the conjunctive category relate to its typicality in each of the conjoined categories? This problem has become known as the 'guppy' problem, after Osherson and Smith's seminal article of 1981 in which they explored the difficulties inherent in the process.[5] Given that a guppy is typical to degree x as a pet, and typical to degree y as a fish, how typical should it be as a pet fish?

---

[4] There are of course many other ways in which complex concepts can be formed, including the formation of non-intersectional compounds like APARTMENT DOG (Kamp and Partee, 1995; Wisniewski, 1997). For simplicity, we do not consider them here.

[5] A version of Stigler's Law of Eponymy (Stigler, 1980) could apply here, since Storms et al. (1998a) discovered that the guppy does not actually show the guppy effect. Plenty of other examples do, however. We will continue to use the guppy example here, since it is the case most often cited.

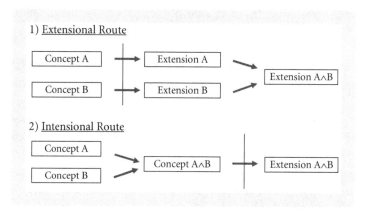

FIGURE 18.1 Two routes to determine the reference of A∧B

There are two ways in which an answer can be derived. The first is to try to find a function that would compute the typicality of an instance for the conjunction directly from its typicality in the constituent parts, by way of, for instance, recruiting fuzzy set theory (Zadeh, 1965). The second is to form a new prototype from the parts of the complex concept and then use that to generate the typicality rating (Cohen and Murphy, 1984; Hampton, 1987, 1988*b*). Fig. 18.1 illustrates the two approaches, which we have labelled the extensional and the intensional routes.

Osherson and Smith (1981) quickly identified major failings with the extensional route. The difficulty they suggested is that whereas a guppy may be an atypical fish (it is not caught in nets and served up with French fries) and may be an atypical pet (it cannot be stroked and petted), it is yet a very typical pet fish. This intuition is at odds with either of the fuzzy logic rules for forming a conjunction, for which membership in a conjunction can never be greater than membership in either constituent set. (Quite reasonably the statement '*p* AND *q*' should never be more true than just '*p*').

In fact the typicality of an item in the conjunctive class cannot be derived in any simple way from its typicality in each of the individual classes. Osherson and Smith (1982) made this point very forcefully with a demonstration concerning a figure that was half way between a circle and a square. They pointed out that even though the shape may be considered just as good a circle as it is a square, it is not equally good as a round circle versus a round square, being a much better example of a round square than a round circle. This demonstration clearly implies that a search for compositional rules that will take degree of membership (or typicality) in each constituent and derive a value for degree of membership (or typicality) in the conjunction is doomed. The shape has equal membership in the constituents [square] and [circle], but when the identical additional conjunct [round] is added to each, the results are no longer equal.

The conclusions drawn by Smith and Osherson (1984, see also Osherson and Smith, 1997) were that category membership and category typicality were two very different issues. Category membership should follow logical rules so that a creature should only be a pet fish if it is both a pet and a fish. On the other hand typicality has to be derived by means of the intensional route which takes account of the interaction between the contents of each concept. In the case of the round circle and the round square, the concept of 'round circle' reduces to the concept of 'circle', whereas 'round square' involves integrating the two concepts to generate a representation of something that is part round and part square—and so a good match to the actually presented shape. Similarly, Cohen and Murphy (1984) and Hampton (1987, 1988b) suggested that the reason that a guppy is a better pet fish than it is a pet or a fish is that the two concepts are first integrated into a single composite concept. Some of the features of pets and of fish will not be carried through to the new complex concept, and so it is quite possible for an instance (such as a guppy) to match the complex prototype better than it does either of the original constituents.[6]

While the intensional route provides a promising way to understand typicality, it appears too unconstrained as a general theory of how concepts should be combined. In particular, the intensional route is unable to rule out logical inconsistencies in category membership assignments, as in the case where 'x is A' is false whereas 'x is both A and B' is true. Effectively, conjunction via the intensional route does not have to correspond to conjunction as it is normatively defined (i.e. as corresponding to the operation of set intersection).

To illustrate the point, let us first consider the case of the conjunction of two concepts that are well-defined (for the sake of argument). Neither suffers from vagueness. Suppose that BACHELOR is represented as the conjunction of the features [male, adult, unmarried, human] and DOCTOR is represented as the conjunction of the features [MD qualification, practises medicine]. Then a simple aggregation or pooling of the two sets of features via the intensional route gives us [male, adult, unmarried, human, MD qualification, practises medicine] as the necessary set of features for defining a bachelor doctor. Aggregation gives us the appropriate truth table for conjunction, provided there is no vagueness.[7]

Even if one concept is well-defined but the other is vague, there is still no logical problem for conjunction via the intensional route. A 'bald bachelor' will have the features that define bachelor coupled with a vague predicate 'is bald', and one can expect that a person would only be considered a bald bachelor if they were both bald and a bachelor.[8]

The problems arise (and the intensional route diverges from logical norms) when both concepts are subject to vagueness at their borderlines. Consider the concepts 'red'

---

[6] There might also be information—extensional feedback—available from actual experience with pet fish that influence the representation corresponding to the complex concept. See below.

[7] As a first pass one can also suppose that the two prototypes simply compose—the bachelor doctor will be interested in dating girls and have illegible handwriting just like other bachelors and other doctors.

[8] Some dimensional adjectives such as 'big' work differently. A big ant is smaller than a small dog. We assume here that 'bald for a bachelor' has the same baldness criterion as 'bald for a married man'.

and 'ripe' as applied to apples. Both redness and ripeness come in degrees, and the decision as to where to draw the line of what counts as red and what counts as ripe is to an extent arbitrary and vague. The extensional route would proceed as follows: (i) a decision is made whether the apple is red, and (ii) a decision is made whether the apple is ripe, and (iii) a truth table rule is applied to the results of (i) and (ii) so that the object is a red ripe apple only if the two decisions are positive. So far, so simple. The extensional route accords with logical norms.

How about the intensional route? There are two main proposals for how intensions of vague concepts might be represented, One is the notion of a prototype described above, and the rest of our chapter will focus on this proposal. However, an alternative has also been proposed—namely that concepts are represented as collections of labelled exemplars (Heit and Barsalou, 1996; Medin and Schaffer, 1978; Storms et al. 2000). It is possible that the concept of Sport is represented by a set of individual sports, and that of Game by a set of individual games. The conjunctive concept Sports that are Games could then be similarly represented by the set intersection of these exemplar sets. No detailed model has been proposed for how this might work however, and there are good reasons, as will become apparent, for supposing that such a model would have limited value. In particular, accounting for phenomena such as the process of conflict resolution leading to attribute inheritance failure is not straightforward with this approach.

Let us turn, then, to how prototypes might combine through a merging of attribute information. First a prototype representation of the conjunctive concept is formed by aggregating the feature [red] with the feature [ripe]. Any instance is then judged to belong in the conjunction on the basis of its overall similarity to this composite representation. If redness and ripeness are true of an apple to differing degrees, then of necessity there will be compensation between membership in one constituent category and membership in the other. Consider two red apples, both equally on the verge of ripeness to the point where they are neither clearly ripe nor clearly unripe. Suppose also that they are both clearly red—membership in the class 'red apples' is not in doubt—but that apple A is actually redder than B. Both are red, but A is more typically red, being closer to the prototype shade of red than is B. That means that A will be a better match to the prototypical red ripe apple than B, and as a result should be more likely to be categorized as such. The degree of redness can compensate for the lack of ripeness. That will mean that an apple may be considered unripe *simpliciter*, but because it is very red it may yet be classified as a red ripe apple. Hence '*p*' is false, but '*p* AND *q*' is true.[9]

Fig. 18.2 illustrates the problem. Redness and ripeness are represented as the two axes, with the category borderlines represented as dotted lines passing through the centre of each scale. A conjunctive concept defined by logical class intersection would therefore have the boundary represented by the bold L-shaped line that encloses the top right

---

[9] Alternatively if the threshold for 'red ripe apple' is raised so as to exclude these cases, it will necessarily also exclude other cases that have in fact passed the threshold for each separate constituent with the result that '*p*' and '*q*' are true, but '*p* AND *q*' is false.

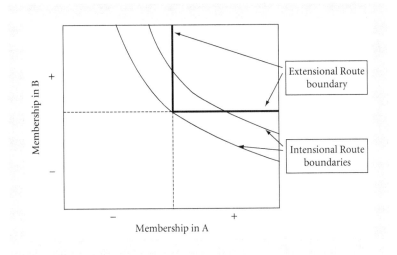

FIGURE 18.2 Boundary for conjunction of A and B

quadrant where both concept memberships are positive. However, the intensional route will mean that membership in the conjunction is a function of distance from the top right corner (the prototype for the conjunction) and hence the category boundary for the conjunction will be a line with negative slope.[10]

In the case of feature-based prototypes the same problem can be readily illustrated. Fig. 18.3 illustrates the case of combining two prototypes with 'polymorphous' membership rules requiring that any two out of three features be present in order to belong to a category (Dennis, Hampton, and Lea, 1973). The composite prototype is constructed by amalgamating the six features, possession of any four of which is now sufficient for category membership. Item 1, which has two A features and two B features is therefore in the conjunctive set. But so is Item 2 which has three A features and only one B feature. Item 2 is therefore in the category A∧B, but is not a member of the category B.[11]

Osherson and Smith (1997) took this undesirable feature of intensional combination processes as good reason to reject the notion that category membership is based on similarity to a prototype. Explaining typicality judgements requires an intensional combination mechanism, but category membership judgements need to respect the rules of logic. They were led to the conclusion that category membership could not be based on the notion of typicality in the way that prototype theory would propose. Hence category membership and typicality must be separable aspects of conceptual structure,

---

[10] Billings and Marcus (1983) review similar compensatory rules in the wider context of decision making.

[11] Composite prototype concepts do not always have to show these effects. If it is the case that each concept has a single feature that is alone sufficient to reach criterion, and the sum of other features is insufficient on their own to reach criterion, then the two concepts will appear to be well-defined, and their conjunction will likewise be intersective (Hampton, 1995).

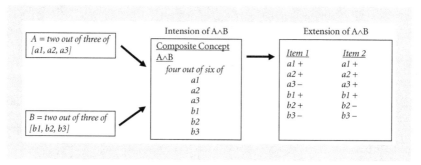

FIGURE 18.3 Conjunctions of prototype concepts based on polymorphous rules. The composite concept is generated by pooling the features of each concept and requiring a similar level of feature match (66% match). Whereas Item 1 correctly belongs in A and B and in A∧B, Item 2 belongs to A∧B but *not* to B. Weak membership in B has been compensated for by high typicality in A.

and must require different theoretical treatments (see also Hampton, 2007; Kamp and Partee, 1995).

18.3 NON-LOGICAL REASONING

The story so far suggests that we need to stick to the extensional route if we are to 'safeguard ... classical logic, with its limpid and sensible rules for deriving truth-values of many compound statements from the truth-values of their parts' (Osherson and Smith, 1997). However, a psychological account of concepts need not of necessity produce rules for combination that agree with classical logic. Being an empirical theory, we need first to discover what people actually do when asked to classify items into conjunctive concepts with vague boundaries. Research on reasoning (Evans, 1982; Evans and Over, 1996) has found that people's reasoning often falls short of all but the most simple of logical rules. Non-logical reasoning is not random or arbitrary, but follows its own heuristic rules with particular adaptive value (Gigerenzer et al., 1999; Chater and Oaksford, 1999).

In the case of concept conjunctions there is ample evidence that people engage in non-logical behaviour. More strikingly, this behaviour is exactly in line with the type of effect just described, in which membership in a conjunction is not a simple logical combination of membership in each individual category, but instead reflects average similarity to each constituent.

In a series of papers, the first author has shown that there is a complex, yet very systematic, set of processes by which prototypes are combined (Hampton, 1987, 1988a, 1988b, 1991, 1996, 1997a, 1997b). The studies considered people's judgements of both extensional and intensional aspects of concept conjunction—the extensional aspect concerning what people consider to belong in a particular category, and the intensional aspect concerning what properties people consider are generally true of a particular category. In both cases, people were asked to provide data for pairs of constituent categories (for example SPORTS and GAMES) and then for their conjunction (SPORTS THAT ARE ALSO GAMES).[12] Extensive further work on this problem has also been conducted by Gert Storms and his colleagues at the Katholik University of Leuven (e.g. Storms et al., 1996, 1998a, 1998b, 1999).

Studies of extensions led to the discovery of three main phenomena. First, as expected from the problem analysis presented in Fig. 18.2, people did not follow the logical conjunctive boundaries corresponding to the Extensional Route. Instead they tended to overextend their conjunctive categories. Fig. 18.4 illustrates the phenomenon with data from Hampton (1988b). The vertical axis shows the degree to which people judged that an instance was a member of the Head noun category (the first mentioned concept), and the horizontal axis shows the same measure for the Qualifier noun category (the concept in the relative clause). The boundary of the conjunction is shown by the contour line. It is clear that the conjunction borderline passes close to the origin in the centre of the diagram. An item that was exactly on the borderline for each constituent would also be borderline for the conjunction. As a consequence there are regions in the diagram where items that are not in one or other of the constituents are nevertheless in the conjunction. Analysis of individual membership judgements confirmed this pattern— both using ratings of membership averaged across participants and using frequencies of making a positive judgement. Regression analysis, using an interaction term to capture the curvature, was able to predict 90–95 per cent of the variance in conjunctive membership on the basis of degree of membership in each category alone. The same pattern was found when participants judged all three category memberships, (Hampton, 1988b) or when different groups made the judgements (Hampton, 1997a). This overextension effect is nicely captured in a quote from Rebecca Goldstein's excellent novel *The Mind–Body Problem* in which the protagonist writes:

> *My intelligence, like my beauty, has always been overpraised, misperceived. The conjunction favors both conjuncts. I am beautiful for a brainy woman, brainy for a beautiful woman, but objectively speaking, neither beautiful nor brainy.*
> (Goldstein, 1983: 164)[13]

The other two phenomena are quickly described. Fig. 18.4 clearly shows an asymmetry in that the area of overextension is greater in the lower right quadrant than in the top left quadrant. This asymmetry reflected the fact that in regressions predicting conjunctive membership from constituent membership, greater weight was accorded to the qualifier noun, resulting in fewer overextensions of the qualifier than of the head. Finally, over and above this asymmetry there was a further asymmetry in that one of the concepts in each pair tended to have greater weight in the regression than the other—an effect referred to as concept dominance. Further research by Storms et al. (1996) suggests that dominance may relate to category size, with smaller categories being more dominant.

---

[12] A relative clause construction was chosen as a way of making the intersective interpretation quite explicit. Storms et al. (1998b), however, have shown that the precise form of the conjunctive expression has no effect on the extent of the non-logical phenomena observed.

[13] We thank Greg Murphy for drawing this passage to our attention.

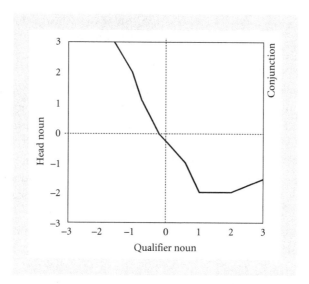

FIGURE 18.4 Overextension pattern seen in Hampton (1988)
The line drawn on the figure is the boundary for the conjunction.

Another possibility is that dominance relates to some notion of category coherence. For example, Patalano, Chin-Parker, and Ross (2006) reported that in conjunctions of social categories, people consider that a member of a conjunction will inherit any arbitrary property from a more coherent category in preference to a less coherent category.

The other line of research on conjunctions considered how concept intensions are combined. People were asked to offer descriptions of the conceptual 'contents' of individual concepts like SPORTS or GAMES, and then to describe the properties of the conjunction 'Sports that are also games'. To improve reliability, a second set of participants were then given a list of all the properties generated to any of the concepts. Different groups judged the extent to which each property could be considered true of each constituent or of the conjunction. In this way the pattern of attribute inheritance was explored, using an analogy of the conjunction as the offspring of the two constituent parents.

Unlike the extensional task, there are generally no hard logical constraints that can be 'broken' in the attribute judgements. The only hard constraint arises when people consider that a feature or property is a necessary attribute of a category, in which case it should also be necessary for conjunctively defined subsets of the category. The results (Hampton, 1987) suggested that people are in fact aware of this general constraint. The rating scale asked for judgements of 'how important' an attribute is for a concept, with the top of the scale labelled 'Necessary'. When an attribute was given a 'necessary' rating for one or more constituents, then it also tended generally to be given a necessary rating for the conjunction. A similar constraint was seen at the bottom of the scale, where an attribute could be judged 'impossible' for a concept. Attributes that were impossible for a constituent also tended to be impossible for conjunctions (the one exception being pet birds, where it was judged impossible for birds to talk, but not impossible for pet birds to talk).

The detailed story of how attribute inheritance works requires a fairly lengthy description. At a first level, regression equations suggested that importance of an attribute for the conjunction could be approximated quite accurately in terms of a weighted average of its importance for each constituent. Furthermore the same categories that were dominant for determining membership were also dominant for determining attribute importance (hence once again implicating the role of conceptual coherence in the process). There were exceptions to this general rule, including the case of impossible and necessary features already mentioned. The two main sources of exceptions to simple averaging of attribute importance came from the retrieval of facts about the world from long-term memory, and the detection of inconsistencies among inherited attributes. Since both of these exceptions require access to knowledge that is external to the concepts being combined, they can be termed non-compositional.

The first of these, dubbed 'extensional feedback', showed up in the presence of 'emergent attributes' in the conjunction which were not present in either constituent concept. For example pet birds are judged to live in cages, but neither pets nor birds typically do this. The attribute is clearly made available by people recalling visits to pet shops or to friends' homes where they have seen pet birds. (Alternatively people might use their 'background theories' to guess that if a bird was not kept in a cage, it would not remain a pet for very long.) Although the occurrence of emergent features complicates the process of exhaustively predicting the prototypes corresponding to complex expressions—since exhaustively detailing what extensional feedback a subject has been exposed to is practically impossible—it does not prevent the development and testing of the model against empirical data.

The second source of variation from simple attribute inheritance came from conflicting attributes. Pets are warm and cuddly, while fish are cold and slimy. It is not possible for something to be simultaneously warm and cold, and it seems hard to imagine cuddling a cold slimy fish. The result is that one or other of the features has to be dropped—attribute inheritance fails on this occasion. Hampton (1987) found evidence that (at least in the case of Pet Birds) the choice of which feature to drop is determined by trying to maximize coherence (reduce conflicts) through the minimum amount of change (see also Thagard, 1983).

We have summarized research into concept conjunctions quite briefly. There is also evidence that conjunctive concept judgements may show compensation with the typicality of membership in one category influencing the degree to which a borderline member of the other category belongs in the conjunction (Hampton, 1996). There is also evidence (Hampton, 1997a) that the effects observed with conjunctions carry over to negated conjunctions (Sports that are not Games) with increased effect size. Work has also been done on disjunctive combinations (Hampton, 1988a), on attribute inheritance with negation (Hampton, 1997a), and on emergent attributes in a wider range of concept conjunctions (Hampton, 1997b). In addition to the forms of non-logical thinking that have been described here, many other forms of reasoning deviating from logical norms have been reported, including: the conjunction fallacy (Tversky and Kahneman, 1983), the inverse conjunction fallacy (Jönsson and Hampton, 2006), the inclusion fallacy

(Shaffir, Smith, and Osherson, 1990), the premise specificity effect, and the inclusion similarity effect (Sloman, 1993). As with the effects described in this section, all of these effects are most naturally explained by reference to prototype-like representations and the operation of similarity-based reasoning.

18.4 THE NON-COMPOSITIONALITY OF THE INTENSIONAL ROUTE

We noted earlier that since the treatment of conceptual conjunctions within prototype theory deviates from the norms of classical logic it has been held to be an incomplete or even erroneous theory of concepts (Osherson and Smith, 1997). This purported incompleteness has been used to promote frameworks where concepts are understood to be something quite different from prototypes. For instance, Fodor (1998) and Connolly et al. (2007) favour a model—the classical model[14]—where concepts are atomic, that is have no internal structure. On this view, conceptual combination is a process where 'concepts remain inert under combination' and 'all you get from your concepts and combinatorics is output denoting relations among sets, properties, or individuals (depending on the ontology assumed)' (Connolly et al., 2007: 2–4). So in contrast with prototype theory, the classical model does not hold that the result of combining two concepts is some amalgamate of their prototypes. Instead, the result of combination is a simple structure having the original concepts as proper parts. This difference can be illustrated in the following way for a conjunctive combination ('sports that are also games' for instance).

The classical model: $A_1, A_2 \rightarrow A_1 \wedge A_2$
Prototype Theory: $P_1, P_2 \rightarrow P_3$

As we have seen above, the ways in which prototypes combine via the intensional route is not such that only the things falling under P_1 and P_2 fall under P_3. This constraint is however guaranteed on the classical model, by the definition of '$\wedge$'. By being able to account for our conviction that only, say, things that are sports *and* that are games are sports that are also games, the classical model seems to be able to do something which prototype theory is unable to do. It is thus concluded that prototypes cannot be concepts, or at least that two different kinds of concepts need to be invoked. But there might be good reasons to resist this conclusion.

When expressions have a syntactic form that makes their logical form explicit, people are often ready to assent to the validity of simple arguments on the basis of form alone.

---

[14] We will call it the classical model, although as detailed in Smith and Medin's (1981) seminal work, the classical model proposed that concepts have defining features. In contrast Fodor's account eschews definitions, and simply proposes that concepts as they play a role in mental life are unanalysed atomic symbols.

Thus *modus ponens* arguments such as (18.1) may be accepted as valid without any information regarding the meaning of the unfamiliar terms

(18.1) If all lokies pling then all maks flug.
        All lokies do pling,
        Therefore all maks must flug.

Similarly, people may assent to arguments involving the simplification of conjunction in the same way.

(18.2) *x* is a flug which is also a loki
        Therefore *x* is a flug

Hence, the intuition that '*x* is a sport which is also a game' entails '*x* is a sport' might be judged valid on the basis of its form alone. Violation of form would explain why we feel that there is something wrong with saying, for instance, that chess might be a sport which is also a game, but that it is not a sport. This formal explanation of our logical intuitions can then be set alongside the alternative explanation of why people are in fact prepared to give inconsistent judgements when form is over-ridden by content.

Another, semantic explanation of our logical intuitions is in terms of logical composition rules for prototypes. There is nothing about prototypes that prevent them from being just as amenable to logical combination as are atoms. It was the kind of composition rules used rather than the fact that concepts were treated as atoms that was key to the explanation of our logical intuitions. Hence, prototype theory could match the explanatory ability of the classical model with respect to logical intuitions by borrowing its composition rules without thereby admitting atomistic concepts. On this view the concept corresponding to 'sports that are also games' might be derived in two different ways. On the one hand that concept could correspond to a single prototype as detailed above, on the other hand that concept could correspond to a conjunctive frame having both the atomic prototypes as parts.

$$P_1, P_2 \rightarrow P_1 \wedge P_2$$
$$P_1, P_2 \rightarrow P_3$$

In this way we again get an explanation of why certain categorization decisions that we make are felt to be inconsistent since something falling under P_3 is not equivalent to it falling under P_1 and P_2.[15] If this is correct, then even though we now have two kinds of composition rule, there is no reason to multiply kinds of concepts. With the application of one kind of rule the prototypes mesh—and non-logical reasoning results; with the application of the other kind they remain inert—and logical reasoning results. But in neither case did we need to make reference to any other form of concept than a prototype.

---

[15] Note that even if a prototype is used in order to determine (via a threshold on the similarity scale) which things fall under the concept, it is still the case that the logical combination of prototypes is 'truth preserving' in the sense that if something is universally true of members of the category corresponding to one of the conjuncts it is true of all members of the conjunctive category since the conjunctive category will be a subclass of the categories of the conjuncts.

If this last proposal is correct then there is at least one way that prototypes can combine that is in accordance with compositionality and is thus 'truth preserving'.[16] However, if compositionality requires that the content of a complex concept is determined by the constituent contents plus the mode of combination, *and nothing else*, then the majority of prototype combinations are clearly not compositional. The occurrence of emergent attributes and of inheritance failures through conflict resolution requires that a much wider range of knowledge and belief is brought to bear on the process of understanding a conjunctive concept. This extra input clearly breaks the constraints of compositionality.

The general non-compositionality of prototypes has been a source of philosophical criticism and we take this opportunity to address some of these broader critiques. Fodor and Lepore (1996), for instance, argue that concepts cannot be prototypes since, supposedly, many complex concepts don't have prototypes.

> However, although 'isn't a cat' [has a definite semantic interpretation] it pretty clearly has no stereotype; and nor do indefinitely many other Boolean complex concepts. There isn't any stereotypic nonprime number, and there isn't anything that is stereotypically pink if it's square. (Fodor and Lepore, 1996: 260–1)

The claim that the listed concepts do not have a prototype is true on an *extensional* understanding of 'prototype'. They clearly don't have instances such that they could serve as 'centres' for their categories. But the common conception of a prototype which we have been assuming in this chapter does not equate a prototype with such an instance. Rather, a prototype is understood intensionally in terms of a structured set of weighted features possibly embedded in a causal schema.

There are several possible ripostes to the 'concepts without prototypes' argument. First, psychologists have never claimed that ALL concepts are represented in the mind as prototypes. Mathematical concepts such as i, the 'imaginary' root of -1, are clearly not represented as prototypes, and no one has ever claimed that they are. Second, it has been shown that while some familiar concepts have strong single prototypes, others are better thought of as being represented by collections of prototypes at a more specific level (Smits et al., 2002). The typical human face, for example, is probably represented by separate prototypes of a male and a female face, rather than a single sexless prototype. Such issues require empirical verification. But the claim made by prototype theory is not that all concepts must have prototypes, or that a single prototype is all that is needed to represent all concepts. The situation is more complex than that.

A third possibility that has been suggested in the literature, is that, for instance, 'cat' and 'not a cat' invoke the same prototype but that the similarity measure is used in a different way when deriving typicality judgements for the two categories (not being a

---

[16] Horwich (1997, 2001) provides a good relevant discussion of the possibility of dropping 'the uniformity assumption', i.e. the assumption that if something is/engenders the meanings of simple expressions, the same kind of thing must be/engender the meaning of complex expressions, in order to preserve compositionality.

cat is then a matter of being sufficiently dissimilar to the cat prototype).[17] There is little empirical work on this, but it is plausible to suppose that a theorem would be considered a much better example of not being a cat than would a dog. Yet without similarity-based reasoning and prototypes, there is of course no way to account for such intuitions.

Finally, one can point out the close correspondence between the existence of a prototype and the naturalness of a concept (Osherson, 1978). Fodorian examples such as 'pink if it's square' are allegedly concepts without prototypes. But equally they are concepts with no likelihood of gaining ground in our conceptual repertoire. What is more, if they did turn out to be valuable for conceptual thinking or communicative purposes, one can suppose that the intensional route would kick in, and additional inferences and prototypical features would start to accumulate. Conditionals are not ruled out from prototype concepts—'dangerous if male' might apply to a range of mammals, (just as 'dangerous if female' might apply to spiders). Negation is not ruled out either. Dead is 'not alive' and impossible means 'not possible'. But most of our negative concepts relate to binary oppositions, so that being dead or being impossible have as many typical entailments as do their opposites.

The point is that Boolean expressions can be as meaningless as you like, and as long as they remain meaningless they are prototype-less. Add in a meaningful context and a prototype will appear. 'Not a cat' is not meaningful out of context, but in a given context (e.g. Christmas presents, pets, road kill) it brings probabilistic entailments that go beyond the simple Boolean expression. As mentioned in Section 18.3, Hampton (1997a) investigated prototypes for expressions such as Building that is not a dwelling, or Vehicle that is not a machine, and revealed some of the complex but systematic effects of how negation operates on prototypes within a given context.

Fodor and Lepore have also advanced variants of the guppy problem—the problem which we have already shown faced the extensional route—against prototype theory in general.

> The problem here is . . . that . . . an object's similarity to the prototype for a complex concept seems not to vary systematically as a function of its similarity to the prototypes of the constituent concepts. So, for example, a goldfish is a poorish example of a fish, and a poorish example of a pet, but it's quite a good example of a pet fish. (Fodor and Lepore, 1996: 262)[18]

The point seems to be that what constitutes a prototype for a complex expression depends on what we believe about the world. If we believe that all brown cows are dangerous the feature 'is dangerous' is going to receive a high weight in the prototype for 'brown cow' regardless of the weights the features corresponding to 'brown' and 'cow' receive. However, it is not clear why this dependency is supposed to be a problem. Once it is recognized that the derivation of prototypes for complex expressions via the

---

[17] See, for instance, Kamp and Partee (1995) and Prinz (2002).

[18] This seems to be more or less the same problem that Fodor and Lepore (1991) have advanced elsewhere against variants of inferential role semantics.

intensional route recruits general knowledge the guppy 'problem' is simply a statement of this dependency. And many theories of the composition of prototypes have been constructed in full awareness of this. The concept specialization model (Murphy, 1988) and the composite prototype model (Hampton, 1988*b*) both make explicit reference to general knowledge. Naturally, too heavy an emphasis on general knowledge could render a psychological account vacuous since our minimal understanding of general cognition would mean that predictions would no longer be available. But as has been illustrated repeatedly (and exemplified above) this is not the case with prototype theory. It is in virtue of its predictions concerning categorization, typicality effects and non-logical reasoning that it remains an attractive model. In addition to the examples already cited, further regularities were revealed by Jönsson and Hampton (2011) pertaining to modifier–noun constructions. One of their results concerned sequences of sentences with increasingly modified head nouns such as 'Ravens are black', 'Young ravens are black' and 'Young jungle ravens are black', or 'Sofas have backrests', 'Uncomfortable sofas have backrests', and 'Uncomfortable handmade sofas have backrests'. Replicating an effect reported by Connolly et al. (2007) they observed that the judged likelihood of such sentences decreases with an increase in the number of atypical modifiers. However, they also found significant correlations between the relative likelihoods of properties being true of modified and unmodified subject nouns, indicating that the strength of a feature for the unmodified prototype was predictive of its strength for the modified version. If property A is more true of a concept than property B, then it turns out that A is also more true of the modified concept that is B. Jönsson and Hampton took this as evidence that information from the concept prototype is imported directly into the modified concept, as would be expected from the operation of the intensional route.[19]

Finally, we consider whether the desiderata of a compositional theory could equally be provided by prototype theory. The two main planks of the argument for compositionality are productivity and systematicity. We will consider each in turn.

To account for productivity—how a system of representation can contain 'an infinite amount of syntactically and semantically distinct symbols' (Fodor and Lepore, 2002: 1)—a theory needs to specify recursive rules for combining concepts. It is the recursion that is critical for productivity, rather than the nature of the concepts. Most of the intensional prototype models do embody recursive rules; the composite prototype model for instance can be applied recursively to generate a concept such as 'Recreations that are games, hobbies, sports, and dangerous activities'. Wisniewski's (1997) model for noun–noun combinations can generate chains of concepts such as 'Apartment dog', 'Apartment dog coat', 'Apartment dog coat cleaner appointment cancellation notification ticket stub residue', and so forth. So there is no barrier to prototype combinations being productive.

---

[19] See Jönsson and Hampton's (2008) for other remarks pertaining to the effect first reported by Connolly et al. (2007).

A conceptual system being 'systematic' amounts to it containing 'such families of syntactically and semantically related but distinct expressions such as "John loves Mary", "Mary loves John", "John loves John" and so forth' (Fodor and Lepore, 2002: 2). There is again nothing that prevents prototype models of concept combination from capturing this intuition. The composite prototype model, for instance, would imply that anyone who can understand 'Sports that are also Games' should be able to understand 'Games that are also Sports', or 'Sports that are also Sports' and so on. Having a fixed set of syntactic combination rules applied to a finite set of atomic elements is sufficient to account for productivity and systematicity. But it is by no means necessary. Productivity and systematicity are a byproduct of a compositional semantics, but they may also be found with non-compositional systems.

Productivity and systematicity do not favour either model of concepts. In fact, it might even be the case that prototype theory has the explanatory upper hand pertaining to these phenomena. It can be remarked, for instance, that systematicity doesn't hold to the same extent for all complex concepts. Where 'Mary loves John' and 'John loves Mary' are both unproblematic it is much easier to understand 'Mary loves Ice-cream' than 'Ice-cream loves Mary'. Given a conception of concepts according to which they have sublexical semantic content, the differences can be explained. But on the classical model where concepts are taken to be atomic no such explanation is possible. Since there are many instances where systematicity is constrained in this way (for instance 'brown cow' and 'prime number' are straightforward, 'brown number' and 'prime cow' are less so), the explanatory scope of the classical theory is more limited. The theory states that for any expression such as 'Mary loves John' there will be at least some other expression in which each concept plays the same semantic role ('Mary hates Peter', 'Joan loves Jill' or 'John plays tennis'). But it has nothing to contribute to the question of where the limits of systematicity lie. On the other hand, a satisfactory prototype account of the concept of 'love' will provide an answer to just that question. What sorts of things can love, what kinds of love are possible between what sorts of things, and what sorts of things can be loved in what ways are all important parts of the concept, and each in its turn will be subject to typicality effects. Mary is a typical subject for the verb, a plant is a less typical subject ('the dahlia loves a sunny aspect'), while an inanimate artifact is more atypical again ('my car loves the open road').

18.5 CONCLUSION

We have tried to illustrate the many ways in which a prototype-based approach to conceptual combination has been successful in providing explanations and predictions pertaining to our use of language and to our conceptual competence. The approach is non-compositional in the sense of principle (PC), since the content of a complex concept is not completely determined by the contents of its parts and their mode of combination but depends also on general knowledge as in principle (PC′). This does not entail, we have argued, any explanatory shortcomings of the approach when compared to compositional alternatives. Instead, it is clear that if we adopt an account based on the basic tenets of prototype theory a wealth of phenomena pertaining to typicality effects, vagueness, and instances of non-logical reasoning can be explained that would otherwise have remained mysterious.

....

CHAPTER 19

EMERGENCY!!!! CHALLENGES TO A COMPOSITIONAL UNDERSTANDING OF NOUN–NOUN COMBINATIONS

....

EDWARD J. WISNIEWSKI AND JING WU

TRADITIONALLY, compositionality refers to how a complex expression is made up of its parts on the basis of grammatical rules, and derives its meaning from these parts. For example, by putting words together we produce phrases. In turn, by putting phrases together we produce sentences. In the context of cognitive linguistics, compositionality allows us to put simple concepts together to produce more complex ones. Composition arises from naming a new entity or situation. When we encounter a new thing or situation which requires more than one concept to describe, we combine concepts together to compose a complex one and express it with the corresponding symbols, leading to the production of a new and larger unit of expression. As a result, compositionality leads to productivity. That is, we have the ability to create an indefinitely large number of sentences from a finite set of grammatical rules and lexical components. Correspondingly, we are able to create an indefinite number of thoughts and concepts from a finite number of these entities. Compositionality also leads to systematicity. That is, there are predictable patterns of lexical components or thoughts that we can understand. For example, anyone who can understand a sentence or thought such as 'Matt likes Marcella', can in turn understand 'Marcella likes Matt'. Some scholars argue that compositionality is essential to concepts (e.g. Fodor and Pylyshyn, 1998).

However, drawing on experimental evidence about how people interpret novel noun–noun combinations (e.g. zebra football, kiwi pie), we show that the meanings of such phrases are generally not a straightforward function of the meanings of their constituents. Instead, the meaning of a novel combination often arises from an *interaction* of the meanings of its constituents, which results in an *emergent feature* (i.e. a feature that is not represented in either constituent). As we detail later, this feature arises from a constructive, integrative process that reflects aspects of both the modifier and head noun but also results in a *unique* feature (Wisniewski, 1997, 1998, 1999). (In a noun–noun combination, the first or left most constituent is called the modifier noun and the second or right most constituent is called the head noun.) It is also likely that other aspects of language understanding involve the creation of emergent features (e.g. sentence comprehension).

In this chapter we first describe what cognitive scientists typically mean by emergent features and present our own view which contrasts with the typical one. We then describe the different types of interpretations that characterize novel noun–noun combinations, based on analyses of two languages that are quite different from each other: American English and Chinese. Our examination of these different languages evaluates the generality of how novel combinations are interpreted. Next, we describe how people understand novel combinations in the context of our multiple-process model of conceptual combination (Wisniewski, 2004). We then address how our multiple-process model can be extended to account for the construction of emergent features. Finally, we contrast our extended model with other models of conceptual combination and metaphor in cognitive science (e.g. Brachman, 1978; Estes and Glucksberg, 2000; Finin, 1980; Gagné and Shoben, 1997; Murphy, 1988).

19.1 EMERGENT FEATURES

In general, emergent features are not initially present in concepts but arise when these concepts are combined. For example, Hampton (1997b) found that 'pets that are also birds' were judged to have the properties 'live in cages and talk' that were false of pets or birds, considered separately (see Hampton, 1988a, 2000; Medin and Shoben, 1988; Murphy, 1988, for more evidence). The source of these emergent features is explained by extensional feedback (Hampton, 1988a; Murphy, 1988; Rips, 1995). In this example, when people think of 'pets that are also birds', they recall examples of birds that are also pets, such as parrots, which highlight the emergent features. As another example, people judge 'overturned chair' to have the feature 'is on a table', but judge neither 'things that are overturned' nor 'chair' to have this feature, when considered separately (Murphy, 1988). In this example, it is likely that an overturned chair reminds them of chairs that they have seen on tables.

Although there is strong evidence for emergent features that arise from extensional feedback, there is another type of emergent feature that is common, although it has not received much attention in cognitive science. These emergent features are constructed or created from existing features represented in the modifier and head noun (Wisniewski, 1997, 1998, 1999, cf. Hampton, 1997*b*). As a simple illustration, consider a novel combination 'zebra football', interpreted as 'a striped football'. Clearly, a zebra football cannot literally be a football with the stripes of a zebra. Instead, people may understand this phrase by imagining stripes that are somewhat different from those of a zebra. Compared to the stripes of a zebra, a zebra football would probably have smaller stripes with smaller between-stripe widths, and perhaps even alternating black and white 'rings' around the football that decrease in diameter as the rings approach the two ends. Thus, the stripes of a zebra football differ from those of a zebra because they apply to a football whose shape and size affect the types of stripes it can have. At the same time, the zebra football has stripes that resemble to some extent those of a zebra (otherwise, it is unclear why one would refer to it as a zebra football). For example, the zebra football has an alternating black and white pattern with stripes on its exterior (just as zebras do). This example also illustrates that emergent features result from an interaction between the representations of the modifier and head noun.

Actual examples of emergent features found in studies of novel combinations include: 'roller coaster dinner' which is often interpreted as 'a series of courses that alternate from tasting good to tasting bad', 'rake pencil' which is sometimes interpreted as a 'pencil with multiple lead points', and 'porcupine mushroom' which is often interpreted as 'a mushroom with prickly protrusions on the cap of the mushroom or on both cap and stem' (Wisniewski, 1997; Wisniewski and Middleton, 2002). Also, in the Chinese language, the creation of novel combinations with emergent features are common (Wu, 2006). For example, consider a recently coined novel combination '豆饼干部' (soybean-cake cadre). This combination refers to leading cadres who are in the middle of a hierarchy in between the top leaders and their staff and unable to please both ends. This emergent feature is derived from a property of soybean cake. These cakes contain soybean in the middle of two layers of bread, much like a sandwich. Later, we provide evidence for the ubiquity of these emergent features and describe cognitive processes that may explain how these features are constructed. To our knowledge, models of conceptual combination and metaphor do not address these processes.

Another way to view emergent features is in terms of *processing stages*. In the earliest stage, understanding a novel combination is initially a compositional process in which features of the constituents are activated (see McElree, Murphy, and Ochoa, 2006*a*; Moss, Tyler, Dalrymple, and Hampton, 1997; Swinney, Love, Walenski, and Smith, 2007 for evidence of this stage in the processing of adjective–noun combinations). In a middle stage, we propose that our multiple-process model constructs emergent features from these compositional features (described later). Finally, some researchers suggest that after comprehending a novel combination, people elaborate the meaning with emergent features based on extensional feedback. For example, Murphy (1988) implies that a person may first comprehend 'apartment dog' by using a compositional constraint-based role-filling process to derive the meaning 'a dog that lives in an apartment'. However, a person may subsequently use a non-compositional *post-comprehension process*, elaborating the meaning of dog to include additional features such as 'yappy and neurotic' based on memories they experience of dogs in apartments.

19.2 CONCEPTUAL COMBINATION—THE INTERPRETATION OF NOVEL NOUN–NOUN PHRASES

People frequently combine familiar concepts to express new ideas, refer to new situations, name innovations, and so on. Language use is a prototypical example of conceptual combination. Virtually every sentence you have heard corresponds to a novel combination of concepts. In cognitive psychology, there has been much interest in novel noun phrases, such as noun–noun combinations and adjective–noun combinations. Typically, researchers who study conceptual combination are interested in identifying and specifying the underlying cognitive processes used to create a new meaning from a novel combination of familiar concepts. Examples of novel combinations of familiar concepts that have appeared recently in print include: the aforementioned 'boomerang flu', 'seafood sausage' ('sausage made out of seafood'), and 'bait car' ('car used to catch car thieves'). Once produced, a combination may become a familiar phrase used by many people in a language community as in 'space shuttle' and 'computer virus'. In many languages, the creation of such combinations is an important mechanism that speakers use to expand their language. In American English, the creation of novel noun phrases is ubiquitous, especially in newspaper and magazine articles, and also involve combinations of nouns, adjectives, and acronyms. (e.g. confident FBI shoe print expert) (Wisniewski and Clancy, 2003).

19.3 DIFFERENT TYPES OF INTERPRETATIONS

Psychological experiments on conceptual combination have identified four basic types of interpretations that people produce for novel noun–noun combinations (Costello and Keane, 2001; Wisniewski, 1996, 1998; Wisniewski and Love, 1998; Wu, 2006). Three of these types can be illustrated by contrasting hypothetical meanings of the novel combination 'robin hawk', shown in Table 19.1.

Interpretation A illustrates a relation interpretation. 'Prey' is a *relation* with two arguments, 'hawk' and 'robin' (the referents of the head and modifier nouns, respectively). The two arguments play different roles in the relation. 'Hawk' plays the predator role and 'robin' the prey role. In contrast, interpretation B illustrates a property interpretation.

Table 19.1 Illustration of three basic types of meanings for 'robin hawk'

Type of interpretation	Example
A. Relation	hawk that preys on a robin
B. Property	hawk with a red breast
C. Hybrid	bird that is a cross between a hawk and a robin

In this case, the modifier 'robin' refers to a *property* of robin (i.e. red breast) rather than to a robin. 'Red breast' is a property of robin that characterizes robin hawks. To intuitively understand the difference between relation and property interpretations consider the referents of interpretation A vs. interpretation B. If one pictures a robin hawk, interpreted with a relation, one imagines a hawk preying on a robin. In contrast, if one pictures a robin hawk interpreted with a property, one sees only a hawk (with a red breast). Meaning C illustrates a *hybrid* interpretation. Robin hawk refers to a bird with characteristics of both a robin and a hawk. This interpretation also implies that a robin hawk is not a hawk but rather a novel bird comprised of a 'mixture' of the characteristics of a robin and a hawk. Hybrid interpretations are related to conjunctive interpretations, such as chef scholar. The latter can be interpreted as 'a scholar who is also a chef'. In contrast to hybrid interpretations, the referent of a conjunctive interpretation refers to dual entities.

Studies have demonstrated that these four kinds of interpretations tend to characterize most of the meanings of familiar and novel combinations. However, relation interpretations are very common, property interpretations somewhat common, and hybrids and conjunctives not very common (for evidence, see Wisniewski, 1996; Wisniewski and Love, 1998). These types of interpretation and their distributions also characterize Chinese noun–noun combinations. Wu (2006) analysed a large sample of relatively novel noun–noun combinations taken from the *Dictionary of Contemporary Chinese New Words* (Qu and Han, 2004). Similar to the study of combinations in American English, Wu found that relation interpretations were very common, property interpretations were less common, and hybrid and conjunctive interpretations were very rare. Novel Chinese combinations with relation interpretations included, '吧姐' (bar sister, 'a woman who works in a bar'), '彩电墙' (colour TV wall, 'a wall containing a giant TV'), and '母乳银行' (mother's milk bank, 'a bank for storing mothers' milk'). Examples of novel combinations with property interpretations include '泡沫经济' (bubble economy, 'an economy that won't last long'), '蛤蟆镜' (toad glasses, 'eyeglasses that make the wearer's face resemble that of a toad'), and '电影小说' (movie novel, 'a novel that applies techniques from movies to the style of novel, such as a flashback'). Examples of some familiar conjunctive combinations included '男演员' (man actor) and '女作家' (woman writer).

Although most nouns have a dominant referent (e.g. dog typically refers to a canine), people flexibly interpret noun referents during conceptual combination. Property interpretations are a good example of this flexibility: people construe or re-conceptualize the modifier noun as referring to a property of the thing named by the noun, rather than to the thing itself (cf. interpretation B above). In what we have termed representation construal (Wisniewski, 1997), people use a noun to refer to a representation of a thing rather than to the thing itself. For example, car box is interpreted as 'a box that contains a toy car', and 'stone squirrel' is interpreted as an 'ornamental squirrel made of stone'. In metonymic construal, people interpret nouns as referring to things associated with a constituent of the combination. For example, in artist collector, artist is construed as 'the works of an artist', (yielding the interpretation, 'a collector of the works of an artist'). In robin termite, robin is interpreted as 'a robin's nest', (yielding the interpretation, 'termite that eats robins' nests').

Chinese also has combinations that reflect representation construal and metonymic construal. The combination '石狮子' (stone lion) refers to a statue of a lion, carved out of stone and hence is a representation of a lion. There are many novel combinations in Chinese with the modifier '电子' (electronic) which refer to a representation. For example, '电子宠物' (electronic pet) refers to a cartoon pet that people can raise and care for by using electronic devices. Examples of metonymic construal include '笔友' (pen friend) and '菜篮子工程' (vegetable-basket project). In the former combination, '笔 (pen)' refers to the action of writing (and is similar conceptually to the American English phrase 'pen pal'). In the latter, 'vegetable-basket project' refers to a project carried out by the Chinese government to provide a greater variety of food to people besides basic staples (e.g. rice). In this case, '菜篮子' (vegetable basket) refers to a group of food products contained in the basket, such as vegetables, fish, fruit, and meat from farms.

19.4 PROCESSES AND KNOWLEDGE USED TO INTERPRET NOVEL COMBINATIONS

Research suggests that people use multiple processes and sources of knowledge to interpret novel combinations. We first contrast different processes assumed to occur for relation interpretations (e.g. robin hawk: 'hawk that *preys on* robins') vs. property interpretations (e.g. robin hawk: 'hawk with a *red breast*').

Many psychological accounts of conceptual combination assume that relation interpretations arise from a constraint-based role-filling process (e.g. Brachman, 1978; Finin, 1980; Murphy, 1988; Wisniewski, 1997). To illustrate this process, consider 'computer soap', typically interpreted as 'soap for cleaning a computer'. Reading this phrase typically activates a characteristic-distinctive relation associated with soap (i.e. cleaning). A characteristic-distinctive relation associated with a category applies to most members of the category and few other categories. Thus, 'cleaning' is a characteristic-distinctive relation of soap because virtually all members of the soap category are used for cleaning, and relatively few other categories are used for cleaning. More formally, a characteristic relation of a category is one for which P (relation | the category) is high and a distinctive relation is one for which P (the category | relation) is high. Following the activation of a cleaning relation, a person's basic knowledge about the cleaning relation indicates that it has at least two roles, each played by a different entity. Soap plays the role of the entity that 'does the cleaning' and computer plays the role of the entity that is 'cleaned.' In this case, soap meets the constraints or preconditions for filling the cleaning role (e.g. people know that soap is used to clean things). Likewise, computer meets the preconditions for filling the 'thing to be cleaned' role (e.g. people know that many entities become dirty and require cleaning from time to time and computers are no exception). As another example, understanding robin hawk should activate the characteristic-distinctive 'preys on' relation associated with hawk. Basic knowledge about robins and hawks allows a person to infer that hawk plays the role of the predator and that robin plays the role of the prey. In this case, hawks meet the preconditions for being a predator (e.g. hawks are known predators) and robins meet the preconditions for being prey (e.g. robins are edible, smaller than hawks, and perhaps fly more slowly).

In contrast to the constraint-based role-filling process, evidence suggests that property interpretations arise from alignment and integration processes involving a characteristic-distinctive property of the modifier (Wisniewski, 1997; Wisniewski and Middleton, 2002). The alignment process was originally developed to account for the understanding of metaphors and analogies (e.g. Gentner, 1983). In conceptual combination, this process puts into correspondence (i.e. aligns) similar aspects of the head noun and modifier which help to indicate how the modifier property is to be integrated into the combination. For example, understanding 'zebra horse' should activate a characteristic-distinctive property (i.e., stripes) that forms the basis for the interpretation of zebra horse. To construct this interpretation, properties in the modifier zebra are aligned with those in the head noun horse because those parts are similarly shaped and share similar spatial relations to similar components. For instance, people may place 'body of zebra' and 'body of horse' into correspondence because they are similarly shaped and are both connected to similarly-shaped necks and legs above and below the body, respectively. For analogous reasons, people would align the neck and legs of zebra with the neck and legs of horse, respectively. Loosely speaking, these correspondences indicate 'where' the stripes go on a zebra horse. In particular, they extend along its body, neck, and legs just as the stripes of a zebra extend along its body, neck, and legs. Thus, the alignment process integrates the property associated with the modifier (i.e. stripes) into the noun–noun combination.

Both property and relation interpretations may also arise from *memory-based processes*. In this case, a novel combination may index an experience of a person that provides an interpretation of the combination. For instance, reading 'computer soap' may remind a person of an incident in which someone washed a computer with soap, leading the person to interpret computer soap as 'soap for cleaning computers' (a relation interpretation). Likewise, reading zebra clam may remind someone of a clam with stripes seen on beach (a property interpretation). Property and relation interpretations can also arise from a reminding-based analogical process involving familiar noun–noun phrases. For example, reading 'kiwi pie' may remind a person of familiar combinations such as apple pie, blueberry pie, and lemon pie. As a result, the person may interpret kiwi pie as 'pie made of kiwis', based on analogy to the meanings of these familiar phrases (a relation interpretation; see Gerrig and Murphy (1992) for evidence). Likewise, reading 'zebra clam' may remind a person of a zebra fish. As a result, the person may interpret zebra clam as a 'clam with stripes', based on analogy to the meaning of this familiar phrase (a property interpretation). A number of experiments show that people use memory-based processes to interpret noun–noun phrases when reading text (e.g., Gagné and Spalding, 2004; Gerrig, 1989; Gerrig and Murphy, 1992; Murphy, 1990).

19.5 LOCAL REPRESENTATIONS RESULT IN EMERGENT FEATURES

The claim that conceptual combination often results in emergent features that are created or constructed (rather than recalled from memory) is based on several key assumptions about predicates. We first describe these assumptions and explain how they result in constructed emergent features.

A key assumption in our view of conceptual combination is that predicates are represented *locally* (cf. Halff, Ortony, and Anderson, 1976; Solomon and Barsalou, 2004; Wisniewski, 1999). For example, the representation of the predicate *stripes* has a different manifestation or instantiation in the concepts of zebra, barber pole, American flag, and pin-striped pants. Even though we may use the same word 'stripes' to refer to these entities, the corresponding predicates do not have the same representations. That is, there is not a *single* representation of the predicate stripes common to all entities with stripes but rather multiple representations of stripes. Each representation corresponds to a different instantiation that is local and typically unique to an entity characterized by stripes. (For ease of discussion, we focus on predicates that are properties such as 'stripes' as opposed to relations such as 'contains', although later we address local representations of relations.)

A second important assumption is that the local representation of a predicate is characterized by various parameters and their values. For example, possible parameters associated with stripes include number, length, width, spatial extent, width between stripes, colour, orientation, location on the object, texture, etc. The values of these parameters typically depend on other predicates. For example, the values of the length and spatial extent of stripes in a zebra are determined to some extent by other predicates such as the size and shape of zebra (Wisniewski, 1999).

Given these assumptions, it follows that the creation of emergent features is a process that *typically occurs* during conceptual combination. Concepts differ from each other and the dependencies which constrain the parameter values of a predicate will not be identical between the modifier and the head noun. Thus, a predicate in the modifier noun generally cannot be straightforwardly transferred or copied to the noun–noun combination. For example, the use of zebra to refer to stripes in noun–noun combinations is quite productive in American English (e.g. zebra mussel, zebra crossing, zebra fish, zebra finch, zebra cake, zebra wood, and zebra butterfly). Recall the previous example of zebra football, interpreted as 'a football with stripes'. Clearly, one cannot simply copy the local representation of stripes in zebra to zebra football. One must construct a unique, local representation of stripes in zebra football. Constrained by parameters such as size, shape, and texture, a zebra football might have circular stripes whose diameters systematically decrease as they approach each end of the football.

Psychological studies show that a predicate typically consists of local representations rather than a single representation that applies to all entities characterized by the predicate. Solomon and Barsalou (2004) observed that although some entities have similar instantiations of a property (e.g. horses and ponies have similar manes) other entities have different instantiations of that property (e.g. horses and tigers have different manes). They took advantage of these observations to test the local representation hypothesis. In a property verification experiment, participants were presented with a series of trials in which they read the name of an object (e.g. bus) followed by the name of a property (e.g. seat) and verified whether the property was true of the object. Then, they read the name of a second object (e.g. truck) followed by the same property (i.e. seat). Verification time for the property of the second object was facilitated if the property had the same form in the second object. For example, having previously verified that seat is a property of bus, participants more quickly verified that seat was a property of truck (as the seat of the bus is similar to the seat of a truck). However, this benefit was not obtained when verifying that seat was a property of bicycle after previously verifying that seat was a property of bus (as the seat of a bicycle is different from the seat of a truck). This finding is incompatible with the view that a predicate such as seat has a single representation as it would predict that verifying a property as true for one object should facilitate its verification for any other object with that property.

Wisniewski (1998) also provided evidence for local representations during conceptual combination. If a property of an entity is locally represented then its instantiation should depend on parameters of that entity (recall that zebra stripes depend on parameters such as the size, texture, and shape of a zebra). Thus, the instantiation of that property in another concept should differ to the extent that the concepts are dissimilar. For example, the stripes of a zebra clam should differ from those of a zebra but the stripes of a zebra horse should be similar to those of a zebra. In these examples, zebra stripes depend on parameter values that differ in clams but are similar in horses. In one experiment, participants were presented with novel combinations that had either similar constituents (e.g. porcupine pig) or dissimilar constituents (e.g. porcupine dandelion). They then rated how similar the property in the modifier was to that of the property in a novel combination. For example, participants rated how similar the 'prickliness of a porcupine' was to the 'prickliness of a porcupine pig' and how similar the prickliness of a porcupine was to the 'prickliness of a porcupine dandelion'. Participants overwhelmingly rated a property of a modifier as more similar to the property in a similar combination than in a dissimilar combination.

In another experiment, participants read pairs of these combinations and their corresponding property interpretations (e.g. they read, 'a porcupine pig is a prickly pig', and 'a cactus pig is a prickly pig', respectively). For each pair, subjects selected the interpretation which sounded more natural to them. Participants strongly preferred property interpretations of similar combinations to those of dissimilar combinations. For example, participants preferred 'a porcupine pig is a prickly pig' over 'a cactus pig is a prickly pig' but preferred 'a cactus dandelion is a prickly dandelion' over 'a porcupine dandelion is a prickly dandelion'.

This result provides support for the local representation view. When participants read an interpretation of a combination that refers to a property of the modifier, they instantiate that property in the combination. In general, the representation of a property in the combination will match its representation in the modifier of the combination when the modifier is similar to the head noun. Thus, the modifier in a similar combination will more appropriately capture the sense or meaning of its referent, leading to a preference for interpretations of similar combinations. For example, the referent of porcupine pig is a pig whose prickliness is similar to the prickliness of a porcupine. In contrast, the referent of cactus pig is a pig whose prickliness is less similar to the prickliness of a cactus. As a result, porcupine better captures the local representation of prickliness in the referent of porcupine pig than in the referent of cactus pig—leading to a preference for 'a porcupine pig is a prickly pig'. This finding is not predicted by the common representation view. If two combinations contain common representations of the same property then people should not prefer one combination over another with the same head noun (e.g. they should not favour the interpretation of 'a porcupine pig is a prickly pig' over 'a cactus pig is a prickly pig'). In summary, there is strong evidence that nominally identical predicates have different representations whose manifestations are a function of different parameters. When combining a predicate of one concept with another concept, emergent features are likely to occur unless the two concepts have similar representations (cf. zebra horse vs. zebra football). This observation raises the question of how emergent features are constructed.

19.6 HOW ARE EMERGENT FEATURES CREATED?

Within the disciplines of Cognitive Science, there has been a renewed interest in perceptual representations and a move away from traditional representational formalisms such as predicate calculus, feature lists, vectors, and schemata or frames (e.g. Barsalou,

1993, 1999; Barsalou and Prinz, 1997; Gibbs, 1994; Glenberg, 1997; Lakoff and Johnson, 1980; Langacker, 1986, 1987*b*; Talmy, 1988; Zwaan, 2004). Barsalou (1999) has shown that perceptually based representations have the strengths of traditional formalisms such as productivity and the ability to distinguish types from tokens while also overcoming limitations of these formalisms (e.g. neural implausibility and the failure to account for symbol grounding). Some work also suggests that abstract concepts (e.g. truth) can be accounted for by this representational approach (Barsalou, 1999; Langacker, 1986, 1987*b*).

Most importantly, a perceptually based approach to representation and processing leads to a very natural account of how new representations are constructed. Mental representations may be primarily perceptually based with constructive processes closely related to perceiving entities and physically interacting with them. Entities may be represented as a number of basic components with specifications of the spatial relationships between those components together with their orientation, relative size, colour, texture, and so on (Barsalou, 1999; Biederman, 1987; Marr, 1982; Zwaan, Stanfield, and Yaxley, 2002). These characteristics are analogues to the physical characteristics of actual entities in the world. For example, as alluded to earlier, the representation of a zebra might include a spatial layout indicating that the legs were below and perpendicular to body, that the tail was connected to the end of body and relatively much smaller than the body, that the neck was connected at an angle to the front of body, and that stripes were spread out across the exterior of parts of the zebra body.

People would use a variety of processes to operate on these representations which also have physical analogues in the real world. These processes include the mental rotation translation, expansion, and contraction of entities or their components. A vast body of work on mental imagery has established that people use these and other related processes (see Finke (1989) for an extensive review). These and other processes could be involved in the construction of emergent features. To take a speculative example, a person might interpret zebra clam as 'a clam with stripes' by aligning the exteriors of zebra and clam and mentally contracting the stripes of a zebra, translating them along the entire exterior of the clam, just as they are spread along the exterior of the zebra. The next step in providing an account of conceptual combination and metaphor is to develop a computational model that creates emergent features.

19.7 CONSTRUCTING EMERGENT FEATURES

To illustrate the processes that might occur in producing emergent features during conceptual combination, consider the previous examples of the novel combinations 'roller-coaster dinner', 'rake pencil', 'porcupine mushroom'. In 'roller-coaster dinner' one-third of participants interpreted this novel phrase with the emergent feature, 'a series of courses that alternated from tasting good to tasting bad'. (One-quarter of the participants interpreted this phrase with the emergent feature, 'a dinner in which the conversation of the diners alternated between positive emotions and negative emotions', though we focus on the former example). In the alternating courses interpretation, the predicate describing the repeating and alternating subevent of 'going up then going down' is activated because it is characteristic and distinctive of roller coaster. This temporal predicate might be aligned with another characteristic-distinctive predicate of the head noun, the temporal predicate, 'a series of courses'. To construct the emergent predicate, the values 'up' and 'down' in the spatial dimension are used to align and create alternating values of 'good' and 'bad' in the taste dimension. This process involves the alignment of non-identical predicates (Wisniewski (1997) discusses how this type of alignment might occur). In this example, people's background knowledge may also contribute to the construction of the emergent predicate. For example, based on knowledge of dining and roller coaster rides, people may infer that the time between the good and bad courses will be less than the time to ascend and descend in the roller coaster.

In another experiment, participants were asked to draw a porcupine mushroom that was prickly. In this interpretation, the characteristic-distinctive predicate was provided by the experimenter. A number of participants drew a mushroom with prickly protrusions on the cap of the mushroom. This finding suggests that participants aligned the mushroom cap with the back of a porcupine, based on their similar relative locations. Participants may have created this emergent feature by imagining sharp protrusions reduced in size, length, and spatial extent relative to the size, length, and spatial extent of the quills of a porcupine (using alignment, along with mental contraction) Also, based on their background knowledge, participants likely changed the composition of the prickly protrusions (we doubt that they literally interpreted the protrusions as porcupine quills).

A third example of emergent features in conceptual combination is illustrated by interpretations of 'rake pencil'. In another experiment, more than one-third of the participants described the referent as, 'a pencil with multiple lead points'. In this novel combination, a characteristic-distinctive predicate is the 'teeth' attached to the end of the rake. The 'teeth' and pencil point are aligned with each other based on similar features and spatial layout (e.g. both pencil points and rake teeth are sharp and are located at the 'same end'). People then create a structure at the 'pencil point' end of the pencil which resembles a rake but is much smaller, made out of wood and involves multiple lead points (though fewer in number than the teeth of a rake). People's background knowledge may constrain the number of lead points because a pencil with the same number of lead points as rake teeth might not be practical or because they can imagine another function for this novel pencil (e.g. one participant suggested that a pencil with four lead points could be used for drawing the lines of music paper).

These three examples of emergent features in conceptual combination involve property interpretations. However, it is not too difficult to contrive examples of emergent relations. For example, consider the novel combinations 'baby scarf' vs. 'giraffe scarf'. Relative to the typical scarf, a giraffe scarf is likely to be very long and wrapped a number of times around the giraffe's neck whereas the baby scarf is likely to be much smaller and wrapped fewer times around the baby's neck. In these examples, the emergent relation is 'wrapped around' which varies as a function of its argument or role filler (i.e. scarf and type of animate being).

As another example, the containment relations that form the basis of the interpretations of 'ladder box' and 'silver dollar box' are likely to refer to boxes that mirror the size and dimensions of what they contain. Thus, compared to the average box, a ladder box will be much longer in one dimension but a silver dollar box will be very small in all dimensions. As one more example, the 'depicts' relations that form the basis of the interpretations of 'elephant photograph' and 'elephant mural' are likely to involve two-dimensional representations of elephants (rather than actual elephants) with the former referring to a smaller representation of an elephant than the latter.

Some readers may object that most of our examples of novel combinations are unusual, uncommon, or metaphorical. Hence, these examples do not characterize typical language use. However, American English and Chinese contain a *very large number* of 'unusual' combinations (e.g. mushroom anchor, butterfly chair, liquid nails, scorpion fly, snake light, toilet duck, peninsula table, rake comb, guitar fish, shoe tree, oven bird, alphabet soup). (See Wisniewski and Love, 1998; Wu, 2006, for more examples.) Non-literal, metaphorical language is ubiquitous (Gibbs, 1994). Reading American English very carefully reveals many examples of non-literal, figurative language: 'The baby sitter kept an eye on the child', 'The White House disputed the New York Times report', 'I'm going to run up to the store', and so on. Much of language use is not literally true and one could not successfully function in society without being able to understand unusual, non-literal, metaphorical language.

19.8 THE STATUS QUO: MODELS OF CONCEPTUAL COMBINATION AND METAPHOR

We have suggested that concepts are typically combined by selecting a characteristic-distinctive predicate from one concept and integrating into the second concept. As a result, the characteristic distinctive predicate is modified, sharing aspects of both concepts but resulting in a unique feature. This process results in the construction or creation of an emergent feature. Specifying and understanding the construction of emergent features is not well understood. Nor has it been seriously addressed. Thus, it is not surprising that many models of conceptual combination and metaphor do not postulate mechanisms for the construction of emergent features. Instead, these models interpret novel combinations or metaphors by selecting predicates and literally copying them from one concept to another. Consequently, these models are strictly compositional. For example, the interactive property attribution model (Estes and Glucksberg, 2000) assumes that property interpretations occur when a salient predicate of the modifier coincides with a relevant dimension of the head noun. For example, 'light' is a salient predicate characterizing the weight of a feather, whereas 'weight' is a relevant dimension that characterizes luggage (Estes and Glucksberg, 2000). Thus, people recognize the correspondence between 'light' and 'weight' and interpret feather luggage as light luggage. Although this model selects predicates that form the basis of an interpretation of a noun–noun combination, it does not construct emergent features from these predicates. In this example, 'light' is a relative predicate whose meaning changes somewhat depending on the referent of the head noun (e.g. light luggage weighs more than a light pen). More generally, the interactive activation model could select a predicate such as 'stripes' but cannot instantiate different, emergent versions of the predicate (e.g. zebra football vs. zebra horse).

As another example, in the 'competition among relations in nominals (CARIN) model' (Gagné and Shoben, 1997) the modifier noun activates a relation that is used to link the modifier and head noun concepts together to form an interpretation. For example, in 'chocolate ostrich' the modifier activates the relation 'made of', resulting in the interpretation 'ostrich made of chocolate'. However, as noted earlier, relations can have emergent meanings depending on their arguments. People probably assume that a chocolate ostrich is composed completely of chocolate. However, in an unpublished study, we found that 'chocolate grapes' were typically interpreted as 'grapes with melted chocolate poured over them', and 'chocolate ravioli' as 'ravioli with chocolate inside the ravioli'. However, the CARIN model assumes that 'made of' (as well as other relations) only function to link the modifier and head noun in forming an interpretation of a novel combination. One model that is not strictly compositional is Murphy's concept specialization model. This model addresses emergent features at the post-compehension stage but has not focused on the construction of emergent features as we have described them.

A number of models of analogy, simile, and metaphor understanding are strictly compositional. In these models, researchers explicitly refer to a *copy process* that literally transfers predicates from one concept to another (Falkenhainer, Forbus, and Gentner, 1989; Holyoak and Thagard, 1989; Hummel and Holyoak, 1998; Keane, Ledgeway, and Duff, 1994). For example, Holyoak and Thagard (1989) suggest that 'the general form of analogical transfer is to find correspondences among elements of the source and target, and then construct candidate inferences about the target by essentially copying over propositions from the source.' As another example, Gentner (1989) suggests that the understanding of an analogy such as 'the atom is like the solar system', includes copying the predicate revolves from solar system to atom and substituting the arguments planets and sun in the solar system with electrons and the nucleus.

19.9 CONCLUSION AND SUMMARY

We have suggested that conceptual combination typically results in the creation of emergent features and have provided some evidence for such features. We have also described how integrative, constructive, and alignment processes might lead to the creation of these features. This account presents a serious challenge to current compositional models of conceptual combination and metaphor. Our account is also problematic for models that only assume that emergent features arise from a post-comprehension process based on extensional feedback. In our view, researchers and scholars must reconceptualize the problem of how people understand metaphors and combine concepts. More generally, language understanding emerges through interactions between concepts that often lead to the creation of emergent features.

CHAPTER 20

CAN PROTOTYPE REPRESENTATIONS SUPPORT COMPOSITION AND DECOMPOSITION?

LILA R. GLEITMAN,
ANDREW C. CONNOLLY, AND
SHARON LEE ARMSTRONG

Tho' a particular colour, taste, and smell, are qualities all united together in this apple, 'tis easy to perceive they are not the same, but are at least distinguishable from each other.

(David Hume, Treatise, Book I)

Red is any of a number of similar colors evoked by light consisting predominantly of the longest wavelengths of light discernible by the human eye, in the wavelength range of roughly 625–740 nm.

(Wikipedia)

Red hair (also referred to as auburn, ginger or titian) varies from a deep orange-red through burnt orange to bright copper.

(Wikipedia)

20.1 INTRODUCTION

Concepts have always been central to theories of cognition, and yet even in the modern era there is considerable disagreement about just what they are. Early theories often treated concepts as icons (something like a mental image, e.g., Hume, 1739). A more recent view has been that a concept is a definition, something like a set of necessary and sufficient conditions for a thing to fall under the concept (e.g. Frege, 1892; Miller and

Johnson-Laird, 1976). So, for example, to satisfy the APPLE concept ('to be an apple. . .'), a thing must exhibit *roundness, edibility, redness, fruitiness,* and so on. Such theories have been touted partly on the grounds that they are said to yield a classification of the objects, properties, events, and relations in which human cognition traffics, and to explain the resemblances that hold across the set of concepts. For instance, apples resemble fire engines by sharing the characteristic of *redness,* they resemble balls by sharing *roundness,* and peaches by being *edible.* However, this theory of concept structure has lost much of its popularity, largely because apples, although most often red, are not necessarily so (there are Granny Smith apples and spoilt brown apples); they are usually but not necessarily round (there are oval and squashed apples); and they are occasionally inedible or at least indigestible (remember Eve and wicked step-mothers). In response to these manifest differences among category members, the dominant positions in psychology and cognitive science today hold that concepts are prototypes (something like a set of weighted properties which things that fall under the concept typically have or are believed to have; Rosch, 1978; Rosch and Mervis, 1975; Smith and Medin, 1981; Prinz, 2002).[1]

In the present chapter, we review two kinds of experimental evidence from our laboratories that challenge the adequacy of prototypes for representing human concepts. First, we will review experiments suggesting that prototype theory does not distin-guish adequately among concepts of maximally variant types, such as formal (e.g. ODD NUMBER) vs. natural kind and artifact (e.g. APPLE and HOCKEY) concepts (Armstrong, Gleitman, and Gleitman, 1983). Second, we will review a more recent experimental line demonstrating how theories of conceptual combination with lexical prototypes fail to predict actual phrasal interpretations, such as language users' doubts as to whether Lithuanian apples are likely to be as edible as apples (Connolly, Fodor, Gleitman, and Gleitman, 2007). We should emphasize at the outset that these studies in no way chal-lenge the view that many concepts have prototypes. Rather, we take our findings to support a distinction between concepts' *having* prototypes and *being* prototypes. Before introducing the experiments, we want to sketch the relation, as we see it, between the varying views of what concepts are and the problem of compositionality that is the more general topic of the present volume.

20.2 FEATURES, PROTOTYPES, AND THE PROBLEM OF COMPOSITIONALITY

Most people who have thought about the meanings of common words assume that the vast majority of them are complex, composed by conjoining several simpler (primitive) concepts, sometimes called features or attributes. We regard this view as the Humean

---

[1] Throughout we will follow the notational convention of referring to properties or features using *italics,* to mentioned words and phrases using 'single quotes', and to concepts using small CAPS. For example, the concept RED represents or denotes the property of *redness,* for which the English word is 'red'.

status quo, though we do not necessarily endorse it. After all, as there are only finitely many words in a speaker-listener's repertoire, it is possible to believe that our elementary concepts are at about the same level and grain as the word/morpheme (e.g. Fodor, 1981), although to be sure in a minority of cases languages draw their lexical boundaries in different places. Nevertheless the idea that lexical-level concepts are compositions out of simpler formatives has been attractive for several reasons, among them the possibility of reducing the number and types of hypothesized mental primitives, and—as we remarked earlier—explaining the resemblances among concepts as a matter of feature overlap (why and how apples and peaches are more alike than either of these is to, say, pencils).[2]

While there is debate as to whether lexical-level concepts are compositional, it is a truism that understanding language requires the compositionality of word meanings (Frege, 1914). Whatever the concepts expressed by the words 'apple', 'red', etc., the standard view is that these must be the ultimate constituents of compositional mental representations for the meanings of phrases such as 'red apple', 'purple apple', and 'Chinese apple'. It follows that these complex (phrasal) representations resemble each other in meaning by component overlap: They have something in common, namely that the concept APPLE is a constituent of each. According to conventional wisdom, then, we can understand each of these phrases because we have the concept referred to by 'apple', which in turn is composed of *roundness, edibility*, and so forth. In sum, the compositional properties of phrasal concepts would seem to be necessary so as to explain the productivity and systematicity of thought, and thus by-and-by, how we are able to produce and understand more than one word at a time. Thus, a theory of concepts must satisfy the compositionality constraint:

Compositionality Constraint (CC): The meaning of a complex expression is determined by the meanings of its constituents plus the syntactic rules used to combine them.[3]

Consider as a further example the descriptions of 'red' and 'red hair' in the prefatory quotes to this chapter. Classical theories of concepts hold that RED denotes a certain

---

[2] To the extent that something like Fodor's view is correct, APPLE is an elementary concept and composition applies to it *tout court* as a constituent of complex concepts such as PURPLE APPLE and POISONED APPLE. This position in no way denies our knowledge about characteristics shared (necessarily or probabilistically) by apples, denying only that this knowledge is constituitive of or (in some cases) even relevant to the concept itself.

[3] That the principle of compositionality is exceptional in several respects is well-known, e.g. former senators are not senators, decoy ducks aren't ducks, and stone lions aren't lions (see Kamp and Partee, 1995 for discussion). Another class of difficulties has to do with the context dependence of indexicals and pronouns such as 'here' and 'it'. Exactly what the principle of compositionality requires of meanings and concepts is, for these and related reasons, a matter of open debate. To be sure, the arguments made in this chapter would be strengthened if a strong form of the compositionality constraint turned out to be true, especially one requiring that **reverse compositionality** holds as well (e.g. Fodor, 1998*b*; Fodor and Lepore, 2002; Pagin, 2003; see Robbins, 2005, and Patterson, 2005, for counter-arguments). However, the findings we report and our interpretations of them require only that over an important (and indefinitely large) subset of phrasal-level concepts, the standard formulation of CC holds.

range of hues without regard to the frequency with which any one component hue might have been observed or to its position within the range of reds (whether at the centre around wavelengths 700 nm or at the margin where red meets, say, brown). 'Red hair' is compositional because its being a noun phrase is entirely determined by the fact that 'red' is an adjective, 'hair' is a noun, and AN structures are NPs in English; its meaning is fully determined by the fact that 'red' expresses the property *red* and 'hair' denotes the range of follicular mammalian skin coverings, together with the principle that AN representations denote the intersection of the As and the Ns. Thus 'red hair' means *hair that is red*. The crucial assumptions are that

(1) a concept expresses the full range of variation allowed for instances that fall under it;
(2) the syntactic and semantic properties of the constituents of complex concepts are context independent.

In virtue of these strictures, the classical concept descriptions are hard-edged (all or none): 'red' applies to all and only *redness*, 'hair' to all and only *hair*, and their combination covers all and only the cases that would be correctly considered as actual or possible members of the extension of the phrase, 'red hair'. Such a theory affords the flexibility and abstractness needed to account for all interpretive possibilities. For example, you wouldn't be likely to guess, upon learning that someone you haven't met has red hair, that the particular hair-hue was vibrant fire-engine red. But as anyone who has been to Manhattan's East Village can attest, this is certainly possible. Conceptualization has to allow for bizarre entities and events. For the same reasons, context independence properly bounds conceptual combination, in the sense of assuring for example, that 'red cheeks' not be interpretable as *cheeks that are green* or *elbows that are red*.

Nevertheless, the fact that this theory does not address the question of plausibilities may be taken as a defect. Consider again the concept RED. The colours of cherries and apples seem 'better', more typical, or more central instances of reds than do the colours of human hair, but the classical theory fails to account for such effects. In fact, under combination the typicality facts in this case reverse such that the expected hue for a human redhead (or a red fox) is not prototypical red at all.[4] This appears to be context dependence *par excellence*, an ominous potential violation of (2), itself a non-negotiable

---

[4] It is an embarrassment to any theory of concepts we know of (except the one that says 'red hair' is an idiom) that several typical hues of human red hair (auburn, ginger, titian) as referred to by Wikipedia turn out to be hues that the same source describes as among the browns rather than among the reds. (See the prefatory quotes to this chapter.) Another embarrassing instance is that the dog often called a Miniature Collie (because it looks just like a miniature collie) turns out to be another breed altogether (the Sheltie) and no Collie at all. Such cases are common. This argues either that the compositionality constraint is too strong (see again fn. 3) or that there are more phrasal idioms than you might have thought.

property of the classical theory. Insofar as traditional concept theories attend to such issues, it is by assuming that the recovery of meaning from the concept descriptions and their combinatorics is only a first step in the real business of everyday understanding. A second, and also crucial, step is the application of a further set of pragmatic-inferential processes that draw on general knowledge of the world. These latter processes supply the plausibility facts.

An alternative set of views, collectively termed **prototype** approaches, were introduced in the mid 1970s by Eleanor Rosch and her colleagues, and today these and related probabilistic perspectives dominate theories of concepts in the psychological literature (Rosch, 1973, 1978; Rosch and Mervis, 1975; Smith and Medin, 1981; Lakoff, 1987a; Hampton, 1993; Barsalou, 1999; Murphy, 2002; Prinz, 2002). The general properties of prototype theories are, as the saying goes, too well-known to require much introduction, but we will mention a few highlights that are important for our further discussion.

Rosch and later theorists allied with the prototype tradition assert that concepts are internally organized roughly as a set of weighted components or features, held together in a family-resemblance structure (following earlier suggestions from Wittgenstein, 1953). What this means is that the set of features that comprise a concept and establish membership in it is not all-or-none, but graded. The conditions for membership in a concept are satisfied for some item when it exhibits a number of these features, but by no means necessarily all of them. As well, the features themselves may bear different weights within the category such that an item's partaking of the heavily weighted features also counts toward its position within the category. Centrality or typicality in the category, for any potential item, is computed as some composite of the number and weighting of the concept features the item exhibits, with high scores being the measure of typicality of an instance.

Consider for example the concept BIRD. Typical properties of birds presumably are that they *fly*, *have wings*, *feathers*, *claws*, *lay eggs*, and have certain *body proportions*. Ostriches lack a heavily weighted property of the bird category (they do not fly) which relegates them to marginal status. Pelicans lose some typicality points too owing to their ungainly proportions but at least they can fly (though awkwardly, it is said). A robin, embodying many heavily weighted bird-properties—a good flier of graceful birdy proportions—is a central or prototypical member. In sum, the all-or-none property of the classical theory is relaxed under prototype theory with category membership a matter of degree. On the matter of conceptual combination, the prototype views further part company with tradition by allowing some degree of context dependence. Thus while the classical analysis of a concept such as HAIR makes no distinction as to colour, a HAIR-prototype may very well incorporate this very distinction, representing and weighting the typical range of mammalian or human hair colours. Such an analysis provides the first components of an explanation for the differential hue-expectations for hair, cheeks, and apples: the *redness* range for hair could be specified along a colour dimension within the representation of HAIR, the *redness* range for cheeks within the representation of CHEEK, and so forth (Katz, 1964; Kamp and Partee, 1995; Osherson and Smith, 1981).

20.2.1 Summary and prospectus

As we see it, the fundamental idea behind prototype theory is, as much as possible, to build the facts about typicality and plausibility directly into the representations of the concepts themselves and, consequently, into the combinatorics for complex concepts and the phrases that express them. Though most prototype theorists acknowledge that a partly separate inferential-pragmatic theory incorporating our general knowledge of the world is a crucial part of human understanding, the idea behind the prototype approach is to develop a theory in which the concept representations themselves will bear as much of the interpretive burden as possible. In the experiments that we now discuss, we will explore the adequacy of prototype theory in terms of two questions: (1) Are lexical concepts represented as prototypes? and (2) to the extent that they are, could such prototypicality representations compose lawfully into phrases?

20.3 ARE CONCEPTS PROTOTYPES?

An extensive body of empirical research seems to provide evidence for the psychological validity of the prototype position. For example, the left hand column of Table 20.1 shows two everyday superordinate categories—FRUIT and VEHICLE—and some exemplars of each (e.g. apple, fig for FRUIT). In an influential study, Rosch (1975) asked subjects to indicate how good an example each exemplar was of its category by use of an appropriate rating scale. It is worth quoting part of the instructions that were used in this experiment:

> This study has to do with what we have in mind when we use words which refer to categories. . . . Think of dogs. You all have some notion of what a 'real dog', a 'doggy dog' is. To me a retriever or a German Shepherd is a very doggy dog while a Pekinese is a less doggy dog. Notice that this kind of judgment has nothing to do with how well you like the thing. . . . You may prefer to own a Pekinese without thinking that it is the breed that best represents what people mean by dogginess. On this form you are asked to judge how good an example of a category various instances of the category are . . . (Rosch, 1975: 198).

Notice then that the instructions assent to the membership of both these animals in the category DOG but then equivocate ('doggy dog') about how the subject is to make distinctions among the class members, a matter to which we will return later. In any case, subjects now rated each instance of each category using response templates of this approximate sort:

FRUIT

apple

1	2	3	4	5	6	7
good					poor	

It turns out that given instructions of this kind and stimulus presentations of this form, people will say that apples are commendable examples of FRUIT, and deserve the lower-numbered ratings (that is, the 1s and 2s rather than 5s and 7s), while figs and olives are poor exemplars and deserve the higher-numbered ratings. Moreover, agreement among subjects is remarkably high with split-half correlations between subject group rankings of approximately .97.[5]

The left-hand column of means in the top half of Table 20.1 shows a successful replication of these effects by Armstrong et al. (1983). Notice that if these subjects were successfully ranking, for example, the apples and the figs for their membership in the category FRUIT, their performance appears to be incompatible with the classical theory of concepts. This is because that theory holds that membership in a category depends on having vs. not having some specified necessary and sufficient set of features. An item lacking any one of these features would be out of the category altogether (off the bottom of the scale at 7+), while those having them—from apples to olives—would be equally FRUITY (rated uniformly as 1s). In short, a coherent ranking of concept membership should have been impossible if subjects thought that membership in the FRUIT and VEHICLE categories is all or none.

Rosch and her colleagues interpreted these findings as evidence that category membership is graded and thus inconsistent with the standard classical theory. Dozens of experiments in the concept literature during the subsequent thirty or so years have achieved the same kinds of results and thus seem to bolster this interpretation of concept structure in general. For instance, asked to name members of a category, subjects reliably list the more stereotypical ones first; subjects can name more attributes/features and agree on more of them for prototypical members than for marginal members (Cree and McRae, 2003); and subjects respond faster in a verification task to items with high exemplariness ratings (e.g. 'A robin is a bird') than to those with lower ones ('An ostrich is a bird') with appropriate controls for word frequency (Rips, Shoben, and Smith, 1973; Rosch, 1975).

---

[5] There has been some objection to the adequacy of the split-half statistical procedure used by Rosch and colleagues to assess cross-subject reliability in these ratings tasks, although this method was state of the art at the time these investigators used it (see Barsalou, 1987). Armstrong et al. (1983) and the report thereof in the present chapter continue to use this relatively weak assessment tool, for comparability with prior findings and reports.

Table 20.1 Exemplar ratings

Categories, category exemplars, and mean exemplariness ratings for prototype and well-defined categories for subjects who were asked only to give exemplariness ratings (Experiment I) compared to subjects who were asked first whether it made sense to rate items for degree of membership within the category and then to give exemplariness ratings (Experiment II).

	Experiment I (all 31 subjects)		Experiment II (the subjects who said NO out of N = 21)	
	n	M	n	M
Prototype categories				
Fruit	31		9	
Apple		1.3		1.3
Strawberry		2.1		1.7
Plum		2.5		1.9
Pineapple		2.7		1.3
Fig		5.2		3.3
Olive		6.4		4.2
Vehicle	31		5	
Car		1.0		1.0
Boat		3.3		1.6
Scooter		4.5		3.8
Tricycle		4.7		2.6
Horse		5.2		2.8
Skis		5.6		5.2
Well-defined categories				
Odd number	31		21	
3		1.6		1.0
7		1.9		1.0
23		2.4		1.3
57		2.6		1.5
501		3.5		1.8
447		3.7		1.9
Female	31		18	
Mother		1.7		1.1
Housewife		2.4		1.8
Princess		3.0		2.1
Waitress		3.2		2.4
Policewoman		3.9		2.9
Comedienne		4.5		3.1

Only data for subjects who said NO to this question are included here. Lower numbers correspond to ratings of comparative goodness of the exemplar, e.g. apples were judged as better fruits (mean rating 1.3) than olives (mean rating 6.4).

Source: (adapted from Armstrong et al. (1983).

Seemingly related typicality effects are found again and again in almost every domain of human existence and relation. There have been prototype-like analyses of cultures (Sinha, 2002), of social structures and groupings (Hess, Pullen, and McGee, 1996), of the profiles of drinkers and smokers (Spijkerman and van den Eijnden, 2004), of love (Aron and Westbay, 1996), and of mobile telephone users (Walsh and White, 2007), to name just a few. In the light of the reliability and domain-generality of such findings, one might well conclude, as have many cognitive psychologists, that the psychological validity of the prototype descriptions of human concepts and categories has been demonstrated beyond reasonable doubt.

But perhaps these victories for prototype theory have been wrested too cheaply. The basis for claiming that certain categories have a prototypical, non-definitional, feature structure has always been the finding of graded responses to their exemplars in various experimental paradigms. But this is only half of the required demonstration, for the truth of the contrapositive has been left implicit rather than being tested directly: If you believe certain concepts are non-definitional because of graded responses to their exemplars, that must be because you also believe that if the categories were all-or-none in character, the graded responses would not have been achieved. Thus a necessary part of the proof requires finding some categories that do have definition-like, categorical, descriptions, showing as well that subjects patently know and assent to these definitions; and, finally, showing that these new category types do not yield the graded outcomes.

Armstrong et al. (1983) attempted to carry out this further part of the required experimental programme by repeating some of Rosch's original procedures, but adding putatively well-defined categories (EVEN NUMBER, ODD NUMBER, FEMALE, and PLANE GEOMETRY FIGURE) to those that had previously been studied (such as FRUIT, FURNITURE, VEHICLE, SPORT). One replication was of the exemplar-rating procedure. In addition to the previously studied categories, they added the formal ones, and presented all of them using the original instructions devised by Rosch (reproduced in the present chapter on p. 423), and the original response templates, for example:

ODD NUMBER
501

1	2	3	4	5	6	7
good					poor	

The findings for ODD NUMBER and FEMALE are shown in the bottom half of Table 20.1. The exemplars of the well-defined categories elicited differential ratings much as had categories such as FRUIT, and at high levels of reliability (rank order split-half correlations were .94, .81, .92, and .92, for EVEN NUMBER, ODD NUMBER, FEMALE, and PLANE GEOMETRY FIGURE, respectively). Keep in mind that these subjects were being asked, for example, to distinguish among odd numbers for their oddity, and common sense asserts one cannot do so. But the subjects could and did: They judged 3 a better ODD NUMBER than 501—and Mother a better FEMALE than comedienne.

One trivializing response to these findings has been that the subjects were knowingly responding in different ways to the two types of stimuli, despite the task instructions. For the categories studied by Rosch, perhaps, they answered with their true assessments of the prototypical organization of, say, FRUIT; but for the formal categories, they responded as though answering silly questions with silly answers. To assess this interpretation, Armstrong et al. (1983) also replicated earlier verification tasks (Rips et al. 1973; Rosch, 1975) which are not as susceptible to such a disclaimer because the requirement for speeded responses discourages self-conscious consideration of category types. Subjects were presented with sentences of the form *An A is a B* in which *B* was a category of which *A* was said to be an exemplar, for both formal and everyday categories. Half of the sentences were true (e.g. 'An orange is a fruit') and half were false ('An orange is a vehicle'). The subjects' task was to answer (by a key press) true or false to each such statement as rapidly as possible. Items with higher exemplariness ratings were verified more quickly than those with lower ratings. This was true for both the putative prototype categories studied by Rips et al. (1973) and Rosch (1975) and for the formal categories (e.g. 'A circle is a plane geometry figure' vs. 'A circle is an odd number').

Some responses to these demonstrations have been to the effect that perhaps concepts such as ODD NUMBER and FEMALE are prototype-like in the same manner as FRUIT and VEHICLE (e.g. Lakoff, 1987a). Exactly what would be implied by such a move is hard to fathom, for clearly notions like ODD NUMBER have definitions that are known to their users and pattern within a theory of arithmetic whose organization cannot be rendered in prototype theory.

Armstrong et al. (1983) reasoned that the many demonstrations of prototype theory are relevant to the exemplariness of instances of a concept rather than to membership (see also Rey (1983) for an important discussion). Good exemplars exhibit the surface features that are most frequently associated with a concept and thus they are easily recognizable as members, but this recognition function need not bear straightforwardly on the issue of category membership. Mammals that swim (such as whales) and albino tigers are atypical and thus easily misclassified, but in the end they are nevertheless whales and tigers respectively. And similarly, as Wanner (1979) showed, people's judgements of prototypical prime numbers are those that go through certain heuristic decision procedures easily. Indeed when we examine the instructions in the Rosch exemplar rating task, we see a number of confusing and perhaps contradictory phrases ('a very doggy dog', 'the breed that best represents what people mean by dogginess', 'how good an example of a category various instances of the category are') that sometimes allude to the category itself and sometimes to attributes of its members.

Armstrong et al. (1983) explored this distinction between concept membership and concept exemplariness in a final experiment. Subjects were asked straight out 'Does it make sense to rate items in this category for *degree of membership* in the category?'

Subjects clearly distinguished formal categories from prototype categories in this paradigm: 100 percent judged that it was nonsensical to rate instances of EVEN NUMBER, ODD NUMBER, and PLANE GEOMETRY FIGURE as to 'how good' they were as members of their respective classes, and a substantial percentage (86 per cent) said the same of FEMALE. Percentages for 'everyday' categories were much lower, with FRUIT, SPORT, VEGETABLE, and VEHICLE being judged all-or-none by 43, 71, 33, and 24 per cent of subjects, respectively.

A crucial further task was then presented to these same subjects: They performed the Rosch exemplar ratings task for instances of all the categories including the formal ones. The results are shown in the bottom half of Table 20.1. Note particularly the response characteristics of those subjects (those in the right-hand columns of the table) who had previously averred that rating degree of membership in the specified category made no sense at all, for example those who said that being a FRUIT or being a FEMALE was all-or-none. Yet subsequently presented with the Rosch instructions to distinguish 'doggy dogs' from less doggy ones, these subjects provided differential rankings, judging 'really odd odd numbers' better than 'less odd ones'. For instance they rated 3 better than 501, among the odd numbers. Indeed it is true, as Table 20.1 shows, that these subjects used less of the scale for the formal categories than they did for the everyday categories (rating no odd number as worse than a 2, on a scale of ODDity that ranged from 1 to 7). But even so! No person who knows and states that all odd numbers are equally odd should rate some of them more odd than any others, even by a smidgen.

Arguably the subjects in the two parts of this experiment did not contradict themselves at all, despite first appearances. Rather, their differential behaviour reflects the fact that the instructions assigned them two different tasks. In part 1 of the experiment, they were asked to (and did) consider the issue of category membership which in the case of formal categories was judged to be all-or-none. But in part 2 they were asked to consider the issue of exemplariness of an item for its category, not at all the same thing. The implications of this disconnect present problems for the usual interpretation of the tasks asking subjects to rate items within categories. It cannot be assumed that the results of ratings tasks reveal concept membership or structure.

In sum, the psychological literature contains scores of demonstrations that people distinguish between typical and marginal members of a concept or class. Plausibly the prototypical instances are those that exhibit several properties (features) that are quite regularly observed in members of that category. These properties represent things we know are true of most, for example, tigers we have seen, and therefore serve as rough and ready clues that some new creature we are viewing is probably also a tiger. Indeed it might be very difficult to recognize a tame, albino, three-legged, toothless tiger as a tiger, and easy to judge that it is a sorry example of a tiger. All the same, it is likely an error to conclude that these surface features are constituitive of the TIGER concept. Armstrong et al., in the work just reviewed, studied this difference between *having a prototype* and *being a prototype* with formal concepts where the distinction arises starkly: nine is a prototypical odd number, probably because in addition to being an integer not divisible by two without remainder it is low in cardinality, familiar, and 'looks primey' (cf., Wanner, 1979), All the same, to claim that 9 is odder than 99 is to be risibly ignorant of the facts about addition and subtraction, systems on which the concepts of NINE and NINETY-NINE are defined. These exclude factors such as low cardinality.

20.4 DO PROTOTYPES COMPOSE?

In the previous section, we raised some doubts as to whether everyday human concepts are represented prototypically as much theorizing in psychology has suggested. The argument was an indirect one for in fact all that was shown was that formal concepts with known internal structure exhibit typicality effects that are at odds with that structure in the psychological laboratory. This bears relevantly on the adequacy of typicality (or measures of typicality) for assessing the structure of concepts, but does not by itself force us to reject (or accept) some variant of a prototype theory. We now ask the same question about concept representation in a more direct way. Suppose that concepts really were prototype-style mental representations; could these representations underlie our actual interpretation of the phrasal concepts, thus satisfying the compositionality constraint? For example, assuming the prototypes of RED and APPLE as the constituents of the complex concept RED APPLE, we must assume that these compose to a prototypical apple that is prototypically red. But is this the desired outcome, the one that comports with how people understand phrases expressing these complex concepts?

A pessimistic argument from Fodor (e.g. Fodor and Lepore, 1996) considers as a test case the phrase 'pet fish'.[6] Perhaps there is a widely shared image that comes to mind for 'pet fish', something like the guppies that typically inhabit home aquariums. This example, among countless others, shows us that complex concepts can have stereotypes. Prototype theory says that the concept PET is itself represented as the set of stereotypic properties of pets and FISH is represented as the stereotypic properties of fish. Compositionality under prototype theory thus entails that to understand the linguistic

---

[6] Several commentators have claimed that the failure of the prototype theory for 'pet fish' may be dismissed on grounds that this phrase is idiomatic in the sense that the stereotype is set not through composition over stereotypes, but rather through direct experience of pet fish in the world (a.k.a., 'extensional feedback', see Hampton, 1988a; Rips, 1995). But notice that the same arguments Fodor and Lepore (1996) made for pet fish can be made just as well for brown cows. For it could very well be the case that brown cows are not prototypically brown (rather, they might always or usually be a reddish brown) or prototypical cows (rather, they might be especially large, robust, or cantankerous). Furthermore, notice that the combinatorics of PET FISH are exactly as one would expect in the classical theory, i.e. something that is necessarily a PET and a FISH. Suppose that the king of South Dakota kept a Great White Shark in his aquarium for the amusement of his guests and himself. Then this creature is a pet fish, though hardly a stereotypical one. In contrast idiomatic phrases fail the test of compositionality which is why they are called idioms in the first place. For instance the idiomatic green thumb is neither green nor a thumb, but rather a person who disports in the garden. On the compositional interpretation, a green thumb is something that is both green and a thumb. To count as an idiom, the phrase 'pet fish' would similarly have to have two disjoint interpretations, and it does not.

expression 'pet fish' we must compute the prototype as a function of the prototypes for 'pet' (i.e. something like a golden retriever) and 'fish' (i.e. something like a trout). Given these prototypes, the derivation of the prototype for 'pet fish', which is neither dog-like nor trout-like, appears on its face to be intractable (though Hampton (1988a), attempts such a derivation for 'pet fish' in his composite prototype model which we will discuss later in this section). If this problem generalizes, it presents a major challenge for prototype theory. We believe it does generalize and we next review experimental evidence in support of this position from Connolly et al. (2007).

An obvious reason to believe that the pet fish problem is general is that we modify nouns when speaking just in those cases where we are talking about something other than the typical case. We say 'green lime' and 'orange carrot' very rarely just because these are the stereotypic colours of these edibles and therefore the modifier seems superfluous, hence odd to utter under Gricean conventions (Grice, 1975). It follows that the stereotypical properties and inferences assumed to be true of unmodified nouns are likely to apply less to modified nouns in general simply because the act of modification is ordinarily a mapping away from the typical case. This fact is problematic for using the prototypes of the simples to compose the complex concepts just because the prototype would seem less relevant within the context of combination. Nevertheless, there have been several attempts to reconcile prototypes with the requirements of compositionality.

One of the most well-specified and widely cited models of prototype-based composition is the **selective modification model** of Smith, Osherson, Rips, and Keane (1988b). A diagram of how their model works to accomplish conceptual combination for Hume's iconic APPLE instance is shown as Fig. 20.1. Notice that the model avoids proliferating and uncontrolled context dependence by assuming that almost all features of the constituent elements retain their original (prototypical) values under combination, the only revision for RED APPLE being the feature dimension explicitly influenced by the combination; namely, its colour. While the specification for APPLE gives some weight ('votes') to colours other than red, the rules of combination shift all the colour weights to red and boost the valence on the colour dimension. They leave the other feature specifications (shape and texture) unchanged. These simply retain the stereotypical weightings they had when unmodified: they default to their stereotype.

In detail, the aspects of the model just stated are what allow it to work. A key aspect of selective modification, as Smith et al. (1988b) emphasized, is the selectivity itself. Thus 'a purple apple' is an atypical apple—in the combinatorics—solely by virtue of its atypical colour. But the compositionality constraint requires that the concept APPLE be a proper part of that combination; and further, under prototype theory, that it be represented as the APPLE-prototype. It is the prototype, therefore, that gives the APPLE concept its identity, and thus it is the prototype that confers APPLEness on the phrasal conjunction.[7] Preserving the structure of the prototype as much as one can is therefore necessary for this position to be internally consistent. Such preservation is possible if the

---

[7] Denying this claim is simply to deny that concepts should be equated with prototypes. Thus, for example, a hybrid theory wherein a concept consists of its prototype plus its denotation may be free to discount or disregard the prototype under combination while contributing its denotation to the complex.

	APPLE		RED APPLE
	APPLE		**RED APPLE**
	RED 25		RED 30
1 *colour*	GREEN 5	2 *colour*	GREEN 0
	BROWN 0		BROWN 0
	...		...
0.5 *shape*	ROUND 15	0.5 *shape*	ROUND 15
	SQUARE 0		SQUARE 0
	CYLINDRICAL 5		CYLINDRICAL 5
	...		...
0.25 *texture*	SMOOTH 25	0.25 *texture*	SMOOTH 25
	ROUGH 5		ROUGH 5
	BUMPY 0		BUMPY 0
	...		...

FIGURE 20.1 Illustration of Smith et al. (1988*b*) selective modification model for deriving a prototype for the combined concept *purple apple* by modifying the colour dimension of the *apple* prototype. Crucially, dimensions not directly affected by the modification process are inherited as defaults

prototype of the head noun of a NP is only minimally modified, where the dimension picked out by the modifier is altered selectively, preserving the values along other feature dimensions (i.e. *roundness, crunchiness*, and so forth). Connolly et al. (2007) entitled this preservation of other dimensions, built in to the Smith et al. apparatus, as *the default to the compositional stereotype strategy* (henceforth DS).

DS says that barring information to the contrary, assume that the typical adjective–noun combination satisfies the noun stereotype. Thus, when pressed, one should judge a purple apple just as likely to be as crunchy or as sweet as any regular apple, 'purple' having selected only the colour for modification. Connolly et al. (2007) tested this prediction by having subjects judge sentences of four types, as exemplified below:

A. Ducks have webbed feet.
B. Quacking ducks have webbed feet.
C. Baby ducks have webbed feet.
D. Baby Peruvian ducks have webbed feet.

The subjects' task was to judge how likely each sentence was to be true on a 10-point scale. The head noun ('ducks') of the subject noun phrase and the predicate ('have webbed feet') were held constant while the number and character of the modifiers were altered according to the four conditions (A–D). In the baseline condition A, an unmodified noun appears with a predicate that is true for typical instances of the noun. Condition B introduces a prototypical modifier—a modifier that is true of typical instances of the head noun. Condition C replaces the prototypical modifier with a

However, such a theory is not in our sights. We take it that the prototype bears the entire compositional burden according to the prototype purist (see also Armstrong et al. (1983) who discuss but discard such a 'dual theory' for reasons related to the present ones).

non-prototypical (but not bizarre or contradictory) modifier, and condition D adds an additional modifier to the one in condition C. The predicates ('have webbed feet') and the prototypical modifiers of condition B ('quacking') were chosen because they appeared with high frequency on a list of feature norms for the associated head noun (Cree and McRae, 2003).

DS predicts that there should be no differences between these conditions in judged likelihood of the truth of these statements. That is to say, if we assume the inheritance of features from the head noun that are not directly implicated in the modification, 'baby Peruvian ducks' should be judged just as likely to have webbed feet as 'quacking ducks', and so on. Listeners react with scepticism to this idea because it is implausible on the face of it, and indeed the results of this experiment show that experimental subjects did not react at all according to the prediction. Fig. 20.2 shows the average subject ratings for the four conditions. While DS predicted that there would be no change from the baseline condition (A) across our experimental conditions, there was in fact a systematic deviation away from this baseline. Condition (B) produced judgements that were reliably lower than those of the baseline despite the fact that the modifiers in this condition belonged to the stereotypes of the head nouns. The introduction of one (C) and two (D) non-prototypical modifiers caused subjects to become progressively less certain as to the applicability of the predicates to the head nouns.

These results (see Fig. 20.2) show that our subjects did not use DS in judging the sentences. That is, they do not conform to this crucial aspect of the model shown in Fig. 20.1. Rather, they reflect the commonsense intuition that noun modification involves entertaining ideas other than what is typically assumed in the generic case. This is what one should expect because persistence in DS invites indefinitely many bad bets (for more argumentation along these lines see Fodor (1998b)). There is no reason, in fact, to assume that a typical purple apple will be a typical apple that is typically purple. It could very well be (and so, apparently, our subjects reasoned) that purple apples are, in nature, some especially livid shade of purple and they might as a group be especially little and shrivelled (or especially huge and bloated) apples. That is, the prototypical features, unless explicitly specified, do not carry over into the complex combination. This is exactly the pet fish problem, now examined quantitatively.

Smith et al. (1988b) in fact anticipated and discussed the failure of the model's DS predictions (and related issues) in their original paper and so cautioned that the selective modification model could not handle all types of conceptual combination. For example, the model deals only with simple feature dimensions such as *colour* and *shape* that might plausibly be represented in the prototype, as opposed to dimensions picked out by more exotic possible modifiers as in 'Chinese apple', or 'elephant apple'. Thus a large range of potential modifiers was left out of the equation, the major intent of Smith et al.'s demonstration being to expose some first principles of a successful model though temporarily sacrificing full coverage. It was also acknowledged at the time that emergent features resulting from some combinations, such as the largeness of wooden spoons, and the fatness of the tyres on a beach bicycle, were problematic for the model, or indeed for any model that posits the inheritance of features of the head noun in forming

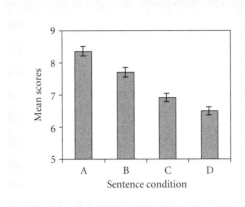

FIGURE 20.2 Grand means for subjects' plausibility judgements on a scale from 1 (highly unlikely) to 10 (most likely), for four sentence types. (A) e.g. Ducks have webbed feet. (B) Quacking ducks have webbed feet. (C) Baby ducks have webbed feet. (D) Baby Peruvian ducks have webbed feet. Error bars show the standard error for the subject means

composite prototypes (see Hampton, 1987). The principle of selectivity captures the primary assumption about the composition of prototypes that we have identified as DS. The contribution of the experimental findings (see again Fig. 20.2) is to show that DS fails generally.

Recently Jönsson and Hampton's (2008) challenged the interpretations of these findings as presented in Connolly et al. (2007). They argue, on the one hand, that experimental subjects do in fact follow the DS strategy (most of the time) and cite their earlier findings that purport to support this claim (Jönsson and Hampton, 2006), and on the other hand, they argue that models of prototype composition, Smith et al. (1988b) included, need not entail DS anyhow. We reserve comment for now on their experimental findings, but we will address here their claim that DS is *not* assumed by models of prototype combination, including both Smith et al. (1988b) and Hampton (1987, 1988a).

In the case of selective modification, Jönsson and Hampton's (2008) claim that DS is not assumed by selective modification is based more on a proviso provided by Jönsson and Hampton than by the original presentation of the model. Returning again to Fig. 20.1, it depicts what happens to the APPLE prototype when it is modified by *red*. According to the model, only the colour dimension is modified by switching all the weights (votes) to the *red* attribute (moving 5 from *green* to *red*) and boosting the diagnosticity of the colour dimension from 1 to 2 (that is, the colour dimension of the head noun concept becomes more prominent when it is modified with a colour concept). The model embodies DS by keeping the weights on all unmentioned dimensions, for example *shape* and *texture*, unchanged. Jönsson and Hampton's (2008) emphasize that relative to the colour dimension, however, the other dimensions are in fact diminished.

Of course, *relative* to the colour dimension, we agree that the value on the other dimensions is necessarily less. But this isn't the pertinent relation. Relative to the overall prototype representation, those values are in fact, unchanged. If the total *proportion* of weights was intended to matter, the sum of the weights should sum to a set total, but they do not: in the unmodified prototype the weights sum to 1.75 and in the modified representation, they sum to 2.75. Changing the model to reflect a set total in diagnosticity may be a reasonably minor change, but the only motivation for doing so appears to be to account for results similar to what we have reported in Connolly et al. (2007). For example, according to the revised model, a 'very red apple' will be expected to be less *crunchy* than a 'red apple', and a 'very very red apple' will be less *crunchy* still. This is a counter-intuitive prediction, especially if one is ignorant of the outcome of Connolly et al. (2007). More importantly, adopting a reflexive demotion of corollary features as a modification to the Smith et al. (1988*b*) model amounts to a denial of DS, which the selective character of the model was supposed to preserve, thus accounting for the compositionality of prototypes. The new model would entail not only selective boosting of feature dimensions, but also non-selective squelching of corollary dimensions. The result would be a model that captures the intuition: *as more and more modifiers are heaped onto a complex phrase, the prototype of the head noun becomes less and less relevant to its meaning.* In our opinion, the intuition is correct, but it does not lend support for prototypes as the input to a compositional semantics. As we will next see, similar strategies to demote the properties built into prototype representations have been offered to accommodate to the fact that prototypes don't seem to compose.

In addition to the Smith et al. model, Jönsson and Hampton point to another widely cited and empirically successful model of prototype composition, the **composite prototype model** (CPM, Hampton 1987, 1988*a*) as another that does not entail DS. We disagree, and contend that it does in fact entail DS in its first step. The 6-step model (from Jönsson and Hampton's, 2008: 917) is reproduced here:

1. a composite prototype is formed by the union of the features of the conjuncts;
2. all features with centrality so high that they are deemed necessary for either conjunct (e.g. fish have gills) will also be necessary for the conjunction;
3. other features are assigned the average of their weights for each of the conjuncts, (a feature is given a weight of zero for a conjunct if it is not part of that prototype);
4. features with low resulting weights are eliminated;
5. a consistency checking procedure is run (informed by general knowledge), possibly resulting in the elimination and addition of further features in order to improve coherence;
6. examples of the conjunction may also be retrieved from memory, and features of these may be added.

Thus, all features of the conjuncts are inherited by the complex concept as step 1. We take this to be an example of DS. In subsequent steps the model advocates pruning features, adding features, and adjusting weights, in effect undoing or fixing up what was done in step 1. This is analogous to the process advocated in Jönsson and Hampton's's (2008) suggested revision of the Smith et al. (1988*b*) model: First inherit the features, then ratchet them down because they are likely to be misleading or irrelevant. Arguably, step (5) acknowledges that offending prototypical features have to be revised or eliminated under conceptual combination lest the output not be coherent. To return to the *pet fish* example, one wants to be sure to get rid of the *furriness* and *waggy-tailed* properties of prototypical pets in talking about fish, but preserving some other properties of convenient size and friendliness so as to exclude hammerhead sharks as good cases of pet fish. Just how to do this, however, remains obscure. While it is undeniable that models such as CPM can and do account for a good deal of data concerning subjects' intuitions about the features of combined concepts (e.g. Hampton, 1987, 1988*a*), our concern is that this is not because it is a good model of lexical conceptual semantics, but, rather, because it is a good predictor of general pragmatic-inferential cognition. The model is under-constrained to the point that it blurs the line between conceptual and general knowledge. Indeed, it is also a familiar criticism of prototype theory in general that the criteria for what counts as a feature or property are similarly under-constrained.

To summarize, subjects do not appear to default to the stereotypes of the conjuncts of a combined concept when interpreting a novel combination. This is hardly surprising because *the more words/concepts combine, the less likely it becomes that they refer to things that satisfy their stereotypes*. We typically use adjectival modifiers in noun phrases when we are talking about something *other than* typical instances of the head noun. As this necessarily implies, any combinatorial scheme whose constituents are prototypes will therefore have to scramble to remove such typicality specifications as a condition for getting the interpretations of the complex concepts anywhere near the mark. Whether there is a general way of doing this is as much in doubt as it was when Hume (1739) and especially Locke (1690) discussed this very problem. In contrast, traditional theories of concept combination avoid this backtracking by not representing constituent concepts as stereotypes in the first place.

20.5 SUMMARY AND FINAL THOUGHTS

> The necessity of communication by language brings men to an agreement in the signification of common words within some tolerable latitude that may serve for ordinary conversation and so a man cannot be supposed wholly ignorant of the ideas which are annexed to words by common use in a language familiar to him. But common use being but an uncertain rule, which reduces itself at last to the ideas of particular men, proves often but a very variable standard.
>
> (John Locke, 1690, Book 3.XI.25)

This discussion has focused on the question of how well the theory of prototypes can serve as the representational basis for human concept structure and understanding. The findings of Armstrong et al. (1983), while never challenging the probabilistic feature-based views of concepts that have been ascendant in psychology and some schools of philosophy during the past thirty or so years, simply asked whether these representations were specific and nuanced enough to differentiate among central categories of human thought that are palpably different at their cores, say, between the concept SEVEN and such concepts as RHUBARB or SKATE-BOARD. Experimental review of this question suggested that the experimental techniques widely taken to reveal prototypical concept structure failed even to render these fundamental distinctions among concept types. Such results cast doubt on the explanatory power of prototype and exemplar-based representations as those that feed conceptual combination, or at least on the empirical literature in psychology that purported to support this view. Connolly et al. (2007) explored the same kind of question from the other way around, asking about the composition rather than the decomposition of concepts. Specifically, they asked whether the compositional rules operate over stereotypical representations of their constituents. The results suggest that prototypical properties associated with these constituents do not figure prominently under composition, but are systematically demoted. That is to say—and this is a tautology—compositionality must fail if there is context dependence: if the combinatorics alter the nature of the constituent elements.

The reasonable retort from prototype theory is that, after all, there *is* context dependence in the interpretation of complex concepts and it is manifest in our everyday understanding. Purple apples not only are purple (as the standard combinatorics tells us) but probably won't keep the doctor away, won't be appreciated by the teacher, and aren't good ingredients for American pies. Any theory of human conceptualization that does not answer to these facts is a failure on the face of it. On such grounds, it is a fair question whether the classical theory of compositionality avoids error only by abandoning hope of predicting almost anything at all about complex concepts. Our answer has been to the contrary. The classical combinatorics does a limited but absolutely required initial job in supporting concept combination and inference. It predicts what every English speaker knows and must know to understand words more than one at a time: *Purple apples are purple and they are apples.* It predicts as well that increasing the string of modifiers will have no effect on such inferences as *Large purple apples are purple, Large purple apples are apples,* and so forth, both of which are warranted by the compositional structure that a classical semantics assigns. But modification may well affect such prototypical inferences as *If it's an apple then it probably grew in the state of Washington and is sold in supermarkets.* These latter inferences derive not from the combinatorics but from our typical past experience with apples, Washington, and supermarkets.[8]

[8] We thank Jerry A. Fodor and Henry Gleitman, who were co-authors on the research reviewed here, and Dan Osherson for helpful conversation. We also thank James Hampton and an anonymous reviewer for penetrating comments that led to significant revisions of the manuscript. Writing of this chapter was partially funded by NIH grant R01-HD37507 to Lila R. Gleitman and John C. Trueswell and by NIH grant R01-MH67008 to Sharon L. Thompson-Schill. Authorship is in reverse alphabetical order.

....

CHAPTER 21

REGAINING COMPOSURE: A DEFENCE OF PROTOTYPE COMPOSITIONALITY

....

JESSE J. PRINZ

In the late 1960s, psychologists began to challenge the definitional theory of concepts. According to that theory, a concept is a mental representation comprising representations of properties (or 'features') that are individually necessary and jointly sufficient for membership in a category. In place of the definitional view, psychologists initially put forward the prototype theory of concept, according to which concepts comprise representations of features that are typical, salient, and diagnostic for category membership, but not necessarily necessary. The prototype theory gained considerable support in the 1970s, but came under attack in the 1980s. One objection, most forcefully advanced by Jerry Fodor, is that prototypes do not combine compositionally. Compositionality is said to be an adequacy condition on a theory of concepts. If prototypes don't compose, then prototypes are not concepts. Or so the argument goes.

In this chapter, I will argue that prototypes are sufficiently compositional to overcome the objection. I will not, however, advance the claim that prototypes *are* concepts. Rather, I will say they are very important components of concepts, components that play a privileged role in our mental lives. An adequate theory of how prototypes combine is, therefore, an important part of any adequate theory of thought. I will sketch such a theory, drawing on proposals that I develop in Prinz (2002: ch. 11). In the final section, I will critically evaluate a line of experimental evidence designed to challenge theories of this kind.

21.1 WHAT ARE PROTOTYPES?

Prototype theory emerged out of two main sources. First, research on perceptual category learning suggested that people spontaneously abstract representations of the statistical central tendency when they are exposed to a range of similar images. The abstracted representation corresponds to the average or prototype for a range of training images and can be used to classify future examples. Examples are recognized faster if they are similar to average, even if an average instance has never actually been seen (Posner and Keele, 1968). The second source was philosophical. Wittgenstein (1953) had gained notoriety for railing against the standard approach to philosophical analysis. He rejected the view that ordinary concepts (those expressed by words in ordinary language) have underlying definitions—an assumption that had been central to philosophical practice since Plato. If the definitional theory were right, the entities in the extension of a concept should share a unifying essence. Wittgenstein tried to show that this is not the case. Concepts often refer to sets of things that are unified by family resemblance, not essence; any two items in the set will share some features in common, but the features shared by one pair will not necessarily be the features shared by another. This idea inspired Eleanor Rosch and Carolyn Mervis to seek out empirical support for Wittgenstein's conjecture. Over the following years, they found substantial evidence (Rosch and Mervis, 1975; Rosch, 1978; see also Hampton, 1979; Smith and Medin, 1981). When people list features corresponding to their concepts, the items they come up with are not necessary, but merely typical.

Rosch and others established that typical features are actively used categorization. Category instances that have more of the typical features are rated as better instances than less typical ones (Mervis, Catlin, and Rosch, 1976). These typical members are produced faster during category production tasks (Smith, Shoben, and Rips, 1974; Rosch, 1978), and they are learned earlier in development (Rosch, 1973). The categories that are most salient to us are the ones whose instances share many typical features in common and differ in typical features from categories at the same level of analysis (Rosch, Mervis, Gray, Johnson, and Boyes-Bream, 1976). For example, we are more likely to identify something as a DOG than as a POODLE or an ANIMAL, even if it falls under all three categories.

The term 'prototype' was introduced to explain results like these. For Rosch (1978), the term refers to the class of behavioural effects, not to an underlying mental structure, but most other theorists have assumed that prototypes are mental representations. On most theories, they are conceptualized as collections of representations corresponding to typical category features. So a bird prototype might include components representing a beak, wings, feathers, flight, and two taloned legs. These features are highly typical (most birds have them), highly salient (they can be seen), and highly diagnostic (something that has one or more of these features is likely to be a bird). But they are not necessary: one could pluck a bird, clip its beak, and sever its legs and wings without transforming it into something other than a bird. For many categories, the prototype will include features that are not only contingent, but also far from universal in the category: apples are prototypically red, chairs prototypically have four legs, and dogs prototypically have ears that hang down.

Beyond this general characterization, there are different, more specific theories of how prototypes are represented. On some versions, the prototypical features are organized into structured lists, which divide into such subheadings as physical attributes, means of locomotion, and perhaps diet. In a connectionist framework, a prototype might be a collection of weighted feature-representing nodes, or, more graphically, points in a multidimensional space, whose dimensions correspond to nodes in the network. On an empiricist approach, prototypical features might be interpreted as components of structured mental images, and imagistic simulations of prototypical activities. A bird prototype might be an image of a bird together with images of how birds move and how they fly. For what follows, the exact format of these representations need not concern us.

21.2 PROTOTYPES AND CONCEPTS

Rosch and others found overwhelming evidence that prototypes are used in categorization and other cognitive tasks. They also found evidence that prototypes are pervasive. Almost every public language expression shows prototype effects, suggesting that words are grasped by means of prototypes. This pattern of findings led naturally to the conjecture that concepts are constituted by prototypes. A concept is a mental representation of a category. Concepts are postulated to explain categorization and comprehension of language. Concepts are also presumed to be the building blocks of thoughts. They are the primary representational tools used in cognition. The discovery that prototypes are pervasively used in cognitive tasks can be taken as direct evidence for the view that concepts are prototypes. By the early 1980s, this was the new orthodoxy in psychology.

But doubts began to emerge as well. Some of these doubts had to do with the fact that psychologists were discovering evidence for some other kinds of mental representations that also seemed to play important roles in cognition. Two of these were particularly well demonstrated. First, there is good evidence that people store mental records of previously experienced category exemplars (Brooks, 1978; Medin and Schaffer, 1978; Nosofsky, 1986). Prototypes are representations of average category instances that are acquired by abstracting over encounters with specific objects. But the specific objects are also internally represented and stored, and these records play a role in categorization. For example, if you encounter an unusual chair, you might store an image of it, and use that image to recognize similarly unusual chairs in the future.

Second, evidence accumulated for the view that people construct theories corresponding to the categories they are familiar with (Carey, 1988; Murphy and Medin, 1985; Keil, 1989; Rips, 1989). A theory can be understood as a set of principles corresponding to causal or explanatory relations between observed features, including the postulation of hidden mechanisms that cannot be readily observed. A theory of birds might tell us that wings are used for flying and that digestion is achieved via organs that are hidden from view. Theory theorists showed that we sometimes categorize something on theoretical grounds, even if it does not resemble a category's prototype.

By the mid 1980s, it seemed that theoreticians had a difficult choice to make: they had to decide whether concepts are prototypes, sets of exemplars, or theories. Simply equating concepts with prototypes no longer seemed tenable because there was good evidence for these other kinds of psychological structures. But the assumption that a choice needed to be made was based on a mistake. In reality, there is no need to choose. Each of these psychological entities may contribute to a theory of concepts.

One framework for integration is suggested by Barsalou (1987). He argues that concepts are temporary constructions in working memory, rather than fixed and enduring entities in long-term memory. What we have in long-term memory is a sizeable body of knowledge associated with each familiar category, and only small subsets of that knowledge matters for any given task. On any given occasion, we generate an active representation that contains features relevant to task performance. The body of knowledge associated with a category contains prototypes, exemplar representations, and theoretical beliefs. Each of these can contribute depending on context. Barsalou reserves the term 'concept' for the temporary constructions in working memory. One motivation for this is that the information in long-term memory is too varied and too inclusive to do the work that concepts are supposed to do. Concepts are supposed to be concise summaries of category knowledge that can serve as components of judgements and other occurrent propositional attitudes. The large storehouses of category knowledge are just too cumbersome, but we can call their contents 'conceptual knowledge' because these storehouses are used to construct concepts.

Using this terminology, we can see that the theorist need not decide what kinds of mental entities our concepts are. On some occasions, the concept corresponding to a given category may be an exemplar, on others it may include theoretical features, and on others it may be a prototype. Exemplars may be valuable when faced with tasks that require unusual instances of a category, such as 'exotic fruit' or 'dangerous pets' or 'beach shoes'. Theoretical features may be most valuable in situations where one must reflect on an unusual application of a category. For example, 'a fruit that resists insect attacks' or 'a pet that can help with house chores' or 'shoes to wear when escaping a burning building'. Notice that these examples all involve concept combination. That is, when one concept is combined with others, a context is created that may influence which aspects of conceptual knowledge we tap into.

If different kinds of representations can contribute to the construction of concepts, then the question about prototypes is not *whether* they are concepts but *when* they are concepts. I think the most plausible answer is that prototypes are our default conceptual representations (see the discussion of 'default proxytypes' in Prinz (2002)). If we are presented with either no conceptual information, or a typical context, or a context that does not bring to mind any unusual constraints, we will represent a category using prototypical features. The idea is this. Since a prototype is generated by averaging across all or most of the ways we represent a category, it captures what typical category instances are like, or at least how they typically strike us. It makes sense, then, that proto-types would be used as default representation unless we have reason to think things are not typical. Prototypes exclude hidden features since these are not salient to us, and we do not typically represent what is not salient. Thus, we don't represent hidden features by default. And, there would be no reason to use exemplar representations by default, since these include very exotic category instances, and there is no reason to draw these up from memory without prior reason to think the context is unusual. Indeed the proposal that the prototypes are used as defaults follows almost directly from what prototypes are. Prototypes do not include all typical features: dogs typically have spleens, but having a spleen is not part of the dog prototype. Rather, prototypes comprise features that are typically noticed when we encounter instances of the category. Thus, prototypical features are features that we typically represent. The features we represent typically on encounters will also be the ones that are most strongly encoded and easily accessed. So prototypes are likely to be the default representations of their corresponding categories. So concepts are prototypes by default, and that suggests that concepts are prototypes most of the time.

21.3 THE COMPOSITIONALITY OBJECTION

As we've just seen, the hypothesis that concepts are prototypes has been challenged by appeal to evidence that other kinds of representations can contribute to conceptual tasks. This led me to conclude that concepts are *usually* prototypes. This qualified con-jecture is the most defensible version of prototype theory. But it faces another objection that is sometimes considered fatal. The objection stems from the allegation that proto-types do not combine compositionally.

Compositionality can be defined as a property that a system of representations has if the content of a compound representation is determined as a function of the contents of its component parts and syntax. For our purposes, we can operationally define a compound as a representation corresponding to a phrase of English and the parts of the compound can be defined as the representations corresponding to the words that make up a phrase. So a phrase with the form ADJECTIVE–NOUN will be a compound with two parts, corresponding to the adjective and the noun. A system of concepts is compositional if the content of phrasal concepts (concepts expressed with phrases) is determined as a function of the content of the component lexical concepts (concepts expressed with single words) and syntax.

Jerry Fodor has argued vigorously that concepts must be compositional (Fodor 1981). He has emphasized two motivations for this requirement (Fodor and Pylyshyn 1988). First, compositionality explains our apparent *productivity*, that is, the ability to think an unbounded number of distinct thoughts despite having a finite conceptual repertoire (this is what Chomsky sometimes calls 'creativity' in his work on syntax). You have probably never thought about the category of pink tennis balls silkscreened with portraits of Hungarian clowns, but you have no difficulty grasping what these would be. The concept, PINK TENNIS BALLS SILKSCREENED WITH PORTRAITS OF HUNGARIAN CLOWNS, is perfectly intelligible because we are familiar with its component concepts. We can grasp the compound by combining these. The content of the whole derives from its parts. If the content did not derive from its parts, there would be no explanation of how we understood it. More generally, if compounds were not functions of their parts, each compound would have to be learned independently by, for example, being presented with category instances. That would mean we couldn't grasp novel, uninstantiated concepts. It would also mean we couldn't acquire novel thoughts by recombining concepts we already possess. Given the frequency with which we have novel thoughts and the ease with which we grasp novel concepts, it seems overwhelmingly likely that concepts compose.

Fodor's second reason for insisting that concepts compose is that compositionality explains the *systematicity* of thought. If one can entertain a thought of the form aRb, then one can entertain a thought of the form bRa. For example, if I can conceive of Obama beating Clinton in an election, I should also be able to conceive of Clinton beating Obama. Compositionality explains this systematicity by saying that such related formulas can be produced using the same concepts and rules of combination. My concept of electoral victory can be freely combined with my concepts of individuals, allowing me to conceptualize what it would mean for any one individual to beat any other. It would be bizarre to the point of absurdity to imagine someone who could conceive of one victory without being able to conceive of any other. Some victories may seem more likely or more desirable or more imaginable, but all are conceivable in the sense that we know what it would mean to say, of any person, that she or he won an election. This suggests a compositional system at work.

Fodor and his collaborators argue that prototypes cannot satisfy the compositionality requirement. I will focus on the presentation of this objection in Fodor and Lepore (1996). Fodor and Lepore point out that prototypes of compound concepts are often not derived from the prototypes of their component concepts. A feature that is prototypical for a compound might not be prototypical for the concepts that comprise it. Evidence for such *emergent features* is widespread in the psychological literature (Osherson and Smith, 1981; Murphy, 1988; Medin and Shoben, 1988; Kunda, Miller, and Claire, 1990). For example, people say that pet fish prototypically live in bowls even though this feature is prototypical for neither PETS nor FISH; the prototype for WOODEN SPOONS has LARGE as one of its features, unlike its components; and the prototype of HARVARD GRADUATED CARPENTERS is judged to have the feature NON-MATERIALISTIC unlike HARVARD GRADUATES or CARPENTERS considered in isolation.

Emergent features come from somewhere other than the prototypes corresponding to the parts of a compound. Thus, the way we acquire the prototype for a compound is not a compositional process. This gives rise to the following argument:

P1.   All concepts are compositional
P2.   Prototypes are not compositional (shown by emergent features)
C.   Therefore, concepts are not prototypes (P1, P2, Leibniz's Law)

On the face of it, this looks like a powerful objection against prototype theory.

21.4 COMPOSITIONALITY REGAINED

On closer inspection, however, the foregoing argument is invalid. It turns on a failure to clarify the modality of the compositionality requirement. Fodor and Lepore (1996) express the requirement in terms of the content of concept combinations, saying that the content of the whole is a function of the concepts of the parts. This implies that when two concepts are combined, they combine compositionally: there is some process that takes two concepts as inputs and generates an output from the two that integrates the content of each according to some combination algorithm, and does not introduce content coming from any other source of knowledge. But, so stated, the compositionality requirement is a generic generalization: concepts combine compositionally. Like any generic, this is ambiguous. Do concepts always combine compositionally? Does the demand for compositionality entail that they must do so? There are two possibilities to consider. First, consider:

Mandatory Compositionality
When two concept tokens are combined, they *necessarily* combine compositionally.

This seems to be what Fodor and Lepore (1996) are presupposing. Or, at least, they are suggesting that concepts necessarily combine within the boundary conditions that circumscribe the normal, well-functioning generation of conceptual compounds (i.e. barring performance errors). If Mandatory Compositionality were an accurate characterization of the compositionality requirement, the emergent features objection would be successful. However, Mandatory Compositionally can be contrasted with a weaker alternative:

Potential Compositionality
When two concept tokens are combined, they must *be capable of* combining compositionally.

This requirement says that this is an algorithm for taking any two concept tokens and generating a compound without consulting any other knowledge, but is does not require that the algorithm is always used. Thus, the phenomenon of emergent features does not rule out Potential Compositionality. The fact that compound prototypes sometimes contain features not derived from the prototypes of their components does not show that there is no way to generate a prototype for a compound by a compositional procedure. So the question we need to answer is, must concepts necessarily compose or is it enough that they have this potential?

To answer this question, recall that compositionality is postulated to explain productivity and systematicity. Potential Compositionality is all we need to explain these two phenomena. Saying thought is productive means we are *capable of* generating an unbounded number of distinct thoughts. Saying thought is systematic means we are *capable of* forming certain thoughts given that we possess certain others. Notice the modality here. Productivity and systematicity are capabilities. We don't actually generate an unbounded number of thoughts, or entertain every thought that is systematically related to the ones we already possess. But we could in principle. These capabilities require only that we be *capable of* computing novel compounds on the basis of their components; they require only Potential Compositionality. We can be systematic and productive simply by having compositional mechanisms at our disposal *even if we don't generally use those mechanisms or if we regularly supplement them with other methods of combination.*

The existence of emergent features shows only that prototypes are not always combined compositionally. To refute the theory that some concepts are prototypes, Fodor and Lepore (1996) would have to demonstrate that those prototypes *cannot* be combined compositionally. Not only do they fail to do this, but there is every reason to believe that prototypes *can* combine compositionally. It is easy to come up with a method. The simplest possibility is to simply pool features together. For example, a CHIMP DETECTIVE might be a typical looking chimpanzee in a trench coat solving whodunit murder cases by careful deduction from the evidence. In some cases, compounds may be generated by swapping a prototypical feature for a new value. A PINK TENNIS BALL will be represented as pink and not yellow, but this transformation of the tennis ball prototype can be generated using a compositional procedure. In other cases, a compound prototype might be generated by introducing a relation between two prototypes. A STRENGTH PILL might be conceived as a typical pill (say, a capsule) that improves strength as typically identified (say, lifting weights).

These informal proposals have been fleshed out in the form of more formal theories. The literature on prototypes includes a number of compositional models. For example Smith, Osherson, Rips, and Keane (1988*b*) have developed a model in which prototypes are selectively modified in accordance with principles that are consistent with compositionality: prototypes for compounds are computed on the basis of their component concepts. Hampton (1991) has a model in which prototype features are pooled together and weights on those features are systematically adjusted. Wisniewski (1997) has a model in which hybrid prototypes are formed, in some cases, and relations are introduced in others in accordance with reliable rules. These models demonstrate that prototypes can be integrated compositionally.

There is also empirical support for this conclusion. Research has exposed systematic patterns in the ways we integrate prototypes. For example, Smith et al. (1988*b*) show that we increase the diagnosticity rating of an attribute dimension in a nominal concept when it is combined with an adjectival concept corresponding to a value along that dimension. Such predictable patterns suggest that compositional mechanisms are at work.

These considerations expose an equivocation in Fodor and Lepore's (1996) argument. They invoke compositionality in two premises. P1 says concepts are compositional. As we have seen, this is only true if 'compositional' is interpreted as 'Potentially Compositional'. P2 says prototypes are not compositional, and this is supported by the presence of emergent features. But we have seen that feature emergence only demonstrates that prototypes do not combine compositionally *of necessity*. Therefore, the argument should be reconstructed as follows:

P1.   All concepts are Potentially Compositional
P2.   Prototypes are not Mandatorily Compositional (shown by emergent features)
C.   Therefore, concepts are not prototypes (P1, P2, Leibniz's Law)

This argument is invalid because the properties mentioned in its first and third premises are distinct.

The basic idea I have been advancing is that prototypes *can* be combined compositionally, even if they aren't always combined that way. One can put the point by saying that compositionality is a fallback method of combining concepts. If we are presented with a novel compound, we can generate a prototype from the parts if we need to. This could be done for any pair prototypes, even PET and FISH. Using compositional algorithms, one would represent a pet fish as a medium sized, furry, scaled, quadruped, that lives both in a body of water and in the home, and gets taken for walks. Of course, this absurd, Boschian compound will immediately be discarded by any one with a bit of background knowledge. And that's just the point. If a compound is familiar, there is no need to use a compositional procedure. We can simply use our memories of the pet fish we have encountered to generate a PET FISH prototype without bothering to imagine what it would be like if we integrated the prototypes of its parts. This leads one to propose that we deploy compositional methods of combination only when we have no knowledge of the things that fall in their extensions. When such *extensional knowledge* exists, we get emergent features; when it does not, we combine compositionally. Call this the Extensional Knowledge Proposal (also suggested by Hampton, 1987; Rips, 1995).

21.5 Is the Extensional Knowledge Proposal irrational?

Fodor and Lepore (1996) consider the Extensional Knowledge Proposal and reject it. They think such a method of combining concepts would be irrational. Here is their argument. They begin with the Extensional Knowledge Proposal in order to prove that it leads to an absurd conclusion:

P1.   We combine prototypes compositionally only when we lack extensional knowledge (Proposal)

Fodor and Lepore notice that extension knowledge tends to diminish with complexity. Consider the concept BROWN COWS OWNED BY PEOPLE WHOSE NAMES BEGIN WITH 'W'. This is a very complex concept, and, because it combines so many elements, it designates a small and obscure category, one with which we are unlikely to have firsthand experience. Thus,

P2.   The more complex a compound is, the *less* you are likely to have extensional knowledge of it.

But complexity *also* tends to reduce prototypicality. For example, pet fish who live in Armenia and have recently swallowed their owners are unlikely to be prototypical pets. Thus,

P3.   The more complex a compound is, the *less* likely we are to be able to predict its prototypical features on the basis of its components.

P1 and P2 entail:

P4.   The more complex a compound is, the more likely it is to be compositionally combined.

But when combined with P3, this leads to the following unhappy conclusion:

C.   The more likely we are to combine prototypes compositionally, the less likely we are to be able to predict its prototypical features on the basis of its components.

This conclusion is taken to demonstrate that the assumption on which it is predicated is an irrational method of combining concepts: we combine prototypes compositionally when doing so is least useful. This gives us reason to think P1 can't be right, and, if P1 is false, the story about prototype combination that I am defending cannot be right. Moreover, the irrationality of combining prototypes compositionally can be used as direct evidence against the claim that we represent complex compounds using prototypes, and that would be a blow to prototype theory.

The problem with this argument is exposed when we notice that there is a tension between the two examples Fodor and Lepore (1996) invoke to support its major premises. Both BROWN COWS OWNED BY PEOPLE WHOSE NAMES BEGIN WITH 'W' and PET FISH WHO LIVE IN ARMENIA AND HAVE RECENTLY SWALLOWED THEIR OWNERS are both complex compounds for which we lack extensional knowledge. But there is a difference. The brown cow example lacks emergent features, and the killer pet fish example seems to have them in abundance; killer pet fish are presumably gigantic, vicious, and voracious. In both cases we lack knowledge of the extensions, but there are emergent features in the second case, and not in the first. This suggests that there is a problem with P1, the premise that was set up for Fodor and Lepore's *reductio*. That premise implies that we will rely on purely compositional algorithms whenever we lack extensional knowledge but this clearly isn't the case. Thus, P1 needs to be revised, because it does not completely specify the conditions under which we resort to compositionality. The necessary revision is worth exploring, because it can help us see what is wrong with the *reductio*.

To see what is missing in P1, we must determine why features emerge in the killer pet fish case. The answer seems to be that we perceive a conflict between its components. A typical pet fish could not possibly swallow its owner. The recognition and resolution of this conflict depends, not on familiarity with killer pet fish, but on basic background knowledge. We reason that a pet fish could only have swallowed its owner if it were gigantic. In the brown cow case, features don't emerge because there are no perceived conflicts between components. Putting this in more general terms, features don't emerge in this case because we lack relevant background knowledge. This suggests a revision in the proposal Fodor and Lepore (1996) criticize:

P1'.   We combine prototypes compositionally only when we lack extensional knowledge *and relevant background knowledge* (Proposal)

This amendment undermines their argument. Arguably, the more complex a concept is, the more likely we are to have relevant background knowledge. Therefore, complexity tends to promote emergent features. This leads to the right prediction. We are less likely to use compositional mechanisms in cases where those mechanisms are less likely to predict prototypical features. The case of BROWN COWS OWNED BY PEOPLE WHOSE NAMES BEGIN WITH 'W' may be an exception. Arguably, we *do* represent that concept by pooling together prototypes, however spare some of those prototypes may be. Doing so might be the reasonable strategy. After all, absent any conflicting knowledge, such cows are likely to be typical brown cows and they are likely to be owned by typical people with W names (which is to say typical people with typical W names). Fodor's reason for denying that such prototypes exist in this argument is based on the putative irrationality of constructing them, but there is absolutely nothing irrational about doing so. If you tell me to go out in the field and find the brown cow owned by a guy named William, I would be well advised to use my prototypes to find William and his cow.

Fodor and Lepore (1996) fail to demonstrate that using compositional mechanisms as a backup strategy is irrational. In fact, this policy is paradigmatically rational in the brown case. And, likewise, it is rational to go beyond compositional procedures in some cases. When we construct a prototype to represent a compound concept, we often possess relevant exemplar memories and background knowledge that allow us to infer that things falling under its two component concepts have important properties not shared by things falling under just one of those concepts. When this information is available, we should use it. For example, if we know that red plants are poisonous, we should incorporate this feature into our RED PLANT concept even if it is not possessed by plants or red things in general. Failing to incorporate this knowledge would needlessly place us in harm's way. This reasoning predicts a priori what is evidenced empirically: purely compositional combination will only be used when no relevant memories or knowledge is available.

21.6 THE RCA MODEL

I have mentioned three things that can contribute to the composition process: compositional mechanisms, memories of exemplars, and background knowledge. It is worth saying something a bit more specific about how these are coordinated. Elsewhere I propose the following three-stage model of concept combination (Prinz, 2002). When we are given two concepts to combine, we first search memory for relevant knowledge. In some cases, we will have stored concepts corresponding to the compound (these often correspond to lexicalized phrases, for example DOG HOUSE, GRAY MATTER, RUSH HOUR). We can also look for stored exemplar representations that can be cross-listed under the two target concepts. WOODEN SPOON and PET FISH might fall under this category. If we find cross-listed exemplars, we can use them to create a prototype for the compound on the fly. I call this the *retrieval stage*.

If the retrieval stage bears no fruit, we move on to a *composition stage*. This is when compositional combination rules kick in to compute a compound prototype. As suggested above, prototypes can be compositionally integrated in a number of ways. The strategy chosen may be dictated by the concepts in question. For example, if one concept contains a feature of a particular type (e.g. a typical colour) and the modifying concept designates another feature of that type (e.g. a colour that isn't prototypical for the first concept), then a prototype for the compound will replace the feature in the first concept with the one designated by the modifier concept. In PINK TENNIS BALL, the usual yellow colour is replaced by a prototypical pink. If both concepts represent objects and the objects in question are similar in form, then we may simply pool features together. For example, a BEER-BARREL END-TABLE may look like a typical beer barrel and serve the function of a typical end table. In cases where there are two object concepts that are too dissimilar in form to integrate, a relation may be introduced between them (Wisniewski, 1997). For example a SNEAKER WASHING-MACHINE may be conceptualized as a washing machine for shoes, rather than a washing machine that one wears on one's feet. Wisniewski hypothesizes that different combination strategies may be applied in parallel and generate various competing interpretations. The strategy that yields results fastest or seems less odd may win.

The composition stage is then followed up by an *analysis stage*, in which background information is used to fill gaps, explain relations, and resolve conflicts between the new collection of features. For example, we resolve a perceived conflict between HARVARD GRADUATE and CARPENTER by introducing NON-MATERIALISTIC, and we can resolve the conflict between PET FISH and SWALLOWED OWNER by introducing GIGANTIC. This stage is non-compositional and requires reasoning. In some cases, an emergent feature is almost compulsory because certain solutions to conflicting concepts are particularly obvious. For example, the compound PAPER RAINCOAT must be modified in some way to avoid the fact that ordinary paper cannot function as a raincoat, because it dissolves in water. Features such as LAMINATED or WAXED are likely to emerge, because they are salient examples of water resistant paper.

In sum, the model has three stages: Retrieval, Composition, and Analysis. I call it the RCA model. It is not intended as a competitor for other accounts in the prototype literature. Rather, it is a way of capturing what any model that allows for emergent features should include. The main thing to notice in the present context is that, if relevant memories and background knowledge are unavailable, this model predicts that we will fall back on purely compositional combination. Since such information generally *is* available, this will happen only rarely. But to explain productivity and systematicity, the mere possibility of compositional combination is all we need.

Before closing this section, it is worth nothing that all stages of the RCA model can be said to draw on conceptual knowledge, according to the approach to concepts that I endorsed earlier. If concepts were always to be identified prototypes, then the retrieval stage and the analysis stage might be described as drawing on non-conceptual knowledge. But I suggested that all knowledge we have of a category, including stored exemplars and theoretical beliefs, count as conceptual. Thus, there is a further sense in which the present model is compositional. Emergent features are not typically features that are drawn from cognitive resources that rely on something outside our knowledge of the categories in question. They are just drawn from components of conceptual knowledge that we don't use by default. In other words, the model concedes that proto-types do not always combine compositionally (a compound prototype often has features not contained in the prototypes of its parts) but there is a sense in which it generally preserves the idea that concepts combine compositionally: the content of a compound is generally derived from the conceptual knowledge associated with words corresponding to each component concept. It is possible that, under some circumstances, we transcend those bodies of conceptual knowledge during the analysis stage. The point is simply that, on the account of concepts endorsed above, many emergent features derive from resources that can be characterized as conceptual. This is a further sense in which we should not see the phenomenon of emergence as a major threat to compositionality. Let me now put this point to one side and consider one final objection from Fodor and his colleagues.

21.7 IS THE FALLBACK PROPOSAL EMPIRICALLY FALSE?

Earlier I considered one objection to the suggestion that prototypes combine composi-tionally as a fallback strategy: the objection is that such a strategy would be irrational. I argued that this objection is mistaken; it is paradigmatically rational to depart from compositional procedures when we have relevant background knowledge or relevant exemplar knowledge. In this final section, I want to consider another objection: Con-nolly, Fodor, Gleitman, and Gleitman (2007) have argued that the view I am defending is empirically false. They have data that they take to show that we do not resort to compositional methods as a fallback plan in cases where we lack relevant knowledge. I will summarize their findings here and explain why they do not pose a threat to the RCA model (for more critical discussion, see Jönsson and Hampton's, 2008).

In the study, all subjects were given large lists of sentences, and asked to rate on a scale of 1–10, how likely it is that each sentence is true (0 = 'very unlikely' and 10 = 'very likely'). The sentence included four different kinds of cases, in random order. Some sentences contained familiar nouns without modifiers and asked about prototypical features (e.g. 'Squirrels eat nuts'), some added prototypical modifiers (e.g. 'Tree dwelling squirrels eat nuts'), some added non-typical modifiers (e.g. 'Nicaraguan squirrels eat nuts'), and some added pairs of non-typical modifiers (e.g. 'Black Nicaraguan squirrels eat nuts'). These non-typical modifiers were chosen because they are not associated with familiar exemplars and they do not create conflicts that require deployment of background knowledge. They are precisely the kinds of modifiers that should promote a compositional strategy for concept combination if the RCA model is right. Without background knowledge or exemplar knowledge, people should rely on the composition stage, and there should be no emergent features. Connolly et al. (2007) say that the RCA model and others like it make the following prediction: each sentence should be judged to be equally likely to be true. If prototypes are used in all cases, then the modifiers should not diminish likely truth. There should be a null effect. But, Connolly at al. did not get null effects. Instead they found that assessments of likely truth diminished significantly for each of the four sentence types just mentioned: unmodified sentences where given the highest ratings of likely truth, followed by sentences with prototypical modifiers, then came sentences with atypical modifiers, followed by sentences with two atypical modifiers.

Connolly et al. explain the results as follows. They say that when categories become less familiar we should withhold judgement of what their instances are like. If we've never seen a Nicaraguan squirrel, we shouldn't assume it's like a North American squirrel. We should withhold judgement. We should recognize that we really don't have a clue what Nicaraguan squirrels are typically like. Thus, our confidence about their diet should diminish. Implicit in this empirical argument is a further objection to prototype theory, which was already forecast in the argument for irrationality above. The authors conjecture that we don't bother to generate prototypes for unfamiliar compounds, because such prototypes would be of little value. This harks back to an objection that Fodor first advanced years ago. Fodor (1981) argues that, when we encounter complex compounds that refer to unfamiliar categories, we don't generate prototypes at all. He would probably say there is no prototype for the concept BLACK NICARAGUAN SQUIRRELS and this is all the more so for the concept BROWN DUCKS THAT LIVE IN BANGKOK AND EAT SPOTTED EELS. This is another way in which prototypes are not strictly compositional, and it cannot be explained on the RCA model.

The Connolly et al. (2007) experiment looks like a direct empirical refutation of the RCA model, but closer analysis tells otherwise. I think the study suffers from several individually fatal flaws.

First, the study may merely reflect pragmatic effects. If I ask you to tell me about Nicaraguan squirrels, I conversationally imply that they may be different from the squirrels with which you are more familiar. Why else would I ask? If the answer were obvious, the question would be foolish. If I were to ask you whether Baltic whales are mammals, I imply that they might not be ordinary whales—they might not be whales at all. So you should modulate your guesses about them accordingly. In fact, asking any seemingly obvious question tips a listener off that the answer may not be obvious. If I ask whether sea-dwelling whales are mammals, you might think it's a trick question in some subtle way. This would explain why subjects in the experiment were not as confident about tree dwelling squirrels eating nuts, even though squirrels typically live in trees. The experimental results reveal that pragmatic factors are at work. A better design would explicitly eliminate such effects by telling subjects that they should not assume that the categories described are unusual even if they are found in unfamiliar places.

Second, Connolly et al. (2007) use an anachronistic measure of prototype structure when they ask subjects to report on 'likely truth'. The vast literature on prototypes contains various measures for prototypical structure: feature listing, reaction times, typicality judgements, and so on. 'Likely truth' is not among these measures, and there is good reason for this. Prototype features are not necessarily true, they are just typical, and there is no straightforward inference from typicality to likely truth. Estimating likelihood requires a procedure over-and-above prototype formation. One procedure would be to directly read a likelihood off the prototype. So if bees are represented as prototypically stinging, I might guess that a random chosen bee is very likely to sting. But nothing about prototype theory entails that this is the procedure I follow, much less that it is the only procedure I follow or that I follow it on every occasion. For example, if a bee were swarming around me, I might over-estimate the likelihood that it stings, but, if you asked me whether I would bet $1,000 that a particular bee stings, my confidence might diminish. The demands of estimating truth can vary, and we have many resources and biases that can be brought to bear on that task. The RCA model makes predictions about how we represent a category—what features we include and how we weigh them. It is not a model of how we form beliefs about probabilities, though it might play a role in such a model. Thus, asking subjects to estimate probabilities is not an ideal measure for detecting prototype structure. To see whether Nicaraguan squirrels are represented using prototypical features, we would need another kind of test. One option is to use the standard feature listing or typicality tests (controlling for pragmatic implicatures). Another option would be to look at implicit measures. If asked whether Hungarian bees sting, I might say I have no clue, but if I encountered a bee in Hungary, I would surely avoid it. That would show that prototypes are being used, despite the fact that I don't consult them (at least not exclusively) when asked to reflect on probabilities. Likewise, if told to find squirrels in Nicaragua I might show facilitation effects for recognition of squirrel-typical features, such as fluffy tails and nuts. In sum, Connolly et al. (2007) chose a bad measure with no solid track record of testing for prototype structure.

Third, Connolly et al. (2007) tried to pick adjectives that would not promote theoretical analysis on the part of their subjects, but they may not have succeeded. Take the squirrel case. One thing we know about speciation is that geography makes a difference. Squirrels in one region often differ biologically from squirrels in another. So, when we hear about Nicaraguan squirrels, there is reason to think they may be a different subspecies. Likewise for color. If a squirrel is black, there is reason to think it's a different subspecies. Subjects may subject these compounds to the analysis stage. They may explicitly reason that squirrels with different morphological features and habitats may have different diets. The majority of Connolly et al.'s examples suffer from this problem; the majority are natural kind concepts with adjectives that could be interpreted as indicating membership in separate subspecies. Similar problems confound their artifact concepts. For examples, subjects are asked how likely it is that 'Handmade saxophones are made out of brass'. They may reason that brass is difficult to craft by hand. In some case, they may also have relevant extensional knowledge. Subjects are asked whether 'Commercial refrigerators are used for storing food'. If they recall that some commercial refrigerators are used in hospitals, they may judge that this sentence is less likely to be true than the sentence 'Refrigerators are used for storing food'.

Fourth, the data are actually consistent with the hypotheses that people use prototypes for unfamiliar cases. All the judgements about 'likely truth' were well above the midline. Subjects were not given the option to say 'I don't have a clue, so I won't guess'. They seem to have no trouble guessing, and they always think the prototypical feature is preserved in unfamiliar compounds. Their certainty goes down a bit, but this is unsurprising, for reasons I have mentioned.

Fifth, reduction in certainty is actually predicted by some models of prototype combination. Hampton's (1991) feature pooling model and Smith et al.'s (1988a) selective modification model both assume that feature weights are adjusted systematically when prototypes are combined (see Jönsson and Hampton's, 2008). A model could even build in an algorithm for reducing feature weights when atypical adjectives are applied. Or perhaps it is an attentional effect. When an adjective is introduced it draws attention towards one dimension of the category away from others, and this impacts access to the other features. Connolly et al. (2007) respond to a similar suggestion, saying it is a departure from the very proposal that prototype theorists are trying to defend, namely the principle that the compounds inherit prototypes from their parts. But it is no departure. Models that systematically adjust feature weights still qualify as compositional, because compound prototypes are generated as a function of component prototypes. The main point, as far as the RCA, Hampton's (1991), and Smith et al.'s (1988a) models are concerned, is that features of the compound are inherited.

In sum, the Connolly et al. (2007) study is inconclusive at best. It is not well designed to test for prototype structure and it actually lends support to the view that prototype features are inherited. Future studies may provide more decisive evidence (see Jönsson and Hampton, 2011; Sabo and Prinz, in progress). Moreover, to revisit an earlier theme, the inheritance models make good practical sense. If I send you to Nicaragua to find squirrels, it's overwhelmingly likely your squirrel prototype will be the primary tool (probably the only tool) you use in your quest to find them. That prototype will serve as a template that can be used to recognize novel cases. Until you've seen the novel cases, the existing prototype can serve as a reliable means for picking out the category. Of course, you can't be sure that Nicaraguan squirrels are typical, and this uncertainty might be expressed in judgements about likely truth, but if the question is, how will you imagine a Nicaraguan squirrel prior to seeing one, the answer is obviously that you will draw on your prototype.

21.8 CONCLUSION

I have argued that prototypes are the default representations we use when thinking about categories; they serve as our concepts most of the time. Concept combination sometimes requires us to use other sources of conceptual knowledge, especially theories and exemplars. But, when such knowledge is not relevant, we can use prototypes to generate compound representations compositionally. That's all the compositionality we need to explain the productivity and systematicity of thought.

CHAPTER 22

....

SIMPLE HEURISTICS FOR
CONCEPT COMBINATION

....

EDOUARD MACHERY AND
LISA G. LEDERER

In psychology, concepts are typically characterized as those bodies of knowledge that are used by default in the psychological processes underlying numerous higher cognitive competences, such as categorization, induction, language understanding, analogy-making, and so on (Machery, 2009). These cognitive competences include concept combination, the capacity to produce new concepts out of pre-existing concepts—for instance, the capacity to produce the concept of a Harvard graduate who is a carpenter out of the concepts of a Harvard graduate and of a carpenter (Kunda, Miller, and Claire, 1990). The outcome of this process is said to be a 'complex concept', while the concepts permanently stored in long-term memory are said to be 'simple concepts'.[1]

Psychologists interested in concepts have studied at length the psychological phenomena associated with concept combination in order to better understand the cognitive processes underlying concept combination (for an overview, see Murphy, 2002: ch. 12). However, psychological research on concept combination has failed to yield any consensus about the nature of these processes. In this article, we will critically review the main theories of concept combination that have been developed since the 1980s. This review will set the stage for some new hypotheses about the cognitive processes underlying concept combination, which emphasize their diversity and their ecological rationality.

Here is how we will proceed. In the first three sections, we consider three important models of concept combination—Smith and colleagues' Selective Modification Model (Section 22.1), Hampton's Composite Prototype Model (Section 22.2), and Costello and

---

[1] It is noteworthy that the distinction between simple and complex concepts does not exactly map onto the distinction between simple and complex expressions. A complex expression, such as 'soccer moms', can express a concept permanently stored in long-term memory, thus a simple concept, according to the terminology used in this chapter.

Keane's C³ model (Section 22.3).[2] In Section 22.4, we contrast these models with the insights about cognitive processing that emerge from Gigerenzer and colleagues' 'Fast and Frugal Heuristics' research programme. In Section 22.5, we apply these insights to concept combination to propose several new hypotheses about the processes underlying the creation of complex concepts.

22.1 THE SELECTIVE MODIFICATION MODEL OF CONCEPT COMBINATION

22.1.1 The Selective Modification Model

Smith and colleagues' famous model of concept combination combines a model for producing complex concepts out of simple concepts with a prototype model of concept representation and a metric for computing the typicality of objects with respect to those concepts (Smith, Osherson, Rips, and Keane, 1988*b*). We consider the first two components in turn.

Prototypes, roughly, are bodies of statistical knowledge about classes of physical objects, types of events, or substances. Smith and colleagues' version of the prototype theory of concepts distinguishes attributes from values. In substance, attributes are kinds of property, while values are properties. *Colour* is an attribute, while *red* and *blue* are values. Smith and colleagues propose that for each attribute it represents, a concept stores some knowledge about the distribution of properties among the members of its extension (Figure 22.1). For example, the prototype of apples is assumed to store some knowledge about how often apples are red, how often apples are blue, how often apples are green, and so on.[3] Each value has a certain number of 'votes' reflecting its salience, which in turn is supposed to reflect its subjective frequency. If someone assumes that 80 per cent of apples are red, then the value *red* for the attribute *colour* should have 80 per cent of the sum of the votes for the attribute *colour*. Attributes vary in their diagnosticity, which is defined as 'a measure of how useful the attribute is in discriminating instances of the concept from instances of contrasting concepts' (Smith et al., 1988*b*: 487).

The model of concept combination proposed by Smith and colleagues applies only to modifier–head complex concepts. In the case of a modifier–head complex concept, a

---

[2] Because some of these models are further described in other chapters of the *Oxford Handbook of Compositionality*, we only focus on their most important properties. For further detail, the reader should consult Prinz's Chapter 21, Hampton and Jönsson's Chapter 18, and Gleitman, Connolly, and Armstrong's Chapter 20. For the sake of space, Wisniewski's Dual-Process Model is not described here, but many of the points made in this chapter also apply to it (see Wisniewski and Wu's Chapter 19).

[3] Smith et al. (1988*b*) do not specify whether the represented values include only those values that have actually been encountered (e.g. the value *red* for the apples) or all of the values that are conceivable (e.g. the value *blue* for the apples).

APPLE			
Attributes		**Values**	
Color	1	Red	27
		Green	3
		Brown	–
Shape	0.5	Round	25
		Cylindrical	5
		Square	–
Texture	0.25	Smooth	24
		Rough	4
		Bumpy	2

FIGURE 22.1

concept such as BLUE modifies a head concept, such as APPLE, forming the complex con-cept BLUE APPLE.[4] Smith and colleagues propose that concept combination consists in modifying the representation of the head concept according to the following procedure. Modifications are limited to the attribute that corresponds to the property expressed by the modifier concept. The remainder of the representation remains unchanged (except for the fact that the relative diagnosticity of the other attributes decreases—see below). For instance, for the complex concept BLUE APPLE, the modifications of the concept APPLE are limited to the attribute *colour*. As we saw, the concept APPLE represents the various colours of apples, each colour's votes corresponding to its subjective frequency (see Fig. 22.1). By contrast, the concept BLUE APPLE represents all the members of its extension (all blue apples) as being blue. That is, all the values for the attribute *colour* in the concept APPLE are replaced with a single value—viz., *blue*. The number of votes for the value *blue* in the complex concept BLUE APPLE is then equal to the sum of the votes for all the colour values in the simple concept APPLE (see Fig. 22.2). The diagnosticity of the modified attribute *colour* is also increased.

Above and beyond the details and mechanics of the Selective Modification Model, it is worthwhile highlighting the key insights about concept combination it incorporates. The central idea is that people assume that members of the extension of a modifier-head complex concept are just like the members of the extension of the head concept but for one respect (corresponding to the property expressed by the modifier). Thus, according to this model, people take blue apples to be just like apples, except that all of

---

[4] We use small caps to name concepts and italics to name properties. We also use the symbol 'A∧B' to name the complex concept produced by combination of the concepts A and B.

GREEN APPLE			
Attributes		**Values**	
Color	2	Green	30
Shape	0.5	Round	25
		Cylindrical	5
		Square	–
Texture	0.25	Smooth	24
		Rough	4
		Bumpy	2

FIGURE 22.2

them are blue (while some apples are red, green, etc.). If people believe that most apples are sour, they should believe, according to the Selective Modification Model, that most blue apples are sour. The second insight built into this model is that when we reason with a complex concept (including when we categorize something as an instance of a complex concept), the attribute corresponding to the modifier is more important than when we reason with the original head concept. For instance, when we decide whether to categorize an object as a blue apple, the colour of this object is more important than when we merely decide whether to categorize it as an apple. The greater diagnosticity of the modified attribute captures this insight.

22.1.2 Empirical adequacy

The Selective Modification Model successfully explains various findings about objects' perceived typicality with respect to the classes denoted by simple and complex concepts (Smith et al., 1988b). According to this model, an object's typicality with respect to the extension of a concept is an increasing function of the properties that are both possessed by the object and represented by the concept (e.g. the redness of a red apple), and a decreasing function of the properties that are represented by the concept (e.g. green for the attribute *colour*), but not possessed by the object (the red apple), weighted by the vote of each value (e.g. *red* and *green*) and the diagnosticity of each attribute (e.g. *colour*). Thus, the model predicts (1) that a brown apple will be judged to be less typical of green apples than of apples and (2) that a green apple will be judged to more typical of green apples than of apples. People's judgements of typicality confirm these predictions.

22.1.3 Empirical objections against the Selective Modification Model

The empirical shortcomings of the Selective Modification Model have been extensively studied. Medin and Shoben (1988) and Murphy (1988) have provided evidence against the hypothesis that an instance of a modifier–head complex concept is taken to be identical to an instance of the head concept in every respect but one (corresponding to the property expressed by the modifier). In particular, Medin and Shoben have shown that combining a head concept, for example SPOON, with a modifier concept, for example WOODEN, does not simply affect the attribute corresponding to the property expressed by the modifier concept (viz. *material*), but other attributes as well. The Selective Modification Model predicts that the representation of wooden spoons should be identical to the representation of spoons, except for the material attribute; the *size* attribute should not be affected. However, while people found large spoons, compared to small spoons, to be more typical of wooden spoons, they found small spoons to be more typical of spoons in general (for other findings, see Medin and Shoben, 1988; Murphy, 1988; Murphy, 1990).

22.1.4 Theoretical objections against the Selective Modification Model

It is clear that the scope of the Selective Modification Model is limited. It bears only on complex concepts that combine a modifier concept with a head concept. Nothing is said about other types of complex concepts, in particular, the complex concepts expressed by noun–noun complex expressions such as 'apartment dog' or 'house bird' (Murphy, 1988) and the modifier + head complex concepts, in which the modifier concept, unlike BLUE, does not specify the same attribute when paired with all head concepts. For example, like all concepts expressed by non-predicating adjectives, the concept expressed by 'corporate' modifies differently the head concepts LAWYER and BUILDING (Levi, 1978; Murphy, 1988, 1990). We can also combine head concepts with modifier concepts that express properties for which the head concept does not have any relevant attribute. Consider for instance the complex concept expressed by 'summer smile': it is unlikely that SMILE has any attribute with values corresponding to the four seasons.

Furthermore, some aspects of the Selective Modification Model are left unspecified. When we produce a complex concept such as BLUE APPLE, we are supposed to increase the diagnosticity of the attribute colour. However, Smith and colleagues do not specify how diagnosticity is to be increased, even though the empirical adequacy of the model depends on how exactly it is increased. This increase has to be sufficiently large so that a strange blue apple (say, a squarish blue apple) is a better example of a blue apple than a typical green apple is. Simultaneously, however, it has to be sufficiently small so that a blue pear is a worse example of a blue apple than of a pear.

22.2 HAMPTON'S COMPOSITE PROTOTYPE MODEL OF CONCEPT COMBINATION

22.2.1 The Composite Prototype Model

Hampton's model of concept combination includes, along with a qualitative description of the process resulting in complex concepts, a model of concepts, a model of categorization, and a model of typicality judgement (Hampton, 1982, 1987, 1988b, 1996, 1997a, 1997c; Storms, de Boeck, Hampton, and van Mechelen, 1999).[5] We will focus mostly on the first two components of this model. Just like Smith and colleagues, Hampton assumes that concepts are prototypes. In his prototype model of concepts, a concept consists simply of a list of weighted properties (Fig. 22.3). Like the values of Smith and colleagues' model, properties are weighted more heavily as their subjective frequency among members of the relevant category becomes greater. A property's weight is thus a measure of its typicality.

For Hampton, concept combination consists in the inheritance of typical properties from the combined concepts (say, GRANDMOTHER and SPY) by the complex concept (GRANDMOTHER SPY). That is, when they produce a complex concept, people assume by default that the properties they judge to be typical of the classes represented by the combined concepts are also typical of the class represented by the complex concept.

VEHICLE
1 Carries people or things
2 Can move
3 Moves along
4 Has wheels
5 Is powered, has an engine, uses fuel
6 Is self-propelled, has some means of propulsion
7 Is used for transport
8 Is steered, has a driver controlling direction
9 Has a space for passengers or goods
10 Moves faster than a person on his own
11 Man-made

FIGURE 22.3

[5] This model has inspired Prinz's (2002) and Machery's (2005) models of concept combination.

Thus, the properties that are judged to be typical of grandmothers and of spies are by default judged to be typical of grandmother spies. Hampton calls this characteristic of concept combination 'attribute inheritance'. Attribute inheritance is related to Smith and colleagues' idea that an instance of a modifier + head concept is similar to an instance of a head concept in all respects but one (corresponding to the dimension of the head concept modified by the modifier concept). Both models assume that by default, we view a blue apple as having the typical properties of apples.

In Hampton's model, property inheritance obeys some constraints. First, in some combinations, the typical properties of one of the combined concepts are more likely to be inherited by the complex concept than the typical properties of the other combined concept. In such cases, an instance of a complex concept $A^\wedge B$ is judged to be an instance of one of the combined concepts (say, A) that has a few of the characteristic properties of the instances of the concept B. Hampton calls this 'the concept dominance effect'. Second, not every property that is typical of a combined concept is inherited by the complex concept. When a property that is typical of the instances of one of the combined concepts is judged to be incompatible with membership in the class represented by the other one, this property is not inherited by the complex concept. Third, properties judged to be necessary for membership in the class represented by one of the combined concepts are always inherited by the complex concept.

In addition, Hampton also proposes that complex concepts represent what he calls 'emergent properties', viz. properties represented by the complex concept that are not derived from either of the combined concepts. For instance, Harvard graduates who are carpenters might be judged to be idealistic, even though neither Harvard graduates nor carpenters are judged to be idealistic (Kunda et al., 1990). Such emergence derives from two sources. In some cases, people who produce a complex concept are already familiar with some members of its extension and assume that most instances of the complex concept possess the same properties as these members (a process called 'extensional feedback' by Hampton). For example, when they produce the complex concept PET FISH, people might rely on their memories of specific pet fish. In other cases, people might reason about why something would be an instance of the complex concept. Thus, people might reason about why a Harvard graduate might become a carpenter by hypothesizing that she was idealistic (Kunda et al., 1990; Hastie, Schroeder, and Weber, 1990).

22.2.2 Empirical adequacy

This model successfully explains a large number of empirical findings (for further detail, see Hampton and Jönsson's chapter in this volume). Hampton (1987) asked participants to list the properties that were typical of the instances of two concepts (A and B) as well as the properties that were typical of the instances of the resulting complex concept. He then asked other participants to evaluate how important each of the listed properties was for categorizing an object as a member of the classes denoted by A, B, and $A^\wedge B$.

As predicted by the Composite Modification Model, he found that the importance of a given property with respect to A$^\wedge$B, according to participants' evaluations, was a positively increasing function of its importance with respect to A and to B.

This model also explains various puzzling characteristics of concept combination. Overextension might be the most striking characteristic (Hampton 1982, 1988b, 1996): people sometimes judge that an object that is not an instance of a concept A is an instance of the complex concept A$^\wedge$B. For instance, people tend to judge that blackboards are not pieces of furniture, while judging that they are pieces of school furniture. This finding follows from the Composite Prototype Model on the assumption that a blackboard is not similar enough to the prototype of a piece of furniture for people to decide that a blackboard is a piece of furniture, while being similar enough to the prototype of a piece of school furniture for people to decide that it is a piece of school furniture.

22.2.3 Empirical objections against the Composite Prototype Model

Connolly, Fodor, Gleitman, and Gleitman (2007; see also Gleitman et al.'s chapter in this volume) have recently challenged what they see as a central idea of Hampton's and of Smith and colleagues' models—that is the hypothesis that people assume that properties typical of the instances of concept A are equally typical of the instances of the complex concept A$^\wedge$B. If Hampton's and Smith and colleagues' models were right, Connolly and colleagues argue, then adding a modifier to a noun (or a noun phrase) should not affect the judged typicality of any properties of its extension that have not been changed explicitly. As they show, however, people judge instances of nouns alone (e.g. 'ducks') to be more likely than instances of modifier + noun combinations (e.g. 'baby ducks') to possess certain typical properties (e.g. *having webbed feet*). People also judge instances of modifier + noun combinations (e.g. 'baby ducks') to be more likely than instances of double modifier + noun combinations (e.g. 'Peruvian baby ducks') to possess these properties.

Importantly, however, Jönsson and Hampton's (2008) argue that Connolly et al., (2007) study does not provide evidence against either Hampton's or Smith and colleagues' models. As we saw, Smith et al., (1988b) specify that the weight of the attribute that is modified by the modifier concept is increased. This shift in weighting entails that all other attributes, whether or not they are related to the modifier, are relatively *less* weighted. Thus, creating the complex concept BABY DUCK results both in the *age* attribute in the prototype DUCK being more heavily weighted and in the *foot type* attribute being less heavily weighted. The Selective Modification Model is thus compatible with Connolly and colleagues' finding that people judge baby ducks less likely than ducks to have webbed feet. Similarly, in the Composite Prototype Model, the weight of a property in a complex concept is an increasing function of its weight in *each* combined concept. When a head concept is modified, the weights of all its properties are impacted by the corresponding weights in the modifier concept. In Connolly and colleagues' experiment, because instances of BABY only rarely have webbed feet, participants would expect baby ducks to be less likely than ducks to have webbed feet.

22.3 Costello and Keane's C^3 Model of Concept Combination

22.3.1 The C^3 Model

Costello and Keane (2000, 2005) propose a computational model and an algorithmic model of concept combination (for details about the algorithmic model, see Costello and Keane, 2000). They focus on the conceptual combination involved in interpreting novel noun–noun compounds, such as 'street knife'. At the computational level of description, concept combination consists of the optimal satisfaction of three constraints: diagnosticity, plausibility, and informativeness. According to the diagnosticity constraint, the complex concept should be better expressed by the uttered noun–noun compound than by other noun–noun compounds; the more the complex concept represents its instances as having some properties that are diagnostic of the combined concepts, the more this constraint is met. According to the plausibility constraint, the complex concept expressed by a noun–noun compound should refer to objects that are plausible in light of previous knowledge. According to the informativeness constraint, both nouns are necessary and sufficient to convey the information the speaker intends to convey. Costello and Keane argue that these three constraints are derived from the pragmatic rules governing successful communication. To satisfy them, concept combination can appeal to any body of knowledge stored in long-term memory: 'the constraint theory proposes that the combination process has direct access to the full contents of memory' (Costello and Keane, 2000: 305).

22.3.2 Empirical adequacy

Costello and Keane (2000) have shown that C^3 is consistent with several characteristics of the interpretation of novel noun–noun compounds, such as the existence of several forms of interpretation, the polysemy of these compounds, and the richness of the interpretations people propose. One form of interpretation of noun-noun compounds that Costello and Keane (2001b) focus on is called 'property interpretation' (Wisniewski, 1996). In property interpretation, the listener supposes that the first noun in the noun–noun compound (e.g. 'whale' in 'whale boat') is used to ascribe a property to the referents of the second noun; for instance, a whale boat might be a very big boat. As C^3

predicts, the properties ascribed to the referents of the second noun are typically highly diagnostic of the concept expressed by the first noun.

22.3.3 Theoretical objections

Although this is not the place to criticize C^3 at length, we note that Costello and Keane focus on a single context in their account of concept combination, viz. linguistic communication, and they propose a single computation-heavy process for the task of combining concepts. We will come back to these two points in the next section.

22.4 FAST AND FRUGAL HEURISTICS AND CONCEPT COMBINATION

22.4.1 Fast and Frugal Heuristics

Gigerenzer and colleagues have developed an attractive picture of the cognitive processes underlying various cognitive competences, such as choice under uncertainty or categorization (e.g. Gigerenzer, Todd, and the ABC Research Group, 1999). According to Gigerenzer and colleagues, these cognitive processes are simple, fast, and frugal. Their speed and their simplicity result from their frugality: they do not take into account all the cues that could be relevant to make a judgement or a decision. Rather, they typically take into account a few cues and sometimes a single one (in which case they are called 'one-reason decision rules'). As an example of a simple and frugal process, consider the recognition heuristic (Gigerenzer and Goldstein, 1996; Goldstein and Gigerenzer, 2002). It is a decision rule that applies to choices between two (or more) options. For choices among two options, the heuristic can be described as follows:

> Recognition heuristic: If one of two objects is recognized and the other is not, then infer that the recognized object has the higher value with respect to the criterion. (Goldstein and Gigerenzer, 2002: 76)

Suppose that someone has to decide whether San Jose or San Diego has the larger population. San Jose and San Diego are the two options and the city size is the criterion. Suppose also that, being a European relatively unfamiliar with American cities, she only recognizes San Diego. If she were to apply the recognition heuristic, she would conclude correctly that San Diego is bigger than San Jose. The recognition heuristic is a simple and frugal one-reason decision rule, since it takes into account a single cue—whether or not the options (e.g. San Diego or San Jose) are recognized.

A second working hypothesis is that these rules are paired with specific environments in which they perform as well, and sometimes better, than more complex rules. These rules are said to be ecologically rational in these environments. Consider again the recognition heuristic. It works well when recognition is correlated with the criterion (viz. size in the example above). Because the larger an American city's size, the more likely it is to be recognizable by someone relatively unfamiliar with American cities, the recognition heuristic is ecologically rational in this case for such a person (but not for one familiar with many American cities).

A third working hypothesis is that we possess numerous rules for making judgements, for making choices, and for drawing inferences. For instance, proponents of the Fast and Frugal Heuristics research programme propose that besides the recognition heuristic, there are other heuristics that can be used to decide which of two (or more) options has the highest value with respect to a criterion, for instance, which of two cities has the larger population. Take-the-Best is one of them. Take-the-Best is supposed to be used to choose between two options that are ranked with respect to a criterion, on the basis of cues that are more or less valid. The validity of a cue is defined as the relative frequency with which options with a positive cue have a higher value with respect to the criterion than options with a negative cue. Take-the-Best is a one-reason decision rule. We look for the most valid cue that discriminates between the two options, and we decide on the basis of this cue, thereby neglecting less valid cues. For example, a person using Take-the-Best may decide whether Bonn or Dresden has the larger population based on the cue of having a soccer team in the Bundesliga. The validity of this cue is defined as the relative frequency with which cities with a soccer team in the Bundesliga are larger than cities without a soccer team in the Bundesliga. Its validity is imperfect, because it happens that the smaller of two cities has a soccer team in the Bundesliga while the larger does not. If having a soccer team is the most valid cue, and if Bonn has a soccer team while Dresden does not, a person using Take-the-Best would decide that Bonn has the larger population. If both Bonn and Dresden have a team in the Bundesliga or if neither does, the person would move to the next cue. As Gigerenzer and colleagues put it, our cognitive processes form a toolbox of simple heuristics. They propose that for a given task, we can use several heuristics. If we do not recognize one of the options, we might use the recognition heuristic. If we do recognize both options, we might use Take-the-Best or other heuristics in the toolbox.

Proponents of the Fast and Frugal Heuristics research programme have not studied the process of concept combination; so, it is unknown whether some processes of concept combination can be understood as fast and frugal heuristics. In Section 22.5, we will consider various hypotheses about concept combination inspired by this research programme. What we want to do in the remainder of this section is to examine critically the past research on concept combination in light of the ideas summarized above. We will argue that past research has systematically overlooked the insights about cognitive processing that inspire the Fast and Frugal Heuristics research programme.

22.4.2 A toolbox of ecologically rational heuristics

Psychologists working on concept combination sometimes recognize that there are several distinct processes of concept combination, each of which is meant to produce a distinct kind of complex concept. As we saw in Section 22.1, Smith et al.'s (1988*b*) Selective Modification Model is meant to apply only to modifier + head complex concepts, such as BLUE APPLE, and they suggest that other processes might be involved in producing other types of complex concepts. Hampton (1997*c*) distinguishes two processes—a process described by the Composite Prototype model (see Section 22.2) and a process involved in the interpretation of novel noun–noun compounds, such as 'trumpet olive' (see also Wisniewski, 1996, 1997).

However, psychologists' acknowledgement that there are several processes of concept combination does not go far enough. To see why, we need to remember that complex concepts are always produced *for a purpose* (Downing, 1977; Wisniewski, 1997; Costello and Keane, 2000). Complex concepts are used to categorize, they are used to make inductive inferences, they are used to draw analogies, and so on. In fact, complex concepts are probably used in most tasks whose solution involves retrieving concepts from long-term memory. We now consider in more detail some of these contexts.

In a communicational context, complex concepts are often produced to understand the assumptions and inferences made by a speaker or writer about the instances of the complex concept (see Costello and Keane (2000, 2005) on this point). Consider, for instance, the following extract from James Ellroy's novel *The Black Dahlia*:

> I dumped my grip on the dresser, and as a precaution on the way out, yanked two hairs from my head and spit-glued them across the door–doorjamb juncture. If the fascisti prowled the pad, I would know. (Ellroy, 1987: 218)

To make sense of this passage, the reader has to assume that spit-gluing (viz. gluing with spit) has by and large the same effects as gluing and thus that the hairs that are spit-glued will remain spit-glued except if the door is open (as we saw, this idea is built into the Selective Modification Model, the Composite Prototype Model, and the C^3 Model).

Concept combination also happens for merely referential purposes. For instance, a hearer might have to identify the referent of a complex linguistic compound. Nunberg's (1979) famous 'ham sandwich' example illustrates this situation: a waitress might have to identify the referent of 'ham sandwich' when she is told, 'The ham sandwich at the corner table wants another root beer.' In this case, in contrast to the situation described earlier, the point of concept combination is not to understand the assumptions and inferences made by a speaker or writer about the instances of a complex concept; the point for the cognizer is simply to identify an object in the environment.

Complex concepts are also produced for non-linguistic purposes. One might produce a complex concept for the purpose of categorization. For instance, one might go to the market to buy some Chinese cabbage called for in a recipe. If one does not already have a concept of Chinese cabbage, then one needs to produce one in order to be able to select the correct vegetable. The concept combination process might vary with the particular selection task. It is one thing to decide whether to classify a single object as a Chinese cabbage (as would, e.g., a person deciding whether to buy a particular vegetable that might or might not be a Chinese cabbage); it is another to decide whether to select any of several vegetables; it is yet another to decide which of several objects to select when one knows that one of the objects must be selected. Time constraints also matter. It is one thing to make a selection without any time constraint and another to have to decide quickly whether an object belongs to a given class.

The idea that concepts are combined for various specific purposes might seem trivial, but it is important to keep it in mind when one attempts to understand concept combination. We hypothesize that the cognitive processes underlying concept combination also vary, depending on the reason why concepts are combined, and not only depending on the type of the complex concepts that are produced, as many psychologists have assumed. That is, concepts might be combined differently when the complex concept is used to understand the assumptions or inferences made by a writer, when it is merely used to identify an object in one's environment, when it is used to categorize something in a category one is not familiar with, and so on. This hypothesis follows from Gigerenzer and colleagues' idea that a cognitive process 'fits' its environment, in the sense that its structure results in satisfying outcomes in this environment (but might fail to yield any satisfying outcomes in other environments). We hypothesize that for the processes underlying concept combination, the relevant environments are defined by the goals for which complex concepts are created.

22.4.3 'Sketchy' complex concepts vs. 'comprehensive' complex concepts

Most models of concept combination assume that people can, and often do, access their whole background knowledge during concept combination (a property called 'isotropy').[6] For example, in Hampton's Composite Prototype Model (Section 22.2), emergence is explained by people accessing their knowledge about the world (extensional feedback) and engaging in causal reasoning, and no limit is put on the knowledge that is ultimately accessed.[7] Thus, when people judge that Harvard graduates who are carpenters are idealistic, they are supposed to appeal to causal generalizations linking character traits and behaviour.

---

[6] Not all the models considered above assume that the processes of concept combination are isotropic. The Selective Modification Model does not require people to access their background knowledge to produce a complex concept.

[7] In the Composite Prototype Model, concept combination involves two stages: during the first stage, the processes of concept combination have a restricted access to the knowledge stored in long-term memory, since only the information stored in prototypes is accessible; during the second stage, however, all the knowledge in long-term memory is accessible. By contrast, in C^3, the process of concept combination accesses simultaneously the whole knowledge base in long-term memory.

The hypothesis that concept combination is underwritten by simple heuristics implies, however, that having access to our total background knowledge during concept combination is the exception rather than the rule because in many environments it is ecologically rational to access only a limited amount of knowledge. For instance, when a reader or listener encounters two words that have previously been associated, efficiency might only require her to retrieve information already associated with that word pair, instead of all background information associated with the individual words (see the Exemplar Heuristic below).[8] Studies of reading text have shown that when people encounter word combinations, they preferentially access information that is sufficient for understanding those combinations (e.g. Tabossi, 1988). Thus, cognitive processes that do not depend on accessing any background knowledge at all, such as the process described by Smith et al.'s Selective Modification Model, might be more common than is suggested by the general rejection of this model in the literature on concept combination (e.g. Gagné and Shoben's (1997) CARIN model).

Notably, such limited knowledge access leads only to 'sketchy' or partial complex concepts, while most models of concept combination assume that people can produce 'comprehensive' complex concepts—that is concepts that represent a large amount of information about their extension. For example, Costello and Keane insist on what they call 'the semantic richness of conceptual combination':

> People's interpretations for novel noun–noun phrases are often semantically rich, containing detailed knowledge drawn from various, apparently semantically distant, parts of world knowledge. (Costello and Keane, 2000: 303)

One way to build the idea of 'sketchy' concept production into a model of concept combination is to assume that a stopping rule governs the production of complex concepts. The production of a complex concept might be interrupted as soon as we have gathered enough information about its extension to fulfil the purpose for which this complex concept was needed.

22.5 A TOOLBOX OF SIMPLE HEURISTICS FOR CONCEPT COMBINATION

Section 22.4 was mostly critical: we argued that past research on concept combination overlooked the main ideas of the Fast and Frugal Heuristics research programme. In the final section of this chapter, we develop some specific hypotheses about the simple heuristics that may underlie concept combination.

---

[8] This is true even if the two words do not form a lexical item like 'goldfish'.

22.5.1 The Exemplar Heuristic

Many researchers have argued that people's acquaintance with specific members of the extensions of complex concepts plays an important role in concept combination (e.g. Hampton, 1987; Medin and Shoben, 1988; Murphy, 1988; Gray and Smith, 1995; Prinz, 2002). For instance, our acquaintance with some pet fish (e.g. goldfish) explains why we judge that pet fish have few of the properties that we take to be typical of pets and of fish. We concur that people's acquaintance with specific members of the extension of complex concepts plays such an important role, but we contend that the Fast and Frugal Heuristic research programme puts this role in a new light.

In Hampton's Composite Prototype Model and in Costello and Keane's C³ Model, the retrieval of knowledge about specific members of the extension of a complex concept is only one step in the process of concept combination. This knowledge is integrated with other sources of knowledge. By contrast, we propose that whenever retrieving the memory of an instance of a complex concept fulfils the purposes of concept combination, it exhausts the process of concept combination; this memory is simply used as the complex concept. We call this hypothesized process 'the Exemplar Heuristic' (for a similar idea, see Prinz (2002)).[9] To illustrate, suppose that we are acquainted with a Harvard graduate who is a carpenter and suppose that we are asked whether Harvard graduates who are carpenters are idealistic. According to the Exemplar Heuristic, we retrieve the memory of this individual from long-term memory, and we answer positively if our acquaintance is idealistic and negatively if she is not.[10] The Exemplar Heuristic is a simple process that does not require integrating our knowledge about a specific member of the extension of a complex concept with any other potential source of information about this extension, such as relevant prototypes (e.g. the prototype of a Harvard graduate) or the outcome of causal reasoning.

This heuristic is ecologically rational in various environments. For instance, when we are asked generic questions about the instances of a complex concept (e.g. 'Are Harvard graduates who are carpenters idealistic?'), answering on the basis of a memory of a specific instance is a reliable strategy, provided that this instance is a typical member (which will usually be true). For the same reason, the heuristic is also ecologically rational when we are asked for a judgement of probability. Since Juslin and Persson (2002) have shown that people rely on exemplars to make judgements of probability about the instances of simple concepts, it is plausible that they might rely on the Exemplar Heuristic for complex concepts.

One of us (L. Lederer) has recently gathered some evidence consistent with the use of the Exemplar Heuristic in tasks involving the production of complex concepts from uncommon adjective–noun and noun–noun phrases. In the simple-concept condition, participants were given a list of predicative questions involving a noun and a predicate

---

[9] In the psychology of concepts, 'exemplar' refers to the representations of individual category members (e.g. Medin and Schaffer, 1978).

[10] We might also retrieve multiple instances of the complex concept.

(e.g. 'There is a bird. What is the likelihood that it can fly?'), and they were asked to answer using a 10-point scale. In the exemplar condition, participants were given a list of predicative questions involving a noun phrase and a predicate (e.g. 'There is an Antarctic bird. What is the likelihood that it can fly?'). The noun phrases were created by modifying the nouns used in the simple-concept condition and the predicates were identical to the predicates used in the simple-concept condition. In the complex-concept condition, participants were given a list of predicative questions involving the noun phrases used in the exemplar condition, but modified by an additional adjective (e.g. 'There is a mountain-dwelling Antarctic bird. What is the likelihood that it can fly?').

Importantly, in the exemplar condition, but not in the complex-concept condition, Lederer expected participants to be able to retrieve representations of instances of the complex concepts expressed by the noun phrases. Furthermore, she expected these representations to constitute counterexamples to the predicative sentences participants had to consider. Thus, it was expected that upon reading the noun phrase 'Antarctic bird' in the exemplar condition, but not upon reading the phrase 'mountain-dwelling Antarctic bird' in the complex concept condition, participants would immediately think about specific instances of penguins, which would constitute a counterexample to the predicative sentence 'Antarctic birds can fly' and lead them to give it a lower likelihood rating. Lower ratings given to sentences in the exemplar condition by comparison to the ratings in the two other conditions would suggest that participants indeed retrieved instances of the noun phrases (Fig. 22.4).

By contrast, if participants did *not* retrieve any exemplar in the exemplar condition, but instead decided according to the Selective Modification model or Hampton's Prototype Combination model, their average rating in the exemplar condition should have fallen between their ratings in the two other conditions. According to the Selective Modification Model, both the modifier ANTARCTIC and the modifier MOUNTAIN-DWELLING should have decreased the weight of the BIRD prototype's *locomotion* attribute (i.e. the attribute containing *flying*) only slightly, since neither modifier affected it explicitly. This would have led participants to give the exemplar condition item a lower rating than the simple condition item, but a higher one than the complex concept condition item. Similarly, according to Hampton's Prototype Composition Model, because few Antarctic things or mountain-dwelling things can fly, the weight of the item's *can fly* property would have decreased in the exemplar and complex-concept conditions. Participants would again have given a lower rating to the exemplar condition item and the lowest to the complex concept condition item.[11]

As expected, participants judged items in the exemplar condition to be substantially less likely than items in the simple concept condition ($F(1, 59) = 82.54$, $p < .000$, Cohen's $d = 2.73$), but also to be substantially less likely than items in the complex concept condition ($F(1, 58) = 35.05$, $p = .006$, Cohen's $d = 1.39$) (Fig. 22.4)

---

[11] Here we neglect the fact that Hampton acknowledges the role of exemplars in concept combination. Since in Hampton's model, exemplars have only been used to account for emergent properties, it is unclear what prediction his model would make in the experiment described here.

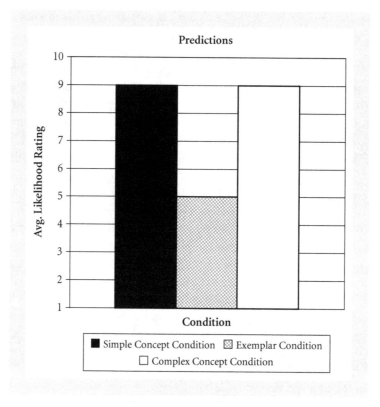

FIGURE 22.4

suggesting that they did in fact access exemplar information during the process of concept combination. This is consistent with the Exemplar Heuristic.

22.5.2 The No-Combination Heuristic

Suppose that you have to decide whether any of several objects or which of several objects belongs to a class you are not familiar with. For instance, you might have to select a Chinese cabbage from the vegetable section in a grocery store. You do not already have a simple concept CHINESE CABBAGE. According to the view on concept combination developed in this chapter, to perform the task of concept combination, you would rely on a simple strategy likely to give you a successful result, given the context you are in. That is, your strategy would result in your selecting a Chinese cabbage. We propose that in this kind of context, a simple and efficient strategy would be to retrieve only one of the concepts from long-term memory (in this case, the head concept CABBAGE) and to use this concept to categorize the candidate vegetables. The simple concept then stands as a proxy for the complex one. If we had to decide which of several vegetables was a

Chinese cabbage, we might choose the vegetable that was most similar to our concept (maybe to our prototype) of cabbage, provided this similarity is above some threshold. We call the practice of using a concept A as proxy for a complex concept A^B 'the No-Combination Heuristic'. The No-Combination Heuristic is simpler than any of the processes of concept combination suggested in the literature because it consists simply in retrieving a concept from long-term memory. It is ecologically rational whenever we have to decide whether an object is an instance of A^B and instances of A^B are similar to instances of A. So far, there is no evidence that people use the No-Combination Heuristic, but we speculate that asking participants to speak aloud in tasks where a simple concept A would be a good proxy for A^B might provide evidence for the use of this hypothesized heuristic.

22.5.3 The Elimination-by-Typicality Heuristic

Suppose that you have to decide which of two objects (x and y) belongs to a class you are not familiar with (the extension of A^B). Suppose also that x and y are similar both to A and to B. Thus, you can use neither the Exemplar Heuristic nor the No-Combination Heuristic. An alternative strategy goes as follows. Consider the typical properties of instances of A and of instances of B. Take the property that is the most typical (either of the instances of A or of the instances of B). If one of the two objects does not possess this property, then eliminate it and conclude that the other object is an instance of A^B. If both objects have this property or if none has it, then repeat this process with the second most typical property. We call this strategy 'the Elimination-by-Typicality Heuristic.'

For instance, suppose you have to decide whether chess or solitaire is a game that is a sport. If you believe that *involving a competition* is the most typical property of sports and that it is more typical of sports than any property is of games, then you might consider whether chess or solitaire involves a competition. Because the former does, while the latter does not, you judge that chess is a game that is a sport. If you had had to discriminate between chess and tic-tac-toe, then you would have to consider the property of sports or of games with the second highest degree of typicality, because both chess and tic-tac-toe are competitive games.

The Elimination-by-Typicality Heuristic is simple in the sense that in contrast with the processes considered in the psychological literature on concept combination, the process of concept combination is not assumed to result in a comprehensive complex concept. Rather, an instance of the complex concept is merely represented as possessing the most typical property (or the second most typical property, etc.) of the instances of one of the two combined concepts. It is also ecologically rational whenever an instance of an A^B is likely to have the typical properties of the instances of A and of B.

22.5.4 The Modality-Specific Heuristic

Many researchers (e.g. Yeh and Barsalou, 2006) have noted the importance of context in interpreting the meaning of a word. This is also true of concept combination. The goal of concept combination is often simply to comprehend a speaker or writer's meaning in discourse or in a written narrative, as in the 'spit-glue' example above. When this is the case, the complex phrase to be comprehended is almost always embedded in a discourse or narrative context that specifies its intended modality—that is, the discourse or narrative context specifies the modality, or perceptual sense, to which its meaning is relevant. In these cases, the cognizer might only represent those properties of the head concept that are related to that modality. For instance, when producing a complex concept HALF GRAPEFRUIT in order to draw a still life, the cognizer might represent the property *pink*, but not the property *sour*. When producing a complex concept HALF GRAPEFRUIT in order to follow a recipe, on the other hand, the cognizer might represent the property *sour*, but not the property *pink*. We call this strategy for producing complex concepts 'the Modality-Specific Heuristic.' It produces sketchy concepts, rather than comprehensive concepts, and it is tailored to specific purposes.

22.6 CONCLUSION

In this article, we have reviewed three of the most important models of concept combination developed in psychology since the 1980s—Smith and colleagues' Selective Modification Model, Hampton's Composite Prototype Model, and Costello and Keane's C^3 Model. We have contrasted these models with the insights about cognitive processing that emerge from Gigerenzer and colleagues' Fast and Frugal Heuristics research programme. We have speculated that the processes underlying concept combination might form a toolbox of simple heuristics that are tailored to the specific circumstances in which concepts are combined. We have described several possible heuristics— the Exemplar Heuristic, the No-Combination Heuristic, the Elimination-by-Typicality Heuristic, and the Modality-Specific Heuristic—and we have provided some tentative evidence for the existence of the Exemplar Heuristic. We acknowledge the speculative nature of our proposal, but we believe that the perspective on concept combination presented in this article is worth exploring further.

PART VI

··

EVOLUTIONARY
AND
COMMUNICATIVE
SUCCESS

··

....

CHAPTER 23

COMPOSITIONALITY AND BEYOND: EMBODIED MEANING IN LANGUAGE AND PROTOLANGUAGE

....

MICHAEL A. ARBIB

23.1 BEING COMPOSITIONAL VS. HAVING COMPOSITIONALITY

....

The meaning of an utterance in a human language can often be gleaned from the meanings of the words in the sentence together with the grammatical constructions whereby the words were combined. In this sense, the language has a *compositional semantics*. However, not all meaning is compositional in this way. The meaning of neither *kick* nor *bucket* contribute to the meaning *he died* of *he kicked the bucket*. Thus language meaning is not entirely compositional, but language *has* compositionality in the sense that the compositional structure of a sentence will often provide cues to the meaning of the whole—though in many cases these cues must be resolved with the aid of further cues concerning our situation as embodied actors in the physical and social world. I will show that a formal view of compositional semantics is helpful both for what it reveals about the structure of language and also for what it omits, including context, the use of compositionality to index rather than define meaning, and the role of idioms. I then show how Construction Grammar allows one to incorporate idioms in a framework in which compositionality may sometimes use familiar sequences of words as atoms when the meanings of single words do not themselves contribute to the meaning of the whole. Schema Theory shows what is meant by embodied meaning, and the way it is embedded in social experience.

The final third of the chapter then uses this framework to illuminate a debate about the nature of a protolanguage, a precursor of human language that contains an open set of 'protowords' but lacks syntactic structure. The debate is then between

(1) the *compositional view* that *Homo erectus* communicated by a protolanguage in which a communicative act comprises a few nouns and verbs strung together without syntactic structure. Then languages evolved from protolanguages simply by 'adding syntax'; and

(2) the *holophrastic view* that in much of protolanguage, a complete communicative act involved a 'unitary utterance' or 'holophrase' whose parts had no independent meaning. On this view, words co-evolved culturally with syntax.

I will review the case for each view but will show why I support the holophrastic view.

23.2 TWO CASE STUDIES

Two very different examples of language use will ground discussion of the extent to which language is compositional.

23.2.1 Emily Dickinson in Parma

While visiting the home of a friend in Parma, I was struck by a painting on her living room wall which contained the words 'Emily Dickinson' and (placed horizontally) the letters

WHEREEVERYBIRDISBOLDTOGOANDBEESABASCHLES

It seemed that this could be segmented as

Where every bird is bold to go and be esabaschles

or

Where every bird is bold to go and bees abaschles

but since there was no way to segment either esabaschles or abaschles into words of English, I Googled '*where every bird is bold*', and thus retrieved poem 1758 by Emily Dickinson:

> *Where every bird is bold to go*
> *And bees abashless play,*
> *The foreigner before he knocks*
> *Must thrust the tears away.*

Although 'abashless' was not a word in my lexicon, my knowledge of English word formation let me infer that it meant 'without bashfulness'.

23.2.2 Language as embedded in embodied communication

The second example shows language use embedded in a larger framework of embodied communication.

> At my train station, the level of the tracks is far below the street level. To get to them one must either take an elevator or descend two long, steep flights of stairs. One morning when the elevator was not working, I found a young mother at the top of the stairs with a two-year old child asleep in a stroller, obviously perplexed as to how to get down the stairs, so I asked 'Would you like to carry the child while I carry the stroller?' She said 'Yes', but then proceeded to lift one end of the stroller. Rather than (compositionally) extracting the full meaning of the utterance, she had extracted an offer of help and then had signalled her idea of how that help could be rendered by grasping one end of the stroller. Receiving this non-verbal message, I chose not to correct her misinterpretation of my words since the essential offer of help had been understood, and instead showed my agreement non-verbally by lifting the other end of the stroller and then proceeding to carefully negotiate the stairs with her without dislodging the child.

23.2.3 Implications for compositionality

The Parable of the Parma Painting was introduced to make three points:

1. Inferring the meaning of an utterance of language need not be a simple, direct translation from 'syntactic form' to 'semantic form' but may be an active process calling on diverse 'knowledge sources' to negotiate what appears to be a satisfactory interpretation. Certainly, had I started with the poem itself and not the painting, much of this would have been avoided—but in everyday language use, what we hear may be fragmentary and distorted and so such completion processes would still apply. Moreover, we may use our *estimate* of the overall meaning of an utterance to *guess* the meaning of a novel word therein, possibly guided by the internal structure of the word.
2. There is real compositionality at work in understanding the above four lines of poetry, both in putting words together and in pulling one word apart in searching for the meaning of an item not in my lexicon.
3. Nonetheless, having a firm purchase on the meaning of each line, I cannot claim to know what Emily Dickinson intended to convey. This suggests that the overall meaning of the poem is far from compositional.

The Story of the Stairs makes four further points:

4. What the speaker intends is not always what the hearer understands. Thus my meaning for 'Would you like to carry the child while I carry the stroller?' was

essentially compositional, while the mother's interpretation was not. Indeed, that interpretation may have depended more on my posture and tone of voice in the context of her predicament rather than on the words themselves.

5. In its normal use, language is often embedded in a larger context of embodied communication. Such embedding is crucial to the process whereby a young child acquires the language of its community, and I posit that it was essential to the processes of biological and cultural evolution that led to the human ability to acquire and use language when raised in an appropriate environment.

6. Meaning is highly context dependent—what is the meaning of reaching for the wheels of a stroller?

7. Finally, we see that meanings may be captured not so much by any formal compositional structure as by the far richer dimensionality of acting within the worlds of matter and social relations.

Thus, to the extent that some form of compositionality is involved in the meaning of an utterance, it may be necessary to incorporate into the utterance the bodily cues that accompany it as well as relevant properties of the immediate physical and mental worlds of the participants in a conversation. Even when we read a text, where no bodily or intonational cues are present, our interpretation of a sentence may depend on the 'mental world' created by the preceding sentences of the text, as well as expectations about the author's intentions in creating the text.

All this argues for a blurring or eradication of the putative distinctions between syntax, semantics, and pragmatics. Note, though, the difference between language use in daily interaction and the writing of essays to be read in different times and places. Here, reliance on gesture is nil, and on context is much reduced—thus the addition of explanatory phrases which repair potential gaps in the reader's knowledge and enhance compositionality. As discussed below, Construction Grammar (CG) offers a framework for the integration of syntax and semantics in the elements of grammar which is rich enough to handle idioms as well as 'regular' compositionality. Complementing this, the notion of 'cooperative computation' in the brain suggests how diverse sources of knowledge may be brought to bear on the processes of perception, whether in vision, language, or the planning of action (Arbib and Caplan, 1979; Arbib and Liaw, 1995). While some argue that the semantic interpretation of a sentence must precede the integration of pragmatic information (world knowledge), the polysemy of words may require invocation of pragmatic cues to establish which word meanings are relevant (Clark, 1996; Jackendoff, 2002). Hagoort et al. (2004) tested these ideas by looking at electroencephalographic responses to sentences with semantic and world knowledge violations. If semantic interpretation precedes verification against world knowledge, the responses to semantic violations should be earlier—but this proved not to be the case (Baggio, Van Lambalgen, and Hagoort, this Handbook, offer related discussion).

23.3 COMPOSITIONALITY *IS* A CRUCIAL FEATURE OF LANGUAGE BUT NOT ALL LANGUAGE USE IS COMPOSITIONAL

23.3.1 Compositionality within a formal framework

This Handbook has much to say about formal models of compositionality. As a foil for our later discussion, it will be useful to briefly recall the formal model offered by Werning (2005*b*) which abstracts from the changing systems espoused by Chomsky as models for the syntax of human languages. Werning defines the *grammar* G of a language L as a pair $G = (T, \Sigma)$ where T is the set of *terms* of L and Σ is the list of *basic syntactic operations* $a_1, \ldots, a_j$ of L. The set T is the closure of a set A of atomic terms with regard to recursive application of the syntactic operations, while the set GT(G) of *grammatical terms* is the set of terms whose leaves do not contain any variables. Werning (2005*b*) then defines the notion of a compositional meaning function in a form which I paraphrase as follows:

Definition. *A* **meaning function** μ *for a language is a function that maps certain grammatical terms to a set M of meanings. A grammatical term of the language is called μ-* **meaningful** *if the term is in the domain of the meaning function μ. μ is called* **compositional** *iff*

(a) *every syntactic part of a μ-meaningful term is μ-meaningful and*
(b) *for every syntactic operation a of G, there is a function μ_a such that for every non-atomic μ-meaningful term $a(t_1, \ldots, t_n)$ we have $\mu(a(t_1, \ldots, t_n)) = \mu_a(\mu(t_1), \ldots, \mu(t_1))$.*

Such a language is called **compositional** *just in case it has a total compositional meaning function.*

This definition is incomplete in two ways:

1. We must add a *readout function* h which reads off a string of symbols from each grammatical term. Let us call the result a *phrase*, with certain phrases designated to be *sentences*. *Parsing* is the process of inferring from a sentence the possible terms for which it is the readout. The sentence s is *ambiguous* if $s = h(t_1)$ and $s = h(t_2)$ but $\mu(h(t_1)) \neq \mu(h(t_2))$, but such ambiguity is not considered an argument against compositionality.
2. We also need to add the notion that the language comes with a set W of words. To make our formalism better match the intuition of what makes a language

compositional, we must block possibilities such as having a string of words—like *he kicked the bucket*—be the readout of an atomic term.

a. Let $\hat{W}$ be the set of disambiguated words which associates each word w with a finite set of atoms $(w,1)$, $(w,2)$, ..., (w,n_w), one for each distinct sense of w. μ then allows us to extract each meaning $\mu(w,m)$ of w, for $1 \leq m \leq n_w$.

b. We next define the number of times $n(a,t)$ an atom a occurs in a term t: if $t = a$ then $n(a, t) = 1$, but if $t = b$ for an atom $b \neq a$ then $n(a, t) = 0$. Recursively, then, if $t = a(t_1, \ldots, t_n)$ then $n(a, t) = n(a, t_1) + \ldots + n(a \, t_n)$.

c. With this, we can capture our intuition that compositionality requires that the meaning of a sentence must be built up from the meanings of its words. Let s be a sentence whose meaning is given as the meaning of a term t which provides a parse of s, $s = h(t)$. Then for each word w in s, the number of occurrences of atoms a in t for which $a = \mu(w, m)$ for $1 \leq m \leq n_w$ must equal the number of occurrences of w in s, and no atom a in t must fail to be of the form (w,m) for some w in s.

An even more subtle formalism would also address the fact that some words are themselves composed of morphemes. It would also discriminate the roles of function words like determiners and prepositions from those of content words like nouns and verbs. But we can ignore these additional subtleties here.

With these refinements, our definition now captures the key idea of a compositional semantics: knowing certain words, we can put them together in novel ways to convey novel meanings, so long as our hearer shares with us something of the meanings of the words and the constructions used to put the words together.

However, compositional semantics does not exhaust the meanings of sentences. What follows is not a critique of Werning. Rather, like Werning, I use his definition as a springboard for further discussion.

23.3.2 Beyond compositionality 1. Context and private memories

The above definition views μ as a function only of the grammatical term with no dependence on the context or the current discourse state of speaker and hearer. It might be argued that we could address this by positing a set C of contexts, then introducing a different meaning function μ^c for each $c \in C$, but this is just an empty formalism, though it might apply to the use of essentially syntactic context to, for example, resolve anaphor. In other cases, syntax cannot resolve the anaphor—Is 'he' *Jim* or *Jon*? Well, it's very unlikely that Jon would act that way so *he* must be *Jim*. Moreover, our earlier discussion of Hagoort et al. (2004) suggests that the pragmatics will in general be integrated with parsing and semantic processing.

23.3.3 Beyond compositionality 2. Using compositionality to index rather than define meaning

We can also see the limits of compositionality in the simple English habit of combining two nouns to get a new noun. We can combine *boat* and *house* to get *houseboat* and *boathouse*, and seek to infer a compositional rule from the definitions 'a houseboat is a boat used as a house' and 'a boathouse is a house for boats'. The first definition suggests the rule 'An XY is a Y used as an X' whereas the second suggests that 'An XY is a Y for X's'. The first definition might then suggest that 'a housecoat is a coat used as a house', in other words, a tent. An attempt to save this would be to say that each XY is short for XRY where the relation R is hidden, and that the meaning of XY can then be read compositionally from XRY. But this is unsatisfactory. Unlike the case for parsing where the hidden relations come from a small, inferable set, here the missing R is specific to one's prior knowledge of the XY compound. Thus, the most we can say to unify these examples is 'an XY is a Y (possibly in a somewhat metaphorical sense) that has something to do with X's'—in other words, X and Y are like search terms limiting the meaning of XY, rather than components whose meaning can be combined in a standard way to yield the meaning of XY. We may say that XY is an 'indexed holophrase' rather than having a composite meaning. Here, I use *index* in a manner suggested by the index in a book—the occurrence of a term in the index does not give you the crucial information about the term, but gives you a pointer to finding that information. An *indexed holophrase* then falls between a string of words to which compositionality applies and a pure *holophrase* in which the parts of the holophrase offer no clues at all about the meaning of the whole.

In general, then, compositionality yields but a first approximation to both the meaning intended by the speaker and the meaning extracted by the hearer. Language offers many devices, such as metaphor and metonymy whereby a new sentence can 'infect' a word with new meaning. And, dramatically, a new sentence can change the meaning of a word (recall our Parable of the Parma Painting), such as when the child is told for the first time 'A whale is a mammal, not a fish'—causing a number of conceptual changes since, till then, the child may have identified the concepts of 'whale' and 'very big fish'. Yet, intriguingly, this very blow against compositionality—the sentence 'A whale is a mammal, not a fish' is false if the child retains its original meaning of *whale*—is also a testament to the power of compositionality, its ability to redefine constituent meanings if an overall sentence is taken to be true (in this case, on parental authority).

23.3.4 Beyond compositionality 3. From idioms to Construction Grammar

As noted in the introduction, a particular challenge to the view that all meaning of terms above the word level is compositional is afforded by idiomatic expressions like *kick the bucket*. Should we consider their meanings as a supplement to the general rules of syntax and semantics? Instead of this, Fillmore, Kay, and O'Connor (1988) suggested that the tools they used in analysing idioms could form the basis for *construction grammar* as a new model of grammatical organization, with constructions ranging from lexical items to idioms to rules of quite general applicability. On this view the grammar of each language is given by a more or less language-specific set of constructions which combine *form* (how to aggregate words) with *meaning* (how the meaning of the words constrains the meaning of the whole). In the case of an idiom like *he kicked the bucket* it is the construction itself, rather than the meanings of the words that comprise it, that determines the overall meaning. This is to be contrasted with a grammar in which autonomous syntactic rules put words together in very general ways without regard for the meaning of the result. Linguists working within Construction Grammar (CG), with its close relations to Cognitive Grammar, have teased out the rule-governed and productive linguistic behaviours specific to each family of constructions (Croft and Cruse, 2005).

In some sense, compositionality is regained in CG by replacing a small set of generally applicable rules by a very large, language specific set of constructions, and recognizing that what appears a compound may be, essentially, an atomic term. For example, in CG, *He kicked the bucket* is ambiguous because it has two parsings. The former yields a form t_1 of the general formula *He X'd the Y* whose overall meaning varies with the values of $\mu(X)$ and $\mu(Y)$; whereas the latter yields t_2 as, essentially, an atomic term in which no substitutions can be made for X and Y and $\mu(t2)$ has no relation to $\mu(kick)$ or $\mu(bucket)$.

The rules of generative grammar have 'slots' that can be filled with any item that belongs to a very broad syntactic category. By contrast, the set of fillers for a given slot in a construction may vary from a single word (one cannot replace *bucket* even by *pail* in the idiomatic use of *he kicked the bucket*) to a narrowly defined semantic category, to a broadly-defined semantic category, to a syntactic category which cuts across constructions, but which may do so in a highly language-specific way (Croft, 2001).

Intriguingly, Werning (2005*b*) notes that Husserl (1970) developed the notion of *Bedeutungskategorie*, or *semantic category*. For any two expressions of the same category, says Husserl, one expression can replace the other in any non-ambiguous meaningful context without making the context nonsensical, but if two expressions are of different categories, there will be at least some cases where the replacement of one expression will turn a meaningful statement into a nonsensical one. To some extent, this is Construction Grammar *avant la lettre*, but for Construction Grammar we must note that semantic categories may be very much construction-specific and for some constructions may shade into syntactic categories. A word might be used in construction C_1 because it belongs to some category S_1 of slot fillers, yet be used in construction C_2 because it belongs to a *different* category S_2 of slot fillers.

In short, language gets great power from compositionality, but not every utterance exploits this to the same degree.

23.4 SCHEMA THEORY AND EMBODIED MEANING

The previous section leaves unspecified the set of meanings M which forms the codomain of μ, but gives the impression that there is some basic set of meanings from which all other meanings can be built up. Note that this base set will be a subset of the set $\{\mu(a) \mid a \in A\}$ of meanings of atoms, but could be much smaller. This is because sense j of word w might be explicitly defined in the dictionary by a sentence $s_{w,j}$ so that $\mu(w, j) = \mu(s_{w,j})$. However, this only works if the dictionary has a property that no extant dictionary has: that there are no loops. In other words, there must be a way of arranging the words in the dictionary (assuming separate entries for different meanings of a word, which can thus be spaced far apart) in an order for which, for each entry, the word's corresponding meaning is either in the base set, or uses words with meanings defined elsewhere in the dictionary.

My argument, then, is that an account of meaning based on interpreting logical forms from a discrete set of atomic meanings is, at best, a crude first approximation to semantics. My counterclaim is that we gain our ability to understand a new sentence by locating it in the double context of words and experience. Then, when new words are put together in a new way, we interpret the result in a new situation by a process of 'dynamic interaction' between the words and the context—where context may include the situation in the physical and social world as well as the flow of words of which the sentence is part. In this section, I suggest how embodiment may ground an account of such meanings, very different from 'logical form', in terms of a version of *schema theory*.

Much of my work has sought to analyse 'schemas' as the 'distributed programmes' of the brain, at a level above, but reducible to, the functioning of neural networks. For example, we have *perceptual schemas* recognizing apples and doors, and *motor schemas* for peeling apples and opening doors. Each of these schemas constitutes a psychological reality and we can combine them into coordinated control programmes and schema assemblages (Arbib, 1981; Arbib, Érdi, and Szentágothai, 1998) to define complex realms of experience and courses of action.

The notion of *coordinated control programme* is basically compositional, building up complex skills from available perceptual and motor schemas (where the perceptual schemas may register the external environment, or the degree of achievement of goals and subgoals), and includes both specification of how data are to be transferred between schemas and how schemas are to be activated and deactivated. In the case of robots, this can yield a complete programme for embodied, perceptually-guided behaviour (Lyons and Arbib, 1989). However, such a compositional account yields only a first approximation to most human skills. Consider learning to drive. Verbal instructions like 'pull on the wheel with your left hand to turn left' and 'press your foot on the brake to slow down' provide but a starting point. Only much experience in driving will tune each schema and the patterns of coordination between schemas to the point that it is reasonably safe for the novice to drive in fast heavy traffic. Here the 'mental level' of explicit analysis of driving skills must be complemented by the 'neural level' of tuning of, for example, cerebellar and basal ganglia circuitry to develop the well-tuned schema for the new overall skill. Intriguingly, then, what starts off as compositional may, with learning, become a new 'atomic' skill for which the original description may serve at best as an index. But this skill is not a discrete atom but a complex function which can adjust to a multitude of different traffic conditions.

Similarly, the notion of *schema assemblage* relates to the observation that the perception of a scene may be modelled as invoking instances of perceptual schemas for certain aspects of the scene. To that extent the assemblage is compositional, though now the 'atomic elements' are no longer single symbols but instead each schema instance has parameters related to size, location, and other features of the represented element of the scene. However, what blocks simple compositionality is that the emerging pattern of schema instances which comes to represent the scene (and thus give it its current meaning to the observer) may result from extensive processes of competition and cooperation in the schema network which invoke schemas beyond those initially associated with the scene. Much will depend on what 'catches' the observer's attention, and this will in turn be a function of prior experience and current motivation. The Story of the Stairs was designed to convey the way in which the meaning of a sentence may depend as much on context as on the meanings of the words that comprise it, with the result reflecting possibly continuous ranges of variation that can only be indexed, but not exhausted, by composition of a discrete set of atoms.

23.5 LANGUAGE AS A SOCIAL SCHEMA: DEVELOPMENT AND EVOLUTION

In *The Construction of Reality* (Arbib and Hesse, 1986), Mary Hesse and I sought to integrate and reconcile an epistemology based on mental schemas and brain mechanisms 'in the head' with an epistemology addressing the ideas shared by a community. The upshot was to extend schema theory to embrace 'social schemas' constituted by collective patterns of behaviour in a society. The latter may provide an external reality for a person's acquisition of schemas 'in the head'. Conversely, it is the collective effect of behaviours which express schemas within the heads of many individuals that constitutes, and changes, this social reality.

Each of us has a somewhat different vocabulary and may disagree from time to time on whether or not a given string of words is a 'good' sentence of English. How then does a young child normally acquire a modern-day language? The child is not exposed to a language as a unified external reality, but rather as part of interactions with other people which may be associated with pragmatic or emotional consequences. The child thus comes to interiorize that language as a set of schemas for words and constructions and the pragmatics of use that allow the child to become a member of the community. The Story of the Stairs makes clear that the schemas so mastered may not relate to words alone but may link words to more explicitly embodied forms of communication. Indeed, the first words of the young child are normally coupled with manual gestures, of which pointing is especially important (Capirci and Volterra, 2008). A child's utterance which contains a point is like a sentence which contains a word like *that*. One may either ascribe such a sentence in itself a rather vague meaning through compositionality (where the reference of *that* is unspecified) or refine the meaning of the overall sentence by using context to infer what it is to which *that* refers.

Various authors (Arbib and Hill, 1988; Tomasello, 2003) have argued that Construction Grammar is more hospitable than Universal Grammar, at least in the form that has a predefined range of principles and parameters (Baker, 2001; Chomsky and Lasnik, 1993), to accounts of language acquisition. Hill (1983) showed that the child may first acquire what the adult perceives as two-word utterances as holophrases (e.g. 'want-milk') whose parts initially have no distinct meanings for the child. Subsequently, the child develops a more general construction (e.g. 'want *x*') in which '*x*' can be replaced by the name of any 'wantable thing' (recall Husserl's notion of *Bedeutungskategorie*). Further experience will yield more general constructions in which semantic categories give way to word classes like 'noun' defined by their syntactic roles in a range of constructions rather than by their semantics. The child may thus proceed 'down' from the overall meaning to gain the meaning of parts as well as 'up' from constituents to the meaning of the whole. The Parable of the Parma Painting showed how, having learned various rules of a language we may tease apart the pieces in a word like *abashless* to infer the meaning of the whole. However, in other cases, lacking morphological clues one might simply use the context to seek a word meaning that would yield an acceptable meaning for the whole sentence. In this case one might wrongly conclude that 'abashless' was a synonym for 'boldly'—but such a mechanism can work well if one refines the estimated meaning through meeting the word in enough different sentences.

- The relevance of Construction Grammar extends also to the study of how languages emerge and change over time (see, e.g., Croft, 2000). Such ideas are also relevant to the study of language evolution. Ontogeny does not in this case recapitulate phylogeny. Adult hunters and gatherers had to communicate about situations outside the range of a modern 2-year old, and protohumans were not communicating with adults who already used a large lexicon and set of constructions to generate complex sentences. Elsewhere (Arbib, 2005a, 2005b, and other papers), I have argued that biological evolution first gave early humans *complex imitation*—the ability to form schema assemblages to characterize who is doing what and how, and the ability to transform such an assemblage into a coordinated control programme which will underwrite the observer's acquisition of the observed skill.
- Complex imitation, extended from praxis to communication, then made the use of *pantomime* possible to yield an open-ended (but non-compositional) semantics;

- *protosign* thereafter emerged from pantomime through processes of ritualization, simplification, and disambiguation which led to a variety of conventionalized gestures; whence
- *protolanguage* emerged as novel vocal symbols (*protospeech*) became integrated with protosign in an expanding spiral which rested on evolutionary changes of both brain and body. Here protolanguage refers to an open system of communication used by a particular hominid grouping which was a precursor of, but not an example of, 'true' language.

Protolanguage emerges as symbols (whether gestures or vocalizations) become linked in patterns of competition and cooperation to schema assemblages of varied complexity. However, it has been argued (see the next section for the debate pro and con) that in early protolanguages, few utterances will reflect the compositionality of the schemas which constitute the assemblages to which they are linked. By contrast, language provides mechanisms (the grammar) that can, but need not, reflect some of this compositional structure.

23.6 THE HOLOPHRASIS–COMPOSITIONALITY DEBATE FOR PROTOLANGUAGE

Much of the debate over the notion of protolanguage focuses on whether it was compositional or holophrastic:

- **The compositional view** (Bickerton, 1995; Tallerman, 2007) hypothesizes that *Homo erectus* communicated by a protolanguage in which a communicative act comprises a few nouns and verbs strung together without syntactic structure. On this view, the 'protowords' (in the evolutionary sense) were so akin to the words of modern languages that languages evolved from protolanguages simply by 'adding syntax'.
- **The holophrastic view** (Arbib, 2005a; Wray, 1998, 2002a) holds that in much of protolanguage, a complete communicative act involved a 'unitary utterance' or 'holophrase' whose parts had no independent meaning. On this view, words co-evolved culturally with syntax: as 'protowords' were fractionated or elaborated to yield words for constituents of their original meaning, so were constructions developed to arrange the words to reconstitute those original meanings and (the advantage of this transition) many more besides.[1]

---

[1] Much of the present section is based on (Arbib, 2008), which is just one of the papers in a special issue of *Interaction Studies* (since republished as Arbib and Bickerton, 2010) which debates the two opposing views on the nature of protolanguage.

Note that the holophrastic view does *not* say 'Protolanguage was only and always a collection of holophrases.' The crucial claim is that the earliest protolanguages were in great part holophrastic, and that as they developed through time, each protolanguage retained holophrastic strategies while making increasing use of compositional strategies. Moreover, I claim that the same basic mechanisms may have served both protohumans inventing language and modern children acquiring the existing language of their community. These mechanisms comprise

1. The ability to create a novel gesture or vocalization and associate it with a communicative goal.
2. The ability both to perform and perceive such a gesture or vocalization. This would improve with experience as its use spread within the community, as would sharpening of the perception of occasions of use by members of the community.
3. Commonalities between two structures could yield to 'fractionation', the isolation of that commonality as a gesture or vocalization betokening some shared 'semantic component' of the event, object, or action denoted by each of the two structures (see Wray (2000) for how this might have operated in protohumans and Kirby (2000) for a related computer model; more on this below). This could in time lead to the emergence of a construction for 'putting the pieces back together', not only allowing recapture of the meanings of the original structures, but also with the original pieces becoming instances of an ever wider class of slot fillers (Arbib, 2005*a*).

To get some feel for holophrases, consider that biological evolution yielded a repertoire of primate calls including those which describe a 'situation'. The 'leopard call' of the vervet monkey is emitted first by a monkey who has seen a leopard; the call triggers further calling and appropriate escape behaviour by others (Cheney and Seyfarth, 1990). The leopard call's meaning might be paraphrased by: 'There is a leopard nearby. Danger! Danger! Run up a tree to escape—and spread the (proto)word.' To this one might respond (Bridgeman, 2005), 'It's only one word, because "leopard" is enough to activate the whole thing.' However, once one moves from species-specific calls to protolanguage one might add new 'protowords' to convey meanings like 'There is a dead leopard. Let's feast upon it.' or 'There is a leopard. Let's hunt it so we can feast upon it.'—and we clearly cannot use the leopard alarm call as the word for *leopard* in either of these utterances without triggering an innate and inappropriate response. Thus, on the *holophrastic view*, early protolanguage proceeded first by adding holophrases expressing such meanings. It was then a major innovation to gain expressive power by beginning to replace such holophrases by compounds that did indeed *fractionate* some of the semantic components of the utterance.

The existence of primate vocalizations has suggested to some authors (e.g. Cheney and Seyfarth, 2005; MacNeilage and Davis, 2005) that language evolved purely in the vocal-auditory domain. However, Arbib, Liebal, and Pika (2008) find little evidence of manual gesture in monkeys but widespread use of such gesture in apes. Moreover, whereas monkey calls rest on innately specified motor programmes, a good number of the gestures used by an ape species will vary from group to group, suggesting that some of these gestures are learned. Some appear to be formed by taking a praxic action and reducing it to a form which stands in for the original action—just as beckoning with the finger is a reduced form of grasping someone and pulling them closer. This grounds the hypothesis that the common ancestor of apes and humans could exploit simple imitation not only to acquire praxic skills but also to share novel communicative gestures within their group.

It is then argued (Arbib, 2005a) that complex imitation—which in primates only emerged in the hominid line—builds on this ancestral capability to provide the break-through *towards* protolanguage made possible by the use of pantomime to provide an open-ended semantic range (Stokoe, 2001). Much of pantomime is holophrastic. If I pantomime 'he is opening the door' there will (contra Stokoe, 2001) be no natural separation of pantomiming *door* and *open*. However, as we move from such simple cases, it may be hard for an observer to understand what is being pantomimed. More-over, a pantomime may be quite long and energetically costly. This paved the way for *protosign* to emerge as pantomimes were replaced increasingly by more economical, less ambiguous conventionalized gestures. As a result, many protowords would have been holophrastic, with no natural separation of noun and verb. But, thanks to the flexibility of pantomime, the set of such protowords was open, whereas the set of primate calls was closed. The price for the transition from pantomime is that these protowords must be learned within a group—though pantomime continues to be available to supplement the protosign repertoire. I thus hypothesized (Arbib (2005a), as Wray (1998) did much ear-lier) that—responding to 'cultural selection' rather than 'natural selection'—the users of the first protolanguages created novel protowords for *complex* situations that met a key condition that they were *frequently important* to the tribe. This is the *holophrastic view*.

Kirby and Wray (Kirby, 2000; Wray, 1998, 2000) showed how fractionation of pro-towords might occur through chance occurrence of shared 'substrings' (whether similar parts of two gestures or two vocalizations) in two holophrases. Imagine (Arbib, 2005a) that a tribe has protowords *reboofalik* and *balikiwert* which could be paraphrased as 'The fire burns' and 'The fire cooks the meat' and which, by chance, contain similar substrings which become regularized as *falik* so that for the first time there is a sign for 'fire'. The utterances become 'reboofalik' and 'falikiwert' as *falik* replaces the two similar but different substrings. I do *not* imply that the tribe at this stage had developed a phonology. The notations *reboofalik* and *balikiwert* are not composed of a fixed stock of phonemes—rather, they are just two sound patterns with parts that are similar but not identical. However, the sort of regularization involved in merging *falik* and *balik* into a common sound pattern may be seen as a move towards creating a phonological stock for the emerging protolanguage.

Eventually, some tribe members regularize the complementary gestures in the first string to get a sign for *burns*; later, others regularize the complementary gestures in the second string to get a sign for *cooks meat*. However, the placement of the gestures that have come to denote 'burns' relative to 'fire' differs greatly from those for 'cooks meat'. It thus requires a further invention to regularize the placement of the gestures in both utterances—localized 'constructions' emerge to maintain and, as new protowords come to be used as slot fillers, extend the earlier set of meanings. Concomitantly, words get categorized by their ability to 'fill the slots' in a certain range of constructions.

This 'Wray–Kirby mechanism' is part of the answer but not the whole one. A tribe might have developed different signs for 'sour apple', 'ripe apple', 'sour plum', 'ripe plum', etc., because the appropriate behaviours ('leave to ripen' vs. 'pick and eat') are so salient that they became expressed in the protolanguage. Occasionally, someone will eat a piece of sour fruit by mistake and make a characteristic face and intake of breath. Another step toward compositionality (Arbib, 2005a) is exemplified by someone getting the idea of mimicking this act as a warning to someone that the fruit he is about to eat is sour. If a conventionalized variant of this gesture becomes accepted by the community, then a sign for 'sour' has extended the protolanguage. A further step would be taken when, for each kind X of fruit, people begin to combine the sign for 'sour' and the sign for 'ripe X' to replace the sign for 'sour X': $2n$ words become replaced by $n + 1$ words and one specialized construction. This exemplifies the role of embodied meaning in shaping core elements of a protolanguage and the languages that will emerge from it.

A third mechanism is the transition from constructions based on the use of a new word in the protolanguage to generalization across a whole set of constructions. A sign such as that for 'sour' could be added to the protovocabulary before any 'adjective mechanism' existed. It might take hundreds of such discoveries before someone could regularize their constructions and invent a general construction with a slot defining the precursor of what we would now call adjectives. Such a construction would be a step toward the emergence of a true language from the protolanguage. However, development of this theme lies outside the scope of this chapter. Instead, see Arbib (2012: chs. 10, 13).

However, not all those who write on language evolution accept the above scenario. Indeed, if a vote were taken, the majority would favour the compositional view of protolanguage (CPL) over the holophrastic view of protolanguage (HPL). Let us thus address some key criticisms of HPL, first those that also apply to CPL and then those that apply to CPL alone.

23.6.1 Criticisms applicable to both the compositional and holophrastic views of protolanguage

How do proponents of HPL deal with the fact that primate calls are essentially affective, involuntary vocalizations, whereas protowords are presumably voluntary vocalizations? In arguing that the transition from monkey-like vocalizations to speech is indirect, Arbib (2005b) extends the above scenario to sketch the way in which voluntary control of gesture came to support protospeech. Work on CPL has not offered a more convincing solution.

Why would any species bother to isolate a situation as the basis for a protoword unless, like the situations that trigger vervet alarm calls, that situation was of life-or-death importance or close thereto? This militates just as strongly against CPL: Why would 'any species bother to isolate an object or action unless that situation was of life-or-death importance or close thereto?' Human sentences rarely involve life-or-death importance. But we have wants and desires, and so may benefit if we have new ways to communicate them. This raises a chicken-and-egg problem of why others would want to satisfy our desires. But, as Dunbar (1996) notes, other primates exhibit behaviours like grooming that may underlie more general forms of reciprocity, while de Waal (2006) provides examples of altruism in apes.

Tallerman objects that

> holistic utterances must be stored by memorizing each complex propositional event and learning which unanalysable string is appropriate at each event. This task is harder, not simpler, than learning words as symbols, and therefore less suitable for an early protolanguage scenario. [In] protolanguage, holistic strings would relate to nothing except an entire message.... How many, then, would it be reasonable to assume that a hominid with a smaller brain... could learn and recall? (Tallerman, 2006: 448)

However, an emotionally charged event like feasting after a successful hunt could be more memorable than the distinction between, say, a plum and an apple, and distinguishing a plum from an apple is no more or less 'complexly propositional' than recognizing a festive occasion. Indeed, acquiring an HPL-protolexicon raises no demands that must not also be met in acquiring a CPL-lexicon. Moreover, modern languages show that a word in one language may require a phrase or even far more to translate it into another.

Bickerton (2005) responds to the scenario where two protowords concerning fire contain, by chance, similar substrings by noting that similar substrings might also occur in protowords that have nothing to do with fire. This problem confronts the compositional account as well—we view 'tar' as a semantic unit within 'get tar' but do not register it as part of 'target'. For the child learning a modern language, prosody may provide relevant clues—but such considerations were unlikely to apply to early protolanguages. Indeed prosody might well have emerged with fractionation in a gestural or vocal performance since the shift from the unfractionated to the fractionated string would have to be signalled in some way. Such signals might have been quite idiosyncratic at first, but in due course conventions would have emerged for marking them.

23.6.2 Criticisms unique to the holophrastic view of protolanguage

Bickerton (2005) asserts that it is 'questionable whether any species could isolate "a situation" from the unbroken, ongoing stream of experience unless it already had a language with which to do so.' But we have seen that biological evolution yielded a repertoire of primate calls each describing a 'situation', and so the association of protowords with salient situations becomes highly plausible.

Tallerman (2007) observes, correctly, that it is highly unlikely that protohumans could have a protoword for the message 'Go and hunt the hare I saw five minutes ago behind the stone at the top of the hill' (from Mithen, 2005: 172). However, this does not rebut my notion that protowords might correspond to complex situations. Mithen's example fails my key criterion that a protoword symbolize *frequently occurring* situations since his 'protoword' would have to specify a precise time interval and the relation of an arbitrary pair of objects. When I posit (Arbib, 2005a) that there could be a protoword for 'The alpha male has killed a meat animal and now the tribe has a chance to feast together. Yum, yum!', I do not claim that (at first) there were protowords for variations like 'The alpha male has killed a meat animal but its too scrawny to eat. Woe is we.' or 'The alpha male has killed a meat animal but is keeping it for himself.' Rather, protohumans would initially have a small stock of protowords that would increase over the generations.

Tallerman (2006) is concerned that the English paraphrase of my hypothetical pro-toword involves many clauses and then asks 'If modern speakers engage in conceptual planning only at the level of a single clause—a mental proposition—how could early hominids possibly have had the lexical capacity to store, retrieve (and execute) a single lexical concept which corresponds to several clauses' worth of semantic content?' (2006: 447). But if we define 'eat' as 'Take a substance whose ingestion is necessary for your survival, place it in your mouth, masticate it and then swallow it', then saying 'eat' is no more simple than uttering my protowords (cf. Smith, 2008). The issue is whether members of the group can recognize the similarity across many situations and associate them with a 'protoword' uttered on these occasions.

Tallerman asserts that

> Nouns and verbs more or less invent themselves....Other word classes follow by grammaticalization, just as in the history of well-documented existing languages....
> To propose [a holophrastic] strategy involving fractionation is to ignore the known processes by which words come into being in language—and, I suggest, in protolan-guage. (Tallerman, 2007: 580)

Here Tallerman commits the error of conflating processes operative in modern lan-guages with those we try to infer as operative when protolanguages emerged with increasing complexity. HPL holds that protolanguage did not start with any set of uni-versal syntactic categories, whether nouns and verbs or others, but rather that syntactic categories were an emerging property as protolanguages grew in complexity.

Although a strong proponent of HPL, Wray (1998: 48) has concerns about what use an evolving grammar could be: '[T]here is a critical level of complexity that must obtain for a creative grammar to be useful in expressing propositions.... [I]t is difficult to imagine what advantage a primitive, half-way grammar would have for its users, over the highly successful interactional systems of other primates'. This is, I think, a misimpression that derives from viewing a grammar as comprising a rather small set of general rules, rather than a large, flexible system of constructions. Wray's objection loses its force because constructions have 'standalone utility'. It is only the merging of categories from different constructions that may blur the original semantic cues as to what entered into the earlier constructions, yielding syntactic categories by default. But such categories are often more language-specific than universal. Cross-linguistically, prototypical nouns specify objects and prototypical verbs specify actions. However, such 'prototypes' are but the starting point for the variety of syntactic categories that can be revealed only by analysing the diverse constructions in any one modern language (Croft, 2001).

23.7 CONCLUSION

This chapter has two parts. The first recognizes the value of compositionality in underwriting the immense expressive power of language, but shows that there is more to meaning than is given by a formal characterization of the meaning of a phrase as built up compositionally from the meanings of its words. Both the embedding of language in embodied communication and the importance of context decree that the cooperative computation of grammar (posited to integrate clusters of form and meaning in constructions) and pragmatics serve to discriminate between alternative compositional analyses of a given sentence and to augment what can be derived from the sentence considered in isolation.

The second part applies these concepts to an ongoing debate about the nature of protolanguage. The compositional view is that the initial protowords of protolanguages were already akin to the words—especially nouns and verbs—of modern languages. Syntactic categories predated syntax! The holophrastic view is that few if any protowords were akin to nouns or verbs, but rather referred to 'important' situations. The emergence of languages from their precursors in the protolanguage spectrum was marked by the increasing importance of compositionality. Nonetheless, the ability to coin new words, metaphors, idioms, and constructions has always added the power to boldly go where compositionality cannot take us without complex and cumbersome circumlocution.

CHAPTER 24

COMPOSITIONALITY AND LINGUISTIC EVOLUTION

KENNY SMITH AND SIMON KIRBY

24.1 COMPOSITIONALITY, DESIGN, AND THE PROBLEM OF LINKAGE

What distinguishes language from the communication systems of other animals? In an early attempt to answer this question, Hockett (1960) lists 13 *design features* of language. Hockett identifies *productivity* ('the capacity to say things that have never been said or heard before and yet to be understood by other speakers of the language', Hockett, 1960: 6) as one of the few design features unique to language, and highlights the importance of accounting for this feature in explaining the evolutionary origins of language.

The productivity of language is subserved by two structural properties: language is *recursive*, which allows the creation of an infinite number of utterances, and language is *compositional*, which makes the interpretation of novel utterances possible—in a recursive compositional system, if you know the meaning of the basic elements and the effects associated with combining elements, you can deduce the meaning of any utterance in the system.

Why is language designed like this? This at first seems like a fairly trivial question to answer: language is recursively compositional because this is useful. First, it offers open-ended expressivity: a population of individuals sharing a recursively compositional system can in principle communicate with each other about anything they choose, including survival-relevant issues such as where to find food and shelter, how to deal with predators and prey, how social relationships are to be managed, and so on. Second, recursive compositionality is an efficient means of achieving productivity, in that it only requires a finite (and fairly small) set of cognitive resources. This combination of attributes is neatly summarized by Krifka (2001):

> In some form, compositionality is a virtually necessary principle, given the fact that natural languages can express an infinity of meanings and can be learned by humans with finite resources. Essentially, humans have to learn the meanings of basic expressions, the words in the lexicon (in the magnitude of 10^5), and the meaning effects of syntactic combinations (in the magnitude of 10^2 ...). With that they are ready to understand an infinite number of syntactically well-formed expressions. Thus, compositionality is necessary if we see the language faculty, with Wilhelm von Humboldt, as making infinite use of finite means. (Krifka, 2001: 152)

However, the fact that recursive compositionality makes good design sense in various ways does not explain how language came to have these properties: to truly answer the question 'why is language designed like this?' we need to establish the *mechanisms* which explain this fit between function and form. The *problem of linkage* remains: given an observation regarding the structure of language (language is compositional) and a corresponding functional preference (compositionality is useful), we are still required to explain how the functional motivation gives rise to the observed structure (Kirby, 1999*a*). In other words, how did the manifest advantages of compositionality become realized in language as a system of human behaviour?

These questions have received some attention in the field of evolutionary linguistics, particularly given the hypothesis that language evolved from a holistic predecessor (as proposed by e.g. Wray, 1998; but see also e.g. Bickerton, 2003). We will review two potential solutions to the problem of linkage for compositionality: one which explains the fit between function and form as arising from the biological evolution of the human language faculty (in Section 24.2), and one which views it as a consequence of the cultural evolution of language itself (in the remainder of the chapter).

24.2 COMPOSITIONALITY AS AN EVOLVED BIOLOGICAL ENDOWMENT

A well-established solution to the problem of linkage in biological systems is that of evolution by natural selection: adaptation (a match between the functional requirements acting on an organism and that organism's phenotype) is a consequence of reproduction and heritable variation in those characteristics that effect an organism's chances of reproducing. Over time, those characteristics that maximize reproductive success come to dominate a population, resulting in a good fit between an organism's characteristics and the functional requirements imposed by the environment.[1]

In a highly influential article, Pinker and Bloom (1990) argue that this well-established solution to the problem of linkage can be applied to language. Following for example Chomsky (1965, 1987), they treat language as a biological capacity. Indeed, they claim '[a]ll modern students of language agree that at least some aspects of language

---

[1] Broadly construed: conspecifics are in this sense part of the environment, and tend to be an important part of the problem an organism must solve to reproduce successfully.

are due to species-specific, task-specific biological abilities' (Pinker and Bloom, 1990: 707). Given the biological nature of language and the primacy of natural selection in explaining adaptation in biological systems, they argue that natural selection should be used to explain adaptation in language: 'It would be natural, then, to expect everyone to agree that human language is the product of Darwinian natural selection. The only successful account of the origin of complex biological structure is the theory of natural selection' (Pinker and Bloom, 1990: 707).

How does this argument work when applied to the evolution of compositionality? First, we must be satisfied that compositionality is an aspect of human biology, imposed on language by the language faculty. Pinker and Bloom provide two sorts of evidence that can be used to support this claim—the universality of a given feature (if a trait is unvarying across populations and across times within a population it can be taken to be innate) and arguments from the poverty of the stimulus (the data from which a particular structure could be learned is not reliably present in the input to learners), both of which we will revisit later in this chapter. Second, we must be satisfied that the conditions for natural selection hold:

1. there must be variation in the extent to which compositionality is pre-specified in the language faculty—minimally, there must be two variants of the language faculty: one which requires language to be compositional, one which does not;
2. that variation is heritable, being transmitted from parent to child during reproduction;
3. the extent to which a language faculty of an individual requires compositionality influences the reproductive success of that individual, with individuals with language faculties which require compositionality enjoying greater reproductive success.

Pinker and Bloom provide several arguments in support of the third requirement, that language in general offers reproductive payoffs. Similar arguments exist for the case of compositionality—as discussed above, compositionality (in combination with recursion) offers open-ended communication, which plausibly might have reproductive consequences. They have less to offer regarding the first two requirements, in variability and heritability, pointing out that there is little evidence on the genetic basis of specific linguistic features.[2]

Nowak, Plotkin, and Jansen (2000) develop this argument in a mathematical model of the evolution of compositionality. They assume two types of language learner: those who learn a holistic (non-compositional) mapping between meanings and signals, and those who learn a simple compositional system. They consider the case of populations of such learners, converged on stable languages, and find that, as expected, populations of compositional learners have higher within-population communicative accuracy than learn-

---

[2] This may, however, be about to change: Dediu and Ladd (2007) highlight a correlation between genes and a particular linguistic feature (tone), and offer an intriguing hypothesis that this correlation may be causal in nature, with certain combinations of genes making this linguistic feature easier to learn.

ers who learn in a holistic fashion, assuming that the number of events that individuals are required to communicate about is relatively large. In other words, under conditions where there are a large number of fitness-relevant situations to communicate about, the productivity advantage of compositional language pays off in evolutionary terms.

24.3 COMPOSITIONALITY AS A CULTURALLY-EVOLVED TRAIT

A second possible explanation for the linkage between the functional properties of compositionality and the compositional structure of language is that this fit arose through *cultural*, rather than biological, evolution. We will discuss several theories along these lines in Sections 24.4 and 24.5: here we cover the preliminaries of what cultural evolution is, and discuss its viability as an alternative to biologically-based theories of language evolution.

Language is a cultural system in as much as it is transmitted from individual to individual by social learning, or learning from the behaviour of others. Individuals acquire some knowledge of language by observing the linguistic behaviour of others, and go on to use this knowledge to produce further examples of linguistic behaviour which others can learn from in turn (see e.g. Andersen, 1973; Hurford, 1990; Kirby, 1999a). This process of cultural transmission is often termed *iterated learning*: learning from the behaviour of another, where that behaviour was itself acquired through the same process of learning (Kirby and Hurford, 2002).

Culturally-transmitted systems of behaviour can undergo evolution, just as biologically-transmitted systems do. For example, cultural systems meet the requirements for a system which will undergo evolution by natural selection, namely (cultural) reproduction, (culturally) heritable variation and differential (cultural) reproduction of competing variants, as a result of the differential survival and reproductive success of individuals with those variants (Boyd and Richerson, 1985; Mesoudi, Whiten, and Laland, 2006). However, the natural selection of cultural variants is not the sole means by which cultural systems evolve: owing to their different mode of transmission, cultural systems are subject to a range of other selection pressures (see Boyd and Richerson, 1985, for a detailed treatment of mechanisms of cultural evolution), some of which we will touch on in Sections 24.4–24.5.

24.3.1 Do cultural accounts have a place?

In order to argue that the compositional structure of language is a product of cultural evolution, we must assume that the fact that language is compositional is socially learned and therefore culturally transmitted. If we assume that compositionality is an aspect of human biology, then cultural explanations have no role to play: if compositionality is hard-wired into the language faculty then cultural accounts of its origins are irrelevant.[3] If, on the other hand, we admit some role for social learning in the transmission of compositionality then cultural evolution has a potential role to play in resolving the problem of linkage.

To what extent is compositionality imposed on language by the language faculty, and to what extent is its acquisition dependent on exposure to utterances drawn from a compositional language? There must be *some* genetic component to compositionality, since examples of compositional communication systems in non-human animals are rare.[4] The question is to what extent this genetic element strictly constrains humans to learning only compositional languages—if it is in principle possible for humans to learn some non-compositional system of communication, then that suffices for cultural explanations to play some role.

In non-human animals, the extent to which a given behaviour requires some element of learning is typically evaluated through cross-fostering or raising in isolation: if an animal still exhibits a species-typical behaviour after being raised by a related species with a different behaviour, or after being raised in isolation, then that behaviour is likely to be innate. Neither experiment has been conducted in the case of compositionality in humans, nor is it likely to be.[5] However, the fact that children successfully acquire *exceptions* to compositionality (irregulars, idioms) suggests that any preference for compositionality cannot be absolute. It has been further argued that even apparently compositional utterances may be learned and processed in a non-compositional (or *holistic*) fashion (Wray, 2002b), casting further doubt on the existence of a strong innate constraint requiring language to be compositional.

[3] Notwithstanding their role in accounts where compositionality is an initially-learned trait which becomes nativized, through e.g. the Baldwin effect (Baldwin, 1896).

[4] Possible cases include the boom–alarm combination call in Campbell's monkeys, where the preceding boom serves to change the meaning of the subsequent alarm call, or reduce its immediacy (Zuberbuhler, 2002), and the dance of the honeybee, where separate components of the dance convey distance and direction to nectar source (von Frisch, 1974).

[5] There are a number of naturally occurring situations which come tantalisingly close, however. Homesigners (deaf children of hearing parents with no access to established sign languages) develop idiosyncratic sign systems which string signs together into (sometimes complex) sentences, with some children differentiating agent and patient by position in the string or by likelihood of omission (agents of transitive verbs being more likely to be omitted than agents of intransitives or patients) (Goldin-Meadow and Mylander, 1998). However, while the signing behaviour of these children goes well beyond the complexity of the gestural system employed by their caregivers in a number of respects, the basic properties of stringing signs together and differentiating agents and patients by omission were evidenced in the gestural behaviour of caregivers (Goldin-Meadow and Mylander, 1998). It is, therefore, possible (and we raise it as no more than a possibility) that the children learned that communication could or should be compositionally structured from the little input they did receive. Similar problems exist with the compositionality of creole languages, the structure of which is often taken as strong evidence for the existence of innate linguistic principles (see e.g. Bickerton, 1984): while the input provided to child language learners in creolization situations is indeed unusual, coming from a pidgin rather than a full-fledged language, it does consist of words combined in strings where manner of combination can be meaningful—again, this might be sufficient evidence to learn socially that language should be compositional.

A less direct source of evidence for the innateness of a particular linguistic feature is universality: if a given feature, such as compositionality, is shared across languages and across large timescales within a population, then the innateness of that feature is a parsimonious explanation. It is not the only possible explanation, however: universal traits may still be socially learned if there is a plausible argument that their universality arises from common ancestry (all languages inherit the feature from their hypothetical extremely distant common ancestor) and/or convergent evolution (all languages share the feature due to pressures acting on the cultural transmission of all languages which tend to introduce and/or protect that feature). Both cases plausibly apply in the case of compositionality: we would argue that compositionality is likely to have evolved early in the history of language, and the pressures which led to its origin pertain today in the transmission of all languages.

It therefore seems to us that there is a case to be made for compositionality being (at least in part) socially-learned. Having made this assumption, and being fully aware that it is at this stage little more than a working hypothesis, we now turn to the question of how compositionality can arise as a consequence of social learning and cultural evolution.

24.4 COMPOSITIONALITY AS A CULTURAL ADAPTATION FOR LEARNABILITY

The data from which language learners learn language is far from ideal in many ways: for instance, it may lack the crucial examples that would be required to learn certain structural generalizations (Chomsky, 1975, but see Pullum and Scholz, 2002). Such *poverty of the stimulus* arguments are typically cited as evidence that aspects of language must be innate—how else could such structures survive transmission through such an impoverished set of learning data, if learners are required to make a lucky guess about the correct underlying structure of a language? However, cultural transmission offers a potential solution to this conundrum that does not require an assumption of innateness—while the poverty of the stimulus poses a challenge for individual learners, language adapts over cultural time so as to minimize this problem, because its survival depends upon it. We have dubbed this process *cultural selection for learnability*:

> in order for linguistic forms to persist from one generation to the next, they must repeatedly survive the processes of expression and induction. That is, the output of one generation must be successfully learned by the next if these linguistic forms are to survive. We say that those forms that repeatedly survive cultural transmission are adaptive in the context of cultural transmission. (Brighton, Kirby, and Smith, 2005a: 303).

Cultural selection for learnability offers a solution to the conundrum posed by the argument from the poverty of the stimulus:

Human children appear preadapted to guess the rules of syntax correctly, precisely because languages evolve so as to embody in their syntax the most frequently guessed patterns. The brain has co-evolved with respect to language, but languages have done most of the adapting. (Deacon, 1997: 122)

24.4.1 Compositionality and the learning bottleneck

How does cultural selection for learnability explain compositionality?[6] As discussed above, languages are infinitely expressive (due to the combination of recursion and compositionality). However, such languages must be transmitted through a finite set of learning data. We call this mismatch between the size of the system to be transmitted and its medium of transmission the *learning bottleneck*. Compositionality provides an elegant solution to this problem: to learn a compositional system, a learner must master a finite set of words and rules for their combination, which can be learned from a finite set of data. This fit between the form of language (it is compositional) and a property of the transmission medium (it is finite but the system passing through it is infinite) is suggestive, but the problem of linkage remains: can cultural evolution account for this goodness of fit? Note that we are appealing to a different notion of function to that discussed in Section 24.2: while Pinker and Bloom (1990) and Nowak et al. (2000) appealed to compositionality as an adaptation for communication, it is also an adaptation for cultural transmission.

To sketch the argument:[7] imagine two alternative linguistic systems being transmitted from individual to individual via a finite set of data. One system is non-compositional, whereas the other is compositional. Both systems are larger (in the sense of providing more meaning–signal pairs) than the set of data they must pass through: this is necessarily the case if the languages are infinitely expressive, but our argument in fact does not require infinitely large languages.

How will these two systems fare over an episode of transmission? The compositional system will be transmitted intact, provided that the finite set of data from which it is to be learned is sufficiently large to allow the component words and rules of combination to be deduced—the learner will learn those rules and reproduce the full language, intact. In contrast, the learner of a non-compositional language will only be able to correctly reproduce those parts of the larger language which were included in the dataset they were exposed to—in a non-compositional system there is no principled means to infer the rest of the language from the finite dataset provided.

---

[6] We will focus here on one possible learnability pressure, arising from the learning bottleneck. There is an alternative pressure, arising from the biases of language learners: as shown by e.g. Griffiths and Kalish (2007), under certain fairly general circumstances, culturally transmitted systems evolve so as to match the inductive biases of their learners. If human learners had some inductive bias favouring compositionality (e.g. arising from their general cognitive system or built in to their language faculty), this would lead to the cultural evolution of a matching system.

[7] This sketch is based around the replicator-based exposition provided in Kirby (2002) and the formal stability analysis provided by Brighton (2002).

What happens to the holistic system at subsequent transmission events? This depends on what a user of the (reduced) holistic language does when they come across a situation for which the language embodied in the data that they learned from provides no means of expression (due to the learning bottleneck). If they remain mute, the holistic system will gradually shrink due to the cumulative loss of utterances, with the rate of shrinkage slowing as the system becomes smaller and smaller and more and more able to fit as a whole through the learning bottleneck. Alternatively, users of the holistic system may attempt to innovate—perhaps by using existing utterances in a novel way or producing novel utterances. In either case they are unlikely to faithfully reproduce the unseen portions of the language they attempted to learn, and consequently the holistic system will change.

This same argument applies within systems which exhibit a mix of compositionality and holism: whereas the compositional components of this system will be stable, the holistic elements will be subject to change. We would therefore expect that, given suffi-cient time, the only systems we will see will be compositional: either holistic systems and holistic parts of systems will be winnowed away to nothing and will disappear, or they will continue to change until they hit upon compositionality and become stable.

In sum, given the learning bottleneck, a language must be learnable (reconstructible) from a subset of itself, and we should therefore see cultural selection for learnability favouring languages which have this property. Compositionality allows an infinite lan-guage to be learned from a finite set of data (or a large language to be learned from a subset), and as such it is likely to be adaptive in the context of cultural transmission through a learning bottleneck. As will be discussed below, compositionality is not the sole possible adaptation to this pressure for *generalizability* introduced by the learning bottleneck.

24.4.2 Models of the cultural evolution of compositionality

This relationship between the learning bottleneck and compositionality has been repeat-edly demonstrated using computational models of the iterated learning process, known as *iterated learning models*. In their simplest form, iterated learning models consist of a chain of simulated language learner/users (known as *agents*). Each agent in this chain learns their language by observing a set of utterances produced by the preceding agent in the chain, and in turn produces example utterances for the next agent to learn from (see Fig. 24.1). In a typical simulation run, the initial agent in the chain will produce some random, and therefore holistic, mapping between meanings and signals.

The treatment of language learning and language production varies from model to model, with similar results having been shown for a fairly wide range of models. For example, in Kirby (2002) (developed from Kirby, 1999b, 2000, 2001), languages are mappings from recursively-embedded predicate–argument structures (meanings) to

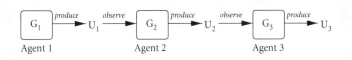

FIGURE 24.1 A simple iterated learning model. Each agent i has a grammar G_i which is used to generate a set of utterances U_i, which the next agent in the chain observes and learns from

strings of characters (forms). Language learning in this model is a process of heuristic grammar induction whereby a context free grammar, with associated semantics, is induced from a set of observed meaning–form pairs. Other iterated learning models are based around heuristic-driven compression of finite state transducers (Brighton, 2003) or neural networks (Kirby and Hurford, 2002; Smith, Brighton, and Kirby, 2003) which capture a given mapping between meaning and signals. In all cases, the crucial feature is that these models of learning are capable of learning *both* holistic and compositional languages: they can memorize a holistic meaning–signal mapping, but they can also generalize to a partially or wholly compositional language when the data they are learning from justifies it. Learners/users are also equipped with a mechanism for innovative production (typically producing holistic utterances): as discussed above, the precise trajectory of linguistic evolution depends on how learners/users deal with gaps in their language.

These models show, as predicted given the stability analysis above, that the presence of a learning bottleneck is a key factor in determining the evolution of compositionality. In conditions where there is no learning bottleneck, the set of utterances produced by one agent for another to learn from covers (or is highly likely to cover) the full space of meanings which any agent will ever be required to produce a signal for—this is of course impossible for human language, where the meaning space is extremely large or infinite. On the other hand, where there is a learning bottleneck, the set of utterances only includes a subset of those meanings—consequently, there is some (typically high) probability that learners/users will subsequently be called upon to produce a signal for a novel meaning, and will therefore be required to generalize. As discussed above, it is this pressure to generalize which leads to the evolution of compositional languages. Fig. 24.2 gives example initial (holistic) and final (compositional) languages from the iterated learning model outlined in Kirby (2002). This final language evolved through repeated transmission through a bottleneck—were there no bottleneck on transmission, the initial holistic language would be entirely stable.

Compositionality can therefore be explained as a cultural adaptation *by language* to the problem of transmission through a learning bottleneck. Note that nowhere in the account above have we appealed to the communicative benefits of compositionality, which play a crucial role in the type of account proposed by Pinker and Bloom (1990), or indeed the representational economy of compositional language highlighted by Krifka (2001). Under the learning bottleneck account, these are both coincidental outcomes of adaptation for language transmission.

(a) Meaning	Form	(b) Meaning	Form
'Mary loves Pete'	k	'Mary loves Pete'	v k g pd c n
'Mary loves Gavin'	bni	'Mary loves Gavin'	v gw g pd c n
'Mary likes Gavin'	ke	'Mary likes Gavin'	v gw g pd z n
'Gavin likes Pete'	qi	'Gavin likes Pete'	v k g gw z n

FIGURE 24.2 Fragments of typical initial (a) and final (b) languages from the iterated learning model described in Kirby (2002, section 6.3.1), with meanings glossed in English. Whereas the initial language in (a) exhibits no structure in the mapping from meaning to form, the final language is compositional—the meaning glossed as 'Agent Predicate Patient' maps to the string 'v Patient g Agent Predicate n'. Note that the spaces in the language (b) have been added to aid clarity, and are not present in the actual language

24.4.3 Compositionality and frequency

Language is not perfectly compositional—rather, while being broadly organized on compositional grounds, it contains numerous instances of non-compositionality in the forms of idioms, irregulars, and so on. As is often noted (e.g. Bybee, 1985, 1995), irregulars are frequent: for example, the ten most frequent verbs of English are irregular (Leech, Rayson, and Wilson, 2001). Frequently-used verbs regularize more slowly than their infrequent counterparts (Lieberman, Michell, Jackson, Tang, and Nowak, 2007). As shown in Kirby (2001), this frequency–regularity interaction naturally falls out of the learning bottleneck account. Signals associated with frequently expressed meanings are likely to be in the data from which each individual learns their language, and frequent meanings are therefore under less pressure to be expressed in a compositional fashion than less frequently-expressed meanings: the learning bottleneck is effectively less of a problem for frequent meanings. The learning bottleneck therefore explains both the general tendency of language to be compositional, and exceptions to this pattern.

24.4.4 A comment on alternative solutions to the generalization problem

The learning bottleneck induces a pressure for language to be generalizable. Compositionality is one way in which language can become generalizable, but there are others, the most obvious of which is generalizability by systematic underspecification of meaning at the lexical level. To give an example: in Fig. 24.2 the compositional final system produced by iterated learning uses a system of lexical items and rules for their combination to convey 125 predicate–argument structures (5 two-place predicates, 5 agents, 5 patients) using a system which requires fewer than 125 exposures to learn. An alternative system which provides similar gains of generalization would be to use a single word for each of the five predicates, regardless of the arguments that predicate applies to—for example, 'Mary loves Pete' and 'Heather loves Gavin' would be associated with the same word. A learner presented with a few examples of each word from this system would soon arrive at the correct generalization, and moreover this generalization requires no syntactic analysis of multi-word constructions. Note that the underspecification must be *systematic*, however: while a system which splits the meanings into five sets, according to predicate, and then associates a word with each such set is eminently generalizable, one which splits the meanings into five sets, arbitrarily and without reference to meaning, and then associates a word with each such set is not a case of systematic underspecification, and is not generalizable.

Systematic underspecification is a potential generalization, and therefore a potential solution to the pressure introduced by the learning bottleneck. Why do iterated learning models discussed above not discover this solution? These models generally include features specifically designed to block ambiguity as an adaptation to the learning bottleneck. Ambiguity is a consequence of underspecification: an utterance with an underspecified meaning picks out several individuals or situations, rather than uniquely identifying one such object or situation. This blocking of ambiguity is achieved by a combination of representational biases and explicit filters on ambiguity (in Kirby, 2002) or learning mechanisms which are biased against acquiring (or cannot acquire) ambiguous mappings (in Smith et al., 2003; Brighton et al., 2005*b*). Without such filters or disadvantages to ambiguity, ambiguity typically swamps compositionality as the response to the learning bottleneck (for examples of this phenomenon, where the penalties for ambiguity are removed, see Smith, 2003; Brighton et al., 2005*b*) with the result that the final languages are of the most ambiguous, most generalizable type, with every meaning being expressed by a single common form.

Needless to say, languages don't exhibit this extreme level of ambiguity, which is why ambiguity is typically penalized in some way in iterated learning models. There is, however, a renewed interest in exploring ambiguity and underspecification of various sorts as an adaptation to cultural transmission (see e.g. Hoefler, 2006 and the discussion of Kirby et al., forthcoming below). There are several reasons for this. First, languages do exhibit systematic underspecification—for example, words picks out a class of objects rather than a single unique object, and word meanings are therefore systematically underspecified in the way described above. Second, arbitrary filters or biases against ambiguity require some justification. There is some evidence that language learners do have expectations that languages should embody a system of lexical contrast and an isomorphic mapping between meaning and form (see e.g. Clark, 1988; Slobin, 1977 and Smith, 2003; Brighton et al., 2005*b* for the relationship between these biases and models of learning in the iterated learning context), but the attested biases of real language learners are at least weaker than those in the models. One area for future study is to understand how these competing adaptations for generalizability interact during cultural evolution. Another is to reconcile the need for such filters on ambiguity with the notion that compositionality can be explained purely in terms of selection for learnability, without reference to function—does the need for blocks on ambiguity fatally undermine this idea and indicate a necessary role for communicative function in explaining compositionality?

24.5 COMPOSITIONALITY AND
LANGUAGE USE

There is a second set of mechanisms by which compositionality can evolve culturally, as a result of the communicative advantages that it offers. First, the biological argument provided by Pinker and Bloom (1990) and supported by, for example, Nowak et al. (2000) has a natural, although not common, cultural interpretation: if we assume that reproduction allows a parent to pass on their language (holistic or compositional) to their offspring, we can relax the assumption that a restrictive language faculty is also transmitted genetically, and still expect to see compositional languages out-compete holistic languages through the natural selection of cultural variants.

There are also several models which explain compositionality as a result of language use and communication, without making the same strong assumptions as Nowak et al. (2000) that grammar type directly influences the reproductive success of individuals and their languages. These models (Batali, 2002; Vogt, 2005; de Beule and Bergen, 2006) are similar to the iterated learning models discussed above, in that they are based around simulated agents learning language from the production of other agents, and in turn producing examples of language use to be learned from—they either adopt the standard iterated learning chain-type population model (as in Vogt, 2005) or a population model where multiple individuals repeatedly interact with one another, taking turns to act as producers and learners of language.

However, unlike the iterated learning models described earlier, these models assume some payoff for expressions which are frequently used and/or frequently used successfully. In Batali (2002), learners/users acquire a set of constructions embodying a mapping between meanings and signals. Each construction has an associated cost, and those costs decrease every time a construction can be used to account for an observed meaning–signal pair during learning. In Vogt (2005) and de Beule and Bergen (2006) each construction or rule of the grammar has a cost which is decreased each time it is used to *successfully* communicate a meaning to an interlocutor. In both cases, the cost dynamic is the same: constructions or rules involved in a compositional system will have more opportunities to be (successfully) used, because they are more productive than non-compositional constructions or rules. The productivity of compositional rules gives them an inherent advantage in a cost-based system such as this. As a result, and even in the absence of a transmission bottleneck (Vogt, 2005),[8] the languages of these popula-

---

[8] The relationship between costs and the learning bottleneck in these models is not actually entirely clear. Due to the population model adopted by Batali (2002), where multiple individuals negotiate a language through repeated reciprocal interactions, quantifying the extent of the learning bottleneck is

tions becomes compositional—each agent produces their preferred linguistic variants, compositional variants are preferentially used when they occur, and repeated learning and production ensures that the population converges on a shared and compositional system. This mechanism has clear parallels in usage-based explanations of language change, which focus on the role of communication-directed innovations by individuals in driving language change (e.g. Croft, 2000).

This cost-based mechanism also potentially offers a less arbitrary means of eliminating widespread ambiguity, that alternative generalization to compositionality. A cost function based on pure re-use, such as that favoured by Batali (2002), would favour systematic ambiguity, and Batali includes penalties for ambiguity to rule this out. However, cost based on *successful* re-use would seem to naturally solve this problem—whereas a system of systematic ambiguity allows a small number of constructions to be repeatedly re-used, the ambiguity of the system ensures that the greater the degree of re-use the less likely each use is to be communicatively successful. While this is a persuasive argument, it remains to be conclusively demonstrated: cost-based accounts (Vogt, 2005; de Beule and Bergen, 2006) which include this success-based dynamic also tend to include mechanisms (similar to those adopted by Batali) which penalize ambiguity directly. It therefore remains to some extent an open question whether compositionality can be explained purely as a cultural adaptation to a pressure arising from a preference for re-use of communicatively successful utterances.

24.6 EXPERIMENTAL MODELS OF THE EVOLUTION OF COMPOSITIONALITY

Computational and mathematical models have proven to be valuable tools in developing our understanding of the types of pressures which will lead to the evolution of compositionality. An exciting new body of work seeks to explore the cultural evolution of communication in the laboratory, using human participants, with the aim of investigating whether the pressures outlined above (learning bottlenecks, communicative functionality) will work in a similar way once we move beyond the idealized world of the formal model. At present, these experiments either involve repeated interaction between pairs of individuals attempting to solve a cooperative task (discussed in Section 24.6.1) or a simpler iterated artificial language learning task (Section 24.6.2).

somewhat difficult: the lack of a clear-cut separation between learners and producers of language makes it difficult to quantify the extent to which individuals are required to generalize, and generalization pressures might change over time. In contrast, Vogt (2005) uses a standard iterated learning model, controlling the presence or absence of the transmission bottleneck, but has a cost-function based on use and success. The safest conclusion from these two models is that either some (possibly very weak) pressure for generalization plus a cost function based on pure reuse can lead to the emergence of compositionality (in Batali, 2002) or no bottleneck plus a cost function based on successful reuse can lead to the emergence of compositionality (in Vogt, 2005).

24.6.1 Experimental studies involving repeated communicative interaction

Galantucci (2005) and Garrod, Fay, Lee, Oberlander, and MacLeod (2007) conduct experiments where pairs of participants repeatedly interact to solve a cooperative task which (explicitly or implicitly) requires communication: a navigation task in Galantucci (2005), a concept identification task in Garrod et al. (2007). In both experiments, participants are provided with a graphical communication channel, and receive explicit or implicit feedback on the success or failure of their communication, and in both experiments we see fleeting glimpses of compositionality in the communication systems that their participants develop.

Participants in the experiment described in Garrod et al. (2007) are required to repeatedly communicate about a number of concepts, by drawing pictures for their partners to identify, as in the parlour game Pictionary. This set of concepts includes four building-related concepts: Art Gallery, Theatre, Museum, and Parliament. Most pairs arrive at holistic symbols which communicate these concept unambiguously: for example, the symbol for Art Gallery may start off as a highly iconic representation of pictures hanging on a wall, and develop into a stylized and simplified representation of a single picture frame. Garrod et al. (2007, specifically, figure 15 and associated discussion) report a single case in which a pair of participants develop a compositional system of representation for these building concepts. The participant pair of interest arrive at a representational system which has internal structure in the symbol for Art Gallery: this comes to be represented by a complex symbol consisting of a symbol for a generic building (a square with windows and a door), a symbol for the containment relationship (similar to the less-than symbol, <), and a simplified representation of a picture frame—this compound sign could be glossed as 'building containing pictures'. Garrod et al. (2007) report that, through further interactions, the building symbol comes to be used by this pair in the representation of the other building concepts. While it is not clear whether the structure of those symbols exactly mirrors the Art Gallery example, this is clearly the potential beginnings of a compositional system of communication.

A similar phenomenon is reported by Galantucci (2005). In this case, participants are required to coordinate their actions so as to meet in a particular location in a multi-room maze (four rooms initially, rising to nine and then sixteen). Participant pairs often develop a system where each room in the smaller maze is numbered (one through four), and the meeting location is conveyed by a graphical representation of that number (given by strokes of the stylus). Upon moving to larger mazes, most participant pairs simply extend this numbering scheme. However, one pair (Pair 7, figure 8, p. 756), developed a system where locations in the larger maze were conveyed by the combination of a 'below' or 'to the right of' symbol (a horizontal or vertical dash), plus the symbol for another room. For example, a room which might otherwise be referred to as room 9 in the sixteen-room maze was referred to instead as (graphically) 'below

3'. Furthermore, the 'below' operator applied recursively (or at least iteratively): another room was referred to as 'below below 3'. Again, this is a fleeting but suggestive glimpse of how a compositional system of communication might be negotiated through repeated, function-driven interaction. A more direct example is provided by the experimental work outlined in Selten and Warglien (2007). In this case, once again involving repeated interaction between individuals, participants were provided with a set of objects to communicate about (differing in shape, colour, and/or inset, e.g. a green triangle with a cross inset, a red pentagon with a star inset) using a set of explicitly symbolic tokens (a limited set of alphabet characters). Again, the goal of the experiment was explicitly communicative, and participants were provided with continual feedback on their success in this task. Selten and Warglien found that a subset of their participants (14 of the 47 pairs who established a common communicative code, from a total of 113 pairs participating in the experiment) developed a communication system which could be classified as compositional: for example, using one letter for each shape, one letter for each inset, and combining them in a fixed order, shape before inset.

Selten and Warglien attribute this evolution of compositional grammars to the pressure for generalizability that their experimental design requires: the set of objects to be communicated about changes rapidly, favouring a productive system like compositionality. While this sounds similar to the learning bottleneck argument above, participants in their experiments received feedback on performance, so communication-based mechanisms may play some role in the eventual form of the emergent communication systems.

24.6.2 Experimental studies of iterated learning

The preceding three experiments speak to the creativity of human participants when thrust into a novel experimental environment requiring communication. However, none of them explicitly address the role of the learning bottleneck in driving the evolution of compositionality. Participants in Garrod et al. (2007) repeatedly interact to communicate the same concepts, and as such there is no bottleneck on transmission—the rarity of compositional representations in their experiment is therefore perhaps unsurprising. Both Galantucci (2005) and Selten and Warglien (2007) find compositionality in situations where there is an incentive for generalizability: the move from small to large mazes in Galantucci (2005), the changing object sets in Selten and Warglien (2007). However, in both cases there is also repeated interaction and feedback, somewhat obscuring the relationship between the structure of the emergent communication systems and the pressure to generalize introduced by novelty. The participants in these experiments are also explicitly attempting to construct a system of communication—outside the lab, while individuals may use their language in innovative ways to meet their communicative goals on a case-by-case basis (Croft, 2000), language is better explained as a product of an 'invisible hand' process (Keller, 1994), lacking in an intentional, intelligent designer.

In part to address these questions, and also to explore a more standard iterated learning approach to transmission, we (in conjunction with Hannah Cornish: Kirby et al., forthcoming) conducted a series of experiments involving the iterated learning of artificial languages. In a standard artificial language learning experiment, participants are trained on some artificial language (in this case, involving a mapping between strings of alphabet characters and coloured geometrical shapes performing certain stereotyped movements), then tested to see how well they recall this language or can identify strings drawn from it (see e.g. Gomez and Gerken, 2000; Hudson Kam and Newport, 2005). In an iterated artificial language learning experiment, as in the classic iterated learning model, a participant's recalled language during testing is simply used as training data for the next individual in the chain. While the application to language is novel, similar transmission studies have been carried out in a number of other cognitive domains (e.g. function learning and categorization: Kalish, Griffiths, and Lewandowsky, 2007; Griffiths, Christian, and Kalish, 2008).

We carried out two variants of this iterated artificial language learning experiment, running several ten-generation iterated learning chains in each condition. In both cases, as in the standard computational iterated learning model, the initial participant was trained on a random, non-compositional meaning–signal mapping, and there was a bottleneck on transmission: participants were trained on a subset of the language produced by the previous individual in the chain, and were required to produce signals for novel meanings. Participants carried out the learning task in isolation, and were not informed of their accuracy levels, or rewarded for accurate learning. In the first condition, the 'filtered' condition, ambiguous strings were removed from the training data passed on to the next individual in the chain: for example, if meanings glossed as 'red square bouncing' and 'blue triangle looping' were both paired with the string 'kimu', then only one such meaning–signal pair would be passed on to the next participant. In the second, unfiltered condition, this filtering process was simply omitted, allowing ambiguity into the learning data. Both experiments therefore had a pressure to generalize acting on transmission, resulting from the learning bottleneck, but differed in whether systematic ambiguity was a viable solution to this transmission problem.

As expected, given our theory of cultural selection for learnability, in both conditions the languages became easier to learn: the average number of errors made during learning by the first individual in each chain was significantly higher than that made by the last individual in each chain, as a consequence of the languages evolving to become more learnable. However, the structure of the evolving languages differed across conditions. In the unfiltered condition, systematic underspecification won out: the number of distinct strings decreased rapidly, and the resulting small number of strings were associated with meanings in a structured way (in one particularly extreme chain, the language reduced down to two words). In contrast, in the filtered condition the population arrived at a compositional system, encoding aspects of the meaning, such as colour, using sub-parts of the string. This results in a language with features reminiscent of natural language morphology. For example, in one run, a word like 'winekuki' can be partially analysed as containing a prefix 'wi-' which consistently refers to black objects, and a suffix '-kuki' which refers to a bouncing movement.

Other recent work explores the frequency–regularity relationship in an iterated artificial language learning context (Beqa, Kirby, and Hurford, 2008). These experimental models provide a basic confirmation that the processes adduced in the computational models can be elicited in human populations, and that the relationship between the transmission bottleneck, the pressure to generalize, and compositionality pertains beyond the computational models.

24.7 CONCLUSIONS

Compositionality can be explained as an adaptation (biological or cultural) to the communicative needs of language users: compositional languages are more functional than their alternatives in situations where open-ended expressivity is required. Alternatively, it can be explained as an adaptation by language itself to the process of its transmission: compositional languages are well designed to be faithfully transmitted despite a learning bottleneck. Computational and mathematical models have proved an invaluable tool in elucidating the precise conditions under which compositionality is favoured and how its evolution might unfold. While much of the basic groundwork in understanding the origins of compositionality has therefore been done, important questions remain to be answered. To what extent is compositionality prefigured in the language faculty, and to what extent is it contingent upon exposure to a compositional language? How does compositionality interact with that other adaptation for learnability, underspecification, and how does language come to exhibit its particular mix of the two? A new generation of computational and (increasingly) experimental models will, we expect, address these questions, further developing our understanding of the origins of compositionality, and the pressures which maintain it today.

CHAPTER 25

....

COMMUNICATION AND THE COMPLEXITY OF SEMANTICS

PETER PAGIN

25.1 INTRODUCTION

....

A celebrated argument for the claim that natural languages are compositional is the *learnability argument*. Briefly: for it to be possible to learn an entire natural language, which has infinitely many sentences, the language must have a compositional semantics. This argument has two main problems: one of them concerns the difference between compositionality and *computability*: if the argument is good at all, it only shows that the language must have a *computable* semantics, which allows speakers to compute the meanings of new sentences. But a semantics may be computable without being compositional (and vice versa). Why would we want the semantics to be compositional over and above being computable? The learnability argument doesn't tell us.

The idea that is developed here is that we get further requirements on semantics by looking at linguistic communication, and in particular at the feature that we manage to convey new contents by means of new sentences *in real time*, that is that a hearer manages to compute the meaning online of an uttered sentence at a speed that matches the speed of speech. It would seem that this can be explained only if the computation steps needed for interpretation are comparatively few and easy. We can even claim that between two semantic theories, if one allows for less complex computation, then it helps to explain online interpretation *better* than its rival. This is elaborated upon in Section 25.3.

In order to justify a particular kind of semantics in this way, we would want to show that a semantics of kind in some respect *minimizes* computational complexity. The relevance of computational complexity for cognition is discussed in Section 25.4. Sections 25.5–25.6 are devoted to selecting an appropriate complexity measure. Section 25.7

discusses the nature of minimal complexity under this measure. Section 25.8, finally, sketches an argument that the class of minimal semantics is derived from standard compositional semantics by means of one restriction and one generalization. The net result is that complexity considerations do give us a new reason for believing that natural language semantics is compositional (in the restricted way), or else has generalized (restricted) compositionality.

Before proceeding with the later sections, we will need to relate the concepts of compositionality, computability, and recursiveness. This is the task of the next section.

25.2 PRELIMINARIES

I shall call a function μ that maps syntactic items on meanings (irrespective of what entities serve as meanings) a *semantic function*. I shall call a function ρ_i that for some n maps meanings $m_1, \ldots, m_n$ on a meaning m a (meaning) *composition function*. A *generalized composition function* ρ is then a function such that, given a language L, for any syntactic operator a in L, $\rho(a)$ is a composition function. Then, a semantic function μ for a language L is *compositional* just in case there is a generalized composition function ρ such that for each operator σ in L and any relevant syntactic items $t_1, \ldots, t_n$ (with μ defined for $\sigma(t_1, \ldots, t_n)$) it holds that

(PC) $\mu(\sigma(t_1, \ldots, t_n)) = \rho(\sigma)(\mu(t_1), \ldots, \mu(t_n))$

Intuitively, (PC) says that the meaning of the complex is a function (ρ) of the meanings of the parts and the mode of composition (σ).[1]

The syntactic items may be expressions, that is surface strings. But in general strings are syntactically ambiguous in that they can be generated in more than one way from atomic expressions and operations. The semantic function must take disambiguated items as arguments (since the meaning may depend on the derivation, not just on the resulting string). Hence, when expressions are ambiguous, expressions cannot (always) be the arguments. Instead, it is common to take the arguments to be *terms*, whose surface syntax reflects the derivation of the string. To give a simple example: where σ is an operation that maps a noun phrase and a verb phrase on a sentence by means of concatenation, we have the string 'John⌣runs' (where '⌣' marks the word space that is part of the string), with the corresponding term 'σ(John, runs)'.

Here I shall be concerned with the syntactic terms and regard the syntactic domain T as a domain of terms. The domain E of *expressions* is derived from T by an evaluation

---

[1] The advantage of this format is that if σ is just the first argument of ρ, the arity of ρ would vary if there are syntactic operators of different arities.

function V. V corresponds, in classical generative grammar, to a mapping from deep structures to surface structures.[2]

Now, it is clear that a compositional semantics need not be recursive. For the semantic function μ is recursive just in case the generalized composition function ρ is recursive, but it is not required in the definition (PC) (or in any common definition of compositionality) that ρ be recursive. It must be a function of the right type, that is with the right arguments and values, that is all. Hence, compositionality does not entail recursiveness.

Neither does recursiveness entail compositionality. In arithmetic, a recursive function is either a projection function that selects an argument from a sequence of arguments, the constant zero function, the successor operation s, or a function defined from these by means of function composition, primitive recursion, or minimization. The counterpart to the successor operator in the syntactic domain is the collection Σ of syntactic operators σ_i. These operators are in general partial. The set of well-formed terms T is defined inductively from a finite set A of primitive expressions by means of the syntactic operations σ_i of Σ. Hence, the semantic function μ differs in one respect from arithmetic functions in that in general the domain is defined by more than one construction type.

The semantic function differs in one other important respect from an arithmetic function, since it maps entities between domains, from a syntactic to an ontic or conceptual domain of meanings (I shall refer to this as *the conceptual domain*). Therefore, to have a recursive semantic function, we need not only recursion over syntax, but also recursion over the conceptual domain. In order for this to make sense, we must regard the meaning domain M as being inductively defined from a finite set B of *basic meanings*, by means of a collection Γ of basic meaning composition functions γ_i. In this case the elements γ_i of Γ correspond to the successor operation of arithmetic. New functions can be defined from B and Γ by means of function composition, primitive recursion, and minimization. Let $\overline{\Gamma}$ be the closure of Γ under these operations.[3]

The situation is in fact more complicated, since what corresponds to the composition functions in the compositional case, the elements of $\overline{\Gamma}$, will take arguments both in the syntactic and the conceptual domain (but their values will be in M). I shall refer to them as *mixed* composition functions. The domain of these functions is the *union* $U = T \cup M$ of the syntactic and the conceptual domains. The semantic function μ is then defined by simultaneous recursion over T and M.

For a function to be recursive over U, it is then required that it be a constant function with a basic meaning as value, a projection function, a member of Σ or Γ, or defined from these by means of function composition, primitive recursion or minimization. In arithmetic, the minimization $\mathrm{Mn}[f](x_1, \ldots, x_n)$ is a function that that gives y as a value if y is the smallest x such that $f(x_1, \ldots, x_n, x) = 0$, with f defined for all $x_1, \ldots, x_n, x$ with $x < y$, and undefined if no such number exists. Since the syntactic and conceptual domains in general contain several minimal elements and several generating operations, there is in general no direct analogy. Rather, we would have to fix one by means of

---

[2] I am by and large using the framework proposed by Wilfrid Hodges and used e.g. in Hodges (2001), Westerståhl (2004), and Pagin (2003).

[3] I shall let the variables 'γ_i' etc. vary over the elements of $\overline{\Gamma}$.

stipulations such as lexicographic orderings. Since this would be arbitrary and since minimization has not played any role in any semantic system I know of, minimization will be ignored. Instead we will consider the counterparts to primitive recursion.

The function composition ingredient generates new functions in accordance with *composition equations* of the following general format:

(FC) $f(\vec{x}) = g(h_1(\vec{x}), \ldots, h_n(\vec{x}))$

where '$\vec{x}$' is short for '$x_1, \ldots, x_m$'. Here the function f is defined by composition from the functions $g, h_1, \ldots, h_n$.

The primitive recursion ingredient instantiate *recursion equations* of the following format for the application of the semantic function μ:

(Rec)   (i) For each simple term $t \in A$ there is a function $\gamma_t \in \overline{\Gamma}$ such that $\mu(t) = \gamma_t(t)$
         (ii) For any n and operation $\sigma_i \in \Sigma$ of arity n there is a function $\gamma_i \in \overline{\Gamma}$ such that for all terms $t_1, \ldots, t_n$, if μ is defined for $\sigma_i(t_1, \ldots, t_n)$, then

$$\mu(\sigma_i(t_1, \ldots, t_n)) = \gamma_i(t_1, \ldots, t_n, \mu(t_1), \ldots, \mu(t_n))$$

Here, it is immediate from the recursive clause, (ii), that μ is directly defined by recursion over T. If γ_i is also defined by means of primitive recursion, this will be recursion over M, or over both T and M.

We can note that the requirement of clause (i) is usually met by a simple list of the values or μ for each simple term t. Second, we can observe that the requirement in clause (ii) that $\gamma_i \in \overline{\Gamma}$, that is that γ_i be recursive over U, imposes a restriction that is not imposed in (PC). Third, the fact that the functions γ_i take the syntactic terms $t_1, \ldots, t_n$ themselves as arguments, has the effect that the compositional substitution laws need not hold. For

$\gamma_i(t_1, t_2, \mu(t_1), \mu(t_2))$

may well differ from

$\gamma_i(t_1, t_3, \mu(t_1), \mu(t_3))$

even if $\mu(t_2) = \mu(t_3)$. Hence, recursiveness does not entail compositionality.[4]

The concept of (effective) *computability* is closely connected to that of recursiveness. Intuitively, for a function f to be effectively computable is for there to be an effective/mechanical procedure p such that for any argument x for which f is defined, p as applied to x terminates after a finite number of steps giving the value of f for x. The paradigm of effective computability is a Turing machine. Arithmetical recursive functions are Turing computable, and Turing computable arithmetic functions are recursive (see e.g. Boolos, Jeffrey, and Burgess, 2002: chs 7–8). The claim that all arithmetic functions that are computable in the general intuitive sense are recursive is known as *Church's Thesis*.

---

[4] As pointed out in Werning (2005b) and developed in Pagin and Westerståhl (2010a, 2010b), we can have a natural recursive semantics for quotation that is not compositional. An example can be found in Potts (2007). Cf. the present Section 25.8.

When we move from arithmetic to the field of natural language semantics, we can satisfy demands of intuitive computability by ensuring that the functions involved are Turing computable. This can be shown directly, in part by showing how the formal substitution operations induced by the recursion equations can be executed.

With these basic concepts in place, I turn to the reason for justifying compositionality by appeal to communication.

25.3 FROM LEARNABILITY TO COMMUNICATION

Almost all of the standard arguments for the claim that natural languages are compositional suffer from severe flaws.[5] I'll take the *learnability* argument as the prime example. This argument was given by Donald Davidson (1965). The argument, applied to some language L, can be presented as follows:

(LA)   (a) There is an infinite set M of meanings.
      (b) Each disambiguated expression in L has at most one meaning.
      (c) For every possible context c, every element in M is the meaning in c of some expression in L.
      (d) Humans can learn at most finitely many basic expression–meaning pairs.
      (e) Humans can learn L.
      (f) Hence, L has a compositional semantics.[6]

The main idea of this argument is that since it is impossible to learn the meanings of all expressions if all expression–meaning pairs are basic, some have to be non-basic, that is derived, and if the meaning of an expression is derivable, the language must be compositional.

There are two main problems with this argument. The first problem is the premise (LAc), for it is a very strong assumption that there are infinitely many meanings expressed, in any context, by sentences of a natural language, say English. Since at any time t, speakers of the language have used at most finitely many sentences, it follows that there are (infinitely many) sentences that have not been used but are nonetheless

---

[5] For a brief survey of arguments for compositionality and a critical discussion, see Pagin and Wester-ståhl (2010b).

[6] Often some of the elements in this arguments are slurred over: it is not enough to say that there are infinitely many meaningful sentences to be learned, for if every sentence has the same meaning, the task of learning the meaning of every sentence is not that hard. Therefore, we need the condition that there are infinitely many expressible meanings. But further, it is not enough to say that there are infinitely many meanings that can be expressed, for with the single sentence 'I am here', infinitely many propositions can be expressed, by using it in different contexts.

meaningful.[7] On what basis do we claim that sentences that no speaker has used are already endowed with a meaning, waiting to be correctly computed by the speakers of English? The most natural justification of this claim would be that English has a compositional semantics, for with such a semantics, the meanings of unused sentences may already be determined. But with such a justification of (LAc), the (LA) argument involves a *petitio principii*. We need either a different justification for (LAc), or a replacement of (LA).

The second problem with (LA) is that the condition of allowing for meanings of some expressions to be *derivable* does not require a compositional semantics. It does require a *computable* semantics. As we saw above, however, a function may be recursive (and hence computable) without being compositional. The learnability requirement therefore, barring the first problem, provides an argument for computability, and therefore (assuming Church's Thesis in the domain of semantics) recursiveness, but not an argument for compositionality. The same problem afflicts several related arguments.[8]

If we turn from learnability to communication, the first problem disappears. The reason is that in each case of linguistic communication, the speaker associates a propositional content with the sentence she uses and the hearer associates a propositional content with that same sentence (on that occasion), and there is or there is not agreement between them in the sense that they associate the same content or at least contents that are sufficiently similar for communication to succeed. Now there is a question of what explains why speaker and hearer associate the same or similar contents with the same sentences. We need not assume that there is any correct or incorrect association of content with a new sentence; all we need care about is the coincidence.

Compositionality enters the picture because it helps to explain the rate of success in linguistic communication when the sentence used or the content communicated is *new*. The first to emphasize this role for compositionality was Gottlob Frege:

> It is astonishing what language can do. With a few syllables it can express an incalculable number of thoughts, so that even a thought grasped by a terrestrial being for the very first time can be put into a form of words which will be understood by somebody to whom the thought is entirely new. This would be impossible, were we not able to distinguish parts in the thought corresponding to the parts of a sentence, so that the structure of the sentence serves as an image of the structure of the thought. (Frege, 1923: opening paragraph)

---

[7] The alternative premise, instead of (LAa), that M is finite but larger than the set of sentences used at t, would work as well, and have the same problem.

[8] Jeff Pelletier (1994a) similarly argues that it is enough if a semantics is what he calls *grounded*. Being grounded in Pelletier's sense is somewhat looser than being recursive: what corresponds to recursion equations in Pelletier's examples allows a clause like $\mu(\sigma(t)) = r(\mu(\beta(t)))$, for some function r, where $\beta(t)$ may be a *successor* of t. In general, derivations with such equations are not guaranteed to terminate. According to Pelletier, it is enough if they in fact do, and only if they do is the semantics grounded. As already shown, however, ordinary recursiveness is enough for exemplifying a semantics that is computable but non-compositional.

This passage is remarkably rich in content. Frege correctly points to the infinite expressive power of a language (rather than its infinite syntax) as the important feature. Frege also draws attention to *communication* as the phenomenon that is crucial for the systematic nature of semantics. In this context, communication has three features that contrast with learnability. First, communication relates two *speakers* who each have an independent interpretation of a sentence. As we saw, this is an advantage compared with the learnability argument.

Second, communication relates a speaker and a hearer, with different roles. The speaker is to find a suitable sentence to express a Thought, while the hearer is to find a suitable Thought for interpreting the uttered sentence, and this asymmetry demands more of semantics than interpretation does by itself.[9] Frege's main claim is that the ability to communicate new thoughts would not be possible without an isomorphism between the sentence and the thought.[10]

There are several problems with this claim, but the most relevant problem concerns computability. In order that the hearer can *compute* the right content from the (parsed) expression, all we need is that the semantic function is recursive. Why would we also want an isomorphism, or that it be compositional?

This question brings us to the third respect in which communication contrasts with learnability: communication takes place in *real time* and under tight time constraints, while learnability has no temporal significance at all and sentence understanding as such (as opposed to the processing of tokens) is not a real time process (at best, the resulting end state of understanding can be assigned a time point).

During oral communication, speaker and hearer have to figure out, respectively, what expression to use and what it means, online, at a high speed. The *complexity* of the cognitive task therefore becomes crucial: the complexity of the articulation and interpretation tasks cannot be too high, on pain of making our near-immediate communication impossible. Computability in principle does not put any upper bound on the (finite) complexity of the computation task. In order to secure a reasonable complexity, we must look for some other property.

The general idea, then is to justify further properties of the semantics by appeal to their role in minimizing complexity. It turns out that compositionality has a role to play in that enterprise. First, we shall need to discuss the cognitive relevance of computational complexity measures.

---

[9] This idea is developed in detail in Pagin (2003).

[10] The isomorphism requirement is stronger than the compositionality requirement in the respect that the semantic function must be one–one, while compositionality only requires many–one. It also requires meanings to be structured (since otherwise there is automatically an isomorphism), while compositionality does not. Taken literally, it is in another respect weaker: that for every sentence s there is an isomorphism between s and its meaning does not entail that there is *one* semantic function μ that for every sentence s is an isomorphism between s and $\mu(s)$.

25.4 COMPUTATIONAL COMPLEXITY AND COGNITIVE TASKS

The speaker has the task of *articulation*, that is of finding and uttering a suitable linguistic expression for conveying her thought content to the hearer, and the hearer has that of *interpretation*, that is of finding a suitable thought content to associate with the expression uttered. Here, I shall focus on the task of the hearer.

We want to know ultimately what properties a semantic function should have so as to be least taxing for the hearer to compute. To this end we want to provide some measure of the complexity of the task. That measure will have to be mathematical in character. But this already introduces a risk of misrepresenting the processes. For whether a certain interpretation task s is more or less complex than a task s' depends not only on obvious differences in some size or other, but also on what happens to be easier for *us*, human language users, given our cognitive architecture. To take an example from the literature, consider the sentences (taken from Gibson (1998: 2)):

(25.1) a. The reporter who attacked the senator admitted the error.
  b. The reporter who the senator attacked admitted the error.

It is well-known in psycholinguistics that certain subordinate constructions are more difficult to process than others. Typically, we find *subject*-extracted relative clauses, as in (25.1a), easier to process than *object*-extracted relative clauses, as in (25.1b). There is no obvious mathematical reason why this should be so. The tree structures of the two complementizer phrases in (25.1) appear to be of about the same complexity, with an equal number of nodes, and resulting from one another by the interchange of the two NP nodes, as shown in Figure 25.1. If anything, the (a) tree is intuitively more complex, since it has five levels while (b) has four. A proposed explanation (cf. Gibson 1998) is that the distance between the relative pronoun 'who' and its corresponding trace t_i is greater in (b) than in (a). Processing from left to right involves keeping elements in mind that

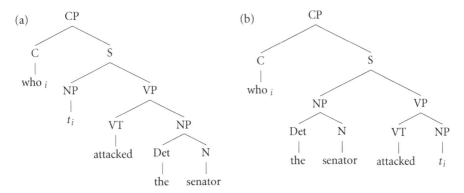

FIGURE 25.1 Complementizer phrases of (25.1)

will be tied to other elements later on, and so the longer it takes before a relative pronoun can be anchored to a position in the subordinate clause, the more heavily short-term memory is taxed.

Whether the explanation is right or wrong, the phenomenon exemplifies the general fact that results that depend on mere intuitive assessments of mathematical complexity are subject to correction by empirical studies. Nevertheless, the difficulty in this case can be modelled and measured by a mathematical property—the left-to-right distance (in the tree/term) between the relative pronoun and the coordinated empty position in the relative clause. That property might seem to be completely unrelated to composi-tionality, since the left–right order of expressions, as opposed to the constituency order, is in principle irrelevant to the structure of the underlying syntactic term. However, minimizing left-to-right distance between a surface element and the last further surface element needed to process it is an example of a general complexity principle that John Hawkins (e.g. in Hawkins, 2003: 144) has called *Maximize On-Line Processing*. Accord-ing to that principle, grammatical systems of natural languages tend to be organized so as to minimize the effort of processing elements online, that is when and where they are encountered in an utterance or a text. As we shall see, minimizing general complexity is closely connected with maximizing online processing. The example suggests that we have reason to be optimistic about the cognitive relevance of general computational measures of complexity.

25.5 COMPLEXITY AND EFFICIENCY

In computational complexity theory, three types of measure have been studied exten-sively, all defined in terms of Turing machines:

- The *time complexity* of a problem P (relative to a way of describing P) with respect to an algorithm A, is the maximum number of computation steps that are needed for a Turing machine that implements A to solve a problem instance of the same *size* as P (cf. Garey and Johnson, 1979: 6, 26).
- The *space complexity* of a problem P (relative to a way of describing P) with respect to an algorithm A, is the maximum number of distinct tape squares visited by a Turing machine that implements A to solve a problem instance of the same *size* as P (cf. Garey and Johnson, 1979: 170).
- The *Kolmogorov complexity* of a problem P (relative to a way of describing P) is the size (relative to a linear encoding of Turing machines) of the smallest Turing machine needed to solve P (cf. Li and Vitányi, 1997: 93–8).

In these contexts, a 'problem' is usually a problem *type*, and what is solved in each particular case is an *instance* of that problem type. Such a problem type is for example

The Traveling Salesman: a salesman is to visit a number of cities exactly once and then return home, and the task is to find a visiting order that minimizes the total distance travelled. The number of cities is the *size* of the instance.

Depending on the choice of complexity measure and on the choice of method for solving problems of a chosen type, a particular problem instance gets assigned a natural number as the complexity of that instance, numbering, for example, the squares that a chosen Turing machine has visited for computing the solution. One is interested not only and not primarily in the complexity of individual instances, but in the *maximal complexity* of instances of the same *size*: given, for example, a number of cities to visit (disregarding further information), what is the maximal number of steps needed to determine the best order? Given a problem type P and a method ψ, one is therefore interested in the *complexity function* $C_{P,\psi}$ from natural numbers to natural numbers which, for a given argument k gives as value the maximal complexity of P-instances of size k.

Suppose we can hold P constant. We can then simply associate each *method* ψ with a complexity function C_ψ. When each method is associated with a complexity function, we can compare methods with respect to *efficiency*: if for all k it holds that $C_\psi(k) < C_\epsilon(k)$, then we can say that method ψ is more *efficient* than method ϵ. In general, the efficiency comparison is less straightforward, since one method may be more efficient than another only in the long run. The most natural way of capturing this idea is to require that from some size onwards, the *sum* of the C values are lower for the one than for the other:

(EC) ψ is more efficient than ϵ iff there is an n such that

$$\forall k > n \left[\sum_{i=1}^{k} C_\epsilon(i) - C_\psi(i) > 0 \right]$$

We are interested in finding out the properties of those interpretation methods, that is semantic functions, that are *most efficient* in this sense. As we shall see below, however, this comparison is significant only for large differences.

25.6 MEASURES OF COMPLEXITY

We turn now to the question of selecting an appropriate complexity measure. Which of the three aforementioned types of complexity are relevant to an intuitive measure of the difficulty of the cognitive task? Time complexity appears to be most directly relevant, since considerations of time pressure motivated looking at complexity in the first place. The general idea of time complexity is that we count the number of steps that have to be taken for completing a process. It is plausible to assume that by and large, an increase of the number of steps required in the formal computation corresponds to an increase of the real time needed for human processing. I shall assume so. Hence, we will in the first place want to minimize time complexity of individual tasks, and therefore to maximize efficiency of semantic functions with respect to time complexity.

The next questions to answer are: What is the character of the relevant problem type? How do we measure the size of an instance? What constitutes an individual step of the computation process?

It would be very natural at first to take maximizing efficiency to consist in finding the most efficient semantic function for a given language L and a given domain M of meanings, where L is understood purely syntactically. That is, measure the size of the problem instance as the size of the term, and look for the longest computation needed for a term of that size. But although this question makes sense, there is a good reason to look at the issue differently. For with some choices of L and M, semantic interpretation becomes *intractable*, whatever the semantic function. To see this, consider the following example of *Lisa*.

We have a language L consisting of a and the successor operator $'$ as basic elements. So L consists of the terms a, a', a'', etc. Then we have a conceptual domain consisting of the object l (Lisa) and the two conceptual functions f (father) and m (mother). So M consists of $l, m(l), f(l), m(m(l)), m(f(l)), f(m(l)), f(f(l))$, etc. Let the *size* of an object of either domain consist in its number of basic elements (basic object plus number of function/operator occurrences), and let the *size* n of a domain be the number of elements of at most size n it contains. The *growth rate* of the domain is a rate of increase of the function $g(n)$ that maps a number n on the number of elements of domain with size n or lower. In these terms, we have a conceptual domain with a growth rate of $g(n+1) = 2g(n) + 1$ and a syntactic domain with a growth rate of $g(n+1) = g(n) + 1$.

In order that the semantic function μ for each element m in M up to size n maps a term t on m, $2^{n+1} - 1$ distinct terms will be needed, since there are that many elements of M of size n or lower. Therefore, there will be at least one element m_i and one term t_j of L such that $\mu(t_j) = m_i$ and the size of t_j is $2^{n+1} - 1$ or greater. Assuming that exactly one computation step is needed for processing each element of a term t, at least $2^{n+1} - 1$ steps are needed to compute t_j.[11] Hence, the maximal number of steps needed to process a term referring to an object of a certain size grows *exponentially* with the size of the object, regardless of the choice of semantic function. In terms of computational complexity theory, using L for referring to M in the *Lisa* example is a strictly *intractable* task. When tasks are considered tractable, the increase in time complexity (number of steps needed) is at most a polynomial function.

More precisely, we get the intractability result if we regard the *problem type* as the type of understanding the expression of a concept, for then the size of a problem instance is the size of that concept. If by contrast we regard the problem type as that of processing a *term*, then the size of the problem instance is the size of the term. The time complexity

---

[11] This assumption is made for ease of exposition. It does not matter much. It will in any case hold that there is a finite number k such that *in the long run*, at most k elements can be computed in each step. Then there is still exponential growth.

function, under the assumption above, is then simply x: as many steps are needed as there are elements in the term. From that point of view, the semantic function appears very efficient. For the same conceptual domain M we could have a more appropriate language L' and a semantic function μ' mapping L' on M that would require, say, terms that are twice as large as the concepts they are mapped on. With the same assumption of one step per element of the term, μ would be as efficient as μ' if the problem type is that of processing terms, but exponentially less efficient if the problem type is that of arriving at contents. The latter is clearly what is cognitively more relevant: $L + \mu$ form an intractably cumbersome combination for talking about or expressing M, while the alternative $L' + \mu'$ would be manageable. The upshot is that the problem type should be that of *interpreting expressions of content*, and that hence the measure of the size of the instance of that problem simply is the size of the content. That is the invariant factor in the comparison between methods.[12] We have to take account not only of the efficiency of the mapping from code to concepts, but also of the efficiency of the encoding itself, that is the size of the code.[13]

But how do we measure the size of contents? Does it make sense to say that one concept or one proposition is larger than another? There is no immediate way of making a relevant sense of that idea, but it does not matter so much. Computations can anyway not be defined over contents, only over symbols. What we can and must do, then, is to measure the size of *representations* of content. We shall need a formal language where we give *canonical* representations of conceptual contents. With such a formal, unambiguous language of canonical representations, we can again count the number of symbols in its expressions for determining the relevant size of contents represented.

The final question concerns the nature of the computation steps that are to be counted. As mentioned above, standard time complexity takes the number of operations of Turing machines as the measure. If that were the choice, we would have to settle for some

[12] A further reason not to use the term size as the size of the problem instance is that we can make terms arbitrarily much larger by throwing in junk constituents that are not needed for the semantics and therefore do not add to computation complexity. With a lot of junk in the terms, a semantic function can appear to be more efficient, which is again counterintuitive.

[13] This aspect of the issue shows the similarity with questions of efficient encoding handled in Mathematical Information Theory, as originated in Shannon (1949). There are also important differences, however. An encoding E is efficient in the information theoretic sense if the average rate of information sent over an information channel and encoded by E is high. In that context, a signal conveys more information if the fact that it reports is less probable. States of affairs that are highly probable will in the long run occur more often, and should be reported by means of shorter codes. So the efficiency of an encoding depends on the matching between the distribution of lengths of codes and the distribution of probabilities, over the same possible states of affairs.

In the present case, the questions of truth or falsity of sentences used or the probabilities of facts reported on, do not arise. We are only concerned with the expressive power and the efficiency of the interpretation. In the information theoretic case, questions of efficient encoding arise even if there is only a small finite number of signal types (sentences) used over and over. In the present context, having only a finite number of sentences would reduce the interpretation problem to triviality, since then the meaning of all sentences could be given by a finite list. This would reduce the total number of processing steps needed for any sentence to exactly 1.

particular *kind* of Turing machine, whether a standard single-tape machine with a tape that is infinite in both directions, or something else. There is no uniquely right choice, and no absolute measure. Turing machine operations will involve steps needed in order to find the relevant information (on other tape squares) and moving symbols in order to make room for others, etc., and how many such operations are needed will depend on the choice of machine. Therefore, these operations are to some extent arbitrary, and to that extent less essential to the complexity measure.

There is a natural alternative, which is to employ the *equation system* used for defining a function as a method for computing the function. Take as a simple example, Donald Davidson's (1967*b*: 17–18) *Annette*:

(25.2)   (i) Ref('Annette') = Annette.
          (ii) Ref('the father of'⌢t) = the father of Ref(t).

This simple definition provides a method for deriving the interpretation of 'the father of the father of the father of Annette' in four steps of substitution. Let 'F' be the object language father operator and 'F' its analogue in the meta-language, and let 'a' be the object language name of Annette. Then we have in four steps with the semantic function μ_a:

(25.3) $\mu_a(F(F(F(a))))$
          $= F(\mu_a(F(F(a))))$
          $= F(F(\mu_a(F(a))))$
          $= F(F(F(\mu_a(a))))$
          $= F(F(F(\text{Annette})))$

where (what corresponds to) the second clause of (25.2) is applied three times and the first clause once.

Each derivation step in (25.3) is a substitution step. Each substitution is performed in accordance with the equations in (25.2). These equations are applied only for substitution from left to right: an instance of the left-hand side is replaced by the corresponding instance of the right-hand side. This makes the system into a so-called *term rewriting system*. Term rewriting systems are sets of *rewrite rules*. Rewrite rules apply to *terms* and license formal *substitutions* of/in those terms. Rewrite rules can contain variables, in which case an *instance* of the left-hand side is allowed to be transformed to the corresponding instance of the right-hand side. Clause (ii) of (25.2) can be regarded as such a rule, with the variable t occurring once on each side. Relative to some rewriting system R, when no rule of R applies to a term u, u is said to be in *normal form*. The little derivation in (25.3) transforms the initial term '$\mu_a(F(F(F(a))))$' to its normal form '$F(F(F(\text{Annette})))$' in four steps.

Transforming terms to normal form by means of a sequence of rewrite rule applications is a completely general form of computation. It has been shown that any both-way infinite one-tape Turing machine can be simulated by a term rewriting system such that each rule of the rewriting system corresponds to a machine transition and each machine transition is represented by at least one rewrite rule (cf. Baader and Nipkow, 1998: 94–7). In virtue of this relation it is not only very convenient but also well motivated to use the count of rewrite rule applications as a measure of time complexity.

Then, for each non-normal rewriting term s, we consider the shortest derivation by which s is normalized. Only normal terms correspond to full interpretation, that is to our representations of the world; other terms only have a role in deriving the normal terms. Let *input terms* of the rewriting system be terms of the form '$\mu(t)$', with t a syntactic term. For a *normal* term s we consider the *shortest* derivation by which some input term $\mu(t)$ is normalized to s.[14] Let that be the *term complexity* $Ct_R(s)$ of s relative to R. The time complexity $C_R(k)$ for the size k relative to the system R is then the *maximal* $Ct_R(s)$ such that s has size k.

With this much of background, I turn to characterizing the main ideas of minimizing time complexity.

25.7 MINIMIZING COMPLEXITY

In this section and the next I shall very briefly sketch the ideas and the reasoning that lead up to the results about compositionality and complexity. Because of space limitations, the presentation must be largely informal, and full precision is not possible here.[15]

In general, a rewriting system R is a set of rewrite rules of the form

$$F(\overrightarrow{x}) \rightarrow G(\overrightarrow{y})$$

(where the arrows over the variables indicate that it is a sequence of variables).[16] An example would be

$$h(x_1)bx_2 \rightarrow g(x_1, c)bd$$

where 'b', 'c', and 'd' are constants. A derivation is a sequence of applications where a term (often a subterm of a larger term) that is an instance of the lhs (left-hand side) is replaced (in the containing term, in case it is a subterm) by the corresponding instance of the rhs. An instance of term s is any term s' resulting from s by uniform substitution by terms for rewrite variables. Thus, '$h(s_7)bf(s_9)$' is an instance of the lhs above.

A rewriting system R is said to *terminate* iff every derivation eventually leads to a term in normal form (to which no rule applies). R is said to be *confluent* iff it holds for any terms s_1, s_2, s_3 such that s_2 and s_3 can both be derived from s_1, that there is a term

---

[14] There need not be any longest derivation, since it is possible that there is no upper bound to the size of terms that reduce to the same normal form.

[15] It is formally developed in Pagin (2008b).

[16] For an excellent introduction to term rewriting, see Baader and Nipkow (1998).

s_4 such that s_4 can be derived from both s_2 and s_3. R is *convergent* iff R both terminates and is confluent.

Not all term rewriting systems terminate and not all are confluent, and neither property is in general decidable. However, the systems we are concerned with, that satisfy the format of primitive recursion equations, involve substitutions of a very restricted kind. It is straightforward to show that these systems are convergent.

Furthermore, it can be shown that every derivation terminates with a canonical term. Given that the set of canonical terms is the fragment of the formal language that represents the conceptual domain, every derivation ends with a term representing the conceptual domain. This means that every such rewriting system, when the rules are stated as equations, has the format for defining a semantic function.

We can call these systems 'μ systems'. A μ system R for a language L is then such that for every (meaningful) grammatical term t of L, there is a rule $r \in R$ such that the rewrite term '$\mu(t)$' instantiates the lhs of r. And a grammatical term occurs in an instance of the lhs of a rule only as a subterm of a larger rewrite term, since it can only occur as an argument to a function.

μ systems have four properties that are crucial for complexity. A fifth property is peculiar to *direct* μ systems:

(RS)   a. Every μ system has a finite number of rules.
     b. No term in the formal language of the μ system (as opposed to terms occurring in the rule formulations) contains any rewrite variables.
     c. For any rule r of the μ system, the set of rewrite variables on the rhs of r is a subset of the set of rewrite variables occurring on the lhs of r.
     d. In a μ system R, no rewrite term containing a terminal symbol instantiates the lhs of any rule $r' \in R$.
     e. Every rule of a *direct* μ system is an output rule. In an output rule a terminal symbol occurs on the rhs, and any symbol on the rhs that does not occur on the lhs is a terminal symbol.

Properties (RSc) and (RSd) have the combined effect that terminal symbols cannot be produced by means of instantiating variables. Any terminal symbol occurring in a term is produced by means of a rule where it is explicitly used on the rhs. At most finitely many terminal symbols can occur on the rhs of any rule. Since the rule system is finite, there is a largest number w of terminal symbol occurrences that can be produced in any single rule application. This is the MaxApp number of the system. It is immediate that the smallest number of application steps needed to produce a term s of size k in a μ system R is $[k/\omega]$, where ω is the MaxApp number of R and $[z]$ is the smallest whole number at least as great as z. Since there are infinitely many terms of normal form, the ratio $[k/\omega]$ will be an upper limit of efficiency in the long run. Hence, no μ rule system R can be faster than having a linear time complexity function C_R.

The real efficiency may be much lower. If rules that produce new non-terminal symbols are present, the upper limit of efficiency may be an exponential function of the size of the canonical terms. If the rule system is *direct*, every new symbol on the rhs of a rule is a terminal symbol. In virtue of property (RSd) of μ systems, that term cannot itself be an argument, that is instantiate the lhs of a rule. Only its proper subterms can. In μ systems, substitutions are only performed on subterms that do not contain terminal symbols. Because of this, μ systems that are direct are guaranteed to transform terms to normal form in an incremental fashion, in each step replacing non-terminal by terminal symbols, until only terminal symbols remain.

Let the MinApp of a μ system be the minimal number of terminal symbol occurrences that are produced by any single rule application. Hence, for a direct system R, $\mathrm{MinApp}(R) \geq 1$. This means that for a direct rule system R, we can estimate the complexity function C_R as

$$\lceil k/\omega \rceil \leq C_R(k) \leq \lceil k/a \rceil$$

where ω is $\mathrm{MaxApp}(R)$ and a is $\mathrm{MinApp}(R)$. Since $a \geq 1$, it follows that $C_R(k) \leq k$ if R is a direct rule system. I shall say that systems with such a complexity function are *maximally time efficient*.

Clearly, since there is no finite upper bound to the value of ω, there is no highest efficiency value. It still makes sense to speak of maximal time efficiency, for the reason that rewriting computation can be sped-up by more than any finite factor. Where we have a system R_μ that computes a function μ we can devise a system R'_μ that computes the same function μ at roughly twice the speed. We do this by creating more complex rules, that is rules that apply to larger terms. Such rules are more specialized, and hence more such rules are needed for having an equivalent system.[17]

We have already seen that a direct rule system is maximally time efficient. Because of the possibility of speed-up, the simple converse, that a system with maximal time efficiency is direct, doesn't hold. We can, however, define a notion *maximal efficiency simpliciter* in a way that excludes ad hoc speed-up features. This allows proving the following claim:

(ED)   If R is maximally efficient, then R is direct.

We have connected efficiency with directness. The second major step will be to connect the directness of a rule system with the nature of the semantic functions that be defined by the corresponding equation systems.

---

[17] This corresponds to speed-up transformations of Turing machines. For a given Turing machine M we can e.g. devise a machine M' that is twice as fast by letting the new one process two tape squares at a time (cf. Hartmanis and Stearns, 1965).

25.8 COMPOSITIONALITY AND MINIMAL COMPLEXITY

In order to see how minimal complexity connects with the question of compositionality, we must inquire into the *form* of maximally efficient systems. It can be shown that

(DH)   If R is a maximally efficient rule system, and r is a rule of R with a lhs of the form $\mu(\sigma(x_1, \ldots, x_n))$, then the rhs has the form $\rho(\mu(x_1), \ldots, \mu(x_n))$.

Proof: Suppose for *reductio* that R is a maximally efficient μ system that contains a rule r of the form

(25.4) $\mu(\sigma(t_1, \ldots, t_n)) \rightarrow p(t_1, \ldots, t_n, \mu(t_1), \ldots, \mu(t_n))$

where p is simple or complex. Suppose we have an instance q of the rhs of r. Since p is a simple or complex *new* symbol and R is maximally efficient, and therefore by (ED) direct, by (RSe) p can only consist of terminal symbols. Hence, by (RSd), neither q, nor any subterm q' of q that contains any constituent of p, instantiates the lhs of any rule r' of R. Only the $\mu(t_i)$ or the t_i do. But μ systems don't have rules where the grammatical terms themselves instantiate the lhs. And since the t_i are not themselves terminal symbols, q contains non-terminal symbols that cannot be eliminated, which is impossible.[18]   □

Instead, the rules for complex terms in a maximally efficient μ system must be of the form

(25.5) $\mu(\sigma(t_1, \ldots, t_n)) \rightarrow p(\mu(t_1), \ldots, \mu(t_n))$

This means that the corresponding equation format for defining a semantic function is

(25.6) $\mu(\sigma(t_1, \ldots, t_n)) = p(\mu(t_1), \ldots, \mu(t_n))$

which conforms to the homomorphism format of compositionality.

The format is, however, stricter than what compositionality requires, since p is required to be a simple or complex *terminal* (operator) symbol. Hence, either p is a simple operator or else a *polynomial term* $g(h_1(\vec{x}), \ldots, h_n(\vec{x}))$ *over* simple operators and (rewrite) variables. If we look at it as a specification of a semantic function, this means that either p denotes a simple function on the conceptual domain which therefore belongs to the set Γ of basic meaning composition functions, or else it denotes a function definable from basic meaning composition functions by means of function

---

[18] In order to keep the proof simple, it must here be required that atomic terms are distinct from the corresponding atomic expressions. Otherwise quotation will produce examples where some atomic grammatical terms in fact are terminal symbols, but this is an inessential complication.

composition, that is the schema (FC). Let's say that semantic functions that comply with this restriction are *polynomially compositional*.[19]

If a semantic function is polynomially compositional, it is specifiable by a direct rule system, and hence by a maximally time efficient rule system. To the extent we can speak of a semantic function itself as having a degree of complexity, we may say that such a semantic function has minimal time complexity. It does not hold for compositional semantics in general, only for the polynomial kind.

The converse does not follow immediately, however.[20] The most important reason is that we can have *other functions* from terms to values that behave well with respect to computational complexity. If we add a *quotation* operator to a language L, we will make another function relevant: the function V from terms to the *expressions* of L. Somewhat oversimplified, with κ as quotation operator, we have

(25.7) $\mu(\kappa(t)) = \text{`}V(t)\text{'}$

(this is a simplified formulation; assume here that substitutions within quotes are allowed). For familiar reasons, clause (25.7) induces non-compositionality: $V(t) \neq V(u)$ even if $\mu(t) = \mu(u)$. However, this need have no adverse effect on time complexity. If the V function itself is a homomorphism, so that for every operator σ there is some simple or polynomial expression operator ϵ such that for any terms $t_1, \ldots, t_n$ for which σ is defined it holds that

(25.8) $V(\sigma(t_1, \ldots, t_n)) = \epsilon(V(t_1), \ldots, V(t_n))$

then semantic processing can continue with the same time efficiency as before. To accommodate a quotation operator, we would need to add expressions to the conceptual domain, so that they can serve as values to the semantic function, but this is not in itself a problem.

In fact, the situation generalizes. Let's say that a set Δ of functions from the syntactic domain T to the (enriched) conceptual domain M is *jointly-compositional* just in case, for any $\delta \in \Delta$ and any operator σ that there is a meaning composition function ρ and functions $\delta_1, \ldots, \delta_n \in \Delta$, not necessarily distinct, such that for all terms $t_1, \ldots, t_n$ (with δ is defined for $\sigma(t_1, \ldots, t_n)$) it holds that

---

[19] Interestingly, this is the intuitively simplest and most natural version of compositionality. It imposes a strong similarity between the syntactic and conceptual algebras. Theo Janssen (1986, 1997) has insisted on the restriction to polynomially defined algebras for the intermediate logical language, in cases when the semantics is defined indirectly, via translation into an intermediary logical language, although for quite different reasons. The restriction has been criticized by Herman Hendriks (2001) as not essential to compositionality and as imposing conditions that are sometimes impossible to meet. The present considerations agree with Hendriks in principle, but also provide separate reasons why approximating polynomial compositionality is nevertheless desirable.

[20] One reason for this that I shall not elaborate on is that it follows only if the meta-language itself has a well-behaved semantics.

(25.9) $\delta(\sigma(t_1,\ldots,t_n)) = \rho(\delta_1(t_1),\ldots,\delta_n(t_n))$

If in each clause of this kind in the semantic system ρ is polynomial, time complexity will still be minimal, since the relevant $\delta_i \in \Delta$ are read off from the clause, and need not be further computed. The system is not compositional in the normal sense. I'll refer to this as *generalized compositionality*. It retains the two features that are crucial for time complexity: meaning composition is polynomial and only δ values for immediate subterms matter. The limiting case is standard polynomial compositionality, where there is only one δ_i, the main semantic function μ itself. Strictly speaking, then, what is motivated from complexity considerations is not standard compositionality, but this generalized form.[21]

The general trend is clear: a drive to minimizing complexity is a drive to compositionality, more particularly to polynomial compositionality, and less particularly to generalized polynomial compositionality. Under certain restrictive conditions, compositionality is entailed, but these conditions tend not to be met in natural language. There are reasons to suspect that syntactic complications and widespread context dependence make (generalized) polynomial compositionality impossible.[22] Hence, in the end, no strict argument for compositionality is forthcoming.

Cognitively, generalized polynomial compositionality allows semantic processing, both in interpretation and in production, to proceed in what is intuitively the simplest possible way: by mere association of atomic terms with atomic concepts, and syntactic modes of composition with conceptual modes of composition. This in turn, allows the speaker/hearer to efficiently process the input online, that is to incrementally construct the output while the input is being observed (in the case of the hearer) or itself constructed (in the case of the speaker). For the speaker, incremental production allows articulation of one part of a Thought to take place in advance of detailed plans about later parts. For the hearer, incremental interpretation allows the semantics to bear on the parsing process, thereby reducing under-determination in the transition from string to structure (cf. e.g. Mahesh, Eiselt, and Holbrook, 1999).[23] What we have a reason to

---

[21] Alternatively, this can be presented as a system with one semantic function $\mu(t,c)$ that takes contextual arguments. Cf. Pagin and Westerståhl (2010a).

Generalized compositionality is also suitable for modal contexts (cf. Glüer and Pagin, 2006, 2008), propositional attitude contexts and quotation contexts (Pagin and Westerståhl 2010c).

[22] This holds e.g. in the architecture of the Principles and Parameters system: here a syntactic phrase structure term is mapped on a syntactic LF term before semantic interpretation can take place. For objections to such an architecture, see e.g. Jacobson (2002) and the conception of so-called *direct compositionality*. This is related to but distinct from what is here called *polynomial compositionality* and differently motivated.

[23] In both cases, preliminary decision are subject to later corrections, as studied especially as regards parsing, with garden-path sentences.

believe, therefore, is that actual semantics of natural languages nonetheless *approximate* the computationally optimal format, since it helps to explain our communicative capacities.[24]

[24] The final text is improved thanks to comments from two anonymous referees. I have also benefited from discussing these issues with Martin Jönsson and Ken Shan at Rutgers, Alasdair Urquhart in Toronto, and over several years with Kathrin Glüijer and Dag Westerståhl. An earlier version was presented at the Rutgers Compositionality series, spring 2007, and a still earlier version in the Compositionality Workshop in Paris 2004 (from where I am grateful for comments by Tim Fernando and Wilfrid Hodges). The research has been supported by grants from the Tercentenary Foundation of the Swedish National Bank, from The Swedish Research Council, and from the Spanish Ministry of Science and Education during a research stay in Barcelona (in the programme *Profesores e investigadores extranjeros de acreditada experiencia, en régimen de año sabático en España*).

CHAPTER 26

....

PROTOTYPES AND THEIR COMPOSITION FROM AN EVOLUTIONARY POINT OF VIEW

....

GERHARD SCHURZ

26.1 INTRODUCTION: NORMIC LAWS AND PROTOTYPICAL PROPERTIES

....

Normic laws are general conditionals of the form

(26.1)   As are normally Bs, here formalized as: $A \Rightarrow B$.

(the terminology is due to Scriven, 1959). They are not strict (i.e. strictly universal), but admit of exceptions (i.e. As which aren't Bs). Normic laws have been investigated in the areas of *philosophy of science* and of *non-monotonic reasoning* (cf. Schurz, 2004). They have an obvious bearing on the prototype theory of concepts, insofar as the normic law (26.1) can be equivalently rephrased as follows:

(26.1*)   B is a prototypical property of As (in the *wide* sense of 'prototypical').

A more narrow sense of 'prototypical properties' will be introduced in Section 26.2.
   In the 1950s, philosophers of science discovered that there are almost no strict laws to be found in the 'higher' non-physical sciences. Rather, the typical explanations in these disciplines make use of *normic* laws, such as the following:

(26.2)   People's actions are normally goal-oriented (folk psychology).

(26.3)   Birds normally can fly (biology). or

(26.4)   Turning the ignition key normally turns on the engine of my car (technology).

In this and the next section I will develop an evolution-theoretic explanation of the omnipresence of normic laws and prototypical properties in everyday life and in the non-physical sciences. My explanation consists of two parts. First, I will argue that reasoning with normic laws is efficient and reliable. Second, I will show that humans' environment is populated by evolutionary systems which obey normic laws, which explains why human cognition is well adapted to prototypicality structures.

In order to enable reliable reasoning, the concept of (prototypical) normality must have an *objective* meaning which connects it with statistical probability, in the sense that if B is a prototypical property of As, then most As are Bs. The thesis that normic laws entail a numerically unspecific statistical *majority* claim is henceforth called the:

Statistical consequence thesis (SC): A $\Rightarrow$ B implies that the conditional statistical probability of B given A, $P(B|A)$, is high.

The statistical consequence thesis does *not* imply that normic laws can be *replaced* by numerical conditional probabilities. The numerical probabilities associated with prototypical properties are typically highly context-sensitive, so that we are unable to specify them without specifying the context. For example, what percentage of all birds can fly (when?, where?). All that one knows or assumes—according to the statistical consequence thesis—is that these probabilities are *high*.

Early philosophers of science as well as founders of non-monotonic reasoning have *doubted* that normic laws have objective meaning—they suggested that normic laws would be similar to linguistic conventions (cf. Dray, 1957: 132; Scriven, 1959: 466; McCarthy, 1986; Reiter, 1987). The crucial problem of this position is, of course, that if normic laws are taken as conventions, then nothing guarantees that reasoning from prototypical properties is *reliable*, that is leads to true predictions in a high majority of cases. In other words, the reliability of normic laws requires an objective characterization of prototypical properties which connects them with statistical reliability (cf. Hempel, 1965; Pearl, 1988: 477–80).[1] But the question is: why should such a connection hold? Why should the objective probability distributions over the properties of complex 'living' systems possess so many high (conditional) probability peaks, rather than being more or less flat? As long as we do not have an *explanation* of the statistical consequence thesis, the force of those doubts will remain strong among those who maintain that the omnipresence of normic laws, instead of being the result of *objective feature* of reality, is merely the product of our *subjective framing* of a world whose complexity exceeds our cognitive limitations.

In the next section I will present one such explanation which has been developed in Schurz (2001a). It is based on an evolution-theoretic understanding of prototypical properties as the result of evolutionary adaptations which establish a connection between prototypicality and high statistical probability on *nomological* reasons. This explanation has the following advantages:

---

[1] An alternative proposal to 'objectify' normic laws is to reconstruct them as *ceteris paribus* laws. Various problems of this account are discussed in Schurz (2002).

1. it makes the statistical consequence thesis plausible;
2. it is needed to defend the statistical consequence thesis against the objections of philosophers of biology (e.g. Millikan, 1984; Laurier, 1996; Wachbroit, 1994); and
3. based on (1) and (2), it yields a deeper understanding of the achievements as well as the limitations of prototype semantics.

26.2 GENERALIZED EVOLUTION-THEORY AS A FOUNDATION OF NORMIC LAWS AND PROTOTYPICAL PROPERTIES

All 'higher' sciences, from biology upwards, are concerned with *living systems* or with their *cultural* and *technical products*. What these systems have in common is the characteristic capacity of *self-regulation* under the permanent pressure of their environment. So this is my first thesis:

Thesis E1: Normic laws describe the properties of self-regulatory systems. According to the framework of *cybernetics* (cf. Ashby, 1961), the identity of self-regulatory systems is governed by certain prototypical *norm* states (or properties) which these systems constantly try to achieve and maintain with the help of *regulatory mechanisms* which compensate for *disturbing influences* of the environment.

But what explains the omnipresence of self-regulatory systems in our world? And what explains their proper functioning most of the time? The answer is contained in my next thesis:

Thesis E2: Almost all self-regulatory systems are *evolutionary systems* in the generalized 'Darwinian' sense. They have evolved through a recursive (natural *or* cultural/technical) process of reproduction, variation, and selection. Their prototypical norm states and self-regulatory mechanisms have been gradually selected in their evolution history according to their contribution to reproductive success.

Evolution theory explains why evolutionary systems obey normic laws which imply high conditional statistical probabilities. The self-regulatory capacities of evolutionary systems are limited. Dysfunctions may occur, hence their normic behaviour may have various *exceptions*. Yet it must be the case that these systems are in their prototypical norm states most of their time—for otherwise, they would not have *survived* in evolution. Green plants, for example, can normally perform photosynthesis. Of course it is possible that due to a catastrophic event, all green plants lose this ability. But then (with high probability), they will become extinct after a short period of evolution. For similar reasons, electric devices normally work, for they are constructed in that way, and if this were not so, they could not survive in the economic market. Put in a nutshell, *prototypical normality and statistical normality are connected by the law of evolutionary selection*.

Various refinements of this rather crude presentation of my evolution-theoretic foundation of normic laws can be found in Schurz (2001*a*). For example, to be applicable to normic laws of all higher sciences, the account has to be based on the *generalized* theory of evolution in the sense of Dawkins (1989: ch. 11). Generalized evolution theory does not reduce evolution to the evolution of *genes* as the reprotypes of biological evolution, but assumes in addition an independent level of so-called *memes* (acquired cognitive abilities) as the reprotypes cultural evolution.[2] The *reprotypes* which underly a kind of evolution are those entities which get directly reproduced, while the so-called *phenotypes* are the 'prototypical' properties which are *produced* by the reprotypes in the given environments and which are the target of selective forces. The following three points illustrate how my evolutionary account can explain normic laws without entailing excessive adaptationism:

1. Whenever an evolutionary system (species) S conatins two competing (heritable) traits P, P' such that the P-variants have a higher reproductivity ('fitness') than the P'-variants, then after sufficiently many generations the frequencies will be driven to almost 100 per cent for P-variants and almost 0 per cent for P'-variants, *independently* of the initial frequencies of P-variants and P'-variants. In this way, the normic law 'Ss are normally Ps' originates from *standard* evolutionary selection conditions. But note that selectively advantageous properties are never driven to *strict fixation*: a small remnant of 'abnormal' variants is constantly produced by spontaneous variations. This small percentage of 'abnormal' species members is not superfluous but highly important for the persistence of the species under sudden changes of environmental fitness conditions (cf. Ridley, 1993: 204ff).

2. Not all properties are positively or negatively prototypical, i.e. are either possessed by the majority or by the minority of the species members, on two reasons:

   2.1 Only biologically or culturally *reproduced* (inherited) properties can count as prototypical; properties whose existence depend on contingent constellations of the environment cannot.

   2.2 Among the reproduced properties there may exist cases of so-called *polymorphisms* with arbitrary (e.g. uniform) probability distributions.

   However, such polymorphisms occur only under *non-standard* selection conditions (such as multiple niche polymorphism, heterozygotic superiority, or negative frequency-dependence; cf. Ridley, 1993: ch. 2). In standard evolutionary scenarios, property distributions will acquire prototypicality structure as explained in (1) above.

3. Not all prototypical properties are functional in the sense of having conferred a selective advantage. To take a much debated example (Bigelow and Pargetter, 1987),

---

[2] An excellent overview of generalized evolution theory is found in Mesoudi et al. (2006).

circulating the blood is a proper function of the vertebrate heart, while the typical sound of the heart beat is a mere side effect of it—but still it is prototypical for vertebrates' hearts to make this sound. A subtle example of this sort are Gould and Lewontin's (1979) 'spandrels', which are prototypical side-effects of complex structural-anatomical architectures which were selected for independent reasons. To cover this difference, I distinguish between *fundamental* vs. *derived* prototypical traits (see definition (P) below): while the former confer a direct selective advantage, the latter are mere causal side-effects of the former.

In Schurz (2001*a*) I arrived at the following definition of prototypical normality in the evolution-theoretic sense:

Definition (P):

1. P is a *prototypical property* of members of a class of evolutionary systems S *i.w.s. (in the wide sense)* iff P is produced by a reprotype R and in the evolutionary history of S there was *overwhelming* selection in *favour* of R.
2. If the selection mentioned in (1) took place *because* of R's producing P, P is called a *fundamental* prototypical property, and otherwise (i.e. if P is just a side-effect of R) P is called a *derived* prototypical property.

Millikan's (1984: ch. 1) concept of an (evolutionary) *proper function* can be derived from this definition as follows: if a fundamental prototypical trait of S-members consists in the possession of item (organ) X with effect F, then F is called a proper function of item X of S-members. The major objection against the statistical consequence thesis given by Millikan (e.g. 1984: 4f, 34) and Laurier (1996: 29–31) points out that many items perform their functions not frequently but just often enough to get selected. For example, living up to the reproductive age is the major proper function of biological organisms, although only a small minority of babies of most species stay alive. This objection is resolved as follows: prototypical properties do not consist in the *actual* performance of a function. Actual performances—for example, whether a baby survives or not—depend on accidental circumstances; they are not reproduced (herited) and, hence, cannot be claimed to be prototypical. What is prototypical is rather the *capacity* to perform the functional behaviour under certain triggering circumstances (which themselves need not be frequent). These capacities are the fundamental prototypical properties which are reproduced and selected as the result of the genetic (or memetic) constitution of S-members; with the result that under standard selection scenarios their frequencies will be driven to almost-fixation.

   In Schurz (2001a: 494f) I gave a proof that the statistical consequence thesis of Section 26.1 is a logical consequence of definition (P) together with a mild assumption about evolution. Let me illustrate definition (P) by way of some examples. It is a prototypical capacity of matches to light when struck because they have been selected for this effect. It is a prototypical side-effect of matches that their flame sometimes burns one's fingers. But it is not prototypical for matches to have a certain colour, etc. It is a fundamental prototypical trait of human noses to smell and to stick out from the face. It is also prototypically normal for human noses to get cold at their top in the winter, but merely in the derived sense. Having legs, clearly, is prototypically normal for humans (in the fundamental biological sense), but not having short or long legs, because there was no dominant biological selection for short vs. long legs.

Prototypical normality applies not only to 'species' but also to higher order classes of evolutionary systems. For example, flying-ability is (fundamentally) prototypically normal within the entire class of birds, although for certain (exceptional) species of birds, such as emus or penguins, *lack* of flying-ability is prototypically normal. This is not a logical conflict, but just illustrates the *non-monotonicity* of prototypical properties— they admit exceptions, *not* only at the level of abnormal individuals (a bird with defective wings) but also at the level of abnormal subspecies whose selection conditions have been significantly different from those of the super-species or S. Penguins, for example, have changed their ecological niche from air-living to water-living creatures with the evolutionary effect that their wings have been gradually reshaped by selection into swimming instead of flying organs (a process which is called ex-adaptation).

One may ask, why do we then still categorize penguins as birds? Given that we base our categorization on prototypical properties, the answer is that penguins still have sufficiently many prototypical properties in common with birds to be classified as an (exceptional) bird-species. One may also ask, what would happen if in some distant future the frequency of birds without flying ability increased up to a value of 50 per cent? In that distant future, flying ability could no longer be called a prototypical property of birds, because there is no longer overwhelmingly positive selection in favour of flying ability among birds. This point highlights the *historical* character of prototypicality in evolution. The historical character is more salient in cultural evolution which proceeds much more rapidly—for example, the prototypical properties of farms two centuries ago (with horses, ploughs, etc.) are completely different from contemporary farms.

The relation between super- and subclasses of evolutionary systems is connected with the important distinction between prototypical properties in the *wide* sense (i.w.s.) and in the *narrow* sense (i.n.s.). Definition (P) identifies prototypical properties in the *wide* sense as those properties of an evolutionary system S which were selectively advantageous for the evolutionary persistence of S. While some of these properties are *indicative* for S, some others are shared by S with many evolutionary 'sibling' species of S which derive from a common ancestor species. The prototypical properties of S *i.n.s.* are *by definition* those prototypical properties of S i.w.s. which are indicative for S, that is which are *not* also prototypical properties of evolutionary sibling species of S. For example, having wings is a prototypical property i.n.s. of birds, but it is merely prototypical i.w.s. (and not i.n.s.) for sparrows or other special kind of birds, because it does not discriminate sparrows from other kinds of birds. Likewise, tasting sweet and being juicy is a prototypical property i.n.s. of fruit which is also a prototypical property i.w.s. but not i.n.s. of ripe apples, because most other kinds of ripe fruit have this property, too. These examples show that the use of 'prototypical properties' is systematically ambiguous between i.w.s. and i.n.s.—whence I suggest distinguishing between these two senses. If one emphasizes the *discriminative* value of prototypical properties (cf. Rosch and Mervis, 1975; Kleiber, 1998: 48ff), one means the *narrow* sense, while if one assumes the default inheritance of prototypical properties from super-categories to sub-categories (cf. Collonny et al., 2007) then one means the *wide* sense of prototypical properties.

The overall picture of my evolution-theoretic account is this: our natural, cultural, or technical environment is full of different kinds evolutionary systems, organisms, and artifacts, each of them characterized by a list of prototypical properties which have played a decisive role in their selection history. Given that humans' environment is full evolutionary systems whose behaviour is governed by prototypical properties, it should be expected that human reasoning is *fit* in reasoning with prototypes. In Schurz (2005a) I set up two criteria of fitness of human reasoning with prototypes: normic (prototype) reasoning must be (i) *statistically reliable* and (ii) *feasible by algorithms of low complexity*. I tried to show that the inference rules of the system **P** of *probabilistic default reasoning* (which are described in Section 26.8) satisfy both criteria. Moreover, in several psychological experiments it has been confirmed that the basic inference rules of the system **P** are well entrenched in people's intuitive reasoning (cf. Schurz, 2007; Pfeifer and Kleiter, 2005, 2008; Evans et al., 2003). In the next sections I extend this line of argument: given my description of evolutionary systems is correct, it should also be expected that the *concepts* by which humans describe evolutionary systems reflect their prototypicality structure. This brings me to the evolution-theoretic account of the prototype theory of concepts, which is described in the next sections.

26.3 THE PROTOTYPE THEORY OF CONCEPTS

The prototype theory of concepts was developed in the 1970s by E. Rosch in order to overcome certain difficulties in the classical theory of the meaning. Several versions of the prototype theory have been developed since then (for an overview cf. Kleiber, 1998; Margolis and Laurence, 1999), and they have the following in common:

1. The prototype theory refutes the *classical theory* of concepts according to which the meaning of a concept (or extensionally: a category) is defined by a list of individually necessary and jointly sufficient properties or conditions which an individual must possess in order to instantiate that concept (to be a member of the corresponding category). In fact, most of everyday language concepts do not have definitions by necessary and sufficient conditions. Nobody has ever given a definition of a bird, a dog, or a chair. All that can be given are prototypical

properties of birds, dogs, or chairs which are not necessary but allow of exceptional instantiations. For example, prototypical birds can fly, but penguins cannot; prototypical chairs have four legs, but some chairs have three legs, etc. The prototype theory of concepts identifies the meaning of a concept with a certain *prototype*— which is either a *prototypical exemplar* of the category, or a list (or structure) of *prototypical properties* of the category.

2. The prototype theory differs from the *theory-theory* of concepts according to which the meaning of a concept is provided by a given *background theory*. The theory-theory is adequate for two kinds of domains: (i) theoretical concepts of scientific theories, and (ii) certain anthropologically universal common sense concepts such as 'inanimate' vs. 'animate' being, 'cause' and 'effect', 'person', 'animal', 'plant', etc., which seem to be provided by inborn theories (cf. Margolis and Laurence, 1999: 43ff; Spelke, 1990; Carey, 1985). However, for the majority of everyday language concepts such as 'bird', 'chair', or 'fruit', common sense lacks background theories of this sort.

Generally speaking I support a *pluralistic* meaning theory: the meaning of *some* concepts is given by explicit definitions, that of others is given by background theories— and prototype theory seems to be the right semantic approach for those concepts whose meaning is given by common sense experience. Various experimental evidence supports the mental reality of prototypes. For example, the ratings of the degree of typicality of exemplars or subkinds of a concept—for example the typicality of a sparrow or a pelican as representative for a bird—are surprisingly coherent among different test persons. Moreover these typicality ratings are positively correlated to the speed and negatively to the error rate with which test persons classify given exemplars as a member of the respective category (cf. Smith and Medin, 1981; Osherson and Smith, 1981: 263; Smith et al., 1988b: 356; Kleiber, 1998: 32). Prototype theory is also supported by recent semantic theories which stress the *perceptual* content of concepts, since memorized visual images focus on prototypical properties (cf. Barsalou, 1999; Prinz, 2002).

In earlier versions of prototype theory (e.g. Heider (= Rosch), 1971; Rosch, 1975) the prototype was understood as a typical exemplar or subkind of the given concept. For example, a 'sparrow' is frequently judged to be the prototype of a bird, or 'apple' to be the prototype of a fruit. The *degree of typicality*, in short $d^{typ}(x:C)$, in which an exemplar x is an instance of the concept C, was *identified* with the *degree of membership*, that is with a *fuzzy measure* of the degree in which x is a member of C's extension. However, in a seminal paper Osherson and Smith (1981) have demonstrated that the distance function of fuzzy set theory does *not* adequately model prototypes. The major obstacle is the so-called *conjunction effect*: an individual x (e.g. a given brown apple) may be a bad member of a super-ordinate category A (for apple) but still a good member of a non-prototypical subcategory B&A (for brown apple) (cf. Hampton, 1982; Smith and Osherson, 1984; Smith et al., 1988b: 357). In this case, $d^{typ}(x:A\&B)$ would have to be greater than $d^{typ}(x:A)$, which is *impossible* for fuzzy set theory, since according to the *min-rule* of fuzzy set theory, $d^{typ}(x:A\&B) = \min(\{d^{typ}(x:A), d^{typ}(x:B)\})$.

In reaction to this problem, other authors have suggested understanding the prototype of a concept as a list of its prototypical properties.[3] An elaborated model of this kind has been developed and experimentally confirmed by Smith et al. (1988*b*). These authors represent a prototype by a *prototype frame*. Frames decompose properties (such as 'red', 'green') into attributes (e.g. colour) and values (red, green . . .); they represent concepts by lists of attributes together with their admitted values. Prototype frames assign, in addition, to each admitted value of an attribute its number of 'votes' which measures the typicality of this value for the prototype and is correlated with the *frequency* in which the value occurs among perceived instances (Smith et al., 1988*b*: 358). Moreover, to each attribute a second number is assigned, the so-called *diagnosticity* of this attribute, which measures the usefulness of this attribute in *discriminating* instances of the concept from instances of contrasting concepts (the importance of diagnosticity has been experimentally confirmed by Rosch and Mervis (1975)).

In the remaining sections of this chapter I will focus on prototype frames because they are a rather advanced version of prototype theory which is especially suited for my purposes, in particular because their votes are connected with the statistical frequencies of the attribute-values of evolutionary systems. For example, the prototype frame of 'apple' is modelled by Smith et al. (1988*b*: 358) as follows:

Prototype frame of 'apple':

attribute (diagnosticity):	values (votes):		
colour (1)	red (25)	green (5)	brown (0)
shape (0.5)	round (15)	square (0)	cylindrical (5)
texture (0.25)	smooth (25)	rough (5)	bumpy (0)

. . .

Further attributes may be taste (sweet 20, sour 5), consistency (juicy 20, dry 5), etc. The degree of typicality of a given instance I is computed as

$$(26.5) \quad d^{typ}(I : Apple) = \Sigma_{i \in Att} \quad \delta_i \cdot (v_i(P \cap I) - v_i(P - I) - v_i(I - P)),$$

where δ_i is the diagnosticity of attribute i, $v_i(P \cap I)$ is the number of votes for values of attribute i which the prototype P and the instance I have in common, $v_i(P-I)$ is the number of votes for values of attribute i which are unique for P, and likewise for $v_i(I-P)$. For example, if I is a particular apple with 30 votes for red, 20 for round, and 30 for smooth, while votes for all other values of attributes are zero, then $d^{typ}(I : Apple) = 1 \cdot (25-5-5) + 0.5 \cdot (15-5-5) + 0.25 \cdot (25-5-5) = 15 + 2.5 + 3.75 = 21.25$ (see Smith et al., 1988*b*: 358f).

---

[3] Also Rosch (1978) had modified her original position.

26.4 FIVE OBJECTIONS AGAINST PROTOTYPE THEORY

In this section I present five objections against prototype theory which have been discussed in the literature.

26.4.1 The problem of analyticity and intersubjective meaning stability

Fodor (1984: 26f) has defended the distinction between semantic (analytic) and empirical (synthetic) information against the attack of Quine (1951) by pointing out that a central function of this demarcation is to enable reasonable communication between speakers having different background beliefs. For if radical meaning holism were true then two speakers with different opinions about, say, priests would mean different things when talking about priests. To be sure, neither Fodor nor myself support a traditional (Frege–Carnapian) view of meaning postulates—all that I need to assume is that every adequate theory of meaning has to assume *some* sort of semantic-factual-demarcation.

Now, the prototypical frame of a concept does not only contain purely semantic information; it also contains world-knowledge, that is factual information (cf. Kleiber, 1998: 48–54). For example, it is empirical information that most apples are yellow and red, but unripe apples are green. But the empirical background knowledge of different people is different. So the question arises how the meanings of concepts as represented by prototypes can be intersubjectively stable? According to Wierzbicka (1985: 40f, 115), the prototype of a concept should not contain expert knowledge but only common sense knowledge. But the problem of intersubjective (in)stability arises also for common sense knowledge. As an example, consider the process of *concept acquisition* in childhood: some children may learn the prototype of a bird at hand of sparrows, because there are sparrows in their vicinity, while other children may learn the bird prototype at hand of pigeons or crows, etc. How does it come to be that, as a matter of fact, subjects agree in their concept of bird to such a high degree, in spite of the differences in their history of learning the concepts via prototypical exemplars?

26.4.2 Typicality vs. vague membership

Many authors have pointed out that degrees of typicality have to be sharply distinguished from degrees of vague membership: $d^{typ}(x{:}C) \neq d^{memb}(x{:}C)$. Only vague membership leads to a fuzzification of the *categorization problem*, insofar as it entails a fuzzification of the membership relation, while degrees of typicalities are compatible with strict categorization. For example, ducks, vultures, or pelicans are rather untypical birds; but they are *no less* birds than sparrows (cf. Kamp and Partee, 1995: 133f; Lakoff, 1986: 43, 1987*a*; Kleiber, 1998: 106ff.). While for Kamp and Partee (1995: 169), $d^{typ}(x{:}C) = d^{memb}(x{:}C)$ holds at least for some concepts, for example for 'chair' or 'red', Osherson and Smith (1997: 192) argue convincingly that even for the latter concepts, $d^{typ}(x{:}C)$ and $d^{memb}(x{:}C)$ diverge: for example, a 'chair made of gold' is untypical but still clearly a chair, and according to Berlin and Kay (1969, Appendix I: 119), the wavelength spectrum of 'unambiguously red' is much more comprehensive than that of 'prototypical red'.

26.4.3 What is the semantic (or cognitive) function of prototypes?

If it is not the function of prototypes to provide criteria for categorization (i.e. concept-membership), what is their semantic or cognitive function? Some authors have argued in favour of a *dual theory* of meaning, according to which each concept possesses a certain *core meaning*, which is purely semantic (or analytic), and a certain portion of (synthetic) world-knowledge about prototypical properties.[4] The core meaning is compositional (see below) and provides *necessary* conditions for the membership-relation. For example, whatever belongs to the category 'lion' *must* be an animal; 'stone lions', although they have several prototypical properties in common with true lions, are *not* lions. The semantic core meaning is also responsible for another important task which, according to Fodor (1999: 176), a semantic theory should fulfil, namely the specification of satisfaction conditions for sentences: these are derivable from the conditions for membership relations together with the meaning of logical operators.

Even if one accepts the dual theory of meaning, the question concerning the semantic or cognitive function of the second meaning component, the prototype, remains. For Lakoff (1987*a*), prototypes are a mere 'side product' of categories whose members bear a *family resemblance* to each other (cf. Kleiber, 1998: 113). In any case, the question of the precise function of prototypes becomes pressing. Note that this problem has two sides: (i) what is the *cognitive* function of prototypes (if any), and (ii) can this cognitive function be regarded as a *semantic* function?

26.4.4 Concepts without prototypes

Many concepts do not possess prototypes at all (cf. Margolis and Laurence, 1999: 36, 44). For example, the following two kinds of concepts do not possess prototypes because

---

[4] Cf. Osherson and Smith (1981: 277), Landau (1982). The position according to which there don't exist sufficient but at least necessary semantic conditions for membership is called the *neoclassical* theory (cf. Margolis and Laurence, 1999: 52ff.).

their range of instances is too *heterogeneous*: (i) *metric concepts*: for example there is no prototype of objects which are longer than one meter, or hotter than 100 degree Celsius; and (ii) *negative* or *disjunctive concepts* such as 'being not a bird', or 'being a bird or a table'. Other kinds of concepts do not possess prototypes because they are (iii) *too abstract* (e.g. 'dimension'), or they are (iv) *too theoretical* (e.g. 'mass' and 'force' in classical physics). Even some primitive kinds of concepts may become so heterogeneous in linguistic evolution that they *lose* their common prototype. An example of this sort is Lakoff's *mother-* example (cf. 1987b: 400): there is no common prototype underlying all present linguistic uses of 'mother'—such as genetic mother, birth mother (giving birth to the child, nowadays not necessarily identical with the genetic mother), foster mother, adoptive mother or stepmother. All these counterexamples imply that the prototype theory of concepts has a *restricted* domain of applications. How can we describe these restrictions in a *non ad-hoc* way?

26.4.5 Major problem: the non-compositionality of prototypes

Fodor and Lepore (1996) have fundamentally criticized the prototype theory because of its apparent non-compositionality. The principle of compositionality requires that the meaning of a complex expression is fully determined by the meaning of its primitive syntactic constituents together with the (semantic composition functions underlying the)[5] syntactic rules by which it is composed from these constituents. In many examples, however, the prototype of a complex expression does not appear to be determined by the prototypes of its constituents. In Fodor and Lepore's famous example, the prototype of a 'pet fish' (for example, a goldfish) is neither prototypical for a pet nor prototypical for a fish. Prototype theorists have tried to rescue compositionality for prototypes by modelling the semantic composition function as a more complex operation than *mere conjunction*—but it is still hard to see how *any* purely semantic composition function could succeed in retrieving the prototypical properties of 'pet fish' from the prototypical properties of 'pet' and 'fish' (more on this in Section 26.7).

The requirement of compositionality is usually justified by the argument that any theory of meaning must be able to explain the following two fundamental features of natural language (cf. Fodor and Lepore, 1996: 28; Robbins, 2002: 315; Connolly et al., 2007: 2):

---

[5] In the literature, the principle of compositionality is usually stated without the brackets (e.g. Fodor and Lepore, 1996: 29, fn. 3; Robbins, 2002: 314; Connolly et al., 2007: 3), but in more technical papers it is stated with the refinement in brackets (cf. Hodges, 2001). Assuming that the relation between syntactic rules and their corresponding semantic composition functions is one-to-one, both versions are equivalent.

1. *productivity*: a competent speaker can understand indefinitely many complex expressions based on *finitely many* primitive meaningful terms and primitive syntactic operations, and
2. *systematicity*: what a competent speaker understands is closed under forming *new combinations* (e.g. 'red chair') from the constituents of already understood expressions (e.g. 'red table' and 'white chair').

Defenders of compositionality argue that every adequate meaning theory must satisfy compositionality because compositionality is the *only* or at least the *best* explanation of productivity and systematicity. Margolis and Laurence (1999: 42) assert that the criticism of non-compositionality has no force against the *dual theory* of meaning explained in Section 26.4.3. However, the problem cannot be solved so easily: although according to the dual theory the analytic core meaning of expressions is still compositional, the extended prototype meaning is not compositional. So the dual theorist would have to conclude that productivity and systematicity hold only in a restricted form: we can retrieve the meaning of newly heard complex expressions from their well-understood constituents only *partially* but not fully.

26.5 EVOLUTION-THEORETIC FOUNDATION OF PROTOTYPE THEORY

In spite of the objections discussed in Section 26.4, prototype semantics is nevertheless adequate if its domain is restricted to common sense concepts describing evolutionary systems, and if its function is considered from an evolutionary viewpoint. In other words, the purpose of this paper is not a universal defence of prototype theory, but the attempt to give prototype theory its natural place in a pluralistic theory of meaning. The consequences of my evolution-theoretic account (recall Section 26.2) for prototype semantics can be summarized in the following two theses:

Thesis P1: One (if not *the*) major evolutionary function of cognition is efficient *predictive* reasoning (inferring the effects of practically important causes) and *diagnostic* reasoning (inferring the causes of practically important effects). *Categorization* is a *necessary condition* of predictive and diagnostic reasoning, but categorization *per se* is not evolutionarily advantageous because not every categorization is predictively and diagnostically efficient.

Thesis P1 contrasts with those cognitive scientists who consider categorization per se as the major task of cognition (cf. Lakoff, 1987a: XI; Kleiber, 1998: 4f). For example, the manifold systems of mythical categorizations in animistic and early religious worldviews are neither predictively nor diagnostically efficient. The category 'bayi' of Australasian aborigines which covers 'man, cangarooh, bats, most snakes, ... boomerang, certain spears . . .' (Kleiber, 1998: 122) may be fascinating for anthropologists but is predictively hopelessly inefficient; categories of that sort can hardly survive in the evolution of cognition.[6] Systems of categorization are predictively and diagnostically efficient if they possess computationally simple categories which figure as junctions in a dense system of lawlike connections (cf. also Rosch, 1978).

Thesis P2: The proper domain of prototype theory is evolutionary systems (as described in Section 26.2). In this domain predictive and diagnostic efficiency is achieved because (following from Section 26.2) evolutionary systems obey the following principles:

P2.1 Each *species* (or kind) S of an evolutionary system is characterized by a bundle of prototypical properties *i.w.s.* which have been selected during the evolution of (ancestors of) S and which S-members possess with a high statistical frequency.

P2.2 A certain subset of these prototypical properties i.w.s.—namely the prototypical properties *i.n.s.*—are highly discriminative vis-à-vis sibling species of S, because each kind of evolutionary system had its *specific* adaptation history to the selection requirements of its environment.

P2.3 All kinds of evolutionary systems include *exceptional* exemplars or subkinds, which deviate from the prototype pattern of the kind.

Theses P2.1–2 entail that the statistical distribution function over the total multidimensional property space will have several sharp peaks corresponding to evolutionary kinds, with low and broad valleys between these peaks. In other words, only certain combinations of properties have been produced by evolution and not arbitrary combinatorial variations in between them. There are no dogs with wings or birds with teeth, etc. This is the reason why reasoning with prototypes is so fast and predictively so efficient, although by thesis P2.3 the laws of evolutionary systems are never strict but merely high majority laws. One prototypical property i.n.s. is usually sufficient to identify an individual as a member of an evolutionary (natural, cultural) kind with high statistical reliability, and from this identification we can predict instantly a variety of other prototypical properties i.n.s. or i.w.s. Since we use all the information we can have, *every* prototypical property i.n.s. can be used as a means of *identifying* an evolutionary kind. For example, members of a primitive tribe hear a prototypical sound, or see a prototypical footprint, and instantly predict there is a predator nearby. Or, they see a prototypical shape in a landscape and instantly predict there is a river (etc.).

---

[6] Some aspects of mythical and religious categorizations can be explained by their 'generalized placebo effect' (Taylor, 1989; Schurz, 1998) or by their effects on promoting altruistic behaviour (Wilson, 2002).

A further clarification is important: since human prototype reasoning is more or less unconscious (Schurz 2007: 629), it may of course happen that humans also apply prototype reasoning to entities which are *not* evolutionary systems—for example they even speak of prototypical 'prime numbers' (cf. Armstrong, Gleitman, and Gleitman, 1983)—but whenever they do this prototype semantics and prototype reasoning loses its efficiency.

Some authors argue that the function of prototypes does not consist in categorization per se, but in (heuristic rules for) *fast* categorization (cf. Machery in this volume). This is true, but it is just one half of my story. To enable efficient predictions, prototypes must enable fast categorization—that is the inference from a prototypical property P_i i.n.s. to the category C ($P_i \Rightarrow C$) must be computationally easy and reliable—but in addition, categories must figure as junctions in a network of correlated prototypical properties, that is the inference from C to many (further) prototypical properties i.w.s. ($C \Rightarrow P_j$, for $j \neq i$) must be computationally easy and reliable, too. From the two inferences $P_i \Rightarrow C$ and $C \Rightarrow P_j$, the direct predictive or diagnostic inference from P_i to P_j ($P_i \Rightarrow P_j$) follows as explained in Section 26.3. If there are n prototypical properties i.w.s. and $m < n$ prototypical properties i.n.s., then the category C figures as *mediator* in a network of $m \cdot (n-1)$ direct predictive or diagnostic inferences $P_i \Rightarrow P_j$.

The *cue validity* of a property P *for* a category C is measured as the statistical probability of P among C-members divided through the statistical probability of P among members of the super-category C^+ in the underlying classification tree (cf. Rosch and Mervis, 1975; Kleiber, 1998: 52). Thus, the properties with high cue validity for category C are precisely the prototypical properties of C *i.n.s.* The cue validity of a category is defined as the sum of the cue validities of its prototypical properties i.n.s. It follows that the *cue validity of a category* C increases with the number of its prototypical properties i.n.s. (cf. Rosch et al., 1976b; Kleiber, 1998: 63f). It was observed by Rosch et al. (1976b) that the categories with highest cue validity are usually categories at a *medium level* of generality. These categories are called *base categories*—here are some examples (cf. Kleiber, 1998: 62):

Superordinate categories: animal, fruit, furniture
Base categories: dog, apple, chair
Subordinate categories: poodle, golden delicious, folding chair

That categories with high cue validity such as 'dog' have medium level generality has the following evolution-theoretic explanation: their branch of ancestors in the tree of evolutionary descendance has a *long, homogenous,* and *category-specific* selection history which produced many prototypical properties i.n.s. The selection history of more *specific* categories such as 'poodles' was too short to produce many prototypical properties i.n.s. of 'poodles'. In contrast, the selection history of 'animals' was very long but much too heterogeneous to produce many prototypical properties i.n.s. of 'animals'. Likewise for fruit and furniture.

In the remainder of this section I want to show how objections one to four of Section 26.4 can be (dis)solved by an evolution-theoretic understanding of prototypes. The major objection, number five, the problem of non-compositionality, is treated in the final Sections 26.6–26.9.

26.5.1 Analyticity and intersubjective meaning stability

The problem of intersubjective meaning stability need not be solved by us; it is solved 'by nature'. If the environment has prototypicality structure, then there is no need to define kinds by an exhaustive list of properties. Indicating some prototypical properties (e.g. 'have wings') is sufficient for grasping the underlying kind ('bird') and discriminate it from other kinds ('mammal', 'fish') by the cognitive operations of induction and abstraction. Even if the process of concept acquisition via prototypes is different from person to person it will nevertheless lead to intersubjectively stable meanings without any analytic definitions or conventions—at least *in most cases*. This is only true because nature has shaped the property-distribution of evolutionary systems in the way of sharp peaks as described below theses P2.1–2. As a thought experiment, imagine that there really exist a multitude of borderline cases between different evolutionary species—say, pigeons with a tail and teeth and four legs, dogs with wings and feathers, fish with wings and tails, etc. In such a possible world the process of concept learning by prototype semantics would be hopelessly inefficient.

26.5.2 Typicality and membership—reasons for the dual theory of meaning

There will always be exceptional instances whose membership to a category is not clearly decided because they *lack* some (or even many) of the prototypical properties of the category. In order to handle these more-or-less *atypical* cases, or *transition* cases between different categories, one has to single out an *analytic core* meaning of the concept. For example, in order to decide whether swimming viviparous animals (whales, etc.) are mammals or fish, we need to fix an analytic core meaning of 'fish' and 'mammal'.

Singling out an analytic core meaning is certainly *not* the task of prototypes. For the functioning of prototypes it is sufficient that exception cases are statistically *rare*—and this is granted by their evolutionary basis. Fixing an analytic core meaning is partially achieved by common sense conventions, in order to stabilize communication. Only in rare cases can the analytic core meaning be fixed by explicit definitions; much more often it is fixed, at least partially, by so-called *ostensive* 'definitions' ('this is a fish'),[7] or by necessary semantic conditions ('mammals can't be fish'). In a more advanced way, fixing the meaning and deciding semantic borderline cases is the task of scien-

---

[7] This is closely related to Fodor's suggestion (1998c: 95) that semantic 'Fido'-Fido-principles ('dog' denotes dogs, etc.) are analytic.

tific *theories*. For example, the classification of species in modern biology is no longer expressed in terms of their prototypical properties, but in terms of their phylogenetic genealogy. This theoretical classification system is more coherent and unified; it agrees in many cases with the prototype classifications of common sense, but there also exist several differences which have caused many controversies in biology (cf. Ridley, 1993: 369f).

The above argument is a clear reason for advocating the *dual* theory of meaning explained in Section 26.4. Adopting this dual theory leads us to the next objection.

26.5.3 The cognitive and semantic function of prototypes

The cognitive function of prototypes has already been worked out: they enable fast and efficient predictive and diagnostic reasoning about evolutionary systems. The remaining question to be discussed is whether and why this cognitive function of prototypes should be understood as a *semantic* function, that is as being part of the *meaning* of a concept. I agree with Quine (1951) that in natural languages the separation between an analytic core meaning and a synthetic (world-dependent) knowledge about the concept's extension is neither sharp nor clear. Of course, one may *insist* that the meaning of a concept should be totally independent of world-knowledge, but such a decision would deprive the resulting notion of 'meaning' much of its psychological content. If one wants a psychologically realistic notion of meaning, which reflects that content which natural language speakers immediately associate when parsing the utterances of linguistic expressions (cf. Springer and Murphy, 1992), then prototypes *should* be regarded as *part* of the meaning. Prototypes are also important for two further tasks which according to Fodor (1999: 176) a semantic theory should fulfil: they should be preserved by good translations, and they should be contained in a notion of content which is adequate for purposes of intentional explanation.

26.5.4 Concepts without prototypes

Heterogeneous concepts of the sort explained in Section 26.4.4 do not belong to the domain of evolutionary systems. Because of the restriction of the domain of prototype theory to evolutionary systems, these concepts are no longer a problem of prototype theory.

One may object that my evolution-theoretic account of prototypes now has the *inverse* problem: it is *too restrictive*. For example, not only kind concepts but also property concepts such as 'colour' have prototypes. However, in these cases there is usually a hidden evolutionary explanation in the background. For example, the similarity space of colours in human vision has its explanation in terms of the colour perception system of the human eye—which is, of course, an evolutionary system.

26.6 FORMAL VS. PROCEDURAL
COMPOSITIONALITY

We now turn to the problem of the compositionality of prototypes. Since not every complex concept has a prototype, we ask the question of compositionality in the following restricted form: provided a complex concept has a prototype at all, is the complex prototype (e.g. 'brown apple') compositionally determined by the prototypes of the constituent concepts ('brown' and 'apple') together with the syntactic operation (here, the adjective–noun combination)? Before we can answer this question, we have to make an important distinction between *formal* and *procedural* compositionality.

Let E be an assumed set of *grammatical expressions* e ∈ E of a given language L which are built up from a set of atomic expressions $A \subset E$ by a set Σ of syntactic rules of the form s: $E^n \rightarrow E$. Let $\mu{:}E{\rightarrow}M$ be a *meaning* function which assigns meanings $m \in M$ to all grammatical expressions of L, and assigns a corresponding meaning function μ_s to each syntactic rule s. Then the principle of *compositionality* can be expressed by the following equation (cf. Hodges 2001):

$$(PC){:}\ \mu(s(e_1,\ldots,e_n)) = \mu_s(\mu(e_1),\ldots,\mu(e_n)), \quad \text{for all } e_1,\ldots,e_n \in E \text{ and } s \in \Sigma.$$

A given language L together with a given *partial* meaning function for L's sentences $\mu{:}\text{Sent}(L){\rightarrow}M$ is called *formally compositional* if there *exists* a total compositional meaning function μ for L's expressions which preserves the meaning of L's sentences. This idea of formal compositionality is based on Frege's context principle, according to which the meaning of a term (or atomic expression) of a language is determined by the term's contribution to the meaning of sentences containing it. It follows from the first extension theorem of Hodges (2001) that *every language L whose sentence meanings are semantically functional, that is are preserved under substitution of synonymous subexpressions, is formally compositional.*[8]

Several authors have observed that formal compositionality is a rather weak condition (Zadrozny, 1994), though it is certainly not *empty* (Westerståhl, 1998). A counterexample to formal compositionality is only given when we encounter an *idiomatic*

---

[8] *Proof*: Hodges 1st extension theorem states that for every subclass of expressions $E^* \subset E$ which is cofinal in E (i.e. every $e \in E$ is subexpression of some $e^* \in E^*$) and which has a meaning function $\mu^*{:}E^*{\rightarrow}M$ which is '1-compositional' and 'husserlian', there exists an extended meaning function $\mu{:}E{\rightarrow}M$ which coincides with μ^* over E^*, is fully compositional and is unique up to isomorphism. We apply this theorem by letting E^* be the set of all sentences Sent(L). Then Hodges condition of '1-compositionality' coincides with the condition of preservation of sentence meanings under substitution of synonymous subexpressions of the same grammatical category (i.e. $\mu(e) = \mu(e') \Rightarrow \mu(S) = \mu(S[e'/e])$). Hodges second condition of 'husserlianity' requires that replacing synonymous subexpression preserves meaningfulness; this condition is met because 1-compositionality is assumed to hold for *all* sentences, i.e. whenever $S \in \text{Sent}(L)$, then also $S[e'/e] \in \text{Sent}(L)$, whence meaningfulness of S implies meaningfulness of $S[e'/e]$ by 1-compositionality.

expression such as 'red herring': although 'herring' and 'an exemplar of Clupeidae' are semantically equivalent, 'a red exemplar of Clupeidae' means something different than 'a red herring'. In contrast, the typical problem of compositionality with prototypes, as exemplified in the *pet fish problem*, has nothing to do with formal compositionality. As long as 'pet fish' has a unique prototype, call it *protopetfish*, we can make μ formally compositional for 'pet fish' simply by setting $\mu(\text{'pet fish'}) = \mu_{AN}(\mu(\text{'pet'}), \mu(\text{'fish'})) := protopetfish$ (where μ_{AN} is the meaning function underlying adjective–noun combinations). However, the so-defined meaning function need not be at all computable.

To understand the *pet fish problem*, we need the stronger notion of procedural compositionality: a formally compositional meaning function μ is called *procedurally compositional if μ is computable (i.e. recursive)—or even stronger, computable in a reasonable (i.e. polynomial) time.*[9] It is the violation of this condition which was the target of the criticism of prototype's non-compositionality. For example, the prototypical pet fish cannot be computed in an obvious way from the prototype of a fish and that of a pet.

26.7 REFINED ACCOUNTS TO PROTOTYPE COMPOSITION AND THEIR LIMITATIONS

In many cases of adjective–noun combinations, the adjective does not correspond to a conjunctive term but functions as a *modifier* of the noun. For example, that x is a skilful F does not mean that x is an F and x is skilful, but rather that x is an F with special F-skills. Several authors have attempted to construct compositional meaning functions which model the meaning of adjective–noun combinations by certain modifications of the noun meaning. An advanced account of this sort is the *selective modification model* of Smith et al. (1988b).[10] Recall the prototype frame of the noun 'apple' as explained in Section 26.4. If the noun 'apple' is combined with an adjective such as 'red', then the prototype of the combined concept 'red apple' is obtained by the following modification operation on the prototype frame of 'apple': (i) the adjective 'red' shifts all votes in the corresponding attribute 'colour' to its own value, (ii) it increases the diagnosticity of

---

[9] For a similar suggestion cf. Kracht (2001). A second condition for procedural compositionality was introduced in Schurz (2005b, 282). This condition requires that the given algorithm computes μ in a *bottom-up* fashion. This is needed for handling the semantics of theoretical terms, but not for prototype semantics. Procedural compositionality becomes equivalent with *epistemic compositionality* in the sense of Bonnay (2005: 43) if the algorithm A is used by the epistemic subject.

[10] Another account is the adjective–noun calibration theory of Kamp and Partee (1995: 164f), which has been criticized by Osherson and Smith (1997: 197f), and the adjective–noun combination model of Wisniewski (1997). Hampton (1987) has developed a concept integration theory which includes the influence of world-knowledge.

the colour attribute, and finally (iii) it leaves the structure of all the other attributes unchanged:

Prototype frame of 'red apple' (modified values in bold):

attribute (diagnosticity)	values (votes)		
colour (2)	red (30)	green (0)	brown (0)
shape (0.5)	round (15)	square (0)	cylindrical (5)
texture (0.25)	smooth (25)	rough (5)	bumpy (0)

It has been experimentally confirmed by Smith et al. (1988*b*: 364ff) that this model works in many cases, but not in all. The major restriction of any selective modification model of this sort is the following: *the modifying adjective must not express an exceptional property*. Otherwise the rule of *default-inheritance* of the remainder prototypical properties which is assumed in condition (iii) of the selective retention model may get violated. For example, it is a prototypical property of apples to have smooth texture, and this prototypical property is inherited by normal (red or yellow) apples, but brown apples[11] have rough texture; or it is a prototypical property of apples to taste sweet, and this prototypical property is inherited by red or yellow apples, but green apples are usually not ripe and hence taste sour. To give another example, birds usually can fly, and this prototypical property is inherited by all *normal* birds, but birds in the Antarctic do not fly because they are penguins.

 In conclusion, whenever the modifying adjective expresses an exceptional property, then the rule of default-inheritance may be violated, because the exceptional property causes *shifts* in the frequency-distributions over the values of the *other* attributes, in a way which is *not* solely determined by the meaning of the noun and the adjective but depends on specific pieces of world-knowledge, such that brown apples have a rough surface, green apples are usually unripe, and almost all birds in the Antarctic are penguins who cannot fly. It follows that the prototypes of complex nouns whose adjectives express exceptional properties are not (fully) compositional in the procedural sense (although they are formally compositional as long as compound prototypes are functionally unique). This fact is also acknowledged by Smith et al. (1988*b*: 386f) and further supported by Hampton and Jönsson (this volume). A further problem of the selective modification model arises when the modifying adjective is 'new' in the sense that it does not belong to any of the value spaces of the prototypical attributes in the noun frame. Smith et al. (1988*b*: 386ff) suggest that in cases in which the new adjective is 'neutral', an appropriate attribute may be added to the prototype frame of the noun. In cases in which the new adjective expresses an exceptional property, it will again change the value frequencies of the other attributes (e.g. 'killer dog'). The exceptional adjective may even necessitate the inclusion of further attribute-values in the frame of the compound noun phrase (e.g. 'victims of a killer dog').

---

[11] Contrary to Smith et al. (1988*b*: 360f), 'brown apples' exist; their German name is 'leather apples'.

26.8 EXPLAINING THE COMPOSITION OF PROTOTYPES BY PROBABILISTIC DEFAULT REASONING

All of the discussed logical properties of prototypes can be explained by the rules of *probabilistic default reasoning*, in short: PDR. These rules, which are summarized in the system **P**, go back to Adams (1975) and have been further developed by various researchers on non-monotonic logic. Instead of presenting system **P** in all of its variants (for overviews cf. Schurz, 1998, 2005*a*) I explain only those aspects which are important for prototypes. Three general features of PDR are the following:

1. PDR interprets normic conditions 'A ⇒ B' as *high conditional probabilities* 'P(B|A) = high' (recall Section 26.1). In the evolution-theoretic understanding 'P' is regarded as a *statistical* (rather than a merely subjective) probability (recall Section 26.2). The so-called *uncertainty* of A⇒B, U(B|A), is defined as $1 - P(B|A)$.

2. The rules of PDR infer normic (conclusion) conditionals from given (premise) conditionals; thus these rules have the format 'A₁⇒B₁, A₂⇒B₂, .../Aₙ⇒Bₙ' (the stroke '/' separates the premises from the conclusion). The PDR-rules for normic conditionals (⇒) are *weaker* than the classical rules for strict (exceptionless) conditionals (→). For example, normic conditionals merely satisfy the rule of cautious transitivity 'A⇒B, A&B⇒C/A ⇒ C', while strict conditionals satisfy full transitivity 'A→B, B→C/A→C'.

3. The semantic criterion of *correctness* which underlies the rules of PDR is the *preservation of high conditional probability*. Although high conditional probability is qualitatively preserved by PDR, a certain probability loss is unavoidable. This probability loss increases with the *number* of premises, but it is *controlled* by the following (mathematically proved) condition: a (conclusion) conditional can be inferred in calculus **P** from given (premise) conditionals if and only if in all probability models the uncertainty of the conclusion conditional is less-than-or-equal-to the sum of the uncertainties of the premise conditionals. For example, for cautious transitivity this means that if $P(B|A) \geq 1-\varepsilon_1$, and $P(C|A\&B) \geq 1-\varepsilon_2$, then $P(C|A) \geq 1-\varepsilon_1-\varepsilon_2$. Similar probabilistic inequalities hold for *all* inferences which can be drawn within system **P**; in other words, the system **P** is under full probabilistic control.

Three central aspects of reasoning with prototypes can be explained by PDR as follows.

26.8.1 Predictive and diagnostic reasoning with prototypes

A prototypical property *i.w.s.* P_i of an underlying category C supports normic conditionals of the form (i) $C \Rightarrow P_i$. A prototypical property *i.n.s.* P_k supports in addition to (ii) $C \Rightarrow P_k$ also the inverse conditional (iii) $P_k \Rightarrow C$—that is, the prototypical property i.n.s. P_k is *indicative* for the corresponding category. From (i), (ii), and (iii) the *direct predictive inference* (iv) $P_k \Rightarrow P_i$ can be inferred by PDR in the following subtle way. Neither full transitivity ($P_k \Rightarrow C, C \Rightarrow P_i / P_k \Rightarrow P_i$) nor full monotonicity ($C \Rightarrow P_i / C \& P_k \Rightarrow P_i$) are rules of the system **P**. However, from (i) and (ii), (v): $C \& P_k \Rightarrow P_i$ follows by the **P**-rule of cautious monotonicity; and from (iii) and (v), the intended conclusion (iv) follows by the above-mentioned **P**-rule of cautious transitivity. In other words, predictive and diagnostic reasoning based on prototypical properties is *only* reliable as long as those properties which are used as *indicators* for the corresponding category (iii) are at the same time prototypical i.w.s., that is are statistically frequent (ii).

26.8.2 Default inheritance of prototypes—a correction of Connolly et al. (2007)

The rule of default inheritance of prototypical properties (or default-to-prototype, in short DP), says formally that $C \Rightarrow P$ implies $CA \Rightarrow P$, where CA is a sub-kind of the category C which obtained by a modifying adjective A. Logically speaking, the sub-kind CA can always be equivalently represented as a conjunction 'C&X' for *some* X. Therefore the rule (DP) is nothing but an unrestrained monotonicity rule ($C \Rightarrow P / C \& A \Rightarrow P$). It is clear that the rule (DP) *cannot* be generally probabilistically safe, because of the well-known fact that conditional probabilities are *non-monotonic*, that is a high value of $P(B|A)$ does not entail a high value of $P(B|A\&C)$. However, this does not mean that this rule is generally unreliable, as Connolly et al. (2007) have argued. It is true that the prior probability that an arbitrary object x is a CA is *smaller-than-or-equal-to* the probability that an arbitrary object x is a C. But this does of course not imply, that 'the probability that an arbitrary AN is a *good* instance of N is smaller-than-or-equal-to the probability that an arbitrary N is a good instance of N', which is the claim of Connolly et al. (2007: 8). That an arbitrary AN is a good instance of N means that 'if something is an AN; then is a GN', where 'GN' stands for 'good N' and means the possession of many prototypical properties of Ns. If the conditional (if X, then Y) is interpreted as a material implication ($\neg X \vee Y$), then the probabilistic relation would even be the inverse of what is claimed by Connolly et al. (2007)—then P(if AN, then GN) $\geq$ P(if N, then GN) would hold. However, the conditional assertion has to be interpreted not as a material conditional but as a high conditional probability, and in this case, there exists no general world-independent relation between the value of P(GN|N) and P(GN|AN): depending on the facts of the world, P(GN|AN) can be greater, smaller or equal to P(GN|N).[12]

26.8.3 Default inheritance and the rule of rational monotonicity

There exists a PDR-rule of the extended system $\mathbf{P}^{+}$ (cf. Schurz, 1998) which expresses precisely what we have worked out before, namely that default-inheritance by sub-kinds is *reliable* if these sub-kinds are non-exceptional in the statistical sense. This is the rule of rational monotonicity which says the following:

Rational monotonicity (RM): From C ⇒ P and ¬(C ⇒ ¬A) infer C&A ⇒ P.
In words: if P is a prototypical property of C, and the subcategory CA is not exceptional (i.e. Cs are *not* normally not CAs), then P is probabilistically inherited to the subcategory CA.

Rational monotonicity (RM) is stronger than the rule of 'cautious monotonicity' '(CM): from C ⇒ P and C ⇒ A infer C&A ⇒ P', because the second premise of (RM) is much weaker than the second premise of (CM).[13] The (RM) rule satisfies the probabilistic inequality U(P|C&A) ≤ U(P|C)/P(A|C); that is if P(A|C) is not small then U(P|C&A) will not be much greater than U(P|C).

Rule (RM) tells us that when the subclass-forming property is not statistically rare, the rule (DP) is reliable. But recall from Section 26.8.2 that the inverse direction does not generally hold: not all statistically rare properties cause exceptions, that is to say induce changes in other prototypical properties—those which don't are called 'neutral'. For example 'living in Düsseldorf' is a statistically rare but neutral property of Europeans. Nevertheless, it hard to see how a semantic computation mechanism could discern, without any empirical information, those cases of statistically rare subclasses which cause exceptions from those which are neutral. Therefore I conclude that general composition procedures are reliable only when the modifying adjectives to which they are applied are not statistically rare.

The (RM) rule also explains the experimental results of Connolly et al. (2007: 10ff). Very briefly, Connolly et al. (2007) found out that the test persons' estimations of the likelihood with which members of a given kind have a prototypical property (e.g. ducks have webbed feet) *decreases* if the kind is constrained by more and more neutral adjectives (e.g. baby Peruvian ducks have webbed feet). Assuming the evolution-theoretic hypothesis of Section 26.2, that humans are quite fit in reasoning with normic conditionals, the probabilistic explanation of this result is as follows: the more adjectives

---

[12] Connolly et al. (2007) call the rule (DP) 'DS' for 'default to stereotypes'. The inequality P(GN|AN) ≤ P(GN|N) holds for the *special* probability distribution by which Connolly et al. illustrate their claim (2007: 9); but it does not hold in general, as they assume.
[13] ¬(C⇒¬A) requires that P(A|C) is not small, while C⇒A requires that P(A|C) is high.

A_1A_2... modify the noun C, the smaller the conditional probability $P(A_1A_2...|C)$ gets, whence rule (DP) becomes more and more unreliable. There is nevertheless a correlation between a property P being prototypical for a given category C and its tendency to be inherited to restricted subcategories CA, but this correlation *sinks* within increasing specificity of the CA-subcategory (cf. Hampton and Jönsson, this volume).

26.9 CONCLUSION: PROTOTYPES ARE SEMI-COMPOSITIONAL

The foregoing considerations support the conjecture that prototypes are *semi-compositional* in the following sense: there exist unboundedly (i.e. potentially infinitely) many combinations of nouns with non-exceptional adjectives which satisfy the rule (DP) and hence are compositional, but presumably there also exist unboundedly many combinations of nouns with exceptional adjectives which violate (DP) and hence are non-compositional. Although I do not have a proof that there exist unboundedly many exceptional adjectives I can think of no principled reason why their number should be finitely bounded, because exceptional properties can be conjoined with other (non-exceptional or exceptional) properties to form new exceptional properties, iteratively up to unbounded complexity. What does this imply for the explanation of the facts of productivity and systematicity of meaning in natural language, for which compositionality was claimed to be the best if not the only explanation?

An insightful analysis of the connection between productivity (systematicity) and compositionality has been suggested by Robbins (2002). He argues that for the explanation of productivity one need not assume that conceptual meanings (contents) always compose—it is enough that they compose in in(de)finitely many cases (2002: 317, 321f). According to the hypothesis of semi-compositionality, this is indeed the case. So we can conclude that semi-compositionality yields an equally good explanation of productivity and hence is not refuted by Fodor's arguments. On the other hand, since semi-compositionality entails the existence of unboundedly many non-compositional cases, non-compositionality cannot be dealt away with a finite list of idiomatic exceptions, but is a genuine feature of prototype semantics in natural language.

PART VII

NEURAL MODELS OF
COMPOSITIONAL
REPRESENTATION

....

CHAPTER 27

CONNECTIONISM, DYNAMICAL COGNITION, AND NON-CLASSICAL COMPOSITIONAL REPRESENTATION

....

TERRY HORGAN

I will address the issue of compositionality of mental representations from the perspective of a foundational framework for cognitive science that is described and defended in Horgan and Tienson (1996). The *dynamical cognition* framework (or DC framework), as John Tienson and I call it, is inspired partially by connectionism and partially by the persistence of the problem of relevance within classical computational cognitive science. The DC framework treats cognition in terms of the mathematics of dynamical systems: total occurrent cognitive states are mathematically/structurally realized as points in a high-dimensional dynamical system, and these mathematical points are physically realized by total-activation states of a neural network with specific connection weights. The framework repudiates the classicist assumption that cognitive-state transitions conform to a tractably computable transition function over cognitive states. I will explain how the DC framework makes conceptual space for the possibility of systematically content-sensitive cognitive-state transitions that (i) automatically accommodate lots of relevant information without explicitly representing it during cognitive processing, and (ii) are too subtle to conform to any tractably computable cognitive transition function. I will then describe the kind of compositionality exhibited by mental representations (according to the framework), which is non-classical in at least three ways:

1. formal/syntactic compositionality and semantic compositionality are too intimately intertwined to be separable;

2. compositional structure in the system of representations need not be tractably computable;
3. compositional structure does not require separately tokenable constitutent-representations.

27.1 THE RELEVANCE PROBLEM AND ITS APPARENT MORALS

Tienson and I maintain that a strong case can be made for the claim that much of human cognition is too complex and subtle to be explainable within the confines of the classical computational theory of mind in cognitive science. Jerry Fodor, a long-time fan of the computational approach with respect to *parts* of human cognition, is also a long-time sceptic about its potential for explaining *all* of human cognition—even though he also thinks that the computational approach is the best that anyone has yet been able to devise. He holds that many centrally important cognitive processes, like those involved in forming and updating one's beliefs, and those involved in decision making and planning, are unlikely to conform to the computational theory of mind. He has recently articulated the case for scepticism in Fodor (2000).

Tienson and I share Fodor's doubts about the prospects of the computational approach, and our reasons for doubting it are much like his own. We argue the case in some detail in our book, in places quoting approvingly from Fodor (1983) and elaborating upon some of the points he makes in the passages we quote. Here I want to briefly reiterate the case for scepticism, by citing the more recent articulation of it in Fodor (2000).

According to the Computational Theory of Mind (CTM), observes Fodor, the causal role of a mental representation is syntactically determined. But this idea of syntactic determination of causal role is ambiguous, between a weaker and stronger reading. On the strong construal, the causal role of a mental representation is entirely determined by *its own* syntax. This assumes the following principle:

Principle E: Only essential properties of a mental representation can determine its causal role.

Fodor uses the label 'E(CTM)' for this version of CTM. On the weak construal, however, the causal role of a mental representation can be determined more holistically, albeit still syntactically. This view he calls the *Minimal* Computational Theory of Mind, M(CTM). He expresses it this way:

M(CTM): The role of a mental representation in cognitive processes supervenes on some syntactic facts or other.

The classical computational account of cognitive architecture faces a dilemma, with respect to the task of accommodating *context-dependent* properties of mental representations—that is, properties whose possession by a mental representation depends on features of the overall cognitive system, above and beyond the intrinsic nature of the mental representation itself. One such property is *simplicity*. The first horn of the dilemma involves the apparent untenability of E(CTM). Fodor articulates the problem this way, using simplicity as an example:

> Simplicity is, I think, a convincing example of a context-dependent property of mental representations to which cognitive processes are responsive. It's part of rationality to prefer the simpler of two competing beliefs, ceteris paribus; and, likewise, it's part of practical intelligence to prefer the simpler of two competing plans for achieving a goal.... [S]implicity is an *intrinsic* (i.e., *context-invariant*) property of thoughts if and only if each thought contributes a constant increment (/decrement) to the overall simplicity of whatever theory you conjoin it to. Pretty clearly, however, the contribution of a thought to determining the simplicity of a theory is not context invariant by this criterion. Rather, what effect adding a new belief has on the overall simplicity of one's prior epistemic commitments depends on *what one's prior epistemic commitments are....* The long and short is: The complexity of a thought is not intrinsic; it depends on the context. But the syntax of a representation is one of its essential properties and so doesn't change when the representation is transported from one context to another. *So how could the simplicity of a thought supervene on its syntax?....* Inferences in which features of an embedding theory affect the inferential-cum-causal roles of their constituent beliefs are what philosophers sometimes call 'global' or 'abductive' or 'holistic' or 'inferences to the best explanation.'.... What they have in common, from the point of view of E(CTM), is that they are presumptive examples where the determinants of the computational role of a mental representation can shift from context to context; hence where the computational role of a mental representation is *not* determined by its individuating properties; hence where the computational role of a mental representation is not determined by its syntax. That is: what they have in common, from the point of view of E(CTM), is that they are all presumptive counterexamples. (Fodor, 2000: 25–8)

The second horn of the dilemma arises for the weaker version of the computational theory, M(CTM). Here the problem is the apparent computational intractability associated with the need to accommodate all relevant background epistemic commitments that are potentially relevant to the contextually appropriate causal role of a context-dependent mental representation. Fodor puts the problem this way:

> Notice that, strictly speaking, M(CTM) is compatible with everything I've said so far about the importance of globality, abduction, and the like for the life of the cognitive mind.... [I]t's still wide open that simplicity is…a syntactic property. All that requires, according to M(CTM) is that, *given the syntax of the representation R and of the other representations in the embedding theory T*, the simplicity of R relative to T is fully determined.... But that is smallish comfort for the thesis that the architecture of cognition is classical. For it is enormously plausible, in the typical case, that the representations over which mental processes are actually defined are *much shorter*

than whole theories.... *Whole theories* can't be the units of computation.... [So] [t]he effects that global features of belief systems appear to have on cognitive processes is a problem for the Classical computational account of mental architecture—that remains true *even if it's assumed that all of the global features of belief systems that have such effects are syntactic.* M(CTM) (unlike E(CTM)) allows *in principle* for abductive inferences to be exhaustively syntactically driven.... But as far as anybody knows, Classical psychological theorizing can exploit this loophole only at the price of a ruinous holism; that is, by assuming that the units of thought are much bigger than they could possibly be. (Fodor, 2000: 29–33)

In light of this dilemma, Fodor maintains, the disappointing track record of artificial intelligence (AI) is no surprise. Here is his bleak assessment of the current situation of AI and the CTM:

[T]he failure of artifical intelligence to produce successful simulations of routine commonsense cognitive competence is notorious, not to say scandalous. We still don't have the fabled machine that can make breakfast without burning down the house; or the one that can translate everyday English into everyday Italian; or the one that can summarize texts; or even the one that can learn anything much except statistical generalizations.... It does seem to me that there's a pattern to the failures. Because of the context sensitivity of many parameters of quotitidan abductive inferences, there is typically no way to delimit a priori the considerations that may be relevant to assessing them. In fact, there's a familiar dilemma: Reliable abduction may require, in the limit, that the whole background of epistemic commitments be somehow brought to bear in planning and belief fixation. But feasible abduction requires, in practice, that not more than a small subset of even the relevant background beliefs is actually consulted. How to make abductive inferences that are both reliable and feasible is what they call in AI the frame problem.... In the general case, it appears that the properties of a representation that determine its causal-cum-inferential role, though they may be exhaustively syntactic, needn't be either local or insensitive to context. As things now stand, Classical architectures know of no reliable way to recognize such properties short of exhaustive searches of the background of epistemic commitments. I think *that's* why our robots don't work. (Fodor, 2000: 37–8)

What Fodor calls the 'frame problem', using this expression broadly, is what I am here calling the *relevance* problem. Briefly, it is the problem of understanding how human cognition manages to quickly and efficiently accomplish cognitive-state transitions that are suitably sensitive to enormous amounts of relevant background information—and to do so without first searching for and explicitly representing all that background information during cognitive processing. This appears to be an in-principle problem for the classical conception of cognition as *computation*, as Fodor himself is here arguing (and as he has argued in earlier writings, such as Fodor (1983)), and as Tienson and I argue in Horgan and Tienson (1996). Fodor's considered conclusion is this:

Computational nativism is clearly the best theory of the cognitive mind that anyone has thought of so far (vastly better than, for example, the associationistic empiricism that is the main alternative); and there may indeed be aspects of cognition about which computational nativism has got the story more or less right. But it's nonetheless quite plausible that computational nativism is, in large part, not true. (Fodor, 2000: 3)

What it seems is needed is a fundamentally different theory of the cognitive mind, in place of the CTM. Fodor evidently thinks so, and Tienson and I think so too.

Well, if the mind doesn't work *that* way—viz., via the *computational* manipulation of mental representations—then how *does* it work? More generally, how is it even *possible* for physical systems like human brains to appropriately accommodate, and appropriately bring to bear, vast amounts of contextually relevant background information in the course of cognitive processing? If indeed the task is not—and cannot be—accomplished via *computation* over mental representations, this means that the relevant cognitive-state transitions *are not tractably computable*. So we have the following 'How Possibly?' question:

HP: How is it possible for physical-state transitions in a human brain, or in a brain-like neural network, both (1) to systematically subserve cognitive-state transitions that do not conform to a tractably computable transition function, and (2) to do so in a way that automatically accommodates vast amounts of relevant background information that does not get explicitly represented during processing?

Can connectionism perhaps illuminate this question? Fodor, as is well-known, is a philosophical arch-enemy of connectionism. In essence, this is because he sees connectionism as a return to associationistic empiricism, and because he construes connectionist networks as essentially just devices for computing statistical inferences. Associative/statistical processing, he maintains, just cannot capture the systematic semantic coherence of rational thought.

Tienson and I agree with Fodor's pessimistic assessments of both 'computational nativism' and 'associationistic empiricism'. We also agree with Fodor that many extant connectionist models do indeed appear to engage in associative-statistical information processing, and hence are not likely to scale up from 'toy' cognitive tasks to tasks such as real-life belief-formation or real-life action-planning. In our view, what is evidently needed is a fundamentally *new* foundational approach to cognitive architecture.

Unlike Fodor, however, Tienson and I believe that there are ideas to be found in connectionism that potentially point the way forward, toward an approach to cognition that is indeed genuinely novel. This non-classical framework for cognitive science, which we call the *dynamical cognition* framework (the DC framework), repudiates the idea that cognition is always *computation* over mental representations. (It does not repudiate the idea that mental representations are language-like, although its approach to representational compositionality is very different from the classicist approach—as I will discuss later in the chapter.)

I have not argued in detail that the CTM is incapable, in principle, of solving the relevance problem. All I have offered is a brief summary, mainly by way of selected quotation, of Fodor's most recent articulation of the argument. The case for this pessimistic conclusion is more fully elaborated both in Fodor's own writings and in my book with Tienson. But let me now add this: even if one is not persuaded by such arguments—even if one doubts that there are convincing arguments for the conclusion that the CTM *cannot possibly* handle the relevant problem—one should still be open to the possibility that there is a fundamentally different, non-computational, foundational framework for understanding how the cognitive mind handles abductive inference and related cognitive tasks. The DC framework is just that.

The plan for the rest of this chapter is as follows. In Section 27.2 I will briefly sketch some key salient features of the DC framework. In Section 27.3 I will describe an overall answer to the HP question that arises within the DC framework—an answer that Tienson and I think should be taken very seriously within cognitive science. Then in Section 27.4 I will turn to the issue of compositionality, from the perspective of the DC framework with its proposed answer to the HP question. Although the framework posits representations that I think deserve to be called compositional, the kind of compositionality in question will turn out to be different in several important ways from the compositional representations posited by the classical computational conception of mind.

27.2 THE *DYNAMICAL COGNITION* FRAMEWORK: KEY IDEAS

To characterize a physical device mathematically as a dynamical system is to describe mathematically its full behavioural *potentiality profile*—its full profile of potential temporal evolutions from one total physical state to another. Each separate magnitude that is a component of the physical device's total physical state, at any time, is assigned a separate mathematical dimension in the dynamical system's state space. Each potential total physical state of the physical device is thus mathematically represented as a point in the state space. Think now of an n-dimensional state–space as a n-dimensional *surface*, topologically 'moulded' in $n+1$ dimensional space in such a way that steepest descent 'downhill' on the surface corresponds to the way the physical device would evolve through time from any initial total physical state (as represented by a point on the landscape) to successive subsequent states (as represented by successive points on the steepest descent downhill trajectory). This high dimensional 'temporal landscape' is the dynamical system describing all the potential temporal evolutions of the physical device, from any initial physical state it might be in to subsequent physical states.

For an n-node neural network with fixed weights on its connections, the network's physical potentiality-profile is naturally describable mathematically via a dynamical system that is an 'activation-landscape': an n-dimensional surface oriented horizontally in $n + 1$ dimensional space (with a separate dimension in this surface corresponding to each node of the network), with 'downhill' being the direction of time.

For a *self-modifying* physical device that contains a neural network with n nodes and m inter-node connections, and that also contains internal mechanisms that somehow alter connection-strengths diachronically—that is, a physical device that automatically and internally modifies the weights of its own weighted connections—a dynamical system describing the device's physical potentiality profile would be an $n+m$ dimensional 'weight/activation landscape' oriented horizontally in $(n+m)+1$ dimensional space, with 'downhill' on the landscape again being the direction of time.

A fact that needs stressing is that high-dimensional dynamical systems can have enormously complex, and exquisitely subtle, mathematical structure—especially if elements of nonlinearity are at work in the physical devices these dynamical systems describe. (Connectionist networks employ nonlinear activation functions: the new activation of a node is a nonlinear function of the nodes's current activation and its current inputs.) This mathematical structure corresponds physically not to the *intrinsic* physical structure of either the physical device or the physical states of the device, but rather to the device's overall pattern of *physical dispositions*—its full profile of potential temporal evolutions from one physical state to another. One important idea that emerges from connectionism is that this very mathematical structure—the structure of the physical device's physical potentiality profile—can be exploited in nature's evolutionary design of cognitive architecture. Classical computational cognitive science, on the other hand, looks elsewhere for the kind of structure that it seeks to exploit in cognitive architecture—viz., to the *intrinsic* structure of the physical device, and/or to the intrinsic structure of current internal *states* of the device. This difference from classicism is important, because of the much greater structural richness that can be exhibited by a physical device's physical-potentiality profile—the structure describable mathematically by the corresponding high-dimensional dynamical system. If that structure can be suitably exploited in the design of a cognitive engine—and if it does get exploited in nature's design of human cognizers—then this may help get past the limitations of classicism.

Explicit representations in a connectionist network are activation patterns over the network's nodes. The total occurrent cognitive state subserved by a network at a time (for short, the TCS) is realized *mathematically* by a point on the network's high-dimensional activation landscape; and this point, in turn, is realized *physically* by a total activation state of the network itself. Different cognitive components of a TCS need not be separately physically realized by activations over different nodes of the network; rather, every potential cognitive state—no matter how simple or complex in its overall representational content—might be physically realized by a fully distributed activation pattern.

Trained-up connectionist networks typically do information processing in a way that implicitly accommodates certain background information without explicitly representing it during the course of processing—information that is 'in the weights', as connectionists like to say (rather than being explicitly represented via the activation patterns that occur during processing). From the dynamical-systems perspective, the automatic accommodation of this background information is a matter of the *contours on the activation landscape*: the landscape is so shaped that trajectories along it, from one TCS-realizing point to another, are appropriate to the relevant background information. Tienson and I call such background information *morphological content*. The reason for this label is to capture the idea that the content is embodied in long-term structure, rather than in the short-term structure of occurrent physical states of the network. (The structure in question, of course, is not the network's intrinsic structure, but rather the high-dimensional topological structure of the network's physical-potentiality profile.) Perhaps such morphological content, subserved by high-dimensional landscape topography, can be directly exploited in the design of a cognitive engine—and *does* get directly exploited in nature's design of human cognizers—as a way of handling the problem of relevant background information, which makes so much trouble for classicism.

Learning, for connectionist networks, is a matter of following a trajectory through weight space, until the network reaches a point in weight space at which its information processing is systematically appropriate to the to-be-learned content. As the weights get progressively altered during learning, the network's activation landscape gets progressively *moulded*: morphological content gets instilled into the landscape topography. Concurrently, the realization relation from TCSs to points on the activation landscape gets progressively refined: TCSs get repositioned on the landscape, and perhaps certain TCSs get realized on the landscape that were not initially realizable by the network at all (i.e. the cognitive agent becomes capable of explicitly representing information that it could not explicitly represent before). The upshot of learning is that temporal trajectories from one TCS-realizing point to another end up being systematically content-appropriate, relative not only to the content of the explicit representations themselves but also to the content of the background morphological content.

In many extant connectionist models, learning occurs in a supervised way—for example via external application of the 'back propagation' algorithm (cf. Rumelhart, Hinton, and Williams, 1986*a*). But perhaps there are internal weight-change mechanisms that can be grafted onto a neural network in such a way that the self-modifying device's physical potentiality profile—its profile of dispositions to evolve temporally from one point in *activation/weight* space to another—automatically and simultaneously subserves diachronic learning (in addition to synchronic information-processing). A temporal trajectory along the activation/weight landscape from any initial TCS-realizing point would simultaneously lead both (i) to a suitable new TCS-realizing point in *activation* space, and (ii) to a suitable new point in *weight* space—a weight-space point subserving a new activation landscape whose topography morphologically embodies the newly learned information. Indeed, perhaps nature has discovered such internal weight-change mechanisms in the course of human evolution, and has installed them as part of the innate structure of the human brain. If so, then the physical-potentiality profile of the human brain would subserve a high-dimensional activation/weight landscape that is so shaped that trajectories along it constitute not only (i) content-appropriate *synchronic information-processing* that is automatically sensitive to *current* background morphological content, but also (ii) content appropriate *diachronic learning* that automatically results in progressively better-moulded activation landscapes that incorporate an increasingly richer background of morphological content.

Notice that I have not said anything about associative/statistical processing. Although neural networks certainly *can* be used to implement such processing, and although it is plausible that this is how many trained-up connectionist models actually do perform the relatively modular and constrained tasks they have been trained to perform, nothing in the ideas I have been sketching in this section limits neural networks to that kind of processing.

What we are looking for is not a return to associationism, but rather a way to get beyond both associationism and the view that cognition is computation—a way to harness the ideas I have been sketching in an answer to the 'How Possibly?' question posed in Section 27.1. I return now to that question.

27.3 DYNAMICAL COGNITION AND THE 'HOW POSSIBLY?' QUESTION

It will be useful to address the question by conducting a thought experiment. Imagine a god-like being who sets herself the task of creating intelligent creatures much like humans who are to inhabit a planet much like Earth and are to have bodies much like ours. Since this goddess is a stand-in for evolution, I will call her Eva. She imposes various constraints upon herself concerning the physical resources she can employ in designing and creating these intelligent agents, including the following ones. (Some of these constraints could be relaxed in various ways without affecting the substance of the following discussion, but formulating them the way I do will simplify exposition and will make certain key points especially vivid.) First, the cognitive state-transitions are to be implemented in each humanoid via a neural network, with no more than some 10 to 100 billion nodes (roughly the number of actual neurons in actual human brains); the nodes in the network are to be fully connected to one another (although connections will be allowed to have zero connection-weights). Second, the neural network is to be discrete in various ways, so that its transitions from one total-activation state to another will be tractably computable. (For instance, the nodes update their activations in discrete time steps.) Third, she assigns in advance a fixed pool of nodes in the neural network as sensory nodes, and she establishes in advance certain hardwired input-connections from sensory organs to the sensory nodes; likewise, she establishes in advance another fixed pool of nodes as motor nodes, and she establishes in advance certain hardwired output-connections from motor-control nodes to muscles of the humanoid body. (Thus, she imposes in advance the way activation patterns over the sensory nodes will code various sensory stimulations of the body, and the way activation patterns over the motor nodes will code various motor-control instructions.) Fourth, she requires that each total cognitive state (TCS) instantiable by a humanoid creature will be realizable by only one total activation of the creature's neural network; thus, the realization relation from TCSs to total-activation states must be a realization *function*. Fifth, she requires that for each TCS instantiable by a humanoid creature, there will be a unique successor TCS that is instantiable; so cognitive transitions will be *deterministic*, and thus will conform to a cognitive-state transition *function*.

Suppose Eva approaches in two stages the task of designing and building an intelligent humanoid. In stage 1, she will assume a fixed body B of background information, which is to figure as morphological content in the cognitive state-transitions of the creature she is designing. This morphological content will not change, as the creature's mental processes unfold. In stage 2, Eva will introduce into the creature the kind of learning that constitutes altered morphological content.

Let us focus for awhile on stage 1. The cognitive transition function (the CTF, for short) that Eva seeks to implement in the humanoid she is designing is not a *tractably computable* function. (It cannot be, as she realizes, since the Computational Theory of Mind cannot handle the relevance problem.) But she can easily conceive this CTF nonetheless, because of her own divine mental capacity: she conceives it in the form of an enormous, non-recursively specifiable, *list*. She holds the whole list before her divine mind at once. Each item on the list is a pair of TCSs $< S_i, S_i^* >$, where the second element of the pair is the uniquely appropriate immediate cognitive successor to the first member.

Eva also holds before her divine mind another gigantic list: the set of pairs $< W_i, AL_i >$, where W_i is a point in the weight space of the neural network N she is working with, and AL_i is the dynamical system (the activation landscape) describing the physical potentiality profile that N would possess if its connections had the weights specified by W_i. Call this list the *landscape function*, for the network N.

Eva's task of 'cognitive engineering', at stage 1, is to search the landscape function to find a specific activation landscape AL_r of N, as determined by a specific weight setting W_r of N's connections, such that AL_r *subserves* the CTF she has in mind. In order to subserve the CTF, AL_r must be an activation landscape that satisfies the following constraint:

There is a (unique) *realization function* R, from the set of TCSs specified in the CTF into the set of points on AL_r, such that for each pair of TCSs $< S_i, S_i^* >$ in the CTF, the temporal trajectory along AL_r that emanates at point $R(S_i)$ leads to a point P on AL_r such that

1. $R(S_i^*) = P$, and
2. there is no intermediate point Q, in the trajectory along AL_r that leads from $R(S_i)$ to P, such that for some TCS S_j in the the CTF, $R(S_j) = Q$. (Although there can be intermediate points along the trajectory, they must not be points that realize TCSs. S_i^* is thus the immediate *cognitive* successor-state of S_i.)

Eva now achieves her cognitive-design goal by setting the weights on the connections of the network N to the weight-values that jointly constitute point W_r in N's weight space.[1] Under this weight setting, there is a class of total-activation states of the network— viz., those specified by the points on AL_r that are in the range of the function R— such that these total-activation states all have *precisely the right causal roles* vis-à-vis the humanoid's sensory inputs, vis-à-vis its behavioural outputs, and vis-à-vis one another that they need to have in order for them to be realizers of the TCSs to which they are assigned by the realization function R. Collectively these total-activation states really do *realize* the TCSs to which they are assigned by the realization function R, since they perform the causal jobs required of such realizing states. So the humanoid as thus designed will do what Eva wants it to do: its actual and potential temporal evolutions from one TCS to another will all conform to the CTF Eva started with—a cognitive transition function, recall, that is *not tractably computable*.

'But wait a minute!' someone might protest. 'It was specified at the start that the neural network N is *discrete* in various ways, and that its temporal transitions from one total-activation state to another are tractably computable. How then could its *cognitive*-state transitions fail to be tractably computable too?' Well, in fact, this is perfectly possible mathematically: as long as the realization function R is *itself* not tractably computable, then tractably computable state-transitions over total-activation states might well realize state-transitions over TCSs that are *not* tractably computable. Tractable computability of state-transitions is not a feature that is automatically 'transferred upward', via realization, from a lower theoretical level of description to a higher level. On the contrary: such transference via realization will only happen when the realization function itself meets certain constraints; what exactly these constraints are is an important and (I think) insufficiently discussed issue; but surely *one* such constraint is that realization itself must be tractably computable. Eva never imposed *that* resource constraint on herself. On the contrary, the realization function at work in her cognitive-engineering design will certainly *not* be tractably computable—precisely because what she is doing is finding a way to set up a neural network so that its tractably computable transitions over total-activation states will subserve a cognitive transition function that is not tractably computable. (See also Horgan and Tienson (1996: section 4.4) and Horgan (1997).)

It bears emphasis that the rich and subtle topological structure of the activation landscape AL_r figures centrally, as the reason why there actually could exist a suitable realization function R, from the TCSs in the CTF to points on AL_r (corresponding to total-activation states of the neural network), such that under R, tractably computable updating of total-activation states subserves cognitive-state transitions that are not

---

[1] Here I am assuming, of course, that there does exist a realization function R that satisfies the constraints just specified. The existence of such a function is a coherent *conceptual* possibility, and thus the answer being proposed to our 'How Possibly' question consists in setting forth a conceptually possible scenario. (Admittedly, some conceptual possibilities—e.g. the completeness of elementary number theory—turn out not to be mathematically possible.) Also, if Eva were to relax some of her resource constraints—e.g. by allowing herself the use of neural networks that update themselves continuously rather than in discrete time-steps—then yet further possibilities would arise for physically implementing a cognitive transition function that is not tractably computable.

tractably computable. Eva's design for a cognitive agent thus accords with what Tienson and I call *The Fundamental Principle of Cognitive Design*:

> The high-dimensional topography of the activation landscape and the positioning of TCS-realizing points on that landscape are jointly just right to subserve content-appropriate cognitive transitions for the whole vast range of potential TCSs the cognitive system has the capacity to instantiate. (Horgan and Tienson, 1996: 154)

The cognitive transitions are appropriate not only to the explicit content of the TCSs, but also to the specific body B of total background information that Eva had in mind when she laid down the TCF in the first place. This background information is implicitly, morphologically, embodied in the contours of the activation landscape—contours that determine how the cognitive trajectories evolve from one TCS to another.

Let us now consider stage 2 of Eva's design project. The CTF she implemented in stage 1 was *synchronic* with respect to background information: that information was held fixed and constant, rather than being changed and updated during cognitive processing. But what she really seeks to implement, in the humanoid she is designing, is a *diachronic* cognitive-transition function (for short, a DCTF): one that incorporates content-appropriate transitions not only in total occurrent cognitive *states*, but also in the total background information. This DCTF, like the original synchronic CTF she implemented in stage 1, will be a transition function that is not tractably computable, and also is not recursively specifiable. Eva, employing her divine mental capacity, brings before her mind the entire DCTF she seeks to implement, in the form of a gigantic *list* of specific cognitive transitions. Each item on the list is a pair of the form $<<S_i, B_j>, <S_i^*, B_j^*>>$, where S_i and S_i^* are each a total occurrent cognitive state, and B_j and B_j^* are each a total body of background information. Thus, each entry $<<S_i, B_j>, <S_i^*, B_j^*>>$ in Eva's list-specification of the DCTF says that if the cognitive agent is in TCS S_i and has total background information B_j, then the agent should next go into TCS S_i^* and have total background information B_j^*.

Once again Eva turns to the range of eligible high-dimensional dynamical systems, in order to find one that will subserve the DCTF she seeks to implement. Each of these dynamical systems is a *weight/activation* landscape: a landscape on which temporal trajectories progress from one point in weight-plus-activation space to another. These landscapes describe a range of physical-potentiality profiles that could be possessed by the self-modifying brain-like device that Eva might install in the humanoid she is designing—where each eligible internal-control system consists of both (i) the neural network N she plans to install, and (ii) some specific weight-change mechanism (perhaps another neural network) that she might couple to the network N. Using her divine mental capacities, she surveys the vast range of eligible dynamical systems, and she finds a weight/activation landscape WAL_r that *subserves* the DCTF she has in mind. In order to subserve the DCTF, WAL_r must be a weight/activation that satisfies the following constraint:

There is a (unique) *realization function* R, from the set of items in the domain and range of the DCTF into the set of points on WAL$_r$, such that for each pair $<<S_i, B_j>, <S_i{}^*, B_j{}^*>>$ in the DCTF, the temporal trajectory along WAL$_r$ from point $R(<S_i, B_j>)$ leads to a point P on WAL$_r$ such that

1. $R(< S_i{}^*, B_j{}^* >) = P$, and
2. there is no intermediate point Q, along the trajectory along AL$_r$ that leads from $R(S_i)$ to P, such that for some pair $<S_k, B_k>$ in the DCTF, $R(<S_k, B_k>) = Q$. (Although there can be intermediate points along the trajectory, they must not be points that realize items in the DCTF. $<S_i{}^*, B_j{}^*>$ is thus the immediate *cognitive* successor-state of $<S_i, B_j>$.)

As I said at the beginning of this section, our thought-experimental goddess Eva is a stand-in for evolution. The blind forces of natural selection might have carried out the design task just described as stage 2. (There would not necessarily be a stage 1 along the way. I introduced stage 1 for expository purposes: it is easier to convey the whole picture by starting with the special case of a synchronic cognitive transition function.) So the Dynamical Cognition framework for cognitive science provides an answer to the 'How Possibly?' question.

27.4 NON-CLASSICAL COMPOSITIONALITY

Let us return to Fodor's dilemma about how the mind works. Suppose, with classicism, that the essence of a mental representation is its intrinsic compositional structure. It syntactically encodes content in virtue of this kind of structure. The structure is entirely *local* to the representation itself, and is context-invariant. The first horn of the dilemma is that a representation cannot play the kind of causal role that is context-sensitive, in a way that is responsive to global aspects of the cognitive agent's background epistemic commitments, if the representation's causal role is determined solely by *its own* syntactic structure—structure that is local and intrinsic, and hence context-invariant. The second horn is this: insofar as the causal role of a local representation depends on the syntactic structure of a whole *host* of representations all of which have the same kind of local, intrinsic, compositional structure, this makes it computationally intractable to accommodate global aspects of the background of epistemic commitments.

Part of the problem is the assumption that the processing needs to be *computation* over mental representations—manipulation of mental representations on the basis of *programmable rules* that operate on the syntactic structure of the representations. The DC framework jettisons that. But another part of the problem is the kind of structure that is relied upon in the system of representations: classical compositionality, which is local and intrinsic, and thus is context-invariant. In order to implement content-sensitive cognitive processing that accommodates global aspects of the agent's background epistemic commitments, the cognitive system needs the right kind of formal/mathematical structure in its system of representations. (This retains a core good idea from classicism: suitably content-sensitive processing is a matter of suitably *structure-sensitive* processing, where the structure in question somehow *encodes* the relevant content.)

Is there compositionality in the representational system posited by the DC framework? Well, not *classical* compositionality, certainly—a kind of syntactic structure that is local and intrinsic to the representations. (Mathematically, after all, TCSs are realized as *points* in a high-dimensional state-space—structureless mathematical objects.[2]) But consider the etymology of the term 'compositional'. It comes from the verb 'compose', which means 'put together'—as does the Latin predecessor 'componere'. What is structurally crucial about all the representations potentially instantiable by a cognitive agent (all the TCS-realizing points in weight/activation space), according to the DC framework, is *how they are collectively positioned, relative to one another, on a suitably shaped weight/activation landscape.*

So it is certainly true, within the DC framework, that potentially-instantiable mental representations need to be *collectively* 'put together' just right, in terms of the mathematical structure of the representational system: the TCSs need to be realized by points that are suitably *positioned* just right relative to one another, on a weight/activation that itself is suitably *shaped* so that cognitive trajectories along the landscape are automatically appropriate not only to the TCSs that get instantiated in the trajectory, but also to implicit background epistemic commitments. I will call this holistic kind of 'put-together-ness' of representations *non-classical compositionality*. It is the sort of compositionality that seems to be needed in a cognitive system, in order to solve the relevance problem—that is, in order to subserve the holistic aspects of abductive inference, belief formation, planning, and other such forms of cognition.

There are very substantial differences between non-classical compositionality and classical compositionality. I have already stressed that non-classical compositional structure is largely or entirely non-intrinsic and thus non-local: it accrues to mental representations (i.e. TCS-realizing points) not by virtue of their intrinsic mathematical structure—points don't *have* intrinsic mathematical structure, after all—but rather by virtue of their positional *relations* to one another on a suitably shaped weight-activation landscape. But there are a number of further important differences too, that result from the relationality of non-classical compositionality and/or from the extent to which tractable computability is eschewed within the DS framework. I will mention several, by way of their contrasts with classicism.

---

[2] This is not to deny that there can be relations among points in a state-space that closely mimic classical compositional operations on structured representations—for instance, relations corresponding to mathematical operations like addition or multiplication of vectors. Such relations are exploited in the format for connectionist representations proposed by Smolensky (1990); for discussion of Smolensky's tensor product representations in relation to the DC framework, see Horgan and Tienson (1996: sections 5.1.2 and 9.3.2).

In classicism, the class of representations is recursively specifiable, and the syntactic categories and syntactic modes of composition are independently characterizable—all without any recourse to semantics. Dynamical updating of these representational states can also be characterized purely in formal, non-semantic terms, viz., via programmable representation-level rules that advert only to the syntax of the representations and not to their content. On the classicist picture, this autonomous regime of syntactic structure and formal symbol-manipulation *mirrors the semantic regime*: the semantically compositional contents of intentional mental states are encoded via the compositional syntax of the mental representations that possess these contents, and content-sensitivity in the dynamical updating of intentional mental states is achieved via structure-sensitivity in the formal symbol-manipulation. (Syntactic transformations implement coherent thought because the purely formal symbol-manipulation rules encode exceptionless dynamical transition rules governing intentional mental states themselves.) At the physical level, constituents are separately tokened, and algorithmic operations over classical compositional structure are implemented physically by suitable physical operations on the physically distinct constituent-representations of the structurally complex physical representations.

The DC framework, in contrast, eschews each of the following classicist ideas: (i) the recursive specifiability of representational states; (ii) the idea that state-transitions are tractably computable and therefore conform to exceptionless, programmable, symbol-manipulation rules; and (iii) the idea of an autonomous syntactic regime. Syntactic structure is *not* eschewed, however, although it is conceived quite differently than in classicism. The DC framework features an intimate intertwining or entanglement of syntactic and semantic compositionality—an interpenetration so thorough that the formal/mathematical features that count as syntactic only do so by virtue of the systematically content-appropriate cognitive processing they subserve. There is thus no clean autonomy of syntax and semantics. Rather, what makes certain points on an activation landscape count as representations in the first place, and likewise what makes for compositionality in the overall system of such representations, is the way these specific points—as so positioned on the (suitably shaped) landscape vis-à-vis each other, figure in dynamical trajectories that constitute content-appropriate cognitive processing.[3] There is indeed a non-classical kind of compositional *syntax* within the system of representations, because certain representational jobs get accomplished via

---

[3] One kind of argument for syntactic compositionality is that it provides an explanation of the fact that thought is *systematic*—where systematicity roughly amounts to this: for any relational predicate R and any singular expressions a, b, c, and d, if a cognitive system can instantiate intentional states whose contents are aRb and cRd, then it can also instantiate states whose contents are cRb and aRd. (See, for instance, Fodor and Pylyshyn (1988), Fodor and McLaughlin (1990).) One might think, however, that the systematicity of thought cannot be explained this way unless compositional syntax is identifiable autonomously; otherwise, it looks as though content-systematicity is being presupposed as a partial determinant of holistic syntactic compositionality, rather than being explained by compositional syntax. Perhaps this is so. But that would be a problem only if there is no other plausible way to explain content-systematicity than by appeal to autonomous compositional syntax. In Horgan and Tienson (1996), an alternative explanation is offered: viz., (i) that real-world cognizers, in order to get on in the world, need a representational repertoire so vast that its implementation requires compositional syntax, and

the positional relations of the pertinent points—jobs like *naming* and *predicating*. But such syntactic structure is a matter of the position-based *commonality of causal roles in thought* of representational states: commonalities appropriate to reference to the same specific individual (the name-role), and to the attribution of the same specific property or relation (the predicate role). (See Horgan and Tienson (1996: ch. 5 and section 9.3 of ch. 9), where this non-classical approach to syntax is elaborated in more detail and is applied to elucidate the non-classical compositional syntax exhibited by connectionist representations like the tensor-product representations of Smolensky (1988*b*, 1990) and the recursive distributed representations of Pollack (1990) and Berg (1992).)

Within the DC framework, non-classical compositional structure is not tractably computable. There are no algorithms for determining the kind of compositional structure being envisioned here. This is closely related, of course, to the fact that the relevant kinds of cognitive-state transitions subserved by the formal/mathematical structure are themselves not tractably computable. The compositional structure need not be tractably computable, since the system does not operate by executing programmable rules that *operate* on tractably computable classical compositional structure (as do classical systems).

In the DC framework there is no need for separately tokenable constituent representations. Physically speaking, representations with complex content can be fully-distributed activation-patterns over large pools of neuron-like units (corresponding mathematically to points in a dynamical system's state-space), and there need not be physically distinct *parts* of these activation patterns that constitute semantic constituent-representations. Distinct representations, physically realized as activation-patterns over the nodes of a neural network, can be physically superimposed over the same nodes. The total-activation state that results from such a superimposition of activation-patterns will physically realize a new point on the activation landscape, suitably positioned to initiate a dynamical trajectory that is appropriate to the total intentional content of this activation state (and is also appropriate to the background content that is morphologically embodied in the topological contours of the activation landscape). Representational constituency, for total-activation states, is not a matter of the intrinsic physical structure of those states, because a total-activation state is the physical implementation of a structureless point in a dynamical system. Rather, constituency is a matter of how the various points with representational content are positioned relative to one another in the dynamical system, and how the slopes on the activation landscape subserve dynamical trajectories from one total cognitive state to another.

(ii) that compositional syntax yields content-systematicity as a byproduct. (See Horgan and Tienson (1996: sections 5.2–5.4 and section 9.3.1), where systematicity and productivity are addressed from the perspective of the DC framework.) Although this alternative explanation still invokes compositional syntax, it does not require syntactic structure to be autonomously characterizable, independently of content.

27.5 CONCLUSION

I have motivated and described the non-classical framework that Tienson and I recommend for serious consideration within cognitive science—a framework that addresses the relevance problem by eschewing the idea that cognitive processing conforms to algorithmic rules of symbol-manipulation, and instead seeks to exploit the rich mathematical structure of high-dimensional dynamical systems. I have also sketched a new and different notion of *compositionality* for mental representation that goes naturally with this framework—and thus that also deserves serious consideration within cognitive science.

Given the conception of cognitive processing here set forth, it may well turn out that much of human cognition is so exquisitely subtle and complex that it is not possible for us humans ever to understand *in detail* how it works. Weather prediction comes to mind, as a basis for comparision. The evolution of weather on Earth is so complex that typically it is not possible to predict in detail how weather systems will develop over periods of time longer than a day or two. But in important ways the prospects for understanding cognition in detail look bleaker than weather prediction. At least we can hope to articulate and understand the *general physical laws* that govern the evolution of weather systems, even if we cannot *use* these laws to accurately predict the weather over very long periods of time. In the case of cognitive processes like human abductive inference, however, there probably do not even *exist* fully general and exceptionless laws or rules governing competent cognitive-state transitions—this is what is suggested by the relevance problem, and by the picture of human cognitive-state transitions as not conforming to any tractably computable cognitive-transition function.

But even if it should turn out that we can never hope to understand in complete detail how the human cognitive system manages the holistic aspects of cognition, there is still surely lots that we *can* learn and *can* understand—including, perhaps, what the right answer is to the 'How Possible?' question, and why the details of holistically content-appropriate processing might be too complex to lend themselves to traditional forms of scientific explanation.

CHAPTER 28

THE DUAL-MECHANISM DEBATE

MARTINA PENKE

28.1 INTRODUCTION

How inflected words are composed and represented in the mind has inspired a heated and long-standing debate not only in the field of linguistics but in the cognitive sciences in general. In brief the controversy centres on the issue of whether regular inflected word forms such as the English past tense form *laughed* are composed by a mental rule that combines a word stem (*laugh*) with an affix (*-ed*) or whether they are stored like simple words in the mental lexicon. This might seem an idle question to pursue and hardly interesting to anyone outside the field of linguistics. However, at the heart of the debate is the question of whether or not mental rules that operate on language specific abstract categories or symbols—such as an inflectional rule 'V + -ed$_{[PAST]}$ → *past tense*'—are part of cognitive processing (cf. e.g. Rumelhart and McClelland, 1986b; Rumelhart et al., 1986b; Elman et al., 1996; Pinker, 1999; Marcus, 2001). The symbolic view of cognitive processing assumes that complex word forms are structurally composed out of component parts by application of a mental rule that combines components displaying the right abstract features such as [+V] or [+PAST]. An anti-symbolic view is in contrast expressed in connectionism, a branch of the cognitive sciences where human behaviour is simulated in artificial network models.[1] Based on modelling data such connectionist approaches deny that regular inflection is based on a compositional mental operation that combines a verbal stem and an affix. Instead, regular (e.g. *laughed*) and irregular inflected forms (e.g. *sang*) are stored just as simple words in an associative network

---

[1] Connectionism is not tied to the anti-symbolic view (cf. e.g. Hinton, 1990; Shastri and Ajjanagadde, 1993; Marcus, 2001); however, it is the anti-symbolic, often called eliminativist, school of connectionisms that is relevant for the Dual-Mechanism debate. In the following, I will, therefore, use the term connectionism only to refer to anti-symbolic, eliminativist connectionist approaches.

structure. Hence, in representation and processing, inflected forms are structurally non-compositional.

Debates between proponents of symbolic and anti-symbolic views have also been led in other fields of cognitive science, for instance in the areas of human categorization or reasoning where instance-based models are opposed to rule- and feature-based models (cf. e.g. Pothos, 2005). However, the debate on the representation and processing of inflected forms such as *laughed* and *sang* has played a central role in this larger controversy about symbolic or anti-symbolic positions on human cognition, since the cognitive mechanisms underlying regular and irregular inflection seem easy to investigate. On the one hand, distinct cognitive operations are overtly reflected by different word forms for regular and irregular inflected forms. On the other hand, potential interfering factors are controlled for since regular and irregular inflected forms share important properties: they comprise only a word, they have the same categorical status in grammar (both being verb forms for instance), and they realize the same morphosyntactic features (for example [PAST]). Steven Pinker has therefore claimed that regular and irregular inflected forms could play the same important role for cognitive science as the fruitfly has played for genetics:

> Perhaps regular verbs can become the fruitflies of the neuroscience of language—their recombining units are easy to extract and visualize, and they are well studied, small, and easy to breed. (Pinker, 1997: 548)

In contrast to most other contributions to this handbook, the focus of this chapter is not on compositionality as such, but on the issue of whether complex regular inflected word forms are structurally compositional or not. In what follows, I will provide a brief overview of the debate that has sparked off this issue by tracing the development of the debate, sketching the two opposing positions (Sections 28.2 and 28.3), and highlighting some of the critical issues pursued in the debate (Section 28.4).

28.2 Starting the debate

Since the cognitive turn in linguistics set off by the work of Noam Chomsky (1957, 1959; cf. Gardner, 1985),[2] language is conceived of as a mental knowledge system that is independent of other cognitive domains (i.e. domain-specific)[3] and that contains abstract linguistic categories (symbols) such as [+V] or [+N] and combinatorial cognitive operations which serve to combine those categories to hierarchically structured representations. Regular inflected words have also been conceived of as the product

---

[2] Chomsky's (1957) *Syntactic Structures* and his criticism of Skinner's behaviouristic approach to language (Skinner, 1957; Chomsky, 1959) are regarded as milestones in the development of a mentalistic approach to cognitive science. For an historical overview on the researchers and ideas preparing the cognitive turn in science and particularly linguistics see Gardner (1985) and Newmeyer (1980).

[3] The term 'domain-specific' is often used as a substitute for the notions of modularity and autonomy (Fodor, 1983) in the recent literature.

of such a combinatorial symbolic operation which combines an affix expressing a specific grammatical information with a word stem of a specific grammatical category.
Over-regularization errors in language acquisition were considered as providing clear
evidence for this view.

28.2.1 Over-regularization errors—an example case for mental rule application

Over-regularization errors such as *singed* (instead of *sang*) where the regular inflectional
pattern is overapplied to a verb that is irregular inflected in the target language are one
of the striking phenomena in child language. Consider as an example the acquisition of
German participle inflection.[4] In German, participles consist of a prefix *ge-*, a verb stem,
and an ending. Regular participles such as *getanzt* ('danced') are built with the basic verb
stem and are suffixed with -*t*. In contrast, irregular participles such as *gesungen* ('sung')
are built with a participle stem that often shows a change in the stem vowel (e.g. stem
sing 'sing') and always take the ending -*n*.[5]

The acquisition of irregular participle forms displays a very characteristic u-shaped
developmental curve (see Fig. 28.1). As exemplified here by longitudinal data from the
German child Eva, the first irregular participles produced by children are typically correct. This stage is followed by a stage where children overapply the regular inflectional
pattern to stems that have irregular inflected participle forms in the target language.
Such an over-regularization error would, for example, result in the participle form
*gesingt instead of the correct irregular form *gesungen*. The weeding out of such over-
regularization errors takes some time in language acquisition, during which correctness
scores for irregular participles rise again and finally reach the adult correctness level
(cf. Marcus et al., 1992).

Regular inflected participle forms, in contrast, do not display a u-shaped developmental curve (cf. Fig. 28.1). Correctness scores are high throughout development and
irregularized forms such as **getanzen*, where the irregular pattern of participle formation is overapplied to a regular verb (stem *tanz*, correct regular participle form *getanzt*
'danced'), are very rare. Whereas the mean over-regularization rate in Eva's data is at
37.1 per cent during the observation period, the mean irregularization rate is at only
4.2 per cent (for similar data cf. Marcus et al., 1992; Clahsen and Rothweiler, 1993).

[4] Most research on the Dual-Mechanism debate has centred on the English past tense (cf. Pinker,
1999 for an overview). In English, regular past tense forms are formed with the suffix -*ed* (e.g. *laugh—
laughed*), irregular past tense forms, in contrast, often only display a change of the stem vowel (e.g. *sing—
sang*). Hence, there is only a regular ending (-*ed*), but there is no ending that always appears on irregular
inflected forms. As a consequence, the regularity or irregularity of inflected forms is confounded with the
presence or absence of an inflectional ending in English. Due to this confound, English is not ideally suited
to investigate issues deriving from the Dual-Mechanism debate. Therefore, languages such as German
where irregular inflected forms have typical inflectional endings too have come into focus (cf. Clahsen,
1999; Penke, 2006 for an overview).
[5] I will henceforth ignore the prefix *ge-* which is phonologically conditioned and of no importance in
the Dual-Mechanism debate.

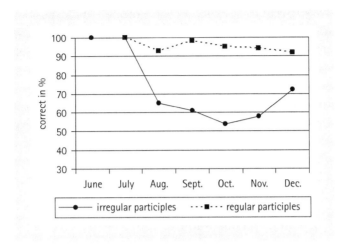

FIGURE 28.1 Correctness scores for regular and irregular participle forms in the data of the German child Eva (cf. Penke, 2006: 54)

These data show that the regular inflectional pattern is much more productive than the irregular one in child language. Until 1986 researchers working in the generative linguistic paradigm regarded this greater productivity of the regular inflectional pattern as clear evidence that the child acquires a regular inflectional rule, that is a mental operation that combines a verb stem and an affix (here the participle affix -t). This affix is identified and generalized during acquisition as more and more pairs of stem and participle form are acquired and form and meaning relationships are extracted. Once this affix is established, affixation can freely apply to any instance of the category verb for which no irregular participle form has been learned and stored in the mental lexicon yet—and over-regularization errors result.[6]

28.2.2 Connectionist networks challenge the symbolic view to regular inflection

In 1986, however, Rumelhart and McClelland published a very influential article (Rumelhart and McClelland, 1986b) in which they set out to seriously challenge the

[6] An alternative view in linguistics attributes over-regularizations as *gesingt and over-irregularizations as *getanzen to analogical extensions of existing patterns in the language. Note, however, that analogical extension of irregular inflectional patterns requires that the involved words display a certain overlap in phonological form (e.g. sing—sung: spling—?), whereas over-regularizations do not require a similarity in phonological form but apply freely to all instances of a specific category, even if these instances display no similarity to any word of the language (e.g. past tense of ploamph: ploamphed). This difference has been taken as evidence against the view that a single mechanism (i.e. analogical extension) underlies over-regularizations and over-irregularizations and has been claimed to suggest a qualitative distinction between stored irregular inflected forms and compositional affix-based regular inflection (cf. Prasada and Pinker, 1993; Penke, 2006).

view that over-regularizations in child language are due to the acquisition of a symbolic mental operation and that, hence, regular inflected forms are structurally composed out of a stem and an affix morpheme. They constructed a connectionist network model that—so they claimed—was able to simulate the acquisition of the English past tense inflection without abstracting a symbolic mental rule.

Connectionist networks, such as the Rumelhart and McClelland network, consist of several layers of simple computational units that are interconnected by weighted connections. The incoming activation that reaches a unit through its connections to other units is summed up and computed by the unit according to a specific implemented transfer function. The activation resulting from this computation, the output activation, is then transferred to other units of the network to which the unit is connected. During learning the connectionist network has to modify the activation weights connecting the units of the network in such a way as to produce a desired correct output activation at the output layer of the network for any given input activation presented at the input layer of the net. To achieve this goal, during learning the output activation generated by the network for a given input activation is compared to the desired correct output activation. A learning algorithm then modifies the connection weights in the network in such a way as to further approximate the desired output activation. Such learning cycles are repeated until the network does no longer achieve any progress (cf. Hinton, 1992; Elman et al., 1996; Marcus, 2001 for an overview on the architecture and functioning of connectionist networks). Thus in a connectionist network, learning, representation, and processing of knowledge are based on simple associative connections between units of the input and the output layer.

The Rumelhart and McClelland model was trained to associate the phonological representation of a given verb stem with the phonological representation of its respective past tense form. After 200 learning cycles, the network was not only able to produce correct past tense forms for the learned verbs, but it could also produce past tense forms for verbs new to the network. Moreover, during learning the network went through a stage where it produced over-regularizations of the regular past tense ending -ed to irregular verbs, similar to over-regularizations in language acquisition. Rumelhart and McClelland were thus able to demonstrate that learning based on associative mechanisms is not unproductive. The activation weights of the network's connections are influenced by factors such as the frequency with which a particular (phonological) activation pattern occurs or the similarity (phonological) activation patterns display. Confronted with a new verb the network would react with the most frequent (phonological) output activation pattern or it would use a (phonological) similarity in the input activation patterns between a new verb and already learned verbs to produce an output activation pattern. Over-regularizations of the regular past tense pattern resulted because during this learning stage the output pattern representing the -ed ending was the most frequent one presented to the network. Based on this simulation Rumelhart and McClelland concluded:

> We have, we believe, provided a distinct alternative to the view that children learn the rules of English past-tense formation in any explicit sense. We have shown

that a reasonable account of the acquisition of past tense can be provided without recourse to the notion of a 'rule' as anything more than a *description* of the language. (Rumelhart and McClelland, 1986*b*: 267) (emphasis as in original)

As this quotation indicates, the goal of Rumelhart and McClelland was not only to provide evidence against the view that regular inflected forms are composed out of a stem and an affix morpheme, but also to challenge the reality of mental symbolic rules in general. According to their view, learning and knowledge representations that are based on associative connections are sufficient to capture and explain human cognition. Representations making use of abstract symbols (such as [+V]) or rules operating over such symbols (such as 'V + -ed → *past tense*') are considered to be simply descriptive artefacts (cf. Rumelhart and McClelland, 1986*b*; Rumelhart et al., 1986*b*; Elman et al., 1996, and for an extensive discussion of the anti-symbolic position expressed in this school of connectionism Marcus, 2001).

28.3 THE DUALISTIC VIEW TO INFLECTION

In reaction to the connectionist network model presented by Rumelhart and McClelland (1986*b*), Steven Pinker and colleagues presented a dualistic model to capture the representation and processing of inflected word forms (cf. Pinker and Prince, 1988; Pinker, 1999). Whereas in connectionist models all inflected forms, regular and irregular ones, are represented in an associative, non-compositional network structure, Pinker's *Dual-Mechanism Model* states that the representations and the mechanisms involved in the processing of regular and irregular inflectional forms are fundamentally different. Regular inflected forms (e.g. past tense forms like *laughed*) are built on the fly by a compositional operation combining a word stem (e.g. the verb stem *laugh*) with an affix (e.g. the past tense affix -*ed*). Irregular inflected forms such as the past tense form *sang* are, in contrast, not built by a combination of stem and affix, but are stored as whole word forms in an associative network structure in the mental lexicon—just as in connectionist network models.[7] Since two qualitatively different cognitive mechanisms are responsible for regular and irregular inflected forms, approaches such as Pinker's Dual-Mechanism Model are called dualistic and they are opposed to unitary approaches to inflection such as connectionist network models that assume a single non-compositional network structure for both regular and irregular inflected forms (cf. Pinker and Prince, 1988; Pinker, 1999, and for an overview and discussion of connectionist models of the past tense Marcus, 2001).[8]

[7] A theoretical spell-out of the dualistic view is given in the morphological framework of Minimalist Morphology (Wunderlich, 1996*b*).

[8] An opposing unitary view of inflectional morphology is advocated by approaches which claim that regular and irregular inflectional morphology are both structurally compositional and consist of stem and affix morpheme (e.g. Chomsky and Halle, 1968; Halle and Marantz, 1993). Naturally, researchers advocating this type of unitary approach to inflection have also opposed dualistic accounts of inflection

Dualistic approaches to inflection assume that different representations and mental operations are involved in regular and irregular inflection, whereas connectionist network models advocate a similar, non-compositional representation for regular and irregular inflected forms. Therefore, proponents of the dualistic view of inflection have set out to provide evidence for their claim that the mechanisms and representations involved in regular and irregular inflection are indeed qualitatively distinct. This goal has inspired psycho- and neurolinguistic research over the last 20 years. During this time a number of different experimental effects and techniques have been used to test the different predictions that derive from these two approaches. An overview of the extensive research that has been carried out on the representation and computation of inflectional morphology until now is beyond the scope of this chapter (see Clahsen, 1999; Pinker, 1999; Penke, 2006 for an overview). Instead, my aim is to present some of the core evidence that has been brought forward as evidence for a qualitative difference between regular and irregular inflected forms.

28.3.1 Evidence that regular and irregular inflection are subserved by independent modules

Underlying the dualistic view to inflection—and also language in general—is the assumption that the human language capacity is autonomous from other cognitive domains or modules (i.e. it is domain-specific) and consists of task-specific and independent submodules carrying out different types of computations on different types of representations (*autonomy* and *modularity*, cf. Fodor, 1983). Under this view, regular and irregular inflection are dependent on two independent modules of the human language faculty: a computational component where affixation is carried out and a component in which stored information is retrieved from the mental lexicon.[9] If this view is correct, than brain damage can in principle result in the selective impairment of

(e.g. Embick and Marantz, 2005). However, both unitary rule-based models and dualistic models of inflection stress the importance of compositional symbolic operations in producing inflected forms. In this they are united against the anti-symbolic connectionist view that claims all inflected forms to be non-compositional in structure. Since the focus of this article is on the debate between symbolic and anti-symbolic views on inflectional morphology, I will not further discuss the debate between unitary and dualistic symbolic approaches to inflection.

Note also that a related debate between dualistic and unitary compositional and non-compositional views of morphology has, meanwhile, been led with regard to semantically transparent (e.g. *airmail* or *government*) vs. semantically opaque word formations (e.g. *blackmail* or *department*). As in the debate on the structural composition of inflected word forms that is the focus of this article, the debate on the compositionality of derived and compound words has waged over the issue of whether and which complex words are decomposed into their constituent parts or stored as unanalysed whole word forms in the mental lexicon (see e.g. Plaut and Gonnerman, 2000; Schreuder and Baayen, 1995; McQueen and Cutler, 1998).

[9] In a broader perspective, the distinction between regular and irregular inflected forms has been argued to exemplify the distinction between a mental lexicon where words are stored together with learned idiosyncratic information and a mental grammar component that contains the rules to generate

specific submodules of the language capacity, such as the ones underlying regular and irregular inflection (*fractionation* assumption, cf. Caramazza, 1984). Thus, we should find language disorders that either selectively affect the regular inflectional component with the irregular inflectional module spared or, vice versa, selectively affect the irregular inflectional component leaving the regular submodule unimpaired. A failure in finding such selective deficits would, on the other hand, weaken the dualistic view on inflection. Whether or not language disorders can be found that selectively affect specific language submodules has, thus, been seen as a test for the dualistic approach to inflection.

Indeed, research during the last ten years has provided ample evidence that deficits with inflectional morphology might selectively affect only regular or only irregular inflection. Consider for example Broca's aphasia, a language impairment caused by strokes that predominantly affect left frontal brain regions and that leads to pronounced problems with the production of inflectional morphology. In an experiment conducted with thirteen German Broca's aphasic speakers, we elicited participle forms for thirty-nine regular and thirty-nine irregular verbs, carefully matched for word and participle frequency as well as phonological complexity (Penke and Westermann, 2006). A comparison of the correctness scores for regular and irregular participles revealed that regular inflection was largely spared in the thirteen aphasic subjects. On average, 91.2 per cent of the regular inflected participles were produced correctly. In contrast, the correctness score for irregular inflected participles was at only 67 per cent, and thus significantly lower ($t(12) = 4.057$, $p = .002$). These data indicate that irregular participle formation can be selectively impaired in German Broca's aphasics, while regular inflection is not affected.[10]

The observation that language deficits might selectively affect only regular or only irregular inflection has been taken as evidence against unitary accounts to inflection since it seems hard to explain how a unitary mechanism can be distorted in such a way as to only affect one type of inflected forms, but not the other (e.g. Pinker, 1999; Ullman et al., 1997, but see Penke and Westermann, 2006). Accordingly, selective impairments

composite structures such as sentences and complex words out of the stored elements in the mental lexicon (cf. Pinker, 1999; Clahsen, 1999).

[10] Deficits that selectively affect only regular or only irregular inflection have meanwhile been observed across languages in a number of acquired and developmental language disorders such as agrammatic Broca's aphasia (Ullman et al., 1997; Penke et al., 1999), progressive semantic aphasia (Patterson et al., 2001), Specific Language Impairment (Gopnik and Crago, 1991; van der Lely and Ullman, 2001), or Williams syndrome (Clahsen and Almazan, 1998; Penke and Krause, 2004; see Penke, 2006, 2008 for an overview). Note, however, that whether regular or irregular inflection is impaired in a specific language disorder is language-dependent. Thus, whereas English-speaking individuals with agrammatic Broca's aphasia or Specific Language Impairment display a selective vulnerability of regular inflection, affected speakers of languages that display richer inflectional systems (such as Catalan, Dutch, German, or Spanish) do not show an impairment of regular but of irregular inflection (e.g. Clahsen and Rothweiler, 1993; Penke et al., 1999; de Diego Balaguer et al., 2004; Penke and Westermann, 2006). These language-specific differences in the effects of particular language disorders have been attributed to differences in the importance morphological markers have in different languages (see Penke, 2006, 2008; Penke and Westermann, 2006 for overview and discussion).

of regular or irregular inflection are considered to provide evidence that regular and irregular inflection are due to two different cognitive mechanisms that can be selectively affected by brain damage.

28.3.2 Evidence for the morphological decomposition of regular forms

Selective deficits of regular or irregular inflection have been taken as evidence that regular and irregular inflection represent two different modules in the human mind/brain. According to dualistic approaches to inflection regular inflected forms are combined via productive affixation of an inflectional affix to a word's stem, whereas irregular inflected forms are not composed out of component morphemes but are stored as fully inflected forms in the mental lexicon (cf. Pinker, 1999; Wunderlich, 1996b). Evidence that regular inflected forms are composed out of a stem and an affix, whereas irregular inflected forms are not, comes from psycholinguistic studies making use of the priming effect.

The priming effect occurs, for instance, in lexical-decision tasks where subjects have to decide as quickly as possible whether a visually or auditorily presented word is an existing word or not. The time required to make this decision is measured. If the same word is presented again during the experiment, the lexical-decision time for this word is shorter compared to its first presentation. The difference in decision time observed for the first and second presentation of a given word is called the priming effect. Priming is explained as follows: the activation of a lexical entry lowers the activation threshold for this entry. Therefore, lexical-access times are quicker when the word is presented again (for a thorough discussion of the priming effect see Balota, 1994).

Sonnenstuhl, Eisenbeiss, and Clahsen (1999) used the cross-modal priming paradigm to investigate whether or not regular and irregular inflected German participles are decomposed into stem and affix. They made use of the observation that a shorter reaction time is also observed when inflected forms such as the German verb form *plane* ('plan$_{[1SG]}$') are presented for a second time in a lexical-decision experiment. In their experiment, they compared lexical-decision times for 1st person singular forms such as *plane* that were either preceded by an identical verb form (1st presentation *plane*, 2nd presentation *plane* = identity condition) or by a participle form (1st presentation *geplant* 'planned', 2nd presentation *plane* = morphological condition) (cf. Fig. 28.2).

In the identity condition, the reaction time for the inflected 1st person singular form (e.g. *plane*) is shorter when the form is presented the second time compared to its first presentation. The reaction time for the second identical presentation of the inflected 1st person singular form can thus be used as a baseline to establish whether a priming effect is also induced in the morphological test condition. In this condition, Sonnenstuhl et al. first presented a regular participle form such as *geplant* before they presented the critical 1st person singular form *plane*. Again they measured the time it took their subjects to decide that the 1st person singular form *plane* is a German word. Sonnenstuhl et al.

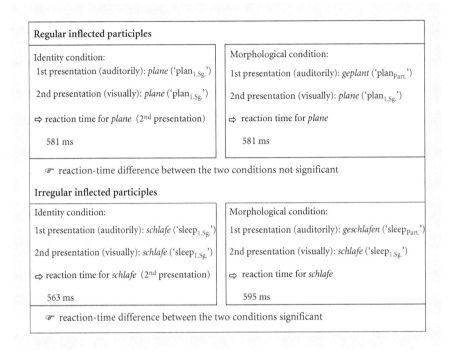

FIGURE 28.2 Exemplification of the experimental design of Sonnenstuhl et al. (1999)

(1999) found that the mean reaction time for the 1st person singular form *plane* in the morphological condition (581 ms) did not differ from the identity condition where the form *plane* was presented twice (581 ms). This observation indicates that a regular participle form such as *geplant* is as good a prime for the inflected form *plane* as is the form *plane* itself.

What if an irregular participle such as *geschlafen* ('slept') precedes its regular inflected 1st person singular form (e.g. *schlafe*)? In this case, the mean lexical-decision time for the 1st person singular form *schlafe* in the morphological condition (1st presentation *geschlafen*, 2nd presentation *schlafe*, mean reaction time for *schlafe* 595 ms) is significantly longer compared to the corresponding identity condition where *schlafe* is presented twice (mean reaction time for 2nd presentation of *schlafe* 563 ms). This result indicates that an irregular participle such as *geschlafen* does not prime the inflected form *schlafe* as effectively as a regular participle such as *geplant* primes the inflected form *plane*.

Under the dualistic view of inflection, the explanation for these findings is straightforward. A regular participle such as *geplant* is decomposed into its constituent parts, the stem *plan* and the participle affix -*t*, during lexical access. The stem *plan* then activates its entry in the mental lexicon. Due to this activation, the activation threshold for this entry is lowered. When the regularly inflected form *plane* is presented subsequently, this form, too, is decomposed into the stem *plan* and the 1st person singular affix *-e*. Since the stem *plan* has already been activated before and its activation threshold has been lowered, the access to this stem's entry is now faster—a priming effect occurs. Irregular inflected participles such as *geschlafen*, in contrast, are not decomposed into stem and affix since they are stored as whole word forms in the mental lexicon. Thus, the presentation of the irregular participle *geschlafen* does not lead to a direct activation of the stem entry *schlaf*. Subsequent presentation of the regular inflected form *schlafe*, which is decomposed into stem and affix, does not lead to a comparable priming effect, since the stem *schlaf* has not been directly activated by the participle presented before.

Summarizing, the priming task suggests that irregular participles do not prime inflected forms as effectively as regular participles. The priming effect observed for regular participles indicates that regular inflected forms are decomposed into stem and affix and, hence, consist of two independent components as assumed in dualistic approaches to inflection. The finding that irregular participles do not display a similar priming effect is compatible with the dualistic assumption that irregular inflected forms, in contrast, are not composed out of stem and affix by productive affixation, but are stored as whole word forms in the mental lexicon.

28.3.3 Evidence for the storage of irregular inflected forms

Whereas regular inflected forms are composed out of stem and affix according to the dualistic view to inflection, irregular inflected forms are assumed to be stored as fully inflected word forms in the mental lexicon. This assumption allows for another prediction that can be experimentally tested. If irregular forms are stored in the mental lexicon, we should find evidence for this full-form storage. Conversely, if regular inflected forms are not stored as whole word forms, no indication of storage effects should be observable. An experimental effect that is generally seen as indicative of lexical storage is the frequency effect that can, for instance, be measured in a lexical-decision experiment.

In a lexical-decision experiment, subjects have to decide as quickly and accurately as possible whether a presented item is an existing word or not. The reaction time required to carry out this word/non-word discrimination task is measured. Lexical-decision times are affected by frequency (see Balota, 1994; Lively, Pisoni, and Goldinger, 1994 for review), that is subjects take less time to decide that a frequent item (such as *Katze* 'cat') is an existing word than they take for infrequent words (such as the phonologically similar word *Tatze* 'paw'). This effect reflects the assumption that memory traces get stronger with each exposure, making frequent forms easier to access than infrequent ones.

The lexical-decision technique has been used to provide evidence for a dualistic distinction between regular and irregular inflected forms. According to dualistic approaches, irregular inflected forms should show effects of word form frequency in a lexical-decision experiment, since they are stored as fully inflected forms in the mental lexicon. Regular inflected forms, in contrast, are not stored but are formed on the fly by a process of affixation and should therefore not be subject to word form frequency effects in lexical-decision experiments.

In a lexical-decision task Clahsen, Eisenbeiss, and Sonnenstuhl (1997) presented infrequently and frequently occurring German participles and measured how long it took their subjects to decide whether the presented participle was a German word or not. Clahsen et al. obtained a clear frequency effect for irregular participles: whereas their subjects took 652 ms (mean reaction time) to decide that an infrequent irregular participle was an existing word, the mean reaction time for frequent irregular participles was only 593 ms. For regular participles, however, no such frequency effect occurred. The mean decision times for infrequent (613 ms) and frequent (617 ms) regular participles did not differ significantly.

That a frequency effect can be obtained for irregular participles but does not occur for regular participles indicates that irregular inflected forms are stored as whole forms in the mental lexicon whereas regular participles are not—as is assumed in dualistic approaches to inflection.

28.3.4 Summary

Psycho- and neurolinguists adopting the dualistic stance have argued that findings such as the ones discussed above provide sound evidence for a fundamental difference between regular and irregular inflected forms. Regular and irregular inflection can be selectively affected in language disorders, indicating that they are subserved by two qualitatively different modules in the human mind/brain. The processing of irregular inflected forms is affected by the frequency of the irregular form, providing evidence for full-form storage of these inflected forms in an associative memory structure. The lack of a frequency effect in regular inflected forms, in contrast, is seen as evidence against full-form storage of these inflected forms. Moreover, that regular inflected forms prime their stem, whereas a similar priming effect was not observed for irregular inflected forms, indicates that regular inflected forms are structurally composed out of stem and affix. The picture emerging from these findings has been argued to fully support dualistic approaches to inflection which assume that irregular inflected forms are stored in the mental lexicon, whereas regular inflected forms are not stored but are composed out of stem and affix.

28.4 A BRIEF SKETCH OF THE DEBATE

The dualistic view and the evidence on which this view is based have, however, not gone undisputed. Proponents of unitary approaches to inflection have set out to show that the above described differences between regular and irregular inflected forms are just artefacts that are due to different distributional properties of regular and irregular verbs in the language or to a specific experimental design chosen. Thus, for example, the different productivity of regular vs. irregular inflection in overgeneralization errors (see Section 28.2.1) or in experiments where novel verbs have to be inflected (e.g. Prasada and Pinker, 1993) has been attributed to the fact that the regular English past-tense inflection applies to many more verb types than the irregular past tense inflection (95 per cent of verb types in English are regular, Marcus et al., 1995). Regular past tense inflection, thus, is the most frequent pattern displayed in English past tense forms and, hence, is preferred in participle production when no irregular form is available (see the discussion in Marcus et al., 1995; Clahsen, 1999). Pursuing a similar goal, Bird et al. (2003) provided evidence that a selective deficit for the production of regular past tense forms apparent in ten English-speaking subjects with Broca's aphasia disappeared when the tested verbs were controlled for phonological complexity.

A particularly important refutation of dualistic approaches to inflection has come from connectionist network models of inflection. Building up on the original work of Rumelhart and McClelland, connectionist modellers have set out to construct a multitude of different network models that claim to adequately simulate the different behaviour observed for regular and irregular inflected forms in experimental research, although both regular as well as irregular inflected forms are represented and processed in a single associative network by identical mechanisms (see Marcus, 2001 for an overview on such models). The last twenty years have seen a heated contest between proponents of dualistic approaches to inflection and connectionist modellers. In this contest, dualists have tried to come up with ever new evidence for a qualitative distinction between regular and irregular inflected forms. These efforts have been countered by ever new connectionist models aiming to simulate the newly discovered aspects of the acquisition, processing, neural representation, or impairment of inflected forms in a unitary non-compositional associative network structure where regular and irregular inflected forms are treated identically. The number of book publications on this issue (e.g. Rumelhart and McClelland, 1986b; Pinker and Mehler, 1989; Macdonald and Macdonald, 1995; Elman et al., 1996; Pinker, 1999; Marcus, 2001; Penke, 2006) and the ardent discussions that regularly ignite in scientific journals (cf. e.g. *The Behavioral and Brain Sciences* 1999: No. 22, *TRENDS in Cognitive Sciences* 2002: No. 6, *Brain and Language* 2003: No. 85, *Brain and Language* 2005: No. 93) give proof of the liveliness of this debate.

The aim of the connectionist stance in this debate is twofold. For one, connectionists want to show that a non-compositional associative network structure is sufficient to adequately simulate human behaviour with respect to regular and irregular inflected forms. In addition, the more general goal behind a successful simulation is to argue against the symbolistic view of language and, ultimately, human cognition. Consequently, the debate between dualistic und unitary connectionist approaches to inflection has been conducted on different levels.

28.4.1 Are connectionist models able to simulate human behaviour with respect to regular and irregular inflected forms?

Most of the research fuelling the Dual-Mechanism debate has dealt with the issue whether or not a specific network model is able to simulate the data collected on the acquisition, processing, and representation of regular and irregular inflected forms (cf. e.g. Pinker and Prince, 1988; Marcus, 2001). The literature is much too extensive to discuss it here even cursorily and the specifics that are dealt with in such discussions are not easily presented in an overview article such as this, nor easily understood by a layperson. Therefore, I will treat this discussion rather globally and refer the interested reader to Marcus (2001) for an overview and detailed discussion of relevant connectionist simulations.

Since the original network model of Rumelhart and McClelland (1986b), the Dual-Mechanism debate has been fuelled by the efforts of psycho- and neurolinguists adopting the dualistic stance to discover and present ever new evidence for the assumption that regular inflected words are not stored as full forms but are composed by affixing an inflectional ending to a word stem. These attempts have then been countered by new connectionist network models claiming to model the reported data without resort to a compositional mental operation. In this competition, connectionist simulations have sometimes been dismissed somewhat hastily and cursorily. Thus, a criticism has been made for instance that connectionists would come up with models specifically tailored to simulate just one type of data, while no model would be able to simulate the whole range of data collected in neuro- and psycholinguistic research (e.g. Marcus, 1998a: 171). However, models have been developed that successfully simulate more than just one type of data. For example, the constructivist network model of Westermann is able to simulate the acquisition of regular and irregular English past tense forms, the different productivity of regular and irregular past tense forms in novel verb experiments (cf. Westermann, 1998, 2000), or the selective impairment of irregular inflected forms evidenced in German Broca's aphasia (cf. Penke and Westermann, 2006).

Westermann's constructivist network consists of an input-layer, an output-layer, and a hidden-layer that initially only contains two units. During learning, the network gradually inserts new units in the hidden layer when adjusting the connection weights of the present units does not improve the network's performance any further. The idea behind this constructivist learning approach is that the network builds up more structure only when this is required by the learning task. Consider Fig. 28.3 as an illustration. The figure shows the hidden layer at the start of the learning regimen. Initially (a) the same unit of the hidden layer responds to both German verbs *hören* and *schwören* ('hear' and 'swear'). Another unit of the hidden layer responds to the German verbs *lachen* and *machen* ('laugh' and 'make'). For the latter unit no problem arises because both verbs are regular in German. Thus, the unit at the hidden layer can react to both verbs in the same way producing the same output pattern for both verbs. However, *hören* has a

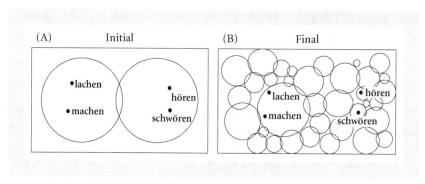

FIGURE 28.3 Illustration of the development of an experience-dependent architecture in a constructivist neural network (Penke and Westermann, 2006)

regular inflected participle form (*gehört*), whereas *schwören* takes the irregular participle inflection (*geschworen*). Thus, both verbs activating the same unit at the hidden layer will lead to output error. Therefore, this hidden unit is split during the process of learning (b). The insertion of a new unit, in effect, leads to a more fine-grained resolution in that area of the input space: whereas one unit of the hidden layer is required to process the regular inflected verb *hören*, a different unit, producing a different output, is needed for the similar sounding irregular inflected verb *schwören*.

In the model, more structural resources are allocated where they are required to distinguish similar sounding but differently behaving verbs. In consequence, the model develops a more fine-grained structure for irregular inflected verbs, whereas fewer hidden units are involved in the processing of regular inflected verbs. Unlike previous connectionist models, Westermann's model contains separate pathways with different representations for verbs. In the direct input–output pathway verbs have distributed representations that overlap between similar-sounding verbs. In the developing hidden-unit pathway representations are quasi-localist: one hidden unit responds to a small subset of verbs. However, unlike in the Dual-Mechanism view, in the model both pathways are involved in the production of all past tense forms, albeit to different degrees, and the structure of the model (hidden layer size and network weight settings) develops through the interaction of both pathways.[11]

In this network, a selective deficit with irregular inflection—as is typically observed in German speakers with Broca's aphasia—arises from a global impairment of the network by which connection weights between units are randomly removed. Since most of the network's resources are allocated for the processing of irregular inflected forms, a random removal of connection weights throughout the network primarily affects irregular inflected verbs. Thus, a selective deficit of one type of inflection does not necessarily

---

[11] As a result of the constructivist learning process the representations developing in the hidden layer are as localist as necessary, and as distributed as possible, to solve the inflection task. The developing multiple representations for each verb (in the hidden-unit pathway and the input–output pathway) take into account that similarity of inputs is not always linked to similarity of outputs (such as in *sing—sang, ring—rang,* but *blink—blinked*), which is a bias that purely distributed connectionist systems struggle to overcome.

presuppose two qualitatively distinct modules, mechanisms, or processes that can be selectively affected by brain damage (Penke and Westermann, 2006).

With his model, Westermann was able to show that the differences regular and irregular inflected forms display with respect to frequency or their selective affectedness in language disorders (see Section 28.3.1 above) also emerge in a network that assumes a unitary non-compositional mechanism and are due to the different distributional properties these different verb types display. Thus, it is fair to conclude that network models such as Westermann's model have indeed been quite successful in simulating at least some of the behavioural data. In doing so, they have highlighted the influence of factors such as frequency and phonological similarity in language processing and representation. What to conclude from a successful simulation is, however, disputable.

28.4.2 What to conclude from a successful simulation?

A model is a system that is put into an experimental situation in which its performance is compared with human subjects. Equivalence of performance is then taken as evidence for the equivalence of representations and processing mechanisms by proponents of connectionism. Two arguments are invoked by connectionists for preferring a successful connectionist model to a dualistic account of inflection. For one, connectionists complain that (psycho-)linguistic theories, such as the Dual-Mechanism Model, are largely underspecified with respect to the exact mechanisms invoked in the representation and processing of inflected forms. A model, in contrast, has to be precise on these issues, if the model is to work at all. Because of its higher degree of explicitness and specificity a successful model is said to be preferable to a theory (Westermann, 2000). Moreover, according to the heuristic maxim called Occam's razor, if two theories such as the unitary and the dualistic view to inflection compete with each other, the simpler, more economic, and parsimonious theory is to be preferred (e.g. McClelland and Plaut, 1999; Westermann, 2000). Since the unitary approach to inflection invokes only a single non-compositional associative mechanism to capture regular and irregular inflected forms, whereas the dualistic approach proposes two qualitatively different mechanisms, a storage component and a compositional rule component, the unitary approach is, hence, to be preferred.

Note, however, that the parsimony of connectionist models vis-à-vis dualistic accounts has been challenged since there are no established criteria to measure the parsimony or simplicity of one theory vis-à-vis another one. Thus, for instance Marcus (1998b) has argued that the large number of parameters—such as the number of layers and nodes, the chosen learning algorithms, and transfer functions etc.—that have to be specified in a connectionist model call the purported parsimony of such models into question. Moreover, a distinction should be drawn between storage and computational economy. Storage and computational economy are the two facets of Occam's razor and pull in different directions (cf. Bierwisch, 1997; Stiebels, 2002: section 1): computation minimizes storage, storage minimizes computation. With respect to computational economy, the unitarists' assumption that all inflected forms are stored and not computed is certainly more parsimonious than the dualistic assumption, since no computation is required at all. With respect to storage economy, however, the storage of every inflected word form that is assumed in unitary accounts is not economical at all but requires huge storing capacities. The dualistic account which assumes that regular inflected forms are not stored but computed is, hence, more economical with respect to storage economy than the connectionist approach (Penke, 2006). Occam's razor does, thus, not provide a simple answer to the Dual-Mechanism debate. A successful simulation of the behavioural data and effects observed in research on the acquisition, processing, and representation of regular and irregular inflected word forms in a unitary associative connectionist network is no proof for the correctness of the unitary connectionist view to inflection, but it indicates that the existing data are compatible with both theoretical approaches—the unitary and the dualistic one.

28.4.3 A new challenge to connectionist networks—problems at morpheme boundaries

Whereas a successful simulation is no proof of the connectionist view to inflection, a failure to simulate behavioural data reflecting a distinction between regular and irregular inflected forms in connectionist network models is taken as evidence against unitary approaches to inflection by the dualist side. Therefore, while connectionist networks have succeeded with some types of data, proponents of dualistic approaches to inflection have sought out ever new types of experimental effects and data over the last twenty years, hoping that these data might turn out to be impossible to simulate in a connectionist network (Pinker, 1999; Clahsen, 1999; Penke, 2006 for an overview). Being a dualist myself, I want to follow this tradition here and issue a new challenge to connectionist network models by presenting some new piece of evidence for a compositional view on regular inflection that comes from my own research on participle production in German child language.

Under a dualistic view of inflection, German regular participle forms such as *getanzt* ('danced') are structurally composed by adding the participle affix -*t* to a verbal stem. But now consider a verb like *husten* ('cough'). Suffixing the verbal stem *hust* with the participle affix -*t* would result in a participle form *gehustt* where two identical segments, the stem final [t] and the affix -*t*, directly follow each other. Sequences of two adjacent identical elements are, however, generally avoided in languages (Yip, 1998). To avoid such a sequence, in German an epenthetic *Schwa* vowel is inserted between the stem final [t] and the inflectional suffix -*t*. Thus, the regular participle form for the stem *hust* is *gehustet*. Another option is chosen in Dutch, for instance, where regular past participles are formed by adding a suffix -*d* to a verbal stem. When the stem ends in a coronal stop /t/ or /d/, as in the Dutch verb *land* ('land'), only one of the two stops is realised (*land* + -*d* → *geland*).

In language acquisition, German children have to find out which solution to this tt-problem is chosen by the language they are learning. In an investigation of German child data (Grijzenhout and Penke, 2005), we found that German children go through a stage in language acquisition where they are engaged in finding out the 'German' solution to this problem. During this stage they display considerable problems in producing regular -*t* inflected participle forms for verbs with a verbal stem that already ends in a coronal stop /t/ or /d/. These problems are exceptionally clear in the data of Naomi, a monolingual German child acquiring standard German. In Naomi's speech the first -*t* inflected forms for verbal stems ending in a coronal stop [t] appear at 1:9.18 (year:month.day). From that age onwards until the last of the weekly speech recordings available to us at age 2:1.20, Naomi varies between the different possible realizations of -*t*-inflected forms for verbs with stem final coronal stop: (i) she produces incorrect forms such as *gehust* where only one of the [t] segments is realized (in 71.4 per cent of the 91 relevant contexts, e.g. (28.1a)),[12] (ii) she produces incorrect forms such as *gehustt* where the two [t] segments directly follow each other (11 per cent, e.g. (28.1b)), and (iii) she produces correct target forms such as *gehustet* that display Schwa epenthesis (6.6 per cent, e.g. (28.1c)):[13]

(28.1)   Naomi's realization of regular German past participles

	Spelling	Adult form	Child's form	(age)	Gloss
a.	angeguckt	[angəkʊkt]	[tʊt][14]	(1;11.24)	look at[PART]
b.			[anətʊtt]	(2;1.03)	
c.			[tʊtət]	(1;9.18)	

Why are these data interesting for the Dual-Mechanism debate? They exemplify that children are faced with a problem they have to solve, namely how to avoid clashes of two identical [t] segments in regular participle forms for verbs such as *husten*. While they are engaged in finding out the solution to this problem, German children experiment with different possible solutions to the problem—and hence produce incorrect forms such as *gehust* or *gehustt*. These errors are interesting, since in trying to solve the problem the children creatively produce forms that they have never heard in their input. The relevant point however is this: the problem German children like Naomi are trying to solve only arises because two morphemes (a stem and an affix) are combined to produce

---

[12] For an analysis of why forms such as *gehust* are the initially preferred solution for German children see Grijzenhout and Penke (2005).

[13] Note that these problems are neither due to articulatory problems, nor to problems with the -*t* inflection per se. For verbs not ending in stem final /t/ or /d/, the -*t* inflection is correctly realized in 82.1 per cent of the relevant contexts (465 out of 566) compared to 6.6 per cent of correctly -*t* inflected forms for verbs with stem final /t/ or /d/. Also, whereas the omission rate of the -*t* inflection after stem final /t/ or /d/ is 71.4 per cent, the omission rate for the affix -*t* in verbs without stem final /t/ or /d/ is only 6.4 per cent (36 of 566).

[14] Naomi pronounces velar [g] and [k] as [t], thus the verb *guck* ('look') is pronounced as [tʊt] by Naomi.

a participle form. It is precisely the composition of a participle form by a stem ending in a coronal stop /t/ or /d/ and a participle affix -t that leads to the phonologically problematic tt-sequence in the first place. This problematic sequence has then to be dealt with in the phonological component. If there were no composition of stem and affix, as suggested in unitary approaches to inflection where regular inflected forms are stored in the mental lexicon, there would be no clash of identical segments at the boundary between stem and affix and, hence, no tt-problem to solve in the first place. In this case, children would simply store and retrieve the participle forms they encounter in their input (i.e. *gehustet*). However, under this assumption, the production of non-standard forms like *gehustt* or *gehust*—which the child has never heard in the input and which clearly indicate that the child is engaged in solving the phonological tt-problem—cannot be explained.

Summarizing, the data exemplified under (28.1) show that in language acquisition German children such as Naomi are faced with a morpho-phonological problem that results from the composition of a stem ending in a coronal stop /t/ or /d/ and an affix -t. The incorrect forms, especially the very marked tt-forms such as *gehustt*, that are produced during this stage provide strong evidence that affixes such as the regular participle suffix -t are independent units of the language system that are added to a stem by a compositional affixation process. Whether or not a unitary connectionist model will succeed in simulating this acquisitional stage and the error patterns observed in this stage is an empirical question and connectionists are right to remind us that arguments of the type 'the models will never be able to do this' might be outdated by a new model just tomorrow (Seidenberg, 1994: 398). However, since the problem exemplified in this data only arises due to the structural composition of a stem morpheme and an affix morpheme, it is difficult to imagine how a non-compositional connectionist network model, in which the composition of inflected forms out of component morphemes is denied, could simulate this stage in language acquisition.

28.4.4 Symbolism and domain-specificity—the broader issues at stake

Underlying the question of whether or not connectionist networks will be able to simulate human behaviour with respect to regular inflection in simple associative networks are two broader, interrelated issues: (i) are symbols manipulated in human cognition (see Section 28.2.2)?; and (ii) is human cognition partitioned into domain-specific knowledge systems? With respect to these issues, connectionism opened up a 'Pandora's box' which generative linguists had assumed to be safely shut since the cognitive turn, initiated by Chomsky's refutation of the up-to-then prevailing behaviouristic approach to language and cognition (Chomsky, 1959; cf. Gardner, 1985 for overview).

In opposition to the behaviouristic claim that mental processes cannot be the object of scientific research, Chomsky argued that the human language faculty is due to a specialized, domain-specific language organ situated in the mind/brain that is part of our biological endowment and thus genetically specified (e.g. Chomsky, 1980, 2002). According to Chomsky, the productivity of the human language capacity, that is the capacity to produce, understand, or judge the grammaticality of sentences and phrases, is in principal unlimited. Such unlimited productivity can only be achieved in a system that has the property of *discrete infinity* (Chomsky, 1988): discrete abstract symbols (e.g. categories such as [+V] or [+N]) can be combined by potentially recursive mental operations (such as *merge*) to build more complex, hierarchically organized structures. While the mental operations combining symbols might well be domain-general, the symbols (or categories) manipulated by these operations are assumed to be specific to language (cf. Wunderlich, 2007; Chomsky, 2005 for discussion).

The assumption that the human language capacity is domain-specific and innate is based on the classical *logical problem of language acquisition*.[15] This problem states that the input for a child is underdetermined in two crucial ways: (i) It is quantitatively underdetermined, that is the child receives a finite set of input data, but must be able to produce and understand a non-finite set of data after acquisition. (ii) The input is also qualitatively underdetermined, that is the child is exposed to spoken utterances, but has to induce abstract rules of grammar (in order to be able to produce and understand a non-finite set of data after acquisition) (Fanselow and Felix, 1987). Given the underdetermination of the input, a simple inductive learning mechanism based on positive input data will run into problems since any given set of data is compatible with indefinitely many generalizations (Gold, 1967; Scholz and Pullum, 2002). A particularly severe problem will occur in those cases where the child induces a rule that generates all the possible structures of her/his native language plus additional ones not allowed by the grammar of this language (the *subset–superset problem*, cf. Pinker, 1989). In these cases, only negative evidence, that is explicit information on the ungrammaticality of these illicit structures, could inform the child about the incorrectness of her or his generalization. Negative evidence that could prevent the child from incorrect generalizations is, however, not available to all children and therefore cannot be necessary for language acquisition (cf. Pinker, 1994). Under these conditions, language acquisition has to fail. However, it does not. According to generative linguistics, children master language acquisition despite the logical problem of language acquisition because of their innate predisposition for

---

[15] The logical problem of language acquisition is based on the *poverty-of-the-stimulus* argument invoked in Chomsky's earlier writings (Chomsky, 1980). The poverty-of-the-stimulus argument, sometimes also called *Plato's problem*, states that there is a strong discrepancy between the sparseness and the poverty of the input data children receive during language acquisition, and the complexity and uniformity of the acquired grammatical knowledge. This rather vague formulation has led to various interpretations as to what this argument actually refers to and to discussions of whether or not the child's input is indeed impoverished (see Pullum and Scholz, 2002). Research on language acquisition has shown that the input children receive during language acquisition is not as depleted, poor, and ungrammatical as originally claimed by Chomsky. As a consequence, the poverty-of-the-stimulus argument has been reformulated into the logical problem of language acquisition, which states that the input data for a child is still underdetermined in two crucial ways, i.e. quantitatively and qualitatively.

learning grammar, that is Universal Grammar (UG) which inherently constrains the set of possible generalizations the child might entertain.

Chomsky's conception of an innate domain-specific language capacity has been discarded in other non-generative theoretical paradigms such as functionalism (e.g. Bates and MacWhinney, 1982), emergentism (e.g. O'Grady, 2008), constructivism (e.g. Piaget, 1980; Quartz and Sejnowski, 1997; Westermann et al., 2007), or cognitive linguistics (e.g. Langacker, 1990) that see language as part and parcel of our general cognitive make-up and, hence, not as independent from general cognitive capacities (see Penke and Rosenbach, 2007 for discussion). The advent of connectionism has considerably revived the debate about whether the innate human language capacity is due to domain-specific or domain-general principles shared with other cognitive modules (see e.g. Elman et al., 1996; Seidenberg and MacDonald, 1999; Pinker, 1994, 2002; Chater and Manning, 2006).[16] It is the merit of connectionism to have shown how successful simple associative learning mechanisms based on frequency distributions, similarity of features, and statistical correlations in the input data can be in learning aspects of language. Research during recent years has provided evidence that such learning mechanisms do indeed play an important role in some aspects of language acquisition, for instance in segmenting the speech stream into words (cf. e.g. Saffran, Aslin, and Newport, 1996; Jusczyk, 2001; Gómez and Gerken, 2001). Thus, the advent of connectionism has forced generative linguists to rethink the issue of which aspects of the human capacity to learn and use language are specific to language and which are domain-general. As a consequence, the amount of innate knowledge assumed to be language-specific has been considerably reduced in research over the last fifteen years (cf. Bierwisch, 1997; Fanselow, 1993; Chomsky, 1995; Hauser et al., 2002; Kayne, 1994; Eisenbeiss, 2002; Wunderlich, 2007).[17]

28.5 CONCLUSION

The Dual-Mechanism debate, concerned with the issue of how to represent regular inflected forms in the human mind, is relevant to much broader issues on the nature of human language and cognition. Whether symbols specific for a particular cognitive

---

[16] It is by now widely accepted that humans are the only species capable of learning and using language on the basis of the input available to children during language acquisition (Elman et al., 1996; Pinker, 2002; Elman, 2005). That the language capacity is species-specific, therefore part of the human genetic endowment and in this sense innate, is no longer controversial.

[17] For example, the X-bar-scheme has been replaced by the simple operation *merge* (Chomsky, 1995). Word order parameters such as the *head parameter* have been replaced by general principles stating that all structures are right-branching (Kayne, 1994) and that heads should be placed consistently (Fanselow, 1993; Eisenbeiss, 2002). And domain-specific principles such as the *Elsewhere principle* have been replaced by domain-general principles such as the *Specificity principle* which captures the relationship between regular processes and exceptions in other cognitive domains as well (cf. Eisenbeiss, 2002; Wunderlich, 2007).

domain are manipulated in human cognition, or whether knowledge is acquired by and represented in associative network structures by making use of domain-general principles of knowledge acquisition and representation are questions that ultimately go back to the two opposing scientific schools of Aristotelean empiricism and Platonean rationalism. The Dual-Mechanism debate on the representation of regular inflected words was considered to be a model case to solve the long-standing opposition between these two scientific schools (cf. Pinker, 1999). The issues invoked by the Dual-Mechanism debate are empirical questions that are, in principal, solvable by further scientific research. In practice, however, it has turned out to be quite difficult to reject one of the opposing views. A successful connectionist simulation, for instance, does not serve to falsify the opposing dualistic view if this can also account for the data (see Section 28.4.2). Conversely, a failure to simulate a particular piece of data in a connectionist network might not be counted as conclusive counter-evidence to the connectionist view but might be left to future models, hopefully able to simulate these data. Taking this into account and considering that the underlying debate between rationalist and empiricist positions to human cognition has remained unresolved since the birth hour of scientific research, it is certain that the Dual-Mechanism debate (and related debates in other fields of cognitive science) will continue over the years to come. This is, however, no reason to despair, nor to discard the debate as fruitless since no consensus is to be reached. On the contrary, the Dual-Mechanism debate has been an inspiration to researchers over the last twenty years and the research conducted in the course of this debate has considerably enlarged and sharpened our knowledge of human cognition—and it will certainly continue to do so during the years to come.[18]

---

[18] I am grateful to three anonymous reviewers for their valuable comments and to Gert Westermann for a number of very lively debates and his never ending enthusiasm in explaining to me that connectionist networks are superior to dualistic accounts of inflection.

CHAPTER 29

....

COMPOSITIONALITY AND BIOLOGICALLY PLAUSIBLE MODELS

....

TERRENCE STEWART AND
CHRIS ELIASMITH

29.1 INTRODUCTION

....

The breadth of this Handbook demonstrates the diversity of approaches to compositionality that characterize current research. Understanding how structured representations are formed and manipulated has been a long-standing challenge for those investigating the complexities of cognition. Fodor and Pylyshyn (1988) and Jackendoff (2002) have provided detailed discussions of the problems faced by any theory purporting to describe how such systems can occur in the physical brain. In particular, neural cognitive theories must not only identify how to neurally instantiate the rapid construction and transformation of compositional structures, but also provide explanatory advantages over classical symbolic approaches.

Traditionally, cognitive theories have expressed their components using an artificial symbolic language, such as first-order predicate logic, for example chased(dog, boy). The atoms in such representations are non-decomposable letter strings, for example dog, chased, and boy. Fodor and Pylyshyn (1988) call this a classical symbol system or classical cognitive architecture, and the defining characteristic is that the individual atoms explicitly appear in any overall structure in which they participate. This sense of 'classical architecture' is used throughout this article.

The technical problem of how symbolic representations, and the relations between such representations, can be accounted for in a neural approach has driven much of the discussion of neurally-inspired compositional models. The specific approaches discussed in this paper have all been shown to meet Jackendoff's challenges (van der Velde and de Kamps, 2006; Gayler, 2003), which highlight potential difficulties for neural systems that are easily accounted for by a traditional classical system. However, each of these approaches continues to face two main criticisms: (i) the architecture is uninteresting because it is an implementation of a classical system; (ii) the architecture is not biologically plausible. We take it as important to understand how the brain implements a classical system (if it indeed does), but agree that none of the past proposals are sufficiently biologically plausible. In this chapter, we first discuss why implementation details may, in fact, be important for understanding cognitive behaviour. We then review the past approaches and present concerns about biological plausibility. We conclude by presenting a new architecture that is not an implementation of a classical architecture, is able to explain the relevant behaviour, and is biologically plausible.

29.1.1 The purpose of neural models

Fodor and McLaughlin (1990) suggest that if a neural theory merely demonstrates how to implement a classical symbol system using neurons, then this is actually an argument *against* the importance of the neural description. The fact that symbol systems are physically instantiated in neurons becomes a mere implementational detail, since there is a direct way to translate from the symbolic description to the more neurally plausible one. It might then be argued that, while the neural aspects of the theory identify *how* behaviour arises, they are not fundamentally important for understanding that behaviour. Classical symbol systems would continue to be seen as the right kinds of description for psychological processes.

However, it seems clear that there are explanatory advantages to having the neural level of description in addition to the purely classical one. A realistic neural explanation opens the door to a wealth of new methods for analysing and investigating cognitive behaviour, such as fMRI, EEG, single-cell recordings, and the rest of modern neuroscience. Without such an explanation, there is no way to generate rigorous constraints from such evidence, and no way to create testable neurological predictions. Cutting ourselves off from this empirical data because of our theoretical commitments (e.g. that cognitive systems are classical) is a case of putting the cart before the horse. Indeed, a neural implementation of a classical system would strengthen the plausibility of the view enormously. However, this means that the biological realism of the proposed neural implementation is of the utmost importance: if the biological constraints are unrealistic then all that remains is a neurally implausible implementation of a classical architecture, of which there are many examples already.

It is also important to entertain the possibility that a neural cognitive theory might *not* be an implementation of a classical symbol system. Perhaps implementational details force us to reconsider our prior theoretical commitments. That is, while our best implementation may exhibit compositional behaviour in its ability to rapidly manipulate structures, it may not have certain properties that are fundamental to the classical symbol system approach: for example in classical symbol systems a structured representation contains, as constituents, explicit representations of each of its components (Fodor and Pylyshyn, 1988; Fodor and McLaughlin, 1990). Notably, some of the Vector

Symbolic Architectures (VSAs) we discuss below do not meet this criteria, while still providing the compositional characteristics required for explaining cognitive behaviour. Indeed, the neural theory we subsequently present (based on VSAs) not only provides interesting neurological constraints, it also relies on non-classical theoretical commitments.

29.1.2 Evaluating neural models

A cognitive model of compositionality can be analysed at any of a number of levels, including the molecular, cellular, network, systems, behavioural, social, etc. levels. For the purposes of this discussion, however, we focus on two levels in particular (though we take the theories to be analysable at many of these levels): the behavioural and the neural levels. We have chosen to narrow our focus in this way because these particular levels of analysis make clear the distinctions between available alternative theories.

Starting with behavioural constraints, we note that while compositionality is clearly a fundamental component of cognitive activity, it is equally clear that compositional behaviour is neither perfect nor unlimited. Complex nested ideas and long conjunctions of concepts are difficult or impossible for people to process all at once. The idea of *cognitive load* is extensively used in behavioural psychology to increase task difficulty until performance errors gradually increase to the desired level. Importantly, this tends to be a gradual effect; people do not perform perfectly well at one moment, only to fail completely in a slightly harder situation.

In the classical symbol system approach, this is considered to be an issue of 'competence' versus 'performance' (after Chomsky, 1965). That is, the underlying theory provides the capacity for arbitrarily complex compositions, but the limitations of the human cognitive system lead to less than perfect performance. This suggests that the best way to understand human compositional activity is to consider it to be an approximation of an ideal theoretical construct, much as modern computers are considered to be approximations of ideal Turing machines.

If a theory does not follow the classical approach, it may incorporate limits on compositionality at the theoretical level (i.e. regardless of implementational considerations). For example, some VSAs combine components in lossy, imperfect ways, while still maintaining the accuracy needed for structured, organized cognition, in many cases. This 'inaccuracy' is introduced at the theoretical level—it is a consequence of how representations and their processing are formally characterized—as opposed to being an implementational detail.

For both classical and non-classical approaches, similar constraints are provided by considerations of neural implementation. Modern neuroscience has led to a wealth of knowledge about the details of neurons in various regions of the brain. We know that neurons are limited in terms of their firing rate, exhibit a great deal of random variation in their firing, are generally highly promiscuous in terms of their connections, and are limited to about 100 billion in the human brain. Neural systems are also known to be highly robust, as neuron death occurs regularly without catastrophic consequences to the overall system.

Neural cognitive theories should conform to these constraints. This is especially true for classical theories, since the only advantage they have over non-neural theories involves comparison to measurements made on real physical neurons. The remainder of this chapter examines four different cognitive theories in terms of how well they conform to these known biological limitations, and how neural implementation leads to constraints on overall compositional behaviour. As will be seen, the classical symbolic approaches are problematic, while a non-classical Vector Symbolic Approach accounts for behavioural limitations via realistic neural constraints.

29.2 CLASSICAL ARCHITECTURES

The three methods for implementing classical symbol systems in a neural architecture discussed here are all capable of meeting Jackendoff's criteria for compositionality. That is, they are able to represent symbols and relations between symbols using a connectionist approach. These models generally do this by explicitly representing each component within a structure, and then adding representations of the relations between these components.

29.2.1 LISA: Learning and Inference with Schemas and Analogies

Hummel and Holyoak have presented a series of papers describing their LISA model (Hummel and Holyoak, 2003; Hummel, Burns, and Holyoak, 1994; Hummel and Holyoak, 1998). Their model is meant to account for various aspects of analogical reasoning, using a schema-based approach. This is common in classical symbol systems, and so their main contribution is showing how neurons can implement this classical architecture. The neural plausibility of the proposal is thus essential to its contribution to our understanding of cognition.

In LISA, a structured representation is constructed out of at least four levels of distributed and localist representations. The first level consists of localist *subsymbols* (e.g. animal, furry, human, etc.). The second level consists of localist units connected to a distributed network of subsymbols relevant to defining the semantics of the second level *symbols* (e.g. dog is connected to furry, animal, etc.). The third level consists of localist *subproposition* nodes that bind roles to objects (e.g. dog + chase-agent to indicate that the dog is the chaser, not the entity being chased). The fourth and final level consists of localist proposition nodes that bind subpropositions to form whole

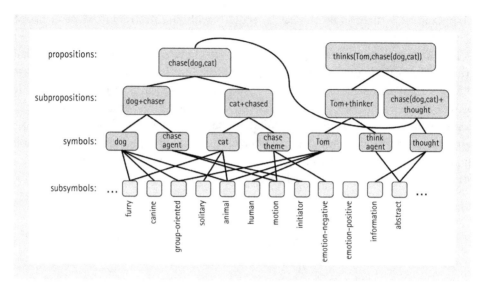

FIGURE 29.1 The LISA architecture. Each box is a single neural group. Shown are just those neural groups required to represent *dogs chase cats* and *Tom thinks that dogs chase cats*.

Source: Based on (Hummel and Holyoak, 2003: Figure 1)

propositions (e.g. **dog** + **chaser** combined with **cat** + **chased** results in chase(dog, cat)) (Fig. 29.1).

Hummel and Holyoak (2003) are careful to note that each of their localist units is intended to be a population of neurons: 'we assume that the localist units are realized neurally as small populations of neurons (as opposed to single neurons), in which the members of each population code very selectively for a single entity' (2003: 223). Each such population only represents one subsymbol, symbol, subproposition, or proposition. They do not provide details as to how the neurons in this neural group interact to form this representation.

The simplest analysis in terms of neurological plausibility that can be done on this system is to determine how many neurons would be required to represent a reasonably complex language. If we suppose that there are 4,000 nouns and 2,000 verbs (relations) in our language,[1] this suggests we need 6,000 populations to represent the basic concepts (i.e. at the second level of LISA's representational hierarchy). Assuming only two-place relations, we then need $4,000 \times 2,000 \times 2 = 16,000,000$ populations to represent the third level (subpropositions), that is each noun playing agent or theme roles for each verb. At the fourth level (propositions) we need $2,000 \times 4,000 \times 4,000 = 32,000,000,000$ populations to be able to represent the possibility that, for each verb, any noun could be either an agent or a theme. Thus, to be able to represent any simple propo-

---

[1] Estimates for the size of the vocabulary of English speakers vary between about 40,000–100,000. For instance, Crystal (2003) estimates that the average college graduate has 60,000 active words. While there are more nouns than verbs, there are about 11,000 verbs in English. As a result, the estimates we are using are very conservative.

sition of the form `relation(agent, theme)` requires around thirty billion neural groups, while only 100 billion neurons exist in the human brain. If higher order relations are desired as well (e.g. `knows (loves(agent, theme))`, `sees(hates(agent, theme))`, etc.), we need that same number of groups again for each such higher order relation.

Importantly, LISA does not fail gracefully when limited to a more reasonable number of neurons. If particular neural groups are not present in the architecture, then the corresponding structures *cannot be represented*. Even if some other mechanism were added that could identify neural groups that were not being used and adjust their connections to be able to represent the desired new concept, this would require adjusting synaptic connection weights between multiple neurons, a process which cannot occur in the few seconds it may take to read a novel sentence.

Another key aspect of the LISA model is its use of neural synchronization. At any given time, a few different propositions can be encoded in a LISA model. This is done by having the neurons corresponding to each proposition fire together, but at a different time from the other neurons. This idea is based on the currently heated debated among neuroscientists about the observations of such synchronized firing seen in physical brains. Since this bursting firing pattern is observed to have a period of around 25 msec, and since neuron firing precision is considered to be around 5 msec, this means that only five separate propositions can be encoded at the same time. Hummel and Holyoak take this to be a limit on human working memory.

However, the kind of synchronization used in LISA is not like that being argued for in biological brains. In LISA, synchronization occurs because there are inhibitory populations connected to each subproposition which set up an oscillatory behaviour when the proposition they are connected to is given a constant input. That oscillation is then reflected in all units that are excitatorily connected to these subpropositions (i.e. propositions and objects/relations). Usually, synchronization in the neurobiological literature is considered functional only if it is not explainable by common input. In LISA binding is established first by construction of subproposition units and that binding then results in synchronization. In the neurobiological literature, synchronization is supposed to *result* in binding (Engel, Fries, and Singer, 2001). Consequently, the neural plausibility of LISA is not supported by current work on synchronization. This severely challenges the claims to neural plausibility or realism made by the model's proponents. Our concern is that, if LISA adopted neurally plausible units, most of the explanatory mechanisms would fail to operate as they do in the much simplified cases explored to date.

LISA is able to represent complex nested structures, and it does so in a classical manner with populations of neurons that represent the sub-components of the overall structure. However, it is limited in terms of the depth of structures that can be represented. This limit is a hard, fixed limit that can be increased only by vastly increasing the number of neurons used. Indeed, even simple structures like `relation(agent,theme)` require more neurons than exist in the human brain. Furthermore, the neurons in this model are extreme idealizations and cannot be directly compared to real neurons.

Although the synchronization aspect of LISA is inspired by neural evidence, it uses a mechanism that is at odds with the neurobiological literature. We believe these problems make LISA a poor candidate for neural explanations of cognitive behaviour.

29.2.2 Neural blackboard architectures

Many of the difficulties of the LISA model derive from the exponential growth in the number of neurons required. This problem is greatly reduced in van der Velde and de Kamps's (2006) neural blackboard architecture. This architecture consists of neural groups that can be temporarily bound to particular atomic concepts, and these neural groups can then be combined to form structures. Since structures are only built out of a restricted number of these temporary processors, this approach does not encounter the exponential growth problem of connecting every possible relation to every possible noun. By reuse of the structure assemblies, neural blackboard architectures can build much more complex structures than the fixed LISA approach with the same number of neural groups.

This approach uses a fixed number of *noun assemblies* and *verb assemblies* (plus separate assemblies for determiners, adjectives, prepositions, clauses, etc.). Any of these assemblies can be connected to any of its associated words. That is, a particular noun assembly might at one time be bound to **boy**, while at another time it may be bound to **dog**. This binding is not done by forming new neural connections, as this would be implausible on a fast time scale. Instead, binding is accomplished via a complex mesh of carefully designed interacting neural groups (Fig. 29.2b) that connect every noun assembly to every noun. This mesh requires eight neural groups for every noun/assembly pair (Fig. 29.2c). That is, if there are 4,000 nouns and we have twenty noun assemblies, $20 \times 4,000 \times 8 = 640,000$ neural groups are required. Similar calculations can be done for each of the other types of word assemblies.

Once these words are bound to particular assemblies in the blackboard, a separate set of neural structures is used to allow these atoms to bind together. This is done by having each of the assemblies also have connections to separate neural groups (called sub-assemblies) representing the *role* of the term. Thus each noun assembly has both an agent sub-assembly and a theme sub-assembly, which can be made active or non-active based on a control system that interacts with a gating assembly between the two. Each of these sub-assemblies are connected to each other similar sub-assembly in the same manner as every noun assembly is connected to every noun. Given this system, it is possible to adjust the activations of the binding and gating systems to allow complex structures to be represented.

Unfortunately, this capability comes at a significant cost in terms of complexity. Notably, each gating circuit and memory circuit consists of eight or nine carefully arranged neural groups. The number of neurons needed for each group is not defined, but due to the degree of accuracy required in this complex structure, we estimate a

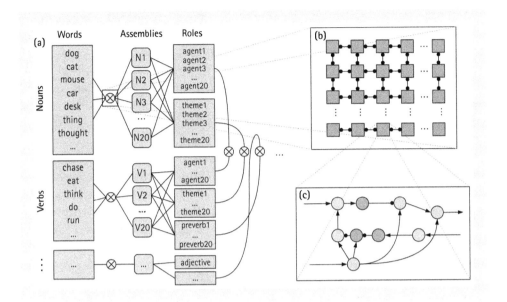

FIGURE 29.2 The neural blackboard architecture. Groups in (a) are connected by mesh grids (b) consisting of multiple copies of a complex system of neural groups (c). Excitatory connections are shown with arrows and inhibitory connections with circles.

Source: For more details, see (van der Velde and de Kamps, 2006).

minimum of about 100 neurons would be required per group, which would provide a signal to noise ratio of about 100:1, and a reasonably stable dynamics over about 2–5 s (Eliasmith and Anderson, 2003). If we allow twenty assemblies for each word type and a total vocabulary (including nouns, verbs, adjectives, adverbs, etc.) of 50,000 words,[2] over 8,000,000 neural groups are required.[3] Given our estimate of at least 100 neurons per neural group, the architecture demands about in 800,000,000 neurons, or approximately 50 cm^2 of cortex. While this is considerably less than is required by LISA, this is still a very large area of the brain (about the size of all language areas combined). And, this is the area that is required merely to *represent* a structure, it does not include the systems for controlling how sentences are encoded into this format, semantic connections between the words (encoded as subsymbols in LISA), methods for manipulating these structures, and so on.

Notably, the architecture depicted in Fig. 29.2 has extremely dense inter-connectivity between neural groups. As far as we are aware, there is no evidence that such a dense connection arrangement is common across language areas of cortex. The evidence cited

---

[2] See footnote 1 for references to typical vocabulary sizes in English.

[3] The neural requirements come from the two types of meshes shown in Fig. 29.2. The first set of meshes binds words to assemblies and requires 50,000 × 20 connections, each of which requires 8 neural groups. The second set of internal meshes bind particular roles to each other to form the represented structure. For 20 different roles, this results in 20 × 20 × 20 × 8 neural groups. 50,000 × 20 × 8 + 20 × 20 × 20 × 8 = 8,064,000 neural groups.

by van der Velde and de Kamps (2006) to support these structures demonstrates that some individual inhibitory cells in visual cortex synapse on other inhibitory cells in the same layer (Gonchar and Burkhalter, 1999)—it is not clear how this renders their architecture plausible in its details. After all, the blackboard architecture necessitates that all noun assemblies and all verb assemblies are connected, and that all nouns are connected to all noun assemblies. This demands very long distance, and highly complete connectivity, which is not observed in the brain. Most cortical connections are local and somewhat sparse (Song et al., 2005).

Furthermore, the highly complex binding and gating systems require thousands of intricately organized mutually dependent neural groups. This ensures that word assemblies are only bound to a single word at a time, and that various different possible structures involving the same words can be distinguished. If some of these neurons are removed, or if they are not connected in exactly the right manner, then it is unclear what behaviour will occur. Word assemblies could be stuck representing one particular word, or a particular noun assembly might become unable to connect to a particular verb assembly. This is not the sort of error generally associated with compositionality performance limitations.

The neural blackboard architecture also introduces a hard constraint on the number of noun, verb, and other word assemblies that exist. That is, if there are only ten noun assemblies, then structures with exactly ten nouns will be represented without difficulty, but a structure with eleven nouns will be impossible. This is not a pattern observed in human behaviour. To deal with this problem, NBA can increase the number of word assemblies to some sufficiently large number (50 or 100 has been suggested). This approximately linearly increases the number of neurons required (to 136 cm^2 or 277 cm^2). With this large a number of assemblies, it is possible that neural failure and timing issues may account for human performance limitations, although it is unclear to us how this occurs. However, this will require significantly more neural hardware than is associated with the language areas of the cortex.

The neural blackboard architecture is an improvement over LISA in that it has reduced the number of neurons required (though not necessarily to a plausible limit). However, the added complexity which allows this reduction does not seem to correspond to existing neural structures, and it is unclear what would happen to the system if neurons are removed or slightly mis-wired. In short, the system does not convincingly abide by neural-level constraints.

29.2.3 Tensor products

Both LISA and the neural blackboard architecture follow a similar approach to representing classical structures: particular neural groups are set to represent the atoms, and neural connections of various forms represent how they are related. A radically different approach that employs *tensor products* was developed by Smolensky (1990).

Considerable debate has arisen over whether this method is, in fact, equivalent to a classical symbol system. McLaughlin (1995) has convincingly argued that since the tensor product binding vectors (described below) can be chosen so that the representations of the atomic constituents are present in the representation of the complete structure, tensor products should be considered to be implementations of classical symbol systems. It should be noted that Smolensky (1990) does not refer to his architecture as a classical system, but he seems to be employing a different, less common, definition than the one we have adopted in this chapter. Our definition of a classical symbol system as one which explicitly represents the constituents of a structure when representing that structure is consistent with the proposals of Fodor (1998a), McLauglin (1995), and Jackendoff (2002).

The core idea behind the tensor product approach is to make use of a vector representation for the atomic components and to build up structures using algebraic manipulations. That is, instead of a particular neuron (or small neural group) representing **dog** and another neuron representing **cat** (as in LISA and neural blackboard architectures), a pattern of activity over many neurons forms the representation. For example, **dog** might be represented by the vector [0.4, 0.4, 0.5, 0.3, −0.4, . . .], while **cat** might be [0, −0.9, −0.2, 0.3, 0.2, . . .]. For technical reasons, these vectors are all fixed to have a magnitude of one, and thus lie on the unit hypersphere. We refer to the number of values in a vector as the *dimension* of that vector.

This vector representation can encode sub-symbols or semantic information about terms. In the simplest approach, the values in the vector might be various possible properties of the term, such as whether or not it is a living thing, whether it is furry, and so on. This is similar to the sub-symbols used in LISA, but any distributed representation scheme can be used. Importantly, the advantage offered by the tensor products approach is to define how such representations can be *combined* to form a structure. To create a structure representing `chase(dogs,cats)`, we perform the following calculation:

`dog⊗agent+chase⊗verb+cat⊗theme`

To do this, the ⊗ operation is defined as the *tensor product* (i.e., outer product). This involves multiplying each element in the two vectors together to form a matrix of values, as shown in Fig. 29.3.

Importantly, with this technique the original components of the structure can later be extracted. That is, if we only have the overall representation matrix, we can determine what the original **agent** was by performing the *inner product* of the matrix with the value for **agent**. To complete our example, this can also be done for the **verb** and **theme** values, and the results summed to give the final matrix. In other words, this matrix is a representation of the entire structure, since the individual components can be recovered or decoded.

Although this approach is typically described in terms of vectors and algebraic manipulations, it can also be interpreted in terms of neurons. The values in the vectors or matrices can be encoded by the firing of a neural group, so a representation consists of a

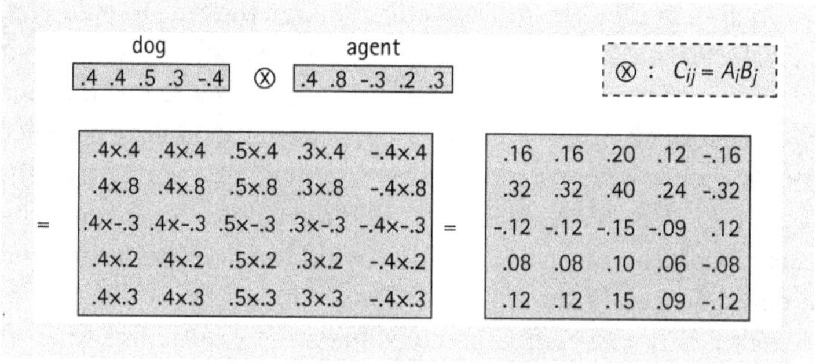

FIGURE 29.3 Binding values via tensor products

set of neural groups. The pattern of activation across the neural groups is the represented value. Encoding and decoding structure can be done by connecting groups together so that they calculate the outer or inner product. Since this requires multiplication of two values from different neural groups, there must be a neural mechanism capable of performing this nonlinear computation. There is some evidence that certain neurons can compute nonlinearities directly (e.g. Mel, 1994; Koch and Poggio, 1992), but it is currently a matter of considerable debate how common such mechanisms are in cortical neurons. However, it is also possible to use the Neural Engineering Framework (Elaismith and Anderson, 2003) discussed later in this chapter to organize highly typical cortical neurons to perform this multiplication.

The tensor product approach also takes into account a fundamental property of physical neurons: the fact that they are *noisy*. Because of the variability in spiking patterns and influences from the rest of the brain, it has been shown that the signal to noise ratio for a typical neuron is 10:1, meaning that it can only represent a value to within 10 per cent accuracy (Rieke et al., 1997). If this constraint is taken into account when evaluating the tensor product approach, we find that it *degrades gracefully*. That is, it will slowly become less accurate, rather than suddenly failing like the architectures we previously considered. To demonstrate this, consider a case with 25,000 atomic terms in the language where we are representing a structure of the form relation(agent,theme). We measure the accuracy of the representation by decoding the agent and determining which of the 25,000 atomic terms is closest to the resulting value. The accuracy shown in Fig. 29.4 indicates how often the correct decoding occurs. We can see from this figure that twenty dimensions (i.e. twenty values per vector) is sufficient to represent relation(agent,theme) with 95 per cent accuracy, while thirty dimensions is required for more complex situations like relation(A,B,C,D) to be represented equally well.

This smooth degradation of accuracy leads to behaviour where more errors are made the more complex a task is. This is a common pattern seen in behavioural psychology, where the cognitive load of a task is often increased specifically to cause errors in subject performance. In other words, tensor products fail in a manner similar to that of

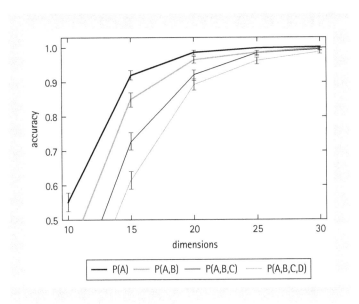

FIGURE 29.4 Decoding accuracy for relations of different complexities and number of dimensions, assuming representation noise of 10 per cent

human behaviour, unlike the catastrophic failures seen for LISA and neural blackboard architectures.

However, tensor products encounter difficulties when creating more complex nested structures. In particular, for twenty dimensional vectors, at least twenty neurons are needed to represent a single atomic value, but 400 (20 × 20) are needed to represent the matrix for A⊗B, 8,000 (20 × 20 × 20) are needed for A⊗B⊗C, and so on. In other words, the maximum depth of the structure is fixed by the number of neurons used, and this value grows exponentially. For two levels (e.g. 'The cat that the dog chased likes the mouse'), with 100 neurons per dimension (as for the blackboard architecture) and 3,500 dimension per vector,[4] 1.2 billion neurons are required for each sentence. Clearly we will not be able to represent structures of sufficient complexity with the available neurons in the brain.

Tensor products are more realistic in terms of their behavioural limitations on compositionality, since attempting to build more and more complex structures leads to a gradual increase in error. Furthermore, when they are implemented using neurons, there is a natural way to model how the randomness of neural firing affects the high-level behaviour of the system. However, tensor products require unrealistic numbers of neurons to represent deep structures, which makes them problematic as a neural theory of compositionality.

---

[4] See the section on Holographic Reduced Representations for the choice of this number of dimensions. Essentially, 3,500 neurons are needed to effectively code for 50,000 words.

29.3 NON-CLASSICAL ARCHITECTURES

The previous three approaches are all implementations of classical symbol systems. That is, their representations can be directly mapped to the standard symbolic approach to compositionality, where representations of the atomic components are constituents of the representation of the overall structure, just as **dog**, **chase**, and **cat** are constituents of chase(dog,cat). The tensor product approach disguises this fact in its matrix representation, but it is possible to exactly extract those original components (ignoring implementation details such as neuron noise).

Recently, a number of new approaches have been developed which are similar to the tensor product approach, but which abandon the idea of being able to perfectly extract the original components. This family of approaches (including tensor products) are known as Vector Symbolic Architectures (VSAs; Gayler, 2003), and they all share the basic principle of representing their atomic constituents via a numerical vector. They differ, however, in terms of what values are allowed, how vectors are combined together, and how the original values are extracted.

For the purposes of this article, we will focus on the VSA known as Holographic Reduced Representation (HRR; Plate, 2003). This makes use of atomic representation vectors of the same form as that used in the tensor product approach discussed above: vectors of numbers with a total length of one. Other VSAs, such as Binary Splatter Codes, only allow the values 0 and 1 for each dimension. Most of our discussion about how to form neural models will apply to any VSA. Plate (2003) provides a detailed overview of the algorithmic differences between numerous VSAs.

29.3.1 Holographic Reduced Representations

The key difference between HRRs and the tensor product approach is that in HRRs, *everything* is a vector with a fixed length. That is, instead of A⊗B producing a large matrix, it produces a vector of the same size as the original vectors. The operation used to do this is *cyclic convolution*, diagrammed in Fig. 29.5.

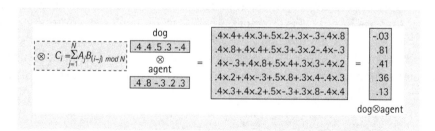

FIGURE 29.5 Binding values via Holographic Reduced Representations

Since the result is of the same dimension as the original vectors, we can make a representation as deep as is desired, while still requiring only a fixed number of neurons. However, this is accomplished at the expense of accuracy: as the complexity of the structure increases, the expected accuracy of the decoding will decrease.

Decoding is accomplished by performing a cyclic convolution with the inverse of a value. The inverse is defined simply by rearranging the values in a vector so that, for example, [a,b,c,d,e] becomes [a,e,d,c,b]. The result is a close approximation of the originally bound value. For example, if we have the representation

dog⊗agent+chase⊗verb+cat⊗theme,

we can perform the calculation shown in Fig. 29.6 to determine what the value that was originally bound to **agent**.

This works because of two fundamental properties of HRRs (and VSAs in general):

A⊗B⊗inverse(B)≈A and A+B≈A.

In words, the convolution of a product of vectors with the inverse of one element is approximated equal to the other element, and the superposition of two elements is somewhat similar to either element. As a consequence, elements can be bound and superposed multiple times and still be recoverable from the resulting vector.

Plate (2003) determined how many dimensions are required to accurately represent and recover structures of this sort. For a fixed number of atomic values in the language (m) and a given maximum number of terms to be combined (k), and a certain probability of error (q), the following formula can be used to determine the number of dimensions needed (n).

$$n=3.16(k - 0.25) \ln \left(\frac{m}{q^3} \right)$$

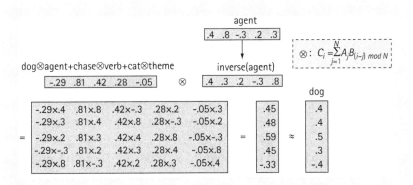

FIGURE 29.6 Extracting structure from an HRR representation. The combined structure is convolved with the inverse of **agent**, resulting in an output value that is an approximation of the original value for **dog**

Given this, we can represent structures with up to 100 terms out of a vocabulary of 50,000 words with 99 per cent accuracy using 3,500 dimensions. Since HRRs are non-classical representation systems, this limitation on accuracy will be a part of any theoretical discussion, even before considering the issues involved in implementing HRRs in neurons. However, using the estimate of 100 neurons per dimension, 350,000 realistic spiking neurons with properties typical to those found in the cortex would be sufficient. This requires less than $2\,mm^2$ of cortical area, significantly less than the neural blackboard architecture, LISA, or tensor products. Indeed, this is many orders of magnitude fewer neurons than the other approaches. However, when implemented in noisy, realistic neurons, with complex structures and atomic vectors that are not randomly distributed, more dimensions are likely to be required to achieve this degree of accuracy. Exactly how much more depends on the neurophysiological details of the neurons involved. It should also be noted that current neural simulations have used 100 dimensions. Efforts are underway to scale this up.

29.3.2 Neural Engineering Framework

Given that HRRs have the best plausibilty of scaling appropriately, here we consider how to implement the necessary operations to construct HRRs in biologically realistic networks. While these methods can be applied to the other approaches, their initial implausibility regarding the use of neural resources makes it unclear what value there is in pursuing that possibility.

Examing the implementation of HRRs in detail allows an analysis of how (or if) realistic neurons can perform the necessary calculations, and what effects different sorts of neurotransmitters, firing rates, and the other diverse features of real physical neurons might have on these representations. The approach we adopt is the Neural Engineering Framework (NEF; Eliasmith and Anderson, 2003), and has been used to model a wide variety of real neural systems, including the barn owl auditory system (Fischer, 2005), the rodent navigation system (Conklin and Eliasmith, 2005), escape and swimming control in zebrafish (Kuo and Eliasmith, 2005), working memory systems (Singh and Eliasmith, 2006), and the translational vestibular ocular reflex in monkeys (Eliasmith, Westover, and Anderson, 2002).

As in the discussions of the previous models, neurons are divided into neural groups. However, in NEF, a neural group can represent a complete vector, rather than just one value within a vector. The neurons within a group are assumed to be *heterogeneous* (as observed in cortex) in that they all have different maximum firing rates and tuning curves, and possibly a variety of receptors and other physiological properties. The pattern of firing across these neurons can be characterized as a representation of a particular value, such as [0, −0.9, −0.2, 0.3, 0.2, . . .] (used above to represent the symbol cat). Notably, the number of dimensions in the vector is *not* the same as the number of neurons in the neural group. By adding more neurons, we increase the representation accuracy, counteracting the effects of random noise in neuron firing patterns.

To define a mapping from a particular value we want to represent to the population firing pattern, each neuron in the neural group is assigned an 'encoding vector', which can be inferred from experimental data characterizing the tuning curve of a neuron if it is available. This encoding vector is a vector in the represented space for which the neuron will fire the strongest. This kind of characterization captures the observed behaviour of neurons in many areas of the brain, where such preferred direction vectors are generally found to cover all possible directions in the space being represented. For our purposes, we choose these to be random vectors for each neuron.

The details of how the encoding vector affects the firing of the neuron will vary depending on the type of neuron and the degree of accuracy to which the neuron is being simulated. In general, the activity a (i.e. the spike train) of a particular neuron i to represent a value x is:

$$a_i = G_i \left(a_i \tilde{\phi}_i \cdot x + J_i^{bias} \right)$$

Here, a is the neuron gain or sensitivity, $\tilde{\phi}$ is the encoding vector, and J^{bias} is a fixed current to model background neural activity. G is the response function, which is determined by what sort of neuron is being modelled, including its particular resistances, capacitances, maximum firing rate, and so on. In this work, we use the response function for the leaky integrate-and-fire (LIF) model, which is widely used for its reasonable trade-off between realism and computational requirements. NEF can make use of more detailed models by changing this response function.

Using this approach, we can directly translate from a particular value that we want to represent (x) to the steady-state firing rates of each neuron in the group (a_i). The value being represented is distributed across all of the neurons. This allows for any vector of a given length to be represented, and any value for each dimension within that vector, including negative numbers (which are problematic to encode just by naively considering the firing rates of neurons).

If we have the firing pattern for a neural group, we can also determine what value is currently being represented: the reverse of the encoding process. This is more complex than encoding, and in general it is impossible to perfectly recover the original value from the firing pattern. However, we can determine an *optimal linear decoder*, ϕ, to give a high quality estimate (Eliasmith and Anderson, 2003), $\hat{x}$:

$$\hat{x} = \sum_i \phi_i a_i \quad \phi = \Gamma^{-1} \Upsilon \quad \Gamma_{ij} = \int a_i a_j dx \quad \Upsilon_j = \int a_j x dx$$

This decoder can be constructed to be robust to random variations in the firing rates of neurons (and to neuron death). The representations can thus be made as accurate as desired by increasing the number of neurons used.

Since any theory of compositionality requires the ability to combine and extract information from the representational structures, we also need to determine how to manipulate these representations using neurons. This must be done via the synaptic connections between neural groups. We do not assume that it is possible to perform multiplication between two different values via a synaptic connection; instead, NEF shows how this can be performed using standard linear weighted connections.

Let us begin by considering the simplest case of a transformation that computes the identity function $f(x) = x$. That is, if we have two neural groups (A and B), and we set the value of group A to be x, we want group B to also represent x. This can be seen as the direct transmission of information from one location in the brain to another. For this situation, the optimal connection weights between each neuron i in group A and each neuron j in group B are (this can be seen by substituting the optimal decoding for neurons in A into the encoding equation for neurons in B):

$$\omega_{ji} = a_j \tilde{\phi}_j \cdot \phi_i$$

If this formula is used to determine the strength of the synaptic connection between the neural groups, then group B will be driven to fire such that it represents the same value as group A. As noted in the previous section, the accuracy of this representation will be dependent on the number of neurons in the groups. This system works even though none of the neurons in the two neural groups will have exactly the same encoding vector (and thus firing pattern). That is, there will generally not be a one-to-one correspondence between any neurons in the groups.

We can also connect neural groups in such a way as to transform the value from A to B. That is, we can set the synaptic weights so that B represents a vector that is, for example, twice the vector in A, or the sum of the values in the A, or any other desired function $f(x)$. This is done using the same formula as above, but the decoding vectors ϕ are replaced by an *optimal linear function decoder* determined using the following formulae:

$$f(\hat{x}) = \sum_i \phi_i a_i \quad \phi = \Gamma^{-1} \Upsilon \quad \Gamma_{ij} = \int a_i a_j dx \quad \Upsilon_j = \int a_j f(x) dx$$

Using this approach, we can determine the neural connection weights needed to compute the circular convolution of two input vectors. Thus, we can bind together the values in different neural groups to create any HRR structure. We have previously shown how this approach can be used to represent rule-following behaviour in different contexts by modelling the Wason card-flipping task (Eliasmith, 2005). This involved over 20,000 spiking neurons organized to perform cyclic convolution on values stored in an associative memory. In other words, not only can arbitrary structures be represented, but also manipulations of these structures can be represented and applied using this approach. This allows for fully compositional behaviour, as necessary to meet Jackendoff's (2002) challenges.

An important feature of the Neural Engineering Framework is that the methods for generating connection weights and representations continue to be applicable no matter how detailed the underlying models of single neurons is. It can be applied to rate neurons, leaky integrate-and-fire (LIF) neurons, adaptive LIF neurons, and even the highly complex compartmental models that require supercomputers to simulate the firing pattern of a single neuron. This means that as we obtain more information about particular neurons involved in a cognitive behaviour, we can add relevant information into the cognitive model and determine the effects of those insights on the overall model. Furthermore, simulations can first be done using a simplistic neural model requiring less computing power, and then once a suitable cognitive model is created a more detailed neural model can be used to generate precise predictions about firing patterns, representational accuracy, etc.

An example of adding increased biological detail involves the synaptic connection weights. In general, the approach described above results in both positively and negatively weighted connections. This is not consistent with what is sometimes called 'Dale's Principle', the observation that in real brains positive (excitatory) and negative (inhibitory) weights use different neurotransmitters and are attributable to distinct types of neurons. Parisien, Anderson, and Eliasmith (2008) show a related approach to determining weights which separates excitatory and inhibitory connections as needed, though with a slight increase in the number of neurons. This biological detail can be added to any NEF model, without disrupting the original function of the model.

Being able to incorporate whatever biological detail is deemed relevant for understanding the system allows the NEF to be a flexible tool for modelling neural systems. Coupling the NEF with the HRR approach leads to a neural model of compositionality that is consistent with available modern neuroscientific evidence as to the capabilities and limitations of real physical neurons.

29.3.3 Evaluating NEF HRRs

The result of implementing Holographic Reduced Representations using the Neural Engineering Framework is a detailed, biologically plausible model of compositionality. Unlike LISA and the neural blackboard architecture, an HRR-based system gradually becomes less accurate as the complexity of the structures increases. This matches the observed gradual increase in error as cognitive load increases. Like tensor products, similar behaviour is observed if neurons are destroyed in the NEF model. The NEF approach to representing values by encoding them in neuron firing patterns is highly robust both to increased noise and the loss of neurons. For example, in our model of the Wason card task (Eliasmith, 2005), on average a full third of the neurons could be removed from the HRR representation before the system became incapable of correctly decoding and applying structured rules. This is a side effect due to the system being designed to deal with realistic spiking neurons and neural variability.

The NEF provides a direct method for designing neural systems that can transmit HRR representations from one location in the brain to another, something not considered by the other approaches. Also, the algebraic manipulations of HRRs can all be implemented by calculating the connection weights between neural groups. For example, the operation A ⊗ B = C can be implemented by having a neural group representing A, a neural group representing B, an intermediate combined representation, and an final neural group representing C. The total number of neurons required is five times the number of neurons needed for a single representation. Given our previous calculations, this means about 1.4 million neurons would be needed ($9\,mm^2$ of cortex). However, this same population of neurons can be used for every binding and unbinding operation, so there is no need to scale the network as structures become more complex, or as the number of possible elements increase. This allows the model to extract required parts of structures and to build up new structures as needed. All of these systems inherit the NEF's capacity for graceful degradation of performance as structure complexity increases.

Finally, since models created using the NEF can be made to be as realistic as possible (in terms of accurately modelling neural behaviour), the results of such models can be directly compared to available neuroscientific evidence. Such comparisons could be based on patterns of connectivity, variability in firing rates, dendritic activity, and so on. This provides a potentially rich source of evidence for testing and comparing theories of compositionality.

However, this is not to say that our approach represents a full and complete theory of compositionality. Indeed, there are many unanswered questions that are topics of ongoing research. For one, there are questions about constructing appropriate vector representations corresponding to the underlying symbols in our system. We do not follow the standard approach of having particular neural groups represent particular symbols (i.e. 'grandmother cells'), but instead we claim that symbols correspond to distributed patterns of activation. However, this raises the question of how these particular patterns come into such correspondence, and how various parts of the brain maintain common representations. It should be noted that although we have assumed random patterns in this paper, we take these patterns to often include semantic similarity, so that the patterns for cat and dog would be similar in some important ways. Furthermore, our approach allows the dimensionality of the representation to change across different regions of the brain—certain regions need less accuracy or a less broad range of symbols. Exactly how this is accomplished is an open question.

The most important question, however, is how such a compositional system can be controlled. In this paper we have focused entirely on the question of representation, and ensuring that the representation would support compositional structure manipulations. To make use of such a system within a full cognitive architecture it is important to specify how this facility is used to answer questions, process complex embedded sentences, form new grounded representations, and so on. Although we have made some progress in this direction, including using this approach to implement a production system associated with the basal ganglia (Stewart and Eliasmith, 2008), more work needs to be done. That said, we believe that the approach of combining Vector Symbolic Architectures with the Neural Engineering Framework resolves many implementation issues and offers an alternative perspective from a purely classical approach (see Eliasmith (in press) for a detailed suggestion of how to answer these questions).

29.4 SUMMARY

We believe that neurobiological constraints can, and should, inform theory choice when evaluating theories of compositionality. In particular, we find that by examining how a particular theory would be implemented neurally we can identify whether a model is implausible in terms of neural requirements (i.e. too many neurons, implausible connectivity, etc.). We can also determine whether the high-level behaviour of a model due to neural restrictions is comparable to the performance limitations of compositionality observed in humans.

Examining LISA and neural blackboard architectures suggests that a direct implementation of a classical symbol system will inevitably be unrealistic. LISA requires many orders of magnitude more neurons than are found in the human brain. The neural blackboard approach requires fewer neurons, but in a highly complex and intricate arrangement that is unlikely to be robust. More importantly, neither approach exhibits the gradual degradation of performance as complexity increases that is characteristic of human behaviour.

Moving away from the directly classical approaches, the tensor product approach and VSAs in general (including HRRs) provide exactly the graceful degradation that is desired. Tensor products (which are arguably isomorphic to classical symbol systems), however, require an unrealistic number of neurons to capture the necessary structures found in language. Holographic Reduced Representations provide the best of both worlds: realistic neural limitations and realistic performance limitations.

Although HRRs exhibit compositional behaviour, they are not classical symbol systems. Even if the implementational details are ignored, a theoretical investigation of HRRs will diverge from classical theories of compositionality. In particular, the representations of the constituents of a structure are not present in the representation of the structure itself. Instead, noisy versions of these constituents must be extracted via algebraic manipulating: that is, extraction will always merely provide an approximation of the original constituents.

This new theory of compositionality also provides new avenues for evaluation. Numerical comparisons can be made between the accuracy of this system as complexity increases and the accuracy observed in people. The model can also be used to generate predictions of what sorts of firing patterns would be observed in neurons performing this sort of task, what connectivity they would have, and even the amount of time it would take to perform structure manipulations. We believe that exploiting these sources of evidence will be fruitful for evaluating theories of human compositional behaviour.

CHAPTER 30

....

NEURONAL ASSEMBLY
MODELS OF
COMPOSITIONALITY

....

ALEXANDER MAYE AND
ANDREAS K. ENGEL

30.1 INTRODUCTION

....

The neurons of a brain act in concert. The large number of connections between neurons
renders it very likely that the firing of any given neuron will influence several downstream cells. Other signalling mechanisms, like those involving humoral or modulatory
substances, have the inherent function to affect even larger populations of neurons.
Apparently, the loss of single neurons does not eliminate a certain brain function completely, but degrades it at worst. The implication is that most brain functions are carried
out by ensembles of neurons which have the capability to compensate for the loss.
While the distributed nature of neural processing is obvious, it is currently unresolved
how large neuronal populations can dynamically be coordinated to accomplish their
function.

Since the discovery of neurons as the basic functional units of the brain an eminent
question is that of the neuronal codes, that is, which functional property of a neuron
encodes the information processed in the respective circuit. The prevailing theory holds
that the information is encoded in the level of activity of a neuron, its average firing
rate. With regard to cell assemblies, evidence is accumulating for the hypothesis that
the temporal relation between the signals of neurons carries information (von der
Malsburg, 1981; Abeles, 1982). In principle, firing rate and synchrony constitute two
independent dimensions in which information can be encoded. Often, however, these
two aspects of neural firing change in conjunction. This occurs, for instance, during
episodes of oscillatory activity, which are frequently found when recording neuronal
activity in-vivo and in-vitro (Engel et al., 1992; Engel et al., 2001).

A popular hypothesis about the function of these oscillations considers them as a mechanism for dynamically linking the activity of spatially dispersed neurons and composing neuronal assemblies (von der Malsburg, 1981; Engel et al., 1992; Singer, 1999; Engel et al., 2001). In this chapter we will review theories explaining the formation of neuronal assemblies, the functions that assemblies can have, present computational models of oscillatory neural networks, and show how they can carry information.

30.2 NEURONAL ASSEMBLY THEORY

In 1949 Hebb published the cell assembly model, in which the co-instantiation of features by an object causes a co-activation of neurons that respond to these features and results in a stronger synaptic coupling between the respective neurons (Hebb, 1949). If we encounter red squares in our environment, neurons that respond to the colour red and neurons responding to the edges of the square will get stimulated together frequently. This co-activation will strengthen the synaptic connections between colour-sensitive neurons responding to red and edge-sensitive neurons responding to the shape of a square, thus forming a cell assembly that is specifically activated by the presentation of a red square. The strong connections between the neurons of an assembly mediate the activation of the whole ensemble even if only part of the neurons receive appropriate sensory stimulation. This function is the basis for associative memory and invariant encoding (Hopfield, 1982). This implies, for instance, that the red square can be recognized even if it is partly occluded.

The advantage of the assembly model is that a single cell can be part of several assemblies which circumvents the problem of the prohibitively large number of neurons required if object memory were carried by single—'gnostic'—cells (Konorski, 1967; Gross, 2002). Moreover, the assembly model in principle permits the decomposition of the whole set of cells forming the assembly into smaller subsets, reflecting the constituent parts into which a complete object could be decomposed. What is lost in the classical Hebb model, however, is information about the syntactic configuration of constituents that led to the activation of this assembly. Looking at a picture of a man, for example, it makes a big difference for us if his head is between his shoulders or under his arm. Another problem is known as the superposition catastrophe (von der Malsburg, 1987) and concerns the question how the properties of an object, signalled by the simultaneous activity of the respective property indicative neurons, is assigned to individual objects. For example, looking at a scene with a red square and a green circle activates neurons responding to the colours red and green and neurons responding to the edges of the square and the circle. A scene with a juxtaposition of the properties, that is a red circle and a green square, would generate the same activation pattern. If there were no mechanism that binds the information about the colour of an object together with the shape of this object we would not be able to distinguish both scenes. This problem is known as the 'binding problem' (Engel et al., 1992; Singer, 1994).

The problems of Hebb's original version of the assembly theory can be alleviated by making the formation of cell assemblies more dynamic and introducing a temporal binding mechanism that can distinguish assemblies. Several computational models have been developed to explain the formation of such dynamic assemblies in the brain. One of the first was probably the synfire-chain model by Abeles (1982). It assumes a network of spiking neurons with converging and diverging feed-forward connections between a large number of layers. The synchronous firing of a group of neurons activates a group on the next layer. The network can show dynamically stable, reproducible activity propagating from layer to layer (Diesmann et al., 1999). This establishes a dynamic link or 'chain' between the participating neurons, and distinguishes them from the uncorrelated background activity of others. Which neurons get linked depends on the input to the lowest level and the coupling strength between the neurons, which can change during learning. Each neuron can participate in several chains, allowing for a combinatorially huge number of dynamic patterns generated by the network. This also solves the binding problem for the case of distinct objects sharing the same property, since the neurons responding to this property can be members of distinct cell assemblies simultaneously.

Another influential model is the 'correlation theory of brain function' by von der Malsburg (1981). The basic idea is that within a network of anatomical connections smaller topological networks—cell assemblies in other words—can develop by means of synaptic modulation. This modulation is supposed to occur on two different timescales. Correlated activation of a set of neurons activates the synaptic connections between these neurons, while uncorrelated activation deactivates them. Activation and deactivation in this context refer to a modulation of synaptic weights on a short timescale, typical for short-term memory, the physiological mechanisms of which are not specified. In this manner a network can shape its connectivity according to the correlation statistics of the input. Activated connections define topological networks which signal the simultaneous presence of features in the input to which the neurons of the respective network respond. The activation states of short-term connections transfer to a more permanent weight change on a longer time-scale, representing long-term memory. These slowly changing connections within a topological network allow the activity from parts of the network to invade previously inactive parts, thereby activating the whole topological network even if the input is incomplete. This property solves the invariance problem, which concerns the question of how the memory trace of an object can be activated independently of irrelevant properties of the particular sensory stimulation such as, for instance, lighting conditions, distance, or orientation.

The correlation theory is neutral with regard to the neurophysiological types of correlated activity. The original idea refers to correlations between irregular spike trains or bursts of single neurons. A special case is the temporal correlation of rhythmic, or oscillatory, activity, which can be observed on the single neuron level (e.g. chattering cells (Gray and Viana Di Prisco, 1997)) as well as on the macroscopic level (e.g. Local Field Potentials, LFPs, (Engel et al., 2001)). Recent accounts of the correlation theory consider the phase relation between synchronized oscillatory neuronal populations as a mechanism for interaction and transmission of information (Womelsdorf et al., 2007). Oscillatory activity might not be only the expression of a temporal code, but could also impose specific time windows for functional modifications of neurons. If these time windows are aligned between two populations of synchronized neurons, the modifications concern both populations, if not, only one or none of them. This mechanism can not only be used to shape the effective connectivity in networks of neurons with synchronized activity, but also to gate the flow of information (Salinas and Sejnowski, 2001).

In the past two decades numerous studies using multi-electrode recordings or non-invasive recordings of brain activity using EEG or MEG have provided support for the 'correlation theory' (for review, see Engel et al., 1992; Singer, 1999; Engel et al., 2001). These studies have shown that global stimulus properties are reflected in the synchronization of sensory neurons (Gray et al., 1989; Kreiter and Singer, 1994) and, moreover, that synchrony in thalamocortical systems can relate to changes of perceptual contents (Fries et al., 1997; Castelo-Branco et al., 2000), to attention (Steinmetz et al., 2000; Fries et al., 2001; Womelsdorf et al., 2006; Siegel et al., 2008), and expectation (Riehle et al., 1997; von Stein et al., 2000). Beyond individual sensory systems, a relevance of temporal correlations for complex processes such as multi-sensory integration (Senkowski et al., 2008), sensorimotor interactions (Roelfsema et al., 1997), memory formation (Herrmann et al., 2004), language (Bastiaansen et al., 2005), and consciousness (Engel and Singer, 2001) has been suggested.

30.3 COMPOSITIONALITY AND PART–WHOLE RELATIONSHIPS

As has been argued by Fodor and Pylyshyn (1988), a neural coding scheme supposed to account for structured mental activity should exhibit a set of crucial features, including systematicity, productivity, and compositionality. Systematicity refers to the observation that intentional capacities with similar contents are correlated. With regard to the computational model we will discuss later, an example for systematicity would be that if one has the capacity to think of a red vertical and a green horizontal object, one has the capacity to think of a green vertical and a red horizontal object as well. Productivity describes the potential of the mind to allow for an infinite number of concepts. Very likely, it is the combinatorial power of composing concepts into more complex concepts that underlies this capacity.[1]

According to Fodor and Pylyshyn's view, classical neural network architectures, such as those developed by mid-1980s connectionism (Rumelhart and McClelland,

---

[1] Still systematicity and productivity do not presuppose compositionality. For linguistic arguments as well as more thorough definitions of the three terms, see Werning (2005b).

1986*a*), are not able to account sufficiently for these features, because such models are essentially based on association embodied by learning connection weights, and they lack genuine combinatorial structure. As a consequence, such models (i) do not distinguish between structurally atomic and structurally complex activity patterns, (ii) the semantic contents of a distributed pattern is not a function of its syntactic parts and their interrelations, and (iii) processes operating upon such patterns are not sensitive to their structure. As we will argue in the remainder of this chapter, fast temporal dynamics may be a way to endow distributed networks with exactly these properties, because synchrony, or coherence of activity, allows specific relations to be established between network elements and, thus, may enable some type of 'proto-syntax'.

Introducing synchronization between several synfire chains, Bienenstock (1995) suggested that these models can exhibit compositionality. Abeles et al. (2004) extended this idea by considering hierarchies of synfire chains. If the synfire chains on a lower level of the hierarchy get activated by primitive concepts like colour or shape, the synchronization between these chains represents the conjunction of primitive features. The synchronized chains on the low level trigger a chain on a higher level in the hierarchy, which then represents the particular combination of features that characterize the current stimulus.

The same principle could be reiterated at a larger scale, where the constituents of a topological network are not neurons any more, but topological networks themselves. By this generalization a hierarchy of networks of correlated activities could be defined that reflects the hierarchical structure of natural objects. The level in the hierarchy corresponds to the strength of the correlation of the activity, with the networks on the lower levels expressing the strongest correlation, and weaker correlations between networks on higher levels. Alternatively, hierarchical binding at multiple levels could be achieved by utilizing different frequency bands. For instance, fast oscillations could be employed to bind information locally within object parts, whereas slower oscillations might serve for embedding constituents into a more global context. We suggest that such a scheme of dynamic hierarchical binding might be seen as a potential model for compositionality.

30.4 COMPUTATIONAL MODELS OF DYNAMIC BINDING

Using similar formalisms, oscillatory activity can be modelled at different scales, ranging from a single neuron with oscillatory activity to networks of coupled oscillators. The mathematical approaches to studying the dynamics and functionality of such networks differ with respect to the amount of biological realism they exhibit and the type of oscillation they describe. Relaxation oscillators (Example 30.1) are used to model the discontinuous dynamics of single spikes or bursts. So-called Wilson–Cowan oscillators (Example 30.2) can generate harmonic oscillations and are more appropriate for describing continuous dynamics like that of the average firing rates of neuronal populations or local field potentials. A simplified version are phase-coupled oscillators, which we use to investigate the interactions between oscillation phase, amplitude, and frequency (Example 30.3).

Example 30.1 Relaxation oscillators describe oscillatory spiking

The activity of a relaxation oscillator (van der Pol, 1926; FitzHugh, 1961) is characterized by long phases with small state changes, the silent phase, and intermittent, short, active phases with rapid state changes. A mechanistic analogy of the two phases is the slow accumulation of potential energy during the silent phase and the sudden release of this energy during the active phase. This can be used to model repetitive firing of single spikes by a neuron or the envelope of oscillatory burst activity.

In a generalized form the oscillator model is given by

$$\frac{dx}{dt} = f(x, y) + I$$

$$\frac{dy}{dt} = \epsilon g(x, y)$$

which describes the dynamics of the two state variables x and y. Here, I is the input to the oscillator. The numerically small parameter ϵ causes y to change on a slow timescale, while x can change more rapidly. Specific implementations of this model have been used to demonstrate figure–ground segmentation (Termann and Wang, 1995) and auditory stream segregation (Wang, 1996).

If several oscillators are coupled, they mutually perturb their dynamics and complex phenomena can arise. In the following we describe a network that we used to model a Gestalt-based grouping of features and binding across feature domains for visual stimuli (Maye and Werning, 2004). The network depicted in Fig. 30.1 consists of oscillators that are arranged in a three-dimensional, rectangular grid. The connectivity is local, that is every oscillator has connections to its neighbours within a sphere of radius r. Connection strength decreases with distance. The connection type is anisotropic. Neighbouring oscillators within a layer are connected by synchronizing connections. Oscillators in different layers have desynchronizing connections. In this model synchronization is mediated by excitatory, and desynchronization by inhibitory connections. If conduction delays in the connectivity are considered, this mapping can change (König and Schillen, 1991; Schillen and König, 1991). This scheme has been chosen to account for two of the Gestalt laws of perception (Wertheimer, 1958), according to which elements that are spatially proximal and similar have the tendency to be grouped together.

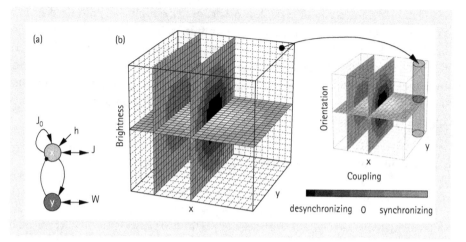

FIGURE 30.1 (a) A neuronal oscillator consisting of two populations of excitatory (x) and inhibitory neurons (y) with recurrent coupling. Each oscillator is coupled to its neighbours either via their excitatory (J) or inhibitory neurons (W). **(b)** A feature module is composed of a three-dimensional arrangement of oscillators (represented by small cubes). Slices with grey levels visualize connection type and strength of the oscillator at the centre of the feature module. The figure shows two feature modules, one brightness module and one orientation module. They model retinotopic maps of brightness and orientation sensitive neurons in the visual cortex of mammalian brains. The arrow between the feature modules symbolizes synchronizing connections between a single oscillator at the origin and all oscillators with the same receptive field position in the other feature module (visualized by a cylinder). This connection scheme is applied to all other positions as well. Using the same pattern, other feature maps (for, e.g., disparity, direction of motion) can be integrated into the model. Note that we do not assume a monotonic change of values along the feature axes.

Example 30.2 Wilson–Cowan oscillators model activity at the population level

Starting from two populations of cells, one of excitatory and the other of inhibitory neurons with recurrent connections between them, Wilson and Cowan (1972) developed a mathematical description of the dynamics of the average firing rate of the two populations. If the activity of a population of excitatory neurons is denoted by x and that of an inhibitory population by y, the dynamics of the system can be described by a system of coupled differential equations:

$$\tau_x \frac{dx_i}{dt} = -x_i - g_y(y_i) + J_0 g_x(x_i) + \sum_j J_{ij} g_x(x_j) + h_i + \eta_x \tag{1}$$

$$\tau_y \frac{dy_i}{dt} = -y_i + g_x(x_i) - \sum_j W_{ij} g_y(y_j) + \eta_y. \tag{2}$$

In these equations $g()$ denotes transfer functions that map the activation of the respective cell population to an output value, J_0 is some self-excitation to obtain stable limit-cycle

(continued)

Example 30.2 Continued

oscillations of the otherwise dissipative system, and the time constants τ can be adjusted to match the oscillation frequency to physiological values. The noise terms η model the variability in neuronal responses, and h_i is the input that this oscillator gets from the stimulus. The sum term in equation (1) describes the input that the excitatory population gets from other excitatory populations. Likewise the sum term in equation (2) is the input to the inhibitory population from the inhibitory populations of coupled oscillators. The coupling between excitatory populations has a synchronizing effect, a coupling between inhibitory populations of two oscillators desynchronizes their oscillations.

Within one layer all oscillators are selective for similar values of a feature at the respective position in the visual field. This models the retinotopic maps of feature sensitive neurons in primary visual cortex. These maps consist of neurons responding to visual features such as, for example, the orientations of edges, disparities, directions of movement, colour hues, and brightness values (Felleman and van Essen, 1991). The connection scheme facilitates the synchronization of neighbouring oscillators that are stimulated by similar features and likely by the same object in the visual field. At the same time oscillators activated by different feature values, and which are located in distinct layers of the network, will desynchronize their activity. This network binds the activity of oscillators with compatible features, and separates it from oscillators that are responding to distinct features. This is shown in the snapshots of the network dynamics upon stimulation with a dark grey, vertical bar and a light grey, horizontal bar (see Fig. 30.2). All neurons that respond to the orientation or brightness of one bar get activated together, but the activity patterns for the two bars are desynchronized, that is, are out of phase.

Example 30.3 Phase-coupled oscillator models make the types of interactions between oscillators explicit

If the coupling between two Wilson–Cowan oscillators is weak, the interactions of the amplitudes of both oscillators can be neglected, and they interact via their phase difference only. This leads to a simplified model (Schuster and Wagner, 1990) in which the output o of a model neuron i is described by a sine function multiplied by an amplitude value a:

$$x_i = a_i sin(\phi_i)$$

$$\frac{d\phi_i}{dt} = \omega + f(\phi_i, \phi_j)$$

ω is the base frequency of the uncoupled oscillator. The coupling function models the effect of (the phase of) a coupled oscillator j on the phase of the oscillator i. If f yields positive
(continued)

Example 30.3 Continued

---

values, the phase is advanced, while for negative values it is recessed. A typical choice for f is

$$f(\phi_i, \phi_j) = -\sin(\phi_i - \phi_j).$$

The advantage of the phase model is that each oscillator is described by only one state variable, its current phase, instead of two in the Wilson–Cowan model. Nonetheless we are free to extend the phase-coupled model by equations that explicitly describe additional interactions between the oscillators. If we want to model phase, amplitude, and frequency interactions, a general description can be given by

$$\frac{d\phi}{dt} = \omega(t) + f(\phi, a, \omega)$$

$$\frac{da}{dt} = g(\phi, a, \omega)$$

$$\frac{d\omega}{dt} = h(\phi, a, \omega)$$

By choosing functions f, g, and h, the effects of different types of interactions can be investigated. For the simulations described in this chapter we used the model

$$\frac{d\phi_i}{dt} = \omega_i(t) - \sum_j J_p s_{ij} a_j \sin(\phi_i - \phi_j) + \eta_i \tag{3}$$

$$\frac{da_i}{dt} = -a_i + \sum_j J_k s_{ij} a_j + h_i \tag{4}$$

$$\omega_i(t) = a_i(t) \tag{5}$$

In this model the phase interaction is weighted by the coupling strength s_{ij} and the current amplitude a_j of the afferent oscillators j. The coupling matrix s_{ij} is used to model the decaying coupling strength with increasing distance between oscillators i and j, while the parameter J_p controls the overall strength of phase coupling. Similarly, J_k controls the strength of the amplitude coupling. The three equations describe the interactions of the phases and the amplitudes of connected oscillators, and the relation between frequency and amplitude of an oscillator. One important point to note is that equation 5 introduces a frequency modulation by the amplitude. The particular choice of an increasing frequency with increasing oscillation amplitude is arbitrary, and in fact the opposite choice, a decreasing frequency with increasing amplitude (e.g. $\omega_i(t) = 1/a_i(t)$, $\omega_i(t) = a_{max} - a_i(t)$) does not change the results qualitatively.

The connection scheme is generic in the sense that every oscillator makes the same connection pattern in its local neighbourhood (apart from oscillators at or close to the border). Whether any set of oscillators synchronizes its activity or not, is determined by the stimulus properties.

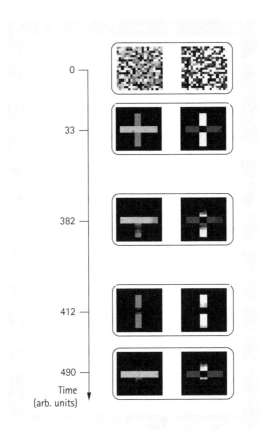

0

33

382

412

490

Time
(arb. units)

FIGURE 30.2 Dynamics of the network upon stimulation with a dark grey, vertical bar and a light grey, horizontal bar (see Fig. 30.3a). At each time point the left panel shows a snapshot of the activity in the brightness module, and the right panel in the orientation module. From the initially random state ($t = 0$) the network first activates all neurons that receive input ($t = 33$). After several cycles the two bars get separated in time. All neurons activated by a bar oscillate in synchrony. This demonstrates how the responses of neurons can be bound together within each feature domain and between different feature modalities. The oscillations for the two bars are desynchronized, though, representing the distinction between them.

The network topology is based on previous models, in which the synchronization properties depending on the type and delay of the coupling between oscillators were investigated (König and Schillen, 1991; Schillen and König, 1991). In a similar model (Li, 2000) a biologically plausible connection topology was employed based on another Gestalt law of perception: elements that constitute a good continuation are perceived together. Beside contour integration, this model exhibits a number of features of the primary processing levels of the human visual system, like texture segregation, contour enhancement and completion, and the pop-out effect. Binding across separate modules, encoding features such as orientation, colour, and disparity information by synchronized oscillations in a network of Wilson–Cowan oscillators, has also been demonstrated (Schillen and König, 1994).

30.5 EIGENMODES DISPLAY ALTERNATIVE INTERPRETATIONS OF THE STIMULUS

Upon stimulation the network exhibits a temporal dynamics in which the oscillators establish certain phase relations between them. If these phase relations stay fixed over time, we consider the dynamics as stable. The stable phase relations are adopted by the oscillators after a transient period in which the effects due to the initialization of the network or switching on the stimulation decay. Depending on the parameters, the network can also undergo unstable dynamics like chaos (van Vreeswijk and Sompolinsky, 1996). However, here we want to limit ourselves to the dynamically stable case. We are interested in analysing the phase relations between oscillators. The prevalent method is to compute cross-correlograms (Example 30.4), which can be used to analyse temporal relations between oscillators in a pairwise manner.

Example 30.4 Cross-correlograms analyse the phase relation of a pair of oscillators

---

The classical method for analysing the synchronization of two oscillators is to compute the cross-correlogram. It shows the cross-correlation $R_{xy}(\tau) = \sum_{t=1}^{T-\tau} x(t)y(t+\tau)$ of two time series x and y depending on the temporal shift τ in time between the two series. Normalization with respect to the means μ and variances σ of x and y of the cross-correlation yields the correlation coefficient: $C_{xy}(\tau) = (R_{xy}(\tau) - \mu_x\mu_y)/\sigma_x\sigma_y$.

The peaks of the cross-correlogram give information about the phase relation of the activities of two oscillators. If the peak is at τ ms, the two oscillators are perfectly synchronous. If the maximum is at another time difference, one of the time-series has to be shifted by that delay in order to bring the two series into perfect synchrony. This means, that one oscillator leads or lags the other by exactly this delay. If there are no peaks in the cross-correlogram, the two time-series are desynchronized. The figure below shows how the binding of two objects is reflected in the cross-correlogram. Note that the activity of neurons 1–2, 3–4, and 5–6 is synchronized even though there is no direct connection between them.

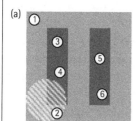

The cross-correlation technique is widely used to analyse the synchronization properties of multi-electrode recordings of brain signals. It analyses the signals pairwise, which is appropriate if the number of channels is low.

a) The stimulus consists of two bars of the same shade of gray in front of a lighter background. The hatched disc shows the coupling range of an oscillator located in the center of the disc. b) Cross-correlograms for the oscillator pairs at positions 1–2, 3–4, and 5–6 revealing synchronization. c) The cross-correlogram of pairs 1–3, 3–5, and 5–1 shows a delay, therefore their oscillations are not synchronized.

(continued)

Example 30.4 Continued

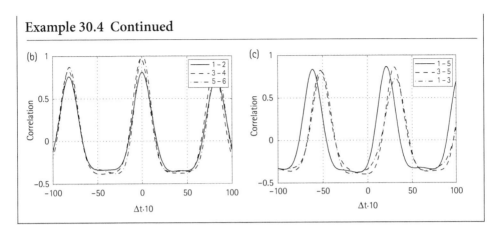

In contrast to experiments in biological brains, the number of 'recording channels' in computational models (e.g. the number of oscillators to be analysed) is potentially large and limited by computing power only. Analysing the dynamics of large networks by pairwise measures is highly ineffective, if not impossible. Rather, a method is required that considers all signals at one time. In physics a number of methods to analyse the dynamics of large systems of coupled elements have been developed. A common approach is to determine the eigenmodes of the dynamics and their temporal evolution (Example 30.5). It is equivalent to principal component analysis (PCA) often applied to multi-dimensional data in biology. Effectively, the eigenmode analysis decomposes the network dynamics into a set of static eigenmodes, that allow the spatial relations of the network activity to be assessed, and the associated characteristic functions, which describe the activation of each eigenmode over time.

In the case of the networks discussed here, the interpretation of eigenmodes is straightforward. All oscillators having positive values in an eigenmode are activated together and are, therefore, synchronized. By the same token, all oscillators with negative values are deactivated together and hence, also synchronized. The two populations of oscillators with positive and negative values are in an anti-phase relation, which we consider as desynchronized. If the value of an oscillator is zero in an eigenmode, this oscillator makes no contribution to this mode.

Example 30.5 Eigenmode analysis considers the joint activity of all oscillators

In mathematical terms, eigenmodes are the eigenvectors of the covariance matrix C of the data X:

$$C = XX^T$$

$$V \Lambda V^{-1} = C$$

The eigenvectors v_i are the columns of matrix V. Reshaping them to the three-dimensional layout of the oscillator network allows the spatial layout of each mode to be visualized. To obtain the time-course of activation of a mode, $c_i(t)$, the network activity can be projected into the space of eigenvectors:

(continued)

Example 30.5 Continued

$$c_i(t) = x(t)^T v_i$$

This corresponds to a rotation of the dynamics in N-dimensional* hyperspace so that the directions of large variances are aligned with the new coordinate axes, the eigenmodes. We will call the scalar functions $c_i(t)$ characteristic functions since they correspond to indexical concepts (see Chapter 31 by Markus Werning, this volume) and hence, object identities. In dynamical systems terms they are called order parameters (Haken, 1990). To reconstruct the original dynamics, all eigenmodes have to be multiplied by their associated characteristic function and summed up, i.e.:

$$x(t) = \sum_i c_i(t) v_i.$$

* N is the number of oscillators in the network.

Using this approach we can describe simulation results obtained with the architecture described above. The eigenmode analysis clearly demonstrates object-specific synchronization if the network of coupled oscillators is activated with two stimuli (cf. Fig. 30.2). As shown in Fig. 30.3, the sign of the elements in each eigenmode clusters oscillators into groups.[2] The third eigenmode,[3] for example, groups the oscillators in the layer with dark-grey-sensitive neurons of the brightness feature module into two groups. The oscillators that are stimulated by the dark grey, vertical bar get activated together and hence, oscillate in synchrony. Likewise, the oscillators that are stimulated by the light grey horizontal also get activated together and are in synchrony as well. But the opposite sign shows the anti-phase relation of the two populations. In our terms this means that the two populations are desynchronized. The remaining oscillators show values at or close to zero, because they are not activated by the stimulus. As in the cross-correlation analysis, we observe that the spatial extent of synchronization exceeds the range of physical connections that each oscillator has with its neighbours.

Comparing the activations between the two feature modules in the eigenmode we see that the dark-grey-sensitive neurons are synchronized with the vertical-sensitive neurons. The same holds for the light-grey- and horizontal-sensitive neurons. This demonstrates how synchrony binds the signals of neurons that are stimulated by different properties of the same object. The interpretation of the third eigenmode is that it shows two distinct objects, a dark grey vertical and a light grey horizontal. Applying the same interpretation to the first eigenmode we arrive at the conclusion that here only one object is present, that is a cross. The second and fourth eigenmodes dissect the bars into left/right and upper/lower parts. Interestingly these eigenmodes correspond to the way a human observer could interpret the stimulus, which can appear perceptually as a cross with two different parts, or as two separate, shaded objects. We have tested

---

[2] The absolute values could provide a grouping, too, but here we consider the sign only.
[3] I.e., the one with the third largest eigenvalue.

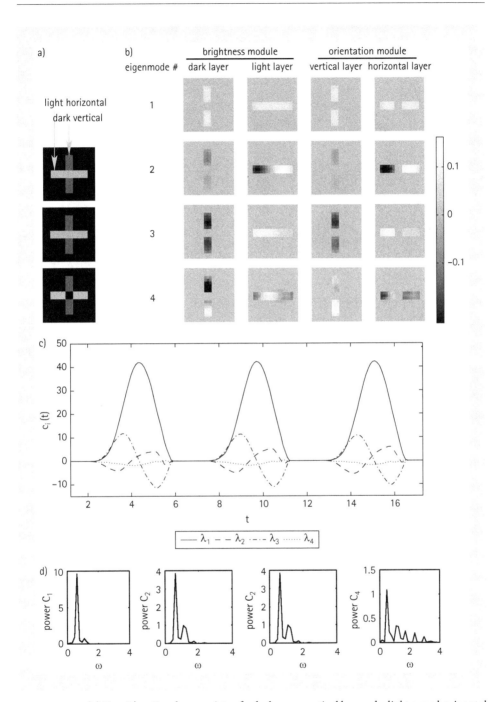

FIGURE 30.3 (a) Top: The stimulus consists of a dark grey, vertical bar and a light grey, horizontal bar. Middle: Activation of oscillators in the brightness module. Bottom: Activation of oscillators in the orientation module. (b) First four eigenmodes of the network layers that get activated by the stimulus, sorted by decreasing eigenvalues from top to bottom. For the interpretation see text. (c) Characteristic functions of the first four eigenmodes. Note that the first function constitutes an envelope for its successors. (d) Frequency spectra of the first four characteristic functions.

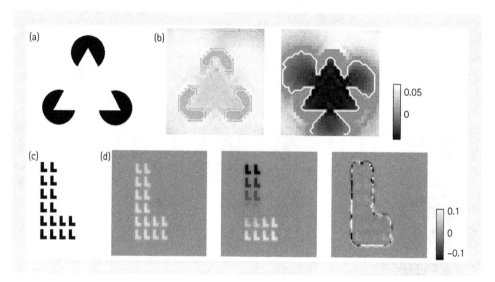

FIGURE 30.4 Selected eigenmodes of a unimodal oscillator network (brightness module only) of other example stimuli. (a) The stimulus shows the Kanisza triangle with illusory contours. (b) The first eigenmode (left panel) shows a simultaneous activation of the triangle and the background. This is a reasonable interpretation because they share the same intensity. In the second eigenmode (right panel) the triangle and the background are separated. Since the network does not employ edge detectors but brightness sensitive neurons only, the phase 'flows out' at the imaginary contours. The white contour lines visualize the level of zero activity. (c) A Navon stimulus. (d) The first eigenmode (left panel) represents the perception at the coarse level, i.e. a large letter 'L'. The second eigenmode (middle panel) shows the two (coarse-level) constituents of the L, the horizontal and the vertical bar. The fourth eigenmode (right panel) shows that the oscillators at the outline build up a separate activation.

many other simple stimuli as well as stimuli showing illusory figures (cf. Fig. 30.4) and always found that the strongest eigenmodes reflect alternative interpretations of the stimulus.

30.6 CHARACTERISTIC FUNCTIONS CAN REFLECT HIERARCHICAL OBJECT STRUCTURE

Fig. 30.3c shows that the characteristic function for the first eigenmode constitutes an envelope for the characteristic functions associated with the second and third eigenmodes. Based on this observation we hypothesize that the characteristic functions put a hierarchical structure on the otherwise unstructured stimulus interpretations given by the eigenmodes. The idea is that the eigenmode associated with the characteristic function with the lowest frequency, the top-most 'envelope', reflects the interpretation of the stimulus on the object level. Eigenmodes associated with subordinate characteristic functions dissect the objects into their constituent parts.

The envelope relation between characteristic functions corresponds to differences in the frequency spectrum of the characteristic functions. As shown in Fig. 30.3d, the top-level envelope contains only low frequencies. For subordinate characteristic functions the fraction of high-frequency signal components increases. From this observation a prediction about brain function can be made: perceiving an object at the global level, that is as a whole, should involve low frequencies in the neuronal oscillatory pattern. The perception of object parts and the focusing on details should entail higher frequencies. Interestingly, some experimental support for this hypothesis seems to exist (Eckhorn et al., 1991).

30.7 Conclusions

We consider synchronized activity as the expression of a functional coupling between neurons, which not necessarily derives in a 1:1 manner from a corresponding anatomical connection. Our modelling results have shown how this functional coupling can integrate the activity of neurons responding to the different properties of an object into a coherent functional entity. The different interpretations of a stimulus configuration emerging in the network dynamics, which we have visualized by the eigenmode analysis, suggests that neuronal synchronization is also a key mechanism at the perceptual level. Here, synchronization could be the neural mechanism that allows for productivity and compositionality of perceptual states.[4]

Moreover, temporal correlations can, in principle, allow for 'structure-sensitive' operations on neural activity patterns. We propose that, in principle, correlation or coherence at different frequencies may allow for dynamic hierarchical binding, accounting for the hierarchical structure of real-world objects. Our modelling results suggest that on top of synchronized, low-frequency oscillations, which may encode the holistic aspects of the object, neurons also synchronize at high frequencies to represent the object's parts.

Of course, much work has to be done to ground this hypothesis in neurophysiological experiments. The current experimental literature provides many examples in which perception co-varied with changes in the strength and layout of functional connectivity. These studies are based on the analysis of coherence or phase-locking (Lachaux et al., 1999) of the activity in different brain areas. Partial directed coherence (Baccalá and Sameshima, 2001) and directed transfer functions (Kamiński et al., 2001) try to estimate the direction of information flow based on the coherent activation of brain regions.

---

[4] The realization of compositional structures by neuronal synchronization has originally been proposed in (Werning, 2005a) and will be explained in the following chapter by Markus Werning in more detail.

What is completely lacking, at this point, is evidence for a context- or action-dependent hierarchical encoding of objects by changes in the correlation structure of neural activity patterns.

The search for experimental evidence for compositional activity patterns has to be parallelled by further development of the theories that account for the computational relevance of such mechanisms. A key question that still remains unresolved is that of 'read-out', that is, the question of how other brain regions can effectively make use of the information encoded in the temporal relations. It seems highly plausible that downstream neuronal populations can detect changes in the level of coherence of neural inputs because it is well established that neurons can act as coincidence detectors under natural input regimes (König et al., 1996). Furthermore, plausible hypotheses have been put forward on how temporal patterns can facilitate the selective routing of signals through distributed networks (Salinas and Sejnowski, 2001; Fries, 2005). However, it remains to be studied whether oscillatory firing patterns containing coupling at multiple frequency ranges could be 'read' by downstream assemblies, and whether the eigen-modes described above merely correspond to 'observer categories' or can themselves adopt biological relevance by being exploited in neural computation. This may require mechanisms that could switch both, the spatial scale and the temporal window width for parallel interactions between assemblies in a context- and action-dependent manner.

Finally, it seems important to emphasize that synchronization as a mechanism for structuring neural activity patterns is unlikely to implement a 'syntax' in the sense of 'Language of thought' models (Fodor, 1975). Clearly, the available experimental findings suggest a high degree of context-sensitivity of oscillatory dynamics. This suggests that the 'coherence model' described here possibly could implement some form of 'weak compositionality' that allows for context-sensitive, but not completely invariant, con-stituency relations. Thus, while grounding syntax in biologically plausible mechanisms for combinatorial encoding, and possibly contributing to explaining the composition-ality of mental states, the coherence model does not (and does not intend to) rescue the 'Language of thought' in its fully fledged classical form.

CHAPTER 31

NON-SYMBOLIC COMPOSITIONAL REPRESENTATION AND ITS NEURONAL FOUNDATION: TOWARDS AN EMULATIVE SEMANTICS

MARKUS WERNING

31.1 COMPOSITIONALITY AND CONSTITUENCY

Throughout its history the principle of compositionality, a widely acknowledged cornerstone for any theory of meaning, has been closely associated with what one might call the principle of semantic constituency. The latter characterizes the subclass of the symbolic theories of meaning. In this chapter a neurobiologically motivated theory of meaning as internal representation will be developed that holds on to the principle of compositionality, but negates the principle of semantic constituency. It is in this sense non-symbolic. The approach builds on neurobiological findings regarding topologically structured cortical feature maps and the mechanism of object-related binding by neuronal synchronization. It incorporates the Gestalt principles of psychology and is implemented by recurrent neural networks. The semantics to be developed is structural analogous—yes, in fact isomorphic—to some variant of model-theoretical semantics, which likewise is compositional and non-symbolic. However, unlike standard model-theoretical semantics, it regards meanings as set-theoretical constructions not of denotations, but of their neural counterparts or, as we will say, their emulations. The semantics to be developed is a neuro-emulative model-theoretical semantics of a first-order language.

The association between the two principles can already be found in what is often regarded as Frege's classical formulation of compositionality:

> With a few syllables [language] can express an incalculable number of thoughts.... This would be impossible, were we not able to distinguish parts in the thoughts corresponding to the parts of a sentence, so that the structure of the sentence serves as the image of the structure of the thought. (Frege, 1923/1976: 55)

The compositionality of meaning today is typically captured by the following principle (Hodges, 2001; Werning, 2004):

Principle 1 (Compositionality of meaning). *The meaning of a complex term is a syntax-dependent function of the meanings of its syntactic parts.*

If one identifies Fregean thoughts with the meanings of sentences, regards sentences as instances or evaluations of complex terms and specifies the parts of sentences as syntactic parts and their structure as a syntactic structure, the last subclause of the quotation can indeed be regarded as echoing the modern principle of compositionality. One only has to presume that Frege, when he spoke of an image, had in mind a homomorphism between two algebraic structures: the syntactic structure of terms and the semantic structure of meanings.

However, the preceding subclause expresses an idea that is in fact distinct therefrom. It postulates a correspondence relation between the part–whole relation in the linguistic domain and some part–whole relation on the level of meanings. One might capture this idea as the principle of semantic constituency:

Principle 2 (Semantic constituency). *There is a semantic part–whole relation on the set of meanings such that for every two terms, if the one is a syntactic part of the other, then the meaning of the former is a semantic part of the meaning of the latter.*

In accordance with a widely used terminology, for a language the *syntactic structure of terms*—sometimes also called term algebra or simply syntax—is regarded as a pair $\langle T, \Sigma_T \rangle$. Here T is the set of terms of the language and Σ_T is a finite set of syntactic operations that reflect syntactic rules of the language. Each syntactic operation $\sigma \in \Sigma_T$ is a partial function from some Cartesian product T^n of the set of terms into the set of terms.

A term s is called an *immediate syntactic part* of a term t just in case there is a syntactic operation σ that may render t as value when s is one of its arguments, in other words: $t = \sigma(\ldots, s, \ldots)$. Any term s is recursively defined to be a *syntactic part* of a term t—in symbols $s \sqsubseteq_T t$—just in case s is either identical to t, an immediate syntactic part of t or an immediate syntactic part of some syntactic part of t. A term is called atomic if it does not have any syntactic parts but itself. It is assumed that there are only finitely many atomic terms.

For the language, the set of meanings M is the range of some meaning function μ defined on T (or a subset thereof). The compositionality condition now comes down to the claim that M can be supplemented by a set of semantic operations Σ_M such that μ is a homomorphism from the syntax $\langle T, \Sigma_T \rangle$ into the structure $\langle M, \Sigma_M \rangle$, called the semantics or semantic structure of the language. In other words:

Definition 1 (Formal Compositionality). *Given a language with the syntax $\langle T, \Sigma_T \rangle$, a meaning function $\mu : T \to M$ is called compositional just in case, for every n-ary syntactic operation $\sigma \in \Sigma_T$ and any sequence of terms $t_1, .., t_n$ in the domain of σ, there is a partial function m_σ defined on M^n such that*

$$\mu(\sigma(t_1, .., t_n)) = m_\sigma(\mu(t_1), \ldots, \mu(t_n)).$$

A semantics induced by a compositional meaning function will be called a compositional semantics of the language.

The principle of semantic constituency makes a statement about the correspondence of two part–whole relations. The weakest conditions one may set upon a part–whole relation $\sqsubseteq$ is that it be reflexive, transitive, and anti-symmetric:

Definition 2 (Part–whole Relation). *A relation $\sqsubseteq$ defined on a set X is called a part–whole relation on X just in case, for all $x, y, z \in X$ the following holds:*[1]

(i) $x \sqsubseteq x$ *(reflexivity).*
(ii) $x \sqsubseteq y \wedge y \sqsubseteq x \to x = y$ *(anti-symmetry).*
(iii) $x \sqsubseteq y \wedge y \sqsubseteq z \to x \sqsubseteq z$ *(transitivity).*

The notion of a part–whole relation can be strengthened in various ways. One may, for example, assume that parts are always co-tokened with their wholes (McLaughlin, 1993) or that parts are spatially contained in the respective wholes. However, our definition is unanimously accepted as a minimal condition on parts and moreover consistent with the definition of a syntactic part.

31.2 SYMBOLIC AND NON-SYMBOLIC THEORIES OF MEANING

As we will illustrate by two examples below, the principle of semantic constituency is the hallmark of all symbolic theories of meaning. These theories regard meanings themselves as symbols. They can be characterized as follows:

---

[1] The definition of a proper part negates the reflexivity condition.

Definition 3 (Symbolic Semantics). *Given a language with the syntax* $\langle T, \Sigma_T \rangle$, *a thereon defined syntactic part–whole relation* $\sqsubseteq_T$ *and a meaning function* $\mu : T \rightarrow M$, *then its semantics* $\langle M, \Sigma_M \rangle$ *is symbolic if and only if there is a part–whole relation* $\sqsubseteq_M$ *defined on M such that for all terms* $s, t \in T$ *the following holds:*

$$s \sqsubseteq_T t \rightarrow \mu(s) \sqsubseteq_M \mu(t).$$

In other words, what's common to all symbolic theories of meaning is that the part–whole structure on the syntactic level is mirrored on the semantic level. The best known example for a symbolic theory of meaning is Fodor's (1975, 2008) Language of Thought. Here meanings are identified with mental concepts and modelled as entries on the tape of a Turing computer. From a finite alphabet of primitive concepts, say {DOG, CAT, BARKS, MEOWS, FIDO, TOM, NOT, . . .}, complex concepts are built as sequences or strings. The semantic part–whole relation is identified with the relation of being a substring. Since *LOT* is a symbolic theory of meaning, it is guaranteed that whenever a syntactically complex expression contains a less complex one as a syntactic part, as happens to be the case with the sentences *Fido is not a dog* and *Fido is a dog*, the meaning of the syntactic part, that is DOG FIDO is a substring of the meaning of the whole, NOT DOG FIDO.[2]

However, a computational or serial format is not required for a theory of meaning to be symbolic. Motivated by the many shortcomings the *LOT* approach was accused of when the aim is to provide a psychologically and neurobiologically realistic theory of representation (see Horgan and Tienson, 1996; Horgan, this volume), connectionists have proposed so-called Vector Symbolic Architectures (VSAs) (see Smolensky, 1995b; Plate, 2003; Stewart and Eliasmith, this volume): meanings or representations are conceived of as vectors rendering a certain pattern of activity in a connectionist network. In contrast to conventional parallel distributed processing architectures, representations in VSA networks can realize part–whole relations and thus do provide a symbolic account of meaning.

VSAs employ operations of binding $\otimes$ and merging $\oplus$ and so allow meanings of complex terms to be generated from the meanings of their syntactic parts, viz. by the combination of role and filler vectors. Given the sentence *Mary loves John* with a certain underlying syntactic structure, its meaning would, for example, be identified with a vector **p** generated in the following way:

$$\mu(Mary\ loves\ John) = \mathbf{p} \tag{31.1}$$

$$= \mathbf{event} \otimes \mathbf{loves} \oplus \mathbf{agent} \otimes \mathbf{mary} \oplus \mathbf{patient} \otimes \mathbf{john}. \tag{31.2}$$

The role vectors **event**, **agent**, and **patient** stand for certain semantic roles. These are bound to the filler vectors **mary**, **loves**, and **john**, which are identified with the meanings of the words *Mary*, *loves*, and *John*. The operations of binding and merging are recursively applicable. VSAs can be made compositional by choosing role and filler

---

[2] We assume that the language of thought is structurally analogous to a first-order language or some extension thereof, so that the two thoughts have the logical form *Fa* and, respectively, ¬*Fa*.

vectors such that the semantic structure is a homomorphic image of the syntactic structure of the language. In early examples of VSAs (Smolensky, 1995b) tensor multiplication was used for binding and vector addition for merging. This led to a dimensional explosion of the network and had a number of technical disadvantages. In the more recent holographic approach of Plate and Stewart and Eliasmith, circular convolution is used for binding. Here the N components of a vector $\mathbf{u}$ resulting from a circular convolution of a vector $\mathbf{v}$ with a vector $\mathbf{w}$ are given as: $u_i = \sum_{j=1}^{N} v_j w_{(i-j)\bmod N}$. This keeps dimensions low and more importantly allows an inverse $\mathbf{z} = inv(\mathbf{u})$ with $z_i = u_{(N-i)\bmod N}$ to be defined. This gives us an operation of unbinding. Any filler vector is now approximately recoverable. For the above example one would get:

$$\mathbf{p} \otimes inv(\mathbf{agent}) \approx \mathbf{mary}. \tag{31.3}$$

In this approach the semantic part-whole relation is identified with the relation of being recoverable by an algorithm of unbinding. VSA semantics with an operation of unbinding is not only compositional, but also symbolic.

To see that a compositional semantics need not be symbolic, let us turn to standard model-theoretical semantics, which is a paradigmatic example for a compositional semantics. The details of such a semantics are given elsewhere (see Partee, ter Meulen, and Wall, 1990; Kracht, this volume). For our purposes it suffices to mention that in standard model-theoretical semantics the meaning of a sentence ϕ is the set of its models. Now, the sentence ϕ is a syntactic part of $\neg\phi$, which in turn is a syntactic part of $\neg\neg\phi$. If standard model theoretical semantics were symbolic, these part–whole relations should be reflected on the semantic level in the following way:

$$\mu(\phi) \sqsubseteq_M \mu(\neg\phi) \sqsubseteq_M \mu(\neg\neg\phi). \tag{31.4}$$

However, the double negation $\neg\neg\phi$ has exactly the same models as ϕ and consequently exactly the same meaning. Therefore:

$$\mu(\phi) \sqsubseteq_M \mu(\neg\phi) \sqsubseteq_M \mu(\phi). \tag{31.5}$$

Using the anti-symmetry of the part–whole relation we derive the contradiction:

$$\mu(\phi) = \mu(\neg\phi). \tag{31.6}$$

For model-theoretical semantics there is no semantic part–whole relation that fulfils the principle of semantic constituency. We have thus shown that the principle of compositionality and the principle of semantic constituency logically fall apart. This is so even though many compositional theories of meaning are in fact symbolic. The model-theoretic counterexample should be remembered when we develop our neuro-emulative semantics, since both are structurally analogous to each other.

Unlike the language of thought or vector symbolic architectures, model-theoretical semantics is merely denotational. It does not imply anything about the structures of the mind or the underlying neural mechanisms that enable us to produce and comprehend meaningful expressions. For many explanatory purposes—the learning, production, or comprehension of language, the underlying biological resources, their evolution and development and eventual disorders—a purely denotational account of meaning remains vacuous. In this chapter I will therefore appeal to a mentally or neurally realistic view of meaning. It characterizes the triangle between language, mind, and world as follows: linguistic expressions are expressions of meaning. Those meanings are to be identified with mental or otherwise internal representations. An internal representation *qua* being a representation essentially has an external content. This external content in turn is responsible for the fact that the expression in question has the denotation it has. The relation between a mental representation and its content is some form of causal-informational covariation (Fodor, 1992). This view is captured by our last semantic principle:[3]

Principle 3 (Content covariation). *An expression has the denotation it has because the meaning it expresses is an internal representation that reliably co-varies with a content that is identical to the expression's denotation.*

In what is to come we will do the following: for a given first-order language we will introduce a neural structure that will then be identified with an internal semantic structure. The neural structure is derived from an algebraic description of the topology and dynamics of oscillatory networks, a member of the recurrent connectionist network family. The topology of those networks closely follows the topological organization of neurobiologically well studied cortical feature maps for various attributes such us colour, orientation, direction of movement, etc. Feature maps of this kind are ubiquitous throughout the sensory cortices of the brains of humans and many other mammals. The dynamics of oscillatory networks is designed to reflect the well-studied mechanisms of object-related neural synchronization (see Maye and Engel, this volume). We will demonstrate that the neural structure provides a compositional semantics of the language. Compositionality of meaning will hence be achieved. It will become obvious that this semantics is non-symbolic in the sense defined above. The principle of semantic constituency is negated. We will also show that the elements of the neural structure are internal representations that reliably co-vary with external contents. These external contents are identical with the standard model-theoretical denotations for the language. The covariation with content is achieved. It will finally become clear that the covariation is one-to-one such that the neural structure can be regarded as isomorphic to the external denotational structure. These results justify us to call the neural structure an emulative semantics. This is to say that each denotation of an expression in our language has a potential counterpart neural state that co-varies with the denotation. An oscillatory network thus generates an algebraic emulation of what it represents. The neural structure is a compositional, non-symbolic, emulative semantics of a first-order language.

---

[3] Philosophically, the principle may strike one as over simplifying rather complex dependency relation between contents and denotations. It certainly needs some fine-tuning. Its impact and elegance for the purposes of this text will, however, become clear below. I conceive of denotation in a broad sense as modal denotation. The denotation of a sentence might, for example, be identified with a proposition (eventually modelled as a set of models or possible worlds). See Werning (2011).

31.3 CORTICAL FEATURE MAPS, NEURONAL SYNCHRONIZATION, AND THE GESTALT PRINCIPLES

The architecture of oscillatory networks, which lays the ground for our emulative semantics, is motivated by empirical findings that regard the existence of topologically structured cortical feature maps, the neural mechanism of object-relative synchronization, and the Gestalt principles of perception. Given that these findings justify the biologically and psychologically adequateness of our network model, I will briefly recapitulate the findings here.

31.3.1 Feature maps

For many attributes (colour, orientation, direction, size, etc.) involved in the course of visual processing one can anatomically identify so-called neuronal feature maps (Hubel and Wiesel, 1968). These are parts of the cortex that exhibit a two-fold topological organization: a receptor topology and a feature topology. Each (pyramidal) neuron x of the feature map has a specific receptive field $r(x)$ on the receptor (in vision, the retina) and a specific feature selectivity $f(x)$. The receptive field is a geometrically convex region on the receptor. The feature selectivity is characterized by a convex region in the attribute space associated with the feature map. A specific neuron in an orientation map, for instance, will fire if a stimulus object, say a bar projected on the retina, is located in the receptive field of the neuron and its orientation has a value in an interval of angles for which the neuron is selective. By speaking of a receptor topology we mean that the synaptic connectivity of neurons within a feature map reflects the geometry of the receptor. The density of synaptic connectivity introduces a topology among the neurons of a feature map. A neuron counts as closer to a reference neuron as compared to a third neuron if the connectivity density between the first and the reference neuron is greater than that between the third and the reference neuron. In humans and many other mammals this connectivity topology is roughly congruent to the topography of the feature maps given by the actual physical distances between neurons (see Fig. 31.1). In the case of vision we say that those feature maps are retinotopic. With some idealizations we can formulate the principle that having a receptive field r is a topologically continuous mapping from the connectivity topology of the feature map into the geometry of the receptor: given a certain neuron in the feature map, all neurons close to it have receptive fields that are close to the receptive field of the given neuron. A second topological principle holds for the feature selectivities of the neurons in a feature map: having a certain feature selectivity f is a topologically continuous mapping from the connectivity topology of the feature map into the topology of the attribute space. Or in other words: given a certain

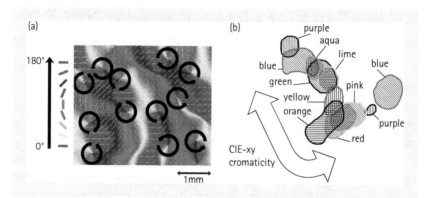

FIGURE 31.1 Cortical feature maps. (a) Fragment of the neural feature map for the attribute orientation of cat primary visual cortex (adapted from Shmuel and Vald, 2000). The arrows indicate the polar topology of the orientation values represented within each hypercolumn. Hypercolumns are arranged in a retinotopic topology. (b) Colour band (*ca.* 1 mm²) from the thin stripes of macaque secondary visual cortex (adapted from Xiao et al., 2003). The values of the attribute colour are arranged in a topology that follows the similarity of hue as defined by the Commission Internationale de l'Eclairages (xy-cromaticity). The topology among the various colour bands of the thin stripes is retinotopic. Both in (a) and (b) the synaptic connectedness is reflected by the cortical topography.

neuron in the feature map, all neurons close to it have feature selectivities that are similar to the feature selectivity of the given neuron.[4] Fig. 31.1 shows fragments of cortical feature maps for the attributes orientation and colour. In the orientation map (Fig. 31.1a) one finds pinwheel-like structures for particular receptive fields. These structures are called hypercolumns. Each hypercolumn typically has an extent of about 1 mm². The receptive fields of overlapping hypercolumns overlap. Within each hypercolumn, neurons for the entire spectrum of values of the attribute, that is angles of orientation, fan out around a pin-wheel centre realizing a polar topology. Neurons of a hypercolumn with a tuning for the same attribute value form a so-called minicolumn. The colour map in the thin stripes of the secondary visual cortex (Fig. 31.1b), in contrast, shows a linear topology. The neurons of neighbouring stripes have neighbouring or overlapping receptive fields. More than 80 so organized cortical areas are experimentally known to be involved in the visual processing of the monkey (Felleman and van Essen, 1991). It should be noted that cortical areas with a feature topology can also be found in higher cortical areas involved in vision, whereas the receptor topology seems to be characteristic only for the cortical areas carrying out early visual processes. Cortical maps with a

---

[4] Having defined a metric d_c on the connectivity topology, a metric d_r for distances between regions on the receptor, and a metric d_f for distances between regions in the attribute space, the receptor and feature topology of feature maps can be formally characterized as follows. Receptor topology: for any choice of $\epsilon > 0$ there is a $\delta > 0$ such that for all neurons x, y of the feature map with $d_c(x, y) < \delta$ it holds that $d_r(r(x), r(y)) < \epsilon$. Feature topology: for any choice of $\epsilon > 0$ there is a $\delta > 0$ such that for all neurons x, y of the feature map with $d_c(x, y) < \delta$ it holds that $d_f(f(x), f(y)) < \epsilon$.

feature topology can also be found in the auditory and somatosensory cortices, where they exhibit tonotopic (Bendor and Wang, 2005) or somatotopic topologies (DiCarlo and Johnson, 2000).

31.3.2 Neural synchronization

The fact that feature values which belong to different attributes, but may be properties of the same stimulus object are processed in distinct regions of the cortex, poses the problem of how this information is integrated in an object-specific way. How can it be that the horizontality and the redness of a red horizontal bar are represented in distinct regions of cortex, but are still part of the representation of one and the same object? This is the binding problem in neuroscience (Treisman, 1996).

A prominent and experimentally well supported solution postulates neuronal synchronization as a mechanism for binding (von der Malsburg, 1981; Gray et al., 1989; Maye and Engel, this volume): neurons that are selective for different properties show synchronous activation when the properties indicated are instantiated by the same object in the perceptual field; otherwise they are firing asynchronously. Synchrony, therefore, might be regarded as fulfilling the task of binding together various property representations in order to form the representation of an object as having these properties. Object-specific synchrony has been measured within minicolumns, within and across hypercolumns, across different feature maps, even across the two hemispheres and on a global scale (for a review see Singer, 1999).

31.3.3 The Gestalt principles

The rules that govern the constitution of objects in perception—that is the rules according to which we perceive a group of stimulus elements as one object—have been studied in perceptual psychology. These studies led to the formulation of the Gestalt principles (Wertheimer, 1924/1950). Fig. 31.2a illustrates the Gestalt principle of similarity of colour: all things being equal, the more similar neighbouring elements of the stimulus are with respect to colour, the more likely they are to be perceptually grouped together into one object. Fig. 31.2b gives an analogous example for the Gestalt principle of similarity of orientation. Those principles are instances of a more general principle that can be expressed as follows: there are a number of attributes (colour, orientation, size, gradient, direction, etc.) that govern the perceptual grouping of stimulus elements into objects such that, all things being equal, the more similar the values of neighbouring stimulus elements are with respect to those attributes, the more likely those elements are perceptually grouped into one object. These Gestalt principles are formulated as *ceteris paribus* rules (see Palmer, 1999, for review). Trade-offs between similarities with respect to various attributes may occur.

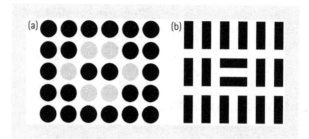

FIGURE 31.2 Illustration of Gestalt principles. (a) Similarity of colour. Neighbouring stimulus elements of light grey colour are perceptually grouped into one object. (b) Similarity of orientation. A square made up of two vertical bars pops out as one object.

31.4 OSCILLATORY NETWORKS

The neurobiological facts on neuronal feature maps and object-relative neural synchronization together with the psychological principles of Gestalt perception allow us to regard oscillatory networks (see Fig. 31.3) as a plausible model of informational processes in the visual cortex.

Oscillatory networks are recurrent neural networks whose basic units are oscillators each consisting of an excitatory and inhibitory node. The oscillators are arranged on a three-dimensional grid forming a module (Fig. 31.3c) that is associated with a certain attribute (colour, orientation, etc.). Each oscillator is first characterized by a receptive field whose coordinates are given relative to the two dimensional XY-plane. It is secondly characterized by its feature selectivity, represented on the Z-axis. Both the receptor and the feature topology of cortical feature maps are honoured by the network topology.

The *Gestalt* principles are implemented in oscillatory networks by the following mechanism: oscillators with neighbouring receptive fields and similar feature selectivities tend to synchronize (light shading), whereas oscillators with neighbouring receptive fields and different feature selectivities tend to desynchronize. As a consequence, oscillators selective for proximal stimulus elements with like properties tend to form a synchronous oscillation when stimulated simultaneously. This oscillation can be regarded as one object representation. In contrast, inputs that contain proximal elements with unlike properties tend to cause anti-synchronous oscillations, that is different object representations. This result is in line with the findings of object-related neural synchronization.

In our model a single oscillator (Fig. 31.3a) consists of two mutually coupled excitatory and inhibitory nodes. They are assigned the variables x and y, which statistically represent the electrical discharge behaviour of a minicolumn of a cortical feature map (typically about 80 to 120 biological cells).

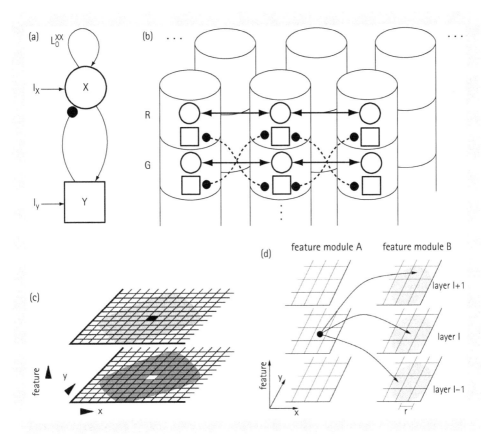

FIGURE 31.3 Oscillatory network. (a) A single oscillator consists of an excitatory (x) and an inhibitory (y) node. Each node represents the average activity of a cluster of biological cells. L_0^{xx} describes the self-excitation of the excitatory neuron. I_x and I_y amounts to external input. (b) Synchronizing connections (solid) are realized by mutually excitatory connections between the excitatory nodes and hold between oscillators within one layer. Desynchronizing connections (dotted) are realized by mutually inhibitory connections between the inhibitory nodes and hold between different layers. 'R' and 'G' denote the red and green channel. The cylinder segments correspond to minicolumns, whole cylinders to hypercolumns. (c) A module for a single feature dimension (e.g. colour) consists of a three-dimensional topology of oscillators. There is one layer per feature and each layer is arranged to reflect a two-dimensional retinotopic structure. The shaded circles visualize the range of synchronizing (light grey) and desynchronizing (dark grey) connections of an oscillator in the top layer (black pixel). (d) Two coupled feature modules are shown schematically. The single oscillator in module A has connections to all oscillators in the shaded region of module B. This schema is applied to all other oscillators and feature modules.

Source: Reprinted from Werning (2005*b*) and Maye (2004).

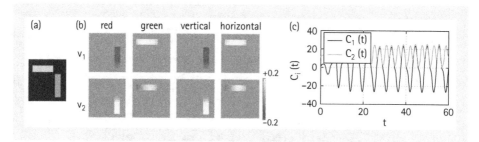

FIGURE 31.4 (a) Stimulus: one vertical red bar and one horizontal green bar. It was presented to a network with 32 × 32 × 4 oscillators. (b) The two stable eigenmodes. The eigenvectors v_1 and v_2 are shown each in one line. The four columns correspond to the four feature layers. Dark shading signifies negative, grey zero and light shading positive components. (c) The characteristic functions for the two eigenmodes.

Synchronizing (resp. de-synchronizing) connections between two oscillators are realized by mutually excitatory (inhibitory) connections between the excitatory (inhibitory) nodes of both oscillators (Fig. 31.3b). Feature modules for different feature dimensions, for example colour and orientation, can be combined by establishing synchronizing connections between oscillators of different modules in case they code for the same stimulus region (Fig. 31.3d).

Populations of recurrently coupled excitatory and inhibitory neurons can be found in the primary visual cortex. Here, excitatory (pyramidal) cells in layers 2 and 3 are tightly coupled to local inhibitory neurons in layers 2–6. If the number of excitatory and inhibitory biological cells is large enough, the dynamics of each oscillator can be statistically described by the temporal evolution of the variables x and y according to differential equations that describe limit-cycle oscillations (for an explicit mathematical description see Maye (2003), Maye and Werning (2004, 2007)).

Stimulated oscillatory networks characteristically show object-specific patterns of synchronized and de-synchronized oscillators within and across feature dimensions. In Fig. 31.4 the network dynamics for a stimulus consisting of a red vertical and a green horizontal bar is shown. Oscillators that represent properties of the same object synchronize, while oscillators that represent properties of different objects desynchronize. We observe that for each represented object a certain oscillation spreads through the network. The oscillation pertains only to oscillators that represent the properties of the object in question.

31.5 ALGEBRAIC NETWORK ANALYSIS

An oscillation function $x(t)$ of an oscillator is the activity of its excitatory node as a function of time during a time window $[0, T]$. Mathematically speaking, activity functions can be conceived of as vectors in the Hilbert space $L_2[0, T]$ of functions that are square-integrable in the interval $[0, T]$. Thus, a precise measure of synchrony can be established and a powerful algebraic framework for the semantic interpretation of the network will be provided. The Hilbert space has the inner product

$$\langle x(t) | x'(t) \rangle = \int_0^T x(t)\, x'(t)dt. \tag{31.7}$$

The degree of synchrony between two oscillations lies between -1 and $+1$ and can now be defined as their normalized inner product

$$\Delta(x, x') = \frac{\langle x|x' \rangle}{\sqrt{\langle x|x \rangle \langle x'|x' \rangle}}. \tag{31.8}$$

The dynamics of complex systems is often governed by a few dominating states, the eigenmodes. The corresponding eigenvalues designate how much of the dynamics is accounted for by that mode. The two stable eigenmodes of a stimulated network are shown in Fig. 31.4b. The overall dynamics of the network is given by the Cartesian vector $x(t) = (x_1(t), \ldots, x_k(t))^T$ that contains the excitatory activities of all k oscillators as components. The network state at any instant is considered as a superposition of the temporally constant, but spatially variant eigenvectors v_i weighted by the corresponding spatially invariant, but temporally evolving characteristic functions $c_i(t)$ of Fig. 31.4c:

$$x(t) = \sum c_i(t)v_i. \tag{31.9}$$

The eigenmodes, for any stimulus, can be ordered along their eigenvalues so that each eigenmode can be signified by a natural number i beginning with 1 for the strongest (v_i is the corresponding eigenvector).

The Hilbert space analysis allows us to interpret the dynamics of oscillatory networks in semantic terms. Since oscillation functions reliably co-vary with objects, they may be assigned to some of the individual terms a, b, ..., x, y, ... $\in$ Ind of a predicate language by the partial function

$$a : \text{Ind} \rightarrow L_2[0, T]. \tag{31.10}$$

The sentence a $=$ b expresses a representational state of the system (i.e. the representation of the identity of the objects denoted by the individual terms a and b) to the degree the oscillation functions $a(a)$ and $a(b)$ of the system are synchronous. The degree to which a sentence ϕ expresses a representational state of the system, for any eigenmode i, can be measured by the value $d_i(\phi) \in [-1, +1]$. In case of identity sentences we have:

$$d_i(\text{a} = \text{b}) = \Delta(a(a), a(b)). \tag{31.11}$$

When we take a closer look at the eigenvector of the first eigenmode in Fig. 31.4b, we see that most of the vector components are exactly zero (grey shading). However, few components in the greenness and the horizontality layers are positive (light shading) and few components in the redness and the verticality layers are negative (dark shading). We may interpret this by saying that the first eigenmode represents two objects as distinct from one another. The representation of the first object is the characteristic function $+c_1(t)$ and the representation of the second object is its mirror image $-c_1(t)$ (Because of the normalization of the Δ-function, only the signs of the eigenvector components matter). These considerations justify the following evaluation of non-identity:[5]

$$d_i(\neg a = b) = \begin{cases} +1 \text{ if } d_i(a = b) = -1, \\ -1 \text{ if } d_i(a = b) > -1. \end{cases} \qquad (31.12)$$

A great advantage of the eigenmode analysis is that object representations are no longer identified with the actual oscillatory behaviour of neurons, but with the eigenmode-relative characteristic functions. In this approach the representation of objects does not require strict synchronization of neural activity over long cortical distances, but tolerates a travelling phase change as it has been observed experimentally (Eckhorn et al., 2001) as well as in our network simulation.

Feature layers function as representations of properties and thus can be expressed by predicates $F_1, \ldots, F_p$, that is, to every predicate F a diagonal matrix $\beta(F) \in \{0, 1\}^{k \times k}$ can be assigned such that, by multiplication with any eigenvector v_i, the matrix renders the sub-vector of those components that belong to the feature layer expressed by F. To determine to which degree an oscillation function assigned to an individual constant a pertains to the feature layer assigned to a predicate F, we have to compute how synchronous it maximally is with one of the oscillations in the feature layer. We are, in other words, justified to evaluate the degree to which a predicative sentence Fa (read: 'a is F', e.g. 'This object is red') expresses a representational state of our system, with respect to the eigenmode i, in the following way (the f_j are the components of the vector $\mathbf{f}$):

$$d_i(Fa) = \max\{\Delta(\alpha(a), f_j) | \mathbf{f} = c_i(t)\beta(F)\mathbf{v}_i\}. \qquad (31.13)$$

If one, furthermore, evaluates the conjunction of two sentences $\phi \wedge \psi$ by the minimum of the value of each conjunct, we may regard the first eigenvector $\mathbf{v}_1$ of the network dynamics resulting from the stimulus in Fig. 31.4a as a representation expressible by the sentence

This is a red vertical object and that is a green horizontal object.

We only have to assign the individual terms *this* ($= a$) and *that* ($= b$) to the oscillatory functions $-c_1(t)$ and $+c_1(t)$, respectively, and the predicates *red* ($= R$), *green* ($= G$), *vertical* ($= V$), and *horizontal* ($= H$) to the redness, greenness, verticality, and horizontality layers as their neuronal meanings. Simple computation then reveals:

$$d_1(Ra \wedge Va \wedge Gb \wedge Hb \wedge \neg a = b) = 1. \qquad (31.14)$$

---

[5] The negation is sharp: it allows only -1 and $+1$ as values. In its definition we follow Gödel's (1932) intuitionist min-max-system. Double negation digitalizes the semantic value of the original sentence. The deeper reasons for this choice of the negation lie in systematic considerations concerning the envisaged calculus and the proof of completeness and compositionality theorems (Werning, 2005c).

Co-variation with content can always be achieved if the individual assignment a and the predicate assignment β are chosen to match the network's perceptual capabilities.

31.6 EIGENMODES AS ALTERNATIVE PERCEPTUAL POSSIBILITIES

So far I have concentrated on a single eigenmode only. The network, however, generates a multitude of eigenmodes. We tested the representational function of the different eigenmodes by presenting an obviously ambiguous stimulus to the network. The stimulus shown in Fig. 31.5a can be perceived as two red vertical bars or as one red vertical grating. It turned out that the network was able to disambiguate the stimulus by representing each of the two perceptual possibilities in a stable eigenmode of its own (see Fig. 31.5b).

Eigenmodes, thus, play a similar role for neuronal representation as possible worlds known from Lewis (1986) or Kripke (1980) play for semantics. Like possible worlds, eigenmodes do not interfere with each other because they are mutually orthogonal.

We now see that both of the two stable eigenmodes shown in Fig. 31.5b can be expressed by a disjunctive sentence if we semantically evaluate disjunction as follows:[6]

$$d(\phi \vee \psi, i) = \max\{d(\phi, i), d(\psi, i)\}, \tag{31.15}$$

for any sentences ϕ and ψ of $PL^=$ and any eigenmode i. Either of the two eigenmodes $i = 1, 2$ makes $d(\phi, i)$ assume the value $+1$ if ϕ is set to the following disjunctive sentence, which says that there is one red vertical object—denoted by a—or two red vertical objects—denoted by b and c:

$$(Ra \wedge Va) \vee (Rb \wedge Rc \wedge Vb \wedge Vc \wedge \neg b = c).$$

One only needs to make the following assignments of individual constants to oscillation functions:

$$a(a) = +c_1(t), \ a(b) = +c_2(t), \ a(c) = -c_2(t).$$

---

[6] The choice of the maximum as the semantic evaluation of disjunction is the primary reason for me to prefer the Gödel system over alternative systems of many-valued logic. The reason is that it is the only continuous evaluation of disjunction, a so-called t-conorm, that always takes the value of one of the disjuncts as the value of the disjunction. Other continuous t-conorms would hence not allow us to treat eigenmodes as independent alternative possibilities. We would not be able to say that a certain disjunction is true because a possibility (i.e. an eigenmode) expressed by one of its disjuncts exists (see Werning, 2005c).

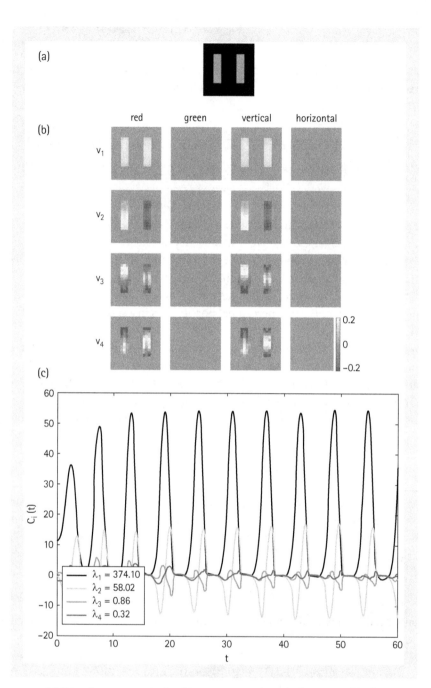

FIGURE 31.5 (a) Stimulus: two vertical red bars or one red vertical grating. (b) The eigenvectors $v_1, \ldots, v_4$ of the four eigenmodes $1, \ldots, 4$ with the largest eigenvalues are shown in one line. The first mode represents the stimulus as one red vertical object, while the second mode represents it as two red vertical objects. (c) The characteristic functions show the temporal evolution of the first four modes. Only the first two are non-decreasing and thus belong to stable eigenmodes. The left box gives the eigenvalues of the respective eigenmodes and their characteristic functions. The eigenvalues correspond to the relative contribution of the eigenmode to the variability of the overall network dynamics.

Source: Reprinted from Werning (2005*a*).

31.7 MAKING SYNTAX AND SEMANTICS EXPLICIT

We are leaving the heuristic approach now and turn to a formally explicit description of the neuronal semantics realized by oscillatory networks. Let the oscillatory network under consideration have k oscillators. The network dynamics is studied in the time window $[0, T]$. For any stable eigenmode $i \in \mathbb{N}$, it renders a determinate eigenvector v_i, a characteristic function $c_i(t)$, and an eigenvalue λ_i after stimulation. The language to be considered is a monadic first-order predicate language with identity ($PL^=$). Let Ind be the set of individual terms and let $Pred$ be the set of predicates. The alphabet of $PL^=$ furthermore contains the logical constants $\wedge, \vee, \rightarrow, \neg, \exists, \forall$, and the binary predicate $=$. As already introduced, we have a constant individual assignment α, that is a partial function from Ind into $L_2[0, T]$. We also have a predicate assignment $\beta : Pred \rightarrow \in \{0,1\}^{k \times k}$. Now, the union $\gamma = \alpha \cup \beta$ is a comprehensive assignment of $PL^=$. The individual terms in the domain of α are individual constants, those not in the domain of α are individual variables. The syntactic operations of the language $PL^=$ and the set SF of sentential formulae as their recursive closure can be defined as follows, for arbitrary a,b,z $\in$ Ind, F $\in$ Pred, and $\phi, \psi \in SF$:

$$\sigma_= : (a, b) \mapsto a = b; \quad \sigma_{pred} : (a, F) \mapsto Fa; \quad \sigma_\neg : \phi \mapsto \neg\phi;$$
$$\sigma_\wedge : (\phi, \psi) \mapsto \phi \wedge \psi; \quad \sigma_\vee : (\phi, \psi) \mapsto \phi \vee \psi; \quad \sigma_\rightarrow : (\phi, \psi) \mapsto \phi \rightarrow \psi; \quad (31.16)$$
$$\sigma_\exists : (z, \phi) \mapsto \exists z\phi; \quad \sigma_\forall : (z, \phi) \mapsto \forall z\phi.$$

The set of terms of $PL^=$ is the union of the sets of individual terms, predicates, and sentential formulae of the language. A sentential formula in SF is called a *sentence* with respect to some constant assignment γ if and only if, under assignment γ, all and only individual terms bound by a quantifier are variables. Any term of $PL^=$ is called γ-*grammatical* if and only if, under assignment γ, it is a predicate, an individual constant, or a sentence. Taking the idea at face value that eigenmodes can be treated like possible worlds (or more neutrally speaking: like models), the relation 'i neurally models ϕ to degree d by constant assignment γ', in symbols

$$i \models_\gamma^d \phi,$$

for any sentence ϕ and any real number $d \in [-1, +1]$, is then recursively given as follows:

Identity: Given any individual constants a,b $\in$ Ind $\cap$dom(γ), then $i \models_\gamma^d a = b$ iff $d = \Delta(\gamma(a), \gamma(b))$.

Predication: Given any individual constant a $\in$ Ind $\cap$ dom(γ) and any predicate F $\in$ Pred, then $i \models_\gamma^d$ Fa iff $d = \max\{\Delta(\gamma(a), f_j) | f = \gamma(F)v_i c_i(t)\}$.

Conjunction: Provided that ϕ, ψ are sentences, then $i \models_\gamma^d \phi \wedge \psi$ iff $d = \min\{d', d'' | i \models_\gamma^{d'} \phi$ and $i \models_\gamma^{d''} \psi\}$.

Disjunction: Provided that ϕ, ψ are sentences, then $i \models^d_\gamma \phi \vee \psi$ iff $d = \max\{d', d'' \mid i \models^{d'}_\gamma \phi$ and $i \models^{d''}_\gamma \psi\}$.

Implication: Provided that ϕ, ψ are sentences, then $i \models^d_\gamma \phi \rightarrow \psi$ iff $d = \sup\{d' | \min\{d', d''\} \leq d'''$ where $i \models^{d''}_\gamma \phi$ and $i \models^{d'''}_\gamma \psi\}$.

Negation: Provided that ϕ is a sentence, then $i \models^d_\gamma \neg\phi$ iff (i) $d = 1$ and $i \models^{-1}_\gamma \phi$ or (ii) $d = -1$ and $i \models^{d'}_\gamma \phi$ where $d' < 1$.

Existential Quantifier: Given any individual variable $z \in$ Ind $\setminus$ dom(γ) and any sentential formula $\phi \in SF$, then $i \models^d_\gamma \exists z\phi$ iff $d = \sup\{d' \mid i \models^{d'}_{\gamma'} \phi$ where $\gamma' = \gamma \cup \{\langle z, c\rangle\}$ and $c \in L_2[0, T]\}$.

Universal Quantifier: Given any individual variable $z \in$ Ind $\setminus$ dom(γ) and any sentential formula $\phi \in SF$, then $i \models^d_\gamma \forall z\phi$ iff $d = \inf\{d' \mid i \models^{d'}_{\gamma'} \phi$ where $\gamma' = \gamma \cup \{\langle z, c\rangle\}$ and $c \in L_2[0, T]\}$.

Let me briefly comment on these definitions: Most of them should be familiar from previous sections. The degree d, however, is no longer treated as a function, but as a relatum in the relation $\models$.

The semantic evaluation of negation has previously only been defined for negated identity sentences. The generalized definition, here, is a straightforward application of the Gödel system.[7] An interesting feature of negation in the Gödel system is that its duplication digitalizes the values of d into $+1$ and -1.

The evaluation of implication, too, follows the Gödel system.[8] Calculi for our semantics have been developed in the literature. The calculi are in principle those of intuitionist logic (Gottwald, 2001; Werning, 2005c).

To evaluate existentially quantified formulae, the well-known method of cylindrification (Kreisel and Krivine, 1976) is adjusted to the many-valued case. The supremum (sup) takes over the role of existential quantification in the meta-language and can be regarded as the limit case of the maximum-function in an infinite domain. This is analogous to the common idea of regarding the existential quantifier as the limit case of disjunction over an infinity of domain elements. It should be noted that the value of an existentially quantified sentence of the form

$(\exists z)(Fz)$

measures whether the oscillators in the feature layer expressed by F oscillate.

For the evaluation of universally quantified formulae, the method of cylindrification is used and adjusted again. This time the infimum (inf) assumes the role of universal quantification in the metalanguage. It can be regarded as the limit case of the minimum for infinite domains in the same way as one might think of the universal quantifier as

---

[7] In t-norm based many-valued logics a function $n : [-1, +1] \rightarrow [-1, +1]$ is generally said to be a negation function if and only if n is non-increasing, $n(-1) = 1$ and $n(1) = -1$ (cf. Gottwald, 2001).

[8] The deeper rationale behind this definition is the adjointness condition, which relates the evaluation of implication to the t-norm ($=$ min, by our choice). The adjointness condition relates the evaluation of implication, the function $i : [-1, +1]^2 \rightarrow [-1, +1]$, to the t-norm t by the following bi-conditional (cf. Gottwald, 2001): $d' \leq i(d'', d''') \Leftrightarrow t(d', d'') \leq d'''$.

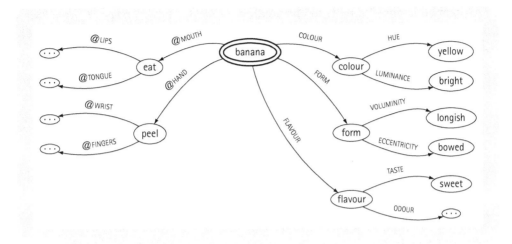

FIGURE 31.6 Hypothetical fragment of the frame for the representation of a banana. The substance representation to be decomposed is marked by a double circle as the referring node of the frame. The labelled arrows denote attributes, the nodes their values. Based on linguistic and neurobiological evidence (e.g. Pulvermüller, 2005), we assume that the representations of substances are linked to body-part related motor programmes. It could be theoretically shown how such a frame might translate into a complex pattern of synchronization where the peripheral attributes of the frame correspond to neuronal feature maps.

the limit case for infinite conjunction. To mention a concrete example, the value of a universally quantified implication of the form

$$(\forall z)(Fz \rightarrow F'z)$$

can be viewed as providing a measure for the overall synchronization between feature layers expressed by the predicates F and F'.

Werning (2003b) extends this semantics from an ontology of objects to an ontology of events. Werning (2003a) integrates relation like the in-relation. Using frame theory, Petersen and Werning (2007) and Werning (2008, 2010) show how our neuronal semantics deals with substance representations that decompose into attributive representations (see Fig. 31.6).

31.8 COMPOSITIONALITY AND EMULATIVE SEMANTICS

In this section I will finally prove that the principle of the compositionality of meaning is fulfilled for oscillatory networks. The work done so far leads us directly to the following theorem:

Theorem 1 (Compositionality of Meaning). *Let L be the set of terms of a PL$^=$-language, SF the set of sentential formulae and $\models$ the neuronal model relation. The function μ with domain L is a compositional meaning function of the language if μ, for every $t \in L$, is defined in the following way:*

$$\mu(t) = \begin{cases} \{\langle \gamma, \gamma(t)\rangle\} \ if \ t \notin SF, \\ \{\langle \gamma, i\rangle \,|\, i \models^1_\gamma \phi\} \ if \ t \in SF. \end{cases}$$

To simplify notation, we may stipulate for any γ-grammatical term t:

$$\mu_\gamma(t) = \begin{cases} \gamma(t) \ if \ t \ is \ not \ a \ sentence, \\ \{i \,|\, \langle \gamma, i\rangle \in \mu(t)\} \ if \ t \ is \ a \ sentence. \end{cases} \tag{31.17}$$

Proof: To prove the theorem, one has to show that for any of the syntactic operations σ in (31.16), there is a semantic operation m_σ that satisfies the equation:

$$\mu(\sigma(t_1, ..., t_n)) = m_\sigma(\mu(t_1), ..., \mu(t_n)). \tag{31.18}$$

To do this for the first six operations, one simply reads the bi-conditionals in the definition of $\models$ as the prescriptions of functions:

$$m_= : (\mu(a), \mu(b)) \mapsto \{\langle \gamma, i\rangle \,|\, 1 = \Delta(\mu_\gamma(a), \mu_\gamma(b))\};$$

$$m_{pred} : (\mu(a), \mu(F)) \mapsto$$
$$\{\langle \gamma, i\rangle \,|\, 1 = \max\{\Delta(\mu_\gamma(a), f_j) \,|\, f = m_\gamma(F)v^i c_i(t)\}\};$$

$$m_\wedge : (\mu(\phi), \mu(\psi)) \mapsto \mu(\phi) \cap \mu(\psi);$$

etc.

To attain semantic counterpart operations for $\sigma_\exists$ and $\sigma_\forall$, we have to apply the method of cylindrification:

$$m_\exists : \mu(\phi(z)) \mapsto$$
$$\{\langle \gamma, i\rangle \,|\, \exists \gamma' : \mathrm{dom}(\gamma') = \mathrm{dom}(\gamma) \cup \{z\} \ and \ \langle \gamma', i\rangle \in \mu(\phi(z))\};$$

$$m_\forall : \mu(\phi(z)) \mapsto$$
$$\{\langle \gamma, i\rangle \,|\, \forall \gamma' : \mathrm{dom}(\gamma') = \mathrm{dom}(\gamma) \cup \{z\} \Rightarrow \langle \gamma', i\rangle \in \mu(\phi(z))\}.$$

One easily verifies that the compositionality condition is satisfied. □

Theorem 1 proves that the dynamics of oscillatory networks provides a compositional semantics for a first-order language. The proof demonstrates that the method of defining a semantics is completely analogous to what one usually does in standard model-theoretical semantics. It follows that the neuronal structure

$$\mathcal{N} = \langle \{\mu_\gamma[L_\gamma], \{\mathrm{m}_=, \mathrm{m}_{pred}, \mathrm{m}_\neg, \mathrm{m}_\wedge, \mathrm{m}_\vee, \mathrm{m}_\rightarrow, \mathrm{m}_\exists, \mathrm{m}_\forall\}\rangle$$

is a compositional semantics for a language with the syntax

$$\langle L_\gamma, \{\sigma_=, \sigma_{pred}, \sigma_\neg, \sigma_\wedge, \sigma_\vee, \sigma_\rightarrow, \sigma_\exists, \sigma_\forall\}\rangle.$$

The meaning $\mu_\gamma(\mathrm{a})$ of an individual constant a can be regarded as an internal object representation. It is an oscillation that co-varies with an object in the stimulus. The stimulus object is to be identified with the denotation of the constant a. The content of the internal object representation expressed by the constant a is hence identical with the denotation of the constant. We should note that a is best conceived of as an indexical that tracks the object. Recall that the construction scheme of the network was chosen to implement the *Gestalt* principles for object perception: whatever yields an oscillation in the network must be regarded as an object of perception. Network simulations with ambiguous and illusionary stimuli support this view (Werning and Maye, 2006; Salari and Maye, 2008).

The meaning $\mu_\gamma(\mathrm{F})$ of a predicate F is identified with an internal predicative representation. It is the matrix that identifies a specific feature layer of a module. The activities of the layer, by construction, co-vary with instantiations of a certain property in the stimulus. We may denote this property by the predicate F. The content of the internal predicative representation expressed by the predicate F is identical with the denotation of the predicate.

The meaning of a sentence is a set of eigenmodes. We can regard it as an internal propositional representation. Since the meanings of constants and predicates are internal representations and co-vary with what they denote, the sets of eigenmodes can be mapped one–to–one to sets of models or possible worlds built from the denoted objects and properties. If one takes propositions to be sets of models or possible worlds, as is commonly done, and if one assumes that propositions are the denotations of sentences, we have a one–to–one mapping between the internal propositional representations of the network and the denotations of the sentences that express them. We may hence infer that the principle of content co-variation is fulfilled for the triples <constant term, internal object representation = oscillation, denoted object>, <predicate, internal object representation = feature layer, denoted property>, <sentence, internal propositional representation = set of eigenmodes, denoted proposition>.

The co-variation between the internal representations generated by the network and expressed by the terms of the language, on the one side, and the denotations of the expressions, on the other side, are one-to-one. Moreover, the semantic operations used to construct our neuronal semantics are also completely analogous to those used in the denotational semantics of standard model theory. It can thus be immediately shown that the neuronal structure $\mathcal{N}$, which provides a semantics of internal representations of our language, is strictly isomorphic to the denotational semantics one would get in the standard model-theoretical approach.[9] This isomorphism justifies the claim that

---

[9] The proof is analogous to the one given in Werning (2005c).

the neuronal structure is an emulative semantics of a first-order language. It is non-symbolic because it is isomorphic to a denotational semantics as provided by standard model theory and thus violates the principle of semantic constituency. Each element of a denotational semantics for the perceptual expressions used in our language has a counterpart in the neuronal structure: its emulation.

31.9 CONCLUSION

Oscillatory networks show how a structure of the cortex can be analysed so that elements of this structure can be identified with internal representations. These cortical states can be regarded as the neuronal meanings of the expressions in a perceptual predicative language. As meanings they form a compositional semantics for such a language. As internal representations they co-vary with external content. The emulative semantics developed in this chapter is biologically realistic. It builds on neurobiological findings regarding cortical feature maps and object-relative synchronization. It also incorporates the Gestalt principles of perception.

Compared to connectionist alternatives (Smolensky, 1991/1995a; Shastri and Ajjana-gadde, 1993; Plate, 1995; van der Velde and de Kamps, 2006; Stewart and Eliasmith, this volume), the architecture proposed here as a model for large parts of the cortex is advantageous in that it not only implements a compositional semantics of meanings, but shows how internal representations can co-vary with external contents. As a consequence it becomes transparent how internal representation can have content and how they thereby mediate between expressions and their denotations.

Oscillatory networks and their biological correlates may be assigned a central role at the interface between language and mind, and between mind and world. This is due to the quasi-perceptual capabilities of oscillatory networks, which alternative connectionist models for semantic implementations lack. Linking oscillatory networks to mechanisms for the production of phonological sequences remains a challenge for future investigations.

The theory developed here amounts to a new mathematical description of the time-structure the cortex is believed to exhibit. Neuronal synchronization plays an essential role not only for binding, but, generally, for the generation of compositional representations in the brain.

According to our approach meanings are non-symbolic, but emulative. In contrast to symbolic theories there is no part–whole relation defined on meanings that reflects the part–whole relations of syntax. Instead, the denotational structure of linguistic expressions is emulated. A main aspect of Fodor's Language of Thought approach is to identify meanings with mental concepts and so 'duplicate' language. The principal idea of emulative semantics is that meanings 'duplicate' the world where duplication is taken to be neuronal emulation.

CHAPTER 32

··

THE PROCESSING
CONSEQUENCES OF
COMPOSITIONALITY

··

GIOSUÈ BAGGIO, MICHIEL VAN
LAMBALGEN, AND PETER HAGOORT

32.1 INTRODUCTION

··

It is often argued that the principle of compositionality is formally vacuous: any grammar can be given a compositional semantics (Janssen, 1986; Zadrozny, 1994),[1] which implies the principle is also empirically vacuous: if a compositional analysis of any linguistic structure can be given, compositionality is always upheld by the data. To be sure, the meaning of any complex expression can be viewed as a function of the meanings of its constituents and the syntactic mode of combination, *provided enough complexity is built into the structures involved*, that is the lexicon and the syntax. These are not motivated on independent grounds, as their characterization serves the sole purpose of yielding a compositional theory (Groenendijk and Stokhof, 1991).

The need for an independent motivation of theories of syntax and lexical semantics is precisely the issue here. Our aim is to show that, even though there often is a way to salvage compositionality in the face of empirical data, the choices one has to make in order to do so have consequences which may be implausible given the cognitive and neural constraints on language comprehension, production, and acquisition. Let us start with the most basic of questions: *why* compositionality? We will now give a sketch of the main arguments, which will be refined in the course of the discussion.

---

[1] See Kazmi and Pelletier (1998) and Westerståhl (1998) among others for a critical discussion.

32.1.1 The productivity argument

A familiar argument in favour of compositionality starts from a perceived tension between the infinity of language and the finiteness of the brain. There are infinitely many sentences in any natural language, but the brain has only finite storage capacity, and it therefore falls to syntax to provide a finitely describable procedure for generating an infinite class of sentences. Furthermore, so the argument goes, a speaker of any language is able to understand a sentence she has never heard before, or to express a meaning she has never expressed before, and in that sense she knows the infinitely many different meanings of the infinitely many sentences of that language. Therefore, semantics is also under the obligation to come up with a finitely describable engine that generates all possible sentence meanings for the given language (Katz and Fodor, 1963).

Compositionality provides a seemingly efficient way to satisfy these desiderata. There are only finitely many words in the lexicon and syntax can have only finitely many rules of combination. Here compositionality comes into play:

Principle of Compositionality *The meaning of an expression is a function of the meanings of its parts and of the way they are syntactically combined.*

If meanings are generated in such a way that compositionality is satisfied, then it seems that all possible sentence meanings can be finitely generated. Now, although compositionality is a guiding principle of *formal* semantics, the standard motivation as sketched above partly appeals to the *psychological* notions of comprehension and production, while at the same time invoking the patently non-psychological infinity of language. A quick way to dismiss the argument from productivity is therefore to deny that language is infinite, even in the sense of *potential* infinity. A moment's reflection shows, however, that the issue is not really about infinity: substituting a large finite number for infinity does not change the essence of the productivity argument, which is that not every sentence that can be understood or produced given human cognitive limitations is stored. So, while there is no reason to have a semantic theory that explains comprehension of nested centre embeddings of arbitrary depth, it is also not the case that all sentences with centre embeddings with depth, say, ≤ 6 can be stored. In other words, psychologically speaking, the real issue is about 'the balance between storage and computation', and the role compositionality plays there. And it might seem that compositionality always leads to the most efficient architecture in this respect.

That this is not necessarily so can be illustrated using an example from Keenan (1979). In an adjective–noun construction, the noun is the argument fed into the adjective, which is viewed as a function. Keenan observes that the interpretation of the function word seems to be determined by its argument: compare for instance the different meanings of the adjective 'flat' in 'flat tyre', 'flat beer', 'flat note', etc. It is of course technically possible, as Keenan notes, to replace the single function 'flat' by a disjunctively defined function, where each of the disjuncts corresponds to a separate meaning for 'flat', with suitable selection restrictions on the argument. However, this technical solution is surely paradoxical: compositionality was invoked to account for productivity, which seemed hard to explain in terms of storage only; but, in this case, compositionality can apparently be salvaged only by *increasing* the demand on storage! From a processing perspective, it would be much better if there were a single computational mechanism generating the meaning of a *flat + noun* construction, starting from a single basic meaning of 'flat'. These considerations show that the principle of compositionality is affected by its ambiguous status: as a formal desideratum on the one hand, and a processing hypothesis on the other.

32.1.2 The systematicity argument

A second argument in favour of compositionality is based on the observation that languages are systematic, that is, the ability to understand certain utterances is connected to the ability to understand certain others. For instance, any native speaker of English that understands 'John loves Mary' also understands 'Mary loves John'.

Systematicity *Anyone who understands the complex expressions e and e' built up through the syntactic operation F from the constituents $e_1, \ldots, e_n$ and $e'_1, \ldots, e'_n$ respectively, can thereby also understand any other expression e'' built up through F from expressions among $e_1, \ldots, e_n, e'_1, \ldots, e'_n$.*

Systematicity seems to entail compositionality, but the issue here is whether languages are systematic in the sense above. For instance, anyone who understands 'The dog is asleep' and 'The cat is awake' can certainly understand 'The dog is awake' and 'The cat is asleep'. However, would everyone who understands 'within an hour' and 'without a watch' also understand 'within a watch' and 'without an hour'? The definition presupposes that e'' is a meaningful expression and that $e_1, \ldots, e_n, e'_1, \ldots, e'_n$ can be freely combined and substituted while keeping F constant. But the fact that we can hardly make sense of 'within a watch' and 'without an hour' suggests that this is not the case, thus languages are not systematic in the sense of the definition above. Now, let us suppose for a moment that this difficulty can be overcome. Would then systematicity force compositionality upon us? It seems not, for systematicity says that, given the sentences 'The dog is asleep' and 'The cat is awake', from the meanings of 'the dog', 'the cat', 'is asleep', and 'is awake' plus the syntax, one is able to understand the meaning of 'The dog is awake'. Compositionality, however, makes a stronger claim, namely that the meanings of 'the dog' and 'is awake' plus the syntax are sufficient to do that. So, even if systematicity held, it would not buy compositionality (see Johnson (2004*a*), Szabó (2007), Pullum and Scholz (2007) for a discussion and further issues).

32.1.3 The methodological argument

A third argument is that compositionality is needed as a constraint on doing semantics, as an essential part of the explanatory enterprise (Janssen 1997; Dever 1999). For instance, if one has to explain why in the 'donkey sentence'

(32.1)   If a farmer owns a donkey, he beats it.

the DP 'a donkey' has universal force, it will not do to say: 'well, in this context it simply has universal force'. An account that starts out with the existential reading of the DP, and then shows how its being embedded in the antecedent of a conditional changes its interpretation from existential to universal, has at least the appearance of an explanation.

The trouble with the methodological argument is that compositionality is highly theory dependent (Partee et al., 1990). Ideally, when looking for an explanation of a given linguistic phenomenon, one takes the syntax and the semantics to be fully specified formal systems. It is then a definite question whether that phenomenon allows for a compositional treatment. If it does not, one may take this as a cue for changing the semantics. In practice, however, the explanation of a new phenomenon of interest often leads to changes in *both* syntax and semantics. Compositionality then becomes a soft constraint indeed.

It seems to us the much-needed methodological constraints have to be sought elsewhere, in a tighter regimentation of syntactic and semantic theories. From our perspective, these constraints should be cognitively motivated, in the sense that formal theories of syntax and semantics should be viewed as 'computational level theories' (Marr, 1982) of actual syntactic and semantic mechanisms (Baggio and van Lambalgen, 2007; Baggio et al., 2012). In the ideal case, it then becomes an empirical question whether syntax and semantics communicate as compositionality says they do. This leads us to the third argument, in which the status of compositionality as a processing principle becomes more prominent.

32.1.4 The modularity argument

A fourth argument leading to compositionality is suggested by a view of the language faculty as a 'cognitive module'. Fodor (1983) lists nine properties characterizing modular systems: domain specificity, fast and mandatory operation, limited central access to modular representations, informational encapsulation, shallow outputs, fixed neural architecture, specific breakdown patters, and characteristic ontogenic pace and sequencing. Of these, the most relevant for our purposes is *informational encapsulation*. This is the idea that perceptual systems—language included—are relatively impenetrable to the bulk of the knowledge internally represented by the organism. Informational encapsulation says that there are tight constraints on the flow and handling of extramodular information *within* the module *prior to* the production of an output.

To a certain extent, informational encapsulation is assumed by any cognitive model of language—which is not to say that all component-based architectures (Jackendoff, 1997) are modular in Fodor's sense. Fodor's (and Chomsky's) original view of modularity is that a grammar's generative power can be captured by a *single* module, which comprises a finite repository of lexical meanings and a finite repertoire of syntactic rules.[2] Rules for *semantic* computation (inference is a paradigmatic case) fall within the province of central systems. It can be easily seen that the computations performed by this kind of modular machine are those regimented by compositionality: the output produced by the module (the meaning of a complex expression) is a function of the knowledge accessible to the module (the lexicon and the syntax). But this is not the only modular architecture supporting compositionality. For instance, one could postulate *two* modules: a module which produces syntactic analyses of clauses, which are then fed into another module containing meanings for the lexical items and combination procedures corresponding to syntactic operations, and outputs a semantic representation of the clause.[3] Compositionality would then constrain the kind of traffic that can occur between the two modules.

So regardless of one's choice of modular architecture, compositionality remains relevant insofar as it acts as a counterpart of information encapsulation at the level of the description of linguistic structure. The link between compositionality and informational encapsulation can be made more explicit: if the composition of meanings is not affected by extra-modular knowledge, then one can characterize the meaning of any complex expression as a function of the meanings of its constituents and syntactic rules *only*, all of which are readily available within the module.[4] Clearly, this hinges very much on what one assumes is contained in the module(s)—and this will be a recurrent theme in this chapter. What bears some emphasis here is that the degree to which a system is informationally encapsulated can be determined only based on empirical data. Hence, with this 'argument from modularity' in place, it also becomes possible to treat compositionality as a processing principle, that is, as a constraint on the range of data structures involved in language processing.

32.2 COMPOSITIONALITY AS A PROCESSING PRINCIPLE

32.2.1 A first approximation

The issue which we set ourselves to address is how to constrain and refine compositionality based on experimental data and cognitive considerations. One may start from the

---

[2] The module also contains mechanisms for phonological decoding, but we ignore these for simplicity.

[3] For a modular view of semantics, see among others Borg (2004) and Robbins (2007) for a critical discussion.

[4] Jackendoff (1997) makes the same point: 'The hypothesis of syntactically transparent semantic composition has the virtue of theoretical elegance and constraint. Its effect is to enable researchers to isolate the language capacity—including its contribution to semantics—from the rest of the mind, as befits a modular conception.'

observation that 'function' in the definition of compositionality needs to refer to some computable input-to-output mapping, and that inputs—lexical meanings and syntactic rules or constraints—must be given incrementally:

Incremental composition *The meaning of a complex expression at some processing stage σ is computed based on the constituent expressions processed at σ and of the syntactic structure built up at σ.*[5]

This definition is silent as to whether meaning assembly involves the lexicon and the syntax *only*, or whether other sources of information could enter the composition process. For this we need another definition, which can be combined with the former:

Simple composition *(i) The meanings of elementary expressions are the only constraints on content in the computation of the meaning of a complex expression. (ii) The syntax of elementary expressions is the only constraint on structure in the computation of the meaning of a complex expression.*

The notion of 'weak' or 'enriched composition' (Pustejovsky, 1995; Jackendoff, 1997) follows from allowing further constraints on content and structure. The distinction between content and structure is admittedly vague, and can only be made clearer based on particular formal theories of syntax and semantics—recall compositionality's theory-dependence (Partee et al., 1990). We could go even further and observe that, at least in formal approaches to grammar, the distinction vanishes, and one is left with a purely syntactic analysis of meaning in some logical language. However, it remains a distinction worth keeping, especially because the brain appears to honour it, as is reflected by the different electrophysiological traces left by morphosyntactic and semantic manipulations (see Section 32.3.3 below). Let us now see how two of the arguments for compositionality presented above fare in light of the new definitions.

32.2.2 Productivity and modularity reconsidered

Compositionality's plausibility is usually argued for by means of a rhetorical question, such as 'what other mechanism could explain the productivity of language?', as if posing the question would already dictate the answer. To address this point, it pays to be more precise regarding the exact technical implications of simple composition. Consider two supposed consequences, due to Hintikka (1983):

Context independence thesis *The meaning of an expression should not depend on the context in which it occurs.*
Inside-out principle *The proper direction of a semantic analysis is from the inside out—that is, from the bottom up, or from elementary to complex meanings.*

---

[5] For simplicity, we may assume that each word corresponds to a processing stage, and vice versa. An important theoretical question is whether assuming finer-grained processing steps would lead to local inconsistencies between incrementality and compositionality.

Together, these consequences suggest that we ought to take the notion of a 'function' in the formulation of the principle very seriously. Semantic computation of complex expressions is function application, so *the meanings of simple expressions are not changed by virtue of the fact that they occur as arguments of the function.*[6] This shows that the principle of compositionality is tied to one very particular form of linguistic productivity, exemplified by the usual rules: if S is a sentence, one can form a new sentence 'I think that S'; if S_1, S_2 are sentences, one can form 'S_1 and S_2'; etc. But there exist other forms of productivity in natural languages, which do not have this function-like character. An example is the progressive construction in English when applied to stative verbs (Croft, 1998):

(32.2)   a. She resembles her mother.
          b. *She is resembling her mother.
          c. She is resembling her mother more and more every day.

'Resemble' is a stative verb, and this seems to be clinched by (32.2b), which clearly shows that the progressive is not applicable. Still, in a suitable context the progressive *is* applicable, as in (32.2c), where it imposes a dynamic meaning upon 'resemble': resemblance now comes in degrees that can change over time. Therefore, the meaning of 'resemble' depends upon the context in which it occurs, contradicting context independence. This variability of meaning can still be predicted once one assumes that the progressive construction has a meaning of its own, which it imposes upon that of the verb. This imposition of meaning is moreover productive in that it applies to many stative verbs. Simple composition as made precise by Hintikka can account for this particular form of productivity only by assuming multiple meanings of stative verbs, where the progressive selects for a dynamic meaning (recall the analysis of 'flat' in Section 32.1.1).

While compositionality can be salvaged formally, experiments on language processing might rule out such *ad hoc* manoeuvres. There is a very different computational account of what goes on in comprehending sentences such as (32.2c) that emphasizes the recomputation of the meaning of 'resemble' which takes place when the adverbial phrase 'more and more every day' is processed (van Lambalgen and Hamm, 2004; ch. 11). The two accounts thus differ in their processing consequences: simple composition in the Hintikka sense leads to search and selection of the appropriate meaning but not to recomputation, as in the second account. These operations might give rise to different neurophysiological responses (Baggio et al., 2008), so in principle the two accounts can be tested experimentally.

If recomputation were to be supported, where would that leave compositionality and the work it is supposed to do? The strict reading as embodied in Hintikka's principles presents semantic composition as entirely inside-out/bottom-up. The recomputation account is also partially outside-in/top-down. In theory, this has the consequence that the meaning which is assigned to an expression is always provisional, a situation that

---

[6] Just as the number 2 has the same meaning, whether it occurs as argument in the function 3^x or in the function $3 + x$. This is obvious in mathematics, but not in natural language, as we shall see.

cannot occur on a literal reading of compositionality (but see Section 32.3.1). However, there is room for both accounts, because the productivity of language is a two-dimensional phenomenon. On the vertical dimension, there is productivity due to increased syntactic complexity; here simple composition has an important role to play. There is, however, also a horizontal dimension to productivity—here it is not so much the syntactic complexity that increases, but new meanings of a given clause are produced by varying syntactic or semantic aspects of other clauses. Thus, if we replace the adverbial 'more and more every day' in (32.2c) with 'in broad daylight', the progressive is no longer felicitous, because the verb 'resemble' then has its default stative meaning. The horizontal dimension of productivity seems to call for some form of enriched composition, that is, ways of combining meaning that allow top-down influences and recomputation.

Two forms of top-down computation seem consistent with informational encapsulation, and therefore with its analogue compositionality. First, the information fed back comes from and remains within the module, as when it is stored in the lexicon. Second, information is fed back into the module from another module or from a central system *after* the production of an output. This is a rather trivial way to preserve informational encapsulation in the face of top-down computation. The former can be dismissed using an argument due to Hodges (2006), which is based on what we might call 'top-down composition'. It takes its cue from the following principle (Frege, 1884):

Context principle *Elementary expressions do not have meaning in isolation, but only in the context of (as constituents of) complex expressions.*

In the briefest outline, Hodges' proposal is this. The syntax is defined in terms of constituent structure in such a way that, if e is an expression occurring in a sentence S, then S can be viewed as $G(e)$, where $G(x)$ is a syntactic frame with open slot x. Now define an equivalence relation $\sim$ on expressions by putting

$e \sim f$ iff for all $G(x)$: $G(e)$ is a sentence iff $G(f)$ is, and $G(e)$ is acceptable in the same contexts as $G(f)$.

The *Fregean value* of e is the equivalence class of e modulo $\sim$. Hodges shows that taking the Fregean value of e as its meaning yields a compositional semantics. Therefore, if we assume that the module contains all Fregean values, modularity is restored. Moreover, this notion of meaning is pleasingly context-sensitive. Hodges gives the example of sentences which have different social connotations, for instance 'he is intoxicated' vs. 'he is pissed' (Hodges, 2006). The contexts in which these sentences are acceptable are very different. In this sense, these two sentences have different meanings in Hodges' semantics, whereas they would be treated as synonymous with 'he is drunk' in a more standard framework.

Although Hodges' proposal formally restores compositionality, it does so in a way that upsets the balance between storage and computation, and renders it unclear how meanings can be acquired. The Fregean value of e is defined by means of all possible uses of e, and it is doubtful that these are available to a young language learner. In other words, learning meanings is a gradual process, so Fregean values should be partial objects, in the sense of being defined by means of a subset of all possible uses of e, and being subject to update and revision as learning proceeds, which is not what Hodges suggests. The point can be amplified by considering what it means to *know* the Fregean value of e. There seem to be two components to this:

1. one must know which f are equivalent to e, which means that for all $G(x)$ such that $G(e)$ is a sentence iff $G(f)$ is, $G(f)$ is acceptable in exactly the same contexts as $G(e)$— this requires one to know for all sentences $G(e)$ and all contexts C, whether $G(e)$ is acceptable in C;
2. one must know which f are not equivalent to e, which means that for all G such that $G(e)$ and $G(f)$ are sentences, one must know a context in which $G(e)$ is acceptable and $G(f)$ is not, or vice versa.

Natural (as opposed to formal) languages may not incorporate the concise representations generating the knowledge required. This implies that the storage component must already contain a great deal of information about the sentences that can be constructed from e, and the contexts in which these are acceptable. Intuitively, this goes against the purpose of a modular architecture, and it also goes against the original motivation for compositionality as easing the burden on storage—recall the argument from productivity. We therefore tend to read Hodges' result, when applied to natural languages, as showing the implausibility of an architecture in which context sensitivity is achieved by storing extra information within the module, rather than by relaxing informational encapsulation to allow cross-module talk. In brief, the a priori arguments considered here show that simple composition is not enough to account for the full range of factors which make language productive. Let us now ask if similar considerations are suggested by experimental work bearing on compositionality.

32.3 EXPERIMENTAL DATA BEARING ON COMPOSITIONALITY

32.3.1 Semantic illusions

One assumption that underlies many semantic theories is that full lexical meanings are used in the composition process. In most formal semantics, this choice is forced by the ontology: a lexical meaning is just a placeholder for a typed entity, and this explains why inputs cannot be partial objects; consequently, meaning assembly amounts to type composition, and this accounts for the fact that the inputs are still recognizable in the end product. In lexical semantics, by contrast, lexical meanings are complex, yet compact representations, such as algorithms (Miller and Johnson-Laird, 1976), feature or conceptual structures (Jackendoff, 1983), and the like. One possible refinement of compositionality is to allow partial representations to be recruited during processing.

Relevant to this issue is the well-known 'Moses illusion' (Erickson and Matteson, 1981). When asked 'How many animals of each sort did Moses put on the ark?', subjects tend to respond 'two' without questioning the (false) presupposition that Moses was the biblical character who did that. Similar results have been obtained with questions such as 'After an air-crash, where should the survivors be buried?' (Barton and Sanford, 1993) or 'Can a man marry his widow's sister?' (Sanford, 2002). Hearers seem to be processing these sentences superficially enough to miss the false presuppositions. Ferreira et al. (2002) and Ferreira and Patson (2007) suggest that these data challenge compositionality. Consider the Moses question. It would seem that the meaning computed by hearers and the meaning derived compositionally are in some important respect different. If the former were a function of the meanings of the constituents and the syntax, 'Moses' would mean Moses and hearers would notice the false presupposition. This seems an instance of a non-compositional process.

One might argue against this conclusion by emphasizing that these data just show that each word in a sentence does not contribute its full meaning (Sanford and Sturt, 2002). The 'full meaning' of 'Moses' need not be retrieved, only some feature made salient by the context (Sanford and Sturt, 2002; Sanford, 2002). This might be 'biblical character', 'patriarch' or some other feature responsible for the semantic proximity of 'Noah' and 'Moses' (van Oostendorp and de Mul, 1990). Feature sharing is thus what gives rise to the illusion. Nonetheless, the fact that the lexicon may be a locus of shallow processing (or retrieval, as the case may be) does not speak against compositionality. Simple composition entails that the lexicon is the only provider of content for complex meanings, though not that *full* lexical representations must be used. The latter seems too strong a requirement to press upon either simple or enriched composition. For if there are such entities as 'full lexical meanings'—and there are reasons to be sceptical about that—they can hardly be used on most processing tasks, because of the massive amount of information, presumably continuous with non-lexical knowledge, that would be fed into the composition process. Incremental, context-sensitive feature selection during the retrieval of word meaning would thus be the default. Semantic illusions would become a special case, in which some critical semantic feature is shared between the word triggering a true presupposition ('Noah') and the word triggering a false presupposition ('Moses'). In summary, compositionality can be refined to accommodate semantic illusions, by allowing composition to make use of partial lexico-semantic representations.

32.3.2 Misinterpretations

Ferreira and colleagues investigated cases of misinterpretation in language processing. Some of these involve garden-path sentences:

(32.3)   While Anna dressed the baby played in the crib.

The 'garden-path model' (Frazier, 1987) hypothesizes that 'the baby' is initially parsed and interpreted as the direct object of 'dressed'. Only when the verb 'played' is encountered are the syntactic and semantic representations revised to the effect that 'the baby' is the subject of 'played'. One question here is whether the initial representation, featuring 'the baby' as a direct object, is at all maintained in memory. Christianson et al. (2001) show that, while readers correctly respond in the affirmative to 'Did the baby play in the crib?', they also give a positive answer to 'Did Anna dress the baby?' No grammar or parser on the market would allow for the same token NP to play two functional roles, subject and direct object. And yet, this appears to be precisely the interpretation computed by readers. Ferreira et al. (2002) take this as 'clear evidence that the meaning people obtain for a sentence is often not a reflection of its true content'—that is, it is not built up compositionally.

Does the existence of 'lingering misinterpretations' demonstrate that the processing of garden-path sentences is non-compositional, as suggested by Ferreira and colleagues? There are at least two ways of accounting for the data, from which different answers ensue. On one account, the last interpretation subjects come up with is that while Anna dressed, the baby played in the crib, which corresponds to the revised parse whereby 'the baby' is the subject of 'played', and is no longer the direct object of 'dressed'. Interpretation is therefore non-monotonic, that is, allowing for revisions on earlier structures. This, however, requires a refinement of compositionality that was introduced earlier on—incremental composition. On this view, both the initial and the revised interpretations can be derived compositionally, and simple composition seems enough in this case. The persisting misinterpretation would be rather an effect of memory architecture or neural implementation. One aspect of the data of Christianson et al. (2001) which supports this story is that misinterpretations are more frequent when the head of the misanalysed phrase occurs early. That is, misinterpretations are more likely to persist the longer they have been part of the initial discourse model.

On the second account, the final interpretation is that Anna dressed the baby while the baby played in the crib. This meaning can hardly be derived compositionally. First, because there is only one token of 'the baby' among the constituents of the sentence, while the final interpretation we have assumed involves two occurrences of it: one as the recipient of the dressing action, the other as the agent of the playing activity—hence the 'constituent parts' aspect of the definition of compositionality is out. Second, because syntax does not allow a phrase to play two distinct functional roles simultaneously— hence the 'syntax' part of the definition is out. To derive the meaning above, one needs a mechanism that copies the token 'the baby' and makes both instances available for interpretation. Such a mechanism does make processing non-compositional (Ferreira et al., 2002; Ferreira and Patson, 2007). In brief, misinterpretations of garden-path sentences challenge compositionality, unless we assume that early semantic material lingers in memory during later stages, but is not part of the discourse model computed on the basis of the revised syntactic analysis.

32.3.3 Interlude: event-related brain potentials (ERPs)

One aspect of enriched composition is that the stored meanings of elementary expressions are not the only source of content for complex meanings. It can be suggested that this challenges informational encapsulation, if one can demonstrate that such additional semantic information is handled by the module (or component) before an output is produced (Fodor, 1983). Some experimental techniques in cognitive neuroscience allow one to make timing inferences, the most sensitive and direct of which is based on event-related brain potentials (ERPs) (Van Berkum, 2004).

The post-synaptic currents generated by the neocortex (electroencephalography, or EEG) can be recorded by placing a number of electrodes on the scalp, amplifying the signal, and plotting the observed voltage changes as a function of time (Luck, 2005). ERPs are defined as electrical potentials time-locked to some event of interest, such as the onset of a stimulus. Averaging over a relatively large number of trials of the same condition is the most widely used approach to obtaining ERPs.

An ERP component that is particularly relevant here is the N400. This is a negative shift starting around 250 ms after word onset, peaking at 400 ms, and lasting until approximately 550 ms. Every content word elicits an N400, but the amplitude of the component, relative to a control condition, is dependent upon the degree of semantic relatedness of the given word with its sentence (Kutas and Hillyard, 1980; Kutas and Hillyard, 1984; Hagoort and Brown, 1994) or discourse context (van Berkum et al., 1999; van Berkum et al., 2003). There is evidence that the N400 does not just reflect lexical access, but the *integration* of a word's meaning into the unfolding semantic representation (see Brown and Hagoort (1993) and Li et al. (2008) among others for experimental data and Hagoort et al. (2009) for a discussion and a comparison with alternative accounts of the N400). The N400 can be seen as an index of the complexity of initial attempts to combine the meaning of the given word with the meanings of the expressions already processed.

Another ERP effect that will be of interest here is the P600. This is a positive shift starting around 500 ms following the onset of the word and lasting for about 500 ms (Osterhout and Holcomb, 1992; Hagoort et al., 1993). Larger P600 effects are elicited by sentences containing violations of syntactic constraints (such as phrase structure, subcategorization, agreement), temporarily syntactically ambiguous sentences, garden-path sentences, and constructions which show high syntactic complexity (Hagoort et al., 2001; Friederici, 2002; Hagoort, 2003). In relation to incremental composition, we can regard the P600 as an index of the time and resources involved in attaching a given word in the syntactic representation computed thus far (Hagoort, 2003). How do N400 and P600 data bear on compositionality?

32.3.4 World knowledge

Relevant to this question is an ERP study by Hagoort et al. (2004), using true (32.4a), false (32.4b) and semantically anomalous (32.4c) sentences:[7]

(32.4)   a. Dutch trains are yellow and very crowded.
         b. Dutch trains are white and very crowded.
         c. Dutch trains are sour and very crowded.

The words 'white' and 'sour' evoked very similar N400s, in both cases larger than the N400 elicited by 'yellow'. Integrating the meanings of 'white' and 'sour' in the ongoing semantic representation is thus relatively hard. This suggests that, upon encountering 'Dutch trains', features are retrieved which code for the colour of Dutch trains—typically yellow-blue—and are responsible for the additional processing costs associated with 'white'.

While it is notoriously hard to define 'core' semantic features, separating linguistic from world knowledge, it is nevertheless possible to identify features which are *invariant* across the individuals and communities using the relevant word. That 'sour' cannot be applied to (Dutch) trains seems a piece of invariant knowledge, and in that sense is a fact of linguistic predication ('linguistic knowledge'). However, trains differ in colour and other properties in space and time, hence that 'white' cannot be applied to Dutch trains reflects a contingent state of affairs which not all users of the expressions 'train' or 'Dutch train' may be aware of ('world knowledge'). The N400 data of Hagoort et al. (2004) show that 'white' is hard to integrate in the sentence context, which in turn suggests there is something in the meaning of 'Dutch trains' which makes integration hard. This must be knowledge that Dutch trains are yellow and blue, and not white. It thus seems that during processing meanings are computed—for instance, of the compound 'Dutch trains'—encompassing invariant *and* community-specific semantic information, that is, linguistic *and* world knowledge. As for compositionality, this may mean two things, depending on one's view of the lexicon: either the lexicon includes declarative memory in its entirety, and then simple composition seems enough to account for the similarity between the N400 effects, or the lexicon includes invariant meanings only, and then enriched composition—the thesis that the lexicon is not the only source of semantic content—is necessary to explain the observed N400s.[8]

32.3.5 Co-speech gestures

At least one other ERP study reporting modulations of the N400 seems relevant for our discussion. Özyürek et al. (2007) show that larger N400s are elicited by co-speech

---

[7] The stimuli were in Dutch and participants were native Dutch speakers.

[8] For other results bearing on the issue of world knowledge and on-line meaning composition, see Münte et al. (1998), Ferretti et al. (2007), and Baggio et al. (2008), among others.

gestures which do not match with the semantic content of the accompanying sentence. This demonstrates that semantic information from different modalities—speech and gesture, in this case—is integrated in the same time frame. The choice mentioned above between two views of the lexicon applies here too. If schematic representations of gestures are stored in declarative memory, which is assumed to be entirely contained in the lexicon, simple composition seems enough to explain the data. However, there exist experimental data showing that subjects attribute different meanings to a given iconic gesture, providing evidence for the non-conventionalized nature of gesture meanings (Chauncey et al., 2004). If indeed gesture schemes are not part of the lexicon, some form of enriched composition must occur, such that the semantics of elementary expressions is just one source of content for complex meanings. This choice between two views of the lexicon, and its consequences for the status of compositionality, shows how severe is the problem of compositionality's theory-dependence, and how pressing the need for realistic constraints on the components of the grammar.

32.3.6 Fictional discourse

The data we have seen so far may not speak directly to the issue of the empirical evidence for or against compositionality, but they reveal the existence of richer meanings including world knowledge and perceptual cues. Experimental research suggests that discourse is not only another source of content beyond strict, invariant lexical meanings, but can even add and subtract core features to elementary meanings themselves. One such extreme case of context-sensitivity can be found in fictional discourse. Nieuwland and van Berkum (2005) show that sentences which are otherwise sensible, like

(32.5)   The peanut was salted.

appear anomalous if they are embedded in a context in which the inanimate subject ('the peanut') is attributed animate features. In a narrative in which the peanut danced, sang, and met an almond it liked, 'salted' in (32.5) resulted in a *larger* N400 compared to 'in love' in (32.6)

(32.6)   The peanut was in love.

This is taken to show that discourse can over-ride even such deep-rooted semantic features as animacy. These findings can also be read as a challenge to Hintikka's principles, for they seem to show that meaning is context-dependent, and semantic composition can proceed from the outside-in, that is, from the discourse to lexical meaning.

Processing sentences such as (32.6) in a fictional context might therefore involve some form of top-down composition which, if it cannot resort to the mental lexicon as a repository of contextual values of expressions (recall Hodges' argument), then it must adopt some form of enriched composition—or give up a share of informational encapsulation, which is the same. However, there seems to be another way out for compositionality. One may ask, not what changes in the meaning of 'peanut' in a context in which it is depicted as animate, but what is preserved of the original (invariant, as we called it) meaning of the word. Animacy aside, there is no evidence that any of the other semantic features is maintained. Therefore, the word form 'peanut' in the fictional context considered here may just be used as a label for an animate subject or, more precisely, a proper name with a reference but no (or perhaps very little) sense. This could easily be handled in a compositional manner. Processing the adjective 'salted', given the plausible combination with 'peanut', might recover its original sense, and this would explain the larger N400. This does not detract from the interest of the data, nor from the interpretation chosen by Nieuwland and van Berkum. It does exemplify, however, the kind of problems one encounters when trying to put compositionality to the test, and in particular the exceptional elbow room compositionality leaves to its application. It is precisely this resilience which has been taken by many as empirical vacuity.

32.3.7 Semantic attraction

A strict reading of compositionality implies that only two sorts of constraints can interact to produce complex meanings: syntax and the lexicon. A further assumption is that the syntax is an analysis of the sentence *as is given*, for instance a formal decomposition into constituents.[9] This is all there is to the input for semantic composition. Combining lexical meanings (representations or types, depending on the ontology) based on the syntactic structure will in turn produce an input for the interpretation. In this sense, semantics is often said to be dependent on syntax. Kim and Osterhout (2005) designed an ERP study to test the extent to which syntax is actually in control of the composition process. They presented participants with sentences such as

(32.7) a. The hearty meal was devouring the kids.
         b. The hearty meal was devoured by the kids.

and found that 'devouring' in (32.7a) elicited a larger P600 compared to 'devoured' in (32.7b). If the syntax were taken as is given in the sentence—in well-formed sentences, that is—and if it were only proposing input to the semantics, an N400 to 'devouring' should be expected: indeed (32.7a) is syntactically well-formed, whereas a semantic constraint (animacy) appears to be violated. The P600 indicates that (32.7a) is perceived as a syntactic violation, originating from the impossibility at 'devouring' of building a passive construction. At the verb's stem 'devour-', the passive is the only continuation compatible with a plausible meaning for the sentence, as is testified by (32.7b). The data therefore show not only that semantic attraction to a more plausible interpretation is an important source of constraints in sentence processing—which could also be concluded if 'devouring' induced a larger N400—but also that such constraints can override syntactic cues as these are given in the input—which is what the P600, as a syntax-related effect, shows. Compositionality can be salvaged only by assuming that semantic

---

[9] The extent to which a syntactic analysis is allowed to deviate from the surface form of an expression is a matter of considerable debate. For a discussion, see Culicover and Jackendoff (2005, 2006).

attractors, such as 'kids devour hearty meals', are configurations of the lexical network and not, as would seem more intuitively appealing, the result of inference. But this move is once again paradoxical: compositionality was introduced to explain productivity, and therefore to *ease* the burden on storage; now it seems we need a growing inventory of stored semantic facts to maintain compositionality.

32.3.8 Coercion

A phenomenon that has often been taken as a challenge to compositionality is complement coercion. Consider the following sentences

(32.8)   a. The journalist began the article after his coffee break.
         b. The journalist wrote the article after his coffee break.

The intuitive difference between the two is that, while 'wrote the article' asserts the relevant activity (writing), 'began the article' does not. So if a full event sense is to be recovered from (32.8a), the activity must be inferred based on other semantic cues present in the sentence and stored knowledge. One candidate analysis (Pustejovsky, 1995) focuses on the interpretation of the NP. For instance, 'the article' is an entity-denoting expression, which combined with verbs such as 'begin' denotes an event. Coercion is thus an instance of type-shifting, where types lay out a basic ontology of entities, events, etc. An alternative analysis assumes richer event structures (van Lambalgen and Hamm, 2004). Each VP is semantically represented by a quadruple $< f_1, f_2, e, f_3 >$, where f_1 represents a force being exerted, f_2 the object or state driven by the force, e the goal toward which the exertion of the force is directed, and f_3 the state of having achieved that goal. Some slots in the quadruple may be empty, depending on the *Aktionsart* of the VP. Accomplishments such as 'write an article' feature a full event structure, while achievements such as 'begin an article' include only a punctual event e (the beginning of a yet unspecified activity relating to the article) and a consequent state (having begun the activity). Coercion is seen as a transition to a richer event structure, in which the activity f_1 is also represented. Both analyses rely on some form of enriched composition, as in both cases an operation of meaning assembly that is not syntactic in nature (type-shifting or enrichment of the event structure) is postulated.

   An interpretation of (32.8a) in which the activity remains unspecified is conceivable, and it therefore falls to experimental research to provide evidence for or against the existence of complement coercion. A series of studies have shown that coercing sentences such as (32.8a) result in increased processing costs compared to controls such as (32.8b) (McElree et al., 2001; Traxler et al., 2002; Traxler et al., 2005; McElree et al., 2006b; Pylkkänen et al., 2007; Baggio et al., 2010; Kuperberg et al., 2010). This can be taken as evidence against simple composition.[10] However, a compositional analysis may still be

[10] Evidence for enriched composition in cases of aspectual coercion has also been found. See Piñango et al. (1999) and Piñango et al. (2006).

possible if the operation which is responsible for generating the enriched meaning (say, type-shifting) is incorporated in the syntax. This choice can be criticized on different grounds. On empirical grounds, it predicts that (32.8a) would elicit a P600 (which, as we have seen, correlates with syntactic complexity), while the available neural data reveal a different effect than the P600 (Pylkkänen et al., 2007, Baggio et al., 2010; Kuperberg et al., 2010). On theoretical grounds, a syntactic reduction of complement coercion requires syntactic representations which resemble less and less a formal decomposition into constituents (Culicover and Jackendoff, 2005): the simplicity and theoretical elegance which are gained by reintroducing compositionality are lost at the level of syntactic structure.

32.4 CONCLUSIONS

In this chapter we have tried to show that compositionality, properly operationalized, can be tested against empirical data. We have also seen that behavioural and neurophysiological data undermine compositionality (simple composition), unless the balance between storage and computation is upset in favour of storage. It now seems appropriate to ask whether there is any interesting sense in which compositionality can be said to hold.

Compositionality (simple composition) remains effective as an explanation of cases in which processing complexity increases due to syntactic factors only. However, it falls short of accounting for situations in which complexity arises from interactions with the sentence or discourse context, perceptual cues, and stored knowledge. The idea of compositionality as a methodological principle is appealing, but imputing the complexity to one component of the grammar or another, instead of enriching the notion of composition, is not always an innocuous move, leading to fully equivalent theories. One may be tempted to believe that equivalent theories in this sense are *in principle* indistinguishable in the face of empirical data. However, neuroscience grants us (restricted) selective access to linguistic processes and representations in the brain, as exemplified by the difference between N400 and P600. Therefore, there is at least a chance that what appear to be neutral methodological choices are in fact controvertible given the data. Compositionality also sets an upper bound on the degree of informational encapsulation that can be posited by modular or component-based theories of language: simple composition ties in with a strongly modular take on meaning assembly, which is seen as sealed off from information streams other than the lexicon and the syntax. Empirical data seem to suggest that the upper bound is not always attainable. This implies a weakening of one's notion of compositionality, but also more complex traffic either within a module or between modules. So compositionality is also crucial for issues of architecture of, and connectivity within, the language system. Perhaps the most important of these issues is the balance between storage and computation: compositionality can often be rescued by increasing the demand on the storage component of the architecture, whereas it must be abandoned if one puts more realistic constraints on storage. In the latter case, of course, the demand on the computational component is increased.[11]

[11] We wish to thank Wilfrid Hodges, Karl Magnus Petersson and two anonymous reviewers for comments on earlier versions of this chapter. We are grateful to the Netherlands Organization for Scientific Research for support under grant 051.04.040.

REFERENCES

Abaelardus, P. 1970. *Dialectica*, ed. L. De Rijk, Assen: Van Gorcum.

Abeles, M. 1982. *Local Cortical Circuits: An Electrophysiological Study*, Springer, Berlin.

Abeles, M., G. Hayon, and D. Lehman. 2004. Modeling compositionality by dynamic binding of synfire chains, *Journal of Computational Neuroscience* 17, 179–201.

Adams, E. W. 1975. *The Logic of Conditionals*, Dordrecht: Reidel.

Aissen, J. 2003. Differential object marking: iconicity vs. economy. *Natural Language and Linguistic Theory* 21: 435–83.

Ammonius 1897. *In Aristotelis De Interpretatione Commentarius*, ed. A. Busse, Berlin: Reimer.

Andersen, H. 1973. Abductive and deductive change, *Language* 40: 765–93.

Angelelli, I. (ed.) 1967. *Gottlob Frege. Kleine Schriften*, Hildesheim: Olms.

Apresjan, J. D. 1973. Synonymy and synonyms, in F. Kiefer (ed.), *Trends in Soviet Theoretical Linguistics*, Dordrecht: Reidel, 173–99.

Arad, M. 2005. *Roots and Patterns: Hebrew Morpho-syntax*, New York: Springer.

Arbib, M. A. 1981. Perceptual structures and distributed motor control. In V. B. Brooks (ed.), *Handbook of Physiology—The Nervous System II. Motor Control*, American Physiological Society, 1449–80.

Arbib, M. A. 2005*a*. From monkey-like action recognition to human language: an evolutionary framework for neurolinguistics (with commentaries and authors response), *Behavioral and Brain Sciences* 28: 105–67.

Arbib, M. A. 2005*b*. Interweaving protosign and protospeech: Further developments beyond the mirror, *Interaction Studies: Social Behavior and Communication in Biological and Artificial Systems* 6: 145–71.

Arbib, M. A. 2008. Holophrasis and the protolanguage spectrum, *Interaction Studies: Social Behavior and Communication in Biological and Artificial Systems* 9 (1): 151–65.

Arbib, M. A. 2012. *How the Brain Got Language: The Mirror System Hypothesis*. Oxford: Oxford University Press.

Arbib, M. A. and D. Bickerton (eds). 2010. *The Emergence of Protolanguage: Holophrasis vs compositionality*. Philadelphia, Amsterdam: John Benjamins Publishing Company.

Arbib, M. A. and D. Caplan. 1979. Neurolinguistics must be computational. *Behavioral and Brain Sciences* 2: 449–83.

Arbib, M. A. and J. C. Hill. 1988. Language acquisition: Schemas replace universal grammar. In J. A. Hawkins (ed.), *Explaining Language Universals*, Oxford: Basil Blackwell, 56–72.

Arbib, M. A. and J.-S. Liaw. 1995. Sensorimotor transformations in the worlds of frogs and robots, *Artificial Intelligence* 72: 53–79.

Arbib, M. A. and M. B. Hesse. 1986. *The Construction of Reality*, Cambridge: Cambridge University Press.

Arbib, M. A., K. Liebal, and S. Pika. 2008. Primate vocalization, ape gesture, and human language: An evolutionary framework, *Current Anthropology* 49 (6).

Arbib, M. A., P. Érdi, and J. Szentágothai. 1998. *Neural Organization: Structure, Function, and Dynamics*, Cambridge, MA: The MIT Press.

Armstrong, S. L., L. R. Gleitman, and H. Gleitman. 1983. What some concepts might not be, *Cognition* 13, 263–308.

Arnold, K. and K. Zuberbühler. 2006. Semantic combinations in primate calls, *Nature* 441(18): 303.

Aron, A. and L. Westbay. 1996. Dimensions of the prototype of love, *Journal of Personality and Social Psychology* 70 (3): 535–51.

Ashby, W. R. 1961. *An Introduction to Cybernetics*, London: Chapman & Hall.

Asher, N. and A. Lascarides. 2003. *Logics of Conversation*, Cambridge: Cambridge University Press.

Atkins, B. T., J. Kegl, and B. Levin. 1988. Anatomy of a Verb Entry: From Linguistic Theory to Lexicographic Practice, *International Journal of Lexicography* 1: 84–126.

Austin, J. L. 1961. Truth. In J. O. Urmson and G. J. Warncock (eds), *Philosophical Papers*, oxford: Oxford University Press.

Baader, F. and T. Nipkow. 1998. *Term Rewriting and All That*, Cambridge: Cambridge University Press.

Baccalá, L. and K. Sameshima. 2001. Overcoming the limitations of correlation analysis for many simultaneously processed neural structures, *Progress in Brain Research* 130, 33–47.

Bach, E. 1968. Nouns and noun phrases, in E. Bach and R. T. Harms (eds), *Universals of Linguistic Theory*, New York: Holt, Rinehart, and Winston, 91–24.

Bach, E. 1979. Control in Montague Grammar, *Linguistic Inquiry* 10: 515–31.

Bach, E. 1980. In defense of passive, *Linguistics and Philosophy* 3: 297–341.

Bach, E. and D. Wheeler. 1983. Montague phonology: a first approximation. In W. Chao and D. Wheeler (eds), *Problems of Linguistic Metatheory*, no. 7 in University of Massachussetts Occasional Papers.

Bach, K. 1982. Semantic non-specificity and mixed quantifiers, *Linguistics and Philosophy* 4: 593–605.

Baggio, G., T. Choma, M. van Lambalgen, and P. Hagoort. 2010. Coercion and compositionality, *Journal of Cognitive Neuroscience* 22, 2131–2140.

Baggio, G., and M. van Lambalgen. 2007. The processing consequences of the imperfective paradox, *Journal of Semantics* 24, 307–30.

Baggio, G., M. van Lambalgen, and P. Hagoort. 2008. Computing and recomputing discourse models: An ERP study, *Journal of Memory and Language* 59, 36–53.

Baggio, G., M. van Lambalgen, and P. Hagoort. 2012. Language, linguistics and cognition. In M. Stokhof and J. Groenendijk (eds), *Handbook of Philosophy of Linguistics*, Amsterdam-New York: Elsevier.

Baker, G. and P. Hacker. 1980. *Wittgenstein: Understanding and Meaning*, Oxford: Oxford University Press.

Baker, G. and P. Hacker. 1984. *Language, Sense and Nonsense*, Oxford: Blackwell.

Baker, M. 1988. *Incorporation*, Chicago: University of Chicago.

Baker, M. 1997. Thematic roles and grammatical categories. In L. Haegeman (ed.), *Elements of Grammar*, Dordrecht: Kluwer, 73–137.

Baker, M. 2001. *The Atoms of Language: The Minds Hidden Rules of Grammar*, New York: Basic Books.

Baker, M. 2003. *Lexical Categories*, Cambridge: Cambridge University Press.

Baker, M., K. Johnson, and I. Roberts. 1989. Passives raised. *Linguistic Inquiry* 20: 219–51.

Baldwin, J. M. 1896. A new factor in evolution, *American Naturalist* 30: 441–51.

Balota, D. A. 1994. Visual word recognition: The journey from features to meaning. In M. A. Gernsbacher (ed.), *Handbook of Psycholinguistics*, San Diego: Academic Press, 303–58.

Bar-Hillel, Y. 1964. A demonstration of the nonfeasibility of fully automatic high quality translation, in Y. Bar-Hillel, *Language and Information: Selected Essays on their Theory and Application*, Reading, MA: Addison-Wesley, 174–9.

Barsalou, L. W. 1987. The instability of graded structure: Implications for the nature of concepts. In U. Neisser (ed.), *Concepts and Conceptual Development*, Cambridge: Cambridge University Press.

Barsalou, L. W. 1992. Frames, concepts, and conceptual fields, in A. Lehrer and E. F. Kittay (eds), *Frames, Fields, and Contrasts: New essays in semantic and lexical organization*. Hillsdale, NJ: Lawrence Erlbaum Associates, 21–74.

Barsalou, L. W. 1993. Flexibility, structure, and linguistic vagary in concepts: Manifestations of a compositional system of perceptual symbols. In A. C.Collins, S. E. Gathercole, M. A. Conway and P. E. M. Morris (eds), *Theories of memory*, Hillsdale, NJ: Lawrence Erlbaum Associates.

Barsalou, L. W. 1999. Perceptual symbol systems, *Behavioral and Brain Sciences* 22: 577–660.

Barsalou, L. W. and C. R. Hale. 1993. Components of conceptual representation: from feature lists to recursive frames, in I. van Mechelen, J. A. Hampton, R. S. Michalski, and P. Theuns (eds), *Categories and Concepts: Theoretical Views and Inductive Data Analysis*, London: Academic Press, 97–144.

Barsalou, L. W. and J. J. Prinz. 1997. Mundane creativity in perceptual symbol systems. In T. B. Ward, S. M. Smith, and J. Vaid (eds), *Creative Thought: An investigation of conceptual structures and processes*, Washington, DC: American Psychological Association, 267–307.

Barss, A. and H. Lasnik. 1986. A note on anaphora and double objects, *Linguistic Inquiry* 17: 347–54.

Barton, S. and A. Sanford. 1993. A case study of anomaly detection: Shallow semantic processing and cohesion establishment, *Memory and Cognition* 21, 477–87.

Barwise, J. 1987. Noun phrases, generalized quantiers and anaphora. In P. Gärdenfors (ed.), *Generalized Quantiers*, Studies in Language and Philosophy, Dordrecht: Reidel, 1–30.

Barwise, J. and J. Etchemendy. 1987. *The Liar: An Essay on Truth and Circularity*, New York: Oxford University Press.

Barwise, J. and J. Perry. 1983. *Situations and Attitudes*, Cambridge, MA: MIT Press.

Barwise, J. and R. Cooper. 1981. Generalized quantifiers and natural language, *Linguistics and Philosophy* 4: 159–219.

Bastiaansen, M., M. van der Linden, M. Ter Keurs, T. Dijkstra, and P. Hagoort. 2005. Theta responses are involved in lexical-semantic retrieval during language processing, *Journal of Cognitive Neuroscience* 17, 530–41.

Batali, J. 2002. The negotiation and acquisition of recursive grammars as a result of competition among exemplars. In E. Briscoe (ed.), *Linguistic Evolution through Language Acquisition: Formal and Computational Models*, Cambridge: Cambridge University Press, 111–72.

Bates, E. and B. MacWhinney. 1982. Functionalist approaches to grammar, in E. Wanner, and L. R. Gleitman (eds), *Language Acquisition: The State of the Art*, Cambridge: Cambridge University Press, 173–218.

Beaver, D. and B. Clark. 2003. Always and only. Why not all focus sensitive operators are alike, *Natural Language Semantics* 11(4): 323–62.

Beaver, D. 1997. Presupposition. In J. van Benthem and A. ter Meulen (eds), *Handbook of Logic and Language*, Amsterdam: Elsevier, 939–1008.

Beck, S. and K. Johnson. 2004. Double objects again, *Linguistic Inquiry* 35(1): 97–123.

Belvin, R. S. 1996. Inside Events: The Non-Possessive Meanings of Possession Predicates and the Semantic Conceptualization of Events. Doctoral dissertation. Los Angeles: University of Southern California.

Bendor, D. and X. Wang. 2005. The neuronal representation of pitch in primate auditory cortex, *Nature* 4367054: 1161–5.

Beqa, A., S. Kirby, and J. R. Hurford. 2008. Regular morphology as a cultural adaptation: Non-uniform frequency in an experimental iterated learning model. In A. D. M. Smith, K. Smith, and R. Ferrer i Cancho (eds), *The Evolution of Language: Proceedings of the 7th International Conference*, Singapore: World Scientific, 401–2.

Berg, G. 1992. A connectionist parser with recursive sentence structure and lexical disambiguation, *AAAI-92: Proceedings of the Tenth National Conference on Artificial Intelligence*, Cambridge, MA: MIT Press.

Berlin, B. and P. Kay. 1969. *Basic Colour Terms: Their Universality and Evolution*, Berkeley/CA: University of California Press.

Bickerton, D. 1984. The language bioprogram hypothesis, *Behavioral and Brain Sciences* 7: 173–221.

Bickerton, D. 1995. *Language and Human Behavior*, Seattle: University of Washington Press.

Bickerton, D. 2003. Symbol and structure: A comprehensive framework for language evolution. In M. H. Christiansen and S. Kirby (eds), *Language Evolution*, Oxford: Oxford University Press, 77–93.

Bickerton, D. 2005. Beyond the mirror neuron—the smoke neuron? *Behavioral and Brain Sciences* 28 (2): 126.

Biederman, I. 1987. Recognition by components: A theory of human image understanding, *Psychological Review* 94: 115–47.

Bienenstock, E. 1995. A model of neocortex, *Network: Computation in neural systems* 6: 179–224.

Bierwisch, M. 1983. Semantische und konzeptuelle Repräsentationen lexikalischer Einheiten. In R. Ruzicka and W. Motsch (eds), *Untersuchungen zur Semantik*, Berlin: Akademie Verlag, 61–99.

Bierwisch, M. 1989. The semantics of gradation, in M. Bierwisch and E. Lang (eds), *Dimensional Adjectives. Grammatical structure and conceptual interpretation*. Berlin: Springer, 71–262.

Bierwisch, M. 1997. Lexical information from a minimalist point of view. In C. Wilder, H.-M. Gärtner, and M. Bierwisch (eds), *The Role of Economy Principles in Linguistic Theory*, Berlin: Akademie Verlag, 227–66.

Bierwisch, M. 2002. A case for CAUSE. In I. Kaufmann and B. Stiebels (eds), *More than Words*, Berlin: Akademie Verlag, 327–53.

Bierwisch, M. and E. Lang (eds). 1989. *Dimensional Adjectives. Grammatical structure and conceptual interpretation*. Berlin: Springer.

Bigelow, J. and R. Pargetter. 1987. Function, *Journal of Philosophy* 84 (4): 181–96.

Billings, R. S. and S. A. Marcus. 1983. Measures of compensatory and noncompensatory models of decision behavior: Process tracing versus policy capturing, *Organizational Behavior and Human Performance* 31: 331–52.

Bird, H., M. A. Lambon Ralph, M. Seidenberg, J. L. McClelland, and K. Patterson. 2003. Deficits in phonology and past-tense morphology: What's the connection? *Journal of Memory and Language* 48: 502–26.

Bloom, P. 2000. *How Children Learn the Meanings of Words*, Cambridge, MA: MIT Press.

Bloomfield, L. 1933. *Language*, London: George Allen & Unwin.

Bolinger, D. 1972. *Degree Words*. Den Haag: Mouton.

Bonnay, D. 2005. Compositionality and molecularism. In M. Werning, E. Machery, and G. Schurz (eds), *The Compositionality of Meaning and Content. Vol. I*. Frankfurt: Ontos-Verlag, 41–62.

Boodin, J. 1939. *The Social Mind: Foundations of Social Philosophy*, New York: Macmillan Co.

Boolos, G. 1998. *Logic, Logic, and Logic*, Cambridge, MA: Harvard University Press.

Boolos, G. S., R. C. Jeffrey, and J. P. Burgess. 2002. *Computability and Logic* 4th edn, Cambridge: Cambridge University Press.

Borer, H. 2005. *Structuring Sense* (volumes I and II), Oxford: Oxford University Press.

Borg, E. 2004. *Minimal Semantics*, Oxford: Oxford University Press.

Borschev, V. and B. H. Partee. 2001. Genitive modifiers, sorts, and metonymy, *Nordic Journal of Linguistics* 242: 140–60.

Bouillon, P. and F. Busa (eds). 2001. *The Language of Word Meaning*, Cambridge: Cambridge University Press.

Boyd, R. and P. J. Richerson, P. J. 1985. *Culture and the Evolutionary Process*, Chicago, IL: University of Chicago Press.

Brachman, R. J. 1978. A structural paradigm for representing knowledge, in BBN Report No. 3605, Cambridge, MA.

Brennan, J. and L. Pylkkänen. 2008. Processing events: Behavioral and neuromagnetic correlates of aspectual coercion, *Brain and Language* 106: 132–43.

Bresnan, J. 2001. *Lexical-Functional Syntax*, Malden, MA: Blackwell.

Bresnan, J. and T. Nikitina. 2007. The gradience of the dative alternation. In L. Uyechi and L. Hee Wee (eds), *Reality Exploration and Discovery: Pattern interaction in language and life*, Stanford: CSLI Publications.

Bridgeman, B. 2005. Action planning supplements mirror systems in language evolution, *Behavioral and Brain Sciences* 28: 129–30.

Brighton, H. 2002. Compositional syntax from cultural transmission, *Artificial Life* 8: 25–54.

Brighton, H. 2003. Simplicity as a driving force in linguistic evolution, PhD Thesis, The University of Edinburgh.

Brighton, H., K. Smith, and S. Kirby. 2005b. Language as an evolutionary system, *Physics of Life Reviews* 2: 177–226.

Brighton, H., S. Kirby, and K. Smith. 2005a. Cultural selection for learnability: Three principles underlying the view that language adapts to be learnable. In M. Tallerman (ed.), *Language Origins: Perspectives on Evolution*, Oxford: Oxford University Press, 291–309.

Briscoe, E. (ed.) 2002. *Linguistic Evolution through Language Acquisition: Formal and Computational Models*, Cambridge: Cambridge University Press.

Brogaard, B. 2009. Introduction to *Relative Truth*, *Synthese*, 166(2): 215–29 (online 2007).

Brooks, L. R. 1978. Nonanalytic concept formation and memory for instances. In E. Rosch and B. B. Lloyd (eds), *Cognition and Categorization*, Hillsdale, NJ: Lawrence Erlbaum Associates.

Brown, C. and P. Hagoort. 1993. The processing nature of the N400: Evidence from masked priming, *Journal of Cognitive Neuroscience* 5, 34–44.

Buchanan, R. and G. Ostretag (2005) Has the problem of incompleteness rested on a mistake? *Mind* 114: 889–913.

Bullinaria, J. and J. Levy. 2007. Extracting semantic representations from word co-occurrence statistics: a computational study, *Behavior Research Methods* 39: 510–26.

Burge, T. 1973. Reference and proper names, *Journal of Philosophy* 70: 425–39.

Burris, S. and H. P. Sankappanavar. 1981. *A Course in Universal Algebra*, no. 78 in Graduate Texts in Mathematics. Berlin: Springer.

Butt, M. 1997. Complex predicates in Urdu. In A. Alsina, J. Bresnan, and P. Sells (eds), *Complex Predicates*, Stanford, CA: CSLI Publications, 107–49.

Bybee, J. L. 1985. *Morphology: a study of the relation between meaning and form*, vol. 9 of *Studies in Language*, Amsterdam: John Benjamins.

Bybee, J. L. 1995. Regular mophology and the lexicon, *Language and Cognitive Processes* 10: 425–55.

Bynum, T. W.(ed.) 1972. *Gottlob Frege. Conceptual notation and related articles*, Oxford: Oxford University Press.

Caicedo, X., F. Dechesne, and T. M. V. Janssen. 2009. Equivalence and quantifier rules for logics with imperfect information, *Logic Journal of the IGPL* 17: 91–129.

Calcagno, M. 1995. A sign-based extension to the Lambek Calculus for discontinuous constituents. *Bulletin of the IGPL* 3: 555–78.

Cameron, P. J. and W. Hodges. 2001. Some combinatorics of imperfect information, *Journal of Symbolic Logic* 66: 673–84.

Cangelosi, A., A. D. M. Smith, and K. Smith. (eds) 2006. *The Evolution of Language: Proceedings of the 6th International Conference*, Singapore: World Scientific.

Capirci, O. and Volterra, V. 2008. Gesture and speech. The emergence and development of a strong and changing partnership, *Gesture* 8 (1): 22–44.

Cappelen, H. 2008. The creative interpreter: content relativism and assertion, *Philosophical Perspectives*, 22: 23–46.

Cappelen, H. and J. Hawthorne. 2009. *Relativism and Monadic Truth*, Oxford: Oxford University Press.

Cappelen, H. and E. Lepore. 2004. *Insensitive Semantics*, Oxford: Blackwell.

Caramazza, A. 1984. The logic of neuropsychological research and the problem of patient classification in aphasia, *Brain and Language* 21: 9–20.

Carey, S. 1985. *Conceptual Change in Childhood*, Cambridge/MA: MIT Press.

Carey, S. 1988. Conceptual differences between children and adults, *Mind and Language* 3: 167–81.

Carlson, G. 1984. Thematic roles and their role in semantic interpretation, *Linguistics* 22: 259–79.

Carnap, R. 1947. *Meaning and Necessity: a study in semantics and modal logic*. Chicago, IL: University of Chicago Press.

Carpenter, B. 1992. *The Logic of Typed Feature Structures*. Cambridge: Cambridge University Press.

Carrier, J. and J. H. Randall. 1992. The argument structure and syntactic structure of resultatives, *Linguistic Inquiry* 23: 173–234.

Carruthers, P. 2002. The cognitive functions of language, *Behavioral and Brain Sciences* 25: 6.

Casati, R. and A. Varzi. 1994. *Holes and Other Superficialities*, Cambridge, MA: MIT Press.

Castañeda, H. 1967. Comments. In N. Rescher (ed.), *The Logic of Decision and Action*, Pittsburgh: Pittsburgh University Press.

Castelo-Branco, M., R. Goebel, S. Neuenschwander, and W. Singer. 2000. Neural synchrony correlates with surface segregation rules, *Nature* 4058: 685–91.

Chater, N. and C. D. Manning. 2006. Probabilistic models of language processing and acquisition, *TRENDS in Cognitive Science* 10: 335–44.

Chater, N. and M. Oaksford. 1999. Ten Years of the rational analysis of cognition, *Trends in Cognitive Science* 3: 57–65.

Chauncey, K., A. Ozyürek, P. Hagoort, and S. Kita. 2004. Recognition of iconic gestures: A first gating study. Unpublished manuscript.

Cheney, D. L. and R. M. Seyfarth. 1990. *How Monkeys See the World: Inside the mind of another species.* Chicago, IL: University of Chicago.

Cheney, D. L. and R. M. Seyfarth. 2005. Constraints and preadaptations in the earliest stages of language evolution, *The Linguistic Review* 22: 135–59.

Chierchia, G. 2004. Scalar implicatures, polarity pphenomena, and the syntax/pragmatics interface, in A. Belletti (ed.), *Structures and Beyond.* Oxford: Oxford University Press, 39–103.

Chierchia, G. and S. McConnell-Ginet. 1990. *Meaning and Grammar.* Cambridge: MIT Press.

Chiswell, I. and W. Hodges. 2007. *Mathematical Logic,* Oxford: Oxford University Press.

Chomsky, N. 1957. *Syntactic Structures,* 'S-Gravenhage: Mouton.

Chomsky, N. 1959. A review of B. F. Skinner's *Verbal Behavior, Language* 35: 26–58.

Chomsky, N. 1965. *Aspects of the Theory of Syntax,* Cambridge, MA: MIT Press.

Chomsky, N. 1970. Remarks on nominalization. In R. Jacobs and R. Rosenbaum (eds), *Readings in English Transformational Grammar,* Waltham: Ginn.

Chomsky, N. 1975a. *The Logical Structure of Linguistic Theory,* New York: Plenum Press.

Chomsky, N. 1975b. *Reflections on Language,* New York, NY: Pantheon.

Chomsky, N. 1976. Conditions on rules of grammar, *Linguistic Analysis* 2: 303–51.

Chomsky, N. 1980. Rules and representations, *Behavioral and Brain Sciences* 3: 1–14.

Chomsky, N. 1986. *Knowledge of Language,* New York: Praeger.

Chomsky, N. 1987. *Knowledge of Language: Its Nature, Origin and Use,* Dordrecht: Foris.

Chomsky, N. 1988. *Language and Problems of Knowledge: The Managua Lectures,* Cambridge, MA: MIT Press.

Chomsky, N. 1995. *The Minimalist Program,* Cambridge, MA: MIT Press.

Chomsky, N. 2000. *New Horizons in the Study of language and Mind.* Cambridge: Cambridge University Press.

Chomsky, N. 2002. *On Nature and Language,* Cambridge: Cambridge University Press.

Chomsky, N. 2005. Three factors in language design, *Linguistic Inquiry* 36(1): 1–22.

Chomsky, N. 2008. On Phases. In C. Otero et al. (eds), *Foundational Issues in Linguistic Theory,* Cambridge, MA: MIT Press.

Chomsky, N. and M. Halle. 1968. *The Sound Pattern of English,* New York: Harper and Row.

Chomsky, N. and H. Lasnik. 1993. The theory of principles and parameters. In J. Jacobs, A. v. Stechow, W. Sternefeld, and T. Vennemann, (eds), *Syntax: An International Handbook of Contemporary Research,* De Gruyter, 506–56. (Reprinted in N. Chomsky, *The Minimalist Program,* Cambridge, MA: MIT Press, 1995.)

Christianson, K. A. Hollingworth, J. Halliwell, and F. Ferreira. 2001. Thematic roles assigned along the garden path linger, *Cognitive Psychology* 42: 368–407.

Church, A. 1941. *The Calculus of Lambda Conversion,* Princeton: Princeton University Press.

Churchland, P. M. 1984. *Matter and Consciousness,* Cambridge, MA: MIT Press.

Churchland, P. S. 1986. *Neurophilosophy.* Cambridge, MA: MIT Press.

Clahsen, H. 1999. Lexical entries and rules of language: A multidisciplinary study of German inflection, *Behavioral and Brain Sciences* 22: 991–1060.

Clahsen, H. and M. Almazan. 1998. Syntax and morphology in Williams syndrome, *Cognition* 68: 167–98.

Clahsen, H. and M. Rothweiler. 1993. Inflectional rules in children's grammars: Evidence from the development of participles in German, *Yearbook of Morphology* 1992: 1–34.

Clahsen, H., S. Eisenbeiss, and I. Sonnenstuhl. 1997. Morphological structure and the processing of inflected words, *Theoretical Linguistics* 23: 201–49.

Clark, E. 1988. On the logic of contrast, *Journal of Child Language* 15: 317–35.

Clark, H. 1975. Bridging. In R. Schank and B. Nash-Webber (eds), *Theoretical Issues in Natural Language Processing*, Cambridge: MA: MIT Press.

Clark, H. H. 1996. *Using Language*, Cambridge: Cambridge University Press.

Cohen, B. and G. L. Murphy. 1984. Models of concepts, *Cognitive Science* 8: 27–58.

Cohen, L. J. 1986. How is conceptual innovation possible? *Erkenntnis* 25: 221–38.

Collins, P. 1995. The indirect object constructions in English: an informational approach, *Linguistics* 33: 35–49.

Comrie, B. 1976. *Aspect*. Cambridge: Cambridge University Press.

Comrie, B. 1981. *Language Universals and Linguistic Typology: Syntax and Morphology*. Chicago: University of Chicago Press.

Conklin, J. and C. Eliasmith. 2005. An attractor network model of path integration in the rat. *Journal of Computational Neuroscience*, 18: 183–203.

Connolly, A. C., J. Fodor, L. Gleitman, and H. Gleitman. 2007. Why Stereotypes Don't Even Make Good Defaults, *Cognition* 103(1); 1–22.

Cooper, L. A. 1975. Mental rotation of random two-dimensional shapes, *Cognitive Psychology*, 7: 20–43.

Cooper, R. 1975. Montague's Semantic Theory and Transformational Syntax. PhD thesis, University of Massachussetts, Amherst.

Cooper, R. 2005. Austinian truth, attitudes and type theory, *Research on Language and Computation* 3(4): 333–62.

Copestake, A. 1992. *The Representation of Lexical Semantic Information*, CSRP 280, University of Sussex.

Copestake, A. 1993. Defaults in the LKB. In T. Briscoe and A. Copestake (eds), *Default Inheritance in the Lexicon*, Cambridge: Cambridge University Press.

Copestake, A. and E. Briscoe. 1992. Lexical operations in a unification-based framework. In J. Pustejovsky and S. Bergler (eds), *Lexical Semantics and Knowledge Representation*, New York: Springer Verlag.

Copestake, A. and T. Briscoe. 1995. Semi-productive polysemy and sense extension, *Journal of Semantics*, 15–67.

Cormack, A. 1984. VP anaphora: variables and scope, in F. Landman and F. Veltman (eds), *Varieties of Formal Sematnics*, Dordrecht: Reidel, 81–102.

Costello, F. J. and M. T. Keane. 2001a. Efficient creativity: Constraint-guided conceptual combination, *Cognitive Science* 24: 299–349.

Costello, F. J. and M. T. Keane. 2001b. Testing two theories of conceptual combination: Alignment versus diagnosticity in the comprehension and production of combined concepts, *Journal of Experimental Psychology: Learning, Memory, and Cognition* 27: 255–71.

Costello, F. J. and M. T. Keane. 2005. Compositionality and the pragmatics of conceptual combination, in E. Machery, M. Werning, and G. Schultz (eds), *The Compositionality of Meaning and Content, II: Applications to Linguistics, Psychology and Neuroscience*. Frankfort: Ontos, 203–16.

Couturat, L. 1903. *Opuscules et Fragments Inédits de Leibniz*, Paris: Alcan.

Covington, M. 2009. *Syntactic Theory in the High Middle Ages: Modistic Models of Sentence Structure*, Cambridge: Cambridge University Press.

Crain, S. and P. Pietroski. 2001. Nature, nurture, and universal grammar, *Linguistics and Philosophy* 24: 139–86.

Cree, G. S. and K. McRae. 2003. Analyzing the factors underlying the structure and computation of the meaning of chipmunk, cherry, chisel, cheese, and cello and many other such concrete nouns, *Journal of Experimental Psychology: General*, 132: 163–201.

Cresswell, M. J. 1973. *Logics and Languages*, London: Methuen.

Croft, W. 1998. The structure of events and the structure of language. In M. Tomasello (ed.), *The New Psychology of Language: Cognitive and Functional Approaches to Language Structure*, Mahwah, NJ: Lawrence Erlbaum Associates, 67–92.

Croft, W. 2000. *Explaining Language Change: An Evolutionary Approach*, Harlow, UK: Longman.

Croft, W. 2001. *Radical Construction Grammar: Syntactic theory in typological perspective*, Oxford: Oxford University Press.

Croft, W. and D. A. Cruse. 2005. *Cognitive Linguistics*, Cambridge: Cambridge University Press.

Crystal, D. 2003. *Cambridge Encyclopedia of the English Language*, Cambridge University Press. Cambridge.

Culicover, P. and R. Jackendoff. 2005. *Simpler Syntax*, Oxford: Oxford University Press.

Culicover, P. and R. Jackendoff. 2006. The simpler syntax hypothesis, *Trends in Cognitive Sciences* 109: 413–18.

Currie, G. 1982. *Frege: An introduction to his philosophy*, nr. 11 in Harvester studies in philosophy, Brighton, Sussex: Harvester Press.

Davidson, D. 1965. Theories of meaning and learnable languages, in Y. Bar-Hillel (ed.), *Proceedings of the 1964 Internatonal Congress for Logic, Methodology and Philosophy of Science* (Tel-Aviv), North Holland, 383–94. Reprinted in Davidson 2001, 3–15.

Davidson, D. 1967a. The logical form of action sentences. In N. Rescher (ed.), *The Logic of Decision and Action*, University of Pittsburgh Press, 81–95.

Davidson, D. 1967b. Truth and meaning, *Synthese* 17: 304–23. Reprinted in Davidson 2001, 17–36.

Davidson, D. 1968. On saying That, *Synthese* 19, 130–46. Reprinted in Davidson 2001, 93–108.

Davidson, D. 1973. In defense of convention T, in H. Leblanc (ed.), *Truth, Syntax and Modality*, Amsterdam: North Holland, 76–85. Reprinted in Davidson 2001, 65–75.

Davidson, D. 1984. *Inquiries into Truth and Interpretation*. Oxford: Oxford University Press.

Davidson, D. 1985. Adverbs of action. In B. Vermazen, and M. Hintikka (eds), *Essays on Davidson: Actions and Events*, Oxford: Clarendon Press.

Davidson, D. 2001. *Inquiries into Truth and Interpretation*, Oxford: Clarendon Press.

Davis, W. 2003. *Meaning, Expression, and Thought*, Cambridge: Cambridge University Press.

Dawkins, R. 1989. *The Selfish Gene* 2nd edn, Oxford: Oxford University Press.

de Beule, J. and B. K. Bergen. 2006. On the emergence of compositionality, In A. Cangelosi, A. D. M. Smith, and K. Smith (eds), *The Evolution of Language: Proceedings of the 6th International Conference*, Singapore: World Scientific, 35–42.

de Diego Balaguer, R., A. Costa, N. Sebastián-Galles, M. Juncadella, and A. Caramazza. 2004. Regular and irregular morphology and its relationship with agrammatism: evidence from two Spanish–Catalan bilinguals, *Brain and Language* 91: 212–22.

de Groote, P. 2001. Towards abstract Categorial Grammars. In Association for Computational Linguistics, 39th Annual Meeting and 10th Conference of the European Chapter, Toulouse, 148–55.

de Roever, W.-P., F. de Beer, U. Hanneman, J. Hooman, Y. Lakhnech, M. Poel, and J. Zwiers. 2001. Concurrency verification. An introduction to compositional and non compositional methods, nr. 54 in W.-P. de Roever, F. de Boer, U. Hanneman, J. Hooman, Y. Lakhnech, M. Poel, and J. Zwiers (eds), *Cambridge Tracts in Theoretical Computer Science*, Cambridge: Cambridge University Press.

de Roever, W.-P., Langmaack, H. and Pnueli, A. (eds). 1998. Compositionality: the significant difference, nr. 1536 in 'Lecture notes in computer science', COMPOS '97, Bad Malente, Germany, Berlin: Springer.

de Waal, F. B. M. 2006. *Primates and Philosophers: How Morality Evolved (with further contributions by Robert Wright, Christine M. Korsgaard, Philip Kitcher, and Peter Singer; Edited and introduced by Stephen Macedo and Josiah Ober)*, Princeton: Princeton University Press.

Deacon, T. 1997. *The Symbolic Species*, London: Penguin.

Dediu, D. and D. R. Ladd. 2007. Linguistic tone is related to the population frequency of the adaptive haplogroups of two brain size genes, *aspm* and *microcephalin*, *Proceedings of the National Academy of Sciences, USA* 104: 10944–9.

Den Dikken, M., R. K. Larson, and P. Ludlow. 1997. Intensional 'transitive' verbs and concealed complement clauses, *Rivista di Linguistica* 8: 29–46.

Dennis, I., J. A. Hampton, and S. E. G. Lea. 1973. New problem in concept formation, *Nature* 243: 101–2.

Dever, J. 1999. Compositionality as methodology, *Linguistics and Philosophy* 22: 311–26.

Dever, J. 2006. Compositionality. In E. Lepore and B. Smith (eds), *The Oxford Handbook of Philosophy of Language*, Oxford: Oxford University Press.

DiCarlo, J. J. and K. O. Johnson. 2000. Spatial and temporal structure of receptive fields in primate somatosensory area 3b: effects of stimulus scanning direction and orientation, *Journal of Neuroscience* 201: 495–510.

Diesmann, M., M.-O. Gewaltig, and A. Aertsen. 1999. Stable propagation of synchronous spiking in cortical neural networks, *Nature* 402: 529–33.

Dijkstra, E. W. 1969. EWD 264, Unpublished note, available at http://www.cs.utexas.edu/EWD/, last acccessed 13 June 2011.

Dölling, J. 1992. Flexible Interpretationen durch Sortenverschiebung. In I. Zimmermann and A. Strigen (eds), Fügungspotenzen, Berlin: Akademie Verlag.

Downing, P. 1977. On the creation and use of English compound nouns, *Language* 53: 810–42.

Dowty, D. 1979. *Word Meaning and Montague Grammar: The semantics of verbs and times in Generative Semantics and in Montague's PTQ*. Dordrecht: Reidel.

Dowty, D. 1982. Grammatical relations in Montague Grammar, in P. Jacobson and G. K. Pullum (eds), *The Nature of Syntactic Representation*, Dordrecht: D. Reidel, 79–130.

Dowty, D. R. 1986. The effects of aspectual class on the the temporal structure of discourse: Semantics or pragmatics, *Linguistics and Philosophy* 9(1).

Dowty, D. 1991. Thematic proto-roles and argument selection, *Language* 67: 547–619.

Dowty, D. 2007. Compositionality as an empirical problem, in C. Barker and P. Jacobson (eds), *Direct Compositionality*, nr. 14 in Oxford Studies in Theoretical Linguistics, Oxford: Oxford University Press, 23–101.

Dowty, D. R., R. E. Wall, and S. Peters. 1981. *Introduction to Montague Semantics*, no. 11 in Synthese Library. Dordrecht: Reidel.

Dray, W. 1957. *Laws and Explanation in History*, Oxford: Oxford University Press.

Duhem, P. 1906. *The Aim and Structure of Physical Theory*, Princeton: Princeton University Press. 1954 translation of *La théorie physique, son objet et sa structure*, by P. Wiener.

Dummett, M. 1973. *Frege. Philosophy of language*, London: Duckworth. Second edition 1981.

Dummett, M. 1981*a*. *Frege: Philosophy of Language*, 2nd edn, Cambridge, MA: Harvard University Press.

Dummett, M. 1981*b*. *The Interpretation of Frege's Philosophy*, London: Duckworth.

Dunbar, R. 1996. *Grooming, Gossip and the Evolution of Language*, London: Faber and Faber Ltd

Eckhorn, R., A. Bruns, M. Saam, A. Gail, A. Gabriel, and H. J. Brinksmeyer. 2001. Flexible cortical gamma-band correlations suggest neural principles of visual processing, *Visual Cognition* 83–5: 519–30.

Eckhorn, R., T. Schanze, M. Brosch, W. Salem, and R. Bauer. 1991. Stimulus-specific synchronizations in cat visual cortex: Multiple microelectrode and correlation studies from several cortical areas. In E. Basar and T. H. Bullock (eds), *Induced Rhythms in the Brain*, Berlin: Birkhuser.

Eisenbeiss, S. 2002. *Merkmalsgesteuerter Grammatikerwerb: eine Untersuchung zum Erwerb der Struktur und Flexion vonNominalphrasen* [Feature-Driven Grammar Acquisition: An Investigation on the Acquisition of NP Structure and Inflection]. Doctoral dissertation, University of Duesseldorf. http://privatewww.essex.ac.uk/~seisen/my%20dissertation.htm.

Elbourne, P. 2005. *Situations and Individuals*, Cambridge, MA: MIT Press.

Eliasmith, C. 2005. Cognition with neurons: A large-scale, biologically realistic model of the Wason task. In G. Bara, L. Barsalou, and M. Bucciarelli (eds), *Proceedings of the 27th Annual Meeting of the Cognitive Science Society*, Stresa, Italy.

Eliasmith, C. in press. *How to Build a Brain: A neural architecture for biological cognition*. Oxford: Oxford University Press.

Eliasmith, C. and C. H. Anderson. 2003. *Neural engineering: Computation, representation and dynamics in neurobiological systems*, Cambridge, MA: MIT Press.

Eliasmith, C., M. B. Westover, and C. H. Anderson. 2002. A general framework for neurobiological modeling: An application to the vestibular system, *Neurocomputing*, 46: 1071–6.

Ellroy, J. 1987. *The Black Dahlia*, New York: Vintage Books.

Elman, J. 2005. Connectionist models of cognitive development: where next?, *TRENDS in Cognitive Science* 9: 111–17.

Elman, J., E. Bates, M. Johnson, A. Karmiloff-Smith, D. Parisi, and K. Plunkett. 1996. *Rethinking Innateness: A Connectionist Perspective on Development*, Cambridge, MA: MIT Press.

Embick, D. and A. Marantz. 2005. Cognitive neuroscience and the English past tense: comments on the paper by Ullman et al., *Brain and Language* 93: 243–7.

Engel, A. K. and W. Singer. 2001. Temporal binding and the neural correlates of sensory awareness, *Trends in Cognitive Sciences* 5: 16–25.

Engel, A. K., P. König, A. K. Kreiter, T. B. Schillen, and W. Singer. 1992. Temporal coding in the visual cortex: new vistas on integration in the nervous system, *Trends in Neurosciences* 15: 218–26.

Engel, A. K., P. Fries, and W. Singer. 2001. Dynamic predictions: Oscillations and synchrony in top-down processing, *Nature reviews: Neuroscience* 210: 704–16.

Estes, W. K. 1994. *Classification and Cognition*, Oxford: Oxford University Press.

Estes, Z. and S. Glucksberg. 2000. Interactive property attribution in concept combination, *Memory and Cognition* 28: 28–34.

Evans, F. 1988. Binding into anaphoric verb phrases, in J. Powers and K. de Jong (eds), *Proceedings of ESCOl 5*, Columbus: Ohio State University, 122–9.

Evans, G. 1982. *Varieties of Reference*, Oxford: Oxford University Press.

Evans, G. 1985. Does tense logic rest on a mistake? In *Collected Papers*, Oxford: Clarendon Press, 343–63.

Evans, J. St. B. T. 1982. *The Psychology of Deductive Reasoning*, London: Routledge Kegan and Paul.

Evans, J. St. B. T. and D. E. Over. 1996. *Rationality and Reasoning*, Hove: Psychology Press.

Evans, J. St., J. H. Simon, and D. E. Over. 2003. Conditionals and conditional probability, *Journal of Experimental Psychology: Learning. Memory, and Cognition* 29/2: 321–35.

Falkenhainer, B., K. D. Forbus, and D. Gentner. 1989. The structure mapping engine: Algorithm and examples. *Artificial Intelligence* 41: 1–63.

Fanselow, G. 1993. Instead of preface: some reflections on parameters. In G. Fanselow (ed.), *The Parametrization of Universal Grammar*, Amsterdam: Benjamins, vii–xvii.

Fanselow, G. and S. W. Felix. 1987. *Sprachtheorie: Eine Einführung in die Generative Grammatik. Bd. I. [Linguistic Theory: An Introduction into Generative Grammar, Volume I]*, Tübingen: Francke.

Feferman, S. 1975. A language and axioms for explicit mathematics. In J. N. Crossley (ed.), *Algebra and Logic*, LNM 450. Berlin: Springer.

Felleman, D. J. and D. C. van Essen. 1991. Distributed hierarchical processing in the primate cerebral cortex, *Cerebral Cortex* 1: 1–47.

Fernando, T. 2001. Conservative generalized quantiers and presupposition. In *Proceedings of Semantics and Linguistic Theory XI*, Ithaca: Cornell University, 172–91.

Fernando, T. 2005. Compositionality inductively, co-inductively and contextually, in M. Werning et al. (eds), *The Compositionality of Meaning and Content, Volume 1: Foundational Issues*. Frankfurt: Ontos Verlag. 87–96.

Fernando, T. and D. Westerståhl. 2001. ESSLLI 2001 lecture notes at www.helsinki.fi/esslli/courses/CaC.html.

Ferreira, F. and N. Patson. 2007. The good enough approach to language comprehension, *Language and Linguistics Compass* 1: 71–83.

Ferreira, F., V. Ferraro, and K. Bailey. 2002. Good-enough representations in language comprehension, *Current Directions in Psychological Science* 11: 11–15.

Ferretti, T., M. Kutas, and K. McRae. 2007. Verb aspect and the activation of event knowledge, *Journal of Experimental Psychology: Learning, Memory and Cognition* 33: 182–96.

Fiengo, R. and R. May. 1994. *Indices and Identity*, Cambridge, MA: MIT Press.

Fillmore, C. J., P. Kay, and M. K. O'Connor. 1988. Regularity and idiomaticity in grammatical constructions: the case of let alone, *Language and Cognitive Processes* 64: 501–38.

Fine, K. 2007. *Semantic Relationism*, Oxford: Blackwell.

Finin, T. 1980. The semantic interpretation of nominal compounds, in *Proceedings of the First Annual National Conference on Artificial Intelligence*, Stanford, CA.

Finke, R. A. 1989. *The Principles of Mental Imagery*, Cambridge, MA: MIT Press.

Fischer, B. 2005. A model of the computations leading to a representation of auditory space in the midbrain of the barn owl. PhD thesis. Washington University in St. Louis.

FitzHugh, R. 1961. Impulses and physiolological states in theoretical models of nerve membrane, *Biophysical Journal* 1, 445–66.

Fodor, J. 1970. Three reasons for not deriving 'kill' from 'cause to die', *Linguistic Inquiry* 1: 429–38.

Fodor, J. 1975. *The Language of Thought*. New York: Crowell.

Fodor, J. 1981*a*. The current status of the innateness controversy. In *Representations: Philosophical essays on the foundations of cognitive science*, Cambridge, MA: MIT Press.

Fodor, J. 1981*b*. The present status of the innateness controversy. In *Representations: Philosophical essays on the foundations of cognitive science*, Cambridge, MA: MIT Press.

Fodor, J. 1983: *The Modularity of Mind*, Cambridge, MA: MIT Press.

Fodor, J. 1984. Observation reconsidered, *Philosophy of Science* 51: 23–43.

Fodor, J. 1986: *Psychosemantics*, Cambridge, MA: MIT Press.

Fodor, J. 1990. *A Theory of Content and Other Essays*, Cambridge, MA: MIT Press.

Fodor, J. 1992. *A Theory of Content and Other Essays*, Cambridge, MA: MIT Press.

Fodor, J. 1998*a*. *Concepts: Where Cognitive Science Went Wrong*. New York: Oxford University Press.

Fodor, J. 1998*b*. There are no recognitional concepts—not even RED, Part 2: The plot thickens. In *In Critical Condition*, Cambridge, MA: MIT Press, 49–62.

Fodor, J. 1999. All at sea in semantic space, *Journal of Philosophy* 96/8. Reprinted in J. Fodor and E. Lepore, *The Compositionality Papers*, Oxford: Oxford University Press, 174–200 (page numbers refer to reprint).

Fodor, J. 2000. *The Mind Doesn't Work that Way: The Scope and Limits of Computational Psychology*, Cambridge, MA: MIT Press.

Fodor, J. 2003. *Hume Variations*, Oxford: Oxford University Press.

Fodor, J. 2008. *LOT2. The Language of Thought Revisited*. Oxford: Oxford University Press.

Fodor, J. and E. Lepore. 1991. Why meaning probably isn't conceptual role, *Mind and Language* 6: 329–43.

Fodor, J. and E. Lepore. 1992. *Holism: A Shopper's Guide*. Oxford: Blackwell.

Fodor, J. and E. Lepore. 1996. The pet fish and the red herring: Why concepts still can't be prototypes, *Cognition* 58 (2): 253–70.

Fodor, J. and E. Lepore. 1998. The emptiness of the lexicon: Reflections on James Pustejovsky's *The Generative Lexicon*, *Linguistic Inquiry* 29: 269–88. Reprinted in J. Fodor and E. Lepore, *The Compositionality Papers*, Oxford: Oxford University Press, (89–119).

Fodor, J. and E. Lepore. 1999. Impossible words? *Linguistic Inquiry* 30: 445–53.

Fodor, J. and E. Lepore. 2002. *The Compositionality Papers*. Oxford: Oxford University Press.

Fodor, J. and E. Lepore. 2005. Morphemes matter; the continuing case against lexical decomposition Or: Please don't play that again, Sam. Rutgers Centre for Cognitive Science Technical Report, MS Rutgers University.

Fodor, J. and B. McLaughlin. 1990. Connectionism and the problem of systematicity: Why Smolensky's solution doesn't work, *Cognition* 35: 183–204.

Fodor, J. and Z. Pylyshyn. 1988. Connectionism and cognitive architecture: A critical analysis, *Cognition* 28: 3–71.

Fodor, J., M. F. Garrett, E. C. T. Walker, and C. H.Parkes. 1980. Against definitions, *Cognition* 8, 263–7.

Folli, R., H. Harley, and S. Karimi. 2005. Determinants of event structure in Persian complex predicates, *Lingua* 115(10): 1365–401.

Forbes, G. 2000. Objectual attitudes, *Linguistics and Philosophy* 23: 141–83.

Forbes, G. 2006. *Attitude Problems. An Essay on Linguistic Intensionality*, Oxford: Oxford University Press.

Frazier, L. 1987. Sentence processing: A tutorial review. In M. Coltheart (ed.), *Attention and Performance*, Volume XII, Hillsdale, NJ: Lawrence Erlbaum Associates, 559–86.

Freeze, R. 1992. Existentials and other locatives, *Language* 68(3): 553–95.

Frege, G. 1879. *Begriffsschrift, eine der arithmetischen nachgebildeten Formelsprache des reinen Denkens*, Halle: Nebert. Reprinted in Angelelli 1967, 89–93.

Frege, G. 1884. *Die Grundlagen der Arithmetik. Eine logisch-mathematische Untersuchung über den Begriff der Zahl*, Breslau: W. Koebner. Reprint published by Georg Olms, Hildesheim, 1961; translation by J. L. Austin (with original text): *The Foundations of Arithmetic. A logico-mathematical enquiry into the concept of number*, Oxford Basil Blackwell, 1953.

Frege, G. 1891. *Function und Begriff*. Jena. Translated by P. Geach as: 'Function and Concept'. In P. Geach and M. Black (eds), *Translations from the Philosophical Writings of Gottlob Frege*. Oxford: Blackwell, 1952, 21–41.

Frege, G. 1892. Über Sinn und Bedeutung, *Zeitschrift für Philosophie und Philosophische Kritik* 100: 25–50. Reprinted in Angelelli (1967), pp. 143–62. Translated by Geach and Black as 'On sense and reference' in Geach and Black 1952, 56–78.

Frege, G. 1914. Logic in mathematics. In H. Hermes, F. Kambartel, and F. Kaulbach (eds), *Gottlob Frege: Posthumous Writings*, Chicago: University of Chicago Press, 72–84. Trans P. Long and R. White.

Frege, G. 1923. Logische Untersuchungen. Dritter Teil: Gedankengefüge, in 'Beiträge zur Philosophie des Deutschen Idealismus', Vol. III, pp. 36–51. Reprinted in Angelelli (1967), 378–94. Translated as 'Compound thoughts' in Geach and Stoothoff 1977, 55–78 and *Mind* 72, 1–17.

Frege, G. 1976. Compound thoughts. In P. Geach and R. H. Stoothoff (eds and trans), *Logical investigations. Gottlob Frege*, Oxford: Basil Blackwell, 55–78. Original work published 1923.

Frege, G. 1980. Brief an Jourdain. In G. Gabriel, F. Kambartel, and C. Thiel (eds), *Gottlob Freges Briefwechsel mit D. Hilbert, E. Husserl, B. Russell, sowie ausgewählte Einzelbriefe Freges*, Hamburg: Felix Meiner Verlag, 110–12; also in G. Gabriel et al. (eds), *Philosophical and Mathematical Correspondence*, Chicago: Chicago University Press, 1980: 78–80 (Original work published 1914.)

Friederici, A. 2002. Towards a neural basis of auditory sentence processing, *Trends in Cognitive Sciences* 6: 78–84.

Fries, P. 2005. A mechanism for cognitive dynamics: neuronal communication through neuronal coherence, *Trends in Cognitive Sciences* 9: 474–80.

Fries, P., J. Reynolds, A. Rorie, and R. Desimone. 2001. Modulation of oscillatory neuronal synchronization by selective visual attention, *Science* 291: 1560–3.

Fries, P., P. R. Roelfsema, A. K. Engel, P. König, and W. Singer. 1997. Synchronization of oscillatory responses in visual cortex correlates with perception in interocular rivalry, *Proceedings of the National Academy of Sciences USA* 94: 12699–704.

Gabriel, G., H. Hermes, F. Kambartel, C. Thiel, and A. Veraart (eds). 1976. *Gottlob Frege. Wissenschaftlicher Briefwechsel*, Hamburg: Felix Meiner.

Gabriel, G., H. Hermes, F. Kambartel, C. Thiel, and A. Veraart (eds). 1980. *Gottlob Frege. Philosophical and mathematical correspondence*, Oxford: Basil Blackwell. Abridged by McGuiness and translated by H. Kaal.

Gagné, C. L. and E. J. Shoben. 1997. Influence of thematic relations on the comprehension of modifier–noun combinations, *Journal of Experimental Psychology: Learning, Memory, and Cognition* 23: 71–87.

Gagné, C. L. and Spalding. 2004. Effect of relation availability on the interpretation and access of familiar noun-noun compounds, *Brain and Language* 90 (1–3).

Galantucci, B. 2005. An experimental study of the emergence of human communication systems, *Cognitive Science* 29: 737–67.

Gallistel, C. 1990. *The Organization of Learning*, Cambridge, MA: MIT Press.

Gallistel, C. and J. Gibbon. 2002. *The Symbolic Foundations of Conditioned Behavior*, Mahwah, NJ: Lawrence Erlbaum.

Gamerschlag, T. 2005. *Komposition und Argumentstruktur komplexer Verben*. Berlin: Akademie Verlag.

García-Carpintero, M. and J. Macia (eds). 2006. *Two-dimensional Semantics: Foundations and Applications*, Oxford: Oxford University Press.

García-Carpintero, M. and M. Kölbel (eds). 2008. *Relative Truth*. Oxford: Oxford University Press.

Gardner, H. 1985. *The Mind's New Science. A History of the Cognitive Revolution*, New York: Basic Books.

Garey, M. R. and D. S. Johnson. 1979. *Computers and Intractability. A Guide to the Theory of NP-Completeness*, New York: W. H. Freeman and Company.

Garfinkel, A. 1981. *Forms of Explanation*, New Haven, CT: Yale University Press.

Garrod, S., N. Fay, J. Lee, J. Oberlander, and T. MacLeod. 2007. Foundations of representation: Where might graphical symbol systems come from? *Cognitive Science* 31: 961–87.

Gayler, R. 2003. Vector symbolic architectures answer Jackendoff's challenges for cognitive neuroscience, *ICCS/ASCS International Conference on Cognitive Science*, Sydney, Australia: University of New South Wales, 133–8.

Gazdar, G. 1979. *Pragmatics*. New York: Academic Press.

Gazdar, G., E. Klein, G. Pullum, and I. Sag. 1985. *Generalized Phrase Structure Grammar*, Oxford: Basil Blackwell.

Geach, P. 1972. A program for syntax. In D. Davidson and G. Harman (eds), *Semantics for Natural Language*, no. 40 in Synthese Library. Dordrecht: Reidel.

Geach, P. T. 1962. *Reference and Generality*. Ithaca, NY: Cornell University Press.

Geach, P. T. and M. Black (eds). 1952. *Translations from the Philosphical Writings of Gottlob Frege*, Oxford: Basil Blackwell.

Geach, P. T. and R. Stoothoff (eds). 1977. *Logical Investigations. Gottlob Frege*, Oxford: Basil Blackwell.

Gentner, D. 1983. Structure-mapping: A theoretical framework for analogy, *Cognitive Science* 7: 155–70.

Gentner, D. 1989. The mechanisms of analogical learing. In S. Vosniadou and A. Ortony (eds), *Similarity, Analogy, and Thought*, Cambridge: Cambridge University Press, 199–241.

Gerrig, R. J. 1989. The time-course of sense creation, *Memory and Cognition* 17: 194–207.

Gerrig, R. J. and G. L. Murphy. 1992. Contextual influences on the comprehension of complex concepts, *Language and Cognitive Processes* 7: 205–30.

Gerrig, R. J. and H. Bortfeld. 1999. Sense creation in and out of discourse contexts, *Journal of Memory and Language*, 41: 457–68.

Giannakidou, A. and M. Stavrou. 1999. Nominalization and ellipsis in the Greek DP, *The Linguistic Review* 16: 295–332.

Gibbs, R. W. 1994. *The poetics of mind: Figurative thought, language, and understanding*. New York: Cambridge University Press.

Gibson, E. 1998. Linguistic complexity: Locality of syntactic dependencies, *Cognition* 68: 1–76.

Gigerenzer, G. and D. G. Goldstein. 1996. Reasoning the fast and frugal way: Models of bounded rationality, *Psychological Review* 103: 650–69.

Gigerenzer, G., P. M. Todd, and the ABC Research Group. 1999. *Simple Heuristics that Make us Smart*. New York: Oxford University Press.

Gillon, B. 2007. Pāṇini's *Aṣṭādhyāyī* and linguistic theory, *Journal of Indian Philosophy* 35, 445–68.

Ginzburg, J. and R. Cooper. 2004. Clarication, ellipsis, and the nature of contextual updates in dialogue, *Linguistics and Philosophy* 27(3): 297–365.

Ginzburg, J. and Sag, I. 2000. *Interrogative Investigations: The Form, Meaning and Use of English Interrogatives*, Stanford: CSLI Publications.

Glanzberg, M. 2009. Semantics and truth relative to a world, *Synthese*, 166(2): 281–307, (online 2007).

Gleitmann, L. 1990. The structural sources of verb meanings, *Language Acquisition* 1: 3–55.

Glenberg, A. M. 1997. What memory is for, *Behavioral and Brain Sciences* 20: 1–55.

Glucksberg, S. and Z. Estes. 2000. Feature accessibility in conceptual combination: Effects of context-induced relevance, *Psychonomic Bulletin and Review* 7: 510–15.

Glüer, K. and P. Pagin. 2006. Proper names and relational modality, *Linguistics and Philosophy* 29: 507–35.

Glüer, K. and P. Pagin. 2008. Relational modality, *Journal of Logic, Language and Information* 17: 307–22.

Goddard, C. and A. Wierzbicka (eds). 2002. *Meaning and Universal Grammar*. Amsterdam: Benjamins.

Gödel, K. 1932. Zum intuitionistischen Aussagenkalkül. Anzeiger Akademie der Wissenschaften Wien, 69 Math.-nat. Klasse. 65–6.

Gödel, K. 1944. Russell's Mathematical Philosophy. In P. A. Schilpp (ed.), *The Philosophy of Bertrand Russell*, Evanston and Chicago: North-Western University Press, 125–53.

Gold, E. 1967. Language identification in the limit, *Information and Control* 16: 447–74.

Goldberg, A. E. 1995. *Constructions: A Construction Grammar Approach to Argument Structure*, Chicago: University of Chicago Press.

Goldin-Meadow, S. and C. Mylander. 1998. Spontaneous sign systems created by deaf children in two cultures, *Nature* 391: 279–81.

Goldstein, D. G. and G. Gigerenzer. 2002. Models of ecological rationality: The recognition heuristic, *Psychological Review* 109: 75–90.

Goldstein, R. 1983. *The Mind–Body Problem*. New York: Penguin Books.

Goldstone, R. L. 1994. Similarity, interactive activation and mapping, *Journal of Experimental Psychology: Learning, Memory, and Cognition* 20: 3–28.

Gómez, R. L. and L. Gerken. 2000. Infant artificial language learning and language acquisition, *Trends in Cognitive Sciences* 4: 178–86.

Gómez, R. L. and L. A. Gerken. 2001. Infant artificial language learning and language acquisition, in M. Tomasello and E. Bates (eds), *Language Development: The Essential Readings*, Malden, MA: Blackwell, 42–8.

Gonchar, Y. and A. Burkhalter. 1999. Connectivity of GABAergic calretinin-immunoreactive neurons in rat primary visual cortex, *Cerebral Cortex* 9: 683–96.

Gopnik, M. and M. B. Crago. 1991. Familial aggregation of a developmental language disorder, *Cognition* 39: 1–50.

Gottwald, S. 2001. *A Treatise on Many-valued Logics*, Baldock: Research Studies Press.

Gould, S. J. and R. C. Lewontin. 1979. The spandrels of San Marco and the Panglossian Paradigm: a critique of the adaptationist programme, *Proceedings of the Royal Society of London* B 205: 581–98.

Gray, C. M. and G. Viana Di Prisco. 1997. Stimulus-dependent neuronal oscillations and local synchronization in striate cortex of the alert cat, *Journal of Neuroscience* 179: 3239–53.

Gray, C., P. König, A. K. Engel, and W. Singer. 1989. Oscilliatory responses in cat visual cortex exhibit inter-columnar synchronization which reflects global stimulus properties, *Nature* 338: 334–7.

Gray, K. C. and E. E. Smith. 1995. The role of instance retrieval in understanding complex concepts, *Memory and Cognition* 23: 665–74.

Green, G. M. 1974. *Semantics and Syntactic Regularity*, Bloomington: Indiana University Press.

Grice, H. P. 1969. Utterer's meaning and intentions, *Philosophical Review*, 78: 147–77.

Grice, H. P. 1975. Logic and conversation. In P. Cole and J. L. Morgan (eds), *Syntax and semantics, Vol. 3: Speech acts*, New York: Academic Press, 41–58.

Griffiths, T. L. and M. L. Kalish. 2007. Language evolution by iterated learning with Bayesian agents, *Cognitive Science* 31: 441–80.

Griffiths, T. L., B. R. Christian, and M. L. Kalish. 2008. Using category structures to test iterated learning as a method for revealing inductive biases, *Cognitive Science* 32: 68–107.

Grijzenhout, J. and M. Penke. 2005. On the interaction of phonology and morphology in language acquisition and German and Dutch Broca's aphasia: the case of inflected verbs, *Yearbook of Morphology* 2005: 49–81.

Grimshaw, J. and A. Mester. 1988. Light verbs and theta-marking, *Linguistic Inquiry* 192: 205–32.

Groenendijk, J. and M. Stokhof. 1982. Semantic analysis of wh-complements, *Linguistics and Philosophy* 5: 175–233.

Groenendijk, J. and M. Stokhof. 1991. Dynamic predicate logic, *Linguistics and Philosophy* 14, 39–100.

Gross, C. 2002. Genealogy of the 'grandmother cell', *Neuroscientist* 8512. 512–18.

Grosz, B. and Sidner, C. 1986. Attention, intentions, and the structure of discourse, *Computational Linguistics* 12(3): 175–204.

Gruppe, O. F. 1834. *Wendepunkt der Philosophie in neunzehnten Jahrhundert*, Berlin: Reimer.

Guerssel, M., K. Hale, M. Laughren, B. Levin, and J. White Eagle. 1985. A cross-linguistic study of transitivity alternations. In W. H. Eilfort et al. (eds), *Papers from the Parasession on Causatives and Agentivity*, Chicago Linguistic Society, 48–63.

Haaparanta, L. 1985. *Frege's Doctrine of Being*. Helsinki: Acta Philosophica Fennica 39.

Hacker, P. M. S. 1979. Semantic holism, in C. Luckhardt (ed.), *Wittgenstein. Sources and perspectives*, Ithaca, NY: Cornell University Press, 213–42.

Hagoort, P. 2003. How the brain solves the binding problem for language: A neurocomputational model of syntactic processing, *Neuroimage* 20: S18–S29.

Hagoort, P. and C. Brown. 1994. Brain responses to lexical ambiguity resolution and parsing. In C. Clifton, L. Frazier, and K. Rayner (eds), *Perspectives on Sentence Processing*, Hillsdale, NJ: Lawrence Erlbaum Associates, 45–81.

Hagoort, P., C. Brown, and J. Groothusen. 1993. The syntactic positive shift SPS. as an ERP measure of syntactic processing, *Language and Cognitive Processes* 8: 439–83.

Hagoort, P., C. Brown, and L. Osterhout. 2001. The neurocognition of syntactic processing. In C. M. Brown and P. Hagoort (eds), *The Neurocognition of Language*, Oxford: Oxford University Press, 273–307.

Hagoort, P., G. Baggio, and R. Willems. 2009. Semantic unification. In M. Gazzaniga (ed.), *The New Cognitive Neurosciences*, Canbridge, MA: MIT Press.

Hagoort, P., L. Hald, M. Bastiaansen, and K. M. Petersson. 2004. Integration of word meaning and world knowledge in language comprehension, *Science* 304 (5669): 438–41.

Haida, A. 2007. The Indefiniteness and Focusing of *Wh*-Words. Dissertation, Humboldt-Universität Berlin 2007. http://amor.cms.hu-berlin.de/~haidaand/download/Haida2007 Diss.pdf.

Haken, H. 1990. *Synergetik*, 3rd edn, Berlin: Springer Verlag.

Hale, K. and S. J. Keyser. 1992. The syntactic character of thematic structure. In I. M. Roca (ed.), *Thematic Structure: Its Role in Grammar*, Berlin: Foris, 107–44.

Hale, K. and S. J. Keyser. 1993. On argument structure and the lexical expression of syntactic relations. In K. Hale and J. Keyser (eds), *The View from Building 20*, Cambridge, MA: MIT Press.

Hale, K. and S. J. Keyser. 1997. On the complex nature of simple predicators. In A. Alsina, J. Bresnan, and P. Sells (eds), *Complex Predicates*, Stanford: CSLI Publications, 29–65.

Hale, K. and S. J. Keyser. 2002. *Prolegomena to a Theory of Argument Structure*, Cambridge, MA: MIT Press.

Halff, H. M., A. Ortony, and R. C. Anderson. 1976. A context sensitive representation of word meanings, *Memory and Cognition* 4: 378–83.

Halle, M. and A. Marantz. 1993. Distributed morphology and the pieces of inflection, in K. Hale and S. J. Keyser (eds), *The View from Building 20*, Cambridge, MA: MIT Press, 111–76.

Halliday, M. A. K. and R. Hasan. 1976. *Cohesion in English*, London: Longman.

Hamm, F. and T. E. Zimmermann. 2002. Quantifiers and anaphora. In F. Hamm and T. E. Zimmermann (eds), *Semantics*. Hamburg: Buske, 137–72.

Hamm, F., H. Kamp, and M. van Lambalgen. 2006. There is no opposition between formal and cognitive semantics, *Theoretical Linguistics* 32(1): 1–40.

Hampton, J. A. 1979. Polymorphous concepts in semantic memory, *Journal of Verbal Learning and Verbal Behavior* 18: 441–61.

Hampton, J. A. 1982. A demonstration of intransitivity in natural categories, *Cognition* 12: 151–64.

Hampton, J. A. 1987. Inheritance of attributes in natural concept conjunctions, *Memory and Cognition* 15, 55–71.

Hampton, J. A. 1988a. Disjunction of natural concepts, *Memory and Cognition* 16: 579–91.

Hampton, J. A. 1988b. Overextension of conjunctive concepts: Evidence for a unitary model of concept typicality and class inclusion, *Journal of Experimental Psychology: Learning, Memory, and Cognition* 14: 12–32.

Hampton, J. A. 1991. The combination of prototype concepts, in P. J. Schwanenflugel (ed.), *The Psychology of Word Meanings*, Hillsdale: Lawrence Erlbaum Associates, 91–116.

Hampton, J. A. 1993. Prototype models of concept representation. In I. Van Mechelen, J. Hampton, R. Michalski, and P. Theuns (eds), *Categories and Concepts: Theoretical Views and Inductive Data Analysis*, New York: Academic Press, 67–95.

Hampton, J. A. 1995. Testing the prototype theory of concepts, *Journal of Memory and Language*, 34: 686–708.

Hampton, J. A. 1996. Conjunctions of visually based categories: Overextension and compensation, *Journal of Experimental Psychology: Learning, Memory, and Cognition* 22: 378–96.

Hampton, J. A. 1997a. Conceptual combination: Conjunction and negation of natural concepts, *Memory and Cognition* 25: 888–909.

Hampton, J. A. 1997b. Emergent attributes in conceptual combinations. In T. B. Ward, S. M. Smith, and J. Viad (eds), *Creative Thought: An Investigation of Conceptual Structures and Processes*, Washington DC: American Psychological Association Press, 83–110.

Hampton, J. A. 1997*c*. Conceptual combination. In K. Lamberts and D. Shanks (eds), *Knowledge, Concepts, and Categories*, Cambridge, MA: MIT Press, 133–60.

Hampton, J. A. 1998. Similarity-based categorization and fuzziness of natural categories, *Cognition* 65: 137–65.

Hampton, J. A. 2000. Concepts and prototypes, *Mind and Language* 15: 299–307.

Hampton, J. A. 2006. Concepts as prototypes, in B. H. Ross (ed.), *The Psychology of Learning and Motivation: Advances in Research and Theory, Vol. 46*. Amsterdam: Elsevier, 79–113.

Hampton, J. A. 2007. Typicality, graded membership and vagueness, *Cognitive Science* 31: 355–83.

Hardt, D. 1993. VP Ellipsis: Form, Meaning, and Processing. PhD Dissertation, University of Pennsylvania, Philadelphia, PA.

Harel, D. 1984. Dynamic logic. In D. Gabbay and F. Guenthner (eds), *Handbook of Philosophical Logic*, vol. 2, Dordrecht: Reidel, 497–604.

Harley, H. 1995. Subjects, Events and Licensing. Doctoral dissertation, Cambridge, MA: Massachusetts Institute of Technology.

Harley, H. 2003. Possession and the double object construction. In P. Pica and J. Rooryck (eds), *The Linguistic Variation Yearbook 2*, Amsterdam: John Benjamins, 29–68.

Harley, H. 2004. Wanting, having, and getting: A note on Fodor and Lepore 1998, *Linguistic Inquiry* 352: 255–67.

Harley, H. 2005. How do verbs get their names? Denominal verbs, Manner Incorporation and the ontology of verb roots in English, in N. Erteschik-Shir and T. Rapoport (eds), *The Syntax of Aspect*, Oxford: Oxford University Press, 42–64.

Harley, H. 2006. The morphology of nominalizations and the syntax of vP. In A. Giannakidou, and A. Rathert (eds), *Quantification, Definiteness, and Nominalization*, Oxford: Oxford University Press.

Harley, H. 2011. Lexical decomposition, this volume.

Harman, G. 1974. Meaning and semantics. In M. Munitz and P. Unger (eds), *Semantics and Philosophy*, New York: SUNY Press, 1–16.

Harrell, M. 1996. Confirmation holism and semantic holism. *Synthese* 109, 63–101.

Hartmanis, J and R. E. Stearns. 1965. On the computational complexity of algorithms, *Transactions of the American Mathematical Society* 117: 285–306.

Harves, S. and R. Kayne. 2008. Having need and needing have in Indo-European. Ms, Pomona College and New York University.

Hastie, R., C. Schroeder, and R. Weber. 1990. Creating complex social conjunction categories from simple categories, *Bulletin of the Psychonomic Society* 28: 242–7.

Hauser, M. D., N. Chomsky, and W. T. Fitch. 2002. The faculty of language: What is it, who has it, and how did it evolve? *Science* 298: 1569–79.

Hausser, R. R. 1984. *Surface Compositional Grammar*, Munich: Wilhelm Finck Verlag.

Hawkins, J. A. 2003. Efficiency and complexity in grammars: Three general principles. In by J. Moore and M. Polinsky (eds), *The Nature of Explanation in Linguistic Theory*, Stanford, CA: CSLI Publications, 121–52.

Hay, J., C. Kennedy, and B. Levin. 1999. Scalar structure underlies telicity in 'degree achievements', in T. Mathews and D. Stolovitch (eds), *Proceedings of SALT IX*. Ithaca: CLC Publications, 127–44.

Heal, J. 1994. Semantic holism: Still a good buy, *Proceedings of the Aristotelian Society* 94, 325–39.

Hebb, D. O. 1949. *The Organization of Behavior*, New York: Wiley.

Heck, R. 2001. Do demonstratives have senses? *Philosophers' Imprint*, 2(2): 1–33.

Heider (= Rosch), E. 1971. Focal colour areas and the development of colour names, *Developmental Psychology* 4: 447–55.

Heim, I. 1982. The Semantics of Definite and Indefinite Noun Phrases. Dissertation, University of Massachusetts.

Heim, I. and A. Kratzer. 1998. *Semantics in Generative Grammar*, Oxford: Blackwell Publishers.

Heit, E. and L. W. Barsalou. 1996. The instantiation principle in natural categories, *Memory* 4: 413–51.

Hempel, C. 1950. Problems and changes in the empiricist criterion of meaning, *Revue Internationale de Philosophie* 4, 41–63.

Hempel, C. G. 1965. *Aspects of Scientific Explanations*, New York: Free Press.

Hendriks, H. 1993. Studied Flexibility. Categories and Types in Syntax and Semantics. PhD thesis, University of Amsterdam.

Hendriks, H. 2001. Compositionality and model-theoretic interpretation, *Journal of Logic, Language and Information* 10: 29–48.

Henkin, L. J. D. Monk, and A. Tarski. 1971. Cylindric algebras. Part I, nr. 64 in *Studies in logic and the foundations of mathematics*, Amsterdam: North Holland.

Hermes, H., F. Kambartel, and F. Kaulbach (eds). 1969. *Gottlob Frege. Nachgelassene Schriften*, Hamburg: Felix Meiner.

Hermes, H., F. Kambartel, and F. Kaulbach (eds). 1979. *Gottlob Frege. Posthumous writings*, Oxford: Basil Blackwell, transl. by P. Long and R. White.

Herrmann, C. S., M. H. J. Munk, and A. K. Engel. 2004. Cognitive functions of gamma-band activity: Memory match and utilization, *Trends in Cognitive Sciences* 8: 347–55.

Hess, T. M., S. M. Pullen, and K. A. McGee. 1996. Acquisition of prototype-based information about social groups in adulthood, *Psychology and Aging* 11 (1), 179–90.

Higginbotham, J. 1983. The logical form of perceptual reports, *Journal of Philosophy* 80: 100–27.

Higginbotham, J. 1985. On semantics, *Linguistic Inquiry* 16: 547–93.

Higginbotham, J. 2007. Some consequences of compositionality, in G. Ramchand and C. Reiss (eds), *The Oxford Handbook of Linguistic Interfaces*, Oxford: Oxford University Press, 425–44.

Higginbotham, J. no date. Some consequences of compositionality, manuscript.

Hill, J. C. 1983. A computational model of language acquisition in the two-year-old, *Cognition and Brain Theory* 6: 287–317.

Hintikka, J. 1980. On the any-thesis and the methodology of linguistics, *Linguistics and Philosophy* 4, 101–22.

Hintikka, J. 1983. *The Game of Language. Studies in Game-Theoretical Semantics and its Applications*, Synthese Language Library, Dordrecht: Reidel.

Hintikka, J. 1984. A hundred years later: The rise and fall of Frege's influence in language theory, *Synthese* 59, 27–49.

Hintikka, J. 1996. *The Principles of Mathematics Revisited*, Cambridge: Cambridge University Press.

Hintikka, J. and G. Sandu. 1989. Informational independence as a semantical phenomenon. In J. E. Fenstad et al. (eds), *Logic, Methodology and Philosophy of Science VIII*, Amsterdam: Elsevier Science, 571–89.

Hintikka, J. and G. Sandu. 1997. Game-theoretical semantics. In J. van Benthem and A. ter Meulen (ed.), *Handbook of Logic and Language*, Amsterdam: Elsevier, 361–410.

Hintikka, J. and G. Sandu. 1999. Tarski's guilty secret: compositionality, in J. Wolenski and E. Köhler (eds). *Alfred Tarski and the Vienna circle*, Dordrecht: Kluwer, 217–30.

Hinton, G. (ed.), 1990. Special issue on connectionist symbol processing, *Artificial Intelligence* 46.

Hinton, G. 1992. How neural networks learn from experience, *Scientific American* 11: 145–51.

Hinzen, W. 2006*a*. *Mind Design and Minimal Syntax*, Oxford: Oxford University Press.

Hinzen, W. 2006*b*. Dualism and the atoms of thought, *Journal of Consciousness Studies* 13(9): 25–55.

Hinzen, W. 2007. *An Essay on Naming and Truth*, Oxford: Oxford University Press.

Hinzen, W. 2008. Succ + Lex = Language?, in Grohmann, K. (ed.), *InterPhases:Phase-Theoretic Investigations of Linguistic Interfaces*, Oxford: Oxford University Press, 25–47.

Hinzen, W. 2009. Hierarchy, Merge, and Truth. In M. Piattelli-Palmarini, P. Salaburu, and J. Uriagereka (eds), *Of Minds and Languages*, Oxford: Oxford University Press, 123–41.

Hinzen, W. and J. Uriagereka. 2006. On the metaphysics of linguistics, *Erkenntnis* 65(1): 71–96.

Hobbs, J. R. 1979. Coherence and coreference, *Cognitive Science* 3(1): 67–90.

Hobbs, J. 1985. Ontological promiscuity. *Proceedings, 23rd Annual Meeting of the Association for Computational Linguistics*, Chicago, Illinois, July, 61–9.

Hockett, C. F. 1960. The origin of speech, *Scientific American* 203: 88–96.

Hodges, W. 1997*a*. Compositional semantics for a language of imperfect information, *Logic Journal of the IGPL* 5(4): 539–63.

Hodges, W. 1997*b*. Some strange quantifiers, in J. Mycielski et al. (eds), *Structures in Logic and Computer Science*, Lecture Notes in Computer Science 1261, Berlin: Springer, 51–65.

Hodges, W. 1998. Compositionality is not the problem, *Logic and Logical Philosophy* 6: 7–33.

Hodges, W. 2001. Formal features of compositionality, *Journal of Logic, Language and Information* 10: 7–28.

Hodges, W. 2005. A context principle, in R. Kahle (ed.), *Intensionality*, Wellesley, MA: Association for Symbolic Logic and A. K. Peters, 42–59.

Hodges, W. 2006*a*. Two doors to open. In D. Gabbay, S. Goncharov, and M. Zakharyaschev (eds), *Mathematical Problems from Applied Logic I: New Logics for the 21st Century*, New York: Springer, 277–316.

Hodges, W. 2006*b*. From sentence meanings to full semantics. Unpublished manuscript.

Hodges, W. 2007. Logics of imperfect information: Why sets of assignments?, in J. van Benthem et al. (eds), *Interactive Logic, Selected Papers from the 7th Augustus De Morgan Workshop*, London and Amsterdam: Amsterdam University Press, 117–33.

Hodges, W. 2008*a*. From sentence meanings to full semantics, in A. Gupta et al. (eds), *Logic at the Crossroads: An Interdisciplinary View I*, New Delhi, Allied Publishers, 399–416.

Hodges, W. 2008*b*. Tarski's theory of definition, in D. E. Patterson (ed.), *New Essays on Tarski and Philosophy*, Oxford: Oxford University Press, 94–132.

Hodges, W. Submitted. Requirements on a theory of sentence and word meanings, in R. Schantz (ed.), *Prospects for Meaning*, New York: de Gruyter.

Hoefler, S. 2006. Why has ambiguous syntax emerged? In A. Cangelosi, A. D. M. Smith, and K. Smith (eds), *The Evolution of Language: Proceedings of the 6th International Conference*, Singapore: World Scientific, 123–30.

Holyoak, K. J. and P. Thagard. 1989. Analogical mapping by constraint satisfaction, *Cognitive Science* 13: 295–355.

Hopfield, J. 1982. Neural networks and physical systems with emergent collective computational abilities, *Proceedings of the National Academy of Sciences, USA* 79: 2554–8.

Horgan, T. 1997. Modelling the noncomputational mind: Reply to Litch, *Philosophical Psychology* 10: 365–71.

Horgan, T. and J. Tienson. 1996. *Connectionism and the Philosophy of Psychology*, Cambridge, MA: MIT Press.

Hornstein, N. and P. Pietroski. 2009. Basic operations, *Catalan Journal of Linguistics* 8: 113–39.

Horty, J. 2007. *Frege on Definitions: A Case Study of Semantic Content*. Oxford: Oxford University Press.

Horwich, P. 1997. The composition of meanings, *Philosophical Review* 106: 503–32.

Horwich, P. 1998. *Meaning*, Oxford: Clarendon Press.

Horwich, P. 2001. Deflating compositionality, *Ratio* 14: 369–85.

Huang, J. T. 1995. Logical form. In G. Webelhuth (ed.), *Government and Binding Theory and the Minimalist Program*. Oxford: Blackwell.

Hubel, D. H. and T. N. Wiesel. 1968. Receptive fields and functional architecture of monkey striate cortex, *Journal of Physiology* 195: 215–43.

Hudson Kam, C. L. and E. L. Newport. 2005. Regularizing unpredictable variation: The roles of adult and child learners in language formation and change, *Language Learning and Development* 1: 151–95.

Hume, D. 1739. A treatise of human nature: Being an attempt to introduce the experimental method of reasoning into moral subjects. In D. F. Norton and M. J. Norton (eds), Cambridge: Oxford Philosophical Texts.

Hummel, J. E. and Holyoak, K. J. 1998. Distributed representations of structure: A theory of analogical access and mapping, *Psychological Review* 104: 427–66.

Hummel, J. E. and K. J. Holyoak. 2003. A symbolic-connectionist theory of relational inference and generalization, *Psychological Review* 110(2), 220–64.

Hummel, J. E., B. Burns, and K. J. Holyoak. 1994. Analogical mapping by dynamic binding: Preliminary investigations. In K. J. Holyoak and J. A. Barnden (eds), *Advances in Connectionist and Neural Computation Theory: Analogical connections*, Norwood, NJ: Ablex.

Hung, H.-K. and J. I. Zucker. 1991. Semantics of pointers, referencing and dereferencing with intensional logic, in *Proceedings of the 6th annual IEEE symposium on Logic in Computer Science*, Los Almolitos, CA: IEEE Computer Society Press, 127–36.

Hurford, J. R. 1990. Nativist and functional explanations in language acquisition. In I. M. Roca (ed.), *Logical Issues in Language Acquisition*, Dordrecht: Foris, 85–136.

Hurford, J. R. 2007. *The Origins of Meaning*. Oxford: Oxford University Press..

Husserl, E. 1900. *Logische Untersuchungen*, band ii. Berlin: Halle. Section references to the translation (of the 1913 2nd edn) by J. M. Findlay, 1970, as *Logical Investigations*, Vol. 2, London: Routledge and Kegan Paul.

Ibn Sīnā 1970. *Al-shifā': Al-mantiq III, Al-ʿʿibāra*, M. El-Khodeiri (ed.), Cairo: Dar El-Katib al-ʿArabi.

Ibn Sīnā 2002. *Al-'ishārāt wa-l-tanbiyyāt*, ed. M. Zāreʾi (ed.), Qum: Būstān-e ketab-e Qom.

Inati, S. 1984. Ibn Sina on single expressions, in M. Marmura (ed.), *Islamic Theology and Philosophy: Studies in Honor of George F. Hourani*, Albany NY: State University of New York Press, 148–59.

Israel, D. and J. Perry. 1996. Where monsters dwell. In J. Seligman and D. Westerståhl (eds), *Logic, Language, Computation*, Stanford: CSLI Publications, 303–16.

Jackendoff, R. 1972. *Semantic Interpretation in Generative Grammar*, Cambridge, MA: MIT Press.

Jackendoff, R. 1983. *Semantics and Cognition*, Cambridge, MA: MIT Press.

Jackendoff, R. 1990. *Semantic Structures*. Cambridge: MIT Press.

Jackendoff, R. 1992. Babe Ruth Homered his way into the hearts of America, in T. Stowell and E.Wehrli (eds), *Syntax and the Lexicon*, Academic Press, San Diego, 155–78.

Jackendoff, R. 1996. Semantics and cognition. In S. Lappin (ed.), *The Handbook of Contemporary Semantic Theory*, Oxford: Blackwell, 539–59.

Jackendoff, R. 1997. *The Architecture of the Language Faculty*, MIT Press, Cambridge, MA.

Jackendoff, R. 2002. *Foundations of Language: Brain, Meaning, Grammar, Evolution*, New York: Oxford University Press.

Jacobsen, W. M. 1981. Transitivity in the Japanese Verbal System. Doctoral dissertation. Chicago: University of Chicago.

Jacobson, P. 1987. Phrase structure, grammatical relations, and discontintinuous constitute-unts, in G. Huck and A. Ojeda (eds), *Syntax and Semantics 20: Discontinuous Constituency*, New York: Academic Press, 27–69.

Jacobson, P. 1992*a*. Flexible categorial grammars: Questions and prospects, in R. Levine (ed.), *Formal Grammar: Theory and Implementation*, Oxford: Oxford University Press, 129–67.

Jacobson, P. 1992*b*. Antecedent contained deltion in a variable-free semantics, in C. Barker and D. Dowty (eds), *Proceedings of the Second Conference on Sematnics and Linguistic Theory*, Columbus: Ohio State Working Papers in Linguistics, 193–213.

Jacobson, P. 1999. Towards a variable free semantics, *Linguistics and Philosophy* 22: 117–84.

Jacobson, P. 2002. The (dis)oganizaiton of the grammar: 25 years, *Lingusitics and Philosophy* 25(5–6): 601–26.

Jacobson, P. 2003. Binding without pronouns (and pronouns without binding), in G.-J. Kruiff and R. Oerhle (eds), *Binding and Resource Sensitivity*, Dordrecht: Kluwer Academic Publishers, 57–96.

Jacobson, P. 2007. Direct compositionality and variable-free semantics: The case of antecedent contained deletion, in K. Johnson (ed.), *Topics in Ellipsis*, Cambridge: Cambridge University Press.

Jacobson, P. 2009. Do representations matter or do meanings matter: The case of antecedent containment. In E. Hinrichs and J. Nerbonne (eds), *Theory and Evidence in Semantics: Papers in Honor of David R. Dowty*, Stanford: CSLI Publications, 81–107.

Jäger, G. and Blutner, R. 2000. Against lexical decomposition in syntax. In A. Z. Wyner (ed.), *Proceedings of the Fifteenth Annual Conference, of the Israeli Association for Theoretical Linguistics*, Haifa: University of Haifa. Downloadable at http://semanticsarchive.net/Archive/mRkMTJiO/rbgjIATL15.pdf. Reprinted in R. Blutner and G. Jäger (eds), *Studies in Optimality Theory*, University of Potsdam, 5–29.

Janssen, T. 1983. *Foundations and Applications of Montague Grammar*, Amsterdam: Mathematisch Centrum.

Janssen, T. M. V. 1986. *Foundations and Applications of Montague Grammar. Part 1: Philosophy, framework, computer science*, no. 19 in CWI tracts, Amsterdam: Centre for Mathematics and Computer Science.

Janssen, T. M. V. 1997. Compositionality (with an appendix by B. Partee), in J. van Benthem and A. ter Meulen (eds), *Handbook of Logic and Language*. Amsterdam: Elsevier, 417–73.

Janssen, T. M. V. 2001. Frege, contextuality and compositionality, *Journal of Logic, Language and Information* 10(1): 115–36.

Janssen, T. M. V. and P. van Emde Boas. 1977*a*. The expressive power of intensional logic in the semantics of programming languages, in J. Gruska (ed.), *Mathematical foundations of computer science 1977* (Proceedings of the 6th symposium Tatranska Lomnica), no. 53 in Lecture notes in computer science, Berlin: Springer, 303–11.

Janssen, T. M. V. and P. van Emde Boas. 1977*b*. On the proper treatment of referencing, dereferencing and assignment, in A. Salomaa and M. Steinby (eds), *Automata, languages and programming* (Proceedings of the 4th coll. Turku), no. 52 in Lecture notes in computer science, Berlin: Springer, 282–300.

Jelinek, E. 1998. Voice and transitivity as functional projections in Yaqui. In M. Butt and W. Geuder (eds), *The Projection of Arguments: Lexical and Compositional Factors*, Stanford: CSLI, 177–206.

Johnson, K. 2004*a*. On the systematicity of language and thought, *Journal of Philosophy* 101, 111–39.

Johnson, K. 2004*b*. From impossible words to conceptual structure: the role of structure and processes in the lexicon, *Mind and Language* 19(3): 334–58.

Jönsson, M. L. 2008. On Compositionality: Doubts about The Structural Path to Meaning, PhD Thesis, Department of Philosophy, Lund University.

Jönsson, M. L. and J. A. Hampton. 2006. The inverse conjunction fallacy, *Journal of Memory and Language* 55, 317–34.

Jönsson, M. L. and J. A. Hampton. 2008. On prototypes as defaults (Comment on Connolly, Fodor, Gleitman and Gleitman, 2007). *Cognition* 106, 913–23.

Jönsson, M. L. and J. A. Hampton. 2011. The modifier effect in within-category induction: Default inheritance in complex noun phrases. *Language and Cognitive Processes*, 26, (forthcoming).

Jusczyk, P. W. 2001. Finding and remembering words: Some beginnings by English-learning infants, in M. Tomasello and E. Bates (eds), *Language Development: The Essential Readings*, Malden, MA: Blackwell, 19–25.

Juslin, P., and M. Persson. 2002. PROBabilities from EXemplars (PROBEX): a 'Lazy' Algorithm for Probabilistic Inference from Generic Knowledge, *Cognitive Science* 26: 563–607.

Kalish, M. L., T. L. Griffiths, and S. Lewandowsky. 2007. Iterated learning: Intergenerational knowledge transmission reveals inductive biases, *Psychonomic Bulletin and Review* 14: 288–94.

Kamiński, M., M. Ding, W. Truccolo, and S. Bressler. 2001. Evaluating causal relations in neural systems: Granger causality, directed transfer function and statistical assessment of significance, *Biological Cybernetics* 85, 145–57.

Kamp, H. 1971. Formal properties of 'now', *Theoria* 37: 227–74.

Kamp, H. 1975. Two theories of adjectives. In E. Keenan (ed.), *Formal Semantics of Natural Language*, Cambridge: Cambridge University Press.

Kamp, H. 1979. Events, instants and temporal reference. In R. Bäuerle, U. Egli, and A. von Stechow (eds), *Semantics from Different Points of View*, Berlin: Springer, 27–54.

Kamp, H. 1981. A theory of truth and semantic representation, in J. Groenendijk, T. Janssen and M. Stokhof (eds), *Formal Methods in the Study of Language*, Amsterdam: CWI, 1–14. Reprinted in J. Groenendijk, T. Janssen, and M. Stokhof (eds), *Truth, Interpretation and Information*, Dordrecht: Foris, 1984, 115–43, and in Portner and Partee 2002, 189–222.

Kamp, H. 1990. Prolegomena to a structural account of belief and other attitudes. In C. A. Anderson and J. Owens (eds), *Propositional Attitudes*, CSLI Lecture Notes Number 20, Stanford: CSLI Publications.

Kamp, H. and B. Partee. 1995. Prototype theory and compositionality. *Cognition* 57 (2): 129–91.

Kamp, H. and U. Reyle. 1993. *From Discourse to Logic*. Dordrecht: Kluwer.

Kant, I. 1781. *Kritik der reinen Vernunft*, Berlin: Reimer.

Kaplan, D. 1975. How to Russell a Frege-Church, *Journal of Philosophy* 72: 716–29.

Kaplan, D. 1977. Demonstratives, presented at the 1977 meeting of the Pacific Division of the American Philosophical Association.

Kaplan, D. 1979. On the logic of demonstratives, *Journal of Philosophical Logic*, 8(1).

Kaplan, D. 1989. Demonstratives: An essay on the semantics, logic, metaphysics, and episte-mology of demonstratives and other indexicals. In J. Almog, J. Perry, and H. Wettstein (eds), *Themes from Kaplan*. Oxford: Oxford University Press, 481–566.

Kaplan, R. and J. Bresnan. 1982. Lexical-Functional Grammar: a formal system for grammatical representation, in J. Bresnan (ed.), *The Mental Representation of Grammatical Relations*, Cambridge, MA: MIT Press, 173–281.

Karttunen, L. 1976. Discourse referents. In J. McCawley (ed.), *Syntax and Semantics 7: Notes from the Linguistic Underground*, New York: Academic Press, 363–85.

Katz, J. 1964. Semantic theory and the meaning of good, *Journal of Philosophy* 61 (23): 739–66.

Katz, J. 1966. *The Philosophy of Language*, London: Harper and Row.

Katz, J. 1972. *Semantic Theory*, New York: Harper & Row.

Katz, J. 1994. Names without bearers, *Philosophical Review* 103: 1–39.

Katz, J. and J. Fodor. 1963. The structure of a semantic theory, *Language* 39, 170–210.

Kaufmann, I. 1995*a*. *Die Kombinatorik lokaler Verben und prädikativer Argumente*, Tübingen: Niemeyer.

Kaufmann, I. 1995*b*. What is an impossible verb? Restrictions on Semantic Form and their consequences for argument structure, *Folia Linguistica* 29: 67–103.

Kaufmann, I. and D. Wunderlich. 1998. Cross-linguistic patterns of resultatives. *Working Papers SFB 282 Theory of the Lexicon*, #109. University of Düsseldorf.

Kayne, R. 1993. Towards a modular theory of auxiliary selection, *Studia Linguistica* 47(1): 3–31.

Kayne, R. 1994. *The Antisymmetry of Syntax*, Cambridge, MA: MIT Press.

Kayne, R. 2008. Antisymmetry and the Lexicon. Ms. New York University. Downloadable at http://ling.auf.net/lingBuzz/000598.

Kazmi, A. and F. Pelletier 1998. Is compositionality formally vacuous? *Linguistics and Philosophy* 21: 629–33.

Keane, M. T., T. Ledgeway, and S. Duff. 1994. Constraints on analogical mapping: A comparison of three models, *Cognitive Science* 18: 387–438.

Keefe, R. and P. Smith. 1997. Theories of vagueness, in R. Keefe and P. Smith (eds), *Vagueness: A Reader*, Cambridge: MIT Press, 1–57.

Keenan, E. 1979. On surface form and logical form, *Studies in the Linguistic Sciences* 8: 163–203.

Keenan, E. L. and L. L. Faltz. 1985. *Boolean Semantics for Natural Language*, Dordrecht: Reidel.

Keenan, E. and E. Stabler. 2003. *Bare Grammar*, Stanford: CSLI.

Kehler, A. 2002. *Coherence, Reference, and the Theory of Grammar*, Stanford: CSLI Publications.

Keil, F. C. 1989. *Concepts, Kinds, and Cognitive Development*, Cambridge, MA: MIT Press.

Keller, R. 1994. *On Language Change: the Invisible Hand in Language*, London: Routledge.

Kempson, R. and A. Cormack. 1981. Ambiguity and quantification, *Linguistics and Philosophy* 4: 259–309.

Kennedy, C. 1999. Gradable adjectives denote measure functions, not partial functions, *Studies in the Linguistic Sciences* 29(1).

Kennedy, C. and L. McNally. 2005. Scale structure, degree modification, and the semantics of gradable predicates, *Language* 81: 345–81.

Kim, A. and L. Osterhout. 2005. The independence of combinatory semantic processing: Evidence from event-related potentials, *Journal of Memory and Language* 52: 205–25.

King, J. C. 2003. Tense, modality, and semantic values. In J. Hawthorne and D. Zimmerman, (eds), *Philosophical Perspectives 17: Language and Philosophical Linguistics*, 195–246.

King, J. C. 2011. Structured propositions. In Edward N. Zalta (ed.), *The Stanford Encyclopedia of Philosophy*. URL = http://plato.stanford.edu/archives/fall2011/entries/propositions-structured/, Fall.

King, J. C. and J. Stanley. 2005. Semantics, pragmatics, and the role of semantic content. In Zoltan Szabó (ed.), *Semantics versus Pragmatics*, Oxford: Oxford University Press, 111–64.

Kiparsky, Paul. 1997. Remarks on denominal verbs. In A. Alsina, J. Bresnan, and P. Sells (eds) *Complex Predicates*, Stanford: CSLI Publications, 473–99.

Kirby, S. 1999a. *Function, Selection and Innateness: The emergence of language universals*, Oxford: Oxford University Press.

Kirby, S. 1999b. Syntax out of learning: The cultural evolution of structured communication in a population of induction algorithms. In D. Floreano, J. D. Nicoud, and F. Mondada (eds), *Advances in Artificial Life: Proceedings of the 5th European Conference on Artificial Life*, Berlin: Springer, 694–703.

Kirby, S. 2000. Syntax without natural selection: How compositionality emerges from vocabulary in a population of learners. In C. Knight, M. Studdert-Kennedy, and J. Hurford (eds), *The Evolutionary Emergence of Language: Social Function and the Origins of Linguistic Form*, Cambridge: Cambridge University Press, 303–23.

Kirby, S. 2001. Spontaneous evolution of linguistic structure: An iterated learning model of the emergence of regularity and irregularity, *IEEE Transactions on Evolutionary Computation* 5: 102–10.

Kirby, S. 2002. Learning, bottlenecks and the evolution of recursive syntax. In E. Briscoe (ed.), *Linguistic Evolution through Language Acquisition: Formal and Computational Models*, Cambridge: Cambridge University Press, 173–203.

Kirby, S. and J. R. Hurford. 2002. The emergence of linguistic structure: An overview of the iterated learning model. In A. Cangelosi and D. Parisi (eds), *Simulating the Evolution of Language*, Springer Verlag, 121–47.

Kirby, S., H. Cornish, and K. Smith. 2008. Cumulative cultural evolution in the laboratory: An experimental approach to the origins of structure in human language, *Proceedings of the National Academy of Sciences*, 105 (31): 10681–6.

Kirschbaum, I. 2002. Schrecklich nett und voll verrückt. Muster der Adjektiv-Intensivierung im Deutschen. Dissertation. Heinrich-Heine-Universität Düsseldorf. http://deposit.ddb.de/cgi-bin/dokserv?idn=969264437.

Kleiber, G. 1998. *Prototypensemantik*, Tübingen: Gunter Narr.

Klein, E. and I. A. Sag. 1985. Type-driven translation, *Linguistics and Philosophy* 8: 163–201.

Kobele, G. 2006. Generating Copies: An Investigation into Structural Identity in Language and Grammar. PhD thesis, Department of Linguistics, UCLA.

Koch, C. and T. Poggio. 1992. Multiplying with synapses and neurons. In T. McKenna, J. Davis, and S. F. Zornetzer (eds), *Single Neuron Computation*, Boston, MA: Academic Press.

Kölbel, M. 2004. Faultless disagreement, *Proceedings of the Aristotelian Society*, 104: 53–73.

König, P. and T. B. Schillen. 1991. Stimulus-dependent assembly formation of oscillatory responses: I. Synchronization, *Neural Computation* 3: 155–66.

König, P., A. K. Engel, and W. Singer. 1996. Integrator or coincidence detector? The role of the cortical neuron revisited, *Trends in Neurosciences* 19: 130–7.

Konorski, J. 1967. *Integrative Activity of the Brain; An Interdisciplinary Approach*, Chicago: University of Chicago Press.

Koopman, H. and D. Sportiche 1991. The position of subjects, in *Lingua*, 85(1): 211–58.

Koster-Moeller, J., J. Varvoutis, and M. Hackl. 2006. Processing evidence for quantifier raising: The case of antecedent contained deletion, in *Proceedings of the 17th Conference on Semantics and Linguistic Theory*, Cornell University: CLS Publications.

Kracht, M. 2001. Strict compositionality and literal movement grammar. In M. Moortgat (ed.), *Logical Aspects of Computational Linguistics*, Berlin: Springer LNAI.

Kracht, M. 2003. *The Mathematics of Language*, Berlin: Mouton de Gruyter.

Kracht, M. 2007. Compositionality: the very idea, *Research on Language and Computation* 5: 287–308.

Kracht, M. 2011. *Interpreted Language and Compositionality*, Berlin and Heidelberg: Springer.

Kratzer, A. 1993. On external arguments, *University of Massachusetts Amherst Occasional Papers* 17. Amherst, MA: GLSA, University of Massachusetts, 103–30.

Kratzer, A. 1996. Severing the external argument from its verb. In J. Rooryck and L. Zaring (eds), *Phrase Structure and the Lexicon*, Dordrecht: Kluwer Academic Publishers.

Kreisel, G. and J. Krivine. 1976. *Elements of Mathematical Logic. Model Theory*, no. 2 in Studies in logic and the foundations of mathematics, Amsterdam: North Holland.

Kreiser, L. 2001. *Gottlob Frege. Leben-Werk-Zeit*, Hamburg: Felix Meiner.

Kreiter, A. K. and W. Singer. 1994. Global stimulus arrangement determines synchronization of neuronal activity in the awake macaque monkey, Supplement *European Journal of Neuroscience* 7: 153.

Krifka, M. 1989. Nominal reference, temporal constitution, and quantification in event semantics. In J. van Benthem, R. Bartsch, and P. van Emde Boas (eds), *Semantics and Contextual Expression*, Dordrecht: Foris, 75–115.

Krifka, M. 1992a. Definite NPs aren't quantifiers, *Linguistic Inquiry* 23: 157–62.

Krifka, M. 1992b. Thematic relations as links between nominal reference and temporal constitution, in I. Sag and A. Szabolcsi (eds), *Lexical Matters*, CSLI Lecture Notes, Chicago, IL: University of Chicago Press.

Krifka, M. 1999. At least some determiners aren't determiners, in K. Turner (ed.), *The Semantics/Pragmatics Interface from Different Points of View*, Amsterdam: Elsevier Science B.V., 257–91.

Krifka, M. 2001a. Compositionality. In R. A. Wilson and F. Keil (eds), *The MIT Encyclopaedia of the Cognitive Sciences*, Cambridge, MA: MIT Press, 152–3.

Krifka, M. 2001b. For a structured meaning account of questions and answers. In C. Fery and W. Sternefeld (eds), *Audiatur Vox Sapientia. A Festschrift for Arnim von Stechow*, Berlin: Akademie Verlag, 287–319.

Krifka, M. 2004. Lexical representations and the nature of the dative alternation, *Korean Jounal of English Language and Linguistics* 4: 1–32.

Kripke, S. 1976. Is there a problem about substitutional quantification?, in G. Evans and J. H. McDowell (eds), *Truth and Meaning. Essays in semantics*, Oxford: Clarendon Press, 325–419.

Kripke, S. 1979. Speaker's reference and semantic reference, *Midwest Studies* 2: 255–76.

Kripke, S. 1980. *Naming and necessity*, Cambridge, MA: Harvard University Press.

Kuhn, W. 1990. *Untersuchungen zum Problem der seriellen Verben*, Tübingen: Niemeyer.

Kunda, Z., D. T. Miller, and T. Claire. 1990. Combining social concepts: The role of causal reasoning, *Cognitive Science* 14, 551–77.

Kuo, D. and C. Eliasmith. 2005. Integrating behavioral and neural data in a model of zebrafish network interaction, *Biological Cybernetics* 933: 178–87.

Kuperberg, G. R., A. Choi, N. Cohn, M. Paczynski and R. Jackendoff. 2010. Electrophysiological correlates of complement coercion, *Journal of Cognitive Neuroscience* 22, 2685–701.

Kupffer, M. 2008. An unintentional defense of the indeterminacy of meaning?, *Erkenntnis* 68: 225–38.

Kutas, M. and S. Hillyard. 1980. Reading senseless sentences: Brain potentials reflect semantic incongruity, *Science* 207: 203–5.

Kutas, M. and S. Hillyard. 1984. Brain potentials during reading reflect word expectancy and semantic association, *Nature* 307, 161–3.

Lachaux, J.-P., E. Rodriguez, J. Martinerie, and F. Varela. 1999. Measuring phase synchrony in brain signals, *Human Brain Mapping* 8, 194–208.

Lahav, R. 1989. Against compositionality: The case of adjectives, *Philosophical Studies* 57: 261–79.

Lakoff, G. 1970. Linguistics and natural logic, *Synthese* 22: 151–271.

Lakoff, G. 1971. On generative semantics, in D. Steinberg and L. Jakobovits (eds), *Semantics*, Cambrdige: Cambridge University Press, 232–96.

Lakoff, G. 1986. Classifiers as a reflection of the mind. In C. Craig (ed.), *Noun Classes and Categorization*, Amsterdam: Benjamin, 13–51.

Lakoff, G. 1987a. *Women, Fire, and Dangerous Things: What categories reveal about the mind*, Chicago: University of Chicago Press.

Lakoff, G. 1987b. Cognitive models and prototype theory. In E. Margolis, and S. Laurence (eds), *Concepts: Core Readings*, Cambridge, MA: MIT Press, 391–424.

Lakoff, G. and M. Johnson. 1980. *Metaphors we Live by*, Chicago, IL: University of Chicago Press.

Landau, B. 1982. Will the real grandmother please stand up? The psychological reality of dual meaning, *Journal of Psycholinguistic Research* 11: 47–62.

Langacker, R. W. 1986. An introduction to cognitive grammar,*Cognitive Science* 10: 1–40.

Langacker, R. W. 1987a. *Foundations of Cognitive Grammar: Vol. 1 Theoretical Prerequisites*. Stanford: Stanford University Press.

Langacker, R. W. 1987b. Nouns and verbs, *Language* 63: 53–94.

Langacker, R. W. 1990. *Concept, Image, and Symbol. The Cognitive Basis of Grammar*, Berlin: Mouton de Gruyter.

Larson, R. 1988. On the double object construction, *Linguistic Inquiry* 19: 335–91.

Larson, R. and G. Segal. 1995. *Knowledge of Meaning: An Introduction to Semantic Theory*, Cambridge: MIT Press.

Lasersohn, P. 2005. Context dependence, disagreement, and predicates of personal taste, *Linguistics and Philosophy*, 28: 643–86.

Laurier, D. 1996. Function, normality, and temporality. In M. Marion and R. S. Cohen (eds), *Québec Studies in the Philosophy of Science*, Dordrecht: Kluwer, 25–52.

Lawrence, S. and E. Margolis. 1999. Review of Jerry A. Fodor 'Concepts: Where Cognitive Science Went Wrong', *British Journal of Philosophy of Science* 50: 487–91.

Leech, G., P. Rayson, and A. Wilson. 2001. *Word Frequencies in Written and Spoken English: based on the British National Corpus*, London: Longman.

Lefebvre, C. and A.-M. Brousseau. 2002. *A Grammar of Fongbe*, Berlin: Mouton de Gruyter.

Leitgeb, H. 2005. Hodges' theorem does not account for determinacy of translation: a reply to Werning, *Erkenntnis* 62: 411–25.

Leslie, A. 1984. Spatiotemporal continuity and the perception of causation in infants, *Perception* 13: 287–305.

Levi, J. N. 1978. *The Syntax and Semantics of Complex Nominals*, New York: Academic Press.

Levin, B. 1993. *English Verb Classes and Alternations*, Chicago, IL: University of Chicago Press.

Levin, B. and M. Rappaport Hovav. 1991. Wiping the slate clean, *Cognition* 41: 123–51.

Levin, B. and M. Rappaport Hovav. 1995. *Unaccusativity: At the Syntax–Semantics Interface*, Cambridge, MA: MIT Press.

Levin, B. and M. Rappaport Hovav. 1999. Two structures for compositionally derived events. In T. Matthews and D. Strolovich (eds) *Semantics and linguistic theory* =SALT 9, Ithaca: Cornell Linguistics Circle Publishing, 199–223.

Levin, B. and M. Rappaport Hovav. 2005. *Argument Realization*, Cambridge: Cambridge University Press.

Levin, B. and M. Rappaport Hovav. 2007. Reflections on the complementarity of manner and result. Talk at ZAS Berlin, 21 November.

Lewis, D. 1970. General Semantics, *Synthese* 22: 18–67, reprinted in B. H. Partee (ed.)n *Montague Grammar*, New York: Academic Press Inc, 1976, 1–50.

Lewis, D. 1973. *Counterfactuals*, Cambridge, MA: Harvard University Press.

Lewis, D. K. 1975. Adverbs of quantification. In E. L. Keenan (ed.), *Formal Semantics of Natural Language*, Cambridge: Cambridge University Press, 3–15.

Lewis, D. 1979. Scorekeeping in a language game, *Journal of Philosophical Logic*, 8: 339–59.

Lewis, D. 1980. Index, context, and content. In S. Kanger and S. Öhman (eds), *Philosophy and Grammar*, Dordrecht: Reidel; reprinted in Lewis 1998, 21–44.

Lewis, D. 1986. *On the Plurality of Worlds*, Oxford: Blackwell.

Lewis, D. 1998. *Papers in Philosophical Logic*, Cambridge: Cambridge University Press.

Lewis, D. and S. Lewis. 1970. Holes, *Australasian Journal of Philosophy* 48, 206–12.

Lewis, D. and S. Lewis. 1996. Review of Casati and Varzi (1994), *Philosophical Review* 105, 77–9.

Li, Ming and Vitányi. 1997. *An Introduction to Kolmogorov Complexity and its Applications* 2nd edn, New York: Springer.

Li, X., P. Hagoort, and Y. Yang. 2008. Event-related potential evidence on the influence of accentuation in spoken discourse comprehension in Chinese, *Journal of Cognitive Neuroscience* 20: 906–15.

Li, Z. 2000. Pre-attentive segmentation in the primary visual cortex, *Spatial Vision* 131: 25–50.

Lieberman, E., J.-B. Michell, J. Jackson, T. Tang, and M. A. Nowak. 2007. Quantifying the evolutionary dynamics of language, *Nature* 449: 713–16.

Lively, S. E., D. B. Pisoni, and S. D. Goldinger. 1994. Spoken word recognition: Research and theory, in M. A. Gernsbacher (ed.), *Handbook of Psycholinguistics*, San Diego: Academic Press, 265–301.

Löbner, S. 1979. *Intensionale Verben und Funktionalbegriffe. Untersuchung zur Syntax und Semantik von* wechseln *und den vergleichbaren Verben des Deutschen*, Tübingen: Narr.

Löbner, S. 1987. Natural language and generalized quantifier theory, in P. Gärdenfors (ed.), *Generalized Quantifiers: linguistic and logical approaches*, Dordrecht: Reidel, 181–201.

Löbner, S. 1990. *Wahr neben Falsch. Duale Operatoren als die Quantoren natürlicher Sprache*, Tübingen: Niemeyer.

Löbner, S. 2000. Polarity in natural language: predication, quantification and negation in particular and characterizing sentences, *Linguistics and Philosophy* 23: 213–308.

Locke, J. 1968. *An essay concerning human understanding*, Cleveland, Ohio: World Publishing Co. Original publication 1690.

Longobardi, G. 1994. Reference and proper names, *Linguistic Inquiry* 25: 609–65.

Lotze, H. 1874. *Logik*, Leipzig: Hirzel. second edition 1880.

Luck, S. 2005. *An Introduction to the Event-Related Potential Technique*, Cambridge, MA: MIT Press.

Lyons, D. M. and M. A. Arbib. 1989. A formal model of computation for sensory-based robotics, *IEEE Transactions on Robotics and Automation* 5: 280–93.

Macdonald, C. and G. Macdonald. (eds), 1995. *Connectionism: Debates on Psychological Explanation*. Vol. 2. Oxford: Blackwell.

MacFarlane, J. 2003. Future contingents and relative truth. *The Philosophical Quarterly*, 53(212): 321–36.

MacFarlane, J. 2005. Making sense of relative truth, *Proceedings of the Aristotelian Society*, 105: 321–39.

MacFarlane, J. 2007. Relativism and disagreement, *Philosophical Studies*, 132(1): 17–31.

MacFarlane, J. 2008. Truth in the garden of forking paths. In García-Carpintero and Kölbel, 2008, 81–102.

MacFarlane, J. 2009. Nonindexical contextualism. *Synthese*, 166(2): 231–50.

Machery, E. 2005. Concepts are not a natural kind, *Philosophy of Science* 72: 444–67.

Machery, E. 2009. *Doing without Concepts*. New York: Oxford University Press.

MacNeilage, P. F. and B. L. Davis. 2005. The frame/content theory of evolution of speech: Comparison with a gestural origins theory, *Interaction Studies: Social Behavior and Communication in Biological and Artificial Systems* 6: 173–99.

Mahesh, K. I., K. P. Eiselt, and J. K. Holbrook. 1999. Sentence *Processing in Understanding: Interaction and Integration of Knowledge Sources*. In A. Ram and K. Moorman (ed.), *Understanding Language Understanding*, Cambridge, MA: MIT Press.

Mann, W. C. and S. A. Thompson. 1988. Rhetorical structure theory: Toward a functional theory of text organization, *Text* 8(3): 243–81.

Marantz, A. 1984. *On the Nature of Grammatical Relations*, Cambridge, MA: MIT Press.

Marantz, A. 1996. Cat as a phrasal idiom MS, MIT.

Marantz, A. 1997. No escape from syntax: Don't try morphological analysis in the privacy of your own lexicon, *University of Penn Working Papers in Linguistics*, 4(2).

Marcus, G. F. 1998a. Can connectionism save constructivism?, *Cognition* 66: 153–82.

Marcus, G. F. 1998b. Rethinking eliminative connectionism, *Cognitive Psychology* 37: 243–82.

Marcus, G. F. 2001. *The Algebraic Mind: Integrating Connectionism and Cognitive Science*, Cambridge, MA: MIT Press.

Marcus, G. F., S. Pinker, M. Ullman, M. Hollander, T. J. Rosen, and F. Xu. 1992. *Overregularization in Language Acquisition*, Chicago: University of Chicago Press.

Marcus, G. F., U. Brinkmann, H. Clahsen, R. Wiese, and S. Pinker. 1995. German inflection: The exception that proves the rule, *Cognitive Psychology* 29: 189–256.

Marcus, R. 1962. Interpreting quantification, *Inquiry* 5, 252–9.

Margolis, E. and S. Laurence. 1999*a*. *Concepts: Core Readings*, Cambridge, MA: MIT Press.

Margolis, E. and S. Laurence. 1999*b*. Concepts and cognitive science. In E. Margolis and S. Laurence (eds), *Concepts: Core Readings*, Cambridge, MA: MIT Press, 3–82.

Markman, A. B. and D. Gentner. 1993. Splitting the differences: A structural alignment view of similarity, *Journal of Memory and Language* 32: 517–35.

Marr, D. 1982. *Vision: A Computational Investigation into the Human Representation and Processing of Visual Information*, San Francisco: Freeman and Company.

Mates, B. 1950. Synonymity, *University of Calfornia Publications in Philosophy* 25, 201–226. Reprinted in L. Linsky (ed.) *Semantics and the Philosophy of Language*, Urbana: University of Illinois Press, 1952.

Mateu, J. 2005. Impossible primitives. In M. Werning et al. (eds), *The Compositionality of Meaning and Content: Foundational Issues*. Frankfurt: Ontos Press, 213–29.

Matushansky, O. 2006. Why rose is the rose: on the use of definite articles in names, *Empirical Issues in Syntax and Semantics* 6: 285–307.

May, R. 1977. The Grammar of Quantification. PhD Dissertation, Cambridge, MA: MIT.

Maye, A. 2003. Correlated neuronal activity can represent multiple binding solutions, *Neurocomputing* 52–54: 73–7.

Maye, A. and M. Werning. 2004. Temporal binding of non-uniform objects, *Neurocomputing* 58–60: 941–8.

Maye, A. and M. Werning. 2007. Neuronal synchronization: From dynamic feature binding to object representations, *Chaos and Complexity Letters* 22/3. 315–25.

Mazurkiewicz, A. 1975. Parallel recursive program schemes, in J. Becvar (ed.), *Mathematical Foundations of Computer Science* (4th. coll., Marianske Lazne), no. 32 in Lecture notes in computer science, Berlin: Springer, 75–87.

McCarthy, J. 1986. Application of circumscription to formalizing common-sense knowledge, *Artificial Intelligence* 13: 89–116.

McCawley, J. D. 1968. Lexical insertion in a transformational grammar without deep structure/*Chicago Linguistic Society* 4: 71–80.

McCawley, J. 1970. Where do noun phrases come from?", in R. Jacobs and P. Rosenbaum (eds), *Readings in English Transformational Grammar*, Waltham, MA: Ginn & Co., 166–83.

McCawley, J. D. 1971. Prelexical syntax. In R. O'Brien (ed.), *Report on the 22nd Roundtable Meeting on Linguistics and Language Studies*, Washington, DC: Georgetown University Press, 19–33.

McCawley, J. D. 1974. On identifying the remains of deceased clauses, *Language Research* 9: 73–85.

McCawley, J. 1981. The syntax and semantics of English relative clauses, *Lingua* 53: 99–149.

McClelland, J. L. and D. C. Plaut. 1999. Does generalization in infant learning implicate abstract algebra-like rules? *TRENDS in Cognitive Sciences* 3: 166–8.

McElree, B., M. Traxler, M. Pickering, R. Seely, and R. Jackendoff. 2001. Reading time evidence for enriched composition, *Cognition* 780010-0277 Print: B17–25.

McElree, B., G. Murphy, and T. Ochoa. 2006*a*. Time course of retrieving conceptual information: A speed–accuracy trade-off study, *Psychonomic Bulletin and Review* 13: 848–53.

McElree, B., L. Pylkkanen, M. Pickering, and M. Traxler. 2006*b*. A time course analysis of enriched composition, *Psychonomic Bulletin and Review* 131: 53–59.

McGinnis, M. 2002. On the systematic aspect of idioms, *Linguistic Inquiry* 33(4): 665–72.

McGonigle, B. O. and M. Chalmers. 2006. Ordering and executive functioning as a window on the evolution and development of cognitive systems, *International Journal of Comparative*

Psychology. Special issue on Development, Evolution and Comparative Psychology and development of cognitive systems 19, 241–67.

McLaughlin, B. 1992. The rise and fall of British emergentism. In A. Beckermann, H. Flohr, and J. Kim (eds), *Emergence or Reduction?*, Berlin: Walter de Gruyter, 49–93.

McLaughlin, B. P. 1993. The connectionism/classicism battle to win souls, *Philosophical Studies* 71: 163–90.

McLaughlin, B. 1995. Classical constituents in Smolensky's ICS Architecture. In M. L. D. Chiara, K. Doets, D. Mundici, and J. van Bentham (eds), *Structures and Norms in Science*, Dordrecht: Kluwer Academic Publishers.

McQueen, J. M. and A. Cutler. 1998. Morphology in word recognition. In A. Spencer and A. M. Zwicky (eds), *Handbook of Morphology*, Oxford: Blackwell, 406–27.

Medin, D. L. and M. M. Schaffer. 1978. Context theory of classification learning, *Psychological Review* 85: 207–38.

Medin, D. L. and E. J. Shoben. 1988. Context and structure in conceptual combination, *Cognitive Psychology* 20: 158–90.

Medin, D. L., R. L. Goldstone, and D. Gentner. 1993. Respects for similarity, *Psychological Review* 100: 254–78.

Mel, B. W. 1994. Information processing in dendritic trees, *Neural Computation*, 66: 1031–85.

Mervis, C. B., J. Catlin, and E. Rosch. 1976. Relationships among goodness-of-example, category norms and word frequency, *Bulletin of the Psychnomic Society* 7: 268–84.

Mesoudi, A., A. Whiten, and K. N. Laland. 2006. Towards a unified science of cultural evolution, *Behavioral and Brain Sciences* 29: 329–83.

Mill, J. S. 1843. *A system of logic, ratiocinative and inductive, being a connected view of the principles of evidence and the methods of scientific investigation*, London: Parker, Son, and Bourn. Reprinted in J. M. Robson (ed.), intro. by R. F. McRae, *Collected works of John Stuart Mill*, vol. 7–8, Toronto: University of Toronto Press, and London: Routledge & Kegan Paul, 1973–74. German translation: Mill 1877.

Mill, J. S. 1877. *System der deductiven und inductiven Logik : eine Darlegung der Principien wissenschaftlicher Forschung, insbesondere der Naturforschung* (2 vol.), Braunschweig. German transl. by J. Schiel.

Miller, G. and P. N. Johnson-Laird. 1976. *Language and Perception*, Cambridge, MA: Belknap Press of Harvard University Press.

Millikan, R. G. 1984. *Language, Thought, and Other Biological Categories*, Cambridge, MA: MIT Press.

Milner, H. J. 1975. Processes: a mathematical model of computing agents, in H. E. Rose and J. C. Shepherdson (eds), *Logic colloquium '73* (Bristol), no. 80 in Studies in logic and the foundations of mathematics, Amsterdam: North Holland, 157–73.

Mithen, S. 2005. *The Singing Neanderthals: The Origins of Music, Language, Mind and Body*, London: Weidenfeld and Nicholson.

Mohanan, T. 1997. Multidimensionality of Representation: NV Complex Predicates in Hindi, in A. Alsina, J. Bresnan, and P. Sells (eds), *Complex Predicates*, Stanford: CSLI, 431–71.

Monk, J. D. 1976. *Mathematical logic*, no. 37 in Graduate texts in mathematics, Berlin: Springer.

Montague, R. 1960. On the nature of certain philosophical entities, *The Monist* 53: 159–94. Reprinted in Montague 1974, 148–87.

Montague, R. 1968. Pragmatics. In R. Klibansky (ed.), *Contemporary Philosophy: A Survey*, Florence: La Nuova Italia Editrice, 102–22, Reprinted in Montague 1974, 95–118.

Montague, R. 1969. On the nature of certain philosophical entities, *Monist* 53: 159–95. Reprinted in Montague, 1974, 149–87.

Montague, R. 1970*a*. English as a Formal Language. In B. Visentini (ed.), *Linguaggi nella Società a nella Tecnica*. Mailand, 189–223. Reprinted in Montague, 1974, 188–221.

Montague, R. 1970*b*. Universal grammar. *Theoria* 36: 373–298. Reprinted in Montague, 1974, 222–46.

Montague, R. 1973. The Proper Treatment of Quantification in Ordinary English. In J. Hintikka, J. Moravcsik, and P. Suppes (eds), *Approaches to Natural Language*. Dordrecht: Reidel. Reprinted in Montague 1974, 247–270, and in Portner and Partee 2002, 17–35.

Montague, R. 1974. *Formal Philosophy: Selected Papers of Richard Montague*, New Haven and London: Yale University Press, ed. by Richmond H. Thomason.

Moortgat, M. 1993. Generalized quantifiers and discontinuous type constructors. In W. Sijtsma and A. van Horck (eds), *Discontinuous Constituency*, Berlin: Mouton de Gruyter.

Moravcsik, J. M. 1975. Aitia as generative factor in Aristotle's philosophy, *Dialogue*, 14: 622–36.

Moravcsik, J. M. 1990. *Thought and Language*, London: Routledge.

Morgan, J. 1969. On arguing about semantics. *Papers in Linguistics* 1: 49–70.

Moro, A. 2000. *Dynamic Antisymmetry*. Cambridge, MA: MIT Press.

Morrill, G. V. 1994. *Type Logical Grammar. Categorial Logic of Signs*, Dordrecht: Kluwer Academic Publishers.

Moss, H. E., L. K. Tyler, K. A. Dalrymple, and J. A. Hampton. 1997. When do rotten bananas go black? The time course of conceptual combination in noun phrases. Paper presented at the annual meeting of the Experimental Psychology Society, Oxford.

Müller-Olm, M. 1997. *Modular Compiler Verification*, no. 1283 in Lecture notes in computer science, Berlin: Springer.

Münte, T., K. Schiltz, and M. Kutas. 1998. When temporal terms belie conceptual order, *Nature* 395: 71–3.

Murphy, G. L. 1988. Comprehending complex concepts, *Cognitive Science* 12: 529–62.

Murphy, G. L. 1990. Noun phrase interpretation and conceptual combination, *Journal of Memory and Language* 29: 259–88.

Murphy, G. L. 2002. *The Big Book of Concepts*, Cambridge, MA: MIT Press.

Murphy, G. L. and D. L. Medin. 1985. The role of theories in conceptual coherence, *Psychological Review* 92: 289–316.

Muskens, R. 1989. A relational reformulation of the theory of types, *Linguistics and Philosophy* 12: 325–46.

Muskens, R. 1995. *Meaning and Partiality*. Stanford, CA: CSLI.

Muskens, R. 2001. Lambda Grammars and the syntax–semantics interface. In R. van Rooy and M. Stokhof (eds), *Proceedings of the Thirteenth Amsterdam Colloquium*, Amsterddam: ILLC/University of Amsterdam, 150–5.

Neale, S. 1995. The Philosophical Significance of Gödel's Slingshot. *Mind* 104: 761–825.

Neuholt, E. (ed.). 1978. Formal description of programming language concepts, Proceedings of the IFIP working conference on formal description of programming concepts, St. Andrews, Canada 1977, Amsterdam: North Holland.

Newmeyer, F. J. 1980. *Linguistic Theory in America: The First Quarter-Century of Transformational Generative Grammar*, New York: Academic Press.

Newmeyer, F. J. 1996. *Generative Linguistics. A historical perspective.*, London: Routledge.

Nida, E. A. 1951. A system for the description of semantic elements, *Word* 7: 1–14.

Nieuwland, M. and J. van Berkum. 2005. When peanuts fall in love: N400 evidence for the power of discourse, *Journal of Cognitive Neuroscience* 18, 1098–111.

Nosofsky, R. M. 1986. Attention, similarity, and the identification–categorization relationship, *Journal of Experimental Psychology: General* 115: 39–57.

Nowak, M. A., J. B. Plotkin, and V. A. A. Jansen. 2000. The evolution of syntactic communication, *Nature* 404: 495–8.

Nunberg, G. 1979. The non-uniqueness of semantic solutions: Polysemy, *Linguistics and Philosophy* 3: 143–84.

Nunberg, G., I. A. Sag, and T. Wasow. 1994. Idioms, *Language* 70: 491–538.

O'Connor, T. and H. Y. Wong. 2006. Emergent properties. In E. N. Zalta (ed.), *The Stanford Encyclopedia of Philosophy*.

O'Grady, W. 2008. The emergentist program, *Lingua* 118: 447–64.

Oehrle, R. 1976. *The Grammatical Status of the English Dative Alternation*, Doctoral dissertation, Cambridge, MA: MIT.

Oehrle, R. T. 1988. Multi-dimensional compositional functionsas a basis for grammatical analysis. In E. Bach, R. T. Oehrle, and D. Wheeler (eds), *Categorial Grammars and Natural Language Structures*, Dordrecht: Reidel, 349–89.

Okasha, S. 2000. Holism about meaning and about evidence: In defence of W. V. Quine, *Erkenntnis* 52, 39–61.

Osgood, C., G. Suci, and P. Tannenbaum. 1957. *The Measurement of Meaning*. Urbana: University of Illinois Press.

Osherson, D. N. 1978. Three conditions on conceptual naturalness, *Cognition* 6: 263–89.

Osherson, D. N. and E. E. Smith. 1981. On the adequacy of prototype theory as a theory of concepts, *Cognition* 9: 35–58.

Osherson, D. N. and E. E. Smith. 1982. Gradedness and conceptual conjunction, *Cognition* 12: 299–318.

Osherson, D. N. and E. E. Smith. 1997. On typicality and vagueness, *Cognition* 64: 189–206.

Osterhout, L. and P. Holcomb. 1992. Event-related brain potentials elicited by syntactic anomaly, *Journal of Memory and Language* 31: 785–806.

Ouattara, K., A. Lemasson, and K. Zuberbühler. 2009. Campbell's Monkeys Use Affixation to Alter Call Meaning. *PLoS ONE* 4(11): e7808.

Ozyürek, A., R. Willems, S. Kita, and P. Hagoort. 2007. On-line integration of semantic information from speech and gesture: Insights from event-related brain potentials, *Journal of Cognitive Neuroscience* 19: 605–16.

Pagin, P. 1997. Is compositionality compatible with holism? *Mind and Language* 12, 11–33.

Pagin, P. 2003. Communication and strong compositionality, *Journal of Philosophical Logic* 32: 287–322.

Pagin, P. 2005. Compositionality and context. In G. Preyer and G. Peter (eds), *Contextualism in Philosophy: Knowledge, Meaning, and Truth*, Oxford: Clarendon Press, 303–48.

Pagin, P. 2006. Meaning holism. In E. Lepore and B. Smith (eds), *The Oxford Handbook of Philosophy of Language*, Oxford: Oxford University Press, 213–31.

Pagin, P. 2008a. Belief sentences and quotation with generalized compositionality. Presentation at the Logos Seminar, Barcelona.

Pagin, P. 2008b. Compositionality, computability, and complexity. Draft. Earlier version presented at the Compositionality Series of lectures, Rutgers University, 2007.

Pagin, P. and J. Pelletier. 2007. Context, content and composition. In G. Preyer and G. Peter (eds), *Context-Sensitivity and Semantic Minimalism*, Oxford: Clarendon Press, 25–62.

Pagin, P. and D. Westerståhl. 2010*a*. Compositionality I: Definitions and Variants, *Philosophy Compass* 5(3): 250–64.

Pagin, P. and D. Westerståhl. 2010*b*. Compositionality II: Arguments and Problems, *Philosophy Compass* 5: 265–82.

Pagin, P. and D. Westerståhl. 2010*c*. Pure quotation and general compositionality, *Linguistics and Philosophy* 33: 381–415.

Palmer, S. 1999. *Vision Science: Photons to phenomenology*, Cambridge, MA: MIT Press.

Parisien, C. C., H. Anderson, and C. Eliasmith. 2008. Solving the problem of negative synaptic weights in cortical models, *Neural Computation* 20: 1473–94.

Parsons, T. 1970. Some problems concerning the logic of grammatical modifiers, *Synthese* 21: 320–34.

Parsons, T. 1990. *Events in the Semantics of English*, Cambridge, MA: MIT Press.

Partee, B. 1974. Opacity and scope. In M. K. Munitz and P. K. Unger (eds), *Semantics and Philosophy*, New York: New York University Press, 81–101.

Partee, B. H. 1975. Comments on C. J. Fillmore's and N. Chomsky's Papers. In R. Austerlitz (ed.), *The Scope of American Linguistics*, Lisse: Peter de Ridder Press, 197–209.

Partee, B. H. 1976. Some transformational extensions of Montague Grammar, in B. Partee (ed.), *Montague Grammar*. New York: Academic Press, 51–76.

Partee, B. H. 1984. Compositionality, in F. Landman and F. Veltman (eds), *Varieties of Formal Semantics*, no. 3 in GRASS, Dordrecht: Foris, 281–311. Reprinted in Partee 2004, 153–81.

Partee, B. H. 1986. Noun phrase interpretation and type-shiftingrules. In J. Groenendijk, D. de Jong, and M. Stokhof (eds), *Discourse Representation Theory and the Theory of Generalized Quanifiers*, Dordrecht: Foris, 115–43.

Partee, B. H. 2004. *Compositionality in Formal Semantics. Selected papers by Barbara H. Partee*, no. 1 in Explorations in semantics, Malden, USA: Blackwell.

Partee, B. and E. Bach. 1981. Quantification, pronouns, and VP anaphora, in J. Groenendijk, T. Janssen, and M. Stokhof (eds), *Formal Approaches to the Study of Language: Proceedings of the Third Amsterdam Colloquium*, Amsterdam: Mathematisch Centrum, 445–81.

Partee, B. and M. Rooth. 1983. Generalized conjunction and type ambiguity, in R. Bauerle et al. (eds), *Meaning, Use, and the Interpretation of Language*, Berlin: de Gruyter, 361–83.

Partee, B., A. ter Meulen, and R. Wall. 1990. *Mathematical Methods in Linguistics*, Dordrecht: Kluwer Academic Publishers.

Patalano, A. L., S. Chin-Parker, and B. H. Ross. 2006. The importance of being coherent: Category coherence, cross-classification, and reasoning, *Journal of Memory and Language* 54: 407–24.

Patterson, D. E. 2005. Learnability and compositionality, *Mind and Language* 20 (3): 326–52.

Patterson, K., M. A. Lambon Ralph, J. R. Hodges, and J. L. McClelland. 2001. Deficits in irregular past-tense verb morphology associated with degraded semantic knowledge, *Neuropsychologia* 39: 709–24.

Pearl, J. 1988. *Probabilistic Reasoning in Intelligent Systems*, Santa Mateo: Morgan Kaufmann.

Pelletier, F. J. 1994*a*. The principle of semantic compositionality, *Topoi* 13, 11–24. Reprinted, with additions, in S. Davis and B. Gillon, *Semantics: A Reader*, Oxford University Press, Oxford, 2004, 133–56.

Pelletier, F. J. 1994*b*. Semantic compositionality: The argument from synonymy. In R. Casati, B. Smith, and G. White (eds), *Philosophy and the Cognitive Sciences*, Vienna: Hölder-Pichler-Tempsky, 283–95.

Pelletier, F. J. 2000*a*. Did Frege believe Frege's principle? *Journal of Logic, Language, and Information* 10, 87–114. See www.sfu.ca/jeffpell, extended version of Pelletier 2001, last accessed 1 February 2009.

Pelletier, F. J. 2000*b*. Semantic compositionality: Free algebras and the argument from ambiguity. In M. Feller, S. Kaufmann, and M. Pauly (eds), *Formalizing the Dynamics of Information*, Stanford: CSLI Press, pp. 207–18.

Pelletier, F. J. 2001. Did Frege believe Frege's principle?, *Journal for Logic, Language and Information* 10(1): 87–114.

Pelletier, F. J. 2003. Context-dependence and compositionality, *Mind and Language* **18**: 148–61.

Penke, M. 2006. *Flexion im mentalen Lexikon*. [Inflectional Morphology in the Mental Lexicon], Tübingen: Niemeyer.

Penke, M. 2008. Morphology and language disorder. In M. Ball, M. Perkins, N. Mueller, and S. Howard (eds), *The Handbook of Clinical Linguistics*, Oxford: Blackwell, 212–27.

Penke, M. and M. Krause. 2004. Regular and irregular inflectional morphology in German Williams syndrome. In S. Bartke, and J. Siegmüller (eds), *Williams Syndrome across Languages*, Amsterdam: Benjamins, 245–70.

Penke, M. and A. Rosenbach. 2007. What counts as evidence in linguistics? An Introduction. In M. Penke, and A. Rosenbach (eds), *What Counts as Evidence in Linguistics—the Case of Innateness*, Amsterdam: Benjamins, 1–50.

Penke, M. and G. Westermann. 2006. Broca's area and inflectional morphology: Evidence from Broca's aphasia and computer modeling, *Cortex* 42: 563–76.

Penke, M., U. Janssen, and M. Krause. 1999. The representation of inflectional morphology: evidence from Broca's aphasia, *Brain and Language* 68: 225–32.

Perry, J. 1986. Thought without representation, *Supplementary Proceedings of the Aristotelian Society* 60: 137–52, Reprinted in Perry, *The Problem of the Essential Indexical and Other Essays*, Oxford: Oxford University Press, 1993, 205–18.

Pesetsky, D. 1995. *Zero Syntax: Experiencers and Cascades*, Cambridge, MA: MIT Press.

Petersen, W. 2007. Decomposing concepts with frames, in J. Skilters, F. Toccafondi, and G. Stemberger (eds), *Complex Cognition and Qualitative Science. The Baltic International Yearbook of Cognition, Logic and Communication*, University of Latvia. Vol. 2, 151–70.

Petersen, W. and M. Werning. 2007. Conceptual fingerprints: Lexical decomposition by means of frames—a neuro-cognitive model. In U. Priss, S. Polovina, and R. Hill (eds), *Conceptual Structures: Knowledge architectures for smart applications LNAI 4604*, Heidelberg: Springer-Verlag, 415–28.

Pfeifer, N., and G. D. Kleiter. 2005. Coherence and non-monotonicity in human reasoning, *Synthese* 146 (1–2): 93–109.

Pfeifer, N. and G. D. Kleiter. 2008. The conditional in mental probability logic, to appear in: M Oaksford (ed.), *The Psychology of Conditionals*, Oxford University Press, Oxford, 153–73.

Phillips, D. 1976. *Holistic Thought in Social Science*, Stanford: Stanford University Press.

Philosophical Perspectives. 2008. Special issue: Philosophy of Language, vol. 22.

Piaget, J. 1980. The psychogenesis of knowledge and its epistemological significance. In M. Piattelli-Palmarini (ed.), *On Language and Learning: The Debate between Jean Piaget and Noam Chomsky*, London: Routledge and Kegan Paul, 23–34.

Pierce, B. 2002. *Types and Programming Languages*, Cambridge, MA: MIT Press.

Pietroski, P. 1998. Actions, adjuncts, and agency, *Mind* 107: 73–111.

Pietroski, P. 2002. *Events and Semantic Architecture*, Oxford: Oxford University Press (2nd edition 2005).

Pietroski, P. 2003. Small verbs, complex events. In L. Antony and H. Hornstein (eds), *Chomsky and His Critics*, New York: Blackwell.

Pietroski, P. 2005. *Events and their Architecture*, Oxford: Oxford University Press.

Pietroski, P. 2006*a*. Interpreting concatenation and concatenates, *Philosophical Issues* 16: 221–45.

Pietroski, P. 2006*b*. Induction and comparison, *Maryland Working Papers in Linguistics*, 15: 157–90.

Pietroski, P. 2011. Minimal semantic instructions. In C. Boeckx (ed.), *The Oxford Handbook of Linguistic Minimalism*, Oxford: Oxford University Press, 472–98.

Pietroski, P. Forthcoming. Lexicalizing and combining.

Piñango, M., E. Zurif, and R. Jackendoff. 1999. Real-time processing implications of enriched composition at the syntax–semantics interface, *Journal of Psycholinguistic Research* 28: 395–414.

Piñango, M., A. Winnick, R. Ullah, and E. Zurif. 2006. The time course of semantic composition: The case of aspectual coercion, *Journal of Psycholinguistic Research* 35: 233–44.

Pinker, S. 1984. *Language Learnability and Language Development*. Cambridge, MA: Harvard University Press.

Pinker, S. 1989. *Learnability and Cognition*, Cambridge, MA: MIT Press.

Pinker, S. 1994. *The Language Instinct: How the Mind Creates Language*, New York: William Morrow and Company.

Pinker, S. 1997. Words and rules in the human brain, *Nature* 387: 547–8.

Pinker, S. 1999. *Words and Rules*, New York: Basic Books.

Pinker, S. 2002. *The Blank Slate: The Modern Denial of Human Nature*, New York: Viking.

Pinker, S. and Bloom, P. 1990. Natural language and natural selection. *Behavioral and Brain Sciences* 13(4): 707–84.

Pinker, S. and J. Mehler (eds). 1989. *Connections and Symbols*, Cambridge, MA: MIT Press.

Pinker, S. and A. Prince. 1988. On language and connectionism: Analysis of a parallel distributed processing model of language acquisition, *Cognition* 28: 73–193.

Plate, T. 1995. Holographic reduced representations, *IEEE Transactions on Neural Networks*, 63: 623–41.

Plate, T. 2003. *Holographic Reduced Representations*, Stanford, CA: CSLI Publication.

Plaut, D. C. and L. G. Gonnerman. 2000. Are non-semantic morphological effects incompatible with a distributed connectionist approach to lexical processing? *Language and Cognitive Processes* 15: 445–85.

Polanyi, L. 1985. A theory of discourse structure and discourse coherence. In W. H. Eilfort, P. D. Kroeberger, and K. L. Peterson (eds), *Papers from the General Session at the Twenty-First Regional Meeting of the Chicago Linguistics Society*, Chicago.

Pollack, J. 1990. Recursive distributed representations, *Artificial Intelligence* 46: 77–105.

Pollard, C. 1984. Generalized Phrase Structure Grammars, Head Grammars, and Natural Language. PhD Dissertation, Stanford University, Stanford, CA.

Pollock, J. 1989. Verb movement, Universal Grammar, and the structure of IP, *Linguistic Inquiry* 20: 365–424.

Portner, P. and Partee, B. (eds). 2002. *Formal Semantics: the essential readings*, Oxford: Blackwell.

Posner, M. I. and S. W. Keele. 1968. On the genesis of abstract ideas, *Journal of Experimental Psychology* 77: 353–363.

Pothos, E.M. 2005. The rules versus similarity distinction, *Behavioral and Brain Sciences* 28: 1–49.

Potts, C. 2007. The dimensions of quotation. In C. Barker and P. Jacobson (eds), *Direct Compositionality*, Oxford: Oxford University Press, 405–31.

Prasada, S. and S. Pinker. 1993. Generalization of regular and irregular morphological patterns, *Language and Cognitive Processes* 8: 1–51.

Pratt, V. R. 1979. Dynamic logic, in J. W. de Bakker and J. van Leeuwen (eds), *Foundations of computer science III, part 2, Languages, logic, semantics*, no. 100 in CWI Tracts, Amsterdam: Centre for Mathematics and Computer science, 53–82.

Prinz, J. J. 2002. *Furnishing the Mind: Concepts and their perceptual basis*. Cambridge, MA: MIT Press.

Prosoporov, O. 2005. Compositionality and contextuality as adjoint principles, in E. Machery, M. Werning and G. Schurz (eds), *The Compositionality of Meaning and Content*. Vol. II Applications to linguistics, psychology and neuroscience, Frankfurt: Ontos Verlag, 149–75.

Pullum, G. and B. Scholz. 2007. Systematicity and natural language syntax, *Croatian Journal of Philosophy* 7, 375–402.

Pullum, G. K. and B. C. Scholz. 2002. Empirical assessment of stimulus poverty arguments, *The Linguistic Review* 19: 9–50.

Pulvermüller, F. 2005. Brain mechanisms linking language and action, *Nature Reviews Neuroscience* 67. 576–82.

Pustejovsky, J. 1991a. The generative lexicon, *Computational Linguistics* 17: 409–41.

Pustejovsky, J. 1991b. The syntax of event structure, *Cognition* 41: 47–81.

Pustejovsky, J. 1995. *The Generative Lexicon*. Cambridge, MA: MIT Press.

Pustejovsky, J. 2011. *The Multiplicity of Meaning*, Cambridge, MA: MIT Press.

Pustejovsky, J. and E. Jezek. 2008. Semantic coercion in language: Beyond distributional analysis, *Italian Journal of Linguistics* 20(1): 181–214.

Pustejovsky, J. and A. Rumshisky. 2008. Between chaos and structure: Interpreting lexical data through a theoretical lens, *International Journal of Lexicography* 21(3): 337–55.

Pustejovsky, J. and A. Rumshisky. 2010. Mechanisms of sense extensions in verbs, in G.-M. de Schryver (ed.) *A Way with Words: Recent Advances in Lexical Theory and Analysis. A Festscrhift for Patrick Hanks*, Gent, Kampala: Menha Publishers.

Putnam, H. 1954. Synonymity, and the analysis of belief sentences, *Analysis* 14: 114–22.

Pylkkäen, L., R. Llinas, and B. McElree. 2007. An MEG study of silent meaning, *Journal of Cognitive Neuroscience* 19(11): 1905–21.

Qu, Wei and Ming an Han. 2004. *Dictionary of Contemporary Chinese New Words*, Beijing: China Encyclopedia Publishing House.

Quartz, S. R. and T. J. Sejnowski. 1997. The neural basis of cognitive development: a constructivist manifesto, *Behavioral and Brain Sciences* 20: 537–96.

Quine, W. V. O. 1951. Two dogmas of empiricism, *Philosophical Review* 60, 20–43.

Quine, W. V. O. 1956. Quantifiers and propositional attitudes, *Journal of Philosophy* 53: 177–87.

Quine, W. V. O. 1960. *Word and Object*, Cambridge, MA: MIT Press.

Quine, W. V. O. 1963. On what there is. In *From a Logical Point of View*, New York: Harper and Row.

Ramchand, G. 2008. *Verb Meaning and the Lexicon: A first phase syntax*, Cambridge: Cambridge University Press.

Ranta, A. 1994. *Type-Theoretical Grammar*, Oxford: Oxford University Press.

Rapp, I. and A. von Stechow. 1999 Fast 'almost' and functional heads, *Journal of Semantics* 16: 149–204.

Rappaport Hovav, M. and B. Levin. 2008. The English dative alternation: The case for verb sensitivity, *Journal of Linguistics* 44: 129–67.

Recanati, F. 2004. *Literal Meaning*. Cambridge: Cambridge University Press.

Recanati, F. 2007. *Perspectival Thought. A Plea for (Moderate) Relativism*, Oxford: Oxford University Press.

Recanati, F. 2011. Compositionality, flexibility, and context-dependence. In this volume.

Reichenbach, H. 1947. *Elements of Symbolic Logic*, London: Macmillan.

Reiter, R. 1980. A logic for default reasoning, *Artificial Intelligence* 13: 81–132.

Reiter, R. 1987. Non-monotonic reasoning, *Annual Review of Computer Science* 2: 147–86.

Rescher, N. (ed.) 1967. *The Logic of Decision and Action*, Pittsburgh: Pittsburgh University Press.

Resnik, M. D. 1967. The context principle in Frege's philosophy, *Philosophy and Phenomenological Research* 27: 356–65.

Resnik, M. D. 1976. Frege's context principle revisited, in M. Schirn (ed.), *Studien zu Frege III: Logik und Semantik*, Stuttgart: Frommann-Holzboog, 35–49.

Resnik, M. D. 1979. Frege as idealist and then realist, *Inquiry* 22: 350–7.

Rey, G. 1983. Concepts and stereotypes, *Cognition* 15, 237–62.

Richards, N. 2001. An idiomatic argument for lexical decomposition, *Linguistic Inquiry* 321: 183–92.

Ridley, M. 1993. *Evolution*, Oxford: Blackwell Scientific Publications.

Riehle, A., S. Grün, and A. Aertsen. 1997. Spike synchronization and rate modulation differentially involved in motor cortical functions, *Science* 278: 1950–3.

Rieke, F., D. Warland, R. de Ruyter van Steveninick, and W. Bialek. 1997. *Spikes: Exploring the neural code*, Cambridge, MA: MIT Press.

Rips, L. J. 1975. Inductive judgements about natural categories, *Journal of Verbal Learning and Verbal Behavior* 14: 665–81.

Rips, L. J. 1989. Similarity, typicality, and categorization. In S. Vosniadou and A. Ortony (eds), *Similarity and Analogical Reasoning*, Cambridge: Cambridge University Press.

Rips, L. J. 1995. The current status of research on conceptual combination. *Mind and Language* 10: 72–104.

Rips, L. J., F. J. Shoben, and E. F. Smith. 1973. Semantic distance and the verification of semantic relations, *Journal of Verbal Learning and Verbal Behavior* 12, 1–20.

Robbins, P. S. 2002. How to blunt the sword of compositionality, *Noûs* 36: 313–34.

Robbins, P. 2005. The myth of reverse compositionality, *Philosophical Studies* 125: 251–75.

Robbins, P. 2007. Minimalism and modularity. In G. Preyer and G. Peter (eds), *Context-Sensitivity and Semantic Minimalism*, Oxford: Oxford University Press.

Roelfsema, P. R., A. K. Engel, P. König, and W. Singer. 1997. Visuomotor integration is associated with zero time-lag synchronization among cortical areas, *Nature* 385, 157–61.

Rooth, M. 1985. Association with focus. Dissertation, University of Massachusetts, Amherst.

Rosch, E. R. 1973. On the internal structure of perceptual and semantic categories. In T. E. Moore (ed.), *Cognitive Development and the Acquisition of Language*, New York: Academic Press.

Rosch, E. R. 1975. Cognitive representations of semantic categories, *Journal of Experimental Psychology: General* 104: 192–232.

Rosch, E. R. 1978. Principles of categorization. In E. Rosch and B. B. Lloyd (eds), *Cognition and Categorization*, Hillsdale, NJ: Erlbaum.

Rosch, E. R. and C. B. Mervis. 1975. Family resemblances: studies in the internal structure of categories, *Cognitive Psychology* 7: 573–605.

Rosch, E. R., C. Simpson, and R. S. Miller. 1976a. Structural bases of typicality effects, *Journal of Experimental Psychology: Human Perception and Performance* 2: 491–502.

Rosch, E., C. B. Mervis, W. D. Gray, D. M. Johnson, and P. Boyes-Bream. 1976b. Basic objects in natural categories, *Cognitive Psychology* 8: 382–429.

Rosen, C. 1997. Auxiliation and serialization: On discerning the difference. In A. Alsina, J. Bresnan, and P. Sells (eds), *Complex Predicates*, Stanford, CA: CSLI Publications, 175–202.

Rosier-Catach, I. 1999. La notion de translation, le principe de compositonalité et l'analyse de la prédiction aceidentelle chez Abélard, in J. Biard (ed.), *Langage, Sciences, Philosophie au XIIe siècle*, Paris: Vrin, 125–64.

Ross, J. R. 1969. Auxiliaries as main verbs, in W. Todd (ed.), *Studies in Philosophical Linguistics* (Series 1), Evanston, Ill: Great Expectations Press.

Ross, J. R. 1972. Act. In D. Davidson and G. Harman (eds), *Semantics of Natural Language*, Dordrecht: Reidel, 70–126.

Ross, J. R. 1976. To have have and to not have have, in M. A. Jazayery, E. C. Polomé and W. Winter (eds), *Linguistic and Literary Studies in Honor of Archibald A. Hill I*, The Hague: Mouton, 263–70.

Rott, H. 2000. Fregean elucidations, *Linguistics and Philosophy* 23: 621–41.

Rumelhart, D. 1979. Some problems with the notion of literal meanings. In A. Ortony (ed.), *Metaphor and Thought*, Cambridge: Cambridge University Press (2nd edn, 1993), 71–82.

Rumelhart, D. E. and J. L. McClelland. 1986a. PDP models and general issues in cognitive science, in D. Rumelhart, J. L. McClelland, and PDP Research Group (eds), *Parallel Distributed Processing: Explorations in the Microstructure of Cognition, Vol. 1: Foundations*, Cambridge, MA: MIT Press.

Rumelhart, D. E. and J. L. McClelland. 1986b. On learning the past tenses of English verbs, in D. E. Rumelhart, J. L. McClelland, and the PDP Research Group (eds), *Parallel Distributed Processing: Explorations in the Microstructure of Cognition. Vol. 2: Psychological and Biological Models*, Cambridge, MA: MIT Press, 216–71.

Rumelhart, D. E., G. E. Hinton, and R. J. Williams. 1986a. Learning Internal Representations by Error Propagation. In D. E. Rumelhart, J. L. McClelland, and the PDP Research Group, *Parallel Distributed Processing*, Volume 1 Cambridge, MA: MIT Press. 318–62.

Rumelhart, D. E., J. L. McClelland, and the PDP Research Group (eds). 1986b. *Parallel Distributed Processing: Explorations in the Microstructure of Cognition*. Vols 1 and 2. Cambridge, MA: MIT Press.

Russell, B. 1905. On denoting, *Mind*, 14. Reprinted in A. P. Martinich (ed.), *The Philosophy of Language* 4th edn. Oxford: Oxford University Press, 2001: 212–20.

Russell, B. 1918. Lectures on logical atomism. In R. Marsh (ed.), *Logic and Knowledge: Essays 1901–1950*, London: Allen & Unwin. Marsh collection published 1956; page references to those in Marsh.

Russell, B. 2006. Against grammatical computation of scalar implicatrues, *Journal of Semantics* 23: 361–82.

Ryle, G. 1957. The theory of meaning, in C. A. Mace (ed.), *British Philosophy in the Mid-century*, Allen & Unwin, 239–64.

Sabo, W. D. and J. J. Prinz, in progress. When are prototypes compositional? University of North Carolina, Chapel Hill.

Saffran, J. R. R. N. Aslin, and E. L. Newport. 1996. Statistical learning by eight-month-old infants, *Science* 274: 1926–8.

Sag, I. 1976. Deletion and Logical Form. PhD Dissertation, MIT, Cambrdige, MA.

Sag, I. 1981. Formal semantics and extralinguistic context. In P. Cole (ed.) *Radical Pragmatics*, New York: Academic Press, 273–94.

Salari, N. and A. Maye. 2008. *Brain Waves: How synchronized neuronal oscillations can explain the perception of illusory objects*, Hamburg: VDM Verlag.

Salinas, E. and T. J. Sejnowski. 2001. Correlated neuronal activity and the flow of neural information, *Nature Reviews Neuroscience* 2, 529–50.

Sandu, G. and J. Hintikka. 2001. Aspects of compositionality, *Journal of Logic, Language and Information* 10: 49–61.

Sanford, A. 2002. Context, attention and depth of processing during interpretation, *Mind and Language* 17: 188–206.

Sanford, A. and P. Sturt. 2002. Depth of processing in language comprehension: Not noticing the evidence, *Trends in Cognitive Sciences* 6, 382–6.

Saussure, F. de. 1916. Cours de linguistique générale. Translated by Roy Harris as F. de Saussure: *Course in General Linguistics*, Chicago: Open Court, 1986. Page references to this translation.

Schank, R. C. 1972. Conceptual dependency: A theory of natural language understanding, *Cognitive Psychology* 3, 532–631.

Schein, B. 1993. *Plurals*, Cambridge, MA: MIT Press.

Schein, B. 2001. Adverbial, descriptive reciprocals. In R. Hastings et al., *Proceedings of Semantics and Linguistic Theory XI*, Ithaca: CLC Publications.

Schein, B. Forthcoming. *Conjunction Reduction Redux*, Cambridge, MA: MIT Press.

Schiffer, S. R. 1987. *The Remnants of Meaning*, Cambridge, MA: The MIT Press.

Schiffer, S. R. 2003. *The Things we Mean*, Oxford: Oxford University Press.

Schillen, T. B. and P. König. 1991. Stimulus-dependent assembly formation of oscillatory responses: II. Desynchronization, *Neural Computation* 3: 167–78.

Schillen, T. B. and P. König. 1994. Binding by temporal structure in multiple feature domains of an oscillatory neuronal network, *Biological Cybernetics* 70, 397–405.

Schlenker, P. 2003. A plea for monsters, *Linguistics and Philosophy*, 26: 29–120.

Schlick, M. 1918. *General Theory of Knowledge*, New York: Springer-Verlag. Translated by A. E. Blumberg; published 1974.

Scholl, B. and P. Tremoulet. 2000. Perceptual causality and animacy, *Trends in Cognitive Science* 4: 299–309.

Scholz, B. C. and G. K. Pullum. 2002. Searching for arguments to support linguistic nativism, *The Linguistic Review* 19: 185–223.

Scholz, O. R. 1999. *Verstehen un Rationalität. Untersuchungen zu den Grundlagen von Hermeneutik und Sprachphilosophie*, no. 76 in Philosophische Abhandlungen, Frankfurt am Main, Klostermann.

Scholz, O. R. 2001*a*. Jenseits der Legende—Auf Suche nach den genuinen Leistungen Schleiermachers für die allgemeine Hermeneutik, in J. Schröder (ed.), *Theorie der Interpretation van Humanismus bis zur Romantik—Rechtswissenschaft, Pilosophie, Theologie*, Stuttgart: Franz Steiner, 168–88.

Scholz, O. R. 2001*b*. Wittgensteins Holismus: Sätze, Sprachspiele, Lebensformen, in U. Meixner and A. Newen (eds), *Grundlagen der analytische Philosophy*, Vol. 4 of Philosophiegeschichte und logische Analyse/Logical analysis and history of philosophy, Paderborn: Mentis, 173–88.

Schreuder, R. and H. Baayen. 1995. Modeling morphological processing, in L. B. Feldman (ed.), *Morphological Aspects of Language Processing*, Hillsdale, NJ: Lawrence Erlbaum, 131–54.

Schubert, L. 2000. The situations we talk about. In J. Minker (ed.), *Logic-Based Artificial Intelligence*, Dordrecht: Kluwer Academic Publishers, 407–39.

Schütte, K. 1977. *Proof Theory*, no. 225 in Grundlehren der mathematische wissenschaften, Berlin: Springer.

Schurz, G. 1998. Probabilistic semantics for Delgrande's Conditional Logic, *Artificial Intelligence* 102: 81–95.

Schurz, G. 2001a. What is normal? An evolution-theoretic foundation of normic laws and their relation to statistical normality, *Philosophy of Science* 28: 476–97.

Schurz, G. 2001b. Kinds of rationality and their role in evolution. In B. B. Brogaard and B. Smith (eds), *Rationality and Irrationality*, Vienna: öbv and hpt, 301–10.

Schurz, G. 2002. Ceteris paribus laws: Classification and deconstruction, *Erkenntnis* 57: 351–72.

Schurz, G. 2004. Normic laws, nonmonotonic reasoning, and the unity of science. In S. Rahman (eds), *Logic, Epistemology, and the Unity of Science*, Kluwer: Dordrecht, 181–211.

Schurz, G. 2005a. Non-monotonic reasoning from an evolutionary viewpoint: Ontic, logical and cognitive foundations, *Synthese* 146: 37–51.

Schurz, G. 2005b. Semantic holism and (non-)compositionality in scientific theories. In M. Werning, E. Machery, and G. Schurz (eds), *The Compositionality of Meaning and Content. Vol. 1: Foundational Issues*, Frankfurt: Ontos Verlag, 271–84.

Schurz, G. 2007. Human conditional reasoning explained by non-monotonicity and probability: An evolutionary account. In S. Vosniadou et al. (eds), *Proceedings of EuroCogSci07. The European Cognitive Science Conference 2007*, New York: Lawrence Erlbaum Assoc., 628–33.

Schuster, H. G. and P. Wagner. 1990. A model for neuronal oscillations in the visual cortex, *Biological Cybernetics* 64: 77–82.

Schwarz, B. 2006. Attributive *wrong*. In D. Baumer et al. (eds), *Proceedings of the 25th West Coast Conference on Formal Linguistics*. Somerville, MA, 362–70. http://www.lingref.com/cpp/wccfl/25/paper1469.pdf.

Scott, D. 1970. Advice on modal logic. In Karel Lambert (ed.), *Philosophical Problems in Logic*, Dordrecht: D. Reidel, 143–73.

Scriven, M. 1959. Truisms as grounds for historical explanations. In P. Gardiner (ed.), *Theories of History*, New York: The Free Press.

Searle, J. 1980. The background of meaning. In J. Searle, F. Kiefer, and M. Bierwisch (eds), *Speech Act Theory and Pragmatics*, Dordrecht: Reidel, 221–32.

Searle, J. 1992. *The Rediscovery of the Mind*, Cambridge, MA: MIT Press.

Sedivy, J., M. Tanenhaus, C. Chambers, and G. Carlson. 1999. Achieving incremental semantic interpretation through contextual representation, *Cognition* 71: 109–47.

Sedlak, P. A. S. 1975. Direct/indirect object word order: a cross-linguistic analysis, *Working Papers on Language Universals* 18: 117–64. Stanford University.

Segal, G. 2001. Two theories of names, *Mind and Language* 5: 547–63.

Segerberg, K. 1973. Two-dimensional modal logic, *Journal of Philosophical Logic*, 2: 77–96.

Seidenberg, M. S. 1994. Language and connectionism: The developing interface, *Cognition* 50: 385–401.

Seidenberg, M. S. and M. C. MacDonald. 1999. A probabilistic constraints approach to language acquisition and processing, *Cognitive Science* 23: 569–88.

Sekular R. and D. Nash. 1972. Speed of size scaling in human vision, *Psychonomic Science* 27: 93–4.

Selten, R. and M. Warglien. 2007. The emergence of simple languages in an experimental coordination game, *Proceedings of the National Academy of Sciences, USA* 104: 7361–6.

Senkowski, D., T. R. Schneider, J. J. Foxe, and A. K. Engel. 2008. Crossmodal binding through neural coherence: implications for multisensory processing, *Trends in Neurosciences* 31, 401–9.

Shaffir, E., E. E. Smith, and D. N. Osherson. 1990. Typicality and reasoning fallacies, *Memory and Cognition* 18: 229–39.

Shan, Chung-chieh. 2005. Linguistic side efects, Dissertation, Harvard University.

Shannon, C. E. 1949. themathematical theory of communication. In C. E. Shannon and W. Weaver (eds), *The Mathematical Theory of Communication*, The University of Illinois Press.

Shastri, L. and V. Ajjanagadde. 1993. From simple associations to systematic reasoning: A connectionist representation of rules, variables and dynamic bindings using temporal synchrony, *Behavioral and Brain Sciences* 16: 417–49.

Shepard, R. N. and J. Metzler. 1971. Mental rotation of three-dimensional objects, *Science* 171: 701–3.

Shieber, S., 1985. Evidence against the context-freeness of natural language, Lingusitics and Philosophy 8: 333–43.

Shmuel, A. and A. Grinvald. 2000. Coexistence of linear zones and pinwheels within orientation maps in cat visual cortex, *Proceedings of the National Academy of Sciences*, 97: 5568–73.

Siegel, M., T. H. Donner, R. Oostenveld, P. Fries, and A. K. Engel. 2008. Neuronal synchronization along the dorsal visual pathway reflects the focus of spatial attention, *Neuron* 60: 709–19.

Singer, W. 1994. Time as coding space in neocortical processing. In R. Buzsaki, W. Singer, A. Berthoz, and Y. Christen (eds), *Temporal Coding in the Brain*, New York: Springer Verlag, 51–79.

Singer, W. 1999. Neuronal synchrony: A versatile code for the definition of relations? *Neuron* 24: 49–65.

Singh, R. and C. Eliasmith. 2006. Higher-dimensional neurons explain the tuning and dynamics of working memory cells, *Journal of Neuroscience* 26: 3667–78.

Sinha, A. K. 2002. Prototype theory and the conceptualisation of culture, *Psychology and Developing Societies* 14 (1): 45–54.

Skinner, B. F. 1957. *Verbal Behavior*, Acton: Copley Publishing Group.

Slobin, D. I. 1977. Language change in childhood and history. In J. Macnamara (ed.), *Language Learning and Thought*, London: Academic Press, 185–221.

Sloman, S. A. 1993. Feature-based induction, *Cognitive Psychology* 25: 231–80.

Sluga, H. D. 1971. Review of Frege's Nachgelassene Schriften, *The Journal of Philosophy* 68: 265–72.

Sluga, H. D. 1975. Frege and the rise of analytic philosophy, *Inquiry* 18: 471–98. Review discussion of Bynum (1972) and Dummett (1973).

Sluga, H. D. 1977. Frege's alleged realism, *Inquiry* 20: 227–42.

Sluga, H. D. 1980. *Gottlob Frege*, London: Routledge & Kegan Paul.

Smith, A. D. M. 2008. Protolanguage reconstructed. *Interaction Studies: Social Behavior and Communication in Biological and Artificial Systems* 9 (1): 100–16.

Smith, E. E. and D. L. Medin. 1981. *Categories and Concepts*, Cambridge, MA: Harvard University Press.

Smith, E. E. and D. N. Osherson. 1984. Conceptual combination with prototype concepts, *Cognitive Science* 8: 337–61.

Smith, E. E., E. Shoben, and L. Rips. 1974. Structure and process in semantic memory: a featural model for semantic decisions, *Psychological Review* 81: 214–41.

Smith, E. E., D. L. Medin, L. J. Rips, and M. Keane. 1988a. Combining prototypes: A selective modification model, *Cognitive Science* 12: 485–527.

Smith, E. E., D. N. Osherson, L. J. Rips, and M. Keane. 1988b. Combining concepts: A selective modification model, *Cognitive Science* 12, 485–527.

Smith, K. 2003. The Transmission of Language: Models of biological and cultural evolution, PhD Thesis, The University of Edinburgh.

Smith, K., H. Brighton, and S. Kirby. 2003. Complex systems in language evolution: the cultural emergence of compositional structure, *Advances in Complex Systems* 6: 537–58.

Smits, T., G. Storms, Y. Rosseel, and P. De Boeck. 2002. Fruits and vegetables categorized: An application of the generalized context model, *Psychonomic Bulletin and Review* 9: 836–44.

Smolensky, P. 1988a. On the proper treatment of connectionism, *Behavioral and Brain Sciences* 11: 1–74.

Smolensky, P. 1988b. The constituent structure of connectionist mental states: A reply to Fodor and Pylyshyn, *Southern Journal of Philosophy* 26: Supplement: *Spindel Conference 1987: Connectionism and the Philosophy of Mind*, 137–61. Reprinted in T. Horgan and J. Tienson (eds), *Connectionism and the Philosophy of Psychology*, Dordrecht: Kluwer, 1991.

Smolensky, P. 1990. Tensor product variable binding and the representation of symbolic structures in connectionist systems, *Artificial Intelligence* 46: 159–216. Reprinted in G. Hinton (ed.), *Connectionist Symbol Processing*, Cambridge, MA: MIT Press, 1991.

Smolensky, P. 1995a. Connectionism, constituency and the language of thought. In C. Macdonald and G. Macdonald (eds), *Connectionism* Cambridge, MA: Blackwell, 164–98. Original work published 1991.

Smolensky, P. 1995b. Reply: Constituent structure and explanation in an integrated connectionist/symbolic cognitive architecture. In C. Macdonald and G. Macdonald (eds.), *Connectionism*, Oxford: Wiley/Blackwell, 223–90.

Smuts, J. 1926. *Holism and Evolution*, London: Macmillan.

Solomon, K. O. and L. W. Barsalou. 2004. Perceptual simulation in property verification, *Memory and Cognition* 32: 244–59.

Song, S., P. J. Sjostrom, M. Reigl, S. Nelson, and D. B. Chklovskii. 2005. Highly nonrandom features of synaptic connectivity in local cortical circuits, *PLoS Biology*, 33.

Sonnenstuhl, I., S. Eisenbeiss, and H. Clahsen, 1999. Morphological priming in the German mental lexicon, *Cognition* 72: 203–36.

Spelke, E. 1990. Principles of object perception, *Cognitive Science* 14: 29–56.

Spelke, E. 2002. Developing knowledge of space: Core systems and new combinations. In S. Kosslyn and A. Galaburda (eds), *Languages of the Brain*, Cambridge, MA: Harvard University Press.

Spijkerman, R. and R. J. J. M. van den Eijnden. Addiction Research Institute, Rotterdam, S. Vitale, and R. C. M. E. Engels. 2004. Explaining adolescents smoking and drinking behavior: The concept of smoker and drinker prototypes in relation to variables of the theory of planned behavior, *Addictive Behaviors* 29 (8): 1615–22.

Springer, K. and G. L. Murphy. 1992. Feature availability in conceptual combination, *Psychological Science* 3: 111–17.

Stalnaker, C. R. 1970. Pragmatics, *Synthese* 22: 272–89, reprinted in C. R. Stalnaker *Context and Content*, Oxford: Oxford University Press, 1999.

Stalnaker, C. R. 1978. Assertion. In P. Cole (ed.), *Syntax and Semantics 9: Pragmatics*. New York: Academic Press, 315–32.

Stalnaker, C. R. 1999. *Context and Content*, Oxford: Oxford University Press.

Stanley, J. 2005. *Knowledge and Practical Interests*, Oxford: Oxford University Press.

Stanley, J. and Z. G. Szabó. 2000. On quantifier domain restriction, *Mind and Language* 15: 219–61.

Stechow, A. von. 1995. Lexical decomposition in syntax, in U. Egli, P. E. Pause, C. Schwarze, A. v. Stechow, and G. Wienold (eds), *Lexical Knowledge in the Organization of Language*, Amsterdam: John Benjamins, 81–118.

Stechow, A. von. 1996. The different readings of wieder 'again': A structural account, *Journal of Semantics* 13: 87–138.

Stechow, A. von. 2003. How are results represented and modified? Remarks on Jäger & Blutner's anti-decomposition, in E. Lang et al. (eds), *Modifying Adjuncts*, Berlin: Mouton de Gruyter, 417–51.

Stechow, A. von and T. E. Zimmermann. 1984. Term answers and contextual change, *Linguistics* 22: 3–40.

Steedman, M. 1987. Combinatory Grammars and Parasitic Gaps, *Natural Language and Linguistic Theory* 5: 403–39.

Steedman, M. 1990. Gapping as constituent coordination, *Linguistics and Philosophy* 13: 207–63.

Steedman, M. 1997. The productions of time. Draft, ftp://ftp.cogsci.ed.ac.uk/pub/steedman/temporality/temporality.ps.gz, July 2000. Subsumes Temporality, in J. van Benthem and A. ter Meulen (eds), *Handbook of Logic and Language*, Amsterdam: Elsevier North Holland, 895–935.

Steinmetz, P. N., A. Roy, P. J. Fitzgerald, S. S. Hsiao, K. O. Johnson, and E. Niebur. 2000. Attention modulates synchronized neuronal firing in primate somatosensory cortex, *Nature* 404: 187–90.

Stewart, O. T. 2001. *The Serial Verb Construction Parameter*, New York: Garland.

Stewart, T. C. and C. Eliasmith. 2008. Building production systems with realistic spiking neurons. In B. C. Love, K. McRae, and V. M. Sloutsky (eds), *Proceedings of the 30th Annual Meeting of the Cognitive Science Society*, Austin, TX: Cognitive Science Society, 1759–64.

Stiebels, B. 1996. *Lexikalische Argumente und Adjunkte*, Berlin: Akademie Verlag.

Stiebels, B. 1998. Complex denominal verbs in German and the morphology-semantics interface. In G. Booij and J. van Marle (eds), *Yearbook of Morphology 1997*, Dordrecht: Kluwer. 265–302.

Stiebels, B. 2002. *Typologie des Argumentlinkings: Ökonomie und Expressivität* [Typology of Argument Linking: Economy and Expressivity]. Berlin: Akademie-Verlag.

Stigler, S. M. 1980. Stigler's law of eponymy. In T. F. Gieryn (ed.), *Science and social structure: a festchrift for Robert K. Merton*, New York: New York Academy of Sciences, 147–57.

Stokoe, W. C. 2001. *Language in Hand: Why Sign Came Before Speech*, Washington, DC: Gallaudet University Press.

Storms, G., P. De Boeck, I. van Mechelen, and W. Ruts. 1996. The dominance effect in concept conjunctions: Generality and interaction aspects, *Journal of Experimental Psychology: Learning, Memory, and Cognition* 22: 1–15.

Storms, G., P. De Boeck, I. van Mechelen, and W. Ruts. 1998a. Not guppies, nor goldfish, but tumble dryers, Noriega, Jesse Jackson, panties, car crashes, bird books, and Stevie Wonder, *Memory and Cognition* 26: 143–45.

Storms, G., W. Ruts, and A. Vandenbroucke. 1998b. Dominance, overextensions, and the conjunction effect in different syntactic phrasings of concept conjunctions, *European Journal of Cognitive Psychology* 10: 337–72.

Storms, G., P. de Boeck, J. A. Hampton, and I. van Mechelen. 1999. Predicting conjunction typicalities by component typicalities, *Psychonomic Bulletin and Review* 6: 677–84.

Storms, G., P. De Boeck, and W. Ruts. 2000. Prototype and exemplar based information in natural language categories, *Journal of Memory and Language* 42: 51–73.

Sundholm, G. 1986. Proof theory and meaning. In D. Gabbay and F. Guenthner (eds), *Handbook of Philosophical Logic*, vol. 3, Dordrecht: Reidel, 471–506.

Swinney, D., T. Love, M. Walenski, and E. Smith. 2007. Conceptual combination during sentence comprehension, *Psychological Science*, 18: 397–400.

Synthese. 2009. Special issue: Relative Truth, vol. 166(2).

Szabó, Z. G. 2000a. *Problems of Compositionality.* New York: Garland.

Szabó, Z. G. 2000b. Compositionality as supervenience, *Linguistics and Philosophy* 23: 475–505.

Szabó, Z. G. 2003. Believing in things, *Philosophy and Phenomenological Research* 66: 584–611.

Szabó, Z. G. 2004. Review of J. Fodor and E. Lepore *The Compositionality Papers, Mind* 113: 340–4.

Szabó, Z. G. 2007. Compositionality. *Stanford Enclyclopedia of Philosophy.*

Tabossi, P. 1988. Effects of context on immediate interpretation of unambiguous nouns, *Journal of Experimental Psychology: Learning, Memory, and Cognition* 14: 153–62.

Tallerman, M. 2006. A holistic protolanguage cannot be stored, cannot be retrieved. In: A. Cangelosi, A. D. M. Smith, and K. Smith (eds), *The Evolution of Language: Proceedings of the 6th International Conference (EVOLANG6)*, World Scientific, 447–8.

Tallerman, M. 2007. Did our ancestors speak a holistic protolanguage? *Lingua* 117: 579–604.

Talmy, L. 1985. Lexicalization patterns: semantic structure in lexical forms. In T. Shopen (ed.), *Language Typology and Syntactic Description*, vol. 3, Cambridge: Cambridge University Press, 136–49.

Talmy, L. 1988. Force dynamics in language and cognition, *Cognitive Science* 12: 49–100.

Talmy, L. 2000. *Toward a Cognitive Semantics*, Vols. I and II, Cambridge, MA: MIT Press.

Tarski, A. 1931. Sur les ensembles définissables de nombres réels. I, *Fundamenta Mathematicae* 17: 210–39.

Tarski, A. 1933. *Pojcie prawdy w jezykach nauk dedukcyjnych*, Prace Towarzystwa naukowego Warszawsiego. Wydzial III, 34. German translation with added postscript: Der Wahrheitsbegriff in den formalisierten Sprachen, *Studia Philosophica* 1: 261–405, 1935. English translation of the German text: The concept of truth in formalized languages, in: J. Woodger (ed.) *Logic, Semantics, Metamathematics. Papers from 1923 to 1938*, Oxford: Clarendon Press, 1956; revised second edition, J. Corcoran (ed.), Indianapolis: Hackett, 1983, 152–278.

Tarski, A. 1983. *Logic, Semantics, Metamathematics: papers from 1923 to 1938*, ed. J. Corcoran, Indianapolis, IN: Hackett Publishing Company.

Taylor, B. 1985. *Modes of Occurrence*, Oxford: Blackwell.

Taylor, J. R. 2003. *Linguistic Categorization* 3rd edn, Oxford: Oxford University Press.

Taylor, S.E. 1989. *Positive Illusions*, New York: Basic Books Inc.

Tenny, C. 1992. The aspectual interface hypothesis. In I. A. Sag and A. Szabolcsi (eds), *Lexical Matters*, Stanford, CA: Center for the Study of Language and Information, 1–27.

Tenny, C. and J. Pustejovsky. 2000. *Events as Grammatical Objects*, Stanford, CA: CSLI Publications.

Termann, D. and D. Wang. 1995. Global competition and local cooperation in a network of neural oscillators, *Physica D* 81: 148–76.

Thagard, P. 1983. Conceptual combination: a frame-based theory, Paper presented to the Annual Meeting of the Society for Philosophy and Psychology, Wellesley, June.

Thomason, R. 1974. Introduction in R. Montague 1974, 1–69.

Tomasello, M. 2003. *Constructing a Language: A Usage-Based Theory of Language Acquisition*, Cambridge, MA: Harvard University Press.

Travis, L. 2000. Event structure in syntax. In C. Tenny and J. Pustejovsky (eds), *Events as Grammatical Objects: The Converging Perspectives of Lexical Semantics and Syntax*, Stanford, CA: CSLI Publications, 145–85.

Traxler, M., M. Pickering, and B. McElree. 2002. Coercion in sentence processing: Evidence from eye-movements and self-paced reading, *Journal of Memory and Language* 47, 530–47.

Traxler, M., B. McElree, R. Williams, and M. Pickering. 2005. Context effects in coercion: Evidence from eye movements, *Journal of Memory and Language* 53, 1–25.

Treisman, A. 1996. The binding problem, *Current Opinion in Neurobiology* 6: 171–8.

Trendelenburg, A. 1840. *Logische Untersuchungen*, Berlin: Bethge,.

Troelstra, A. S. and H. Schwichtenberg. 2000. *Basic Proof Theory*, 2nd edn, Cambridge: Cambridge University Press.

Tsujimura, N. 2001. Degree words and scalar structure in Japanese, *Lingua* 111: 29–52.

Tversky, A. and D. Kahneman. 1983. Extensional versus intuitive resoning: The conjunction fallacy in probability judgement, *Psychological Review* 90: 293–315.

Ullman, M. T., S. Corkin, M. Coppola, G. Hickok, J. Growdon, W. Koroshetz, and S. Pinker. 1997. A neural dissociation within language: evidence that the mental dictionary is part of declarative memory, and that grammatical rules are processed by the procedural system, *Journal of Cognitive Neuroscience* 9: 266–76.

Uriagereka, J. 1995. Warps. University of Maryland Working Papers in Linguistics.

Uriagereka, J. 2002. *Derivations*, London: Routledge.

Uriagereka, J. 2008. *Syntactic Anchors*, Cambridge: Cambridge University Press.

van Benthem, J. 1986. The Logic of Semantics, in *Essays on Logical Semantics*, Dordrecht: D. Reidel, 198–214.

van Benthem, J. 1995. *Language in Action*, Cambridge, MA: MIT Press.

van Benthem, J. and A. ter Meulen. 1997. *Handbook of Logic and Language*, Amsterdam: Elsevier and Cambridge MA: MIT Press.

van Berkum, J. 2004. Sentence comprehension in a wider discourse: Can we use ERPs to keep track of things? In M. Carreiras and C. Clifton (eds), *The On-line Study of Sentence Comprehension: Eyetracking, Erps and Beyond*, New York: Psychology Press, 229–70.

van Berkum, J., P. Hagoort, and C. Brown. 1999. Semantic integration in sentences and discourse: Evidence from the N400, *Journal of Cognitive Neuroscience* 11: 657–71.

van Berkum, J., P. Zwitserlood, P. Hagoort, and C. Brown. 2003. When and how do listeners relate a sentence to the wider discourse? Evidence from the N400 effect, *Cognitive Brain Research* 17: 701–18.

van der Lely, H. and M. T. Ullman. 2001. Past tense morphology in specifically language impaired and normally developing children, *Language and Cognitive Processes* 16: 177–217.

van der Pol, B. 1926. On 'relaxation-oscillations', *The London, Edinburgh, and Dublin Philosophical Magazine and Journal of Science* Series 7 (2): 978–92.

van der Sandt, R. A. 1992. Presupposition projection as anaphora resolution, *Journal of Semantics* 9(4): 333–77.

van der Velde, F. and M. de Kamps. 2006. Neural blackboard architectures of combinatorial structures in cognition, *Behavioral and Brain Sciences*, 29, 37–70.

van Eijck, J. and H. Kamp. 1997. Representing discourse in context, in van Benthem and ter Meulen 1997, 179–237.

van Lambalgen, M. and F. Hamm. 2004. *The Proper Treatment of Events*, Oxford: Blackwell.

van Oostendorp, H. and S. de Mul. 1990. Moses beats Adam: A semantic relatedness effect on a semantic illusion, *Acta Psychologica* 74: 35–46.

van Vreeswijk, C. and H. Sompolinsky. 1996. Chaos in neuronal networks with balanced excitatory and inhibitory activity, *Science* 274, 1724–6.

Vendler, Z. 1967. Verbs and times, in Z. Vendler, *Linguistics in Philosophy*, Ithaca: Cornell University Press, 97–121.

Vijay-Shanker, K., D. Wier and A. Joshi. 1986. Adjoining, wrapping, and headed strings, in *Proceedings of the 24th Meeting of the Association for Computaitonal Linguistics*, New York: ACL.

Vogt, P. 2005. The emergence of compositional structures in perceptually grounded language games, *Artificial Intelligence* 167: 206–42.

von der Malsburg, C. 1981. The correlation theory of brain function, Internal Report 81-2, Max-Planck-Institute for Biophysical Chemistry, Göttingen.

von der Malsburg, C. 1987. Synaptic plasticity as basis of brain organization. In J. Changeux and M. Konishi (eds), *The Neural and Molecular Bases of Learning*, Chichester: John Wiley and Sons Ltd., 411–31.

von Frisch, K. 1974. Decoding the language of the bee, *Science* 185: 663–8.

von Stein, A., C. Chiang, and P. König, 2000. Top-down processing mediated by interareal synchronization, *Proceedings of the National Academy of Sciences, USA* 9726: 14748–53.

Wachbroit, R. 1994. Normality as a Biological Concept, *Philosophy of Science* 61: 579–91.

Walsh, S. P. and K. M. White. 2007. Me, my mobile, and I: The role of self- and prototypical identity influences in the prediction of mobile phone behavior, *Journal of Applied Social Psychology* 37 (10), 2405–34.

Wang, D. 1996. Primitive auditory segregation based on oscillatory correlation, *Cognitive Science* 20: 409–56.

Wanner, E. 1979. False identification of prime numbers. Paper presented at the 1979 meeting of The Society for Philosophy and Psychology, New York.

Washio, R. 1997. Resultatives, compositionality and language variation, *East Asian Journal of Linguistics* 6: 1–49.

Weatherson, B. 2006. Intrinsic and extrinsic properties, *Stanford Encyclopedia of Philosophy*, Edward N. Zalta (ed.), URL =<http://plato.stanford.edu/entries/intrinsic-extrinsic/>.

Webber, B., M. Stone, A. Joshi, and A. Knott. 2003. Anaphora and discourse structure, *Computational Linguistics* 29(4): 545–88.

Wechsler, S. 1995. *The Semantic Basis of Argument Structure*, Stanford: CSLI Publications.

Wechsler, S. 2008. Idioms, light verbs and lexical decomposition. Talk presented at the NORMS Workshop on Argument Structure, University of Lund, Sweden, 5–6 February.

Weinreich, U. 1972. *Explorations in Semantic Theory*, The Hague: Mouton.

Weiskopf, D. 2007. Compound nominals, context, and compositionality *Synthese* 156: 161–204.

Wells, R. 1947. Immediate constituents, *Language* 23: 81–117.

Werning, M. 2003*a*. Synchrony and composition: Toward a cognitive architecture between classicism and connectionism. In B. Löwe, W. Malzkorn, and T. Raesch (eds), *Applications of Mathematical Logic in Philosophy and Linguistics*, Dordrecht: Kluwer, 261–78.

Werning, M. 2003*b*. Ventral vs. dorsal pathway: The source of the semantic object/event and the syntactic noun/verb distinction, *Behavioral and Brain Sciences* 263: 299–300.

Werning, M. 2004. Compositionaltity, context, categories and the indeterminacy of translation, *Erkenntnis* 60(2): 145–78.

Werning, M. 2005*a*. The temporal dimension of thought: Cortical foundations of predicative representation, *Synthese* 146(1/2): 203–24.

Werning, M. 2005*b*. Right and wrong reasons for compositionality. In M. Werning, E. Machery, and G. Schurz (eds), *The Compositionality of Meaning and Content* Vol. I: Foundational Issues, Frankfurt: Ontos Verlag, 285–309.

Werning, M. 2005*c*. Neuronal synchronization, covariation, and compositional representation. In E. Machery, M. Werning, and G. Schurz (eds), *The Compositionality of Meaning and Content Vols. II: Applications to Linguistics, Philosophy and Neuroscience*, Frankfurt: Ontos Verlag, 283–312.

Werning, M. 2008. The complex first paradox: Why do semantically thick concepts so early lexicalize as nouns? *Interaction Studies* 9: 67–83.

Werning, M. 2010. Complex first? On the evolutionary and developmental priority of semantically thick words. *Philosophy of Science 77*: 1096–1108.

Werning, M. 2011. The compositional brain: A unification of conceptual and neuronal perspectives. Paderborn: Mentis Verlag (in press).

Werning, M. and A. Maye. 2006. The neural basis of the object concept in ambiguous and illusionary perception. In R. Sun and N. Miyake (eds), *Proceedings of the Twenty-Eighth Annual Conference of the Cognitive Science Society*, London: Erlbaum, 876–81.

Wertheimer, M. 1950. Gestalt theory. In W. D. Ellis (ed.), *A Sourcebook of Gestalt Psychology*, New York: The Humanities Press, 1–11. Original work published 1924.

Wertheimer, M. 1958. Principles of perceptual organization. In D. G. Beardslee and M. Wertheimer (eds), *Readings in Perception*, Princeton: Van Nostrand.

Westermann, G. 1998. Emergent modularity and u-shaped learning in a constructivist neural network learning the English past tense, *Proceedings of the 20th Annual Conference of the Cognitive Science Society*, Hillsdale, NJ: Erlbaum, 1130–5.

Westermann, G. 2000. Constructivist Neural Network Models of Cognitive Development, PhD thesis, University of Edinburgh.

Westermann, G., D. Mareschal, M. H. Johnson, S. Sirois, M. W. Spratling, and M. S. C. Thomas. 2007. Neuroconstructivism, *Developmental Science* 10: 75–83.

Westerståhl, D. 1998. On mathematical proofs of the vacuity of compositionality, *Linguistics and Philosophy* 21: 635–43.

Westerståhl, D. 2004. On the compositional extension problem, *Journal of Philosophical Logic* 33, 549–82.

Westerståhl, D. 2011. Compositionality in Kaplan style semantics. This volume.

Wierzbicka, A. 1972. *Semantic Primitives*, Frankfurt a.M.: Athenäum.

Wierzbicka, A. 1985. *Lexicography and Conceptual Analysis*, Ann Arbor: Karoma Publishers.

Wierzbicka, A. 1996. *Semantics: Primes and Universals*, New York: Oxford University Press.

Williams, A. 2005. Complex Causatives and Verbal Valence. Doctoral Dissertation: University of Pennsylvania.

Williams, A. 2007. Patients in Igbo and Mandarin. In J. Dölling and T. Heye-Zybatow (eds), *Event Structures in Linguistic Form and Interpretation*, Berlin: Mouton de Gruyter.

Williams, J. R. G. 2005. The Inscrutability of Reference. Dissertation, University of St Andrews. https://webspace.utexas.edu/deverj/personal/test/inscrutabilityofreference.pdf.

Wilson, C. 1989. *Leibniz's Metaphysics*, Princeton: Princeton University Press.

Wilson, D.S. 2002. *Darwin's Cathedral*, Chicago: University of Chicago Press.

Wilson, H. R. and J. D. Cowan. 1972. Excitatory and inhibitory interactions in localized populations of model neurons, *Biophysical Journal* 121.

Winograd, T. 1972. *Understanding Natural Language*, New York: Academic Press.

Wisniewski, E. J. 1996. Construal and similarity in conceptual combination, *Journal of Memory and Language*, 35: 434–53.

Wisniewski, E. J. 1997. When concepts combine, *Psychonomic Bulletin and Review* 4: 167–83.

Wisniewski, E. J. 1998. Property instantiation in conceptual combination, *Memory and Cognition* 26: 1330–47.

Wisniewski, E. J. 1999. The copying machine metaphor. in D. L. Medin (ed.), *The Psychology of Learning and Motivation*, New York: Academic Press, 39: 129–62.

Wisniewski, E. J. 2004. Multiple processes in conceptual combination. Paper presented at the twenty-sixth Annual Conference of the Cognitive Science Society, Symposium on the Diversity of Conceptual Combination Chicago, Illinois.

Wisniewski, E. J. and E. J. Clancy. 2003. You don't need a weatherman to know which way the wind blows: The role of discourse context in conceptual combination. Unpublished Manuscript.

Wisniewski, E. J. and B. C. Love. 1998. Relations versus properties in conceptual combination, *Journal of Memory and Language* 38: 177–202.

Wisniewski, E. J. and E. L. Middleton. 2002. Of bucket bowls and coffee cup bowls: Spatial alignment in conceptual combination, *Journal of Memory and Language* 46: 1–23.

Wittgenstein, L. 1921. Tractatus logico-philosophicus. Logisch-philosphische Abhandlung, in Ostwald (ed.), *Annalen der Naturphilosphie*. Reprint Oxford: Blackwell, 1959.

Wittgenstein, L. 1953. *Philosophical Investigations*, Oxford: Blackwell.

Womelsdorf, T., P. Fries, P. Mitra, and R. Desimone, 2006. Gamma-band synchronization in visual cortex predicts speed of change detection, *Nature* 4399: 733–6.

Womelsdorf, T., J.-M. Schoffelen, R. Oostenveld, W. Singer, R. Desimone, A. K. Engel, and P. Fries. 2007. Modulation of neuronal interactions through neuronal synchronization, *Science* 316, 1609–12.

Wray, A. 1998. Protolanguage as a holistic system for social interaction, *Language and Communication* 18: 47–67.

Wray, A. 2000. Holistic utterances in protolanguage: The link from primates to humans. In C. Knight, M. Studdert-Kennedy, and J. Hurford (eds), *The Evolutionary Emergence of Language: Social function and the origins of linguistic form*, Cambridge: Cambridge University Press, 285–02.

Wray, A. 2002a. *The Transition to Language*, Oxford: Oxford University Press.

Wray, A. 2002b. *Formulaic Language and the Lexicon*, Cambridge: Cambridge University Press.

Wu, Jing. 2006. Schema Theory and the Interpretation of Noun–Noun Compounds in Contemporary Chinese: A Database-Driven Study. Dissertation submitted to Shanghai International Studies University.

Wunderlich, D. 1996a. Models of lexical decomposition. In E. Weigand and F. Hundsnurscher (eds), *Lexical Structures and Language Use*, vol. 1, Tübingen: Niemeyer, 169–83.

Wunderlich, D. 1996*b*. A minimalist model of inflectional morphology. In C. Wilder, H.-M. Gärtner, and M. Bierwisch (eds), *The Role of Economy Principles in Linguistic Theory*, Berlin: Akademie-Verlag, 267–98.

Wunderlich, D. 1997*a*. Cause and the structure of verbs, *Linguistic Inquiry* 28: 27–68.

Wunderlich, D. 1997*b*. Argument extension by lexical adjunction, *Journal of Semantics* 14: 95–142.

Wunderlich, D. 2000. Predicate composition and argument extension as general options. In B. Stiebels and D. Wunderlich (eds), *Lexicon in Focus*, Berlin: Akademie Verlag, 247–70.

Wunderlich, D. 2001. Prelexical syntax and the voice hypothesis. In C. Féry and W. Sternefeld (eds), *Audiatur Vox Sapientiae. A Festschrift for Arnim von Stechow*, Berlin: Akademie Verlag, 487–513.

Wunderlich, D. 2006*a*. Towards a structural typology of verb classes. In D. Wunderlich (ed.), *Advances in the Theory of the Lexicon*, Berlin: Mouton de Gruyter, 57–166.

Wunderlich, D. 2006*b*. Argument hierarchy and other factors determining argument realization. In I. Bornkessel et al. (eds), *Semantic Role Universals and Argument Linking*, Berlin: Mouton de Gruyter, 15–52.

Wunderlich, D. 2007. Why assume UG? In M. Penke and A. Rosenbach (eds), *What Counts as Evidence in Linguistics—the Case of Innateness*, Amsterdam: Benjamins, 147–74.

Wunderlich, D. and R. Fabri. 1995. Minimalist Morphology: An approach to inflection. *Zeitschrift für Sprachwissenschaft* 14: 236–94.

Wundt, W. 1880. *Logik. Eine Untersuchung der Principien der Erkenntnis und der Methoden wissenschafliche Forschung, Vol. I. Erkentnisslehre*, 2 vols Stuttgart: Ferdinand Enke.

Wundt, W. 1893. *Logik. Eine Untersuchung der Principien der Erkenntnis und der Methoden wissenschafliche Forschung, Vol. I. Erkentnisslehre*, 2nd edn, 2 vols Stuttgart: Ferdinand Enke.

Xiao, Y., Y. Wang, and D. J. Felleman. 2003. A spatially organized representation of colour in macaque cortical area V2, *Nature*, 421: 535–9.

Yeh, W. and L. Barsalou. 2006. The situated nature of concepts, *American Journal of Psychology* 119: 349–84.

Yip, M. 1998. Identity avoidance in phonology and morphology, in S. Lapointe, D. Brentari, and P. Farrell (eds), *Morphology and its Relation to Phonology and Syntax*, Stanford, CA: CSLI Publications, 216–46.

Zadeh, L. A. 1965. Fuzzy sets, *Information and Control* 8: 338–53.

Zadrozny, W. 1994. From compositional to systematic semantics, *Linguistics and Philosophy* 17: 329–42.

Zagona, K. 1995. Temporal argument structure: Configurational elements of construal, in P. M. Bertinetto et al. (eds), *Temporal Reference, Aspect and Actionality, Vol. 1: Semantic and Syntactic Perspectives*, Torino: Rosenberg & Sellier, 397–410.

Zeevat, H. 1989. A compositional approach to Discourse RepresentationTheory, *Linguistics and Philosophy* 12: 95–131.

Zimmermann, F. 1981. *Al-Farabi's Commentary and Short Treatise on Aristotle's De Interpretatione*, Oxford: Oxford University Press.

Zimmermann, M. 2003. Pluractionality and complex quantifier formation, *Natural Language Semantics* 11: 249–87.

Zimmermann, T. E. 1985. Remarks on Groenendijk and Stokhof's Theory of Indirect Questions, *Linguistics and Philosophy* 8: 431–48.

Zimmermann, T. E. 1991. Kontextabhängigkeit. In: A. v. Stechow and D. Wunderlich (eds), *Semantik. Semantics*. Berlin/New York: de Gruyter, 156–229.

Zimmermann, T. E. 1999. Meaning postulates and the model-theoretic approach to natural language semantics, *Linguistics and Philosophy* 22: 529–61.

Zimmermann, T. E. 2010. What it takes to be *missing*. In: T. Hanneforth and G. Fanselow (eds), *Language and Logos. Studies in Theoretical and Computational Linguistics* Berlin: Akademie Verlag, 255–65.

Zimmermann, T. E. 2011. Model-theoretic semantics. In K. von Heusinger et al. (eds), *Semantics: An International Hanbook of Natural Language Meaning*. Berlin/New York, 762–802.

Zimmermann, T. E. Forthcoming. Equivalence of Semantic Theories. In G. Schantz (ed.), *Prospects of Meaning*. Berlin.

Zuberbuhler, K. 2002. A syntactic rule in forest monkey communication, *Animal Behaviour* 63: 293–9.

Zwaan, R. A. 2004. The immersed experiencer: Toward an embodied theory of language comprehension. In B.H. Ross (ed.), *The Psychology of Learning and Motivation*, New York: Academic Press, 44: 35–62.

Zwaan, R. A., R. A. Stanfield, and R. H. Yaxley. 2002. Do language comprehenders routinely represent the shapes of objects? *Psychological Science* 13: 168–71.

INDEX

Note: page numbers followed by *fn* refer to mentions in the footnotes.

logical inference 51
logical language vs. natural language 52
logical problem of language acquisition 595
logical types 225
Logik (Lotze, 1874) 24–5
Logik (Wundt, 1880) 25–6
Logik (Wundt, 1893) 30–2
Logische Untersuchungen (Trendelenburg, 1840) 22–3
Lotze, H. 24–5

M extensions 196
MacFarlane, J. 194*fn*, 198*fn*, 199*fn*, 213–14
Machery, E. 454
Malagasy, change of state verbs 347
Mandatory Compositionality 443, 445
manner vs. result 326
Marcus, G. F. 38, 589, 591
Margolis, E. and S. Laurence 544
Martin-Löf type theory 293–4, 297
Mateu, J. 312
mathematical function of compositionality 160
Mathematical InformationTheory 523*fn*
mathematics, objective truth 26
Maximize On-Line Processing principle 520
Maye, A. 645
Mazurkiewicz, A. 43
McCawley, J. 119, 308
McGinnis, M. 349*fn*
McLaughlin, B. 607
meaning
    analytic core 547–8
    Aristotelian theory 245–9
    change in context 249, 255–6, 358
    and compositionality 480
    concepts of 161
    of constituents 68–71
    dimensions of 152
    embodied 485–6
    extended 376–7
    vs. fregean values 259–61
    function 67–8, 151, 161, 481–2
        and context 482
    and Generative Semantics 55–6
    and hybrid content hypothesis (HCH) 304
    inferences 120–1

intrinsicness 72–3
as label for concepts 129
and the learnability argument (LA) 516–18
and logic 253–4
and Logical Form (LF) 111
modulated 189–91
occasion meaning 187
    vs. standing meaning 179–85, 195
parts of 248
polysemy 255–9, 310, 357–9, 371–2, 480
postulates 62–3, 309
and primitive items 312
in progressive constructions 663–4
and prototypes 399
in PTQ (proper treatment of quantification) 48–9
in quantifiers 66
vs. representation 128
semantic vs. speaker's 188
and semantic flexibility 176–9, 182–3
sentences vs. words 249–50, 256–9
standing meaning 185–7
    vs. occasion meaning 179–85, 195
and tree structures 110–11
truth conditional in discourse 280–4
and understanding 74–7
and Universal Grammar 51–4
vs. values 162–5
Meaning and Necessity (Carnap, 1947) 35–6
meaningful expressions 264–5
meaningfulness and grammaticality 250–1
Medin, D. L. and E. J. Shoben 458
membership, category 422–9
    overextension in 393–4
    and typicality effects 388–92, 547–8
memory
    and the cell assembly model 619
    and concepts 440
    and stored concepts 448
memory-based processes 409–10
mental representations 439–40
metaphor of unsaturedness 23
methodological argument for compositionality 659–60
metonymic construal 408
Mill, J. S. 26–7, 39
Millikan, R. G. 536

CPSIA information can be obtained
at www.ICGtesting.com
Printed in the USA
BVHW011025141019
560917BV00012BA/60/P